Western Europe

Catherine Le Nevez, Kerry Christiani, Gregor Clark, Mark Elliott, Duncan Garwood, Korina Miller, Nicola Williams, Neil Wilson

Isabel Albiston, Kate Armstrong, Alexis Averbuck, Oliver Berry, Cristian Bonetto, Jean-Bernard Carillet, Fionn Davenport, Marc Di Duca, Belinda Dixon, Anthony Ham, Paula Hardy, Damian Harper, Anita Isalska, Ali Lemer, Virginia Maxwell, Hugh McNaughtan, Isabella Noble, John Noble, Lorna Parkes, Christopher Pitts, Leonid Ragozin, Kevin Raub, Simon Richmond, Daniel Robinson, Brendan Sainsbury, Andrea Schulte-Peevers, Helena Smith, Regis St Louis, Andy Symington, Benedict Walker, Greg Ward

PLAN YOUR TRIP

ON THE ROAD

TANGMAN PHOTOGRAPHY/GETTY IMAGES ©

HOUSES OF PARLIAMENT (P110), LONDON

MASSIMO SANTI/SHUTTERSTOCK ©

REIMS P208

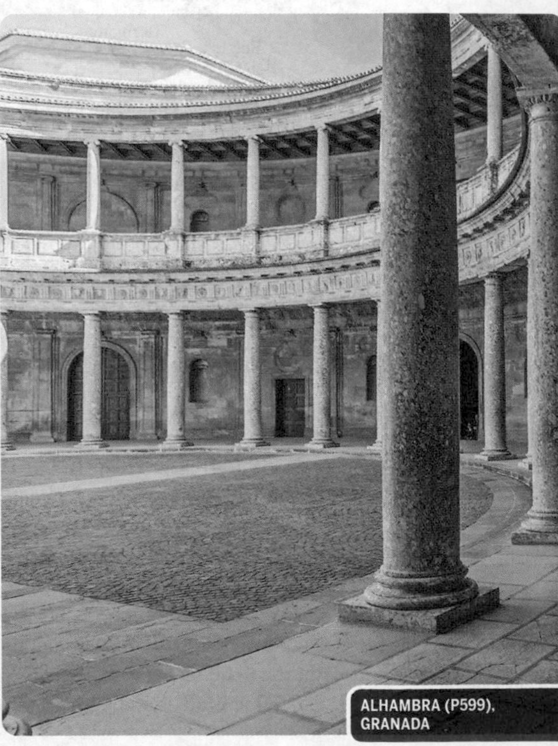

JOHN ROBERTS IMAGES/SHUTTERSTOCK ©

ALHAMBRA (P599), GRANADA

Contents

ON THE ROAD

TRABANTOS/SHUTTERSTOCK ©

MALLORCA P589

Contents

COVID-19

We have re-checked every business in this book before publication to ensure that it is still open after the COVID-19 outbreak. However, the economic and social impacts of COVID-19 will continue to be felt long after the outbreak has been contained, and many businesses, services and events referenced in this guide may experience ongoing restrictions. Some businesses may be temporarily closed, have changed their opening hours and services, or require bookings; some unfortunately could have closed permanently. We suggest you check with venues before visiting for the latest information.

Right: Florence (p452)

RASTISLAV SEDLAK SK/SHUTTERSTOCK ©

WELCOME TO

Western Europe

I love that you only have to travel a short distance in Western Europe to find yourself in a completely different environment. From the language, streetscapes, street food, music and fashion to the climate, topography, natural landscapes and even the rhythm of daily life, there's an astonishing diversity in this compact area that's easily accessible thanks to its fantastic transport network. What I love most, though, isn't the countries' differences but the similarities that unite them – above all, a passion for the quality of life here and a community spirit that transcends individual borders.

By Catherine Le Nevez, Writer

For more about our writers, see p672

Western Europe's Top Experiences

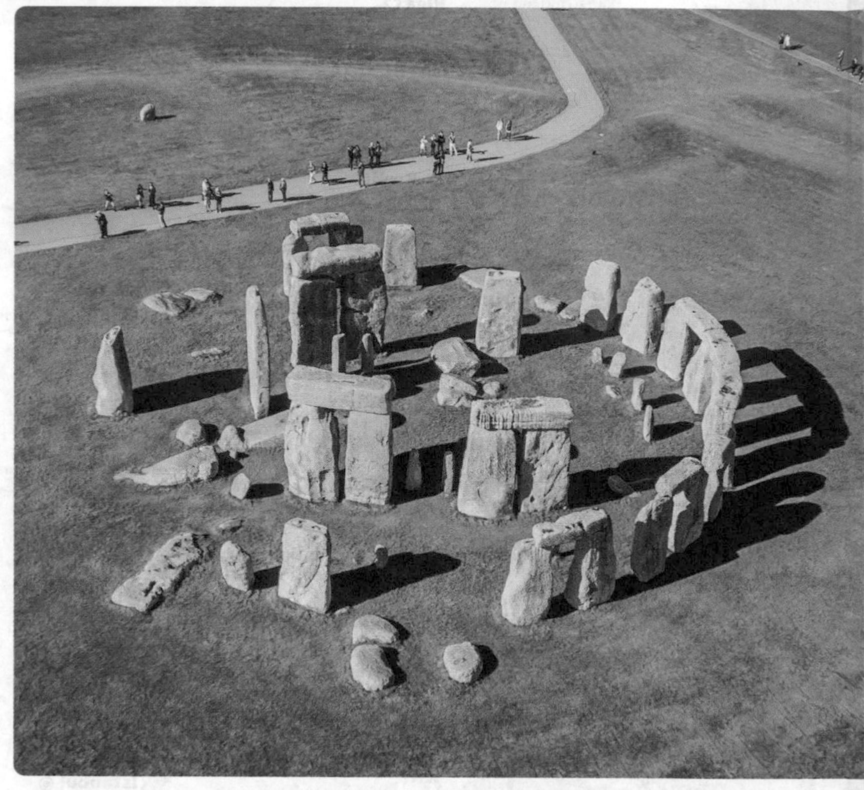

1 HANDS-ON HISTORY

History is everywhere in Western Europe: prehistoric Cro-Magnon caves, mystical passage tombs and stone circles, the remains of Greek temples and Roman bathhouses, monumental buildings where geopolitical boundaries were shaped and reshaped, beautiful Renaissance towns, stately city streets, and poignant sites including the D-Day beaches, confronting Nazi concentration camps, remnants of the Berlin Wall and political murals of West Belfast that are vital to understanding these countries today.

Above: Stonehenge (p136)

DAVID BUFFINGTON/GETTY IMAGES ©

Greek Antiquity

In Greece, you can embark on the path of history in its capital, Athens, where the crumbling remains of ancient wonders include the Acropolis, crowned by the Parthenon, Ancient Agora and the Temple of Olympian Zeus. p329

Right: Erechtheion at the Acropolis (p329)

DRONEMYBUSINESS/SHUTTERSTOCK ©

NICK15/SHUTTERSTOCK ©

S.BORISOV/SHUTTERSTOCK ©

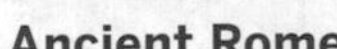

Ancient Rome

The Roman Forum (pictured above) contains the remains of temples, basilicas and public spaces. This was the social, political and commercial hub of the Roman empire, where Romulus supposedly founded the city and emperors lived in unimaginable luxury. Adjacent is the gladiatorial Colosseum. p405

Amsterdam's Canal Ring

The Dutch capital made its fortune in maritime trade, and its Canal Ring was constructed during Amsterdam's 17th-century Golden Age. Soak up the sight of its hump-backed bridges, narrow, gabled houses and thousands of houseboats. Come nightfall, glowing lights reflect in the water. p487

Above: Canal in Amsterdam

2 ARCHITECTURAL LANDMARKS

Across Western Europe, the built environment is as diverse as the continent itself. An architectural heritage spanning seven millenniums of progressive innovation has given rise to splendid structures that are synonymous with their locations – Big Ben immediately brings to mind London, the Brandenburg Gate, Berlin, and the leaning tower, Pisa. Alongside icons from varying eras, styles and celebrated architects' designs, you will also discover lesser-known treasures and visionary contemporary additions.

Eiffel Tower

Initially intended as a temporary exhibit for the 1889 Exposition Universelle (World's Fair), the art-nouveau design of Paris' Eiffel Tower (pictured right) has become the defining fixture of the French capital's skyline. Visit at dusk for the best views of the glittering City of Light. p178

K_SAMURKAS/SHUTTERSTOCK ©

ALIAKSANDR ANTANOVICH/SHUTTERSTOCK ©

SHUANG LI/SHUTTERSTOCK ©

La Sagrada Família

Begun in 1882, the Modernista brainchild of Antoni Gaudí remains a work in progress. Wildly fanciful and deeply profound, inspired by nature and barely restrained by a Gothic style, Barcelona's La Sagrada Família (pictured above) climbs skyward: the highest of its 18 towers reaching 172.5 metres. p567

Bath

Georgian architecture incorporating sweeping crescents, grand town houses, and Palladian mansions (not to mention Roman remains, a beautiful abbey and 21st-century spa) make novelist Jane Austen's former hometown, Bath, the belle of Britain's ball. p136

Left: Royal Crescent (p137)

3 CASTLES & PALACES

Strategically conceived castles and colossal palaces in extravagant grounds provide a portal into centuries of royal and military powerplays, from Wales' Conwy Castle with its defensive towers and Luxembourg City's extraordinary fortifications along the Chemin de la Corniche pedestrian promenade, to the opulence of France's Château de Versailles with its Hall of Mirrors and fountained gardens and Germany's Disney inspiration, Schloss Neuschwanstein.

OLIVER HALLER/500PX ©

ANNA KUCHEROVA/SHUTTERSTOCK ©

SKANDARAMANIA/SHUTTERSTOCK©

Hofburg

At the heart of Austria's capital, Vienna, the Hofburg (pictured above) whisks you back to the age of empires as you marvel at the treasury's imperial crowns, the equine ballet of the Spanish Riding School and the chandelier-lit apartments. p42

Alhambra

Below the snow-dusted Sierra Nevada peaks in Spain's sultry southern city of Granada is the Alhambra (pictured bottom right). The world's most refined example of Islamic art, this palatial World Heritage–listed site with its red fortress towers is the enduring symbol of 800 years of the Moorish rule of Al-Andalus. p599

Edinburgh Castle

Built upon the brooding, black crags of Castle Rock, the most easily defended hilltop on the invasion route between England and Scotland, used by armies from the Roman legions on, Edinburgh Castle (pictured top) remains a striking presence silhouetted against the sky. p156

4 ARTISTIC SHOWCASES

Western Europe's incredible artistic legacy draws on the expressive environment that has brought about momentous advances in every aspect of society. The home turf of masters from Michelangelo to Monet, da Vinci to Dalí, Rubens to Rembrandt, Botticelli to Banksy continues to inspire new generations of creators. A cache of museums, galleries and countless public spaces, particularly in the region's great art cities, are the backdrops for their incomparable works.

Musée du Louvre

Paris' *pièce de résistance*, the Musée du Louvre (pictured below), occupies a labyrinthine former fortress that became a royal palace and then France's first national museum. Among its priceless collections are antiquities including the *Venus de Milo*, sculptures such as Michelangelo's *The Dying Slave* and paintings, most famously da Vinci's *Mona Lisa*. p182

KRZYSZTOF DYDYNSKI/LONELY PLANET ©

EVGENII IAROSHEVSKII/SHUTTERSTOCK ©

TAKASHI IMAGES/SHUTTERSTOCK ©

Galleria degli Uffizi

In the resplendent capital of Italy's Tuscany region, Florence's Galleria degli Uffizi (pictured top right) contains the world's greatest collection of Italian Renaissance art, bequeathed to the city by the Medici family in 1743, including a room of Botticelli masterpieces. p452

Museo del Prado

Part of Madrid's golden mile – one of Europe's richest art concentrations – the extraordinary Museo del Prado (pictured top left) holds royal paintings by Velázquez, Pinturas negras (Black Paintings) by Goya, and thousands of other works. p546

5 EPICUREAN ADVENTURES

Every corner of Western Europe has unique specialities made using locally honed techniques, recipes and ingredients: olive oils and sun-ripened vegetables in the hot south, rich cream and butter in the north, fresh seafood along the coastlines, and meat and cheeses from fertile mountains and pastures. Whet your appetitein street markets laden with seasonal produce, before heading to memorable restaurants.

MAGDANATKA/SHUTTERSTOCK ©

French Baking

All across France, *boulangeries* (bakeries) turn out still-warm, crusty baguettes and richer treats like buttery croissants. *Pâtisseries* (pastry shops) are generally more upmarket, with jewel-like pastries such as éclairs, fruit-topped tarts, macarons and exquisite cakes. p175

Below: French bread and pastries

RIVER THOMPSON/LONELY PLANET ©

SAMI SERT/GETTY IMAGES ©

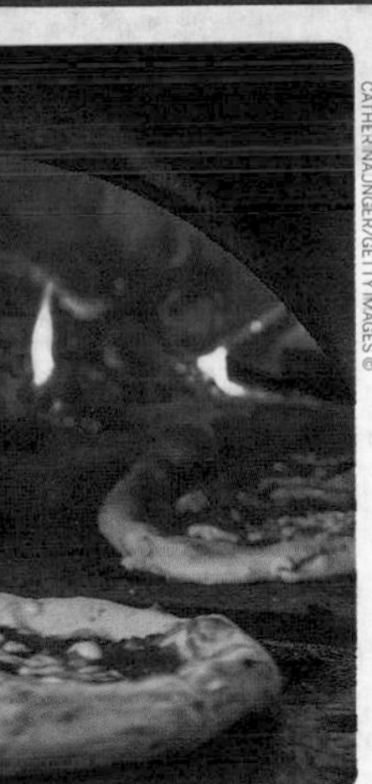

CATHERINE NAJUNGER/GETTY IMAGES ©

Spanish Tapas

Many places across Western Europe have their own version of small sharing plates. In Spain, it's tapas: little dishes of every description, such as cured Iberian ham, a perfect stuffed olive, *tortilla* (Spanish omelette; pictured above) or *patatas bravas* (fried potatoes with spicy tomato sauce). p543

Italian Pizza

The influence of Italy's cuisine extends far beyond the country's borders, and perhaps the most beloved dish of all is pizza (pictured left). The best are wood fired, whether Roman (with a thin, crispy base) or Neapolitan (higher, doughier base). p403

6 SIGNATURE DRINKS

Virtually every European region has at least one distinctive tipple. Vineyards ribbon undulating landscapes, producing wines like France's renowned Bordeaux reds, Italy's Tuscan Chianti, Germany's classic white Riesling and Portugal's rich port – and the basis of Spain's spicy, fruity sangria. English ales, Irish stouts and ubiquitous beers and ciders are part of the social fabric, as are spirits such as barrel-aged Scottish whisky, anise-flavoured Greek ouzo, and fiery Austrian schnapps.

Belgian Brews

Belgium's staggering variety of lagers, white beers, tangy spontaneously fermented lambics, abbey beers and monastery-brewed Trappist beers are each served in their own special glass. Sip a selection in timeless art nouveau cafes in the historic centre of Brussels. p71

Above: Belgian beers

KRZYSZTOF DYDYNSKI/LONELY PLANET ©

Champagne Tasting

Some of Champagne's best liquid gold is made by small-scale vignerons (winemakers) in picturesque villages. Dozens welcome visitors for a taste and the chance to shop at producers' prices along the French region's scenic driving routes. p175

Left: Champagne tasting in Paris

Bavarian Beers

The southern German state of Bavaria is legendary for brewing. Its capital, Munich, plays host to the rollicking Oktoberfest festival, and is the home of famous beer halls complete with oompah bands, traditional breweries and high-spirited beer gardens where you can enjoy a frothy, refreshing stein. p284

Left and below: Oktoberfest

ANANDOART/SHUTTERSTOCK ©

NIKADA/GETTY IMAGES ©

7 ALPINE HIGHS

While Western Europe has many majestic mountain ranges, the highest and most extensive are the Alps, stretching some 1200km across France, Switzerland, Monaco, Italy, Liechtenstein, Austria and Germany (and eastwards into Slovenia). Skiing, snowboarding, mountaineering, trekking, tobogganing, canyoning, rafting, lake-diving, you name it – amid these towering peaks, you'll find it all and more. After an action-packed day, wood-panelled chalets are atmospheric places for a revitalising drink and hearty mountain cuisine.

NATALIYA NAZAROVA/SHUTTERSTOCK ©

DITTY_ABOUT_SUMMER/SHUTTERSTOCK ©

Innsbruck

Even if you're visiting in mid-summer, you can still hit the slopes. Head to the glaciers near Austria's alpine city Innsbruck (pictured above) for year-round downhill action. p64

Chamonix

Take the vertiginous Téléphérique de l'Aiguille du Midi cable car (pictured top left) from chic French resort Chamonix to the top of Aiguille du Midi and marvel at the unfolding Alpine scenery. p222

Zermatt

In this Swiss village, the snow-capped peak of the Toblerone package-famed Matterhorn (pictured above) soars skywards. Strap on skis or walk alpine paths as cowbells clink in the distance. p621

8 SUN, SEA & SHORELINES

JOYFULL/SHUTTERSTOCK ©

KARSTEN/GETTY IMAGES ©

Baleal

Portugal is renowned among board riders for the pumping surf along its Atlantic coastline. An ideal place to catch some waves is Baleal (pictured left), where you'll find surf schools and chilled bar-restaurants. p527

St-Tropez

Plage de Pampelonne, near the historic Mediterranean fishing village of St-Tropez, is studded with some of the most glamorous drinking and dining haunts along the French Riviera. p244

Bottom left: Plage de Pampelonne (p244)

Beaches abound in Western Europe, from white Mediterranean sand lapped by turquoise waters, secluded coves beneath wind-carved cliffs, pebbled shores flanked by grand promenades to idyllic islands with villages perched on the hillsides, wildlife-filled nature reserves, windswept dunes beside the North Sea and pounding Atlantic surf. Look for the Blue Flag ecolabel, which is awarded to beaches and marinas that meet strict environmental criteria.

9 HIKING & CYCLING

Trails fan out across Western Europe. Lace up your boots for a leisurely stroll, an all-day ramble through picturesque landscapes, or stock up your backpack and head off on a multiday hike on one of the many long-distance routes. If you prefer to get around on two wheels, there are also a welter of cycling paths and plenty of places where you can hire bikes (classic and electric) to explore.

Hiking the Causeway Coast

This otherworldly route takes in inspiring Northern Ireland coastal scenery, including the Giant's Causeway geological formation, with 40,000 dramatic hexagonal basalt columns, and the nerve-testing challenge of the swaying Carrick-a-Rede rope bridge. p397

Below left: The Giant's Causeway (p397)

RICKFORDUK/SHUTTERSTOCK ©

Cycling in the Netherlands

Pedal past the creaking windmills, canals and, in springtime, fields of tulips in the gloriously flat Dutch countryside. p499

Top right: Cyclists in the Dutch countryside

Walking in England

The English countryside is tailor-made for walking, with rolling hills, beautiful woodlands, riverside trails and chocolate-box villages home to cosy pubs with crackling open fires.

Bottom right: Walkers in England

10 MUSIC FOR EVERYONE

SOPOTNICK/SHUTTERSTOCK ©

Whatever your favourite musical genre – orchestral symphonies, traditional folk, flamenco, jazz, rock, pop, hip-hop, rap, and electro beats at pulsating clubs – you'll find your niche in Western Europe's wide-ranging music scene. Along with spectacular opera houses, theatres and intimate venues like Paris' medieval cellars or Ireland's atmosphere-steeped pubs, there are many other opportunities to catch live performances, such as festivals, outdoor concerts and buskers providing a soundtrack to city streets.

Lisbon

The narrow alleyways of Lisbon's Alfama neighbourhood are an evocative setting for the melancholy, nostalgic songs of Portuguese fado. p519

Above: Fado singers in Lisbon

Salzburg

Salzburg's baroque old town looks much as it did when Mozart lived here. Classical concerts are a treat here, as are the Sound of Music tributes to the enduring musical. p57

London

Catch the Proms at the Royal Albert Hall, an East End singalong around a pub piano, a grand-scale production in the West End, a DJ set at a thumping club, or an up-and-coming band at a local boozer. p129

Need to Know

For more information, see Survival Guide (p639)

Currency

Euro (€) Austria, Belgium, France, Germany, Greece, Republic of Ireland, Italy, Luxembourg, the Netherlands, Portugal, Spain

Pound (£; also called 'pound sterling') Britain, Northern Ireland

Swiss franc (CHF, also Sfr) Switzerland

Visas

Generally not required for stays of up to 90 days; by the end of 2022, non-EU nationals will need prior authorisation under the ETIAS system for Schengen area travel.

Money

ATMs are widespread. Visa and MasterCard most widely accepted.

Time

Greenwich Mean Time/UTC UK, Ireland, Portugal

Central European Time (GMT/UTC plus one hour) Austria, Belgium, France, Germany, Italy, Luxembourg, the Netherlands, Spain, Switzerland

Eastern European Time (GMT/UTC plus two hours) Greece

When to Go

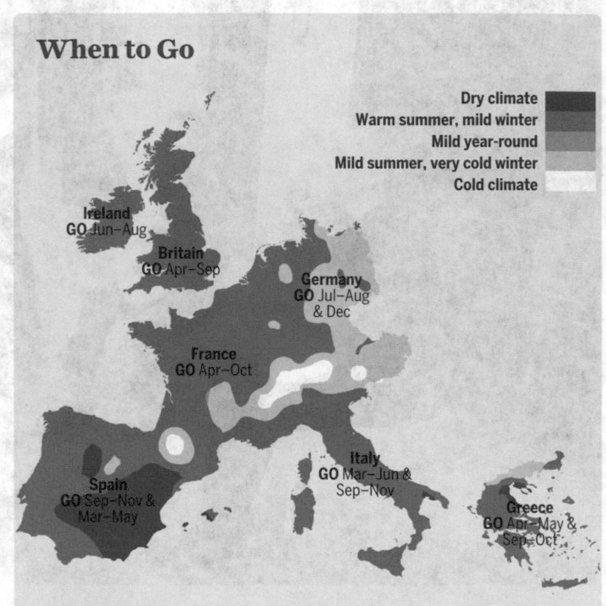

High Season
(Jun–Aug)

➡ Visitors arrive and Europeans hit the road; prices peak.

➡ Beautiful weather means that everybody is outside at cafes.

➡ Businesses in major cities often have seasonal closures around July/August.

Shoulder
(Apr, May, Sep & Oct)

➡ Moderate weather with frequent bright, clear days.

➡ Almost everything is open.

➡ Considered high season in some places such as Italy's big art cites (Rome, Florence and Venice).

Low Season
(Nov–Mar)

➡ Apart from ski resorts and Christmas markets, much is closed in regional areas.

➡ Perfect for enjoying major cities where indoor attractions and venues stay open.

➡ Prices often plummet.

Useful Websites

Lonely Planet (www.lonelyplanet.com/europe) Destination info, hotel reviews, traveller forums and more.

The Man in Seat 61 (www.seat61.com) Comprehensive information about travelling Europe by train.

Ferrylines (www.ferrylines.com) Excellent portal for researching ferry routes and operators throughout Europe.

Michelin (www.viamichelin.com) Calculates the best driving routes and estimates toll and fuel costs.

Europa (www.europa.eu) Official website of the EU.

BBC News (www.bbc.co.uk/news) Find out what's happening before you arrive.

Important Numbers

EU-wide general emergency	☎112
UK general emergency	☎999

Tipping

Tipping varies between Western European countries, but generally is not expected. Ask locally for guidance.

Taxis Optional. Most people round up the fare.

Hotels Tip porters modestly at high-end hotels.

Restaurants Service charges are typically included in restaurant bills, though many people add 5% to 10% of the bill if pleased with the waitstaff.

Bars Optional. If drinks are brought to your table, tip as you would in a restaurant.

Daily Costs

Budget: Less than €100

- Dorm bed: €20–50
- Double room in budget property per person: €40–65
- Restaurant mains under €12
- Local bus/train tickets: €5–10

Midrange: €100–250

- Double room in midrange hotel per person: €65–125
- Restaurant mains €12–25
- Museum admission: free–€15
- Short taxi trip: €10–20

Top End: More than €250

- High-end hotel per person: from €125
- Destination restaurant three-course meal with wine per person: from €65
- Prime tickets to a performance in a grand opera house per person: from €60

What to Take

Phrasebook for rewarding experiences interacting with locals

Earplugs to sleep peacefully in the heart of boisterous cities

Travel plug (adaptor)

Pocket knife with corkscrew as corked wine bottles are the norm; screw caps are rare (just remember to pack it in your checked-in luggage)

Arriving in Western Europe

Schiphol Airport (p495; Amsterdam) Trains (20 minutes) to the centre.

Heathrow Airport (p132; London) Trains (15 minutes) and tube (one hour) to the centre.

Aéroport de Charles de Gaulle (p198; Paris) Many buses (one hour) and trains (50 minutes) to the centre.

Frankfurt Airport (p304; Frankfurt) Trains (15 minutes) to the centre.

Leonardo da Vinci Airport (p426; Rome) Buses (one hour) and trains (30 minutes) to the centre.

Getting Around

Air Cheap airfares make it easy to fly from one end of the continent to the other.

Bicycle From coasting along the flat Netherlands landscape alongside canals to tackling mountainous trails in Italy, Western Europe is ideal for cycling. Bike-rental outlets abound.

Boat Relax at sea on board ferries between Ireland and Britain, France and Spain; Northern Ireland and Britain; England and the continent; France and Italy; Spain and Italy; and Italy and Greece.

Car In the UK and Ireland, drive on the left; in continental Europe, drive on the right. Car hire is readily available throughout Western Europe. Non-EU citizens might consider leasing a vehicle, which can work out cheaper.

Train Trains go almost everywhere; they're often fast and usually frequent.

For much more on **getting around**, see p649

Month by Month

TOP EVENTS

Carnevale, Venice, February

Edinburgh International Festival, August

Notting Hill Carnival, London, August

Oktoberfest, Munich, September

Christmas Markets, December

January

Chilly and in some places snowy, the first month of the year isn't Western Europe's most festive. But museum queues are non-existent, cosy cafes have crackling fireplaces and it's a great time to ski.

Hogmanay

An enormous, raucous Edinburgh street party, Hogmanay sees in the new year in Scotland. It's replicated Europe-wide as main squares resonate with champagne corks and fireworks.

Vienna Ball Season

If you've dreamed of waltzing at Vienna's grand balls, you won't want to miss the Austrian capital's ball season, when 300 or so balls are held in January and February. The most famous is the lavish Opernball (Opera Ball). (p48)

February

Carnival in all its manic glory sweeps through Catholic regions of continental Europe – cold temperatures are forgotten amid masquerades, street festivals and general bacchanalia. Couples descend on romantic destinations such as Paris for Valentine's Day.

Carnaval

Pre-Lent is celebrated with greater vigour in Maastricht than anywhere else in northern Europe. While the rest of the Netherlands hopes the canals will freeze for ice-skating, this Dutch corner cuts loose with a celebration that would have done its former Roman residents proud. (p506)

Carnevale

In the pre-Lent period before Ash Wednesday (2 March 2022; 22 February 2023), Venice goes mad for masks: costume balls, many with traditions centuries old, enliven the social calendar like no other event. Even those without a coveted invite are swept up in the pageantry. (p445)

Karneval

Germany doesn't leave the pre-Lent season solely to its neighbours. Karneval (Fasching) is celebrated with abandon in the traditional Catholic regions of the country including Cologne, much of Bavaria, along the Rhine and deep in the Black Forest.

March

Leaves start greening city avenues and festivities begin to flourish.

St Patrick's Day

Parades and celebrations are held on 17 March in Irish towns big and small to honour St Patrick. While elsewhere the day is a commercialised romp of green beer, in his home country it's a time to celebrate with friends and family.

April

Spring arrives with a burst of colour, from the glorious bulb fields

of the Netherlands to the blossoming orchards of Spain. On the southernmost beaches it's time to shake the sand out of the umbrellas.

Feria de Abril

The southern Spanish city of Seville's beautiful old squares come alive during this week-long party held in late April to counterbalance the religious peak of Easter. (p593)

Greek Easter

The most important festival in the Greek Orthodox calendar. The emphasis is on the Resurrection so it's a celebratory event – the most significant part is midnight on Easter Saturday (23 April 2022; 15 April 2023) when fireworks explode. The night before, candlelit processions hit the streets.

Koningsdag (Kings's Day)

On 27 April (26 April if the 27th is a Sunday) the Netherlands celebrates Koningsdag (King's Day), the birthday of King Willem-Alexander. There are events nationwide but especially in Amsterdam, where – uproarious partying, music and outrageous orange get-ups aside – there's a giant flea market. (p490)

Semana Santa

Procession of penitents and holy icons take place in Spain, notably in Seville, during Easter week (from 10 April 2022; 2 April 2023). Throughout the week thousands of members of religious brotherhoods parade in traditional garb. (p593)

Settimana Santa

Italy celebrates Holy Week with processions and passion plays. By Holy Thursday (14 April 2022; 6 April 2023), Rome is thronged with hundreds of thousands of faithful flocking to the Vatican and St Peter's Basilica. (p410)

Mostra delle Azalee

From mid-April to early May in Rome, the Spanish Steps are decorated with hundreds of vases of blooming, brightly coloured azaleas.

May

Outdoor activities and cafe terraces come into their own. The weather is especially pleasant in the south throughout the Mediterranean regions. Yachts ply the harbours while beautiful people take to the sunloungers.

Brussels Jazz Weekend

Three fabulous evenings of free, nonstop jazz, blues and zydeco concerts take place on the last weekend of the month, on stages and in pubs all over Brussels (www.brujazzwe.be).

Cannes Film Festival

Celebrities, would-be celebrities and plenty of starstruck spectators hit the French Riviera's glitziest seafront, La Croisette, during Cannes' famous film festival, held over two weeks in May. (p243)

Queima das Fitas

Fado fills the air in the Portuguese town of Coimbra, whose annual highlight is this boozy festival of traditional music and revelry during the first week in May, when students celebrate the end of the academic year. (p530)

Karneval der Kulturen

This joyous street carnival celebrates Berlin's multicultural tapestry with parties, food and a fun parade of flamboyantly costumed dancers, DJs, artists and musicians over four days in mid-May.

June

The huge summer travel season hasn't started yet, but the sun has burst through the clouds, the weather is gorgeous, and long daylight hours peak during the summer solstice (between 20 and 22 June).

LGBTIQ+ Pride

European LGBTIQ+ Pride celebrations take place on a summer weekend usually in late June but at times as late as August. Amsterdam hosts the world's only waterborne pride parade.

Festa de Santo António

The lively Festa de Santo António (Festival of Saint Anthony), in mid-June, is celebrated with fervour in Lisbon's Alfama and Madragoa districts, with feasting, drinking and dancing in some 50 *arraiais* (street parties).

Festa de São João

Live music on Porto's plazas and merrymaking take place in Portugal's second city. Squeaky plastic hammers (available for sale everywhere) come out for the custom of whacking one another. Everyone is fair game – don't expect mercy. (p532)

Glastonbury Festival

One of England's favourite outdoor events is Glastonbury's long, muddy weekend of music, theatre and New Age shenanigans. Tickets usually go on sale in autumn, and always sell out within minutes. (p143)

Luxembourg National Day

Luxembourg National Day is the Grand Duchy's biggest event – a celebration of the birth of the Grand Duke (though it has never fallen on a Grand Ducal birthday). Festivities begin the day before and include a torchlight procession and fireworks.

July

Visitors have arrived from around the world, and outdoor cafes, beer gardens and beach clubs are hopping. Expect beautiful – even scorching – weather anywhere you go.

Bastille Day

Fireworks and military processions mark France's national day, 14 July. It's celebrated in every French town and city, with the biggest festivities in Paris, where the storming of the Bastille prison kick-started the French Revolution. (p178)

Gentse Feesten

The charming Belgian city of Ghent is transformed into a 10-day party of music and theatre; a highlight is a vast techno celebration. (p89)

Il Palio

Siena's great annual event is the Palio (2 July and 16 August), a pageant culminating in a bareback horse race round Il Campo. The city is divided into 17 *contrade* (districts), of which 10 compete for the *palio* (silk banner). (p461)

Montreux Jazz Festival

It's not just jazz: big-name rock acts also hit the shores of Lake Geneva during this two-week festival. The cheaper music festival Paleo (http://yeah.paleo.ch) takes place in Nyon, between Geneva and Lausanne, in the second half of July. (p620)

Sanfermines (aka 'Running of the Bulls')

From 6 to 14 July, Pamplona, Spain, hosts the famous Sanfermines festival (aka Encierro or 'Running of the Bulls'). Serious injuries are common, and the bulls are destined to die in the bullring; animal welfare groups condemn the spectacle as a cruel tradition.Two days earlier is the anti-bullfighting event, the Running of the Nudes. (p583)

Festival d'Avignon

In France's lavender-scented Provence region, hundreds of artists take to the stage and streets of Avignon during July's world-famous Festival d'Avignon. The fringe Festival Off (www.avignonleoff.com) runs in parallel. (p237)

August

Everybody's on the move as major European city businesses shut down and residents head off to enjoy the traditional month of holiday. If it's near the beach, from Germany's Baltic to Spain's Balearic, it's mobbed.

Edinburgh International Festival

Three weeks of innovative drama, comedy, dance, music and more, held in Edinburgh. Two weeks overlap with the celebrated 3½-week Fringe Festival (www.edfringe.com), which draws innovative acts from around the globe. Catch cutting-edge comedy, drama and productions that defy description. (p157)

Notting Hill Carnival

For three days during the last weekend of August, London's Notting Hill echoes to the beats of calypso, ska, reggae and soca at London's most vibrant outdoor carnival, where the local Caribbean community shows the city how to party.

Salzburg Festival

Austria's renowned Salzburger Festspiele attracts

international stars in July and August when it stages some 200 productions spanning theatre, classical music and opera. (p60)

Street Parade

In Switzerland, it's Zürich's turn to let its hair down with an enormous techno parade. All thoughts of high finance are forgotten as bankers and everybody else parties to deep-bass thump, thump, thump.

September

It's cooling off in every sense, from the northern countries to the romance started on an Ibiza dance floor. But it's often the best time to visit, with sparkling days and reduced crowds.

Festes de la Mercè

Barcelona knows how to party until dawn and it outdoes itself around 24 September for the Festes de la Mercè: four days of concerts, dancing, *castellers* (human-castle builders), fireworks and *correfocs* – a parade of firework-spitting dragons and devils. (p570)

Oktoberfest

Germany's legendary beer-swilling party originates from the marriage celebrations of Crown Prince Ludwig in 1810. Munich's Oktoberfest runs for the 15 days before the first Sunday in October. Millions descend for whopping 1L steins of beer and carousing that has no equal. (p284)

Venice International Film Festival

The Mostra del Cinema di Venezia is Italy's top film festival and one of the world's top indie film fests. Judging is seen as an indication of what to look for at the next year's Oscars. (p445)

Galway International Oyster & Seafood Festival

Oyster-opening championships are just the start of this spirited seafood festival in Ireland's colourful west-coast city of Galway, which also has tastings, talks, cooking demonstrations and plenty of live music and merrymaking. (p391)

October

October heralds an autumnal kaleidoscope, along with bright, crisp days, cool, clear nights and excellent cultural offerings, with prices and visitor numbers way down.

Belfast International Arts Festival

Belfast hosts one of the UK's biggest arts festivals – and the city's largest cultural event – over three weeks in late October/early November. (p393)

November

Leaves have fallen and snow is about to in much of Europe. Even in the temperate zones around the Mediterranean it can get chilly, rainy and blustery. Most seasonal attractions have closed for the year.

December

Twinkling lights, brightly decorated Christmas trees and shop windows, and outdoor ice-skating rinks make December an enchanting month to be in Western Europe, where every region has its own traditions.

Christmas Markets

Christmas markets are held across many European counties, particularly Germany and Austria. Germany's best is Nuremberg's Christkindlesmarkt. Warm your hands through your mittens holding a hot mug of mulled wine and find that special present. (p293)

Natale

Italian churches set up an intricate crib or *presepe* (nativity scene) in the lead-up to celebrating Christmas. Some are quite famous, most are works of art and many date back hundreds of years and are venerated for their spiritual ties.

Itineraries

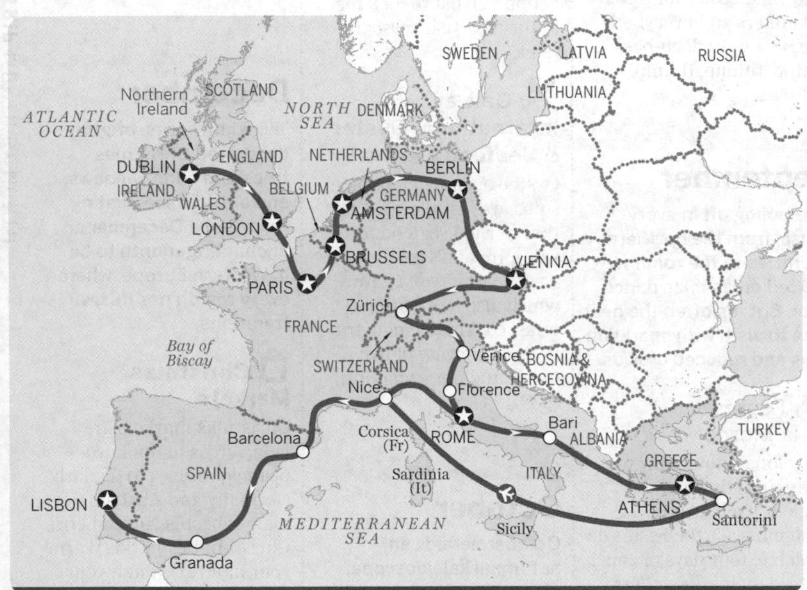

Ultimate Europe

Have limited time but want to see a bit of everything? Hit the highlights on this trip.

Start in **Dublin**, soaking up its vibrant pubs and rich literary history. From Ireland, fly to **London** for great theatre. Then catch the Eurostar train through the English Channel tunnel to beautiful **Paris**.

Travel north to **Brussels** for famed beer and chocolate, then further north to free-spirited **Amsterdam**, making time to cruise its canals. Go east, stopping for a cruise on the Rhine, and explore the legendary nightlife in **Berlin**. Next, visit **Vienna** for architectural and classical-music riches. Zip west to **Zürich** and the Swiss Alps for awe-inspiring ski slopes and vistas.

Head to canal-laced **Venice**, art-filled **Florence** and historic **Rome**. Train it to **Bari**, take a ferry to Patras, and head east to **Athens**, then explore island beaches, starting with the stunning **Santorini**. Connect by air or by ferry and train to the French Riviera (aka the Côte d'Azur) to check out quintessential Mediterranean destinations such as **Nice**. Continue to **Barcelona**, then the Moorish towns of southern Spain like **Granada**. End your trip in the hilly quarters of **Lisbon**, toasting your grand journey with Portugal's port wine.

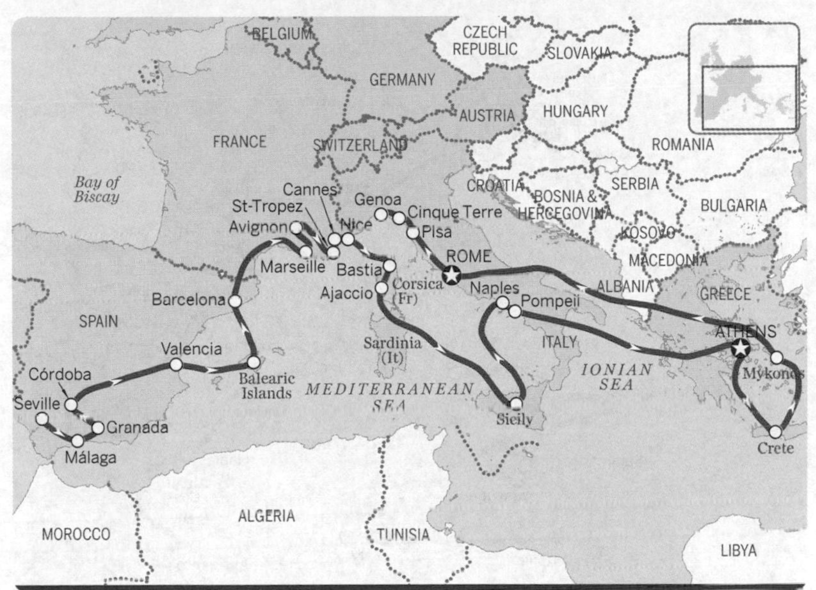

Mediterranean Europe

Beautiful weather and breathtaking scenery are the draws of this comprehensive tour that takes in famous towns and cities from antiquity to the present.

Start in southern Spain in orange-blossom-scented **Seville** and soak up the architecture, sunshine and party atmosphere. Make your way up the eastern coast past the Moorish town of **Málaga** and on to **Granada** and **Córdoba**. Then it's back to the coast at **Valencia**, home of Spain's famous rice-dish paella, for a ferry hop to the parties and beaches of the **Balearic Islands**.

Back on the mainland, **Barcelona** brims with the architecture of Gaudí. From here, head into France's fabled Provence region, where in **Marseille** you can see the fortress that was inspiration for the novel *The Count of Monte Cristo*. Then leave the sea for Provence's lush hills and lavender-scented towns around the rampart-hooped city of **Avignon**, and on to the **French Riviera** and its playground for the rich and famous, **St-Tropez**. The charming seaside city **Nice** is a perfect jumping-off point for other nearby coastal hot spots such as glamorous **Cannes**.

Cruise by ferry to Corsica and experience the traditional lifestyle of quiet fishing villages. Hit the bustling old port of **Bastia**, Napoléon Bonaparte's home town **Ajaccio**, then the glittering harbour of Bonifacio to hop on a ferry south to Sardinia and on to **Sicily** to visit its colossal temples and famous volcano, Mt Etna.

Catch a ferry to **Naples**, on the Italian mainland, and take a trip to **Pompeii**. Move east to Brindisi for a ferry to Greece that passes rocky coasts seen by mariners for millennia. Head to **Athens** to wonder at the Greek capital's ancient treasures before boarding a plane or ferry to magical islands such as **Crete** and **Mykonos**. Return to Italy, taking time to wander amid the ruins and piazzas of **Rome**. Continue north through Tuscany, stopping at **Pisa** to see its famous 'leaning tower'. Finish up along the Ligurian coast, travelling via the brightly coloured coastal villages making up the **Cinque Terre**, strung between plunging cliffs and vine-covered hills, to the port city of **Genoa**.

Backroads of Europe

The far west of Ireland is rugged and uncrowded; start in bohemian **Galway**, with its colourful shopfronts and sensational music-filled pubs. Then travel to Northern Ireland – **Belfast** in particular. Catch a ferry to reach the dynamic Scottish city of **Glasgow** and check out the art nouveau architecture, along with a trove of museums. Swing south to the atmospheric walled English city of **York**. Hop across to the Netherlands, where buzzing **Rotterdam** is a veritable open-air gallery of modern and cutting-edge architecture.

Travel to the dynamic eastern German cities of **Leipzig** and **Dresden**, whose historic core has been restored to its 18th-century glory. Turn south via the stunning Bavarian student hub of **Regensburg**, to the temperate Swiss town of **Lugano**. Cross into Italy and stop at the cultured city of **Turin**, followed by beautiful Umbria spots such as **Orvieto**, with its hilltop-perched medieval centre. In Italy's south, explore frenetic **Naples** and the winding **Amalfi Coast**. Scoot over to the sun-baked Mediterranean island of **Sicily**. Marvel at the Grecian Valley of the Temples in **Agrigento**, which rivals anything in Greece itself.

France & Iberia

Start in **Paris**, discovering the magnificent monuments and hidden backstreet bistros of the City of Light. Visit the chateaux of the **Loire Valley**, then take the fast TGV train to Brittany. Walk the 17th-century ramparts encircling **St-Malo** and sample authentic Breton cider. Track south along the Atlantic coast, where red wine reaches its pinnacle around **Bordeaux**. Cross the border to the Basque city of **Bilbao**, best known for the magnificent Guggenheim Museum, before continuing to the pilgrimage shrine of **Santiago de Compostela**.

Spain's art-rich capital, **Madrid**, is prime for night owls: an evening of tapas and drinks in tiny bars can postpone dinner until midnight. Spend a day exploring the Roman aqueduct and storybook castle in beautiful **Segovia**. And don't skip the sandstone splendour of lively **Salamanca**. Plan on using a car to explore the many hill towns of Andalucía, where narrow, winding roads traverse sunburnt landscapes and olive orchards. Finally, go west via **Seville** to Portugal's pretty Algarve region, finishing in **Faro** to explore the Parque Natural da Ria Formosa's lagoons, salt pans and sandy islands.

Top: Acueducto, Segovia (p559), Spain

Bottom: Ponte dell'Accademia, Venice (p440), Italy

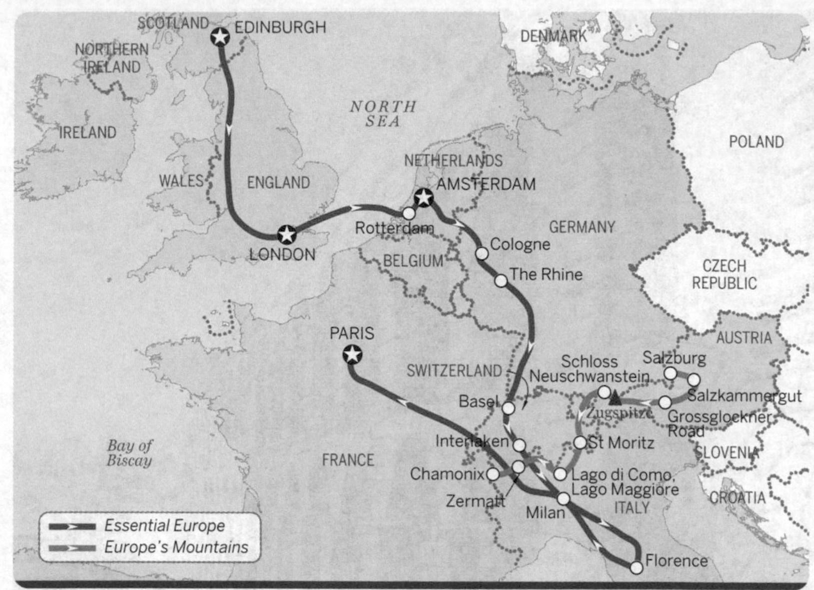

Europe's Mountains

From the storybook Austrian city of **Salzburg**, head east to the mountain-ringed, jewel-like lakes of the **Salzkammergut** region. To the south is the heart-in-mouth **Grossglockner Road**, with 36 switchbacks over 48km as it traverses Austria's highest peak, the 3798m-high Grossglockner. Northwest, on the Austrian–German border, lies the 2962m-high Zugspitze, Germany's tallest mountain, adjacent to swish ski resort Garmisch-Partenkirchen in the Bavarian Alps. From here it's a short jaunt to Füssen, crowned by King Ludwig II's fairy-tale castle **Schloss Neuschwanstein**.

Swing southwest to one of Switzerland's ritziest ski resorts, **St Moritz**, where you can ride the Bernina Express mountain railway. Continue southwest into Italy to the sparkling lakes of **Lago di Como** and **Lago Maggiore** beneath the towering peaks. Zigzag northwest back into Switzerland to **Zermatt**, with dress-circle views of the 4478m-high Matterhorn. Then make your way southwest to mighty Mont Blanc – Western Europe's highest peak at 4809m – and its feted ski resort **Chamonix** across the border in France, by the Mer de Glace glacier.

Essential Europe

Watching Europe from the window of a train or gazing at the sea rolling past the handrail of a ferry is the way generations of travellers have explored the continent. Hit the region's most unmissable highlights on this two-week itinerary.

Start in the engaging Scottish capital **Edinburgh**, where highlights include its dramatic castle, then take the train to pulsating **London** and on to Harwich for a ferry crossing to Hoek van Holland. From here, trains connect to the contemporary Dutch city of **Rotterdam** and the gabled Golden Age canal-scapes of **Amsterdam**. Take a fast train to cathedral-crowned **Cologne** and then relax on a river cruise down the vineyard-ribboned **Rhine**. Alight at Mainz and connect by train through **Basel** to picturesque **Interlaken** for the slow-moving local trains and trams that wend through the majestic Alps. Then take a train past soaring mountain scenery to stylish **Milan**. From Milan, fast trains zip to Tuscany's resplendent capital, **Florence**, a veritable Renaissance time capsule. Connect in Milan to snuggle up on the night train to **Paris**, feeling the romance in the rhythm of the rails.

On the Road

Ireland
p372

Britain
p106

The Netherlands
p484

Germany
p251

Belgium & Luxembourg
p70

France
p174

Switzerland
p612

Austria
p38

Italy
p402

Portugal
p510

Spain
p542

Greece
p326

Austria

POP 8.8 MILLION

Includes ➡

Best Places to Eat

- Vollpension (p49)
- Der Steirer (p56)
- Esszimmer (p61)
- Restaurant zum Salzbaron (p63)
- Die Wilderin (p65)

Best Places to Stay

- Hotel am Domplatz (p54)
- Haus Ballwein (p60)
- Magdas (p48)
- Hotel Weisses Kreuz (p65)
- Hotel Wiesler (p56)

Why Go?

For such a small country, Austria is ridiculously large on inspiration. This is the land where Mozart was born, Strauss taught the world to waltz and Julie Andrews grabbed the spotlight with her twirling entrance in *The Sound of Music*. It's where the Habsburgs ruled over their spectacular, sprawling 600-year empire.

These past glories still shine in the resplendent baroque palaces and chandelier-lit coffee houses of Vienna, Innsbruck and Salzburg, but beyond its storybook cities, Austria's allure is one of natural beauty and outdoor adventure. Whether you're schussing down the legendary slopes of Kitzbühel, climbing high in the Alps of Tyrol or cycling the banks of the mighty Danube, you'll find the kind of landscapes to which no well-orchestrated symphony or singing nun could ever quite do justice.

When to Go

Vienna

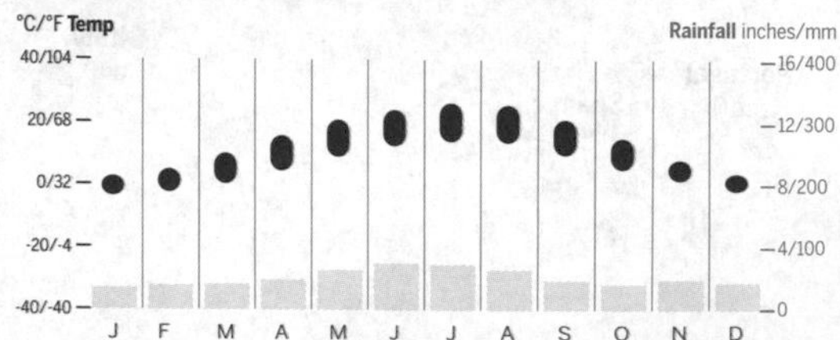

Jul–Aug Alpine hiking in Tyrol, lake swimming in Salzkammergut and lots of summer festivals.

Sep–Oct New wine in vineyards near Vienna, golden forest strolls and few crowds.

Dec–Jan Christmas markets, skiing in the Alps and Vienna waltzing into the New Year.

Entering the Country

Austria is well connected to the rest of the world. Vienna and several regional capitals are served by no-frills airlines (plus regular airline services). Europe's extensive bus and train networks criss-cross the country and there are major highways from Germany and Italy. It's also possible to enter Austria by boat from Hungary, Slovakia and Germany. Trains from Vienna run to many Eastern European destinations, including Bratislava, Budapest, Prague and Warsaw; there are also connections south to Italy via Klagenfurt and north to Berlin. Salzburg is within sight of the Bavarian border, with many Munich-bound trains. Innsbruck is on the main rail line from Vienna to Switzerland, and two routes also lead to Munich. Look out for the fast, comfortable RailJet services to Germany and Switzerland.

ITINERARIES

Two Days

Make the most of Vienna (p42), spending your first day visiting the Habsburg palaces and Stephansdom before cosying up in a *Kaffeehäus* (coffee house). At night, check out the pumping bar scene.

One Week

Plan for two long and lovely days in Vienna, plus another day exploring the Wachau (Danube Valley; p53) wine region, a day each in Salzburg (p57) and Innsbruck (p64), a day in Kitzbühel (p66) hiking or skiing, and then a final day exploring the Salzkammergut (p62) lakes.

Essential Food & Drink

Make it meaty Go for a classic Wiener schnitzel, *Tafelspitz* (boiled beef with horseradish sauce) or *Schweinebraten* (pork roast). The humble *Wurst* (sausage) comes in various guises.

On the side Lashings of potatoes, either fried *(Pommes)*, roasted *(Bratkartoffeln)*, in a salad *(Erdapfelsalat)* or boiled in their skins *(Quellmänner)*; or try *Knödel* (dumplings) and *Nudeln* (flat egg noodles).

Kaffee und Kuchen Coffee and cake is Austria's sweetest tradition. Must-tries: flaky apple strudel, rich, chocolatey *Sacher Torte* and *Kaiserschmarrn* (sweet 'scrambled' pancakes with raisins).

Wine at the source Jovial locals gather in rustic *Heurigen* (wine taverns) in the wine-producing east, identified by an evergreen branch above the door. Sip crisp Grüner Veltliner whites and spicy Blaufränkisch wines.

Cheese fest Dig into gooey *Käsnudeln* (cheese noodles) in Carinthia, *Kaspressknodel* (fried cheese dumplings) in Tyrol and *Käsekrainer* (cheesy sausages) in Vienna. The hilly Bregenzerwald is studded with dairies.

AT A GLANCE

Area 83,871 sq km

Capital Vienna

Country Code ☎43

Currency euro (€)

Emergency ☎112

Language German

Time Central European Time (GMT/UTC plus one hour)

Visas Schengen rules apply

Sleeping Price Ranges

The following price ranges refer to a double room with a bathroom for two people, including breakfast.

€ less than €80

€€ €80–200

€€€ more than €200

Eating Price Ranges

The following price ranges refer to the cost of a two-course meal, excluding drinks.

€ less than €15

€€ €15–30

€€€ more than €30

Resources

Embassy of Austria (www.austria.org)

Lonely Planet (www.lonelyplanet.com/austria)

Österreich Werbung (www.austria.info)

Tiscover (www.tiscover.com)

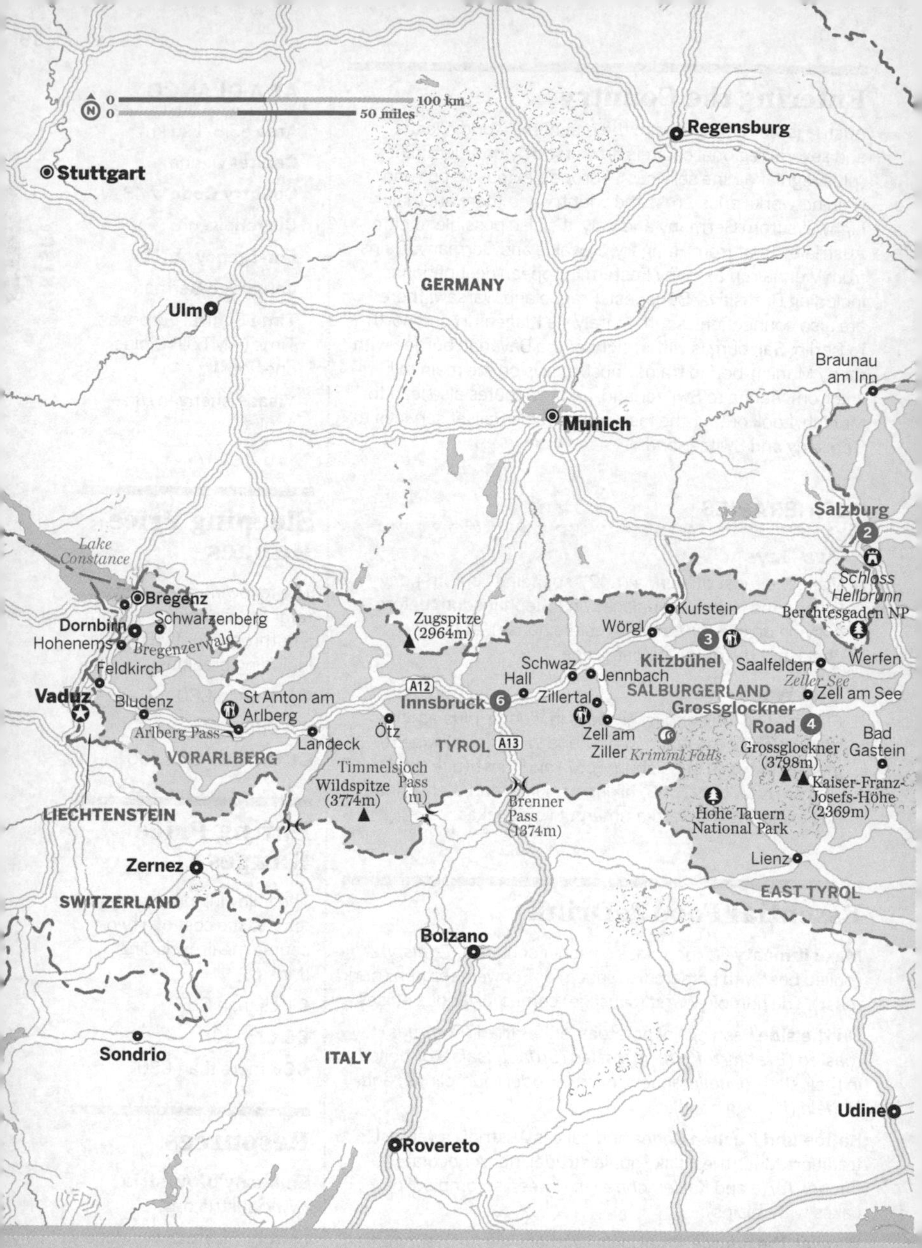

Austria Highlights

1 **Vienna** (p42) Discovering opulent Habsburg palaces, coffee houses and cutting-edge galleries.

2 **Salzburg** (p57) Surveying the baroque cityscape from the giddy heights of 900-year-old Festung Hohensalzburg.

3 **Kitzbühel** (p66) Sending your spirits soaring from peak to peak hiking and skiing.

4 **Grossglockner Road** (p67) Buckling up for a rollercoaster ride of Alps and glaciers on one of Austria's greatest drives.

5 Salzkammergut (p62) Diving into the crystal-clear lakes of Austria's summer playground.

6 Innsbruck (p64) Whizzing up to the Tyrolean Alps in Zaha Hadid's space-age funicular.

7 Danube Valley (p53) Exploring the romantic Wachau and technology trailblazer Linz.

VIENNA

☎01 / POP 1.9 MILLION

Few cities in the world waltz so effortlessly between the present and the past like Vienna. Its splendid historical face is easily recognised: grand imperial palaces and bombastic baroque interiors, revered opera houses and magnificent squares. But Vienna is also one of Europe's most dynamic urban spaces. A stone's throw from Hofburg (the Imperial Palace), the MuseumsQuartier houses provocative and high-profile contemporary art behind a striking basalt facade. In the Innere Stadt (Inner City), up-to-the-minute design stores sidle up to old-world confectioners, and Austro-Asian fusion restaurants stand alongside traditional *Beisl* (small taverns).

Sights

Vienna's magnificent series of boulevards, the Ringstrasse, encircles the Innere Stadt, with many of the city's most famous sights situated on or within it, including the monumental Hofburg palace complex. Just outside the Ringstrasse are exceptional museums including the Kunsthistorisches Museum and the ensemble making up the MuseumsQuartier, while attractions further afield include the sumptuous palaces Schloss Schönbrunn and Schloss Belvedere.

★Hofburg — PALACE

(Imperial Palace; www.hofburg-wien.at; 01, Michaelerkuppel; adult/child €13.90/8.20; 9am-5.30pm; 1A, 2A Michaelerplatz, D, 1, 2, 46, 49, 71 Burgring, U Herrengasse) Nothing symbolises Austria's resplendent cultural heritage more than its Hofburg, home base of the Habsburgs from 1273 to 1918. The oldest section is the 13th-century **Schweizerhof** (Swiss Courtyard), named after the Swiss guards who used to protect its precincts. The Renaissance **Swiss gate** dates from 1553. The courtyard adjoins a larger courtyard, **In der Burg**, with a monument to Emperor Franz II adorning its centre. The palace now houses the Austrian president's offices and a raft of museums.

★Kaiserappartements — PALACE

(Imperial Apartments; ☎01-533 75 70; www.hofburg-wien.at; 01, Michaelerplatz; adult/child €13.90/8.20, incl guided tour €16.90/9.70; 9am-6pm Jul & Aug, to 5.30pm Sep-Jun; U Herrengasse) The Kaiserappartements, once the official living quarters of Franz Josef I and Empress Elisabeth, are dazzling in their chandelier-lit opulence. The highlight is the **Sisi Museum**, devoted to Austria's most beloved empress, which has a strong focus on the clothing and jewellery of Austria's monarch. Multilingual audio guides are included in the admission price. Guided tours take in the Kaiserappartements, the Sisi Museum and the **Silberkammer** (Silver Depot), whose largest silver service caters for 140 dinner guests.

★Kaiserliche Schatzkammer — MUSEUM

(Imperial Treasury; www.kaiserliche-schatzkammer.at; 01, Schweizerhof; adult/child €12/free; 9am-5.30pm Wed-Mon; U Herrengasse) The Hofburg's Kaiserliche Schatzkammer contains secular and ecclesiastical treasures (including devotional images and altars, particularly from the baroque era) of priceless value and splendour – the sheer wealth of this collection of crown jewels is staggering. As you walk through the rooms you'll see magnificent treasures such as a golden rose, diamond-studded Turkish sabres, a 2680-carat Colombian emerald and, the highlight of the treasury, the imperial crown.

★Stephansdom — CATHEDRAL

(St Stephen's Cathedral; www.stephanskirche.at; 01, Stephansplatz; tours adult/child €6/2.50; 6am-10pm Mon-Sat, 7am-10pm Sun, tours 10.30am Mon-Sat; U Stephansplatz) Vienna's Gothic masterpiece Stephansdom – or Steffl (Little Stephan), as it's ironically nicknamed – is Vienna's pride and joy. A church has stood here since the 12th century, and reminders of this are the Romanesque **Riesentor** (Giant Gate) and **Heidentürme** (Towers of the Heathens). From the exterior, the first thing that will strike you is the glorious tiled roof, with its dazzling row of chevrons and Austrian eagle. Inside, the magnificent Gothic stone pulpit presides over the main nave, fashioned in 1515 by Anton Pilgrim.

★Kunsthistorisches Museum Vienna — MUSEUM

(KHM, Museum of Art History; www.khm.at; 01, Maria-Theresien-Platz; adult/child incl Neue Burg museums €15/free; 10am-6pm Fri-Wed, to 9pm Thu; U Museumsquartier, Volkstheater) One of the unforgettable experiences of any trip to Vienna is a visit to the Kunsthistorisches Museum Vienna, brimming with works by Europe's finest painters, sculptors and artisans. Occupying a neoclassical building as sumptuous as the art it contains, the museum takes you on a time-travel treasure hunt from Classical Rome to Egypt and the Renaissance. If your time's limited, skip straight to the **Picture**

Gallery, where you'll want to dedicate at least an hour or two to the Old Masters.

★Neue Burg Museums MUSEUM

(☎01-525 240; www.khm.at; 01, Heldenplatz, Hofburg; adult/child €12/free; ⏲10am-6pm Wed-Sun; 🚋D, 1, 2, 71 Burgring, Ⓤ Herrengasse, Museumsquartier) The Neue Burg is home to the three Neue Burg Museums. The **Sammlung Alter Musik Instrumente** (Collection of Ancient Musical Instruments) contains a wonderfully diverse array of instruments. The **Ephesos Museum** features artefacts unearthed during Austrian archaeologists' excavations at Ephesus in Turkey between 1895 and 1906. The **Hofjägd und Rüstkammer** (Arms and Armour) museum contains armour dating mainly from the 15th and 16th centuries. Admission includes the Kunsthistorisches Museum Vienna (p42) and all three Neue Burg museums. Audio guides cost €4.

★Staatsoper NOTABLE BUILDING

(www.wiener-staatsoper.at; 01, Opernring 2; tour adult/child €9/4; Ⓤ Karlsplatz) Few concert halls can hold a candle to the neo-Renaissance Staatsoper, Vienna's foremost opera and ballet venue. Even if you can't snag tickets to see a tenor hitting the high notes, you can get a taste of the architectural brilliance and musical genius that have shaped this cultural bastion by taking a 40-minute guided tour. Tours (in English and German) generally depart on the hour between 10am and 4pm.

★MuseumsQuartier MUSEUM

(Museum Quarter; MQ; www.mqw.at; 07, Museumsplatz; ⏲information & ticket centre 10am-7pm; Ⓤ Museumsquartier, Volkstheater) The MuseumsQuartier is a remarkable ensemble of museums, cafes, restaurants and bars inside former imperial stables designed by Fischer von Erlach. This breeding ground of Viennese cultural life is the perfect place to hang out and watch or meet people on warm evenings. With over 90,000 sq metres of exhibition space – including the Leopold Museum, MUMOK, **Kunsthalle** (Arts Hall; ☎01-521 890; www.kunsthallewien.at; adult/child €8/free; ⏲11am-7pm Tue, Wed & Fri-Sun, to 9pm Thu), **Architekturzentrum** (Vienna Architecture Centre; ☎01-522 31 15; www.azw.at; adult/child €9/2.50; ⏲architecture centre 10am-7pm, library 10am-5.30pm Mon, Wed & Fri, to 7pm Sat & Sun) and **Zoom** (☎01-524 79 08; www.kindermuseum.at; exhibition adult/child €6/free, activities child €5-7, accompanying adult free; ⏲12.45-5pm Tue-Sun Jul & Aug, 8.30am-4pm Tue-Fri, 9.45am-4pm Sat & Sun Sep-Jun, activity times vary; 👪) – the complex is one of the world's most ambitious cultural hubs.

★MUMOK GALLERY

(Museum Moderner Kunst; Museum of Modern Art; www.mumok.at; 07, Museumsplatz 1; adult/child €12/free; ⏲2-7pm Mon, 10am-7pm Tue, Wed & Fri-Sun, 10am-9pm Thu; 🚋49 Volkstheater, Ⓤ Volkstheater, Museumsquartier) The dark basalt edifice and sharp corners of the Museum Moderner Kunst are a complete contrast to the MuseumsQuartier's historical sleeve. Inside, MUMOK contains Vienna's finest collection of 20th-century art, centred on fluxus, nouveau realism, pop art and photo-realism. The best of expressionism, cubism, minimal art and Viennese Actionism is also represented in a collection of 9000 works that are rotated and exhibited by theme – but note that sometimes all this Actionism is packed away to make room for temporary exhibitions.

★Leopold Museum MUSEUM

(www.leopoldmuseum.org; 07, Museumsplatz 1; adult/child €13/8; ⏲10am-6pm Fri-Wed, to 9pm Thu; Ⓤ Volkstheater, Museumsquartier) Part of the MuseumsQuartier, the Leopold Museum is named after ophthalmologist Rudolf Leopold, who, after buying his first Egon Schiele for a song as a young student in 1950, amassed a huge private collection of mainly 19th-century and modernist Austrian artworks. In 1994 he sold the lot – 5266 paintings – to the Austrian government for €160 million (individually, the paintings

SPIN OF THE RING

One of the best deals in Vienna is a self-guided tour on tram 1 or 2 of the monumental **Ringstrasse** boulevard encircling much of the Innere Stadt, which turns 150 in 2015. For the price of a single ticket you'll take in the neo-Gothic **Rathaus** (City Hall; ☎01-502 55; www.wien.gv.at; 01, Rathausplatz 1; ⏲tours 1pm Mon, Wed & Fri Sep-Jun, 1pm Mon-Fri Jul & Aug; 🚋D, 1, 2 Rathaus, Ⓤ Rathaus) FREE, the Greek Revival–style parliament, the 19th-century **Burgtheater** (National Theatre; ☎01-514 44 4440; www.burgtheater.at; 01, Universitätsring 2; seats €10-61, standing room €3.50; ⏲box office 9am-5pm Mon-Fri; 🚋D, 1, 2 Rathaus, Ⓤ Rathaus) and the baroque Karlskirche (p47), among other sights.

Central Vienna

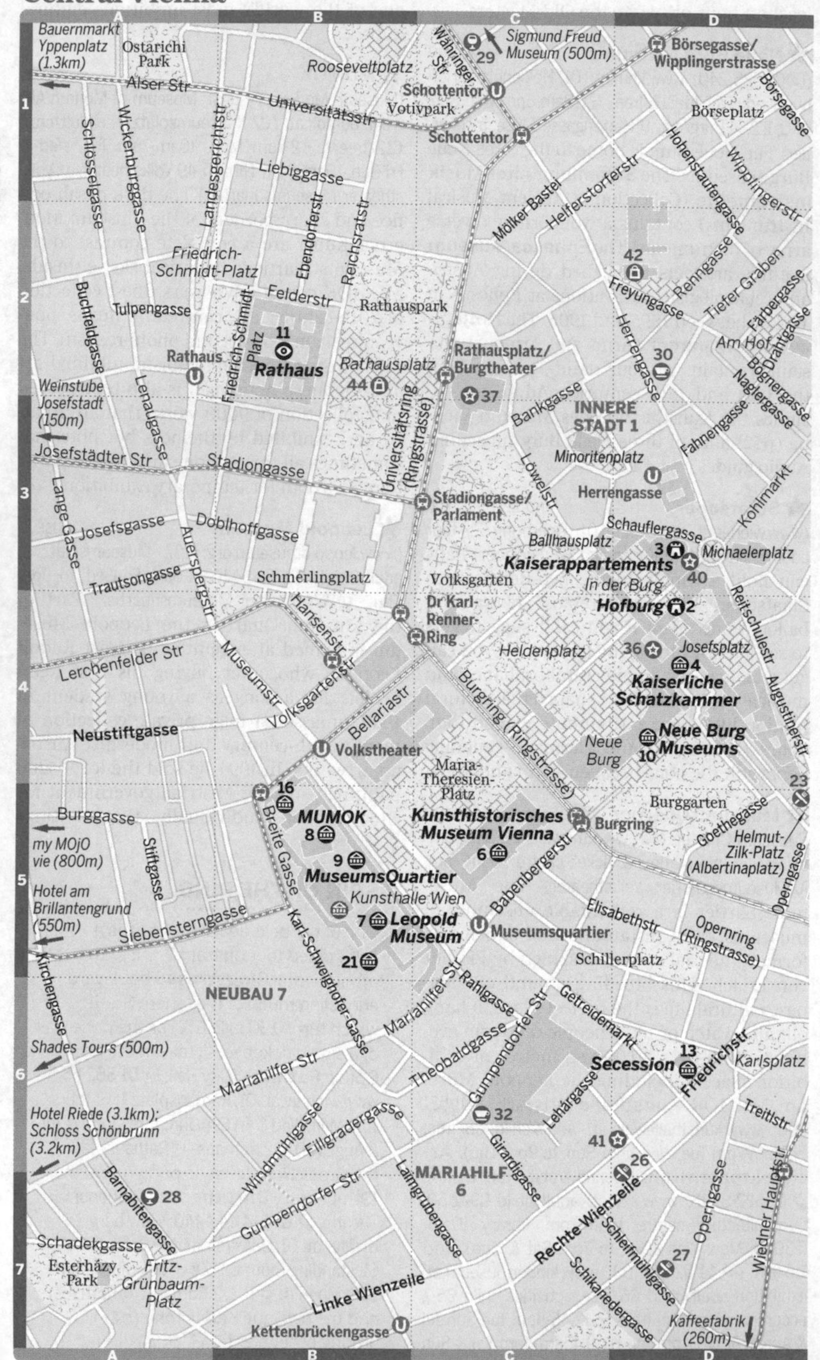

Bauernmarkt Yppenplatz (1.3km)
Ostarichi Park
Alser Str
Universitätsstr
Rooseveltplatz
Währinger Str
29
Sigmund Freud Museum (500m)
Börsegasse/ Wipplingerstrasse
Schottentor
Votivpark
Börseplatz
Börsegasse
Schlösselgasse
Wickenburggasse
Landesgerichtstr
Liebiggasse
Ebendorferstr
Reichsratstr
Mölker Bastei
Helferstorferstr
Hohenstaufengasse
Wipplingerstr
Friedrich-Schmidt-Platz
Felderstr
Rathauspark
42
Freyungasse
Renngasse
Tiefer Graben
Färbergasse
Drahtgasse
Buchfeldgasse
Tulpengasse
Friedrich-Schmidt-Platz
11
Rathaus
Rathausplatz
44
Rathausplatz/ Burgtheater
Herrengasse
30
Am Hof
Bognergasse
Naglergasse
Weinstube Josefstadt (150m)
Lenaugasse
Universitätsring (Ringstrasse)
37
Bankgasse
INNERE STADT 1
Fahnengasse
Josefstädter Str
Stadiongasse
Minoritenplatz
Löwelstr
Stadiongasse/ Parlament
Herrengasse
Kohlmarkt
Lange Gasse
Josefsgasse
Doblhoffgasse
Auerspergstr
Schauflergasse
Ballhausplatz
3
Michaelerplatz
Trautsongasse
Schmerlingplatz
Volksgarten
Kaiserappartements
40
In der Burg
Hofburg
2
Dr Karl-Renner-Ring
Hansenstr
Reitschulestr
Lerchenfelder Str
Museumstr
Heldenplatz
36
Josefsplatz
4
Volksgartenstr
Kaiserliche Schatzkammer
Bellariastr
Burgring (Ringstrasse)
Augustinerstr
Neustiftgasse
Neue Burg
Neue Burg Museums
10
Volkstheater
Maria-Theresien-Platz
23
16
Burggasse
MUMOK
8
Kunsthistorisches Museum Vienna
Burgring
Burggarten
Goethegasse
Helmut-Zilk-Platz (Albertinaplatz)
my MOjO vie (800m)
Breite Gasse
Stiftgasse
9
MuseumsQuartier
6
Babenbergerstr
Operngasse
Hotel am Brillantengrund (550m)
Kunsthalle Wien
7
Leopold Museum
Museumsquartier
Elisabethstr
Opernring (Ringstrasse)
Siebensterngasse
Karl-Schweighofer-Gasse
21
Schillerplatz
Kirchengasse
NEUBAU 7
Mariahilfer Str
Rahlgasse
Getreidemarkt
Gumpendorfer Str
Theobaldgasse
13
Secession
Friedrichstr
Karlsplatz
Shades Tours (500m)
Mariahilfer Str
Lehárgasse
Treitlstr
Hotel Riede (3.1km); Schloss Schönbrunn (3.2km)
32
Fillgradergasse
Windmühlgasse
Girardigasse
41
26
Laimgrubengasse
MARIAHILF 6
Barnabitengasse
28
Gumpendorfer Str
Rechte Wienzeile
Schleifmühlgasse
Operngasse
Wiedner Hauptstr
Schadekgasse
27
Esterházy Park
Fritz-Grünbaum-Platz
Linke Wienzeile
Schikanedergasse
Kettenbrückengasse
Kaffeefabrik (260m)
AUSTRIA

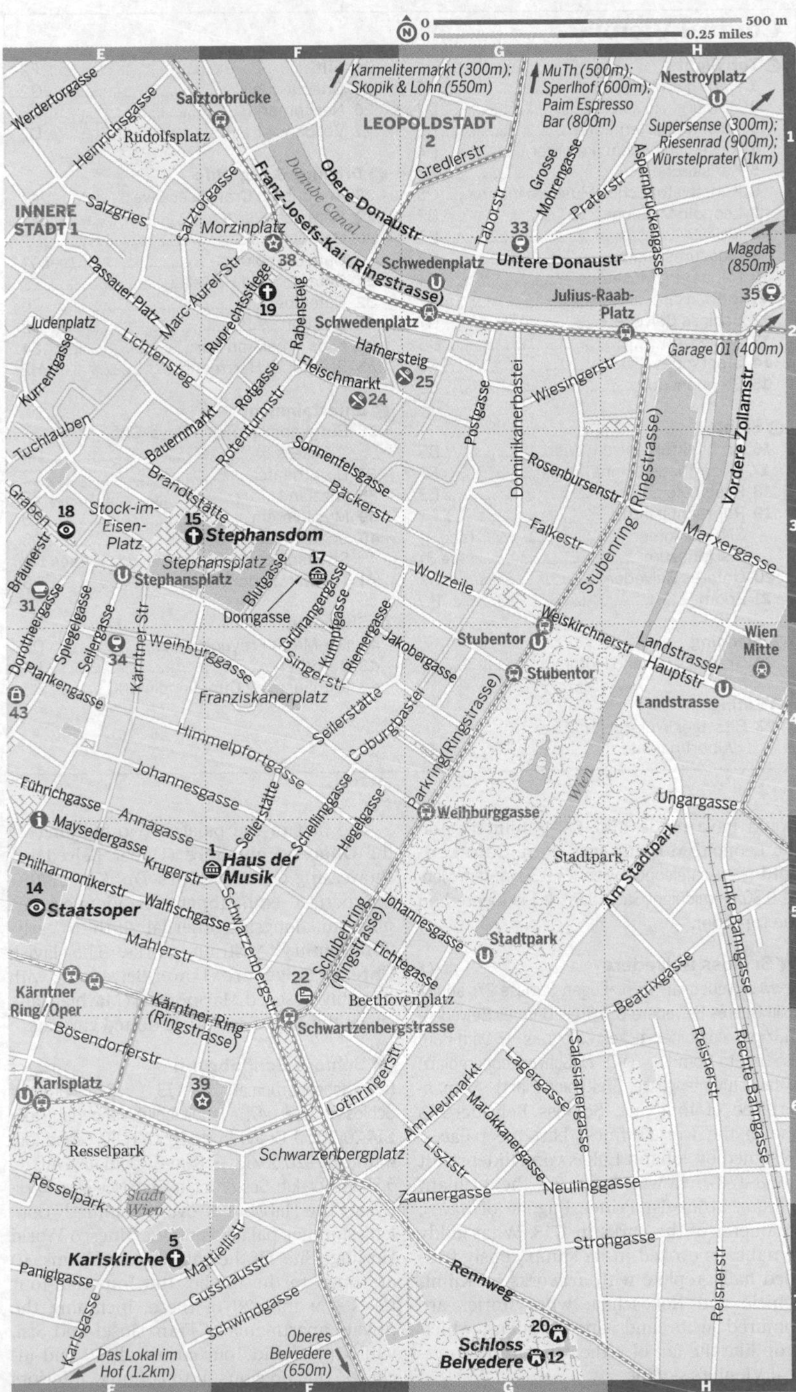

0 500 m
0 0.25 miles
E
F
G
H
Karmelitermarkt (300m); Skopik & Lohn (550m)
MuTh (500m); Sperlhof (600m); Paim Espresso Bar (800m)
Nestroyplatz
Supersense (300m); Riesenrad (900m); Würstelprater (1km)
LEOPOLDSTADT 2
INNERE STADT 1
Werdertorgasse
Heinrichsgasse
Rudolfsplatz
Salztorbrücke
Salzgries
Salztorgasse
Morzinplatz
Franz-Josefs-Kai (Ringstrasse)
Danube Canal
Obere Donaustr
Gredlerstr
Taborstr
Grosse Mohrengasse
Praterstr
Aspernbrückengasse
Untere Donaustr
Schwedenplatz
Julius-Raab-Platz
Magdas (850m)
Garage 01 (400m)
Passauer Platz
Marc-Aurel-Str
Ruprechtsstiege
Rabensteig
Judenplatz
Lichtensteg
Hafnersteig
Fleischmarkt
Kurrentgasse
Rotgasse
Rotenturmstr
Postgasse
Dominikanerbastei
Wiesingerstr
Tuchlauben
Bauernmarkt
Sonnenfelsgasse
Bäckerstr
Rosenbursenstr
Stubenring (Ringstrasse)
Vordere Zollamstr
Brandstätte
Graben
Stock-im-Eisen-Platz
Stephansdom
Stephansplatz
Blutgasse
Domgasse
Falkestr
Marxergasse
Wollzeile
Bräunerstr
Dorotheergasse
Spiegelgasse
Seilergasse
Kärntner Str
Weihburggasse
Grünangergasse
Kumpfgasse
Riemergasse
Singerstr
Jakobergasse
Weiskirchnerstr
Stubentor
Landstrasser Hauptstr
Landstrasse
Wien Mitte
Plankengasse
Franziskanerplatz
Seilerstätte
Coburgbastei
Himmelpfortgasse
Parkring (Ringstrasse)
Wien
Johannesgasse
Führichgasse
Maysedergasse
Annagasse
Schellinggasse
Hegelgasse
Weihburggasse
Ungargasse
Krugerstr
Haus der Musik
Stadtpark
Am Stadtpark
Philharmonikerstr
Staatsoper
Walfischgasse
Schwarzenbergstr
Schubertring (Ringstrasse)
Linke Bahngasse
Mahlerstr
Fichtegasse
Beethovenplatz
Beatrixgasse
Kärntner Ring/Oper
Kärntner Ring (Ringstrasse)
Schwartzenbergstrasse
Bösendorferstr
Salesianergasse
Reisnerstr
Rechte Bahngasse
Lagergasse
Karlsplatz
Lothringerstr
Am Heumarkt
Marokkanergasse
Lisztstr
Resselpark
Schwarzenbergplatz
Neulinggasse
Zaunergasse
Stadt Wien
Mattiellistr
Strohgasse
Karlskirche
Paniglgasse
Gusshausstr
Rennweg
Karlsgasse
Schwindgasse
Oberes Belvedere (650m)
Schloss Belvedere
Das Lokal im Hof (1.2km)
AUSTRIA

Central Vienna

Top Sights
1 Haus der Musik F5
2 Hofburg D4
3 Kaiserappartements D3
4 Kaiserliche Schatzkammer D4
5 Karlskirche E7
6 Kunsthistorisches Museum Vienna C5
7 Leopold Museum B5
8 MUMOK B5
9 MuseumsQuartier B5
10 Neue Burg Museums D4
11 Rathaus B2
12 Schloss Belvedere G7
13 Secession D6
14 Staatsoper E5
15 Stephansdom E3

Sights
16 Architekturzentrum Wien B5
17 Mozarthaus Vienna F3
18 Pestsäule E3
19 Ruprechtskirche F2
Silberkammer (see 3)
Sisi Museum (see 3)
20 Unteres Belvedere G7
21 Zoom B5

Sleeping
22 Grand Ferdinand Hotel F5

Eating
23 Bitzinger Würstelstand am Albertinaplatz D5
24 ef16 F2
25 Griechenbeisl G2
26 Naschmarkt D6
27 Vollpension D7

Drinking & Nightlife
28 Ammutson Craft Beer Dive A7
29 Botanical Gardens C1
30 Café Central D2
Café Leopold (see 7)
31 Café Leopold Hawelka E3
32 Café Sperl C6
33 Das Loft G2
34 Loos American Bar E4
35 Strandbar Herrmann H2

Entertainment
36 Burgkapelle Vienna Boys' Choir Tickets D4
37 Burgtheater C2
38 Jazzland F2
39 Musikverein E6
40 Spanish Riding School D3
Staatsoper (see 14)
41 Theater an der Wien D6

Shopping
42 Bio-Markt Freyung D2
43 Dorotheum E4
44 Rathausplatz Christkindlmarkt B2

would have made him €574 million), and the Leopold Museum was born. **Café Leopold** (www.cafeleopold.wien; 9.30am-1am Mon-Fri, 9.30am-midnight Sat & Sun;) is located on the top floor.

★Schloss Belvedere PALACE
(www.belvedere.at; Prinz-Eugen-Strasse 27; adult/child Oberes Belvedere €15/free, Unteres Belvedere €13/free, combined ticket €22/free; 9am-6pm Sat-Thu, to 9pm Fri; D, 71 Schwarzenbergplatz, U Taubstummengasse, Südtiroler Platz) A masterpiece of total art, Schloss Belvedere is one of the world's finest baroque palaces. Designed by Johann Lukas von Hildebrandt (1668–1745), it was built for the brilliant military strategist Prince Eugene of Savoy, conqueror of the Turks in 1718. What giddy romance is evoked in its sumptuously frescoed halls, replete with artworks by Klimt, Schiele and Kokoschka; what stories are conjured in its landscaped gardens, which drop like the fall of a theatre curtain to reveal Vienna's skyline.

The first of the palace's two buildings is the **Oberes Belvedere** (Upper Belvedere), showcasing Gustav Klimt's *The Kiss* (1908), the perfect embodiment of Viennese art nouveau, alongside other late-19th- to early-20th-century Austrian works. The lavish **Unteres Belvedere** (Lower Belvedere), with its richly frescoed Marmorsaal (Marble Hall), sits at the end of sculpture-dotted gardens.

★Schloss Schönbrunn PALACE
(www.schoenbrunn.at; 13, Schönbrunner Schlossstrasse 47; adult/child Imperial Tour €14.20/10.50, Grand Tour €17.50/11.50, Grand Tour with guide €20.50/13; 8am-6.30pm Jul & Aug, to 5.30pm Apr-Jun, Sep & Oct, to 5pm Nov-Mar; U Hietzing) The Habsburgs' overwhelmingly opulent summer palace is now a Unesco World Heritage Site. Of the palace's 1441 rooms, 40 are open to the public; the Imperial Tour takes you into 26 of these, including the private apartments of Franz Josef and Sisi, while the Grand Tour covers all 40 and includes the precious 18th-century interiors

from the time of Maria Theresia. These mandatory tours are done with an audio guide or, for an additional charge, a tour guide.

★Haus der Musik MUSEUM

(www.hausdermusik.com; 01, Seilerstätte 30; adult/child €13/6, incl Mozarthaus Vienna €18/8; 10am-10pm; ; 2, 71 Schwarzenbergplatz, U Karlsplatz) The Haus der Musik explains the world of sound and music to adults and children alike in an amusing and interactive way (in English and German). Exhibits are spread over four floors and cover everything about how sound is created, from Vienna's Philharmonic Orchestra to street noises. The staircase between floors acts as a piano; its glassed-in ground-floor courtyard hosts musical events. Admission is discounted after 8pm.

Mozarthaus Vienna MUSEUM

(01-512 17 91; www.mozarthausvienna.at; 01, Domgasse 5; adult/child €11/4.50, incl Haus der Musik €18/8; 10am-7pm; U Stephansplatz) The great composer spent 2½ happy and productive years at this residence between 1784 and 1787. Exhibits include copies of music scores and paintings, while free audio guides recreate the story of his time here. Mozart spent a total of 11 years in Vienna, changing residences frequently and sometimes setting up his home outside the Ringstrasse in the cheaper *Vorstädte* (inner suburbs) when his finances were tight. Of these the Mozarthaus Vienna is the only one that survives.

★Prater PARK

(www.wiener-prater.at; ; U Praterstern) Spread across 60 sq km, central Vienna's biggest park comprises woodlands of poplar and chestnut, meadows and tree-lined boulevards, as well as children's playgrounds, a swimming pool, a golf course and a race track. Fringed by statuesque chestnut trees that are ablaze with russet and gold in autumn and frilly with white blossom in spring, the central Hauptallee avenue is the main vein, running straight as a die from the Praterstern to the **Lusthaus** (01-728 95 65; 02, Freudenau 254; mains €13-20; noon-11pm Mon-Fri, to 6pm Sat & Sun, shorter hours winter; ; 77A).

Twirling above the **Würstelprater** (Prater 7; rides €1.50-5; 10am-midnight; ; U Praterstern) amusement park is one of the city's most visible icons, the **Riesenrad** (www.wienerriesenrad.com; 02, Prater 90; adult/child €12/5; 9am-11.45pm, shorter hours winter; ; U Praterstern). Built in 1897, this 65m-high Ferris wheel of *The Third Man* fame affords far-reaching views of Vienna.

Sigmund Freud Museum MUSEUM, HOUSE

(www.freud-museum.at; 09, Berggasse 19; adult/child €12/4; 10am-6pm; 1, D Schlickgasse, U Schottentor, Schottenring) Sigmund Freud is a bit like the telephone – once he happened, there was no going back. This is where Freud spent his most prolific years and developed the most significant of his groundbreaking theories; he moved here with his family in 1891 and stayed until forced into exile by the Nazis in 1938.

★Secession MUSEUM

(www.secession.at; 01, Friedrichstrasse 12; adult/child €9/6; 10am-6pm Tue-Sun; U Karlsplatz) In 1897, 19 progressive artists swam away from the mainstream Künstlerhaus artistic establishment to form the *Wiener Secession* (Vienna Secession). Among their number were Gustav Klimt, Josef Hoffman, Kolo Moser and Joseph M Olbrich. Olbrich designed the new exhibition centre of the Secessionists, which combined sparse functionality with stylistic motifs. Its biggest draw is Klimt's exquisitely gilded *Beethoven Frieze*. Guided tours in English (€3) lasting one hour take place at 11am Saturday. An audio guide costs €3.

★Karlskirche CHURCH

(St Charles Church; www.karlskirche.at; 04, Karlsplatz; adult/child €8/4; 9am-6pm Mon-Sat, noon-7pm Sun; U Karlsplatz) Built between 1716 and 1739, after a vow by Karl VI at the end of the 1713 plague, Vienna's finest baroque church rises at the southeast corner of Resselpark. It was designed and commenced by Johann Bernhard Fischer von Erlach and completed by his son Joseph. The huge elliptical copper **dome** reaches 72m; the highlight is the lift to the cupola (included in admission) for a close-up view of the intricate frescoes by Johann Michael Rottmayr.

Pestsäule MEMORIAL

(Plague Column; 01, Graben; U Stephansplatz) Graben is dominated by the twisting outline of this gold-topped baroque memorial, designed by Fischer von Erlach in 1693 at the behest of Emperor Leopold I to commemorate the 75,000 Viennese victims of the Black Death, the bubonic plague epidemic that swept through Vienna in 1679.

Activities & Tours

Vienna steps effortlessly between urban and outdoors. The Wienerwald to the west is criss-crossed with hiking and cycling trails, while the Danube, Alte Donau, Donauinsel and Lobau to the east offer boating, swimming, cycling and inline skating. There are over 1200km of cycle paths, and the city is dotted with parks, some big (Prater), some small (Stadtpark).

★Space & Place WALKING
(☎0680 125 43 54; http://spaceandplace.at; walking tours €10, Coffeehouse Conversations €11) For the inside scoop on Vienna, join Eugene on one of his fun, quirky tours. The alternative line-up keeps growing: from Vienna Ugly tours, homing in on the capital's ugly side, to Smells Like Wien Spirit, a playful exploration of the city through smell, and the sociable Coffeehouse Conversations. See the website for dates, further details and meeting points.

Shades Tours WALKING
(☎01-997 19 83; www.shades-tours.com; Impact Hub Vienna, Lindengasse 56; walking tours €18) A world apart from the bog-standard city tour, Shades reveals central Vienna from a unique perspective, with two-hour walks guided by formerly homeless residents. Offered in English and German, the tours are a real eye-opener. It also provides integration-aimed tours led by refugees. See the website for dates, bookings and meeting points.

Festivals & Events

★Christkindlmärkte CHRISTMAS MARKET
(www.wien.info/en/shopping-wining-dining/markets/christmas-markets; mid-Nov–24 Dec) Vienna's much-loved Christmas market season runs from around mid-November to Christmas Eve. Magical *Christkindlmärkte* set up in streets and squares, with stalls selling wooden toys, holiday decorations and traditional food such as *Wurst* (sausages) and *Glühwein* (mulled wine). The centrepiece is the **Rathausplatz Christkindlmarkt** (www.christkindlmarkt.at; D, 1, 2 Rathaus, U Rathaus).

Donauinselfest MUSIC
(https://donauinselfest.at; late Jun) FREE Held over three days on a weekend in late June, the Donauinselfest features a feast of rock, pop, folk and country performers, and attracts almost three million onlookers. Best of all, it's free!

Wiener Festwochen ART
(Vienna Festival; www.festwochen.at; mid-May–mid-Jun) A wide-ranging program of theatrical productions, concerts, dance performances and visual arts from around the world, the month-long Wiener Festwochen takes place from mid-May to mid-June at various venues city-wide.

Opernball CULTURAL
(www.wiener-staatsoper.at; Feb; U Karlsplatz) Of the 300 or so balls held in January and February, the Opernball (Opera Ball) is number one. Held in the Staatsoper (p51) on the Thursday preceding Ash Wednesday, it's a supremely lavish affair, with the men in tails and women in shining white gowns.

Sleeping

my MOjO vie HOSTEL $
(☎0676 551 11 55; www.mymojovie.at; 07, Kaiserstrasse 77; dm/d/tr/q €25/80/100/120, s/d/tr/q with shared bathroom €44/60/80/100; U Burggasse-Stadthalle) An old-fashioned cage lift rattles up to these design-focused backpacker digs. Everything you could wish for is here – well-equipped dorms with two power points per bed, a self-catering kitchen, tablets for surfing, guidebooks for browsing and musical instruments for your own jam session. There's no air-con but fans are available in summer.

Hotel am Brillantengrund HOTEL $
(☎01-523 36 62; www.brillantengrund.com; 07, Bandgasse 4; s/d/tr/q from €59/69/89/109; @; 49 Westbahnstrasse/Zieglergasse, U Zieglergasse) In a lemon-yellow building set around a sociable courtyard strewn with potted palms, this community linchpin works with local artists and hosts regular exhibitions, along with DJs, live music and other events such as pop-up markets and shops. Parquet-floored rooms are simple but decorated with vintage furniture, and variously incorporate local artworks, funky wallpapers and retro light fittings. Breakfast included.

Hotel Riede B&B $$
(☎01-813 85 76; www.hotelriede.at; Niederhofstrasse 18; s €65-76, d €70-100; P; U Niederhofstrasse) Around a 15-minute stroll east of Schönbrunn, this family-run hotel in a gorgeous art nouveau building has a spiral staircase curling up to parquet-floored rooms that are simple but spacious, comfortable and well kept. Tots can stay free in their parents' room. Bring cash as credit cards aren't accepted.

★Magdas BOUTIQUE HOTEL $$
(☎01-720 02 88; www.magdas-hotel.at; 02, Laufbergergasse 2; d €70-150; U Praterstern) How

clever: the Magdas is a hotel making a difference as the staff who welcome guests are refugees. The former retirement home turned boutique hotel opened its doors in 2016 and hit the ground running. The rooms are retro cool, with one-of-a-kind murals, knitted cushions and upcycling. The pick of them have balconies overlooking the Prater, just around the corner.

Grand Ferdinand Hotel DESIGN HOTEL **$$**
(☎01-918 80; www.grandferdinand.com; 01, Schubertring 10-12; dm/d/ste from €30/180/600; ; 2, 71 Schwarzenbergplatz) An enormous taxidermied horse stands in the reception area of this ultrahip hotel, which is shaking up Vienna's accommodation scene by offering parquet-floored dorms with mahogany bunks alongside richly coloured designer rooms with chaise longues and chandeliered suites with private champagne bars. Breakfast (€29) is served on the panoramic rooftop terrace, adjacent to the heated, open-air infinity pool.

Eating

Würstelstande (sausage stands) are great for a cheap bite on the run, and the city also has a booming international restaurant scene and many multi-ethnic markets. Self-caterers can stock up at central Hofer, Billa and Spar supermarkets. Some have delis that make sandwiches to order.

★**Vollpension** CAFE **$**
(www.vollpension.wien; 04, Schleifmühlgasse 16; dishes €4.60-8.90; 9am-10pm Tue-Sat, to 8pm Sun; ; U Karlsplatz) This white-painted brick space with mismatched vintage furniture, tasselled lampshades and portraits on the walls is run by 15 *omas* (grandmas) and *opas* (grandpas) along with their families, with more than 200 cakes in their collective repertoire. Breakfast, such as avocado and feta on pumpernickel bread, is served until 4pm; lunch dishes include a vegan goulash with potato and tofu.

Das Lokal in Hof INTERNATIONAL **$**
(☎01-971 91 41; https://daslokal.at; Viktorgasse 22; mains €11.90-19.90, lunch special €6.90-7.90; 11am-11pm Mon-Fri; U Hauptbahnhof) Snuggled away in the courtyard of an old dairy is this cracking cafe-restaurant, with a stripped-back interior and open kitchen. Robert and Barbara run the place with love and an imaginative eye, serving food that is honest, generous and delicious – be it pumpkin gnocchi with lingonberries and cashews or black pudding spring roll with apple mousse and chive sauce.

> **MORE FOR YOUR MONEY**
>
> The **Vienna Card** (Die Wien-Karte; 24/48/72 hr €17/25/29) offers you unlimited travel plus discounts at selected museums, cafes and shops as well as the City Airport Train (CAT). It's available from hotels and the tourist office.

Bitzinger Würstelstand am Albertinaplatz STREET FOOD **$**
(www.bitzinger-wien.at; 01, Albertinaplatz; sausages €3.50-4.70; 8am-4am; D, 1, 2, 71 Kärntner Ring/Oper, U Karlsplatz, Stephansplatz) Behind the Staatsoper, Vienna's best sausage stand has cult status. Bitzinger offers the contrasting spectacle of ladies and gents dressed to the nines, sipping beer, wine or Joseph Perrier Champagne (€19.90 for 0.2L) while tucking into sausages at outdoor tables or the heated counter after performances. Mustard comes in *süss* (sweet, ie mild) or *scharf* (fiercely hot).

ef16 AUSTRIAN **$$**
(☎01-513 23 18; www.ef16.net; Fleischmarkt 16; mains €16.50-32.50; 5.30-11.30pm; 1, 2, 31 Schwedenplatz, U Schwedenplatz) What a joy it is to step into this quirkily named restaurant and wine bar, where you'll dine by candlelight in a vaulted, red-walled space. In summer, the vine-rimmed *Schanigarten* (courtyard-garden) is among Vienna's prettiest. The beautifully presented food reveals profound flavours in such dishes as venison carpaccio with black nuts and cranberry mayonnaise, and guinea fowl with olive polenta.

Skopik & Lohn EUROPEAN **$$**
(☎01-219 89 77; www.skopikundlohn.at; 02, Leopoldsgasse 17; mains €13-28; 6pm-1am Tue-Sat; U Taborstrasse) The spidery web of scrawl that creeps across the ceiling at Skopik & Lohn gives an avant-garde edge to an otherwise French-style brasserie – all wainscoting, globe lights, cheek-by-jowl tables and white-jacketed waiters. The menu is modern European with a Mediterranean slant, delivering spot-on dishes like slow-braised lamb with mint-pea purée, almonds and polenta, and pasta with summer truffle and monkfish.

Griechenbeisl BISTRO **$$**
(☎01-533 19 77; www.griechenbeisl.at; 01, Fleischmarkt 11; mains €15-28; 11.30am-11.30pm; ;

DON'T MISS

FOOD MARKET FINDS

The sprawling **Naschmarkt** (06, Linke & Rechte Wienzeile; 6am-7.30pm Mon-Fri, to 6pm Sat; U Karlsplatz, Kettenbrückengasse) is the place to *nasch* (snack) in Vienna. Stalls are piled high with meats, fruits, vegetables, cheeses, olives, spices and wine. There are also plenty of cafes dishing up good-value lunches, along with delis and takeaway stands.

Bio-Markt Freyung (www.biobauernmarkt-freyung.at; 01, Freyungasse; 9am-6pm Fri & Sat; U Herrengasse, Schottentor) sells farm-fresh produce, as does the bustling **Karmelitermarkt** (02, Karmelitermarkt; 6am-7.30pm Mon-Fri, to 5pm Sat; 2 Karmeliterplatz, U Taborstrasse). Head to the Saturday farmers market at the latter for brunch at one of the excellent deli-cafes or, if you like your markets with a little more edge, head to **Bauernmarkt Yppenplatz** (16, Yppenplatz; 9am-1pm Sat; 44 Yppengasse, U Josefstädter Strasse).

1, 2, 31 Schwedenplatz, U Schwedenplatz) Dating from 1447 and frequented by Beethoven, Brahms, Schubert and Strauss among other luminaries, Vienna's oldest restaurant has vaulted rooms, wood panelling and a figure of Augustin trapped at the bottom of a well inside the front door. Every classic Viennese dish is on the menu, along with three daily vegetarian options. In summer, head to the plant-fringed front garden.

Drinking & Nightlife

★Das Loft BAR
(www.dasloftwien.at; 02, Praterstrasse 1; noon-2am; 2 Gredlerstrasse, U Schwedenplatz) Wow, what a view! Take the lift to Das Loft on the Sofitel's 18th floor to reduce Vienna to toytown scale. From this slinky, glass-walled lounge, you can pick out landmarks such as the Stephansdom and the Hofburg over a tonka bean sour or mojito. By night, the backlit ceiling swirls with an impressionist painter's palette of colours.

Botanical Gardens COCKTAIL BAR
(www.botanicalgarden.at; 09, Kolingasse 1; 6pm-2am Tue-Thu, to 3am Fri & Sat; U Schottentor) A subterranean mirror of Cafe Stein's sunny spaces above, Botanical Gardens makes for a cosy, magical retreat once Vienna's weather turns chilly. A dark nautical theme ticks all the cocktail-revival-scene boxes, but with enough local eccentricity to keep things interesting.

Weinstube Josefstadt WINE BAR
(08, Piaristengasse 27; 4pm-midnight Apr-Dec; U Rathaus) Weinstube Josefstadt is one of the loveliest *Stadtheurigen* (city wine taverns) in Vienna. A leafy green oasis nestled between towering residential blocks, its tables of friendly, well-liquored locals are squeezed in between the trees and shrubs looking onto a pretty, painted *Salettl* (wooden summerhouse). Wine is local and cheap, and food is typical, with a buffet-style meat and fritter selection.

Strandbar Herrmann BAR
(www.strandbarherrmann.at; 03, Herrmannpark; 10am-2am Apr-early Oct; ; O Hintere Zollamstrasse, U Schwedenplatz) You'd swear you're by the sea at this hopping canalside beach bar, with beach chairs, sand, DJ beats and hordes of Viennese livin' it up on summer evenings. Cocktail happy hour is from 5pm to 6pm. Cool trivia: it's located on Herrmannpark, named after picture-postcard inventor Emanuel Herrmann (1839–1902).

Loos American Bar COCKTAIL BAR
(www.loosbar.at; 01, Kärntner Durchgang 10; noon-4am; U Stephansplatz) Loos is *the* spot in the Innere Stadt for a classic cocktail such as its signature dry martini, expertly whipped up by talented mixologists. Designed by Adolf Loos in 1908, this tiny 27-sq-metre box (seating just 20 or so patrons) is bedecked with onyx and polished brass, with mirrored walls that make it appear far larger.

Ammutson Craft Beer Dive BAR
(0664 479 91 30; www.facebook.com/Ammutson; 06, Barnabitengasse 10; 4pm-1am Mon, to 2am Tue & Wed, to 4am Thu-Sat, 2pm-midnight Sun; U3 Neubaugasse) Tucked into a cobbled alley, Ammutson is a welcoming bar with simple wooden communal bench seating and quirky art on its white brick walls. Twelve taps pour 'proudly independent' brews from Austrian and European craft beer makers. Come for the chatty, laid-back atmosphere fostered by owner Misho and his passionate team.

✩ Entertainment

Vienna is, was and will always be the European capital of opera and classical music. The line-up of music events is never-ending and even the city's buskers are often classically trained musicians. Box offices generally open from Monday to Saturday and sell cheap (€3 to €6) standing-room tickets around an hour before performances. For weekly listings, visit Falter (www.falter.at), while Tourist Info Wien (http://events.wien.info/en) lists concerts up to 18 months in advance.

★ Staatsoper — OPERA

(☎01-514 44 7880; www.wiener-staatsoper.at; 01, Opernring 2; tickets €13-239, standing room €3-4; U Karlsplatz) The glorious Staatsoper is Vienna's premier opera and classical-music venue. Productions are lavish, formal affairs, where people dress up accordingly. In the interval, wander the foyer and refreshment rooms to fully appreciate the gold-and-crystal interior. Opera is not performed here in July and August (but tours still take place). Tickets can be purchased up to two months in advance.

Musikverein — CONCERT VENUE

(☎01-505 81 90; www.musikverein.at; 01, Musikvereinsplatz 1; tickets €25-105, standing room €7-15; ⊙box office 9am-8pm Mon-Fri, to 1pm Sat Sep-Jun, 9am-noon Mon-Fri Jul & Aug; U Karlsplatz) The opulent Musikverein holds the proud title of the best acoustics of any concert hall in Austria, which the Vienna Philharmonic Orchestra embraces. The lavish interior can be visited by 45-minute guided tour (in English; adult/child €8.50/5) at 1pm Tuesday to Saturday. Smaller-scale performances are held in the Brahms Saal. There are no student tickets.

Theater an der Wien — THEATRE

(☎01-588 85; www.theater-wien.at; 06, Linke Wienzeile 6; tickets €5-148; ⊙box office 10am-6pm Mon-Sat, 2-6pm Sun; U Karlsplatz) The Theater an der Wien has hosted some monumental premiere performances, including Beethoven's *Fidelio,* Mozart's *Die Zauberflöte* and Strauss Jnr's *Die Fledermaus.* These days, besides staging musicals, dance and concerts, it's re-established its reputation for high-quality opera. Student tickets go on sale 30 minutes before shows; standing-room tickets are available one hour prior to performances.

Jazzland — LIVE MUSIC

(☎01-533 25 75; www.jazzland.at; 01, Franz-Josefs-Kai 29; cover €11-20; ⊙7pm-2am Mon-Sat mid-Aug–mid-Jul, live music from 9pm; 🚋1, 2, 31 Schwedenplatz, U Schwedenplatz) Buried in a former wine cellar beneath **Ruprechtskirche** (St Rupert's Church; ☎01-535 60 03; www.ruprechtskirche.at; 01, Ruprechtsplatz 1; ⊙10am-noon Mon & Tue, 10am-noon & 3-5pm Wed, 10am-5pm Thu & Fri, 11.30am-3.30pm Sat), Jazzland is Vienna's oldest jazz club, dating back nearly 50 years. The music covers the whole jazz spectrum, and features both local and international acts. Past performers have included

DON'T MISS

COFFEE HOUSE CULTURE

Vienna's legendary *Kaffeehäuser* (coffee houses) houses rank on the Unesco list of Intangible Cultural Heritage, which defines them as 'places where time and space are consumed, but only the coffee is found on the bill'. Grand or humble, poster-plastered or chandelier-lit, this is where you can join the locals for coffee, cake and a slice of living history.

Café Central (www.cafecentral.wien; 01, Herrengasse 14; ⊙7.30am-10pm Mon-Sat, 10am-10pm Sun; 📶; U Herrengasse)

Café Leopold Hawelka (www.hawelka.at; 01, Dorotheergasse 6; ⊙8am-midnight Mon-Thu, to 1am Fri & Sat, 10am-midnight Sun; U Stephansplatz)

Café Sperl (www.cafesperl.at; 06, Gumpendorfer Strasse 11; ⊙7am-10pm Mon-Sat, 10am-8pm Sun; 📶; U Museumsquartier, Kettenbrückengasse)

Sperlhof (02, Grosse Sperlgasse 41; ⊙4pm-1.30am; 📶; U Taborstrasse)

Supersense (02, Praterstrasse 70; 2-course lunch €10, breakfast €3.80-9.20; ⊙9.30am-7pm Tue-Fri, 10am-5pm Sat; U Praterstern)

IMPERIAL ENTERTAINMENT

The world-famous Vienna Boys' Choir performs on Sunday at 9.15am (late September to June) in the **Burgkapelle** (Royal Chapel) in the Hofburg (p42). **Tickets** (☎01-533 99 27; www.hofmusikkapelle.gv.at; 01, Schweizerhof; tickets €11-37; Ⓤ Herrengasse) should be booked around six weeks in advance. The group also performs on Friday afternoons at the **MuTh** (☎01-347 80 80; www.muth.at; 02, Obere Augartenstrasse 1e; Vienna Boys' Choir Fri tickets €39-89; ⏲4-6pm Mon-Fri & 1 hour before performances; Ⓤ Taborstrasse).

Another Habsburg legacy is the **Spanish Riding School** (Spanische Hofreitschule; ☎01-533 90 31-0; www.srs.at; 01, Michaelerplatz 1; tickets €25-217; ⏲hours vary; 🚌1A, 2A Michaelerplatz, Ⓤ Herrengasse), where Lipizzaner stallions gracefully perform equine ballet to classical music. For morning training sessions, same-day tickets are available at the nearby visitor centre.

Ray Brown, Teddy Wilson, Big Joe Williams and Max Kaminsky.

Shopping

With a long-standing history of craftsmanship, in recent years this elegant city has spread its creative wings in the fashion and design world. Whether you're browsing for hand-painted porcelain in the Innere Stadt, new-wave streetwear in Neubau or epicurean treats in the Freihausviertel, you'll find inspiration, a passion for quality and an attentive eye for detail.

Dorotheum ANTIQUES
(www.dorotheum.com; 01, Dorotheergasse 17; ⏲10am-6pm Mon-Fri, 9am-5pm Sat; Ⓤ Stephansplatz) The Dorotheum is among the largest auction houses in Europe, and for the casual visitor it's more like a museum, housing everything from antique toys and tableware to autographs, antique guns and, above all, lots of quality paintings. You can bid at the regular auctions held here; otherwise just drop by (it's free) and enjoy browsing.

Information

Most hostels and hotels in Vienna offer free wi-fi, called WLAN (pronounced vee-lan) in German. As well as 400 city hotspots that can be found at www.wien.gv.at/stadtplan, cafes, coffee houses and bars also offer free wi-fi; check locations at www.freewave.at/en/hotspots.

Tourist Info Wien (☎01-245 55; www.wien.info; 01, Albertinaplatz; ⏲9am-7pm; 📶; 🚋D, 1, 2, 71 Kärntner Ring/Oper, Ⓤ Stephansplatz) Vienna's main tourist office has free maps and racks of brochures.

Getting There & Away

AIR

Located 19km southwest of the city centre, **Vienna International Airport** (VIE; ☎01-700 722 233; www.viennaairport.com; 📶) operates services worldwide. The fastest transport into the centre is **City Airport Train** (CAT; www.cityairporttrain.com; single/return €12/21), which runs every 30 minutes and takes 16 minutes between the airport and Wien Mitte; book online for a discount. The cheaper but slower S7 suburban train (€4.20, 37 minutes) does the same journey.

BUS

Eurolines (☎01-798 29 00; www.eurolines.at; 03, Erdbergstrasse 200; ⏲office 6.30am-9pm; Ⓤ Erdberg) has basically tied up the bus routes connecting Austria with the rest of Europe. Its main terminal is at the U3 U-Bahn station Erdberg, but some buses stop at the U6 and U1 U-Bahn and train station Praterstern, and at Südtiroler Platz by Vienna's *Hauptbahnhof*.

CAR & MOTORCYCLE

The Gürtel is an outer ring road that joins up with the A22 on the north bank of the Danube and the A23 southeast of town. All the main road routes intersect with this system, including the A1 from Linz and Salzburg, and the A2 from Graz.

TRAIN

Austria's train network is a dense web reaching the country's far-flung corners. The system is fast, efficient, frequent and well used. **Österreiche Bundesbahn** (ÖBB; www.oebb.at) is the main operator, and has information offices at all of Vienna's main train stations. Tickets can be purchased online, at ticket offices or from train-station ticket machines. Long-distance train tickets can be purchased on board but incur a €3 service charge. Tickets for local, regional and intercity trains must be purchased before boarding.

Getting Around

BICYCLE

Citybike Wien (Vienna City Bike; www.citybikewien.at; 1st/2nd/3rd hour free/€1/2, per hour thereafter €4) has more than 120 bicycle stands across the city. A credit card and €1 registration fee is required to hire bikes; swipe your card in the machine and follow the multilingual instructions.

PUBLIC TRANSPORT

Vienna's unified public transport network encompasses trains, trams, buses, and underground (U-Bahn) and suburban (S-Bahn) trains. Free maps and information pamphlets are available from **Wiener Linien** (01-7909-100; www.wienerlinien.at). All tickets must be validated at the entrance to U-Bahn stations and on buses and trams (except for weekly and monthly tickets).

THE DANUBE VALLEY

The stretch of Danube between Krems and Melk, known locally as the Wachau, is arguably the loveliest along the entire length of this long, long river. Both banks are dotted with ruined castles and medieval towns, and lined with terraced vineyards. Further upstream is the industrial city of Linz, Austria's avant-garde art and new technology trailblazer.

Krems an der Donau

02732 / POP 24,610

Sitting on the northern bank of the Danube against a backdrop of terraced vineyards, Krems marks the beginning of the Wachau. It has an attractive cobbled centre, some good restaurants and the gallery-dotted Kunstmeile.

Sights & Activities

Kunsthalle Krems GALLERY

(www.kunsthalle.at; Franz-Zeller-Platz 3; €10; 10am-6pm Tue-Sun) The flagship of Krems' Kunstmeile, an eclectic collection of galleries and museums, the Kunsthalle has a program of changing exhibitions. These might be mid-19th-century landscapes or hardcore conceptual works, but are always well curated. Guided tours (€3) run on Sundays at 2pm.

Weingut der Stadt Krems WINE

(www.weingutstadtkrems.at; Stadtgraben 11; 9am-noon & 1-5pm Mon-Fri, 9am-noon Sat) This city-owned vineyard yielding 200,000 bottles per year, with almost all Grüner Veltliner and riesling, offers a variety of wine for tasting and purchase.

Sleeping

Arte Hotel Krems DESIGN HOTEL $$

(02732-711 23; www.arte-hotel.at; Dr-Karl-Dorrek-Strasse 23; s/d €109/161; P) The art of the title might be a stretch, but what you do get here are large, well-designed rooms with open-plan bathrooms, all scattered with '60s-tilting furniture and big, bright patterns.

Information

Krems Tourismus (02732-826 76; www.krems.info; Utzstrasse 1; 9am-6pm Mon-Fri, 11am-6pm Sat, 11am-4pm Sun, shorter hours winter) Helpful office well stocked with info and maps.

Getting There & Away

For boats, the **river station** is near Donaustrasse, about 1.5km west of the train station.

Frequent daily trains connect Krems with Vienna (€18.40, 70 minutes).

Melk

02752 / POP 5529

With its blockbuster abbey-fortress set high above the valley, Melk is a high point of any visit to the Danube Valley. Separated from the river by a stretch of woodland, this pretty town makes for an easy and rewarding day trip from Krems or even Vienna. Post abbey visit, you'll find plenty of restaurants and cafes with alfresco seating line the Rathausplatz. **Melk Tourist Office** (02752-511 60; www.stadt-melk.at; Kremser Strasse 5; 9.30am-6pm Mon-Sat, 9.30am-3.30pm Sun May-Sep, shorter hours rest of year) should be your first port of call.

★Stift Melk ABBEY

(Benedictine Abbey of Melk; www.stiftmelk.at; Abt Berthold Dietmayr Strasse 1; adult/child €12.50/6.50, with guided tour €14.50/8.50; 9am-5.30pm, tours 10am-4pm Apr-Oct, tours only 11am & 2pm Nov-Mar) Of the many abbeys in Austria, Stift Melk is the most famous. Possibly Lower Austria's finest, the monastery church dominates the complex with its twin spires and high octagonal dome. The interior is baroque gone barmy, with regiments of smirking cherubs, gilt twirls and polished faux marble. The theatrical high-altar scene, depicting St Peter and St Paul (the church's two patron saints), is by Peter Widerin. Johann Michael Rottmayr created most of the ceiling paintings, including those in the dome.

Getting There & Away

Boats leave from the canal by Pionierstrasse, 400m north of the abbey. There are regular train services to Melk from Vienna (€18.40, 50 minutes, twice hourly).

UPPER AUSTRIA

Linz

0732 / POP 204,846

'It begins in Linz' goes the Austrian saying, and it's true. The technology trailblazer and European Capital of Culture 2009 is blessed with a leading-edge cyber centre and world-class contemporary-art gallery.

Sitting astride the Danube, Linz also harbours a charming Altstadt filled with historic baroque architecture.

Sights

★Lentos GALLERY

(www.lentos.at; Ernst-Koref-Promenade 1; adult/child €8/4.50, guided tours €3; 10am-6pm Tue, Wed & Fri-Sun, 10am-9pm Thu) Overlooking the Danube, the rectangular glass-and-steel Lentos is strikingly illuminated by night. The gallery guards one of Austria's finest modern-art collections, including works by Warhol, Schiele, Klimt, Kokoschka and Lovis Corinth, which sometimes feature in the large-scale exhibitions. There are regular guided tours in German and 30-minute tours in English at 4pm on the first Saturday of the month. Alternatively, download Lentos' app from the website.

★Ars Electronica Center MUSEUM

(www.aec.at; Ars-Electronica-Strasse 1; adult/child €9.50/7.50; 9am-5pm Tue, Wed & Fri, 9am-7pm Thu, 10am-6pm Sat & Sun;) The technology, science and digital media of the future are in the spotlight at Linz' biggest crowd-puller. In the labs you can interact with robots, animate digital objects, print 3D structures, turn your body into musical instruments, and (virtually) travel to outer space. Kids love it. Designed by Vienna-based architectural firm Treusch, the centre resembles a futuristic ship by the Danube after dark, when its LED glass skin kaleidoscopically changes colour.

Mural Harbour PUBLIC ART

(www.muralharbor.at; Industriezeile 40; guided tours €15-25) Street art comes into its own on the graffiti-blasted industrial facades in Linz' harbourside Hafenviertel. You'll find eye-catching, larger-than-life, Instagrammable works from the likes of Roa (Belgium), Lords (USA), Aryz (Spain) and a host of ballsy Austrian artists. For more insider info, join one of the regular walks, workshops or cruises. Visit the website for times and dates.

Sleeping & Eating

★Hotel am Domplatz DESIGN HOTEL $$

(0732-77 30 00; www.hotelamdomplatz.at; Stifterstrasse 4; d €114-178, ste €310-350;) Adjacent to the neo-Gothic **Mariendom** (Neuer Dom; Herrenstrasse 26; 7.30am-7pm Mon-Sat, 8am-7.15pm Sun) (ask for a room overlooking the cathedral), this glass-and-concrete cube filled with striking metal sculptures has streamlined, Nordic-style pristine-white and blond-wood rooms with semi-open bathrooms. Wind down with a view in the rooftop spa. In fine weather the cathedral-facing terrace is a prime spot for breakfast (€19), which includes a glass of bubbly.

★Cafe Jindrak CAFE $

(www.jindrak.at; Herrenstrasse 22; dishes €3-8.80; 8am-6pm Mon-Sat, 8.30am-6pm Sun;) Join the cake-loving locals at this celebrated cafe – the original shop (1929) of a now nine-strong chain that produces over 100,000 of its famous *Linzer Torte* each year made to its family recipe. You'd need a huge fork (and appetite) to tackle the torte that set a Guinness World Record in 1999, measuring 4m high and weighing 650kg.

Information

Tourist Information Linz (0732-7070 2009; www.linztourismus.at; Hauptplatz 1; 9am-7pm Mon-Sat, 10am-7pm Sun May-Sep, 9am-

> **LINZ CARD**
>
> The **Linz Card** (one day adult/child €18/15, three days €30/25) grants unlimited use of public transport, entry to major museums, plus discounts on other sights, city tours and river cruises.

5pm Mon-Sat, 10am-5pm Sun Oct-Apr) Upper Austria information as well as brochures and accommodation listings.

Getting There & Away

Ryanair flies to the **Blue Danube Airport** (LNZ; 07221-60 00; www.linz-airport.com; Flughafenstrasse 1, Hörsching), 13km southwest of Linz. An hourly shuttle bus (€3.20, 22 minutes) links the airport to the main train station.

Linz is on the main rail route between Vienna (€36.20, 1½ hours) and Salzburg (€27.50, 1¼ hours); express trains run twice hourly in both directions.

THE SOUTH

Austria's southern states often feel worlds apart from the rest of the country, both in climate and attitude. Styria (Steiermark) is a blissful amalgamation of genteel architecture, rolling green hills, vine-covered slopes and soaring mountains. Its capital, Graz, is one of Austria's most attractive cities. A glamorous crowd heads to sun-drenched Carinthia (Kärnten) in summer. Sidling up to Italy, its sparkling lakes and pretty lidos are as close to Mediterranean as this landlocked country gets.

Graz

0316 / POP 286,292

Austria's second-largest city is relaxed and good-looking, with ample green spaces, red rooftops and a narrow, fast-flowing river gushing through its centre. Architecturally, Graz hints at nearby Italy with its Renaissance courtyards and baroque palaces. But there's a youthful, almost Eastern European energy too, with a handful of edgily modern buildings, a vibrant arts scene and great nightlife (thanks in part to its large student population).

Sights

Graz' most compelling sights can easily be seen in a day or two and are easily accessible by foot or a quick tram ride.

★**Kunsthaus Graz** GALLERY

(0316-8017 92 00; www.museum-joanneum.at; Lendkai 1; adult/child €9.50/3.50; 10am-5pm Tue-Sun; 1, 3, 6, 7 Südtiroler Platz) Designed by British architects Peter Cook and Colin Fournier, this world-class contemporary-art space is known as the 'friendly alien' by locals. The building is signature Cook, a photovoltaic-skinned sexy biomorphic blob that is at once completely at odds with its pristine historic surroundings but sitting rather lyrically within it as well. Exhibitions change every three to four months.

Schlossberg VIEWPOINT

(one way €2.40; 4, 5 Schlossbergplatz) FREE Rising to 473m, Schlossberg is the site of the original fortress where Graz was founded and is marked by the city's most visible icon – the **Uhrturm** (Clock Tower; 4, 5 Schlossplatz/Murinsel) FREE. Its wooded slopes can be reached by a number of bucolic and strenuous paths, but also by lift or Schlossbergbahn funicular. It's a brief walk or take tram 4 or 5 to Schlossplatz/Murinsel for the lift.

★**Schloss Eggenberg** PALACE

(0316-8017 95 32; www.museum-joanneum.at; Eggenberger Allee 90; adult/child €15/6; tours hourly 10am-4pm, except 1pm Tue-Sun Apr-Oct, exhibitions 10am-5pm Tue-Sun Apr-Oct; 1 Schloss Eggenberg) Graz' elegant palace was created for the Eggenberg dynasty in 1625 by Giovanni Pietro de Pomis (1565–1633) at the request of Johann Ulrich (1568–1634). Admission is via a highly worthwhile guided tour during which you learn about the idiosyncrasies of each room, the stories told by the frescoes and about the Eggenberg family itself.

★**Neue Galerie Graz** GALLERY

(0316-8017 91 00; www.museum-joanneum.at; Joanneumsviertel; adult/child €9.50/3.50; 10am-5pm Tue-Sun; 1, 3, 4, 5, 6, 7 Hauptplatz) The Neue Galerie is the crowning glory of the three museums inside the Joanneumsviertel complex. The collection of works on level 0 is the highlight, which is regularly curated from visual arts works since 1800. It also has changing exhibitions on level 1, and a section about Styrian artists; finally, the Bruseum (a separate museum) on level 0 is dedicated to the Styrian artist Günter Brus and his followers.

Sleeping & Eating

Graz does fine dining with aplomb, but you'll also find plenty of cheap eats near Universität Graz, particularly on Halbärthgasse, Zinzendorfgasse and Harrachgasse.

Stock up for a picnic at the farmers markets on Kaiser-Josef-Platz and Lendplatz. For fast-food stands, head for Hauptplatz and Jakominiplatz.

Hotel Daniel HOTEL $

(☎0316-71 10 80; www.hoteldaniel.com; Europaplatz 1; d €75-350; P ⊖ ❄ @ 🛜; 🚊1, 3, 6, 7 Hauptbahnhof) The Daniel's rooms are well designed and super-simple, and while its small 'smart' rooms scrape into budget territory, it also offers the super-exclusive loft cube on the roof if you're looking for something out of the ordinary. The lobby area is a lot of fun – a great space in which to work or just hang out.

★ **Hotel Wiesler** HOTEL $$

(☎0316-70 66-0; www.hotelwiesler.com; Grieskai 4; d €141-246; P ⊖ @ 🛜; 🚊1, 3, 6, 7 Südtiroler Platz) The riverside Wiesler, a *Jugenstil* (art nouveau) gem from 1901, has been transformed into Graz' most glamorous hotel, complete with oriental-style spa. Hotelier Florian Weltzer has shaken up everything, including the notion of room categories, and ensured that this is a luxury experience that is far from stuffy.

OFF THE BEATEN TRACK

STYRIAN TUSCANY

Head south of Graz to what's known as *Steirische Toskana* (Styrian Tuscany), for lush wine country that's reminiscent of Chianti: gentle rolling hills cultivated with vineyards or patchwork farmland, dotted with small forests where deer roam. Apart from its stellar whites, it's also famous for Kürbiskernöl, the rich pumpkin-seed oil generously used in Styrian cooking. The picturesque 'capital' of **Ehrenhausen**, on the road to the Slovenian border, makes a fine base for wine tasting and exploring.

Kunsthauscafé INTERNATIONAL $

(☎0316-71 49 57; www.kunsthauscafe.co.at; Südtirolerplatz 2; mains €7-16.50; ⏲9am-midnight Mon-Thu, to 2am Fri & Sat, to 8pm Sun; 🚊1, 3, 6, 7 Südtiroler Platz) A happy, young crowd fills the long tables here for a menu that incorporates burgers (from big beef to chickpea), creative salads and international flavours from noodle bowls to steak tartare with skinny fries. It's very very loud – but fun if you're in the mood. The lunch special goes for just €6.80.

★ **Der Steirer** AUSTRIAN, TAPAS $$

(☎0316-70 36 54; www.der-steirer.at; Belgiergasse 1; weekday lunch menu €8.90, mains €11.50-24; ⏲11am-midnight; ✎; 🚊1, 3, 6, 7 Südtiroler Platz) This neo-*Beisl* (bistro pub) and wine bar has a beautiful selection of Styrian dishes, including great goulash, crispy *Backhendl* (fried breaded chicken) and seasonal game dishes, all done in a simple, contemporary style. Its Styrian tapas concept is a nice way to sample local flavours.

Aiola Upstairs INTERNATIONAL $$

(☎0316-81 87 97; http://upstairs.aiola.at; Schlossberg 2; pasta €16-17.50, mains €19.90-34; ⏲9am-midnight; 🛜✎; 🚊4, 5 Schlossbergplatz/Murinsel (for lift)) This cracking restaurant atop Schlossberg (p55) has fabulous views from both its glass box interior and summer terrace. Even better, the cooking up here is some of the city's best, with chefs putting a novel spin on regional, seasonal and global ingredients, along the lines of blueberry and chanterelle risotto or wild brook trout with aubergines, fresh cheese and tomato salsa.

Drinking & Nightlife

The bar scene in Graz is split between three main areas: around the university; east of the Kunsthaus in hipster Lend; and on Mehlplatz and Prokopigasse (dubbed the 'Bermuda Triangle').

Blendend COFFEE

(☎0660 4714 753; www.blendend.at; Mariahilferstrasse 24; ⏲6pm-2am Mon-Fri, 9am-2am Sat, 9am-midnight Sun; 🛜; 🚊1, 3, 6, 7 Südtiroler Platz) A rambling, warm and endearingly boho addition to Lend's usual line-up of grungy bars, Blendend is a great drinking and snacking spot during the week and then turns all-day cafe on weekends with beautiful homemade cakes and desserts competing with the spritzs and excellent local beers. In warmer weather all the action happens at the courtyard tables.

Freiblick Tagescafe ROOFTOP BAR
(☎0316-83 53 02; http://freiblick.co.at; Kastner & Öhler, Sackstrasse 7-11; ⏱9.30am-7pm Mon-Fri, to 6pm Sat; ; 1, 3, 4, 5, 6, 7 Hauptplatz) This huge terrace cafe-bar tops the Kastner & Öhler department store and has the best view in the city. Enjoy the clouds and rooftops over a breakfast platter and coffee or a lunchtime soup or salad. Or stop by in the afternoon for something from the Prosecco spritz menu or a Hugo Royal – Moët Chandon splashed with elderflower (€15).

Information

Graz Tourismus (☎0316-807 50; www.graztourismus.at; Herrengasse 16; ⏱10am-5pm Jan-Mar & Nov, to 6pm Apr-Oct & Dec; ; 1, 3, 4, 5, 6, 7 Hauptplatz) Graz' main tourist office, with loads of free information on the city and helpful and knowledgeable staff.

Getting There & Away

Graz airport (GRZ; ☎0316-290 21 72; www.flughafen-graz.at) is 10km south of the centre and is served by carriers including easyJet, Austrian Airlines, KLM, Eurowings and Lufthansa.

Trains to Vienna depart hourly (€39, 2½ hours), and five daily go to Salzburg (€58 to €69, four to 5½ hours). International train connections from Graz include Ljubljana (€31.90, 3½ hours) and Budapest (€56.40 to €79, 5½ hours).

Klagenfurt

☎0463 / POP 100,369

With its captivating location on Wörthersee and its beauty more Renaissance than baroque, Klagenfurt has a distinct Mediterranean feel and is surprisingly lively. Carinthia's capital makes a handy base for exploring Wörthersee's lakeside villages and elegant medieval towns to the north.

Sights & Activities

Boating and swimming are usually possible from May to September.

Europapark PARK
() The green expanse and its *Strandbad* (beach) on the shores of the Wörthersee are centres for aquatic fun and especially great for kids. The park's biggest draw is **Minimundus** (www.minimundus.at; Villacher Strasse 241; adult/child €19/10; ⏱9am-6pm Mar, Apr, Oct & Nov, to 7pm May-Sep;), a 'miniature world' with 140 replicas of the world's architectural icons, downsized to a scale of 1:25. To get here, take bus 10, 11, 12 or 22 from Heiligengeistplatz.

Sleeping & Eating

Das Domizil APARTMENT **$$**
(☎0664 843 30 50; www.das-domizil.at; Bahnhofstrasse 51; apt €92; P) This large, light and sweetly decorated apartment is in a grand 19th-century building just beyond the historic centre's ring. It's extremely well equipped with a full kitchen, laundry facilities and lots of space. Owner Ingo Dietrich is a friendly and fashionable young local who is generous with his insider tips and time. Courtyard parking is €12 per day extra.

Information

Tourist Office (☎0463-287 46 30; www.visitklagenfurt.at; Neuer Platz 5; ⏱9am-5pm Mon-Fri, 10am-3pm Sat) Sells Kärnten Cards and books accommodation.

Getting There & Away

Klagenfurt's **airport** (KLU; www.klagenfurt-airport.com; Flughafenstrasse 60-66) is 3km north of town. Eurowings flies from here to a number of destinations including London Heathrow and Cologne-Bonn in Germany.

Two-hourly direct trains run from Klagenfurt to Vienna (€54.40, four hours) and Salzburg (€41.20, three hours). Trains to Graz depart every two to three hours (€42, 2¾ hours). Trains to western Austria, Italy, Slovenia and Germany go via Villach (€8.10, 25 to 40 minutes, two to four per hour).

SALZBURG

☎0662 / POP 150,887

The joke 'If it's baroque, don't fix it' is a perfect maxim for Salzburg: the tranquil Old Town nested between steep hills looks much as it did when Mozart lived here 250 years ago.

A Unesco World Heritage Site, Salzburg's overwhelmingly 17th-century Altstadt (old

Salzburg

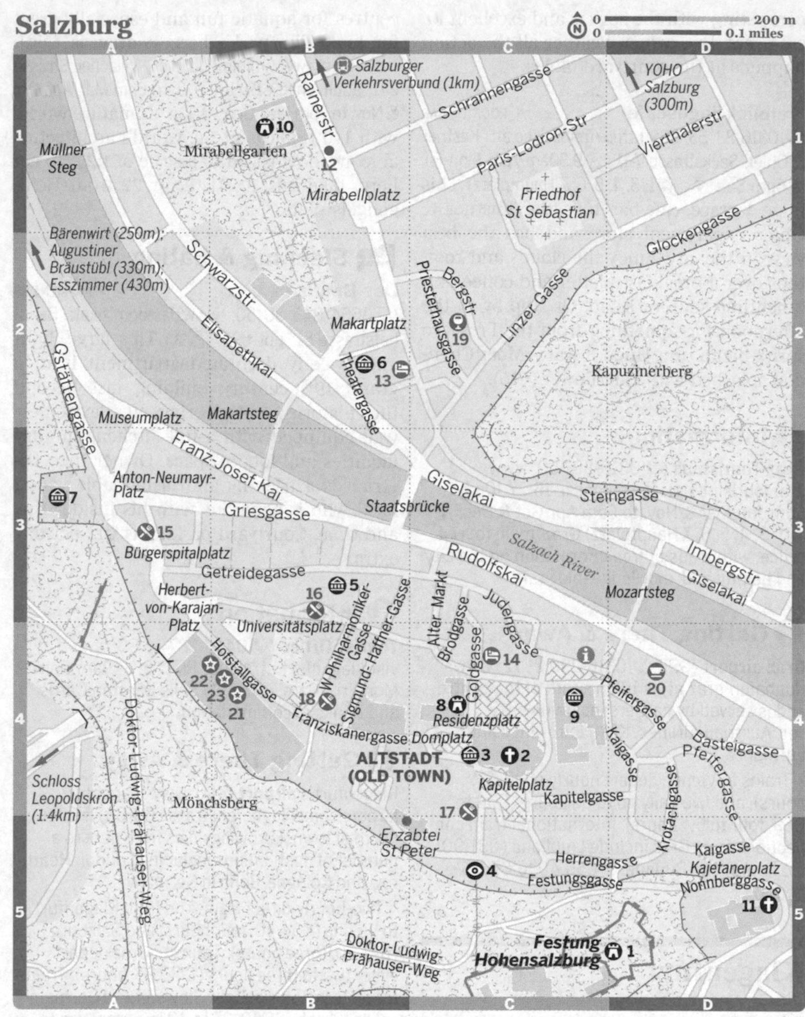

town) is entrancing both at ground level and from Hohensalzburg fortress high above. Across the fast-flowing Salzach River rests Schloss Mirabell, surrounded by gorgeous manicured gardens. You can of course, bypass the baroque grandeur and head straight for kitsch-country via a tour of *The Sound of Music* film locations.

Sights

★ Festung Hohensalzburg — FORT

(www.salzburg-burgen.at; Mönchsberg 34; adult/child/family €9.40/5.40/20.90, incl funicular €12.20/7/27.10; ⌚9.30am-5pm Oct-Apr, 9am-7pm May-Sep) Salzburg's most visible icon is this mighty, 900-year-old clifftop fortress, one of the biggest and best preserved in Europe. It's easy to spend half a day up here, roaming the ramparts for far-reaching views over the city's spires, the Salzach River and the mountains. The fortress is a steep 15-minute walk from the centre or a speedy ride up in the glass **Festungsbahn** (Festungsgasse 4; one way/return adult €6.90/8.60, child €3.70/4.70; ⌚9am-8pm May-Sep, to 5pm Oct-Apr) funicular.

Residenz — PALACE

(www.domquartier.at; Residenzplatz 1; DomQuartier ticket adult/child €13/8; ⌚10am-5pm Wed-

Salzburg

Top Sights
1 Festung Hohensalzburg........D5

Sights
2 Dom........C4
3 Dommuseum........C4
4 Festungsbahn........C5
5 Mozart's Geburtshaus........B3
6 Mozart-Wohnhaus........B2
7 Museum der Moderne........A3
8 Residenz........C4
9 Salzburg Museum........C4
10 Schloss Mirabell........B1
11 Stift Nonnberg........D5

Activities, Courses & Tours
12 Fräulein Maria's Bicycle Tours........B1

Sleeping
13 Arte Vida........B2
14 Hotel am Dom........C4

Eating
15 Afro Café........A3
16 Grünmarkt........B3
17 Stiftsbäckerei St Peter........C4
18 Triangel........B4

Drinking & Nightlife
19 Enoteca Settemila........C2
20 Kaffee Alchemie........D4

Entertainment
21 Felsenreitschule........B4
22 Grosses Festpielhaus........A4
23 Haus für Mozart........B4

Mon Sep-Jun, 10am-5pm Thu-Tue, to 8pm Wed Jul & Aug) The crowning glory of Salzburg's DomQuartier, the Residenz is where the prince-archbishops held court until Salzburg became part of the Habsburg Empire in the 19th century. An audio-guide tour takes in the exuberant **state rooms**, lavishly adorned with tapestries, stucco and frescoes by Johann Michael Rottmayr. The 3rd floor is given over to the **Residenzgalerie**, where the focus is on Flemish and Dutch masters. Must-sees include Rubens' *Allegory on Emperor Charles V* and Rembrandt's chiaroscuro *Old Woman Praying*.

Museum der Moderne GALLERY
(www.museumdermoderne.at; Mönchsberg 32; adult/child €8/6; 10am-6pm Tue-Sun, to 8pm Wed;) Straddling Mönchsberg's cliffs, this contemporary glass-and-marble oblong of a gallery stands in stark contrast to the fortress, and shows first-rate temporary exhibitions of 20th- and 21st-century art. The works of Alberto Giacometti, Dieter Roth, Emil Nolde and John Cage have previously been featured. There's a free guided tour of the gallery at 6.30pm every Wednesday. The **Mönchsberg Lift** (Gstättengasse 13; one way/return €2.40/3.70, incl gallery entry €9.10/9.70; 8am-11pm Jul & Aug, 8am-7pm Mon, to 9pm Tue-Sun Sep-Jun) whizzes up to the gallery year-round.

Salzburg Museum MUSEUM
(www.salzburgmuseum.at; Mozartplatz 1; adult/child €8.50/3; 9am-5pm Tue-Sun;) Housed in the baroque Neue Residenz palace, this flagship museum takes you on a fascinating romp through Salzburg past and present. Ornate rooms showcase everything from Roman excavations to royal portraits. There are free guided tours at 6pm every Thursday.

Stift Nonnberg CONVENT
(Nonnberg Convent; Nonnberggasse 2; 7am-dusk) FREE A short climb up the Nonnbergstiege staircase from Kaigasse or along Festungsgasse brings you to this Benedictine convent, founded 1300 years ago and made famous as the nunnery in *The Sound of Music*. You can visit the beautiful rib-vaulted **church**, but the rest of the convent is off limits. Take €0.50 to switch on the light that illuminates the beautiful **Romanesque frescoes**.

Dom CATHEDRAL
(Cathedral; 0662-804 77 950; www.salzburger-dom.at; Domplatz; 8am-7pm Mon-Sat, from 1pm Sun May-Sep, shorter hours Oct-Apr) Gracefully crowned by a bulbous copper dome and twin spires, the Dom stands out as a masterpiece of baroque art. Bronze portals symbolising faith, hope and charity lead into the cathedral. In the nave, both the intricate stucco and Arsenio Mascagni's ceiling frescoes recounting the Passion of Christ guide the eye to the polychrome dome.

Mozart's Geburtshaus MUSEUM
(Mozart's Birthplace; www.mozarteum.at; Getreidegasse 9; adult/child €11/3.50; 8.30am-7pm Jul & Aug, 9am-5.30pm Sep-Jun) Wolfgang Amadeus Mozart, Salzburg's most famous son, was born in this bright yellow townhouse in 1756, and spent the first 17 years of his life here. Today's museum harbours a collection of instruments, documents and portraits. Highlights include the mini-violin he played as a toddler, plus a lock of his hair and buttons from his jacket.

Mozart-Wohnhaus MUSEUM
(Mozart's Residence; www.mozarteum.at; Makartplatz 8; adult/child €11/3.50; 8.30am-7pm Jul & Aug, 9am-5.30pm Sep-Jun) Tired of the cramped living conditions on Getreidegasse, the Mozart family moved in 1773 to this roomier abode, where the prolific Wolfgang composed works such as the *Shepherd King* (K208) and *Idomeneo* (K366). Emanuel Schikaneder, a close friend of Mozart and the librettist of *The Magic Flute*, was a regular guest here. An audio guide accompanies your visit, serenading you with opera excerpts. Alongside family portraits and documents, you'll find Mozart's original fortepiano.

Tours

Fräulein Maria's Bicycle Tours CYCLING
(www.mariasbicycletours.com; Mirabellplatz 4; adult/child €30/18; 9.30am Apr-Oct, plus 4.30pm Jun-Aug;) Belt out *The Sound of Music* faves as you pedal on one of these jolly 3½-hour bike tours, taking in locations from the film including the **Mirabellgarten** (Mirabellplatz 4; Marble Hall 8am-4pm Mon, Wed & Thu, from 1pm Tue & Fri, gardens 6am-dusk) FREE, Stift Nonnberg (p59), **Schloss Leopoldskron** (www.schloss-leopoldskron.com; Leopoldskronstrasse 56-58) and Hellbrunn. No advance booking is necessary; just turn up at the meeting point on Mirabellplatz.

Festivals & Events

Salzburg Festival CULTURAL
(Salzburger Festspiele; www.salzburgerfestspiele.at; Jul & Aug) The absolute highlight of the city's events calendar is the Salzburg Festival. It's a grand affair, with some 200 productions – including theatre, classical music and opera – staged in the impressive surrounds of the **Grosses Festpielhaus** (0662-804 50; Hofstallgasse 1), **Haus für Mozart** (House for Mozart; 0662-804 55 00; www.salzburgerfestspiele.at; Hofstallgasse 1) and the baroque **Felsenreitschule** (Summer Riding School; Hofstallgasse 1). Tickets vary in price between €11 and €430; book well ahead.

SALZBURG CARD

If you're planning on doing lots of sightseeing, save by buying the **Salzburg Card** (1-/2-/3-day card €29/38/44). The card gets you entry to all of the major sights and attractions, unlimited use of public transport (including cable cars) and numerous discounts on tours and events. The card is half-price for children and €3 cheaper in the low season.

The card can be purchased at the airport, tourist office, most hotels and online at www.salzburg.info.

Sleeping

★ **Haus Ballwein** GUESTHOUSE $
(0662-82 40 29; www.haus-ballwein.at; Moosstrasse 69a; s €55-65, d €72-85, tr €85-90, q €90-100; P) With its bright, pine-filled rooms, mountain views, free bike hire and garden, this place is big on charm. The largest, quietest rooms face the back and have balconies and kitchenettes. It's a 10-minute trundle from the Altstadt; take bus 21 to Gsengerweg. Breakfast is a wholesome spread of fresh rolls, eggs, fruit, muesli and cold cuts.

Yoho Salzburg HOSTEL $
(0662-87 96 49; www.yoho.at; Paracelsusstrasse 9; dm €20-26, d €70-88; @) Free wi-fi, secure lockers, comfy bunks, plenty of cheap beer and good-value schnitzels – what more could a backpacker ask for? Except, perhaps, a merry singalong with *The Sound of Music* screened daily (yes, *every* day). The friendly crew can arrange tours, adventure sports such as rafting and canyoning, and bike hire.

Arte Vida GUESTHOUSE $$
(0662-87 31 85; www.artevida.at; Dreifaltigkeitsgasse 9; d €110-145, apt €170-220;) Arte Vida has the boho-chic feel of a Marrakech *riad*, with its lantern-lit salon, communal kitchen and serene garden. Asia and Africa have provided the inspiration for the rich colours and fabrics that dress the individually designed rooms. Affable hosts Herbert and Karoline happily give tips on Salzburg and its surrounds, and can arrange massages and private yoga sessions.

Hotel am Dom BOUTIQUE HOTEL $$
(0662-84 27 65; www.hotelamdom.at; Goldgasse 17; s €109-219, d €149-349;) Antique meets boutique at this Altstadt hotel, where the original vaults and beams of the 800-year-old building contrast with razor-sharp design features. Artworks inspired by the musical legends of the Salzburg Festival grace the rooms, which sport caramel-champagne colour schemes, funky lighting, velvet throws and ultra-glam bathrooms.

★ **Villa Trapp** HOTEL $$$
(0662-63 08 60; www.villa-trapp.com; Traunstrasse 34; s €65-130, d €114-280, ste €290-580;

P) Marianne and Christopher have transformed the original von Trapp family home into a beautiful guesthouse (for guests only, we might add). The 19th-century villa is elegant, if not *quite* as palatial as in the movie, with tasteful wood-floored rooms and a balustrade for sweeping down à la Baroness Schräder.

Eating

Self-caterers can find picnic fixings at the **Grünmarkt** (Green Market; Universitätsplatz; 7am-7pm Mon-Fri, to 3pm Sat).

Stiftsbäckerei St Peter BAKERY $

(Kapitelplatz 8; 8am-5.30pm Mon & Tue, 7am-5.30pm Thu & Fri, 7am-1pm Sat) Next to the monastery, where the watermill turns, this 700-year-old bakery turns out Salzburg's best sourdough loaves from a wood-fired oven.

Bärenwirt AUSTRIAN $$

(0662-42 24 04; www.baerenwirt-salzburg.at; Müllner Hauptstrasse 8; mains €12-20; 11am-11pm) Sizzling and stirring since 1663, Bärenwirt is Austrian through and through. Go for hearty *Bierbraten* (beer roast) with dumplings, locally caught trout or organic wild-boar bratwurst. A tiled oven warms the woody, hunting-lodge-style interior in winter, while the river-facing terrace is a summer crowd-puller. The restaurant is 500m north of Museumplatz.

Triangel AUSTRIAN $$

(0662-84 22 29; Wiener-Philharmoniker-Gasse 7; mains €12-38; 11.30am-10pm Tue-Sat) The menu is market-fresh at this arty bistro, where the picture-clad walls pay tribute to Salzburg Festival luminaries. It does gourmet salads, a mean Hungarian goulash with organic beef, and delicious house-made ice cream. Lunch specials go for just €7.90.

Afro Café INTERNATIONAL $$

(www.afrocafe.at; Bürgerspitalplatz 5; lunch €8.90, mains €14-19; 9am-11pm Mon-Thu, to midnight Fri & Sat) Hot-pink walls, butterfly chairs and artworks made from beach junk…this Afro-chic cafe is totally groovy. Staff keep the good vibes and food coming – from breakfasts to ostrich burgers, and from samosas to steaks sizzling hot from the grill. It also does a good line in coffee, rooibos teas, juices and cakes.

★**Esszimmer** FRENCH $$$

(0662-87 08 99; www.esszimmer.com; Müllner Hauptstrasse 33; 3 course lunch €45, tasting menus €79-128; noon-2pm & 6.30-9.30pm Tue-Sat) Andreas Kaiblinger puts an innovative spin on market-driven French cuisine at Michelin-starred Esszimmer. Eye-catching art, playful backlighting and a glass floor revealing the Almkanal stream keep diners captivated, as do gastronomic show-stoppers such as Arctic char with calf's head and asparagus. Buses 7, 21 and 28 to Landeskrankenhaus stop close by.

DOMQUARTIER

Salzburg's DomQuartier (www.domquartier.at) showcases the most fabulous baroque monuments and museums in the historic centre. A single ticket (adult/child €13/8) gives you access to the Residenz (p58) state rooms and gallery, the upper galleries of the Dom (p59), the **Dommuseum** (www.domquartier.at; Domplatz; DomQuartier ticket adult/child €13/8; 10am-5pm Wed-Mon) and **Erzabtei St Peter** (St Peter's Abbey; www.stift-stpeter.at; Sankt-Peter-Bezirk 1-2; catacombs adult/child €2/1.50; church 8am-noon & 2.30-6.30pm, cemetery 6.30am-7pm, catacombs 10am-6pm). The free multilingual audio guide whisks you through the quarter in 90 minutes, though you could easily spend half a day absorbing all of its sights. For an insight into the DomQuartier's history and architecture, you can download the audioguide to your phone, tablet or PC from the website before you visit.

Drinking & Nightlife

★**Augustiner Bräustübl** BREWERY

(www.augustinerbier.at; Augustinergasse 4-6; 3-11pm Mon-Fri, from 2.30pm Sat & Sun) Who says monks can't enjoy themselves? Since 1621, this cheery, monastery-run brewery has served potent homebrews in beer steins, in the vaulted hall and beneath the chestnut trees of the 1000-seat beer garden. Get your tankard filled at the foyer pump and visit the snack stands for hearty, beer-swigging grub including *Stelzen* (ham hock), pork belly and giant pretzels.

Kaffee Alchemie CAFE

(www.kaffee-alchemie.at; Rudolfskai 38; 7.30am-6pm Mon-Fri, from 10am Sat & Sun) Making coffee really is rocket science at this vintage-cool cafe by the river, which spotlights high-quality, fair-trade, single-origin beans. Talented baristas make spot-on espressos (on a Marzocco GB5, in case you wondered), cappuccinos and speciality coffees, which go nicely with the selection of cakes and brownies. Not a coffee fan? Try the super-smooth coffee-leaf tea.

Enoteca Settemila WINE BAR
(www.facebook.com/enotecasettemila; Bergstrasse 9; ⏲5-11pm Wed-Sat) This bijou wine shop and bar brims with the enthusiasm and passion of Rafael Peil and Nina Corti. Go to sample their well-curated selection of wines, including Austrian, organic and biodynamic ones, with *taglieri* – sharing plates of cheese and *salumi* (salami, ham, prosciutto and the like) – from small Italian producers.

Information

Most hotels and bars offer free wi-fi, and there are several cheap internet cafes near the train station. *Bankomaten* (ATMs) are all over the place.

Tourist Office (☎0662-88 98 73 30; www.salzburg.info; Mozartplatz 5; ⏲9am-6pm Apr-Sep, 9am-6pm Mon-Sat Oct-Mar) Helpful tourist office with a ticket-booking service (www.salzburgticket.com) in the same building.

Getting There & Away

Flights from the UK and the rest of Europe, including low-cost airlines **Ryanair** (www.ryanair.com) and **easyJet** (www.easyjet.com) service **Salzburg airport** (SZG; ☎0662-858 00; www.salzburg-airport.com; Innsbrucker Bundesstrasse 95; 📶), a 20-minute bus ride from the centre.

Salzburger Verkehrsverbund (☎24hr hotline 0662-63 29 00; www.svv-info.at) buses depart from just outside the Hauptbahnhof on Südtiroler Platz.

Trains leave frequently for Vienna (€54.10, 2½ to three hours) and Linz (€27.50, 1¼ hours). There is a two-hourly express service to Klagenfurt (€41.20, three hours).

Getting Around

A Velo (☎0676-435 59 50; Mozartplatz; bicycle rental half-day/full day/week €12/18/55, e-bike €18/25/120; ⏲9.30am-5pm Apr-Jun & Sep, to 7pm Jul & Aug) is just across the way from the tourist office.

Bus routes are shown at bus stops and on some city maps; buses 1 and 4 start from the Hauptbahnhof and skirt the pedestrian-only Altstadt. Bus drivers sell single (€2.60), 24-hour (€5.70) and weekly tickets (€16). Single tickets bought in advance from machines are slightly cheaper.

WORTH A TRIP

SCHLOSS HELLBRUNN

A prince-archbishop with a wicked sense of humour, Markus Sittikus built Italianate **Schloss Hellbrunn** (www.hellbrunn.at; Fürstenweg 37; adult/child/family €12.50/5.50/26.50, gardens free; ⏲9am-9pm Jul & Aug, to 5.30pm Apr-Jun, Sep & Oct; 👪) as a 17th-century summer palace and an escape from his Residenz functions. While the whimsical palace interior is worth a peek, the eccentric **Wasserspiele** (trick fountains) are the big draw in summer. Be prepared to get soaked in the mock Roman theatre, the shell-clad Neptune Grotto and the twittering Bird Grotto. In the palace gardens, look out for *The Sound of Music* pavilion of 'Sixteen Going on Seventeen' fame. Bus 25 (€2, every 20 minutes) runs to Hellbrunn, 4.5km south of Salzburg, from Mozartsteg/Rudolfskai in the Altstadt.

THE SALZKAMMERGUT

A wonderland of deep blue lakes and tall craggy peaks, the Lake District has long been a favourite holiday destination for Austrians, luring a throng of summertime visitors to sail, fish, swim, hike or just laze on the shore. Bad Ischl is the region's hub, but Hallstatt is its true jewel.

Information

For info visit **Salzkammergut Tourismus** (☎06132-2400 051; www.salzkammergut.co.at; Götzstrasse 12, Bad Ischl; ⏲9am-6pm Mon-Fri, 9am-2pm Sat & Sun, closed Sun Sep-Jun). The Salzkammergut Card (€4.90, available May to October) provides up to 30% discounts on sights, ferries, cable cars and some buses.

Hallstatt

☎06134 / ☎778

With pastel-coloured houses that cast shimmering reflections onto the glassy waters of the lake and with towering mountains on all sides, Hallstatt is a beauty with a great backstory. Now a Unesco World Heritage Site, Hallstatt was settled 4500 years ago and over 2000 Iron Age graves have been discovered in the area, most of them dating from 1000 to 500 BC.

Sights & Activities

Salzwelten MINE

(☎06132-200 24 00; www.salzwelten.at; Salzbergstrasse 21; funicular return & tour adult/child/family €34/17/71; ⊙9.30am-2.30pm early Mar-late Mar & late Sep–mid-Dec, to 4.30pm late-Mar-late Sept) The fascinating *Salzbergwerk* (salt mine) is situated high above Hallstatt on Salzberg (Salt Mountain) and is the lake's major cultural attraction. The bilingual German-English tour details how salt is formed and the history of mining, and takes visitors down into the depths on miners' slides – the largest is 60m (on which you can get your photo taken).

Beinhaus CHURCH

(Bone House; Kirchenweg 40; adult/child €1.50/0.50; ⊙10am-5pm May-Oct, 11.30am-3.30pm Wed-Sun Nov-Apr) This small ossuary contains rows of neatly stacked skulls, painted with decorative designs and the names of their former owners. Bones have been exhumed from the overcrowded graveyard since 1600, and although the practice waned in the 20th century, the last joined the collection in 1995. It stands in the grounds of the 15th-century Catholic **Pfarrkirche** (parish church), which has some attractive Gothic frescoes and three winged altars inside.

Sleeping & Eating

Pension Sarstein GUESTHOUSE $$

(☎06134-82 17; Gosaumühlstrasse 83; d €110, apt for 2/3/4 people €140/180/210, breakfast €8 per person;) The affable Fischer family takes pride in its little guesthouse, a few minutes' walk along the lakefront from central Hallstatt. The old-fashioned rooms are not flash, but they are neat, cosy and have balconies with dreamy lake and mountain views. Family-sized apartments come with kitchenettes. Doubles can be rented for a night, but apartments only for three or more (five in summer). Wi-fi is not in the rooms themselves.

★**Halstätt Hideaway** BOUTIQUE HOTEL $$$

(☎0677 617 105 18; www.hallstatt-hideaway.com; Dr. Friedrich-Morton-Weg 24; ste €270-480;) Six splendidly modern, beautifully textured private suites make up what is the region's most stylish accommodation choice. While prices reflect the varying sizes and facilities of each of the suites, they all have their own particular appeal – be that alpine charm, a stuccoed ceiling or contemporary design pieces and killer terraces with hot tub in the penthouse.

> WORTH A TRIP
>
> ### OBERTRAUN
>
> Across the lake from the Hallstatt throngs, down-to-earth Obertraun is the gateway for some geological fun. The many 1000-year-old caves of the **Dachstein Rieseneishöhle** (www.dachstein-salzkammergut.com; All cable car sections plus caves adult/child €48.20/26.60, one section plus caves €42.60/23.40; ⊙9.20am-3.30pm late Apr–mid Jun & mid-Sep–Oct, to 4pm mid late Jun, to 5pm late Jun–mid-Sep) extend into the mountain for almost 80km in places.
>
> From Obertraun it's also possible to catch a cable car to **Krippenstein** (www.dachstein-salzkammergut.com; cable car return adult/child €32/17.60; ⊙mid-Jun–Oct), where you'll find the freaky but fabulous **5 Fingers viewing platform**, which protrudes over a sheer cliff face – not for sufferers of vertigo.

Restaurant zum Salzbaron EUROPEAN $$

(☎06134-82 63 0; www.gruenerbaum.cc; Marktplatz 104; mains €21.90-32.90; ⊙noon-10pm;) One of the best gourmet acts in town, the Salzbaron is perched alongside the lake inside the **Seehotel Grüner Baum** (s €150, d €250-380, ste €450;) and serves a seasonal pan-European menu – the wonderful local trout features strongly in summer.

Getting There & Away

Ferry excursions (☎06134-82 28; www.hallstattschifffahrt.at) do the circuit of Hallstatt Lahn via Hallstatt Markt, Obersee, Untersee and Steeg return (€10, 90 minutes) three times daily from July to early September.

Trains connect Hallstatt and Bad Ischl (€5.20, 20 minutes, hourly). Hallstatt Bahnhof (train station) is across the lake from the village, and boat services (€2.50, 10 minutes, last ferry to Hallstatt Markt 6.50pm) coincide with train arrivals.

TYROL

Tyrol is as pure Alpine as Austria gets, with mountains that make you want to yodel out loud and patchwork pastures chiming with cowbells. After the first proper dump of snow in winter, it's a Christmas-card scene, with snow-frosted forests and skiers whizzing down some of the finest slopes in

Europe. Summer is lower key: hiking trails thread high to peaks and mountain huts, while folk music gets steins swinging down in the valleys.

Innsbruck

☎0512 / POP 132,493 / ELEV 574M

Tyrol's capital is a sight to behold. Jagged rock spires are so close that within 25 minutes it's possible to travel from the heart of the city to over 2000m above sea level. Summer and winter outdoor activities abound, and it's understandable why some visitors only take a peek at Innsbruck proper before heading for the hills. But to do so is a shame, for Innsbruck is in many ways Austria in microcosm, with an authentic late-medieval Altstadt (Old Town), inventive architecture and a vibrant student-driven nightlife.

Sights

★Hofkirche CHURCH

(www.tiroler-landesmuseum.at; Universitätsstrasse 2; adult/child €7/free; 9am-5pm Mon-Sat, 12.30-5pm Sun) Innsbruck's pride and joy is the Gothic Hofkirche, one of Europe's finest royal court churches. It was commissioned in 1553 by Ferdinand I, who enlisted top artists of the age such as Albrecht Dürer, Alexander Colin and Peter Vischer the Elder. Top billing goes to the empty **sarcophagus of Emperor Maximilian I** (1459–1519), a masterpiece of German Renaissance sculpture, elaborately carved from black marble.

Schloss Ambras PALACE

(www.schlossambras-innsbruck.at; Schlosstrasse 20; palace adult/child €10/free, gardens free; palace 10am-5pm, gardens 6am-dusk, closed Nov;) Picturesquely perched on a hill and set among beautiful gardens, this Renaissance pile was acquired in 1564 by Archduke Ferdinand II, then ruler of Tyrol, who transformed it from a fortress into a palace. Don't miss the centrepiece **Spanische Saal** (Spanish Hall), the dazzling **Armour Collection** and the gallery's Velázquez and Van Dyck originals.

Hofburg PALACE

(Imperial Palace; www.hofburg-innsbruck.at; Rennweg 1; adult/child €9/free; 9am-5pm) Grabbing attention with its pearly white facade and cupolas, the Hofburg was built as a castle for Archduke Sigmund the Rich in the 15th century, expanded by Emperor Maximilian I in the 16th century and given a baroque makeover by Empress Maria Theresia in the 18th century. The centrepiece of the lavish rococo state apartments is the 31m-long **Riesensaal** (Giant's Hall).

Goldenes Dachl MUSEUM

(Golden Roof; Herzog-Friedrich-Strasse 15; museum adult/child €4.80/2.40; 10am-5pm May-Sep, 10am-5pm Tue-Sun Oct & Dec-Apr) Innsbruck's golden wonder and most distinctive landmark is this Gothic oriel, built for Holy Roman Emperor Maximilian I (1459–1519), lavishly decorated with murals and glittering with 2657 fire-gilt copper tiles. It is most impressive from the exterior, but the museum is worth a look – especially if you have the Innsbruck Card – with an audio guide whisking you through the history. Keep an eye out for the grotesque tournament helmets designed to resemble the Turks of the rival Ottoman Empire.

Bergisel VIEWPOINT

(www.bergisel.info; adult/child €9.50/4.50; 9am-6pm Jun-Oct, 10am-5pm Wed-Mon Nov-May) Rising above Innsbruck like a celestial staircase, this glass-and-steel ski jump was designed by much-lauded Iraqi architect Zaha Hadid. It's 455 steps or a two-minute funicular ride to the 50m-high **viewing platform**, with a breathtaking panorama of the Nordkette range, Inntal and Innsbruck. Tram 1 trundles here from central Innsbruck.

Activities

Nordkettenbahnen CABLE CAR

(www.nordkette.com; single/return to Hungerburg €5.40/9, to Seegrube €18.60/31.10, to Hafelekar €20.70/34.50; Hungerburg 7.15am-7.15pm Mon-Fri, 8am-7.15pm Sat & Sun, Seegrube 8.30am-5.30pm daily, Hafelekar 9am-5pm daily) Zaha Hadid's space-age funicular runs every 15 minutes, whizzing you from the Congress Centre to the slopes in no time. Walking trails head off in all directions from **Hungerburg** and

FREE GUIDED HIKES

From late May to October, Innsbruck Information (p65) arranges daily guided hikes from Monday to Friday, including sunrise walks, lantern-lit strolls and half-day mountain jaunts, which are, incredibly, free to anyone with an Innsbruck guest card. Pop into the tourist office to register and browse the program.

Seegrube. For more of a challenge, there is a downhill track for mountain bikers and two fixed-rope routes *(Klettersteige)* for climbers.

Inntour ADVENTURE SPORTS
(www.inntour.com; Leopoldstrasse 4; ⊙9am-6pm Mon-Sat) Inntour arranges guided cycling and mountain biking trips, including routes along the Inn River.

Sleeping & Eating

Nepomuk's HOSTEL **$**
(☎0512-58 41 18; www.nepomuks.at; Kiebachgasse 16; dm/d from €24/58; 📶) Could this be backpacker heaven? Nepomuk's sure comes close, with its Altstadt location, well-stocked kitchen and high-ceilinged dorms with nice touches like CD players. The delicious breakfast in attached Cafe Munding, with homemade pastries, jam and fresh-roasted coffee, gets your day off to a grand start.

★ **Hotel Weisses Kreuz** HISTORIC HOTEL **$$**
(☎0512-594 79; www.weisseskreuz.at; Herzog-Friedrich-Strasse 31; s €66-105, d €100-180; P @ 📶) Beneath the arcades, this atmospheric Altstadt hotel has played host to guests for 500 years, including a 13-year-old Mozart. With its wood-panelled parlours, antiques and twisting staircase, the hotel oozes history with every creaking beam. Rooms are supremely comfortable, staff are charming and breakfast is a lavish spread.

Breakfast Club BREAKFAST **$**
(www.breakfast-club.at; Maria-Theresien-Strasse 49; breakfast €5-13; ⊙8am-4pm; 📶✍) Hip, wholesome and nicely chilled, the Breakfast Club does what it says on the tin: all-day breakfast and brunch. And boy are you in for a treat: free-range eggs, Tyrolean mountain cheese, organic breads, homemade spreads, cinnamon-dusted waffles with cranberries and cream, French toast, Greek omelettes – take your pick. It also does fresh-pressed juices and proper Italian coffee.

Die Wilderin AUSTRIAN **$$**
(☎0512-56 27 28; www.diewilderin.at; Seilergasse 5; mains €12.50-20; ⊙5pm-midnight Tue-Sun) Take a gastronomic walk on the wild side at this modern-day hunter-gatherer of a restaurant, where chefs take pride in local sourcing and using top-notch farm-fresh and foraged ingredients. The menu sings of the seasons, be it asparagus, game, strawberries or winter veg. The vibe is urbane and relaxed.

> **CITY SAVERS**
>
> The **Innsbruck Card** allows one visit to Innsbruck's main sights and attractions, a return journey on lifts and cable cars, three hours' bike rental, a guided city walk and unlimited use of public transport. It's available at the tourist office and costs €43/50/59 for 24/48/72 hours (half-price for children).

Il Convento ITALIAN **$$**
(☎0512-58 13 54; www.ilconvento.at; Burggraben 29; mains €13.50-25, 2-course lunch €17.50-18.50; ⊙10am-3pm & 5pm-midnight Mon-Sat) Neatly tucked into the old city walls, this Italian job is run with passion by Peppino and Angelika. It's a winner, with its refined look (white tablecloths, wood beams, Franciscan monastery views from the terrace) and menu. Dishes such as clam linguine, braised veal and salt-crusted cod are cooked to a T and served with wines drawn from the well-stocked cellar.

Drinking & Nightlife

Moustache BAR
(www.cafe-moustache.at; Herzog-Otto-Strasse 8; ⊙11am-2am Tue-Sat, 10am-1am Sun; 📶) Playing Spot-the-Moustache (Einstein, Charlie Chaplin and co) is the preferred pastime at this retro bolthole, with table football and a terrace overlooking pretty Domplatz. The bartenders knock up a mean pisco sour.

Tribaun CRAFT BEER
(www.tribaun.com; Museumstrasse 5; ⊙6pm-1am Mon-Thu, to 3am Fri & Sat) This cracking bar taps into craft-beer culture, with a wide variety of brews – from stouts and porters to IPA, sour, amber, honey and red ales. The easygoing vibe and fun-loving crew add to its appeal.

360° BAR
(Rathaus Galerien; ⊙10am-1am Mon-Sat) Grab a cushion and drink in 360-degree views of the city and Alps from the balcony that skirts this spherical, glass-walled bar. It's a nicely chilled spot for a coffee or sundowner.

Information

Innsbruck Information (☎0512-598 50, 0512-535 60; www.innsbruck.info; Burggraben 3; ⊙9am-6pm Mon-Sat, 10am-4.30pm Sun) Main tourist office with truckloads of info on the city and surrounds, including skiing and walking.

Getting There & Away

EasyJet flies to **Innsbruck Airport** (INN; ☎0512-22 52 50; www.innsbruck-airport.com; Fürstenweg 180), 4km west of the city centre. Buses depart every 15 or 20 minutes from Maria-Theresien-Strasse (16 minutes).

The A12 and the parallel Hwy 171 are the main roads heading west and east. The B177, to the west of Innsbruck, continues north to Germany and Munich while the A13 toll road (€9.50) runs south through the Brenner Pass to Italy.

Fast trains depart daily every two hours for Bregenz (€38.90, 2½ hours) and Salzburg (€47.20, 1¾ hours). From Innsbruck to the Arlberg, the best views are on the right-hand side of the train. Two-hourly express trains serve Munich (€42.60, 1¾ hours) and Verona (€43, 3½ hours). Direct services to Kitzbühel also run every two hours (€15.80, 1¼ hours).

Getting Around

Single tickets on buses and trams cost €3 from the driver or €2.40 if purchased in advance. If you plan to use the city's public transport frequently you're better off buying a 24-hour ticket (€5.60).

Kitzbühel

☎05356 / POP 8272 / ELEV 762M

Ever since Franz Reisch slipped on skis and whizzed down the slopes of Kitzbüheler Horn way back in 1893, so christening the first alpine ski run in Austria, Kitzbühel has carved out its reputation as one of Europe's foremost ski resorts. It's renowned for the white-knuckled Hahnenkamm downhill ski race in January and the reliable excellence of its slopes.

Activities

Downhill skiers flock here for the 185km of slopes that are mostly intermediate and focused on Hahnenkamm-Pengelstein. Kitzbüheler Horn is much loved by beginners. If you're an intermediate skiier, pick a good day to cruise the unforgettable 35km **Ski Safari**. Anyone wanting to up the fear ante should brave the heart-stopping World Cup **Streif**. Kitzbühel makes a terrific base for walking in summer, with scores of well-marked trails, including the 15km **Kaiser Trail** with superlative views of the jagged Kaisergebirge massif. All cable cars are covered by ski passes in winter and by the **Summer Card** (adult three/seven days €52.50/73.50) in summer. The card is sold at cable-car base stations.

Sleeping & Eating

Rates leap by up to 50% in the winter season.

Snowbunny's Hostel HOSTEL $
(☎0676 794 02 33; www.snowbunnys.com; Bichlstrasse 30; dm €24-48, d €66-146;) This friendly, laid-back hostel is a bunny-hop from the slopes. Dorms are fine, if a tad dark; breakfast is DIY-style in the kitchen. There's a TV lounge, a ski storage room and cats to stroke.

★**Villa Licht** HOTEL $$
(☎05356-622 93; www.villa-licht.at; Franz-Reisch-Strasse 8; d apt €130-580;) Pretty gardens, spruce modern apartments with pine trappings, living rooms with kitchenettes, balconies with mountain views, peace – this charming Tyrolean chalet has the lot, and owner Renate goes out of her way to please. Kids love the outdoor pool in summer.

Huberbräu Stüberl AUSTRIAN $$
(☎05356-656 77; Vorderstadt 18; mains €9-19; 8am-11.30pm Mon-Sat, 9am-11.30pm Sun;) An old-world Tyrolean haunt with vaults and pine benches, this tavern favours substantial portions of Austrian classics, such as schnitzel, goulash and dumplings, cooked to perfection.

Bring cash as cards are not accepted.

Getting There & Away

Trains run frequently from Kitzbühel to Innsbruck (€15.80, 1¼ hours) and Salzburg (€31.50 to €43.80, two to 2½ hours). For Kufstein (€10.20, 51 minutes), change at Wörgl.

Lienz

☎04852 / POP 11,844 / ELEV 673M

The Dolomites rise like an amphitheatre around Lienz, which straddles the Isel and Drau Rivers just 40km north of Italy. The capital of East Tyrol is a scenic staging point for travels through the Hohe Tauern National Park.

Sights & Activities

Lienz is renowned for its 64km of cross-country skiing trails; the town fills up for the annual Dolomitenlauf cross-country race in mid-January. A €47.50 day pass covers the downhill slopes on nearby Zettersfeld and Hochstein peaks.

WORTH A TRIP

KRIMML FALLS

The thunderous, three-tier **Krimmler Wasserfälle** (Krimml Falls; 06564-72 12; www.wasserfaelle-krimml.at; adult/child €4/1; 9am-5pm mid-Apr–Oct) is Europe's highest waterfall at 380m, and one of Austria's most unforgettable sights. The **Wasserfallweg** (Waterfall Trail), which starts at the ticket office and weaves gently uphill through mixed forest, has numerous viewpoints with photogenic close-ups of the falls. It's about a two-hour return-trip walk.

The pretty Alpine village of Krimml has a handful of places to sleep and eat – contact the **tourist office** (06564-72 39; www.krimml.at; Oberkrimml 37; 8am-noon & 2-5pm Mon-Fri, 8.30-11.30am Sat) for more information.

Buses run year-round from Krimml to Zell am See (€10.20, 1¼ hours, every two hours), with frequent onward train connections to Salzburg (€19.60, 1½ hours). The village is about 500m north of the waterfall, on a side turning from the B165. There are parking spaces near the falls.

Sleeping & Eating

Gasthof Schlossberghof HOTEL $$
(04852-632 33; https://schlossberghof.at; Iseltaler Strasse 21, s/d €65/100; P) With rooms revamped in a contemporary style, this rustic, chalet-style guesthouse is a 10-minute stroll from the centre and is watched over by the Dolomites.

Garage EUROPEAN $$
(04852-645 54; www.garage-lienz.at; Südtiroler Platz 2; mains €10-26, lunch special €8.50; 11am-3pm & 6-11pm Tue-Sat) At this garage-style restaurant in the heart of Lienz, the decor is an atmospheric new-old combination of dark beams, monochrome tones, marble-topped tables and vintage picture frames. Alongside faves like organic *Wiener Schnitzel,* you'll find bright flavours in dishes like basil felafel with rocket, five-spice sirloin with rosemary dumplings, and coconut-lemongrass chicken curry.

Information

The **tourist office** (Lienzer Dolimiten; 050 212 212; www.osttirol.com; Mühlgasse 11; 8am-6pm Mon-Fri, 9am-noon & 4-6pm Sat) sells walking (€4) and via ferrate (€1) maps, can advise on the high-altitude trails that thread through the Dolomites' peaks and has brochures on all the adventure sports operators.

Getting There & Away

Most trains to the rest of Austria, including Salzburg (€40.70, 3½ to 4½ hours, hourly), go east via Spittal-Millstättersee, where you usually have to change. Buses to Kitzbühel (€15.80, 1¾ hours) are quicker and more direct than the train, but less frequent.

Hohe Tauern National Park

Straddling Tyrol, Salzburg and Carinthia, this national park is the largest in the Alps; a 1786-sq-km wilderness of 3000m peaks, alpine meadows and waterfalls. At its heart lies Grossglockner (3798m), Austria's highest mountain, which towers over the 8km-long Pasterze Glacier, best seen from the outlook at Kaiser-Franz-Josefs-Höhe (2369m).

The 48km **Grossglockner Road** (www.grossglockner.at; day ticket car/motorbike €36/26; 6am-8pm May, 5am-9.30pm Jun-Aug, 6am-7.30pm Sep & Oct) from Bruck in Salzburgerland to Heiligenblut in Carinthia is one of Europe's greatest Alpine drives. A feat of 1930s engineering, the road swings giddily around 36 switchbacks, passing jewel-coloured lakes, forested slopes and wondrous glaciers.

The major village on the Grossglockner Road is **Heiligenblut**, famous for its 15th-century pilgrimage church. Here the **tourist office** (04824 27 00 20; www.heiligenblut.at; Hof 4; 9am-6pm Mon-Fri, 2-6pm Sat & Sun) can advise on guided ranger hikes, mountain hiking and skiing. The village also has a spick-and-span **Jugendherberge** (04824-22 59; www.oejhv.or.at; Hof 36; dm/s/d €23.50/31.50/58; P).

Bus 5002 runs frequently between Lienz and Heiligenblut on weekdays (€8.70, one hour), and less frequently at weekends. From late June to late September, four buses run from Monday to Friday, and three at weekends between Heiligenblut and Kaiser-Franz-Josefs-Höhe (€5.90, 32 minutes).

SURVIVAL GUIDE

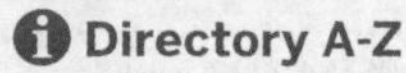

Directory A-Z

ACCOMMODATION

Tourist offices invariably keep lists and details of accommodation; some arrange bookings (free, or for a small fee).

Hotels From budget picks to five-star luxury in palatial surrounds.

B&Bs Also called pensions and *Gasthöfe;* range from simple city digs to rustic mountain chalets.

Private rooms *Privat Zimmer* usually represent great value (doubles go for as little as €50).

Farmstays Well geared towards families. Some only operate during the summer months.

Alpine huts These go with the snow, opening from roughly late June to mid-September. Advance bookings are essential.

Camping Most resorts and cities have campgrounds, usually in pretty, natural settings.

Booking Services

Local city and regional tourist office websites often have excellent accommodation booking functions.

Austrian Hotelreservation (www.austrianhotelreservation.at) Find hotels Austria-wide by theme and/or destination.

Austrian National Tourist Office (www.austria.info) The Austrian National Tourist Office has a number of overseas offices. There is a comprehensive listing on the ANTO website.

Bergfex (www.bergfex.at) Hotels, guesthouses, hostels, B&Bs, farms and huts searchable by region.

Best Alpine Wellness Hotels (www.wellnesshotel.com) The pick of Austria's top family-run spa hotels.

Camping in Österreich (https://www.camping.info/österreich) Search for campgrounds by location, facilities or reviews.

Lonely Planet (lonelyplanet.com/austria/hotels) Recommendations and bookings.

MONEY

- Austria's currency is the euro. An approximate 10% tip is expected in restaurants. Pay it directly to the server; don't leave it on the table.
- ATMs are widely available. Maestro direct debit and Visa and MasterCard credit cards accepted in most hotels and midrange restaurants. Expect to pay cash elsewhere.

OPENING HOURS

Banks 8am or 9am–3pm Monday to Friday (to 5.30pm Thursday)

Cafes 7am or 8am–11pm or midnight; traditional cafes close at 7pm or 8pm

Offices and government departments 8am–3.30pm, 4pm or 5pm Monday to Friday

Post offices 8am–noon and 2–6pm Monday to Friday; some open Saturday morning

Pubs and Bars Close between midnight and 4am

Restaurants Generally 11am–2.30pm or 3pm and 6–11pm or midnight

Shops 9am–6.30pm Monday to Friday (often to 9pm Thursday or Friday in cities), 9am–5pm Saturday

PUBLIC HOLIDAYS

New Year's Day (Neujahr) 1 January

Epiphany (Heilige Drei Könige) 6 January

Easter Monday (Ostermontag) March/April

Labour Day (Tag der Arbeit) 1 May

Whit Monday (Pfingstmontag) 6th Monday after Easter

Ascension Day (Christi Himmelfahrt) 6th Thursday after Easter

Corpus Christi (Fronleichnam) 2nd Thursday after Whitsunday

Assumption (Maria Himmelfahrt) 15 August

National Day (Nationalfeiertag) 26 October

All Saints' Day (Allerheiligen) 1 November

Immaculate Conception (Mariä Empfängnis) 8 December

Christmas Day (Christfest) 25 December

St Stephen's Day (Stephanitag) 26 December

SAFE TRAVEL

Theft Take usual common-sense precautions: keep valuables out of sight (on your person and in parked cars). Pickpockets occasionally operate on public transport and at major tourist sights.

Natural dangers Every year people die from landslides and avalanches in the Alps. Always check weather conditions before heading out; consider hiring a guide when skiing off-piste. Before going on challenging hikes, ensure you have the proper equipment and fitness. Inform someone at your hotel/guesthouse where you're going and when you intend to return.

TELEPHONE

- Austrian telephone numbers consist of an area code followed by the local number.
- Austria's international access code is 00; its country code is 43.
- Phone shops sell prepaid SIM cards from around €15.
- Phone cards in different denominations are sold at post offices and *Tabak* (tobacconist) shops. Call centres are widespread in cities, and many internet cafes are geared for Skype calls.

TOURIST INFORMATION

Austria Info (www.austria.info) is the official tourism website for the low-down on Austria, including hotels, itineraries, activities and excellent information on walking in Austria, from themed day hikes to long-distance treks. Also has details on national parks and nature reserves, hiking villages and special walking packages. Region-specific brochures are available for downloading.

Transport

GETTING THERE & AWAY

Air

Vienna is the main transport hub for Austria, but Graz, Linz, Klagenfurt, Salzburg and Innsbruck all receive international flights. Flights to these cities are often a cheaper option than those to the capital, as are flights to Airport Letisko (Bratislava Airport), which is only 60km east of Vienna, in Slovakia. Bregenz has no airport; there are limited flights to nearby Friedrichshafen in Germany and much better connections at Zürich in Switzerland.

Bus

Buses depart from Austria for as far afield as England, the Baltic countries, the Netherlands, Germany and Switzerland. Most significantly, they provide access to Eastern European cities small and large – from the likes of Sofia and Warsaw to Banja Luka, Mostar and Sarajevo.

Services operated by **Eurolines** (www.eurolines.at) leave from Vienna and from several regional cities.

Car & Motorcycle

There are numerous entry points into Austria by road from Germany, the Czech Republic, Slovakia, Hungary, Slovenia, Italy and Switzerland. All border-crossing points are open 24 hours.

Standard European insurance and paperwork rules apply.

Train

The main services in and out of the country from the west normally pass through Bregenz, Innsbruck or Salzburg en route to Vienna. Trains to Eastern Europe leave from Vienna. Express services to Italy go via Innsbruck or Villach; trains to Slovenia are routed through Graz.

For online timetables and tickets, visit the **ÖBB** (www.oebb.at) website. SparSchiene (discounted tickets) are often available when you book online in advance. **Deutsche Bahn** (www.bahn.com) is also useful.

River

Hydrofoils run to Bratislava and Budapest from Vienna; slower boats cruise the Danube between the capital and Passau.

GETTING AROUND

Air

Flying within a country the size of Austria is rarely necessary. The main exception is to/from Innsbruck (in the far west of Austria).

The national carrier **Austrian Airlines** (www.austrian.com) offers several flights daily between Vienna and Graz, Innsbruck, Klagenfurt, Linz and Salzburg.

Bicycle

- Most regional tourist boards have brochures on cycling facilities and routes within their region.
- Separate bike tracks are common in cities, and long-distance tracks and routes also run along many of the major valleys such as the Danube, Enns and Mur.
- The **Danube cycling trail** is like a Holy Grail for cyclists, following the entire length of the river in Austria between the borders with Germany and Slovakia.

Boat

The Danube serves as a thoroughfare between Vienna and Lower and Upper Austria. Services are generally slow, scenic excursions rather than functional means of transport.

Bus

Rail routes are often complemented by **Postbus** (www.postbus.at) services, which really come into their own in the more inaccessible mountainous regions. Buses are fairly reliable, and usually depart from outside train stations

Car & Motorcycle

- A *Vignette* (toll sticker) is imposed on all motorways. *Vignette* can be purchased at border crossings, petrol stations and *Tabak* shops.
- Winter or all-weather tyres are compulsory from 1 November to 15 April. Carrying snow chains in winter is highly recommended.
- Speed limits are 50km/h in built-up areas, 130km/h on autobahn and 100km/h on other roads.

Train

ÖBB (www.oebb.at) is the main operator, supplemented by a handful of private lines. Tickets and timetables are available online.

- Reservations cost €3.50 for most 2nd-class express services within Austria.
- Fares quoted are for 2nd-class tickets.
- Passengers with disabilities can use the 24-hour 05-17 17 customer number for special travel assistance; do this at least 24 hours ahead of travel (48 hours ahead for international services).

Belgium & Luxembourg

POP 11.4 MILLION/576,000

Includes ➡

Best Places to Eat

- ➡ The Jane (p96)
- ➡ Comme Chez Soi (p79)
- ➡ Le Sud (p101)
- ➡ Arcadi (p79)
- ➡ De Stove (p86)

Best Places to Stay

- ➡ 1898 The Post (p91)
- ➡ Guesthouse Nuit Blanche (p85)
- ➡ Chambres d'Hôtes du Vaudeville (p78)
- ➡ Villa Botanique Guesthouse (p78)
- ➡ La Pipistrelle (p100)

Why Go?

Stereotypes of comic books, chips and sublime chocolates are just the start in eccentric little Belgium. Its self-deprecating people have quietly spent centuries producing some of Europe's finest art and architecture. Bilingual Brussels is the dynamic yet personable EU capital, also sporting what's arguably the world's most beautiful city square. Flat, Dutch-speaking Flanders has many other alluring medieval cities, all easily linked by regular train hops. Much of hilly, French-speaking Wallonia is contrastingly rural – its castles and extensive cave systems easier to reach by car – though fascinating Mons is well connected by public transport. Independent Luxembourg, the EU's richest country, is compact and attractive with its own wealth of castle villages, while its capital city is famed both for banking and for its fairy-tale Unesco-listed Old Town. Meanwhile the brilliant beers of Belgium and the sparkling wines of Luxembourg's Moselle Valley lubricate some of Europe's best dining.

When to Go

Brussels

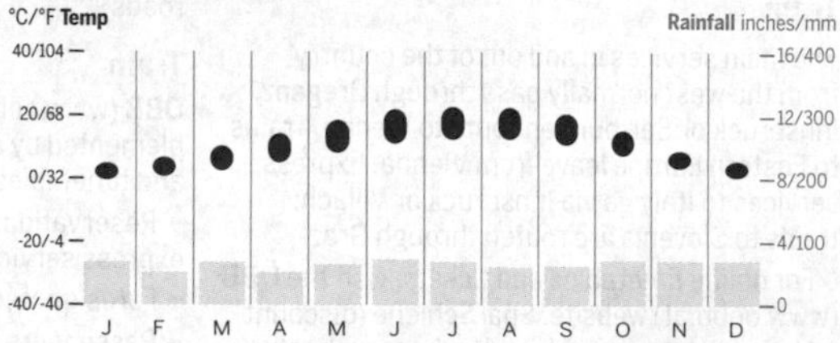

Pre-Easter weekends Belgium hosts many of Europe's weirdest carnivals, not just at Mardi Gras.

Feb–Mar Both countries symbolically burn the spirit of winter on the first weekend after Carnival.

Jul–Aug Countless festivals; hotels are packed in Bruges but cheaper in Brussels and Luxembourg City.

Entering the Country

As part of the Schengen area, there are usually no controls at land borders. The main airport is at Brussels but those at Charleroi, and to a lesser extent Luxembourg, have a good range of budget flights.

ITINERARIES

Four Days

Belgium's four finest 'art cities' all make easy stops or short excursions while you're train-hopping between Paris and Amsterdam. Bruges (p83) is the fairy-tale 'Venice of the north', Ghent (p89) has similar canalside charms without the tourist hordes, Brussels' (p74) incomparable Grand Place is worth jumping off any train for, and cosmopolitan Antwerp (p93) goes one further, adding in fashion and diamonds to its rich artistic and architectural heritage.

Ten Days

Stay longer in each of the above, then return south from Antwerp dropping into lively Leuven (p97), charming Lier (p97) and spiritual Mechelen (p98). From Brussels, visit the world-famous battle site at Waterloo (p82) then take the train across the rolling Ardennes to wealthy little Luxembourg (p100) with its compact Unesco-listed capital and quaint, accessible castle villages.

Essential Food & Drink

Belgium's famous lagers (eg Stella Artois) and white beers (Hoegaarden) are global brands, but what has connoisseurs really drooling are the robust, rich abbey-brewed 'Trappist beers'. Chimay, Rochefort, Westmalle and Orval are widely known, but the one that really counts is ultra-rare Westvleteren XII. Luxembourg's Moselle region produces creditable white wines and excellent *crémants* (bubbles). While top restaurants often have a French-fusion focus, home-style local dishes are making a resurgence. Classics include the following:

Boulettes Meatballs

Chicons au gratin Endives rolled in ham and cooked in cheese/béchamel sauce.

Filet Américain A blob of raw minced beef, typically topped with equally raw egg yolk.

Judd mat gaardebounen Luxembourg's national dish: smoked pork neck in a cream-based sauce with chunks of potato and broad beans.

Mosselen/moules Cauldrons of in-the-shell mussels, typically steamed in white wine with celery and onions and served with a mountain of *frites* (chips).

Paling in 't groen Eel in a sorrel or spinach sauce.

Stoemp Mashed veg-and-potato dish.

Waterzooi A cream-based chicken or fish stew.

AT A GLANCE (BELGIUM/ LUXEMBOURG)

Area 30,528/2586 sq km

Capital Brussels/ Luxembourg City

Country Code ☎+32/+352

Currency euro (€)

Emergency ☎112

Languages Dutch (Flanders), French (Wallonia), both (Brussels); Letzebeurgisch, French and German (Luxembourg)

Time Central European Time (GMT/UTC plus one hour)

Visas Schengen rules apply

Sleeping Price Ranges

The following ranges refer to the cost of a double room in high season.

€ less than €60

€€ €60–140

€€€ more than €140

Eating Price Ranges

The following price ranges refer to the cost of a typical main course.

€ less than €15

€€ €15–25

€€€ more than €25

Resources

Visit Brussels https://visit.brussels/en

Visit Flanders www.visitflanders.com

Visit Luxembourg www.visitluxembourg.com

Belgium & Luxembourg Highlights

❶ Bruges (p83) Visiting on weekdays off-season to appreciate the picture-perfect canal scenes of this medieval city.

❷ Ghent (p89) Being wooed by one of Europe's greatest underappreciated all-round discoveries.

❸ Brussels (p74) Savouring the 'world's most beautiful square', then seeking out remarkable *cafés* (pubs or bars) and chocolate shops.

❹ Antwerp (p93) Following fashion and Rubens to this hip yet historic port city.

❺ Luxembourg City (p100) Spending the weekend in the UNESCO-listed Old Town then heading out to the grand duchy's evocative castle villages.

❻ Waterloo (p82) Tramping across the world-famous battlefield where Napoleon met his Abba song.

❼ Ypres (p87) Pondering the heartbreaking futility of WWI in Flanders' fields.

❽ Lier (p97) Discovering the quaintest Flemish canal city that nobody's heard of.

❾ Moselle Valley (p104) Tasting your way through a range of Luxembourg white wines and sparking *crémants* while watching the Moselle River glide by.

0 30 km
0 20 miles
NETHERLANDS
Tilburg
Roosendaal
Eindhoven
Venlo
A1
N1
A12
Turnhout
A21
Antwerp
4
Antwerp Airport
Herentals
Mol
Neerpelt
Roermond
Mönchengladbach
8 Lier
Fort van Breendonk
E313
GERMANY
National Park Hoge Kempen
Mechelen
Diest
A2
Genk
Hasselt
Bokrijk Openluchtmuseum
E19
Brussels Airport
Leuven
Maastricht
3 Brussels
E313
A2
Aachen
Waterloo
6
A3
E19
Braine l'Alleud
Ottignies
Louvain-la-Neuve
Liège Airport
Liège
Verviers
Hautes Fagnes-Eifel Nature Park
Nivelles
E411
Jehay
Huy
Hautes Fagnes
Remouchamps
Herzogenhugel
Charleroi Airport
E42
Namur
Modave
Hautes Fagnes Nature Reserve
Coo
Stavelot
Charleroi
Durbuy
Barvaux
Godinne
E25
N5
Hotton
Dinant
E421
Marloie
Houyet
Rochefort
Jemelle
La Roche-en-Ardenne
Botte de Hainaut
Lavaux-Ste-Anne
Han-sur-Lesse
Champlon
Clervaux
GERMANY
Chimay
Couvin
E46
Bastogne
Wiltz
E411
ARDENNES
Libramont
Parc Naturel de la Haute Sûre
Vianden
Diekirch
Rochehaut
E46
Ettelbrück
LUXEMBOURG
Echternach
Gutland
Bouillon
Charleville-Mezières
Mersch
Bourglinster
Arlon
Luxembourg Airport
Orval
9
5
Mosell Valley
Luxembourg City
Virton
Rodange
Dudelange

BRUSSELS

POP 1.2 MILLION / ☎ 02

Belgium's capital, and the EU's administrative heart, Brussels is historic yet hip, bureaucratic yet bizarre, self-confident yet unshowy, and multicultural to its roots. All this plays out in a cityscape that swings from majestic to quirky to rundown and back again. Organic art nouveau facades face off against 1960s concrete developments, and regal 19th-century mansions contrast with a Gotham City of brutal glass that forms the EU district. This whole maelstrom swirls out from Brussels' medieval core, where the Grand Place is surely one of the world's most beautiful squares.

Sights

To see a bunch of top sites, consider the **BrusselsCard** (www.brusselscard.be; 24/48/72hr €26/34/42) which includes free city transport. However, avoid buying one for Mondays when much is closed or on the first Wednesday afternoon of each month when many major museums are free.

Central Brussels

★ Grand Place SQUARE

(M Gare Centrale) Brussels' magnificent Grand Place is one of the world's most unforgettable urban ensembles. Oddly hidden, the enclosed cobblestone square is only revealed as you enter on foot from one of six narrow side alleys: Rue des Harengs is the best first approach. The focal point is the spired 15th-century city hall, but each of the antique guildhalls (mostly 1697–1705) has a charm of its own. Most are unashamed exhibitionists, with fine baroque gables, gilded statues and elaborate guild symbols.

Musées Royaux des Beaux-Arts GALLERY

(Royal Museums of Fine Arts; ☎ 02-508 32 11; www.fine-arts-museum.be; Rue de la Régence 3; adult/6-25yr/BrusselsCard €10/3/free, incl Magritte Museum €15; ⏲ 10am-5pm Tue-Fri, 11am-6pm Sat & Sun; M Gare Centrale, Parc) This prestigious museum incorporates the **Musée d'Art Ancien** (ancient art); the **Musée d'Art Moderne** (modern art), with works by surrealist Paul Delvaux and fauvist Rik Wouters; and the purpose-built Musée Magritte. The 15th-century Flemish Primitives are wonderfully represented in the Musée d'Art Ancien: there's Rogier Van der Weyden's *Pietà* with its hallucinatory sky, Hans Memling's refined portraits, and the richly textured *Madonna with Saints* by the anonymous artist known as Master of the Legend of St Lucy.

Musée Magritte GALLERY

(☎ 02-508 32 11; www.musee-magritte-museum.be; Place Royale 1; adult/under 26yr/BrusselsCard €10/3/free; ⏲ 10am-5pm Tue-Fri, 11am-6pm Sat & Sun; M Gare Centrale, Parc) The beautifully presented Magritte Museum holds the world's largest collection of the surrealist pioneer's paintings and drawings. Watch his style develop from colourful Braque-style cubism in 1920 through a Dali-esque phase and a late-1940s period of Kandinsky-like brushwork to his trademark bowler hats of the 1960s. Regular screenings of a 50-minute documentary provide insights into the artist's unconventionally conventional life.

MIM MUSEUM

(Musée des Instruments de Musique; ☎ 02-545 01 30; www.mim.be; Rue Montagne de la Cour 2; adult/concession €10/8; ⏲ 9.30am-5pm Tue-Fri, from 10am Sat & Sun; M Gare Centrale, Parc) Strap on a pair of headphones, then step on the automated floor panels in front of the precious instruments (including world instruments and Adolphe Sax' inventions) to hear them being played. As much of a highlight as the museum itself are the premises – the art nouveau Old England Building. This former department store was built in 1899 by Paul Saintenoy and has a panoramic rooftop *café* (pub/bar) and outdoor terrace.

Galeries St-Hubert ARCHITECTURE

(☎ 02-545 09 90; www.grsh.be; Rue du Marché aux Herbes; M Gare Centrale) When opened in 1847 by King Léopold I, the glorious Galeries St-Hubert formed Europe's very first shopping arcade. Many enticing shops lie behind its neoclassical glassed-in arches flanked by marble pilasters. Several eclectic *cafés* spill tables onto the gallery terrace, safe from rain beneath the glass roof. The arcade is off Rue du Marché aux Herbes.

Musée Mode & Dentelle MUSEUM

(Fashion & Lace Museum; ☎ 02-213 44 50; www.costumeandlacemuseum.brussels; Rue de la Violette 12; adult/child/BrusselsCard €8/free/free; ⏲ 10am-5pm Tue-Sun; M Gare Centrale) Lace making has been one of Flanders' finest crafts since the 16th century. While *kloskant* (bobbin lace) originated in Bruges, *naaldkant* (needlepoint lace) was developed in Italy but was predominantly made in Brussels. This excellent museum reveals lace's applications for underwear and outerwear over the

DON'T MISS

CINQUANTENAIRE & THE EU AREA

While far less famous than the Paris equivalent, Brussels has its very own triumphal arch. It's the centrepiece of the **Parc du Cinquantenaire** (Rue de la Loi & Rue Belliard; M Mérode), built to celebrate 50 years of Belgian independence but only finished in 1905, 25 years late. A surrounding cluster of museums includes the **Musée Art & Histoire** (02-741 73 01; www.artandhistory.museum; Parc du Cinquantenaire 10; adult/child/Brussels-Card €10/4/free; 9.30am-5pm Tue-Fri, from 10am Sat & Sun; M Mérode), chock-a-block with priceless antiquities, and **Autoworld** (www.autoworld.be; Parc du Cinquantenaire; adult/concession/BrusselsCard €10/€7/free; 10am-6pm Apr-Sep, to 5pm Oct-Mar; M Mérode) with its huge collection of vintage cars. Around a kilometre west, the thought-provoking **Musée des Sciences Naturelles** (02-627 42 11; www.naturalsciences.be; Rue Vautier 29; adult/concession/child/BrusselsCard €7/6/4.50/free; 9.30am-5pm Tue-Fri, 10am-6pm Sat & Sun; 38) is a highly interactive science museum featuring a unique 'family' of iguanodons – 10m-high dinosaurs found in a Hainaut coal mine in 1878. The museum is directly south of the **EU Parliament** (02-284 34 57; www.europarl.europa.eu; Rue Wiertz 43; tours 10am & 3pm Mon-Thu, 10am Fri; 38, M Trône) FREE.

centuries, as well as displaying other luxury textiles in beautifully presented exhibitions. There's a new focus here on Belgium's ahead-of-the-curve fashion industry, with changing exhibitions of contemporary textiles.

Manneken Pis MONUMENT
(cnr Rue de l'Étuve & Rue du Chêne; M Gare Centrale) Rue Charles Buls – Brussels' most unashamedly touristy shopping street, lined with chocolate and trinket shops – leads the hordes three blocks from the Grand Place to the Manneken Pis. This fountain-statue of a little boy taking a leak is comically tiny and a perversely perfect national symbol for surreal Belgium. Most of the time the statue's nakedness is hidden beneath a costume relevant to an anniversary, national day or local event: his ever-growing wardrobe is displayed at the **Maison du Roi** (Musée de la Ville de Bruxelles; Grand Place; M Gare Centrale).

Beyond the Centre

Atomium MONUMENT
(02-475 47 75; www.atomium.be; Av de l'Atomium; adult/teen/child €15/8/free; 10am-6pm; M Heysel, 51) The space-age Atomium looms 102m over north Brussels' suburbia, resembling a steel alien from a '60s Hollywood movie. It consists of nine house-sized metallic balls linked by steel tube-columns containing escalators and lifts. The balls are arranged like a school chemistry set to represent iron atoms in their crystal lattice…except these are 165 billion times bigger. It was built as a symbol of postwar progress for the 1958 World's Fair and became an architectural icon, receiving a makeover in 2006.

Cantillon Brewery BREWERY
(Musée Bruxellois de la Gueuze; 02-520 28 91; www.cantillon.be; Rue Gheude 56; €9.50; 10am-5pm Mon, Tue & Thu-Sat; M Clemenceau) Beer lovers shouldn't miss this unique living brewery-museum. Atmospheric and family run, it's Brussels' last operating lambic brewery and still uses much of the original 19th-century equipment. After hearing a brief explanation, visitors take a self-guided tour, including the barrel rooms where the beers mature for up to three years in chestnut wine casks. The entry fee includes two taster glasses of Cantillon's startlingly acidic brews.

Africa Museum MUSEUM
(02-769 52 11; www.africamuseum.be/en/home; Leuvensesteenweg 13, Tervuren; adult €12, concessions free €8; 11am-5pm Tue-Fri, 10am-6pm Sat & Sun, public & school holidays; 44) The revived Africa Museum is a world away from its earlier dusty colonial incarnation. The exhibits are predominantly from former Belgian colony the Congo, and include some beautiful musical instruments, masquerade masks and artfully carved pot lids. Resident artists and a digital project give the space a contemporary focus.

Train World MUSEUM
(02-224 74 98; www.trainworld.be; Place Princesse Elisabeth 5; adult/concession/BrusselsCard €12/9/free; 10am-5pm Tue-Sun; 58, 59, 7, 92, Schaerbeek) Wonderful old engines gleam in the low light of this imaginative and beautiful museum, located in the renovated 1887 Schaerbeek station: exhibits include *Le Belge*, the country's first locomotive. You can climb on board the engines,

Central Brussels

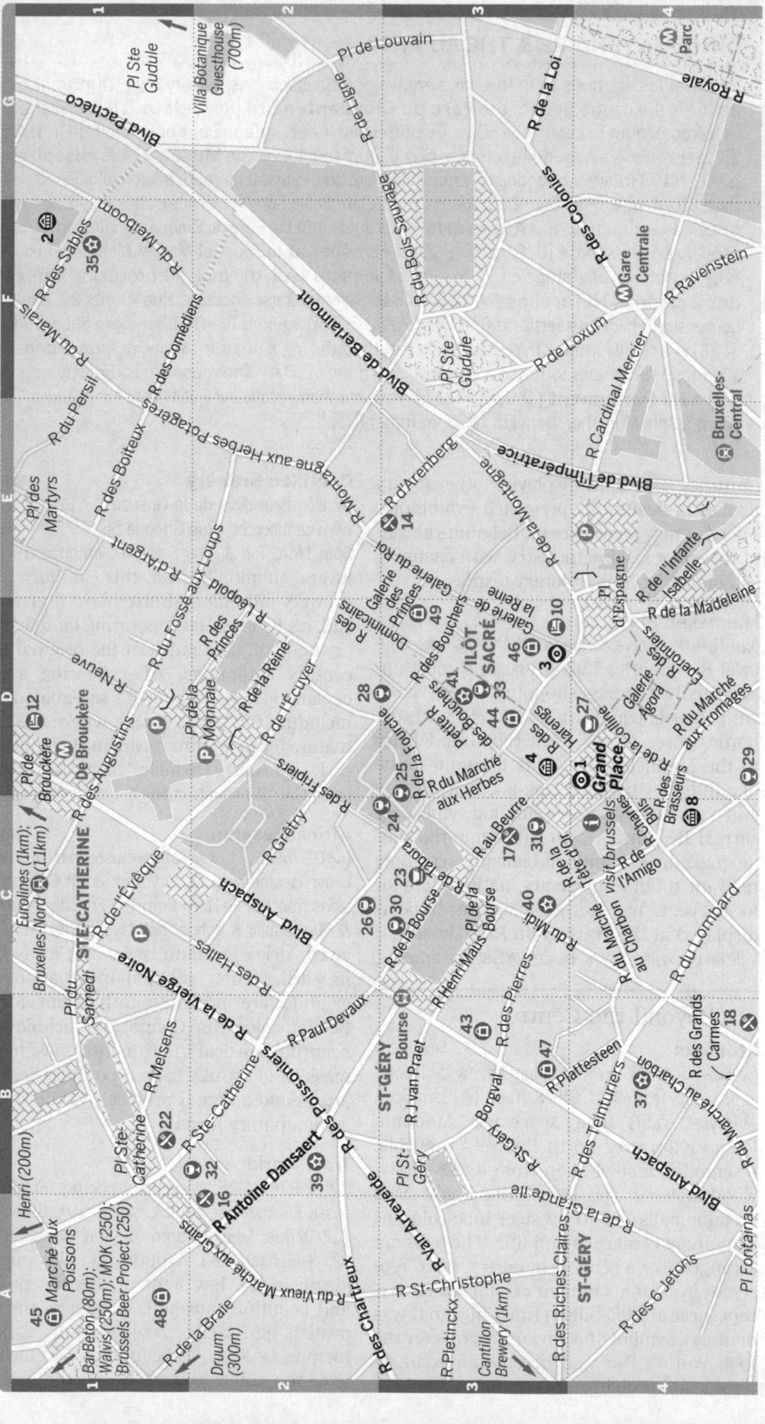

0 200 m
0 0.1 miles

A B C D E F G
1 2 3 4

Henri (200m)
45 Marché aux Poissons
BarBeton (80m); Walvis (250m); MOK (250); Brussels Beer Project (250)
48
R de la Braie
Druum (300m)
R du Vieux Marché aux Grains
R Antoine Dansaert
16
32
Pl Ste-Catherine
22
R Melsens
R Ste-Catherine
39
R des Chartreux
R des Poissoniers
R de la Vierge Noire
Pl du Samedi
STE-CATHERINE
Eurolines (1km); Bruxelles-Nord (1.1km)
Pl de Brouckère
12
De Brouckère
R des Augustins
R de l'Évêque
R des Halles
Blvd Anspach
R Paul Devaux
R Grétry
R Neuve
Pl de la Monnaie
R du Fossé aux Loups
R des Princes
R de la Reine
R de l'Écuyer
R Léopold
R d'Argent
Pl des Martyrs
R du Persil
R du Marais
R des Sables
2
35
R des Boiteux
R des Comédiens
R du Meiboom
Blvd Pachéco
Pl Ste Gudule
Villa Botanique Guesthouse (700m)
R Montagne aux Herbes Potagères
Blvd de Berlaimont
R de Ligne
Pl de Louvain
R du Bois Sauvage
Pl Ste Gudule
R Van Artevelde
ST-GÉRY
Bourse
26
30
23
24
25
28
R des Fripiers
R de la Fourche
R des Dominicains
Galerie des Princes
Galerie du Roi
14
R d'Arenberg
49
R des Bouchers
Pl St-Géry
R J van Praet
R de la Bourse
R de Tabora
R du Marché aux Herbes
Petite R des Bouchers
41
ILÔT SACRÉ
33
44
Galerie de la Reine
R Pletinckx
R St-Christophe
Cantillon Brewery (1km)
43
R Henri Maus
Pl de la Bourse
R au Beurre
17
Borgval
R des Pierres
R St-Géry
40
R du Midi
31
4
R des Harengs
46
3
10
R de la Montagne
Blvd de l'Impératrice
R de Loxum
R des Colonies
R de la Loi
R des Riches Claires
47
R de la Grande Île
ST-GÉRY
R des Teinturiers
R Plattesteen
R de la Tête d'Or
1
Grand Place
27
visit.brussels
R du Marché au Charbon
R de l'Amigo
R Charles Buls
R de la Colline
Galerie Agora
R des Éperonniers
Pl d'Espagne
R de l'Infante Isabelle
R de la Madeleine
R Cardinal Mercier
Gare Centrale
R Ravenstein
R Royale
Parc
R des 6 Jetons
Blvd Anspach
37
R du Marché au Charbon
R des Grands Carmes
18
R du Lombard
R des Brasseurs
8
R du Marché aux Fromages
29
Pl Fontainas
Bruxelles-Central

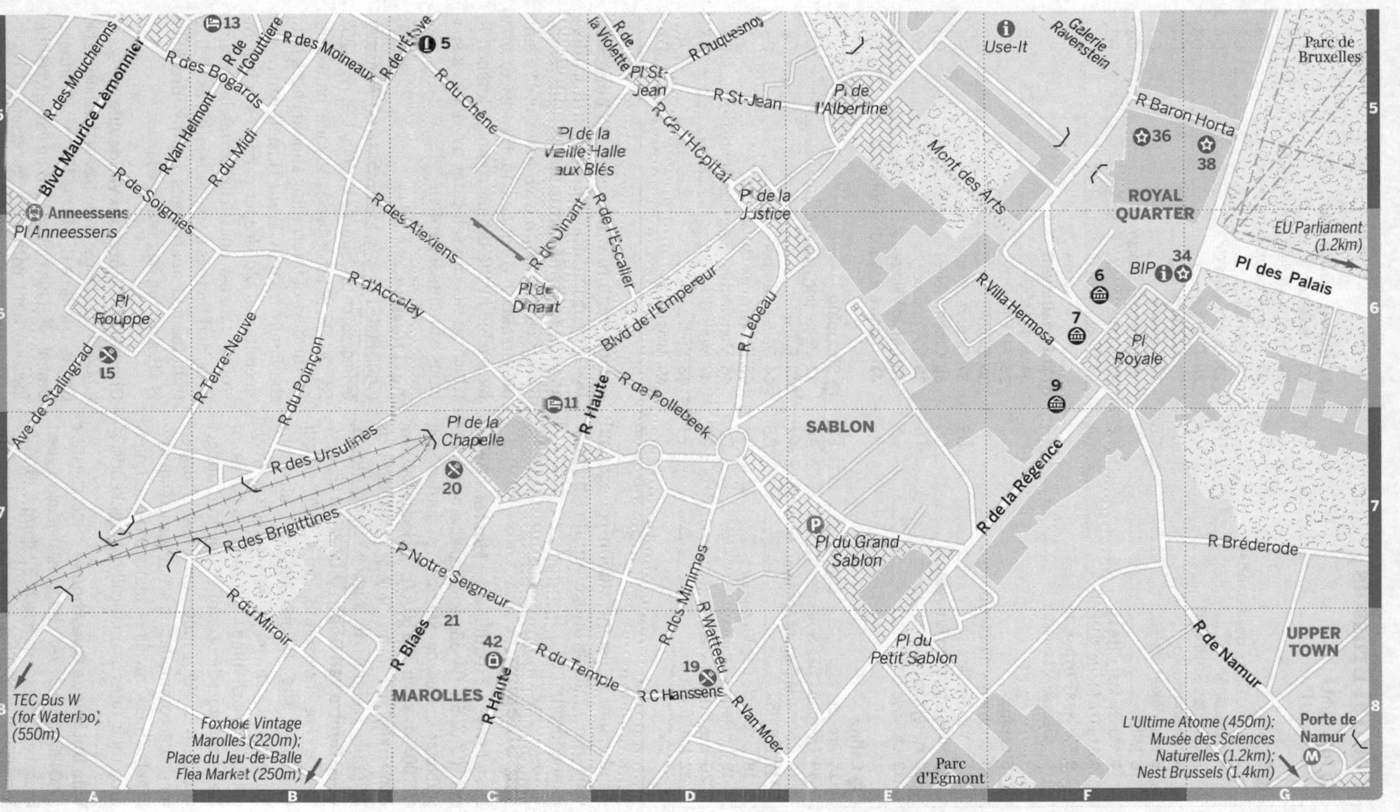

R des Moucherons
Blvd Maurice Lemonnier
R des Bogards
R de l'Gouttière
R des Moineaux
R de l'Étuve
R du Chêne
R de la Violette
Pl St-Jean
R Duquesnoy
R St-Jean
Pl de l'Albertine
Use-It
Galerie Ravenstein
Parc de Bruxelles
R Baron Horta
ROYAL QUARTER
EU Parliament (1.2km)
Pl des Palais
BIP
R Van Helmont
R du Midi
R de Soignies
Anneessens
Pl Anneessens
Pl de la Vieille Halle aux Blés
R de l'Hôpital
Pl de la Justice
Mont des Arts
R des Alexiens
R de Dinant
R de l'Escalier
Pl de Dinant
R d'Accolay
Blvd de l'Empereur
R Lebeau
R Villa Hermosa
Pl Royale
Pl Rouppe
R Terre-Neuve
R du Poinçon
Ave de Stalingrad
R Haute
R de Pollebeek
SABLON
Pl de la Chapelle
R des Ursulines
R de la Régence
R des Brigittines
P Notre Seigneur
Pl du Grand Sablon
R Brederode
R du Miroir
R des Minimes
R Watteeu
R Blaes
R du Temple
R C Hanssens
Pl du Petit Sablon
R de Namur
UPPER TOWN
MAROLLES
R Van Moer
TEC Bus W (for Waterloo; 550m)
Foxhole Vintage Marolles (220m); Place du Jeu-de-Balle Flea Market (250m)
Parc d'Egmont
L'Ultime Atome (450m); Musée des Sciences Naturelles (1.2km); Nest Brussels (1.4km)
Porte de Namur
A
B
C
D
E
F
G
5
6
7
8

Central Brussels

Top Sights
1 Grand Place........D4

Sights
2 Centre Belge de la Bande Dessinée........F1
3 Galeries St-Hubert........D3
4 Maison du Roi........D3
5 Manneken Pis........C5
6 MIM........F6
7 Musée Magritte........F6
8 Musée Mode & Dentelle........C4
9 Musées Royaux des Beaux-Arts........F6

Sleeping
10 Chambres d'Hôtes du Vaudeville........D3
11 HI Hostel John Bruegel........C6
12 Hôtel Métropole........D1
13 La Casa-BXL........B5

Eating
14 Arcadi........E3
15 Comme Chez Soi........A6
16 Cremerie De Linkebeek........A2
17 Dandoy........C3
18 Le Cercle des Voyageurs........B4
19 Le Perroquet........D8
20 Les Brigittines........C7
22 Mer du Nord........B1

Drinking & Nightlife
23 À la Bécasse........C3
24 A l'Imaige de Nostre-Dame........C3
25 Au Bon Vieux Temps........D3
26 Celtica........C2
27 Chaloupe d'Or........D4
28 Délirium Café........D3
29 Goupil le Fol........D4
30 Le Cirio........C3
31 Le Roy d'Espagne........C3
32 Monk........B2
33 Toone........D3

Entertainment
34 Arsène50........F6
35 Art Base........F1
36 BOZAR........F5
37 Cabaret Mademoiselle........B4
38 Cinematek........G5
39 L'Archiduc........B2
40 Music Village........C3
41 Théâtre Royal de Toone........D3

Shopping
42 Belge une fois........C8
43 Brüsel........B3
44 De Biertempel........D3
45 ICON........A1
46 Manufacture Belge de Dentelles........D3
47 Multi-BD........B3
48 Stijl........A1
49 Tropismes........D3

wander into a historic station cottage and walk over a railway bridge. A train simulator is an added bonus.

Sleeping

Hostel-wise, HI-affiliated **Hostel Bruegel** (☎02-511 04 36; www.jeugdherbergen.be/en/brussels; Rue du St-Esprit 2; dm/tw adult €23.90/64, youth €21.60/60; ⏲lockout 10am-2pm, curfew 1am-7am; ⊖@📶; Ⓜ Louise) is helpfully central if rather institutional, while **Centre van Gogh** (☎02-217 01 58; www.chab.be; Rue Traversière 8; dm €22-26, s/tw/tr €35/60/90; @📶; Ⓜ Botanique) has a hip lobby bar but less glamrous rooms (plus a 35-year-old upper age limit). A good network of B&Bs and guesthouses offer fine mid-budget alternatives. With much of Brussels' upper-market accommodation scene aimed squarely at business travellers, many top-end hotels drop their rates dramatically at weekends.

Villa Botanique Guesthouse GUESTHOUSE €
(☎0496 59 93 79; http://villabotaniqueguesthouse.be; Chaussée de Haecht 31; dm/d €30/€60; 📶; Ⓜ Botanique) This idiosyncratic, warmly friendly venture is housed in an impressive 1830s mansion near the botanical gardens and has a mix of dorms and private rooms. Guests connect with each other over a simple breakfast (included in the price) at a long table in the dining room. A kitchen in which guests can self-cater overlooks a spacious communal garden.

Train Hostel HOSTEL €
(☎02-808 61 76; www.trainhostel.be/en; Ave Georges Rodenbach 6; dm/d/ste €18/45/129; 📶; 🚌58, 58, 🚋7, 92, 🚆Schaerbeek) Anyone hankering for the days of interrailing should check in to the family-friendly Train Hostel, where you sleep in real old sleeper carriages, albeit restored and cosy ones. The dorms have bunk beds, and there is a spacious suite, as well as train-themed apartments nearby. Breakfast is €8, sleeping bag rental €15.

Chambres d'Hôtes du Vaudeville B&B €€
(☎0484 59 46 69; www.theatreduvaudeville.be; Galerie de la Reine 11; d from €120; 📶; 🚆Bruxelles Central) 🍃 This classy B&B has an incredible location right within the gorgeous (if reverberant) Galeries St-Hubert (p74). Delectable

decor styles include African, modernist and 'Madame Loulou' (with 1920s nude sketches). Larger front rooms have claw-foot bathtubs and *galerie* views, but can be noisy with clatter that continues all night. Get keys via the art deco–influenced Café du Vaudeville, where breakfast is included.

Druum B&B €€
(☎0472 05 42 40; www.druum.be; Rue du Houblon 63; s/d €105/115; 📶; 🚌51) Brussels' most stylish B&B appeared after the owners gave artists carte blanche to rework the six bedrooms. Now this former pipe factory is a quirky homage to apartment-style living with incredible one-offs like a gigantic concrete bed for four and the cassette tapes of former studio recordings found in the stripped-back HS63 room.

La Casa-BXL B&B €€
(☎0475 29 07 21; www.downtownbxl.com; Rue du Marché au Charbon 16; d €109-119; 🚊Anneessens) Three B&B rooms are decked out in Moroccan-Asian style in a quiet but central location.

Nest Brussels B&B €€
(☎0488 38 80 29; http://bb the-nest.hotelsbrussels.net/en; Rue Wayenberg 24; d €80-110; 📶; 🚌38, Ⓜ Porte de Namur) This beautifully tasteful B&B has subtly coloured Turkish carpets, ikat cushions and Moroccan tiles. Run by a young family, it offers great value in the EU district, and a personal atmosphere. Three rooms; a simple breakfast is provided.

Hôtel Métropole HOTEL €€€
(☎02-217 23 00, reservations 02-214 24 24; www.metropolehotel.com; Place de Brouckère 31; d €170-350, weekend rates from €130; 🅿❄📶; Ⓜ De Brouckère) This 1895 showpiece has a jaw-droppingly sumptuous French Renaissance–style foyer with marble walls, coffered ceiling and beautifully etched stained-glass back windows. The *café* is indulgent and the bar (with frequent live music) features recently 'rediscovered' murals by a student of Horta. One of the lifts is an 1895 original.

✖ Eating

The central area is ideal for classic bar-cafés and good Asian places, while in Ste-Catherine you'll find classy seafood restaurants along with ever-popular fishmonger takeaway-window **Mer du Nord** (Noordzee, www.vishandelnoordzee.be; Rue Ste-Catherine 45; items from €7; ⏲8am-6pm Tue-Fri, to 5pm Sat; Ⓜ Ste-Catherine) and enticing 1902 cheese shop **Cremerie de Linkebeek** (☎02-512 35 10; Rue du Vieux Marché aux Grains 4; items from €5; ⏲9am-3pm Mon, to 6pm Tue-Sat; Ⓜ Ste-Catherine). There are delightful chocolate-shop cafes around the Sablon and some quirky dining choices in the Marolles. Excellent neighbourhood restaurants like **L'Ultime Atome** (☎02-513 13 67; www.ultimeatome.be; Rue St-Boniface 14; mains €11-19; ⏲8.30am-1am Mon-Fri, 10am-1am Sat & Sun; Ⓜ Porte de Namur) abound in Ixelles, though that's a little off the main tourist circuit. For the very finest restaurants like **Comme Chez Soi** (www.commechezsoi.be; Place Rouppe 23; mains from €49; ⏲7-9pm Tue & Wed, noon-1.30pm & 7-9pm Thu-Sat; 🚊Anneessens), you'll generally need to book months in advance.

Arcadi BRASSERIE €
(☎02-511 33 43; www.arcadicafe.be; Rue d'Arenberg 1b; mains €10-15; ⏲8am-11.45pm Tue-Fri, from 7.30am Sat, from 9am Sun; Ⓜ Gare Centrale) The jars of preserves, beautiful cakes and fruit tarts at this classic and charming bistro entice plenty of Brussels residents, as do well-priced meals such as lasagne and steak, all served nonstop by courteous staff. With a nice location on the edge of the Galeries St-Hubert, this is a great spot for an indulgent, creamy hot chocolate.

Le Perroquet CAFE €
(☎02-512 99 22; Rue Watteeu 31; light meals €9-15; ⏲noon-11.30pm; Ⓜ Porte de Namur) Perfect for a drink, but also good for a simple bite (think salads and variations on croque-monsieurs), this art nouveau cafe with its stained glass, marble tables and timber panelling is an atmospheric, inexpensive stop in an area that's light on such places. Popular with expats.

MOK VEGETARIAN €
(☎02-513 57 87; www.mokcoffee.be; Rue Antoine Dansaert 196; mains €10-20; ⏲8.30am-6pm Mon-Fri, from 10am Sat & Sun; 🥗; Ⓜ Comte de Flandre) MOK serves some of the capital's best coffee and offers a wide range of vegan-inspired recipes prepared by Josefien Smets – think crispy tofu and pickled cucumber sandwiches or the legendary avocado toast. A big picture window looks out onto Rue Dansaert.

Dandoy BAKERY €
(☎02-511 03 26; www.maisondandoy.com; Rue au Beurre 31; snacks from €6; ⏲9.30am-7pm Mon-Sat, from 10.30am Sun; 🚊Bourse) Established in 1829, Brussels' best-known *biscuiterie* has five local branches, this one with an attached tearoom. The chocolate for Dandoy's choc-dipped biscuits is handmade by Laurent Gerbaud.

DON'T MISS

BOURSE CAFE CLASSICS

Many of Brussels' most historic drinking holes are within stumbling distance of the Bourse, Brussels' classically columned stock exchange building. Don't miss **Le Cirio** (02-512 13 95; Rue de la Bourse 18; 10am-midnight; Bourse), a sumptuous yet affordable 1866 marvel full of polished brasswork serving great-value pub meals. Three more classics are hidden up shoulder-wide alleys: the medieval yet unpretentious **A l'Imaige de Nostre-Dame** (Rue du Marché aux Herbes 8; noon-midnight Mon-Fri, 3pm-1am Sat, 4-10.30pm Sun; Bourse); the 1695 Rubenseque **Au Bon Vieux Temps** (02-217 26 26; Impasse St-Nicolas; 11am-midnight; Bourse), which sometimes stocks ultra-rare Westvleteren beers; and lambic specialist **À la Bécasse** (02-511 00 06; www.alabecasse.com; Rue de Tabora 11; 11am-midnight, to 1am Fri & Sat; M Gare Centrale) with its vaguely Puritanical rows of wooden tables.

Henri FUSION €€

(02-218 00 08; www.restohenri.be; Rue de Flandre 113; mains €17-24; noon-2pm Tue-Fri & 6-10pm Tue-Sat; M Ste-Catherine) In an airy white space on this street to watch, Henri concocts tangy fusion dishes such as tuna with ginger, soy and lime, artichokes with scampi, lime and olive tapenade, or Argentine fillet steak in parsley. It has an astutely curated wine list and staff who know their stuff.

Les Brigittines FRENCH, BELGIAN €€

(02-512 68 91; www.lesbrigittines.com; Place de la Chapelle 5; mains €16-24; noon-2.30pm & 7-10.30pm Mon-Fri, to 11pm Sat; M Louise) Offering grown-up eating in a muted belle époque dining room, Les Brigittines dishes up traditional French and Belgian food. Its classic (and very meaty) dishes include veal cheek, pigs' trotters and steak tartare. Staff are knowledgeable about local beer and artisanal wines, and can advise on pairing these with your food.

Drinking & Nightlife

In most cities, tourists stop in at cafes in between visiting the sights. Here the cafés are the sights; visiting a museum just gives your liver necessary respite. Beer in multitudinous variety is the main draw.

On the Grand Place itself, 300-year-old gems like **Le Roy d'Espagne** (02-513 08 07; www.roydespagne.be; Grand Place 1; 9.30am-1am; M Gare Centrale) and **Chaloupe d'Or** (02-511 41 61; https://chaloupedor.be/en; Grand Place 24; 11am-1am; M Gare Centrale) are magnificent if predictably pricey. It's just a short stumble to the 'Bourse Classics', to **Délirium** (www.deliriumcafe.be; Impasse de la Fidélité 4a; 10am-4am Mon-Sat, to 2am Sun; M Gare Centrale) for an astonishing brew variety with a party atmosphere, to **Cercle des Voyageurs** (02-514 39 49; www.lecercledesvoyageurs.com; Rue des Grands Carmes 18; mains €15-21; 11am-midnight; Bourse, Anneessens) to sit in settees reading travel books, or to **Celtica** (www.celticpubs.com/celtica; Rue de Marché aux Poulets 55; Bourse) if you just want cheep booze (and maybe a dance). In Ste-Catherine, meet the locals at **Monk** (02-511 75 11; www.monk.be; Rue Ste-Catherine 42; 11am-2am Mon-Sat, from 2pm Sun; M Ste-Catherine), hit **BarBeton** (02-513 83 63; www.barbeton.be; Rue Antoine Dansaert 114; 10am-midnight; M Ste-Catherine) or **Walvis** (02-219 95 32; www.cafewalvis.be; Rue Antoine Dansaert; 11am-2am Mon-Thu & Sun, to 4am Fri & Sat; M Ste-Catherine) for DJ-led hipster minimalism, and **Brussels Beer Project** (02-502 28 56; www.beerproject.be; Rue Antoine Dansaert 188; 2-10pm Thu-Sat; 51) for inventive new microbrewed beers.

Toone BAR

(Rue du Marche des Herbes 66; beer from €2.50; noon-midnight Tue-Sun; M Gare Centrale) At the home to Brussels' classic **puppet theatre** (02-511 71 37; www.toone.be; adult/child €10/7; typically 8.30pm Thu & 4pm Sat), this irresistibly quaint and cosy timber-framed bar serves beers and basic snacks.

Goupil le Fol BAR

(02-511 13 96; www.goupillefol.com; Rue de la Violette 22; 4pm-2am; M Gare Centrale) Overwhelming weirdness hits you as you acid-trip your way through this sensory overload of rambling passageways, ragged old sofas and inexplicable beverages mostly based on madly fruit-flavoured wines (no beer is served). Unmissable.

☆ Entertainment

Home to the National Orchestra, **BOZAR** (www.bozar.be; Palais des Beaux-Arts, Rue Ravenstein 23; Ⓜ Gare Centrale) is a Horta-designed mega-venue with splendid acoustics incorporating **Cinematek** (☎02-507 83 70; www.cinematheque.be) where silent movies are screened with live piano accompaniment. Intimate jazz venues include **Sounds** (☎02 512 92 50; www.soundsjazzclub.be; Rue de la Tulipe 28; ⏰8pm-4am Mon-Sat; Ⓜ Porte de Namur), **Music Village** (☎02-513 13 45; www.themusicvillage.com; Rue des Pierres 50; cover €7.50-20; ⏰from 7.30pm Wed-Sat; 🚋Bourse) and **L'Archiduc** (☎02-512 0652; www.archiduc.net; Rue Antoine Dansaert 6; ⏰4pm-5am; 🚋Bourse) which is free at 5pm on Saturdays...if you can get in. **Art Base** (☎02-217 29 20; www.art-base.be; Rue des Sables 29; ⏰Fri & Sat; Ⓜ Rogier) hosts salon-style gigs, from classical to Greek *rebetiko* to Indian classical while brassy **Cabaret Mademoiselle** (☎0474 58 57 61; www.cabaretmademoiselle.be; Rue du Marché au Charbon 53; ⏰7pm-late Wed-Sat; 🚋Bourse)

is a burlesque cabaret combining drag, circus, comedy and good beer. For extensive listings check www.agenda.be, www.thebulletin.be and http://thewordmagazine.com/neighbourhood-life. Discounted tickets for arts, music and cinema are sold by **Arsène50** (www.arsene50.be; Rue Royale 2; ⏰12.30-5pm; Ⓜ Parc).

Shopping

Supermarkets stock many of the 'standard' Belgian beers, but for rare brews try well-stocked **de Biertempel** (☎02-502 19 06; http://biertempel.wixsite.com/debiertempel; Rue du Marché aux Herbes 56b; ⏰9.30am-7pm; 🚋Bourse).

Gorgeous chocolate boutiques are dotted around the Sablon and in the magical Galleries-St Hubert (p74) shopping passage, though for non conoisseurs, pralines from the ubiquitous Leonidas chain can taste almost as good for around a third of the price.

Brussels is also great for fashion, from funky vintage shops like **Foxhole Vintage Marolles** (☎0477 20 53 36; https://foxholevintage.com; Rue des Renards 6; ⏰10am-6.30pm Thu-Sun; Ⓜ Louise) to chic boutiques on Ave Louise and alternative designer outlets around Rue Antoine Dansaert, notably **Stijl** (☎02-512 03 13; www.stijl.be; Rue Antoine Dansaert 74; ⏰10.30am-6.30pm Mon-Sat; Ⓜ Ste-Catherine) and **ICON** (☎02-502 71 51; www.icon-shop.be; Place du Nouveau Marché aux Grains 5; ⏰10.30am-6.30pm Mon-Sat; 🚋Dansaert).

For unique if downmarket shopping experiences, visit the **Jeu-de-Balle Flea Market** (www.marcheauxpuces.be; Place du Jeu-de-Balle; ⏰6am-2pm Mon-Fri, to 3pm Sat & Sun; Ⓜ Porte de Hal, 🚋Lemonnier) and the vast, multicultural Sunday morning market around the **Gare du Midi**.

Manufacture Belge de Dentelles ARTS & CRAFTS
(☎02-511 44 77; www.mbd.be; Galerie de la Reine 6-8; ⏰9.30am-6pm Mon-Sat, 10am-4pm Sun; Ⓜ Gare Centrale) Excellent stock of antique lace, and staff who love the stuff.

Tropismes BOOKS
(☎02-512 88 52; http://tropismes.com; Galerie des Princes 11; ⏰11am-6.30pm Mon, 10am-

COMIC-STRIP CULTURE

In Belgium, comic strips *(bandes dessinées)* are revered as the 'ninth art'. Dozens of cartoon murals enliven Brussels buildings and serious comic fans might enjoy Brussels' comprehensive **Centre Belge de la Bande Dessinée** (Belgian Comic Strip Centre; ☎02-219 19 80; www.comicscenter.net; Rue des Sables 20; adult/concession €10/7; ⏰10am-6pm; Ⓜ Rogier) in a distinctive Horta-designed art nouveau building.

For an immersive Tintin experience, **Musée Hergé** (☎010-48 84 21; www.museeherge.com; Rue du Labrador 26; adult/child €9.50/5; ⏰10.30am-5.30pm Tue-Fri, 10am-6pm Sat & Sun) is highly recommended, but it's in Louvain-la-Neuve, a €5.50 train ride from Brussels taking around 50 minutes including a quick change at Ottignies.

Comic-book shops include **Brüsel** (www.brusel.com; Blvd Anspach 100; ⏰10.30am-6.30pm Mon-Sat, from noon Sun; 🚋Bourse) and **Multi-BD** (☎02-513 72 35; http://bulledor.blogspot.com; Blvd Anspach 122-124; ⏰10.30am-7pm Mon-Sat, 12.30-6.30pm Sun; 🚋Bourse).

WORTH A TRIP

WATERLOO

Tourists have been swarming to Waterloo ever since Napoleon's 1815 defeat, a pivotal event in European history. Inaugurated for the 2015 bicentenary, **Memorial 1815** (☎02-385 19 12; www.waterloo1815.be; Rte du Lion, Hameau du Lion; adult/child €16/13, with Wellington & Napoleon HQ museums €20/16; ⏲9.30am-6.30pm Apr-Sep, to 5.30pm Oct-Mar) is a showpiece underground museum and visitor centre at the main battlefield area (known as Hameau du Lion). There's a detailed audio guide and some enjoyable technological effects. The climax is an impressive 3D film that sticks you right into the middle of the cavalry charges. It includes admission to various other battlefield attractions, including the **Butte du Lion**, a lion-topped memorial hill from which you can survey the terrain, and the restored **Hougoumont farmhouse** that played a key part in the battle.

Hameau du Lion is 5km south of Waterloo town. Rather than the train, use twice-hourly TEC bus W from Ave Fonsny outside Bruxelles-Midi station (€3.50, one hour).

6.30pm Tue-Thu, 10am-7.30pm Fri, 10.30am-7pm Sat, 1.30-6.30pm Sun; Ⓜ Gare Centrale) With its gold-wreath-encircled columns and ornate gilded ceiling, this is about the prettiest bookshop you could imagine. The literary connections are hot too: this is where the exiled Victor Hugo visited his lover/assistant Juliette Drouet. Some titles are in English.

Belge une fois ARTS & CRAFTS

(☎02-503 85 41; www.belgeunefois.com; Rue Haute 89; ⏲11am-6pm Wed-Sat, 1-6pm Sun; 🚌92, 93) Belge une fois is a concept store selling creations by the eponymous designers' collective. It also sells artefacts, accessories and light fixtures by other Belgian designers. Expect everything from simple postcards and concrete cactus holders to large photographic prints.

ℹ Information

Use-It (☎02-218 39 06; www.brussels.use-it.travel; Galerie Ravenstein 17; ⏲10am-6pm Mon-Sat; 📶; Ⓜ Gare Central) Youth-oriented office with a list of nightly events, great guide-maps and a free city tour.

Visit.Brussels (☎02-513 89 40; www.visit.brussels; Hôtel de Ville, Grand Place; ⏲9am-6pm; 🚌 Bourse) High-quality information on the main square, a booth at Gare du Midi and an office on Rue Royale, where you'll also find **BIP** (☎02-563 63 99; http://bip.brussels/en; Rue Royale 2-4; ⏲9.30am-5.30pm Mon-Fri, 10am-6pm Sat & Sun; Ⓜ Parc) and the **Arsène50** desk for discounted events tickets.

ℹ Getting There & Away

BUS

Eurolines (☎02-274 13 50; www.eurolines.be; Rue du Progrès 80; 🚌 Gare du Nord) and **Flix-Bus** (www.flixbus.co.uk) operate international services to London, Amsterdam, Paris and beyond, mostly starting from Bruxelles-Nord. Pre-book online.

TEC Bus W for Waterloo starts from Ave Fosny outside Buxelles-Midi station.

TRAIN

Bruxelles-Midi (Gare du Midi; luggage office per article per day €4, luggage lockers per 24hr small/large €3/4; ⏲luggage office 6am-9pm; Ⓜ Gare du Midi, 🚆 Bruxelles-Midi) is the only stop for Eurostar, TGV and Thalys high-speed international trains (prebooking compulsory). Other mainline trains also stop at more convenient **Bruxelles-Central** (Gare Centrale). For enquiries consult www.belgiantrain.be/en.

ℹ Getting Around

TO/FROM BRUSSELS AIRPORT

Brussels Airport (https://www.brusselsairport.be/en) is 14km northeast of Brussels.

Airport City Express (tickets €9; ⏲5.30am-12.20am) trains (€10) run four times hourly to the city's three main train stations, Bruxelles-Nord (15 minutes), Bruxelles-Central (20 minutes) and Bruxelles-Midi (25 minutes). Taxis are a very bad idea in rush-hour traffic.

TO/FROM CHARLEROI AIRPORT

Misleadingly known as 'Brussels South', **Charleroi Airport** (www.brussels-charleroi-airport.com) is 46km southeast of the city. It's mainly used by budget airlines, including Ryanair and WizzAir.

Buses to Brussels Gare du Midi leave around half an hour after flight arrivals (€14.20/28.40 one way/return, 1½ hours). Bus-train combination tickets via Charleroi station are also worth considering.

BICYCLE

Villo! (☎078-05 11 10; http://en.villo.be; subscription day/week €1.60/8.20) is a system of 180 automated stations for short-term bicycle rental (under 30/30/60/90/120 minutes free/€0.50/1/1.50/2) with a subscription (€1.60/8.20/32.60 day/week/year), credit or debit-card essential. Read instructions carefully.

For longer bike hires, try **FietsPunt/PointVelo** (02-513 04 09; www.cyclo.org; Carrefour de l'Europe 2; per day/week €15/45; 7am-7pm Mon-Fri; Bruxelles-Central), on the left as you leave Bruxelles-Central station via the day-time-only Madeleine exit. **Maison des Cyclistes** (02-502 73 55; www.provelo.be; Rue de Londres 15; noon-6pm Mon-Fri, 10am-6pm Sat & Sun Apr-Oct; M Trone) also offers bike tours.

PUBLIC TRANSPORT

STIB/MIVB (02-515 20 00; www.stib.be; 10am-6pm Mon-Sat) tickets are sold at metro stations, kiosks, newsagents and on buses and trams. Single-/five-/10-journey tickets cost €2.10/8/14 including transfers, valid for an hour from mandatory validation. Unlimited one-day passes cost €6. Airport buses are excluded. Slightly higher 'jump' fares apply if you want to connect to city routes operated by De Lijn (Flanders bus), TEC (Wallonia bus) or SNCB/NMBS (rail). Children under six travel free.

FLANDERS

Bruges

050 / POP 118,284

If you set out to design a fairy-tale medieval town, it would be hard to improve on central Bruges (Brugge in Dutch). Picturesque cobbled lanes and dreamy canals link photogenic squares lined with soaring towers, historical churches and photogenic old whitewashed almshouses. Of course the secret is already out and during the busy summer months you'll be sharing Bruges' with constant streams of tourists. If you can stand the cold, come midweek in the depths of winter (except Christmas time) to avoid the crowds. And do stay overnight to enjoy the city's stunning nocturnal floodlighting.

Sights

Old-town Bruges is an ambler's dream. At its heart, **Markt** is the old market square, lined with pavement cafes beneath step-gabled facades. The buildings aren't always quite as medieval as they look, but together they create a fabulous scene, and soaring above is the **Belfort** (Belfry; 050-44 87 43; www.visitbruges.be/nl/belfort; Markt 7; adult/child €12/10; 9.30am-6pm), Belgium's most famous belfry. Its iconic octagonal tower is arguably better appreciated from afar than by climbing the 366 claustrophobic steps to the top. Immediately east, **Burg** is a less theatrical but still enchanting square that's been Bruges' administrative centre for centuries and retains several unmissable buildings. To escape the crowds, explore east of pretty Jan van Eykplein and seek out city gateways and windmills around the oval-shaped moat.

Groeningemuseum GALLERY
(050-44 87 11; www.visitbruges.be/en/groeningemuseum-groeninge-museum; Dijver 12; adult/concession/under 18yr €12/10/free; 9.30am-5pm Tue-Sun) Bruges' most celebrated art gallery boasts an astonishingly rich collection that's strong in superb Flemish Primitive and Renaissance works, depicting the conspicuous wealth of the city with glittering realistic artistry. Meditative works include Jan Van Eyck's radiant masterpiece *Madonna with Canon Van der Paele* (1436) and the *Madonna Crowned by Angels* (1482) by the Master of the Embroidered Foliage, where the rich fabric of the Madonna's robe meets the 'real' foliage at her feet with exquisite detail.

Museum Sint-Janshospitaal MUSEUM
(Memlingmuseum; 050-44 87 43; www.visitbruges.be/en/sint-janshospitaal-saint-johns-hospital; Mariastraat 38; adult/concession/under 18yr €12/10/free; 9.30am-5pm Tue-Sun) In the restored chapel of a 12th-century hospital building with superb timber beamwork, this museum shows various torturous-looking medical implements, hospital sedan chairs and a gruesome 1679 painting of an anatomy class. But it's much better known for

> LOCAL KNOWLEDGE
>
> **WHAT'S A BEGIJNHOF?**
>
> Usually enclosed around a central garden, a *begijnhof* (*béguinage* in French) is a pretty cluster of historic houses originally built to house lay sisters. The idea originated in the 12th century when many such women were left widowed by their crusader-knight husbands. Today 14 of Flanders' historic *begijnhoven* have been declared Unesco World Heritage Sites with great examples at Diest, Lier, Turnhout, Kortrijk and Bruges, which also has dozens of smaller *godshuizen* (almshouses).

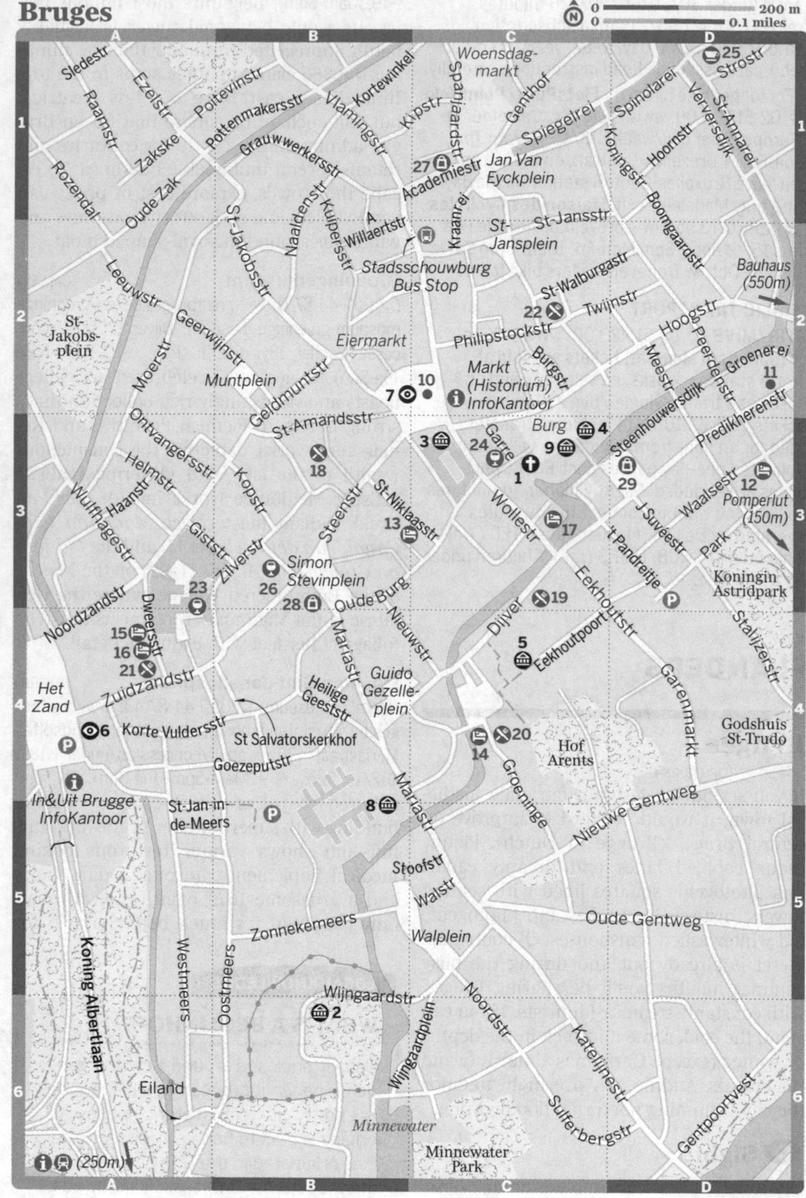

its six masterpieces by 15th-century artist Hans Memling, including the enchanting reliquary of St Ursula. This gilded oak reliquary looks like a miniature Gothic cathedral, painted with scenes from the life of St Ursula, including highly realistic Cologne cityscapes.

Begijnhof HISTORIC BUILDING

(Wijngaardstraat; ⌚6.30am-6.30pm) **FREE** Bruges' delightful *begijnhof* dates from the 13th century. Despite the hordes of summer tourists, it remains a remarkably tranquil haven. Outside the 1776 gateway bridge lies a tempting (if predictably tourist-priced)

Bruges

Sights

1	Basiliek van het Heilig Bloed	C3
2	Begijnhof	B6
3	Belfort	C3
4	Brugse Vrije	C3
5	Groeningemuseum	C4
6	Het Zand Square	A4
7	Markt	B2
8	Museum Sint-Janshospitaal	B5
9	Stadhuis	C3

Activities, Courses & Tours

10	Legends Walking Tours	C2
11	Quasimundo	D2

Sleeping

12	B&B Dieltiens	D3
13	B&B SintNik	B3
14	Guesthouse Nuit Blanche	C4
15	Hotel Bla Bla	A4
16	Passage Bruges	A4
17	Relais Bourgondisch Cruyce	C3

Eating

18	De Stove	B3
19	Den Dyver	C3
20	Den Gouden Harynck	C4
21	Gran Kaffee De Passage	A4
22	Lieven	C2

Drinking & Nightlife

23	Cafédraal	A3
24	De Garre	C3
25	Herberg Vlissinghe	D1
26	't Brugs Beertje	B3

Shopping

27	Bacchus Cornelius	C1
28	Chocolate Line	D3
29	Vismarkt	D3

array of terraced restaurants, lace shops and waffle peddlers.

The classic way to arrive here from Markt is by horse-carriage, but walking allows you to seek out lesser-known almshouses en route. Don't miss a romantic stroll in the **Minnewater Park** around the 'Lake of Love'.

Tours

The city's must-do activity is a 30-minute **canal-boat tour** (adult/child €8/4; 10am-6pm Mar–mid-Nov). Boats depart roughly every 20 minutes from various jetties south of the Burg. Each operator does essentially the same loop for the same price, so just pick the shortest queue. **Legends** (0472 26 87 15; www.legendstours.be/walking-tours-bruges; Markt) FREE conducts wildly popular 'free' (ie tips-based) walking tours – book your slot online. **Quasimundo** (050-33 07 75; www.quasimundo.eu; Predikherenstraat 28; adult/student €28/26; Mar-Oct) leads cycle tours into the countryside around Bruges, with bike rental included.

Sleeping

Bauhaus HOSTEL €

(St Christopher's Hostel; 050-34 10 93; www.bauhaus.be; Langestraat 133-137; dm/d from €21/39;) One of Belgium's most popular hang-outs for young travellers, this backpacker village incorporates a hostel, apartments, a nightclub, internet cafe and a little chill-out room that's well hidden behind the reception and laundrette section at Langestraat 145. Simple and slightly cramped dorms are operated with key cards; hotel-section double rooms have private shower cubicles. Bike hire is also available.

B&B Dieltiens B&B €€

(050-33 42 94; www.bedandbreakfastbruges.be; Waalsestraat 40; s/d/tr from €70/80/90;) Old and new art fills this lovingly restored classical mansion, which remains an appealing real home run by charming musician hosts. Superbly central yet quiet. It also operates a holiday flat (from €75 per night) nearby in a 17th-century house.

Hotel Bla Bla HOTEL €€

(050-33 90 14; www.hotelblabla.com; Dweersstraat 24; s/d incl breakfast from €85/95;) A shuttered and step-gabled building given an elegant makeover, with parquet floors, modern artworks and soothingly pale rooms. Excellent buffet breakfast.

B&B SintNik B&B €€

(050-61 03 08; www.sintnik.be; St-Niklaasstraat 18; s/d from €125/135;) Room 1 has a claw-foot bath and antique glass panel, but it's the other two rooms' remarkable Pisa-like belfry views that make this welcoming B&B so special and popular.

★ **Guesthouse Nuit Blanche** B&B €€€

(0494 40 04 47; www.bb-nuitblanche.com; Groeninge 2; d from €185;) Pay what you like, nowhere else in Bruges can get you a more romantic location than this fabulous B&B, which started life as a 15th-century tannery. It oozes history, retaining original Gothic fireplaces, stained-glass roundels and some historical furniture, while bathrooms and beds are luxury-hotel standard.

Relais Bourgondisch Cruyce BOUTIQUE HOTEL €€€
(☎050-33 79 26; www.relaisbourgondischcruyce.be; Wollestraat 41-47; d from €245; P ❄ 📶) This luxurious little boutique hotel occupies a part-timbered medieval house that's been tastefully updated and graced with art, antiques, Persian carpets and fresh orchids. A special delight is relaxing in the canal-side lounge while envious tourists cruise past on their barge tours.

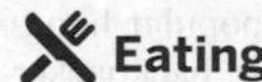

Eating

De Stove INTERNATIONAL €€
(☎050-33 78 35; www.restaurantdestove.be; Kleine St-Amandsstraat 4; mains €19-36, menu with/without wine €69/51; ⏲7-9pm Fri-Tue, noon-1.30pm Sun) Having just 20 seats keeps this gem intimate. Fish caught daily is the house speciality, but the monthly changing menu also includes the likes of wild boar fillet on oyster mushrooms. Everything, from the bread to the ice cream, is homemade. Despite perennially rave reviews, this calm one-room family restaurant remains friendly, reliable and inventive, without a hint of tourist-tweeness.

Lieven BELGIAN €€
(☎050-68 09 75; www.etenbijlieven.be; Philipstockstraat 45; mains €22-34; ⏲noon-10pm Tue-Sun) You'll need to book ahead for a table at this extremely popular, excellent-value Belgian bistro. It works wonders with local ingredients, and is recognised by its peers from around the country. Simple food done well in a trendy but relaxed environment.

Gran Kaffee De Passage BISTRO €€
(☎050-34 02 32; www.passagebruges.com; Dweersstraat 26-28; mains €10-18; ⏲5-11pm Tue-Thu & Sun, noon-11pm Fri & Sat) A mix of regulars and travellers staying at the adjoining **hostel** (d/tr from €64/98; 📶) give this candlelit, alternative art deco–style bistro one of the best atmospheres in town. Its menu of hearty traditional dishes, such as *stoverij* (local meat in beer sauce), as well as filling tofu creations, is a bargain.

Den Dyver BELGIAN €€€
(☎050-33 60 69; www.dyver.be; Dijver 5; mains €23-47, tasting menu €45; ⏲noon-2pm & 6.30-9.30pm Fri-Mon) Den Dyver is a pioneer of fine beer dining where you match the brew you drink with the one the chef used to create the sauce on your plate. This is no pub: beers come in wine glasses served on starched tablecloths in an atmosphere of Burgundian grandeur. The lunch menu includes an *amuse-bouche,* nibbles and coffee.

Den Gouden Harynck INTERNATIONAL €€€
(☎050-33 76 37; www.goudenharynck.be; Groeninge 25; set lunch menu €45, midweek dinner €65, surprise menu €95; ⏲noon-1.30pm & 7-8.30pm Tue-Fri, 7-8.30pm Sat) Behind an ivy-clad facade, this uncluttered Michelin-starred restaurant garners consistent praise and won't hurt the purse quite as severely as some better-known competitors. Its lovely location is both central and secluded. Exquisite dishes might include noisettes of venison topped with lardo and quince purée, or seed-crusted fillet of bream.

BRUGES' BURG

The centrepiece of this tree-shaded central square is Bruges' beautiful 1420 city hall, the **Stadhuis** (City Hall; ☎050-44 87 43; www.visitbruges.be/en/stadhuis-city-hall; Burg 12; adult/concession/under 18yr €6/5/free; ⏲9.30am-5pm). Its exterior is fancifully smothered with statues of the counts and countesses of Flanders – convincing replicas of originals that were torn down in 1792 by French soldiers. Inside, the highlight is the dazzling **Gotische Zaal** (Gothic Hall) with its polychrome ceiling, hanging vaults and romantic murals. Entrance also includes admission to parts of the adjacent **Brugse Vrije** (Liberty of Bruges; ☎050-44 87 11; Burg 11a; €6; ⏲9.30am-noon & 1.30-5pm) where the Renaissancezaal has a remarkable 1531 carved chimneypiece.

The western end of the stadhuis morphs into the **Basiliek van het Heilig Bloed** (Basilica of the Holy Blood; ☎050-33 67 92; www.holyblood.com; Burg 13; €2; ⏲9.30am-noon & 2-5pm, closed Wed afternoons mid-Nov–Mar), a small basilica that takes its name from a phial supposedly containing a few drops of Christ's blood, brought here after the 12th-century Crusades. The right-hand door leads upstairs to a colourfully adorned chapel where the relic is hidden behind a flamboyant silver tabernacle and is brought out for pious veneration at 2pm daily.

Drinking & Nightlife

Beer-specialist *cafés* include **'t Brugs Beertje** (050-33 96 16; www.brugsbeertje.be; Kemelstraat 5; 4pm-midnight Mon, Thu & Sun, to 1am Fri & Sat) and alley-hidden **De Garre** (050-34 10 29; www.degarre.be; De Garre 1; noon-midnight Sun-Thu, to 12.30am Fri, 11am-12.30am Sat) serving its own fabulous 11% Garre house brew. Old-world classic **Herberg Vlissinghe** (050-34 37 37; www.cafevlissinghe.be; Blekersstraat 2; 11am-10pm Wed-Sat, to 7pm Sun) dates from 1515; local legend has it that Rubens once painted an imitation coin on the table here and then did a runner. Eiermarkt, just north of Markt, has many plain but lively bars, with DJs and seemingly endless happy hours. For cocktails try suavely classy **Cafédraal** (050-34 08 45; www.cafedraal.be; Zilverstraat 38; 6pm-1am Tue-Thu, to 3am Fri & Sat).

Shopping

There are morning markets at **Markt** (Wednesday) and **Het Zand** ('t Zand) (Saturday), plus a fish market at colonnaded **Vismarkt** (Fish Market; Vismarkt; 7am-1pm Tue-Fri). Supermarkets stock standard beers (Leffe, Chimay etc), but for rare brews try **Bacchus Cornelius** (050-34 53 38; www.bacchuscornelius.com; Academiestraat 17; 1-6.30pm). Of some 50 chocolate shops, **Chocolate Line** (050-82 01 26; www.thechocolateline.be; Simon Stevinplein 19; per kg €50; 10am-6pm) is among the most experimental, though for great value, ubiquitous Leonidas can save you a packet.

Information

There are three main info locations in Bruges.

Tourist Information Counter (050-44 40 46; www.visitbruges.be; Stationsplein; 10am-5pm Mon-Fri, to 2pm Sat & Sun)

Tourist Office (In&Uit Brugge) (050-44 46 46; www.visitbruges.be; Concertgebouw, 't Zand 34; 10am-5pm Mon-Sat, 10am-2pm Sun)

Markt (Historium) InfoKantoor (050-44 46 46; Markt 1; 10am-5pm)

These places, and hostels, generally stock the excellent free *Use-it* map/guide (www.use-it.be), also available online.

Getting There & Around

Intercity trains and international bus services use Bruges central station, 1.5km south of the Markt – a lovely walk via Minnewater. Both **Eurolines** (www.eurolines.eu) and **Flixbus** (www.flixbus.co.uk) have overnight buses to London. Book online.

Trains run twice-hourly to Brussels (€14.50, one hour) via Ghent (€7, 23 minutes) and hourly to Antwerp (€15.40, 80 minutes). For Ypres (Ieper), take the train to Roeselare then bus 95 via Langemark or 94 via Passendale, Tyne Cot and Zonnebeke, all WWI-related sights that you're likely to want to see anyway.

City buses operate 5.30am to 11pm (€3/8 per one-hour ride/day pass). Services marked 'Centrum' run to Markt. For the station, the most central stop is **Stadsschouwburg** (Vlamingstraat 58).

> **WORTH A TRIP**
>
> **DAMME**
>
> Charming Damme village is little more than a single street plus a historic main square sporting a fine Gothic stadhuis. It's 5km from Bruges via a perfectly straight canal, with a cycleway on one side and a road on the other.
>
> A classic (if somewhat over-rated) way to arrive is using paddle-steamer **Lamme Goedzak** (050-28 86 10; www.bootdamme-brugge.be; Noorweegse Kaai 31; adult/child one way €8.50/6, return €10.50/9.50; 10am-5pm Easter–mid-Oct), taking a dawdling 35 minutes from Bruges' Noorweegse Kaai (every two hours). Cycling is arguably more enjoyable and in summer it's worth continuing beyond Damme to much quieter areas of very beautiful tree-lined canals.

Ypres

057 / POP 34,964

Only the hardest of hearts are unmoved by historic Ypres (Ieper in Dutch). In the Middle Ages it was an important cloth town ranking alongside Bruges and Ghent. In WWI some 300,000 Allied soldiers plus countless more civilians and German troops died in Flanders Fields, aka the 'Salient', a bow-shaped bulge that formed the front line around the town. Ypres remained unoccupied by German forces, but was utterly flattened by bombardment. After the war, the city's beautiful medieval core was convincingly rebuilt and the restored **Lakenhalle** is today one of the most spectacular buildings in Belgium.

 Sights

Central Ypres

In Flanders Fields Museum MUSEUM
(☎057-23 92 20; www.inflandersfields.be; Grote Markt 34; adult/under 26yr/child €9/5/4; 🕒10am-6pm Apr–mid-Nov, to 5pm Tue-Sun mid-Nov–Mar) No museum gives a more balanced yet moving and user-friendly introduction to WWI history. It's a multisensory experience combining soundscapes, videos, well-chosen exhibits and interactive learning stations at which you 'become' a character and follow his or her progress through the wartime period. An electronic 'identity' bracelet activates certain displays.

Ramparts CWGC Cemetery CEMETERY
(Lille Gate Cemetery; Lille Gate) One of Ypres' most attractive military graveyards, this Commonwealth War Graves Commission site is found 1km south of the Grote Markt.

Ypres Salient

Flanders' WWI battlefields are famed for red poppies, both real and metaphorical. From 1914 the area suffered four years of brutal fighting in a muddy, bloody quagmire where the world first saw poison-gas attacks and as thousands of diggers valiantly tunnelled underground to dynamite enemy trenches.

Tourism here still revolves around widely spaced WWI cemeteries, memorials, bunkers and museums. The following are relatively accessible between Bruges and Ypres, all within 600m of Ypres–Roeselare bus routes 94 and 95, which run once or twice hourly on weekdays, and five times daily on weekends.

Having your own wheels makes visits much easier, or join the various half-day guided bus tours organised by **British Grenadier** (☎057-21 46 57; www.salienttours.be; Menenstraat 5; tours from €40; 🕒10am-1.30pm). Its offices are between the Grote Markt and Menin Gate in central Ypres.

Memorial Museum Passchendaele 1917 MUSEUM
(☎051-77 04 41; www.passchendaele.be; Berten Pilstraat 5A, Zonnebeke; €10.50; 🕒9am-6pm Feb–mid-Dec; 🚌94) Within the grounds of Kasteelpark Zonnebeke you'll find this polished WWI museum charting local battle progressions with plenty of multilingual commentaries. The big attraction here is descending into its multiroom 'trench experience', with low-lit, wooden-clad subterranean bunk rooms and a soundtrack. Explanations are much more helpful here than in 'real' trenches elsewhere.

Tyne Cot CWGC Cemetary CEMETERY
(Vijfwegestraat, Zonnebeke; 🕒24hr, visitor centre 10am-6pm Feb-Nov; 🚌94) Probably the most-visited Salient site, this is the world's biggest British Commonwealth war cemetery, with 11,956 graves. A huge semicircular wall commemorates another 34,857 lost-in-action soldiers whose names wouldn't fit on Ypres' Menin Gate. The name Tyne Cot was coined by the Northumberland Fusiliers who fancied that German bunkers on the hillside here looked like Tyneside cottages. Two such dumpy concrete bunkers sit amid the graves, with a third visible through the metal wreath beneath the white Cross of Sacrifice.

Langemark Deutscher Soldatenfriedhof CEMETERY
(Klerkenstraat, Langemark) The Salient's largest German WWI cemetery is smaller than Tyne Cot but arguably more memorable, sited amid oak trees and trios of squat, mossy crosses. Some 44,000 corpses were grouped together here, up to 10 per granite grave slab; four eerie silhouette statues survey the site. Entering takes you through a black concrete tunnel that clanks and hisses with distant war sounds, while four short video montages commemorate the tragedy of war.

DON'T MISS

LAST POST

A block east of Ypres central square lies a huge stone gateway called the **Menin Gate** (Menenpoort; Menenstraat). It's inscribed with 54,896 names: British and Commonwealth casualties of WWI whose bodies were never found. At 8pm daily, traffic through the gateway is halted while buglers sound the **Last Post** (www.lastpost.be; 🕒8pm) FREE in remembrance of the dead, a moving tradition that started in 1928. Every evening the scene is somewhat different, possibly accompanied by pipers, troops of cadets or maybe a military band.

Sleeping & Eating

Ariane Hotel HOTEL €€

(☎057-21 82 18; www.ariane.be; Slachthuisstraat 58; d from €129; P 📶) This peaceful, professionally managed large hotel has a designer feel to its rooms and popular restaurant. Wartime memorabilia dots the spacious common areas.

Main Street Hotel GUESTHOUSE €€€

(☎057-46 96 33; www.mainstreet-hotel.be; Rijselstraat 136; d incl breakfast from €180; 📶) Jumbling eccentricity with historical twists and luxurious comfort, this is a one-off that oozes character. The smallest room is designed like a mad professor's experiment. The breakfast room has a Tiffany glass ceiling.

De Ruyffelaer FLEMISH €€

(☎057-36 60 06; www.deruyffelaer.be; Gustave de Stuersstraat 9; mains €15-26; ⏰11.30am-3.30pm Sun, 5.30-9.30pm Fri-Sun) Traditional local dishes are served in an adorable wood-panelled interior with old chequerboard floors and *brocante* (vintage) decor including dried flowers, old radios and antique biscuit tins.

Information

Tourist Office (☎057-23 92 20; www.toerismeieper.be; Grote Markt 34, Lakenhalle; ⏰9am-6pm Mon-Fri, 10am-6pm Sat & Sun Apr–mid-Nov, to 5pm mid-Nov–Mar) Has an extensive bookshop.

Getting There & Around

Buses depart from Ypres Station, 500m southwest of centre, and also pick up at the Grote Markt bus stop (check the direction carefully).

Trains run hourly to Brussels (€18.40, 1¾ hours) via Ghent and Kortrijk (30 minutes), where you could change for Bruges or Antwerp.

Bike hire is available from **Hotel Ambrosia** (☎057-36 63 66; www.ambrosiahotel.be; D'Hondtstraat 54; bike per day €15; ⏰7.30am-7.30pm).

Ghent

☎09 / POP 248,358

One of Europe's greatest hidden gems, Ghent (Gent in Dutch) is small enough to feel cosy but big enough to stay vibrant. There's a wealth of medieval and classical architecture here, contrasted by large post-industrial areas undergoing urban development, and with a lively student population to inject life. Magical canalside views from Korenmarkt and Graslei give Bruges a run for its money, there's an abundance of quirky bars, and Ghent has some of Belgium's most fascinating museums; altogether this is a city you really won't want to miss.

Sights

The Adoration of the Mystic Lamb GALLERY

(Het Lam Gods; ☎09-269 20 45; www.sintbaafskathedraal.be; St-Baafskathedraal, Sint-Baafsplein; adult/child/audioguide €4/1.50/1; ⏰9.30am-5pm Mon-Sat, 1-5pm Sun Apr-Oct, 10.30am-4pm Mon-Sat, 1-4pm Sun Nov-Mar) Art enthusiasts swarm the **Sint-Baafskathedraal** (⏰8.30am-6pm Mon-Sat, 10am-6pm Sun Apr-Oct, to 5pm Nov-Mar) FREE to glimpse *The Adoration of the Mystic Lamb* (De Aanbidding van het Lams God), a lavish representation of medieval religious thinking that is one of the earliest-known oil paintings. Completed in 1432, it was painted as an altarpiece by Flemish Primitive artists the Van Eyck brothers, and has 20 panels.

Gravensteen CASTLE

(☎09-225 93 06; https://gravensteen.stad.gent/en; St-Veerleplein 11; adult/concession/child €10/6/free; ⏰10am-6pm Apr-Oct, 9am-5pm Nov-Mar) Flanders' quintessential 12th-century stone castle comes complete with moat, turrets and arrow slits. It's all the more remarkable considering that during the 19th century the site was converted into a cotton mill. Meticulously restored since, the interior sports the odd suit of armour, a guillotine and torture devices. The relative lack of furnishings is compensated for by a handheld 15-minute movie guide, which sets a tongue-in-cheek historical costumed drama in the rooms, prison pit and battlements.

Belfort HISTORIC BUILDING

(☎09-375 31 61; www.belfortgent.be; Sint-Baafsplein; adult/concession €8/3; ⏰10am-6pm) Ghent's Unesco-listed 14th-century belfry (91m) is topped by a large dragon weathervane: he's become something of a city mascot. You'll meet two previous dragon incarnations on the 350-stair climb to the top; there are lifts to help some of the way. Enter through the **Lakenhalle**, Ghent's cloth hall that was left half-built in 1445 and only completed in 1903. Hear the carillon at 11.30am Fridays and 11am on summer Sundays.

MSK GALLERY

(Museum voor Schone Kunsten, Museum of Fine Arts Ghent; ☎09-323 67 00; www.mskgent.be; Fernand Scribedreef 1; adult/youth/child €8/2/free; ⏰9.30am-5.30pm Tue-Fri, 10am-6pm Sat &

Central Ghent

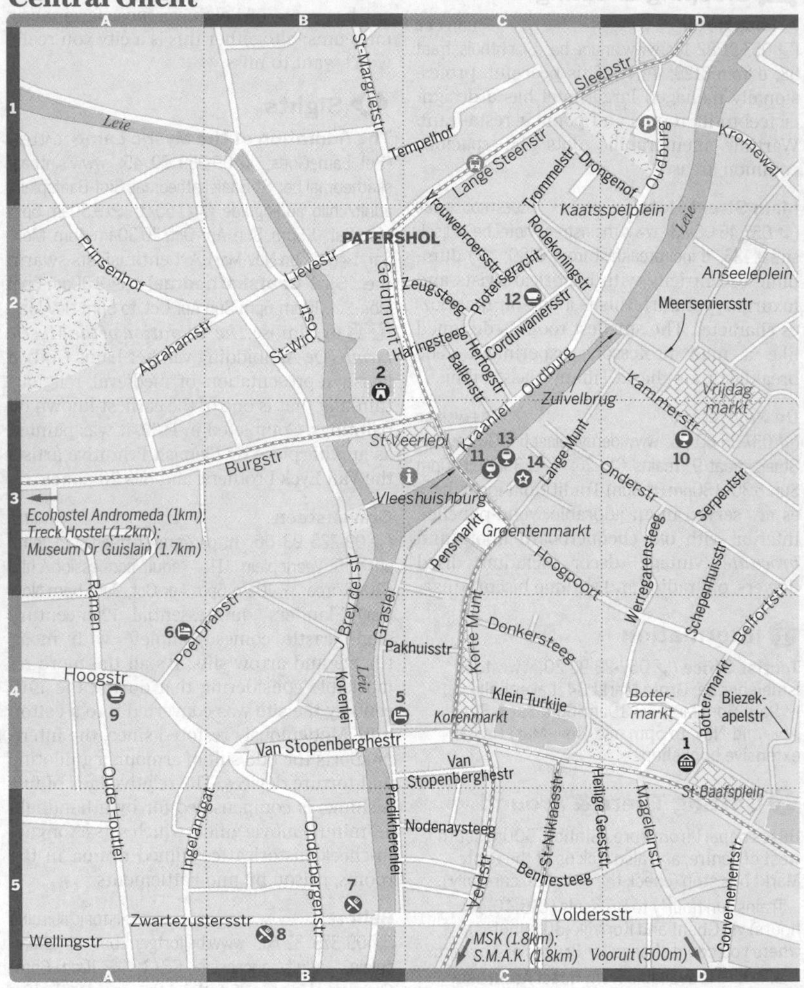

Sun) Styled like a Greek temple, this superb 1903 fine-art gallery introduces a veritable A–Z of great Belgian and other Low Countries' painters from the 14th to mid-20th centuries. Highlights include a happy family of coffins by Magritte, luminist canvases by Emile Claus, and Pieter Brueghel the Younger's 1621 *Dorpsadvocaat* – a brilliant portrait of a village lawyer oozing with arrogance. English-language explanation cards are available in each room.

Museum Dr Guislain MUSEUM

(☎09-398 69 50; www.museumdrguislain.be; Jozef Guislainstraat 43; adult/concession €8/3; ⏲9am-5pm Tue-Fri, 1-5pm Sat & Sun; 🚊1) Hidden away in an 1857 neo-Gothic psychiatric hospital, this enthralling mental-health museum takes visitors on a trilingual, multicultural journey through the history of psychiatry, from gruesome Neolithic trepanning to contemporary brain scans via cage beds, straightjackets, shackles and phrenology. Dr D'Arsonval's extraordinary 1909 radiographic apparatus looks like a Dr Frankenstein creation.

S.M.A.K. GALLERY

(Museum of Contemporary Art; ☎09-240 76 01; www.smak.be; Jan Hoetplein 1; adult/concession/

child €8/2/free; 9.30am-5.30pm Tue-Sun; 5) Ghent's highly regarded Museum of Contemporary Art is one of Belgium's largest. Works from its 3000-strong permanent collection (dating from 1939 to the present) are regularly curated to complement visiting temporary exhibitions of provocative, cutting-edge installations, which sometimes spill out right across the city.

Sleeping

Ghent offers innovative accommodation in all price ranges. There's plenty for budget travellers including a big, central HI Hostel, the recycled barge 'Eco'-hostel **Andromeda** (0486 67 80 33; www.ecohostel.be; Bargiekaai 35; dm/d incl breakfast from €23/68; reception 2-8pm; P; 1) and indoor camping at **Treck Hostel** (09 310 76 20; www.treckhostel.be; Groendreef 51; dm/van from €19/35;). Numerous B&Bs can be found through www.gent-accommodations.be and www.bedandbreakfast-gent.be.

Hotel Erasmus HERITAGE HOTEL €€
(09-224 21 95; www.erasmushotel.be; Poel 25; s/d incl breakfast from €79/99; reception 7am-10.30pm;) A suit of armour guards the breakfast in this creaky 16th-century building. Its 12 guest rooms have a mixture of old and antique furniture, giving it an atmospheric feeling of times gone by.

★**1898 The Post** LUXURY HOTEL €€€
(09-277 09 60; www.zannierhotels.com/1898thepost/en; Graslei 16; d/ste €175/315;) This beautiful boutique offering is housed in Ghent's spectacular twin-turreted former post office. The property's common areas, guestrooms and suites are dark and moody in a wonderful way, with elements of great design at every turn (though note the standard rooms are compact for the price). The hotel also offers fine dining and an ultra-atmospheric bar.

Central Ghent

Sights

1	Belfort	D4
2	Gravensteen	B2
3	Sint-Baafskathedraal	E5
4	The Adoration of the Mystic Lamb	E5

Sleeping

5	1898 The Post	B4
6	Hotel Erasmus	A4

Eating

7	Balls & Glory	B5
8	't Oud Clooster	B5

Drinking & Nightlife

9	Café Labath	A4
10	Dulle Griet	D3
11	Het Waterhuis aan de Bierkant	C3
12	Rococo	C2
13	't Dreupelkot	C3

Entertainment

14	Hot Club Gent	C3

PARTY TIME IN GHENT

Mid-July's raucous **Gentse Feesten** (http://gentsefeesten.stad.gent) is a vast, city-wide festival during which many squares become venues for a variety of street-theatre performances, and there are big associated techno and jazz festivals. Those wanting a merrily boozy party atmosphere will love it. But consider avoiding Ghent at this time if you don't.

Eating

Cosy, upmarket restaurants in the delightful cobbled alleyways of Patershol cover most cuisines. Several eateries jostle for summer terrace space on Graslei's gorgeous canal-side terrace; there's fast food around Korenmarkt, great-value Turkish food on Sleepstraat and numerous vegetarian choices city-wide.

Balls & Glory BELGIAN €
(0486 67 87 76; www.ballsnglory.be; Jakobijnenstraat 6; balls €4.40-6; 10am-9pm Mon-Sat;) This easy-going eatery is popular with students and hipsters for its classy interiors and good value. It serves big meaty or vegetarian balls (a bit like a hybrid of a traditional meatball and an arancini) that you can take away in a box or devour on-site.

't Oud Clooster CAFE €€
(09-233 78 02; www.toudclooster.be; Zwartezusterstraat 5; mains €16-22; 11.45am-2.30pm & 6-10.30pm Mon-Fri, 11.45am-2.30pm & 5.30-10.30pm Sat, 5.30-9.30pm Sun) Mostly candlelit at night, this atmospheric double-level cafe is built into sections of what was long ago a nunnery, hence the sprinkling of religious statues and cherub lamp-holders. Well-priced light meals are presented with unexpected style.

Drinking & Entertainment

Try the snug **Hot Club** (09-256 71 99; www.hotclub.gent; Schuddevisstraatje 2; 3pm-late) for live jazz, gyspy or blues music; **Hotsy Totsy** (09-224 20 12; www.facebook.com/Hotsy.Totsy.Gent; Hoogstraat 1; 6pm-1am Mon-Fri, 8pm-2am Sat & Sun, from 8pm daily Jul & Aug) for free Thursday jazz; and beautifully panelled **Rococo** (09-224 30 35; Corduwaniersstraat 5; 9pm-late Tue-Sun) for candlelit late-night conversation. **Café Labath** (09-225 28 25; www.cafelabath.be; Oude Houtlei 1; 8am-7pm Mon-Fri, 9am-7pm Sat, 10am-6pm Sun) is ideal for a coffee fix, **Dulle Griet** (09-224 24 55; www.dullegriet.be; Vrijdagmarkt 50; noon-1am Tue-Sat, to 7pm Sun, 4.30pm-1am Mon) and **Het Waterhuis aan de Bierkant** (09-225 06 80; Groentenmarkt 9; 11am-1am) are traditional brown-bar gems, with brick-thick beer menus while next door to the latter, **'t Dreupelkot** (09-224 21 20; www.dreupelkot.be; Groentenmarkt 12; 11am-1.30am Mon-Thu, to 2am Fri-Sun) is a timeless jenever bar with a hundred variants on Flemish and Dutch 'gin'.

As a wide-ranging events venue, it's hard to beat **Vooruit** (09-267 28 20; www.vooruit.be; St-Pietersnieuwstraat 23; 10am-1am; 5) whose 1912 building is a visionary architectural premonition of art deco.

Information

CityCard Gent (48-/72-hour €30/35) gives free entrance to all of Ghent's top museums and monuments, and allows unlimited travel on trams and city buses, plus a boat trip. It's excellent value. Buy one at participating museums, major bus offices or the **tourist office** (09-266 56 60; https://visit.gent.be; St-Veerleplein 5; 10am-6pm).

Getting There & Around

Gent-Dampoort Station, 1km west of the old city, is handy for trains to Antwerp (€9.90, fast/slow 42/64 minutes, three per hour) and Bruges (€7, 36 minutes, hourly), and is a pick-up point for international buses. Bigger **Gent-Sint-Pieters Station**, 2.5km south of the centre by tram 1, has many more Bruges-bound trains and twice hourly services to Brussels (€9.40, 36 minutes).

Biker (09-224 29 03; www.bikerfietsen.be; Steendam 16; per day from €9; 9am-12.30pm & 1.30-6pm Tue-Sat) and **De Fiets Ambassade** (The Bike Embassy; 09-242 80 40; https://fietsambassade.gent.be/en; Voskenslaan 27; per half-day/day/week €7/10/30; 7am-7pm Mon-Fri) rent out bicycles.

Antwerp

03 / POP 521,700

Known as Antwerpen in Dutch and Anvers in French, the port city of Antwerp is Belgium's capital of cool. In the mid-16th century it was one of Europe's most important cities and home to baroque superstar painter Pieter Paul Rubens, and today it remains a powerful magnet for everyone from fashion moguls and club queens to art lovers and diamond dealers.

Sights

City Centre

★Onze-Lieve-Vrouwekathedraal CATHEDRAL
(☎03-213 99 51; www.dekathedraal.be; Handschoenmarkt; adult/reduced/under 12yr €6/4/free; ⏰10am-5pm Mon-Fri, to 3pm Sat, 1-5pm Sun) Belgium's finest Gothic cathedral was 169 years in the making (1352–1521). Wherever you wander in Antwerp, its gracious, 123m-high spire has a habit of popping unexpectedly into view and it rarely fails to prompt a gasp of awe. The sight is particularly well framed when looking up Pelgrimstraat in the afternoon light.

Grote Markt SQUARE
As is the case with every great Flemish city, Antwerp's medieval heart is a classic Grote Markt (market square). Here the triangular, pedestrianised space features the voluptuous, baroque **Brabo Fountain** depicting the hero of Antwerp's giant-killing, hand-throwing foundation legend. Flanked on two sides by very photogenic guildhalls, the square is dominated by an impressive Italo-Flemish Renaissance-style **stadhuis** (Town Hall; Grote Markt) completed in 1565.

★Museum Plantin-Moretus MUSEUM, HISTORIC BUILDING
(☎03-221 14 50; www.museumplantinmoretus.be; Vrijdagmarkt 22; adult/reduced/child €8/6/free; ⏰10am-5pm Tue-Sun, last entry 4.30pm) The medieval building and 1622 courtyard garden alone would be worth a visit, but it's the world's oldest printing press, priceless manuscripts and original type sets that justify this museum's Unesco World Heritage status. It's been a museum since 1876 and its other great highlights include a 1640 library, a bookshop dating from 1700 and rooms lined with gilt leather.

Rubenshuis MUSEUM
(☎03-201 15 55; www.rubenshuis.be; Wapper 9-11; adult/reduced €8/6; ⏰10am-5pm Tue-Sun) This delightfully indulgent 1611 mansion was built as a home and studio for celebrated painter Pieter Paul Rubens. It was rescued from ruins in 1937 and has been very sensitively restored with furniture that dates from Rubens' era plus a priceless collection of 17th-century art. There are around a dozen Rubens canvases, most memorably his world-famous hatted self-portrait and a large-scale canvas of Eve glancing lustfully at Adam's fig leaf.

Museum Mayer van den Bergh MUSEUM
(☎03-232 42 37; www.museummayervandenbergh.be; Lange Gasthuisstraat 19; adult/reduced €8/6, with Rubenshuis €10/8; ⏰10am-5pm Tue-Sun) Styled as a 16th-century town house, this superb place was actually constructed in 1904 as one of the first museums in the world built around a single collection. Fritz Mayer van den Bergh's collection is indeed as rich as that of many a national gallery with its notable paintings, sculptures, tapestries, drawings, jewellery and stained-glass windows. The undoubted highlight is the Brueghel Room, whose centrepiece is Pieter Brueghel the Elder's brilliantly grotesque *Dulle Griet* (Mad Meg), painted in 1561 and restored in 2018.

Snijder-Rockoxhuis MUSEUM
(☎03-201 92 50; www.snijdersrockoxhuis.be; Keizerstraat 10-12; adult/reduced €8/6; ⏰10am-5pm Tue-Sun) Combining the impressive 17th-century houses of artist Frans Snijders and of Antwerp lawyer, mayor and Rubens patron Nicolaas Rockox, this recently revamped museum does a superb job of making accessible a fine collection of 16th- and 17th-century masterpieces with a very helpful tablet tour, headphones and two six-minute films.

St-Carolus-Borromeuskerk CHURCH
(www.mkaweb.be/site/english/062.mv; Hendrik Conscienceplein 6; ⏰10am-12.30pm & 2-5pm Mon-Sat) FREE Rubens turned interior designer as part of the team that created this superb 1621 baroque church, designed to give worshippers a very visceral foretaste of heaven's delights. A wonder of its era, the remarkable altarpiece allowed vast canvases to be changed using a series of wire pulleys.

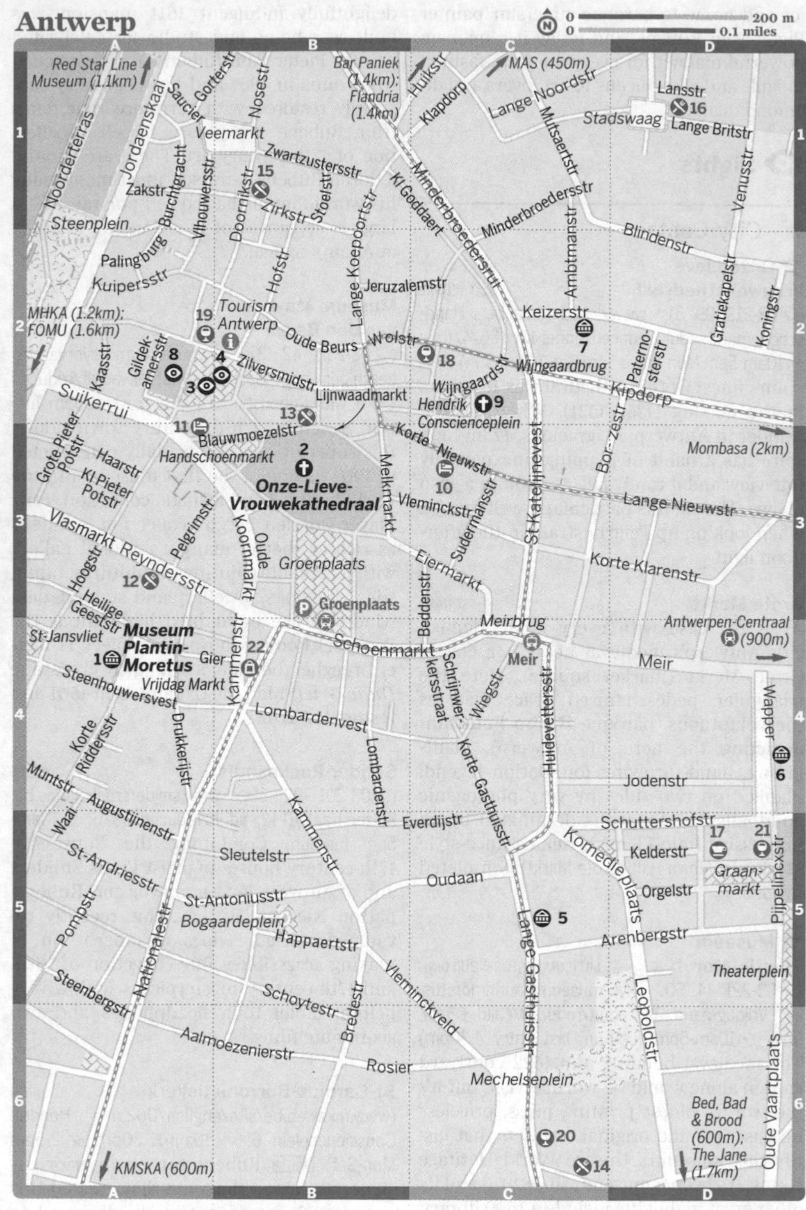

't Zuid & Zurenborg

Heading south from the centre, the Fashion District morphs into 't Zuid, a dining, drinking and museum zone interspersed by some areas of relatively grand urban residences. The highlight here is the world-class gallery, **KMSKA** (www.kmska.be; Leopold de Waelplaats), housed in a monumental neoclassical building topped with winged charioteer statues. There is also an important modern art gallery, **MHKA** (☎03-260 99 99; www.muhka.be; Leuvenstraat 32; some floors free, exhibitions adult/student/under 26yr/child €10/5/1/free; ⏰11am-

Antwerp

Top Sights

1	Museum Plantin-Moretus	A4
2	Onze-Lieve-Vrouwekathedraal	B3

Sights

3	Brabo Fountain	A2
4	Grote Markt	B2
5	Museum Mayer van den Bergh	C5
6	Rubenshuis	D4
7	Snijder-Rockoxhuis	C2
8	Stadhuis	A2
9	St-Carolus-Borromeuskerk	C2

Sleeping

10	Hotel Julien	C3
11	Hotel O	A3

Eating

12	De Groote Witte Arend	A3
13	Elfde Gebod	B2
14	Life Is Art	C6
15	Little Ethiopia	B1
16	Nimmanhaemin	D1

Drinking & Nightlife

17	De Duifkens	D5
18	De Kat	C2
19	Den Engel	A2
20	Korsakov	C6
21	Oud Arsenaal	D5

Shopping

22	Het Modepaleis	D4

6pm Tue-Sun, to 9pm Thu), and photography museum **FoMu** (Fotomuseum; ☎03-242 93 00; www.fotomuseum.be; Waalsekaai 47; adult/pensioner/under 26yr/child €10/5/3/free; ⏲10am-6pm Tue-Sun, last tickets 5.30pm). Further southeast, Zurenborg has a wealth of art nouveau and belle-époch residential architecture, notably around Waterloostraat.

't Eilandje

Starting around 800m north of Grote Markt, 't Eilandje is a regenerated dockland area with a scattering of in-vogue bars, a marina and a parked lightship. From here, the **Flandria** (☎03-472 21 40 56; www.flandria.nu; Kattendijkdok; adult/child €19/3; ⏲noon Thu, Sat & Sun Apr-Nov) makes three-hour cruises of the greater Antwerp harbour area, passing Zaha Hadid's 2016 architectural flight of fancy, the Port House.

MAS MUSEUM

(Museum aan de Stroom; ☎03-338 44 00; www.mas.be; Hanzestedenplaats; viewpoint free, museum adult/reduced €10/8, btwn exhibitions €5/3; ⏲viewpoint 9.30am-11.30pm Tue-Sun, museum 10am-4.45pm Tue-Sun) Opened in 2011, MAS is a 10-storey complex that redefines the idea of a museum-gallery. Floors are designed around big-idea themes using a barrage of media, from old master paintings and tribal artefacts to video installations. But many people come just for the views over the city (no ticket required), which transform as you climb somewhat laboriously by a series of escalators and three flights of stairs (no public lifts).

Red Star Line Museum MUSEUM

(☎03-298 27 70; www.redstarline.be; Montevideostraat 3; adult/reduced €8/6; ⏲10am-5pm Tue-Sun, reservations required on weekends) Over two million passengers sailed from Antwerp on Red Star Line ships between 1873 and 1934, the great majority of them immigrants bound for America. This museum, housed in the very building where those many embarkations took place, is beautifully designed and extremely engaging, telling the story of individual journeys through photographs, recreations and objects, including some gorgeous period model ships.

Sleeping

ABhostel HOSTEL €

(☎0473-57 01 66; www.abhostel.com; Kattenberg 110; dm/tw €25/55; ⏲reception noon-3pm & 6-8pm; 📶; 🚌10, 24 to Drink) 🌿 This adorable, family-run hostel in Borgerhout is a great place to get to know fellow travellers while fixing breakfast from provided ingredients

> **BOLLEKE**
>
> To sound like a local, ask for a *bolleke*. No, that's not an insult, but the nickname for 'little bowl' (ie glass) of De Koninck, Antwerp's favourite brown ale. Timeless old-world places to try one include the following:
>
> **Oud Arsenaal** (Pijpelincxstraat 4; ⏲10am-10pm Wed-Fri, 7.30am-7.30pm Sat & Sun).
>
> **De Kat** (☎03-233 08 92; www.facebook.com/cafeDeKat; Wolstraat 22; ⏲noon-2am Mon-Sat, 5pm-2am Sun).
>
> **Den Engel** (www.cafedenengel.be; Grote Markt 3; ⏲9am-2am)
>
> **De Duifkens** (Graanmarkt 5; ⏲10am-late Mon-Thu, from noon Fri-Sun)

DON'T MISS

THE FASHION DISTRICT

Antwerp may seem far more sartorially laid-back than fashion heavyweights Paris or Milan, but it punches above its weight. Few places in the world have such a covetable concentration of designer boutiques, end-of-line discounters, upmarket vintage stores and designer consignment shops. Most lie within a couple of blocks from Dries Van Noten's iconic flagship store **Het Modepaleis** (www.driesvannoten.be; Nationalestraat 16; ⏰10am-6.30pm Mon-Sat). Browse Nationalestraat, Lombardenvest, Huidevettersstraat and Schuttershofstraat, not missing Kammenstraat for streetwear and up-and-coming designers.

in the kitchen-bar, or relaxing in hammocks in the small yard-garden. Helpful traveller staff are a mine of information to help you make the most of the odd-ball location's opportunities and hot spots.

Bed, Bad & Brood B&B €€
(☎03-248 15 39; www.bbantwerp.com; Justitiestraat 43; s/d/q from €62/76/135; 🚭@) In a 1910, belle époque–era town house near the vast Gerechtshof (former courthouse), this B&B impresses with authentic wooden floors, high ceilings and beautifully eclectic furniture. The three rooms are remarkably spacious and comfortable for the price and rates include a bountiful breakfast.

Hotel O BOUTIQUE HOTEL €€
(☎03-500 89 50; www.hotelokathedral.com; Handschoenmarkt 3; rear s/d from €79/89, d with view €99-154; ❄📶) The immediate selling point of this excellent-value 39-room hotel is its unbeatable location, with oblique views across the square to the cathedral frontage. Expect moody decor with baths or showers in black-framed glass boxes and – in most rooms – giant 17th-century paintings reproduced as either headboards or covering whole walls.

Hotel Julien BOUTIQUE HOTEL €€€
(☎03-229 06 00; www.hotel-julien.com; Korte Nieuwstraat 24; d €184-284, ste €334; ❄@📶) In a grand old mansion with lots of designer detail, this discreet 21-room boutique hotel has a suave, understated elegance, impressive lounge and bar spaces, and a staff attitude that hits the sweet spot between friendly and professional. Every room is different. Choose pricier versions for high ceilings, exposed beams, coffee maker etc. The breathtaking rooftop terrace view is a well-kept secret.

Eating

Locals often head south of centre to dine in 't Zuid, where there are great mid-range choices around Leopold de Waelplaats, Vlaamsekaai and Marnixplaats. Troonplaats is an up-and-coming place to eat, while just one block away, contrastingly ungentrified Brederodestraat has excellent-value Turkish bakeries, kebab shops and Eastern European groceries. More centrally, **Little Ethiopia** (☎03-336 22 93; www.little-ethiopia.be; Zirkstraat 8; mains €9-19.50; ⏰noon-10pm Wed-Mon) serves Ethiopian cuisine in a veritable museum of African artefacts, while **Nimmanhaemin** (☎03-345 35 38; www.nimmanhaemin.be; Stadswaag 9; starters €6-10, mains €13-20; ⏰6-10pm) offers richly flavoured Thai food by a pretty, tree-shaded square.

Elfde Gebod BELGIAN €€
(www.11gebod.com; Torfbrug 10; mains €14-24.50, sandwiches €8.50; ⏰noon-11pm) In the heart of the tourist zone, this ivy-clad medieval masterpiece has an astounding interior decked with angels, saints, pulpits and several deliciously sacrilegious visual jokes.

Life Is Art INTERNATIONAL €€
(www.rebeccavanherck.wixsite.com/lifeisart; St-Jorispoort 21-23; lunch salads €15, starters/mains €13/22; ⏰11am-3pm & 7-10pm Thu & Fri, 10am-10pm Sat & Sun) Loose cushions on bench seats, *brocante* mirrors, an old piano and a dangling canoe-skeleton all conspire to create a casually quirky venue for super-fresh food that changes so regularly that you'll have to ask the waitstaff for details.

De Groote Witte Arend BELGIAN €€
(☎03-233 50 33; www.degrootewittearend.be; Reyndersstraat 18; lunches €8-15, mains €16-26; ⏰noon-9pm Sun-Thu, to 10pm Fri & Sat; 📶) Retaining the Tuscan stone arcade of a 15th-to-17th-century convent building, as well as a little family chapel, this place combines the joys of a good beer bar with the satisfaction of well-cooked, sensibly priced Flemish home cuisine.

★**The Jane** INTERNATIONAL €€€
(☎03-808 44 65; www.thejaneantwerp.com; Paradeplein 1; 12/14 courses €110/130, Upper Room lunch plates €7-22; ⏰7pm, 7.30pm or 8pm Tue-Sat,

bar noon-2am; 🚌9 to Zurenborg) In a stunningly repurposed old military-hospital chapel, the Jane's sublime two-Michelin-star dining is such an overwhelmingly fabulous experience that you'll need to book online exactly three months ahead…on the dot of 8am.

 Drinking & Nightlife

Around Mechelseplein, stylishly unkempt drinking holes like **Korsåkov** (☎0485 46 45 06; www.facebook.com/vokasrov; Mechelseplein 21; ⊙noon-4am Mon-Thu, 2pm-5am Fri & Sat, noon-midnight Sun) open super-late. Less centrally, **Bar Paniek** (Kattendijkdok-Oostkai 21B; ⊙11am-11pm) is an artists' collective bar in old harbour warehouses. The pre-gentrified inner-suburb of Borgerhout has several absolute gems, most notably **Mombasa** (☎0498 52 11 94; Moorkensplein 37; ⊙3pm-2am Tue-Sun).

Information

Tourism Antwerp (☎03-232 01 03; www.visitantwerpen.be; Grote Markt 13; ⊙10am-5pm) sells tram/bus passes and books tickets here. They have a booth at Antwerpen Centraal station (open 9am to 5pm). Ask for the excellent, free *Use It guide maps* (www.antwerp.use-it.travel). For events and offbeat visitor ideas consult www.thisisantwerp.be.

Getting There & Away

An attraction in itself, the gorgeous main station **Antwerpen-Centraal** (Koningin Astridplein 27; ⊙ticket office 5.45am-10pm) has regular IC trains to Amsterdam (from €37.40 booked online, two hours), Bruges (€15.50, 90 minutes), Brussels (€7.70, 46 minutes), Leuven (€7.70, 46 minutes), Lier (€3, 25 minutes) and Mechelen (€4.10, 20 minutes).

Getting Around

Velo-Antwerpen (☎03-200 50 30; www.velo-antwerpen.be; Kievitplein 7; day/week membership €4/10; ⊙11am-5pm Mon-Thu, 9am-3pm Fri) is a super-handy short-hop bike rental service with around 100 docking stations. Sign up online and get the phone app for an interactive map showing availability and spaces.

Cyclant (☎03-232 01 09; www.cyclant.com; Pelikaanstraat 3/1050; per 4/12/24hr €9/12/15; ⊙10am-6pm Sun, Mon, Wed & Thu, to 7pm Fri & Sat) has longer-term bike rental. The shop is tucked into the outer west side of Antwerpen-Centraal.

De Lijn (www.delijn.be) runs an integrated bus and tram service. One ride costs €3 and a day-pass €8 (or €6 if pre-purchased).

Lier

☎03 / POP 35,700

Delightful Lier is one of Flanders' overlooked historical gems. The centre retains a satisfying architectural integrity and is ringed by a circular waterway followed by a walkable green rampart where the city walls once stood. Founded in 1258, the Unesco-listed **Begijnhof** (Sint-Margaretastraat) is one of Belgium's prettiest, a picture-perfect grid of cobbled lanes lined with archetypal houses around the baroque-fronted 1671 St-Margaretakerk. Two blocks away is the intriguing **Zimmertoren** (☎03-800 03 95; www.zimmertoren.be; Zimmerplein; museum adult/child €4.50/2; ⊙10am-noon & 1-5pm Tue-Sun), a partly 14th-century tower incorporating a fanciful 1930 timepiece that's eccentrically overendowed with dials and zodiac signs. On the fine central square, it's worth visiting the **tourist office** (☎03-800 05 55; www.visitlier.be; Grote Markt 58; ⊙9am-4.30pm Mon-Fri, to 4pm Sat & Sun Apr-Oct, 9am-4.30pm Mon-Fri & closed weekends & lunchtimes Nov-Mar) if only to admire the splendid chandeliers, ceiling mural and portrait of Leopold I.

Bed Muzet (☎03-488 60 36; www.vjh.be; Volmolenstraat 65; dm/d €27/62; ⊙check in 4.30-7pm), Lier's swish modern hostel, occupies a repurposed former monastery, while the atmospheric, riverside **Hof van Aragon** (☎03-491 08 00; www.hofvanaragon.be; Mosdijk 6; small s/d €79/94, extra-large s/d/tr €109/124/157; 📶) has a minor maze linking its 20 comfortable rooms in a series of knocked together historic riverside houses.

Grote Markt, Eikelstraat and Zimmerplein are lined with inviting places to eat and drink, with other characterful restaurants scattered in lanes near Lier's huge Gothic church, **St-Gummaruskerk** (www.topalier.be/bezoeken; Kardinaal Mercierplein; treasury €3; ⊙2-4.30pm daily & 10am-noon Tue-Fri, closed Nov-Easter).

Frequent Lier–Antwerp trains (€3) take under 20 minutes.

Leuven

☎016 / POP 101,200

Lively, self-confident Leuven (Louvain in French; www.leuven.be) is Flanders' oldest university town and home to the vast **Stella Artois brewery** (www.breweryvisits.com; Aarschotsesteenweg 22; adult/concession €8.50/7.50; ⊙1pm & 3pm Sat & Sun). Its greatest attraction is the flamboyant 15th-century city hall, the **Stadhuis** (Grote Markt 9; tours €4; ⏲tours 3pm), lavished with intricate exterior statuary. Other architectural attractions are patchy due to heavy damage sustained in 20th-century wars, but the iconic **university library** (www.bib.kuleuven.be; Monseigneur Ladeuzeplein 21; library/library plus tower €2/7; ⏲library 9am-8pm Mon-Thu, to 7pm Fri, 10am-5pm Sat & Sun, tower 10am-7pm Mon-Fri, to 5pm Sat & Sun) has been rebuilt. Twice.

Mirroring the ornate Gothic look of the nearby Stadhuis, **The Fourth** (☎016-22 75 54; www.th4th.com; Grote Markt 5; r from €107, peak times €245-295) is a highly automated, luxury hotel within a 1479 guildhouse. Peaceful **Martin's Klooster Hotel** (☎016-21 31 41; www.martinshotels.com; Onze-Lieve-Vrouwstraat 18; d €115-230, ste €299; @📶) also successfully recycles a medieval building, while for backpackers there's an HI hostel and the homey **Leuven City Hostel** (☎016 84 30 33; www.leuvencityhostel.com; Bogaardenstraat 27; s/d/tr/q with bathroom €70/80/95/120, dm/d/tr without bathroom €22/52/53; ⏲reception 4-8pm; @📶).

Casually stylish restaurants fill flag-decked **Muntstraat,** while low prices and quirky character make **De Werf** (www.dewerf-leuven.be; Hogeschoolplein 5; snacks €5-7, pasta & salads €8-15; ⏲9am-midnight Mon-Fri, kitchen to 9pm) a student dining classic. For the full-on Leuven pub experience, be blown away by the cacophanous overload of **Oude Markt** (Oude Markt; ⏲8am-7am), a whole square packed with drinking revelry that's collectively nicknamed 'Europe's Longest Bar'.

Trains are frequent to Brussels (€5.50, 30 minutes), Lier (€7.20, 45 minutes) and Mechelen (€4.70, 30 minutes).

Mechelen

☎015 / POP 86,140

Belgium's religious capital, Mechelen (Malines in French) is centred on the **St-Romboutskathedraal cathedral** (www.sintromboutstoren.mechelen.be; Grote Markt; church free, tower adult/under 26yr €8/3; ⏲church 9am-5.30pm, tower 1-4.40pm Sun-Fri, 10am-4.40pm Sat) featuring a 97m, 15th-century tower. It soars above a particularly memorable central market square from which IJzerenleen, a street of fine baroque facades, leads south. There are several other splendid churches around town, and along Keizerstraat the courthouse and theatre buildings were once royal palaces in the days when the Low Countries were effectively run from Mechelen. Other top sights include the brilliantly wide-ranging **Speelgoedmuseum** (☎015-55 70 75; www.speelgoedmuseum.be; Nekkerstraat 21; adult/child €9.80/7.30; ⏲10am-5pm Tue-Sun; 👪) toy museum, the harrowing **Kazerne Dossin** (☎015-29 06 60; www.kazernedossin.eu; Goswin de Stassartstraat 153; memorial free, museum adult/reduced/under 21yr €10/8/4; ⏲museum 9.30am-5pm Thu-Tue, memorial from 10am) remembering WWII Nazi deportations, and the contrastingly uplifting **Hof van Busleyden** (☎015-29 40 30; www.hofvanbusleyden.be; Sint-Janstraat 2A; adult/under 26yr/child €11/5/free), a state-of-the-art history museum in a gracious medieval mansion.

The HI **Hostel De Zandpoort** (☎015-27 85 39; www.mechelen-hostel.com; Zandpoortvest 70; dm €23-26, tw €55-58; ⏲check-in 5-10pm; P📶) is handy for budget visitors. For more classy accommodation try stylish **Martins Patershof** (☎015-46 46 46; www.facebook.com/MartinsPatershof; Karmelietenstraat 4; d €100-399; P❄📶) 🍃, set in a 1867 Franciscan monastery.

There's a compact bar-cafe zone on Vismarkt beside the canal, but don't miss **Het Anker** (www.hetanker.be; Guido Gezellelaan 49; ⏲tours 11am Tue-Sun & 1pm Fri-Sun, brasserie 10am-11pm, kitchen 11.30am-9pm), a classic brewery whose brasserie is great for Belgian meals as well as for tasting thier own top-rated Gouden Carolus beers.

Trains from Brussels (€4.70, 30 minutes) and Antwerp (€4.10, 20 minutes) run to Mechelen station. Some slower services also call at conveniently central Mechelen-Nekerspoel.

WALLONIA

Wallonia (La Wallonie) is Belgium's mostly French-speaking southern half. It includes many a pretty rustic village in rolling green countryside, interspersed by a scattering of post-industrial cities. The heavily wooded Ardennes is a major area for outdoors activities, but for those without wheels, the regions's most accessible historic cities are Mons and Tournai.

Mons

☎065 / POP 95,300

Historic Mons (Bergen in Dutch; www.visitmons.be) has a characterful medieval cen-

WORTH A TRIP

BOUILLON

Wallonia and Luxembourg have many magnificent castles in widely scattered rural towns and villages. If you're only going to visit one, a great choice is the **Château de Bouillon** (061-46 62 57; www.bouillon-initiative.be; Rue du Château; adult/senior/student & child €7/6.50/5; 10am-6.30pm Jul & Aug, 10am-5pm or 6pm Mar-Jun & Sep-Nov, see website for winter hours; P), the hefty ruins of Belgium's finest feudal castle dominating a tight loop of the Semois River. Accessed by two stone bridges between crags, the fortress harks back to 988, but is especially associated with the knight Godefroid (Godefroy) de Bouillon who sold it to help fund the 1096 First Crusade. The super-atmospheric castle has many an eerie nook and cranny to explore with dank dripping passageways, musty half-lit cell rooms and rough-hewn stairwells. From March to October, entertaining falconry shows at 11.30am, 2pm and 3.30pm are included in the ticket price.

To reach Bouillon, take a train to Libramont, then bus 8 (€3.50, 45 minutes, roughly hourly weekdays, two-hourly weekends).

tre with a fine **Grand Place** (main square), a Unesco-listed **belfry** (www.beffroi mons.be; Parc du Château; adult/child €9/6; 10am-6pm Tue-Sun) and a large, 15th-century Gothic church, the **Collégiale Ste-Waudru** (www.waudru.be; Place du Chapitre; 9am-6pm). The latter's small treasury displays a sword-slashed skull relic, supposedly that of sainted Merovingian king Dagobert II whose murder in AD 675 was, according to some conspiracy theorists, an attempt to put an end to the 'Jesus bloodline'. Mons received a substantial facelift in 2015 when it was a European Capital of Culture and the legacy includes a handful of modern museums, most notably the superb **Memorial Museum** (065-40 53 20; www.monsmemorialmuseum.mons.be; Blvd Dolez 51; adult/child €9/2; 10am-6pm Tue-Sun) covering the city's experience of two world wars.

Accommodation-wise there's a central **HI hostel** (065-87 55 70; www.lesauberges dejeunesse.be; Rampe du Château 2; dm/d/q incl breakfast €26/56/104; P@) and several midrange hotels set in historic buildings, including **Dream Hôtel** (065-32 97 20; www.dream-mons.be; Rue de la Grand Triperie 17; s €94, d €113-130, ste €180-350; P@) that brings Belgian eccentricity to a revamped 19th-century convent.

Dining is a treat with great bistros like **L'Envers** (065-35 45 10; www.lenvers-mons.be; Rue de la Coupe 20; mains €15-29; noon-2.15pm & 6.15-10.15pm, closed Wed & Sun;) and creative brasserie **Oscar** (065-95 96 12; www.brasserie-oscar.be; Rue de Nimy 14; mains €18-22; noon-2pm & 6-9.30pm Tue-Fri, 6-10pm Sat, noon-2pm Sun;).

Regular trains connect Mons to Brussels (€9.90, 52 minutes), Charleroi (€6.80, 35 minutes) and Tournai (€7.70, 30 to 50 minutes). Free city shuttle buses link the station and the Grand Place.

Tournai

069 / POP 69,600

If you want to go by train between France and Belgium without paying for high-speed services, a good tactic is to transit via Tournai to/from Lille. While you're passing through, don't miss Tournai's particularly splendid five-towered **cathedral** (www.cathedrale-tournai.be; Place de l'Évêché; 9am-6pm Mon-Fri, to noon & 1-6pm Sat & Sun Apr-Oct, to 5pm Nov-Mar) FREE, whose interior shows a fascinating evolution of architectural styles combining an Romanesque nave with an early-Gothic choir whose soaring pillars bend disconcertingly. Tournai's gorgeous triangular main square, the **Grand Place**, is ringed with cafes in fine gable-fronted guildhouses and features Belgium's oldest belfry-tower. Art lovers shouldn't miss the **Musée des Beaux-Arts** (069-33 24 31; www.tournai.be; Enclos St-Martin 3; adult/child €2.60/2.10; 9.30am-12.30pm & 1.30-5pm Wed-Mon Apr-Oct, 9.30am-noon & 2-5pm Mon & Wed-Sat, 2-5pm Sun Nov-Mar), a Horta-designed gallery whose rich collection features work by Monet, Rubens and most notably Rogier Van de Weyden.

Tournai's train station is around 1km northeast of the Grand Place. Regular trains serve **Brussels** (€13.40, 70 minutes), Lille, France (€6.60, 30 minutes) and Mons (€7.70, 30 to 55 minutes).

LUXEMBOURG

Stretching just 82km and 57km at its longest and widest points respectively, diminutive Luxembourg (www.visitluxembourg.com) is a charming slice of northern Europe ruled by its own monarchy. It consistently ranks among the world's top three nations in both wealth and wine consumption. Getting around is easy: wherever you go by public transport within the country the fare is just €2 for up to two hours' journey, €4 for the whole day. Luxembourg has its own language, Lëtzebuergesch, but most Luxembourgers also speak French and German.

Luxembourg City

POP 116,323

The scenic capital has a Unesco-listed old core that's majestically set across the deep gorges of the Alzette and Pétrusse rivers. Some outstanding museums add to a lively drinking and dining scene. Since city accommodation is primarily geared to bankers and Eurocrats, hotel prices drop dramatically at weekends when those folks head home. Sundays can be deathly quiet, but summer Saturday nights see many a festival.

Sights

Chemin de la Corniche STREET

Hailed as 'Europe's most beautiful balcony', this pedestrian promenade winds along the course of the 17th-century city ramparts with views across the river canyon towards the hefty fortifications of the Wenzelsmauer (Wenceslas Wall). The rampart-top walk continues along Blvd Victor Thorn to the **Dräi Tier** (Triple Gate) tower, stretching 600m in total.

Bock Casemates FORTRESS

(www.luxembourg-city.com; Montée de Clausen; adult/child €6/3; 10am-5.30pm mid-Feb–Mar & Oct-early Nov, 10am-8.30pm Apr-Sep) Beneath the Montée de Clausen, the clifftop site of Count Sigefroi's once-mighty fort, the Bock Casemates are an atmospheric honeycomb of rock galleries and passages initially carved by the Spaniards from 1644 onwards. They were extended by French engineer Vauban in the 1680s, and again by the Austrians in the mid-18th century. Over the years the casemates have housed everything from garrisons to bakeries and slaughterhouses; during WWI and WWII they sheltered 35,000 locals. Kids will adore exploring the passageways.

Mudam GALLERY

(Musée d'Art Moderne; 45 37 85 1; www.mudam.lu; 3 Parc Dräi Eechelen; adult/child €8/free; 10am-6pm Thu-Mon, to 9pm Wed) Groundbreaking exhibitions of modern, installation and experiential art take place in this airy architectural icon designed by Pritzker-winning architect IM Pei (best known for his glass pyramid entrance to Paris' Louvre museum). The collection includes everything from photography to fashion, design and multimedia. Regional products are used in local specialities at its glass-roofed cafe, which hosts free concerts on Wednesday evenings.

Musée d'Histoire de la Ville de Luxembourg MUSEUM

(Luxembourg City History Museum; 47 96 45 00; www.citymuseum.lu; 14 Rue du St-Esprit; adult/child €5/free, after 6pm Thu free; 10am-6pm Tue, Wed & Fri-Sun, to 8pm Thu) Hidden within a series of 17th- to 19th-century houses, including a former 'holiday home' of the Bishop of Orval, the city's history museum is engrossing. Permanent collections on its lower levels cover the city's industrial, handicraft and commercial heritage, with models, plans and engravings, textiles, ceramics, posters, photographs and household items. Upper floors host temporary exhibitions. Its enormous glass lift provides views of the rock foundations, the Grund valley and Rham plateau; there's also a lovely garden and panoramic terrace.

Sleeping

Midweek, accommodation can seem dauntingly overpriced. Prices are marginally cheaper around the train station, a slightly sleazy area by Luxembourg's high standards, where the **Hotel Bristol** (48 58 30; www.hotel-bristol.lu; 11 Rue de Strasbourg; s/d/studio incl breakfast from €75/120/130, d without bathroom incl breakfast from €85;) is a decent bet. For budget travellers there's a handily central **HI hostel** (26 27 66 65 0; www.youthhostels.lu; 5 Rue du Fort Olisy; dm €25.15-26.15; P), plus another at attractively rural **Larochette** (26 27 66 550; www.youthhostels.lu; 45 Rue Osterbour; dm/s/d €24.70/39.70/60.40; P), 25km away by Luxembourg–Diekirch bus route 100.

La Pipistrelle B&B €€€

(621 300 351; www.lapipistrelle.lu; 26 Montée du Grund; s/d from €185/220;) Just four sumptuous suites and a charming location mean you'll have to book early to enjoy this inti-

mate B&B-style hotel. Carved into the rock face, the 18th-century property retains period features but the spacious rooms are stylishly rendered with designer fabrics and open bathrooms. Breakfast is an extra €16; bars and restaurants abound close by. A nearby public lift zips you up to the Old Town

Hôtel Le Place d'Armes BOUTIQUE HOTEL €€€
(☎27 47 37; www.hotel-leplacedarmes.com; 18 Place d'Armes; d incl breakfast from €295; ❄📶) On the city's busiest central square, seven 18th-century buildings have been combined into an enchanting labyrinth incorporating part-cave meeting rooms with stone walls, light-touch modern lounges and inner courtyards. Each of the 28 luxurious rooms is different, with details including fireplaces, beams or timber ceilings.

Hotel Les Jardins d'Anaïs BOUTIQUE HOTEL €€€
(☎27 04 83 71; https://jardinsdanais.lu; 2 Place Ste-Cunégonde; s/d from €150/180; P❄📶) Behind an ivy-clad facade, Hotel Les Jardins d'Anaïs's seven rooms spread over two floors, served by an lift. Each has an individual theme, such as sunflower-yellow Provence, Bibliothéque ('library') with a wooden bookcase framing the tartan-quilted bed, and pink-accented Roses with wrought-iron furniture. Its glass-paned, Michelin-starred restaurant opens to a magical garden with a pond and a gazebo.

Eating & Drinking

Cafe and restaurants spill summer tables on to city squares such as leafy Place d'Armes. For atmospheric options, explore the alleys and passages directly behind the Royal Palace, collectively nicknamed 'Ilôt Gourmand'. For inexpensive, if mostly characterless, Asian eateries, search towards the train station. Grund has many great drinking spots, with **Scott's** (www.scotts-pub.com; 4 Bisserweg; ⏲noon-1am Mon-Fri, from 11am Sat & Sun; 📶) perfectly perched overlooking the river. Nightlife is centred on the Rives de Clausen, with numerous bar-resto clubs and a handy night bus running back to the centre.

Am Tiirmschen BISTRO €€
(☎26 27 07 33; www.amtiirmschen.lu; 32 Rue de l'Eau; mains €19-29; ⏲noon-2pm Tue-Fri, 7-10.30pm Mon-Sat) At this cosy restaurant with exposed-stone walls and heavy bowed beams, Luxembourg specialities include *Judd mat Gaardebounen* (smoked pork with broad beans), *Gromperekichelcher* (a spiced potato pancake), *Rieslingspaschtéit* (a loaf-shaped meat pie made with Riesling) and *Kniddelen mam Speck* (flour-based dumplings topped with bacon and served with apple sauce). Wines are predominantly from Luxembourg's Moselle Valley.

ⓘ LUXEMBOURG CARD

The highly worthwhile **Luxembourg Card** (www.visitluxembourg.com; 1-/2-/3-day adult €13/20/28, family €28/48/68) gives free admission to 76 of the country's top attractions, discounts on several others, plus unlimited use of public transport countrywide. Family tickets cover two adults and three children. You'll save money if visiting more than two museums or castles a day. Purchase it online or from tourist offices, museums, campgrounds and hotels.

★Le Sud FRENCH €€€
(☎26 47 87 50; www.le-sud.lu; 8 Rives de Clausen; mains €37-42, 2-/3-course lunch menu €28/32, 5-course dinner menu €78; ⏲kitchen noon-3pm & 7.30-10pm Tue-Fri, 7.30-10pm Sat, noon-3pm Sun, bar 6pm-1am Tue-Thu, 6pm-3am Fri & Sat, 2-6pm Sun; 📶) *Crémant*-poached lobster, brioche-crumbed garlic snails, line-caught John Dory with artichoke mousseline and Grand Marnier soufflé are among the refined French dishes at this stone-walled restaurant in the historic Rives de Clausen neighbourhood. Stupendous views extend over the area's rooftops and wooded hillsides from the bar's panoramic rooftop terrace.

Dipso WINE BAR
(☎26 20 14 14; 4 Rue de la Loge; ⏲5pm-1am Tue-Thu, 5pm-3am Fri, 3pm-1am Sat; 📶) Dating from 1453, this stone building with leaded glass windows incorporates part of the old city walls. Its wines, including 20-plus available by the glass, are accompanied by cheese and charcuterie platters. DJs hit the decks on Friday nights year-round; umbrella-shaded tables set up on its tiny, fight-for-a-seat cobbled terrace in summer.

Brauerei BREWERY
(www.bigbeercompany.lu; 12 Rives de Clausen; ⏲4.30pm-1am Mon-Thu, to 3am Fri & Sat; 📶) Dating from 1511, this vast brick brewery complex retains its copper boilers and steam engines. Beers now brewed at its latest incarnation include blonde, amber and bruin

Luxembourg City

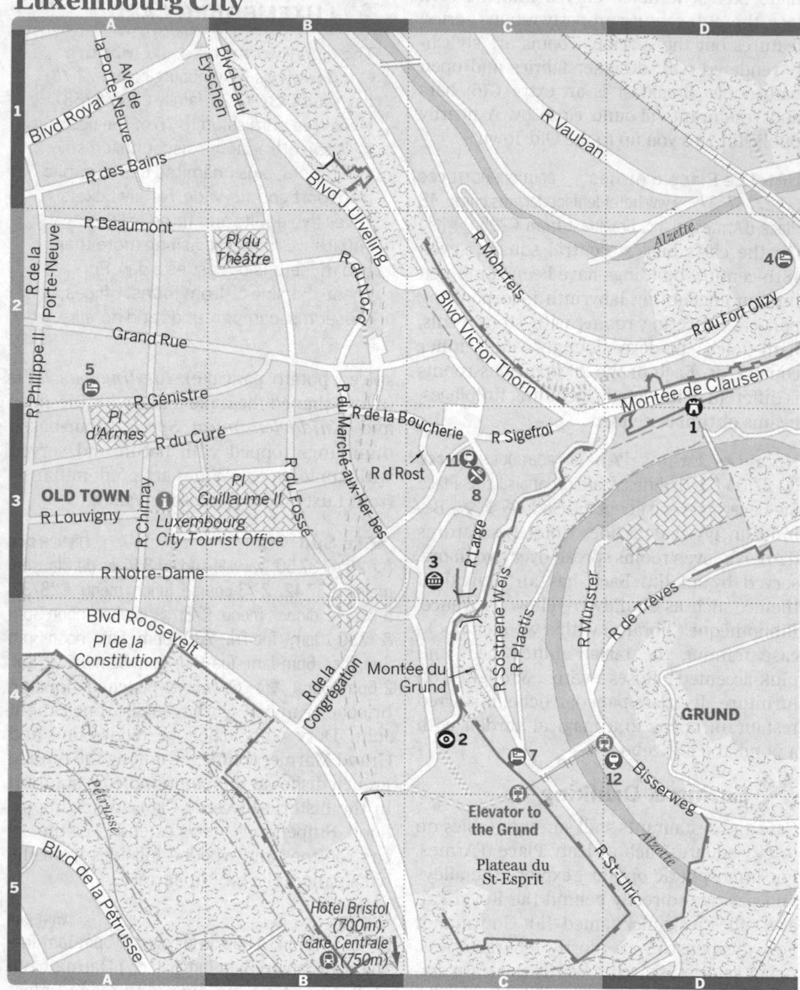

BELGIUM & LUXEMBOURG LUXEMBOURG CITY

varieties. Soak them up with Bavarian specialities such as sausages, pretzels, *Spätzle* (hand-rolled noodles) and sauerkraut. The huge main brewhall reverberates when DJs spin tunes on weekends.

Information

Luxembourg City Tourist Office (LCTO; 22 28 09; www.luxembourg-city.com; 30 Place Guillaume II; 8.30am-7pm Mon-Sat, to 6pm Sun mid-Jul–Aug, 9am-7pm Mon-Sat Apr–mid-Jul & Sep, 9am-6pm Mon-Sat Oct-Mar) Has maps, walking-tour leaflets and event guides.

Getting There & Away

Luxembourg Airport (LUX; www.lux-airport.lu; Rue de Treves), 8km northwest of centre, is well connected to other European cities by national carrier **Luxair** (www.luxair.lu) and other airlines including budget operator EasyJet.

For most overland connections, www.mobiliteit.lu has the timetables including bus 401 from Luxembourg-Kirchberg to Bitburg, Germany (€2, 1¼ hours, up to two per hour) via Echternach (45 minutes).

Pre-bookable **Flibco** (www.flibco.com) buses shuttle from Luxembourg City to German and Belgian airports at Frankfurt, Frankfurt Hahn

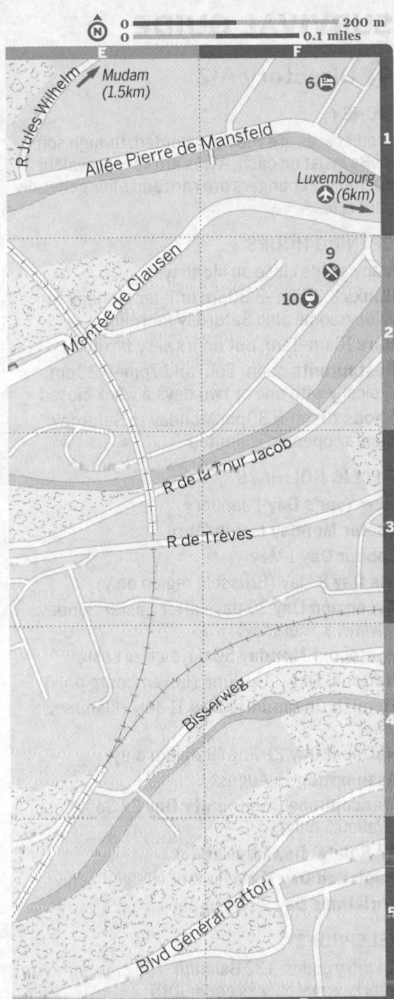

and Charleroi. They leave from the main train station, Gare Centrale, 1km south of the Old City.

Train services (www.cfl.lu) include Brussels (€43.60 to €50.40, 3¾ hours, hourly), Diekirch (€2, 45 minutes, every 30 minutes) via Ettelbrück (35 minutes), and Paris (€92 to €110, 2¼ hours, six daily) via Metz (€18.40, 40 minutes). Trains run hourly to Trier (€19.90 to €24.60, one hour, hourly) but on weekdays it's much cheaper to use commuter bus routes 118/117 from Kirchberg (one hour)/the station (45 minutes).

Luxembourg City

Sights

1	Bock Casemates	D2
2	Chemin de la Corniche	C4
3	Musée d'Histoire de la Ville de Luxembourg	C3

Sleeping

4	Auberge de Jeunesse	D2
5	Hôtel Le Place d'Armes	A2
6	Hotel Les Jardins d'Anaïs	F1
7	La Pipistrelle	C4

Eating

8	Am Tiirmschen	C3
9	Le Sud	F2

Drinking & Nightlife

10	Brauerei	F2
11	Dipso	C3
12	Scott's	D4

Getting Around

Handy lifts link the valleys with the city centre, between **Plateau St-Esprit and Grund** (6am-1am), and between **Montée du Pfaffenthal and Pfaffenthal** (6am-1am).

BICYCLE

Velóh (800 611 00; www.en.veloh.lu; subscription per week €1, 1st 30min free/subsequent hour €1; 24hr) Short-hop shared bike-hire scheme with 683 bikes across 75 docking stations. The initial subscription is payable by credit card at one of 25 special stands; locations are listed online.

Vélo en Ville (47 96 42 71; www.vdl.lu; 8 Bisserweg; per day/week bike hire from €20/75, helmet €3.50/10; 8am-noon & 1-8pm Mon-Fri, 10am-noon & 1-8pm Sat & Sun Apr-Sep, 7am-3pm Mon-Fri Oct-Mar) Hires out city bikes and tandems.

BUS & TRAM

- Tickets (€2/4 per two hours/day) are sold at vending machines, at the train station or from bus drivers. They are valid for trams, buses and domestic trains.
- Route maps are available at www.vdl.lu.
- Buses run from 5.30am to 10pm; trams run till midnight (all night on Saturday evenings).

Northern Luxembourg

Understandably popular as a weekend getaway, magical little **Vianden** (www.vianden-info.lu) is dominated by a vast slate-roofed **castle** (83 41 08; www.castle-vianden.lu; Montée du Château; adult/child €7/2; 10am-4pm Nov-Feb, to 5pm Mar & Oct, to 6pm Apr-Sep) and its impregnable stone walls glow golden in the evening's floodlights. Cobbled Grand Rue descends 700m from there to the riverside tourist office, passing the **HI hostel** (☎26 27 66 80 0; www.youthhostels.lu; 3 Montée du Château; dm/s/d €24.70/39.70/60.40; 📶) and several appealling family hotels, notably **Auberge Aal Veinen** (☎83 43 68; http://vianden.beimhunn.lu; 114 Grand-Rue; s/d €60/90; ⏲closed mid-Dec–mid-Jan; 📶) and **Hôtel Heintz** (☎83 41 55; www.hotel-heintz.lu; 55 Grand-Rue; d/tr/f from €75/110/145; ⏲Easter-Sep; 🅿📶).

Bus 570 (18 minutes) connects at least hourly to **Diekirch**, which is home to **Musée National d'Histoire Militaire** (☎80 89 08; www.mnhm.net; 10 Rue Bamertal; adult/child €5/3; ⏲10am-6pm Tue-Sun), the most comprehensive and visual of many museums commemorating 1944's devastating midwinter Battle of the Ardennes. Diekirch has twice-hourly trains to Luxembourg City (40 minutes) via Ettelbrück (10 minutes). From the latter, bus 545 gets you within 2km of isolated **Château de Bourscheid** (☎99 05 70; http://chateau.bourscheid.lu; Rue du Château; adult/child €5/3; ⏲9.30am-6pm Apr–mid-Oct, 11am-4pm mid-Oct–Mar), Luxembourg's most evocative medieval ruined castle.

Moselle Valley

Smothering the Moselle River's steeply rising banks are the neatly clipped vineyards that produce Luxembourg's balanced Rieslings, fruity rivaners and excellent *crémants* (sparkling *méthode traditionelle* wines). Many wineries offer tastings, but if you choose just one, make it the grand **Caves Bernard-Massard** (☎75 05 45 1; www.bernard-massard.lu; 8 Rue du Pont, Grevenmacher; tour incl 1 glass of wine €6; ⏲tours 9.30am-6pm Tue-Sun Apr-Oct, by reservation Nov-Mar, shop 10am-noon & 1.30-6pm Mon-Fri, 10am-1pm Sat) in central **Grevenmacher** where frequent 20-minute winery tours are multilingual and spiced with humour. Further south at Remerschen near Schengen (where the EU's agreement ensuring free movement of people was signed), don't miss the **Valentiny Foundation** (www.valentiny-foundation.com; 34 Rte du Vin, Remerschen; ⏲2-6pm Tue-Sun) FREE, a 2016 Arctic-white exhibition space featuring displays about modern architecture.

A good way of visiting the area is renting a bicycle from **Rentabike Miselerland** (www.entente-moselle.lu/en/rentabike/presentation; standard/mountain/electric bike hire per day €12/15/20). Pick up at one of 11 points and drop off at another: just make sure that you check closing times and take ID.

SURVIVAL GUIDE

Directory A-Z

MONEY

Credit cards are widely accepted, though some B&Bs insist on cash. ATMs are very prevalent but money changers are rare and offer generally poor rates.

OPENING HOURS

Many sights close on Mondays.

Banks 8.30am–3.30pm or later Monday to Friday, some also Saturday morning

Bars 10am–1am, but hours very flexible

Restaurants noon–2pm and 7pm–9.30pm, typically with one or two days a week closed

Shops 10am–6.30pm Monday to Saturday; Sunday opening is limited

PUBLIC HOLIDAYS

New Year's Day 1 January

Easter Monday March/April

Labour Day 1 May

Iris Day 8 May (Brussels region only)

Ascension Day 39 days after Easter Sunday (always a Thursday)

Pentecost Monday 50 days after Easter

National Day 23rd June (Luxembourg only)

Flemish Community Day 11 July (Flanders only)

National Day 21 July (Belgium only)

Assumption 15 August

Francophone Community Day 27 September (Wallonia only)

All Saints' Day 1 November

Armistice Day 11 November (Belgium only)

Christmas Day 25 December

TELEPHONE

Country codes: +32 Belgium, +352 Luxembourg. International access code 0015.

Getting There & Away

AIR

Brussels Airport (BRU, www.brusselsairport.be) is Belgium's most globally connected airport.

Charleroi Airport (CRL, www.brussels-charleroi-airport.com), sometimes misleadingly called Brussels-South, is a major hub for budget airline RyanAir.

Luxembourg Airport (LUX, www.lux-airport.lu) has a wide range of European connections.

For long-haul flights it can be worth comparing costs with flying into neighbouring countries via Frankfurt, Amsterdam or Paris, then continuing to Belgium overland.

LAND

Bus

Long-distance international bus fares can be remarkable bargains if prebooked well in advance.

Eurolines (www.eurolines.eu) and **Flixbus** (www.flixbus.be) both have very extensive European networks.

Ecolines (www.ecolines.net) specialises in mostly Baltic and Eastern European destinations.

Flibco (www.flibco.com) runs long-distance shuttles between major airports in Belgium, Luxembourg and Germany.

Car & Motorcycle

- Northern Europe is one vast web of motorways, so Belgium is easily accessed from anywhere.
- If driving from the southeast, fill your tank in Luxembourg for Western Europe's lowest petrol prices.
- As in France, the *priorité à droite* rule gives right of way to vehicles emerging from the right even from a small side lane, unless otherwise indicated.
- Motorway speed limits are 120km/h in Belgium and 130km/h in Luxembourg.
- The centres of most larger Flemish cities (especially Bruges and Ghent) are highly pedestrianised making access very awkward for motorists. Use park-and-ride facilities outside town and shuttle in.
- Driving into Antwerp is complicated by its Low Emission Zone (https://lez.antwerpen.be). Read the website carefully and, assuming your car is neither Belgian nor Dutch, allow at 10 days' application time to get the necessary permit (apply online with scans of the vehicle's original registration documents).
- While Belgium's motorway system is extensive and toll-free, traffic often grinds to a halt, especially on the ring roads around Brussels and Antwerp (during rush hour, September to June), on the Brussels–Ghent–Ostend highway (sunny weekends) and on the Ardennes bound E411 (holidays and snowy weekends).

Train

High-speed trains offer easy connections between Brussels and London, and from Belgium to the broader French, Dutch and German networks. Such trains require reservations and can prove expensive, especially if demand is high. Although advance-purchase discounts can be massive, you'll usually forfeit the right to make changes.

Less-publicised ordinary trains run on several international sectors, including Antwerp–Breda–Amsterdam, Antwerp–Roosendaal, Tournai–Lille Flandres, Liège–Maastricht and Luxembourg–Trier–Koblenz. Using these routes combined with domestic tickets is slower but can prove far cheaper than high-speed services for last-minute journeys. There are no assigned seats, but booking online (self-printing or use the e-ticket service) saves a cheeky €6 in-station international ticketing fee for fares ex-Belgium. See www.b-europe.com, Belgian Railways' international site, for details.

SEA

P&O (www.poferries.com) operates a Zeebrugge–Hull service (14 hours, overnight). The quickest way across the channel is via the French port of Calais, around an hour's drive west of Ostend.

Getting Around

BICYCLE

Bicycle on train Free in Luxembourg, ticket required in Belgium (€5/8 for one journey/whole day).

Bike helmets Rarely worn and not a legal requirement.

Cycle paths Very extensive in Belgium, especially Flanders. Most tourist offices sell regional cycling maps, while www.fietsroute.org, http://ravel.wallonie.be and www.randovelo.org are very helpful online resources.

Bike rental Available near most major train stations. Short-hop hire schemes operate in many cities; you'll need a credit card to sign up, then be sure to return the bike to any other automated stand within 30 minutes to avoid extra charges.

BUS

Where bus and train options link the same two cities, the bus is usually cheaper but far slower. Single tickets are valid for transfers for up to an hour after the ticket's validation (or 90 minutes for TEC Horizon) plus however long the final leg of your ride takes.

TRAIN

In Belgium, trains are run by **NMBS/SNCB** (www.belgianrail.be). Tickets should be pre-purchased; buying once aboard incurs a €7 surcharge. Fares a calculated by distance, with return tickets costing twice the price except for over-65-year-olds and for anyone on weekends, when there's a discounted return for travel after 7pm Friday, returning by Sunday night.

For under-26s, a Go-Pass 1 (€6.40) allows any one-way trip within Belgium or, for €8.20, an added border crossing to Roosendaal or Maastricht in the Netherlands.

In Luxembourg, trains (www.cfl.lu) are included in the nationwide flat-fare ticketing system (two hours/all day €2/4).

Britain

POP 66 MILLION

Includes ➡

Best Traditional British Pubs

➡ Ye Olde Mitre (p128)

➡ Turf Tavern (p141)

➡ Old Thatch Tavern (p144)

➡ Blue Bell (p149)

Best Museums

➡ Natural History Museum (p115)

➡ Victoria & Albert Museum (p118)

➡ Ashmolean Museum (p140)

➡ National Railway Museum (p147)

Why Go?

Few places cram so much history, heritage and scenery into such a compact space as Britain. Twelve hours is all you'll need to travel from one end to the other, but you could spend a lifetime exploring – from the ancient relics of Stonehenge and Avebury, to the great medieval cathedrals of Westminster and Canterbury, and the magnificent mountain landscapes of Snowdonia and Skye.

In fact, Britain isn't really one country at all, but three. While they haven't always been easy bedfellows, the contrasts between England, Wales and Scotland make this a rewarding place to visit. With a wealth of rolling countryside, stately cities, world-class museums and national parks to explore, Britain really is one of Europe's most unmissable destinations. And despite what you may have heard, it doesn't rain all the time – but even so, a brolly and a raincoat will certainly come in handy.

When to Go

London

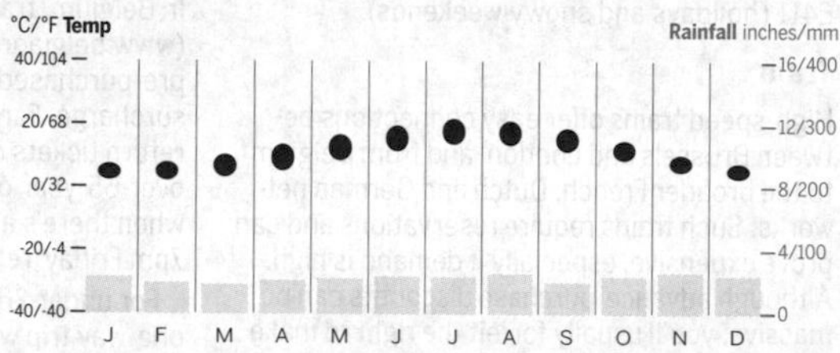

Easter–May Fewer crowds, especially in popular spots like Bath, York and Edinburgh.

Jun–Aug The weather is at its best but the coast and national parks are busy.

Mid-Sep–Oct Prices drop and the weather is often surprisingly good.

Entering the Country

Most visitors reach Britain by air. As London is a global transport hub, it's easy to fly to Britain from just about anywhere.

The other main option for travel between Britain and mainland Europe (and Ireland) is ferry, either port-to-port or combined with a long-distance bus trip, although journeys can be long and financial savings not huge compared with budget airfares.

International trains are much more comfortable and a 'green' option; the Channel Tunnel allows direct rail services between Britain, France and Belgium, with onward connections to many other European destinations.

ITINERARIES

One Week

With just seven days, you're pretty much limited to sights in England. Spend three days seeing the sights in London (p110), then head to Oxford (p139) for a day, followed by a day each at Stonehenge (p136) and historic Bath (p136), before returning for a final day in London.

Two Weeks

Follow the one-week itinerary, but instead of returning to London on day seven, head north to Stratford-upon-Avon (p142) for everything Shakespeare. Continue north with a day in the Lake District (p151), followed by two days in Scotland's capital, Edinburgh (p156). After a day trip to Loch Ness (p167), recross the border for two days to see York (p147) and Castle Howard (p150). Then, stop off in Cambridge (p145) on the way back to London.

Essential Food & Drink

Britain once had a reputation for bad food, but the nation has enjoyed something of a culinary revolution and you can now easily find fine dining based on fresh local produce.

Fish and chips Long-standing favourite, best sampled in coastal towns.

Haggis Scottish icon, mainly offal and oatmeal, traditionally served with mashed 'tatties and neeps' (potatoes and turnips).

Laverbread Laver is a type of seaweed, mixed with oatmeal and fried to create this traditional Welsh speciality.

Roast beef and Yorkshire pudding Traditional lunch on Sunday for the English.

Cornish pasty Savoury pastry; a southwest speciality, now available countrywide.

Real ale Traditionally brewed beer served at room temperature.

Scotch whisky Spirit distilled from malted and fermented barley, then aged in oak barrels for at least three years.

AT A GLANCE

Area 88,500 sq miles

Capitals London (England and the United Kingdom), Cardiff (Wales), Edinburgh (Scotland)

Country Code ☎44

Currency pound sterling (£)

Emergency ☎999 or ☎112

Languages English, Welsh, Scottish Gaelic

Time Greenwich Mean Time (GMT/UTC)

Visas Schengen rules do not apply

Sleeping Price Ranges

The following price ranges refer to a double room with private bathroom in high season (London/elsewhere). Hotels in London are more expensive than the rest of the country, so have different price ranges.

£ less than £100/£65

££ £100–200/£65–130

£££ more than £200/£130

Eating Price Ranges

The following price ranges refer to a main dish (London/elsewhere).

£ less than £12/£10£

££ £12–25/£10–20

£££ more than £25/£20

Britain Highlights

1 **London** (p110) Exploring the streets of one of the world's greatest capital cities.

2 **Bath** (p136) Visiting Roman baths and admiring grand Georgian architecture.

3 **Stratford-upon-Avon** (p142) Enjoying a Shakepeare play in the town where he was born.

4 **Snowdonia National Park** (p155) Marvelling at the mountainous landscape of Wales' first national park.

5 **York** (p147) Delving into the city's history – Roman, Viking and medieval.

6 **Oxford** (p139) Getting lost among the dreaming spires.

7 **Stonehenge** (p136) Stepping back in time while

wandering around the great trilithons of this ancient site.

8 **Edinburgh** (p156) Joining the party in Scotland's festival city.

9 **Skye** (p168) Heading north through the Scottish Highlands to experience the epic scenery of this rugged island.

10 **Lake District National Park** (p151) Following in the footsteps of Romantic poet William Wordsworth.

ENGLAND

POP 53 MILLION

By far the biggest of the three nations that comprise Great Britain, England offers a tempting spread of classic travel experiences, from London's vibrant theatre scene and the historic colleges of Oxford to the grand cathedrals of Canterbury and York and the mountain landscapes of the Lake District.

London

POP 8.8 MILLION

Everyone comes to London with preconceptions shaped by a multitude of books, movies, TV shows and pop songs. Whatever yours are, prepare to have them exploded by this endlessly intriguing city. Its streets are steeped in fascinating history, magnificent art, imposing architecture and popular culture. When you add a bottomless reserve of cool to this mix, it's hard not to conclude that London is one of the world's great cities, if not the greatest.

The only downside is cost: London is Europe's most expensive city for visitors, whatever their budget. But with some careful planning and a bit of common sense, you can find excellent bargains and freebies among the popular attractions. And many of London's finest assets – its wonderful parks, bridges, squares and boulevards, not to mention many of its landmark museums – come completely free.

Sights

The West End

★Westminster Abbey CHURCH

(Map p120; ☎020-7222 5152; www.westminster-abbey.org; 20 Dean's Yard, SW1; adult/child £22/9; ⏰9.30am-3.30pm Mon, Tue, Thu & Fri, to 6pm Wed, to 3pm Sat May-Aug, to 1pm Sat Sep-Apr; U Westminster) A splendid mixture of architectural styles, Westminster Abbey is considered the finest example of Early English Gothic. It's not merely a beautiful place of worship – the Abbey is still a working church and the stage on which history unfolds. For centuries, the country's greatest have been interred here, including 17 monarchs from King Henry III (died 1272) to King George II (1760). Much of the Abbey's architecture is from the 13th century, but it was founded much earlier, in AD 960.

> **BIG BEN**
>
> The Houses of Parliament's most famous feature is the clock tower known as **Big Ben** (Map p120; www.parliament.uk/visiting/visiting-and-tours/tours-of-parliament/bigben; Bridge St; U Westminster). Strictly speaking, however, Big Ben is the tower's 13-ton bell, named after Benjamin Hall, commissioner of works when the tower was completed in 1858.

Houses of Parliament HISTORIC BUILDING

(Map p120; ☎tours 020-7219 4114; www.parliament.uk; Parliament Sq, SW1; guided tour adult/child/under 5yr £28/12/free, audio guide tour £20.50/8.50/free; U Westminster) A visit here is a journey to the heart of UK democracy. The Houses of Parliament are officially called the Palace of Westminster, and its oldest part is 11th-century **Westminster Hall**, one of only a few sections that survived a catastrophic 1834 fire. The rest is mostly a neo-Gothic confection built over 36 years from 1840. The palace's most famous feature is its clock tower, Elizabeth Tower – but better known as Big Ben – recently uncovered after restoration works.

Tate Britain GALLERY

(☎020-7887 8888; www.tate.org.uk/visit/tate-britain; Millbank, SW1; ⏰10am-6pm; U Pimlico) FREE On the site of the former Millbank Penitentiary, the older and more venerable of the two Tate siblings opened in 1892 and celebrates British art from 1500 to the present, including pieces from William Blake, William Hogarth, Thomas Gainsborough and John Constable, as well as vibrant modern and contemporary pieces from Lucian Freud, Barbara Hepworth, Francis Bacon and Henry Moore. The stars of the show are, undoubtedly, the light-infused visions of JMW Turner in the Clore Gallery.

Trafalgar Square SQUARE

(Map p120; U Charing Cross or Embankment) Opened to the public in 1844, Trafalgar Sq, is the true centre of London, where rallies and marches take place, tens of thousands of revellers usher in the New Year and locals congregate for anything from communal open-air cinema and Christmas celebrations to political protests. It is dominated by the 52m-high **Nelson's Column**, guarded by four **bronze lion statues**, and ringed by many splendid buildings, including the National Gallery (p111) and the church of **St Martin-in-the-Fields** (Map p120; ☎020-7766

London

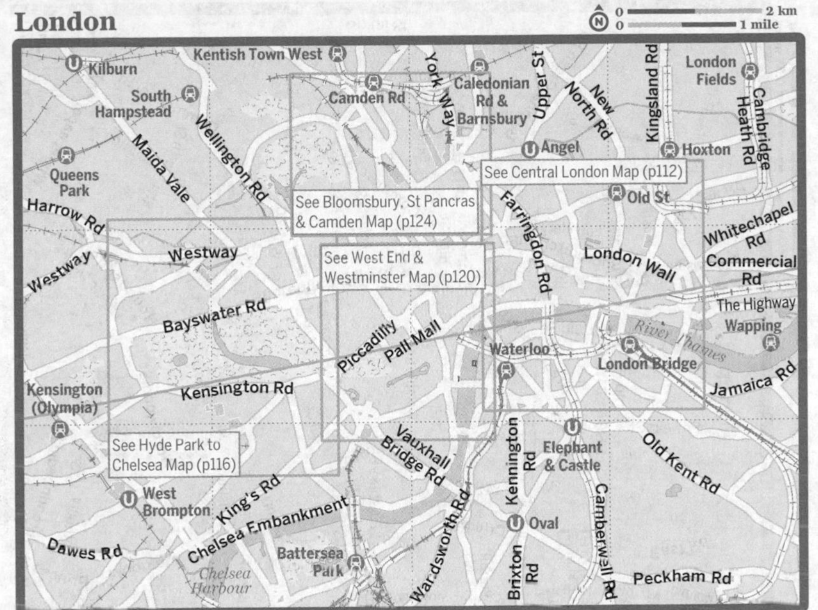

1100; www.stmartin-in-the-fields.org; 8.30am-6pm Mon-Fri, 9am-6pm Sat & Sun).

★National Gallery GALLERY
(Map p120; 020-7747 2885; www.nationalgallery.org.uk; Trafalgar Sq, WC2; 10am-6pm Sat-Thu, to 9pm Fri; U Charing Cross) FREE With more than 2300 European masterpieces in its collection, this is one of the world's great galleries, with seminal works from the 13th to the mid-20th century, including masterpieces by Leonardo da Vinci, Michelangelo, Titian, Vincent van Gogh and Auguste Renoir. Many visitors flock to the eastern rooms on the main floor (1700–1930), where works by British artists such as Thomas Gainsborough, John Constable and JMW Turner, and Impressionist and post-Impressionist masterpieces by Van Gogh, Renoir and Claude Monet await.

Madame Tussauds MUSEUM
(Map p124; 0870 400 3000; www.madame-tussauds.com/london; Marylebone Rd, NW1; adult/child 4-15yr £35/30; 10am-6pm; U Baker St) It may be kitschy and pricey, but Madame Tussauds makes for a fun-filled day. There are photo ops with your dream celebrity (be it Daniel Craig, Lady Gaga, Benedict Cumberbatch, Audrey Hepburn or the Beckhams), the Bollywood gathering (sparring studs Hrithik Roshan and Salman Khan) and the Royal Appointment (the Queen, Harry and Meghan, William and Kate). Book online for much cheaper rates and check the website for seasonal opening hours.

Piccadilly Circus SQUARE
(Map p120; U Piccadilly Circus) Architect John Nash had originally designed Regent St and Piccadilly in the 1820s to be the two most elegant streets in London but, restrained by city planners, he couldn't fully realise his dream. He may be disappointed, but suitably astonished, by Piccadilly Circus today: a traffic maelstrom, deluged by visitors and flanked by flashing advertisement panels.

Buckingham Palace PALACE
(Map p120; 0303 123 7300; www.rct.uk/visit/the-state-rooms-buckingham-palace; Buckingham Palace Rd, SW1; adult/child/under 5yr £25/14/free, incl Royal Mews & Queen's Gallery £45/24.50/free; 9.30am-7pm mid-Jul–Aug, to 6pm Sep; U Green Park or St James's Park) Built in 1703 for the Duke of Buckingham, Buckingham Palace replaced St James's Palace as the monarch's official London residence in 1837. Queen Elizabeth II divides her time between here, Windsor Castle and, in summer, Balmoral Castle in Scotland. If she's in residence, the square yellow, red and blue Royal Standard is flown; if not, it's the Union Flag. The 19 lavishly furnished **State Rooms** are open

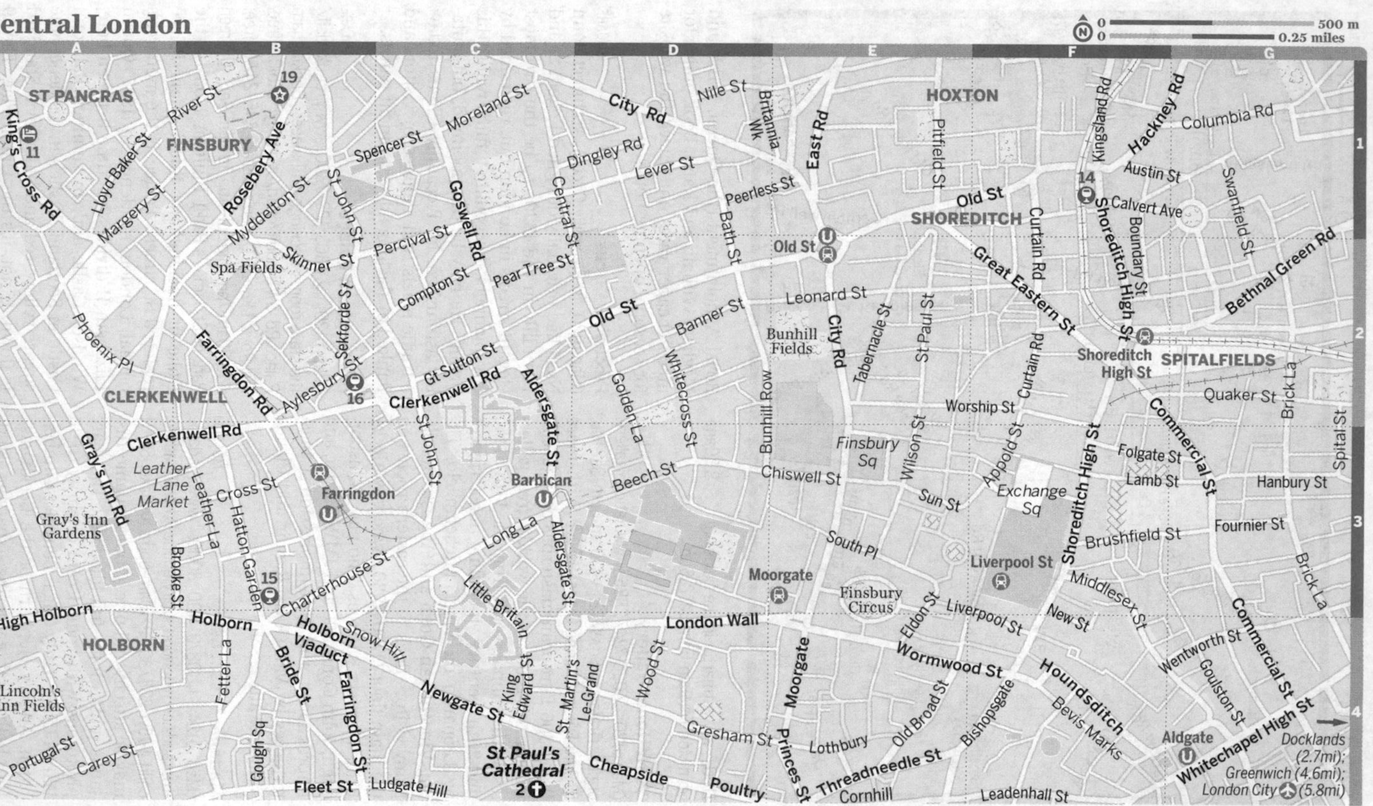
Central London
0 500 m
0 0.25 miles
ST PANCRAS
FINSBURY
CLERKENWELL
HOLBORN
HOXTON
SHOREDITCH
SPITALFIELDS
King's Cross Rd
Lloyd Baker St
Margery St
River St
Rosebery Ave
Myddelton St
Spa Fields
Skinner St
St John St
Spencer St
Moreland St
Percival St
Compton St
Goswell Rd
Central St
Pear Tree St
Dingley Rd
Lever St
City Rd
Nile St
Britannia Wk
East Rd
Peerless St
Bath St
Old St
Pitfield St
Kingsland Rd
Hackney Rd
Columbia Rd
Austin St
Calvert Ave
Boundary St
Swanfield St
Bethnal Green Rd
Curtain Rd
Great Eastern St
Shoreditch High St
Shoreditch High St
Sekforde St
Aylesbury St
Farringdon Rd
Phoenix Pl
Gt Sutton St
Clerkenwell Rd
Aldersgate St
Banner St
Leonard St
Bunhill Fields
Tabernacle St
St Paul St
Golden La
Whitecross St
Bunhill Row
Worship St
Quaker St
Brick La
Spital St
Gray's Inn Rd
Leather Lane Market
Leather La
Cross St
Hatton Garden
Farringdon
Barbican
Beech St
Chiswell St
Finsbury Sq
Wilson St
Sun St
Appold St
Exchange Sq
Folgate St
Lamb St
Commercial St
Hanbury St
Fournier St
Brushfield St
Gray's Inn Gardens
Brooke St
Long La
Charterhouse St
South Pl
Liverpool St
Moorgate
Finsbury Circus
Middlesex St
Little Britain
High Holborn
Holborn
Holborn Viaduct
Snow Hill
London Wall
Eldon St
Liverpool St
New St
Wentworth St
Goulston St
Wormwood St
Houndsditch
Bevis Marks
Fetter La
Bride St
Farringdon St
Newgate St
King Edward St
St Martin's Le-Grand
Wood St
Moorgate
Old Broad St
Bishopsgate
Lincoln's Inn Fields
Portugal St
Carey St
Gough Sq
Fleet St
Ludgate Hill
St Paul's Cathedral
Cheapside
Gresham St
Poultry
Princes St
Lothbury
Threadneedle St
Cornhill
Leadenhall St
Aldgate
Whitechapel High St
Docklands (2.7mi); Greenwich (4.6mi); London City (5.8mi)
11
14
15
16
19
2

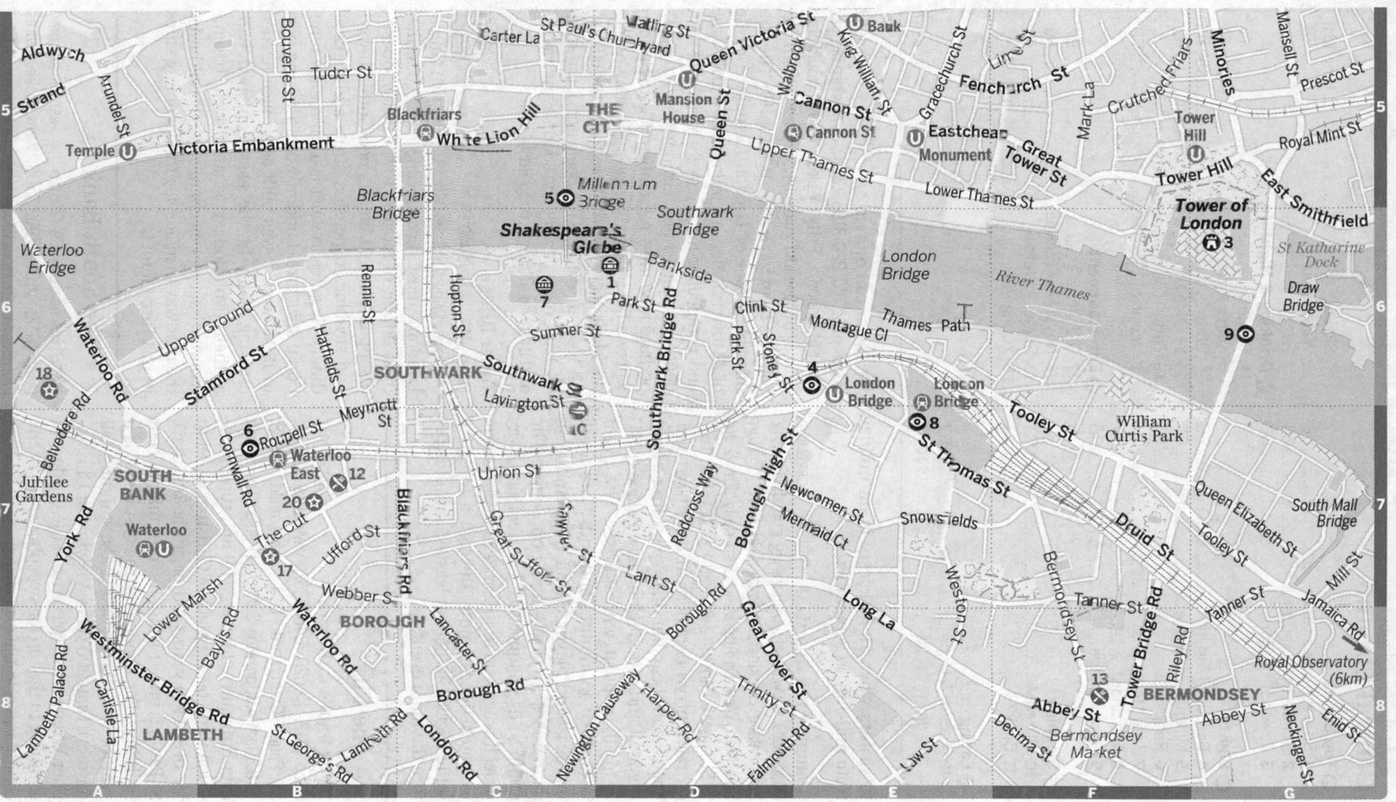

Aldwych
Strand
Arundel St
Bouverie St
Tudor St
Carter La
St Paul's Churchyard
Watling St
Queen Victoria St
Bank
King William St
Walbrook
Gracechurch St
Lime St
Fenchurch St
Mark La
Crutched Friars
Minories
Mansell St
Prescot St
Temple
Victoria Embankment
Blackfriars
White Lion Hill
THE CITY
Mansion House
Queen St
Cannon St
Eastcheap
Monument
Great Tower St
Tower Hill
Royal Mint St
Upper Thames St
Lower Thames St
East Smithfield
Tower of London
3
St Katharine Dock
Draw Bridge
Millennium Bridge
5
Blackfriars Bridge
Southwark Bridge
Shakespeare's Globe
1
Bankside
London Bridge
River Thames
Waterloo Bridge
7
Park St
Clink St
Montague Cl
Thames Path
9
Rennie St
Hopton St
Sumner St
Southwark Bridge Rd
Stoney St
Upper Ground
Waterloo Rd
Stamford St
Hatfields St
SOUTHWARK
Southwark St
4
London Bridge
8
Tooley St
William Curtis Park
18
Belvedere Rd
Lavington St
10
Meymott St
6
Roupell St
Waterloo East
12
Cornwall Rd
Jubilee Gardens
SOUTH BANK
Union St
Borough High St
Redcross Way
Newcomen St
Mermaid Ct
St Thomas St
Snowsfields
Queen Elizabeth St
South Mall Bridge
York Rd
20
The Cut
Waterloo
Blackfriars Rd
Great Suffolk St
Sawyer St
Ufford St
17
Druid St
Tooley St
Lower Marsh
Webber St
Lant St
Weston St
Bermondsey St
Tanner St
Tower Bridge Rd
Riley Rd
Mill St
Jamaica Rd
BOROUGH
Borough Rd
Long La
Lancaster St
Baylis Rd
Westminster Bridge Rd
Royal Observatory (6km)
Lambeth Palace Rd
Carlisle La
13
BERMONDSEY
Abbey St
Borough Rd
Trinity St
Great Dover St
Harper Rd
Newington Causeway
LAMBETH
St George's Rd
Lambeth Rd
London Rd
Falmouth Rd
Law St
Decima St
Bermondsey Market
Neckinger St
Enid St

Central London

Top Sights
1 Shakespeare's Globe............D6
2 St Paul's Cathedral............C4
3 Tower of London............G6

Sights
4 Borough Market............E6
5 Millennium Bridge............C5
6 Roupell St............B7
7 Tate Modern............C6
8 The Shard............E7
9 Tower Bridge............G6

Sleeping
10 citizenM............C7
11 Clink78............A1

Eating
12 Anchor & Hope............B7
Padella............(see 4)
Skylon............(see 18)
13 Watch House............F8

Drinking & Nightlife
14 Cargo............F1
King's Arms............(see 6)
Oblix............(see 8)
15 Ye Olde Mitre............B3
16 Zetter Townhouse Cocktail Lounge............B2

Entertainment
17 Old Vic............B7
18 Royal Festival Hall............A6
19 Sadler's Wells............B1
20 Young Vic............B7

to visitors when Her Majesty is on holiday from mid-July to September.

Changing the Guard CEREMONY
(Map p120; www.royal.uk/changing-guard; Buckingham Palace, Buckingham Palace Rd, SW1; 11am Sun, Mon, Wed, Fri Aug-May, 11am daily Jun & Jul; U St James's Park or Green Park) FREE The full-on pageantry of soldiers in bright-red uniforms and bearskin hats parading down the Mall and into Buckingham Palace (p111) is madly popular with tourists. The event lasts about 45 minutes and ends with a full military band playing music from traditional marches, musicals and pop songs. The pomp and circumstance can feel far away indeed when you're in a row 15 deep, trying to watch the ceremony through a forest of selfie sticks. Get here at least 45 minutes before the main event.

The City

★**St Paul's Cathedral** CATHEDRAL
(Map p112; 020-7246 8357; www.stpauls.co.uk; St Paul's Churchyard, EC4; adult/child £18/8; 8.30am-4.30pm Mon-Sat; U St Paul's) Towering over diminutive Ludgate Hill in a superb position that's been a place of Christian worship for over 1400 years (and pagan before that), St Paul's is one of London's most magnificent buildings. For Londoners, the vast dome is a symbol of resilience and pride, standing tall for more than 300 years. Viewing Sir Christopher Wren's masterpiece from the inside and climbing to the top for sweeping views of the capital is a celestial experience.

★**Tower of London** CASTLE
(Map p112; 020-3166 6000; www.hrp.org.uk/tower-of-london; Petty Wales, EC3; adult/child £26.80/12.70, audio guide £4; 9am-4.30pm Tue-Sat, from 10am Sun & Mon; U Tower Hill) The unmissable Tower of London (actually a castle of 22 towers) offers a window into a gruesome and compelling history. A former royal residence, treasury, mint, armoury and zoo, it's perhaps now most remembered as the prison where a king, three queens and many nobles met their deaths. Come here to see the colourful Yeoman Warders (or Beefeaters), the spectacular Crown Jewels, the soothsaying ravens and armour fit for a *very* large king.

Tower Bridge BRIDGE
(Map p112; 020-7403 3761; www.towerbridge.org.uk; Tower Bridge, SE1; 24hr; U Tower Hill) One of London's most recognisable sights, familiar from dozens of movies, Tower Bridge doesn't disappoint in real life. Its neo-Gothic towers and sky-blue suspension struts add extraordinary elegance to what is a supremely functional structure. London was a thriving port in 1894 when it was built as a much-needed crossing point in the east, equipped with a then-revolutionary steam-driven bascule (counterbalance) mechanism that could raise the roadway to make way for oncoming ships in just three minutes.

The South Bank

★**Shakespeare's Globe** HISTORIC BUILDING
(Map p112; 020-7902 1500; www.shakespearesglobe.com; 21 New Globe Walk, SE1; tours adult/

child £17/10; 9am-5pm; ; Blackfriars or London Bridge) The new Globe was designed to resemble the original as closely as possible, which means having the arena open to the fickle London skies, leaving the 700 'groundlings' (standing spectators) to weather London's spectacular downpours. Visits to the Globe include tours of the theatre (half-hourly) as well as access to the exhibition space, which has fascinating exhibits on Shakespeare, life in Bankside and theatre in the 17th century.

Tate Modern GALLERY
(Map p112; 020-7887 8888; www.tate.org.uk; Bankside, SE1; 10am-6pm Sun-Thu, to 10pm Fri & Sat; ; Blackfriars, Southwark or London Bridge) FREE One of London's most amazing attractions, this outstanding modern- and contemporary-art gallery is housed in the creatively revamped Bankside Power Station south of the **Millennium Bridge** (Map p112; St Paul's or Blackfriars). A spellbinding synthesis of modern art and capacious industrial brick design, Tate Modern has been extraordinarily successful in bringing challenging work to the masses, through both its free permanent collection and fee-paying big-name temporary exhibitions. The stunning **Blavatnik Building** opened in 2016, increasing the available exhibition space by 60%.

London Eye VIEWPOINT
(Map p120; www.londoneye.com; near County Hall; adult/child £28/23; 11am-6pm Sep-May, 10am-8.30pm Jun-Aug; Waterloo or Westminster) Standing 135m high in a fairly flat city, the London Eye affords views 25 miles in every direction, weather permitting. Interactive tablets provide great information (in six languages) about landmarks as they appear in the skyline. Each rotation – or 'flight' – takes a gracefully slow 30 minutes. At peak times (July, August and school holidays) it can feel like you'll spend more time in the queue than in the capsule; book premium fast-track tickets (adult/child £37/32) to jump the line.

Kensington & Hyde Park

★Natural History Museum MUSEUM
(Map p116; www.nhm.ac.uk; Cromwell Rd, SW7; 10am-5.50pm; ; South Kensington) FREE This colossal and magnificent-looking building is infused with the irrepressible Victorian spirit of collecting, cataloguing and interpreting the natural world. The **Dinosaurs Gallery** (Blue Zone) is a must for children, who gawp at the animatronic T-rex, fossils and excellent displays. Adults will love the intriguing Treasures exhibition in the **Cadogan Gallery** (Green Zone), which houses a host of unrelated objects, each telling its own unique story, from a chunk of moon rock to a dodo skeleton.

DON'T MISS

BRITISH MUSEUM

The country's largest museum and one of the oldest and finest in the world, the **British Museum** (Map p120; 020-7323 8000; www.britishmuseum.org; Great Russell St, WC1; 10am-5.30pm Sat-Thu, to 8.30pm Fri; Tottenham Court Rd or Russell Sq) is a famous museum opened in 1759 and boasts vast Egyptian, Etruscan, Greek, Roman, European and Middle Eastern galleries, among others. It's London's most visited attraction, drawing 5.9 million people annually. Don't miss the **Rosetta Stone**, the key to deciphering Egyptian hieroglyphics; the controversial **Parthenon sculptures**, taken from Athens' Acropolis by Lord Elgin (British ambassador to the Ottoman Empire at the time); and the large collection of **Egyptian mummies**.

Science Museum MUSEUM
(Map p116; 020-7942 4000; www.sciencemuseum.org.uk; Exhibition Rd, SW7; 10am-6pm; ; South Kensington) FREE This scientifically spellbinding museum will mesmerise adults and children alike with its interactive and educational exhibits covering everything from early technology to space travel. On the ground floor, a perennial favourite is **Exploring Space**, a gallery featuring genuine rockets and satellites and a full-size replica of the *Eagle,* the lander that took Neil Armstrong and Buzz Aldrin to the surface of the moon in 1969. The **Making the Modern World Gallery** next door is a visual feast of locomotives, planes, cars and other revolutionary inventions.

The 2nd-floor displays cover a host of subjects. The fantastic **Information Age Gallery** showcases how information and communication technologies – from the telegraph to smartphones – have transformed our lives since the 19th century. Standout displays include wireless messages sent by a sinking *Titanic,* the first BBC radio broadcast and a Soviet BESM 1965 supercomputer. The **Clockmaker's Museum** is a fascinating collection of timepieces, while **Mathematics:**

Hyde Park to Chelsea

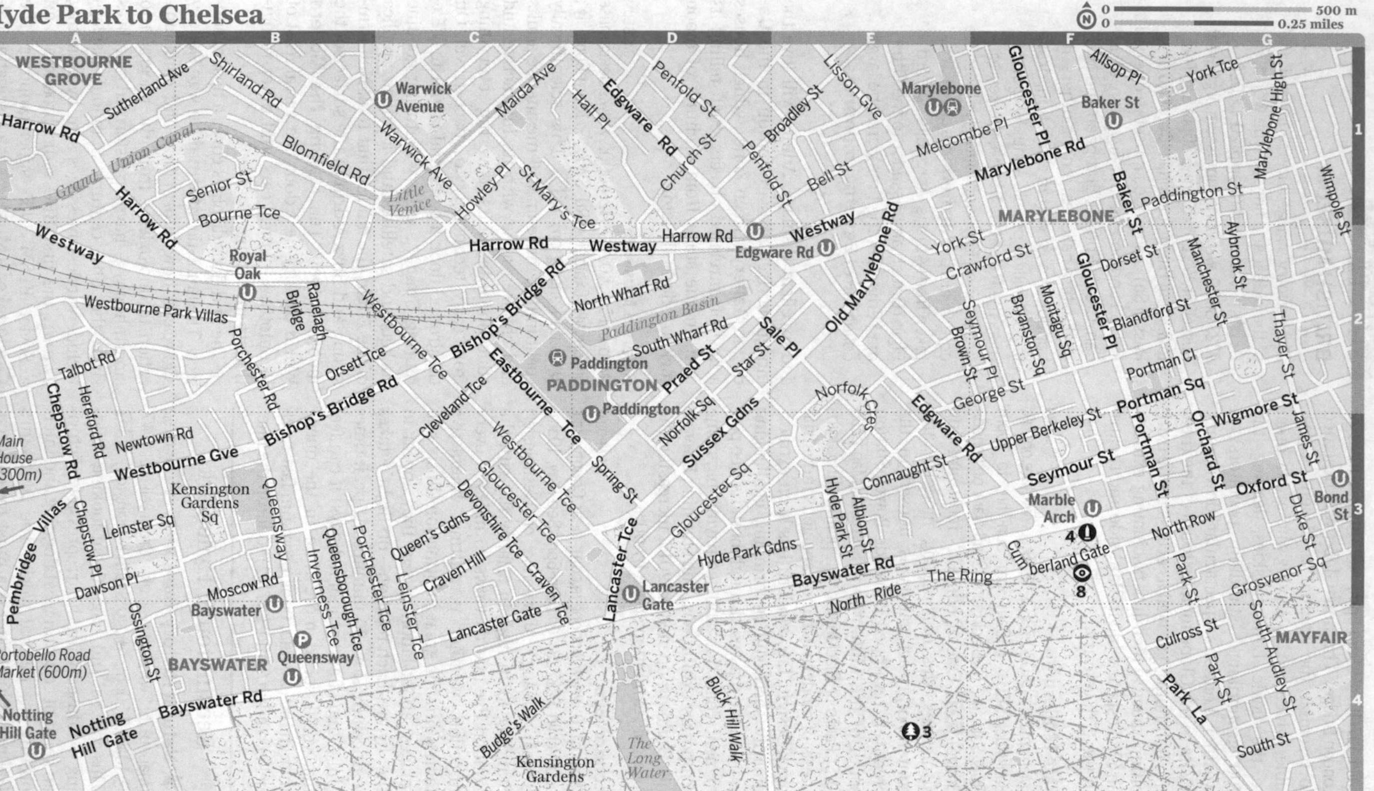

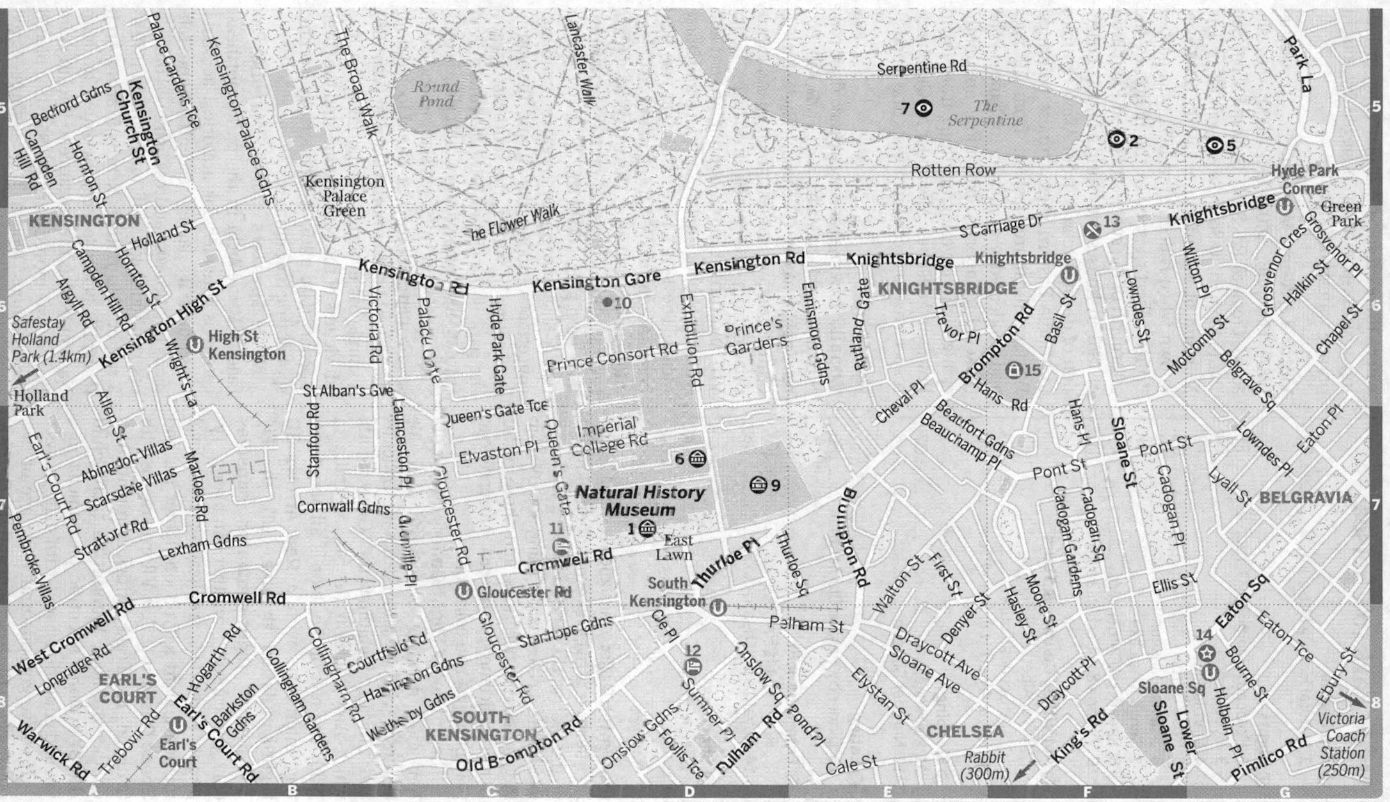
Serpentine Rd
Park La
Round Pond
7
The Serpentine
2
5
Rotten Row
Hyde Park Corner
Green Park
Bedford Gdns
Kensington Church St
Palace Gardens Tce
Kensington Palace Gdns
The Broad Walk
Lancaster Walk
Campden Hill Rd
Hornton St
Kensington Palace Green
The Flower Walk
KENSINGTON
Holland St
S Carriage Dr
13
Knightsbridge
Grosvenor Cres
Grosvenor Pl
Kensington Rd
Knightsbridge
Knightsbridge
Lowndes St
Wilton Pl
Halkin St
Kensington Gore
KNIGHTSBRIDGE
Chapel St
Campden Hill Rd
Hornton St
Argyll Rd
Kensington High St
Victoria Rd
Palace Gate
Hyde Park Gate
10
Exhibition Rd
Ennismore Gdns
Rutland Gate
Prince's Gardens
Trevor Pl
Basil St
Motcomb St
Safestay Holland Park (1.4km)
High St Kensington
Wright's La
Prince Consort Rd
Brompton Rd
15
Belgrave Sq
Holland Park
Allen St
St Alban's Gve
Launceston Pl
Queen's Gate Tce
Cheval Pl
Hans Rd
Hans Pl
Eaton Pl
Earl's Court Rd
Abingdon Villas
Stanford Rd
Elvaston Pl
Queen's Gate
Imperial College Rd
Beaufort Gdns
Beauchamp Pl
Sloane St
Pont St
Lowndes Pl
Scarsdale Villas
Marloes Rd
Gloucester Rd
6
Pont St
Cadogan Pl
Lyall St
Cornwall Gdns
Grenville Pl
Natural History Museum
9
BELGRAVIA
Pembroke Villas
Stratford Rd
Lexham Gdns
11
1
East Lawn
Brompton Rd
Thurloe Sq
Cadogan Gardens
Cadogan Sq
Cromwell Rd
Thurloe Pl
Walton St
First St
Cromwell Rd
Gloucester Rd
South Kensington
Denyer St
Hasley St
Moore St
Ellis St
Eaton Sq
West Cromwell Rd
Hogarth Rd
Collingham Rd
Courtfield Rd
Stanhope Gdns
Cle Pl
Pelham St
Draycott Ave
14
Eaton Tce
Longridge Rd
EARL'S COURT
Barkston Gdns
Collingham Gardens
Harrington Gdns
12
Onslow Sq
Sloane Ave
Elystan St
Draycott Pl
Sloane Sq
Bourne St
Ebury St
Earl's Court Rd
Wetherby Gdns
SOUTH KENSINGTON
Sumner Pl
Holbein Pl
Warwick Rd
Trebovir Rd
Earl's Court
Old Brompton Rd
Onslow Gdns
Foulis Tce
Fulham Rd
Pond Pl
CHELSEA
King's Rd
Lower Sloane St
Victoria Coach Station (250m)
Cale St
Rabbit (300m)
Pimlico Rd
A
B
C
D
E
F
G
5
6
7
8

BRITAIN

Hyde Park to Chelsea

Top Sights
1 Natural History Museum D7

Sights
2 Holocaust Memorial Garden F5
3 Hyde Park E4
4 Marble Arch F3
5 Rose Garden G5
6 Science Museum D7
7 Serpentine Lake E5
8 Speakers' Corner F3
9 Victoria & Albert Museum D7

Activities, Courses & Tours
Royal Albert Hall Behind the Scenes Tours .... (see 10)
10 Royal Albert Hall Grand Tour D6

Sleeping
11 Meininger C7
12 Number Sixteen D8

Eating
13 Dinner by Heston Blumenthal F6

Entertainment
Royal Albert Hall .... (see 10)
14 Royal Court Theatre G8

Shopping
15 Harrods F6

the Winton Gallery, designed by Zaha Hadid Architects, is a riveting exploration of maths in the real world. The **Medicine Galleries** look at the medical world using objects from the museum's collections and those of Sir Henry Wellcome, pharmacist, entrepreneur, philanthropist and collector.

The 3rd floor's **Flight Gallery** (free tours 1pm most days) is a favourite place for children, with its gliders, hot-air balloons and aircraft, including the Gipsy Moth, which Amy Johnson flew to Australia in 1930. The rest of the floor is all about getting interactive, with a **Red Arrows 3D flight-simulation theatre** (£5), the **Fly 360-degree flight-simulator capsules** (£12 per capsule), another simulator, **Typhoon Force** (£5), replicating a low-level mission aboard a Typhoon fighter jet, and **Space Descent** (£7), a VR experience with (a digital) Tim Peake, British astronaut. Also on the 3rd floor, **Wonderlab** (adult/child £10/8) explores scientific phenomena in a fun and educational way, with daily shows.

If you've got kids under the age of five, pop down to the basement and the **Garden**, where there's a fun-filled play zone, including a water-play area, besieged by tots in orange waterproof smocks.

Victoria & Albert Museum MUSEUM
(V&A; Map p116; 020-7942 2000; www.vam.ac.uk; Cromwell Rd, SW7; 10am-5.45pm Sat-Thu, to 10pm Fri; South Kensington) FREE The Museum of Manufactures, as the V&A was known when it opened in 1852, was part of Prince Albert's legacy to the nation in the aftermath of the successful Great Exhibition of 1851. It houses the world's largest collection of decorative arts, from Asian ceramics to Middle Eastern rugs, Chinese paintings, Western furniture, fashion from all ages and modern-day domestic appliances. The (ticketed) temporary exhibitions are another highlight, covering anything from David Bowie and designer Alexander McQueen retrospectives to special materials and trends.

Hyde Park PARK
(Map p116; www.royalparks.org.uk/parks/hyde-park; 5am-midnight; Marble Arch, Hyde Park Corner, Knightsbridge or Queensway) Hyde Park is central London's largest green space, expropriated from the church in 1536 by Henry VIII and turned into a hunting ground and later a venue for duels, executions and horse racing. The 1851 Great Exhibition was held here, and during WWII the park became an enormous potato field. These days it's a place to stroll and picnic, boat on the **Serpentine lake** (Map p116; 020-7262 1330; Lancaster Gate or Knightsbridge), or to catch a summer concert or outdoor film during the warmer months. In winter, the southeast area of the park is the site of **Winter Wonderland** (https://hydeparkwinterwonderland.com), with fairground rides, ice skating and other seasonal attractions. Year-round look out for the **Holocaust Memorial Garden** (Map p116), a simple but evocative memorial to the Jewish victims of the Nazi regime, and the **Rose Garden** (Map p116), a wonderfully scented spot during the summer.

While **Speakers' Corner** (Map p116; Park Lane; Marble Arch) in the park's northeast corner is intended for oratorical acrobats, these days it's largely eccentrics and religious fanatics who address bemused onlookers, maintaining a tradition begun in 1872 as a response to rioting. Nearby **Marble Arch** (Map p116; Marble Arch), designed by John Nash in 1828 as the entrance to Buckingham Palace, was moved here in 1851. It replaced the infamous Tyburn Tree, a three-legged gallows that was the place of execution for up to 50,000 people between 1196 and 1783.

North London

ZSL London Zoo ZOO

(Map p124; www.zsl.org/zsl-london-zoo; Outer Circle, Regent's Park, NW1; adult/child £25/22, discounts if booked in advance online; 10am-6pm Apr-Sep, to 5.30pm Mar & Oct, to 4pm Nov-Feb; ; 274) Opened in 1828, London Zoo is among the oldest in the world. The emphasis nowadays is firmly on conservation, breeding and education, with fewer animals and bigger enclosures. Highlights include **Land of the Lions**, **Gorilla Kingdom**, **Tiger Territory**, the walk-through **In with the Lemurs** and **Penguin Beach**. There are regular feeding sessions and talks, various experiences are available, such as Keeper for a Day, and you can even spend the night in the Gir Lion Lodge.

Regent's Park PARK

(Map p124; www.royalparks.org.uk; 5am-dusk; U Regent's Park, Baker St) The most elaborate and formal of London's many parks, Regent's Park is one of the capital's loveliest green spaces. Among its many attractions are London Zoo, **Regent's Canal** (Map p124), an ornamental lake, and sports pitches where locals meet to play football, rugby and volleyball. **Queen Mary's Gardens**, towards the south of the park, are particularly pretty, especially in June when the roses are in bloom. Performances take place here in an **open-air theatre** (Map p124; 0844 826 4242; www.openairtheatre.org; May-Sep; ; U Baker St) during summer.

Greenwich

An extraordinary cluster of buildings has earned 'Maritime Greenwich' its place on Unesco's World Heritage list. It's also famous for straddling the hemispheres; this is the degree zero of longitude, home of the Greenwich Meridian and Greenwich Mean Time. Greenwich is easily reached on the DLR train (to Cutty Sark station), or by boat – Thames Clippers (p133) depart from the London Eye every 20 minutes.

Royal Observatory HISTORIC BUILDING

(020-8312 6565; www.rmg.co.uk/royal-observatory; Greenwich Park, Blackheath Ave, SE10; adult/child £10/6.50, incl Cutty Sark £20/11.50; 10am-5pm Sep-Jun, to 6pm Jul & Aug; U Greenwich or Cutty Sark) Rising like a beacon of time atop **Greenwich Park** (www.royalparks.org.uk; King George St, SE10; 6am-around sunset; U Greenwich, Maze Hill or Cutty Sark), the Royal Observatory is home to the **prime meridian** (longitude 0° 0′ 0″). Tickets include access to the Christopher Wren-designed **Flamsteed House** (named for the first Royal Astronomer) and the **Meridian Courtyard**, where you can stand with your feet straddling the eastern and western hemispheres. You can also see the Great Equatorial Telescope (1893) inside the onion-domed observatory and explore space and time in the **Weller Astronomy Galleries**.

Cutty Sark MUSEUM

(020-8312 6608; www.rmg.co.uk/cuttysark; King William Walk, SE10; adult/child £13.50/7; 10am-5pm; U Cutty Sark) The last of the great clipper ships to sail between China and England in the 19th century, the *Cutty Sark* endured massive fire damage in 2007 during a £25 million restoration. The exhibition in the hold of the fully restored ship tells its story as a tea clipper. Launched in 1869 in Scotland, it made eight voyages to China in the 1870s, sailing out with a mixed cargo and coming back with tea.

Old Royal Naval College HISTORIC BUILDING

(www.ornc.org; 2 Cutty Sark Gardens, SE10; 10am-5pm, grounds 8am-11pm; U Cutty Sark) FREE Sir Christopher Wren's baroque masterpiece in Greenwich, and indeed Britain's largest ensemble of baroque architecture, the Old Royal Naval College contains the neoclassical **Chapel of St Peter and St Paul** (www.ornc.org/chapel; SE10; 10am-5pm) and the extraordinary **Painted Hall** (020 8269 4799; www.ornc.org; adult/child £12/free; 10am-5pm) FREE. The entire Old Royal Naval College, including the chapel, the **visitor centre** (www.ornc.org/visitor-centre; Pepys Bldg, King William Walk, SE10; 10am-5pm) FREE, and the grounds, can be visited for free. Volunteers lead free 45-minute tours throughout the day from the visitor centre.

National Maritime Museum MUSEUM

(020-8312 6565; www.rmg.co.uk/national-maritime-museum; Romney Rd, SE10; 10am-5pm; U Cutty Sark) FREE Narrating the long, briny and eventful history of seafaring Britain, this excellent museum's exhibits are arranged thematically, with highlights including *Miss Britain III* (the first boat to top 100mph on open water) from 1933, the 19m-long golden state barge built in 1732 for Frederick, Prince of Wales, the huge ship's propeller and the colourful figureheads installed on the

West End & Westminster

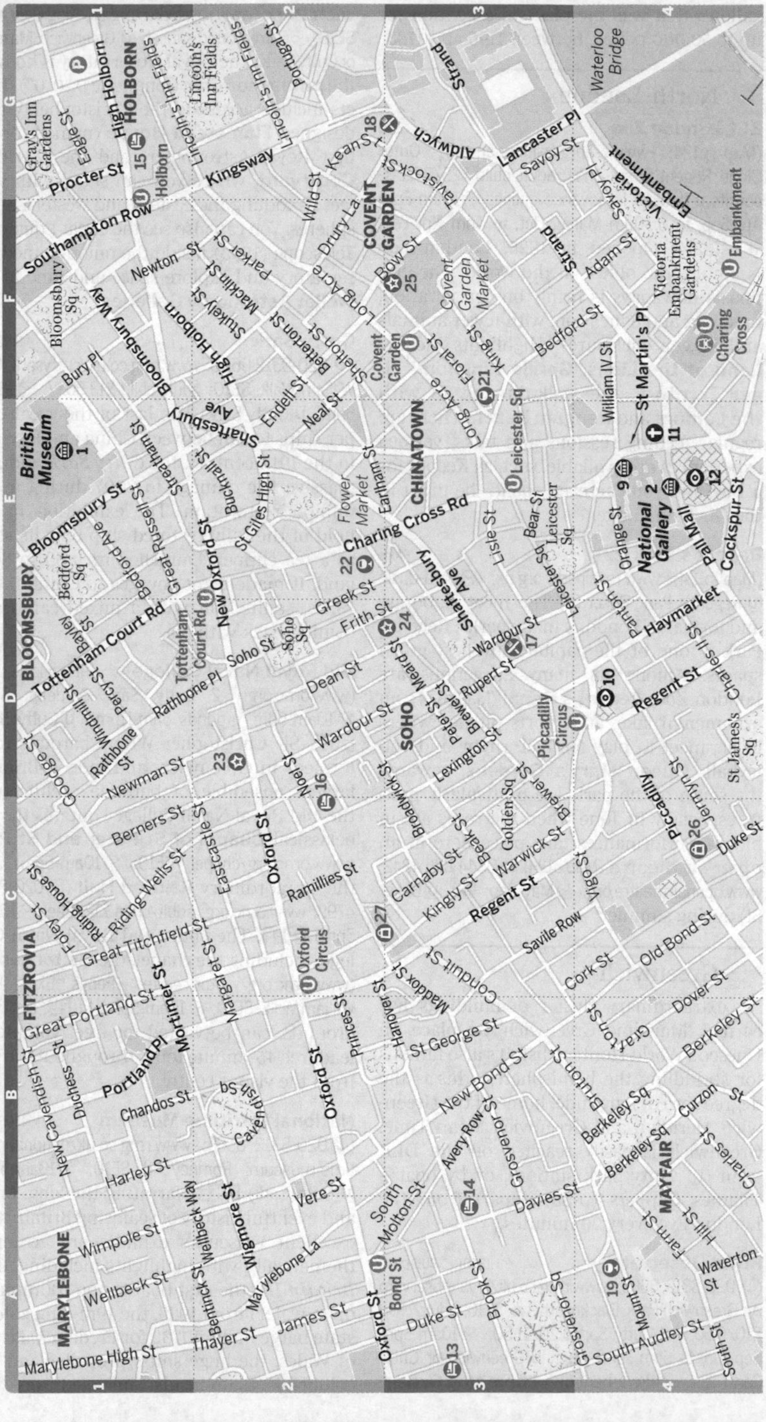

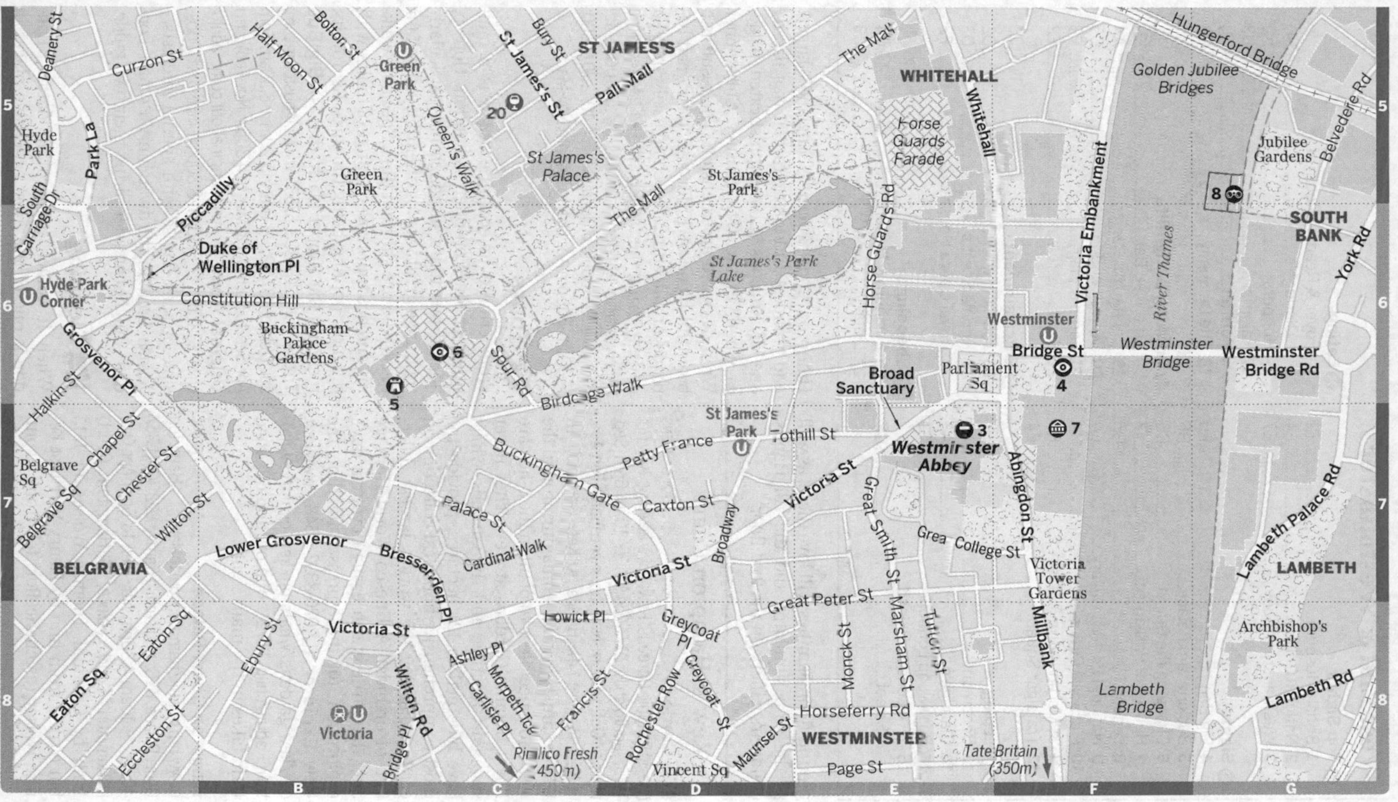
Deanery St
Curzon St
Half Moon St
Bolton St
Green Park
Bury St
St James's St
ST JAMES'S
Pall Mall
20
The Mall
WHITEHALL
Whitehall
Hungerford Bridge
Golden Jubilee Bridges
Belvedere Rd
Hyde Park
Park La
Queen's Walk
St James's Palace
Horse Guards Parade
Jubilee Gardens
South Carriage Dr
Piccadilly
Green Park
St James's Park
8
SOUTH BANK
York Rd
Duke of Wellington Pl
St James's Park Lake
Horse Guards Rd
Victoria Embankment
River Thames
Hyde Park Corner
Constitution Hill
Westminster
Buckingham Palace Gardens
6
Spur Rd
Bridge St
Westminster Bridge
Westminster Bridge Rd
Grosvenor Pl
5
Birdcage Walk
Broad Sanctuary
Parliament Sq
4
Halkin St
St James's Park
Tothill St
3
7
Chapel St
Petty France
Westminster Abbey
Belgrave Sq
Chester St
Buckingham Gate
Victoria St
Abingdon St
Great Smith St
Belgrave Sq
Wilton St
Palace St
Caxton St
Lambeth Palace Rd
Broadway
Great College St
Lower Grosvenor
Bressenden Pl
Cardinal Walk
BELGRAVIA
Victoria St
Victoria Tower Gardens
LAMBETH
Great Peter St
Victoria St
Howick Pl
Greycoat Pl
Eaton Sq
Ebury St
Ashley Pl
Monck St
Marsham St
Tufton St
Millbank
Archbishop's Park
Morpeth Tce
Carlisle Pl
Francis St
Rochester Row
Greycoat St
Eaton Sq
Wilton Rd
Lambeth Bridge
Lambeth Rd
Victoria
Horseferry Rd
Eccleston St
Bridge Pl
Maunsel St
WESTMINSTER
Pimlico Fresh (450m)
Vincent Sq
Page St
Tate Britain (350m)
A
B
C
D
E
F
G
5
6
7
8

West End & Westminster

Top Sights
1 British Museum.....E1
2 National Gallery.....E4
3 Westminster Abbey.....E7

Sights
4 Big Ben.....F6
5 Buckingham Palace.....B6
6 Changing the Guard.....C6
7 Houses of Parliament.....F7
8 London Eye.....G5
9 National Portrait Gallery.....E4
10 Piccadilly Circus.....D4
11 St Martin-in-the-Fields.....E4
12 Trafalgar Square.....E4

Sleeping
13 Beaumont.....A3
14 Claridge's.....A3
15 Rosewood London.....G1
16 YHA London Oxford Street.....C2

Eating
Foyer & Reading Room at Claridge's.....(see 14)
Hoppers.....(see 24)
17 Palomar.....D3
Portrait.....(see 9)
18 The Delaunay.....G3

Drinking & Nightlife
American Bar.....(see 13)
19 Connaught Bar.....A4
20 Dukes London.....C5
21 Lamb & Flag.....F3
22 Swift.....E2

Entertainment
23 100 Club.....D2
24 Ronnie Scott's.....D3
25 Royal Opera House.....F3

Shopping
26 Fortnum & Mason.....C4
27 Liberty.....C3

ground floor. Families will love these, as well as the ship simulator and the 'All Hands' children's gallery on the 2nd floor.

Kew & Hampton Court

Kew Gardens GARDENS
(Royal Botanic Gardens, Kew; www.kew.org; Kew Rd, TW9; adult/child £13.50/4.50; 10am-6pm Sep, to 5pm Oct, to 3pm Nov-Jan, closes later Feb-Aug; Kew Pier, Kew Bridge, Kew Gardens) In 1759 botanists began rummaging around the world for specimens to plant in the 3-hectare Royal Botanic Gardens at Kew. They never stopped collecting, and the gardens, which have bloomed to 121 hectares, provide the most comprehensive botanical collection on earth (including the world's largest collection of orchids). A Unesco World Heritage Site, the gardens can easily devour a day's exploration; for those pressed for time, the **Kew Explorer** (020-8332 5648; www.kew.org/kew-gardens/whats-on/kew-explorer-land-train; adult/child £5/2) hop-on/hop-off road train takes in the main sights.

Hampton Court Palace PALACE
(www.hrp.org.uk/hamptoncourtpalace; Hampton Court Palace, KT8; adult/child/family £22.70/11.35/40.40; 10am-4.30pm Nov-Mar, to 6pm Apr-Oct; Hampton Court Palace, Hampton Court) Built by Cardinal Thomas Wolsey in 1515 but coaxed from him by Henry VIII just before Wolsey (as chancellor) fell from favour, Hampton Court Palace is England's largest and grandest Tudor structure. It was already one of Europe's most sophisticated palaces when, in the 17th century, Christopher Wren designed an extension. The result is a beautiful blend of Tudor and 'restrained baroque' architecture. You could easily spend a day exploring the palace and its 24 hectares of riverside gardens, including a 300-year-old **maze** (adult/child/family £4.40/2.70/12.80; 10am-5.15pm Apr-Oct, to 3.45pm Nov-Mar).

Tours

From erudite to eccentric, there is a multitude of tours on offer in London. Hop-on, hop-off bus tours, although not particularly cool, are a great way for orienting yourself for those who are short on time. Specialist walking and bus tours cover a range of topics, with the most popular being the three Rs: royalty, rock and the Ripper (Jack, that is). **Big Bus Tours** (020-7808 6753; www.bigbustours.com; adult/child £37/19; every 5-20min 8.30am-6pm Apr-Sep, to 5pm Oct & Mar, to 4.30pm Nov-Feb) and **Original Tour** (www.theoriginaltour.com; adult/child £32/15; 8.30am-8.30pm) are two possible options. Those with special interests – Jewish London, birdwatching, Roman London – might consider hiring their own guide.

Sleeping

When it comes to accommodation, London is one of the most expensive places in the world. Budget is pretty much anything below £100 per night for a double; double rooms ranging between £100 and £200 per night are considered midrange; more expensive options fall into the top-end category. Public transport is good, so you don't need to sleep at Buckingham Palace to be at the heart of things.

The West End

The city's major theatres, as well some of its best attractions, dining and drinking, are right on your doorstep here. Though moderately priced hotels are scarce, Bloomsbury is a haven of B&Bs and guesthouses, and Cartwright Gardens, north of Russell Square (within easy walking distance of the West End), has some of central London's best-value small hotels.

Generator London HOSTEL £

(Map p124; 020-7388 7666; www.generatorhostels.com/london; 37 Tavistock Pl, WC1; dm/r from £9/44; ; Russell Sq) With its industrial lines and funky decor, the huge Generator (it has more than 870 beds) is one of central London's grooviest budget spots. The bar, complete with pool tables, stays open until 3am and there are frequent themed parties. Dorm rooms have between four and 12 beds; backing it up are twins and triples.

YHA London Oxford Street HOSTEL £

(Map p120; 020-7734 1618; www.yha.org.uk/hostel/yha-london-oxford-street; 14 Noel St, W1; dm £18-36, tw £50-85; ; Oxford Circus) The most central of London's seven YHA hostels is also one of the most intimate with just 104 beds. The excellent shared facilities include a fuchsia-coloured kitchen and a bright, funky lounge. Dormitories have three or four beds, and there are doubles and twins. The in-house shop sells coffee and beer. Free wi-fi in common areas.

Arosfa Hotel B&B ££

(Map p124; 020-7636 2115; www.arosfalondon.com; 83 Gower St, WC1; s/tw/tr/f from £90/135/155/210, d £140-175; ; Goodge St) The Philippe Starck furniture and modern look in the lounge are more lavish than the decor in the guest rooms, with cabin-like bathrooms in many of them. Fully refurbished, the 16 rooms are small but remain good value. There are a couple of family rooms; room 4 looks on to a small but charming garden in the back.

★**Rosewood London** HOTEL £££

(Map p120; 020-7781 8888; www.rosewoodhotels.com/en/london; 252 High Holborn, WC1; d/ste from £390/702; ; Holborn) What was once the grand Pearl Assurance building (dating from 1914) now houses the stunning Rosewood hotel, where an artful marriage of period and modern styles thanks to designer Tony Chi can be found in its 262 rooms and 44 suites. British heritage is carefully woven throughout the bar, restaurant, deli, lobby and even the housekeepers' uniforms.

The South Bank

Immediately south of the river is good if you want to immerse yourself in workaday London and still be central.

★**citizenM** BOUTIQUE HOTEL ££

(Map p112; 020-3519 1680; www.citizenm.com/london-bankside; 20 Lavington St, SE1; r £89-329; ; Southwark) If citizenM had a motto, it would be 'Less fuss, more comfort'. The hotel has done away with things it considers superfluous (room service, reception, heaps of space) and instead has gone all out on mattresses and bedding (heavenly super-king-sized beds), state-of-the-art technology (everything from mood lighting to TV is controlled through a tablet computer) and superb decor.

Kensington & Hyde Park

This classy area offers easy access to the museums and big-name fashion shops, but at a price that reflects the upmarket surroundings.

Meininger HOSTEL £

(Map p116; 020-3318 1407; www.meininger-hostels.com; Baden Powell House, 65-67 Queen's Gate, SW7; dm £16-50, s/tw from £60/70; ; Gloucester Rd, South Kensington) Housed in the late-1950s Baden Powell House opposite the Natural History Museum, this 48-room German-run 'city hostel and hotel' has spick-and-span rooms – most are dorms of between four and 12 beds, with podlike showers. There is also a handful of private rooms. It has good security and nice communal facilities, including a bar and a big roof terrace, plus a fantastic location.

Lime Tree Hotel BOUTIQUE HOTEL ££

(020-7730 8191; www.limetreehotel.co.uk; 135-137 Ebury St, SW1; s incl breakfast £125-165, d &

Bloomsbury, St Pancras & Camden

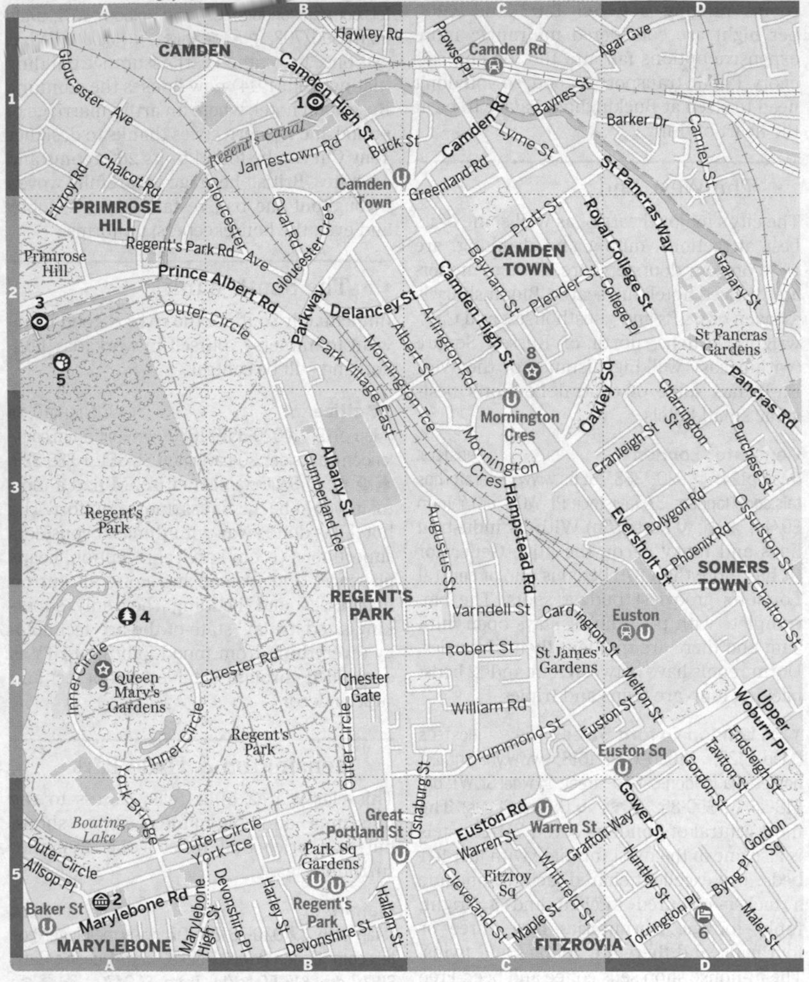

Bloomsbury, St Pancras & Camden

Sights

1	Camden Market	B1
2	Madame Tussauds	A5
3	Regent's Canal	A2
4	Regent's Park	A4
5	ZSL London Zoo	A2

Sleeping

6	Arosfa Hotel	D5
7	Generator London	E4

Entertainment

8	KOKO	C2
9	Regent's Park Open Air Theatre	A4
10	Scala	F3

tw £185-215, tr £240; ; Victoria) Family run for over three decades, this beautiful 25-bedroom Georgian town-house hotel is all comfort, British design and understated elegance. Rooms are individually decorated, many with open fireplaces and sash win-

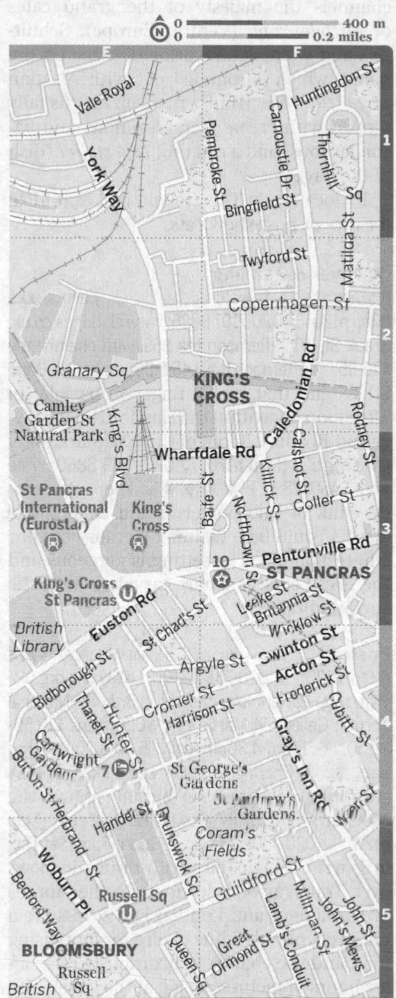

dows, but some are smaller than others, so enquire. There is a lovely back garden for late-afternoon rays (picnics encouraged on summer evenings). Rates include a hearty full English breakfast. No lift. If you don't like climbing stairs, try to secure a room on a lower floor.

★Number Sixteen HOTEL £££
(Map p116; ☎020-7589 5232; www.firmdalehotels.com/hotels/london/number-sixteen; 16 Sumner Pl, SW7; s from £192, d £240-396; ; South Kensington) With uplifting splashes of colour, choice art and a sophisticated-but-fun design ethos, Number Sixteen is simply ravishing. There are 41 individually designed rooms, a cosy drawing room and a fully stocked library. And wait till you see the idyllic, long back garden set around a fountain, or sit down for breakfast in the light-filled conservatory. Great amenities for families.

North London

Sleeping options in North London are concentrated around the King's Cross area, where you'll find the best in both budget and top-end accommodation.

★Clink78 HOSTEL £
(Map p112; ☎020-7183 9400; www.clinkhostels.com/london/clink78; 78 King's Cross Rd, WC1; dm/r incl breakfast from £16/65; ; King's Cross St Pancras) This fantastic 630-bed hostel is housed in a 19th-century magistrates' courthouse where Charles Dickens once worked as a scribe and members of the Clash stood trial in 1978. It features pod beds (including overhead storage space) in four- to 16-bed dormitories. There's a top kitchen with a huge dining area and a busy bar – Clash – in the basement.

West London

West London is well supplied with accommodation choices, from excellent hostels in leafy parks to boutique hotels, family-run B&Bs and apartments. It's so popular with travelling Antipodeans that it's been nicknamed Kangaroo Valley.

Safestay Holland Park HOSTEL £
(☎020-3326 8471; www.safestay.co.uk; Holland Walk, W8; dm £20, r from £60; ; High St Kensington, Holland Park) This fresh place replaced the long-serving YHA hostel that ran here since 1958. With a bright and bold colour design, the hostel has four- to eight-bunk dorm rooms, twin-bunk and single-bunk rooms, free wi-fi in the lobby and a fabulous location in the Jacobean east wing of Holland House in **Holland Park** (Ilchester Pl; 7.30am-dusk), the only part that survived a Luftwaffe onslaught.

★Main House HOTEL ££
(☎020-7221 9691; www.themainhouse.co.uk; 6 Colville Rd, W11; ste £130-150; ; Ladbroke Grove, Notting Hill Gate, Westbourne Park) The four adorable suites at this peach of a

Victorian midterrace house on Colville Rd make this a superb choice. Bright and spacious rooms are excellent value and come with vast bathrooms and endless tea and coffee. Cream of the crop is the uppermost suite, occupying the entire top floor. There's no sign, but look for the huge letters 'SIX'. Minimum three-night stay.

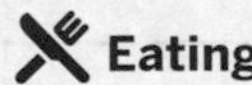

Eating

Once the butt of many a culinary joke, London has transformed itself over the last few decades and today is a global dining destination. World-famous chefs can be found at the helm of several top-tier restaurants, but it is the sheer diversity on offer that is head-spinning: from Afghan to Zambian, London delivers an A to Z of world cuisine.

The West End

Hoppers SRI LANKAN **£**
(Map p120; www.hopperslondon.com; 49 Frith St, W1; dishes £5-21; noon-2.30pm & 5.30-10.30pm Mon-Thu, noon-10.30pm Fri & Sat; Tottenham Court Rd or Leicester Sq) This pint-sized, enormously popular place specialises in the Sri Lankan national dish of hoppers: thin pancakes of rice flour and coconut milk with spices. Eat them (or dosas) with various types of *kari* (curry) or *kothu,* a dish of chopped flatbread with spices and meat, fish, crab or vegetables.

The decor here is Old Ceylon, and the service swift but personable.

★**Palomar** MIDDLE EASTERN **££**
(Map p120; 020-7439 8777; www.thepalomar.co.uk; 34 Rupert St, W1; dishes £7.50-26; noon-2.30pm & 5.30-11pm Mon-Sat, 12.30-3.30pm & 6-9pm Sun; Piccadilly Circus) With a stack of 'restaurant of the year' awards, Palomar is a firm favourite, and the wait for one of the 16 bar stools or 40 seats is testament to that. It celebrates modern Jerusalem cuisine, with flavours stretching from the Levant to the Maghreb. *Kubaneh* (bread dipped in tomato and tahini), 'octo-hummus' and balsamic-glazed chicken livers are a few of the must-orders.

The Delaunay EUROPEAN **££**
(Map p120; 020-7499 8558; www.thedelaunay.com; 55 Aldwych, WC2; mains £14.50-35; 7am-11pm Mon-Fri, from 8am Sat, 9am-10pm Sun; Temple or Covent Garden) This smart spot channels the majesty of the grand cafes of *Mitteleuropa* (Central Europe). Schnitzels and wieners take pride of place on the menu, which is rounded out with Alsatian *tarte flambée* (thin crust pizzas usually topped with *crème fraiche,* onions and bacon lardons) and a rotating *Tagesteller* (dish of the day).

Its location in Theatreland makes it ideal for pre- or post-show eats.

★**Foyer & Reading Room at Claridge's** BRITISH **£££**
(Map p120; 020-7107 8886; www.claridges.co.uk; Brook St, W1; afternoon tea £65, with champagne £75-85; afternoon tea 2.45-5.30pm; Bond St) Extend that pinkie finger to partake in afternoon tea within the classic art deco foyer and Reading Room of the landmark hotel **Claridge's** (Map p120; 020-7629 8860; r/ste from £450/780;), where the gentle clink of fine porcelain and champagne glasses could be a defining memory of your trip to London. The setting is gorgeous and the dress code is smart casual to befit the surroundings.

Portrait MODERN EUROPEAN **£££**
(Map p120; 020-7312 2490; www.npg.org.uk/visit/shop-eat-drink/restaurant; 3rd fl, National Portrait Gallery, St Martin's Pl, WC2; mains £19.50-29.50; 10am-4.30pm daily, 5.30-8.30pm Thu-Sat; Charing Cross or Leicester Sq) This stunningly located restaurant above the excellent **National Portrait Gallery** (Map p120; 020-7306 0055; 10am-6pm Sat-Thu, to 9pm Fri) FREE comes with dramatic views over Trafalgar Sq and down to the Houses of Parliament and London Eye. Prices are a bit steep, but it's a fine choice for tantalising food and the chance to luxuriously relax after hours of picture-gazing at the gallery. It's best to book in advance.

The South Bank

For a feed with a local feel, head to Borough Market or Bermondsey St.

Watch House CAFE **£**
(Map p112; 020-7407 6431; www.thewatchhouse.com; 199 Bermondsey St, SE1; mains from £4.95; 7am-6pm Mon-Fri, 8am-6pm Sat & Sun; Borough or London Bridge) Saying that the Watch House nails the sandwich wouldn't really do justice to this tip-top cafe: the sandwiches really are delicious. There is

also great coffee, and treats for the sweet-toothed. The small but lovely setting is a renovated 19th-century watch-house from where guards kept an eye on the next-door cemetery. No bathroom.

Padella ITALIAN £
(Map p112; www.padella.co; 6 Southwark St, SE1; dishes £4-11.50; noon-3.45pm & 5-10pm Mon-Sat, noon-3.45pm & 5-9pm Sun; ; London Bridge) A fantastic part of the foodie enclave of **Borough Market** (Map p112; www.boroughmarket.org.uk; full market 10am-5pm Wed & Thu, 10am-6pm Fri, 8am-5pm Sat), Padella is a small, energetic bistro specialising in handmade pasta dishes, inspired by the owners' extensive culinary adventures in Italy. The portions are small, which means that, joy of joys, you can (and should!) have more than one dish. Outstanding, but be prepared to queue (no reservations taken).

Anchor & Hope GASTROPUB ££
(Map p112; 020-7928 9898; www.anchorandhopepub.co.uk; 36 The Cut, SE1; mains £12-20; 5-11pm Mon, 11am-11pm Tue-Sat, 12.30-3.15pm Sun; Southwark) The Anchor & Hope is a quintessential gastropub: elegant but not formal, serving utterly delicious European fare with a British twist. The menu changes daily, but could include grilled sole served with spinach, or roast rabbit with green beans in a mustard and bacon sauce. Bookings taken for Sunday lunch only.

Skylon MODERN EUROPEAN £££
(Map p112; 020-7654 7800; www.skylon-restaurant.co.uk; 3rd fl, Royal Festival Hall, Southbank Centre, Belvedere Rd, SE1; 3-course menu grill/restaurant £25/30; grill noon-11pm Mon-Sat, to 10pm Sun, restaurant 12.30-2.30pm & 5-10.30pm Mon-Sat; ; Waterloo) This excellent restaurant inside the Royal Festival Hall (p130) is divided into grill and fine-dining sections by a large bar. The decor is cutting-edge 1950s, with muted colours and period chairs (trendy then, trendier now), while floor-to-ceiling windows bathe you in magnificent views of the Thames and the city. Booking is advised.

Kensington & Hyde Park

Pimlico Fresh CAFE £
(020-7932 0030; 86 Wilton Rd, SW1; mains from £4.50; 7.30am-6pm Mon-Fri, 8.30am-6pm Sat & Sun; Victoria) This friendly two-room cafe will see you right, whether you need breakfast (French toast, bowls of porridge laced with honey or maple syrup), lunch (homemade quiches and soups, 'things' on toast) or just a good old latte and cake.

★**Rabbit** MODERN BRITISH ££
(020-3750 0172; www.rabbit-restaurant.com; 172 King's Rd, SW3; small plates £6-13, set lunch of 2/3 courses £14.50/19.50; noon-midnight Tue-Sat, noon-6pm Sun, 6-11pm Mon; ; Sloane Sq) Three brothers grew up on a farm. One became a farmer, another a butcher, while the third worked in hospitality. So they pooled their skills and came up with Rabbit, a breath of fresh air in upmarket Chelsea. The restaurant rocks the agri-chic look, and the creative, seasonal Modern British cuisine is fabulous.

★**Dinner by Heston Blumenthal** MODERN BRITISH £££
(Map p116; 020-7201 3833; www.dinnerbyheston.com; Mandarin Oriental Hyde Park, 66 Knightsbridge, SW1; 3-course set lunch £45, mains £33-52; noon-2pm & 6-10.15pm Mon-Fri, noon-2.30pm & 6.30-10.30pm Sat & Sun; ; Knightsbridge) Sumptuously presented Dinner is a gastronomic tour de force, taking diners on a journey through British culinary history (with inventive modern inflections). Dishes carry historical dates to convey context, while the restaurant interior is a design triumph, from the glass-walled kitchen and its overhead clock mechanism to the large windows looking onto the park. Book ahead.

Drinking & Nightlife

You need only glance at William Hogarth's *Gin Lane* prints from 1751 to realise that Londoners and alcohol have had more than a passing acquaintance. The metropolis offers a huge variety of venues to wet your whistle in – from cosy neighbourhood pubs to glitzy all-night clubs, and everything in between.

The West End

★**Dukes London** COCKTAIL BAR
(Map p120; 020-7491 4840; www.dukeshotel.com/dukes-bar; Dukes Hotel, 35 St James's Pl, SW1; 2-11pm Mon-Sat, 4-10.30pm Sun; ; Green Park) Sip to-die-for martinis in a gentlemen's club-like ambience at this clas-

sic bar where white-jacketed masters mix up perfect preparations. James Bond fans in particular should make a pilgrimage here: author Ian Fleming used to frequent the place, where he undoubtedly ordered his drinks 'shaken, not stirred'. Smokers can ease into the secluded Cognac and Cigar Garden to light up cigars purchased here.

American Bar BAR

(Map p120; ☎020-7499 1001; www.thebeaumont.com/dining/american-bar; Beaumont, Brown Hart Gardens, W1; ⏰11.30am-midnight Mon-Sat, to 11pm Sun; 📶; Ⓤ Bond St) Sip a bourbon or a classic cocktail in the 1920s art deco ambience of this stylish bar at the hallmark **Beaumont hotel** (Map p120; d/studio/ste from £550/865/1475; ❄📶). It's central, glam and like a private members' club, but far from stuffy. Only a few years old, the American Bar feels like it's been pouring drinks since the days of the flapper and the jazz age.

★Lamb & Flag PUB

(Map p120; ☎020-7497 9504; www.lambandflagcoventgarden.co.uk; 33 Rose St, WC2; ⏰11am-11pm Mon-Sat, noon-10.30pm Sun; Ⓤ Covent Garden) Perpetually busy pint-sized Lamb & Flag is full of charm and history, and has been a public house since at least 1772. Rain or shine, you'll have to elbow your way through the merry crowd drinking outside to get to the bar.

The main entrance is at the top of tiny, cobbled Rose St.

Connaught Bar COCKTAIL BAR

(Map p120; ☎020-7314 3419; www.the-connaught.co.uk/mayfair-bars/connaught-bar; Connaught Hotel, Carlos Pl, W1; ⏰11am-1am Mon-Sat, to midnight Sun; Ⓤ Bond St) Drinkers who know their stuff single out the travelling martini trolley for particular praise, but almost everything at this sumptuous bar at the exclusive and very British Connaught Hotel gets the nod: lavish art deco–inspired lines, faultless and cheerful service, and some of the best drinks in town. Cocktails – classic and those given a thoroughly contemporary twist – start at £18.

Swift COCKTAIL BAR

(Map p120; ☎020-7437 7820; www.barswift.com; 12 Old Compton St, W1; ⏰3pm-midnight Mon-Sat, 3-10.30pm Sun; Ⓤ Leicester Sq or Tottenham Court Rd) One of our favourite spots for a tipple, Swift has a sleek, candlelit Upstairs Bar designed for those who want a quick drink before dinner or the theatre, while the Downstairs Bar is a whisky-lover's dream, with 250 bottles and counting, plus art deco–inspired sofas that invite lounging, especially when live blues and jazz are played on Friday and Saturday nights.

The South Bank

★King's Arms PUB

(Map p112; ☎020-7207 0784; www.thekingsarmslondon.co.uk; 25 Roupell St, SE1; ⏰11am-11pm Mon-Sat, noon-10.30pm Sun; Ⓤ Waterloo) Relaxed and charming, this neighbourhood boozer is found at the corner of Roupell St, a terraced Waterloo backstreet. The large traditional bar area, complete with open fire in winter, serves up a changing selection of ales and bottled beers. It gets packed with after-work crowds between 6pm and 8pm.

★Oblix BAR

(Map p112; www.oblixrestaurant.com; 32nd fl, Shard, 31 St Thomas St, SE1; ⏰noon-11pm; Ⓤ London Bridge) The views from Oblix on the 32nd floor of **the Shard** (Map p112; www.theviewfromtheshard.com; 32 London Bridge St, SE1; adult/child £30.95/24.95; ⏰10am-10pm) aren't quite as impressive as the panoramas from the 69th-floor viewing platform, but you'll still be wowed. Relax with a cocktail (from £13.50) in the stylish bar and enjoy views towards the City, East and South London. Live music or DJ most nights from 7pm. Smart dress recommended.

Clerkenwell, Shoreditch & Spitalfields

Ye Olde Mitre PUB

(Map p112; www.yeoldemitreholborn.co.uk; 1 Ely Ct, EC1; ⏰11am-11pm Mon-Fri; 📶; Ⓤ Farringdon) A delightfully cosy historic pub with an extensive beer selection, tucked away in a backstreet off Hatton Garden, Ye Olde Mitre was originally built in 1546 for the servants of Ely Palace. There's no music, so rooms echo only with amiable chit-chat. Queen Elizabeth I danced around the cherry tree by the bar, or so they say.

★Zetter Townhouse Cocktail Lounge COCKTAIL BAR

(Map p112; ☎020-7324 4545; www.thezettertownhouse.com/clerkenwell/bar; 49-50 St John's Sq,

EC1; ⌚7am-midnight Sun-Wed, to 1am Thu-Sat; 📶; Ⓤ Farringdon) Behind an unassuming door on St John's Sq, this ground-floor bar is decorated with plush armchairs, stuffed animal heads and a legion of lamps. The cocktail list takes its theme from the area's distilling history – recipes of yesteryear plus homemade tinctures and cordials are used to create interesting and unusual tipples.

Cargo CLUB

(Map p112; www.cargo-london.com; 83 Rivington St, EC2; ⌚noon-1am Sun-Wed, to 3am Thu & Fri, to midnight Sat; Ⓤ Shoreditch High St) Cargo has seen better days but still packs in a crowd several nights weekly. Under its brick railway arches, you'll find a dance floor and bar, and there's also an outside terrace with two stencil works by Banksy. Drinks can be insanely overpriced, and the cover charge at peak times is steep – know what you're getting into or be too drunk to care.

☆ Entertainment

Whatever it is that sets your spirits soaring or your booty shaking, you'll find it in London. The city's been a world leader in theatre ever since a young bard from Stratford-upon-Avon set up shop here in the 16th century. And if London started swinging in the 1960s, its live rock and pop scene has barely let up since.

Theatre

A night out at the theatre is as much a must-do London experience as a trip on the top deck of a double-decker bus. London's Theatreland in the dazzling West End – from Aldwych in the east, past Shaftesbury Ave to Regent St in the west – has a concentration of theatres only rivalled by New York's Broadway. It's a thrillingly diverse scene, encompassing Shakespeare's classics performed with old-school precision, edgy new works, raise-the-roof musicals and some of the world's longest-running shows.

Old Vic THEATRE

(Map p112; ☎0844 871 7628; www.oldvictheatre.com; The Cut, SE1; Ⓤ Waterloo) Artistic director Matthew Warchus (who directed *Matilda the Musical* and the film *Pride*) aims to bring eclectic programming to the Old Vic theatre: expect new writing, as well as some dynamic revivals of old works and musicals.

Young Vic THEATRE

(Map p112; ☎020-7922 2922; www.youngvic.org; 66 The Cut, SE1; Ⓤ Southwark or Waterloo) This groundbreaking theatre is as much about showcasing and discovering new talent as it is about people discovering theatre. The Young Vic features actors, directors and plays from across the world, many tackling contemporary political and cultural issues, such as the death penalty, racism or corruption, and often blending dance and music with acting. Discounts are available for children, students and over-60s.

Royal Court Theatre THEATRE

(Map p116; ☎020-7565 5000; www.royalcourttheatre.com; Sloane Sq, SW1; tickets £12-38; Ⓤ Sloane Sq) Equally renowned for staging innovative new plays and old classics, the Royal Court is among London's most progressive theatres and has continued to foster major writing talent across the UK for over 60 years. There are two auditoriums: the main Jerwood Theatre Downstairs, and the much smaller studio Jerwood Theatre Upstairs. Tickets for Monday performances are £12.

Live Music

★ KOKO LIVE MUSIC

(Map p124; www.koko.uk.com; 1a Camden High St, NW1; Ⓤ Mornington Cres) Once the legendary Camden Palace, where Charlie Chaplin, the Goons and the Sex Pistols performed, and where Prince played surprise gigs, KOKO is maintaining its reputation as one of London's better gig venues. The theatre has a dance floor and decadent balconies, and attracts an indie crowd. There are live bands most nights and hugely popular club nights on Saturdays. Check the website to find out what's on, and when to show up.

100 Club LIVE MUSIC

(Map p120; ☎020-7636 0933; www.the100club.co.uk; 100 Oxford St, W1; tickets £8-20; ⌚check website for gig times; Ⓤ Oxford Circus or Tottenham Court Rd) This heritage London venue at the same address since 1942 started off as a jazz club but now leans towards rock. Back in the day it showcased Chris Barber, BB King and the Rolling Stones, and it was at the centre

LGBTIQ+ LONDON

London is a world LGBTIQ+ capital on par with New York and San Francisco, with visible communities and enlightened laws to protect them. It's rare to encounter any problem with sharing rooms or holding hands in the inner city, although it would pay to keep your wits about you at night and be conscious of your surroundings. The West End, particularly Soho, is the visible centre of LGBTIQ+ London, with numerous venues clustered around Old Compton St – but many other areas have their own miniscenes. The easiest way to find out what's going on is to pick up the free press from a venue; the gay section of *Time Out* (www.timeout.com/london/lgbt) is also useful.

of the punk revolution and the '90s indie scene. It hosts dancing gigs, the occasional big name, where-are-they-now bands and top-league tributes.

Ronnie Scott's JAZZ

(Map p120; ☎020-7439 0747; www.ronniescotts.co.uk; 47 Frith St, W1; ⏰6pm-3am Mon-Sat, noon-4pm & 6.30pm-midnight Sun; Ⓤ Leicester Sq or Tottenham Court Rd) Ronnie Scott's jazz club opened in 1959 and became widely known as Britain's best, hosting such luminaries as Miles Davis, Charlie Parker, Ella Fitzgerald, Count Basie and Sarah Vaughan. The club continues to build upon its formidable reputation by presenting a range of big names and new talent. Book in advance, or come for a more informal gig at Upstairs @ Ronnie's.

Scala LIVE MUSIC

(Map p124; ☎020-7833 2022; www.scala.co.uk; 275 Pentonville Rd, N1; Ⓤ King's Cross St Pancras) Opened in 1920 as a salubrious golden-age cinema, Scala slipped into porn-movie hell in the 1970s, only to be reborn as a club and live-music venue in the early 2000s. It's one of the top places in London to catch an intimate gig and is a great dance space too, hosting a diverse range of club nights.

Classical Music, Opera & Dance

★ Royal Albert Hall CONCERT VENUE

(Map p116; ☎0845 401 5034; 020-7589 8212; www.royalalberthall.com; Kensington Gore, SW7; Ⓤ South Kensington) This splendid Victorian concert hall hosts classical music, rock and other performances, but is famously the venue for the BBC-sponsored Proms. Booking is possible, but from mid-July to mid-September Promenaders queue for £5 standing tickets that go on sale one hour before curtain-up. Otherwise, the box office and prepaid-ticket collection counter are through door 12 (south side of the hall).

A variety of tours of the Albert Hall are also available, ranging from a **Grand Tour** (Map p116; adult/child £14/7; ⏰hourly 9.30am-4.30pm), giving a general overview of the building, to a **Behind the Scenes Tour** (Map p116; ☎0845 401 5045; www.royalalberthall.com; adult/children £16/8.75). These can be followed by afternoon tea in the bright, chic Verdi restaurant (£30).

Royal Opera House OPERA

(Map p120; ☎020-7304 4000; www.roh.org.uk; Bow St, WC2; ⏰gift shop & cafe from 10am; Ⓤ Covent Garden) Opera and ballet have a fantastic setting on Covent Garden Piazza, and a night here is a sumptuous affair. Although the program has modern influences, the main attractions are still the classic productions, which feature world-class performers. A recent £50-million revamp opened up new areas to the non-ticketed public for the first time, including a swish cafe.

Sadler's Wells DANCE

(Map p112; ☎020-7863 8000; www.sadlerswells.com; Rosebery Ave, EC1; Ⓤ Angel) A glittering modern venue that was first established in 1683, Sadler's Wells is the most eclectic modern-dance and ballet venue in town, with experimental dance shows of all genres and from all corners of the globe. The Lilian Baylis Studio stages smaller productions.

Royal Festival Hall CONCERT VENUE

(Map p112; ☎020-3879 9555; www.southbankcentre.co.uk; Southbank Centre, Belvedere Rd, SE1; 📶; Ⓤ Waterloo) The Royal Festival Hall is Europe's largest centre for performing and visual arts. The amphitheatre seats 2500 and is one of the best places for catching world- and classical-music artists. The sound is fantastic, the programming impeccable and there are frequent free gigs in the wonderfully expansive foyer.

Shopping

Department Stores

London's famous department stores are an attraction in themselves, even if you're not interested in buying.

★Fortnum & Mason DEPARTMENT STORE

(Map p120; ☎020-7734 8040; www.fortnumandmason.com; 181 Piccadilly, W1; ⏰10am-9pm Mon-Sat, 11.30am-6pm Sun; Ⓤ Green Park or Piccadilly Circus) With its classic eau-de-Nil (pale green) colour scheme, the 'Queen's grocery store' established in 1707 refuses to yield to modern times. Its staff – men and women – still wear old-fashioned tailcoats, and its glamorous food hall is supplied with hampers, marmalade and speciality teas. Stop for a spot of afternoon tea at the Diamond Jubilee Tea Salon, visited by Queen Elizabeth II in 2012.

Harrods DEPARTMENT STORE

(Map p116; ☎020-7730 1234; www.harrods.com; 87-135 Brompton Rd, SW1; ⏰10am-9pm Mon-Sat, 11.30am-6pm Sun; Ⓤ Knightsbridge) Garish and stylish in equal measure, perennially crowded Harrods is an obligatory stop for visitors, from the cash-strapped to the big spenders. The stock is astonishing, as are many of the price tags. High on kitsch, the 'Egyptian Elevator' resembles something out of an Indiana Jones epic, while the memorial fountain to Dodi and Di (lower ground floor) merely adds surrealism.

★Liberty DEPARTMENT STORE

(Map p120; ☎020-7734 1234; www.libertylondon.com; Regent St, entrance on Great Marlborough St, W1; ⏰10am-8pm Mon-Sat, 11.30am-6pm Sun; 📶; Ⓤ Oxford Circus) One of London's most recognisable shops, Liberty department store has a white-and-wood-beam Tudor Revival facade that lures shoppers in to browse luxury contemporary fashion, homewares, cosmetics and accessories, all at sky-high prices. Liberty is known for its fabrics and has a full haberdashery department; a classic London gift or souvenir is a Liberty fabric print, especially in the form of a scarf.

Markets

Perhaps the biggest draw for visitors is the capital's famed markets. A treasure trove of small designers, unique jewellery pieces, original framed photographs and posters, colourful vintage pieces and bric-a-brac, they are the antidote to impersonal, carbon-copy shopping centres.

★Portobello Road Market MARKET

(www.portobellomarket.org; Portobello Rd, W10; ⏰8am-6.30pm Mon-Wed, Fri & Sat, to 1pm Thu; Ⓤ Notting Hill Gate or Ladbroke Grove) Lovely on a warm summer's day, Portobello Road Market is an iconic London attraction with an eclectic mix of street food, fruit and veg, antiques, curios, collectables, fashion and trinkets. The shops along Portobello Rd open daily and the fruit and veg stalls (from Elgin Cres to Talbot Rd) only close on Sunday. But while some antique stalls operate on Friday, the busiest day by far is Saturday, when antique dealers set up shop (from Chepstow Villas to Elgin Cres).

Camden Market MARKET

(Map p124; www.camdenmarket.com; Camden High St, NW1; ⏰10am-late; Ⓤ Camden Town or Chalk Farm) Although – or perhaps because – it stopped being cutting-edge several thousand cheap leather jackets ago, Camden Market attracts millions of visitors each year and is one of London's most popular attractions. What started out as a collection of attractive craft stalls beside Camden Lock on the Regent's Canal now extends most of the way from Camden Town tube station to Chalk Farm tube station.

Broadway Market MARKET

(www.broadwaymarket.co.uk; Broadway Market, E8; ⏰9am-5pm Sat; 🚌394) There's been a market down here since the late 19th century, but the focus these days is artisanal food, handmade gifts and unique clothing. Cafes along both sides of the street do a roaring trade with coffee drinking shoppers. Stock up on edible treats then head to **London Fields** (Richmond Rd, E8; Ⓤ London Fields) for a picnic.

Information

Visit London (www.visitlondon.com) can fill you in on everything from tourist attractions and events (Changing the Guard, Chinese New Year parade etc) to river trips and tours, accommodation, eating, theatre, shopping, children's

MAPS

There was a time when no Londoner would be without a pocket-sized *London A–Z* map-book. It's a great resource if you don't have a smartphone. You can buy them at news stands and shops everywhere. For getting around the London Underground system (the tube), maps are free at underground stations.

activities and LGBTIQ+ venues. Kiosks are dotted about the city and can provide maps and brochures; some branches book theatre tickets.

Getting There & Away

BUS

Long-distance and international buses arrive and depart from **Victoria Coach Station** (164 Buckingham Palace Rd, SW1; Ⓤ Victoria), close to the Victoria tube and rail stations.

TRAIN

Most of London's main-line rail terminals are linked by the Circle line on the tube. The terminals listed here serve the following destinations:

Charing Cross Canterbury

Euston Manchester, Liverpool, Carlisle, Glasgow

King's Cross Gatwick airport, Cambridge, Hull, York, Newcastle, Edinburgh, Aberdeen

Liverpool Street Stansted airport (Express), Cambridge

London Bridge Gatwick airport, Brighton

Marylebone Birmingham

Paddington Heathrow airport (Express), Oxford, Bath, Bristol, Exeter, Plymouth, Cardiff

St Pancras Gatwick and Luton airports, Brighton, Nottingham, Sheffield, Leicester, Leeds, Paris Eurostar

Victoria Gatwick airport (Express), Brighton, Canterbury

Waterloo Windsor, Winchester, Exeter, Plymouth

Getting Around

TO/FROM THE AIRPORTS

Gatwick

National Rail (www.nationalrail.co.uk) Regular train services to/from London Bridge (30 minutes, every 15 to 30 minutes), London King's Cross (55 minutes, every 15 to 30 minutes) and London Victoria (30 minutes, every 10 to 15 minutes). Fares vary, but allow £10 to £20 for a single.

EasyBus (www.easybus.co.uk) Runs 13-seater minibuses to Gatwick every 15 to 20 minutes from Victoria Coach Station (one way from £1.95). The service runs round the clock. Journey time averages 75 minutes.

Heathrow

The Underground (known as 'the tube') is the cheapest way of getting to Heathrow (£6, one hour, every three to nine minutes from around 5am to midnight, all night Friday and Saturday, with reduced frequency). Buy tickets at the station.

Heathrow Express (www.heathrowexpress.com; one way/return £27/42; 📶) and **Heathrow Connect** (☎0343 222 1234; www.tfl.gov.uk; adult single/open return £10.20/12.50), trains run every 30 minutes, to Paddington train station from around 5am and between 11pm and midnight. Heathrow Express trains take a mere 15 minutes to reach Paddington.

London City

Docklands Light Railway (DLR; www.tfl.gov.uk/dlr) stops at the London City Airport station (one way £2.80 to £3.30). Trains depart every eight to 10 minutes from just after 5.30am to 12.15am Monday to Saturday, and 7am to 11.15pm Sunday. The journey to Bank takes just over 20 minutes.

A metered black-cab trip to the City/Oxford St/Earl's Court costs about £25/35/50.

Luton

National Rail (www.nationalrail.co.uk) has 24-hour services (one way from £14, 26 to 50 minutes, departures every six minutes to one hour) from London St Pancras International to Luton Airport Parkway station, where an airport shuttle bus (one way/return £2.20/3.50) will take you to the airport in 10 minutes.

Airbus A1 (www.nationalexpress.com; one way from £11) runs over 60 times daily to London Victoria Coach Station (one way from £5), via Portman Sq, Baker St, St John's Wood, Finchley Rd and Golders Green. It takes around 1½ hours.

OYSTER CARD

The Oyster Card is a smart card on which you can store credit towards 'prepay' fares, as well as Travelcards valid for periods from a day to a year. Oyster Cards are valid across the entire public transport network in London. When entering a station, touch your card on a reader (which has a yellow circle with the image of an Oyster Card on it) and then touch again on your way out. The system will then deduct the appropriate amount of credit from your card. For bus journeys, you only need to touch once upon boarding. The benefit is that fares for Oyster Card users are lower than standard ones. If you are making many journeys during the day, you will never pay more than the appropriate Travelcard (peak or off-peak) once the daily 'price cap' has been reached. Oyster Cards can be bought (£5 refundable deposit required) and topped up at any Underground station, travel information centre or shop displaying the Oyster logo. To get your deposit back along with any remaining credit, simply return your Oyster Card at a ticket booth.

Stansted

Stansted Express (☎ 0345 600 7245; www.stanstedexpress.com; one way/return £17/29) rail service (45 minutes, every 15 to 30 minutes) links the airport and Liverpool St station. From the airport, the first train leaves at 5.30am, the last at 12.30am. Trains depart Liverpool St station from 4.40am (on some days at 3.40am) to 11.25pm.

Airbus A6 (☎ 0871 781 8181; www.nationalexpress.com; one way from £10) runs to Victoria Coach Station (around one hour to 1½ hours, every 20 minutes) via Marble Arch, Paddington, Baker St and Golders Green

EasyBus (www.easybus.co.uk) runs services to Baker St and Old St tube stations every 15 minutes. The journey (one way from £4.95) takes one hour from Old St or 1¼ hour from Baker St.

BICYCLE

Tens of thousands of Londoners cycle to work every day, and it is generally a good way to get around the city, although traffic can be intimidating for less-confident cyclists and it's important to keep your wits about you. The city has tried hard to improve the cycling infrastructure, by opening new 'cycle superhighways' for commuters, while the public bike hire scheme **Santander Cycles** (☎ 0343 222 6666; www.tfl.gov.uk/modes/cycling/santander-cycles) is particularly useful for visitors.

Transport for London (www.tfl.gov.uk) publishes 14 free maps of London's cycle routes.

CAR

Don't. As a visitor, it's very unlikely you'll need to drive in London. If you do, you'll incur an £11.50 per day congestion charge (7am to 6pm weekdays) simply to take a car into central London. If you're hiring a car to continue your trip around Britain, take the tube or train to a major airport and pick it up from there.

PUBLIC TRANSPORT

Boat

Thames Clipper (www.thamesclippers.com; all zones adult/child £9.90/4.95) boats run regular services between Embankment, Waterloo (London Eye), Blackfriars, Bankside (Shakespeare's Globe), London Bridge, Tower Bridge, Canary Wharf, Greenwich, North Greenwich and Woolwich piers from 6.55am to around midnight (from 9.29am weekends).

Bus

London's ubiquitous red double-decker buses operate from 5am to 11.30pm and afford great views of the city, but be aware that the going can be slow, thanks to traffic jams and dozens of commuters getting on and off at every stop.

Cash cannot be used on London's buses. Instead you must pay with an Oyster Card, Travelcard or a contactless payment card. Bus fares are a flat £1.50, no matter the distance travelled.

Underground & DLR

The London Underground ('the tube'; 11 colour-coded lines) is part of an integrated-transport system that also includes the **Docklands Light Railway** (DLR; www.tfl.gov.uk/dlr). It's the quickest and easiest way of getting around the city, if not the cheapest.

The first trains operate from around 5.30am Monday to Saturday and 6.45am Sunday. The last trains leave around 12.30am Monday to Saturday and 11.30pm Sunday.

Additionally, selected lines (the Victoria and Jubilee lines, plus most of the Piccadilly, Central and Northern lines) run all night on Friday and Saturday to get revellers home (on what is called the 'Night Tube'), with trains every 10 minutes or so.

Single fares cost from £2.40/4.90 with/without an Oyster Card.

TAXI

London's famous black cabs are available for hire when the yellow sign above the windscreen is lit; just stick your arm out to signal one. Fares are metered, with the flagfall charge of £2.60 (covering the first 235m during a weekday), rising by increments of 20p for each subsequent 117m.

Minicabs, which are licensed, are (usually) cheaper competitors. Unlike black cabs, minicabs cannot be hailed on the street; they must be hired by phone or directly from one of the minicab offices.

Windsor & Eton

POP 32,184

Facing each other across the Thames, with the massive bulk of Windsor Castle looming above, the twin riverside towns of Windsor and Eton have a rather surreal atmosphere. Windsor on the south bank sees the daily pomp and ritual of the changing of the guards, while schoolboys dressed in formal tailcoats wander the streets of tiny Eton to the north. **Eton College** (www.etoncollege.com) is England's most famous 'public' – as in private and fee-paying – boys' school, and arguably the most enduring symbol of the British class system. High-profile alumni include 19 British prime ministers, countless princes, kings and maharajas, Princes William and Harry, George Orwell, John Maynard Keynes, Bear Grylls and Eddie Redmayne. It can only be visited on guided tours, on summer Fridays, which take in the chapel and the Museum of Eton Life. Book online.

WORTH A TRIP

THE MAKING OF HARRY POTTER

Whether you're a fairweather fan or a full-on Potterhead, this studio **tour** (☎0345 084 0900; www.wbstudiotour.co.uk; Studio Tour Dr, Leavesden, WD25; adult/child £41/33; ⏱8.30am-10pm Jun-Sep, hours vary Oct-May; P 👪) is well worth the admittedly hefty admission price. You'll need to pre-book your visit for an allocated timeslot and then allow two- to three hours to do the complex justice. It starts with a short film before you're ushered through giant doors into the actual set of Hogwarts' Great Hall – the first of many 'wow' moments. It's near Watford, northwest of London.

★Windsor Castle CASTLE
(☎03031-237304; www.royalcollection.org.uk; Castle Hill; adult/child £21.20/12.30; ⏱9.30am-5.15pm Mar-Oct, 9.45am-4.15pm Nov-Feb, last admission 1¼hr before closing, all or part of castle subject to occasional closures; 👪; 🚌702 from London Victoria, 🚆London Waterloo to Windsor & Eton Riverside, 🚆London Paddington to Windsor & Eton Central via Slough) The world's largest and oldest continuously occupied fortress, Windsor Castle is a majestic vision of battlements and towers. Used for state occasions, it's one of the Queen's principal residences; when she's at home, the Royal Standard flies from the Round Tower.

Frequent, free guided tours introduce visitors to the castle precincts, divided into the Lower, Middle and Upper Wards. Free audio tours guide everyone through its lavish State Apartments and beautiful chapels; certain areas may be off limits if in use.

ℹ Information

Tourist Office (☎01753-743900; www.windsor.gov.uk; Old Booking Hall, Windsor Royal Shopping Arcade, Thames St, Windsor; ⏱10am-5pm Apr-Sep, to 4pm Oct-Mar) Tickets for attractions and events, plus guidebooks and walking maps.

ℹ Getting There & Away

The quickest rail route from London connects London Paddington with Windsor & Eton Central, opposite the castle, but you have to change at Slough (£10.50, 30 to 45 minutes). London Waterloo has slower but direct services to Windsor & Eton Riverside, on Dachet Rd (£10.50, 45 minutes to one hour).

Canterbury

☎01227 / POP 55,240

Canterbury tops the charts for English cathedral cities. Many consider the World Heritage–listed cathedral that dominates its centre to be one of Europe's finest, and the town's narrow medieval alleyways, riverside gardens and ancient city walls are a joy to explore.

Sights

★Canterbury Cathedral CATHEDRAL
(www.canterbury-cathedral.org; adult/concession/child £12.50/10.50/8.50, tours adult/child £5/4, audio guide £4/3; ⏱9am-5.30pm Mon-Sat, 12.30-2.30pm Sun) A rich repository of more than 1400 years of Christian history, the Church of England's mother ship is a truly extraordinary place with an absorbing history. This Gothic cathedral, the highlight of the city's World Heritage Sites, is southeast England's top tourist attraction as well as a place of worship. It's also the site of English history's most famous murder: Archbishop Thomas Becket was done in here in 1170. Allow at least two hours to do the cathedral justice.

Sleeping & Eating

Kipp's Independent Hostel HOSTEL £
(☎01227-786121; www.kipps-hostel.com; 40 Nunnery Fields; dm £12.50-24.50, s £22.50-40, d £40-68; @📶) Occupying a century-old red-brick town house in a quietish residential area less than a mile from the city centre, these superb backpacker digs enjoy a homey atmosphere, clean (though cramped) dorms, a good kitchen for self-caterers and a large TV lounge.

★ABode Canterbury BOUTIQUE HOTEL ££
(☎01227-766266; www.abodecanterbury.co.uk; 30-33 High St; r from £64; 📶) The 72 rooms at this super-central hotel, the only boutique hotel in town, are graded from 'comfortable' to 'fabulous' (via 'enviable'), and for the most part live up to their names. They come with features such as handmade beds, chesterfield sofas, tweed cushions and beautiful modern bathrooms. There's a splendid champagne bar, restaurant and tavern too.

Tiny Tim's Tearoom CAFE £
(www.tinytimstearoom.com; 34 St Margaret's St; mains £6-10; ⏱9.30am-5pm Mon-Sat, 10.30am-5pm Sun) It's no mean feat to be declared 'Kent Tearoom of the Year', but this swish 1930s cafe was awarded the accolade in 2015. It offers hungry shoppers big breakfasts

packed with Kentish ingredients, and tiers of cakes, crumpets, cucumber sandwiches and scones plastered in clotted cream. On busy shopping days you are guaranteed to queue for a table.

★Goods Shed MARKET ££
(☎01227-459153; www.thegoodsshed.co.uk; Station Rd West; mains £17.50-20; ⊙market 9am-7pm Tue-Sat, to 4pm Sun, restaurant noon-2.30pm & 6pm-last customer) Aromatic farmers market, food hall and fabulous restaurant rolled into one, this converted warehouse by the Canterbury West train station is a hit with everyone from self-caterers to sit-down gourmets. The chunky wooden tables sit slightly above the market hubbub but in full view of its appetite-whetting stalls. Daily specials exploit the freshest farm goodies the Garden of England offers.

Information

Tourist Office (☎01227-862162; www.canterbury.co.uk; 18 High St; ⊙9am-6pm Mon-Wed & Fri, to 8pm Thu, to 5pm Sat, 10am-5pm Sun; 📶) Located in the Beaney House of Art & Knowledge. Staff can help book accommodation, excursions and theatre tickets.

Getting There & Away

There are two train stations: Canterbury East for London Victoria and Canterbury West for London's Charing Cross/St Pancras stations. Canterbury connections:

London St Pancras (£38.70, one hour, hourly) High speed service.

London Victoria/Charing Cross (£32.60, 1¾ hours, two hourly)

Salisbury

☎01722 / POP 40,300

Centred on a majestic cathedral that's topped by the tallest spire in England, Salisbury makes an appealing Wiltshire base. It's been an important provincial city for more than a thousand years.

Sights

★Salisbury Cathedral CATHEDRAL
(☎01722 555120; www.salisburycathedral.org.uk; The Close; requested donation adult/child £7.50/3; ⊙9am-5pm Mon-Sat, noon-4pm Sun) England is endowed with countless stunning churches, but few can hold a candle to the grandeur and sheer spectacle of 13th-century Salisbury Cathedral. This early English Gothic-style structure has an elaborate exterior decorated with pointed arches and flying buttresses, and a sombre, austere interior designed to keep its congregation suitably pious. Its statuary and tombs are outstanding; don't miss the daily **tower tours** (adult/child £13.50/8.50; ⊙2-5 tours daily, May-Sep) and the cathedral's original, 13th-century copy of the **Magna Carta** (⊙9.30am-5pm Mon-Sat, noon-4pm Sun Apr-Oct, 9.30am-4.30pm Mon-Sat, noon-3.45pm Sun Nov-Mar).

Salisbury Museum MUSEUM
(☎01722-332151; www.salisburymuseum.org.uk; 65 The Close; adult/child £8/4; ⊙10am-5pm Mon-Sat year-round, plus noon-5pm Sun Jun-Sep) The hugely important archaeological finds here include the Stonehenge Archer, the bones of a man found in the ditch near the stone circle – one of the arrows found alongside probably killed him. With gold coins dating from 100 BC and a Bronze Age gold necklace, it's a powerful introduction to Wiltshire's prehistory.

Sleeping & Eating

Cathedral View B&B ££
(☎01722-502254; www.cathedral-viewbandb.co.uk; 83 Exeter St; s £85-95, d £99-140; P📶) Admirable attention to detail defines this Georgian town house, where miniature flower displays and home-baked biscuits sit in quietly elegant rooms. Breakfasts include prime Wiltshire sausages and the B&B's own bread

DON'T MISS

AVEBURY

While the tour buses usually head straight to Stonehenge, prehistoric purists make for **Avebury Stone Circle** (NT; ☎01672-539250; www.nationaltrust.org.uk; ⊙24hr; P) FREE. Though it lacks the dramatic trilithons ('gateways') of its sister site across the plain, Avebury is the largest stone circle in the world and a more rewarding place to visit simply because you can get closer to the giant boulders.

A large section of Avebury village is actually inside the circle, meaning you can sleep, or at least have lunch and a pint, inside the mystic ring.

Take bus 2 from Salisbury to Devizes (£6, one hour, hourly Monday to Saturday), where bus 49 runs hourly to Avebury (£3, 15 minutes).

and jam, while homemade lemon drizzle cake will be waiting for your afternoon tea.

★**Chapter House** INN £££
(☎01722-341277; www.thechapterhouseuk.com; 9 St Johns St; s £115-145, d £135-155; 📶) In this 800-year-old boutique beauty, wood panels and wildly wonky stairs sit beside duck-your-head beams. The cheaper bedrooms are swish but the posher ones are stunning, starring slipper baths and the odd heraldic crest. The pick is room 6, where King Charles is reputed to have stayed. Lucky him.

King's House CAFE £
(☎01722-332151; www.salisburymuseum.org.uk; 65 The Close; snacks from £4; ⏱11am-3pm Tue-Sat) A cafe just made for sightseeing: attached to Salisbury Museum, with fine views of the soaring spire of neighbouring Salisbury Cathedral from the flower-framed garden. A perfect spot to refuel on well-filled sandwiches and decadent cakes.

ℹ Information

Tourist Office (☎01722-342860; www.visitsalisbury.co.uk; Fish Row; ⏱9am-5pm Mon-Fri, 10am-4pm Sat, 10am-2pm Sun; 📶)

ℹ Getting There & Away

BUS

National Express (www.nationalexpress.com) services stop at Millstream Approach, near the train station. Direct services include the following:

Bath (£11, 1¼ hours, one daily)
Bristol (£6, 2¼ hours, one daily)
London Victoria via Heathrow (£10, three hours, three daily Monday to Saturday)

TRAIN

Salisbury's train station is half a mile northwest of the cathedral. Half-hourly connections include the following:

Bath (£10, one hour)
Bristol (£16, 1¼ hours)
London Waterloo (£42, 1½ hours)

Stonehenge

This compelling ring of monolithic stones has been attracting a steady stream of pilgrims, poets and philosophers for the last 5000 years and is easily Britain's most iconic archaeological site.

An ultramodern makeover at ancient **Stonehenge** (EH; ☎0370 333 1181; www.english-heritage.org.uk; near Amesbury; adult/child same-day tickets £19.50/11.70, advance booking £17.50/10.50; ⏱9am-8pm Jun-Aug, 9.30am-7pm Apr, May & Sep, 9.30am-5pm Oct-Mar; Ⓟ) has brought an impressive visitor centre and the closure of an intrusive road (now restored to grassland). The result is a far stronger sense of historical context, with dignity and mystery returned to an archaeological gem.

Stonehenge is one of Britain's great archaeological mysteries: despite countless theories about the site's purpose, ranging from a sacrificial centre to a celestial timepiece, in truth, no one knows for sure what drove prehistoric Britons to expend so much time and effort on its construction. Admission is through timed tickets – secure a place well in advance.

> **ℹ STONE CIRCLE ACCESS VISITS**
>
> Visitors to Stonehenge normally have to stay outside the stone circle. But on **Stone Circle Access Visits** (☎0370 333 0605; www.english-heritage.org.uk; adult/child £38.50/23.10) you get to wander round the core of the site, getting up-close views of the bluestones and trilithons. The walks take place in the evening or early morning, so the quieter atmosphere and the slanting sunlight add to the effect. Each visit only takes 26 people; to secure a place book at least two months in advance.

ℹ Getting There & Away

There is no public transport to the site. The **Stonehenge Tour** (☎01202-338420; www.thestonehengetour.info; adult/child/family £30/20/90) leaves Salisbury's train station half-hourly from June to August, and hourly from September to May.

Bath

☎01225 / POP 88,850

Britain is littered with beautiful cities, but precious few compare to Bath, founded on top of natural hot springs that led the Romans to build a magnificent bathhouse here. Bath's heyday was during the 18th century, when local entrepreneur Ralph Allen and the father-and-son architects John Wood the Elder and Younger turned this sleepy backwater into the toast of Georgian society, and constructed fabulous landmarks such as the Circus and Royal Crescent.

Sights

★Roman Baths HISTORIC BUILDING
(☎01225-477785; www.romanbaths.co.uk; Abbey Churchyard; adult/child/family £17.50/10.25/48; ⏰9.30am-5pm Nov-Feb, 9am-5pm Mar–mid-Jun, Sep & Oct, 9am-9pm mid-Jun–Aug) In typically ostentatious style, the Romans built a bathhouse complex above Bath's 46°C (115°F) hot springs. Set alongside a temple dedicated to the healing goddess Sulis-Minerva, the baths now form one of the world's best-preserved ancient Roman spas, and are encircled by 18th- and 19th-century buildings. To dodge the worst of the crowds avoid weekends, and July and August; buy fast-track tickets online to by-pass the queues. Saver tickets covering the Roman Baths and the Fashion Museum cost adult/child/family £22.50/12.25/58.

Royal Crescent ARCHITECTURE
Bath is famous for its glorious Georgian architecture, and it doesn't get any grander than this semicircular terrace of majestic town houses overlooking the green sweep of Royal Victoria Park. Designed by John Wood the Younger (1728–82) and built between 1767 and 1775, the houses appear perfectly symmetrical from the outside, but the owners were allowed to tweak the interiors, so no two houses are quite the same. **No 1 Royal Crescent** (☎01225-428126; www.no1royalcrescent.org.uk; 1 Royal Cres; adult/child/family £10.30/5.10/25.40; ⏰10am-5pm) offers you an intriguing insight into life inside.

Jane Austen Centre MUSEUM
(☎01225-443000; www.janeausten.co.uk; 40 Gay St; adult/child £12/6.20; ⏰9.45am-5.30pm Apr-Oct, 10am-4pm Sun-Fri, 9.45am-5.30pm Sat Nov-Mar) Bath is known to many as a location in Jane Austen's novels, including *Persuasion* and *Northanger Abbey*. Although Austen lived in Bath for only five years, from 1801 to 1806, she remained a regular visitor and a keen student of the city's social scene. Here, guides in Regency costumes regale you with Austen-esque tales as you tour memorabilia relating to the writer's life in Bath.

Sleeping

Bath YHA HOSTEL £
(☎0345 371 9303; www.yha.org.uk; Bathwick Hill; dm £23, d/q from £49/69; ⏰check-in 3-11pm; P@☎) Split across an Italianate mansion and modern annexes, this impressive hostel is a steep climb (or a short hop on bus U1) from the city. The listed building means the rooms are huge, and some have period features such as cornicing and bay windows.

★Three Abbey Green B&B ££
(☎01225-428558; www.threeabbeygreen.com; 3 Abbey Green; s £108-144, d £120-200, q £240; ☎) Rarely in Bath do you get somewhere as central as this Georgian town house with such spacious rooms. Elegant, 18th-century-style furnishings are teamed with swish wet-room bathrooms, while the opulent Lord Nelson suite features a vast four-poster bed. There's a fabulous vibe here – friendly, family-run and proud of it.

Hill House Bath B&B ££
(☎01225-920520; www.hillhousebath.co.uk; 25 Belvedere; r £115-135; P☎) When you walk through the door here it almost feels like you're staying with friends. The decor is quietly quirky: moustache-themed cushions, retro pictures and objets d'art abound.

Breakfasts are a cut above – how many other B&Bs add dollops of dill crème fraiche to homemade potato cakes, smoked salmon and poached egg?

★Grays Bath B&B £££
(☎01225-403020; www.graysbath.co.uk; 9 Upper Oldfield Park; r £115-245; P☎) Boutique treat Grays is a beautiful blend of modern, pared-down design and family treasures, many picked up from the owners' travels. All the rooms are individual: choose from floral, polka dot or maritime stripes. Perhaps the pick is the curving, six-sided room 12 in the attic, with partial city views.

Eating & Drinking

Sally Lunn's CAFE £
(☎01225-461634; www.sallylunns.co.uk; 4 North Pde Passage; mains £6-17, afternoon tea £8-40;

DON'T MISS

THE THERMAE BATH SPA

Taking a dip in the Roman Baths might be off limits, but you can still sample the city's curative waters at this fantastic modern **spa complex** (☎01225-331234; www.thermaebathspa.com; Hot Bath St; spa £36-40, treatments from £65; ⏰9am-9.30pm, last entry 7pm), housed in a shell of local stone and plate glass. The showpiece attraction is the open-air rooftop pool, where you can bathe with a backdrop of Bath's cityscape – a don't-miss experience best enjoyed at dusk.

Bath

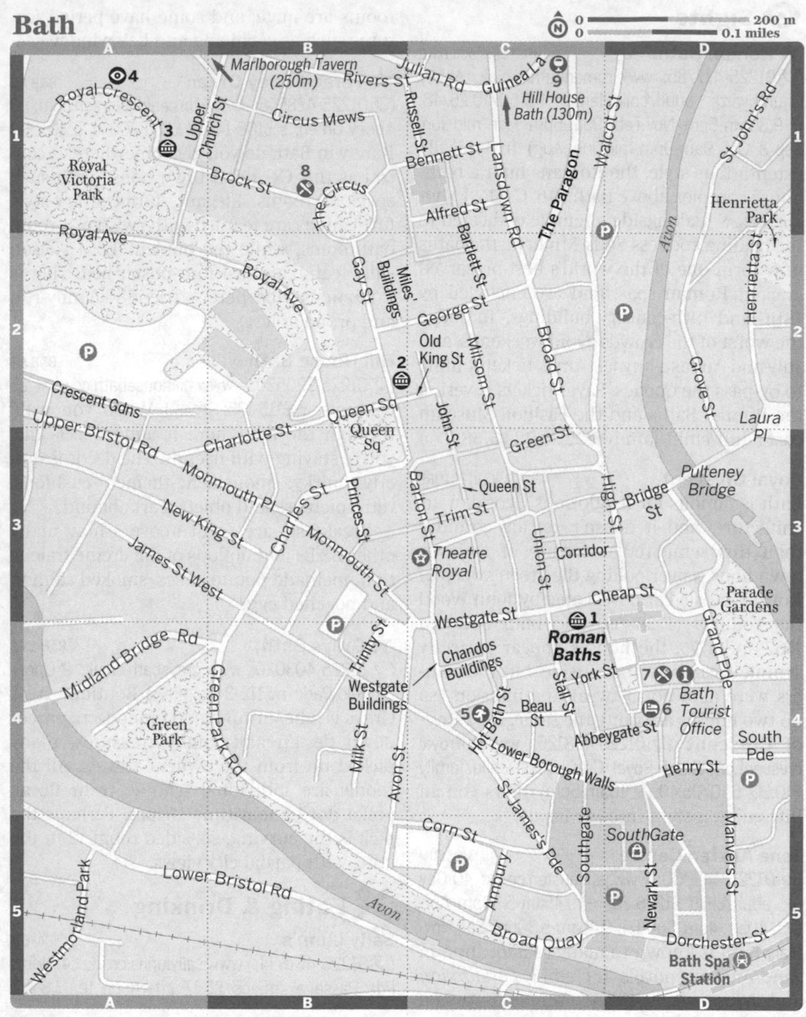

⏲10am-9pm) Eating a bun at Sally Lunn's is a Bath tradition. It's all about proper English tea here, brewed in bone-china teapots, with finger sandwiches and dainty cakes served by waitresses in frilly aprons.

The trademark Sally Lunn's bun is the house speciality – but there are heartier plates too, such as Welsh rarebit and 'Trencher' dishes (with the 'bun' acting as plate).

★The Circus MODERN BRITISH ££

(☎01225-466020; www.thecircusrestaurant.co.uk; 34 Brock St; mains lunch £12-15, dinner £16-23; ⏲10am-midnight Mon-Sat; ✎) Chef Ali Golden has turned this bistro into one of Bath's destination addresses. Her taste is for British dishes with a Continental twist, à la British food writer Elizabeth David: rabbit, Wiltshire lamb and West Country fish are all infused with herby flavours and rich sauces. It occupies an elegant town house near the Circus. Reservations recommended.

Marlborough Tavern GASTROPUB ££

(☎01225-423731; www.marlborough-tavern.com; 35 Marlborough Bldgs; mains £13-25; ⏲bar noon-11pm, food noon-2pm & 6-9.30pm) The queen of Bath's gastropubs has food that's closer to that of a fine-dining restaurant – smoked

Bath

Top Sights

Sights

Activities, Courses & Tours

Sleeping

Eating

Drinking & Nightlife

white-bean purée, and crab and ginger salad rather than bog-standard meat-and-two-veg. Chunky wooden tables and racks of wine behind the bar give it an exclusive, classy feel.

Canny diners head here in the early evening to get 25% off the food bill.

★Menu Gordon Jones MODERN BRITISH £££
(☎01225-480871; www.menugordonjones.co.uk; 2 Wellsway; 5-course lunch £50, 6-course dinner £55; ⏲12.30-2pm & 7-9pm Tue-Sat) If you enjoy dining with an element of surprise, then Gordon Jones' restaurant will be right up your culinary boulevard. Menus are dreamt up daily and showcase the chef's taste for experimental ingredients (expect mushroom mousse and Weetabix ice cream) and eye-catching presentation (test tubes and paper bags). It's superb value given the skill on show. Reservations essential.

★Star PUB
(☎01225-425072; www.abbeyales.co.uk; 23 The Vineyards, off the Paragon; ⏲noon-2.30pm & 5.30-11pm Mon-Fri, noon-midnight Sat, to 10.30pm Sun) Few pubs are registered relics, but the Star is just that, and it still has many of its 19th-century bar fittings. It's the brewery tap for Bath-based Abbey Ales; some ales are served in traditional jugs, and you can even ask for a pinch of snuff in the 'smaller bar'.

Information

Bath Tourist Office (☎01225-614420; www.visitbath.co.uk; 2 Terrace Walk; ⏲9.30am-5.30pm Mon-Sat, 10am-4pm Sun, closed Sun Nov-Jan) Offers advice and information. Also runs an accommodation booking service and sells a wide range of local books and maps.

Getting There & Away

Inter-city bus links through National Express (www.nationalexpress.com) are cheaper than the train – sample connections include those to London (£20, 2½ hours, hourly) and Bristol (£5, 45 minutes, two daily)

Train services are regular and reliable, although some intercity ones require a change at Bristol. Direct connections include those to London Paddington (from £35, 90 minutes, half-hourly), Cardiff Central (£21, one hour, hourly) and Bristol (£8, 15 minutes, half hourly).

Oxford

☎01865 / POP 161,300

One of the world's most famous university cities, Oxford is both beautiful and privileged. It's a wonderful place to wander: the elegant honey-toned buildings of the university's 38 colleges wrap around tranquil courtyards and narrow cobbled lanes where a studious calm reigns. But along with the rich history, tradition and energetic academic life, there is a busy, lively town beyond the college walls.

Sights

Not all of Oxford's colleges are open to the public, and visiting hours vary seasonally; check www.ox.ac.uk for details.

★Bodleian Library LIBRARY
(☎01865-287400; www.bodleian.ox.ac.uk/bodley; Catte St; Divinity School £2, with audio tour £4, guided tours £6-14; ⏲9am-5pm Mon-Sat, from 11am Sun) At least five kings, dozens of prime ministers and Nobel laureates, and luminaries such as Oscar Wilde, CS Lewis and JRR Tolkien have studied in Oxford's Bodleian Library, a magnificent survivor from the Middle Ages. Wander into its central 17th-century quad, and you can admire its ancient buildings for free, while it costs just £1 to enter the most impressive of these, the 15th-century Divinity School. To see the rest of the complex, though, you'll have to join a guided tour.

★Christ Church COLLEGE
(☎01865-276492; www.chch.ox.ac.uk; St Aldate's; adult/child Jul & Aug £10/9, Sep-Jun £8/7; ⏲10am-5pm Mon-Sat, from 2pm Sun, last admission 4.15pm) With its compelling combination of majestic architecture, literary

heritage and double identity as (parts of) Harry Potter's Hogwarts, Christ Church attracts tourists galore. Among Oxford's largest colleges – *the* largest, if you include its bucolic meadow – and proud possessor of its most impressive quad, plus a superb art gallery and even a cathedral, it was founded in 1525 by Cardinal Wolsey. It later became home to Lewis Carroll, whose picnic excursions with the then-dean's daughter gave us *Alice's Adventures in Wonderland*.

Ashmolean Museum MUSEUM
(☎01865-278000; www.ashmolean.org; Beaumont St; ⏰10am-5pm Tue-Sun, to 8pm last Fri of month) FREE Britain's oldest public museum, Oxford's wonderful Ashmolean Museum is surpassed only by the British Museum in London. It was established in 1683, when Elias Ashmole presented Oxford University with a collection of 'rarities' amassed by the well-travelled John Tradescant, gardener to Charles I. A new exhibition celebrates Ashmole's 400th birthday by displaying original treasures including the hat worn by the judge who presided over the trial of Charles I, and a mantle belonging to 'Chief Powhatan', the father of Pocahontas.

Magdalen College COLLEGE
(☎01865-276000; www.magd.ox.ac.uk; High St; adult/child £6/5; ⏰10am-7pm late Jun-late Sep, 1pm-dusk or 6pm late Sep-late Jun) Guarding access to a breathtaking expanse of private lawns, woodlands, river walks and even its own deer park, Magdalen ('mawd-lin'), founded in 1458, is one of Oxford's wealthiest and most beautiful colleges. Beyond its elegant Victorian gateway, you come to its medieval chapel and glorious 15th-century tower. From here, move on to the remarkable 15th-century **cloisters**, where the fantastic grotesques (carved figures) may have inspired CS Lewis' stone statues in *The Chronicles of Narnia*.

MESSING ABOUT ON THE RIVER

An unmissable Oxford experience, punting is all about sitting back and quaffing Pimms (the quintessential English summer drink) as you watch the city's glorious architecture float by. Which, of course, requires someone else to do the hard work – punting is far more difficult than it appears. If you decide to go it alone, a deposit is usually charged. Most punts hold five people including the punter. Hire them from **Magdalen Bridge Boathouse** (☎01865-202643; www.oxfordpunting.co.uk; High St; chauffeured 4-person punts per 30min £32, punt rental per hour £22; ⏰9.30am-dusk Feb-Nov) or **Cherwell Boat House** (☎01865-515978; www.cherwellboathouse.co.uk; 50 Bardwell Rd; punt rental per hour Mon-Fri £17, Sat & Sun £19; ⏰10am-dusk mid-Mar–mid-Oct).

Sleeping

Oxford YHA HOSTEL £
(☎01865-727275; www.yha.org.uk; 2a Botley Rd; dm/r £26/110; 📶) Set in a purpose-built modern building behind the station, Oxford's large YHA is a cut above other local hostels, with the feel of a chain hotel – and the prices too, for a private twin or double. The simple, comfortable four- and six-bed en suite dorms are better value. Abundant facilities include a restaurant, a library, a garden, a laundry, lounges and private lockers.

Tower House GUESTHOUSE ££
(☎01865-246828; www.towerhouseoxford.co.uk; 15 Ship St; s/d £100/125, d without bathroom £110; 📶) In a peaceful central location, this listed 17th-century town house holds eight good-value double rooms, simple but tastefully decorated. Some share bathrooms (not always on the same floor), while larger en suites also have attractive tongue-and-groove panelling. It donates profits to a community charity.

Acorn Guest House B&B ££
(☎01865-247998; www.oxford-acorn.co.uk; 260 Iffley Rd; s/d £50/75; P📶🐾) Spread through two adjoining houses, the friendly Acorn offers eight comfortable rooms at very reasonable prices, close to great pubs and restaurants and a short bus ride from the centre. Single rooms and 'budget' doubles share bathrooms; en suite facilities cost just £5 more. Everything has the feel of a family home, complete with resident labradoodle Annie (visiting dogs welcome).

Head of the River HOTEL £££
(☎01865-721600; www.headoftheriveroxford.co.uk; Folly Bridge, St Aldates; r incl breakfast £189; 📶) A genuine jewel among Oxford hotels, this large and characterful place, at Folly Bridge immediately south of Christ Church, was

DON'T MISS

BLENHEIM PALACE

One of the country's greatest stately homes, **Blenheim Palace** (☎01993-810530; www.blenheimpalace.com; Woodstock; adult/child £26/14.50, park & gardens only £16/7.40; ⏰palace 10.30am-5.30pm, park & gardens 9am-6.30pm or dusk; P) is a monumental baroque fantasy designed by Sir John Vanbrugh and Nicholas Hawksmoor between 1705 and 1722. Now a Unesco World Heritage Site, it's home to the 12th Duke of Marlborough. Highlights include the **Great Hall**, a vast space topped by 20m-high ceilings adorned with images of the first duke in battle; the various grand **state rooms** with their plush decor and priceless china cabinets; and the magnificent 55m **Long Library**. You can also visit the **Churchill Exhibition**, dedicated to the life, work and writings of Sir Winston, who was born at Blenheim in 1874. Blenheim Palace is near the town of Woodstock, a few miles northwest of Oxford. Take Stagecoach bus S3 (£3.20, 30 minutes) from Oxford, which stops outside Blenheim Palace.

originally a Thames-side warehouse. Each of its 20 good-sized rooms is individually decorated with contemporary flair, featuring exposed brickwork and/or tongue-and-groove panelling plus modern fittings, while rates include breakfast cooked to order in the (excellent) **pub** (⏰8am-10.30pm Sun-Thu, to 11.30pm Fri & Sat) downstairs.

Eating

★Edamamé JAPANESE £
(☎01865-246916; www.edamame.co.uk; 15 Holywell St; mains £7-10.50; ⏰11.30am-2.30pm Wed, 11.30am-2.30pm & 5-8.30pm Thu-Sat, noon-3.30pm Sun;) No wonder a constant stream of students squeeze in and out of this tiny diner – it's Oxford's top spot for delicious, gracefully simple Japanese cuisine. Changing noodle and curry specials include fragrant chicken miso ramen, tofu stir-fries, or mackerel with soba noodles; it only serves sushi or sashimi on Thursday evenings. No bookings; arrive early and be prepared to wait.

Covered Market MARKET £
(www.oxford-coveredmarket.co.uk; Market St; ⏰hours vary, some close Sun;) A haven for impecunious students, this indoor marketplace holds 20 restaurants, cafes and takeaways. Let anyone loose here, and something's sure to catch their fancy. Brown's no-frills cafe, famous for its apple pies, is the longest-standing veteran. Look out too for Georgina's, serving quiches and burgers upstairs; Burt's superlative cookies; two excellent pie shops; and good Thai and Chinese options.

Magdalen Arms BRITISH ££
(☎01865-243159; www.magdalenarms.co.uk; 243 Iffley Rd; mains £14-42; ⏰5-11pm Mon, from 10am Tue-Sat, 10am-10.30pm Sun;) A mile beyond Magdalen Bridge, this extra-special neighbourhood gastropub has won plaudits from the national press. A friendly, informal spot, it offers indoor and outdoor space for drinkers, and dining tables further back. From vegetarian specials such as broad-bean tagliatelle to the fabulous sharing-size steak-and-ale pie – well, it's a stew with a suet-crust lid, really – everything is delicious, with gutsy flavours.

Oxford Kitchen MODERN BRITISH £££
(☎01865-511149; www.theoxfordkitchen.co.uk; 215 Banbury Rd; set menus £22.50-65; ⏰noon-2.30pm & 6-9.30pm Tue-Sat) Oxford's not renowned for high-end, cutting-edge cuisine, so if you're crying out for a few foams, mousses, funny-shaped plates and bumpy slates, make haste to Summertown's contemporary Oxford Kitchen.

We jest; its modern British food, served as set menus ranging from £22.50 for a weekday lunch up to the £65 weekend tasting menu, is superb.

Drinking & Nightlife

Turf Tavern PUB
(☎01865-243235; www.turftavern-oxford.co.uk; 4-5 Bath Pl; ⏰11am-11pm;) Squeezed down an alleyway and subdivided into endless nooks and crannies, this medieval rabbit warren dates from around 1381. The definitive Oxford pub, this is where Bill Clinton famously 'did not inhale'; other patrons have included Oscar Wilde, Stephen Hawking and Margaret Thatcher.

Home to a fabulous array of real ales and ciders, it's always pretty crowded, but there's outdoor seating too.

The Perch PUB

(☎01865-728891; www.the-perch.co.uk; Binsey Lane, Binsey; ⏲10.30am-11pm Mon-Sat, to 10.30pm Sun;) This thatched and wonderfully rural 800-year-old inn can be reached by road, but it's more enjoyable to walk half an hour upstream along the Thames Path, then follow an enchanting footpath punctuated by floral pergolas. Its huge willow-draped garden is an idyllic spot for a pint or two of Fullers, but summer crowds can mean a long wait for food.

ℹ Information

Tourist Office (☎01865-686430; www.experienceoxfordshire.org; 15-16 Broad St; ⏲9am-5.30pm Mon-Sat, 10am-4pm Sun Jul & Aug, 9.30am-5pm Mon-Sat, 10am-4pm Sun Sep-Jun) Covers the whole of Oxfordshire and sells Oxford guidebooks, makes reservations for local accommodation and walking tours, and sells tickets for events and attractions.

ℹ Getting There & Away

Oxford's chaotic outdoor **bus station** (Gloucester Green) is in the centre near the corner of Worcester and George Sts. Destinations:

Bath (£11.30, two hours)

Cambridge (X5; £13.50, 3¾ hours)

London Victoria (Oxford Tube/X90; £15, 1¾ hours)

Oxford's main train station is just west of the city centre, roughly 10 minutes' walk from Broad St. Destinations include the following:

London Marylebone (£7 to £29, 1¼ hours)

London Paddington (£9.50 to £26.50, 1¼ hours)

The Cotswolds

Undulating gracefully across six counties, the Cotswolds region is a delightful tangle of golden villages, thatched cottages, evocative churches and honey-coloured mansions. In 1966 it was designated an Area of Outstanding Natural Beauty, surpassed for size in England only by the Lake District.

Travel by public transport requires careful planning and patience; for the greatest flexibility, and the potential to get off the beaten track, having your own car is unbeatable. Alternatively, the **Cotswolds Discoverer One-Day Pass** (www.cotswoldsaonb.org.uk/visiting-and-exploring; adult/child £10/5) gives you unlimited travel on participating bus or train routes.

Stratford-upon-Avon

☎01789 / POP 27,455

The author of some of the most quoted lines ever written in the English language, William Shakespeare was born in Stratford in 1564 and died here in 1616. Experiences linked to his life in this unmistakably Tudor town range from the touristy (medieval recreations and Bard-themed tearooms) to the humbling (Shakespeare's modest grave in Holy Trinity Church) and the sublime (taking in a play by the world-famous Royal Shakespeare Company).

Sights

★Shakespeare's Birthplace HISTORIC BUILDING

(☎01789-204016; www.shakespeare.org.uk; Henley St; adult/child £17.50/11.50; ⏲9am-5pm Apr-Aug, to 4.30pm Sep & Oct, 10am-3.30pm Nov-Mar) Start your Shakespeare quest at the house where the renowned playwright was born in 1564 and spent his childhood days. John Shakespeare owned the house for a period of 50 years. William, as the eldest surviving son, inherited it upon his father's death in 1601 and spent his first five years of marriage here. Behind a modern facade, the house has restored Tudor rooms, live presentations from famous Shakespearean characters and an engaging exhibition on Stratford's favourite son.

★Shakespeare's New Place HISTORIC SITE

(☎01789-338536; www.shakespeare.org.uk; cnr Chapel St & Chapel Lane; adult/child £12.50/8; ⏲10am-5pm Apr-Aug, to 4.30pm Sep & Oct, to 3.30pm Nov-Feb) When Shakespeare retired, he swapped the bright lights of London for a comfortable town house at New Place, where he died of unknown causes in April 1616. The house was demolished in 1759, but an attractive Elizabethan knot garden occupies part of the grounds. A major restoration project has uncovered Shakespeare's kitchen and incorporated new exhibits in a reimagining of the house as it would have been. You can also explore the adjacent Nash's House, where Shakespeare's granddaughter Elizabeth lived.

WORTH A TRIP

GLASTONBURY

To many people, Glastonbury is synonymous with the **Glastonbury Festival of Contemporary Performing Arts** (www.glastonburyfestivals.co.uk; tickets from £238; ⌚Jun or Jul), a majestic (and frequently mud-soaked) extravaganza of music, theatre, dance, cabaret, carnival, spirituality and general all-round weirdness that's been held on farmland in Pilton, just outside Glastonbury, since 1970 (bar the occasional off-year to let the farm recover).

The town owes much of its spiritual fame to nearby **Glastonbury Tor** (NT; ⌚24hr) FREE, a grassy hump about a mile from town, topped by the ruins of St Michael's Church. According to local legend, the tor is said to be the mythical Isle of Avalon, King Arthur's last resting place. It's also allegedly one of the world's great spiritual nodes, marking the meeting point of many mystical lines of power known as ley lines.

There is no train station in Glastonbury, but buses run from Wells (£3.70, 15 minutes, several times per hour) and Taunton (£5.70, 1½ hours, four to seven daily Monday to Saturday).

Shakespeare's School Room HISTORIC SITE
(☎01789-203170; www.shakespearesschoolroom.org; King Edward VI School, Church St; adult/child £8/5; ⌚11am-5pm) Shakespeare's alma mater, King Edward VI School (still a prestigious grammar school today), incorporates a vast black-and-white timbered building, dating from 1420, that was once the town's guildhall, where Shakespeare's father John served as bailiff (mayor). In the Bard's former classroom, you can sit in on mock-Tudor lessons, watch a short film and test yourself on Tudor-style homework.

It's adjacent to the 1269-built **Guild Chapel** (www.guildchapel.org.uk; cnr Chapel Lane & Church St; by donation; ⌚10am-4pm).

Anne Hathaway's Cottage HISTORIC BUILDING
(☎01789-338532; www.shakespeare.org.uk; Cottage Lane, Shottery; adult/child £12.50/8; ⌚9am-5pm Apr-Aug, to 4.30pm Sep & Oct, 10am-3.30pm Nov-Mar) Before tying the knot with Shakespeare, Anne Hathaway lived in Shottery, 1 mile west of the centre of Stratford, in this delightful thatched farmhouse. As well as period furniture, it has gorgeous gardens and an orchard and arboretum, with examples of all the trees mentioned in Shakespeare's plays. A footpath (no bikes allowed) leads to Shottery from Evesham Pl. The **City Sightseeing** (☎01789-299123; www.city-sightseeing.com; adult/child 24hr £16.82/8.41, 48hr £25.52/13; ⌚9.30am-5pm Apr-Sep, to 4pm Oct-Mar) bus stops here.

Holy Trinity Church CHURCH
(☎01789-266316; www.stratford-upon-avon.org; Old Town; Shakespeare's grave adult/child £3/2; ⌚9am-6pm Mon-Sat, 12.30-5pm Sun Apr-Sep, reduced hours rest of year) The final resting place of the Bard, where he was also baptised and where he worshipped, is said to be the most visited parish church in England. Inside are handsome 16th- and 17th-century tombs (particularly in the Clopton Chapel), some fabulous carvings on the choir stalls and, of course, the grave of William Shakespeare, with its ominous epitaph: 'cvrst be he yt moves my bones'.

Sleeping

Stratford-upon-Avon YHA HOSTEL £
(☎0345 371 9661; www.yha.org.uk; Welleshourne Rd, Alveston; dm/d/glamping from £13/58/49; P📶) Set in a large 200-year-old mansion 1.5 miles east of the town centre, this superior 134-bed hostel attracts travellers of all ages. Of its 32 rooms and dorms, 16 are en suite. There's a canteen, bar and kitchen. Buses 6 and X17 (£3.50, 12 minutes, up to two per hour) run here from Bridge St. Wi-fi is in common areas only. Tepee-style glamping tents and hutlike camping pods with kitchenettes are available from April to September.

Townhouse BOUTIQUE HOTEL £££
(☎01789-262222; www.stratfordtownhouse.co.uk; 16 Church St; d incl breakfast from £130; 📶) Some of the dozen rooms at this exquisite hotel have free-standing claw-foot bathtubs, and all have luxurious bedding and Temple Spa toiletries. The building is a centrally located 400-year-old gem with a first-rate **restaurant** (mains £9.50-24; ⌚kitchen noon-3pm & 5-10pm Mon-Fri, noon-10pm Sat, to 8pm Sun,

bar 8am-midnight Mon-Sat, to 10.30pm Sun; 📶). Light sleepers should avoid room 1, nearest the bar. There's a minimum two-night stay on weekends.

Eating & Drinking

Sheep St is rammed with upmarket eating options, mostly aimed at theatre goers (look out for good-value pre-theatre menus). Picnickers will find some delightful spots in the surrounding countryside, including the grounds of Mary Arden's Farm.

Fourteas CAFE £
(☎01789-293908; www.thefourteas.co.uk; 24 Sheep St; dishes £4.60-7.55, afternoon tea with/without Prosecco £20/15; ⏲9.30am-5pm Mon-Sat, 11am-4.30pm Sun) Breaking with Stratford's Shakespearean theme, this tearoom takes the 1940s as its inspiration with beautiful old teapots, framed posters and staff in period costume. As well as premium loose-leaf teas and homemade cakes, there are all-day breakfasts, soups, sandwiches (including a chicken and bacon 'Churchill club') and lavish afternoon teas.

Edward Moon's BRITISH ££
(☎01789-267069; www.edwardmoon.com; 9 Chapel St; mains £12.25-17; ⏲noon-2.30pm & 5-9.30pm Mon-Fri, noon-3pm & 5-10pm Sat, noon-3pm & 5-9pm Sun; 👪) Named after a famous travelling chef who cooked up the flavours of home for the British colonial service, this snug independent restaurant serves hearty English dishes, such as steak-and-ale pie and meltingly tender lamb shank with redcurrant gravy. Kids get a two-course menu for £6.95.

> **SHAKESPEARE HISTORIC HOMES**
>
> Five of the most important buildings associated with Shakespeare – Shakespeare's Birthplace (p142), Shakespeare's New Place (p142), **Hall's Croft** (☎01789-338533; www.shakespeare.org.uk; Old Town; adult/child £8.50/5.50; ⏲10am-5pm Apr-Aug, to 4.30pm Sep & Oct, 11am-3.30pm Nov-Feb), Anne Hathaway's Cottage (p143) and **Mary Arden's Farm** (☎01789-338535; www.shakespeare.org.uk; Station Rd, Wilmcote; adult/child £15/10; ⏲10am-5pm Apr-Aug, to 4.30pm Sep & Oct; 👪) – contain museums that form the core of the visitor experience at Stratford. All are run by the Shakespeare Birthplace Trust (www.shakespeare.org.uk). A Full Story ticket (adult/child £22/14.50) covering all five properties is available online or at the sites and provides up to a 60% discount off individual admission prices.

★Salt BRITISH £££
(☎01789-263566; www.salt-restaurant.co.uk; 8 Church St; 2-/3-course menus lunch £33.50/37, dinner £37/45; ⏲noon-2pm & 6.30-10pm Wed-Sat, noon-2pm Sun) Stratford's gastronomic star is this intimate, beam-ceilinged bistro. In the semi-open kitchen, owner-chef Paul Foster produces stunning creations influenced by the seasons: spring might see glazed parsley root with chicory and black-truffle shavings, onglet of beef with malted artichoke, cured halibut with oyster and apple emulsion, and sea-buckthorn mille-feuille with fig and goat's-milk ice cream.

★Old Thatch Tavern PUB
(www.oldthatchtavernstratford.co.uk; Greenhill St; ⏲11.30am-11pm Mon-Sat, from noon Sun; 📶) To truly appreciate Stratford's olde-worlde atmosphere, join the locals for a pint at the town's oldest pub. Built in 1470, this thatch-roofed treasure has great real ales and a gorgeous summertime courtyard.

Entertainment

★Royal Shakespeare Company THEATRE
(RSC; ☎box office 01789-403493; www.rsc.org.uk; Waterside; tours adult £7-9, child £4.50-5, tower adult/child £2.50/1.25; ⏲tour times vary, tower 10am-5pm Sun-Fri, 10am-12.15pm & 2-5pm Sat mid-Mar–mid-Oct, 10am-4.30pm Sun-Fri, to 12.15pm Sat mid-Oct–mid-Mar) Stratford has two grand stages run by the world-renowned Royal Shakespeare Company – the **Royal Shakespeare Theatre** and the **Swan Theatre** (☎01789-403493; www.rsc.org.uk) on Waterside – as well as the smaller **Other Place** (☎box office 01789-403493; www.rsc.org.uk; 22 Southern Lane). The theatres have witnessed performances by such legends as Lawrence Olivier, Richard Burton, Judi Dench, Helen Mirren, Ian McKellan and Patrick Stewart. Various one-hour guided tours take you behind the scenes.

WORTH A TRIP

WARWICK

Regularly namechecked by Shakespeare, the town of Warwick is a treasure-house of medieval architecture. It is dominated by the soaring turrets of **Warwick Castle** (☎01926-495421; www.warwick-castle.com; Castle Lane; castle adult/child £27/24, castle & dungeon £32/28; ⏲10am-5pm Apr-Sep, to 4pm Oct-Mar; P), founded in 1068 by William the Conqueror, and later the ancestral home of the Earls of Warwick. It's now been transformed into a major tourist attraction by the owners of Madame Tussauds, with family-friendly activities and waxworks populating the private apartments.

Stagecoach bus 18A goes to Stratford-upon-Avon (£4.30, 45 minutes, half-hourly). Trains run to Birmingham (£6.80, 40 minutes, half-hourly), Stratford-upon-Avon (£6.60, 30 minutes, hourly) and London Marylebone (£31.80, 1½ hours, every 20 minutes). Stagecoach bus X18 runs to Stratford-upon-Avon (£5.40, 40 minutes, two per hour Monday to Saturday, hourly Sunday).

Trains run to Stratford-upon-Avon (£6.90, 30 minutes, every two hours) and London Marylebone (£34, 1½ hours, every 30 minutes; some require a change in Leamington Spa).

Information

The **tourist office** (☎01789-264293; www.shakespeares-england.co.uk; Bridge Foot; ⏲9am-5.30pm Mon-Sat, 10am-4pm Sun) is just west of Clopton Bridge.

Getting There & Away

BUS

National Express coaches and other bus companies run from Stratford's Riverside bus station (behind the Stratford Leisure Centre on Bridgeway). National Express services include the following:

London Victoria (£13.10, three hours, two direct services per day)

Oxford (£10.10, 1¼ hours, one per day)

TRAIN

From Stratford-upon-Avon train station, London Midland runs to Birmingham (£8, 50 minutes, two per hour), Chiltern Railways serves London Marylebone (£30.40, 2¾ hours, up to two per hour) with a change in Leamington Spa, and East Midlands runs to Warwick (£6.90, 30 minutes, every two hours).

Cambridge

☎01223 / POP 123,900

Abounding with exquisite architecture, oozing history and tradition, and renowned for its quirky rituals, Cambridge is a university town extraordinaire. The tightly packed core of ancient colleges, the picturesque 'Backs' (college gardens) leading on to the river and the leafy green meadows that surround the city give it a far more tranquil appeal than its historic rival Oxford.

Sights

Cambridge University comprises 31 colleges, though not all are open to the public. Opening hours are only a rough guide, so contact the colleges or the tourist office (p147) for more information.

★King's College Chapel — CHURCH

(☎01223-331212; www.kings.cam.ac.uk; King's Pde; adult/child £9/6; ⏲9.30am-3.15pm Mon-Sat, 1.15-2.30pm Sun term time, 9.30am-4.30pm daily university holidays) In a city crammed with showstopping buildings, this is a scene-stealer. Grandiose 16th-century King's College Chapel is one of England's most extraordinary examples of Gothic architecture. Its inspirational, intricate 80m-long fan-vaulted ceiling is the world's largest and soars upwards before exploding into a series of stone fireworks. This hugely atmospheric space is a fitting stage for the chapel's world-famous choir; hear it sing during the free and magnificent **evensong** in term time (5.30pm Monday to Saturday; 10.30am and 3.30pm Sunday).

★Trinity College — COLLEGE

(☎01223-338400; www.trin.cam.ac.uk; Trinity St; adult/child £3/1; ⏲10am-4.30pm Jul-Oct, to 3.30pm Nov-Jun) The largest of Cambridge's colleges, Trinity offers an extraordinary Tudor gateway, an air of supreme elegance and a sweeping Great Court – the largest of its kind in the world. It also boasts the renowned and suitably musty **Wren Library** (⏲noon-2pm Mon-Fri year-round, plus 10.30am-12.30pm Sat term time) FREE, containing 55,000 books published before 1820 and more than 2500 manuscripts. Works

DON'T MISS

PUNTING ON THE BACKS

Gliding a self-propelled punt along the Backs is a blissful experience – once you've got the hang of it. It can also be a manic challenge for beginners. If you wimp out, you can always opt for a relaxing chauffeured punt.

Punt hire costs around £24 to £30 per hour; 45-minute chauffeured trips of the Backs cost about £14 to £20 per person. One-way trips to Grantchester (1½ hours) start at around £28 per person.

include those by Shakespeare, St Jerome, Newton and Swift – and AA Milne's original *Winnie the Pooh;* both Milne and his son, Christopher Robin, were graduates.

Fitzwilliam Museum MUSEUM
(www.fitzmuseum.cam.ac.uk; Trumpington St; by donation; ⌚10am-5pm Tue-Sat, from noon Sun) FREE Fondly dubbed 'the Fitz' by locals, this colossal neoclassical pile was one of the first public art museums in Britain, built to house the fabulous treasures that the seventh Viscount Fitzwilliam bequeathed to his old university. Expect Roman and Egyptian grave goods, artworks by many of the great masters and some quirkier collections: banknotes, literary autographs, watches and armour.

The Backs PARK
Behind the Cambridge colleges' grandiose facades and stately courts, a series of gardens and parks line up beside the river. Collectively known as the Backs, the tranquil green spaces and shimmering waters offer unparalleled views of the colleges and are often the most enduring image of Cambridge for visitors. The picture-postcard snapshots of student life and graceful bridges can be seen from the riverside pathways and pedestrian bridges – or from the comfort of a chauffeured punt.

Sleeping

Cambridge YHA HOSTEL £
(☎0345-371 9728; www.yha.org.uk; 97 Tenison Rd; dm/d £25/60; @📶) A smart, friendly and deservedly popular hostel with compact dorms and good facilities. Handily, it's very near the train station. The choice of rooms for families is particularly good.

★Varsity BOUTIQUE HOTEL £££
(☎01223-306030; www.thevarsityhotel.co.uk; Thompson's Lane; d £195-360; ❄@📶) In the 44 individually styled rooms of riverside Varsity, wondrous fixtures and furnishings (such as roll-top baths and travellers' trunks) sit beside floor-to-ceiling glass windows, espresso machines and smartphone docks. The views out over the colleges from the roof terrace are utterly sublime. Valet parking costs £20 a night.

Eating & Drinking

Pint Shop MODERN BRITISH ££
(☎01223-352293; www.pintshop.co.uk; 10 Peas Hill; snacks from £5, mains £12-22; ⌚noon-10pm Mon-Fri, 11am-10.30pm Sat, 11am-10pm Sun) Popular Pint Shop's vision is to embrace eating and drinking equally. To this end, it's both a busy bar specialising in draught craft beer and a stylish dining room serving classy versions of traditional grub (dry-aged steaks, gin-cured sea trout, coal-baked fish and meat kebabs). All in all, hard to resist.

Kingston Arms PUB FOOD ££
(☎01223-319414; www.facebook.com/pg/KingstonArms; 33 Kingston St; mains £8-14; ⌚5-11pm Mon-Thu, noon-midnight Fri & Sat, to 11pm Sun; 📶) Great gastropub grub – from roasts to homemade risotto and gourmet sausages – keeps stomachs satisfied at the award-winning Kingston. More than 10 real ales, stacked board games and a students-meet-locals clientele deliver a contemporary Cambridge vibe. It's 1 mile southeast of the centre.

★Midsummer House MODERN BRITISH £££
(☎01223-369299; www.midsummerhouse.co.uk; Midsummer Common; 5/8 courses £69/145; ⌚noon-1.30pm Wed-Sat, 7-9pm Tue-Sat; ☎) At the region's top table, chef Daniel Clifford's double-Michelin-starred creations are distinguished by depth of flavour and immense technical skill. Savour transformations of pumpkin (into velouté), mackerel (with Jack Daniels), quail, sea scallops and grouse, before a coriander white-chocolate dome, served with coconut, mango and jasmine rice.

Eagle PUB

(☎01223-505020; www.eagle-cambridge.co.uk; Bene't St; ⏰11am-11pm Sun-Thu, to midnight Fri & Sat; 📶👪) Cambridge's most famous pub has loosened the tongues and pickled the grey cells of many an illustrious academic, among them Nobel Prize–winning scientists Crick and Watson, who discussed their research into DNA here (note the blue plaque by the door). Fifteenth-century, wood-panelled and rambling, the Eagle's cosy rooms include one with WWII airmen's signatures on the ceiling. The food (mains £10 to 15), served all day, is good too; it includes some thoughtful options for children.

Information

Visit Cambridge (www.visitcambridge.org)

Getting There & Away

Buses run by **National Express** (☎0871 781 8181; www.nationalexpress.com; Parkside; 📶) leave from Parkside. Direct services include the following:

Heathrow (£31, 2¾ hours, hourly)

London Victoria (£11, 2½ hours, every two hours)

Oxford (£14, 3½ hours, hourly)

The train station is 1.5 miles southeast of the centre. Direct services include the following:

London King's Cross (£25, one hour, two to four per hour)

Stansted Airport (£11, 35 minutes, every 30 minutes)

York

☎01904 / POP 152,841

No other city in northern England says 'medieval' quite like York, a city of extraordinary cultural and historical wealth that has lost little of its pre-industrial lustre. A magnificent circuit of 13th-century walls encloses a medieval spider's web of narrow streets. At its heart lies the immense, awe-inspiring York Minster; York's long history and rich heritage is woven into virtually every brick and beam.

Sights

Don't miss the chance to walk York's **City Walls** (www.yorkwalls.org.uk), which follow the line of the original Roman walls and give a whole new perspective on the city. Allow 1½ to two hours for the full circuit of 4.5 miles or, if you're pushed for time, the short stretch from Bootham Bar to Monk Bar is worth doing for the views of the minster.

★York Minster CATHEDRAL

(☎01904-557200; www.yorkminster.org; Deangate; adult/child £10/free, incl tower £15/5; ⏰9am-6pm Mon-Sat, 12.30-6pm Sun, last admission 4.30pm Mon-Sat, 3pm Sun) York Minster is the largest medieval cathedral in northern Europe, and one of the world's most beautiful Gothic buildings. Seat of the archbishop of York, primate of England, it is second in importance only to Canterbury, seat of the primate of *all* England – the separate titles were created to settle a debate over the true centre of the English Church. Note that the quire, east end and undercroft close in preparation for evening service around the time of last admission.

★Jorvik Viking Centre MUSEUM

(☎ticket reservations 01904-615505; www.jorvik-viking-centre.co.uk; Coppergate; adult/child £11/8; ⏰10am-5pm Apr-Oct, to 4pm Nov-Mar) Interactive multimedia exhibits aimed at bringing history to life often achieve exactly the opposite, but the much-hyped Jorvik manages to pull it off with aplomb. It's a smells-and-all reconstruction of the Viking settlement unearthed here during excavations in the late 1970s, experienced via a 'time-car' monorail that transports you through 9th-century Jorvik (the Viking name for York). You can reduce time waiting in line by booking timed-entry tickets online; there is almost always a queue to get in.

★National Railway Museum MUSEUM

(www.nrm.org.uk; Leeman Rd; ⏰10am-6pm Apr-Oct, to 5pm Nov-Mar; P👪) FREE York's National Railway Museum – the biggest in the world, with more than 100 locomotives – is well presented and crammed with fascinating stuff. It is laid out on a vast scale and is housed in a series of giant railway sheds – allow at least two hours to do it justice. The museum also now includes a high-tech simulator experience of riding on the **Mallard** (£4), which set the world speed record for a steam locomotive in 1938 (126mph).

The Shambles STREET

The Shambles takes its name from the Saxon word *shamel,* meaning 'slaughterhouse' – in 1862 there were 26 butcher shops on this street. Today the butchers are long gone, but this narrow cobbled lane, lined with 15th-century Tudor buildings that overhang so much they seem to meet above your head, is the most picturesque in Britain, and one of the most visited in Europe, often filled with visitors wielding cameras.

Yorkshire Museum MUSEUM

(www.yorkshiremuseum.org.uk; Museum St; adult/child £7.50/free; ⏲10am-5pm) Most of York's Roman archaeology is hidden beneath the medieval city, so the superb displays in the Yorkshire Museum are invaluable if you want to get an idea of what Eboracum Roman York was like. There are maps and models, funerary monuments, mosaic floors and wall paintings, and a 4th-century bust of Emperor Constantine. Kids will enjoy the dinosaur exhibit, centred on giant ichthyosaur fossils from Yorkshire's Jurassic coast.

There are excellent galleries dedicated to Viking and medieval York as well, including priceless artefacts such as the beautifully decorated 9th-century York helmet.

Tours

★Brewtown BEER TOUR

(☎01904-636666; www.brewtowntours.co.uk; £60; ⏲11.30am-5pm) These craft-brewery minivan tours are a fuss-free way to get behind the scenes at Yorkshire's smaller breweries, some of which only open to the public for these tours. Owner Mark runs different routes (around York, Malton or Leeds) depending on the day of the week; each tour visits three breweries with tastings along the way, and sometimes even beer-pairing nibbles.

Ghost Hunt of York WALKING

(☎01904-608700; www.ghosthunt.co.uk; adult/child £6/4; ⏲tours 7.30pm) The kids will just love this award-winning and highly entertaining 75-minute tour laced with authentic ghost stories. It begins at the top end of the Shambles, whatever the weather (it's never cancelled), and there's no need to book – just turn up and wait till you hear the handbell ringing…

Sleeping

Beds can be hard to find in midsummer, even with high-season rates. The tourist office offers an accommodation booking service, which costs £4.

Safestay York HOSTEL £

(☎01904-627720; www.safestay.com; 88-90 Micklegate; dm/tw/f from £15/60/75; @📶) Housed in a Grade I Georgian townhouse, this is a large boutique hostel with colourful decor and good facilities including a bar with pool table. Rooms are mostly en suite and have a bit more character than you'd usually find in hostels, with the added intrigue of plaques outside doors describing the history of different rooms in the house.

Fort HOSTEL £

(☎01904-620222; www.thefortyork.co.uk; 1 Little Stonegate; dm/d from £22/85; 📶) This boutique hostel showcases the interior design of young British talents, creating affordable accommodation with a dash of character and flair. There are six- and eight-bed dorms, along with five doubles, but don't expect a peaceful retreat – it's central and there's a lively club downstairs (earplugs are provided!). Towels are included, as well as free tea, coffee and laundry.

★The Lawrance APARTMENT ££

(☎01904-239988; www.thelawrance.com/york/; 74 Micklegate; 1-/2-bed apt from £75/160; ❄📶) Set back from the road in a huddle of old red-brick buildings that once formed a factory, the Lawrance is an excellent find: super-swish serviced apartments with all mod cons on the inside and heritage character on the outside. Some apartments are split-level and all are comfy and spacious, with leather sofas, flatscreen TVs and luxurious fixtures and fittings.

Dairy Guesthouse B&B ££

(☎01904-639367; www.dairyguesthouse.co.uk; 3 Scarcroft Rd; s/d/f from £70/80/100; P📶) This Victorian home offers tasteful rooms that mesh fresh decor and five-star bathrooms with original features like cast-iron fireplaces. The flower- and plant-filled courtyard is a lovely place to pause for a rest after a day of sightseeing. It leads to a pair of cottage-style rooms, which are not as nice as those inside but are more private.

St Raphael B&B ££

(☎01904-645028; www.straphaelguesthouse.co.uk; 44 Queen Anne's Rd; d/tr/q £99/139/169; P📶) Set in a historic house with that distinctively English half-timbered look, this B&B has a great central location, seven bright, airy and simple bedrooms, and the smell of home-baked bread wafting up from the breakfast room.

★**Grays Court** HISTORIC HOTEL £££

(☎01904-612613; www.grayscourtyork.com; Chapter House St; d £190-235, ste £270-290; P📶) This medieval mansion with just 11 rooms feels like a country-house hotel. It's set in lovely gardens with direct access to the city walls, and bedrooms combine antique furniture with modern comfort and design. The oldest part of the building was built in the 11th century, and King James I once dined in the Long Gallery.

Eating & Drinking

★**Mannion & Co** CAFE, BISTRO £

(☎01904-631030; www.mannionandco.co.uk; 1 Blake St; mains £7-12; ⏲9am-5pm Mon-Sat, 10am-4.30pm Sun) Expect to queue for a table at this busy bistro (no reservations), with its convivial atmosphere and selection of delicious daily specials. Regulars on the menu include eggs Benedict for breakfast, a chunky Yorkshire rarebit (cheese on toast) made with home-baked bread, and lunch platters of cheese and charcuterie. Oh, and pavlova for pudding.

Hairy Fig CAFE £

(☎01904-677074; www.thehairyfig.co.uk; 39 Fossgate; mains £5-12; ⏲9am-4.30pm Mon-Sat) This cafe-deli is a standout in York. On the one side you've got the best of Yorkshire tripping over the best of Europe, with Italian white anchovies and truffle-infused olive oil stacked alongside York honey mead and baked pies; on the other you've got a Dickensian-style sweet shop and backroom cafe serving dishes crafted from the deli.

No 8 Bistro BISTRO ££

(☎01904-653074; www.no8york.co.uk/bistro; 8 Gillygate; dinner mains £17-19; ⏲noon-10pm Mon-Fri, 9am-10pm Sat & Sun; 📶👪) 🍃 A cool little place with modern artwork mimicking the Edwardian stained glass at the front, No 8 offers a day-long menu of top-notch bistro dishes using fresh local produce, such as Jerusalem artichoke risotto with fresh herbs, and Yorkshire lamb slow-cooked in hay and lavender. It also does breakfast (mains £6 to £9) and Sunday lunch. Booking recommended.

★**Cochon Aveugle** FRENCH £££

(☎01904-640222; www.lecochonaveugle.uk; 37 Walmgate; 4-course lunch £40, 8-course tasting menu £60; ⏲6-9pm Wed-Sat, noon-1.30pm Sat) 🍃 Black-pudding macaroon? Strawberry and elderflower sandwich? Blowtorched mackerel with melon gazpacho? Fussy eaters beware – this small restaurant with huge ambition serves an ever-changing tasting menu (no à la carte) of infinite imagination and invention. You never know what will come next, except that it will be delicious. Bookings are essential.

★**Blue Bell** PUB

(☎01904-654904; 53 Fossgate; ⏲11am-11pm Mon-Thu, to midnight Fri & Sat, noon-10.30pm Sun; 📶) This is what a proper English pub looks like – a tiny, 200-year-old wood-panelled room with a smouldering fireplace, decor untouched since 1903, a pile of ancient board games in the corner, friendly and efficient bar staff, and weekly cask-ale specials chalked on a board. Bliss, with froth on top – if you can get in (it's often full). Cash only.

Information

York Tourist Office (☎01904-550099; www.visityork.org; 1 Museum St; ⏲9am-5pm Mon-Sat, 10am-4pm Sun) Visitor and transport info for all of Yorkshire, plus accommodation bookings (for a small fee) and ticket sales.

Getting There & Away

York does not have a bus station; intercity buses stop outside the train station, while local and regional buses stop here and also on Rougier St, about 200m northeast of the train station. Services include the following:

Edinburgh (£40, 5½ hours, two daily)

London from (£36, 5½ hours, three daily)

York is a major train hub, with frequent direct services to many British cities, including **Edinburgh** (£70, 2½ hours, two to three per hour) and **London King's Cross** (£80, two hours, every 30 minutes)

Castle Howard

Stately homes may be two a penny in England, but you'll have to try pretty damn hard to find one as breathtakingly stately as **Castle Howard** (☎01653-648333; www.castlehoward.co.uk; adult/child house & grounds £18.95/9.95, grounds only £11.95/7.95; ⌚house 10am-4pm, grounds 10am-5pm, last admission 4pm; P), a work of theatrical grandeur and audacity set in the rolling Howardian Hills. This is one of the world's most beautiful buildings, instantly recognisable from its starring role in the 1980s TV series *Brideshead Revisited* and in the 2008 film of the same name (both based on Evelyn Waugh's 1945 novel of nostalgia for the English age of aristocracy).

Castle Howard is 15 miles northeast of York, off the A64. Bus 181 from York goes to Malton via Castle Howard (£10 return, one hour, four times daily Monday to Saturday year-round).

Chester

☎01244 / POP 118,200

With a red-sandstone Roman wall wrapped around a tidy collection of Tudor and Victorian buildings, Chester is one of English history's greatest gifts to the contemporary visitor. The walls were built when this was Castra Devana, the largest Roman fortress in Britain.

Sights

★City Walls LANDMARK

A good way to get a sense of Chester's unique character is to walk the 2-mile circuit along the walls that surround the historic centre. Originally built by the Romans around AD 70, the walls were altered substantially over the following centuries, but have retained their current position since around 1200. The tourist office's *Walk Around Chester Walls* leaflet is an excellent guide and you can also take a 90-minute guided walk.

★Rows ARCHITECTURE

Besides the City Walls, Chester's other great draw is the Rows, a series of two-level galleried arcades along the four streets that fan out in each direction from the **Central Cross**. The architecture is a handsome mix of Victorian and Tudor (original and mock) buildings that house a fantastic collection of independently owned shops.

Chester Cathedral CATHEDRAL

(☎01244-324756; www.chestercathedral.com; 12 Abbey Sq; ⌚9am-6pm Mon-Sat, 1-4pm Sun) FREE Chester Cathedral was originally a Benedictine abbey built on the remains of an earlier Saxon church dedicated to St Werburgh (the city's patron saint); it was shut down in 1540 as part of Henry VIII's Dissolution frenzy, but reconsecrated as a cathedral the following year. Despite a substantial Victorian facelift, the cathedral retains much of its original 12th-century structure. You can amble about freely, but the **tours** (adult/child full tour £8/6, short tour £6; ⌚full tour 11am & 3pm daily, short tour 12.30pm & 1.15pm Mon-Tue, also 2pm & 4pm Wed-Sat) are excellent, as they take you up to the top of the panoramic bell tower.

Sleeping & Eating

★Edgar House BOUTIQUE HOTEL ££

(☎01244-347007; www.edgarhouse.co.uk; 22 City Walls; ⌚r from £105) These award-winning digs are the ultimate in boutique luxury. This Georgian house has seven rooms, each decorated in its own individual style – some have free-standing claw-foot tubs and French doors that lead onto an elegant terrace. There's beautiful art on the walls and fabulous touches of the owners' gorgeous aesthetic throughout. The superb **Twenty2** (www.restauranttwenty2.co.uk; tasting menu £59; ⌚6-9pm Wed-Sat, afternoon tea noon-4pm Fri-Sun) restaurant is open to nonguests.

Joseph Benjamin MODERN BRITISH ££

(☎01244-344295; www.josephbenjamin.co.uk; 134-140 Northgate St; mains £11-18; ⌚noon-3pm Tue-Sat, also 6-9.30pm Thu-Sat & noon-4pm Sun) A bright star in Chester's culinary firmament is this combo restaurant, bar and deli that delivers carefully prepared local produce to take away or eat in. Excellent sandwiches and gorgeous salads are the mainstay of the takeaway menu, while the more formal dinner menu features fine examples of Modern British cuisine.

★Simon Radley at the Grosvenor MODERN BRITISH £££

(☎01244-324024; www.chestergrosvenor.com; 58 Eastgate St, Chester Grosvenor Hotel; tasting menu/à la carte menu £99/75; ⌚6.30-9pm Tue-Sat) Simon Radley's formal restaurant (you're instructed to arrive 30 minutes early for drinks and canapés) has served near-perfect Modern British cuisine since

1990, when it was first awarded the Michelin star that it has kept ever since. The food is divine and the wine list extensive. It's one of Britain's best, but why no second star? Note that attire must be smart and no children under 12 are permitted.

ℹ Information

Tourist Office (☎01244-402111; www.visitchester.com; Town Hall, Northgate St; ⊙9am-5.30pm Mon-Sat, 10am-5pm Sun Mar-Oct, 9am-5pm Mon-Sat, 10am-4pm Sun Nov-Feb)

ℹ Getting There & Away

National Express (☎08717 81 81 81; www.nationalexpress.com) coaches stop on Vicar's Lane, just opposite the tourist office by the Roman amphitheatre. Destinations include London (£33, 5½ hours, three daily).

The train station is about a mile from the city centre. Destinations include London Euston (£85.90, 2½ hours, hourly).

Lake District National Park

A dramatic landscape of ridges, lakes and peaks, including England's highest mountain, Scafell Pike (978m), the Lake District is one of Britain's most scenic corners. Among the many writers who found inspiration here were William Wordsworth, Samuel Taylor Coleridge, Arthur Ransome and Beatrix Potter. Often called simply the Lakes, the national park and surrounding area attract around 15 million visitors annually. But if you avoid summer weekends it's easy enough to miss the crush, especially if you do a bit of hiking. There's a host of B&Bs and country-house hotels in the Lakes, plus more than 20 YHA hostels, many of which can be linked by foot if you wish to hike.

ℹ Information

The national park's main visitor centre is at **Brockhole** (☎015394-46601; www.brockhole.co.uk; ⊙10am-5pm), just outside Windermere, and there are tourist offices in Windermere, Bowness, Ambleside, Keswick, Coniston and Carlisle.

ℹ Getting There & Around

To get to the Lake District via the main West Coast train line, you need to change at Oxenholme for Kendal and Windermere.

DON'T MISS

HILL TOP

The cute-as-a-button farmhouse of **Hill Top** (NT; ☎015394-36269; www.nationaltrust.org.uk/hill-top; adult/child £10.90/5.45, admission to garden & shop free; ⊙10am-5.30pm Jun-Aug, to 4.30pm Sat-Thu Apr, May, Sep & Oct, weekends only Nov-Mar) is a must for Beatrix Potter fans: it was her first house in the Lake District, and is also where she wrote and illustrated several of her famous tales.

The cottage is in Near Sawrey, 2 miles from Hawkshead. The **Cross Lakes Experience** (☎015394-43360; www.mountain-goat.co.uk/Cross-Lakes-Experience; adult/child return Bowness to Hawkshead £12.75/7.10; ⊙Apr-Oct) provides boat and minibus transport from Bowness, 1.5 miles southwest of Windermere.

There's one daily National Express coach from London to Windermere (£46, eight hours) via Lancaster and Kendal.

Bus 555/556 Lakeslink (£4.70 to £9.80) runs at least hourly every day from Windermere train station to Brockhole Visitor Centre (seven minutes), Ambleside (£4.70, 15 minutes), Grasmere (£7.20, 30 minutes) and Keswick (£9.80, one hour).

Windermere

POP 5423

Stretching for 10.5 miles between Ambleside and Newby Bridge, Windermere isn't just the queen of Lake District lakes – it's also the largest body of water anywhere in England, closer in stature to a Scottish loch. It's been a centre for tourism since the first trains chugged into town in 1847 and it's still one of the national park's busiest spots.

★Windermere & the Islands LAKE

Windermere gets its name from the old Norse, *Vinandr mere* (Vinandr's lake; so 'Lake Windermere' is actually tautologous). Encompassing 5.7 sq miles between Ambleside and Newby Bridge, the lake is a mile wide at its broadest point, with a maximum depth of about 220m. It's a nice place to hire a boat for the afternoon, but it is far and away the busiest of the lakes. **Windermere Lake Cruises** (☎015394-43360; www.windermere-lakecruises.co.uk; tickets from £2.70)

OTHER BRITISH PLACES WORTH A VISIT

Some other places in Britain we recommend for day trips or longer visits:

Cornwall The southwestern tip of Britain is ringed with rugged granite seacliffs, sparkling bays, picturesque fishing villages and white sandy beaches.

Liverpool The city's waterfront is a World Heritage Site crammed with top museums, including the International Slavery Museum and the Beatles Story.

Hadrian's Wall One of the country's most dramatic Roman ruins, this 2000-year-old procession of abandoned forts and towers marches across the lonely landscape of northern England.

Glen Coe Scotland's most famous glen combines those two essential qualities of Highlands landscape: dramatic scenery and deep history.

Pembrokeshire Wales' western extremity is famous for its beaches and coastal walks, as well as being home to one of Britain's finest Norman castles.

offers sightseeing cruises, departing from Bowness Pier.

★Rum Doodle B&B ££

(☎015394-45967; www.rumdoodlewindermere.com; Sunny Bank Rd, Windermere Town; d £95-139; P ☜) Named after a classic travel novel about a fictional mountain in the Himalayas, this B&B zings with imagination. Its rooms are themed after places and characters in the book, with details such as book-effect wallpaper, vintage maps and old suitcases. Top of the heap is the Summit, snug under the eaves with a separate sitting room. Two-night minimum in summer.

The Hideaway B&B ££

(☎015394-43070; www.thehideawayatwindermere.co.uk; Phoenix Way; d £90-170; P ☜) There's a fine range of rooms available at this much-recommended B&B in a former schoolmaster's house. There's a choice for all budgets, from Standard Comfy (simple decor, not much space) all the way to Ultimate Comfy (claw-foot tub, split-level mezzanine, space galore). Regardless which you choose, you'll be treated to spoils such as homemade cakes and afternoon tea every day.

★Mason's Arms PUB FOOD ££

(☎015395-68486; www.masonsarmsstrawberrybank.co.uk; Winster; mains £12.95-18.95) Three miles east of Crosthwaite, near Bowlands Bridge, the marvellous Mason's Arms is a local secret. The rafters, flagstones and cast-iron range haven't changed in centuries, and the patio has to-die-for views across fields and fells. The food is hearty – Cumbrian stewpot, slow-roasted Cartmel lamb – and there are lovely rooms and cottages for rent (£175 to £350). In short, a cracker.

Grasmere

POP 1458

Grasmere is a gorgeous little Lakeland village, all the more famous because of its links with Britain's leading Romantic poet, William Wordsworth.

★Dove Cottage & The Wordsworth Museum HISTORIC BUILDING

(☎015394-35544; www.wordsworth.org.uk; adult/child £8.95/free; ⏲9.30am-5.30pm Mar-Oct, 10am-4.30pm Nov, Dec & Feb) On the edge of Grasmere, this tiny, creeper-clad cottage (formerly a pub called the Dove & Olive Bough) was famously inhabited by William Wordsworth between 1799 and 1808. The cottage's cramped rooms are full of artefacts – try to spot the poet's passport, a pair of his spectacles and a portrait (given to him by Sir Walter Scott) of his favourite dog, Pepper. Entry is by timed ticket to avoid overcrowding and includes an informative guided tour.

The Wordsworth family graves are tucked into a quiet corner of the churchyard at nearby **St Oswald's Church**.

★Forest Side BOUTIQUE HOTEL £££

(☎015394-35250; www.theforestside.com; Keswick Rd; r incl full board £230-400; P ☜) For out-and-out-luxury, plump for this boutique beauty. Run by renowned hotelier Andrew Wildsmith, it's a design palace: chic interiors decorated with crushed-velvet sofas, bird-of-paradise wallpaper, stag heads and 20 swish rooms from 'Cosy' to 'Jolly Good', 'Superb', 'Grand' and 'Master'. Chef Kevin Tickle previously worked at **L'Enclume** (☎015395-36362; www.lenclume.co.uk; Cavendish St; set lunch £59, lunch & dinner menu £155; ⏲noon-1.30pm & 6.30-8.30pm Tue-Sun), and now runs the stellar restaurant here using produce from its kitchen garden.

Keswick

POP 4821

The main town of the north Lakes, Keswick sits beside lovely Derwent Water, a silvery curve studded by wooded islands and crisscrossed by puttering cruise boats, operated by the **Keswick Launch** (017687-72263; www.keswick-launch.co.uk; round-the-lake pass adult/child/family £10.75/5.65/25.50).

Keswick YHA HOSTEL £
(0845 371 9746; www.yha.org.uk; Station Rd; dm £15-35; reception 7am-11pm;) Refurbished after flooding in 2015, Keswick's handsome YHA looks as good as new. Its premium facilities include an open-plan ground-floor cafe, a seriously smart kitchen and cracking views over Fitz Park and the rushing River Greta. The dorm decor is standard YHA, but some rooms have private riverside balconies. What a treat!

★Howe Keld B&B ££
(017687-72417; www.howekeld.co.uk; 5-7 The Heads; s £65-90, d £110-140; P) This gold-standard B&B pulls out all the stops: goose-down duvets, slate-floored bathrooms, chic colours and locally made furniture. The best rooms have views across Crow Park and the golf course, and the breakfast is a pick-and-mix delight. Free parking is available on The Heads if there's space.

★Cottage in the Wood HOTEL £££
(017687-78409; www.thecottageinthewood.co.uk; Braithwaite; d £130-220; restaurant 6.30-9pm Tue-Sat; P) For a secluded indulgence, head for this out-of-the-way bolthole, on the road to Whinlatter Forest, in a completely modernised coaching inn. Elegant rooms survey woods and countryside: the Mountain View rooms overlook the Skiddaw Range, but we liked the super-private Attic Suite and the Garden Room, with its wood floors and wet-room. The restaurant's fantastic too (set dinner menu £45).

WALES

029 / POP 3.1M

Lying to the west of England, Wales is a nation with Celtic roots, its own language and a rich historical legacy. While some areas in the south are undeniably scarred by coal mining and heavy industry, Wales boasts a scenic landscape of wild mountains, rolling hills and rich farmland, and the bustling capital city of Cardiff.

Cardiff

POP 349,941

The capital of Wales since just 1955, Cardiff has embraced the role with vigour, emerging in the new millennium as one of Britain's leading urban centres. Spread between an ancient fort and an ultramodern waterfront, compact Cardiff seems to have surprised even itself with how interesting it has become.

Sights

★Cardiff Castle CASTLE
(029-2087 8100; www.cardiffcastle.com; Castle St; adult/child £13/9.25, incl guided tour £16/12; 9am-6pm Mar-Oct, to 5pm Nov-Feb) There's a medieval keep at its heart, but it's the later additions to Cardiff Castle that really capture the imagination. In Victorian times, extravagant mock-Gothic features were grafted onto this relic, including a clock tower and a lavish banqueting hall. Some but not all of this flamboyant fantasy world can be accessed with regular castle entry; the rest can be visited as part of a (recommended) guided tour. Look for the *trebuchet* (medieval siege engine) and falcons on the grounds.

★National Museum Cardiff MUSEUM
(0300 111 2 333; www.museumwales.ac.uk; Cathays Park; 10am-5pm Tue-Sun; P) FREE Devoted mainly to natural history and art, this grand neoclassical building is the centrepiece of the seven institutions dotted around the country that together form the Welsh National Museum. It's one of Britain's best museums; you'll need at least three hours to do it justice, but it could easily consume the best part of a rainy day. On-site parking, behind the museum, is £6.50.

Wales Millennium Centre ARTS CENTRE
(029-2063 6464; www.wmc.org.uk; Bute Pl, Cardiff Bay; 9am-7pm, later on show nights) The centrepiece and symbol of Cardiff Bay's regeneration is the £106 million Wales Millennium Centre, an architectural masterpiece of stacked Welsh slate in shades of purple, green and grey topped with an overarching bronzed steel shell. Designed by Welsh architect Jonathan Adams, it opened in 2004 as Wales' premier arts complex, housing major cultural organisations such as the Welsh National Opera,

National Dance Company, BBC National Orchestra of Wales, Literature Wales, HiJinx Theatre and Tŷ Cerdd (Music Centre Wales).

Castell Coch CASTLE
(Cadw; www.cadw.gov.wales; Castle Rd, Tongwynlais; adult/child £6.90/4.10; 9.30am-5pm Mar-Jun, Sep & Oct, to 6pm Jul & Aug, 10am-4pm Mon-Sat, from 11am Sun Nov-Feb; P) Cardiff Castle's fanciful little brother sits perched atop a thickly wooded crag on the northern fringes of Cardiff. It was the summer retreat of the third marquess of Bute and, like Cardiff Castle, was designed by oddball architect William Burges in gaudy Gothic-revival style. Raised on the ruins of Gilbert de Clare's 13th-century Castell Coch (Red Castle), the Butes' Disneyesque holiday home is a monument to high camp. An excellent audio guide is included in the admission price.

Sleeping

★River House HOSTEL £
(029-2039 9810; www.riverhousebackpackers.com; 59 Fitzhamon Embankment, Riverside; dm/s/d incl breakfast from £16/33/38; @) Professionally run by a helpful young brother-and-sister team, River House has a well-equipped kitchen, a laundry, a small garden and a cosy TV lounge, and it's right across the Taff from Millennium Stadium. There's a mix of small dorms and private rooms with double beds, all sharing bathrooms, and a free breakfast of cereal, toast, pastries and fruit is provided.

★Lincoln House HOTEL ££
(029-2039 5558; www.lincolnhotel.co.uk; 118-120 Cathedral Rd, Pontcanna; d/penthouses from £125/250; P) Walking a middle line between a large B&B and a small hotel, Lincoln House is a generously proportioned Victorian property with heraldic emblems in the stained-glass windows of its book-lined sitting room, and a separate bar. There are 21 rooms and a loft penthouse sleeping up to four; for added romance, book a four-poster room.

Number 62 GUESTHOUSE ££
(029-2041 2765; www.number62.com; 62 Cathedral Rd, Pontcanna; s/d from £74/83;) The only thing preventing Number 62 from being a B&B is that breakfast is only offered as an add-on (served at the Beverley Hotel across the road). The cosy rooms come with thoughtful extras such as body lotion, make-up wipes and cotton buds, and the front garden is one of the most immaculate of all the houses on this strip.

Park Plaza HOTEL £££
(029-2011 1111; www.parkplazacardiff.com; Greyfriars Rd; s/d £125/175;) Luxurious without being stuffy, the Plaza has all the five-star facilities you'd expect from an upmarket business-oriented hotel, including a gym for guests, a spa, a restaurant and bar (open to all) and Egyptian cotton on the beds. The slick reception has a gas fire blazing along one wall and rear rooms have leafy views over the Civic Centre.

Eating & Drinking

Coffee Barker CAFE £
(029-2022 4575; Castle Arcade; mains £6-7; 8.30am-5.30pm Mon-Wed, to 11pm Thu-Sat, 9.30am-4.30pm Sun;) This cool cafe, a series of rooms at the entrance to one of Cardiff's Victorian arcades, is good for coffee, indulgent pancake stacks, daily soups and thick milkshakes served in glass milk bottles. Despite its size, soft chairs and quirky decor give it a cosy vibe. Usually busy, it also includes a cruisy bar, open until 11pm Thursday to Saturday.

Purple Poppadom INDIAN ££
(029-2022 0026; www.purplepoppadom.com; 185a Cowbridge Rd E, Canton; mains £15-17, 2-course lunch £15; noon-2pm & 5.30-11pm Tue-Sat, 1-9pm Sun) Trailblazing a path for 'nouvelle Indian' cuisine, chef and author Anand George adds his own twist to dishes from all over the subcontinent – from Kashmir to Kerala. Thankfully, the emphasis is on the perfection of tried-and-tested regional delights rather than anything unnecessarily wacky.

Porter's BAR
(029-2125 0666; www.porterscardiff.com; Bute Tce; 5pm-12.30am Sun-Wed, 4pm-3am Thu & Fri, noon-3am Sat) Owned by a self-confessed 'failed actor', this friendly, attitude-free bar has something on most nights, whether it's a quiz, live music, comedy, theatre or a movie screening (there's a little cinema attached). Local drama is showcased in the 'Other Room', the adjoining 44-seat theatre, while under the shadow of the train tracks out the back is a wonderful beer garden.

Information

Tourist Office (029-2087 3573; www.visitcardiff.com; Yr Hen Lyfrgell, The Hayes; 10am-3pm Sun-Thu, to 5pm Fri & Sat)

Getting There & Away

BUS

Cardiff's old central bus station was closed in 2015; its replacement is due to open near the train station in 2023. In the meantime, buses call at temporary stops scattered around the city. See https://www.traveline.cymru for details.

Megabus (http://uk.megabus.com) offers one-way coach journeys from London to Cardiff (via Newport) from as little as £8.30.

National Express (www.nationalexpress.com) coaches depart from **Cardiff Coach Station** (Sophia Gardens) to destinations including Bristol (£8.70, 1¼ hours, six daily) and London (from £15, 3¾ hours, frequent).

TRAIN

Trains from major British cities arrive at Cardiff Central station, on the southern edge of the city centre. Direct services to/from Cardiff include London Paddington (from £62, 2¼ hours, two per hour) and Holyhead (£47, five hours, seven daily). For the latest timetables and bookings, see www.thetrainline.com.

Snowdonia National Park (Parc Cenedlaethol Eryri)

Wales' best-known slice of nature became the country's first national park (www.eryri-npa.gov.uk) in 1951. Every year more than 400,000 people walk, climb or take the train to the 1085m summit of Snowdon, Wales' highest mountain. Yet the park offers much more – its 823 sq miles embrace stunning coastline, forests, valleys, rivers, bird-filled estuaries and Wales' biggest natural lake. The Welsh for Snowdonia is Eryri (*eh*-ruh-ree) – 'highlands'.

Snowdon (Yr Wyddfa)

No Snowdonia experience is complete without coming face-to-face with Snowdon (1085m) – 'Yr Wyddfa' in Welsh (pronounced uhr-with-vuh, meaning 'the Tomb'). On a clear day the views stretch to Ireland and the Isle of Man. Even on a gloomy day you could find yourself above the clouds. At the top is the striking **Hafod Eryri** (https://snowdonrailway.co.uk; ⏲10am-20min before last train departure Easter-Oct; 📶) visitor centre.

Six paths of varying length and difficulty lead to the summit, all taking around six hours return, or you can cheat and catch the **Snowdon Mountain Railway** (☎01286-870223; www.snowdonrailway.co.uk; adult/child return diesel £29/20, steam £37/27; ⏲9am-5pm mid-Mar–Oct), which opened in 1896 and is still the UK's only public rack-and-pinion railway.

However you get to the summit, take warm, waterproof clothing, wear sturdy footwear and check the weather forecast before setting out.

WORTH A TRIP

CONWY CASTLE

On the north coast of Wales, the historic town of Conwy is dominated by the Unesco-designated cultural treasure of **Conwy Castle** (Cadw; ☎01492-592358; www.cadw.wales.gov.uk; Castle Sq; adult/child £9.50/5.70; ⏲9.30am-5pm Mar-Jun, Sep & Oct, to 6pm Jul & Aug, 10am-4pm Mon-Sat, from 11am Sun Nov-Feb; 🅿), the most stunning of all Edward I's Welsh fortresses. Built between 1277 and 1307 on a rocky outcrop, it has commanding views across the estuary and Snowdonia National Park.

YHA Snowdon Ranger HOSTEL £

(☎0845 3719 659; www.yha.org.uk; Rhyd Ddu; dm/tw from £23/50; 🅿📶) On the A4085, 5 miles north of Beddgelert at the trailhead for the Snowdon Ranger Path, this former inn has its own adjoining beach on the shore of Llyn Cwellyn, and is close to the hiking and climbing centres of Llanberis and Beddgelert. It's basic, dependable accommodation within sight of Snowdon.

Pen-y-Gwryd HOTEL ££

(☎01286-870211; www.pyg.co.uk; Nant Gwynant; s/d £58/115; 🅿📶🐾) Eccentric but full of atmosphere, this Georgian coaching inn was used as a training base by the 1953 Everest team, and memorabilia from their stay includes signatures on the restaurant ceiling. TV, wi-fi and mobile-phone signals don't penetrate here; instead, there's a comfy games room, a sauna, and a lake for those hardy enough to swim. Meals and packed lunches are available.

You'll find the hotel below Pen-y-Pass, at the junction of the A498 and A4086.

Getting There & Away

The Welsh Highland Railway (www.festrail.co.uk) and Snowdon Sherpa buses (single/day ticket £2/5) link various places in Snowdonia with the town of Caernarfon, which can be reached by train from London Euston.

SCOTLAND

POP 5.45 MILLION

Despite its small size, Scotland has many treasures crammed into its compact territory – big skies, lonely landscapes, spectacular wildlife, superb seafood and hospitable, down-to-earth people. From the cultural attractions of Edinburgh to the heather-clad hills of the Highlands, there's something for everyone.

Edinburgh

☎0131 / POP 513,210

Edinburgh is a city that just begs to be explored. From the imposing castle to the Palace of Holyroodhouse to the Royal Yacht *Britannia,* every corner turned reveals sudden views and unexpected vistas – green sunlit hills, a glimpse of rust-red crags, a blue flash of distant sea. But there's more to Edinburgh than sightseeing – there are top shops, world-class restaurants and a bacchanalia of bars to enjoy.

Sights

★Edinburgh Castle CASTLE

(☎0131-225 9846; www.edinburghcastle.gov.uk; Castle Esplanade; adult/child £18.50/11.50, audio guide £3.50/1.50; ⌚9.30am-6pm Apr-Sep, to 5pm Oct-Mar, last entry 1hr before closing; 🚌23, 27, 41, 42, 67) Edinburgh Castle has played a pivotal role in Scottish history, both as a royal residence – King Malcolm Canmore (r 1058–93) and Queen Margaret first made their home here in the 11th century – and as a military stronghold. The castle last saw military action in 1745; from then until the 1920s it served as the British army's main base in Scotland. Today it is one of Scotland's most atmospheric and popular tourist attractions.

★National Museum of Scotland MUSEUM

(☎0300 123 6789; www.nms.ac.uk/national-museum-of-scotland; Chambers St; ⌚10am-5pm; 👪; 🚌45, 300) FREE Elegant Chambers St is dominated by the long facade of the National Museum of Scotland. Its extensive collections are spread between two buildings: one modern, one Victorian – the golden stone and striking architecture of the new building (1998) make it one of the city's most distinctive landmarks. The museum's five floors trace the history of Scotland from geological beginnings to the 1990s, with many imaginative and stimulating exhibits. Audio guides are available in several languages. Fees apply for special exhibitions.

Real Mary King's Close HISTORIC BUILDING

(☎0131-225 0672; www.realmarykingsclose.com; 2 Warriston's Close; adult/child £15.50/9.50; ⌚10am-9pm Apr-Oct, reduced hours rest of year; 🚌23, 27, 41, 42) Edinburgh's 18th-century City Chambers were built over the sealed-off remains of Mary King's Close, and the lower levels of this medieval Old Town alley have survived almost unchanged amid the foundations for 250 years. Now open to the public, this spooky, subterranean labyrinth gives a fascinating insight into the everyday life of 17th-century Edinburgh. Costumed characters lead tours through a 16th-century town house and the plague-stricken home of a 17th-century gravedigger. Advance booking recommended.

Palace of Holyroodhouse PALACE

(☎03031237306; www.royalcollection.org.uk/visit/palace-of-holyroodhouse; Canongate, Royal Mile; adult/child incl audio guide £14/8.10; ⌚9.30am-6pm, last entry 4.30pm Apr-Oct, to 4.30pm, last entry 3.15pm Nov-Mar; 🚌6, 300) This palace is the royal family's official residence in Scotland, but is more famous as the 16th-century home of the ill-fated Mary, Queen of Scots. The highlight of the tour is **Mary's Bedchamber**, home to the unfortunate queen from 1561 to 1567. It was here that her jealous second husband, Lord Darnley, restrained the pregnant queen while his henchmen murdered her secretary – and favourite – David Rizzio. A plaque in the neighbouring room marks the spot where Rizzio bled to death.

Scottish Parliament Building NOTABLE BUILDING

(☎0131-348 5200; www.parliament.scot; Horse Wynd; ⌚9am-6.30pm Tue-Thu, 10am-5pm Mon, Fri & Sat in session, 10am-5pm Tue-Thu in recess; 👪; 🚌6, 300) FREE The Scottish Parliament Building, on the site of a former brewery and designed by Catalan architect Enric Miralles (1955–2000), was opened by the Queen in October 2004. The ground plan of the complex is said to represent a 'flower of democracy rooted in Scottish soil' (best seen looking down from Salisbury Crags). Free, one-hour tours (advance bookings recommended) include visits to the Debating Chamber, a committee room, the Garden Lobby and the office of a member of parliament (MSP).

Royal Yacht Britannia SHIP

(www.royalyachtbritannia.co.uk; Ocean Terminal; adult/child incl audio guide £16/8.50; ⌚9.30am-6pm Apr-Sep, to 5.30pm Oct, 10am-5pm Nov-Mar, last entry 1½hr before closing; P; 🚌11, 22, 34, 36,

200, 300) Built on Clydeside, the former Royal Yacht *Britannia* was the British Royal Family's floating holiday home during their foreign travels from the time of its launch in 1953 until its decommissioning in 1997, and is now permanently moored in front of **Ocean Terminal** (☎0131-555 8888; www.oceanterminal.com; Ocean Dr; ⏰10am-8pm Mon-Fri, to 7pm Sat, 11am-6pm Sun; 📶). The tour, which you take at your own pace with an audio guide (available in 30 languages), lifts the curtain on the everyday lives of the royals, and gives an intriguing insight into the Queen's private tastes.

Sleeping

Edinburgh offers a wide range of accommodation options, from moderately priced guesthouses set in lovely Victorian villas and Georgian town houses to expensive and stylish boutique hotels. There are also plenty of chain hotels, and a few truly exceptional hotels housed in magnificent historic buildings. At the budget end of the range, there is no shortage of youth hostels and independent backpacker hostels, which often have inexpensive double and twin rooms.

Code - The Loft HOSTEL **£**
(☎0131 659 9883; www.codehostel.com; 50 Rose St N Lane; dm from £25, d £99; 📶; 🚌Princes St) This upmarket hostel, bang in the middle of the New Town, combines cute designer decor with innovative sleeping pods that offer more privacy than bunks (four to six people per dorm, each with en suite shower room). There's also a luxurious double apartment called the Penthouse, complete with kitchenette and roof terrace.

Safestay Edinburgh HOSTEL **£**
(☎0131-524 1989; www.safestay.com; 50 Blackfriars St; dm £34-40, tw £109; @📶; 🚌300) A big, modern hostel, with a convivial cafe where you can buy breakfast, and mod cons such as keycard access and charging stations for mobile phones, MP3 players and laptops. Lockers in every room, a huge bar and a central location just off the Royal Mile make this a favourite among the young, party-mad crowd – don't expect a quiet night!

★**Two Hillside Crescent** B&B **££**
(☎0131-556 4871; www.twohillsidecrescent.com; 2 Hillside Cres; r from £115; @📶; 🚌19, 26, 44) Five spacious and individually decorated bedrooms grace this gorgeous Georgian town house – it's worth splashing out for the 'superior' room with twin floor-to-ceiling windows overlooking the gardens. Guests take breakfast around a large communal table in a stylishly modern dining room – smoked salmon and scrambled eggs is on the menu – and your hosts could not be more helpful.

14 Hart Street B&B **££**
(☎07795 203414; http://14hartstreet.co.uk; 14 Hart St; s/d £115/125; 📶; 🚌8) Centrally located and child friendly, 14 Hart Street is steeped in Georgian elegance and old Edinburgh charm. Run by a retired couple, the B&B has three generous bedrooms, all en suite, and a sumptuous dining room where guests can enjoy breakfast at a time of their choosing. Indulgent extras include whisky decanters and shortbread in every room.

★**Principal** BOUTIQUE HOTEL **£££**
(☎0131-341 4932; www.phcompany.com/principal/edinburgh-charlotte-square; 38 Charlotte Sq; r from £245; P📶; 🚌all Princes St buses) Arriving in this modern makeover of a classic Georgian New Town establishment (formerly the Roxburghe Hotel) feels like being welcomed into a country-house party. Service is friendly and attentive without being intrusive, and the atmosphere is informal; in the bedrooms, designer decor meets traditional tweed, and breakfast is served in a lovely glass-roofed garden courtyard.

Eating

Scott's Kitchen SCOTTISH, CAFE **£**
(☎0131-322 6868; https://scottskitchen.co.uk; 4-6 Victoria Tce; mains £8-10; ⏰9am-6pm; P📶; 🚌23, 27, 41, 42, 67) Green tile, brown leather and arched Georgian windows lend an elegant feel to this modern cafe, which combines fine Scottish produce with great value. Fill up on a breakfast (served till 11.45am) of eggs Benedict, bacon baps or porridge with honey, banana and almonds, or linger over

FESTIVAL CITY

Edinburgh boasts a frenzy of festivals throughout the year, including the world-famous **Edinburgh Festival Fringe** (☎0131-226 0026; www.edfringe.com), held over 3½ weeks in August. The last two weeks overlap with the first two weeks of the **Edinburgh International Festival** (☎0131-473 2000; www.eif.co.uk). See www.edinburghfestivalcity.com for more.

Central Edinburgh

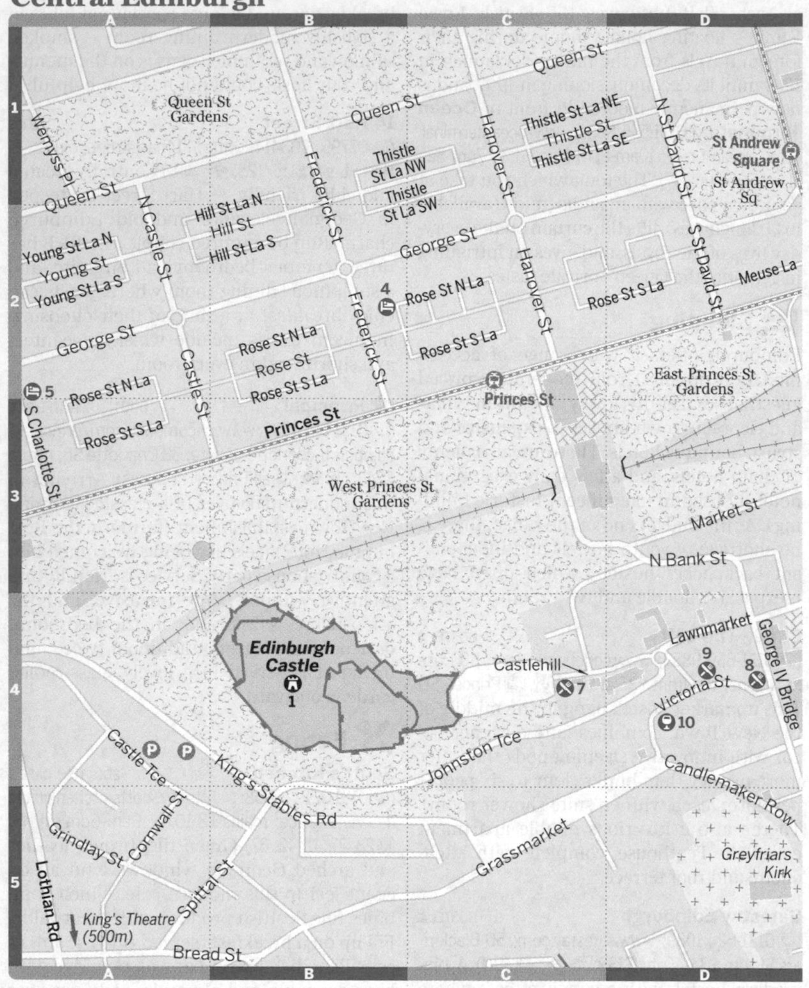

a lunch of Cullen skink (smoked haddock soup), venison casserole or haggis.

★Gardener's Cottage SCOTTISH **££**
(☎0131-558 1221; www.thegardenerscottage.co; 1 Royal Terrace Gardens, London Rd; 4-course lunch £21, 7-course dinner £50; ⊙noon-2pm & 5-10pm Mon-Fri, 10am-2pm & 5-10pm Sat & Sun; 🚌all London Rd buses) This country cottage in the heart of the city, bedecked with flowers and fairy lights, offers one of Edinburgh's most interesting dining experiences – two tiny rooms with communal tables made of salvaged timber, and a set menu based on fresh local produce (most of the vegetables and fruit are from its own organic garden). Bookings essential; brunch served at weekends.

Cannonball Restaurant SCOTTISH **££**
(☎0131-225 1550; www.contini.com/cannonball; 356 Castlehill; mains £15-25; ⊙noon-3pm & 5.30-10pm Tue-Sat; 📶👪; 🚌23, 27, 41, 42) The historic Cannonball House next to Edinburgh Castle's esplanade has been transformed into a sophisticated restaurant (and whisky bar) where the Contini family work their Italian magic on Scottish classics to produce dishes such as haggis balls with spiced pickled turnip and whisky marmalade, and lobster with wild garlic and lemon butter.

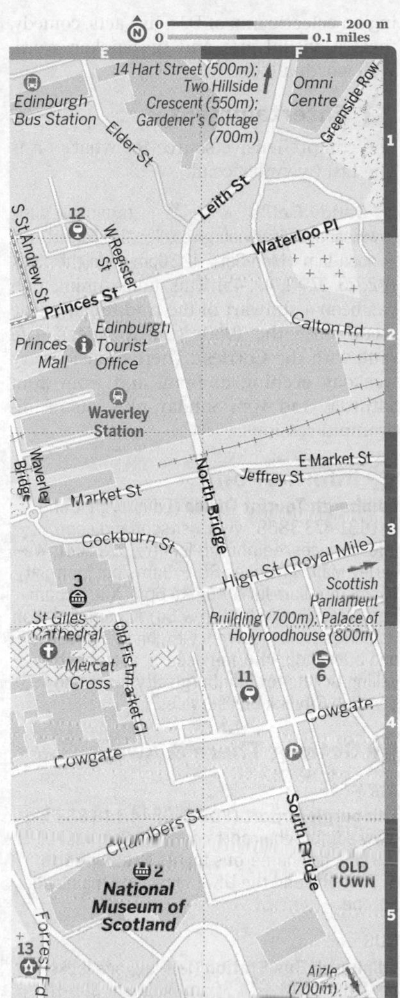

Aizle SCOTTISH ££

(☎0131-662 9349; http://aizle.co.uk; 107-109 St Leonard's St; 5-course dinner £55; ⊙5-9pm Wed-Sat; 📶; 🚌14) If you tend to have trouble deciding what to eat, Aizle (the name is an old Scots word for 'spark' or 'ember') will do the job for you. There's no menu here, just a five-course dinner conjured from a monthly 'harvest' of the finest and freshest local produce (listed on a blackboard), and presented beautifully – art on a plate.

Fishers Bistro SEAFOOD ££

(☎0131-554 5666; www.fishersbistros.co.uk; 1 The Shore; mains £14-25; ⊙noon-10.30pm Mon-Sat, 12.30-10.30pm Sun; 📶; 🚌16, 22, 36, 300) This cosy little restaurant, tucked beneath a 17th-century signal tower, is one of the city's best seafood places. The menu ranges widely in price, from cheaper dishes such as classic fish cakes with lemon-and-chive mayonnaise to more expensive delights such as Fife lobster and chips (£40).

★Ondine SEAFOOD £££

(☎0131-226 1888; www.ondinerestaurant.co.uk; 2 George IV Bridge; mains £18-38, 2-/3-course lunch £19/24; ⊙noon-3pm & 5.30-10pm Mon-Sat; 📶; 🚌23, 27, 41, 42) Ondine is one of Edinburgh's finest seafood restaurants, with a menu based on sustainably sourced fish. Take a seat at the curved Oyster Bar and tuck into oysters Kilpatrick, smoked haddock chowder, lobster thermidor, a roast-shellfish platter or just good old haddock and chips (with minted pea purée, just to keep things posh).

Drinking & Nightlife

★Bennet's Bar PUB

(☎0131-229 5143; www.bennetsbaredinburgh.co.uk; 8 Leven St; ⊙11am-1am; 🚌all Tollcross buses) Situated beside the **King's Theatre** (☎0131-529 6000; www.capitaltheatres.com/kings; 2 Leven St; ⊙box office 10am-6pm), Bennet's (established in 1839) has managed to hang on to almost all of its beautiful Victorian fittings, from the stained-glass windows and the ornate mirrors to the wooden

Central Edinburgh

Top Sights
1 Edinburgh Castle B4
2 National Museum of Scotland E5

Sights
3 Real Mary King's Close E3

Sleeping
4 Code Pod Hostel B2
5 Principal A2
6 Safestay Edinburgh F4

Eating
7 Cannonball Restaurant C4
8 Ondine D4
9 Scott's Kitchen D4

Drinking & Nightlife
10 Bow Bar D4
11 Cabaret Voltaire F4
12 Café Royal Circle Bar E1

Entertainment
13 Sandy Bell's E5

THE QUEENSFERRY CROSSING

The famous Forth Bridge (1890) and Forth Road Bridge (1964), which soar across the Firth of Forth to the west of Edinburgh, have been joined by the impressive Queensferry Crossing, a new road bridge that opened in 2017.

gantry and the brass water taps on the bar (for your whisky – there are over 100 from which to choose).

★Bow Bar PUB
(www.thebowbar.co.uk; 80 West Bow; noon-midnight Mon-Sat, to 11.30pm Sun; 2, 23, 27, 41, 42) One of the city's best traditional-style pubs (it's not as old as it looks), serving a range of excellent real ales, Scottish craft gins and a vast selection of malt whiskies, the Bow Bar often has standing-room only on Friday and Saturday evenings.

Café Royal Circle Bar PUB
(0131-556 1884; www.caferoyaledinburgh.co.uk; 17 W Register St; 11am-11pm Mon-Wed, to midnight Thu, to 1am Fri & Sat, to 10pm Sun; ; Princes St) Perhaps *the* classic Edinburgh pub, the Café Royal's main claims to fame are its magnificent oval bar and its Doulton tile portraits of famous Victorian inventors. Sit at the bar or claim one of the cosy leather booths beneath the stained-glass windows, and choose from the seven real ales on tap.

Roseleaf BAR
(0131-476 5268; www.roseleaf.co.uk; 23-24 Sandport Pl; 10am-1am; ; 16, 22, 36, 300) Cute, quaint and decked out in flowered wallpaper, old furniture and rose-patterned china (cocktails are served in teapots), the Roseleaf could hardly be further from the average Leith bar. The real ales and bottled beers are complemented by a range of speciality teas, coffees and fruit drinks (including rose lemonade), and well-above-average pub grub (served from 10am to 10pm).

★Cabaret Voltaire CLUB
(www.thecabaretvoltaire.com; 36-38 Blair St; 5pm-3am Tue-Sat, 8pm-1am Sun; ; all South Bridge buses) An atmospheric warren of stone-lined vaults houses this self-consciously 'alternative' club, which eschews huge dance floors and egotistical DJ worship in favour of a 'creative crucible' hosting an eclectic mix of DJs, live acts, comedy, theatre, visual arts and the spoken word. Well worth a look.

☆ Entertainment

The comprehensive source for what's on is The List (www.list.co.uk).

★Sandy Bell's TRADITIONAL MUSIC
(www.sandybellsedinburgh.co.uk; 25 Forrest Rd; noon-1am Mon-Sat, 12.30pm-midnight Sun; 2, 23, 27, 41, 42, 45) This unassuming pub has been a stalwart of the traditional-music scene since the 1960s (the founder's wife sang with the Corries). There's music every weekday evening at 9pm, and from 2pm Saturday and 4pm Sunday, plus lots of impromptu sessions.

Information

Edinburgh Tourist Office (Edinburgh iCentre; 0131-473 3868; www.visitscotland.com/info/services/edinburgh-icentre-p234441; Waverley Mall, 3 Princes St; 9am-7pm Mon-Sat, 10am-7pm Sun Jul & Aug, to 6pm Jun, to 5pm Sep-May; ; St Andrew Sq) Accommodation booking service, currency exchange, gift shop and bookshop, internet access, and counters selling tickets for Edinburgh city tours and Scottish Citylink bus services.

Getting There & Away

AIR

Edinburgh Airport (EDI; 0844 448 8833; www.edinburghairport.com), 8 miles west of the city, has numerous flights to other parts of Scotland and the UK, Ireland and mainland Europe.

BUS

Edinburgh Bus Station (left-luggage lockers per 24hr £5-10; 4.30am-midnight Sun-Thu, to 12.30am Fri & Sat; St Andrew Sq) is at the northeastern corner of St Andrew Sq, with pedestrian entrances from the square and from Elder St. For timetable information, contact **Traveline** (0871 200 22 33; www.travelinescotland.com).

Scottish Citylink (0871 266 3333; www.citylink.co.uk) buses connect Edinburgh with all of Scotland's cities and major towns including Glasgow (£7.90, 1¼ hours, every 15 minutes), Stirling (£8.70, one hour, hourly) and Inverness (£32.20, 3½ to 4½ hours, hourly).

It's also worth checking with **Megabus** (0141-352 4444; www.megabus.com) for cheap intercity bus fares (from as little as £5) from Edinburgh to London, Glasgow and Inverness.

TRAIN

The main rail terminus in Edinburgh is Waverley train station, in the heart of the city. Trains arriving from, and departing for, the west also stop at Haymarket station, which is more convenient for the West End.

ScotRail (☎ 0344 811 0141; www.scotrail.co.uk) operates regular train services to Glasgow (£14.40, 50 minutes, every 15 minutes) and Inverness (£40, 3½ hours).

Glasgow

☎ 0141 / POP 596,500

With a population around 1½ times that of Edinburgh, and a radically different history rooted in industry and trade rather than politics and law, Glasgow stands in complete contrast to the capital. The city offers a unique blend of friendliness, energy, dry humour and urban chaos, and also boasts excellent art galleries and museums – including the famous Burrell Collection (due to reopen in 2022) – as well as numerous good-value restaurants, countless pubs, bars and clubs, and a lively performing-arts scene. Just 50 miles to the west of Edinburgh, Glasgow makes an easy day trip by train or bus.

Sights

Glasgow's main square in the city centre is grand **George Square**, built in the Victorian era to show off the city's wealth, and dignified by statues of notable Scots, including Robert Burns, James Watt, John Moore and Sir Walter Scott.

★ Kelvingrove Art Gallery & Museum GALLERY, MUSEUM

(☎ 0141-276 9599; www.glasgowmuseums.com; Argyle St; ⊙10am-5pm Mon-Thu & Sat, from 11am Fri & Sun) FREE A magnificent sandstone building, this grand Victorian cathedral of culture is a fascinating and unusual museum, with a bewildering variety of exhibits. You'll find fine art alongside stuffed animals, and Micronesian shark-tooth swords alongside a Spitfire plane, but it's not mix 'n' match: rooms are carefully and thoughtfully themed, and the collection is of a manageable size. It has an excellent room of Scottish art, a room of fine French impressionist works, and quality Renaissance paintings from Italy and Flanders.

★ Riverside Museum MUSEUM

(☎ 0141-287 2720; www.glasgowmuseums.com; 100 Pointhouse Pl; ⊙10am-5pm Mon-Thu & Sat, from 11am Fri & Sun;) FREE This visually impressive modern museum at Glasgow Harbour owes its striking curved forms to late British-Iraqi architect Zaha Hadid. A transport museum forms the main part of the collection, featuring a fascinating series of cars made in Scotland, plus assorted railway locos, trams, bikes (including the world's first pedal-powered bicycle from 1847) and model Clyde-built ships. An atmospheric recreation of a Glasgow shopping street from the

THE GENIUS OF CHARLES RENNIE MACKINTOSH

Charles Rennie Mackintosh (1868–1928) is to Glasgow what Gaudí is to Barcelona. A designer, architect and master of the art nouveau style, his quirky, linear and geometric designs are seen all over Glasgow.

Many of his buildings are open to the public, though his masterpiece, the **Glasgow School of Art**, was extensively damaged by fires in 2014 and 2018 and remains closed to the public. If you're a fan, be sure to visit the following:

Mackintosh at the Willow (☎ 0141-204 1903; www.mackintoshatthewillow.com; 217 Sauchiehall St; exhibition admission adult/child £5.50/3.50; ⊙ tearoom 9am-5pm, exhibition 9am-5.30pm Mon-Sat, 10am-5pm Sun, last entry 1hr before closing)

Mackintosh House (☎ 0141-330 4221; www.hunterian.gla.ac.uk; 82 Hillhead St; adult/child £6/3; ⊙ 10am-5pm Tue-Sat, 11am-4pm Sun)

House for an Art Lover (☎ 0141-353 4770; www.houseforanartlover.co.uk; Bellahouston Park, Dumbreck Rd; adult/child £6/4.50; ⊙ check online, roughly 10am-4pm Mon-Fri, to noon Sat, to 2pm Sun)

Hill House (☎ 01436-673900; www.nts.org.uk; Upper Colquhoun St, Helensburgh; adult/child £10.50/7.50; ⊙ 11.30am-5pm Mar-Oct)

Glasgow

early 20th century puts the vintage vehicles into a social context. There's also a cafe.

Glasgow Cathedral CATHEDRAL

(HES; ☎0141-552 6891; www.historicenvironment.scot; Cathedral Sq; ⏰9.30am-5.30pm Mon-Sat, 1-5pm Sun Apr-Sep, 10am-4pm Mon-Sat, from 1pm Sun Oct-Mar) Glasgow Cathedral has a rare timelessness. The dark, imposing interior conjures up medieval might and can send a shiver down the spine. It's a shining example of Gothic architecture, and unlike nearly all of Scotland's cathedrals, it survived the turmoil of the Reformation mobs almost intact. Most of the current building dates from the 15th century.

Glasgow Science Centre MUSEUM

(☎0141-420 5000; www.glasgowsciencecentre.org; 50 Pacific Quay; adult/child £11.50/9.50, IMAX, Glasgow Tower or Planetarium extra £2.50-3.50; ⏰10am-5pm daily Apr-Oct, to 3pm Wed-Fri, to 5pm Sat & Sun Nov-Mar; 👪) This brilliant science museum will keep the kids entertained for hours (that's middle-aged kids too!). It brings science and technology alive through hundreds of interactive exhibits on four floors: a bounty of discovery for inquisitive

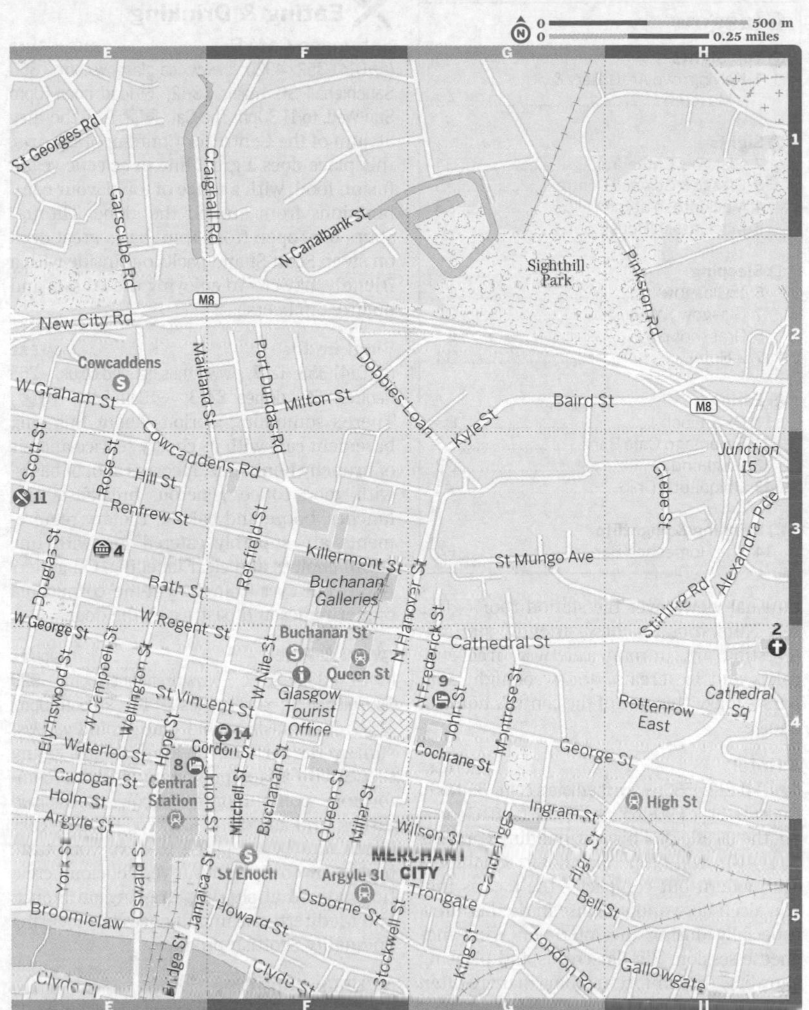

minds. There's also an **IMAX theatre** (see www.cineworld.com for current screenings), a rotating 127m-high **observation tower**, a **planetarium** and a **Science Theatre**, with live science demonstrations. To get here, take bus 89 or 90 from Union St.

Sleeping

Glasgow SYHA HOSTEL £

(☎0141-332 3004; www.hostellingscotland.org.uk; 8 Park Tce; dm/s/tw £29/52/69; @📶) Perched on a hill overlooking Kelvingrove Park in a charming townhouse, this place is one of Scotland's best official hostels. Dorms are mostly four to six beds with padlocked lockers, and all have their own en suite. The common rooms are spacious, plush and good for lounging about in. There's no curfew, it has a good kitchen, and meals are available.

★**Grasshoppers** HOTEL ££

(☎0141-222 2666; www.grasshoppersglasgow.com; 87 Union St; r £90-138; ❄📶🐾) Discreetly hidden atop a time-worn railway administration building alongside Central station, this small, well-priced hotel is a modern, upbeat surprise. Rooms are compact (a few are larger) but well appointed, with

Glasgow

Top Sights
1 Kelvingrove Art Gallery & Museum A2

Sights
2 Glasgow Cathedral H4
3 Glasgow Science Centre A5
4 Mackintosh at the Willow E3
5 Mackintosh House A1

Sleeping
6 15Glasgow C3
7 Glasgow SYHA C2
8 Grasshoppers E4
9 Z Hotel G4

Eating
10 Ox & Finch B3
11 Saramago Café Bar E3
12 Singl-end D3
13 Ubiquitous Chip A1

Drinking & Nightlife
14 The Horseshoe Bar F4

unusual views over the station roof's glass sea. Numerous touches – friendly staff, interesting art, in-room cafetière, free cupcakes and ice cream, and weeknight suppers – make this one of the centre's homiest choices.

Z Hotel HOTEL ££
(0141-212 4550; www.thezhotels.com; 36 North Frederick St; r £90-165;) Just off George Sq, the facade of a historic building conceals a stylish contemporary hotel. Chambers are modern but compact – the idea is that you sleep here and socialise in the bar area, especially during the afternoon wine-and-cheese session. Big flatscreens and pleasing showers add comfort to rooms that are often overpriced but can be great value if advance booked.

★15Glasgow B&B £££
(0141-332 1263; www.15glasgow.com; 15 Woodside Pl; d/ste £130/160;) Glasgow's 19th-century merchants certainly knew how to build a beautiful house, and this 1840s terrace is a sumptuous example. Huge rooms with lofty ceilings have exquisite period detail complemented by attractive modern greys, striking bathrooms and well-chosen quality furniture.

Your welcoming host makes everything easy for you: the in-room breakfast, overlooking the park, is a real treat. They prefer no under-five-year-olds.

Eating & Drinking

Saramago Café Bar CAFE, VEGAN £
(0141-352 4920; www.cca-glasgow.com; 350 Sauchiehall St; mains £8-12; food noon-10pm Sun-Wed, to 11.30pm Thu-Sat;) In the airy atrium of the Centre for Contemporary Arts, this place does a great line in eclectic vegan fusion food, with a range of top flavour combinations from around the globe. The upstairs bar (open from 4pm) has a great deck on steep Scott St and packs out inside with a friendly arty crowd enjoying the DJ sets and quality tap beers.

Singl-end CAFE ££
(0141-353 1277; www.thesingl-end.co.uk; 265 Renfrew St; dishes £7-13; 9am-5pm;) There's something glorious about this long basement cafe with its cheery service and air of brunchy bonhomie. It covers a lot of bases, with good coffee, generous breakfasts and lunches, booze and baking. Dietary requirements are superbly catered for, with fine vegan choices and clear labelling. On a diet? Avert your eyes from the 'eat-me' cornucopia of meringues and pastries by the door.

★Ox & Finch FUSION ££
(0141-339 8627; www.oxandfinch.com; 920 Sauchiehall St; small plates £4-10; noon-10pm;) This fashionable place could almost sum up the thriving modern Glasgow eating scene, with a faux-pub name, sleek but comfortable contemporary decor, tapas-sized dishes and an open kitchen. Grab a cosy booth and be prepared to have your taste buds wowed by innovative, delicious creations aimed at sharing, drawing on French and Mediterreanean influences but focusing on quality Scottish produce.

★Ubiquitous Chip SCOTTISH £££
(0141-334 5007; www.ubiquitouschip.co.uk; 12 Ashton Lane; 2-/3-course lunch £20/24, mains £20-30, brasserie mains £13-16; restaurant noon-2.30pm & 5-11pm Mon-Sat, 12.30-3pm & 5-10pm Sun;) The original champion of Scottish produce, Ubiquitous Chip is legendary for its still-unparalleled cuisine and lengthy wine list. Named to poke fun at Scotland's culinary reputation, it offers a French touch but resolutely Scottish ingredients, carefully selected and following sustainable principles. The elegant courtyard space offers some of Glasgow's best dining, while, above, the cheaper brasserie (open longer hours) offers exceptional value for money.

The Horseshoe Bar PUB
(☎0141-248 6368; www.thehorseshoebarglasgow.co.uk; 17 Drury St; ⊙10am-midnight Sun-Fri, from 9am Sat) This legendary city pub and popular meeting place dates from the late 19th century and is largely unchanged. It's a picturesque spot, with the longest continuous bar in the UK, but its main attraction is what's served over it – real ale and good cheer. Upstairs in the lounge is some of the best-value pub food (dishes £4 to £10) in town.

Information

Glasgow Tourist Office (www.visitscotland.com; 158 Buchanan St; ⊙9am-5pm Mon-Sat, 10am-4pm Sun Nov-Apr, 9am-6pm Mon-Sat, 10am-4pm Sun May, Jun, Sep & Oct, 9am-7pm Mon-Sat, 10am-5pm Sun Jul & Aug;) The city's tourist office is in the centre of town. It opens at 9.30am on Thursday mornings.

Getting There & Away

Glasgow is easily reached from Edinburgh by bus (£7.90, 1¼ hours, every 15 minutes) or train (£14.40, 50 minutes, every 15 minutes).

Loch Lomond & the Trossachs

The 'bonnie banks' and 'bonnie braes' of Loch Lomond have long been Glasgow's rural retreat. The main tourist focus is on the loch's western shore, along the A82. The eastern shore, followed by the **West Highland Way** long-distance footpath, is quieter. The region's importance was recognised when it became the heart of **Loch Lomond & the Trossachs National Park** (☎01389-722600; www.lochlomond-trossachs.org) – Scotland's first national park, created in 2002.

The nearby Trossachs is a region famous for its thickly forested hills and scenic lochs. It first gained popularity in the early 19th century when curious visitors came from across Britain, drawn by the romantic language of Walter Scott's poem *Lady of the Lake,* inspired by Loch Katrine, and his novel *Rob Roy,* about the derring-do of the region's most famous son.

The main centre for Loch Lomond boat trips is Balloch, where **Sweeney's Cruises** (☎01389-752376; www.sweeneyscruiseco.com; Balloch Rd) offers a range of outings, including a one-hour cruise to Inchmurrin and back (adult/child £10.20/7, five times daily April to October, twice daily November to March).

Loch Katrine Cruises (☎01877-376315; www.lochkatrine.com; Trossachs Pier, Loch Katrine; 1hr cruise adult £12-14, child £6.50-7.50) runs boat trips from Trossachs Pier at the eastern end of Loch Katrine; some are aboard the fabulous centenarian steamship *Sir Walter Scott.* One-hour scenic cruises run one to four times daily; there are also departures to Stronachlachar at the other end of the loch (two hours return).

Sleeping & Eating

★Callander Hostel HOSTEL £
(☎01877 331465; www.callanderhostel.co.uk; 6 Bridgend; dm/d £19.50/60; P@) This hostel in a mock-Tudor building has been a

DON'T MISS

STIRLING CASTLE

Hold Stirling and you control Scotland. This maxim has ensured that a fortress of some kind has existed here since prehistoric times. You cannot help drawing parallels with Edinburgh Castle, but many find **Stirling Castle** (HES; www.stirlingcastle.gov.uk; Castle Wynd; adult/child £15/9; ⊙9.30am-6pm Apr-Sep, to 5pm Oct-Mar, last entry 45min before closing; P) more atmospheric – the location, architecture, historical significance and commanding views combine to make it a grand and memorable sight.

The current castle dates from the late 14th to the 16th century, when it was a residence of the Stuart monarchs. The undisputed highlight of a visit is the fabulous **Royal Palace** – during restoration the idea was that it should look brand new, just as when it was constructed by French masons under the orders of James V in the mid-16th century, with the aim of impressing his new (also French) bride and other crowned heads of Europe.

The suite of six rooms – three for the king, three for the queen – is a sumptuous riot of colour. Particularly notable are the fine fireplaces, the **Stirling Heads** – modern reproductions of painted oak discs in the ceiling of the king's audience chamber – and the fabulous series of **tapestries** that have been painstakingly woven over many years. Stirling is 35 miles northwest of Edinburgh, and easily reached by train (£9.10, one hour, half-hourly).

major labour of love by a local youth project and is now a top-class facility. Well-furnished dorms offer bunks with individual lights and USB charge ports, while en suite doubles have super views. Staff are lovely, and it has a spacious common area and share kitchen as well as a cafe and garden.

Oak Tree Inn INN ££
(01360-870357; www.theoaktreeinn.co.uk; Balmaha; s/d £80/100; P) An attractive traditional inn built in slate and timber, this place offers bright, modern bedrooms for pampered hikers, plus super-spacious superior chambers, self-catering cottages and glamping pods with their own deck. The rustic restaurant brings locals, tourists and walkers together and dishes up hearty meals that cover lots of bases (mains £10 to £13; open noon to 9pm). There's plenty of outdoor seating. But it doesn't end there; the Oak Tree is an impressive set-up that brews its own beers, makes its own ice cream (and sells it in an adjacent cafe), and smokes its own fish. In fact, Balmaha basically is the Oak Tree these days.

★**Callander Meadows** SCOTTISH ££
(01877-330181; www.callandermeadows.co.uk; 24 Main St; dinner mains £13-19; 10am-2.30pm & 6-8.30pm Thu-Sun year-round, plus Mon May-Sep;) Informal and cosy, this well-loved restaurant in the centre of Callander occupies the front rooms of a Main St house. It's truly excellent; there's a contemporary flair for presentation and unusual flavour combinations, but a solidly British base underpins the cuisine. There's a great beer/coffee garden out the back, where you can also eat. Lighter lunches such as sandwiches are also available.

Drover's Inn PUB FOOD ££
(01301-704234; www.thedroversinn.co.uk; Inverarnan; bar meals £9-14; 11.30am-10pm Mon-Sat, to 9.30pm or 10pm Sun; P) Don't miss this low-ceilinged howff (drinking den), just north of Ardlui, with its smoke-blackened stone, kilted bartenders, and walls adorned with moth-eaten stags' heads and stuffed birds. The convivial bar, where Rob Roy allegedly dropped by for pints, serves hearty hill-walking fuel and hosts live folk music on weekends.

Getting There & Away

Balloch, at the southern end of Loch Lomond, can be easily reached from Glasgow by bus (£5.30, 1½ hours, at least two per hour) or train (£5.60, 45 minutes, every 30 minutes).

For exploring the Trossachs, your own transport is recommended.

Inverness

01463 / POP 61,235

Inverness, the primary city and shopping centre of the Highlands, has a great location astride the River Ness at the northern end of the Great Glen. It's a jumping-off point for exploring Loch Ness and northern Scotland, with the railway line from Edinburgh branching east to Elgin and Aberdeen, north to Thurso and Wick, and west to Kyle of Lochalsh (the nearest train station to the Isle of Skye). The latter route is one of Britain's great scenic rail journeys.

Eating & Sleeping

Black Isle Bar & Rooms HOSTEL £
(01463-229920; www.blackislebar.com; 68 Church St; dm/s/d £25/55/100;) It's a beer drinker's dream come true – top-quality hostel accommodation in a central location, upstairs from a bar that serves real ales from the local Black Isle Brewery.

Ardconnel House B&B ££
(01463-240455; www.ardconnel-inverness.co.uk; 21 Ardconnel St; r per person £45-50;) The six-room Ardconnel is one of our favourites (advance booking is essential, especially in July and August) – a terraced Victorian house with comfortable en suite rooms, a dining room with crisp white table linen, and a breakfast menu that includes Vegemite for homesick Antipodeans. Kids under 10 years not allowed.

Ach Aluinn B&B ££
(01463-230127; www.achaluinn.com; 27 Fairfield Rd; r per person £40-45; P) This large, detached Victorian house is bright and homey, and offers all you might want from a B&B – a private bathroom, TV, reading lights, comfy beds with two pillows each, and an excellent breakfast. Less than 10 minutes' walk west from the city centre.

★**Trafford Bank** B&B £££
(01463-241414; www.traffordbankguesthouse.co.uk; 96 Fairfield Rd; d £130-150; P) Lots of rave reviews for this elegant Victorian villa, which was once home to a bishop, just a mitre's-toss from the Caledonian Canal and 10 minutes' walk west from the city centre. The luxurious rooms include fresh flowers and fruit, bathrobes and fluffy towels – ask for the Tartan Room, which has a wrought-iron king-size bed and Victorian roll-top bath.

★Café 1 BISTRO ££

(☎01463-226200; www.cafe1.net; 75 Castle St; mains £12-28; ⏰noon-2.30pm & 5-9.30pm Mon-Fri, 12.30-3pm & 6-9.30pm Sat;) Café 1 is a friendly, appealing bistro with candlelit tables amid elegant blond-wood and wrought-iron decor. There is an international menu based on quality Scottish produce, from Aberdeen Angus steaks to crisp pan-fried sea bass and meltingly tender pork belly. There's a separate vegan menu.

Kitchen Brasserie MODERN SCOTTISH ££

(☎01463 259119; www.kitchenrestaurant.co.uk; 15 Huntly St; mains £11-22; ⏰noon-3pm & 5-10pm;) This spectacular glass-fronted restaurant offers a great menu of top Scottish produce with a Mediterranean or Asian touch, and a view over the River Ness – try to get a table upstairs. Offers a great value two-course lunch (£10; noon to 3pm) and early-bird menu (£14; 5pm to 7pm).

Information

Inverness Tourist Office (☎01463-252401; www.visithighlands.com; 36 High St; ⏰9am-5pm Mon & Wed-Sat, from 10am Tue, 10am-3pm Sun, longer hours Mar-Oct;) Accommodation booking service; also sells tickets for tours and cruises.

Getting There & Away

BUS

Services depart from **Inverness bus station** (Margaret St). Most intercity routes are served by **Scottish Citylink** (☎0871 266 3333; www.citylink.co.uk) and **Stagecoach** (☎01463-233371; www.stagecoachbus.com). **National Express** (☎08717 818181; www.nationalexpress.com) has services to London (from £30, 13½ hours, one daily – more frequent services require changing at Glasgow).

Edinburgh (£32.20, 3½ to 4½ hours, seven daily)

Glasgow (£32.20, 3½ to 4½ hours, hourly)

Portree (£26.40, 3¼ hours, two daily)

If you book far enough in advance, **Megabus** (☎0141-352 4444; www.megabus.com) offers fares from as little as £1 for buses from Inverness to Glasgow and Edinburgh, and £10 to London.

TRAIN

Edinburgh (£40, 3½ hours, eight daily)

Kyle of Lochalsh (£20, 2½ hours, four daily Monday to Saturday, two Sunday) One of Britain's great scenic train journeys.

London (£180, eight to nine hours, one daily direct; others require a change at Edinburgh)

Loch Ness

Deep, dark and narrow, Loch Ness stretches for 23 miles between Inverness and Fort Augustus. Its bitterly cold waters have been extensively explored in search of the elusive Loch Ness monster, but most visitors see her only in cardboard cut-out form at the monster exhibitions. The village of **Drumnadrochit** is a hotbed of beastie fever, with two monster exhibitions battling it out for the tourist dollar.

Urquhart Castle CASTLE

(HES; ☎01456-450551; adult/child £9/5.40; ⏰9.30am-8pm Jun-Aug, to 6pm Apr, May & Sep, to 5pm Oct, to 4.30pm Nov-Mar; P) Commanding a superb location 1.5 miles east of Drumnadrochit, with outstanding views (on a clear day), Urquhart Castle is a popular Nessie-hunting hot spot. A huge visitor centre (most of which is beneath ground level) includes a video theatre (with a dramatic 'reveal' of the castle at the end of the film) and displays of medieval items discovered in the castle. The site includes a huge gift shop and a restaurant, and is often very crowded in summer.

Loch Ness Centre & Exhibition MUSEUM

(☎01456-450573; www.lochness.com; adult/child £7.95/4.95; ⏰9.30am-6pm Jul & Aug, to 5pm Easter Jun, Sep & Oct, 10am-4pm Nov-Easter; P) This Nessie-themed attraction adopts a scientific approach that allows you to weigh the evidence for yourself. Exhibits include original equipment – sonar survey vessels, miniature submarines, cameras and sediment coring tools – used in various monster hunts, plus original photographs and film footage of sightings.

You'll find out about hoaxes and optical illusions, as well as learning a lot about the ecology of Loch Ness – is there enough food in the loch to support even one 'monster', let alone a breeding population?

Nessie Hunter BOATING

(☎01456-450395; www.lochness-cruises.com; adult/child £16/10; ⏰Easter-Oct) One-hour monster-hunting cruises, complete with sonar and underwater cameras. Cruises depart from Drumnadrochit hourly (except 1pm) from 10am to 6pm daily.

★Loch Ness Inn INN ££

(☎01456-450991; www.staylochness.co.uk; Lewiston; s/d/f £99/120/140; P) Loch Ness Inn

THE NORTH COAST 500

This 500-mile circuit of northern Scotland's stunning coastline (www.northcoast500.com) has become hugely popular, with thousands of people completing the route by car, campervan, motorbike or bicycle.

ticks all the weary traveller's boxes, with comfortable bedrooms (the family suite sleeps two adults and two children), a cosy bar pouring real ales from the Cairngorm and Isle of Skye breweries, and a rustic restaurant (mains £10 to £20) serving wholesome fare. It's conveniently located in the quiet hamlet of Lewiston, between Drumnadrochit and Urquhart Castle.

Getting There & Away

Stagecoach (p167) buses run from Inverness to Drumnadrochit (£3.70, 30 minutes, six to eight daily, five on Sunday) and Urquhart Castle car park (£4, 35 minutes).

Skye

POP 10,000

The Isle of Skye is the biggest of Scotland's islands (linked to the mainland by a bridge at Kyle of Lochalsh), a 50-mile-long smorgasbord of velvet moors, jagged mountains, sparkling lochs and towering sea cliffs. It takes its name from the old Norse *sky-a*, meaning 'cloud island', a Viking reference to the often mist-enshrouded **Cuillin Hills**, Britain's most spectacular mountain range. The stunning scenery is the main attraction, including the cliffs and pinnacles of the **Old Man of Storr**, **Kilt Rock** and the **Quiraing**, but there are plenty of cosy pubs to retire to when the rainclouds close in.

Portree is the main town, with **Broadford** a close second; both have banks, ATMs, supermarkets and petrol stations.

Sights & Activities

Dunvegan Castle CASTLE

(☎01470-521206; www.dunvegancastle.com; adult/child £14/9; ⏲10am-5.30pm Easter–mid-Oct; P) Skye's most famous historic building, and one of its most popular tourist attractions, Dunvegan Castle is the seat of the chief of Clan MacLeod. In addition to the usual castle stuff – swords, silver and family portraits – there are some interesting artefacts, including the Fairy Flag, a diaphanous silk banner that dates from some time between the 4th and 7th centuries, and Bonnie Prince Charlie's waistcoat and a lock of his hair, donated by Flora MacDonald's granddaughter.

Skye Tours BUS

(☎01471-822716; www.skye-tours.co.uk; adult/child £40/30; ⏲Mon-Sat) Five-hour sightseeing tours of Skye in a minibus, taking in the Old Man of Storr, Kilt Rock and Dunvegan Castle. Tours depart from Kyle of Lochalsh train station at 11.30am, connecting with the 8.55am train from Inverness, and returning to Kyle by 4.45pm in time to catch the return train at 5.13pm.

Sleeping

Portree, the island's capital, has the largest selection of accommodation, eating places and other services.

★**Cowshed Boutique Bunkhouse** HOSTEL £

(☎07917 536820; www.skyecowshed.co.uk; Uig; dm/tw/pod £20/80/70; P) This hostel enjoys a glorious setting overlooking Uig Bay, with superb views from its ultra-stylish lounge. The dorms have custom-built wooden bunks that offer comfort and privacy, while the camping pods (sleeping up to four, but more comfortable with two) have heating and en suite shower rooms; there are even mini 'dog pods' for your canine companions.

Portree Youth Hostel HOSTEL £

(SYHA; ☎01478-612231; www.syha.org.uk; Bayfield Rd; dm/tw £26/78; P) This SYHA hostel (formerly Bayfield Backpackers) was completely renovated in 2015 and offers brightly decorated dorms and private rooms, a stylish lounge with views over the bay, and outdoor seating areas. Its location in the town centre just 100m from the bus stop is ideal.

Ben Tianavaig B&B B&B ££

(☎01478-612152; www.ben-tianavaig.co.uk; 5 Bosville Tce; r £80-98; P) A warm welcome awaits from the Irish-Welsh couple who run this appealing B&B bang in the centre of town. All four bedrooms have a view across the harbour to the hill that gives the house its name, and breakfasts include free-range eggs and vegetables grown in the garden.

Two-night minimum stay April to October; no credit cards.

Eating

★Cafe Sia

CAFE, PIZZERIA ££

(☎01471-822616; www.cafesia.co.uk; Rathad na h-Atha; mains £7-17; ⏲10am-9pm; 📶👪) Serving everything from eggs Benedict and cappuccino to cocktails and seafood specials, this appealing cafe specialises in wood-fired pizzas (also available to take away) and superb artisanal coffee. There's also an outdoor deck with great views of the Red Cuillin. Takeaway coffee from 8am.

Scorrybreac

MODERN SCOTTISH ££

(☎01478-612069; www.scorrybreac.com; 7 Bosville Tce; 3-course dinner £42; ⏲5-9pm Wed-Sun year-round, noon-2pm mid-May–mid-Sep) Set in the front rooms of what was once a private house, and with just eight tables, Scorrybreac is snug and intimate, offering fine dining without the faff. Chef Calum Munro (son of Donnie Munro, of Gaelic rock band Runrig fame) sources as much produce as possible from Skye, including foraged herbs and mushrooms, and creates the most exquisite concoctions.

★Loch Bay

SEAFOOD £££

(☎01470-592235; www.lochbay-restaurant.co.uk; Stein, Waternish; 3-course dinner £43.50; ⏲12.15-1.45pm Wed-Sun, 6.15-9pm Tue-Sat Apr-early Oct; P) This cosy farmhouse kitchen of a place, with terracotta tiles and a wood-burning stove, is one of Skye's most romantic restaurants and was awarded a Michelin star in 2018. The menu includes most things that swim in the sea or live in a shell, but there are non-seafood choices too. Best to book ahead.

Three Chimneys

MODERN SCOTTISH £££

(☎01470-511258; www.threechimneys.co.uk; Colbost; 3-course lunch/dinner £40/68; ⏲12.15-1.45pm Mon-Sat mid-Mar–Oct, plus Sun Easter-Sep, 6.30-9.15pm daily year-round; P📶) Halfway between Dunvegan and Waterstein, the Three Chimneys is a superb romantic retreat combining a gourmet restaurant in a candlelit crofter's cottage with sumptuous five-star rooms (double £345) in the modern house next door. Book well in advance, and note that children are not welcome in the restaurant in the evenings.

Information

Portree Tourist Office (☎01478-612992; www.visitscotland.com; Bayfield Rd; ⏲9am-6pm Mon-Sat, 10am-4pm Sun Jun-Aug, shorter hours Sep-May; 📶) The only tourist office on the island, it provides internet access and an accommodation booking service. Ask for the free *Art Skye – Gallery & Studio Trails* booklet.

Getting There & Away

BOAT

Despite the bridge, there are still a couple of ferry links between Skye and the mainland. Ferries also operate from Uig on Skye to the Outer Hebrides.

The **CalMac** (☎0800 066 5000; www.calmac.co.uk) ferry between Mallaig and Armadale (passenger/car £2.90/9.70, 30 minutes, eight daily Monday to Saturday, five to seven on Sunday) is very popular on weekends and in July and August. Book ahead if you're travelling by car.

The **Glenelg-Skye Ferry** (☎07881 634726; www.skyeferry.co.uk; car with up to 4 passengers £15; ⏲Easter–mid-Oct) runs a tiny vessel (six cars only) on the short Kylerhea to Glenelg crossing (five minutes, every 20 minutes). The ferry operates from 10am to 6pm daily (till 7pm June to August).

BUS

There are buses from Glasgow to Portree (£44, seven hours, three daily), and Uig (£44, 7½ hours, two daily) via Crianlarich, Fort William and Kyle of Lochalsh, plus a service from Inverness to Portree (£26.40, 3¼ hours, three daily).

SURVIVAL GUIDE

Directory A-Z

ACCOMMODATION

Booking your accommodation in advance is recommended, especially in popular holiday areas and on islands (where options are often limited). Summer and school holidays (including half-terms) are particularly busy. Book at least two months ahead for July and August.

B&Bs These small, family-run houses generally provide good value. More luxurious versions are more like boutique hotels.

Hotels British hotels range from half a dozen rooms above a pub to restored country houses and castles, with a commensurate range in rates.

Hostels There's a good choice of both institutional and independent hostels, many housed in rustic and/or historic buildings.

ACTIVITIES

Walking is the most popular outdoor activity in Britain, for locals and visitors alike: firstly, because it opens up some beautiful corners of the country, and secondly, because it can be done virtually on a whim. In fact, compared to hiking and trekking in some other parts of the world, it doesn't take much planning at all.

Good maps and websites include the following:

Ordnance Survey UK's national mapping agency; Explorer series 1:25,000 scale.

Harvey Maps Specially designed for walkers; Superwalker series 1:25,000 scale.

www.walkhighlands.co.uk Superb database for walks of all lengths in Scotland.

www.walkingenglishman.com Short walks in England and Wales.

www.nationaltrail.co.uk Great for specifics on long-distance trails in England and Wales.

www.scotlandsgreattrails.com Long-distance trails in Scotland.

LGBTIQ+ TRAVELLERS

Britain is a generally tolerant place for gays and lesbians. London, Manchester and Brighton have flourishing gay scenes, and in other sizeable cities (even some small towns), you'll find communities not entirely in the closet. That said, you'll still find pockets of homophobic hostility in some areas. Resources include the following:

Diva (www.divamag.co.uk)

Gay Times (www.gaytimes.co.uk)

Switchboard LGBT+ Helpline (0300 330 0630; www.switchboard.lgbt)

MONEY

➡ The currency of Britain is the pound sterling (£). Banknotes come in £5, £10, £20 and £50 denominations, although some shops don't accept £50 notes.

➡ ATMs, often called cash machines, are easy to find in towns and cities.

➡ Most banks and some post offices offer currency exchange.

➡ Visa and MasterCard credit and debit cards are widely accepted in Britain. Nearly everywhere uses a 'Chip and PIN' system (instead of signing).

➡ Smaller businesses may charge a fee for credit-card use, and some take cash or cheque only.

➡ Tipping is not obligatory. A 10% to 15% tip is fine for restaurants, cafes, taxi drivers and pub meals; if you order drinks and food at the bar, there's no need to tip.

SCHOOL HOLIDAYS

Roads get busy and hotel prices go up during school holidays.

Easter holiday Week before and week after Easter.

Summer holiday Third week of July to first week of September.

Christmas holiday Mid-December to first week of January.

There are also three week-long 'half-term' school holidays – usually late February (or early March), late May and late October. These vary between Scotland, England and Wales.

OPENING HOURS

Opening hours may vary throughout the year, especially in rural areas where many places have shorter hours or close completely from October or November to March or April.

Banks 9.30am–4pm or 5pm Monday to Friday; some open 9.30am–1pm Saturday

Pubs and bars Noon–11pm Monday to Saturday (many till midnight or 1am Friday and Saturday, especially in Scotland) and 12.30–11pm Sunday

Restaurants Lunch noon–3pm, dinner 6–9pm or 10pm (or later in cities)

Shops 9am–5.30pm (or to 6pm in cities) Monday to Saturday, and often 11am–5pm Sunday; big-city convenience stores open 24/7

PUBLIC HOLIDAYS

Holidays for the whole of Britain:

New Year's Day 1 January (plus 2 January in Scotland)

Easter March/April (Good Friday to Easter Monday inclusive)

May Day First Monday in May

Spring Bank Holiday Last Monday in May

Summer Bank Holiday Last Monday in August

Christmas Day 25 December

Boxing Day 26 December

If a public holiday falls on a weekend, the nearest Monday is usually taken instead. In England and Wales most businesses and banks close on official public holidays (hence the quaint term 'bank holiday'). In Scotland, bank holidays are just for the banks, and many businesses stay open. Many Scottish towns normally have a spring and autumn holiday, but the dates vary.

On public holidays, some small museums and places of interest close, but larger attractions have their busiest times. If a place closes on Sunday, it'll probably be shut on bank holidays as well.

Virtually everything – attractions, shops, banks, offices – closes on Christmas Day, although pubs open at lunchtime. There's usually no public transport on Christmas Day, and a very minimal service on Boxing Day.

SAFE TRAVEL

Britain is a remarkably safe country, but crime is not unknown – especially in London and other cities.

- Watch out for pickpockets and hustlers in crowded areas popular with tourists, such as around Westminster Bridge in London.
- When travelling by tube, tram or urban train services at night, choose a carriage containing other people.
- Many town centres can be rowdy on Friday and Saturday nights when the pubs and clubs are emptying.
- Unlicensed minicabs – a driver with a car earning money on the side – operate in large cities, and are worth avoiding unless you know what you're doing.

TELEPHONE

The UK uses the GSM 900/1800 network, which covers the rest of Europe, Australia and New Zealand, but isn't compatible with the North American GSM 1900. Most modern mobiles can function on both networks, but check before you leave home just in case.

VISAS

Generally not needed for stays of up to six months. Britain is not a member of the Schengen Zone, so you will need to show your passport when arriving and leaving from a UK border point.

 Getting There & Away

AIR

Visitors to the UK arriving by air generally do so at one of London's two largest airports, Heathrow and Gatwick, which have a huge range of international flights to pretty much all corners of the globe. International flights also serve the capital's three other airports (Stansted, Luton and London City) and regional hubs such as Manchester, Bristol and Edinburgh.

London Airports

The national carrier is **British Airways** (www.britishairways.com).

The main airports are as follows:

Heathrow (www.heathrowairport.com) Britain's main airport for international flights; often chaotic and crowded. About 15 miles west of central London.

Gatwick (www.gatwickairport.com) Britain's number-two airport, mainly for international flights, 30 miles south of central London.

Stansted (www.stanstedairport.com) About 35 miles northeast of central London, mainly handling charter and budget European flights.

Luton (www.london-luton.co.uk) Some 35 miles north of central London, well known as a holiday-flight airport.

London City (www.londoncityairport.com) A few miles east of central London, specialising in flights to/from European and other UK airports.

> **TRAVELINE**
>
> **Traveline** (www.traveline.info) is a very useful information service covering bus, coach, taxi and train services nationwide.

LAND

Bus

You can easily get between Britain and other European countries via long-distance bus or coach. The international network **Eurolines** (www.eurolines.com) connects a huge number of destinations; you can buy tickets online via one of the national operators.

Services to/from Britain are operated by **National Express** (www.nationalexpress.com). Sample journeys and times to/from London include Amsterdam (12 hours), Barcelona (24 hours), Dublin (12 hours), and Paris (eight hours).

If you book early, and can be flexible with timings (ie travel when few other people want to), you can get some very good deals, eg between London to Paris or Amsterdam from about £25 one way (although paying £35 to £45 is more usual).

Train

High-speed **Eurostar** (www.eurostar.com) passenger services shuttle at least 10 times daily between London and Paris (2½ hours) or Brussels (two hours). Buy tickets from travel agencies, major train stations or the Eurostar website.

The normal one-way fare between London and Paris/Brussels costs around £154; advance booking and off-peak travel gets cheaper fares, as low as £29 one way.

Drivers use **Eurotunnel** (www.eurotunnel.com). At Folkestone in England or Calais in France, you drive onto a train, get carried through the tunnel and drive off at the other end.

Trains run about four times an hour from 6am to 10pm, then hourly through the night. Loading and unloading takes an hour; the journey lasts 35 minutes.

Book in advance online or pay on the spot. The standard one-way fare for a car and up to nine passengers is between £75 and £100 depending on the time of day; promotional fares often bring it down to £59 or less.

SEA

The main ferry routes between Great Britain and other European countries are as follows:

- Dover–Calais (France)

- Dover–Boulogne (France)
- Newhaven–Dieppe (France)
- Liverpool–Dublin (Ireland)
- Holyhead–Dublin (Ireland)
- Fishguard–Rosslare (Ireland)
- Pembroke Dock–Rosslare (Ireland)
- Newcastle–Amsterdam (Netherlands)
- Harwich–Hook of Holland (Netherlands)
- Hull–Rotterdam (Netherlands)
- Hull–Zeebrugge (Belgium)
- Cairnryan–Larne (Northern Ireland)
- Portsmouth–Santander (Spain)
- Portsmouth–Bilbao (Spain)

Book direct with one of the operators listed below, or use the very handy www.directferries.co.uk – a single site covering all sea-ferry routes, plus Eurotunnel.

Brittany Ferries (www.brittany-ferries.com)
DFDS Seaways (www.dfdsseaways.co.uk)
Irish Ferries (www.irishferries.com)
P&O Ferries (www.poferries.com)
Stena Line (www.stenaline.com)

Getting Around

Having your own car makes the best use of time and helps reach remote places, but rental, fuel costs and parking can be expensive – so public transport is often the better way to go.

Cheapest but slowest are long-distance buses (called coaches in Britain). Trains are faster but much more expensive.

AIR

If you're really pushed for time, flights on longer routes across Britain (eg London to Inverness) are handy. On some shorter routes (eg London to Edinburgh) trains compare favourably with planes on time, once airport downtime is factored in. On costs, you might get a bargain airfare, but trains can be cheaper if you buy tickets in advance. Some of Britain's domestic airline companies are as follows:

British Airways (www.britishairways.com)
EasyJet (www.easyjet.com)

> **CONNECTIONS**
>
> The quickest way to Europe from Britain is via the Channel Tunnel, which has direct Eurostar rail services from London to Paris and Brussels. Ferries sail from southern England to French ports in a couple of hours; other routes connect eastern England to the Netherlands, Germany and northern Spain, and Ireland from southwest Scotland and Wales.

FlyBe (www.flybe.com)
Loganair (www.loganair.co.uk)
Ryanair (www.ryanair.com)

BUS

If you're on a tight budget, long-distance buses are nearly always the cheapest way to get around, although they're also the slowest – sometimes by a considerable margin. Many towns have separate stations for local buses and long-distance coaches; make sure you go to the right one!

National Express (www.nationalexpress.com) is the main coach operator, with a wide network and frequent services between main centres. North of the border, services tie in with those of **Scottish Citylink** (www.citylink.co.uk), Scotland's leading coach company. Fares vary: they're cheaper if you book in advance and travel at quieter times, and more expensive if you buy your ticket on the spot and it's Friday afternoon. As a guide, a 200-mile trip (eg London to York) will cost £15 to £25 if you book a few days in advance.

Megabus (www.megabus.com) operates a budget coach service between about 30 destinations around the country. Go at a quiet time, book early and your ticket will be very cheap. Book later, for a busy time and... You get the picture.

CAR & MOTORCYCLE

Traffic drives on the left; steering wheels are on the right side of the car. Most rental cars have manual gears (stick shift).

Rental

Compared with many countries (especially the USA), hire rates are expensive in Britain: the smallest cars start at about £130 per week, and it's around £190 and upwards per week for a medium car. All rates include insurance and unlimited mileage, and can rise at busy times (or drop at quiet times).

Main players are as follows:

Avis (www.avis.co.uk)
Budget (www.budget.co.uk)
Europcar (www.europcar.co.uk)
Sixt (www.sixt.co.uk)
Thrifty (www.thrifty.co.uk)

Another option is to look online for small local car-hire companies in Britain that can undercut the international franchises. Generally those in cities are cheaper than in rural areas. Using a rental-broker or comparison site such as **UK Car Hire** (www.ukcarhire.net) or **Kayak** (www.kayak.com) can also help find bargains.

Road Rules

A foreign driving licence is valid in Britain for up to 12 months.

Drink-driving is taken very seriously; you're allowed a maximum blood-alcohol level of 80mg/100mL (0.08%) in England and Wales, and 50mg/100mL (0.05%) in Scotland.

Some other important rules:

➡ Drive on the left.

➡ Wear fitted seatbelts in cars.

➡ Wear helmets on motorcycles.

➡ Give way to your right at junctions and roundabouts.

➡ Always use the left lane on motorways and dual carriageways unless overtaking (although so many people ignore this rule, you'd think it didn't exist).

➡ Don't use a mobile phone while driving unless it's fully hands-free (another rule frequently flouted).

TRAIN

About 20 different companies operate train services in Britain, while Network Rail operates track and stations. For some passengers this system can be confusing at first, but information and ticket-buying services are mostly centralised. If you have to change trains, or use two or more train operators, you still buy one ticket – valid for the whole journey. The main railcards and passes are also accepted by all train operators.

Where more than one train operator services the same route, eg York to Edinburgh, a ticket purchased from one company may not be valid on trains run by another. So if you miss the train you originally booked, it's worth checking which later services your ticket will be valid for.

Classes

There are two classes of rail travel: first and standard. First class costs around 50% more than standard fare (up to double at busy periods) and gets you bigger seats, more leg-room and usually a more peaceful business-like atmosphere, plus extras such as complimentary drinks and newspapers. At weekends some train operators offer 'upgrades' to first class for an extra £5 to £25 on top of your standard class fare, payable on the spot.

Your first stop should be **National Rail Enquiries** (www.nationalrail.co.uk), the nationwide timetable and fare information service. Its website advertises special offers and has real-time links to station departure boards and downloadable maps of the rail network.

Tickets & Reservations

For longer journeys, on-the-spot fares are always available, but tickets are much cheaper if bought in advance. The earlier you book, the cheaper it gets. You can also save if you travel off-peak. Advance purchase usually gets a reserved seat too.

SCOTTISH BANKNOTES

Scottish banks issue their own sterling banknotes. They are interchangeable with Bank of England notes, but you'll sometimes run into problems outside Scotland – shops in the south of England may refuse to accept them. They are also harder to exchange once you get outside the UK, though British banks will always exchange them.

Whichever operator you travel with and wherever you buy tickets, these are the three main fare types:

Anytime Buy anytime, travel anytime – usually the most expensive option.

Off-peak Buy ticket any time and travel off-peak (what is off-peak depends on the journey).

Advance Buy ticket in advance and travel only on specific trains – usually the cheapest option.

For an idea of the (substantial) price differences, an Anytime single ticket from London to York will cost £127 or more, an Off-peak around £109, with an Advance around £44 to £55. The cheapest fares are usually nonrefundable, so if you miss your train you'll have to buy a new ticket.

Mobile train tickets are gradually becoming more common across the network, but it's a slow process – for now printed tickets are still the norm.

Train Passes

If you're staying in Britain for a while, passes known as **Railcards** (www.railcard.co.uk) are worth considering.

16-25 Railcard For those aged 16 to 25, or full-time UK students.

Two Together Railcard For two specified people travelling together.

Senior Railcard For anyone over 60.

Family & Friends Railcard Covers up to four adults and four children travelling together.

Railcards cost £30 (valid for one year; available from major stations or online) and give a 33% discount on most train fares, except those already heavily discounted. With the Family card, adults get 33% and children get 60% discounts, so the fee is easily recouped in a couple of journeys.

For country-wide travel, **BritRail** (www.britrail.net) passes are available for visitors from overseas. They must be bought in your country of origin (not in Britain) from a specialist travel agency. They're available in seven different versions (eg England only; Scotland only; all of Britain; UK and Ireland) for periods from four to 30 days.

France

POP 67.2 MILLION

Includes ➡

Best Places to Eat

- ➡ L'Assiette Champenoise (p209)
- ➡ Restaurant AT (p193)
- ➡ 1741 (p212)
- ➡ Le Musée (p220)

Best Places to Stay

- ➡ Hôtel Ritz Paris (p192)
- ➡ Hôtel Particulier Montmartre (p192)
- ➡ Château Les Crayères (p209)
- ➡ Cour du Corbeau (p211)

Why Go?

France seduces travellers with its iconic landmarks and unfalteringly familiar culture woven around cafe terraces, markets and lace-curtained bistros with their *plat du jour* (dish of the day) chalked on the board. Nowhere else does the simple rhythm of daily life transform everyday rituals into exquisite moments quite like *la belle France:* a coffee and croissant in the Parisian cafe where Jean-Paul Sartre and Simone de Beauvoir met, a stroll through the lily-clad gardens Monet painted, a walk on a beach in Brittany scented with the subtle infusion of language, music and mythology brought by 5th-century Celtic invaders.

France is the world's top tourism destination, attracting some 89 million visitors each year with its exceptional wealth of museums and galleries, world-class art and architecture, tempting cuisine, and incredible bounty of outdoor experiences. Go slowly and enjoy.

When to Go

Paris

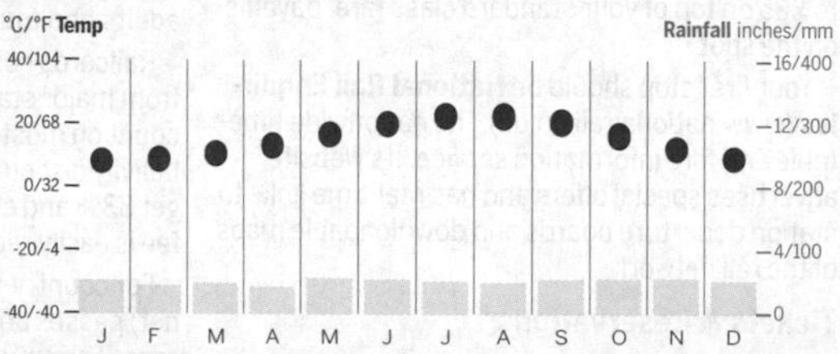

Dec–Mar Christmas markets in Alsace, snow in the Alps and decadent black truffles in the south.

Apr–Jun France is at its springtime best, with good weather and far smaller crowds.

Sep–Oct Cooling temperatures, abundant local produce and the *vendange* (grape harvest).

Entering the Country

Air France (www.airfrance.com) is the national carrier, with plenty of both domestic and international flights in and out of major French airports. Rail services link France with virtually every country in Europe. Eurolines (www.eurolines.eu), a grouping of 32 long-haul coach operators (including the UK's National Express), links France with cities all across Europe, Morocco and Russia.

ITINERARIES

One Week

Start with a couple of days exploring Paris (p178), taking in the Louvre, the Eiffel Tower, Montmartre and a boat trip along the Seine. Day-trip to magnificent Versailles (p200) and then spend the rest of the week in Normandy (p204) to visit WWII's D-Day beaches and glorious Mont St-Michel. Or head east to Champagne (p208) to sample the famous bubbly and visit Reims' (p208) magnificent cathedral.

Two Weeks

With Paris and surrounds having taken up much of the first week, hop on a high-speed TGV to Avignon (p237) or Marseille (p232) and take in the delights of Provence's Roman heritage, its beautiful hilltop villages and its famous artistic legacy. Finish your stay with a few days in Nice (p239), enjoying its glittering Mediterranean landscapes and sunny cuisine. Alternatively, head southwest to elegant Bordeaux (p225) and its world-famous vineyards before pushing inland to the Dordogne (p224) with its hearty gastronomy and unique prehistoric-art heritage.

Essential Food & Drink

Bordeaux and Burgundy wines You'll find France's signature reds in every restaurant; now find out more by touring the vineyards.

Bouillabaisse Marseille's signature hearty fish stew, eaten with croutons and rouille (garlic-and-chilli mayonnaise).

Champagne Tasting in century-old cellars is an essential part of Champagne's bubbly experience.

Foie gras and truffles The Dordogne features goose and 'black diamonds' from December to March. Provence is also good for indulging in the aphrodisiacal fungi.

Fondue and raclette Warming cheese dishes in the French Alps.

Oysters and white wine Everywhere on the Atlantic coast, but especially in Cancale and Bordeaux.

Piggy-part cuisine Lyon is famous for its juicy *andouillette* (pig-intestine sausage), a perfect marriage with a local Côtes du Rhône red.

AT A GLANCE

Area 551,000 sq km

Capital Paris

Country Code ☎33

Currency euro (€)

Emergency ☎112

Language French

Time Central European Time (GMT/UTC plus one hour)

Visas Schengen rules apply

Sleeping Price Ranges

The following price ranges refer to a double room in high season, with private bathroom, excluding breakfast unless noted.

€ less than €90 (€130 in Paris)

€€ €90–190 (€130–250 in Paris)

€€€ more than €190 (€250 in Paris)

Eating Price Ranges

The following price ranges refer to the average cost of a two-course à la carte meal (starter and main, or main and dessert), or a two- or three-course *menu* (set meal at a fixed price).

€ less than €20

€€ €20–40

€€€ more than €40

Resources

France.fr (www.france.fr)

France 24 (www.france24.com/en/france)

France Highlights

❶ **Paris** (p178) Gorging on the iconic sights and sophistication of Europe's most impossibly romantic city.

❷ **Loire Valley** (p212) Reliving the French Renaissance with extraordinary châteaux built by kings and queens.

❸ **Chamonix** (p222) Doing a Bond and swooshing down slopes in the shadow of Mont Blanc.

❹ **Mont St-Michel** (p206) Dodging tides, strolling moonlit sand and immersing yourself in legend at this island abbey.

❺ **Provence** (p232) Savouring ancient ruins, modern art, markets, lavender and hilltop villages.

❻ **Dune du Pilat** (p229) Romping up and down Europe's largest sand dune.

❼ **Épernay** (p210) Tasting bubbly in ancient *caves* (cellars) in the heart of Champagne.

❽ **Lyon** (p217) Tucking into France's piggy-driven cuisine in a traditional *bouchon* (Lyonnais bistro).

❾ **Casino de Monte Carlo** (p245) Hitting the big time in Monaco's sumptuous gaming house.

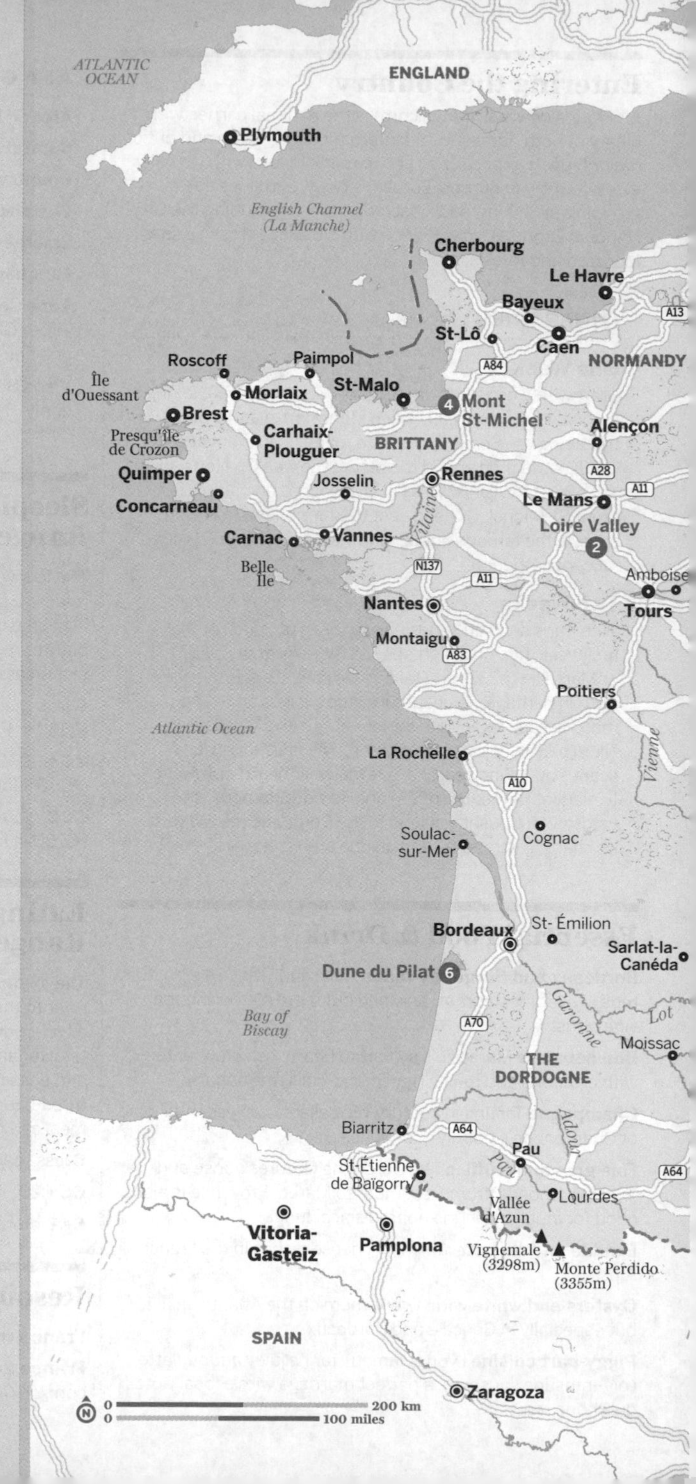

Folkestone
Dunkirk
Calais
Boulogne-sur-Mer
BRUSSELS
NETHERLANDS
BELGIUM
Lille
Meuse
GERMANY
A28
Authie
Somme
Mainz
SOMME
LUXEMBOURG
LUXEMBOURG CITY
A1
Oise
Aisne
A4
Reims
Vernon
Marne
7
Épernay
Metz
Versailles
1
Paris
ALSACE
Stuttgart
Strasbourg
Nancy
Dreux
Seine
Marne
Moselle
A5
Sélestat
Chartres
Troyes
LORRAINE
Épinal
Schnellenbuhl
A10
A6
A31
Katzenthal
BURGUNDY
Orléans
Auxerre
Saône
Beaugency
Chambord
Basel
LIECHTENSTEIN
Blois
Dijon
Besançon
Doubs
VADUZ
AUSTRIA
LA SOLOGNE
CÔTE D'OR
A36
Arc-et-Senans
BERN
Cher
Beaune
SWITZERLAND
Arbois
Métabief
JURA
Loire
Le Creusot
Mont d'Or
Les Rousses
Lausanne
Lake Geneva
A6
A20
Les Portes du Soleil
A71
Chamonix
3
Annecy
Mont Blanc (4810m)
A72
Lyon
Limoges
Clermont-Ferrand
8
Rhône
Chambéry
Milan
LIMOUSIN
Dordogne
A48
FRENCH ALPS
St Étienne
ITALY
Turin
Moissac
Turenne
Puy Mary (1787m)
Allier
A49
Grenoble
Drac
Sestriere
Rhône
Valence
D921
A7
Genoa
Vaison la Romaine
Mt Lozère (1699m)
Durance
Cahors
Mt Ventoux (1912m)
THE LOT
Pont du Gard
Avignon
Tarn
A75
Nîmes
Nice
9
Monaco
Ligurian Sea
Provence
Les Baux-de-Provence
5
Toulouse
Montpellier
Arles
Cannes
Aix-en-Provence
LANGUEDOC
Marseille
St-Tropez
A61
Carcassonne
ROUSILLON
Golfe de Beauduc
Ariège
A9
Île Rousse
Bastia
Perpignan
Calvi
ANDORRA
Monte Cinto (2706m)
ANDORRA LA VELLA
Puig Neulós
Mediterranean Sea
CORSICA
SPAIN
Ajaccio
Bonifacio
Barcelona
ITALY

PARIS

POP 2.2 MILLION

What can be said about the timelessly sexy, sophisticated City of Lights that hasn't already been said myriad times before? Quite simply, this is one of the world's great metropolises – a trendsetter, market leader and cultural capital for over a thousand years and still going strong.

As you might expect, Paris is strewn with historic architecture, glorious galleries and cultural treasures galore. But the modern-day city is much more than just a museum piece: a new wave of multimedia galleries, creative wine bars, design shops and tech start-ups ensure it stays right up-to-the-minute and a delightful place to simply be: stroll the boulevards, shop until you drop, flop riverside or simply do as the Parisians do and watch the city's unique world buzz by from a cafe pavement terrace.

Sights

Most sights offer discounted tickets *(tarif réduit)* for students and seniors (over 60) provided they have valid ID. Children are often free; the cut-off age for 'child' is between six and 18 years. EU citizens under 26 years get in for free at national monuments and museums. The **Paris Museum Pass** (http://en.parismuseumpass.com; two/four/six days €48/62/74) covers admission to 50-plus venues – often via a different entrance to bypass ridiculously long ticket queues. The **Paris Passlib'** (www.parisinfo.com; two/three/five days €109/129/155) pass includes the above plus unlimited public transport in zones 1 to 3, a boat cruise and a one-day hop-on, hop-off open-top bus sightseeing tour around central Paris.

Left Bank

★Eiffel Tower TOWER

(☎08 92 70 12 39; www.toureiffel.paris; Champ de Mars, 5 av Anatole France, 7e; adult/child lift to top €25/12.50, lift to 2nd fl €16/8, stairs to 2nd fl €10/5; ⏲lifts & stairs 9am-12.45am mid-Jun–Aug, lifts 9.30am-11.45pm, stairs 9.30am-6.30pm Sep–mid-Jun; Ⓜ Bir Hakeim or RER Champ de Mars–Tour Eiffel) No one could imagine Paris today without it. But Gustave Eiffel only constructed this elegant, 324m-tall signature spire as a temporary exhibit for the 1889 World's Fair. Luckily, the art nouveau tower's popularity assured its survival. Prebook online to avoid painfully long ticket queues. Lifts ascend to the tower's three floors; change lifts on the 2nd floor for the final ascent to the top. Energetic visitors can climb as far as the 2nd floor via the south pillar's 720 stairs (no prebooking).

★Musée du Quai Branly – Jacques Chirac MUSEUM

(☎01 56 61 70 00; www.quaibranly.fr; 37 quai Branly, 7e; adult/child €10/free; ⏲11am-7pm Tue, Wed & Sun, 11am-9pm Thu-Sat, plus 11am-7pm Mon during school holidays; Ⓜ Alma Marceau or RER Pont de l'Alma) A tribute to the diversity of human culture, Musée du Quai Branly's highly inspiring overview of indigenous and folk art spans four main sections – Oceania, Asia, Africa and the Americas. An impressive array of masks, carvings, weapons, jewellery and more make up the body of the rich collection, displayed in a refreshingly unorthodox interior without rooms or high walls. Look out for excellent temporary exhibitions and performances.

★Hôtel des Invalides MONUMENT, MUSEUM

(www.musee-armee.fr; 129 rue de Grenelle, 7e; adult/child €12/free; ⏲10am-6pm Apr-Oct, to 5pm Nov-Mar; Ⓜ Varenne or La Tour Maubourg) Flanked by the 500m-long Esplanade des Invalides lawns, Hôtel des Invalides was built in the 1670s by Louis XIV to house 4000 *invalides* (disabled war veterans). On 14 July 1789, a mob broke into the building and seized 32,000 rifles before heading on to the prison at Bastille and the start of the French Revolution. Admission includes entry to all Hôtel des Invalides sights (temporary exhibitions cost extra). Hours for individual sites can vary – check the website for updates.

★Musée Rodin MUSEUM, GARDEN

(☎01 44 18 61 10; www.musee-rodin.fr; 79 rue de Varenne, 7e; adult/child €10/free, garden only €4/free; ⏲10am-5.45pm Tue-Sun; Ⓜ Varenne or Invalides) Sculptor, painter, sketcher, engraver and collector Auguste Rodin donated his entire collection to the French state in 1908 on the proviso that it dedicate his former workshop and showroom, the beautiful 1730 Hôtel Biron, to displaying his works. They're now installed not only in the mansion itself, but also in its rose-filled garden – one of the most peaceful places in central Paris and a wonderful spot to contemplate his famous work *The Thinker*. Prepurchase tickets online to avoid queuing.

★Musée d'Orsay MUSEUM

(☎01 40 49 48 14; www.musee-orsay.fr; 1 rue de la Légion d'Honneur, 7e; adult/child €14/free; ⏲9.30am-6pm Tue, Wed & Fri-Sun, to 9.45pm Thu;

Ⓜ Assemblée Nationale or RER Musée d'Orsay) The home of France's national collection from the impressionist, post-impressionist and art nouveau movements spanning from 1848 to 1914 is the glorious former Gare d'Orsay train station – itself an art nouveau showpiece – where a roll-call of masters and their world-famous works are on display. Top of every visitor's must-see list is the painting collection, centred on the world's largest collection of impressionist and post-impressionist art. Allow ample time to swoon over masterpieces by Manet, Monet, Cézanne, Renoir, Degas, Pissarro and Van Gogh.

★ Église St-Germain des Prés CHURCH

(Map p180; ☎ 01 55 42 81 18; www.eglise-saintgermaindespres.fr; 3 place St-Germain des Prés, 6e; ⏰ 9am-8pm; Ⓜ St-Germain des Prés) Paris' oldest standing church, the Romanesque St Germanus of the Fields, was built in the 11th century on the site of a 6th-century abbey and was the main place of worship in Paris until the arrival of Notre Dame. It's since been altered many times. The oldest part, **Chapelle de St-Symphorien**, is to the right as you enter; St Germanus (496–576), the first bishop of Paris, is believed to be buried there.

★ Jardin du Luxembourg PARK

(Map p180; www.senat.fr/visite/jardin; 6e; ⏰ hours vary; Ⓜ Mabillon, St-Sulpice, Rennes, Notre Dame des Champs or RER Luxembourg) This inner-city oasis of formal terraces, chestnut groves and lush lawns has a special place in Parisians' hearts. Napoleon dedicated the 23 gracefully laid-out hectares of the Luxembourg Gardens to the children of Paris, and many residents spent their childhood prodding 1920s wooden **sailboats** (sailboat rental per 30min €4; ⏰ 11am-6pm Apr-Oct) with long sticks on the octagonal **Grand Bassin** pond, watching puppets perform puppet shows at the **Théâtre du Luxembourg** (☎ 01 43 29 50 97; www.marionnettesduluxembourg.fr; tickets €6.40; ⏰ Wed, Sat & Sun, daily during school holidays) and riding the *carrousel* (merry-go-round) or **ponies** (Map p180; ☎ 06 07 32 53 95; www.animaponey.com; 600m/900m pony ride €6/8.50; ⏰ 3-6pm Wed, Sat, Sun & school holidays).

★ Panthéon MAUSOLEUM

(Map p180; ☎ 01 44 32 18 00; www.paris-pantheon.fr; place du Panthéon, 5e; adult/child €9/free; ⏰ 10am-6.30pm Apr-Sep, to 6pm Oct-Mar; Ⓜ Maubert-Mutualité or RER Luxembourg) The Panthéon's stately neoclassical dome is an icon of the Parisian skyline. Its vast interior is an architectural masterpiece: originally an abbey church dedicated to Ste Geneviève and now a mausoleum, it has served since 1791 as the resting place of some of France's greatest thinkers, including Voltaire, Rousseau, Braille and Hugo. A copy of Foucault's pendulum, first hung from the dome in 1851 to demonstrate the rotation of the earth, takes pride of place.

★ Les Catacombes CEMETERY

(☎ 01 43 22 47 63; www.catacombes.paris.fr; place Denfert-Rochereau, 14e; adult/child €13/free, online booking incl audio guide €29/5; ⏰ 10am-8.30pm Tue-Sun; Ⓜ Denfert-Rochereau) Paris' most macabre sight are these skull- and bone-lined underground tunnels. In 1785 it was decided to rectify the hygiene problems of Paris' overflowing cemeteries by exhuming the bones and storing them in disused quarry tunnels, and the Catacombes were created in 1810. After descending 20m (via 131 narrow, dizzying spiral steps), you follow dark, subterranean passages to the ossuary (1.5km in all). Exit up 112 steps via a 'transition space' with gift shop onto 21bis av René Coty, 14e.

The Islands

★ Cathédrale Notre Dame de Paris CATHEDRAL

(Map p180; www.notredamedeparis.fr; 6 Parvis Notre Dame – place Jean-Paul-II, 4e; ⏰ closed indefinitely; Ⓜ Cité) While its interior is closed off to visitors following the devastating fire of April 2019, this masterpiece of French Gothic architecture remains the city's geographic and spiritual heart. It's grand exterior, with its two enduring towers and flying buttresses, is rightly still an alluring attraction to countless visitors.

★ Sainte-Chapelle CHAPEL

(Map p180; ☎ 01 53 40 60 80, concerts 01 42 77 65 65; www.sainte-chapelle.fr; 8 bd du Palais, 1er; adult/child €10/free, joint ticket with Conciergerie €15/free; ⏰ 9am-7pm Apr-Sep, to 5pm Oct-Mar; Ⓜ Cité) Try to save Sainte-Chapelle for a sunny day, when Paris' oldest, finest stained glass is at its dazzling best. Enshrined within the Palais de Justice (Law Courts), this gem-like Holy Chapel is Paris' most exquisite Gothic monument. It was completed in 1248, just six years after the first stone was laid, and was conceived by Louis IX to house his personal collection of holy relics, including the famous Holy Crown.

Central Paris

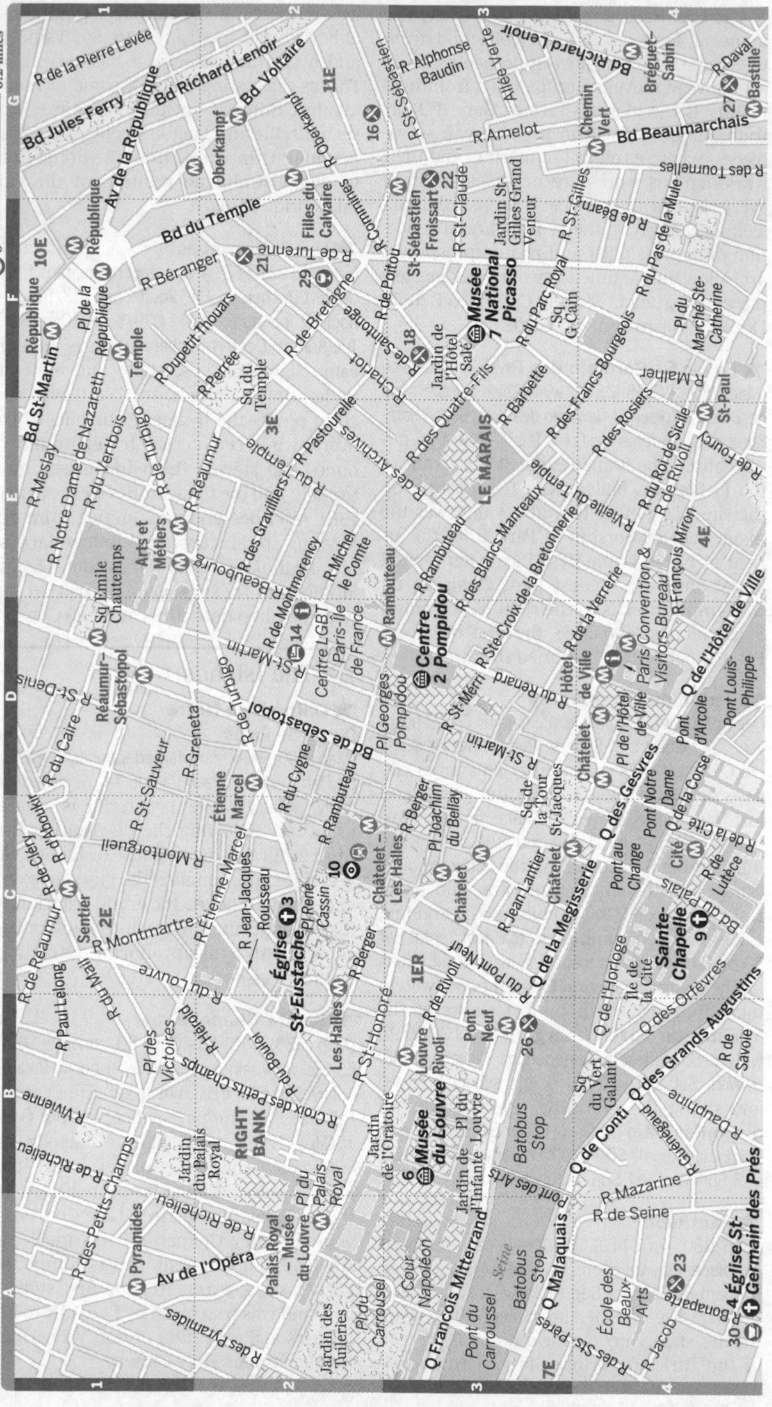

0 400 m
0 0.2 miles

A B C D E F G
1 2 3 4

Pyramides
Av de l'Opéra
R des Pyramides
R des Petits Champs
R de Richelieu
R Vivienne
Jardin du Palais Royal
RIGHT BANK
Palais Royal – Musée du Louvre
Pl du Palais Royal
Jardin des Tuileries
Pl du Carrousel
Cour Napoléon
6 Musée du Louvre
Jardin de l'Oratoire
Jardin de l'Infante
Pl du Louvre
Q Francois Mitterrand
Pont du Carroussel
Seine
Batobus Stop
Batobus Stop
Pont des Arts
7E
Q Malaquais
R des Sts-Pères
École des Beaux-Arts
R Jacob
R Bonaparte
23
30
4 Église St-Germain des Prés
R de Seine
R Mazarine
R Guénégaud
R Dauphine
Q de Conti
Sq du Vert Galant
Q des Grands Augustins
R de Savoie
Q des Orfèvres
Q de l'Horloge
Île de la Cité
Sainte-Chapelle
9
Bd du Palais
R de Lutèce
Cité
R de la Cité
Q de la Corse
Pont au Change
Pont Notre Dame
Pont d'Arcole
Pont Louis-Philippe
Q de l'Hôtel de Ville
R Paul Lelong
R de Réaumur
R de Cléry
R d'Aboukir
Sentier
R du Mail
2E
R Montmartre
Pl des Victoires
R Hérold
R du Louvre
R Croix des Petits Champs
R du Bouloi
R Étienne Marcel
R Jean-Jacques Rousseau
Église St-Eustache 3
Pl René Cassin
Les Halles
R St-Honoré
R Berger
10
Châtelet – Les Halles
Louvre Rivoli
R de Rivoli
1ER
Pont Neuf
26
R du Pont Neuf
Q de la Megisserie
Châtelet
Pl Joachim du Bellay
R Jean Lantier
Châtelet
Sq de la Tour St-Jacques
Châtelet
Q des Gesvres
R Montorgueil
R St-Sauveur
R Greneta
Étienne Marcel
R du Cygne
R Rambuteau
R du Caire
R St-Denis
Réaumur-Sébastopol
Sq Emile Chautemps
Bd de Sébastopol
R de Turbigo
R St-Martin
14
Centre LGBT Paris-Île de France
Pl Georges Pompidou
Rambuteau
Centre 2 Pompidou
R St-Merri
R St-Martin
R du Renard
Hôtel de Ville
Pl de l'Hôtel de Ville
Paris Convention & Visitors Bureau
R de la Verrerie
R Ste-Croix de la Bretonnerie
R des Blancs Manteaux
R Vieille du Temple
R François Miron
R de Rivoli
R du Roi de Sicile
4E
R de Fourcy
R des Rosiers
St-Paul
R Malher
R des Francs Bourgeois
LE MARAIS
R Rambuteau
R Beaubourg
R de Montmorency
R Michel le Comte
R des Gravilliers
R du Temple
3E
R des Archives
R Pastourelle
R des Quatre-Fils
R Barbette
Arts et Métiers
R Réaumur
R de Turbigo
R Meslay
R Notre Dame de Nazareth
R du Vertbois
Bd St-Martin
République
10E
Pl de la République
République
Temple
R Dupetit Thouars
R Perrée
Sq du Temple
R de Bretagne
R Charlot
R de Saintonge
18
Jardin de l'Hôtel Salé
Musée 7 National Picasso
R du Parc Royal
Sq G Cain
R de Poitou
R Béranger
21
R de Turenne
29
Filles du Calvaire
Bd du Temple
St-Sébastien Froissart
22
R St-Claude
Jardin St-Gilles Grand Veneur
R St-Gilles
R de Béarn
R du Pas de la Mule
Pl du Marché Ste-Catherine
R des Tournelles
Bd Beaumarchais
Chemin Vert
R Amelot
R Commines
R Oberkampf
Oberkampf
11E
16
R St-Sébastien
R Alphonse Baudin
Allée Verte
Bd Richard Lenoir
Bréguet-Sabin
27
R Daval
Bastille
Av de la République
Bd Jules Ferry
R de la Pierre Levée
Bd Richard Lenoir
Bd Voltaire

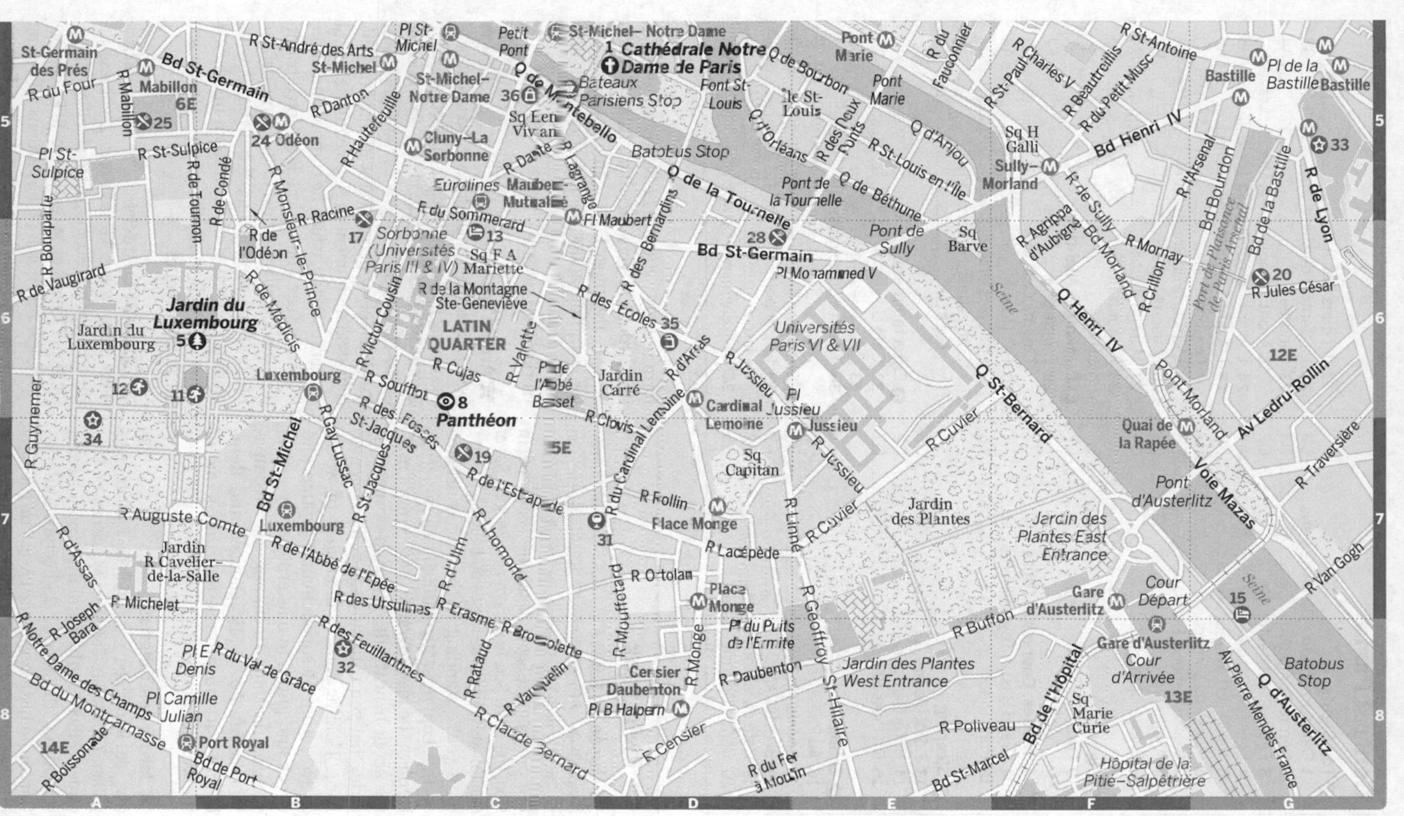

1 Cathédrale Notre Dame de Paris
St-Michel– Notre Dame
Petit Pont
Pl St-Michel
St-Michel
St-Michel–Notre Dame
Q de Montebello
36
Bateaux Parisiens Stop
Sq Rene Viviani
Font St-Louis
Ile St-Louis
Q de Bourbon
Pont Marie
R du Fauconnier
R St-Paul
R Charles V
R Beautreillis
R St-Antoine
R du Petit Musc
Pl de la Bastille
Bastille
Bd Henri IV
Sq H Galli
Sully–Morland
R de Sully
R l'Arsenal
Bd Bourdon
Bd de la Bastille
Port de Plaisance de Paris Arsenal
R de Lyon
33
20
R Jules César
R Agrippa d'Aubigné
Bd Morland
R Mornay
R Crillon
Q d'Orléans
R des Deux Ponts
Q d'Anjou
R St-Louis en l'Île
Q de Béthune
Pont de la Tournelle
Q de la Tournelle
Batobus Stop
Pont de Sully
Sq Barve
Seine
Q Henri IV
Pont Morland
12E
Av Ledru-Rollin
Quai de la Rapée
R Traversière
Voie Mazas
Pont d'Austerlitz
R Van Gogh
15
Cour Départ
Gare d'Austerlitz
Cour d'Arrivée
13E
Av Pierre Mendès-France
Q d'Austerlitz
Batobus Stop
Hôpital de la Pitié–Salpêtrière
Sq Marie Curie
Bd de l'Hôpital
Bd St-Marcel
R Poliveau
R Buffon
Jardin des Plantes East Entrance
Jardin des Plantes
Jardin des Plantes West Entrance
R Cuvier
Q St-Bernard
Universités Paris VI & VII
Pl Mohammed V
Bd St-Germain
28
Pl Maubert
R des Bernardins
R des Écoles
35
R d'Arras
R Jussieu
Pl Jussieu
Jussieu
Cardinal Lemoine
Sq Capitan
R Linné
R Geoffroy St-Hilaire
R Lacépède
Place Monge
R Follin
R du Cardinal Lemoine
R Clovis
Jardin Carré
Pl de l'Abbé Basset
5E
R Ortolan
Pl du Puits de l'Ermite
R Monge
R Daubenton
Censier Daubenton
Pl B Halpern
R Censier
R du Fer à Moulin
R Mouffetard
31
R de l'Estrapade
R Lhomond
R d'Ulm
R Erasme
R Rataud
R Vauquelin
R Broca
R Claude Bernard
R des Ursulines
R des Feuillantines
32
R de l'Abbé de l'Epée
R St-Jacques
R Gay Lussac
Bd St-Michel
Luxembourg
R des Fossés St-Jacques
8 Panthéon
19
R Soufflot
R Cujas
LATIN QUARTER
R Valette
R de la Montagne Ste-Geneviève
Sq F A Mariette
Sorbonne (Universités Paris III & IV)
13
R du Sommerard
Eurolines
Maubert-Mutualité
R Lagrange
R Dante
Cluny–La Sorbonne
R Hautefeuille
R Danton
R St-André des Arts
Bd St-Germain
St-Germain des Prés
R du Four
R Mabillon
Mabillon
6E
25
24 Odéon
R St-Sulpice
Pl St-Sulpice
R de Tournon
R de Condé
R Monsieur-le-Prince
R Racine
17
R de l'Odéon
R Victor Cousin
R Bonaparte
R de Vaugirard
R de Médicis
Jardin du Luxembourg
5
Jardin du Luxembourg
12
11
34
R Guynemer
R Auguste Comte
Jardin R Cavelier-de-la-Salle
R d'Assas
R Michelet
R Joseph Bara
R Notre Dame des Champs
Bd du Montparnasse
Pl E Denis
R du Val de Grâce
Pl Camille Julian
Port Royal
Bd de Port Royal
14E
R Boissonade
A
B
C
D
E
F
G
5
6
7
8

Central Paris

Right Bank

★Musée du Louvre — MUSEUM

(Map p180; ☎01 40 20 53 17; www.louvre.fr; rue de Rivoli & quai des Tuileries, 1er; adult/child €15/free, 6-9.45pm 1st Sat of month free; ⏲9am-6pm Mon, Thu, Sat & Sun, to 9.45pm Wed, Fri & 1st Sat of month; M Palais Royal–Musée du Louvre) It isn't until you're standing in the vast courtyard of the Louvre, with sunlight shimmering through the glass pyramid and crowds milling about beneath the museum's ornate facade, that you can truly say you've been to Paris. Holding tens of thousands of works of art – from Mesopotamian, Egyptian and Greek antiquities to masterpieces by artists such as da Vinci (including his incomparable *Mona Lisa*), Michelangelo and Rembrandt – it's no surprise that this is one of the world's most visited museums.

★Jardin des Tuileries — PARK

(rue de Rivoli, 1er; ⏲7am-9pm Apr-late Sep, 7.30am-7.30pm late Sep-Mar; M Tuileries or Concorde) Filled with fountains, ponds and sculptures, the formal 28-hectare Tuileries Garden, which begins just west of the Jardin du Carrousel, was laid out in its present form in 1664 by André Le Nôtre, architect of the gardens at Versailles. The Tuileries soon became the most fashionable spot in Paris for parading about in one's finery. It now forms part of the Banks of the Seine Unesco World Heritage Site.

★Arc de Triomphe — LANDMARK

(www.paris-arc-de-triomphe.fr; place Charles de Gaulle, 8e; viewing platform adult/child €12/free; ⏲10am-11pm Apr-Sep, to 10.30pm Oct-Mar; M Charles de Gaulle–Étoile) If anything rivals the Eiffel Tower (p178) as the symbol of Paris, it's this magnificent 1836 monument to Napoléon's victory at Austerlitz (1805), which he commissioned the following year. The intricately sculpted triumphal arch stands sentinel in the centre of the Étoile (Star) roundabout. From the viewing platform on top of the arch (50m up via 284 steps and well worth the climb) you can see the dozen avenues.

★Église St-Eustache — CHURCH

(Map p180; www.st-eustache.org; 2 impasse St-Eustache, 1er; ⏲9.30am-7pm Mon-Fri, 10am-7.15pm Sat, 9am-7.15pm Sun; M Les Halles or RER Châtelet–Les Halles) Just north of the gardens adjoining the city's old marketplace, now the **Forum** des Halles (Map p180; www.forumdeshalles.com; 1 rue Pierre Lescot, 1er; ⏲ shops 10am-8pm Mon-Sat, 11am-7pm Sun), is one of the most beautiful churches in Paris. Majestic, architecturally magnificent and musically outstanding, St-Eustache was constructed between 1532 and 1632 and is primarily Gothic. Artistic highlights include a work by Rubens, Raymond Mason's colourful bas-relief of market vendors (1969) and Keith Haring's bronze triptych (1990) in the side chapels.

★Centre Pompidou MUSEUM

(Map p180; ☎01 44 78 12 33; www.centrepompidou.fr; place Georges Pompidou, 4e; museum, exhibitions & panorama adult/child €14/free, panorama only ticket €5/free; ⏲11am-9pm Wed-Mon, temporary exhibits to 11pm Thu; Ⓜ Rambuteau) Renowned for its radical architectural statement, the 1977-opened Centre Pompidou brings together galleries and cutting-edge exhibitions, hands-on workshops, dance performances, cinemas and other entertainment venues, with street performers and fanciful fountains outside. The **Musée National d'Art Moderne**, France's national collection of art dating from 1905 onwards, is the main draw; a fraction of its 100,000-plus pieces – including Fauvist, cubist, surrealist, pop art and contemporary works – is on display. Don't miss the spectacular Parisian panorama from the rooftop.

★Musée National Picasso MUSEUM

(Map p180; ☎01 85 56 00 36; www.museepicassoparis.fr; 5 rue de Thorigny, 3e; adult/child €12.50/free; ⏲10.30am-6pm Tue-Fri, from 9.30am Sat & Sun; Ⓜ Chemin Vert or St-Paul) One of Paris' most treasured art collections is showcased inside the mid-17th-century Hôtel Salé, an exquisite private mansion owned by the city since 1964. The Musée National Picasso is a staggering art museum devoted to Spanish artist Pablo Picasso (1881–1973), who spent much of his life living and working in Paris. The collection includes more than 5000 drawings, engravings, paintings, ceramic works and sculptures by the *grand maître* (great master), although they're not all displayed at the same time.

★Cimetière du Père Lachaise CEMETERY

(☎01 55 25 82 10; www.pere-lachaise.com; 16 rue du Repos & 8 bd de Ménilmontant, 20e; ⏲8am-6pm Mon-Fri, from 8.30am Sat, from 9am Sun mid-Mar–Oct, shorter hours Nov–mid-Mar; Ⓜ Père Lachaise or Gambetta) Opened in 1804, Père Lachaise is today the world's most visited cemetery. Its 70,000 ornate tombs of the rich and famous form a verdant, 44-hectare sculpture garden. The most visited are those of 1960s rock star Jim Morrison (division 6) and Oscar Wilde (division 89). Pick up cemetery maps at the **conservation office** (Bureaux de la Conservation; 16 rue du Repos, 20e; ⏲8.30am-12.30pm & 2-5pm Mon-Fri; Ⓜ Philippe Auguste, Père Lachaise) near the main bd de Ménilmontant entrance. Other notables buried here include composer Chopin, playwright Molière, poet Apollinaire, and writers Balzac, Proust, Stein and Colette.

DON'T MISS

'I LOVE YOU' PARIS-STYLE

Few visitors can resist a selfie in front of Montmartre's 'I Love You' wall, **Le Mur des je t'aime** (www.lesjetaime.com; Sq Jehan Rictus, place des Abbesses ,18e; ⏲8am-9.30pm Mon-Fri, from 9am Sat & Sun mid-May–Aug, shorter hours Sep–mid-May; Ⓜ Abbesses), a public artwork created in a small park by artists Frédéric Baron and Claire Kito in the year 2000. Made from 511 dark-blue enamel tiles, the striking mural features the immortal phrase 'I love you' 311 times in nearly 250 different languages (the red fragments, if joined together, would form a heart). Find a bench beneath a maple tree and brush up your language skills romantic-Paris-style.

★Basilique du Sacré-Cœur BASILICA

(☎01 53 41 89 00; www.sacre-coeur-montmartre.com; Parvis du Sacré Cœur, 18e; basilica free, dome adult/child €6/4, cash only; ⏲basilica 6am-10.30pm, dome 8.30am-8pm May-Sep, 9am-5pm Oct-Apr; Ⓜ Anvers or Abbesses) Begun in 1875 in the wake of the Franco-Prussian War and the chaos of the Paris Commune, Sacré-Cœur is a symbol of the former struggle between the conservative Catholic old guard and the secular, republican radicals. It was finally consecrated in 1919, standing in contrast to the bohemian lifestyle that surrounded it. The view over Paris from its parvis is breathtaking. Avoid walking up the steep hill by using a regular metro ticket aboard the **funicular** (www.ratp.fr; place St-Pierre, 18e; ⏲6am-12.45am; Ⓜ Anvers or Abbesses) to the **upper station** (www.ratp.fr; rue du Cardinal Dubois, 18e; ⏲6am-12.45am; Ⓜ Abbesses).

☞ Tours

A boat cruise down the Seine is the most relaxing way to acquaint or reacquaint yourself with the city's main monuments as you watch

The Louvre

A HALF-DAY TOUR

Successfully visiting the Louvre is a fine art. Its complex labyrinth of galleries and staircases spiralling across three wings and four floors renders discovery a snakes-and-ladders experience. Initiate yourself with this three-hour itinerary – a playful mix of *Mona Lisa*–obvious and up-to-the-minute unexpected.

Arriving in the ❶ **Cour Napoléon** beneath IM Pei's glass pyramid, pick up colour-coded floor plans at an information stand, then ride the escalator up to the Sully Wing and swap passport or credit card for a multimedia guide (there are limited descriptions in the galleries) at the wing entrance.

The Louvre is as much about spectacular architecture as masterful art. To appreciate this, zip up and down Sully's Escalier Henri II to admire ❷ **Venus de Milo**, then up parallel Escalier Henri IV to the palatial displays in ❸ **Cour Khorsabad**. Follow signs for the escalator up to the 1st floor and the opulent ❹ **Napoléon III apartments**. Next traverse 25 consecutive galleries (thank you, floor plan!) to flip conventional contemplation on its head with Cy Twombly's ❺ **The Ceiling**, and the hypnotic ❻ **Winged Victory of Samothrace**, which brazenly insists on being admired from all angles. End with the impossibly famous ❼ **Raft of the Medusa**, ❽ **Mona Lisa** and ❾ **Virgin & Child**.

TOP TIPS

➡ Floor plans for navigating the Louvre's maze of galleries are free from the information desks in the Hall Napoléon.

➡ The Denon Wing is always packed; visit on late nights (Wednesday or Friday) or trade Denon in for the notably quieter Richelieu Wing.

BRIAN KINNEY / SHUTTERSTOCK ©

Napoléon III Apartments
Rooms 544 & 547, 1st Floor, Richelieu
Napoléon III's gorgeous gilt apartments were built from 1854 to 1861, featuring an over-the-top decor of gold leaf, stucco and crystal chandeliers that reaches a dizzying climax in the Grand Salon and State Dining Room.

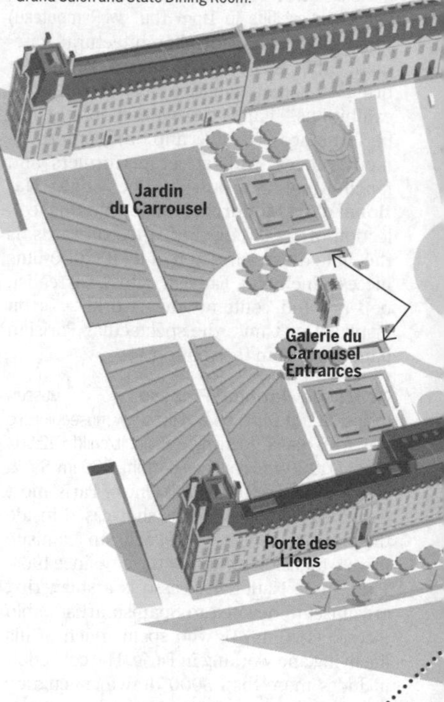

LOUVRE AUDITORIUM

Classical-music concerts are staged several times a week at the Louvre Auditorium (off the main entrance hall). Don't miss the Thursday lunchtime concerts featuring emerging composers and musicians. The season runs from September to April or May, depending on the concert series.

Mona Lisa
Room 711, 1st Floor, Denon
No smile is as enigmatic or bewitching as hers. Da Vinci's diminutive *La Joconde* hangs opposite the largest painting in the Louvre – sumptuous, fellow Italian Renaissance artwork *The Wedding at Cana*.

The Raft of the Medusa
Room 700, 1st Floor, Denon
Decipher the politics behind French romanticism in Théodore Géricault's *Raft of the Medusa*.

Cour Khorsabad
Ground Floor, Richelieu
Time travel with a pair of winged human-headed bulls to view some of the world's oldest Mesopotamian art.
DETOUR» Night-lit statues in Cour Puget.

PRYZMAT / SHUTTERSTOCK ©

The Ceiling
Room 663, Sully
Admire the blue shock of Cy Twombly's 400-sq-metre contemporary ceiling fresco – the Louvre's latest, daring commission.
DETOUR» *The Braque Ceiling*, Room 662.

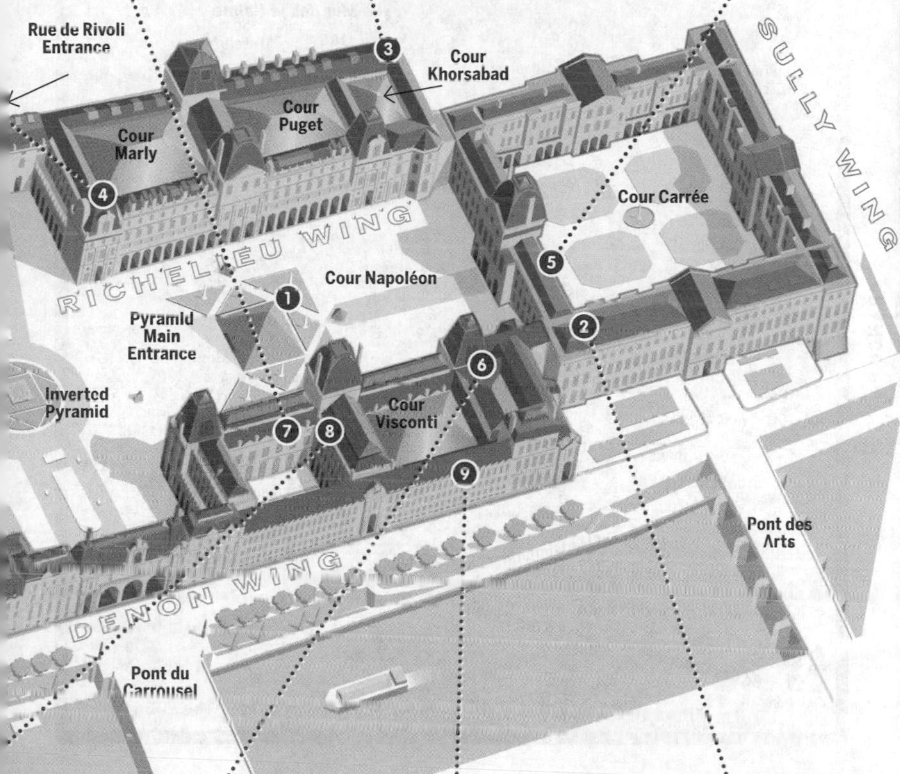

Rue de Rivoli Entrance

Cour Khorsabad

Cour Puget

Cour Marly

SULLY WING

Cour Carrée

RICHELIEU WING

Cour Napoléon

Pyramid Main Entrance

Inverted Pyramid

Cour Visconti

Pont des Arts

DENON WING

Pont du Carrousel

1 2 3 4 5 6 7 8 9

Venus de Milo
Room 346, Ground Floor, Sully
No one knows who sculpted this seductively realistic goddess from Greek antiquity. Naked to the hips, she is a Hellenistic masterpiece.

PRYZMAT / SHUTTERSTOCK ©

Winged Victory of Samothrace
Room 703, 1st Floor, Denon
Draw breath at the aggressive dynamism of this headless, handless Hellenistic goddess.
DETOUR» The razzle-dazzle of the Apollo Gallery's crown jewels.

Virgin & Child
Grande Galerie, 1st Floor, Denon
In the spirit of artistic devotion save the Louvre's most famous gallery for last: a feast of Virgin-and-child paintings by Da Vinci, Raphael, Domenico Ghirlandaio, Giovanni Bellini and Francesco Botticini.

TUTTI FRUTTI / SHUTTERSTOCK ©

Montmartre

Montmartre

Top Sights

1 Basilique du Sacré-Cœur C1
2 Le Mur des je t'aime C2

Sleeping

3 Hôtel Particulier Montmartre B1
4 Hoxton D5

Eating

5 Le Grenier à Pain C2
6 Le Potager de Charlotte D3
7 L'Office D4
8 Richer D4

Drinking & Nightlife

Le Très Particulier .... (see 3)

Entertainment

9 Kiosque Théâtre Madeleine A5
10 Moulin Rouge B2
11 Palais Garnier B5

Paris glide by. **Bateaux-Mouches** (☎01 42 25 96 10; www.bateaux-mouches.fr; Port de la Conférence, 8e; adult/child €14/6; ⊙10am-10.30pm Mon-Fri, 10.15am-9.20pm Sat & Sun Apr-Sep, every 40min 11am-9.20pm Oct-Mar; Ⓜ Alma Marceau) is Paris' largest river-cruise company; boats depart from just east of the Pont de l'Alma on the Right Bank. An alternative to a regular tour is the hop-on, hop-off Batobus (p199).

★Parisien d'un Jour – Paris Greeters WALKING
(www.greeters.paris; by donation) See Paris through local eyes with these two- to three-hour city tours. Volunteers – mainly knowledgeable Parisians passionate about their city – lead groups (maximum six people) to their favourite spots. Minimum two weeks' notice is needed.

Meeting the French CULTURAL, TOURS
(☎01 42 51 19 80; www.meetingthefrench.com; tours & courses from €12) Cosmetics workshops, backstage cabaret tours, fashion-designer showroom visits, French table decoration, art embroidery classes, market tours, baking with a Parisian baker – the repertoire of cultural and gourmet tours and behind-the-scenes experiences offered by Meeting the French is truly outstanding. All courses and tours are in English.

Street Art Paris WALKING
(☎09 50 75 19 92; www.streetartparis.fr; tours €20; ⊙by reservation) Learn about the history of graffiti on fascinating tours taking in Paris' vibrant street art. Tours take place in Belleville and Montmartre and on the Left Bank. If you're inspired to try it yourself, book into a 2½-hour mural workshop (€35).

Sleeping

Left Bank

★Hôtel Diana HOTEL $
(Map p180; ☎01 43 54 92 55; http://hotel-diana-paris.com; 73 rue St-Jacques, 5e; s €78-98, d €105-145, tr €160-195; 📶; Ⓜ Maubert-Mutualité) Footsteps from the Sorbonne, two-star Diana is budget-traveller gold. Owner extraordinaire, Thérèse Cheval, has been at the helm here since the 1970s and the pr ide and joy she invests in the hotel is boundless. Spacious rooms sport a stylish contemporary decor with geometric-patterned fabrics, the odd retro furniture piece, and courtesy tray with kettle and white-mug twinset. Breakfast €10.

★Hôtel Henriette DESIGN HOTEL $$
(☎01 47 07 26 90; www.hotelhenriette.com; 9 rue des Gobelins, 13e; s €69-209, d €79-309, tr €89-339, q €129-499; ❄📶; Ⓜ Les Gobelins) Interior designer Vanessa Scoffier scoured Paris' flea markets to source Platner chairs, 1950s lighting and other unique vintage pieces for the 32 rooms at bohemian Henriette – one of the Left Bank's most stunning boutique addresses. Guests can mingle in the light-flooded glass atrium and adjoining plant-filled patio with wrought-iron furniture.

Off Paris Seine HOTEL $$
(Map p180; ☎01 44 06 62 66; www.offparisseine.com; 85 quai d'Austerlitz, 13e; d from €169; 📶🏊; Ⓜ Gare d'Austerlitz) Should the idea of being gently rocked to sleep take your fancy, check in to Paris' first floating hotel by the highly recommended Parisian Elegancia hotel group. The sleek, 80m-long catamaran-design structure moored by Pont Charles de Gaulle sports sun terraces overlooking the Seine, a chic bar with silver beanbags by a 15m-long dipping pool, a lounge and 58 stunningly appointed rooms and suites.

Right Bank

★Generator Hostel HOSTEL $
(☎01 70 98 84 00; www.generatorhostels.com; 9-11 place du Colonel Fabien, 10e; dm/d from €33/92; ❄@📶; Ⓜ Colonel Fabien) From the 9th-floor rooftop bar overlooking Sacré-Cœur and the stylish ground-floor cafe-restaurant to the vaulted basement bar-club styled like a Paris metro station, and supercool bathrooms with 'I love you' tiling, this ultra-contemporary hostel near Canal St-Martin is sharp. Dorms have USB sockets and free lockers, and the best doubles have fabulous terraces with views. Women only dorms are available.

★Hôtel du Dragon HOTEL $
(☎01 45 48 51 05; www.hoteldudragon.com; 36 rue du Dragon, 6e; d €95-150, tr €130-180; 📶; Ⓜ St-Sulpice) It's hard to believe that such a gem of a budget hotel still exists in this ultrachic part of St-Germain. A family affair for the last five generations, today the ever-charming Roy runs the 28-room Dragon with his children, Sébastien and Marie-Hélène. Spotlessly clean rooms are decidedly large by Paris standards, often with exposed wooden beams and lovely vintage furnishings.

★Hôtel Georgette DESIGN HOTEL $$
(Map p180; ☎01 44 61 10 10; www.hotelgeorgette.com; 36 rue du Grenier St-Lazare, 3e; d from €240;

Versailles

A DAY IN COURT

Visiting Versailles – even just the State Apartments – may seem overwhelming at first, but think of it as a house where people ate, drank, worked, slept and conspired and you'll be on the right path.

Some two decades into his long reign, Louis XIV began turning his father's hunting lodge into a palace large enough to house his entire court (to keep closer tabs on the 6000-strong army of courtiers). Sparing no expense, the Sun King employed the greatest artists and craftspeople of the day and by 1682 he'd created the most extravagant dormitory in history.

The royal schedule was as accurate and predictable as a Swiss watch. Although it's impossible to recreate the king's day on a visit, the following itinerary does allow you to pass all of the rooms of interest. You'll start with the 1 **Royal Chapel**, where morning Mass was held, followed by the 2 **Hercules Drawing Room** and 3 **Diana Drawing Room**, both sites of evening entertainment, while the 4 **King's Library** was visited after lunch. The 5 **Hall of Mirrors** was for the royal procession, and the 6 **Council Chamber** for late-morning meetings with ministers. The day would have begun in the 7 **King's Bedchamber** and the 8 **Queen's Bedchamber**, where the royal couple was roused at about the same time.

VERSAILLES BY NUMBERS

Rooms 700 (11 hectares of roof)

Windows 2153

Staircases 67

Gardens and parks 800 hectares

Trees 200,000

Fountains 50 (with 620 nozzles)

Paintings 6300 (measuring 11km laid end to end)

Statues and sculptures 2100

Objets d'art and furnishings 5000

Visitors 8.1 million per year

VICHIE81 / SHUTTERSTOCK ©

Queen's Bedchamber
Chambre de la Reine
The queen's life was on constant public display and even the births of her children were watched by crowds of spectators in her own bedchamber. **DETOUR »** The Guardroom, with a dozen armed men at the ready.

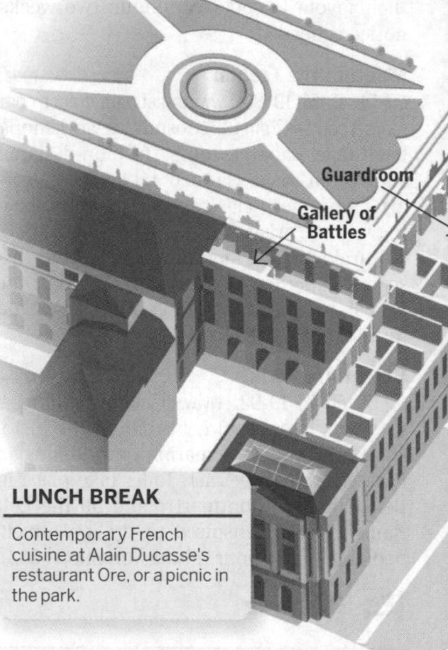

LUNCH BREAK

Contemporary French cuisine at Alain Ducasse's restaurant Ore, or a picnic in the park.

Hercules Drawing Room
Salon d'Hercule
This salon, with its stunning ceiling fresco of the strong man, gave way to the State Apartments, which were open to courtiers three nights a week. **DETOUR»** Apollo Drawing Room, used for formal audiences and as a throne room.

T.W.VAN URK / SHUTTERSTOCK ©

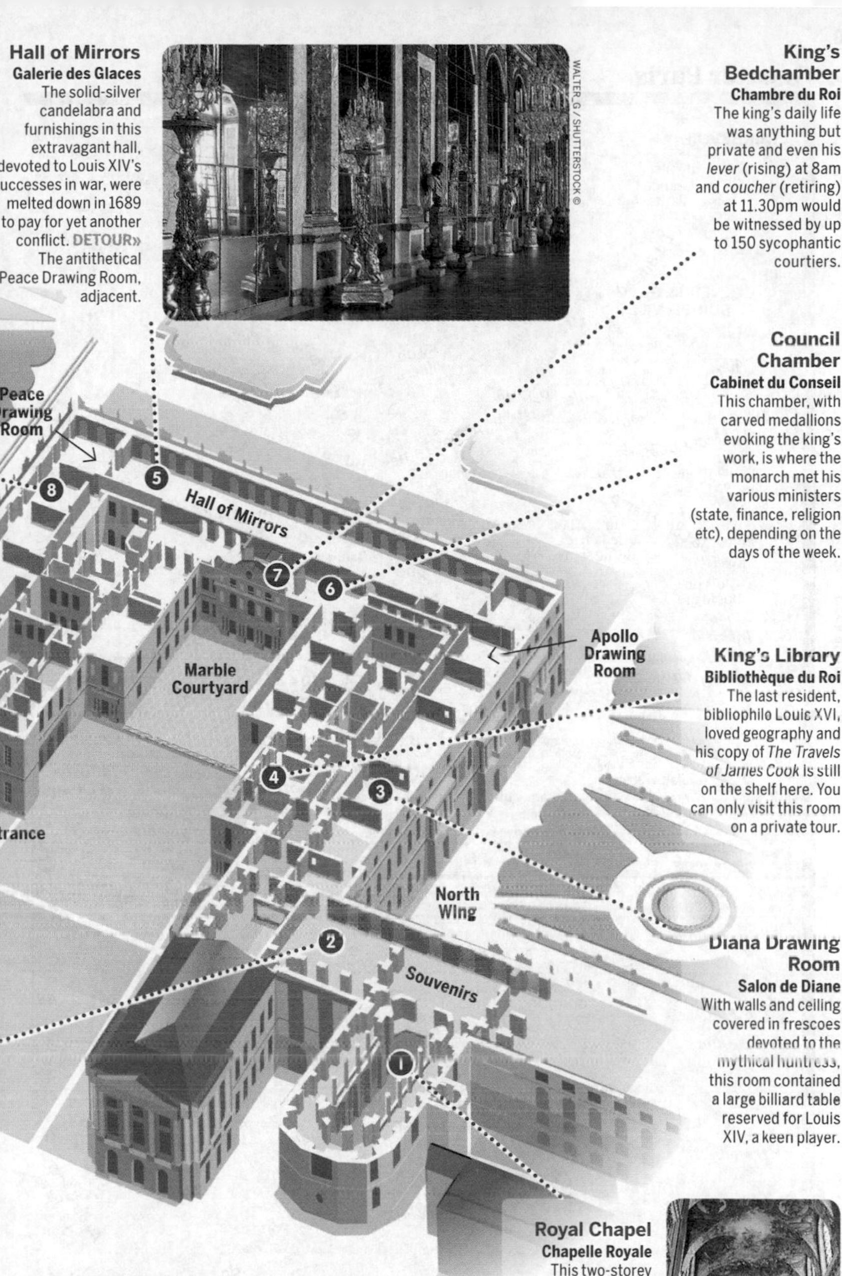

Hall of Mirrors
Galerie des Glaces
The solid-silver candelabra and furnishings in this extravagant hall, devoted to Louis XIV's successes in war, were melted down in 1689 to pay for yet another conflict. **DETOUR»** The antithetical Peace Drawing Room, adjacent.

King's Bedchamber
Chambre du Roi
The king's daily life was anything but private and even his *lever* (rising) at 8am and *coucher* (retiring) at 11.30pm would be witnessed by up to 150 sycophantic courtiers.

Council Chamber
Cabinet du Conseil
This chamber, with carved medallions evoking the king's work, is where the monarch met his various ministers (state, finance, religion etc), depending on the days of the week.

King's Library
Bibliothèque du Roi
The last resident, bibliophile Louis XVI, loved geography and his copy of *The Travels of James Cook* is still on the shelf here. You can only visit this room on a private tour.

Diana Drawing Room
Salon de Diane
With walls and ceiling covered in frescoes devoted to the mythical huntress, this room contained a large billiard table reserved for Louis XIV, a keen player.

Royal Chapel
Chapelle Royale
This two-storey chapel (with gallery for the royals and important courtiers, and the ground floor for the B-list) was dedicated to St Louis, patron of French monarchs. **DETOUR»** The sumptuous Royal Opera.

SAVVY SIGHTSEEING

Avoid Versailles on Monday (closed), Tuesday (Paris' museums close, so visitors flock here) and Sunday, the busiest day. Also, book tickets online so you don't have to queue.

Greater Paris

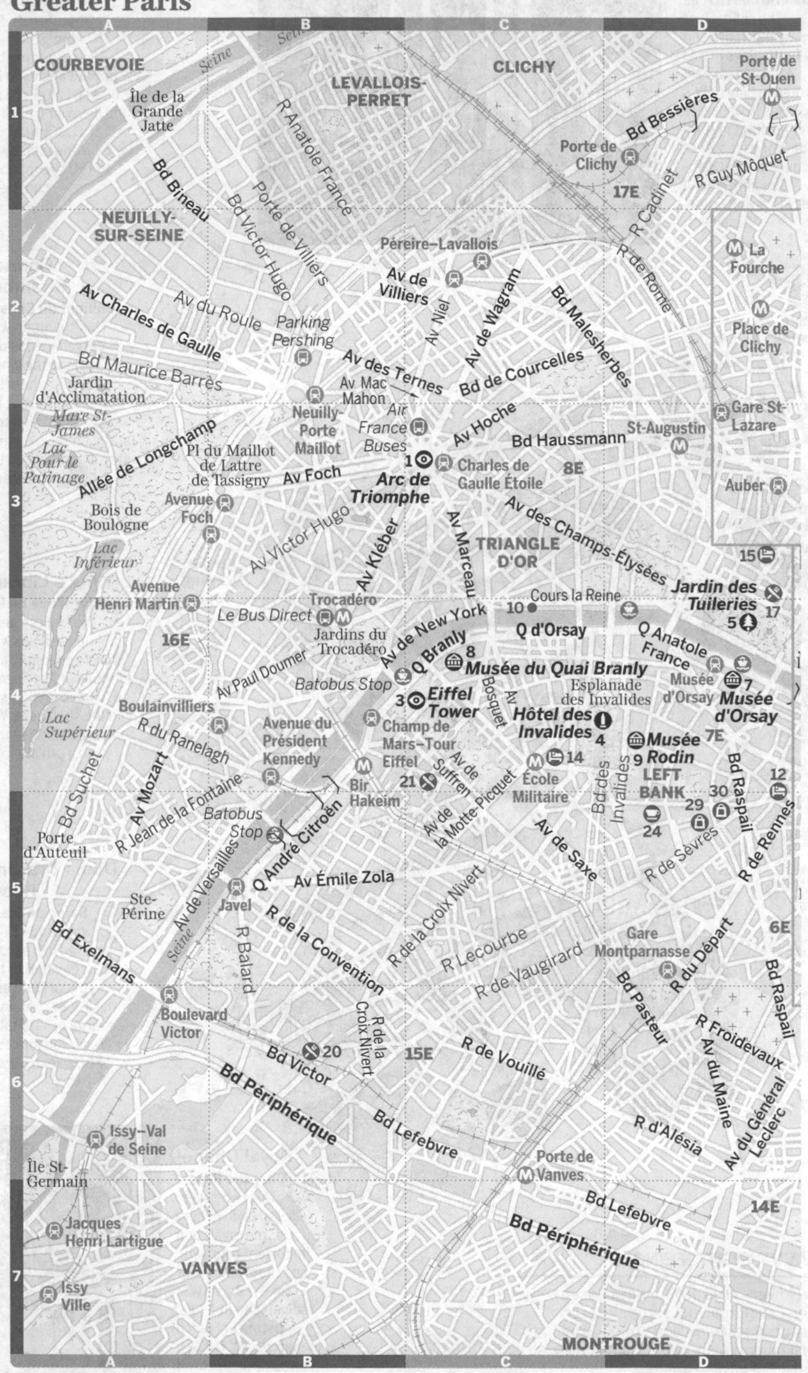
A
B
C
D
1
2
3
4
5
6
7
COURBEVOIE
Seine
Île de la Grande Jatte
LEVALLOIS-PERRET
CLICHY
Porte de St-Ouen
Bd Bessières
Porte de Clichy
R Guy Môquet
17E
R Cadinet
R Anatole France
Bd Bineau
Porte de Villiers
Bd Victor Hugo
NEUILLY-SUR-SEINE
Péreire–Lavallois
R de Rome
La Fourche
Av de Villiers
Av de Wagram
Bd Malesherbes
Place de Clichy
Av Charles de Gaulle
Av du Roule
Parking Pershing
Av Niel
Bd Maurice Barrès
Jardin d'Acclimatation
Av des Ternes
Av Mac Mahon
Bd de Courcelles
Neuilly-Porte Maillot
Air France Buses
Gare St-Lazare
Mare St-James
Lac Pour le Patinage
Allée de Longchamp
Pl du Maillot de Lattre de Tassigny
Av Foch
Av Hoche
Bd Haussmann
St-Augustin
1
Arc de Triomphe
Charles de Gaulle Étoile
8E
Auber
Avenue Foch
Bois de Boulogne
Av Victor Hugo
Av Kléber
Av Marceau
Av des Champs-Élysées
TRIANGLE D'OR
15
Lac Inférieur
Avenue Henri Martin
Trocadéro
Cours la Reine
10
Jardin des Tuileries
17
5
Le Bus Direct
Av de New York
Q d'Orsay
16E
Jardins du Trocadéro
Q Branly
8
Q Anatole France
Av Paul Doumer
Musée du Quai Branly
Esplanade des Invalides
Musée d'Orsay
7
Musée d'Orsay
Batobus Stop
3
Eiffel Tower
Av Bosquet
Boulainvilliers
Lac Supérieur
R du Ranelagh
Avenue du Président Kennedy
Champ de Mars–Tour Eiffel
Hôtel des Invalides
4
Musée Rodin
9
7E
14
Av de Suffren
21
Bir Hakeim
École Militaire
Bd des Invalides
LEFT BANK
Bd Raspail
12
30
29
24
Bd Suchet
Av Mozart
R Jean de la Fontaine
Batobus Stop
Av de la Motte-Picquet
Av de Saxe
R de Sèvres
R de Rennes
Porte d'Auteuil
Av de Versailles
Q André Citroën
Av Émile Zola
Javel
Ste-Périne
R de la Croix Nivert
R de la Convention
R Balard
Bd Exelmans
R Lecourbe
R de Vaugirard
Gare Montparnasse
R du Départ
6E
Bd Pasteur
Bd Raspail
Boulevard Victor
R de la Croix Nivert
20
15E
R de Vouillé
R Froidevaux
Av du Maine
Bd Victor
Bd Périphérique
Bd Lefebvre
R d'Alésia
Av du Général Leclerc
Issy–Val de Seine
Île St-Germain
Porte de Vanves
Bd Lefebvre
14E
Jacques Henri Lartigue
Bd Périphérique
VANVES
Issy Ville
MONTROUGE

FRANCE PARIS

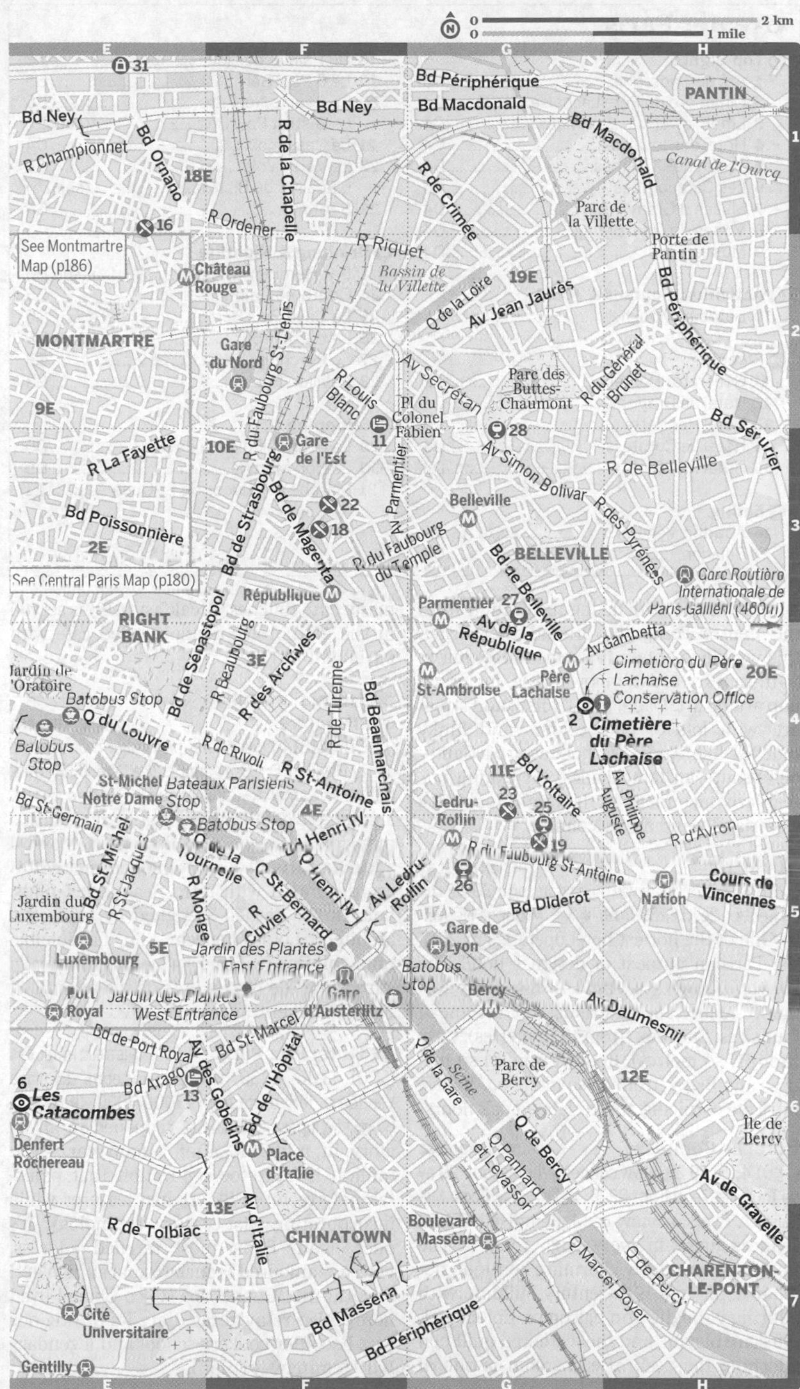
0 2 km
0 1 mile
Bd Périphérique
Bd Ney
Bd Macdonald
PANTIN
R Championnet
Bd Ornano
18E
R de la Chapelle
R de Crimée
Canal de l'Ourcq
R Ordener
Parc de la Villette
Porte de Pantin
R Riquet
See Montmartre Map (p186)
Château Rouge
Bassin de la Villette
19E
Q de la Loire
Av Jean Jaurès
Bd Périphérique
MONTMARTRE
Gare du Nord
R du Faubourg St-Denis
Av Secrétan
Parc des Buttes-Chaumont
R du Général Brunet
R Louis Blanc
Pl du Colonel Fabien
9E
Bd Sérurier
10E
Gare de l'Est
R La Fayette
Av Simon Bolivar
R de Belleville
Av Parmentier
Belleville
Bd Poissonnière
2E
Bd de Strasbourg
Bd de Magenta
R du Faubourg du Temple
R des Pyrénées
BELLEVILLE
Bd de Belleville
Gare Routière Internationale de Paris-Galliéni (460m)
See Central Paris Map (p180)
République
Parmentier
Av de la République
RIGHT BANK
3E
Bd de Sébastopol
R Beaubourg
R des Archives
Av Gambetta
Cimetière du Père Lachaise Conservation Office
Jardin de l'Oratoire
Père Lachaise
St-Ambroise
20E
Batobus Stop
Q du Louvre
R de Turenne
Bd Beaumarchais
Cimetière du Père Lachaise
Batobus Stop
R de Rivoli
R St-Antoine
11E
Bd Voltaire
Av Philippe Auguste
St-Michel Notre Dame
Bateaux Parisiens Stop
4E
Ledru-Rollin
Bd St-Germain
Batobus Stop
Bd Henri IV
R d'Avron
Q de la Tournelle
Bd St Michel
R St-Jacques
R Monge
Q Henri IV
Q St-Bernard
R du Faubourg St-Antoine
Av Ledru-Rollin
Nation
Cours de Vincennes
Jardin du Luxembourg
R Cuvier
Bd Diderot
5E
Jardin des Plantes East Entrance
Gare de Lyon
Luxembourg
Batobus Stop
Port Royal
Jardin des Plantes West Entrance
Gare d'Austerlitz
Bercy
Av Daumesnil
Bd St-Marcel
Bd de Port Royal
Q de la Gare
Seine
Parc de Bercy
12E
Bd Arago
Av des Gobelins
Bd de l'Hôpital
Les Catacombes
Q de Bercy
Île de Bercy
Denfert Rochereau
Place d'Italie
Q Panhard et Levassor
Av de Gravelle
13E
Av d'Italie
R de Tolbiac
CHINATOWN
Boulevard Masséna
Q Marcel Boyer
Q de Bercy
CHARENTON-LE-PONT
Cité Universitaire
Bd Masséna
Bd Périphérique
Gentilly
FRANCE PARIS

Greater Paris

Top Sights
1 Arc de Triomphe ... C3
2 Cimetière du Père Lachaise ... G4
3 Eiffel Tower ... C4
4 Hôtel des Invalides ... C4
5 Jardin des Tuileries ... D4
6 Les Catacombes ... E6
7 Musée d'Orsay ... D4
8 Musée du Quai Branly ... C4
9 Musée Rodin ... D4

Activities, Courses & Tours
10 Bateaux-Mouches ... C4

Sleeping
11 Generator Hostel ... F2
12 Hôtel du Dragon ... D4
13 Hôtel Henriette ... E6
14 Hôtel Le Comtesse ... C4
15 Hôtel Ritz Paris ... D3

Eating
16 Abattoir Végétal ... E1
17 Balagan ... D3
18 Du Pain et des Idées ... F3
19 Le 6 Paul Bert ... G5
20 Le Beurre Noisette ... B6
Le Bistrot Paul Bert ... (see 25)
21 Le Cassenoix ... C4
22 Le Verre Volé ... F3
L'Écailler du Bistrot ... (see 25)
23 Septime ... G4

Drinking & Nightlife
Bar Hemingway ... (see 15)
24 Coutume Café ... D5
25 La Cave Paul Bert ... G5
26 Le Baron Rouge ... G5
27 Le Perchoir ... G3
28 Pavillon Puebla ... G3

Shopping
29 La Grande Épicerie de Paris ... D5
30 Le Bon Marché ... D5
31 Marché aux Puces de St-Ouen ... E1

; Rambuteau) Taking inspiration from the Centre Pompidou around the corner, this vivacious hotel's 19 rooms reflect major 20th-century artistic movements, including pop art, op art, Dada, new realism and street art, with lots of bold colours and funky touches like Andy Warhol–inspired Campbell's-soup-can lampshades. Art exhibitions regularly take place in the bright lobby. It's gay-friendly and all-welcoming.

★ Hoxton DESIGN HOTEL $$
(01 85 65 75 00; www.thehoxton.com; 30-32 rue du Sentier, 2e; d €239-549; ; Bonne Nouvelle) One of the hottest hotel openings of 2017, the Parisian outpost of designer hotel The Hoxton occupies a grand 18th-century former residence. Its 172 striking rooms come in four sizes: Shoebox (from 13 sq metres), Cosy (from 17 sq metres), Roomy (from 21 sq metres) and Biggy (from 32 sq metres). All have intricate cornicing and reclaimed oak floors.

Hôtel Le Comtesse BOUTIQUE HOTEL $$
(01 45 51 29 29; www.comtesse-hotel.com; 29 av de Tourville, 7e; d from €229; @; École Militaire) A five-star view of Mademoiselle Eiffel seduces guests in every single room at The Countess, an utterly charming boutique hotel at home in a 19th-century building with alluring wrought-iron balconies. Colour palettes are playful, and the feathered quill pen adorning the desk in each room is one of many cute touches. Breakfast (€19) is served in the glamorous, boudoir-styled cafe with pavement terrace.

★ Hôtel Particulier Montmartre BOUTIQUE HOTEL $$$
(0153418140; www.hotel-particulier-montmartre.com; Pavillon D, 23 av Junot, 18e; ste €390-590; ; Lamarck–Caulaincourt) Hidden down a stone-paved alley behind a high wall, this mansion is one of the city's most magical addresses. Its five sweeping designer suites are decorated with retro flea-market finds, but it's the garden, designed by landscape architect Louis Benech, and fashionable **cocktail bar** (6pm-2am Tue-Sat) that really stun. Ring the buzzer outside the unmarked black-gated entrance at No 23.

★ Hôtel Ritz Paris HISTORIC HOTEL $$$
(01 43 16 30 30; www.ritzparis.com; 15 place Vendôme, 1er; d/ste from €1000/1900; P@; Opéra) The Ritz reopened in all its glory in mid-2016 after a four-year, €400 million head-to-toe renovation that painstakingly restored its original features while incorporating 21st-century technology. It's once again Paris' most rarefied address, with a manicured French formal garden and a world-first Chanel spa (Coco Chanel lived here). Also reinvigorated are its prestigious Ritz Escoffier cookery school and legendary Bar Hemingway (p196).

Eating

Left Bank

Café de la Nouvelle Mairie CAFE $
(Map p180; ☎01 44 07 04 41; 19 rue des Fossés St-Jacques, 5e; mains €11-17; ⏰8am-12.30am Mon-Fri, kitchen noon-2.30pm & 8-10.30pm Mon-Thu, 8-10pm Fri; Ⓜ Cardinal Lemoine) Shhhh…just around the corner from the Panthéon (p179) but hidden away on a small, fountained square, this hybrid cafe-restaurant and wine bar is a tip-top neighbourhood secret, serving natural wines and delicious seasonal bistro fare from oysters and ribs *(à la française)* to grilled lamb sausage over lentils. It takes reservations for dinner but not lunch – arrive early.

★ **Bouillon Racine** BRASSERIE $$
(Map p180; ☎01 44 32 15 60; www.bouillonracine.fr; 3 rue Racine, 6e; 2-course weekday lunch menu €17.50, 3-course menu €35, mains €17-24.50; ⏰noon-11pm; 🚸; Ⓜ Cluny–La Sorbonne) Inconspicuously situated in a quiet street, this heritage-listed art nouveau 'soup kitchen', with mirrored walls, floral motifs and ceramic tiling, was built in 1906 to feed market workers. Despite the magnificent interior, the food – inspired by age-old recipes – is no afterthought and superbly executed (stuffed, spit-roasted suckling pig, pork shank in Rodenbach red beer, scallops and shrimps with lobster coulis).

Le Beurre Noisette BISTRO $$
(☎01 48 56 82 49; www.restaurantbeurrenoisette.com; 68 rue Vasco de Gama, 15e; 2-/3-course lunch menu €25/34, 3-/5-course dinner menu €38/46, mains €19; ⏰noon-2pm & 7-10.30pm Tue-Sat; Ⓜ Lourmel) *Beurre noisette* (brown butter sauce, named for its hazelnut colour) features in dishes such as tender veal loin with homemade fries and caramelised pork belly tender with braised red cabbage and apple, at pedigreed chef Thierry Blanqui's neighbourhood neobistro. Filled with locals, the chocolate-toned dining room is wonderfully convivial – be sure to book. Fantastic value.

Le Cassenoix MODERN FRENCH $$
(☎01 45 66 09 01; www.le-cassenoix.fr; 56 rue de la Fédération, 15e; 3-course menu €34; ⏰noon-2pm & 7-10.30pm Mon-Fri; Ⓜ Bir Hakeim) The Nutcracker is everything a self-respecting neighbourhood bistro should be. *'Tradition et terroir'* (tradition and provenance) dictate the menu that inspires owner-chef Pierre Olivier Lenormand to deliver feisty dishes such as braised veal chuck with mashed potato and caramelised onions or grilled hake with parsnips and hazelnut-parmesan crumble. Vintage ceiling fans add to the wonderful retro vibe. Book ahead.

★ **Restaurant AT** GASTRONOMY $$$
(Map p180; ☎01 56 81 94 08; www.atsushitanaka.com; 4 rue du Cardinal Lemoine, 5e; 6-course lunch menu €55, 12-course dinner tasting menu €95, with paired wines €170; ⏰12.15-2pm & 8-9.30pm Mon-Sat; Ⓜ Cardinal Lemoine) Trained by some of the biggest names in gastronomy (Pierre Gagnaire included), chef Atsushi Tanaka showcases abstract artlike masterpieces incorporating rare ingredients (charred bamboo, kohlrabi turnip cabbage, juniper berry powder, wild purple fennel, Nepalese Timut pepper) in a blank-canvas-style dining space on stunning outsized plates. Reservations essential.

Right Bank

Marché Bastille MARKET $
(Map p180; bd Richard Lenoir, 11e; ⏰7am-2.30pm Thu, to 3pm Sun; Ⓜ Bastille or Bréguet–Sabin) If you only get to one open air street market

DON'T MISS

TOP THREE PICNIC STOPS

When a light bite for lunch or between sights beckons – be it a pastry, well-filled baguette sandwich or sweet bite – head to one of these favourite *boulangeries* and patisseries.

Ladurée (Map p180; ☎01 44 07 64 87; www.laduree.fr; 34 rue Bonaparte, 6e; ⏰8.30am-7.30pm Mon-Fri, 8.30am-8.30pm Sat, 10am-7.30pm Sun; Ⓜ St-Germain des Prés) One of Paris' oldest patisseries (1862), baking its iconic ganache-filled macarons since the 1930s.

Du Pain et des Idées (www.dupainetdesidees.com; 34 rue Yves Toudic, 10e; breads €1.20-7, pastries €2.50-6.50; ⏰6.45am-8pm Mon-Fri, closed Aug; Ⓜ Jacques Bonsergent) Traditional bakery near Canal St-Martin with an exquisite 1889 interior.

Le Grenier à Pain (www.legrenierapain.com; 38 rue des Abbesses, 18e; pastries €1.10-4.50; ⏰7.30am-8pm Thu-Mon; Ⓜ Abbesses) Perfect Montmartre picnic stop.

in Paris, this one – stretching between the Bastille and Richard Lenoir metro stations – is among the very best. Its 150-plus stalls are piled high with fruit and vegetables, meats, fish, shellfish, cheeses and seasonal specialities such as truffles. You'll also find clothing, leather handbags and wallets, and a smattering of antiques.

★ **Jacques Genin** PASTRIES $
(Map p180; ☎01 45 77 29 01; www.jacquesgenin.fr; 133 rue de Turenne, 3e; pastries €9; ⊙11am-7pm Tue-Fri & Sun, to 7.30pm Sat; M Oberkampf or Filles du Calvaire) Wildly creative *chocolatier* Jacques Genin is famed for his flavoured caramels, *pâtes de fruits* (fruit jellies) and exquisitely embossed *bonbons de chocolat* (chocolate sweets). But what completely steals the show at his elegant chocolate showroom is the *salon de dégustation* (aka tearoom), where you can order a pot of outrageously thick hot chocolate and legendary Genin *millefeuille*, assembled to order.

★ **Breizh Café** CRÊPES $
(Map p180; ☎01 42 72 13 77; www.breizhcafe.com; 109 rue Vieille du Temple, 3e; crêpes & galettes €6.80-18.80; ⊙10am-11pm; M St-Sébastien–Froissart) Everything at the Breizh ('Breton' in Breton) is 100% authentic, including its organic-flour crêpes and *galettes* (savoury buckwheat crêpes) that top many Parisians' lists for the best in the city. Other specialities include Cancale oysters and 20 types of cider. Tables are limited and there's often a wait; book ahead or try its deli, **L'Épicerie** (Map p180; ☎01 42 71 39 44; 111 rue Vieille du Temple, 3e; crêpes & galettes €6.80-18.80; ⊙10am-10pm), next door.

Le Verre Volé BISTRO $
(☎01 48 03 17 34; www.leverrevole.fr; 67 rue de Lancry, 10e; mains €11-22, sandwiches €7.90; ⊙bistro 12.30-2.30pm & 7.30-11.30pm, wine bar 10am-2am; 📶; M Jacques Bonsergent) The tiny 'Stolen Glass' – a wine shop with a few tables – is one of Paris' most popular wine bar–restaurants, with outstanding natural and unfiltered wines and expert advice. Unpretentious, hearty *plats du jour* are excellent. Reserve in advance for meals, or stop by to pick up a gourmet sandwich (such as mustard-smoked burrata with garlic-pork sausage) and a bottle.

Richer BISTRO $
(www.lericher.com; 2 rue Richer, 9e; mains €17-28; ⊙noon-2.30pm & 7.30-10.30pm; M Poissonnière or Bonne Nouvelle) Run by the same team as across-the-street neighbour **L'Office** (☎01 47 70 67 31; www.office-resto.com; 3 rue Richer, 9e; 2-/3-course lunch menus €22/27, mains €22-29; ⊙noon-2pm & 7.30-10.30pm Mon-Fri), Richer's pared-back, exposed-brick decor is a smart setting for genius creations including smoked-duck-breast ravioli in miso broth, and quince-and-lime cheesecake for dessert. It doesn't take reservations, but it serves snacks and Chinese tea, and has a full bar (open until midnight). Fantastic value.

L'Avant Comptoir de la Mer SEAFOOD $
(Map p180; ☎01 42 38 47 55; www.hotel-paris-relais-saint-germain.com; 3 Carrefour de l'Odéon, 6e; tapas €5-25, oysters per 6 €17; ⊙noon-11pm; M Odéon) One of Yves Camdeborde's stunning line-up of St-Germain hors d'oeuvre bars – alongside **Le Comptoir** (Map p180; ☎01 44 27 07 97; 9 Carrefour de l'Odéon, 6e; lunch mains €15-30, dinner menu €60; ⊙noon-6pm & 8.30-11.30pm Mon-Fri, noon-11pm Sat & Sun), **L'Avant Comptoir de la Terre** (Map p180; 3 Carrefour de l'Odéon, 6e; tapas €5.50-13.50; ⊙noon-11pm) and **L'Avant Comptoir du Marché** (Map p180; 15 rue Lobineau, 6e; tapas €5.50-21; ⊙noon-11pm; M Mabillon) – serves succulent Cap Ferret oysters (straight, Bloody Mary–style or with chipolata sausages), herring tartine, cauliflower and trout roe, blood-orange razor clams, roasted scallops and salmon cro-

TOP THREE VEGETARIAN & VEGAN

Abattoir Végétal (www.abattoirvegetal.fr; 61 rue Ramey, 18e; 2-/3-course lunch menu €16.50/19, mains €10-16.50; ⊙9am-6pm Tue, 9am-10.30pm Wed-Fri, 10am-10.30pm Sat, 11am-4.30pm Sun; 📶 ✎; M Jules Joffrin) Plant-filled vegan cafe in Montmartre.

Le Potager de Charlotte (☎01 44 65 09 63; www.lepotagerdecharlotte.fr; 12 rue de la Tour d'Auvergne, 9e; mains €14.50-16, Sunday brunch €29; ⊙7-10.30pm Wed & Thu, noon-2.30pm & 7-10.30pm Fri & Sat, 11am-3pm Sun; ✎; M Cadet) Gourmet vegan restaurant.

Gentle Gourmet Café (Map p180; ☎01 43 43 48 49; https://gentlegourmet.fr; 24 bd de la Bastille, 12e; 2-/3-course lunch menu €23/30, mains €21-25; ⊙noon-2.30pm & 6.30-10pm Tue-Sun; 📶 ✎ 👪; M Quai de la Rapée or Bastille) 🍃 All of the dishes are vegan and most are organic at this light-filled cafe.

LOCAL KNOWLEDGE

TOP THREE FOOD TRUCKS

Street food continues to take the city by storm as food trucks roll out across Paris. Find the day's location online.

Le Camion Qui Fume (https://lecamionquifume.com; burger & fries €13-15) This 'smoking truck' serving gourmet burgers started the local food-truck craze.

KimPop (www.facebook.com/kimpopfoodtruck; dishes €5.50-12.50) Korean food truck KimPop serves soup, pork, beef or tofu *bibimbap* ('mixed rice') salad bowls, *kimbap* (sushi-style rolls) and more.

La Cabane de Cape Cod (www.facebook.com/cabanecapecod; dishes €11-16) Choose from classic fish and chips, salmon gravlax, tuna tataki and other seafood dishes.

quettes, complemented by fantastic artisanal bread, hand-churned flavoured butters, sea salt and Kalamata olives.

★ Au Passage BISTRO **$$**

(Map p180; ☎01 43 55 07 52; www.restaurant-aupassage.fr; 1bis passage St-Sébastien, 11e; small plates €8-18, meats to share €25-70; ⏰7-11pm Tue-Sat, bar to 1.30am Tue-Sat; Ⓜ St-Sébastien–Froissart) Rising star chefs continue to make their name at this *petit bar de quartier* (little neighbourhood bar). Choose from a good-value, uncomplicated selection *of petites assiettes* (small tapas-style plates) of cold meats, raw or cooked fish, vegetables and so on, and larger meat dishes such as slow roasted lamb shoulder or *côte de bœuf* (rib-eye steak) to share. Reservations are essential.

Le Bistrot Paul Bert BISTRO **$$**

(☎01 43 72 24 01; 18 rue Paul Bert, 11e; 3-course menu €41, mains €29; ⏰noon-2pm & 7.30-11pm Tue-Thu, 7.30-11pm Fri, noon-2.30pm Sat, closed Aug; Ⓜ Faidherbe-Chaligny) When food writers list Paris' best bistros, Paul Bert's name consistently pops up. The timeless decor and classic dishes such as *steak-frites* (steak and chips) and hazelnut-cream Paris-Brest pastry reward those booking ahead. Siblings in the same street: **L'Écailler du Bistrot** (☎01 43 72 76 77; 22 rue Paul Bert, 11e; oysters per half-dozen €9-22, mains €32-48, seafood platters per person from €40; ⏰noon-2.30pm & 7.30-11pm Tue-Sat) for seafood; **La Cave Paul Bert** (☎01 58 53 50 92; 16 rue Paul Bert, 11e; ⏰noon-midnight, kitchen noon-2pm & 7.30-11.30pm), a wine bar with small plates; and **Le 6 Paul Bert** (☎01 43 79 14 32; www.le6paulbert.com; 6 rue Paul Bert, 12e; mains €24-34; ⏰noon-2pm & 7.30-11pm Tue-Fri, 7.30-11pm Sat) for modern cuisine.

Maison Maison MEDITERRANEAN **$$**

(Map p180; ☎09 67 82 07 32; www.restaurant-maisonmaison.com; 63 Parc Rives de Seine, 1er; 2-/3-course lunch menu €20/25, small plates €7-16; ⏰kitchen 7-10pm Mon, noon-3pm & 7-10pm Tue-Sun, bar to 2am; Ⓜ Pont Neuf) Halfway down the stairs by Pont Neuf is this wonderfully secret space beneath the *bouquinistes* (used-book sellers), where you can watch the *bateaux-mouches* (river-cruise boats) float by as you dine on creations such as beetroot and pink-grapefruit-cured bonito or gnocchi with white asparagus and broccoli pesto. In nice weather, cocktails at the glorious riverside terrace are not to be missed.

Balagan ISRAELI **$$**

(☎01 40 20 72 14; www.balagan-paris.com; 9 rue d'Alger, 1er; mains €24-34; ⏰7-10.30pm; Ⓜ Tuileries) Cool navy blues and creamy diamond tiling contrast with the chic vibe at this Israeli hot spot. Come here to sample delectable starters – deconstructed kebabs, crispy halloumi cheese with dates, onion confit Ashkenazi chicken liver or a spicy, succulent tuna tartare with fennel, coriander, capers and pistachios – followed by praiseworthy mains such as the sea bream black pasta.

★ Septime GASTRONOMY **$$$**

(☎01 43 67 38 29; www.septime-charonne.fr; 80 rue de Charonne, 11e; 4-course lunch menu with/without wine €80/42, 7-course dinner menu €135/80; ⏰7.30-10pm Mon, 12.15-2pm & 7.30-10pm Tue-Fri; Ⓜ Charonne) The alchemists in Bertrand Grébaut's Michelin-starred kitchen produce truly beautiful creations, served by blue-aproned waitstaff. The menu reads like an obscure shopping list: each dish is a mere listing of three ingredients, while the mystery *carte blanche* dinner *menu* puts you in the hands of the innovative chef. Reservations require planning and perseverance – book at least three weeks in advance.

🍷 Drinking & Nightlife

The line between bars, cafes and bistros is blurred at best. It costs more to sit at a table

LOCAL KNOWLEDGE

BAR-HOPPING STREETS

Prime Parisian streets for a soirée:

Rue Vieille du Temple, 4e Marais cocktail of gay bars and chic cafes.

Rue Oberkampf, 11e Edgy urban hang-outs.

Rue de Lappe, 11e Boisterous Bastille bars and clubs.

Rue de la Butte aux Cailles, 13e Village atmosphere and fun local haunts.

Rue Princesse, 6e Student and sports bars.

than to stand at the counter, more on a fancy square than a backstreet, and more in the 8e than in the 18e. After 10pm many cafes charge a pricier *tarif de nuit* (night rate).

Left Bank

★Coutume Café COFFEE

(☎01 45 51 50 47; www.coutumecafe.com; 47 rue de Babylone, 7e; ⊙8.30am-5.30pm Mon-Fri, 9am-6pm Sat & Sun; 🛜; ⓂSt-François Xavier) The Parisian coffee revolution is thanks in no small part to Coutume, artisanal roaster of premium beans for scores of establishments around town. Its flagship cafe – a light-filled, post-industrial space – is ground zero for innovative preparation methods including cold extraction and siphon brews. Couple some of Paris' finest coffee with tasty, seasonal cuisine and the place is always packed out.

Les Deux Magots CAFE

(Map p180; ☎01 45 48 55 25; www.lesdeuxmagots.fr; 6 place St-Germain des Prés, 6e; ⊙7.30am-1am; ⓂSt-Germain des Prés) If ever there was a cafe that summed up St-Germain des Prés' early-20th-century literary scene, it's this former hang-out of anyone who was anyone. You'll spend substantially more here to sip *un café* (€4.80) in a wicker chair on the pavement terrace shaded by dark-green awnings and geraniums spilling from window boxes, but it's an undeniable piece of Parisian history.

Right Bank

★Bar Hemingway COCKTAIL BAR

(www.ritzparis.com; Hôtel Ritz Paris, 15 place Vendôme, 1er; ⊙6pm-2am; 🛜; ⓂOpéra) Black-and-white photos and memorabilia (hunting trophies, old typewriters and framed handwritten letters by the great writer) fill this snug bar inside the Ritz (p192). Head bartender Colin Peter Field mixes monumental cocktails, including three different Bloody Marys made with juice from freshly squeezed seasonal tomatoes. Legend has it that Hemingway himself, wielding a machine gun, helped liberate the bar during WWII.

★Le Baron Rouge WINE BAR

(www.lebaronrouge.net; 1 rue Théophile Roussel, 12e; ⊙5-10pm Mon, 10am-2pm & 5-10pm Tue-Fri, 10am-10pm Sat, 10am-4pm Sun; ⓂLedru-Rollin) Just about the ultimate Parisian wine-bar experience, this wonderfully unpretentious local meeting place, where everyone is welcome, has barrels stacked against the bottle-lined walls and serves cheese, charcuterie, and oysters in season. It's especially busy on Sunday after the Marché d'Aligre wraps up. For a small deposit, you can fill up 1L bottles straight from the barrel for less than €5.

★Le Perchoir ROOFTOP BAR

(☎01 48 06 18 48; www.leperchoir.tv; 14 rue Crespin du Gast, 11e; ⊙6pm-2am Tue-Sat; 🛜; ⓂMénilmontant) Sunset is the best time to head up to this 7th-floor bar for a drink overlooking Paris' rooftops, where DJs spin on Saturday nights. Greenery provides shade in summer; in winter it's covered by a sail-like canopy and warmed by fires burning in metal drums. It's accessed off an inner courtyard via a lift (or a spiralling staircase).

Candelaria COCKTAIL BAR

(Map p180; www.quixotic-projects.com; 52 rue de Saintonge, 3e; ⊙bar 6pm-2am, taqueria noon-10.30pm Sun-Wed, to 11.30pm Thu-Sat; ⓂFilles du Calvaire) A lime-green *taqueria* serving homemade tacos, quesadillas and tostadas conceals one of Paris' coolest cocktail bars through an unmarked internal door. Phenomenal cocktails made from agave spirits, including mezcal, are inspired by Central and South America, such as a Guatemalan El Sombrerón (tequila, vermouth, bitters, hibiscus syrup, pink-pepper-infused tonic and lime). Weekend evenings kick off with DJ sets.

Pavillon Puebla BEER GARDEN

(www.leperchoir.tv; Parc des Buttes Chaumont, 39 av Simon Bolivar, 19e; ⊙6pm-2am Wed-Fri, from noon Sat, noon-10pm Sun; 🛜; ⓂButtes Chaumont) Strung with fairy lights, this rustic ivy-draped cottage's two rambling terraces in the Parc des Buttes Chaumont evoke a *guinguette* (old-fashioned outdoor tavern/ dance venue), with a 21st-century vibe provided by its Moroccan decor, contemporary furniture, and DJ beats from Thursdays to Saturdays. Alongside mostly French wines and craft beers, cocktails include its signature Spritz du Pavillon (Aperol, Prosecco and soda).

☆ Entertainment

France's Opéra National de Paris and Ballet de l'Opéra National de Paris perform at Paris' two opera houses: the **Palais Garnier** (www.operadeparis.fr; place de l'Opéra, 9e; Ⓜ Opéra) and **Opéra Bastille** (Map p180; ☎ international calls 01 71 25 24 23, within France 08 92 89 90 90; www.operadeparis.fr; 2-6 place de la Bastille, 12e; ⏲ box office 11.30am-6.30pm Mon-Sat, 1hr prior to performances Sun; Ⓜ Bastille). The season runs between September and July.

On the day of performance, theatre, opera and ballet tickets are sold for half price (plus €3.50 commission) at the central **Kiosque Théâtre Madeleine** (www.kiosqueculture.com; opposite 15 place de la Madeleine, 8e; ⏲ 12.30-2.30pm & 3-7.30pm Tue-Sat, 12.30-3.45pm Sun Sep-Jun, closed Sun Jul & Aug; Ⓜ Madeleine). Paris' top listings guide, *L'Officiel des Spectacles* (www.offi.fr; €1), is published in French but is easy to navigate. It's available from news stands on Wednesday, and is crammed with everything that's on in the capital.

★ La Seine Musicale CONCERT VENUE
(☎ 01 74 34 54 00; www.laseinemusicale.com; Île Seguin, Boulogne-Billancourt; Ⓜ Pont de Sèvres) A landmark addition to Paris' cultural offerings, La Seine Musicale opened on the Seine island of Île Seguin in 2017. Constructed of steel and glass, the egg-shaped auditorium has a capacity of 1150, while the larger, modular concrete hall accommodates 6000. Ballets, musicals and concerts from classical to rock are all staged here, alongside exhibitions.

★ Café Universel JAZZ, BLUES
(Map p180; ☎ 01 43 25 74 20; www.facebook.com/cafeuniversel.paris05; 267 rue St-Jacques, 5e; ⏲ concerts from 8.30pm Tue-Sat, cafe 8.30am-3pm Mon, 8.30am-1am Tue-Fri, 4.30pm-1am Sat, 1.30pm-1am Sun; 📶; Ⓜ Censier Daubenton or RER Port Royal) Café Universel hosts a brilliant array of live concerts with everything from bebop and Latin sounds to vocal jazz sessions. Plenty of freedom is given to young producers and artists, and its convivial, relaxed atmosphere attracts a mix of students and jazz lovers. Concerts are free, but you should tip the artists when they pass the hat around.

Moulin Rouge CABARET
(☎ 01 53 09 82 82; www.moulinrouge.fr; 82 bd de Clichy, 18e; show only from €87, lunch & show from €165, dinner & show from €190; ⏲ show only 2.45pm, 9pm & 11pm, lunch & show 1.45pm, dinner & show 7pm; Ⓜ Blanche) Immortalised in Toulouse-Lautrec's posters and later in Baz Luhrmann's film, Paris' legendary cabaret twinkles beneath a 1925 replica of its original red windmill. Yes, it's packed with bus-tour crowds, but from the opening bars of music to the last high cancan kick, it's a whirl of fantastical costumes, sets, choreography and Champagne. Book in advance and dress smartly (no trainers or sneakers).

🛍 Shopping

Paris has it all: broad boulevards lined with international chains, luxury avenues studded with designer fashion houses, famous *grands magasins* (department stores) and fabulous markets. But the real charm lies in strolling the city's backstreets, where tiny speciality shops and quirky boutiques selling everything from strawberry-scented wellington boots to heavenly fragranced candles are wedged between cafes, galleries and churches.

Paris' twice-yearly *soldes* (sales) generally last five to six weeks, starting around mid-January and again around mid-June.

LGBTIQ+ PARIS

Le Marais (4e), especially the areas around the intersection of rue Ste-Croix de la Bretonnerie and rue des Archives, and eastwards to rue Vieille du Temple, has been Paris' centre of gay nightlife for some three decades. The single best source of info is the **Centre Gai et Lesbien de Paris** (Map p180; ☎ 01 43 57 21 47; www.centrelgbtparis.org; 63 rue Beaubourg, 3e; ⏲ centre & bar 3.30-8pm Mon-Fri, 1-7pm Sat, library 6-8pm Mon-Wed, 5-7pm Fri & Sat; Ⓜ Rambuteau), with a large library and happening bar.

DON'T MISS

MARKET SHOPPING

Spanning 9 hectares, **Marché aux Puces de St-Ouen** (www.marcheauxpuces-saintouen.com; rue des Rosiers, St-Ouen; ⏲Sat-Mon; Ⓜ Porte de Clignancourt) is a vast flea market that was founded in 1870 and is said to be Europe's largest. Over 2000 stalls are grouped into 15 *marchés* (markets) selling everything from 17th-century furniture to 21st-century clothing. Each market has different opening hours – check the website for details. There are miles upon miles of 'freelance' stalls; come prepared to spend some time.

★ **Merci** CONCEPT STORE
(Map p180; ☎01 42 77 00 33; www.merci-merci.com; 111 bd Beaumarchais, 3e; ⏲10am-7.30pm Mon-Sat, noon-7pm Sun; Ⓜ St-Sébastien–Froissart) A Fiat Cinquecento marks the entrance to this unique concept store, which donates all its profits to a children's charity in Madagascar. Shop for fashion, accessories, linens, lamps and nifty designs for the home. Complete the experience with a coffee in its hybrid used-bookshop-cafe, a juice at its **Ciné-ma Café** (⏲11am-7pm Mon-Sat) or lunch in its stylish **La Cantine de Merci** (mains €16-21; ⏲noon-5pm Mon-Fri, to 6pm Sat).

★ **Shakespeare & Company** BOOKS
(Map p180; ☎01 43 25 40 93; www.shakespeareandcompany.com; 37 rue de la Bûcherie, 5e; ⏲10am-10pm; Ⓜ St-Michel) Enchanting nooks and crannies overflow with new and secondhand English-language books. The original shop (12 rue l'Odéon, 6e; closed by the Nazis in 1941) was run by Sylvia Beach and became the meeting point for Hemingway's 'Lost Generation'. Readings by emerging and illustrious authors regularly take place and there's a wonderful **cafe** (2 rue St-Julien le Pauvre, 5e; ⏲9.30am-7pm Mon-Fri, to 8pm Sat & Sun; 📶) next door.

★ **Le Bonbon au Palais** FOOD
(Map p180; ☎01 78 56 15 72; www.lebonbonaupalais.com; 19 rue Monge, 5e; ⏲10.30am-7.30pm Tue-Sat; Ⓜ Cardinal Lemoine) Kids and kids-at-heart will adore this sugar-fuelled *tour de France*. The school-geography-themed boutique stocks rainbows of artisanal sweets from around the country. Old-fashioned glass jars brim with treats like *calissons* (diamond-shaped, icing-sugar-topped ground fruit and almonds from Aix-en-Provence), *rigolettes* (fruit-filled pillows from Nantes), *berlingots* (striped, triangular boiled sweets from Carpentras and elsewhere) and *papalines* (herbal liqueur-filled pink-chocolate balls from Avignon).

★ **La Grande Épicerie de Paris** FOOD & DRINKS
(www.lagrandeepicerie.com; 38 rue de Sèvres, 7e; ⏲8.30am-9pm Mon-Sat, 10am-8pm Sun; Ⓜ Sèvres-Babylone) The magnificent food hall of department store **Le Bon Marché** (☎01 44 39 80 00; www.24sevres.com; 24 rue de Sèvres, 7e; ⏲10am-8pm Mon-Wed, Fri & Sat, 10am-8.45pm Thu, 11am-7.45pm Sun; Ⓜ Sèvres-Babylone) sells 30,000 rare and/or luxury gourmet products, including 60 different types of bread baked on-site and delicacies such as caviar ravioli. Its fantastical displays of chocolates, pastries, biscuits, cheeses, fresh fruit and vegetables and deli goods are a sight in themselves. Wine tastings regularly take place in the basement.

ℹ Information

Paris Convention & Visitors Bureau (Paris Office de Tourisme; Map p180; ☎01 49 52 42 63; www.parisinfo.com; 29 rue de Rivoli, 4e; ⏲9am-7pm May-Oct, 10am-7pm Nov-Apr; 📶; Ⓜ Hôtel de Ville) Paris' main tourist office is at the Hôtel de Ville. It sells tickets for tours and several attractions, plus museum and transport passes.

ℹ Getting There & Away

AIR

Aéroport de Charles de Gaulle (CDG; ☎01 70 36 39 50; www.parisaeroport.fr) Most international airlines fly to Aéroport de Charles de Gaulle (also known as Roissy), 28km northeast of central Paris.

Aéroport d'Orly (ORY; ☎01 70 36 39 50; www.parisaeroport.fr) Located 19km south of central Paris.

BUS

Eurolines (Map p180; ☎08 92 89 90 91; www.eurolines.fr; 55 rue St-Jacques, 5e; ⏲10am-1pm & 2-6pm Mon-Fri; Ⓜ Cluny–La Sorbonne) connects all major European capitals to Paris' international bus terminal, **Gare Routière Internationale de Paris-Galliéni** (28 av du Général de Gaulle, Bagnolet; Ⓜ Galliéni). The terminal is in the eastern suburb of Bagnolet; it's about a 15-minute metro ride to the more central République station.

Major European bus company FlixBus (www.flixbus.com) uses western **Parking Pershing** (16-24 bd Pershing, 17e; Ⓜ Porte Maillot).

TRAIN

Paris has six major train stations serving both national and international destinations. For mainline train information, check **SNCF** (www.sncf-voyages.com).

Gare du Nord (www.gares-sncf.com; rue de Dunkerque, 10e; Ⓜ Gare du Nord) Trains to/from the UK, Belgium, Germany and northern France.

Gare de l'Est (www.gares-sncf.com; place du 11 Novembre 1918, 10e; Ⓜ Gare de l'Est) Trains to/from Luxembourg, southern Germany and points further east; TGV Est trains to areas of France east of Paris (Champagne, Alsace and Lorraine).

Gare de Lyon (bd Diderot, 12e; Ⓜ Gare de Lyon) Trains to/from Provence, the Riviera, the Alps and Italy. Also serves Geneva.

Gare d'Austerlitz (bd de l'Hôpital, 13e; Ⓜ Gare d'Austerlitz) Terminus for a handful of trains from the south, including services to/from Toulouse. High-speed trains to/from Barcelona and Madrid also use Austerlitz.

Gare Montparnasse (av du Maine & bd de Vaugirard, 15e; Ⓜ Montparnasse Bienvenüe) Trains to/from the southwest and west (Brittany, the Loire and Bordeaux), Spain and Portugal. Some services will eventually move to Gare d'Austerlitz.

Gare St-Lazare (www.gares-sncf.com; rue Intérieure, 8e; Ⓜ St Lazare) Trains to Normandy.

Getting Around

TO/FROM THE AIRPORTS

Getting into town is straightforward and inexpensive thanks to a raft of public-transport options. Bus drivers sell tickets. Children aged four to 11 years pay half-price on most services.

Aéroport de Charles de Gaulle

RER B line (€11.40, 50 minutes, every 10 to 20 minutes) Stops at Gare du Nord, Châtelet–Les Halles and St-Michel–Notre Dame stations. Trains run from 4.50am to 11.50pm; fewer trains on weekends.

Le Bus Direct line 2 (€17, one hour, every 30 minutes, 5.45am to 11pm) Links the airport with the Arc de Triomphe via the Eiffel Tower and Trocadéro.

Le Bus Direct line 4 (€17, 50 to 80 minutes, every 30 minutes, 6am to 10.30pm from the airport, 5.30am to 10.30pm from Montparnasse) Links the airport with Gare Montparnasse (80 minutes) in southern Paris via Gare de Lyon (50 minutes) in eastern Paris.

RATP bus 350 (€6 or three metro tickets, 70 minutes, every 30 minutes, 5.30am to 11pm) Links the airport with Gare de l'Est.

Taxi (€50 to Right Bank and €55 to Left Bank, plus 15% surcharge between 7pm and 7am and on Sundays) It takes 40 minutes to city centre.

Aéroport d'Orly

RER B and Orlyval (€13.25, 35 minutes, every four to 12 minutes, 6am to 11.35pm) The nearest RER station to the airport is Antony, where you connect on the dedicated Orlyval automatic train.

Le Bus Direct line 1 (€12, one hour, every 20 minutes, 5.50am to 11.30pm from Orly, 4.50am to 10.30pm from the Arc de Triomphe) Runs to/from the Arc de Triomphe (one hour) via Gare Montparnasse (40 minutes), La Motte-Picquet and Trocadéro.

Orlybus (€8.70, 30 minutes, every 15 to 20 minutes, 6am to 12.30am from Orly, 5.35am to midnight from Paris) Runs to/from place Denfert-Rochereau in southern Paris.

Taxi (€30 to the Left Bank and €35 to the Right Bank, plus 15% between 7pm and 7am and on Sundays) It takes 30 minutes to city centre.

BICYCLE

Paris is increasingly bike-friendly, with more cycling lanes and efforts from the City of Paris to reduce the number of cars on the roads.

BOAT

Batobus (www.batobus.com; adult/child 1-day pass €17/8, 2-day pass €19/10; ⏲10am-9.30pm late Apr-Aug, shorter hours Sep-late Apr) runs glassed-in trimarans that dock every 20 to 25 minutes at nine small piers along the Seine: Beaugrenelle, Eiffel Tower, Musée d'Orsay, St-Germain des Prés, Jardin des Plantes/Cité de la Mode et du Design, Hôtel de Ville, Musée du Louvre and Champs-Élysées. (At time of printing, the Notre Dame pier was closed.) Buy tickets online, at ferry stops or at tourist offices.

PUBLIC TRANSPORT

Paris' public transit system is operated by the **RATP** (www.ratp.fr).

➡ The same RATP tickets are valid on the 14-line metro, the RER (for travel on five main lines within the city limits), buses, trams and the Montmartre funicular.

➡ A ticket – white in colour and called *Le Ticket t+* costs €1.90 (half price for children aged four to nine years) if bought individually; a *carnet* (book) of 10 costs €14.90 for adults.

➡ One ticket lets you travel between any two metro stations (no return journeys) for a period of 1½ hours, no matter how many transfers are required. You can also use it on the RER for travel within zone 1, which encompasses all of central Paris.

➡ Keep your ticket until you exit from your station or risk a fine.

Bus

➡ Buses run runs from approximately 5am to 1am Monday to Saturday; services are drastically reduced on Sunday and public holidays.

➡ Normal bus rides embracing one or two bus zones cost one metro ticket; longer rides require two or even three tickets.

➡ Validate your ticket in the ticket machine near the driver. If you don't have a ticket, the driver can sell you one for €2 (correct change required).

Metro & RER

➡ Trains usually start at around 5.30am, with the last train beginning its run between 12.35am and 1.15am (2.15am on Friday and Saturday).

➡ The RER is faster than the metro, but the stops are much further apart. Some attractions, particularly those on the Left Bank (eg the Musée d'Orsay, Eiffel Tower and Panthéon), can be reached far more conveniently by the RER than by the metro.

➡ If you're going out to the suburbs (eg Versailles or Disneyland), ask for help on the platform – finding the right train can be confusing. Also make sure your ticket is for the correct zone.

Tourist Passes

Mobilis Allows unlimited travel for one day and costs from €7.50 (for two zones) to €17.80 (five zones). Buy it at any metro, RER or SNCF station in the Paris region. Depending on how many times you plan to hop on/off the metro in a day, a *carnet* (book of 10 tickets) might work out cheaper.

Paris Visite Allows unlimited travel as well as discounted entry to certain museums, and other discounts and bonuses. The 'Paris+Suburbs+Airports' pass includes transport to/from the airports and costs €25.25/38.35/53.75/65.80 for one/two/three/five days. The cheaper 'Paris Centre' pass, valid for zones 1 to 3, costs €12/19.50/26.65/38.35 for one/two/three/five days. Children aged four to 11 years pay half price.

Navigo If you're staying in Paris more than three or four days, the cheapest and easiest way to use public transport is to get a rechargeable Navigo (www. navigo.fr) pass. A weekly pass costs €22.80 and is valid Monday to Sunday. You'll also need to pay €5 for the Navigo card and provide a passport photo.

TAXI

➡ Flagging down a taxi in Paris can be difficult; it's best to find an official taxi stand.

➡ To order a taxi, call or reserve online with **Taxis G7** (☎01 41 27 66 99, 3607; www.g7.fr) or **Alpha Taxis** (☎01 45 85 85 85; www.alphataxis.fr).

➡ The minimum taxi fare for a short trip is €7.10. The *prise en charge* (flagfall) is €4. Within the city limits, it costs €1.07 per kilometre for travel between 10am and 5pm Monday to Saturday. At night (5pm to 10am), on Sunday from 7am to midnight and in the inner suburbs, the rate is €1.29 per kilometre.

AROUND PARIS

Splendid architecture, including some of the most magnificent châteaux and gardens in the country, are within easy striking distance of the French capital.

Versailles

POP 87,550

Louis XIV transformed his father's hunting lodge into the monumental Château de Versailles in the mid-17th century, and it remains France's most famous and grand palace. Situated in the leafy, bourgeois suburb of Versailles, 22km southwest of central Paris, the baroque château was the kingdom's political capital and the seat of the royal court from 1682 up until the fateful events of 1789 when revolutionaries massacred the palace guard. Louis XVI and Marie Antoinette were ultimately dragged back to Paris, where they were ingloriously guillotined.

Sights

★Château de Versailles PALACE

(☎01 30 83 78 00; www.chateauversailles.fr; place d'Armes; adult/child passport ticket incl estate-wide access €20/free, with musical events €27/free, palace €18/free except during musical events; ⏲9am-6.30pm Tue-Sun Apr-Oct, to 5.30pm Tue-Sun Nov-Mar; Ⓜ RER Versailles-Château–Rive Gauche) Amid magnificently landscaped formal **gardens** (free except during musical events; ⏲gardens 8am-8.30pm Apr-Oct, to 6pm Nov-Mar, park 7am-8.30pm Apr-Oct, 8am-6pm Nov-Mar), this splendid and enormous palace was built in the mid-17th century during the reign of Louis XIV – the Roi Soleil (Sun King) – to project the absolute power of the French monarchy, which was then at the height of its glory. The château has undergone relatively few alterations since its construction, though almost all the interior furnishings disappeared during the Revolution and many of the rooms were rebuilt by Louis-Philippe (r 1830–48).

Eating

Rue de Satory is lined with restaurants and cafes. More local options can be found on and around rue de la Paroisse, where you'll also find Versailles' **markets** (rue de la Paroisse; ⏲food market 7am-2pm Tue, Fri & Sun, covered market 7am-7.30pm Tue-Sat, to 2pm Sun, flea market 11am-7pm Wed, Thu & Sat).

TOP VERSAILLES TIPS

➡ Monday is out for obvious reasons (it's closed).

➡ Arrive early morning and avoid Tuesday, Saturday and Sunday, its busiest days.

➡ Pre-purchase tickets on the château's website or at **Fnac** (08 92 68 36 22; www.fnactickets.com) branches and head straight to **Entrance A** (Château de Versailles).

➡ Versailles is free on the first Sunday of every month from November to March.

➡ Prebook a **guided tour** (01 30 83 77 88; www.chateauversailles.fr; Château de Versailles; tours €10, plus palace entry; English-language tours 11am, 1.30pm & 3pm Tue-Sun) to access areas otherwise off limits.

➡ Try to time your visit for summertime's **Grandes Eaux Musicales** (www.chateauversailles-spectacles.fr; adult/child €9.50/8; 9am-7pm Tue, Sat & Sun mid-May–late Jun, 9am-7pm Sat & Sun Apr–mid-May & late Jun-Oct) or the after-dark **Grandes Eaux Nocturnes** (adult/child €24/20; 8.30-11.30pm Sat mid-Jun–mid-Sep), magical 'dancing water' displays – set to music composed by baroque- and classical-era composers – in the grounds.

★ **Ore** FRENCH **$$**
(01 30 84 12 96; www.ducasse-chateauversailles.com; 1st fl, Pavillon Dufour, Château de Versailles; breakfast menus €12-20, mains €20-36, afternoon-tea platters €35; 9am-6.30pm Tue-Sun Apr-Oct, to 5.30pm Nov-Mar;) Full-length windows frame the Cour d'Honneur and Cour Royale at this resplendent light-flooded restaurant inside the Château de Versailles. Created by superstar chef Alain Ducasse, it offers breakfast (mini pastries, organic eggs), small lunchtime plates (like citrus-marinated mackerel with horseradish crème) and afternoon tea (such as chocolate soufflé with Ducasse's Paris-made bean-to-bar chocolate, or laden platters with tea or coffee)

Information

Tourist Office (01 39 24 88 88; www.versailles-tourisme.com; 2bis av de Paris; 9.30am-6pm Mon, 8.30am-7pm Tue-Sun Apr-Oct, 11am-5pm Mon, 8.30am-6pm Tue-Sun Nov-Mar)

Getting There & Away

Take RER C5 (return €7.10, 40 minutes, frequent) from Paris' Left Bank RER stations to Versailles-Château–Rive Gauche station.

Chartres

POP 41,588

The magnificent 13th-century **Cathédrale Notre Dame** (www.cathedrale-chartres.org; place de la Cathédrale; 8.30am-7.30pm daily year-round, also to 10pm Tue, Fri & Sun Jun-Aug) of Chartres, crowned by two very different spires – one Gothic, the other Romanesque – rises from rich farmland 88km southwest of Paris and dominates the medieval town. The cathedral's west, north and south entrances have superbly ornamented triple portals and its 105m-high **Clocher Vieux** (Old Bell Tower) is the tallest Romanesque steeple still standing. Superb views of three-tiered flying buttresses and the 19th-century copper roof, turned green by verdigris, reward the 350-step hike up the 112m-high **Clocher Neuf** (New Bell Tower; adult/child €7.50/free; 9.30am-12.30pm & 2-4.30pm Mon-Sat, 2-4.30pm Sun).

Inside, 172 extraordinary stained-glass windows, mainly from the 13th century, form one of the most important ensembles of medieval stained glass in the world. The three most exquisite – renowned for the depth and intensity of their tones, famously known as 'Chartres blue' – are above the west entrance and below the rose window.

Information

Tourist Office (02 37 18 26 26; www.chartres-tourisme.com; 8-10 rue de la Poissonnerie; 10am-6pm Mon-Sat, to 5.30pm Sun) Rents 1½-hour English-language audio-guide tours (€5.50/8.50 per one/two) of the medieval city, as well as binoculars (€2), which are fabulous for seeing details of the cathedral close up.

Getting There & Away

Frequent SNCF trains link Paris' Gare Montparnasse (€16, 55 to 70 minutes) with Chartres' **train station** (place Pierre Semard).

Giverny

POP 518

The tiny village of Giverny, 74km northwest of Paris, was the **home of impressionist**

Claude Monet (☎02 32 51 28 21; www.fondation-monet.com; 84 rue Claude Monet; adult/child €9.50/5.50, incl Musée des Impressionnismes Giverny €17/9; ⏲9.30am-6pm Easter-Oct) for the last 43 years of his life. You can visit the artist's pastel-pink house and famous gardens with lily pond, Japanese bridge draped in purple wisteria, and so on. Early to late spring, daffodils, tulips, rhododendrons, wisteria and irises bloom in the flowery gardens, followed by poppies and lilies. By June, nasturtiums, roses and sweet peas are in flower, while September is the month to see dahlias, sunflowers and hollyhocks.

Pre- or post-garden visit, indulge in the inventive Michelin-starred cuisine of chef Eric Guerin's at Le Jardin des Plumes, a gorgeous sky-blue-trimmed address less than 10 minutes' walk from Monet's pad.

ℹ Getting There & Away

The closest train station is at Vernon, from where buses, taxis and cycle/walking tracks run to Giverny. Shuttle buses (www.sngo-giverny.fr; single/return €5/10, 20 minutes, up to five daily Easter to October) meet most trains from Paris' Gare St-Lazare at Vernon (from €9, 45 minutes to one hour).

LILLE & THE SOMME

When it comes to culture, cuisine, beer, shopping and dramatic views of land and sea, the friendly Ch'tis (residents of France's northern tip) and their region compete with the best France has to offer. Highlights include Flemish-style Lille, the cross-Channel shopping centre of Calais, and the moving battlefields and cemeteries of WWI.

Lille

POP 233,900

Lille may be France's most underrated metropolis. Recent decades have seen it transform from an industrial centre into a glittering cultural and commercial hub, with enchanting old town, magnificent French and Flemish architecture, renowned art museums, stylish shopping and a nightlife scene bolstered by 67,000 university students. In 2020, Lille was the World Design Capital.

Sights

The **Lille City Pass** (24/48/72 hours €25/35/45) gets you into almost all the museums in greater Lille and affords unlimited use of public transport; buy it at the tourist office or online.

★ Palais des Beaux Arts MUSEUM
(Fine Arts Museum; ☎03 20 06 78 00; www.pba-lille.fr; place de la République; adult/child €7/4; ⏲2-6pm Mon, 10am-6pm Wed-Sun; Ⓜ République-Beaux-Arts) Inaugurated in 1892, Lille's illustrious Fine Arts Museum claims France's second-largest collection after Paris' Musée du Louvre. Its cache of sublime 15th- to 20th-century paintings include works by Rubens, Van Dyck and Manet. Exquisite porcelain and faience (pottery), much of it of local provenance, is on the ground floor, while in the basement you'll find classical archaeology, medieval statuary and 18th-century scale models of the fortified cities of northern France and Belgium.

Hôtel de Ville HISTORIC BUILDING
(☎03 20 49 50 00; www.lille.fr; place Augustin Laurent CS; belfry adult/child €7/5.50; ⏲belfry 10am-1pm & 2-5.30pm; Ⓜ Mairie de Lille) Built between 1924 and 1932, Lille's city hall is topped by a slender, 104m-high belfry that was designated a Unesco-listed monument in 2004. Climbing 100 steps leads to a lift that whisks you to the top for a stunning panorama over the town. An audio guide costs €2; binoculars are available for €1. Ring the doorbell to gain entry.

★ La Piscine Musée d'Art et d'Industrie GALLERY
(☎03 20 69 23 60; www.roubaix-lapiscine.com; 23 rue de l'Espérance, Roubaix; adult/child €9/6; ⏲11am-6pm Tue-Thu, 11am-8pm Fri, 1-6pm Sat & Sun; Ⓜ Gare Jean Lebas) An art deco municipal swimming pool built between 1927 and 1932 is now an innovative museum showcasing fine arts (paintings, sculptures, drawings) and applied arts (furniture, textiles, fashion) in a delightfully watery environment: the pool is still filled and sculptures are reflected in the water. It reopened in 2018 with a new wing and 2000 sq metres of additional exhibition space. It's 12km northeast of Gare Lille-Europe in Roubaix.

Musée d'Art Moderne, d'Art Contemporain et d'Art Brut – LaM MUSEUM
(☎03 20 19 68 68; www.musee-lam.fr; 1 allée du Musée, Villeneuve-d'Ascq; adult/child €7/5, 1st Sun of month free; ⏲museum 10am-6pm Tue-Sun, sculpture park 9am-6pm Tue-Sun) Colourful, playful and just plain weird works of modern and contemporary art by masters such as Braque, Calder, Léger, Miró, Modigliani and Picasso are the big draw at this re-

nowned museum and sculpture park in the Lille suburb of Villeneuve-d'Ascq, 9km east of Gare Lille-Europe. Take metro line 1 to Pont de Bois, then bus L4 six stops to 'LaM'.

Sleeping & Eating

Dining hot spots in Vieux Lille include rue de Gand, rue de la Monnaie and its side streets, alleys and courtyards. Keep an eye out for *estaminets* (traditional Flemish eateries).

★Hôtel L'Arbre Voyageur DESIGN HOTEL **$$**
(03 20 20 62 62; http://hotelarbrevoyageur.com; 45 bd Carnot; d/f/ste from €119/214/219; ; M Gare Lille-Flandres) Behind a fretted glass-and-steel facade in the former Polish Consulate's post-Soviet building, the 2016-opened Hôtel L'Arbre Voyageur has 48 stylised rooms (including four suites) with custom-made furniture and minibars stocked with free soft drinks, and a bamboo and palm-filled courtyard. Green initiatives span solar panels to a free drink for guests who don't want their linen changed every day.

Papà Raffaele PIZZA **$**
(www.facebook.com/paparaffaelepizzeria; 5 rue St-Jacques; pizza €7.50-14; noon-2pm & 7-10pm Mon-Thu, noon-2pm & 6.30-11pm Fri, noon-3pm & 6.30-11pm Sat & Sun; ; M Gare Lille-Flandres) The queues at Papà Raffaele are as legendary as its pizzas (it doesn't take reservations), so come early or late to this post-industrial space with recycled timber tables, vintage chairs and cured meats hanging from the ceiling. Wood-fired pizzas (like Cheesus Christ, with six cheeses) are made with Naples-sourced ingredients; coffee, craft beers and wine are all Italian. Takeaway is available.

★L'Assiette du Marché FRENCH **$$**
(03 20 06 83 61; www.assiettedumarche.com; 61 rue de la Monnaie; 2-/3-course menus €19.50/25, mains €16-25; noon-2.30pm & 7-10.30pm Mon-Fri, to 11pm Sat & Sun; M Rihour) Entered via a grand archway, a 12th-century aristocratic mansion – a mint under Louis XIV, hence the street's name, and a listed historical monument – is the romantic setting for contemporary cuisine (tuna carpaccio with Champagne vinaigrette, roast duckling with glazed turnips and smoked garlic). Dine under its glass roof, in its intimate dining rooms, or on its cobbled courtyard in summer.

Drinking & Nightlife

Small, stylish bars line rue Royale and rue de la Barre, while university students descend on the bars along rue Masséna and rue Solférino. In warm weather, cafes on place du Général de Gaulle and place du Théâtre spill onto table-filled terraces.

★La Capsule CRAFT BEER
(03 20 42 14 75; www.bar-la-capsule.fr; 25 rue des Trois Mollettes; 5.30pm-1am Mon-Wed, 5.30pm-3am Thu & Fri, 4pm-3am Sat, 5.30pm-midnight Sun; ; M Rihour) Spread across three levels – a vaulted stone cellar, a beamed-ceilinged ground floor and an upper level reached by a spiral staircase – Lille's best craft beer bar has 28 varieties on tap and over 100 by the bottle. Most are French (such as Lille's Lydéric and Paris' BapBap) and Belgian (eg Cantillon), but small-scale brewers from around the world are also represented.

DON'T MISS

WONDERFUL WAFFLES

Meert (03 20 57 07 44; www.meert.fr; 27 rue Esquermoise; waffles & pastries €3-7.60, tearoom dishes €4.50-11.50, restaurant mains €26-32; shop 2-7.30pm Mon, 9.30am-7.30pm Tue-Fri, 9am-7.30pm Sat, 9am-7pm Sun, tearoom 2-7pm Mon, 9.30am-10pm Tue-Fri, 9am-10pm Sat, 9am-6.30pm Sun, restaurant noon-2.30pm & 7.30-10pm Tue-Sat, 11am-2pm Sun; ; M Rihour) Famed for its *gaufres* (waffles) made with Madagascar vanilla, Meert has served kings, viceroys and generals since 1761. The sumptuous chocolate shop's coffered ceiling, painted wooden panels, wrought-iron balcony and mosaic floor date from 1839. Its *salon de thé* (tearoom) is a delightful spot for a morning arabica or a mid-afternoon tea. Also here is a French gourmet restaurant.

Information

Tourist Office (03 59 57 94 00; www.lilletourism.com; 3 rue du Palais Rihour; 9.30am-1pm & 2-6pm Mon-Sat, 10am-12.30pm & 1.15-4.30pm Sun; M Rihour)

Getting There & Around

AIR

Aéroport de Lille (LIL; www.lille.aeroport.fr; rte de L'Aéroport, Lesquin), 11km southeast of the centre, is linked to destinations around France and southern Europe by a variety of low-cost carriers. To get to/from the city centre (Gare Lille-Europe), take a shuttle bus (return €8, 20 minutes, hourly).

WORTH A TRIP

THE SOMME BATTLEFIELDS

The First Battle of the Somme, a WWI Allied offensive waged in the villages and woodlands northeast of Amiens, was designed to relieve pressure on the beleaguered French troops at Verdun. On 1 July 1916, British, Commonwealth and French troops 'went over the top' in a massive assault along a 34km front. But German positions proved virtually unbreachable, and on the first day of the battle an astounding 21,392 British troops were killed and another 35,492 were wounded. By the time the offensive was called off in mid-November, a total of 1.2 million lives had been lost on both sides. The British had advanced 12km, the French 8km.

The battlefields and memorials are numerous and scattered – joining a tour can therefore be a good option, especially if you don't have your own transport. Tourist offices in **Péronne** (03 22 84 42 38; www.hautesomme-tourisme.com; 16 place André Audinot; 9.30am-12.30pm & 1.30-6.30pm Mon-Sat, 10am-noon & 2-5pm Sun Jul & Aug, 9am-12.30pm & 2-6pm Mon-Fri, 9am-noon & 2-6pm Sat Apr-Jun, Sep & Oct, shorter hour Nov-Mar) and **Albert** (03 22 75 16 42; www.tourisme-paysducoquelicot.com; 9 rue Gambetta; 9am-12.30pm & 1.30-6.30pm Mon-Fri, 9am-12.30pm & 2-6.30pm Sat, 9am-1pm Sun May-Aug, 9am-12.30pm & 1.30-5pm Mon-Fri, 9am-noon & 2-5pm Sat Sep-Apr) can help with booking tours and accommodation.

TRAIN

Lille has two main train stations: **Gare Lille-Flandres** for trains to Paris Gare du Nord (€47 to €63, one hour, at least hourly) and intra-regional TER services; and ultramodern **Gare Lille-Europe** for Eurostar trains to London, TGV/Thalys/Eurostar trains to Brussels-Midi, half of the TGVs to Paris Gare du Nord and most province-to-province TGVs. The two stations, 400m apart, are linked by metro line 2 (one stop).

NORMANDY

Famous for cows, cider and Camembert, this largely rural region (www.normandie-tourisme.fr) is one of France's most traditional, and most visited, thanks to world-renowned sights such as the Bayeux Tapestry, the historic D-Day beaches and spectacular Mont St-Michel.

Bayeux

POP 13,900

Bayeux has become famous throughout the English-speaking world thanks to a 68.3m-long piece of painstakingly embroidered cloth: the 11th-century Bayeux Tapestry, with its 58 scenes that vividly tell the story of the Norman invasion of England in 1066.

The town is also one of the few in Normandy to have survived WWII practically unscathed, with a centre crammed with 13th- to 18th-century buildings, timber-framed Norman-style houses, and a spectacular Norman Gothic **cathedral** (rue du Bienvenu; 8.30am-7pm). It makes a great base for exploring D-Day beaches.

Sights

A 'triple ticket' good for all three of Bayeux' outstanding municipal museums costs €15/13.50 for an adult/child (€12/10 for two museums).

★Bayeux Tapestry MUSEUM

(02 31 51 25 50; www.bayeuxmuseum.com; 15bis rue de Nesmond; adult/child incl audio guide €9.50/5; 9.30am-12.30pm & 2-5.30pm Mon-Sat, 10am-1pm & 2-5.30pm Sun Feb, Mar, Nov & Dec, to 6pm Apr-Jun, Sep & Oct, 9am-7pm Mon-Sat, 9am-1pm & 2-6pm Sun Jul & Aug, closed Jan) The world's most celebrated embroidery depicts the conquest of England by William the Conqueror in 1066 from an unashamedly Norman perspective. Commissioned by Bishop Odo of Bayeux, William's half-brother, for the opening of Bayeux' cathedral in 1077, the well-preserved cartoon strip tells the dramatic, bloody tale with verve and vividness as well as some astonishing artistry. Particularly incredible are its length – nearly 70m long – and fine attention to detail.

★Musée d'Art et d'Histoire Baron Gérard MUSEUM

(MAHB; 02 31 92 14 21; www.bayeuxmuseum.com; 37 rue du Bienvenu; adult/child €7.50/5; 9.30am-6.30pm May-Sep, 10am-12.30pm & 2-6pm Oct-Apr, closed 3 weeks in Jan) Make sure you drop by this museum – one of France's most gorgeously presented provincial museums – where exhibitions cover everything from Gallo-Roman archaeology through medieval art to paintings from the Renaissance and on to the 20th century, including a fine work by Gustave Caillebotte. Other highlights include impossibly fine local lace and Bayeux-made porcelain. The museum is housed in the former bishop's palace.

Sleeping & Eating

Local specialities to keep an eye out for include products made from *cochon de Bayeux* (a local heritage pig breed). Near the tourist office, along rue St-Jean and rue St-Martin, there is a variety food shops and cheap eateries.

Hôtel Reine Mathilde HOTEL $
(02 31 92 08 13; www.hotel-bayeux-reinemathilde.fr; 23 rue Larcher; d/ste/studio from €50/90/95;) Occupying a superbly central location, this friendly hotel has comfortable accommodation, with an assortment of sleek and spacious rooms in the annexe, a converted barn by the Aure River. Rooms, named after historic figures, are attractively designed with beamed ceilings, and elegant lines, excellent lighting and modern bathrooms; studios come with a small kitchenette. A decent restaurant is also on-site.

Au Ptit Bistrot MODERN FRENCH $$
(02 31 92 30 08; 31 rue Larcher; lunch menus €17-20, dinner menus €29-35, mains €18-22; noon-2pm & 7-9pm Tue-Sat) Near the cathedral, this friendly, welcoming eatery whips up creative, beautifully prepared dishes that highlight the Norman bounty without pretension. Recent hits include braised beef cheek with red wine, polenta, grapefruit tapenade and vegetables, or roasted pigeon with mushrooms and mashed parsnip. The kids' menu is €11. Reservations essential.

Information

Tourist Office (02 31 51 28 28; www.bayeux-bessin-tourisme.com; Pont St-Jean; 9am-7pm Mon-Sat, 10am-1pm & 2-6pm Sun Jul & Aug, shorter hours rest of year)

Getting There & Away

Direct trains link Bayeux with Caen (€6, 15 to 20 minutes, hourly), from where there are connections to Paris' Gare St-Lazare and Rouen.

D-Day Beaches

Early on 6 June 1944, Allied troops stormed 80km of beaches north of Bayeux, code-named (from west to east) Utah, Omaha, Gold, Juno and Sword. The landings on D Day – called *Jour J* in French – ultimately led to the liberation of Europe from Nazi occupation. For context, see www.normandiememoire.com and www.6juin1944.com.

The most brutal fighting on D Day took place 15km northwest of Bayeux along the stretch of coastline now known as **Omaha Beach**, today a glorious stretch of fine golden sand partly lined with sand dunes and summer homes. **Circuit de la Plage d'Omaha**, a trail marked with a yellow stripe, is a self-guided tour along the beach, surveyed from a bluff above by the huge **Normandy American Cemetery & Memorial** (02 31 51 62 00; www.abmc.gov; Colleville-sur-Mer;

WORTH A TRIP

MODERN ART MUSEUMS

Two of Paris' foremost art institutions, the Louvre and the Centre Pompidou, have satellite outposts in northern France that art lovers won't want to miss.

Centre Pompidou-Metz (www.centrepompidou-metz.fr; 1 parvis des Droits de l'Homme; adult/child €7/free; 10am-6pm Mon & Wed-Thu, to 7pm Fri-Sun) concentrates mainly on abstract and experimental art. The building itself is worth the trip, designed by Japanese architect Shigeru Ban, with a curved roof resembling a space-age Chinese hat. Trains run direct from Paris (€77 to €82, 1½ hours) and Strasbourg (€27.80, 1½ hours).

Louvre-Lens (03 21 18 62 62; www.louvrelens.fr; 99 rue Paul Bert, Lens; temporary exhibitions adult/child €10/5; 10am-6pm Wed-Mon) FREE showcases hundreds of the Louvre's treasures in a purpose-built, state-of-the-art exhibition space in Lens, 35km southwest of Lille. A second building, the glass-walled **Pavillon de Verre**, displays temporary themed exhibits. Free half-hourly shuttle buses link the museum with Lens' train station, linked by regular trains to/from Paris' Gare du Nord (€33, 1¼ hours) and Lille-Flandres (from €8.30, 45 minutes).

⏰9am-6pm mid-Apr–mid-Sep, to 5pm mid-Sep–mid-Apr) FREE. Featured in the opening scenes of Steven Spielberg's *Saving Private Ryan,* this is the largest American cemetery in Europe.

Caen's high-tech, hugely impressive **Mémorial – Un Musée pour la Paix** (Memorial – A Museum for Peace; ☎02 31 06 06 44; www.memorial-caen.fr; esplanade Général Eisenhower; adult/child/family pass €19.80/17.50/51; ⏰9am-7pm Apr-Sep, 9.30am-6pm Oct-Dec, 9am-6pm Feb-Mar, closed 3 weeks in Jan, shut most Mon in Nov & Dec) uses sound, lighting, film, animation and lots of exhibits to graphically explore and evoke the events of WWII, the D-Day landings and the ensuing Cold War.

Lots of local companies offer guided minibus tours of the D-Day beaches; reserve at Bayeux tourist office (p205).

ℹ Getting There & Away

Bus Verts (☎09 70 83 00 14; www.busverts.fr) links Bayeux' train station and place St-Patrice with many of the villages along the D-Day beaches.

Mont St-Michel

POP 44

It's one of France's most iconic images: the slender spires, stout ramparts and rocky outcrops of Mont St-Michel rising dramatically from the sea – or towering over slick, shimmering sands laid bare by the receding tide. The surrounding bay is famed for having Europe's highest tidal variations; the difference between low and high tides – only about six hours apart – can reach an astonishing 15m.

The Mont's one main street, the **Grande Rue**, leads up the slope – past souvenir shops, touristy eateries and a forest of elbows – to the abbey. Be prepared for hundreds of steps.

The Mont's star attraction is the stunning ensemble crowning its top: the **abbey** (☎02 33 89 80 00; www.abbaye-mont-saint-michel.fr/en; adult/child incl guided tour €10/free; ⏰9am-7pm May-Aug, 9.30am-6pm Sep-Apr, last entry 1hr before closing). Most areas can be visited without a guide, but it's worth taking the 1¼-hour tour included in the ticket. Admission is free the first Sunday of the month from November to March. For spectacular views of the bay and people trudging through the mud at low tide, walk along the top of the entire eastern section of the Mont's **ramparts**, from Tour du Nord (North Tower) to the Porte du Roy.

ℹ Information

La Caserne Tourist Office (☎02 14 13 20 15; www.bienvenueaumontsaintmichel.com; La Caserne car park; ⏰10am-6pm)

Mont St-Michel Tourist Office (☎02 33 60 14 30; www.ot-montsaintmichel.com; bd Avancée, Corps de Garde des Bourgeois; ⏰9.30am-7pm Jul & Aug, to 6.30pm Mon-Sat, 9.30am-12.30pm & 1.30-6pm Sun Apr, May, Jun & Sep, shorter hours rest of year; 📶)

ℹ Getting There & Away

For all manner of details on getting to the Mont, see www.bienvenueaumontsaintmichel.com.

Bus 1 (every hour or two, more frequently in July and August), operated by **Transdev** (☎02 14 13 20 15), links La Caserne with the train station in Pontorson (€3.20, 18 minutes); times are coordinated with some trains to/from Caen and Rennes.

BRITTANY

Brittany is for explorers. Its wild, dramatic coastline, medieval towns and thick forests make an excursion here well worth the detour off the beaten track. This is a land of prehistoric mysticism, proud tradition and culinary wealth, where fiercely independent locals celebrate Breton culture, and Paris feels a long way away indeed.

Quimper

POP 66,926

Small enough to feel like a village, with its slanted half-timbered houses and narrow cobbled streets, and large enough to buzz as the troubadour of Breton culture and arts, Quimper (kam-pair) is Finistère's thriving capital. With some excellent museums, standout crêperies, a history of faience (pottery) production, one of Brittany's loveliest old quarters and a delightful setting along the Odet River, Quimper deserves serious exploration. Beside the **Cathédrale St-Corentin**, recessed behind a magnificent stone courtyard, Quimper's superb **Musée Départemental Breton** showcases Breton history, furniture, crafts and archaeology in a former bishop's palace.

Quimper has a bewildering choice of exceptional crêperies centred on place au Beurre and rue du Sallé. The covered market **Halles St-François** (www.halles-cornouaille.com; 16 quai du Stéir; ⏰7am-7.30pm Mon-Sat, to 1pm Sun) has a slew of salad and sandwich options, or dine brasserie-style at one of Quimper's oldest addresses, **L'Épée** (☎02 98 95 28 97; http://cafedelepee.fr; 14 rue du Parc; mains €12-32, menus €15.50-39; ⊙brasserie noon-2.30pm & 7-10.30pm Mon-Sat, cafe 10.30am-midnight Mon-Sat, noon-2.30pm Sun).

Information

Tourist Office (☎02 98 53 04 05; www.quimper-tourisme.bzh; 8 rue Élie Fréron; ⊙9am-7pm Mon-Sat, 10am-12.45pm & 3-5.45pm Sun Jul & Aug, shorter hours rest of year; 📶) Sells the Pass Quimper (€12), which gives admission to four museums, sights or tours from a list of participating organisations.

Getting There & Away

Frequent trains serve Paris' Gare Montparnasse (€67 to €108, 4¾ hours).

St-Malo

POP 46,589

The enthralling mast-filled port of fortified St-Malo is inextricably tied up with the deep briny blue: the town became a key harbour during the 17th and 18th centuries, functioning as a base for merchant ships and government-sanctioned privateers. These days it's a busy cross-Channel ferry port and summertime getaway.

Sights

Walking on top of the sturdy 17th-century ramparts (1.8km) affords fine views of the old walled city known as **Intra-Muros** (Within the Walls), or Ville Close; access the ramparts from any of the city gates.

★Château de St-Malo CASTLE

(place Chateaubriand; ⊙10am-12.30pm & 2-6pm Apr-Sep, 10am-noon & 2-6pm Tue-Sun Oct-Mar) Château de St-Malo was built by the dukes of Brittany in the 15th and 16th centuries, and is now the home of the **Musée d'Histoire de St-Malo** (☎02 99 40 71 57; www.ville-saint-malo.fr/culture/les musees; adult/child €6/3; ⊙10am-12.30pm & 2-6pm Apr-Sep, 10am-noon & 2-6pm Tue-Sun Oct-Mar), which examines the life and history of the city, while the lookout tower offers eye-popping views of the old city.

Ramparts WALLS

Constructed at the end of the 17th century under military architect Vauban, and measuring 1.8km, the ramparts of St-Malo can be accessed from several points, including all the main city gates.

Île du Grand Bé & Fort du Petit Bé ISLAND, CASTLE

(☎06 08 27 51 20; fort guided tours adult/child €6/4; ⊙fort by reservation, depending on tides & weather) At low tide, cross the beach to walk out via Porte des Bés to Île du Grand Bé, the rocky islet where the great St-Malo-born, 18th-century writer Chateaubriand is buried. About 100m beyond Grand Bé is the privately owned, Vauban-built, 17th-century Fort du Petit Bé. Once the tide rushes in, the causeway remains impassable for about six hours; check tide times with the tourist office (p208) so you don't get trapped on the island.

Sleeping & Eating

★Le Valmarin HISTORIC HOTEL $$

(☎02 99 81 94 76; www.levalmarin.com; 7 rue Jean XXIII, St-Servan; s €80-125, d €85-165, f €149-230; 📶) If you're yearning for an aristocratic overlay to your St-Malo experience then this peaceful 18th-century mansion should do the job nicely. It has 12 high-ceilinged rooms dressed in late-19th-century style, and glorious gardens full of flowers and shade trees. Minus: some bathrooms feel a bit dated. It's a soothing escape from the St-Malo hubbub, on the edge of the village-like St-Servan quarter.

Breizh Café CRÊPES $

(☎02 99 56 96 08; www.breizhcafe.com; 6 rue de l'Orme; crêpes €10-15, menu €15.80; ⊙noon-2pm & 7-10pm Wed-Sun) This will be one of your most memorable meals in Brittany, from the delicious menu at this international name to the excellent service. The creative chef combines traditional Breton ingredients and *galette* and crêpe styles with Japanese flavours, textures and presentation, where seaweed and delightful seasonal pickles meet local ham, organic eggs and roast duck.

★Bistro Autour du Beurre BISTRO $$

(☎02 23 18 25 81; www.lebeurrebordier.com; 7 rue de l'Orme; 3-course weekday lunch menu €22, mains €19-26; ⊙noon-2pm & 7-10pm Tue-Sat Jul & Aug, noon-2pm Tue & Wed, plus 7-10pm Thu-Sat Sep-Oct, Apr & Jun, noon-2pm Tue-Thu, plus 7-10pm Fri & Sat Nov-Mar) This casual bistro showcases the cheeses and butters handmade by the world-famous Jean-Yves Bordier; you'll find his **shop** (☎02 99 40 88 79; 9 rue de l'Orme; ⊙9am-1pm & 3.30-7.30pm Mon-Sat, 9am-1pm Sun Jul & Aug, closed Mon Sep-Jun) next door. At the bistro, the butter sampler and bottomless bread basket are just the start to creative, local meals that change with the seasons.

Information

Tourist Office (☎08 25 13 52 00; www.saint-malo-tourisme.com; esplanade St-Vincent; ⏲9am-7.30pm Mon-Sat, 10am-7pm Sun Jul & Aug, shorter hours rest of year; 📶)

Getting There & Away

Brittany Ferries (www.brittany-ferries.com) sails between St-Malo and Portsmouth; Condor Ferries (www.condorferries.co.uk) runs to/from Poole via Jersey or Guernsey.

TGV train services go to Paris' Gare Montparnasse (€74, 2¾ hours, three direct TGVs daily).

CHAMPAGNE

POP 1.3 MILLION

Known in Roman times as Campania, meaning 'plain', the agricultural region of Champagne is synonymous these days with its world-famous bubbly. This multi-million-dollar industry is strictly protected under French law, ensuring that only grapes grown in designated Champagne vineyards can truly lay claim to the hallowed title. The town of Épernay, 30km south of the regional capital of Reims, is the best place to head for *dégustation* (tasting); self-drive **Champagne Routes** (www.tourisme-en-champagne.com) wend their way through the region's most celebrated vineyards.

Reims

POP 186,971

Rising golden and imperious above the city, Reims' gargantuan Gothic cathedral is where, over the course of a millennium (816 to 1825), some 34 sovereigns – among them two dozen kings – began their reigns. Meticulously restored after WWI and again following WWII, Reims is endowed with handsome pedestrian boulevards, Roman remains, art deco cafes and a flourishing fine-dining scene that counts among it four Michelin-starred restaurants.

Sights & Activities

The musty *caves* (cellars) and dusty bottles of the 10 Reims-based Champagne producers (known as *maisons* – literally, 'houses') can be visited on guided tours. Major *maisons* such as **Veuve Clicquot Ponsardin** (☎03 26 89 53 90; www.veuveclicquot.com; 1 place des Droits de l'Homme; public tours & tastings €26-53, private tour & tasting €250; ⏲tours 9.30am, 10.30am, 12.30pm, 1.30pm, 2pm, 3.30pm & 4.30pm Tue-Sat Mar-Dec), **Mumm** (☎03 26 49 59 70; www.mumm.com; 34 rue du Champ de Mars; tours incl tasting €20-39; ⏲tours 9.30am-1pm & 2-6pm daily, shorter hours & closed Sun Oct-Mar) and **Taittinger** (☎03 26 85 45 35; https://cellars-booking.taittinger.fr; 9 place St-Niçaise; tours €19-55; ⏲tours 10am-4.30pm) all have fancy websites, cellar temperatures of 10°C to 12°C (bring warm clothes!) and frequent English-language tours that end, *naturellement*, with a tasting session.

★Cathédrale Notre Dame CATHEDRAL
(☎03 26 47 81 79; www.cathedrale-reims.fr; 2 place du Cardinal Luçon; tower adult/child €8/free, incl Palais du Tau €11/free; ⏲7.30am-7.30pm, tower tours 10am, 11am & 2-5pm Tue-Sat, 2-5pm Sun May-Aug, 10am, 11am & 2-4pm Sat, 2-4pm Sun Sep, Oct & mid-Mar–Apr) Imagine the extravagance of a French royal coronation. The focal point of such pomposity was Reims' resplendent Gothic cathedral, begun in 1211 on a site occupied by churches since the 5th century. The interior is a rainbow of stained-glass windows; the finest are the western facade's great rose window, the north transept's rose window and the vivid Marc Chagall creations (1974) in the central axial chapel. The tourist office (p209) rents out audio guides for self-paced tours.

★Palais du Tau MUSEUM
(www.palais-du-tau.fr; 2 place du Cardinal Luçon; adult/child €8/free, incl cathedral tower €11/free; ⏲9.30am-6.30pm Tue-Sun May–mid-Sep, 9.30am-12.30pm & 2-5.30pm Tue-Sun mid-Sep–Apr) A Unesco World Heritage Site, this lavish former archbishop's residence, redesigned in neoclassical style between 1671 and 1710, was where French princes stayed before their coronations – and where they threw sumptuous banquets afterwards. Now a museum, it displays truly exceptional statuary, liturgical objects and tapestries from the cathedral, some in the impressive, Gothic-style **Salle de Tau** (Great Hall). Treasures worth seeking out include the 9th-century talisman of Charlemagne and St Rémi's golden, gem-encrusted chalice, which dates from the 12th century.

Basilique St-Rémi BASILICA
(place du Chanoine Ladame; ⏲9am-7pm) This 121m-long former Benedictine abbey

church, a Unesco World Heritage Site, mixes Romanesque elements from the mid-11th century (the worn but stunning nave and transept) with early Gothic features from the latter half of the 12th century (the choir, with a large triforium gallery and, way up top, tiny clerestory windows). Next door is the **Musée St-Rémi** (http://musees-reims.fr; 53 rue Simon; adult/child €5/free; ⏲10am-noon & 2-6pm Tue-Sun).

Sleeping

Les Telliers B&B $$
(☎09 53 79 80 74; https://telliers.fr; 18 rue des Telliers; s €68-85, d €80-121, tr €117-142, q €133-163; P 📶) Enticingly positioned down a quiet alley near the cathedral, this bijou B&B extends one of Reims' warmest *bienvenues* (welcomes). The high-ceilinged rooms are big on art deco character, and handsomely decorated with ornamental fireplaces, polished oak floors and the odd antique. Breakfast costs an extra €9 and is a generous spread of pastries, fruit, fresh-pressed juice and coffee.

★**Château Les Crayères** LUXURY HOTEL $$$
(☎03 26 24 90 00; www.lescrayeres.com; 64 bd Henry-Vasnier; d €395-755; P ❄ @ 📶) Such class! If you've ever wanted to stay in a palace, this romantic château on the fringes of Reims is the real McCoy. Manicured lawns sweep to the graceful turn-of-the-century estate, where you can play golf or tennis, dine in two-Michelin-starred finery, and stay in the lap of luxury in exuberantly furnished, chandelier-lit interiors – all at a price, naturally.

Eating & Drinking

A tempting array of delis, patisseries and chocolatiers lines rue de Mars, near **Halles du Boulingrin**. Place du Forum is a great place to watch the world drift languidly by at bistros, cafes and bars with pavement seating.

Le Wine Bar by Le Vintage WINE BAR
(http://winebar-reims.com; 16 place du Forum; ⏲6pm-12.30am Tue-Thu, to 1.30am Fri & Sat) This bijou wine bar is a convivial spot to chill over a glass of wine or Champagne (some 500 are offered) with a tasting plate of charcuterie and cheese. The friendly brothers who own the place are happy to give recommendations.

> **CENT SAVER**
>
> The great-value **Reims City Pass**, costing €22/32/42 for one/two/three days, is available at the tourist office or online at www.reimscitypass.com. It gives you entry to all the major museums and attractions, guided tours of the city and unlimited use of public transport, as well as discounts on activities such as Champagne house visits.

l'Alambic FRENCH $$
(☎03 26 35 64 93; www.restaurant-lalambic.fr; 63 bis rue de Chativesle; mains €14-25; ⏲noon-2pm & 7-9.30pm Tue-Fri, 7-9.30pm Sat & Mon; 👪) Ideal for an intimate dinner, this vaulted cellar dishes up well-prepared French classics – along the lines of home-smoked trout with horseradish, cod fillet with Champagne-laced *choucroute* (sauerkraut), and pigeon served two ways with Reims mustard sauce. Save room for terrific desserts such as crème brûlée with chicory ice cream. The *plat du jour* (dish of the day) is a snip at €11.

★**L'Assiette Champenoise** GASTRONOMY $$$
(☎03 26 84 64 64; www.assiettechampenoise.com; 40 av Paul-Vaillant-Couturier, Tinqueux; menus €95-315; ⏲noon-2pm & 7.30-10pm Thu-Mon) Heralded far and wide as one of Champagne's finest tables and crowned with the holy grail of three Michelin stars, L'Assiette Champenoise is headed up by chef Arnaud Lallemen. Listed by ingredients, his intricate, creative dishes rely on outstanding produce and play up integral flavours – be they Breton scallops or milk-fed lamb with preserved vegetables. One for special occasions.

Information

Tourist Office (☎03 26 77 45 00; www.reims-tourisme.com; 6 rue Rockefeller; ⏲10am-5pm Mon-Sat, 10am-12.30pm & 1.30-5pm Sun; 📶)

Getting There & Away

from Reims train station, 1km northwest of the cathedral, frequent services include Paris Gare de l'Est (€28 to €61, 46 minutes to one hour) and Épernay (€7.20, 30 minutes).

Épernay

POP 24,456

Prosperous Épernay, the self-proclaimed *capitale du Champagne* and home to many of the world's most celebrated Champagne houses, is the best place for touring subterranean cellars and sampling bubbly. The town also makes an excellent base for exploring the Champagne Routes.

Sights & Activities

★ Avenue de Champagne — STREET

Épernay's handsome av de Champagne fizzes with *maisons de champagne* (Champagne houses). The boulevard is lined with mansions and neoclassical villas, rebuilt after WWI. Peek through wrought-iron gates at Moët's private **Hôtel Chandon**, an early-19th-century pavilion-style residence set in landscaped gardens, which counts Wagner among its famous past guests. The haunted-looking **Château Perrier**, a red-brick mansion built in 1854 in neo–Louis XIII style, is aptly placed at number 13! It is home to the Musée du vin de Champagne et d'archéologie régionale d'Epernay as of 2021.

Atelier 1834: Champagne Boizel — WINE

(☎03 26 55 91 49; www.boizel.com; 46 av de Champagne; tours incl 2 Champagne tastings €22-40; ⏲10am-1pm & 2.30-5.30pm Mon-Fri, 10am-1pm & 2.30-6pm Sat) This wonderfully intimate Champagne house is still run with passion and prowess by the Boizel family, with a winemaking tradition dating from 1834. Unlike many of the *maisons* that open their doors to the public, these are still very much working cellars. Hidden away here are the real treasures – several bottles (still drinkable, apparently) hail from 1834.

Moët & Chandon — WINE

(☎03 26 51 20 20; www.moet.com; 20 av de Champagne; 1½hr tour with tasting €25-40, 10-17yr €10; ⏲tours 9.30-11.30am & 2-4.30pm) Flying the Moët, French, European and Russian flags, this prestigious *maison* is the world's biggest producer of Champagne. It has frequent 90-minute tours that are among the region's most impressive, offering a peek at part of its 28km labyrinth of *caves* (cellars).

Sleeping & Eating

Épernay's main eat street is rue Gambetta and adjacent place de la République. For picnic fixings, head to rue St-Thibault.

Hôtel Jean Moët — HISTORIC HOTEL $$

(☎03 26 32 19 22; www.hoteljeanmoet.com; 7 rue Jean Moët; d €168-212, ste €235-265; ❄📶🏊) Housed in a beautifully converted 18th-century mansion, this old-town hotel is big on atmosphere, with its skylit tearoom and revamped antique-meets-boutique-chic rooms. Exposed beams add a dash of romance and there are modern comforts like Nespresso makers. Champagne cellar **C. Comme** (☎03 26 32 09 55; www.c-comme.fr; 8 rue Gambetta; 2-/4-/6-glass Champagne tasting €13/26.60/37.50; ⏲10am-8pm Mon, Tue & Thu, 3-8pm Wed, 10am-midnight Fri & Sat) awaits downstairs.

★ La Grillade Gourmande — FRENCH $$

(☎03 26 55 44 22; www.lagrilladegourmande.com; 16 rue de Reims; lunch menus €21, dinner menus €33-59, mains €20-26; ⏲noon-1.45pm & 7.30-9.30pm Tue-Sat) This chic, red-walled, art-slung bistro is an inviting spot to try chargrilled meats and dishes rich in texture and flavour, such as crayfish pan-fried in Champagne and lamb cooked in rosemary and honey until meltingly tender. Diners spill out onto the covered terrace in the warm months. Both the presentation and service are flawless.

Information

Tourist Office (☎03 26 53 33 00; www.ot-epernay.fr; 7 av de Champagne; ⏲9am-12.30pm & 1.30-7pm Mon-Sat, 10.30am-1pm & 2-4.30pm Sun mid-Apr–mid-Oct, 9.30am-12.30pm & 1.30-5.30pm Mon-Sat mid-Oct–mid-Apr; 📶)

Getting There & Away

The **train station** (place Mendès-France) has direct services to Reims (€7.20, 27 minutes, 14 daily) and Paris Gare de l'Est (€24 to €69, 1¼ to 2¾ hours, seven daily).

LOCAL KNOWLEDGE

TASTE LIKE A PRO

You can taste Champagne anywhere, but you might get more out of the two-hour workshop at **Villa Bissinger** (☎03 26 55 78 78; www.villabissinger.com; 15 rue Jeanson, Ay), home to the International Institute for the Wines of Champagne. Besides covering the basics like names, producers, grape varieties and characteristics, the workshop includes a tasting of four different Champagnes. The institute is in Ay, 3.5km northeast of Épernay. Call ahead to secure your place.

ALSACE & LORRAINE

Teetering on the tempestuous frontier between France and Germany, the neighbouring regions of Alsace and Lorraine are where the worlds of Gallic and Germanic culture collide. Half-timbered houses, lush vineyards and forest-clad mountains hint at Alsace's Teutonic leanings, while Lorraine is indisputably Francophile.

Strasbourg

POP 276,170

Strasbourg is the perfect overture to all that is idiosyncratic about Alsace – walking a fine tightrope between France and Germany and between a medieval past and a progressive future, it pulls off its act in inimitable Alsatian style. Roam the old town's twisting alleys lined with fairy-tale half-timbered houses, feast in snug *winstubs* (Alsatian taverns) by the canals in Petite France, and marvel at how a city that does Christmas markets and gingerbread so well can also be home to the glittering EU Quarter and France's second-largest student population.

Sights

★ **Cathédrale Notre-Dame** CATHEDRAL

(www.cathedrale-strasbourg.fr; place de la Cathédrale; adult/child astronomical clock €3/2, platform €5/3; 9.30-11.15am & 2-5.45pm, astronomical clock noon-12.45pm, platform 9am-7.15pm; Grand'Rue) Nothing prepares you for your first glimpse of Strasbourg's Cathédrale Notre-Dame, completed in all its Gothic grandeur in 1439. The lace-fine facade lifts the gaze little by little to flying buttresses, leering gargoyles and a 142m spire. The interior is exquisitely lit by 12th- to 14th-century **stained-glass windows**, including the western portal's jewel-like rose window. The Gothic-meets-Renaissance **astronomical clock** strikes solar noon at 12.30pm with a parade of figures portraying the different stages of life and Jesus with his apostles.

★ **Grande Île** HISTORIC SITE

(Grand'Rue) History seeps through the twisting lanes and cafe-rimmed plazas of Grande Île, Strasbourg's Unesco World Heritage–listed island bordered by the River Ill. These streets – with their photogenic line-up of wonky, timber-framed houses in sherbet colours – are made for aimless ambling. They cower beneath the soaring magnificence of the cathedral and its sidekick, the gingerbready 15th-century **Maison Kammerzell** (rue des Hallebardes), with its ornate carvings and leaded windows. The alleys are at their most atmospheric when lantern-lit at night.

Petite France AREA

(Grand'Rue) Criss-crossed by narrow lanes, canals and locks, Petite France is where artisans plied their trades in the Middle Ages. The half-timbered houses, sprouting veritable thickets of scarlet geraniums in summer, and the riverside parks attract the masses, but the area still manages to retain its Alsatian charm, especially in the early morning and late evening. Drink in views of the River Ill and the Barrage Vauban from the much-photographed **Ponts Couverts** (Covered Bridges; Musée d'Art Moderne) and their trio of 13th-century towers.

★ **Palais Rohan** HISTORIC BUILDING

(2 place du Château; adult/child per museum €6.50/free, all 3 museums €12/free; 10am-6pm Wed-Mon; Grand'Rue) Hailed as a 'Versailles in miniature', this opulent 18th-century residence is loaded with treasures. The basement **Musée Archéologique** takes you from the Palaeolithic period to AD 800. On the ground floor is the **Musée des Arts Décoratifs**, where rooms adorned with Hannong ceramics and gleaming silverware evoke the lavish lifestyle of the nobility in the 18th century. On the 1st floor, the **Musée des Beaux-Arts'** collection of 14th- to 19th-century art includes El Greco, Botticelli and Flemish Primitive works.

Barrage Vauban VIEWPOINT

(Vauban Dam; viewing terrace 7.15am-9pm, shorter hours winter; Faubourg National) FREE A triumph of 17th-century engineering, the Barrage Vauban bears the architectural imprint of the leading French military engineer of the age – Sébastien Le Prestre de Vauban. The dam has been restored to its former glory and is now free to visit. Ascend to the terrace for a tremendously photogenic view that reaches across the canal-woven Petite France district to the Ponts Couverts and cathedral spire beyond.

Sleeping

It can be tricky to find last-minute accommodation from Monday to Thursday when the European Parliament is in plenary session (see www.europarl.europa.eu for dates).

★ **Cour du Corbeau** BOUTIQUE HOTEL $$

(03 90 00 26 26; www.cour-corbeau.com; 6-8 rue des Couples; r €157-275, ste €220-260;

Porte de l'Hôpital) A 16th-century inn lovingly converted into a boutique hotel, Cour du Corbeau wins you over with its half-timbered charm and its location, just steps from the river. Gathered around a courtyard, rooms blend original touches such as oak parquet and Louis XV furnishings with mod cons including flat-screen TVs.

Hôtel du Dragon HOTEL **$$**
(03 88 35 79 80; www.dragon.fr; 12 rue du Dragon; r €80-154; ; Porte de l'Hôpital) Step through a tree-shaded courtyard and into the, ahhh…blissful calm of this bijou hotel. The Dragon receives glowing reviews for its crisp interiors, attentive service and prime location near Petite France (p211).

Eating

Try canalside Petite France for Alsatian fare and half-timbered romance; Grand'Rue for curb-side kebabs and *tarte flambée* (thin Alsatian-style pizza topped with crème fraiche, onions and lardons); and rue des Veaux or rue des Pucelles for hole-in-the-wall eateries serving the world on a plate.

Winstub S'Kaechele FRENCH **$**
(03 88 22 62 36; www.skaechele.fr; 8 rue de l'Argile; mains €12.50-18.50; 7-9.30pm Mon, 11.45am-1.30pm & 7-9.30pm Tue-Fri; Grand'Rue) Traditional French and Alsatian grub doesn't come more authentic than at this snug, amiable *winstub* (wine tavern), run with love by couple Karine and Daniel. Cue wonderfully cosy evenings spent in stone-walled, lamp-lit, wood-beamed surrounds, huddled over dishes such as escargots oozing Roquefort, fat pork knuckles braised in pinot noir, and *choucroute garnie* (sauerkraut garnished with meats).

★1741 GASTRONOMY **$$$**
(03 88 35 50 50; www.1741.fr; 22 quai des Bateliers; 3-course lunch menus €42, 3-/5-course dinner menus €95/129; noon-2pm & 7-10pm Thu-Mon; Porte de l'Hôpital) A team of profoundly passionate chefs runs the show at this Michelin-starred number facing the River Ill. Murals, playful fabrics and splashes of colour add warmth to the dining room, where waiters bring well-executed, unfussy dishes, such as sea bass with Jerusalem artichoke and Alsatian venison with root vegetables, to the table. Service is excellent, as is the wine list.

Information

Tourist Office (03 88 52 28 28; www.otstrasbourg.fr; 17 place de la Cathédrale; 9am-7pm; Grand'Rue) Buy a money-saving **Strasbourg Pass** (adult/child €21.50/15) here, valid for three consecutive days and covering one museum visit, access to the cathedral platform and astronomical clock, half a day's bicycle rental and a boat tour.

Getting There & Around

AIR

Strasbourg's **airport** (SXB; www.strasbourg.aeroport.fr), 17km southwest of town, is served by major carriers and budget airline Ryanair (London Stansted). A shuttle train links it to Strasbourg train station (€4.30, nine minutes, four hourly).

TRAIN

Train services include the following:
Lille (€128 to €151, four hours, 17 daily)
Lyon (€54 to €194, 4½ hours, 14 daily)
Paris (€90 to €113, 1¾ hours, 19 daily)

THE LOIRE VALLEY

One step removed from the French capital, this valley was historically the place where princes, dukes and notable nobles established their country getaways, and the countryside is littered with some of the most extravagant architecture outside Versailles.

Blois

POP 46,350

Towering above the northern bank of the Loire, Blois' royal château, one-time feudal seat of the powerful counts of Blois, offers a gripping introduction to some key periods in French history and architecture. Parts of the city still have a medieval vibe, and Blois makes an excellent base for visits to the châteaux, villages and towns of the central Loire Valley.

Sights

Billets combinés (combo tickets; €15.50 to €26.50), sold at the château, Maison de la Magie and Fondation du Doute, can save you some cash.

★Château Royal de Blois CHATEAU
(02 54 90 33 33; www.chateaudeblois.fr; place du Château; adult/child €12/6.50, audio guide €4; 9am-6.30pm or 7pm Apr-Oct, 10am-5pm Nov-Mar) Seven French kings lived in Blois' royal château, whose four grand wings were built during four distinct periods in French architecture: Gothic (13th century), Flamboyant

Gothic (1498–1501), early Renaissance (1515–20) and classical (1630s). You can easily spend a half-day immersing yourself in the château's dramatic and bloody history and its extraordinary architecture. In July and August there are free tours in English (at 10.30am, 1.15pm and 3pm).

Maison de la Magie MUSEUM
(☎02 54 90 33 33; www.maisondelamagie.fr; 1 place du Château; adult/child €10/6.50; ⏲10am-12.30pm & 2-6.30pm Apr-Aug & mid-Oct–early Nov, 2-6.30pm daily plus 10am-12.30pm Sat & Sun 1st 2 weeks Sep; 👪) This museum of magic occupies the one-time home of watchmaker, inventor and conjurer Jean Eugène Robert-Houdin (1805–71), after whom the American magician Harry Houdini named himself. Dragons emerge roaring from the windows every half-hour, while inside the museum has exhibits on Robert-Houdin and the history of magic, displays of optical trickery, and several daily magic shows.

Sleeping & Eating

Hôtel Anne de Bretagne HOTEL $
(☎02 54 78 05 38; www.hotelannedebretagne.com; 31 av du Dr Jean Laigret; s/d/tr/q €60/69/76/95, winter s/d €45/55; ⏲reception 7am-11pm; P 📶) This ivy-covered hotel, in a great location midway between the train station and the château, has friendly staff, a cosy piano-equipped *salon* and 29 brightly coloured rooms with bold bedspreads. A packed three-course picnic lunch costs €11.50. Also rents out bicycles (€16) and has free enclosed bike parking.

L'Orangerie du Château GASTRONOMY $$$
(☎02 54 78 05 36; www.orangerie-du-chateau.fr; 1 av du Dr Jean Laigret; menus €40-86; ⏲noon-1.45pm & 7-9.15pm Tue-Sat; P) This Michelin-starred restaurant serves *cuisine gastronomique inventive* inspired by both French tradition and culinary ideas brought from faraway lands. The excellent wine list comes on a tablet computer. For dessert try the house speciality, *soufflé chaud* (hot soufflé).

Information

Tourist Office (☎02 54 90 41 41; www.bloischambord.co.uk; 6 rue de la Voûte du Château; ⏲9am-7pm Apr-Sep, 10am-12.30pm & 2-5pm Mon-Sat, plus Sun school holidays, Oct-Mar)

Getting There & Away

BUS

The tourist office has a brochure detailing public-transport options to nearby châteaux. A *navette* (shuttle bus; €6) run by **Rémi** (☎02 54 58 55 44; www.remi-centrevaldeloire.fr) makes it possible to do a Blois–Chambord–Cheverny–Beauregard–Blois circuit on Wednesday, Saturday and Sunday from early April to 5 November. From early April to August, this line runs daily during school-holiday periods and on public holidays.

TRAIN

Blois-Chambord train station (av Dr Jean Laigret) is 600m west (up the hill) from Blois' château.

Amboise (€7.20, 20 minutes, 15 to 20 daily)

Paris Gare d'Austerlitz (€18 to €32.40, 1½ hours, five direct daily)

Tours (€11.20, 30 to 46 minutes, 16 to 22 daily)

DON'T MISS

A ROOM WITH A VIEW

At home in the Château de Chambord's former kennels in front of the castle, **Relais de Chambord** (☎02 54 81 01 01; www.relaisdechambord.com; place St-Louis, Chambord; d from €165; P ❄ @ 📶) is a four-star hotel that offers larger-than-life views of the château from some rooms and a sensational bar and restaurant terrace. Contemporary rooms are country-chic, dining is modern French and the hotel has a spa. Guests can borrow electric bicycles to cruise around the vast private estate. Rates include breakfast.

Around Blois

The peaceful, verdant countryside around the former royal seat of Blois is home to some of France's finest châteaux.

Sights

★Château de Chambord CHATEAU
(☎info 02 54 50 40 00, tour & show reservations 02 54 50 50 40; www.chambord.org; adult/child €13/free, parking distant/near €4/6; ⏲9am-6pm Apr-Oct, to 5pm Nov-Mar; 👪) One of the crowning achievements of French Renaissance architecture, the Château de Chambord – with 426 rooms, 282 fireplaces and 77 staircases – is the largest, grandest and most visited château in the Loire Valley. Begun in 1519 by François I (r 1515–47) as a weekend hunting retreat, it quickly grew into one of the most ambitious – and expensive – building projects ever undertaken by a French monarch. A French-style **formal garden** opened in 2017.

Château de Chaumont-sur-Loire CHATEAU
(☎02 54 20 99 22; www.domaine-chaumont.fr; adult/child Apr-Oct €18/12, Jan-Mar, Nov & Dec €12/7; ⏲9.30am or 10am-5pm or 6pm Nov-Mar, to 8pm Apr-Oct) Set on a strategic bluff with sweeping views along the Loire, Chaumont-sur-Loire is known for three things: the **château** itself, which has a medieval exterior (cylindrical towers, a sturdy drawbridge) and an interior courtyard that is very much of the Renaissance; world-class exhibitions of striking **contemporary art**; and the **Festival International des Jardins** (⏲late Apr-early Nov), for which 30 magnificent gardens are created each year by jury-selected teams led by visual artists, architects, set designers and landscape gardeners.

Amboise

POP 13,370

Elegant Amboise, childhood home of Charles VIII and final resting place of the incomparable Leonardo da Vinci, is gorgeously situated on the southern bank of the Loire, guarded by a soaring château. With some seriously posh hotels, outstanding dining and one of France's most vivacious weekly markets (on Sunday morning), Amboise is a convivial base for exploring the Loire countryside and nearby châteaux by car or bicycle.

Sights

★**Château Royal d'Amboise** CHATEAU
(☎02 47 57 00 98; www.chateau-amboise.com; place Michel Debré; adult/child €11.70/7.80, incl audio guide €15.70/10.80; ⏲9am-5.45pm Dec-Feb, to btwn 6.30pm & 8pm Mar-Nov, last entry 1hr before closing) Perched atop a rocky escarpment above town, Amboise's castle was a favoured retreat for all of France's Valois and Bourbon kings. Only a few of the château's original structures survive, but you can still visit the furnished **Logis** (Lodge) – Gothic except for the top half of one wing, which is Renaissance – and the Flamboyant Gothic **Chapelle St-Hubert** (1493), where Leonardo da Vinci's presumed remains have been buried since 1863. The ramparts afford thrilling views of the town and river.

Le Clos Lucé HISTORIC BUILDING
(☎02 47 57 00 73; www.vinci-closluce.com; 2 rue du Clos Lucé; adult/child €15.50/11, mid-Nov–Feb €13.50/10.50; ⏲9am-7pm or 8pm Feb-Oct, 9am or 10am-6pm Nov-Jan, last entry 1hr before closing; ♿) It was at the invitation of François I that Leonardo da Vinci (1452–1519), aged 64, took up residence in this grand manor house, built in 1471. An admirer of the Italian Renaissance, the French monarch named Da Vinci 'first painter, engineer and king's architect', and the Italian spent his time here sketching, tinkering and dreaming up ingenious contraptions.

Château Gaillard CHATEAU
(☎02 47 30 33 29; www.chateau-gaillard-amboise.fr; 95-97 av Léonard de Vinci & 29 allée du Pont Moulin; adult/child €12/8; ⏲1-7pm Apr-early Nov) The most exciting Loire château to open to visitors in years, Gaillard is the earliest expression of the Italian Renaissance in France. Begun in 1496, the château was inspired by the refined living that Charles VIII fell in love with during his Italian campaign. The harmonious, Renaissance-style **gardens** were laid out by master gardener Dom Pacello (1453–1534), an Italian Benedictine monk who brought the first orange trees to France.

Sleeping & Eating

L'Écluse FRENCH **$$**
(☎02 47 79 94 91; www.ecluse-amboise.fr; rue Racine; lunch menu €19, other menus €25-39; ⏲noon-1.30pm & 7-9pm Tue-Sat) On the banks of the bubbling L'Amasse (or La Masse) River next to an *écluse* (river lock), L'Écluse has generated enthusiasm and glowing reviews from the moment it opened in 2017. The sharply focused menu is made up of just three starters, three mains and three desserts, expertly prepared with fresh seasonal products from a dozen Loire-area producers.

Information

Tourist Office (☎02 47 57 09 28; www.amboise-valdeloire.co.uk; quai du Général de Gaulle; ⏲9am or 10am-6pm or 7pm Mon-Sat, 10am-1pm & 2-5pm Sun Apr-Oct, 10am-12.30pm & 2-5pm Mon-Sat Nov-Mar; 📶)

Getting There & Away

Amboise's **train station** (bd Gambetta) is 1.5km north of the château, on the opposite side of the Loire.

Blois (€7.20, 20 minutes, 15 to 20 daily)

Paris (€18.50 to €60.50, two hours) A handful of direct trains go to Gare d'Austerlitz, other trains serve Gare Montparnasse.

Around Amboise

A trio of world-class châteaux lies within easy day-trip reach of Amboise. Your own wheels – two or four – is the easiest means of getting around, although the towns of Chenonceaux (€7, 25 minutes, nine to 11 trains daily) and Azay-le-Rideau (€5.90, 26/41 minutes by train/bus, six to eight daily) are both served by public transport to/from the town of Tours.

Sights

★Château de Chenonceau CHATEAU
(☎02 47 23 90 07; www.chenonceau.com; adult/child €14/11, with audio guide €18/14.50; ⏲9am-6.30pm or later Apr-Oct, to 5pm or 6pm Nov-Mar) Spanning the languid Cher River atop a graceful arched bridge, Chenonceau is one of France's most elegant châteaux. It's hard not to be moved and exhilarated by the glorious setting, the formal gardens, the magic of the architecture and the château's fascinating history, shaped by a series of powerful women. The interior is decorated with rare furnishings and an **art collection** that includes works by Tintoretto, Correggio, Rubens, Murillo, Van Dyck and Ribera (look for an extraordinary portrait of Louis XIV).

★Château de Villandry CHATEAU
(☎02 47 50 02 09; www.chateauvillandry.com; 3 rue Principale; chateau & gardens adult/child €11/7, gardens only €7/5, cheaper Dec-Feb, audio guide €4; ⏲9am-5pm or 6.30pm year round, château interior closed mid-Nov–late Dec & early Jan-early Feb) Villandry's six glorious landscaped gardens *à la française* are some of France's finest, with more than 6 hectares of kitchen gardens, cascading flowers, ornamental vines, manicured lime trees, razor-sharp box hedges and tinkling fountains. Try to visit when the gardens – all of them organic – are blooming, between April and October. Tickets are valid all day (get your hand stamped). The website has details on special events.

Château d'Azay-le-Rideau CHATEAU
(☎02 47 45 42 04; www.azay-le-rideau.fr; adult/child €10.50/free, audio guide €3; ⏲9.30am-11pm Jul & Aug, to 6pm Apr-Jun & Sep, 10am 5.15pm Oct-Mar) Romantic, moat-ringed Azay-le-Rideau is celebrated for its elegant turrets, perfectly proportioned windows, delicate stonework and steep slate roofs. Built in the early 1500s on a natural island in the middle of the Indre River, it is one of the Loire's loveliest castles: Honoré de Balzac called it a 'multifaceted diamond set in the River Indre'. The famous, Italian-style **loggia staircase** overlooking the central courtyard is decorated with the salamanders and ermines of François I and Queen Claude.

BURGUNDY

Burgundy (Bourgogne in French) offers some of France's most gorgeous countryside: rolling green hills dotted with mustard fields and medieval villages. Its handsome capital, Dijon, is heir to a glorious architectural heritage and peerless food and wine culture: Burgundy's tantalising vineyards are a treasured Unesco World Heritage Site.

Dijon

POP 159,168

Filled with elegant medieval and Renaissance buildings, dashing Dijon is Burgundy's capital, and the spiritual home of French mustard. Its lively old town is wonderful for strolling and shopping, interspersed with some snappy drinking and dining.

Sights & Activities

English-language minibus tours operated by **Authentica Tours** (☎06 87 01 43 78; www.authentica-tours.com; group tours per person €65-130) introduce the Côte d'Or vineyards. Reserve by phone, internet or via the tourist office.

Palais des Ducs et des États de Bourgogne PALACE
(Palace of the Dukes & States of Burgundy; place de la Libération) Once home to Burgundy's powerful dukes, this monumental palace with a neoclassical facade overlooks place de la Libération, old Dijon's magnificent central square dating from 1686. The palace's eastern wing houses the outstanding Musée des Beaux-Arts (p216), whose entrance is next to the **Tour de Bar**, a squat 14th-century tower that once served as a prison. The remainder of the palace houses municipal offices that are off limits to the public.

★ **Musée des Beaux-Arts** MUSEUM
(☎ 03 80 74 52 09; http://beaux-arts.dijon.fr; 1 rue Rameau; audio guide €4, guided tour €6; ⏲ 10am-6.30pm Jun-Sep, 9.30am-6pm Oct-May, closed Tue year-round) FREE Nearing the end of a nine-year renovation, these sprawling galleries in Dijon's monumental Palais des Ducs are works of art in themselves and constitute one of France's most outstanding museums. The star attraction is the wood-panelled **Salle des Gardes**, which houses the ornate, carved late-medieval sepulchres of dukes John the Fearless and Philip the Bold. Other sections focus on Egyptian art, the Middle Ages in Burgundy and Europe, and six centuries of European painting, from the Renaissance to modern times.

Tour Philippe le Bon TOWER
(place de la Libération; adult/child €3/1.50; ⏲ guided tours every 45min 10.30am-noon & 1.45-5.30pm Tue-Sun Apr–mid-Nov, hourly 2-4pm Tue, 11am-4pm Sat & Sun mid-Nov–Mar) Adjacent to the ducal palace, this 46m-high, mid-15th-century tower affords fantastic views over the city. On a clear day you can see all the way to Mont Blanc. Dijon's tourist office handles reservations.

Sleeping & Eating

Find loads of restaurants on buzzy rue Berbisey, around place Émile Zola, on rue Amiral Roussin and around the perimeter of the covered market. In warm months, outdoor cafes and brasseries (restaurants) fill place de la Libération.

Hôtel Le Chambellan HOTEL $
(☎ 03 80 67 12 67; www.hotel-chambellan.com; 92 rue Vannerie; s €44-59, d €59-66, q from €79, s/d with shared bathroom €37/39; 📶) This renovated budget favourite in the heart of medieval Dijon mixes modern flair (remodelled bathrooms, bold colours, phone-charging ports, spiffy reading lamps) with the three Ps – *poutres, pierre, parquet* (exposed beams, stone and wood floors) – that epitomise owner Christophe Comte's long-standing fondness for the rustic.

★ **L'Age de Raisin** WINE BAR
(☎ 03 80 23 24 82; 67 rue Berbisey; ⏲ 6pm-2am Tue-Sat) Stone walls, red-and-white-checked tablecloths and gracious service set the mood at this cosiest of Dijon wine bars. With late hours and a wealth of local vintages hand-selected by affable owners Jeff and Nadine, it doubles as a bistro, serving fabulous home-cooked *plats du jour* built from locally sourced organic produce. Reserve ahead at dinner time; it fills up fast!

Information

Tourist Office (☎ 08 92 70 05 58; www.destinationdijon.com; 11 rue des Forges; ⏲ 9.30am-6.30pm Mon-Sat, 10am-6pm Sun Apr-Sep, 9.30am-1pm & 2-6pm Mon-Sat, 10am-4pm Sun Oct-Mar; 📶)

Getting There & Away

Transco (☎ 03 80 11 29 29; www.mobigo-bourgogne.com; single ticket/day pass €1.50/6.60) Buses stop in front of the train station. Bus 44 goes to Nuits-St-Georges (45 minutes) and Beaune (1¼ hours).

Frequent rail services from Dijon's train station include the following:

Lyon-Part Dieu (€32 to 37, 1½ to two hours)
Marseille (€81, 3¾ hours)
Paris Gare de Lyon (€35 to €61, 1½ to three hours)

Beaune

POP 22,418

Beaune (pronounced similarly to 'bone'), 44km south of Dijon, is the unofficial capital of the Côte d'Or and wine is its raison d'être. The jewel of its old city hides a subterranean labyrinth of centuries-old wine cellars where some of the world's most prestigious wines repose. The amoeba-shaped old city is enclosed by thick stone ramparts and a stream, which is in turn encircled by a one-way boulevard with seven names. The ramparts, which shelter wine cellars, are lined with overgrown gardens and ringed by a pathway that makes for a lovely stroll. Beaune's flagship sight is the magnificent Gothic **Hôtel-Dieu des Hospices de Beaune** (☎ 03 80 24 45 00; www.hospices-de-beaune.com; 2 rue de l'Hôtel-Dieu; adult/child €7.50/3; ⏲ 9am-6.30pm mid-Mar–mid-Nov, 9-11.30am & 2-5.30pm rest of year), built as a hospital in 1443 and famously topped by stunning turrets and pitched rooftops covered in multicoloured tiles.

The **tourist office** (☎ 03 80 26 21 30; www.beaune-tourisme.fr; 6 bd Perpreuil; ⏲ 9am-6.30pm Mon-Sat, to 6pm Sun Apr-Oct, shorter hours Nov-Mar) has information on wine tasting and visiting nearby vineyards. An annexe opposite the Hôtel-Dieu keeps shorter hours.

WORTH A TRIP

A TRIP BETWEEN VINES

Burgundy's most renowned vintages come from the **Côte d'Or** (Golden Hillside), a range of hills made of limestone, flint and clay that runs south from Dijon for about 60km. The northern section, the **Côte de Nuits**, stretches from Marsannay-la-Côte south to Corgoloin and produces reds known for their robust, full-bodied character. The southern section, the **Côte de Beaune**, lies between Ladoix-Serrigny and Santenay and produces great reds and whites.

Tourist offices provide brochures. The signposted **Route des Grands Crus** (www.road-of-the-fine-burgundy-wines.com) visits some of the most celebrated Côte de Nuits vineyards; mandatory tasting stops for oenophiles seeking nirvana include 16th-century **Château du Clos de Vougeot** (☎03 80 62 86 09; www.closdevougeot.fr; rue de la Montagne, Vougeot; adult/child €7.50/2.50; ⊙9am-6.30pm Sun-Fri, to 5pm Sat Apr-Oct, 10am-5pm Nov-Mar), which offers excellent guided tours, and **L'Imaginarium** (☎03 80 62 61 40; www.imaginarium-bourgogne.com; av du Jura, Nuits-St-Georges; adult incl basic/grand cru tasting €10/21, child €7; ⊙2-7pm Mon, 10am-7pm Tue-Sun, last admission 5pm), an entertaining wine museum in **Nuits-St-Georges**.

Getting There & Away

Bus 44, operated by **Transco** (☎03 80 11 29 29; www.mobigo-bourgogne.com), links Beaune with Dijon (€1.50, 1¼ hours), stopping at Côte d'Or villages.

LYON

POP 514,000

Commanding a strategic spot at the confluence of the Rhône and the Saône Rivers, Lyon has been luring people ever since the Romans named it Lugdunum in 43 BC. As France's third-largest city, it cooks up outstanding museums, a dynamic cultural life, busy clubbing and drinking scenes, fantastic shopping and stupendous gastronomy. Don't leave without sampling some Lyonnais specialities in a *bouchon* (Lyonnais bistro) – it's the quintessential Lyon experience.

Sights

The excellent-value **Lyon City Card** (www.lyoncitycard.com; 1/2/3 days adult €25/35/45, child €17/24/31) offers free admission to every Lyon museum, the roof of Basilique Notre Dame de Fourvière, guided city tours, Guignol puppet shows and river excursions (April to October), along with numerous other discounts. The card also includes unlimited public transport.

Vieux Lyon

Lyon's Unesco-listed old town is a rabbit warren of narrow streets lined with medieval and Renaissance houses, especially on rue du Bœuf, rue St-Jean and rue des Trois Maries. Crane your neck upwards to see gargoyles and other cheeky stone characters carved on window ledges along rue Juiverie, which was home to Lyonnais Jews in the Middle Ages.

Cathédrale St-Jean-Baptiste CATHEDRAL
(www.cathedrale-lyon.fr; place St-Jean, 5e; ⊙cathedral 8.15am-7.45pm Mon-Fri, 8am-7pm Sat & Sun, treasury 9.30am-noon & 2-6pm Tue-Sat; ⓂVieux Lyon) Lyon's partly Romanesque cathedral was built between the late 11th and early 16th centuries. The portals of its Flamboyant Gothic facade, completed in 1480 (and recently renovated), are decorated with 280 square stone medallions. Inside, the highlight is the astronomical clock in the north transept.

Fourvière

More than two millennia ago, the Romans built the city of Lugdunum on the slopes of Fourvière – an **amphitheatre** is all that remains. Footpaths wind uphill from Vieux Lyon, but the funicular is less taxing.

Basilique Notre Dame de Fourvière CHURCH
(☎04 78 25 13 01; www.fourviere.org; place de Fourvière, 5e; rooftop tour adult/child €10/5; ⊙basilica

Lyon

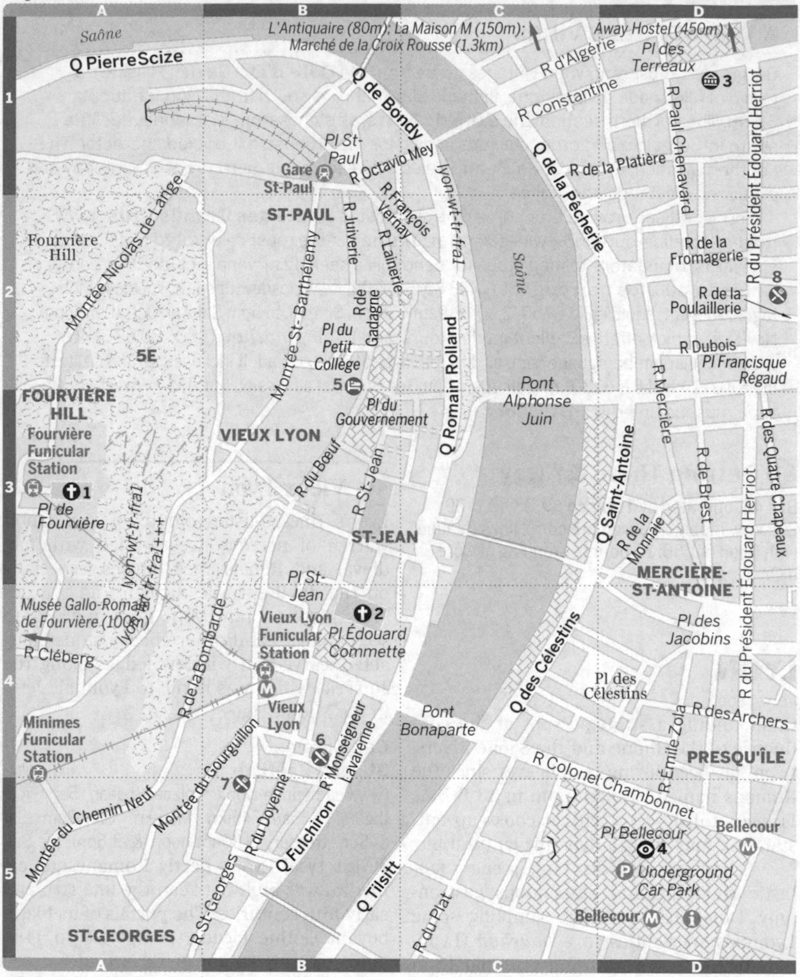

7am-7pm, tours 9am-12.30pm & 2-6pm Mon-Fri, 9am-12.30pm & 2-4.45pm Sat, 2-4.45pm Sun Apr-Nov; Fourvière) Crowning the hill, with stunning city panoramas from its terrace, this superb example of late-19th-century French ecclesiastical architecture is lined with magnificent mosaics. From April to November, free 30-minute discovery visits take in the main features of the basilica and crypt; otherwise, 90-minute rooftop tours ('Visite Insolite') climax on the stone-sculpted roof. Reserve tickets in advance online for the latter.

Musée Gallo-Romain de Fourvière MUSEUM
(04 73 38 49 30; www.museegalloromain.grandlyon.com; 17 rue Cléberg, 5e; adult/child €4/free; 11am-6pm Tue-Fri, from 10am Sat & Sun; Fourvière) For an enlightening historical perspective on the city's past, start your visit at this archaeological museum on the hillside of Fourvière. It hosts a wide-ranging collection of ancient artefacts found in the Rhône Valley as well as superb mosaics.

Presqu'île & Confluence

Lyon's city centre lies on this peninsula, 500m to 800m wide, bounded by the rivers Rhône and Saône, and pierced by **place Bellecour** (Bellecour), one of Europe's largest

Lyon

Sights

1 Basilique Notre Dame de Fourvière A3
2 Cathédrale St-Jean-Baptiste B4
3 Musée des Beaux-Arts D1
4 Place Bellecour D5

Sleeping

5 Cour des Loges B2

Eating

6 Cinq Mains B4
7 La Cuisinerie B5
8 Le Musée D2

public squares. Past Gare de Perrache lies **Lyon Confluence** (www.lyon-confluence.fr) the city's newest neighbourhood.

★Musée des Beaux-Arts MUSEUM

(☎04 72 10 17 40; www.mba-lyon.fr; 20 place des Terreaux, 1er; adult/child €8/free; ⊙10am-6pm Wed, Thu & Sat-Mon, 10.30am-6pm Fri; Ⓜ Hôtel de Ville) This stunning and eminently manageable museum showcases France's finest collection of sculptures and paintings outside of Paris, from antiquity onwards. Highlights include works by Rodin, Monet and Picasso. Pick up a free audio guide and be sure to stop for a drink or meal on the delightful stone terrace off its cafe-restaurant or take time out in its tranquil cloister garden.

★Musée des Confluences MUSEUM

(☎04 28 38 12 12; www.museedesconfluences.fr; 86 quai Perrache, 6e; adult/child €9/free; ⊙11am-7pm Tue, Wed & Fri, to 10pm Thu, 10am-7pm Sat & Sun; 🚊T1) This eye-catching building, designed by the Viennese firm Coop Himmelb(l)au, is the crowning glory of the Confluence, at Presqu'île's southern tip. Lying at the confluence of the Rhône and Saône rivers, this ambitious science-and-humanities museum is housed in a futuristic steel-and-glass transparent crystal. Its distorted structure is one of the city's iconic landmarks.

Sleeping

Lyon's **tourist office** (☎04 72 77 69 69; www.lyon-france.com; place Bellecour, 2e; ⊙9am-6pm; 📶; Ⓜ Bellecour) runs a free reservation service (http://book.lyon-france.com/en/accommodation) and occasionally offers deals like free breakfasts or discounts on multinight stays.

Away Hostel HOSTEL $

(☎04 78 98 53 20; www.awayhostel.com; 21 rue Alsace Lorraine, 1er; dm €25-30, d €95; @📶; Ⓜ Croix-Paquet) One of Lyon's best new budget sleeps, Away Hostel has attractive, sunny rooms with tall ceilings, wood floors and oversized windows. The cafe is a good place to meet other travellers, and there are loads of events going on (walking tours, yoga brunches, communal dinners).

★Mob Hotel BOUTIQUE HOTEL $$

(☎04 58 55 55 88; www.mobhotel.com; 55 quai Rambaud, 2e; d/ste from €120/170; Ⓟ📶; 🚊T1) A stellar new addition to Lyon, the Mob Hotel is a magnet for designers and the creative set. Metal lacework encases the avant-garde building overlooking the Saône, while the

DON'T MISS

LYON'S HIDDEN LABYRINTH

Deep within Vieux Lyon and the hilltop quartier of Croix-Rousse, *traboules* (secret passages) wind their way through apartment blocks, under streets and into courtyards. In all, 315 passages link 230 streets, with a combined length of 50km. Most were constructed by *canuts* (silk weavers) in the 19th century to transport silk in inclement weather.

Vieux Lyon's most celebrated *traboules* include those connecting 27 rue St-Jean with 6 rue des Trois Maries and 54 rue St-Jean with 27 rue du Bœuf (push the intercom button to buzz open the door). Step into Croix-Rousse's underworld at 9 place Colbert, crossing cour des Voraces – renowned for its monumental seven-storey staircase – to 14bis montée St-Sébastien, and eventually emerging at 29 rue Imbert Colomès.

For detailed descriptions and maps, download the free iPhone app **Traboules de Lyon**. Guided walking **tours** (04 72 77 69 69; www.visiterlyon.com; tours adult/child €13/8; by reservation) by Lyon's tourist office also visit *traboules*.

inside is a playful mixture of polished concrete, pale blond woods, artful lighting and subtle pastels. Book a Master Mob room for a balcony and ample space.

Mama Shelter HOTEL **$$**
(04 78 02 58 00; www.mamashelter.com/en/lyon; 13 rue Domer, 7e; r €79-323; P; M Jean Macé) Lyon's branch of this trendy hotel chain has sleek decor, carpets splashed with calli-graffiti, firm beds, plush pillows, modernist lighting and big-screen Macs offering free in-room movies. A youthful crowd fills the long bar in the low-lit restaurant. The residential location 2km outside the centre may feel remote, but it's only three metro stops from Gare de la Part-Dieu and place Bellecour.

★Cour des Loges HOTEL **$$$**
(04 72 77 44 44; www.courdesloges.com; 2-8 rue du Bœuf, 5e; d €250-450, ste €430-580; M Vieux Lyon) Four 14th- to 17th-century houses wrapped around a *traboule* (secret passage) with preserved features such as Italianate loggias make this an exquisite place to stay. Individually decorated rooms draw guests with designer bathroom fittings and bountiful antiques, while decadent facilities include a spa, a Michelin-starred restaurant (*menus* €105 to €145), a swish cafe and a cross-vaulted bar.

Eating

Lyon's famed indoor food market **Les Halles de Lyon Paul Bocuse** (04 78 62 39 33; www.hallespaulbocuse.lyon.fr; 102 cours Lafayette, 3e; 7am-10.30pm Tue-Sat, to 4.30pm Sun; M Part-Dieu) has more than 60 stalls selling their renowned wares and ample spots to squat and quaff freshly shucked oysters. Lyon's premier outdoor food market is the bustling **Marché de la Croix Rousse** (bd de la Croix Rousse, 1er; 6am-1pm Tue-Sun; M Croix Rousse).

La Cuisinerie FUSION **$**
(04 78 60 91 86; www.lacuisinerie.com; 16 rue St-Georges; lunch menu €11-17, small plates €6-13; noon-2pm & 7pm-midnight Mon-Sat; ; M Vieux Lyon) A charming new addition to Vieux Lyon's St-Georges neighbourhood, La Cuisinerie has a deliciously innovative menu of tapas-sized plates with global influences. You can sample a wide range of flavours (including vegetarian dishes) in small plates like chicken and goat's cheese *churros*, crayfish ravioli, or smoked salmon blinis with wasabi cream, among dozens of other options.

★Le Musée BOUCHON **$$**
(04 78 37 71 54; 2 rue des Forces, 2e; lunch mains €14, lunch menus €19-26, dinner menus €23-32; noon-1.30pm & 7.30-9.30pm Tue-Sat; M Cordeliers) Housed in the stables of Lyon's former Hôtel de Ville, this delightful *bouchon* serves a splendid array of meat-heavy Lyonnais classics, including a divine *poulet au vinaigre* (chicken cooked in vinegar). The daily changing *menu* features 10 appetisers and 10 main dishes, plus five scrumptious desserts, all served on cute china plates at long family-style tables.

Cinq Mains NEOBISTRO **$$**
(04 37 57 30 52; www.facebook.com/cinqmains; 12 rue Monseigneur Lavarenne, 5e; menu lunch/dinner €19/33; noon-1.30pm & 7.30-9.30pm; M Vieux Lyon) When young Lyonnais Grégory Cuilleron and his two friends opened this neobistro in early 2016, it was an instant hit. They're working wonders at this cool loft-like space with a mezzanine, serving up tantalising creations based on what they find at

the market. A new generation of chefs, and a new spin for Lyonnais cuisine.

★ **Restaurant Paul Bocuse** GASTRONOMY **$$$**
(04 72 42 90 90; www.bocuse.com; 40 quai de la Plage, Collonges au Mont d'Or; menus €175-275; noon-1.30pm & 8-9pm) Some 7km north of Lyon, this triple-Michelin-starred restaurant was the flagship of the city's most decorated chef, Paul Bocuse. Although Bocuse is no longer around, his recipes continue to dazzle foodies, with the likes of escargots with parsley butter, thyme-roasted rack of lamb and Bocuse's signature *soupe aux truffes noires VGE* (truffle soup created for French president Valéry Giscard d'Estaing in 1975).

Drinking & Nightlife

Vieux Lyon and rue Ste-Catherine behind place des Terreaux sport extraordinary concentrations of British and Irish pubs. Along quai Victor Augagneur on the Rhône's left bank, a string of *péniches* (barges with onboard bars) serve drinks from mid-afternoon onwards; many rock until the wee hours with DJs and/or live bands.

L'Antiquaire COCKTAIL BAR
(06 34 21 54 65; 20 rue Hippolyte Flandrin, 1er; 5pm-1am Tue & Wed, to 3am Thu-Sat, 6.30pm-1am Sun & Mon; M Hôtel de Ville) Old-time jazz, flickering candles and friendly suspenders-wearing barkeeps set the mood in this atmospheric speakeasy-style bar. The painstakingly prepared cocktails are first-rate (try a Penicillin made from scotch, ginger, honey, lemon and peat whisky) and are best sipped slowly at one of the dark wood and leather booths.

La Maison M CLUB
(04 72 00 87 67; http://mmlyon.com; 21 place Gabriel Rambaud, 1er; 7.30pm-4am Wed-Sat; M Hôtel de Ville) A fantastic addition to Lyon's nightlife scene, La Maison M has three separate spaces: a tropical-style bar near the entrance, a dance floor to the left and a cosy lounge off to the right. DJ parties feature nights of samba (with Brazilian cocktails to match), cumbia, hip-hop and new-wave disco.

★ **Le Sucre** LIVE MUSIC
(www.le-sucre.eu; 50 quai Rambaud, 2e; 8.30pm-midnight Wed & Thu, 6.30pm-1am Fri, to 5am Sat, 4-11pm Sun; T1) Down in the Confluence neighbourhood, Lyon's most innovative club hosts DJs, live shows and eclectic arts events on its super-cool roof terrace atop a 1930s sugar factory, La Sucrière.

Information

The tourist office (p219) offers excellent guided tours, many themed.

Getting There & Away

AIR

Lyon-St-Exupéry Airport (LYS; www.lyonaeroports.com) Located 25km east of the city, with 40 airlines (including many budget carriers) serving more than 120 direct destinations across Europe and beyond.

BUS

International bus companies **Eurolines** (08 92 89 90 91; www.eurolines.fr; Gare de Perrache, 2e; 6.30am-9.15pm Mon-Sat, noon-4pm & 8.15-10pm Sun; M Perrache) and **Linebús** (04 72 41 72 27; www.linebus.es; Gare de Perrache; 7am-9pm Mon-Sat, noon-4pm Sun; M Perrache) offer services to Spain, Portugal, Italy and Germany from the Centre d'Échange building at the north end of the Perrache train complex. Follow signs for 'Cars Grandes Lignes' and 'Galerie A: Gare Routière Internationale'.

TRAIN

Lyon has two main-line train stations: **Gare de la Part-Dieu** (place Charles Béraudier, 3e; M Part-Dieu), 1.5km east of the Rhône, and **Gare de Perrache** (cours de Verdun Rambaud, 2e; M Perrache). Destinations by direct TGV include the following:

Marseille (€52, 1¾ hours, every 30 to 60 minutes)

Paris Charles de Gaulle Airport (€88, two hours, at least 11 daily)

Paris Gare de Lyon (€75, two hours, every 30 to 60 minutes)

Getting Around

Buses, trams, a four-line metro and two funiculars linking Vieux Lyon to Fourvière and St-Just are operated by TCL (www.tcl.fr) and run from around 5am to midnight.

DON'T MISS

FESTIVAL OF LIGHTS

Fête des Lumières (Festival of Lights; www.fetedeslumieres.lyon.fr; Dec) Over four days around the Feast of the Immaculate Conception (8 December), magnificent sound-and-light shows are projected onto key buildings, while locals illuminate window sills with candles. This is Lyon's premier festival, and it's so colourful that it's worth timing your trip around it. Note that every hotel will be fully booked.

Tickets cost €1.90 (€16.90 for a *carnet* of 10) and are available from bus and tram drivers as well as machines at metro entrances. Tickets allow two consecutive hours of travel after 9am or unlimited travel after 7pm cost €3, and an all-day ticket costs €5.80. Time-stamp tickets on all forms of public transport or risk a fine.

THE FRENCH ALPS

Hiking, skiing, soul-soaring panoramas – the French Alps have it all when it comes to the great outdoors. But you'll also find excellent gastronomy, good nightlife and plenty of history.

Chamonix

POP 8906 / ELEV 1035M

Mountains loom large almost everywhere you look in Chamonix – France's original winter-sports hub rediscovered as a tourist destination by Brits William Windham and Richard Pococke in 1741. In 1924 Chamonix hosted the first ever Winter Olympics.

Downtown Chamonix hums with life. Streets are lined with Michelin-starred restaurants, sports gear shops and some of the French Alps' fanciest hotels. And if you do the nightlife justice, it'll exhaust you as much as the mountains.

Sights & Activities

The ski season runs from mid-December to mid-April. Summer activities – hiking, biking, canyoning, mountaineering etc – generally start in June and end in September. The **Compagnie des Guides de Chamonix** (04 50 53 00 88; www.chamonix-guides.com; 190 place de l'Église, Maison de la Montagne; 8.30am-noon & 2.30-7.30pm mid-Dec–late Apr & mid-June–mid-Sep, closed Sun & Mon rest of year) is the most famous of all the guide companies and has guides for virtually every activity, whatever the season.

★Aiguille du Midi VIEWPOINT

The great rocky fang of the Aiguille du Midi (3842m), rising from the Mont Blanc massif, is one of Chamonix' most distinctive features. The 360-degree views of the French, Swiss and Italian Alps from the summit are (quite literally) breathtaking. Year-round, you can float via cable car from Chamonix to the Aiguille du Midi on the vertiginous **Téléphérique de l'Aiguille du Midi** (www.compagniedumontblanc.co.uk; place de l'Aiguille du Midi; adult/child return to Aiguille du Midi €61.50/52.30, to Plan de l'Aiguille €32.50/27.60; 1st ascent btwn 6.30am & 8.10am, last btwn 4pm & 5.30pm, mid-Dec–early Nov). Dress warmly: even in summer, temperatures at the top rarely rise above -10°C (in winter prepare for -25°C).

SkyWay Monte Bianco CABLE CAR

(www.montebianco.com; Pointe Helbronner; single/return €37/49; 6.30am-4.30pm Jul & Aug, 8.30am-4pm Sep–mid-Nov & Dec-May, 7.30am-4.20pm Jun) This spectacular, international cable car links France with Italy, from Pointe Helbronner to Courmayeur in the Val d'Aosta. The cars rotate a full 360 degrees, affording peerless views of Mont Blanc, the Matterhorn and Gran Paradiso. To get there, take the Aiguille du Midi and **Télécabine Panoramique Mont Blanc** (04 50 53 22 75; www.montblancnaturalresort.com; Aiguille du Midi; adult/child return from Chamonix €89/75.70; 7.30am-4.30pm Jul & Aug, 8am-4pm Jun, 9am-3.30pm Sep) cable cars.

★Mer de Glace GLACIER

France's largest glacier, the 200m-deep 'Sea of Ice', flows 7km down the northern side of Mont Blanc, scarred with crevasses formed by the immense pressure of its 90m-per-year movement. The **Train du Montenvers** (04 50 53 22 75; www.montblancnaturalresort.com; 35 place de la Mer de Glace; adult/child return €32.50/27.60; 10am-4.30pm late Dec–mid-Mar, to 5pm mid-Mar–Apr), a picturesque, 5km-long cog railway opened in 1909, links Gare du Montenvers with Montenvers (1913m), from where a cable car descends to the glacier and, 420 stairs later, the **Grotte de Glace** FREE. Also worth a visit is the **Glaciorium**, an exhibition on the formation (and future) of glaciers.

Sleeping

Le Vert Hôtel HOTEL $

(04 50 53 13 58; www.verthotel.com; 964 rte des Gaillands; d €55-120, q €85-190; P) This lively hotel has 21 compact rooms – all with new bathrooms and some with fantastic Aiguille du Midi views. There's also a more-than-decent restaurant (dinner *menu* €22.50) and in-house ski rental. In winter, the bar regularly hosts international DJs (Gilles Peterson and Krafty Kuts, to name two). *Navettes* (shuttle buses) to central Chamonix, 2km to the northeast, stop right outside.

Terminal Neige HOTEL $$

(Refuge du Montenvers; 04 50 53 87 70; http://montenvers.terminal-neige.com; Le Montenvers; half-board dm €80-100, d €190-270, tr €275-395, q €360-

500; ⌚Nov-Sep; @📶) There's just one way to access this iconic mountain address, overlooking the shimmering ice of Mer de Glace – by the Train du Montenvers cog railway. Its 20 designer-chic, wood-panelled rooms have glacier views, and hikers and families are well catered for with an insanely stylish 10-bed dorm, cosy duplex rooms for five or seven, and five-person bunk-bed rooms. Rates include dinner and breakfast.

★Grand Hôtel des Alpes HISTORIC HOTEL **$$$**
(☎04 50 55 37 80; www.grandhoteldesalpes.com; 75 rue du Docteur Paccard; d/ste from €175/294; ⌚mid-Dec–mid-Apr & mid-June–late Sep; P📶) Exuding belle époque charm, this buttercup and powder-blue hotel is one of the prettiest buildings in Chamonix. Established in 1840, the hotel's 30 rooms have a classic style: flowing drapes, wood-panelled ceilings and glossy marble bathrooms. There's a glamorous-feeling wellness centre, and in winter a scrumptious teatime cake buffet (4pm to 6pm) greets skiers back from the slopes.

Eating

Pizzeria des Moulins PIZZA **$**
(☎06 68 70 99 82, 06 47 07 75 10; www.facebook.com/pizzeriadesmoulins; 107 rue des Moulins; pizzas from €15; ⌚noon-2.30pm & 6.30-11pm) Cham's best pizzas, piled with buffalo mozzarella, forest mushrooms and Savoyard ham, puff up in the oven of this little gourmet joint. Reservations are essential for dining in, but you can always get takeaway if (or rather, when) they're packed with ravenous diners.

Munchie FUSION **$$**
(☎04 50 53 45 41; www.streamcreek.com/munchie; 87 rue des Moulins; mains €23-29; ⌚7pm-2am winter & summer) Franco-Japanese-Scandinavian fusion may not be the most obvious recipe for success, but this casual, Swedish-skippered restaurant has been making diners happy since 1997. There's a sharing plate concept with sushi plates resembling little works of art, and the excellent seafood and passion-fruit ceviche, teriyaki duck and alcoholic Oreo milkshakes have brought local acclaim. Reservations recommended.

★Le Cap Horn FRENCH, SEAFOOD **$$$**
(☎04 50 21 80 80; www.caphorn-chamonix.com; 74 rue des Moulins; lunch/dinner menus from €23/42; ⌚noon-3pm & 7-10.30pm; 🖉) Housed in a candelit, two-storey chalet decorated with model sailing boats – joint homage to the Alps and Cape Horn – this highly praised restaurant, which opened in 2012, serves French and Asian dishes such as pan-seared duck breast with honey and soy sauce, an ample sushi menu, and a marvellous range of seafood like red tuna *taquitos* and fish stew. Reserve for dinner Friday and Saturday in winter and summer.

Drinking & Nightlife

For a bar crawl, head to central rue des Moulins, where wall-to-wall watering holes keep buzzing until about 1am.

★Chambre Neuf BAR
(☎04 50 53 00 31; www.facebook.com/chambre.neuf; 272 av Michel Croz; ⌚7am-1am; 📶) A favourite among seasonal workers letting off steam, 'Room 9' boasts the most spirited (rather, loudest) après-ski party in Cham (from 3pm or 4pm). There's live rock music (from Sunday to Friday), dancing on the tables, and themed events (if DJ sets or circus-themed parties sound like your jam). Action spills out of the front door, and the terrace opens in spring.

Jekyll & Hyde PUB
(☎04 50 55 99 70; www.facebook.com/jekyllchamonix; 71 rte des Pélerins, Chamonix Sud; ⌚4pm-2am Mon-Fri, opens earlier Sat & Sun; 📶) This British-owned après-ski mainstay has a split personality: upstairs the 'Jekyll' has really good pub food (from seafood tapas and sweet and sour duck to plenty of veggie options), live music, DJs and comedy; check their Facebook page for events. Downstairs, the 'Hyde' is cosier and more relaxed. Both have good Irish beer and a friendly vibe.

MBC MICROBREWERY
(Micro Brasserie de Chamonix; ☎04 50 53 61 59; www.mbchx.com; 350 rte du Bouchet; ⌚4pm-2am Mon-Fri, 10am-2am Sat & Sun) This Canadian-run microbrewery is one of Chamonix' most unpretentious and gregarious watering holes, pouring its own locally made blonde, stout, pale ale, German-style wheat beer and mystery beer of the month. Soaking it up is a menu of huge burgers, poutine (chips with cottage cheese and gravy) and vegetarian choices. Eclectic live music (usually from 9pm) could mean anything from soul to hard rock. Enormously satisfying.

Information

Tourist Office (☎04 50 53 00 24; www.chamonix.com; 85 place du Triangle de l'Amitié; ⌚9am-7pm mid-Jun–mid-Sep & mid-Dec-Apr, 9am-12.30pm & 2-6pm rest of year, closed Sun Oct & Nov; 📶)

Getting There & Away

BUS

Drop by the **bus station** (☎04 50 53 01 15; 234 av Courmayeur, Chamonix Sud; ⊙ticket 8am-noon & 1.15-6.30pm in winter, shorter hours rest of year) for timetables and reservations (highly recommended) or book online with **Ouibus** (www.ouibus.com). Direct daily buses serve Lyon Perrache (from €26, 3½ to 4½ hours) and Geneva in Switzerland (€19, 1½ to two hours). **Savda** (www.savda.it) operates four daily buses to Courmayeur in Italy (€15, 45 minutes), with onward connections to Aosta and Milan.

TRAIN

The scenic, narrow-gauge **Mont Blanc Express** (www.mont-blanc-express.com) glides from the Swiss town of Martigny to Chamonix, taking in Argentière and Vallorcine en route.

For destinations around France, including Lyon, Annecy and Paris, you'll need to change trains at St-Gervais-Le-Fayet first (€11.40, 45 minutes, hourly).

THE DORDOGNE

Tucked into the green southwestern corner of *la belle France,* the Dordogne fuses history, culture and culinary sophistication in one unforgettably scenic package. The region is best known for its sturdy *bastides* (fortified towns), earthy cuisine, clifftop châteaux teetering above the mighty Dordogne River and spectacular prehistoric cave paintings.

Sarlat-la-Canéda

POP 9030

A picturesque tangle of honey-coloured buildings, alleyways and secret squares make up the beautiful town of Sarlat-la-Canéda. Boasting some of the region's best-preserved medieval architecture, it's a popular base for exploring the Vézère Valley, and a favourite location for film directors.

Sights & Activities

Part of the fun of wandering around Sarlat is losing yourself in its twisting alleyways and

DON'T MISS

PREHISTORIC CAVE ART

The Vézère Valley is littered with some of Europe's most impressive prehistoric cave art. The most famous is **Grotte de Lascaux**, 2km southeast of Montignac, which features the largest collection of paintings ever discovered. The original cave has been closed since 1963 to prevent damage, but a perfect replica can be viewed at **Lascaux IV** (International Centre for Cave Art; ☎05 53 50 99 10; www.lascaux.fr; Montignac; adult/child €16/10.40; ⊙8.30am-10pm Jul & Aug, shorter hours rest of year). Using laser technology and 3D printing to re-create the rock paintings in what feels like a real cave – complete with muffled sounds, semi-darkness, damp smells and prehistoric fauna – the whole experience is legitimately spine-tingling. Advance reservations (up to two days in advance online) are highly recommended. Several other caves in the valley remain open to the public; reserve well ahead.

Grotte de Font de Gaume (☎05 53 06 86 00; www.sites-les-eyzies.fr; 4 av des Grottes; adult/child €10/free; ⊙guided tours 9.30am-5.30pm Sun-Fri mid-May–mid-Sep, 9.30am-12.30pm & 2-5.30pm Sun-Fri mid-Sep–mid-May) About 14,000 years ago, prehistoric artists created the gallery of over 230 figures, including bison, reindeer, horses, mammoths, bears and wolves, of which 25 are on permanent display; 1km northeast of Les Eyzies.

Abri du Cap Blanc (☎05 53 59 60 30; www.sites-les-eyzies.fr; adult/child €8/free; ⊙guided tours 10am-6pm Sun-Fri mid-May–mid-Sep, 10am-12.30pm & 2-5.30pm Sun-Fri mid-Sep–mid-May) Showcases an unusual sculpture gallery of horses, bison and deer; 7km east of Les Eyzies.

Grotte de Rouffignac (☎05 53 05 41 71; www.grottederouffignac.fr; Rouffignac-St-Cernin-de-Reilhac; adult/child €7.80/5.10; ⊙9-11.30am & 2-6pm Jul & Aug, 10-11.30am & 2-5pm Apr-Jun, Sep & Oct, closed Nov-Mar) Sometimes known as the 'Cave of 100 Mammoths' because of its painted mammoths. Access to the caves, hidden in woodland 15km north of Les Eyzies, is aboard a trundling electric train.

WORTH A TRIP

PÉRIGUEUX

Founded by Gallic tribes, and later developed by the Romans into the important city of Vesunna, Périgueux, 85km northwest of Sarlat, is the Dordogne's biggest and busiest town. Medieval buildings and Renaissance mansions dot a charming old town, radiating out from the Gothic **Cathédrale St-Front** (place de la Clautre; ⌚8.30am-7pm). In the old Roman quarter of La Cité, the **Gallo-Roman museum** (☎05 53 53 00 92; www.perigueux-vesunna.fr; 20 rue du 26e Régiment d'Infanterie, Parc de Vésone; adult/child €6/4, audioguide €1; ⌚10am-7pm Jul & Aug, shorter hours rest of year), designed by French architect Jean Nouvel around a 1st-century Roman domus (townhouse), is a Dordogne highlight.

Périgueux' wonderful street markets – a prime spot for seasonal black truffles,wild mushrooms and foie gras – explode into action on Wednesday and Saturday. Michelin-starred **L'Essentiel** (☎05 53 35 15 15; www.restaurant-perigueux.com; 8 rue de la Clarté; lunch menus €29-47, dinner menus €45-81; ⌚noon-1.30pm & 7.30-9.30pm Tue-Sat) or down-to-earth, utterly delicious **Café de la Place** (☎05 53 08 21 11; www.cafedelaplace24.com; 7 place du Marché au Bois; mains €9.50-20; ⌚restaurant noon-2.30pm & 7-10.30pm, bar 8am-2am) are memorable lunch spots.

backstreets. Rue Landry, rue de la Liberté and rue Jean-Jacques Rousseau are good starting points.

★**Weekly Markets** MARKET
(place de la Liberté; ⌚8.30am-1pm Wed & Sat) For an introductory French market experience, visit Sarlat's heavily touristed Saturday market, which takes over the streets around Cathédrale St-Sacerdos. Depending on the season, delicacies include local mushrooms and duck- and goose-based products such as foie gras. The Wednesday version is a smaller affair. An atmospheric, largely organic **night market** (place du 14 Juillet; ⌚6-10pm Thu) operates on Thursdays.

Église Ste-Marie MARKET
(place de la Liberté; elevator adult/child €4/1) Église Ste-Marie was ingeniously converted by acclaimed architect Jean Nouvel, whose parents still live in Sarlat, into the town's touristy **Marché Couvert** (Covered Market; place de la Liberté; ⌚8.30am-2pm daily mid-Apr-mid-Nov, closed Mon, Thu & Sun rest of year). Its **panoramic elevator** (buy tickets at tourist office) offers 360-degree views across Sarlat's countryside.

Sleeping & Eating

★**Le Grand Bleu** GASTRONOMY $$$
(☎05 53 31 08 48; www.legrandbleu.eu; 43 av de la Gare; lunch menus €25, dinner menus €54-125; ⌚12.30-2pm Thu-Sun, 7.30-9.30pm Tue-Sat) This eminent Michelin-starred restaurant run by chef Maxime Lebrun is renowned for its creative cuisine, with elaborate *menus* making maximum use of luxury produce: truffles, lobster, turbot and scallops, with a wine list to match. Cooking courses are also available. Located 1.5km south of the centre.

Information

Tourist Office (☎05 53 31 45 45; www.sarlat-tourisme.com; 3 rue Tourny; ⌚9am-7.30pm Mon-Sat, 10am-1pm & 2-6pm Sun Jul & Aug, shorter hours rest of year; 📶)

Getting There & Away

The **train station** (av de la Gare) is 1.3km south of the old city. Services include Bordeaux (€28.20, 2½ hours, three daily) and Périgueux (€16.20, 1¼ to three hours, five daily).

ATLANTIC COAST

With quiet country roads winding through vine-striped hills and wild stretches of coastal sands interspersed with misty islands, the Atlantic coast is where France returns to nature. If you're a surf nut or beach bum, the sandy bays around Biarritz will be right up your alley, while oenophiles can sample the fruits of the vine in the high temple of French winemaking, Bordeaux.

Bordeaux

POP 250,776

An intoxicating cocktail of 18th-century savoir-faire, millennial hi-tech and urban street life, France's sixth largest city is among

Europe's most exciting players. Its art and architecture are utterly sublime (half the city is Unesco-listed), the dining scene is exceptional, and the majestic River Garonne fuels bags of riverside fun and action on its leggy route north past traditional wine-producing châteaux to the Atlantic Ocean. Bordeaux' flagship wine museum and surrounding vineyards make the city a key stop for wine lovers.

Sights & Activities

Consider buying a **Bordeaux Métropole City Pass** (www.bordeauxcitypass.com; 24/48/72hr €29/39/46) online before arrival. The pass covers admission to major museums as well as a free guided tour and unlimited use of public transport

★La Cité du Vin MUSEUM
(☎05 56 16 20 20; www.laciteduvin.com; 134-150 Quai de Bacalan, 1 Esplanade de Pontac; adult/child €20/free; ⏲10am-7pm Apr-Aug, shorter hours rest of year) The complex world of wine is explored in depth at ground-breaking La Cité du Vin, a stunning piece of contemporary architecture resembling a wine decanter on the banks of the River Garonne. The curvaceous gold building glitters in the sun and its 3000 sq metres of exhibits are equally sensory and sensational. Digital guides lead visitors around 20 themed sections covering everything from vine cultivation, grape varieties and wine production to ancient wine trade, 21st-century wine trends and celebrated personalities.

★Cathédrale St-André CATHEDRAL
(☎05 56 44 67 29; www.cathedrale-bordeaux.fr; place Jean Moulin; ⏲2-7pm Mon, 10am-noon & 2-6pm Tue-Sun) FREE The Cathédrale St-André, a Unesco World Heritage Site prior to the city's classification, lords it over the city. The cathedral's oldest section dates from 1096; most of what you see today was built in the 13th and 14th centuries. Enjoy exceptional masonry carvings in the north portal.

Musée d'Aquitaine MUSEUM
(☎05 56 01 51 00; www.musee-aquitaine-bordeaux.fr; 20 cours Pasteur; adult/child €5/free; ⏲11am-6pm Tue-Sun) Gallo-Roman statues and relics dating back 25,000 years are among the highlights at this bright and spacious, well-curated history and civilisations museum. Grab a bilingual floor plan at the entrance and borrow an English-language catalogue to better appreciate the exhibits that span prehistory through to 18th-century Atlantic trade and slavery, world cultures and the emergence of Bordeaux as a world port in the 19th century. Temporary exhibitions cost extra.

★Miroir d'Eau FOUNTAIN
(Water Mirror; place de la Bourse; ⏲10am-10pm summer) FREE A fountain of sorts, the Miroir d'Eau is the world's largest reflecting pool. Covering an area of 3450 sq metres of black granite on the quayside opposite the imposing Palais de la Bourse, the 'water mirror' provides hours of entertainment on warm sunny days when the reflections in its thin slick of water – drained and refilled every half-hour – are stunning. Every 23 minutes a dense foglike vapour is ejected for three minutes to add to the fun (and photo opportunities).

École du Vin de Bordeaux WINE
(Bordeaux Wine School; ☎05 56 00 22 85; www.bordeaux.com; 3 cours du 30 juillet; introductory

DON'T MISS

WINE-TASTING IN SITU

Diminutive neighbour to nearby Château Haut-Brion, which is rated among the top 'first growths' in the 1855 classification, **Château Les Carmes Haut Briond** (☎07 77 38 10 64; www.les-carmes-haut-brion.com; 20 rue des Carmes; 1½hr guided visit incl tasting €30; ⏲9.30am-12.30pm & 2-6pm Mon-Sat) is named after Carmelite monks – Les Carmes – who tended vines here from 1584 until the French Revolution. The 16th-century château is very much intact and contrasts beautifully with its millennial cellars and tasting room designed by French designer Philippe Starck. Resembling a majestic ship, the striking building 'floats' in a pool of water and is accessed by footbridges.

Guided visits include a tour of the 19th-century château gardens and cellar, and end with wine tasting. Advance reservations online or by telephone are essential. The château is 4km southwest of the cathedral, in Pessac. Take tram line A from Hôtel de Ville to the François Mitterrand stop, a 10-minute walk from the château.

workshops €32) Serious students of the grape can enrol at this highly regarded wine school inside the Maison du Vin de Bordeaux (Bordeaux House of Wine). It hosts introductory two-hour workshops the last Saturday of each month and daily from July to September (€32), plus more complex two- to three-day courses from May to October.

Sleeping

Central Hostel HOSTEL $
(http://centralhostel.fr; 2 place Projet; d €19-30, d €90-150) Urban chic dorms and swish doubles with USB plugs aplenty and en suite bathrooms are spread across four floors at this dead-central, designer hostel in Saint-Pierre. Glam to the core, the 97-bed hostel promises a bespoke guest experience, with a bar, sun-drenched terrace designed for summertime chilling and a locally sourced restaurant, open 24 hours.

★ **Hôtel La Cour Carrée** BOUTIQUE HOTEL $$
(05 57 35 00 00; www.lacourcarree.com; 5 rue de Lurbe; d €125-250; P ❄ @) Tucked in an 18th-century house on a quiet side street with little passing traffic, this design-driven boutique hotel oozes natural style and peace. Soft, muted colours and contemporary Scandinavian furnishings complement ancient gold-stone walls in its 16 elegant rooms, and the pièce de résistance is the interior courtyard – a much-appreciated alfresco lounge in summer. Breakfast/parking €12/13.

Mama Shelter DESIGN HOTEL $$
(05 57 30 45 45; www.mamashelter.com/en/bordeaux; 19 rue Poquelin Molière; d/tr from €80/130; ❄ @) With personalised iMacs, video booths and free movies in every room, Mama Shelter is up-to-the-minute. White rooms are small, medium or large; XL doubles have a sofa bed. The ground-floor restaurant (mains €13 to €29) sports the same signature rubber rings strung above the bar as other Philippe Starck–designed hotels. Summertime drinks and dinner are served on the sensational rooftop terrace.

Eating

Timeless dining icons mingle with new openings and cheaper eats in the tasty tangle of pedestrian streets in Saint-Pierre and Saint-Paul. North along the river, quai des Chartons is laced with waterfront restaurants and bars – particularly enchanting at sunset.

Chez Jean-Mi SEAFOOD $
(place des Capucins, Maré des Capucins; breakfast €1-7.50, seafood €6-25; 7am-2.30pm Tue-Fri, to 3.30pm Sat & Sun) If there's one stall at the city's iconic food market that sums up the contagious *joie de vivre* of Les Capus (as locals call the market), it is this *bistrot à huitres* (oyster bar). Jean-Mi greets regulars and first-timers with the same huge smile, and his freshly shucked oysters, fish soup and copious seafood platters are of the finest quality money can buy.

★ **Magasin Général** INTERNATIONAL $
(05 56 77 88 35; www.magasingeneral.camp; 87 quai des Queyries; mains €10-20; 8am-6pm Mon, to 7pm Tue & Wed, to midnight Thu & Fri, 8.30am-midnight Sat, 8.30am-6pm Sun;) Follow the hip crowd across the river to this huge industrial hangar on the right bank, France's biggest and best organic restaurant with a gargantuan terrace complete with vintage sofa seating, ping-pong table and table football. Everything here – from vegan burgers and superfood salads to smoothies, pizzas, wine and French bistro fare is *bio* (organic) and sourced locally. Sunday brunch is a bottomless feast.

Au Bistrot FRENCH $$
(06 63 54 21 14; www.facebook.com/aubistrotbordeaux; 61 place des Capucins; mains €18-24; noon-2.30pm & 7-11pm Wed-Sun) There's nothing flashy or fancy about this hardcore French bistro, an ode to traditional market cuisine with charismatic François front of house and talented French-Thai chef Jacques In'On in the kitchen. Marinated herrings, lentil salad topped with a poached egg, half a roast pigeon or a feisty *andouillette* (tripe sausage) roasted in the oven – 90% of produce is local or from the surrounding Aquitaine region.

★ **Brasserie Le Bordeaux** CAFE $$
(05 57 30 43 46; https://bordeaux.intercontinental.com; 2-5 place de la Comédie; 2-/3-course lunch menu from €29/39, mains €27; 7am-10.30pm) To dine à la Gordon Ramsay without breaking the bank, reserve a table at his elegant belle époque brasserie with an interesting Anglo-French hybrid cuisine – local Arcachon oysters, fish and chips, Gascon pork pie with piccalilli, braised beef chuck, hand-cut tartare – and a parasol-shaded pavement terrace overlooking busy place de la Comédie. Weekend brunch (€68) is a local hot date.

La Tupina FRENCH $$$

(☎05 56 91 56 37; www.latupina.com; 6 rue Porte de la Monnaie; lunch menu €18, dinner menus €44-52, mains €20-32; ⊙noon-2pm & 7-11pm Tue-Sun) Filled with the aroma of soup simmering inside a *tupina* ('kettle' in Basque) over an open fire, this iconic bistro is feted for its seasonal southwestern French fare: calf kidneys with fries cooked in goose fat, milk-fed lamb, tripe and goose wings. Dining is farmhouse-style, in a maze of small elegant rooms decorated with vintage photographs, antique furniture and silver tableware.

Drinking & Nightlife

Medieval Saint-Pierre teems with atmospheric cafe pavement terraces, as do Chartron's riverside quays. Mainstream nightclubs congregate on busy quai du Paladate near the train station.

★Symbiose COCKTAIL BAR

(Old-Fashioned Stories; ☎05 56 23 67 15; www.facebook.com/symbiosebordeaux; 4 quai des Chartrons; ⊙noon-2.30pm Mon, noon-2.30pm & 6.30pm-2am Tue-Fri, 6.30pm-2am Sat) There is something inviting about this clandestine address with a soft green facade across from the river on the fringe of the Chartrons district. This is the secret speakeasy that introduced good cocktails with gastronomic food pairings to Bordeaux. The chef uses locally sourced artisanal products, and cocktails rekindle old-fashioned recipes packed with homemade syrups and 'forgotten', exotic or unusual ingredients.

★Bar à Vin WINE BAR

(☎05 56 00 43 47; http://baravin.bordeaux.com; 3 cours du 30 Juillet; ⊙11am-10pm Mon-Sat) The decor – herringbone parquet, grandiose stained glass depicting the godly Bacchus, and sky-high ceiling – matches the reverent air that fills this wine bar inside the hallowed halls of the Maison du Vin de Bordeaux. Dozens of Bordeaux wines are served by the glass (€3.50 to €8) which, paired with a cheese or charcuterie platter, transport foodies straight to heaven. Gracious sommeliers know their *vin*.

★Night Beach BAR

(https://bordeaux.intercontinental.com; 2-5 place de la Comédie, 7th fl, Grand Hôtel de Bordeaux; ⊙7pm-1am late May-late Sep) There is no finer, more elegant or more romantic rooftop bar in Bordeaux than this achingly hip drinking-and-hobnobbing joint on the 7th floor of the historic Grand Hôtel de Bordeaux. Views of the city, River Garonne and the vineyards beyond are a panoramic 360 degrees. French-chic seating is sofa-style beneath parasols, and DJ sets play at weekends.

LOCAL KNOWLEDGE

BREAKFAST & BRUNCH

Whatever the time of day, **Horace** (☎05 56 90 01 93; 40 rue Poquelin Molière; mains €8-14; ⊙8.30am-6.30pm Mon, to 9.30pm Tue-Fri, 9.30am-9.30pm Sat, 9.30am-6.30pm Sun) can do no wrong. Outstanding speciality coffee roasts (including Oven Heaven beans roasted locally), sophisticated fruit- and veg-packed breakfasts, homemade brioches and breads, and lunch/dinner menus bursting with creativity are the quality hallmarks of this coffee shop, owned by the same talented barista as Bordeaux' **Black List** (☎06 89 91 82 65; www.facebook.com/blacklistcafe; 27 place Pey Berland; ⊙8am-6pm Mon-Fri, 9.30am-6pm Sat). Sunday brunch (€21) is a sell-out every week.

I.Boat CLUB

(☎05 56 10 48 37; www.iboat.eu; quai Armand Lalande, Bassins à Flot 1; ⊙7.30pm-6am) Hip-hop, rock, indie pop, psyche blues rock, punk and hardcore are among the varied sounds that blast out of this fun nightclub and concert venue, on a decommissioned ferry moored in the increasingly trendy, industrial Bassins à Flot district in the north of the city. Live music starts at 7pm, with DJ sets kicking in on the club dance floor from 11.30pm.

Information

Tourist Office (☎05 56 00 66 00; www.bordeaux-tourisme.com; 12 cours du 30 Juillet; ⊙9am-6.30pm Mon-Sat, to 5pm Sun)

Getting There & Away

Aéroport de Bordeaux (Bordeaux Airport; BOD; ☎Information 05 56 34 50 50; www.bordeaux.aeroport.fr) is 10km west of the city centre in the suburb of Mérignac.

Major train services to/from from Bordeaux train station **Gare St-Jean** (Cours de la Marne) include Paris Gare Montparnasse (€69, 3¼ hours, at least 16 daily) and Toulouse (€39, 2¼ hours, hourly).

Biarritz

POP 25,500

Edge your way south along the coast towards Spain and you arrive in stylish Biarritz, which is just as ritzy as its name suggests. The resort took off in the mid-19th century and it still shimmers with architectural treasures from the belle époque and art deco eras. Big waves – some of Europe's best – and a beachy lifestyle are a magnet for Europe's hip surfing set.

Biarritz' raison d'être is its fashionable beaches, particularly central **Grande Plage** and **Plage Miramar**. North of Pointe St-Martin, the adrenaline-pumping surfing beaches of **Anglet** continue northwards for more than 4km. Take bus 10 or 13 from the bottom of av Verdun (just near av Édouard VII).

Sleeping & Eating

Biarritz is a pricey place to sleep, with a massive premium during July and August – although off-season discounts are often available, especially in winter when the town is largely deserted.

Shop for beach-perfect picnic supplies at the covered **Les Halles** (www.halles-biarritz.fr; rue des Halles; ⊙7am-2pm) market.

Auberge de Jeunesse de Biarritz HOSTEL $
(☎05 59 41 76 00; www.hihostels.com; 8 rue Chiquito de Cambo; dm/s incl sheets & breakfast €26/44; ⊙reception 9am-noon & 6-10pm, closed mid-Dec–early Jan;) This popular, well-run place has a lot going for it: clean dorms, a lively cafe-bar and a sunny terrace for summer barbecues. From the train station, follow the railway line westwards for 800m.

★**Hôtel de Silhouette** BOUTIQUE HOTEL $$$
(☎05 59 24 93 82; www.hotel-silhouette-biarritz.com; 30 rue Gambetta; d from €175;) Come here if you want to splash out. It's just steps from the covered market, but is surprisingly secluded thanks to being set back from the street. It's full of fun, from the weird faces on the wallpaper to the odd bear and sheep sculptures, and there's a gorgeous garden. The building dates from 1610, but it's metropolitan modern in style.

Haragia STEAK $$$
(☎05 35 46 68 92; www.facebook.com/haragia64; 26 rue Gambetta; mains €30-50; ⊙8pm-1am Thu-Sun, to 5pm Sun) Tucked back in a tiny alley near the central market, this convivial steakhouse has a few small tables and an open kitchen with the grill on show as the friendly brothers cook up your evening meal. The meat menu is simple – steak, veal and pork – but the wine menu is vast!

Information

Tourist Office (☎05 59 22 37 10; www.tourisme.biarritz.fr; Square d'Ixelles; ⊙9am-7pm Jul–mid-Sep, shorter hours rest of year)

Getting There & Around

AIR

Domestic and international flights leave from **Aéroport Biarritz Pays Basque** (BIQ; ☎05 59 43 83 83; www.biarritz.aeroport.fr). Chronoplus (www.chronoplus.eu) Line C buses run from the train station in Biarritz, while Line 14 leaves from near the Biarritz tourist office. Both run every half-hour or so and take about 10 minutes. A single fare costs €1.

TRAIN

Trains to Biarritz stop at the **train station** (☎08 92 35 35 35; allée du Moura) 3.5km southeast of the town centre. Chronoplus bus 10 runs regularly into the city centre. Services include Paris Gare Montparnasse (€50 to €100, 4¼ hours, five daily) and Bordeaux (€35 to €50, 2¼ hours, 10 daily).

LANGUEDOC-ROUSSILLON

POP 2.7 MILLION

Languedoc-Roussillon comes in three distinct flavours: Bas-Languedoc (Lower

DON'T MISS

DUNE DU PILAT

This colossal **sand dune** (sometimes referred to as the Dune de Pyla because of its location in the resort town of Pyla-sur-Mer), an easy day trip from Bordeaux 65km west, stretches from the mouth of the Bassin d'Arcachon southwards for almost 3km. Already the largest in Europe, it's spreading eastwards at 4.5m a year – it has swallowed trees, a road junction and even a hotel. Take care swimming in this area: powerful currents swirl out to sea from the deceptively tranquil *baïnes* (little bays).

WORTH A TRIP

TOULOUSE

Elegantly set at the confluence of the Canal du Midi and the Garonne River , this vibrant southern city – nicknamed *la ville rose* (the pink city) after the distinctive hot-pink stone used in many buildings – is one of France's liveliest metropolises. Busy, buzzy and bustling with students, this riverside dame has a history stretching back over 2000 years and has been a hub for the aerospace industry since the 1930s.

Lavish **place du Capitole** is the classic starting point to explore Toulouse, before wandering south into the pedestrianised **Vieux Quartier** (Old Quarter). Most of the city's major galleries, museums and **Couvent des Jacobins** (☎05 61 22 23 82; www.jacobins.toulouse.fr; rue Lakanal; cloister adult/child €4/free; ⏰10am-6pm Tue-Sun) are easily accessed from metro stops Esquirol, Jean Jaurès and Jeanne d'Arc, all on the red A line.

The fantastic **Cité de l'Espace** (☎05 67 22 23 24; www.cite-espace.com; av Jean Gonord; adult €21-26, child €15.50-19; ⏰10am-7pm daily Jul & Aug, to 5pm or 6pm Sep-Dec & Feb-Jun, closed Mon in Feb, Mar & Sep-Dec, closed Jan; 👪), on the city's eastern outskirts, brings Toulouse's illustrious aeronautical history to life through hands-on exhibits. Plane-spotters can arrange a guided tour of Toulouse's massive JL Lagardère **Airbus factory** (☎05 34 39 42 00; www.manatour.fr; allée André Turcat, Blagnac; tours adult/child €15.50/13; ⏰Mon-Sat by reservation), near the airport in Blagnac, 10km northwest of the city centre.

When France's sacrosanct aperitif hour beckons, head to **N°5 Wine Bar** (☎05 61 38 44 51; www.n5winebar.com; 5 rue de la Bourse; ⏰6pm-1am Mon-Sat), voted the world's best wine bar in 2017, followed by dinner at always-packed **La Pente Douce** (☎05 61 46 16 91; www.lapentedouce.fr; 6 rue de la Concorde; menus €23-28, mains €18-24; ⏰noon-1.30pm Tue & Wed, noon-1.30pm & 8-9.30pm Thu-Sat).

Toulouse is served by frequent fast TGVs, which run west to Bordeaux (from €17, two hours, 13 daily) and east to Carcassonne (from €16.50, 45 minutes to one hour, up to 23 daily) and beyond.

Languedoc), home to the biggest beaches, rugby and robust red wines; Haut Languedoc (Upper Languedoc), a mountainous, sparsely populated terrain made for lovers of the great outdoors; and Roussillon, to the south, snug against the rugged Pyrenees and frontier to Spanish Catalonia.

Nîmes

This lively city boasts some of France's best-preserved classical buildings, including a famous Roman amphitheatre, although the city is most famous for its sartorial export, *serge de Nîmes* – better known to cowboys, clubbers and couturiers as denim.

Sights

Save money by purchasing a **Pass Nîmes Romaine** (adult/child €13/11), covering admission to a trio of Roman sights (including Les Arènes) and valid for three days.

★Les Arènes ROMAN SITE
(☎04 66 21 82 56; www.arenes-nimes.com; place des Arènes; adult/child incl audio guide €10/8; ⏰9am-8pm Jul & Aug, 9am-6.30pm Apr-Jun & Sep, 9am-6pm Mar & Oct, 9.30am-5pm Jan, Feb, Nov & Dec) Nîmes' twin-tiered amphitheatre is the best preserved in France. Built around 100 BC, the arena once seated 24,000 spectators and staged gladiatorial contests and public executions; it's still an impressive venue for gigs and events. An audio guide provides context as you explore the arena, seating areas, stairwells and corridors (known to Romans as *vomitoria*), and afterwards you can view replicas of gladiatorial armour and original bullfighters' costumes in the museum.

Musée de la Romanité MUSEUM
(☎04 48 21 02 10; 16 bd des Arènes; adult/child €8/3; ⏰10am-8pm Jul & Aug, 10am-7pm Sep-Nov & Apr-Jun, 10am-6pm Wed-Mon Dec-Mar) This futuristic steel-and-glass structure faces Les Arènes right in the heart of the city. Within, the ambitious archaeological museum's permanent exhibitions are devoted to regional archaeology, with more than 5000 artefacts including well-preserved mosaics and ceramics.

Sleeping & Eating

Place aux Herbes, place de l'Horloge and place du Marché are great places to watch the world drift languidly by at bistros, cafes and bars with pavement seating.

Hôtel des Tuileries HOTEL $
(☎04 66 21 31 15; www.hoteldestuileries.com; 22 rue Roussy; d €60-81, tr €70-93, ste €85-118; P ❄ 📶) Run by an English couple, this well-priced 11-room hotel within strolling distance from Les Arènes (p230) features simple yet satisfyingly equipped rooms, some with covered balconies. Breakfast costs €9. Its private parking garage (€10 to €15) is just down the street, but there are only five car spaces, so reserve ahead.

Les Halles MARKET $
(www.leshallesdenimes.com; rues Guizot, Général Perrier & des Halles; ⏲7am-1pm Mon-Sat, to 1.30pm Sun) With over 100 stalls in 3500 sq metres, Nîmes' covered market is the best place for supplies. Look out for local specialities including *picholines* – a local green olive with its own AOP (Appellation d'Origine Protégée) – and *brandade* (salt cod). You'll also find a couple of great eateries.

Getting There & Around

AIR

Aéroport de Nîmes Alès Camargue Cévennes (FNI; ☎04 66 70 49 49; www.aeroport-nimes.fr; St-Gilles) Nîmes' airport, 10km southeast of the city on the A54, is served only by Ryanair. An airport bus (€6.80, 30 minutes) to/from the **train station** (bd Sergent Triaire) connects with all flights.

BUS

From the **bus station** (☎08 10 33 42 73; rue Ste-Félicité), local buses run by Edgard (www.edgard-transport.fr) serve Pont du Gard (Line B21, €1.50, 40 minutes, two or three daily Monday to Saturday).

TRAIN

TGVs run hourly to/from Paris' Gare de Lyon (from €45, three hours) from the train station.

Pont du Gard

Southern France has no shortage of superb Roman sites, but nothing can top the Unesco World Heritage-listed **Pont du Gard** (☎04 00 37 50 99; www.pontdugard.fr; adult/child €8.50/6, Pass Aqueduc incl guided visit of topmost tier €11.50/6; ⏲9am-11pm Jul & Aug, to 10pm Jun & Sep, to 9pm May, to 8pm Apr & Oct, to 6pm Nov-Mar), 21km northeast of Nîmes. One of the most impressive surviving Roman ruins in Europe, this extraordinary three-tiered aqueduct is a definite highlight in any trip to France. It was once part of a 50km-long system of channels built around 19 BC to transport water from Uzès to Nîmes. The scale is huge: the bridge is 48.8m high, 275m long and graced with 52 precision-built arches.

DON'T MISS

CARCASSONNE

Perched on a rocky hilltop and bristling with zigzag battlements, stout walls and spiky turrets, the fortified city of Carcassonne (population 49,400) looks like something out of a children's storybook from afar. A Unesco World Heritage Site since 1997, it's most people's idea of the perfect medieval castle.

Built on a steep spur of rock, Carcassonne's rampart-ringed fortress dates back more than two millennia. The fortified town is encircled by two sets of battlements and 52 stone towers, topped by distinctive 'witch's hat' roofs (added by architect Viollet-le-Duc during 19th century restorations). Inside the gates, cobbled lanes and courtyards in the **Cité Médiévale** (enter via Porte Narbonnaise or Porte d'Aude; ⏲24hr) FREE lead to a bounty of touristy shops and restaurants.

To walk the ramparts and visit the keep built for the viscounts of Carcassonne in the 12th century, buy a **Château et Remparts** (www.remparts-carcassonne.fr; 1 rue Viollet le Duc, Cité Médiévale; adult/child €9/free; ⏲10am-6.30pm Apr-Sep, 9.30am-5pm Oct-Mar) ticket.

The **tourist office** (☎04 68 10 24 30; www.tourisme-carcassonne.fr; impasse Agnès de Montpellier, Cité Médiévale; ⏲9.30am-7pm Jul & Aug, 9am-6pm Apr-Jun, Sep & Oct, 9.30am-1pm & 1.30-5.30pm Nov-Mar) in the Cité Médiévale runs regular 1¼-hour guided walking tours (adult/child €8/6) of the old city in English (Saturdays and Sundays at 1.30pm), French and Spanish (daily).

It was the highest in the Roman Empire. At the visitors centre on the northern bank, there's an impressive, high-tech **museum** featuring the bridge, the aqueduct and the role of water in Roman society.

For a unique perspective on the Pont du Gard, view it from the water afloat the Gard River. Rent kayaks from **Canoë Le Tourbillon** (☎04 66 22 85 54; www.canoeletourbillon.com; 3 chemin du Gardon, Collias; adult/child from €23/17; ⏲9am-7pm Apr-Sep) in Collias, 8km and a two-hour paddle from the Pont du Gard.

PROVENCE

Provence conjures up images of rolling lavender fields, blue skies, gorgeous villages, wonderful food and superb wine. It certainly delivers on all those fronts, but it's not just worth visiting for its good looks – dig a little deeper and you'll also discover the multicultural metropolis of Marseille, the artistic haven of Aix-en-Provence and Roman Arles.

Marseille

POP 861,635

Grit and grandeur coexist seamlessly in Marseille, an exuberantly multicultural port city with a pedigree stretching back to classical Greece and a fair claim to the mantle of France's second city. Track down its vibrant heart and soul in the Vieux Port (old port), mast-to-mast with yachts and pleasure boats; uphill in the ancient Le Panier neighbourhood; and looking out to sea on the contemporary rooftop of its flagship museum, MuCEM.

Sights

The **Marseille City Pass** (www.resamarseille.com; 24/48/72hr €26/33/41) covers admission to city museums and public transport, and includes a guided city tour and a Château d'If boat trip, plus other discounts. It's not necessary for children under 12, as many attractions are greatly reduced or free. Buy it online or at the tourist office.

★Vieux Port PORT

(Old Port; MVieux Port) Ships have docked for millennia at Marseille's birthplace, the vibrant Vieux Port. The main commercial docks were transferred to the Joliette area in the 1840s, but the old port remains a thriving harbour for fishing boats, pleasure yachts and tourist boats. Guarded by the forts **St-Jean** (MVieux Port) and **St-Nicolas** (1 bd Charles Livon; 83), both sides of the port are dotted with bars, brasseries and cafes, with more to be found around place Thiars and cours Honoré d'Estienne d'Orves, where the action continues until late.

★Musée des Civilisations de l'Europe et de la Méditerranée MUSEUM

(MuCEM, Museum of European & Mediterranean Civilisations; ☎04 84 35 13 13; www.mucem.org; 7 promenade Robert Laffont; adult/child incl exhibitions €9.50/free; ⏲10am-8pm Wed-Mon Jul & Aug, 11am-7pm Wed-Mon May-Jun & Sep-Oct, 11am-6pm Wed-Mon Nov-Apr; ; MVieux Port, Joliette) The icon of modern Marseille, this stunning museum explores the history, culture and civilisation of the Mediterranean region through anthropological exhibits, rotating art exhibitions and film. The collection sits in a bold, contemporary building designed by Algerian-born, Marseille-educated architect Rudy Ricciotti, and Roland Carta. It is linked by a vertigo-inducing footbridge to the 13th-century Fort St-Jean, from which there are stupendous views of the Vieux Port and the surrounding sea. The fort grounds and gardens are free to explore.

Le Panier AREA

(MVieux Port) 'The Basket' is Marseille's oldest quarter – site of the original Greek settlement and nicknamed for its steep streets and buildings. Its close, village-like feel, artsy ambience, cool hidden squares and sun-baked cafes make it a delight to explore. Rebuilt after destruction in WWII, its mishmash of lanes hide artisan shops, *ateliers* (workshops) and terraced houses strung with drying washing. Its centrepiece is **La Vieille Charité** (☎04 91 14 58 80; www.vieille-charite-marseille.com; 2 rue de la Charité; museums adult/child €6/free; ⏲10am-6pm Tue-Sun mid-Sep–mid-May, longer hours in summer; MJoliette), which houses several museums.

Basilique Notre Dame de la Garde BASILICA

(Montée de la Bonne Mère; ☎04 91 13 40 80; www.notredamedelagarde.com; rue Fort du Sanctuaire; ⏲7am-8pm Apr-Sep, to 7pm Oct-Mar; 60) Occupying Marseille's highest point, La Garde (154m), this opulent 19th-century Romano-

Byzantine basilica is Marseille's most-visited icon. Built on the foundations of a 16th-century fort, which was itself an enlargement of a 13th-century chapel, the basilica is ornamented with coloured marble, superb Byzantine-style mosaics, and murals depicting ships sailing under the protection of La Bonne Mère (The Good Mother). The campanile supports a 9.7m-tall gilded statue of said Mother on a 12m-high pedestal, and the hilltop gives 360-degree panoramas of the city.

Château d'If CASTLE

(☎06 03 06 25 26; www.if.monuments-nationaux.fr; Île d'If; adult/child €6/free; ⏲10am-6pm Apr-Sep, to 5pm Tue-Sun Oct-Mar) Commanding access to Marseille's Vieux Port, this photogenic island-fortress was immortalised in Alexandre Dumas' 1844 classic *The Count of Monte Cristo*. Many political prisoners were incarcerated here, including the Revolutionary hero Mirabeau and the Communards of 1871. Other than the island itself there's not a great deal to see, but it's worth visiting just for the views of the Vieux Port. **Frioul If Express** (☎04 96 11 03 50; www.frioul-if-express.com; 1 quai de la Fraternité) runs boats (return €11, 20 minutes, up to 10 daily) from Quai de la Fraternité.

Sleeping

★Vertigo Vieux-Port HOSTEL $

(☎04 91 54 42 95; www.hotelvertigo.fr; 38 rue Fort Notre Dame; dm/tw €26/76; 📶; Ⓜ Vieux Port) This award-winning hostel shows a swanky sleep is possible on a shoestring budget – for your euro you can expect breakfast, murals by local artists, vintage furniture, stripped wooden floors and original architectural details such as exposed wooden beams and stone arches. All rooms have their own modern bathrooms, and there are lockers, a good kitchen and a TV lounge.

★Hôtel Edmond Rostand DESIGN HOTEL $$

(☎04 91 37 74 95; www.hoteledmondrostand.com; 31 rue Dragon; s/d/tr €100/110/135; ❄@📶; ⓂEstrangin-Préfecture) Push past the unassuming facade of this great-value hotel in the Quartier des Antiquaires to find a stylish interior in olive-grey and citrus, with a communal lounge area, a cafe and 15 rooms dressed in crisp white and soothing natural hues. Some rooms overlook a tiny private garden and others the Basilique Notre Dame de la Garde.

Mama Shelter DESIGN HOTEL $$

(☎04 84 35 20 00; www.mamashelter.com; 64 rue de la Loubière; d from €113; P❄📶; ⓂNotre Dame du Mont Cours Julien) Part of a funky mini-chain of design-forward hotels, Marseille's Mama Shelter offers 125 Philippe Starck–imagined rooms over five floors. It's all about keeping the cool kids happy here – with sleek white-and-chrome colour schemes, a live stage and bar, and a giant *bubi foot* (foosball) table. Smaller rooms are oddly shaped, however, and it's a walk from the Vieux Port.

Eating

The Vieux Port and surrounding pedestrian streets teem with cafe terraces, but choose carefully (some rely on tourists to pay

WORTH A TRIP

LES CALANQUES

Marseille abuts the wild and spectacular **Parc National des Calanques** (www.calanques-parcnational.fr), a 20km stretch of high, rocky promontories rising from brilliant-turquoise Mediterranean waters.

The sheer cliffs are occasionally interrupted by small idyllic beaches, some impossible to reach without a kayak. Among the most famous are the calanques of Sormiou, Port-Miou, Port-Pin and En-Vau.

From October to June, the best way to see the Calanques is to hike, and the best access is from the small town of Cassis. Its **tourist office** (☎08 92 39 01 03; www.ot-cassis.com; quai des Moulins; ⏲9am-6.30pm Mon-Sat, 9.30am-12.30pm & 3-6pm Sun May-Aug, shorter hours rest of year; 📶) has maps. In July and August, trails close because of fire danger: take a boat tour from Marseille or Cassis; sea kayak with **Raskas Kayak** (☎04 91 73 27 16; www.raskas-kayak.com; impasse du Dr Bonfils, Auberge de Jeunesse Marseille; half/full day €40/70); drive; or take a bus.

too much for average food). For world cuisine, try cours Julien and nearby rue des Trois Mages. For pizza, roast chicken, and Middle Eastern food under €10, nose around the streets surrounding **Marché des Capucins** (Marché de Noailles; place des Capucins; ⏲8am-7pm Mon-Sat; Ⓜ Noailles, Canebière Garibaldi).

★ **L'Arôme** FRENCH $$
(☎04 91 42 88 80; 9 rue de Trois Rois; menus €23-28; ⏲7.30-11pm Mon-Sat; Ⓜ Notre Dame du Mont) Reserve ahead to snag a table at this fabulous little restaurant just off cours Julien. From the service – relaxed, competent and friendly without over familiarity – to the street art on the walls and the memorable food, it's a complete winner. Well-credentialled chef-owner Romain achieves sophisticated simplicity in dishes such as roast duckling served with polenta and a pecorino *beignet* (doughnut).

Drinking & Nightlife

Near the Vieux Port, head to place Thiars and cours Honoré d'Estienne d'Orves for cafes that bask in the sun by day and buzz into the night. Cours Julien is a fine place on a sunny day to watch people come and go. Le Panier, place de Lenche and rue des Pistoles are ideal places to while away an afternoon soaking up the area's boho charms.

★ **Waaw** BAR
(☎04 91 42 16 33; www.waaw.fr; 17 rue Pastoret; ⏲4pm-midnight Wed & Sat, from 6pm Tue, Thu & Fri; Ⓜ Notre Dame du Mont) Marseille's creative chameleon and the heart of the cours Julien scene, Waaw ('What an Amazing World') has everything you could possibly want for a night out, whether that's a cold cocktail, a late-night dancehall DJ set or an innovative dinner made from local market produce. The city's unofficial cultural headquarters also offers music, film, festivals and much more.

★ **La Friche La Belle de Mai** ARTS CENTRE
(☎04 95 04 95 04; www.lafriche.org; 41 rue Jobin; ⏲ticket kiosk 11am-6pm Mon, to 7pm Tue-Sat, from 12.30pm Sun; 49, 52) This 45,000-sq-metre former tobacco factory is now a vibrant arts centre with a theatre, cinema, bar, bookshop, artists' workshops, multimedia displays, skateboard ramps, electro- and world-music parties and much more. Check the program online. The on-site restaurant, **Les Grandes Tables** (☎04 95 04 95 85; www.lesgrandestables.com; mains €16; ⏲noon-2pm Sun-Wed, noon-2pm & 8-10pm Thu-Sat), is a great bet for interesting, locally sourced food.

Information

Tourist Office (☎08 26 50 05 00, box office 04 91 13 89 16; www.marseille-tourisme.com; 11 La Canebière; ⏲9am-6pm; Ⓜ Vieux Port)

Getting There & Around

For local transport information in and around Marseille, see www.lepilote.com.

AIR

Aéroport Marseille-Provence (Aéroport Marseille-Marignane; MRS; ☎08 20 81 14 14; www.marseille.aeroport.fr) is 25km northwest of Marseille in Marignane. There are regular year-round flights to nearly all major French cities, plus major hubs in the UK, Germany, Belgium, Italy and Spain.

Navette Marseille (www.lepilote.com; one way/return €8.30/14; ⏲4.30am-11.30pm) buses link the airport and Gare St-Charles (30 minutes) every 15 to 20 minutes.

The airport's train station has direct services to several cities including Arles and Avignon – a free shuttle bus runs to/from the airport terminal.

BOAT

Gare Maritime de la Major (Marseille Fos; www.marseille-port.fr; Quai de la Joliette; Ⓜ Joliette), the passenger ferry terminal, is just south of place de la Joliette.

Corsica Linea (☎08 25 88 80 88; www.corsicalinea.com; quai du Maroc; ⏲8.30am-8pm) has regular ferries from Marseille to Corsica and Sardinia, plus long-distance routes to Algeria and Tunisia.

TRAIN

Eurostar (www.eurostar.com) offers two to 10 weekly services between Marseille and London (from €213, seven hours) via Lille or Paris. As always, the earlier you book, the cheaper the fare.

Regular and TGV trains serve **Gare St-Charles** (☎04 91 08 16 40; www.rtm.fr; rue Jacques Bory; Ⓜ Gare St-Charles SNCF), which is a junction for both metro lines. The **left-luggage office** (Consignes Automatiques; ⏲8.15am-9pm) is next to platform A. Sample fares:

Avignon (€22, 1¼ hours, hourly)
Nice (€38, 2½ hours, up to six per day)

Paris Gare de Lyon (from €76, 3½ hours, at least hourly)

Aix-en-Provence

POP 142,668

Aix-en-Provence is to Provence what the Left Bank is to Paris: a pocket of bohemian chic crawling with students. It's hard to believe that 'Aix' (pronounced ex) is just 25km from chaotic, exotic Marseille. The city has been a cultural centre since the Middle Ages (two of the town's most famous sons are painter Paul Cézanne and novelist Émile Zola), but for all its polish, it's still a laid-back Provençal town at heart.

Sights

A stroller's paradise, Aix' highlight is the mostly pedestrian old city, **Vieil Aix**. South of cours Mirabeau, the **Quartier Mazarin** was laid out in the 17th century, and is home to some of Aix' finest buildings.

The **Aix City Pass** (http://booking.aixenprovencetourism.com; adult 24/48/72hr €25/34/43, child €17/21/26) covers entry to all the major museums and Cézanne sights, plus public transport and a guided walking tour.

★Musée Granet MUSEUM

(☎04 42 52 88 32; www.museegranet-aixenprovence.fr; place St-Jean de Malte; adult/child €5.50/free; ⏱10am-7pm Tue-Sun mid-Jun–Sep, noon-6pm Tue-Sun Oct–mid-Jun) Aix established one of France's first public museums here, on the site of a former Hospitallers' priory, in 1838. Nearly 200 years of acquisitions (including bequests by the eponymous François Marius Granet, himself a painter of note) have resulted in a collection of more than 12,000 works, including pieces by Picasso, Léger, Matisse, Monet, Klee, Van Gogh and, crucially, nine pieces by local boy Cézanne. This fabulous art museum sits right near the top of France's artistic must-sees.

★Caumont Centre d'Art HISTORIC BUILDING

(☎04 42 20 70 01; www.caumont-centredart.com; 3 rue Joseph Cabassol; adult/child €6.50/free; ⏱10am-7pm May-Sep, to 6pm Oct-Apr) The Caumont is a stellar art space housed inside the Mazarin quarter's grandest 18th-century *hôtel particulier* (mansion). While there are three quality exhibitions each year, plus concerts and other events, it's the building itself that's the star of the show. Built from local honey-coloured stone, its palatial rooms are stuffed with antiques and objets d'art

WORTH A TRIP

VAN GOGH'S ARLES

If the winding streets and colourful houses of Arles seem familiar, it's hardly surprising – Vincent van Gogh lived here for much of his life in a yellow house on place Lamartine, and the town regularly featured in his canvases. His original house was destroyed during WWII, but you can still follow in Vincent's footsteps on the evocative **Van Gogh walking circuit** – the **tourist office** (☎04 90 18 41 20; www.arlestourisme.com; 9 blvd des Lices; ⏱9am-6.45pm Apr-Sep, 9am-4.45pm Mon-Sat, 10am-1pm Sun Oct-Mar; 📶) sells maps (€1). You won't see many of the artist's masterpieces in Arles, however, although the modern art gallery **Fondation Vincent Van Gogh** (☎04 90 93 08 08; www.fondation-vincentvangogh-arles.org; 35ter rue du Docteur Fanton; adult/child €9/free; ⏱10am-7pm Jul & Aug, from 11am Sep-Jun) always has one on show, as well as contemporary exhibitions inspired by the Impressionist.

Two millennia ago, Arles was a major Roman settlement. The town's 20,000-seat amphitheatre, known as **Les Arènes** (Amphithéâtre; ☎08 91 70 03 70; www.arenes-arles.com; Rond-Point des Arènes; adult/child €6/free, incl Théâtre Antique €9/free; ⏱9am-8pm Jul & Aug, to 7pm May, Jun & Sep, shorter hours Oct-Apr), nowadays hosts host outdoor spectacles, concerts, races and the *corrida* – bullfighting that is banned in most parts of France and which has come under intense scrutiny for its cruelty.

There are buses to/from Aix-en-Provence (€11, 1¼ hours) and regular trains to/from Nîmes (€7.50, 30 minutes to one hour), Marseille (€13, one hour) and Avignon (€6, 20 minutes).

attesting to the opulence of the house's aristocratic past.

Atelier Cézanne MUSEUM

(☎04 42 21 06 53; www.atelier-cezanne.com; 9 av Paul Cézanne; adult/child €6.50/free, audio guide €3; ⏲10am-6pm Jun-Sep, 10am-12.30pm & 2-6pm Apr & May, 10.30am-12.30pm & 2-5pm Oct-Mar, closed Sun Dec-Feb; 🚌5, 12) Cézanne's last studio, where he worked from 1902 until his death four years later, has been painstakingly preserved. Some elements have been recreated: not all the tools and still-life models strewn around the room were his. Though the studio is inspiring, and home to periodic exhibitions, none of Cezanne's works actually hang there. It's a leisurely walk to the studio at Lauves hill, 1.5km north of central Aix, or you can take the bus.

Sleeping

★Hôtel les Quatre Dauphins BOUTIQUE HOTEL $$

(☎04 42 38 16 39; www.lesquatredauphins.fr; 54 rue Roux Alphéran; s/d €101/123; ❄📶) This sweet 13-room hotel slumbers in a former 19th-century mansion in one of the loveliest parts of town. Rooms are fresh and clean, decorated with a great eye and equipped with excellent modern bathrooms. Those with sloping, beamed ceilings in the attic are quaint but are not for those who don't pack light – the terracotta-tiled staircase is not suitcase friendly.

★L'Épicerie B&B $$

(☎06 74 40 89 73; 12 rue du Cancel; r from €110; 📶) It's best to connect by phone to this intimate B&B on a backstreet in Vieil Aix. The creation of born-and-bred Aixois lad Luc, the breakfast room re-creates a 1950s grocery store, while the flowery garden out the back is perfect for evening dining and weekend brunch (book ahead for both). Breakfast is a veritable feast. Two rooms accommodate families of four.

Eating

No spot revs up taste buds more than the city's daily **food market** on place Richelme. Restaurant terraces spill out across dozens of charm-heavy old-town squares: place des Trois Ormeaux, place des Augustins, place Ramus and vast Forum des Cardeurs are particular favourites.

★Farinoman Fou BAKERY $

(www.farinomanfou.fr; 3 rue Mignet; bread €1.40-3; ⏲7am-7pm Tue-Sat) To appeal to bread connoisseurs, in Aix as in any part of France, you need to know your dough. Judging by the lines typically spilling out of this shop onto place des Prêcheurs, artisanal *boulanger* Benoît Fradette clearly does. The bakery has no need to invest in a fancy shopfront –the customers jostle for space with the bread ovens and dough-mixing tubs.

Jardin Mazarin FRENCH $$

(☎04 28 31 08 36; www.jardinmazarin.com; 15 rue du 4 Septembre; lunch/dinner menus €23/29; ⏲9am-3pm & 7-10.30pm Mon-Sat) This elegant restaurant is set perfectly on the ground floor of a handsome 18th-century *hôtel particulier* in the Quartier Mazarin. Two salons sit beneath splendid beamed ceilings, but the real gem is the verdant fountain-centred garden, which comes into its own in summer. Expect knowledgeable treatment of local, seasonal produce (such as truffles and asparagus) from the kitchen.

Information

Tourist Office (☎04 42 16 11 61; www.aixenprovencetourism.com; 300 av Giuseppe Verdi, Les Allées; ⏲8.30am-7pm Mon-Sat, 10am-1pm & 2-6pm Sun Apr-Sep, 8.30am-6pm Mon-Sat Oct-Mar; 📶)

Getting There & Around

Consult www.lepilote.com for timetables, fares and itineraries for public transport journeys to/from Aix and www.navetteaixmarseille.com for shuttle buses to/from Marseille.

BUS

Aix' **bus station** (Gare routière; ☎04 42 91 26 80, 08 91 02 40 25; 6 bd Coq) is a 10-minute walk southwest from La Rotonde. Services include Avignon (€18, 1¼ hours, six daily), Marseille (€9, 40 minutes, every 10 minutes Monday to Saturday, fewer on Sunday) and Nice (€30, 2¼ hours, three to five daily).

TRAIN

The **city centre train station** (☎08 00 11 40 23; www.ter.sncf.com/paca; av Maurice Blondel; ⏲5am-1am Mon-Sat, from 6am Sun), at the southern end of av Victor Hugo, serves Marseille (€8.30, 45 minutes).

Aix' **TGV station** (☎0892 35 35 35; www.gares-sncf.com; rte Départementale 9;

⌚5.30am-1am), 15km from the centre, is a stop on the high-speed Paris–Marseille line. Destinations include Avignon (from €13, 25 minutes, one or two per hour) and Lyon (from €33, 1½ hours, around hourly).

Bus 40 runs from the TGV station to Aix' bus station (€4.30, 15 minutes, every 15 minutes).

Avignon

POP 91,250

Hooped by 4.3km of superbly preserved stone ramparts, this graceful city is the belle of Provence's ball. Its turn as the papal seat of power has bestowed Avignon with a treasury of magnificent art and architecture, none grander than the massive World Heritage–listed fortress-cum-palace known as the Palais des Papes. Famed for its annual performing arts festival, these days Avignon is a lively student city and an ideal spot to step out into the surrounding region.

Sights

With the free **Avignon Passion** card, available at the tourist office and museums, pay full price at the first museum or monument you visit, then get a discount at every subsequent site visited.

★Palais des Papes PALACE

(Papal Palace; ☎tickets 04 32 74 32 74; www.palais-des-papes.com; place du Palais; adult/child €12/10, with Pont St-Bénézet €14.50/11.50; ⌚9am-8pm Jul, to 8.30pm Aug, shorter hours Sep-Jun) The largest Gothic palace ever built, the Palais des Papes was erected by Pope Clement V, who abandoned Rome in 1309 in the wake of violent disorder after his election. Its immense scale illustrates the medieval might of the Roman Catholic church.

Ringed by 3m-thick walls, its cavernous halls, chapels and antechambers are largely bare today – but tickets now include tablet 'Histopads' revealing virtual-reality representations of how the building would have looked in all its papal pomp.

Musée du Petit Palais MUSEUM

(☎04 90 86 44 58; www.petit-palais.org; place du Palais; adult/child €6/free; ⌚10am-1pm & 2-6pm Wed-Mon) The archbishops' palace during the 14th and 15th centuries now houses outstanding collections of primitive, pre-Rennaissance, 13th- to 16th-century Italian religious paintings by artists including Botticelli, Carpaccio and Giovanni di Paolo – the most famous is Botticelli's *La Vierge et l'Enfant* (1470).

★Pont St-Bénézet BRIDGE

(☎tickets 04 32 74 32 74; bd de la Ligne; adult/child 24hr ticket €5/4, with Palais des Papes €14.50/11.50; ⌚9am-8pm Jul, to 8.30pm Aug, shorter hours Sep-Jun) Legend says Pastor Bénézet (a former shepherd) had three visions urging him to build a bridge across the Rhône. Completed in 1185, the 900m-long bridge linked Avignon with Villeneuve-lès-Avignon. It was rebuilt several times before all but four of its 22 spans were washed away in the 1600s, leaving the far side marooned in the middle of the Rhône. There are fine (and free) views from Rocher des Doms park, Pont Édouard Daladier and Île de la Barthelasse's chemin des Berges.

Festivals & Events

★Festival d'Avignon PERFORMING ARTS

(☎box office 04 90 14 14 14; www.festival-avignon.com; ⌚Jul) The three-week annual Festival d'Avignon is one of the world's great performing-arts festivals. Over 40 international works of dance and drama play to 100,000-plus spectators at venues around town. Tickets don't go on sale until springtime, but hotels sell out by February.

Sleeping

★Les Jardins de Baracane B&B $$

(☎06 11 14 88 54; www.lesjardinsdebaracane.fr; 12 rue Baracane; r €125-310; P❄☜≋) This 18th-century house near place des Corps Saints is owned by an architect, so it's been sensitively and tastefully renovated. Wood beams, stone walls and period detailing feature in all rooms, but the best are the two suites, which are posh enough for a pope. There's a great pool, and breakfast is served in the garden under a huge wisteria tree.

★Hôtel La Mirande HOTEL $$$

(☎04 90 14 20 20; www.la-mirande.fr; 4 place de la Mirande; d from €450; ❄@☜) The address to sleep in Avignon *en luxe*. It's located literally in the shadow of the palace, and stepping inside feels more like entering an aristocrat's château than a hotel, with oriental rugs, gold-threaded tapestries, marble statues and oil paintings everywhere you look. Rooms are equally opulent, and the best overlook the interior garden where afternoon tea is served.

Eating

Place de l'Horloge is crammed with touristy restaurants that don't offer the best cuisine or value in town. Delve instead into the pedestrian old city where ample pretty squares like place des Châtaignes or place de la Principle tempt.

★Maison Violette BAKERY **$**

(☎06 59 44 62 94; place des Corps Saints; ⊙7am-7.30pm Mon-Sat) We simply defy you to walk into this bakery and not instantly be tempted by the stacks of baguettes, *ficelles* and *pains de campagnes* loaded up on the counter, not to mention the orderly ranks of éclairs, *millefeuilles,* fruit tarts and cookies lined up irresistibly behind the glass. Go on, a little bit of what you fancy does you good, *non*?

Hygge CAFE **$**

(☎04 65 81 06 87; 25 place des Carmes; 2-/3-course lunch €13.90/15.90; ⊙8am-3pm Mon-Wed, 8am-3pm & 6-10pm Thu-Sat) Having worked at a smorgasbord of high-flying restaurants (including Copenhagen's Noma and Avignon's La Mirande), Jacques Pampiri opened his own place in Avignon, and it's a big hit with the locals. Hearty, wholesome organic food is dished up canteen-style to keep costs down, and the mix-and-match thrift-shop decor is great fun. Arrive early for a prime table on the square.

★Restaurant L'Essentiel FRENCH **$$**

(☎04 90 85 87 12; www.restaurantlessentiel.com; 2 rue Petite Fusterie; menus €32-46; ⊙noon-2pm & 7-9.45pm Tue-Sat) In the top tier of Avignon's restaurants for many a year, this elegant restaurant remains (as its name suggests) as essential as ever. First there's the setting: a lovely, honey-stoned *hôtel particulier* (mansion) with a sweet courtyard garden. Then there's the food: rich, sophisticated French dining of the first order, replete with the requisite foams, veloutés and reductions.

Information

Tourist Office (☎04 32 74 32 74; www.avignon-tourisme.com; 41 cours Jean Jaurès; ⊙9am-6pm Mon-Sat, 10am-5pm Sun Apr-Oct, shorter hours Nov-Mar) Guided walking tours, information on boat trips along the River Rhône and wine-tasting trips to nearby vineyards.

Getting There & Around

AIR

Aéroport Avignon-Provence (AVN; ☎04 90 81 51 51; www.avignon.aeroport.fr) is in Caumont, 8km southeast of Avignon, and has direct flights to London, Birmingham and Southampton in the UK.

From the airport, LER bus 22 (www.info-ler.fr; €1.50) goes to the Avignon bus station and TGV station.

BUS

Avignon's **bus station** (bd St-Roch; ⊙information window 8am-7pm Mon-Fri, to 1pm Sat) is a major bus hub for the Vaucluse *département*. Services include Aix-en-Provence (€18, 1¼ hours, two to six daily) and Arles (€7.80, 50 minutes, five daily).

TRAIN

Avignon has two train stations: **Gare Avignon Centre** (42 bd St-Roch), on the southern edge of the walled town, and **Gare Avignon TGV**, 4km southwest in Courtine. Shuttle trains link the two every 15 to 20 minutes (€1.60, six minutes, 6am to 11pm).

Eurostar (www.eurostar.com) services operate one to five times weekly between Avignon TGV and London St Pancras (from €78, 5¾ hours) en route to/from Marseille.

Frequent TGV services include Aix-en-Provence (€12.50 to €21, 25 minutes), Marseille (€12.50 to €19, 40 minutes), Nice (€36 to €62, 3¼ hours) and Paris (€45 to €90, 3½ hours).

THE FRENCH RIVIERA & MONACO

With its glistening seas, idyllic beaches and fabulous weather, the French Riviera (Côte d'Azur in French) screams exclusivity, extravagance and glitz. It has been a favourite getaway for the European jet set since Victorian times and there is nowhere more chichi or glam in France than St-Tropez, Cannes and super-rich, sovereign Monaco.

Nice

POP 342,522

With its mix of real-city grit, old-world opulence, year-round sunshine, vibrant street life and shimmering seaside shores, no place in France compares with Nice. But then this is the queen of the Riviera who truly understand what good living is all about: the very best of Mediterranean food, free museums, exceptional art, and alpine wilderness within an hour's drive.

Sights & Activities

The **French Riviera Pass** (www.frenchrivierapass.com; 1/2/3 days €26/38/56) includes access to a number of sights in Nice and along the Riviera. Buy it online or at the Nice tourist office (p242).

★Promenade des Anglais ARCHITECTURE

(8, 52, 62) The most famous stretch of seafront in Nice – if not France – is this vast paved promenade, which gets its name from the English expat patrons who paid for it in 1822. It runs for the whole 4km sweep of the Baie des Anges with a dedicated lane for cyclists and skaters; if you fancy joining them, you can rent skates, scooters and bikes from **Roller Station** (04 93 62 99 05; www.roller-station.fr; 49 quai des États-Unis; skates, boards & scooters per hour/day €5/15, bicycles €5/18; 9am-8pm Jul & Aug, 10am-7pm May, Jun, Sep & Oct, to 6pm Nov-Apr).

★Vieux Nice HISTORIC SITE

(1 to Opéra-Vieille Ville/Cathédrale-Vieille Ville) Getting lost among the dark, narrow, winding alleyways of Nice's old town is a highlight. The layout has barely changed since the 1700s, and it's now packed with delis, restaurants, boutiques and bars, but the centrepiece remains **cours Saleya**: a massive market square that's permanently thronging in summer. The **food market** (6am-1.30pm Tue-Sun) is perfect for fresh produce and foodie souvenirs, while the **flower market** (6am-5.30pm Tue-Sat, 6.30am-1.30pm Sun) is worth visiting just for the colours and fragrances. A **flea market** (Marché à la Brocante; 7am-6pm Mon) is held on Monday.

Colline du Château PARK

(Castle Hill; 8.30am-8pm Apr-Sep, to 6pm Oct-Mar) FREE For the best views over Nice's red-tiled rooftops, climb the winding staircases up to this wooded outcrop on the eastern edge of the old town. It's been occupied since ancient times; archaeological digs have revealed Celtic and Roman remains, and the site was later occupied by a medieval castle that was razed by Louis XIV in 1706 (only the 16th-century **Tour Bellanda** remains). There are various entrances, including one beside the tower, or you can cheat and ride the free **lift** (Ascenseur du Château; rue des Ponchettes; 9am-8pm Jun-Aug, to 7pm Apr, May & Sep, 10am-6pm Oct-Mar).

Musée Masséna MUSEUM

(04 93 91 19 10; 65 rue de France; museum pass 24hr/7 days €10/20; 10am-6pm Wed-Mon late Jun–mid-Oct, from 11am rest of year; 8, 52, 62 to Congrès/Promenade) Originally built as a holiday home for Prince Victor d'Essling (the grandson of one of Napoléon's favourite generals, Maréchal Massena), this lavish belle époque building is another of the city's iconic architectural landmarks. Built between 1898 and 1901 in grand neoclassical style with an Italianate twist, it's now a fascinating museum dedicated to the history of the Riviera – taking in everything from holidaying monarchs to expat Americans, the boom of tourism and the enduring importance of Carnaval.

Musée d'Art Moderne et d'Art Contemporain GALLERY

(MAMAC; 04 97 13 42 01; www.mamac-nice.org; place Yves Klein; museum pass 24hr/7 days €10/20; 10am-6pm Tue-Sun late Jun–mid-Oct, from 11am rest of year; 1 to Garibaldi) European and American avant-garde works from the 1950s to the present are the focus of this sprawling multilevel museum. Highlights include many works by Christo and Nice's neorealists: Niki de Saint Phalle, César, Arman and Yves Klein. The building's rooftop also works as an exhibition space (with knockout panoramas of Nice to boot).

★Musée Matisse GALLERY

(04 93 81 08 08; www.musee-matisse-nice.org; 164 av des Arènes de Cimiez; museum pass 24hr/7 days €10/20; 10am-6pm Wed-Mon late Jun–mid-Oct, from 11am rest of year; 15, 17, 20, 22 to Arènes/Musée Matisse) This museum, 2km north of the city centre in the leafy Cimiez quarter, houses a fascinating assortment of works by Matisse, including oil paintings, drawings, sculptures, tapestries and Matisse's famous paper cut-outs. The permanent collection is displayed in a red-ochre 17th-century Genoese villa in an olive grove. Temporary exhibitions are in the futuristic

Nice

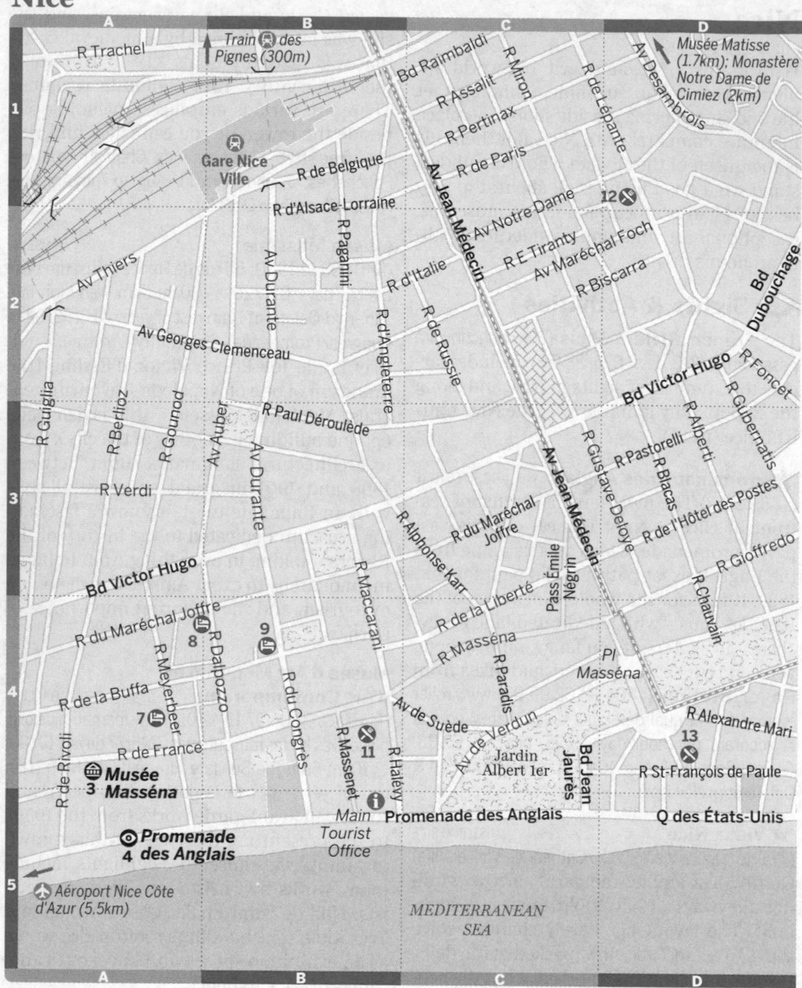

Nice

Top Sights

1 Colline du Château ... F5
2 Musée d'Art Moderne et d'Art Contemporain ... F2
3 Musée Masséna ... A4
4 Promenade des Anglais ... A5
5 Vieux Nice ... E5

Activities, Courses & Tours

6 Roller Station ... E5

Sleeping

7 Hostel Meyerbeer Beach ... A4
8 Hôtel Windsor ... A4
9 Nice Garden Hôtel ... B4

Eating

10 Chez Palmyre ... E4
11 La Femme du Boulanger ... B4
12 Mama Baker ... D1
13 Peixes ... D4

Shopping

14 Cours Saleya Flea Market ... E4
15 Cours Saleya Flower Market ... E4
16 Cours Saleya Food Market ... E4

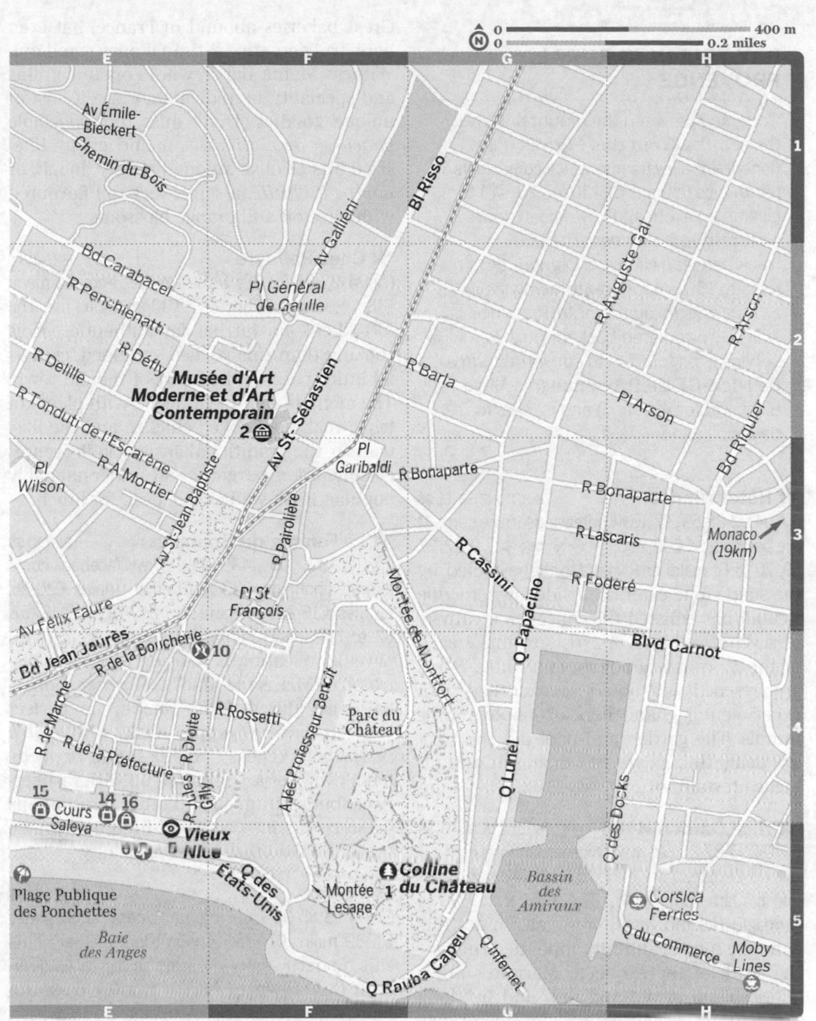

basement building. Matisse is buried in the **Monastère Notre Dame de Cimiez** (place du Monastère; ⏲8.30am-12.30pm & 2.30-6.30pm) cemetery, across the park from the museum.

Festivals & Events

★Carnaval de Nice CARNIVAL

(www.nicecarnaval.com; ⏲Feb-Mar) Held over a two-week period in late February and early March since 1294. Highlights include the *batailles de fleurs* (battles of flowers) and the ceremonial burning of the carnival king on Promenade des Anglais, followed by a fireworks display.

Sleeping

★Hostel Meyerbeer Beach HOSTEL $

(☎04 93 88 95 65; www.hostelmeyerbeer.com; 15 rue Meyerbeer; dm €25-50, s €80-90, d €90-100; 🚌7, 9, 22, 27, 59, 70 to Rivoli) It's easy to see why this cosy little hostel got voted Best in France in 2018. A welcoming mood prevails throughout, thanks to the congenial, international staff of four, a kitchen small enough to make you feel like you're cooking at home, and a cheerful, immaculate mix of private rooms and four- to eight-bed dorms, each with its own en suite bathroom.

OFF THE BEATEN TRACK

DAY TRIP INTO RURAL PROVENCE

Chugging between the mountains and the sea, the **Train des Pignes** (Pine Cone Train; www.trainprovence.com; single/return Nice to Digne €24.10/48.20; 1 to Libération) is one of Provence's most picturesque train rides. The 151km track between Nice and Digne-les-Bains rises to 1000m for breathtaking views as it passes through Haute-Provence's scarcely populated backcountry. The service runs four times daily from **Gare de Nice-CF de Provence** (rue Alfred Binet; 1 to Libération) and is ideal for a day trip inland.

★Hôtel Windsor BOUTIQUE HOTEL $$
(04 93 88 59 35; www.hotelwindsornice.com; 11 rue Dalpozzo; d €92-290; ; 7, 9, 22, 27, 59, 70 to Grimaldi or Rivoli) Don't be fooled by the staid stone exterior: inside, owner Odile Redolfi has enlisted the collective creativity of several well-known artists to make each of the 57 rooms uniquely appealing. Some are frescoed and others are adorned with experimental chandeliers or photographic murals. The garden and pool out the back are delightful, as are the small bar and attached restaurant.

★Nice Garden Hôtel BOUTIQUE HOTEL $$
(04 93 87 35 62; www.nicegardenhotel.com; 11 rue du Congrès; s €75-85, d €110-140; reception 8.30am-9pm; ; 7, 9, 22, 27, 59, 70 to Grimaldi) Behind heavy iron gates hides this gem: the nine beautifully appointed rooms – the work of the exquisite Marion – are a subtle blend of old and new and overlook a delightful garden with a glorious orange tree. Amazingly, all this charm and peacefulness is just two blocks from the promenade. Breakfast costs €9.

Eating

To lunch with locals, grab a pew in the midday sun on one of the many place Garibaldi cafe terraces. There are lots of restaurants on cours Saleya, but quality can be variable.

★Mama Baker BAKERY $
(06 23 91 33 86; www.facebook.com/Mamabakernice; 13 rue de Lépante; items from €2; 7am-2pm & 3-7pm Mon-Fri, 7am-6pm Sat; 4 to Toselli) Great bakeries abound in France, but even here, truly creative artisanal ones stand out. Witness Mama Baker, where organic grains and speciality ingredients go into a host of unique goodies. Don't miss the delectable *bouchées aux olives,* soft and crispy bite-sized bits of olive-studded cheesy dough, or *pompe à l'huile,* a semisweet roll flavoured with olive oil and orange blossoms.

★Chez Palmyre FRENCH $
(04 93 85 72 32; 5 rue Droite; 3-course menu €18; noon-1.30pm & 7-9.30pm Mon, Tue, Thu & Fri) Look no further for authentic Niçois cooking than this packed, cramped, convivial little space in the heart of the old town. The menu is very meat-heavy, with plenty of tripe, veal, pot-cooked chicken and the like, true to the traditional tastes of Provençal cuisine. It's a bargain, and understandably popular. Book well ahead, even for lunch.

★La Femme du Boulanger BISTRO $$
(04 89 03 43 03; www.facebook.com/femmeduboulanger; 3 rue Raffali; mains €20-25, tartines €16-22; 9am-3pm & 7-11pm; 8, 52, 62 to Massenet) This back-alley gem with pavement seating is a vision of French bistro bliss. Mains like duck *à l'orange,* honey-balsamic glazed lamb shank, or perfect *steak au poivre* (pepper steak) with *gratin dauphinois* (cheesy potatoes) and perfectly tender veggies are followed up with raspberry clafoutis, tiramisu and other scrumptious desserts. Tartines on wood-fired homemade bread are the other house speciality.

★Peixes SEAFOOD $$
(04 93 85 96 15; 4 rue de l'Opéra; small plates €12-19, mains €17-35; noon-10pm Tue-Sat) This chic modern seafood eatery is the latest jewel in the crown of Niçois master restaurateur Armand Crespo. All done up in white-and-turquoise nautical decor, with dangling fish eyeball light fixtures and murals of a tentacle-haired mermaid ensnaring a fishing boat, it specialises in fresh local fish turned into delicious ceviches, tartares and Japanese-style tatakis by chefs in the open kitchen.

Information

Tourist Office (04 92 14 46 14; www.nicetourisme.com; 5 Promenade des Anglais; 9am-7pm daily Jun-Sep, to 6pm Mon-Sat Oct-May; ; 8, 52, 62 to Massenet)

Getting There & Around

AIR

Nice-Côte d'Azur Airport (NCE; ☎08 20 42 33 33; www.nice.aeroport.fr; 📶; 🚌98, 99, 🚊2) is France's second-largest airport and has international flights to Europe, North Africa and the USA, with regular and low-cost airlines.

Buses 98 and 99 link the airport's terminal with Promenade des Anglais and Nice train station respectively (€6, 35 minutes, every 20 minutes).

BOAT

Corsica Ferries (☎04 92 00 42 76; www.corsicaferries.com; quai du Commerce; 🚊2 to Port Lympia) and **Moby Lines** (☎08 00 90 11 44; www.mobylines.fr; Quai du Commerce; 🚊2 to Port Lympia) offer regular ferry services from Nice to Corsica. Corsica Ferries also serves Golfo Aranci in Sardinia.

TRAIN

From Nice's train station, 1.2km north of the beach, there are frequent services to Cannes (€7.20, 40 minutes), Marseille (€36 to €42, 2¾ hours), Monaco (€4.10, 25 minutes) and other Riviera destinations.

Cannes

POP 74,285

Most have heard of Cannes and its celebrity film festival. The latter only lasts for two weeks in May, but the buzz and glitz linger all year thanks to regular visits from celebrities who come here to indulge in designer shopping, beaches and the palace hotels of the Riviera's most glam seafront strip, bd de la Croisette.

Sights & Activities

★La Croisette — ARCHITECTURE

The multi-starred hotels and couture shops lining the iconic bd de la Croisette (aka La Croisette) may be the preserve of the rich and famous, but anyone can enjoy strolling the palm-shaded promenade – a favourite pastime among Cannois at night, when it twinkles with bright lights. Views of the Baie de Cannes and nearby Estérel mountains are beautiful, and seafront hotel palaces dazzle in all their stunning art deco glory.

Le Suquet — HISTORIC SITE

Follow rue St-Antoine and snake your way up through the narrow streets of Le Suquet, Cannes' oldest district. Up top you'll find the site of Cannes' medieval castle, place de la Castre, flanked by the 17th-century Église Notre-Dame de l'Esperance. Climb the adjacent ramparts for great views of the bay.

Îles de Lérins — ISLAND

Although just 20 minutes away by boat, Cannes' tranquil islands feel far from the madding crowd. **Île Ste-Marguerite**, where the mysterious Man in the Iron Mask was incarcerated during the late 17th century, is known for its bone-white beaches, eucalyptus groves and small marine museum. Tiny **Île St-Honorat** has been a monastery since the 5th century; you can visit the church and small chapels and stroll through the monks' vineyards.

Boats leave Cannes from quai des Îles on the western side of the harbour. **Trans Côte d'Azur** (☎04 92 98 71 30; www.trans-cote-azur.com; quai Max Laubeuf), **Riviera Lines** (☎04 92 98 71 31; www.riviera-lines.com; quai Max

DON'T MISS

THE CORNICHES

Some of the Riviera's most spectacular scenery stretches east between Nice and Monaco. A trio of *corniches* (coastal roads) hugs the cliffs between the two seaside cities, each higher up the hill than the last. The middle *corniche* ends in Monaco; the upper and lower continue to Menton near the France–Italy border.

Corniche Inférieure (lower) Skimming the glittering, villa-studded shoreline, this road is all about belle époque glamour, the height of which can be seen at the extravagant **Villa Ephrussi de Rothschild** (☎04 93 01 33 09; www.villa-ephrussi.com/en; adult/child €14/11; ⏲10am-6pm Feb-Jun, Sep & Oct, to 7pm Jul & Aug, 2-6pm Mon-Fri, 10am-6pm Sat & Sun Nov Jan) in St-Jean-Cap Ferrat.

Moyenne (middle) Corniche The jewel in the Riviera crown undoubtedly goes to **Èze**, a medieval village spectacularly located on a rocky outcrop with dazzling views of the Med.

Grande (upper) Corniche The epitomy of 'scenic drive', with sublime panoramas unfolding at every bend. Stop in **La Turbie** for dramatic views of Monaco.

Laubeuf) and **Horizon** (☎04 92 98 71 36; www.horizon-lerins.com; quai Laubeuf) all run ferries to Île Ste-Marguerite, while **Planaria** (☎04 92 98 71 38; www.cannes-ilesdelerins.com; quai Max Laubeuf) covers Île St-Honorat.

Sleeping & Eating

Most private beaches have restaurants: expect to pay around €25 to €30 for a main of grilled fish or meat, or gourmet salad. Several streets just inland, such as rue Hoche, are filled with restaurants and bistros. Cheaper eats can be found in and around Cannes' atmospheric food market, **Marché Forville** (11 rue du Marché Forville; ⏰7.30am-1pm Tue-Fri, to 2pm Sat & Sun).

★Hôtel de Provence HOTEL $$
(☎04 93 38 44 35; www.hotel-de-provence.com; 9 rue Molière; s €93-140, d €110-247, ste €246-340; ⏰closed mid-Jan–early Mar; ❄📶) This traditional Provençal townhouse with buttermilk walls, lavender-blue shutters and a palm-lined entryway disguises a minimalist-chic interior. Almost every room sports a balcony, climaxing with a 7th-floor suite with stunning rooftop terrace. The Provence also has self-catering studios in the neighbourhood for three to six people. Breakfast costs €10.80.

★Bobo Bistro MEDITERRANEAN $$
(☎04 93 99 97 33; www.facebook.com/BoboBistro Cannes; 21 rue du Commandant André; pizzas €14-20, mains €18-31; ⏰noon-11pm) Predictably, it's a 'bobo' (bourgeois bohemian) crowd that gathers at this achingly cool bistro in Cannes' fashionable Carré d'Or. Decor is stylishly retro, with attention-grabbing objets d'art including a tableau of dozens of spindles of coloured yarn. Cuisine is local, seasonal and invariably organic: artichoke salad, tuna carpaccio with passion fruit, or roasted cod with mash *fait masion* (homemade).

★Table 22 MODERN EUROPEAN $$$
(Mantel; ☎04 93 39 13 10; www.restaurantmantel.com; 22 rue St-Antoine; menus €39-65, mains €35-46; ⏰noon-2pm Wed-Sun, 7.30-10pm daily) Discover why Noël Mantel is the hotshot of the Cannois gastronomic scene at his refined old-town restaurant. Service is stellar and the seasonally inspired cuisine divine – Mantel's food maximises local ingredients but isn't afraid to experiment with unusual flavours and cooking techniques. Spot the classic film stars on the walls, from Cary Grant to Alfred Hitchcock.

Information

Tourist Office (☎04 92 99 84 22; www.cannes-destination.fr; 1 bd de la Croisette; ⏰9am-7pm Mar-Oct, to 8pm Jul & Aug, 10am-6pm Nov-Feb; 📶)

Getting There & Away

Cannes' gleaming white train station is well connected with other towns along the coast.

Marseille (€33, 2¼ hours, half-hourly)
Monaco (€10, one hour, at least twice hourly)
Nice (€7.20, 40 minutes, every 15 minutes)

St-Tropez

POP 4305

In the soft autumn or winter light, it's hard to believe the pretty terracotta fishing village of St-Tropez is a stop on the Riviera celebrity circuit. It seems far removed from its glitzy siblings further up the coast, but come spring or summer, it's a different world: the population increases tenfold, prices triple and fun-seekers pile in to party till dawn, strut around the luxury-yacht-packed **Vieux Port** and enjoy the creature comforts of exclusive A-listers' beaches in the **Baie de Pampelonne**.

Sights & Activities

About 4km southeast of town is the start of magnificently sandy (and nudist) **Plage de Tahiti** and its continuation, celebrity **Plage de Pampelonne**, studded with legendary drinking and dining haunts.

★Musée de l'Annonciade GALLERY
(☎04 94 17 84 10; www.saint-tropez.fr/fr/culture/musee-de-lannonciade; place Grammont; adult/child €6/free; ⏰10am-6pm daily mid-Jun–Sep, Tue-Sun Oct–mid-Jun) In a gracefully converted 16th-century chapel, this small but famous museum showcases an impressive collection of modern art infused with that legendary Côte d'Azur light. Pointillist Paul Signac bought a house in St-Tropez in 1892 and introduced other artists to the area. The museum's collection includes his *St-Tropez, Le Quai* (1899) and *St-Tropez, Coucher de Soleil au Bois de Pins* (1896). Vuillard, Bonnard and Maurice Denis (the

self-named 'Nabis' group) have a room to themselves.

★La Ponche HISTORIC SITE

Shrug off the hustle of the port in St-Tropez' historic fishing quarter, La Ponche, northeast of the Vieux Port. From the southern end of quai Frédéric Mistral, place Garrezio sprawls east from 10th-century **Tour Suffren** to place de l'Hôtel de Ville. From here, rue Guichard leads southeast to iconic **Église de St-Tropez** (Eglise Notre Dame de l'Assomption; rue Commandant Guichard). Follow rue du Portail Neuf south to **Chapelle de la Miséricorde** (1-5 rue de la Miséricorde; ⌚10am-6pm).

★Citadelle de St-Tropez MUSEUM

(☎04 94 97 59 43; www.saint-tropez.fr/fr/culture/citadelle; 1 montée de la Citadelle; adult/child €3/free; ⌚10am-6.30pm Apr-Sep, to 5.30pm Oct-Mar; 👪) Built in 1602 to defend the coast against Spain, the citadel dominates the hillside overlooking St-Tropez to the east. The views are fantastic, as are the exotic peacocks wandering the grounds. Its dungeons are home to the excellent **Musée de l'Histoire Maritime**, an interactive museum that traces the history of humans at sea through fishing, trading, exploration, travel and the navy. The particular focus, of course, is Tropezienne and Provençal seafarers.

Sleeping & Eating

Celebrity studded St-Trop is no shoestring destination, although campgrounds do sit southeast along Plage de Pampelonne.

Tuesday and Saturday mornings mean market day on place des Lices. Don't leave town without sampling *tarte Tropézienne,* an orange-blossom-flavoured double sponge cake filled with thick cream, created by Polish baker A Mickla in 1955.

★Le Café CAFE $$

(☎04 94 97 44 69; www.lecafe.fr; Traverse des Lices; 2-course lunch menu €18, mains €22-29; ⌚8am-11pm) Wetting whistles since 1789, this historic cafe is where artists and painters preferred to hang out back in the days when St-Trop was still a sleepy port. Happily, it has clung on to its no-nonsense roots - you'll find solid dishes such as pot-roasted chicken, mussels and grilled fish on the menu.

Information

Tourist Office (☎08 92 68 48 28; www.sainttropeztourisme.com; quai Jean Jaurès; ⌚9.30am-1.30pm & 3-7.30pm Jul & Aug, 9.30am-12.30pm & 2-7pm Apr-Jun, Sep & Oct, to 6pm Mon-Sat Nov-Mar) Runs occasional walking tours April to October, and also has a **kiosk** (⌚9am-6pm Jul & Aug) in Parking du Port in July and August.

Getting There & Away

VarLib (☎09 70 83 03 80; www.varlib.fr) Tickets cost €3 from the **bus station** (Gare Routière; ☎04 94 56 25 74; av du Général de Gaulle) for anywhere within the Var département (except Toulon-Hyères airport). Destinations include Ramatuelle (35 minutes, up to six daily) and St-Raphaël (1¼ to three hours, depending on traffic, hourly) via Grimaud and Port Grimaud, and Fréjus.

Buses serve Toulon-Hyères airport (€15, 1½ hours), but some require a transfer.

Monaco

POP 37,550 / TEL +377

Squeezed into just 200 hectares, this confetti principality might be the world's second-smallest country (the Vatican is smaller), but what it lacks in size it makes up for in attitude. Glitzy, glam and screaming hedonism to the core, Monaco is truly beguiling.

It is a sovereign state but has no border control. It has its own flag (red and white) and national holiday (19 November), and it uses the euro even though it's not part of the EU. Renowned as one of the world's most notorious tax havens and home to the annual Formula One Grand Prix, it can easily be visited as a day trip from Nice.

Sights

★Casino de Monte Carlo CASINO

(☎98 06 21 21; www.casinomontecarlo.com; place du Casino; morning visit incl audio guide adult/child Oct-Apr €14/10, May-Sep €17/12, salons ordinaires gaming Oct-Apr €14, May-Sep €17; ⌚visits 9am-1pm, gaming 2pm-late) Peeping inside Monte Carlo's legendary marble-and-gold casino is a Monaco essential. The building, open to visitors every morning, including the exclusive *salons privés*, is Europe's most lavish example of belle époque architecture. Prince Charles III spearheaded the casino's development and in 1866, three years after its inauguration, the name 'Monte Carlo' – Ligurian for 'Mount Charles' in honour of the prince – was coined. To gamble here, visit after 2pm (when a strict over-18s-only admission rule kicks in).

★Musée Océanographique de Monaco AQUARIUM
(☎93 15 36 00; www.oceano.mc; av St-Martin; adult/child high season €16/12, low season €11/7; ⊙9.30am-8pm Jul & Aug, 10am-7pm Apr-Jun & Sep, to 6pm Oct-Mar) Stuck dramatically to the edge of a cliff since 1910, the world-renowned Musée Océanographique de Monaco, founded by Prince Albert I (1848–1922), is a stunner. Its centrepiece is its aquarium with a 6m-deep lagoon where sharks and marine predators are separated from colourful tropical fish by a coral reef. Upstairs, two huge colonnaded rooms retrace the history of oceanography and marine biology (and Prince Albert's contribution to the field) through photographs, old equipment, numerous specimens and interactive displays.

Le Rocher HISTORIC SITE
Monaco Ville, also called Le Rocher, is the only part of Monaco to have retained its original old town, complete with small, windy medieval lanes. The old town thrusts skywards on a pistol-shaped rock, its strategic location overlooking the sea that became the stronghold of the Grimaldi dynasty. There are various staircases up to Le Rocher; the best route up is via Rampe Major, which starts from place d'Armes near the port.

Eating

French and Italian cuisine prevail, though you'll find a full line-up of international fare. Don't miss the quintessential Monégasque speciality, *barbajuans* (deep-fried ravioli). Key restaurant zones include bd des Moulins near the Casino, the Les Condamines port and market, and the narrow streets behind the cathedral in Le Rocher.

★Marché de la Condamine MARKET $
(www.facebook.com/marche.condamine; 15 place d'Armes; ⊙7am-3pm Mon-Sat, to 2pm Sun) For tasty, excellent-value fare around shared tables, hit Monaco's fabulous food court, tucked beneath the arches behind the open-air place d'Armes market. Rock-bottom budget faves include fresh pasta from **Maison des Pâtes** (☎93 50 95 77; pasta €6.40-12; ⊙7am-3.30pm) and traditional Niçois *socca* from **Chez Roger** (☎93 50 80 20; socca €3; ⊙10am-3pm); there's also pizza and seafood from **Le Comptoir**, truffle cuisine from **Truffle Bistrot**, a deli, a cafe, a cheesemonger and more.

★La Montgolfière FUSION $$$
(☎97 98 61 59; www.lamontgolfiere.mc; 16 rue Basse; 3-/4-course menu €47/54; ⊙noon-2pm & 7.30-9.30pm Mon, Tue & Thu-Sat) Monégasque chef Henri Geraci has worked in some of the Riviera's top restaurants, but he's now happily settled at his own establishment down a shady alleyway near the palace. Escoffier-trained, he's faithful to the French classics, but his travels have inspired a fondness for Asian flavours, so expect some exotic twists. The restaurant's small and sought after, so reserve ahead.

Information

Tourist Office (☎92 16 61 16; www.visitmonaco.com; 2a bd des Moulins; ⊙9am-7pm Mon-Sat, 11am-1pm Sun)

Getting There & Away

Trains run about every 20 minutes to Nice (€4.10, 25 minutes). Access to the **station** (av Prince Pierre) is through pedestrian tunnels, lifts and escalators from allée Lazare Sauvaigo, pont Ste-Dévote, place Ste-Dévote and bd de Belgique/bd du Jardin Exotique.

CORSICA

The rugged island of Corsica (Corse in French) is officially a part of France but remains fiercely proud of its own culture, history and language. It's one of the Mediterranean's most dramatic islands, with a bevy of beautiful beaches, glitzy ports and a mountainous, maquis-covered interior to explore, as well as a wild, independent spirit all of its own.

Ajaccio

POP 68,490

Commanding a lovely sweep of bay, the handsome city of Ajaccio has the self-confidence that comes with a starring role in world history. Looming over this elegant port city is the spectre of Corsica's great general: Napoléon Bonaparte was born here in 1769 and the city is dotted with statues and museums relating to him.

Sights & Activities

Kiosks on the quayside at the foot of place du Maréchal Foch sell tickets for seasonal **boat trips** around the Golfe d'Ajaccio and Îles Sanguinaires (adult/child €27/15), and excursions to the Réserve Naturelle de Scandola (adult/child €58/38).

Maison Bonaparte MUSEUM
(☎04 95 21 43 89; www.musees-nationaux-napoleoniens.org; rue St-Charles; adult/child €7/free; ⏲10am-12.30pm & 1.15-5.30pm Tue-Sun Apr-Sep, 10.30am-12.30pm & 1.15-4.30pm Tue-Sun Oct-Mar) Unremarkable from the outside, the old-town house where Napoléon was born and spent his first nine years was ransacked by Corsican nationalists in 1793, requisitioned by English troops from 1794 to 1796, and eventually rebuilt by his mother. It's now preserved as a museum, filled with interesting displays and memorabilia despite the loss of its original furnishings and decor. Highlights include a glass medallion containing a lock of Napoléon's hair.

Palais Fesch – Musée des Beaux-Arts GALLERY
(☎04 95 26 26 26; www.musee-fesch.com; 50-52 rue du Cardinal Fesch; adult/child €8/5; ⏲9.15am-6pm May-Sep, 9am-5pm Oct-Apr) Established by Napoléon's uncle, cardinal Joseph Fesch (1763–1839), Ajaccio's superb art museum holds the largest French collection of Italian paintings outside the Louvre. Masterpieces by Titian, Fra Bartolomeo, Veronese, Bellini and Botticelli – look out for his *Vierge à l'Enfant Soutenu par un Ange* (Mother and Child Supported by an Angel) – are complemented by temporary exhibitions. Several rooms are devoted to Napoléon and his family, with one unlikely painting showing Napoléon atop a dromedary.

Sleeping & Eating

Key spots to linger over a lazy lunch include waterfront quai Napoléon at the old port, the main commercial street cours Napoléon, the car-free place de Gaulle, and the citadel end of beach-bound bd Pascal Rossini.

Hôtel Napoléon HOTEL $$
(☎04 95 51 54 00; www.hotel-napoleon-ajaccio.fr; 4 rue Lorenzo Vero; d €130-150; ❄📶) The warmth of a family-run hotel, coupled with a prime location on a side street in the heart of town, make the Napoléon an excellent midrange choice. Rooms are clean, bright and comfortable, despite their rather uninspiring decor; some of the nicest are on the 7th floor, with high ceilings and tall shuttered windows looking out on a leafy backyard.

★**Hôtel Demeure Les Mouettes** BOUTIQUE HOTEL $$$
(☎04 95 50 40 40; www.hotellesmouettes.fr; 9 cours Lucien Bonaparte; d €170-520; ⏲Apr-Oct; ❄📶🏊) Nestled right at the water's edge, 1.5km west of the old town, this colonnaded, peach-coloured 19th-century mansion is a dream. Views of the bay from its terraces – some rooms have their own private ones – and (heated) pool are exquisite; you may spot dolphins at dawn or dusk. Inside, the decor is elegantly understated and the service superb.

★**Le 20123** CORSICAN $$
(☎04 95 21 50 05; www.20123.fr; 2 rue du Roi de Rome; menu €36.50; ⏲7-11pm Apr-Oct, closed Mon Nov-Mar) This fabulous, one-of-a-kind restaurant originated in the village of Pila Canale (postcode 20123). When the owner moved to Ajaccio, the village came too – water fountain, life-sized dolls, central square and all. That might sound tacky, but it works; lively year-round, it's a charming, characterful night out, where everyone feasts on a seasonal four-course menu that's rich in meaty traditional cuisine.

★**L'Altru Versu** BISTRO $$
(☎04 95 50 05 22; www.facebook.com/mezzacquiresto; rte des Sanguinaires; mains €18-38, menus €29-54; ⏲12.30-2pm & 7.30-10.30pm Thu-Mon, plus 7.30-10.30pm Tue & Wed mid-May–mid-Oct, closed Jan & Feb) At this perennial favourite on Ajaccio's waterfront, 2.5km west of the old town, magnificent sea views complement the exquisite gastronomic creations of the Mezzacqui brothers (Jean-Pierre front of house, David powering the kitchen), from crispy minted prawns with pistachio cream to pork with honey and clementine zest.

Information

Tourist Office (☎04 95 51 53 03; www.ajaccio-tourisme.com; 3 bd du Roi Jérôme;

⌚8am-8pm Mon-Sat, 9am-1pm Sun Jul-Aug, shorter hours Sep-June, closed Sun Nov-Mar; 📶)

Getting There & Around

AIR

The **Aéroport d'Ajaccio Napoléon Bonaparte** (☎04 95 23 56 56; www.2a.cci.fr/Aeroport-Napoleon-Bonaparte-Ajaccio), 6km east of the town centre around the bay, is connected with the French mainland, and in summer with London Stansted, by Air Corsica. It's linked by the hourly bus 8 (€5, 30 minutes) to Ajaccio's train station (bus stop Marconajo). A taxi into town will cost around €25.

BOAT

Corsica Linea (☎04 95 57 69 10, 08 25 88 80 88; www.corsicalinea.com), **Corsica Ferries** (☎08 25 09 50 95; www.corsica-ferries.fr) and **La Méridionale** (☎04 91 99 45 09, 09 70 83 13 20; www.lameridionale.com) sail to the French mainland ports of Toulon (seven to 11 hours), Nice (6¼ to 10 hours) and Marseille (12 hours) from Ajaccio's **Gare Maritime** (☎04 95 51 55 45; quai L'Herminier). Buy tickets before sailings inside the combined bus and ferry terminal.

BUS

Local bus companies have ticket kiosks inside the ferry terminal building, the arrival/departure point for buses. Daily services include Bonifacio (€20, three hours), Porto (€12, two hours) and Porto-Vecchio (€20, 3¼ hours).

TRAIN

Services from the **train station** (☎04 95 23 11 03; www.cf-corse.corsica; place de la Gare), 1km north of the old town and 500m north of the ferry terminal, include the following:

Bastia (€21.60, 3¾ hours, five daily)

Calvi (€25.10, 4¾ hours, two daily; change at Ponte Leccia)

Bastia

POP 43,675

The bustling old port of Bastia has an alluring magnetism. Allow yourself at least a day to drink in the narrow old-town alleyways of Terra Vecchia, the seething Vieux Port, the dramatic 16th-century citadel perched up high, and the compelling history museum.

Sights & Activities

★Terra Vecchia — OLD TOWN

Criss-crossed by narrow lanes, Terra Vecchia is Bastia's heart and soul. Shady place de l'Hôtel de Ville hosts a lively morning market on Saturday and Sunday. One block west, baroque **Chapelle de l'Immaculée Conception** (rue des Terrasses; ⌚8am-7pm), with its elaborately painted barrel-vaulted ceiling, served as the seat of the short-lived Anglo-Corsican parliament in 1795. Further north, **Chapelle St-Roch** (rue Napoléon; ⌚8am-7pm) holds an 18th-century organ and trompe l'œil roof.

★Terra Nova — OLD TOWN

Looming above the harbour, Bastia's stern-walled citadel was built between the 15th and 17th centuries for the city's Genoese masters. Known as the Terra Nova, despite looking much older than the lower town, it's largely residential and uncommercialised. The amber-hued Palais des Gouverneurs now houses the Musée de Bastia, while the majestic **Cathédrale Ste-Marie** (rue de l'Évêché; ⌚8am-noon & 2-6.30pm Mon-Sat, to 5.30pm Oct-Mar, 8am-noon Sun) and the rococo **Église Ste-Croix** (rue de l'Évêché; ⌚9am-noon & 2-6pm Mon-Sat, to 5pm Oct-Mar), home to a mysterious black-oak crucifix found in the sea in 1428, stand side by side a few streets south.

★Vieux Port — HARBOUR

Bastia's Vieux Port is ringed by precariously tall, pastel-coloured tenements and buzzy brasseries, and overlooked by the twin-towered **Église St-Jean Baptiste** (4 rue du Cardinal Viale Préla; ⌚8am-noon & 3-7pm Mon-Sat). The best views of the harbour are from the citadel or the hillside park of Jardin Romieu, reached via a stately old staircase that twists up from the waterfront.

Musée de Bastia — MUSEUM

(☎04 95 31 09 12; www.musee-bastia.com; place du Donjon; adult/child €5/2.50, Oct-Apr free; ⌚10am-6.30pm daily Jul & Aug, Tue-Sun May-Jun & Sep, 9am-noon & 2-5pm Tue-Sat Oct-Apr) Occupying the former palace of Bastia's Genoese governors, set into the formidable walls of the citadel, this museum retraces the city's history from its early days as a Roman trading port. Expect plenty of busts and portraits of local dignitaries such as Louis-Napoleon Mattei, inventor of the Cap Corse aperitif. Admission also gives access to the palace's lovely upper gardens, with views over the port.

Sleeping & Eating

Market stalls packed with local produce spill across place de l'Hôtel de Ville every Saturday and Sunday morning.

★Hôtel-Restaurant La Corniche HOTEL $$
(☎04 95 31 40 98; www.hotel-lacorniche.com; D31, San Martino di Lota; d €88-130; ⏲mid-Feb–Dec; ❄📶🏊) Perched high in the hills, 8km along a tortuous road northwest of Bastia, this veteran family-run hotel makes a brilliant halfway house between city and wilderness. Summertime ushers in dreamy lounging in the bijou back garden, by the pool or on the panoramic terrace – the sea views will leave you smitten.

A Scudella CORSICAN $$
(☎09 51 70 79 46, 06 25 27 26 25; 10 rue Pino; mains €13-18, menu €25; ⏲6-11.30pm Tue-Sat) Tucked down a back alley near the Vieux Port, this is a superb spot to sample traditional mountain cuisine, from appetisers of fine Corsican charcuterie and *beignets de brocciu* (sweet, lemon-scented fritters filled with ricotta-like Brocciu cheese) to *veau aux olives* (stewed veal with olives) and *flan à la châtaigne* (chestnut flan).

Information

Tourist Office (☎04 95 54 20 40; www.bastia-tourisme.com; place St-Nicolas; ⏲8am-8pm Mon-Sat, 8am-1pm & 3-7pm Sun Jul & Aug, 8am-6pm Mon-Sat, to noon Sun May, Jun, Sep & Oct, 8.30am-noon & 2-6pm Mon-Fri Nov-Apr; 📶)

Getting There & Away

BOAT

Ferry companies including **Corsica Ferries** (☎08 25 09 50 95; www.corsica-ferries.fr), **Corsica Linea** (☎08 25 88 80 88; www.corsicalinea.com), **La Méridionale** (☎04 91 99 45 09, 09 70 83 13 20; www.lameridionale.com) and **Moby** (☎09 74 56 20 75, 04 95 34 84 94; www.mobycorse.fr) have information offices at **Bastia Port** (www.bastia.port.fr); they usually open for same-day ticket sales a couple of hours before sailings. Ferries sail to/from Marseille, Toulon and Nice (mainland France), and Livorno, Savona and Genoa (Italy).

TRAIN

Services from the **train station** (www.cf-corse.corsica; av Maréchal Sébastiani) run to Ajaccio (€21.60, 3¾ hours, five daily) via Corte (€10.10, 1¾ hours), and Calvi (€16.40, 3¼ hours, two daily) via Île Rousse (€13.50, 2¾ hours).

Bonifacio

POP 3015

With its glittering harbour, dramatic perch atop creamy white cliffs, and a stout citadel teetering above the cornflower-blue waters of the Bouches de Bonifacio, this dazzling port is an essential stop. Just a short hop from Sardinia, Bonifacio has a distinctly Italianate feel: sun-bleached townhouses, dangling washing lines and murky chapels cram the web of alleyways of the old citadel, while, down below on the harbourside, brasseries and boat kiosks tout their wares to the droves of day trippers.

Sights

★Citadel HISTORIC SITE
(Haute Ville) The great joy of visiting Bonifacio lies in strolling the tangled medieval lanes of the citadel. The paved steps of montée du Rastello and montée St-Roch lead up from the marina to its old gateway, the **Porte de Gênes**, complete with an original 16th-century drawbridge. Immediately inside, the **Bastion de l'Étendard** (adult/child €2.50/free, incl Escalier du Roi d'Aragon €3.50/free; ⏲9am-8pm mid-Apr–Sep, 10am-5pm rest of year) was the main stronghold of the fortified town. Built to hold heavy artillery, it now houses a small museum, and provides access to the ramparts, which offer jaw-dropping views.

Îles Lavezzi ISLAND
(day trips from Bonifacio adult/child €35/17.50) Paradise! If you love to splash in tranquil lapis lazuli waters, this protected clutch of uninhabited islets was made for you. The largest, the 65-hectare Île Lavezzi itself, is the most accessible. In summer, operators based at Bonifacio's marina (and also in Porto-Vecchio) offer boat trips; bring a picnic lunch.

Escalier du Roi d'Aragon HISTORIC SITE
(adult/child €2.50/free, incl Bastion de l'Étendard €3.50/free; ⏲9am-sunset Apr-Oct) Only accessible from the top, this impressive staircase cuts down Bonifacio's southern cliff-face. Legend says that during the siege of 1420, Aragonese troops carved its 187 steep steps from the bottom up in a single night, only to be rebuffed by Bonifacio's defenders at the top. In reality the steps gave access to an underground freshwater well.

Sleeping & Eating

Hôtel Le Colomba HOTEL $$
(☎04 95 73 73 44; www.hotel-bonifacio-corse.fr; 4-6 rue Simon Varsi; d €167; P ❄ 📶) Occupying a tastefully renovated 14th-century building, this hotel enjoys a prime location on a picturesque (steep) street, bang in the heart of the old town. Rooms are simple and smallish, but fresh and decorated with amenities including wrought-iron bedsteads, country fabrics, carved bedheads and/or chequerboard tiles. Other pluses include friendly staff and breakfast served in a medieval vaulted cellar.

★**Kissing Pigs** CORSICAN $
(☎04 95 73 56 09; 15 quai Banda del Ferro; mains €9-23, menus €21-23; ⏰11.30am-2.30pm & 6.30-11pm Tue-Sun) At water's edge beneath the citadel, and festooned with swinging sausages, this seductively cosy and friendly restaurant-cum-wine bar serves wonderfully rich and predominantly meaty Corsican dishes. Hearty casseroles include pork stewed with muscat and chestnuts, while the cheese and charcuterie platters are great for sharing. The Corsican wine list is another hit.

Information

Tourist Office (☎04 95 73 11 88; www.bonifacio.fr; 2 rue Fred Scamaroni; ⏰9am-8pm Jul & Aug, shorter hours rest of year, closed Sat & Sun Nov-Mar; 📶)

Getting There & Around

AIR

Aéroport de Figari-Sud-Corse (☎04 95 71 10 10; www.2a.cci.fr/Aeroport-Figari-Sud-Corse), 20km north of Bonfacio, welcomes domestic flights from France, plus seasonal services from London Stansted on Air Corsica, and London Gatwick on EasyJet. There's no shuttle-bus service to Bonifacio, though **Transports Rossi** (☎04 95 73 11 88; www.corsicabus.org) runs shuttles to Porto-Vecchio. Car rental is available, while a taxi into Bonifacio costs about €45.

BOAT

Italian ferry operators **Moby** (☎04 95 34 84 94, 09 74 56 20 75; www.mobycorse.fr) and **Blu Navy** (☎05 65 26 97 10; www.blunavytraghetti.com) run seasonal boats between Bonifacio and Santa Teresa Gallura (Sardinia); sailing time is 50 minutes.

BUS

Eurocorse Voyages (☎04 95 21 06 30; www.eurocorse.com) runs daily buses to Porto-Vecchio (€8, 30 minutes) and Ajaccio (€20, three hours).

SURVIVAL GUIDE

Directory A–Z

ACCESSIBLE TRAVEL

While France presents evident challenges for *visiteurs handicapés* (disabled visitors), particularly those with mobility issues – think cobblestones, cafe-lined streets that are a nightmare to navigate in a wheelchair *(fauteuil roulant)*, a lack of kerb ramps, older public facilities and many budget hotels without lifts – efforts are being made to improve the situation.

➡ Paris' tourist office runs the excellent 'Tourisme & Handicap' initiative whereby museums, cultural attractions, hotels and restaurants that provide access or special assistance or facilities for those with physical, mental, visual and/or hearing disabilities display a special logo at their entrances. For a list of qualifying places, go to www.parisinfo.com and click on 'Practical Paris'.

Accès Plus (☎03 69 32 26 26, 08 90 64 06 50; www.accessibilite.sncf.com) is a SNCF assistance service for rail travellers with disabilities.

Tourisme et Handicaps (☎01 44 11 10 41; www.tourisme-handicaps.org; 43 rue Marx Dormoy, 18e) isues the 'Tourisme et Handicap' label to tourist sites, restaurants and hotels that comply with strict accessibility and usability standards.

ACCOMMODATION

Be it a fairy-tale château, a boutique hideaway or floating pod on a lake, France has accommodation to suit every taste and pocket.

B&Bs Enchanting properties with maximum five rooms.

Camping Sites range from wild and remote to brash resorts with pools, slides etc.

Hostels New-wave hostels are design-driven, lifestyle spaces with single and double rooms as well as dorms.

Hotels Hotels embrace every budget and taste. Breakfast is rarely included in rates.

Refuges and Gîtes d'Étape Huts for hikers on trails in mountainous areas.

INTERNET ACCESS

➡ Wi-fi (pronounced 'wee-fee' in French) is available at major airports, in most hotels, and at many cafes, restaurants, museums and tourist offices.

➡ In cities free wi-fi is available in hundreds of public places, including parks, libraries and municipal buildings. In Paris look for a purple 'Zone Wi-Fi' sign. To connect, select the 'PARIS_WI-FI_' network. Sessions are limited to two hours (renewable). For complete details and a map of hot spots, see www.paris.fr/wifi.

➡ Tourist offices is some larger cities, including Lyon and Bordeaux, rent out pocket-sized mobile wi-fi devices that you carry around with you, ensuring a fast wi-fi connection while roaming the city.

LEGAL MATTERS

➡ French police have wide powers of search and seizure and can ask you to prove your identity at any time – whether or not there is 'probable cause'.

➡ Foreigners must be able to prove their legal status in France (eg with a passport, visa or residency permit) without delay.

➡ French law does not distinguish between 'hard' and 'soft' drugs; penalties can be severe.

LGBTIQ+ TRAVELLERS

Laissez-faire perfectly sums up France's liberal attitude towards homosexuality and people's private lives in general.

➡ Paris has been a thriving gay and lesbian centre since the late 1970s, and most major organisations are based there today. Bordeaux, Lille and Lyon are among other LGBTIQ-active towns.

➡ Attitudes towards homosexuality tend to be more conservative in the countryside and villages.

➡ France's lesbian scene is less public than its gay male counterpart and is centred mainly on women's cafes and bars.

➡ Same-sex marriage has been legal in France since May 2013.

➡ Gay Pride marches are held in major French cities mid-May to early July.

OPENING HOURS

Banks 9am–noon and 2pm–5pm Monday to Friday or Tuesday to Saturday

Bars 7pm–1am

Cafes 7am–11pm

Clubs 10pm–3am, 4am or 5am Thursday to Saturday

Restaurants Noon–2.30pm and 7pm–11pm six days a week

Shops 10am–noon and 2pm–7pm Monday to Saturday; longer, and including Sunday, for shops in defined ZTIs (international tourist zones)

PUBLIC HOLIDAYS

New Year's Day (Jour de l'An) 1 January

Easter Sunday & Monday (Pâques & Lundi de Pâques) Late March/April

May Day (Fête du Travail) 1 May

Victoire 1945 8 May

Ascension Thursday (Ascension) May; on the 40th day after Easter

Pentecost/Whit Sunday & Whit Monday (Pentecôte & Lundi de Pentecôte) Mid-May to mid-June; on the seventh Sunday after Easter

Bastille Day/National Day (Fête Nationale) 14 July

Assumption Day (Assomption) 15 August

All Saints' Day (Toussaint) 1 November

Remembrance Day (L'onze Novembre) 11 November

Christmas (Noël) 25 December

SAFE TRAVEL

France is generally a safe place, despite a rise in crime and terrorism in recent years.

➡ Never leave baggage unattended, especially at airports or train stations.

➡ At museums and monuments, bags are routinely checked on entry.

➡ Sporadic train strikes and striking taxi drivers can disrupt travel.

➡ France's hunting season is September to February: if you see signs reading *'chasseurs'* or *'chasse gardée'* tacked to trees, don't enter the area.

➡ In the Alps, check the day's avalanche report and stick to groomed pistes. Summer thunderstorms can be sudden and violent.

➡ On the Atlantic Coast watch for powerful tides and undertows; only swim on beaches with lifeguards.

TELEPHONE

➡ French mobile phone numbers begin with 06 or 07.

➡ France uses GSM 900/1800, which is compatible with the rest of Europe and Australia but not with the North American GSM 1900 or the totally different system in Japan (though some North Americans have tri-band phones that work here).

➡ It is usually cheaper to buy a local SIM card from a French provider such as Orange, SFR, Bouygues or Free Mobile, which gives you a local phone number. To do this, ensure your phone is unlocked.

➡ Recharge cards are sold at most *tabacs* (tobacconist-newsagents), supermarkets and online through websites such as Topengo (www.topengo.fr) or Sim-OK (https://recharge.sim-ok.com).

➡ To call France from abroad dial your country's international access code, then 33 (France's country code), then the 10-digit local number without the initial zero.

➡ To call internationally from France dial 00, the country code, the area code (without the initial zero if there is one) and the local number.

Transport

GETTING THERE & AWAY

Air

International airports include the following; there are many smaller ones serving European destinations only.

Aéroport de Charles de Gaulle, Paris (p198)

Aéroport d'Orly, Paris (p198)

Aéroport Lyon-St Exupéry (p221)

Aéroport Marseille-Provence (p234)

Aéroport Nice-Côte d'Azur (p243)

Land

Bus

Eurolines (☎08 92 89 90 91; www.eurolines.eu), a grouping of 32 long-haul coach operators (including the UK's National Express), links France with cities all across Europe, Morocco and Russia.

Flixbus (www.flixbus.com) offers low-cost, intercity bus travel between 27 countries in Europe aboard comfy buses equipped with a toilet, snacks, plug sockets to keep devices charged and free wi-fi, and runs night services too.

Car & Motorcycle

A right-hand-drive vehicle brought to France from the UK or Ireland must have deflectors affixed to the headlights to avoid dazzling oncoming traffic.

A foreign motor vehicle entering France must display a sticker or licence plate identifying its country of registration.

High-speed **Eurotunnel Le Shuttle** (☎France 08 10 63 03 04, UK 08443 35 35 35; www.eurotunnel.com) trains whisk bicycles, motorcycles, cars and coaches in 35 minutes from Folkestone through the Channel Tunnel to Coquelles, 5km southwest of Calais. Shuttles run 24 hours a day, with up to three departures an hour during peak periods. Fares for a car, including up to nine passengers, start at £30 (€37).

Train

Rail services – including a dwindling number of overnight services to/from Spain, Italy and Germany, and Eurostar services to/from the UK – link France with virtually every country in Europe.

➡ Book tickets and get train information from Rail Europe (www.raileurope.com). In the UK contact Railteam (www.railteam.co.uk).

Sea

Regular ferries travel to France from the UK, Ireland and Italy. To get the best fares, check Ferry Savers (www.ferrysavers.com). Several ferry companies ply the waters between Corsica and Italy.

Brittany Ferries (www.brittany-ferries.co.uk) Links between England/Ireland and Brittany and Normandy.

Condor Ferries (www.condorferries.co.uk) Ferries between England/Channel Islands and Normandy and Brittany.

Corsica Linea (www.corsicalinea.com) Sailings to/from France and Sardinia, Tunisia and Algeria.

P&O Ferries (www.poferries.com) Ferries between England and northern France.

GETTING AROUND

Air

France's high-speed train network renders rail travel between some cities (eg from Paris to Lyon, Marseille and Bordeaux) faster and easier than flying.

Air France (www.airfrance.com) and its subsidiaries Hop! (www.hop.com) and Transavia (www.transavia.com) control the lion's share of France's domestic airline industry.

Budget carriers offering flights within France include EasyJet (www.easyjet.com), Twin Jet (www.twinjet.net) and Air Corsica (www.aircorsica.com).

Bicycle

The SNCF does its best to make travelling with a bicycle easy; see www.velo.sncf.com for full details.

Most French cities and towns have at least one bike shop that rents out *vélos tout terrains* (mountain bikes; around €15 a day), known as VTTs, as well as more road-oriented *vélos tout chemin* (VTCs) or cheaper city bikes. You usually have to leave ID and/or a deposit (often a credit-card slip of €250) that you forfeit if the bike is damaged or stolen.

A growing number of cities have automatic bike-rental systems, intended to encourage cycling as a form of urban transport, with computerised pick-up and drop-off sites all over town.

Bus

Buses are widely used for short-distance travel within *départements*, especially in rural areas with relatively few train lines (eg Brittany and Normandy). Unfortunately, services in some regions are infrequent and slow, in part because they were designed to get children to their schools in the towns rather than transport visitors around the countryside.

Some less-busy train lines have been replaced by SNCF buses, which, unlike regional buses, are free if you've got a rail pass.

SNCF TRAIN FARES & DISCOUNTS

The Basics

- 1st-class travel, where available, costs 20% to 30% extra.
- Ticket prices for some trains, including most TGVs, are pricier during peak periods.
- The further in advance you reserve, the lower the fares.
- Children under four travel for free, or for €9 with a *forfait bambin* to any destination if they need a seat.
- Children aged four to 11 travel for half-price.

Discount Tickets

Prem's The SNCF's most heavily discounted, use-or-lose tickets are sold online, by phone and at ticket windows/machines. Prem's are available from Thursday evening to Monday night, for last-minute travel that weekend; Saturday-return Prem's are valid for return travel on a Saturday; and three-month Prem's can be booked a maximum of 90 days in advance.

Intercités 100% Éco can be booked from three months to the day of departure, and offer cheap tickets between any stops, in any direction, on four main lines: Paris–Toulouse, Paris–Bordeaux, Paris–Nantes and Paris–Strasbourg. A single fare costs €15 to €35.

Ouigo (www.ouigo.com) is a low-cost TGV service whereby you can travel on high-speed TGVs for a snip of the usual price. Purchase tickets online from three weeks until four hours before departure.

Discount Cards

Reductions of 25% to 60% are available with several discount cards (valid for one year):

Carte Jeune (€50) Available to travellers aged 12 to 27.

Carte Enfant+ (€75) For one to four adults travelling with a child aged four to 11.

Carte Weekend (€75) For people aged 26 to 59. Discounts on return journeys of at least 200km that either include a Saturday night away or only involve travel on a Saturday or Sunday.

Carte Sénior+ (€60) For travellers over 60.

Car & Motorcycle

A car gives you exceptional freedom and allows you to visit more remote parts of France.

- All drivers must carry a national ID card or passport; a valid driving licence, car-ownership papers, known as a *carte grise* (grey card), and proof of third-party (liability) insurance.
- Many French motorways *(autoroutes)* are fitted with toll *(péage)* stations that charge a fee based on the distance you've travelled; factor in these costs when driving. See www.autoroutes.fr.
- In the cities, traffic and finding a place to park can be a major headache. During holiday periods and bank-holiday weekends, roads throughout France also get backed up with traffic jams *(bouchons)*.
- **Bison Futé** (www.bison-fute.gouv.fr) is also a good source of information about traffic conditions.
- Theft from cars can be a major problem in France, especially in the south.

Train

- France's superb rail network is run by the **SNCF** (Société Nationale des Chemins de fer Français, French National Railway Company; ☎ France 36 35, abroad +33 8 92 35 35 35; http://en.voyages-sncf.com); many rural towns not on the rail network are served by SNCF buses instead.
- Few train stations have *consignes automatiques* (left-luggage lockers). In larger stations you can leave your bags in a *consigne manuelle* (staffed left-luggage facility) where items are handed over in person and X-rayed before being stowed. Charges are around €7 for up to 10 hours and €12 for 24 hours; payment must be made in cash.
- Before boarding the train, paper tickets must be validated *(composter)* by time-stamping them in a *composteur*, a yellow post located on the way to the platform.

Germany

POP 82.3 MILLION

Includes ➡

Best Places to Eat

- Schwein (p270)
- Stadtpfeiffer (p277)
- Fraunhofer (p286)
- Bürgerspital Weinstube (p292)
- Zu den 12 Aposteln (p304)

Best Places to Stay

- 25hours Hotel Bikini (p269)
- Hotel Schloss Eckberg (p275)
- Flushing Meadows (p285)
- Hotel Reikartz Vier Jahreszeiten (p289)

Why Go?

Few countries have had as much impact on the world as Germany. It has given us the printing press, the automobile, aspirin and historical heavyweights from Luther to Bach to Hitler. You'll encounter history in towns where streets were laid out long before Columbus set sail, and in castles that loom above prim, half-timbered villages where flower boxes billow with crimson geraniums. The great cities – Berlin, Munich and Hamburg among them – come in more flavours than a jar of jelly beans, but will all wow you with a cultural kaleidoscope that spans the arc from art museums and high-brow opera to naughty cabaret and underground clubs. Germany's storybook landscapes will also likely leave an even bigger imprint on your memories. There's something undeniably artistic in the way Germany's scenery unfolds from the dune-fringed northern coasts via romantic river valleys to the off-the-charts Alpine splendour.

When to Go

Berlin

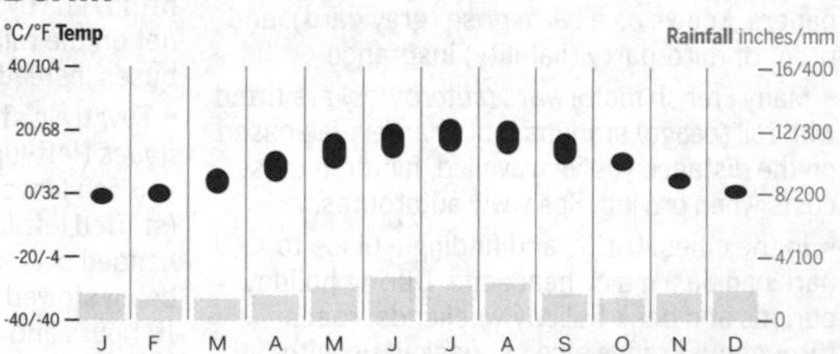

Jun–Aug Warm summers cause Germans to shed their clothes; night never seems to come.

Sep Radiant foliage and often-sunny skies invite outdoor pursuits; festivals galore (Oktoberfest anyone?).

Dec It's icy, it's cold but lines are short and Alpine slopes and twinkly Christmas markets beckon.

Entering the Country

Entering Germany is usually a very straightforward procedure. If you're arriving from any of the 25 other Schengen countries, such as the Netherlands, Poland, Austria or the Czech Republic, you no longer have to show your passport or go through customs in Germany, no matter which nationality you are. If you're coming in from non-Schengen countries, full border procedures apply.

ITINERARIES

Three Days

Come on, is that all you got? If the answer really is yes, drive down the Romantic Road (p290), stopping in Rothenburg ob der Tauber (p291) and Füssen (p289), then spend the rest of your time in Munich (p281).

Five Days

Spend a couple of days in Berlin (p258), head south to Dresden (p274) and Nuremberg (p293) or Bamberg (p294) for half a day each and wrap up your trip in Munich (p281) and surrounds.

One Week

This gives you a little bit of time to tailor a tour beyond the highlights mentioned above. Art fans might want to build Cologne (p308) or Düsseldorf (p311) into their itinerary; romantics could consider Heidelberg (p298), a Rhine cruise or a trip down the Romantic Road (p290), while outdoorsy types are likely to be lured by Garmisch-Partenkirchen (p288), Berchtesgaden (p288) or the Black Forest (p299).

Essential Food & Drink

As in Britain, Germany has redeemed itself gastronomically over the past decade. These days culinary offerings are often slimmed down and healthier as many chefs let seasonal, regional and organic ingredients steer their menus. Of course, if you crave traditional comfort food, you'll still find plenty of pork, potatoes and cabbage on the menus. Here are our top-five classic German culinary treats:

Sausage (Wurst) A favourite snack food, links come in 1500 varieties, including finger-sized Nürnbergers, crunchy Thüringers and tomato-sauce-drowned Currywurst.

Schweinshaxe The mother of all pork dishes, this one presents itself as entire knuckle roasted to crispy perfection.

Königsberger Klopse A simple but elegant plate of golf-ball-sized veal meatballs in a caper-laced white sauce and served with a side of boiled potatoes and beetroot.

Bread Get Germans talking about bread and often their eyes will water as they describe their favourite type – usually hearty and wholegrained in infinite variations.

AT A GLANCE

Area 356,866 sq km

Capital Berlin

Country Code ☎49

Currency euro (€)

Emergency ☎112

Language German

Time Central European Time (GMT/UTC plus one hour)

Visas Schengen rules apply

Sleeping Price Ranges

The following price ranges refer to the cost of a double room with private bathroom, including 7% VAT.

€ less than €80

€€ €80–160

€€€ more than €160

Eating Price Ranges

The following price ranges refer to a standard main course. Unless otherwise stated, 19% tax is included in the price.

€ less than €12

€€ €12–22

€€€ more than €22

Resources

German National Tourist Office (www.germany.travel)

Deutsche Welle (www.dw.com)

Facts About Germany (www.tatsachen-ueber-deutschland.de/en)

Germany Highlights

1 Berlin (p258) Discovering your inner party animal in the capital; save sleep for somewhere else as there's no time here with all the clubs, museums and bars.

2 Munich (p281) Experiencing Oktoberfest, a bacchanale of suds, or just soaking up the vibe in a beer garden.

3 Bamberg (p294) Going slow in Germany's alluring small towns like this gem, with winding lanes, smoked beer and a lack of cliché.

4 Cologne (p308) Comparing the soaring spires of the Dom with the slinky glasses of this city's famous beer.

5 Black Forest (p299) Going cuckoo in the Black Forest, discovering its chilly

crags, misty peaks and endless trails.

6 **Dresden** (p274) Getting into the swing of this city, with a creative culture beyond the restorations.

7 **Hamburg** (p314) Cruising around one of the world's great harbours, then following the trail of the Beatles.

8 **Trier** (p307) Discovering the best-preserved Roman ruins north of the Alps in this delightful wine town on the Moselle.

9 **Schloss Neuschwanstein** (p290) Diving into the mind of a loopy Bavarian monarch at this dreamy palace cradled by the Alps.

10 **Nuremberg** (p293) Tapping into this city's medieval roots, enjoying the famous local sausages, and pondering its Nazi past.

BERLIN

030 / POP 3.71 MILLION

Berlin is a bon vivant, passionately feasting on the smorgasbord of life and never taking things – or itself – too seriously. Its unique blend of glamour and grit is bound to mesmerise anyone keen to connect with its vibrant culture, superb museums, fabulous food, intense nightlife and tangible history.

When it comes to creativity, the sky's the limit in Berlin, Europe's newest start-up capital. In the last 20 years, the city has become a giant lab of cultural experimentation thanks to an abundance of space, cheap rent and a free-wheeling spirit that nurtures and encourages new ideas.

All this trendiness is a triumph for a city that staged a revolution, was headquartered by the Nazis, bombed to bits, divided in two and finally reunited – and that was just in the 20th century! Must-sees and aimless explorations – Berlin delivers it all in one exciting and memorable package.

Sights

Key sights such as the Reichstag, Brandenburger Tor and Museumsinsel cluster in the walkable historic city centre – Mitte – which also cradles the Scheunenviertel, a maze-like hipster quarter around Hackescher Markt. Further north, residential Prenzlauer Berg has a lively cafe and restaurant scene, while to the south loom the contemporary high-rises of Potsdamer Platz. Further south, gritty but cool Kreuzberg and Neukölln are party central, as is student-flavoured Friedrichshain east across the Spree River. Western Berlin's hub is Charlottenburg, with great shopping and a swish royal palace.

Stasi Prison

Victims of Stasi persecution often ended up in this grim remand prison, now a memorial site officially called **Gedenkstätte Berlin-Hohenschönhausen** (Gedenkstätte Berlin-Hohenschönhausen; 030-9860 8230; www.stiftung-hsh.de; Genslerstrasse 66; tours adult/concession €6/3, exhibit free; tours in English 10.30am, 12.30pm & 2.30pm Mar-Oct, 11.30am & 2.30pm Nov-Feb, exhibit 9am-6pm, German tours more frequent; P; M5). Tours – often conducted by former inmates – reveal the full extent of the terror and cruelty perpetrated upon thousands of suspected regime opponents, many utterly innocent. A permanent exhibit uses photographs, objects and a free audioguide to document daily life behind bars and also opens up the offices of the prison administration.

City West & Charlottenburg

★**Schloss Charlottenburg** PALACE
(Charlottenburg Palace; 030-320 910; www.spsg.de; Spandauer Damm 10-22; day pass to all 4 bldgs adult/concession €17/13; hours vary by bldg; M45, 109, 309, U Richard-Wagner-Platz, Sophie-Charlotte-Platz) Charlottenburg Palace is one of Berlin's few sites that still reflect the one-time grandeur of the Hohenzollern clan, which ruled the region from 1415 to 1918. Originally a petite summer retreat, it grew into an exquisite baroque pile with opulent private apartments, richly decorated festival halls, collections of precious porcelain and paintings by French 18th-century masters. It's lovely in fine weather, when you can fold a stroll in the palace park into a day of peeking at royal treasures.

BERLIN IN...

One Day

Book ahead for an early lift ride to the **Reichstag** dome, then snap a picture of the **Brandenburger Tor** before walking quietly through the **Holocaust Memorial** and admiring the contemporary architecture of **Potsdamer Platz**. Ponder Cold War madness at **Checkpoint Charlie**, then head to **Museumsinsel** for an audience with Queen Nefertiti and the Ishtar Gate. Finish up with a night of mirth and gaiety around **Hackescher Markt**.

Two Days

Kick off day two coming to grips with what life was like in divided Berlin at the **Gedenkstätte Berliner Mauer**. Intensify the experience at the **DDR Museum** or on a walk along the **East Side Gallery**. Spend the afternoon soaking up the urban spirit of **Kreuzberg** with its sassy shops and street art, grab dinner along the canal, drinks around Kottbusser Tor and finish up with a night of clubbing.

Berlin

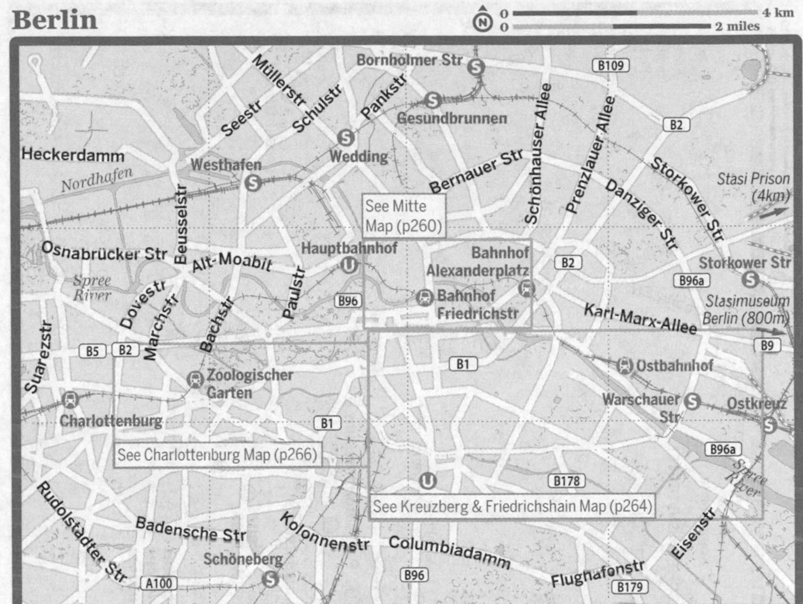

Schlossgarten Charlottenburg PARK
(Charlottenburg Palace Park; ☎030-320 910; www.spsg.de; Spandauer Damm 20-24; ⏱8am-dusk; 🚌M45, 109, 309, Ⓤ Sophie-Charlotte-Platz, Richard-Wagner-Platz) FREE The expansive park behind Schloss Charlottenburg is part formal French, part unruly English and all picturesque playground. Hidden among the shady paths, flower beds, lawns, mature trees and carp pond are two smaller royal buildings, the sombre **Mausoleum** (Spandauer Damm 10-22; €3; ⏱10am-5.30pm Tue-Sun Apr-Oct) and the dainty **Belvedere** (Spandauer Damm 20-24; adult/concession €4/3; ⏱10am-5.30pm Tue-Sun Apr-Oct). It's a lovely place for strolling, jogging or lazing on a sunny day.

Museum Berggruen MUSEUM
(☎030-266 424 242; www.smb.museum/mb; Schlossstrasse 1; adult/concession incl Sammlung Scharf-Gerstenberg €10/5; ⏱10am-6pm Tue-Fri, from 11am Sat & Sun; Ⓟ; 🚌M45, 109, 309, Ⓤ Richard-Wagner-Platz, Sophie-Charlotte-Platz, Ⓢ Westend) Classic modern art is the ammo of this delightful museum where Picasso is especially well represented, with paintings, drawings and sculptures from all his major creative phases. Elsewhere it's off to Paul Klee's emotional world, Henri Matisse's paper cut-outs, Alberto Giacometti's elongated sculptures and a sprinkling of African art that inspired both Klee and Picasso.

Schloss Charlottenburg – Altes Schloss PALACE
(Old Palace; ☎030-320 910; www.spsg.de; Spandauer Damm 10-22; adult/concession €10/7; ⏱10am-5.30pm Tue-Sun Apr-Oct, to 5pm Tue-Sun Nov & Dec, to 4.30pm Tue-Sun Jan-Mar; 🚌M45, 109, 309, Ⓤ Richard-Wagner-Platz, Sophie-Charlotte-Platz) Fronted by Andreas Schlüter's equestrian statue of the *Great Elector* (1699), the baroque living quarters of Friedrich I and Sophie-Charlotte are an extravaganza in stucco, brocade and overall opulence. Highlights include the Oak Gallery, a wood-panelled festival hall draped in family portraits; the charming Oval Hall overlooking the park, Friedrich I's bedchamber, with the first-ever bathroom in a baroque palace; the fabulous Porcelain Chamber, smothered in Chinese and Japanese blue ware; and the Eosander Chapel, with its trompe l'oeil arches.

Friedrichshain

★East Side Gallery LANDMARK
(Map p264; www.eastsidegallery-berlin.de; Mühlenstrasse btwn Oberbaumbrücke & Ostbahnhof; ⏱24hr; Ⓤ Warschauer Strasse, Ⓢ Ostbahnhof, Warschauer Strasse) FREE In 1989, after 28 years, the Berlin Wall, that grim and grey divider of humanity, was finally torn down.

Mitte

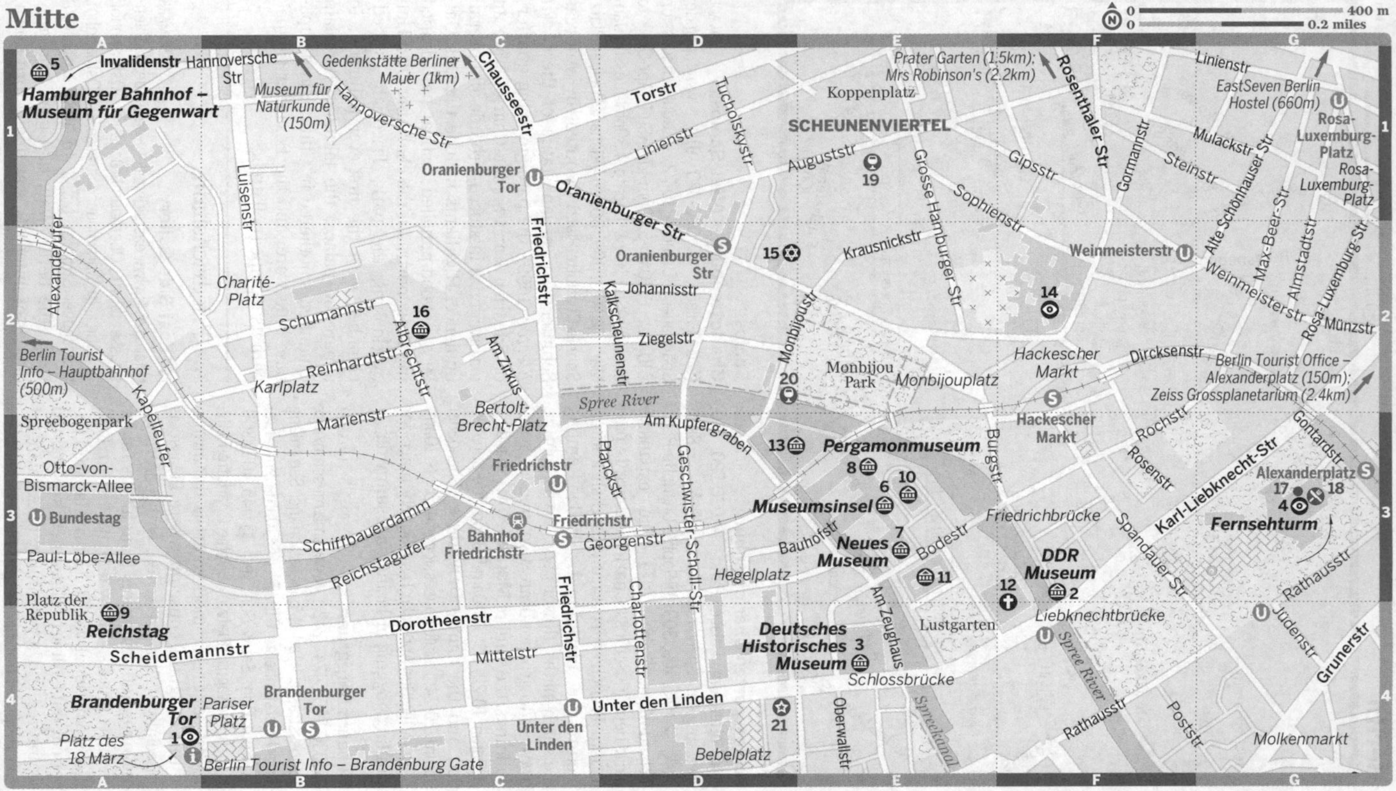

0 400 m
0 0.2 miles
Hamburger Bahnhof – Museum für Gegenwart
5
Invalidenstr
Hannoversche Str
Museum für Naturkunde (150m)
Gedenkstätte Berliner Mauer (1km)
Hannoversche Str
Chausseestr
Torstr
Tucholskystr
Koppenplatz
Prater Garten (1.5km); Mrs Robinson's (2.2km)
Rosenthaler Str
Linienstr
EastSeven Berlin Hostel (660m)
Rosa-Luxemburg-Platz
SCHEUNENVIERTEL
Linienstr
Auguststr
19
Gipsstr
Gormannstr
Mulackstr
Steinstr
Alte Schönhauser Str
Oranienburger Tor
Oranienburger Str
Luisenstr
Friedrichstr
Sophienstr
Grosse Hamburger Str
Max-Beer-Str
Almstadtstr
Rosa-Luxemburg-Str
Weinmeisterstr
15
Krausnickstr
Oranienburger Str
Alexanderufer
Charité-Platz
Johannisstr
14
Weinmeisterstr
Münzstr
16
Schumannstr
Kalkscheunenstr
Ziegelstr
Monbijoustr
Albrechtstr
Am Zirkus
Reinhardtstr
Berlin Tourist Info – Hauptbahnhof (500m)
Karlplatz
Monbijou Park
Monbijouplatz
Hackescher Markt
Dircksenstr
Berlin Tourist Office – Alexanderplatz (150m); Zeiss Grossplanetarium (2.4km)
20
Spree River
Kapelleufer
Marienstr
Bertolt-Brecht-Platz
Am Kupfergraben
Spreebogenpark
13
Pergamonmuseum
Burgstr
Hackescher Markt
Rochstr
Gontardstr
Karl-Liebknecht-Str
Otto-von-Bismarck-Allee
Friedrichstr
Planckstr
Geschwister-Scholl-Str
8
10
6
Rosenstr
Alexanderplatz
17
18
4
Bundestag
Schiffbauerdamm
Friedrichstr
Museumsinsel
Friedrichbrücke
Spandauer Str
Fernsehturm
Bahnhof Friedrichstr
Georgenstr
Bauhofstr
7
Neues Museum
Bodestr
DDR Museum
Paul-Löbe-Allee
Reichstagufer
Hegelplatz
11
12
2
Rathausstr
Platz der Republik
9
Reichstag
Charlottenstr
Am Zeughaus
Lustgarten
Liebknechtbrücke
Jüdenstr
Dorotheenstr
Deutsches Historisches Museum
3
Scheidemannstr
Mittelstr
Schlossbrücke
Spree River
Grunerstr
Brandenburger Tor
Pariser Platz
Brandenburger Tor
Unter den Linden
Unter den Linden
21
Spreekanal
Rathausstr
Poststr
1
Platz des 18 März
Berlin Tourist Info – Brandenburg Gate
Bebelplatz
Oberwallstr
Molkenmarkt

Mitte

Most of it was quickly dismantled, but along Mühlenstrasse, paralleling the Spree, a 1.3km stretch became the East Side Gallery, the world's largest open-air mural collection. In more than 100 paintings, dozens of international artists translated the era's global euphoria and optimism into a mix of political statements, drug-induced musings and truly artistic visions.

Historic Mitte

★ Brandenburger Tor — LANDMARK

(Brandenburg Gate; Map p260; Pariser Platz; S Brandenburger Tor, U Brandenburger Tor) A symbol of division during the Cold War, the landmark Brandenburg Gate now epitomises German reunification. Carl Gotthard Langhans found inspiration in Athens' Acropolis for the elegant triumphal arch, completed in 1791 as the royal city gate.

★ Reichstag — HISTORIC BUILDING

(Map p260; www.bundestag.de; Platz der Republik 1, Visitors Centre, Scheidemannstrasse; lift 8am-midnight, last entry 9.45pm, Visitors Centre 8am-8pm Apr-Oct, to 6pm Nov-Mar; ; 100, S Brandenburger Tor, Hauptbahnhof, U Brandenburger Tor, Bundestag) FREE It's been burned, bombed, rebuilt, buttressed by the Wall, wrapped in fabric and finally turned into the modern home of the German parliament by Norman Foster: the 1894 Reichstag is indeed one of Berlin's most iconic buildings. Its most distinctive feature, the glittering glass dome, is served by a lift and affords fabulous 360-degree views of the city.

For guaranteed access, make free reservations online; otherwise try scoring tickets at the **Reichstag Visitors' Centre** (8am-8pm Apr-Oct, to 6pm Nov-Mar) for the same or next day. Bring ID.

★ Holocaust Memorial — MEMORIAL

(Memorial to the Murdered Jews of Europe; Map p264; 030-2639 4336; www.stiftung-denkmal.de; Cora-Berliner-Strasse 1; audioguide €3; 24hr; S Brandenburger Tor, U Brandenburger Tor) FREE Inaugurated in 2005, this football-field-sized memorial by American architect Peter Eisenman consists of 2711 sarcophagi-like concrete columns rising in sombre silence from the undulating ground. You're free to access this maze at any point and make your individual journey through it. For context visit the subterranean **Ort der Information** (Information Centre; Map p264; 030-7407 2929; www.holocaust-mahnmal.de; audio guide €3; 10am-8pm Tue-Sun Apr-Sep, to 7pm Oct-Mar, last admission 45min before closing) FREE, whose exhibits will leave no one untouched. Audioguides and audio translations of exhibit panels are available.

★ Topographie des Terrors — MUSEUM

(Topography of Terror; Map p264; 030-2545 0950; www.topographie.de; Niederkirchner Strasse 8; 10am-8pm, grounds close at dusk or 8pm at the latest; M41, S Potsdamer Platz, U Potsdamer Platz) FREE In the spot where the most feared institutions of Nazi Germany (including the Gestapo headquarters and the SS central command) once stood, this compelling exhibit chronicles the stages of terror and persecution, puts a face on the perpetrators and details the impact these brutal institutions had on all of Europe. A second exhibit outside zeroes in on how life changed for Berlin and its people after the Nazis made it their capital.

DON'T MISS

MORE MUSEUM ISLAND TREASURES

While the Pergamonmuseum and the Neues Museum are the highlights of Museum Island, the other three museums are no slouches in the treasure department either. Fronting the Lustgarten park the Altes Museum (p263) presents Greek, Etruscan and Roman antiquities. At the northern tip of the island, the Bode-Museum (p265) has a prized collection of European sculpture from the Middle Ages to the 18th century. Finally, there's the Alte Nationalgalerie (p265), whose thematic focus is on 19th-century European painting. A combined day pass for all five museums costs €18 (concession €9).

★Deutsches Historisches Museum MUSEUM
(German Historical Museum; Map p260; ☎030-203 040; www.dhm.de; Unter den Linden 2; adult/concession/child under 18 incl IM Pei Bau €8/4/free; ⌚10am-6pm; 🚌100, 200, U Hausvogteiplatz, S Hackescher Markt) If you're wondering what the Germans have been up to for the past 1500 years, take a spin around the baroque Zeughaus, formerly the Prussian arsenal and now home of the German Historical Museum. Upstairs, displays concentrate on the period from the 6th century AD to the end of WWI in 1918, while the ground floor tracks the 20th century all the way through to the early years after German reunification.

★Gendarmenmarkt SQUARE
(Map p264; U Französische Strasse, Stadtmitte) This graceful square is bookended by the domed German and French cathedrals and punctuated by a grandly porticoed concert hall, the **Konzerthaus** (Map p264; ☎030-203 092 333; www.konzerthaus.de). It was named for the Gens d'Armes, an 18th-century Prussian regiment consisting of French Huguenot refugees.

Kreuzberg & Neukölln

★Jüdisches Museum MUSEUM
(Jewish Museum; Map p264; ☎030-2599 3300; www.jmberlin.de; Lindenstrasse 9-14; adult/concession €8/3, audioguide €3; ⌚10am-8pm; U Hallesches Tor, Kochstrasse) In a landmark building by American-Polish architect Daniel Libeskind, Berlin's Jewish Museum offers a chronicle of the trials and triumphs in 2000 years of Jewish life in Germany. The exhibit smoothly navigates all major periods, from the Middle Ages via the Enlightenment to the community's post-1990 renaissance. Find out about Jewish cultural contributions, holiday traditions, the difficult road to emancipation, outstanding individuals (eg Moses Mendelssohn and Levi Strauss) and the fates of ordinary people.

König Galerie @ St Agnes Kirche GALLERY
(Map p264; ☎030-2610 3080; www.koeniggalerie.com; Alexandrinenstrasse 118-121; ⌚11am-7pm Tue-Sat, from noon Sun; U Prinzenstrasse) FREE If art is your religion, a pilgrimage to this church-turned-gallery is a must. Tucked into a nondescript part of Kreuzberg, this decommissioned Catholic church, designed in the mid-1960s by architect and city planner Werner Düttmann, is a prime example of Brutalist architecture in Berlin. In 2012, it was leased by the gallerist Johann König and converted into a spectacular space that presents interdisciplinary, concept-oriented and space-based art.

Deutsches Technikmuseum MUSEUM
(German Museum of Technology; Map p264; ☎030-902 540; http://sdtb.de/technikmuseum; Trebbiner Strasse 9; adult/concession/child under 18 €8/4/after 3pm free; ⌚9am-5.30pm Tue-Fri, 10am-6pm Sat & Sun; P 👪; U Gleisdreieck, Möckernbrücke) A roof-mounted 'candy bomber' (the plane used in the 1948 Berlin Airlift) is merely the overture to this enormous and hugely engaging shrine to technology. Fantastic for kids, the giant museum includes the world's first computer, an entire hall of vintage locomotives and exhibits on aerospace and navigation in a modern annexe. At the adjacent **Science Center Spectrum** (Map p264; ☎030-9025 4284; www.sdtb.de; Möckernstrasse 26; ⌚9am-5.30pm Tue-Fri, 10am-6pm Sat & Sun; P; U Möckernbrücke, Gleisdreieck), entered on the same ticket, kids can participate in hands-on experiments.

Museumsinsel & Alexanderplatz

★Museumsinsel MUSEUM
(Map p260; ☎030-266 424 242; www.smb.museum; day tickets for all 5 museums adult/concession/under 18 €18/9/free; ⌚varies by museum; 🚌100, 200, TXL, S Hackescher Markt, Friedrichstrasse, U Friedrichstrasse) Walk through ancient Babylon, meet an Egyptian queen, clamber up a Greek

altar or be mesmerised by Monet's ethereal landscapes. Welcome to Museumsinsel (Museum Island), Berlin's most important treasure trove, spanning 6000 years' worth of art, artefacts, sculpture and architecture from Europe and beyond. Spread across five grand museums built between 1830 and 1930, the complex takes up the entire northern half of the little Spree Island where Berlin's settlement began in the 13th century.

★Pergamonmuseum MUSEUM

(Map p260; ☎030-266 424 242; www.smb.museum; Bodestrasse 1-3; adult/concession/under 18yr €12/6/free; ⏰10am-6pm Fri-Wed, to 8pm Thu; 🚌100, 200, TXL, Ⓢ Hackescher Markt, Friedrichstrasse, Ⓤ Friedrichstrasse) Opening a fascinating window on to the ancient world, this palatial three-wing complex unites a rich feast of classical sculpture and monumental architecture from Greece, Rome, Babylon and the Middle East, including the radiant-blue Ishtar Gate from Babylon, the Roman Market Gate of Miletus and the Caliph's Palace of Mshatta. Note that extensive renovations put the namesake Pergamon Altar and several rooms off limits until 2023. Budget at least two hours for this amazing place and be sure to use the free and excellent audio guide.

★Neues Museum MUSEUM

(New Museum; Map p260; ☎030-266 424 242; www.smb.museum; Bodestrasse 1-3; adult/concession/under 18yr €12/6/free; ⏰10am-6pm Fri-Wed, to 8pm Thu; 🚌100, 200, TXL, Ⓢ Hackescher Markt, Friedrichstrasse, Ⓤ Friedrichstrasse) David Chipperfield's reconstruction of the bombed-out Neues Museum is now the residence of Queen Nefertiti, the showstopper of the Egyptian Museum, which also features mummies, sculptures and sarcophagi. Pride of place at the Museum of Pre- and Early History (in the same building) goes to Trojan antiquities, a Neanderthal skull and the 3000-year-old 'Berliner Goldhut', a golden conical hat. Skip the queue by buying your timed ticket online.

★Fernsehturm LANDMARK

(TV Tower; Map p260; ☎030-247 575 875; www.tv-turm.de; Panoramastrasse 1a; adult/child €15.50/9.50, fast track online ticket €19.50/12; ⏰9am-midnight Mar-Oct, 10am-midnight Nov-Feb, last ascent 11.30pm; 🚌100, 200, TXL, Ⓤ Alexanderplatz, Ⓢ Alexanderplatz) Germany's tallest structure, the TV Tower has been soaring 368m high since 1969 and is as iconic to Berlin as the Eiffel Tower is to Paris. On clear days, views are stunning from the observation deck (with bar) at 203m or from the upstairs **Sphere restaurant** (Map p260; ☎030-247 575 875; www.tv-turm.de/en/bar-restaurant; mains lunch €10.50-18, dinner €12.50-28; ⏰10am-11pm; 📶), which makes one revolution per hour.

★DDR Museum MUSEUM

(GDR (East Germany) Museum; Map p260; ☎030-847 123 731; www.ddr-museum.de; Karl-Liebknecht-Strasse 1; adult/concession €9.80/6; ⏰10am-8pm Sun-Fri, to 10pm Sat; 🚌100, 200, TXL, Ⓢ Hackescher Markt) This touchy-feely museum does an insightful and entertaining job of pulling back the iron curtain on daily life in socialist East Germany. You'll learn how kids were put through collective potty training, engineers earned little more than farmers, and everyone, it seems, went on nudist holidays. A perennial crowd-pleaser among the historic objects on display is a Trabi, the tinny East German standard car – sit in it to take a virtual spin around an East Berlin neighbourhood.

Altes Museum MUSEUM

(Old Museum; Map p260; ☎030-266 424 242; www.smb.museum; Am Lustgarten; adult/concession/under 18 €10/5/free; ⏰10am-6pm Tue, Wed & Fri-Sun, to 8pm Thu; 🚌100, 200, TXL, Ⓢ Friedrichstrasse, Hackescher Markt, Ⓤ Friedrichstrasse) A curtain of fluted columns gives way to the Pantheon-inspired rotunda of the grand neoclassical Old Museum, which harbours a prized antiquities collection. In the downstairs galleries, sculptures, vases, tomb reliefs and jewellery shed light on various facets of life in ancient Greece, while upstairs the focus is on the Etruscans and Romans. Top draws include the *Praying Boy* bronze sculpture, Roman silver vessels, an 'erotic cabinet' (over 18s only!) and portraits of Caesar and Cleopatra.

Berliner Dom CHURCH

(Berlin Cathedral; Map p260; ☎ticket office 030-2026 9136; www.berlinerdom.de; Am Lustgarten; adult/concession €7/5; ⏰9am-8pm Apr-Sep, to 7pm Oct-Mar; 🚌100, 200, TXL, Ⓢ Hackescher Markt) Pompous yet majestic, the Italian Renaissance–style former royal court church (1905) does triple duty as house of worship, museum and concert hall. Inside it's gilt to the hilt and outfitted with a lavish marble-and-onyx altar, a 7269-pipe Sauer organ and elaborate royal sarcophagi. Climb up the 267 steps to the gallery for glorious city views.

Kreuzberg & Friedrichshain

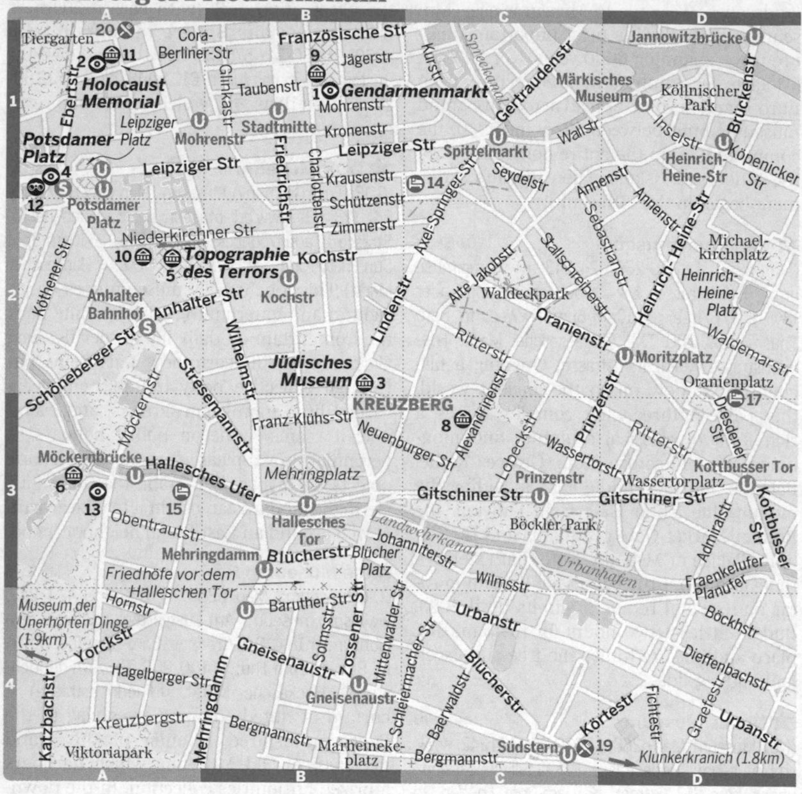

Kreuzberg & Friedrichshain

Top Sights

1 Gendarmenmarkt B1
2 Holocaust Memorial A1
3 Jüdisches Museum B2
4 Potsdamer Platz A1
5 Topographie des Terrors A2

Sights

6 Deutsches Technikmuseum A3
7 East Side Gallery F2
8 König Galerie @ St Agnes Kirche C3
9 Konzerthaus B1
10 Martin-Gropius-Bau A2
11 Ort der Information A1
12 Panoramapunkt A1
13 Science Center Spectrum A3

Sleeping

14 Adina Apartment Hotel Berlin Checkpoint Charlie C1
15 Grand Hostel Berlin Classic A3
16 Michelberger Hotel G2
17 Orania.Berlin D2
18 Plus Berlin G2

Eating

19 Fes Turkish Barbecue C4
20 India Club A1
Michelberger .... (see 16)
21 Silo Coffee H1
22 Sironi E3

Drinking & Nightlife

23 ://about blank H3
24 Berghain/Panorama Bar F1

Entertainment

25 Kantine am Berghain F1

Shopping

Markthalle Neun .... (see 22)

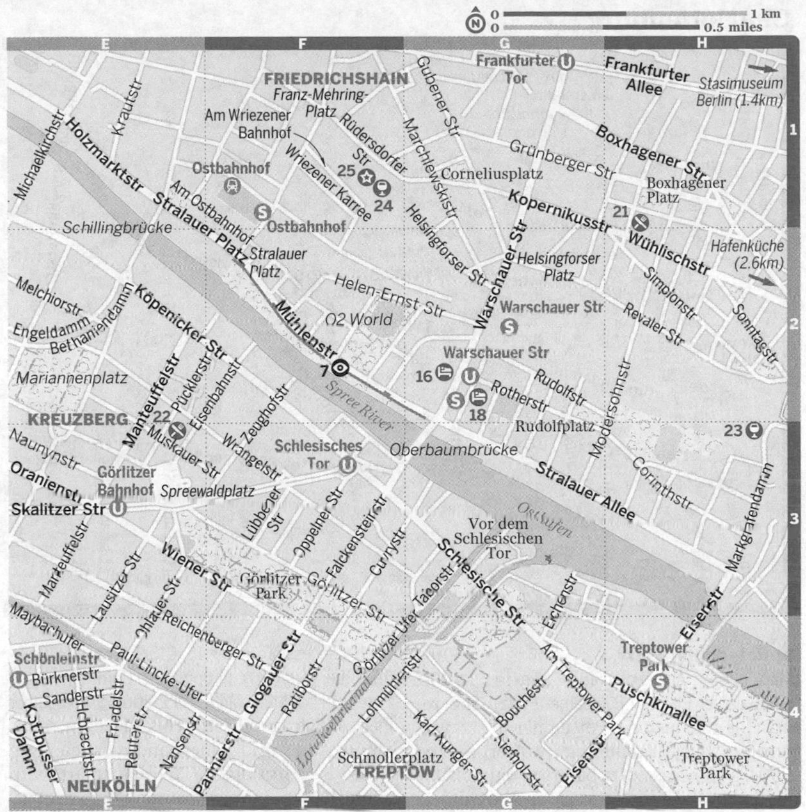

Bode-Museum

MUSEUM

(Map p260; 030-266 424 242; www.smb.museum; cnr Am Kupfergraben & Monbijoubrücke; adult/concession/under 18 €12/6/free; 10am-6pm Tue, Wed & Fri-Sun, to 8pm Thu; Hackescher Markt, Friedrichstrasse) On the northern tip of Museumsinsel, this palatial edifice houses a comprehensive collection of European sculpture from the early Middle Ages to the 18th century, including priceless masterpieces by Tilman Riemenschneider, Donatello and Giovanni Pisano. Other rooms harbour a precious coin collection and a smattering of Byzantine art, including sarcophagi and ivory carvings.

Alte Nationalgalerie

MUSEUM

(Old National Gallery; Map p260; 030-266 424 242; www.smb.museum; Bodestrasse 1-3; adult/concession €10/5; 10am-6pm Tue, Wed & Fri-Sun, to 8pm Thu; 100, 200, TXL, Hackescher Markt) The Greek temple–style Old National Gallery is a three-storey showcase of 19th-century European art. To get a sense of the period's virtuosity, pay special attention to the moody landscapes by Romantic heart-throb Caspar David Friedrich, the epic canvases by Franz Krüger and Adolf Menzel glorifying Prussia, the Gothic fantasies of Karl Friedrich Schinkel, and the sprinkling of French and German impressionists.

Potsdamer Platz & Tiergarten

★Tiergarten

PARK

(Map p266; Strasse des 17 Juni; 100, 200, Potsdamer Platz, Brandenburger Tor, Brandenburger Tor) Berlin's rulers used to hunt boar and pheasants in the rambling Tiergarten until garden architect Peter Lenné landscaped the grounds in the 19th century. Today it's one of the world's largest urban parks, popular for strolling, jogging, picnicking, frisbee tossing and, yes, nude sunbathing and gay cruising (especially around the Löwenbrücke).

Charlottenburg

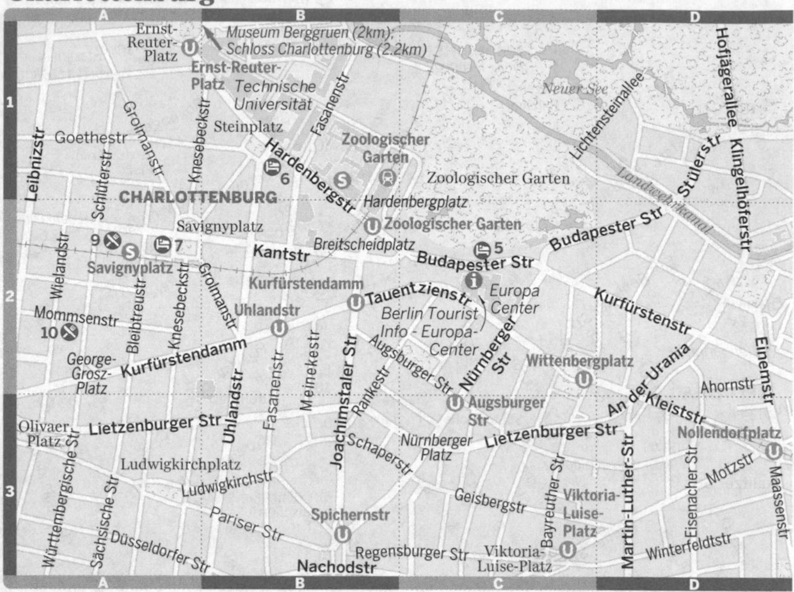

★Potsdamer Platz AREA

(Map p264; Alte Potsdamer Strasse; 🚌200, Ⓢ Potsdamer Platz, Ⓤ Potsdamer Platz) The rebirth of the historic Potsdamer Platz was Europe's biggest building project of the 1990s, a showcase of urban renewal masterminded by such top international architects as Renzo Piano and Helmut Jahn. An entire city quarter sprouted on terrain once bifurcated by the Berlin Wall and today houses offices, theatres and cinemas, hotels, apartments and museums. Highlights include the glass-tented Sony Center and the Panoramapunkt observation deck.

★Sony Center NOTABLE BUILDING

(Map p266; www.potsdamer-platz.net; Potsdamer Strasse; 🚌200, Ⓤ Potsdamer Platz, Ⓢ Potsdamer Platz) Designed by Helmut Jahn, the visually dramatic Sony Center is fronted by a 26-floor, glass-and-steel tower and integrates rare relics from the prewar era of Potsdamer Platz, such as the opulent Kaisersaal. The heart of the Sony Center, though, is a central plaza canopied by a tentlike glass roof with supporting beams radiating like bicycle spokes. The plaza and its many cafes are popular places to hang out and people-watch.

★Gemäldegalerie GALLERY

(Gallery of Old Masters; Map p266; ☎030-266 424 242; www.smb.museum/gg; Matthäikirchplatz; adult/concession/under 18 €10/5/free; ⏲10am-6pm Tue, Wed & Fri, to 8pm Thu, 11am-6pm Sat & Sun; 👪; 🚌M29, M48, M85, 200, Ⓢ Potsdamer Platz, Ⓤ Potsdamer Platz) This museum ranks among the world's finest and most comprehensive collections of European art with about 1500 paintings spanning the arc of artistic vision from the 13th to the 18th century. Wear comfy shoes when exploring the 72 galleries: a walk past masterpieces by Titian, Dürer, Hals, Vermeer, Gainsborough and many more Old Masters covers almost 2km. Don't miss the Rembrandt Room (Room X).

Panoramapunkt VIEWPOINT

(Map p264; ☎030-2593 7080; www.panoramapunkt.de; Potsdamer Platz 1; adult/concession €7.50/6, without wait €11.50/9; ⏲10am-8pm Apr-Oct, to 6pm Nov-Mar; 🚌M41, 200, Ⓢ Potsdamer Platz, Ⓤ Potsdamer Platz) Europe's fastest lift, Panoramapunkt yo-yos up and down the red-brick postmodern Kollhoff Tower in 20 seconds. From the bilevel viewing platform at a lofty 100m, you can pinpoint the sights, make a java stop in the 1930s-style cafe, enjoy sunset from the terrace and check out the exhibit that peels back the layers of the square's history.

Martin-Gropius-Bau GALLERY

(Map p264; ☎030-254 860; www.gropiusbau.de; Niederkirchner Strasse 7; cost varies, usually €10-12, under 16 free; ⏲10am-7pm Wed-Mon; 🚌M41,

Charlottenburg

Top Sights

1 Gemäldegalerie F1
2 Sony Center F1
3 Tiergarten E1

Sights

4 Berliner Philharmonie F1

Sleeping

5 25hours Hotel Bikini Berlin C2
6 Hotel am Steinplatz B1
7 Sir Savigny A2

Eating

8 BRLO Brwhouse F3
9 Kuchenladen A2
10 Schwein A2

Drinking & Nightlife

Bar am Steinplatz .... (see 6)

Entertainment

Berliner Philharmoniker .... (see 4)

S Potsdamer Platz, U Potsdamer Platz) With its mosaics, terracotta reliefs and airy atrium, this Italian Renaissance-style exhibit space named for its architect (Bauhaus founder Walter Gropius' great-uncle) is a celebrated venue for high-calibre art and cultural exhibits. Whether it's a David Bowie retrospective, the latest works of Ai Weiwei or an ethnological exhibit on the mysteries of Angkor Wat, it's bound to be well curated and utterly fascinating.

Prenzlauer Berg

★Gedenkstätte Berliner Mauer MEMORIAL
(Berlin Wall Memorial; ☎030-467 986 666; www.berliner-mauer-gedenkstaette.de; Bernauer Strasse btwn Schwedter Strasse & Gartenstrasse; ⊙visitor & documentation centre 10am-6pm Tue-Sun, open-air exhibit 8am-10pm daily; S Nordbahnhof, Bernauer Strasse, Eberswalder Strasse) FREE For an insightful primer on the Berlin Wall, visit this outdoor memorial, which extends for 1.4km along Bernauer Strasse and integrates an original section of Wall, vestiges of the border installations and escape tunnels, a chapel and a monument. Multimedia stations, panels, excavations and a Documentation Centre provide context and explain what the border fortifications looked like and how they shaped the everyday lives of people on both sides of it. There's a great outlook from the centre's viewing platform.

★Zeiss Grossplanetarium PLANETARIUM
(☎030 4218 4510; www.planetarium.berlin; Prenzlauer Allee 80; adult €8-9.50, concession €6-7.50; 🚋M2, S Prenzlauer Allee) It was the most advanced planetarium in East Germany at its opening in 1987 and after the recent renovation it has upped the scientific, technology and comfort factor ante once again to become one of the most modern in Europe. It's a beautiful space to delve into the mysteries not only of the cosmos but of science in general. Many programs are in English, some are set to music, others are geared to children. Tickets are available online.

Scheunenviertel

★Hamburger Bahnhof – Museum für Gegenwart MUSEUM
(Contemporary Art Museum; Map p260; ☎030-266 424 242; www.smb.museum; Invalidenstrasse 50-51; adult/concession €10/5, free 4-8pm 1st Thu of the month; ⊙10am-6pm Tue, Wed & Fri, to 8pm Thu, 11am-6pm Sat & Sun; 🚋M5, M8, M10, S Hauptbahnhof, U Hauptbahnhof) Berlin's contemporary art showcase opened in 1996 in an old railway station, whose grandeur is a great backdrop for this Aladdin's cave of paintings, installations, sculptures and video art. Changing exhibits span the arc of post-1950 artistic movements – from conceptual

WORTH A TRIP

SCHLOSS & PARK SANSSOUCI

Easily reached in half an hour from central Berlin, the former royal Prussian seat of Potsdam lures visitors to its splendid Unesco-recognised palaces and parks dreamed up by 18th-century King Friedrich II (Frederick the Great).

Headlining the roll call of royal pads is **Schloss Sanssouci** (☎0331-969 4200; www.spsg.de; Maulbeerallee; adult/concession incl tour or audioguide €12/8; ⏲10am-5.30pm Tue-Sun Apr-Oct, to 5pm Nov & Dec, to 4.30pm Jan-Mar; 🚌614, 650, 695), a celebrated rococo palace and the king's favourite summer retreat. Standouts on the audio-guided tour include the whimsically decorated concert hall, the intimate library and the domed Marble Hall. Admission is limited and by timed ticket only; book online (http://tickets.spsg.de) to avoid wait times and/or disappointment. Tickets must be printed out. Tours run by the Potsdam **tourist office** (☎0331-2755 8899; www.potsdam-tourism.com; Potsdam Hauptbahnhof; ⏲9.30am-6pm Mon-Sat; Ⓢ Potsdam Hauptbahnhof) guarantee entry.

Schloss Sanssouci is surrounded by a sprawling park dotted with numerous other palaces, buildings, fountains, statues and romantic corners. The one building not to be missed is the **Chinesisches Haus** (Chinese House; ☎0331-969 4200; www.spsg.de; Am Grünen Gitter; adult/concession €4/3; ⏲10am-5.30pm Tue-Sun May-Oct; 🚌605, 606, 🚋91), an adorable clover-leaf-shaped pavilion whose exterior is decorated with exotically dressed gilded figures shown sipping tea, dancing and playing musical instruments.

Another park highlight is the **Neues Palais** (New Palace; ☎0331-969 4200; www.spsg.de; Am Neuen Palais; adult/concession incl tour or audioguide €8/6; ⏲10am-5.30pm Mon & Wed-Sun Apr-Oct, to 5pm Nov-Dec, to 4.30pm Jan-Mar; 🚌605, 606, 695, Ⓢ Potsdam Charlottenhof) at the far western end. It has built-to-impress dimensions and is filled with opulent private and representative rooms.

Each building charges separate admission; a day pass to all costs €19 (concession €14).

On a nice day, it's worth exploring Potsdam's watery landscape and numerous other palaces on a **boat cruise** (☎0331-275 9210; www.schiffahrt-in-potsdam.de; Lange Brücke 6; ⏲Apr-Oct; 🚌605, 610, 631, 694, 🚋91, 92, 93, 98). The most popular one is the 90-minute Schlösserundfahrt (palace cruise; €16). Boats leave from docks near the Hauptbahnhof.

Regional trains leaving from Berlin-Hauptbahnhof and Zoologischer Garten need only 25 minutes to reach Potsdam Hauptbahnhof. The S-Bahn S7 from central Berlin makes the trip in about 40 minutes. You need an ABC ticket (€3.40) for either service.

art and pop art to minimal art and Fluxus – and include seminal works by such major players as Andy Warhol, Cy Twombly, Joseph Beuys and Robert Rauschenberg.

Sammlung Boros GALLERY
(Boros Collection; Map p260; ☎030-2759 4065; www.sammlung-boros.de; Reinhardtstrasse 20; adult/concession €12/6; ⏲tours 3-6.30pm Thu, 10.30am-6.30pm Fri, 10am-6.30pm Sat & Sun; 🚋M1, Ⓢ Friedrichstrasse, Ⓤ Oranienburger Tor, Friedrichstrasse) This Nazi-era bunker presents one of Berlin's finest private contemporary art collections, amassed by advertising guru Christian Boros who acquired the behemoth in 2003. A third selection of works went live in May 2017 and includes installations by Katja Novitskova, digital paintings by Avery Singer and photo series by Peter Piller. Book online (weeks, if not months, ahead) to join a guided tour (also in English) and to pick up fascinating nuggets about the building's surprising other peacetime incarnations.

Hackesche Höfe HISTORIC SITE
(Hackesche Courtyards; Map p260; ☎030-2809 8010; www.hackesche-hoefe.com; enter from Rosenthaler Strasse 40/41 or Sophienstrasse 6; 🚋M1, Ⓢ Hackescher Markt, Ⓤ Weinmeisterstrasse) The Hackesche Höfe is the largest and most famous of the courtyard ensembles peppered throughout the Scheunenviertel. Built in 1907, the eight interlinked *Höfe* reopened in 1996 with a congenial mix of cafes, galleries, shops and entertainment venues. The main entrance on Rosenthaler Strasse leads to **Court I**, prettily festooned with art nouveau tiles, while Court VII segues to the romantic **Rosenhöfe** with a sunken rose garden and tendril-like balustrades.

Museum für Naturkunde MUSEUM
(Museum of Natural History; 030-2093 8591; www.naturkundemuseum.berlin; Invalidenstrasse 43; adult/concession incl audioguide €8/5; 9.30am-6pm Tue-Fri, 10am-6pm Sat & Sun; ; M5, M8, M10, 12, U Naturkundemuseum) Fossils and minerals don't quicken your pulse? Well, how about Tristan, the T-Rex? His skeleton is among the best-preserved in the world and, along with the 12m-high *Brachiosaurus branchai,* part of the Jurassic superstar line-up at this highly engaging museum. Elsewhere you can wave at Knut, the world's most famous dead polar bear; marvel at the fragile bones of an ultrarare *Archaeopteryx* protobird, and find out why zebras are striped.

Neue Synagoge SYNAGOGUE
(Map p260; 030-8802 8300; www.centrumjudaicum.de; Oranienburger Strasse 28-30; adult/concession €5/4, audioguide €3; 10am-6pm Mon-Fri, to 7pm Sun, closes 3pm Fri & 6pm Sun Oct-Mar; M1, U Oranienburger Tor, S Oranienburger Strasse) The gleaming gold dome of the Neue Synagoge is the most visible symbol of Berlin's revitalised Jewish community. The 1866 original was Germany's largest synagogue but its modern incarnation is not so much a house of worship (although prayer services do take place), as a museum and place of remembrance called **Centrum Judaicum**. The dome can be climbed from April to September (adult/concession €3/2.50).

Schöneberg

Museum der Unerhörten Dinge MUSEUM
(Museum of Unheard of Things; 030-781 4932, 0175 410 9120; www.museumderunerhoertendinge.de; Crellestrasse 5-6; 3-7pm Wed-Fri; U Kleistpark, S Julius-Leber-Brücke) FREE 'Every object tells a story' could be the motto of this kooky collection of curiosities. Find madness nibbling at your psyche as you try to find the meaning in displays about Swiss cowpat-worshippers or Goethe's stone rose. It may all be a mind-bending spoof or a complete exercise in irony by founder Roland Albrecht. But one thing's certain: it will challenge the way you look at museums.

Tours

Berliner Unterwelten TOURS
(030-4991 0517; www.berliner-unterwelten.de; Brunnenstrasse 105; adult/concession €12/10; Dark Worlds tours in English 11am Wed-Sun, 11am & 1pm Mon year-round, 3pm Mon, Wed-Sun, 1pm & 3pm Wed-Sun Apr-Oct; S Gesundbrunnen, U Gesundbrunnen) After you've checked off the Brandenburg Gate and the TV Tower, why not explore Berlin's dark and dank underbelly? Join Berliner Unterwelten on its 1½-hour 'Dark Worlds' tour of a WWII underground bunker and pick your way through a warren of claustrophobic rooms, past heavy steel doors, hospital beds, helmets, guns, boots and lots of other wartime artefacts.

Fat Tire Tours Berlin CYCLING
(Map p260; 030-2404 7991; www.fattiretours.com/berlin; Panoramastrasse 1a; adult/concession/under 12yr incl bicycle from €28/26/14; S Alexanderplatz, U Alexanderplatz) This top-rated outfit runs English-language tours by bike, e-bike and Segway. Options include a classic city spin; tours with a focus on Nazi Germany, the Cold War or 'Modern Berlin'; a trip to Potsdam; and an evening food tour. Tours leave from the Fernsehturm (TV Tower) main entrance. Reservations advised.

Sleeping

City West & Charlottenburg

★ 25hours Hotel Bikini Berlin DESIGN HOTEL €€
(Map p266; 030-120 2210; www.25hours-hotels.com; Budapester Strasse 40; r €110-250; ; 100, 200, S Zoologischer Garten, U Zoologischer Garten) The 'urban jungle' theme of this lifestyle outpost in the iconic 1950s Bikini Haus plays on its location between the zoo and main shopping district. Rooms are thoughtfully cool, and drip with clever design touches; the best face the animal park. Quirks include an on-site bakery, hammocks in the public areas and the 'jungle-sauna' with zoo view.

Sir Savigny BOUTIQUE HOTEL €€
(Map p266; 030-323 015 600; www.hotel-sir savigny.de; Kantstrasse 144; r from €130; ; S Savignyplatz) Global nomads with a hankering for style would be well advised to point their compass to this cosmopolitan crash pad. Each of the 44 rooms exudes delightfully risqué glamour and teems with mod cons and clever design touches. And yes, the beds are fab. If you're feeling social,

report to the book-filled 'kitchen' lounge or the cool bar and burger joint.

Friedrichshain

★Plus Berlin HOSTEL €
(Map p264; ☎030-311 698 820; www.plushostels.com/plusberlin; Warschauer Platz 6; dm/d from €18/90; P❄@📶🏊; U Warschauer Strasse, S Warschauer Strasse) A hostel with a pool, steam room and yoga classes? Yep. Close to Berlin's best nightlife, this flashpacker favourite is like a hostel resort. There's a bar for easing into the night and a tranquil courtyard to soothe that hangover. Spacious dorms have four or six bunks, desks and lockers, while private rooms have TV and air-con. All have en suites.

Historic Mitte

★Adina Apartment Hotel Berlin Checkpoint Charlie APARTMENT €€
(Map p264; ☎030-200 7670; www.adinahotels.com; Krausenstrasse 35-36; studio/1-bedroom apt from €120/145; P❄@📶🏊🐾; U Stadtmitte, Spittelmarkt) Adina's contemporary one- and two-bedroom, stylishly functional apartments with full kitchens are tailor-made for cost-conscious families, anyone in need of elbow room, and self-caterers (a supermarket is a minute away). Roomy studios with kitchenette are also available. The spa area with its 17m-long indoor pool and sauna helps combat post-flight fatigue. Optional breakfast is €19.

Kreuzberg & Neukölln

★Grand Hostel Berlin Classic HOSTEL €
(Map p264; ☎030-2009 5450; www.grandhostel-berlin.de; Tempelhofer Ufer 14; dm €10-44, tw €75-150, tw without bathroom €50-110; 🚭@📶; U Möckernbrücke) Cocktails in the library bar? Check. Free German lessons? Got 'em. Canal views? Yep. Ensconced in a fully renovated 1870s building, the 'five-star' Grand Hostel is one of Berlin's most supremely comfortable, convivial and atmospheric hostels. Breakfast is €7.50.

Orania.Berlin HOTEL €€
(Map p264; ☎030-6953 9680; www.orania.berlin; Oranienstrasse 40; d from €150; 🚭❄📶🐾; U Moritzplatz) This gorgeous hotel in a sensitively restored 1913 building wraps everything that makes Berlin special – culture, class and culinary acumen, infused with a freewheeling cosmopolitan spirit – into one tidy package. Great warmth radiates from the open lobby bar, whose stylish furniture, sultry lighting and open fireplace exude living-room flair. Catch shuteye in 41 comfy rooms that mix retro and modern touches.

Prenzlauer Berg

★EastSeven Berlin Hostel HOSTEL €
(☎030-9362 2240; www.eastseven.de; Schwedter Strasse 7; dm/d from €25/65; 🚭@📶; U Senefelderplatz) An excellent choice for solo travellers, this small indie hostel has personable staff who go out of their way to make all feel welcome. Make new friends while chilling in the lounge or garden (hammocks!), firing up the barbecue or hanging out in the 24-hour kitchen. Brightly painted dorms feature comfy pine beds and lockers. Linen is free, breakfast €3.

Eating

City West & Charlottenburg

Kuchenladen CAFE €
(Map p266; ☎030-3101 8424; www.derkuchenladen.de; Kantstrasse 138; cakes €2.50-4.50; ⏰10am-8pm; S Savignyplatz) Even size-0 locals can't resist the siren call of this classic cafe whose homemade cakes are like works of art wrought from flour, sugar and cream. From cheesecake to carrot cake to the ridiculously rich *Sacher Torte,* it's all delicious down to the last crumb.

★Schwein INTERNATIONAL €€€
(Map p266; ☎030-2435 6282; www.schwein.online; Mommsenstrasse 63; dishes €13-37, 4-/5-course menu €65/75; ⏰6pm-midnight Mon-Fri, to 2am Sat; 📶🍷; S Savignyplatz) This casual fine-dining lair delivers the perfect trifecta – fabulous food, wine and long drinks. Order the multicourse menu to truly experience the genius of kitchen champion Christopher Kümper, who creates globally inspired and regionally sourced symphonies of taste and textures. Or keep it 'casual' with just a bite and a gin and tonic.

Friedrichshain

Silo Coffee CAFE €

(Map p264; www.facebook.com/silocoffee; Gabriel-Max-Strasse 4; dishes €6-12; 8.30am-5pm Mon-Fri, 9.30am-6pm Sat & Sun; ; M10, M13, U Warschauer Strasse, S Warschauer Strasse) If you've greeted the day with bloodshot eyes, get back in gear at this Aussie-run coffee and breakfast joint favoured by Friedrichshain's hip and expat crowds. Beans from Fjord coffee roasters ensure possibly the best flat white in town, while bread from Sironi (Markthalle Neun) adds scrumptiousness to the poached-egg avo toast.

Michelberger INTERNATIONAL €€

(Map p264; 030-2977 8590; www.michelberger hotel.com; Warschauer Strasse 39; 3-course lunch €12, dinner dishes €8-15; 7-11am, noon-2.30pm & 6.30-11pm; ; S Warschauer Strasse, U Warschauer Strasse) Ensconced in one of Berlin's coolest **hotels** (Map p264; Warschauer Strasse 39; d €95-190; P), Michelberger makes creative dishes that often combine unusual organic ingredients (eg wild boar with miso, scallops, cabbage and gooseberry). Sit inside the lofty, white-tiled restaurant or in the breezy courtyard.

Hafenküche INTERNATIONAL €€

(030-4221 9926; www.hafenkueche.de; Zur Alten Flussbadeanstalt 5; lunch €5.50-6.50, dinner mains €12-19; 10am-11pm Mon-Fri, 9pm-11.30 Sat & Sun; , 21) The erstwhile staff restaurant of the adjacent bus operator is now a top address for seasonal and regional cuisine in a dreamy location right on the Spree River. It's a great lunch destination while on riverside bike rides. The dinners are more elaborate and best enjoyed on the romantically lit terrace. In good weather, the waterfront beer garden has cold drinks and grilled meats.

Historic Mitte

India Club NORTH INDIAN €€

(Map p264; 030-2062 8610; www.india-club -berlin.com; Behrenstrasse 72; mains €16-27; 6-10.30pm; ; S Brandenburger Tor) No need to book a flight to Mumbai or London: authentic Indian cuisine has finally landed in Berlin. Thanks to top toque Manish Bahukhandi, these curries are like culinary poetry, the chicken tikka perfectly succulent and the stuffed cauliflower an inspiration. The dark mahogany furniture is enlivened by splashes of colour in the plates, the chandeliers and the servers' uniforms.

Kreuzberg & Neukölln

Sironi BAKERY €

(Map p264; www.facebook.com/sironi.de; Eisenbahnstrasse 42, Markthalle Neun; snacks from €2.50; 8am-8pm Mon-Wed, Fri & Sat, to 10pm Thu; U Görlitzer Bahnhof) The focaccia and ciabatta are as good as they get without taking a flight to Italy, thanks to Alfredo Sironi, who hails from the Boot and now treats Berlin bread lovers to his habit-forming carb creations. Watch the flour magicians whip up the next batch in his glass bakery right in the iconic **Markthalle Neun** (Map p264; 030-6107 3473; www.markthalleneun.de; Eisenbahnstrasse 42-43; noon-6pm Mon-Wed & Fri, noon-10pm Thu, 10am-6pm Sat), then order a piece to take away.

Fes Turkish Barbecue TURKISH €€

(Map p264; 030-2391 7778; http://fes-turkish bbq.de; Hasenheide 58; meze €4-10, meat from €15; 5-10pm Tue-Sun; U Südstern) If you like a DIY approach to dining, give this innovative Turkish restaurant a try. Perhaps borrowing a page from the Koreans, it requires you to cook your own slabs of marinated chicken, beef fillet and tender lamb on a grill sunk right into your table.

Prenzlauer Berg

Mrs Robinson's INTERNATIONAL €€

(030-5462 2839, 01520 518 8946; www.mrs robinsons.de; Pappelallee 29; mains €16-20; 6-11pm Thu-Mon; ; 12, U Schönhauser Allee, S Schönhauser Allee) When Israel transplant Ben Zviel and his partner Samina Raza launched their minimalist parlour

BUS TOUR ON THE CHEAP

Get a crash course in 'Berlinology' by hopping on bus 100 or 200 at Zoologischer Garten or Alexanderplatz and letting the landmarks whoosh by for the price of a standard bus ticket. Bus 100 goes via the Tiergarten and bus 200 via Potsdamer Platz. Without traffic and getting off, trips take about 30 minutes.

(white-brick walls, polished wooden tables) in 2016, they added another rung to Berlin's food ladder. The menu is constantly in flux, but by turning carefully edited ingredients into shareable small and big plates, Ben fearlessly captures the city's adventurous and uninhibited spirit. Casual fine dining at its best.

Schöneberg

BRLO Brwhouse INTERNATIONAL €€
(Map p266; ☎0151 7437 4235; www.brlo-brwhouse.de; Schöneberger Strasse 16; mains from €18; ⏱restaurant 5pm-midnight Tue-Fri, noon-midnight Sat & Sun, beer garden noon-midnight Apr-Sep; 📶👪; U Gleisdreieck) The house-crafted suds flow freely at this shooting star among Berlin's craft breweries. Production, taproom and restaurant are all housed in 38 shipping containers fronted by a big beer garden with a sand box and views of Gleisdreieckpark. Shareable dishes are mostly vegetable-centric, although missing out on the meat prepared to succulent perfection in a smoker would be a shame.

Drinking & Nightlife

★Prater Garten BEER GARDEN
(☎030-448 5688; www.pratergarten.de; Kastanienallee 7-9; snacks €2.50-7.50; ⏱noon-late Apr-Sep, weather permitting; 👪; 🚋M1, 12, U Eberswalder Strasse) Berlin's oldest beer garden has seen beer-soaked days and nights since 1837 and is still a charismatic spot for guzzling a custom-brewed Prater pilsner (self-service) beneath the ancient chestnut trees. Kids can romp around the small play area.

Bar am Steinplatz COCKTAIL BAR
(Map p266; ☎030-554 4440; www.hotelsteinplatz.com; Steinplatz 4; ⏱4pm-late; U Ernst-Reuter-Platz) Christian Gentemann's liquid playground at the art deco **Hotel am Steinplatz** (Map p266; r €100-290; P⊝❄@📶🐾) was crowned 'Hotel Bar of the Year' in 2016 and 2017, and for good reason The drinks here are simply sensational and the ambience is a perfect blend of hip and grown-up. The illustrated cocktail menu teases the imagination by listing ingredients and tastes for each drink instead of just an abstract name.

Berghain/Panorama Bar CLUB
(Map p264; www.berghain.de; Am Wriezener Bahnhof; ⏱Fri-Mon; S Ostbahnhof) Only world-class spin-masters heat up this hedonistic bass-junkie hellhole inside a labyrinthine ex-powerplant. Hard-edged minimal techno dominates the ex-turbine hall (Berghain), while house dominates at Panorama Bar, one floor up. Long lines, strict door, no cameras. Check the website for midweek concerts and record-release parties at the main venue and the adjacent **Kantine am Berghain** (Map p264; admission varies; ⏱hours vary).

Clärchens Ballhaus CLUB
(Map p260; ☎030-282 9295; www.ballhaus.de; Auguststrasse 24; Sun-Thu free, Fri & Sat €5; ⏱11am-late; 🚋M1, S Oranienburger Strasse) Yesteryear is now at this early-20th-century dance hall where groovers and grannies hoof it across the parquet without even a touch of irony. There are different sounds nightly – salsa to swing, tango to disco – and a live band on Saturday. Dancing kicks off from 9pm or 9.30pm. Ask about dance lessons. Tables can only be reserved if you plan on eating.

://about blank CLUB
(Map p264; www.aboutparty.net; Markgrafendamm 24c; ⏱hours vary, always Fri & Sat; S Ostkreuz) At this gritty multifloor party pen with lots of nooks and crannies, a steady line-up of top DJs feeds a diverse bunch of revellers with dance-worthy electronic gruel. Intense club nights usually segue into the morning and beyond. Run by a collec-

ℹ DISCOUNT CARDS

Berlin Welcome Card (www.berlin-welcomecard.de; travel in AB zones 48/72 hours €19.90/28.90, AB zones 72 hours plus admission to Museumsinsel €45) Valid for unlimited public transport for one adult and up to three children under 14 plus up to 50% discount to 200 sights, attractions and tours. Sold online, at the tourist offices, from U-Bahn and S-Bahn station ticket vending machines and on buses.

Museumspass Berlin (adult/concession €29/14.50) Buys admission to the permanent exhibits of about 30 museums for three consecutive days, including big draws like the Pergamonmuseum. Sold at tourist offices and participating museums.

tive, the venue also hosts cultural, political and gender events.

Strandbar Mitte BAR

(Map p260; ☎030-2838 5588; www.strandbar-mitte.de; Monbijoustrasse 3; dancing €4; ⊙10am-late May-Sep; 🚊M1, Ⓢ Oranienburger Strasse) A full-on view of the Spree River and the majestic Bode-Museum combines with a relaxed ambience at Germany's first beach bar (since 2002). A stint here is great for balancing a surfeit of sightseeing stimulus with a reviving drink and thin-crust pizza. At night, there's dancing under the stars with tango, cha-cha, swing and salsa, often preceded by dance lessons.

☆ Entertainment

Staatsoper Berlin OPERA

(Map p260; ☎030-2035 4554; www.staatsoper-berlin.de; Unter den Linden 7; tickets €12-250; 🚌100, 200, TXL, Ⓤ Französische Strasse) After a seven-year exile, Berlin's most famous opera company is once again performing at the venerable neoclassical Staatsoper Unter den Linden, which emerged from a massive refurbishment in 2017. Its repertory includes works from four centuries along with concerts and classical and modern ballet, all under the musical leadership of Daniel Barenboim.

Berliner Philharmoniker CLASSICAL MUSIC

(Map p266; ☎tickets 030-2548 8999; www.berliner-philharmoniker.de; Herbert-von-Karajan-Strasse 1; tickets €21-290; 🚌M29, M48, M85, 200, Ⓢ Potsdamer Platz, Ⓤ Potsdamer Platz) One of the world's most famous orchestras, the Berliner Philharmoniker, is based at the tent-like **Philharmonie** (Map p266; ☎030-2548 8156; tours adult/concession €5/3; ⊙tours 1.30pm Sep-Jun), designed by Hans Scharoun in the 1950s and built in the 1960s. In 2018, Sir Simon Rattle, who had been chief conductor since 2002, passed on the baton to the Russia-born Kirill Petrenko. Tickets can be booked online.

ℹ Information

Alexanderplatz (☎030-250 025; www.visitberlin.de; lobby Park Inn, Alexanderplatz 7; ⊙7am-9pm Mon-Sat, 8am-6pm Sun)

Brandenburg Gate (Map p260; ☎030-250 023; Pariser Platz, Brandenburger Tor, south wing; ⊙9.30am-7pm Apr-Oct, to 6pm Nov-Mar)

Central Bus Station (ZOB) (Masurenallee 4-6; ⊙8am-8pm Mon, Fri & Sat, to 4pm Tue-Thu & Sun; Ⓢ Messe Nord/ICC)

Europa-Center (Map p266; ☎030 2500 2333; Tauentzienstrasse 9, ground fl; ⊙10am-8pm Mon-Sat; 🚌100, 200, Ⓤ Kurfürstendamm, Zoologischer Garten, Ⓢ Zoologischer Garten)

Hauptbahnhof (☎030-250 025; www.visitberlin.de; Hauptbahnhof, Europaplatz entrance, ground fl; ⊙8am-10pm)

LGBTIQ+ BERLIN

Berlin's legendary liberalism has spawned one of the world's biggest and most diverse LGBTIQ+ playgrounds. The historic 'gay village' is near Nollendorfplatz in Schöneberg (Motzstrasse and Fuggerstrasse especially; get off at U-Bahn station Nollendorfplatz), where the rainbow flag has proudly flown since the 1920s. The crowd skews older and leather. Current hipster central is Kreuzberg, where freewheeling party pens cluster along Oranienstrasse. Check *Siegessäule* (www.siegessaeule.de), the weekly freebie 'bible' to all things LGBTIQ+ in town, for the latest happenings.

ℹ Getting There & Away

AIR

Most visitors arrive in Berlin by air. After an eight-year delay, **Berlin Brandenburg Airport** (BER; ☎030 609 160 910; https://ber.berlin-airport.de; Schönefelder Allee), about 27km south of the city centre, finally launched its inaugural flight on 31 October 2020. The previous airports in Tegel and Schönefeld are closed.

BUS

Most long-haul buses arrive at the **Zentraler Omnibusbahnhof** (ZOB, Central Bus Station; ☎030-3010 0175; www.zob-berlin.de; Messedamm 8; Ⓢ Messe/ICC Nord, Ⓤ Kaiserdamm) near the trade fair grounds in far western Berlin. The U2 U-Bahn line links to the city centre. Some bus operators also stop at Alexanderplatz and other points around town.

TRAIN

Berlin has several train stations, but most trains converge at the **Hauptbahnhof** (Main Train Station; Europaplatz, Washingtonplatz; Ⓢ Hauptbahnhof, Ⓤ Hauptbahnhof) in the heart of the city.

Getting Around

TO/FROM THE AIRPORT

The railway station is below Terminal 1. You'll need an ABC ticket (€3.80) for these journeys:

FEX Airport Express Travels every half hour between 4am and midnight between the Hauptbahnhof (main train station) and T1/2 in 30 minutes. Also stops at Gesundbrunnen and Ostkreuz.

Regional Trains Regular Deutsche Bahn trains designated RE7 and RB14 make hourly trips from the city centre to T1/T2 (30 minutes).

S-Bahn S-Bahns run along the same tracks but stop more frequently. The S9 leaves every 20 minutes and needs about 45 minutes to/from the city centre.

PUBLIC TRANSPORT

➡ One ticket is valid on all forms of public transport, including the U-Bahn, buses, trams and ferries. Most rides require a Tariff AB ticket, which is valid for two hours (interruptions and transfers allowed, but not return trips).

➡ Tickets are available from bus drivers, vending machines at U- and S-Bahn stations and on trams and at station offices. Expect to pay cash (change given) and be sure to validate (stamp) your ticket or risk a €60 fine during spot-checks.

➡ Services operate from 4am to 12.30am and all night Friday, Saturday and public holidays.

➡ For trip planning, check the **BVG** (☎ hotline 030-194 49; www.bvg.de) website or call the 24-hour hotline.

SAXONY

POP 4 MILLION

Placed where northern plains abut mountain ranges and German efficiency meets Slavic flamboyance, and packed with elegant hilltop castles and lavish baroque palaces, Saxony is the definition of Central Europe. It was also at the centre of events during the most decisive points in European history, such as the Reformation, the Napoleonic Wars, and the velvet revolutions that dismantled Communist regimes in the late 1980s.

Dresden

☎ 0351 / POP 563,000

Proof that there is life after death, Dresden has become one of Germany's most visited cities, and for good reason. Restorations have returned its historical core to its 18th-century heyday when it was famous throughout Europe as 'Florence on the Elbe'. Scores of Italian artists, musicians, actors and master craftsmen flocked to the court of Augustus the Strong, bestowing countless masterpieces upon the city. The devastating bombing raids in 1945 levelled most of these treasures. But Dresden is a survivor and many of the most important landmarks have since been rebuilt, including the elegant Frauenkirche. Today there's a constantly evolving arts and cultural scene and zinging pub and nightlife quarters, especially in the Outer Neustadt.

Sights

Dresden straddles the Elbe River, with the attraction-studded Altstadt (old town) in the south and the Neustadt (new town) pub and student quarter to the north.

★Zwinger PALACE

(☎ 0351-4914 2000; www.der-dresdner-zwinger.de; Theaterplatz 1; ticket for all museums adult/concession €12/9, courtyard free; ⏲6am-10pm Apr-Oct, to 8pm Nov-Mar) A collaboration between the architect Matthäus Pöppelmann and the sculptor Balthasar Permoser, the Zwinger was built between 1710 and 1728 on the orders of Augustus the Strong, who, having returned from seeing Louis XIV's palace at Versailles, wanted something similar for himself. Primarily a party palace for royals, the Zwinger has ornate portals that lead into the vast fountain-studded courtyard, which is framed by buildings lavishly adorned with evocative sculpture. Today it houses three superb museums within its baroque walls.

★Gemäldegalerie Alte Meister MUSEUM

(Old Masters Gallery; www.skd.museum; Zwinger, Theaterplatz 1; adult/concession €12/9, audioguide €3; ⏲10am-6pm Tue-Sun) This astounding collection of European art from the 16th to 18th centuries houses an incredible number of masterpieces, including Raphael's famous *Sistine Madonna* (1513), which dominates the enormous main hall on the ground floor, as well as works by Titian, Tintoretto, Holbein, Dürer, and Cranach, whose *Paradise* (1530) is particularly arresting. Upstairs you'll find an exquisite display of Rembrandt, Botticelli, Veronese, Van Dyck, Vermeer, Brueghel and Poussin. Finally, don't miss Canaletto's sumptuous portrayals of 18th-century Dresden on the top floor.

★Albertinum GALLERY

(Galerie Neue Meister; ☎ 0351-4914 2000; www.skd.museum; enter from Brühlsche Terrasse or Georg-Treu-Platz 2; adult/concession/child under 17yr €10/7.50/free; ⏲10am-6pm Tue-Sun) The

WORTH A TRIP

SACHSENHAUSEN CONCENTRATION CAMP

A mere 35km north of Berlin, Sachsenhausen was built by prisoners and opened in 1936 as a prototype for other concentration camps. By 1945 some 200,000 people had passed through its sinister gates, most of them political opponents, Jews, Roma people and, after 1939, POWs. Tens of thousands died from hunger, exhaustion, illness, exposure, medical experiments and executions. The camp became a **memorial site** (Memorial & Museum Sachsenhausen; ☎03301-200 200; www.stiftung-bg.de; Strasse der Nationen 22, Oranienburg; ⏰8.30am-6pm mid-Mar–mid-Oct, to 4.30pm mid-Oct–mid-Mar, museums closed Mon mid-Oct–mid-Mar; P; S Oranienburg) FREE in 1961. A tour of the grounds, remaining buildings and exhibits will leave no one untouched. Unless you're on a guided tour, pick up a leaflet (€0.50) or, better yet, an audioguide (€3, including leaflet) at the visitor centre to get a better grasp of this huge site. Between mid-October and mid-March avoid visiting on a Monday when all indoor exhibits are closed. The S-Bahn S1 makes the trip to Oranienburg train station thrice hourly (ABC ticket €3.40, 45 minutes), from where it's a 2km signposted walk or a ride on hourly bus 804 to the site.

Renaissance-era former arsenal is the stunning home of the **Galerie Neue Meister** (New Masters Gallery), which displays an array of paintings by some of the great names in art from the 18th century onwards. Caspar David Friedrich and Claude Monet's landscapes compete with the abstract visions of Marc Chagall and Gerhard Richter, all in gorgeous rooms orbiting a light-filled courtyard. There's also a superb sculpture collection spread over the lower floors.

★Historisches Grünes Gewölbe MUSEUM
(Historic Green Vault; ☎0351-4914 2000; www.skd.museum; Residenzschloss; €12; ⏰10am-6pm Wed-Mon) The Historic Green Vault displays some 3000 precious items in the same fashion as during the time of August der Starke, namely on shelves and tables without glass protection in a series of increasingly lavish rooms. Admission is by timed ticket only, and only a limited number of visitors per hour may pass through the 'dust lock'. Get advance tickets online or by phone, since only 40% are sold at the palace box office for same-day admission.

Frauenkirche CHURCH
(☎0351-6560 6100; www.frauenkirche-dresden.de; Neumarkt; audioguide €2.50, cupola adult/student €8/5; ⏰10am-noon & 1-6pm Mon-Fri, weekend hours vary) The domed Frauenkirche – Dresden's most beloved symbol – has literally risen from the city's ashes. The original church graced the skyline for two centuries before collapsing after the February 1945 bombing, and was rebuilt from a pile of rubble between 1994 and 2005. A spitting image of the original, today's structure may not bear the gravitas of age but that only slightly detracts from its beauty, inside and out. The altar, reassembled from nearly 2000 fragments, is especially striking.

Neues Grünes Gewölbe MUSEUM
(New Green Vault; ☎0351-4914 2000; www.skd.museum; Residenzschloss; adult/under 17yr incl audioguide €12/free; ⏰10am-6pm Wed-Mon) The New Green Vault presents some 1000 objects in 10 modern rooms. Key sights include a frigate fashioned from ivory with wafer-thin sails, a cherry pit with 185 faces carved into it, and an ensemble of 132 gem studded figurines representing a royal court in India. The artistry of each item is dazzling. To avoid the worst crush of people, visit during lunchtime.

Festivals & Events

Striezelmarkt CHRISTMAS MARKET
(Altmarkt) In December, sample the famous Dresdner Stollen (fruit cake) at one of Germany's oldest and best Christmas markets.

Sleeping & Eating

The Neustadt has oodles of cafes and restaurants, especially along Königstrasse and the streets north of Albertplatz. The latter is also the centre of Dresden's nightlife. Altstadt restaurants are more tourist-geared and pricier.

★Hotel Schloss Eckberg HOTEL €€
(☎0351-809 90; www.schloss-eckberg.de; Bautzner Strasse 134; d Kavaliershaus/Schloss from €99/134; P❄️📶) This romantic castle set in its own riverside park east of the Neustadt is a breathtaking place to stay. Rooms in the Schloss itself are pricier and have oodles of historic flair, but staying in the modern Kavaliershaus lets you enjoy almost as many amenities and the same dreamy setting.

WORTH A TRIP

MEISSEN

Straddling the Elbe around 25km upstream from Dresden, Meissen is the cradle of European porcelain, which was first cooked up in 1710 in its imposing castle, the **Albrechtsburg** (☎03521-470 70; www.albrechtsburg-meissen.de; Domplatz 1; adult/concession incl audioguide €8/6.50, with Dom €11/8; ⏰10am-6pm Mar-Oct, to 5pm Nov-Feb). An exhibit on the 2nd floor chronicles how it all began. Highlights of the adjacent **cathedral** (☎03521-452 490; www.dom-zu-meissen.de; Domplatz 7; adult/concession €4.50/3, with Albrechtsburg €11/8; ⏰9am-6pm Apr-Oct, 10am-4pm Nov-Mar) include medieval stained-glass windows and an altarpiece by Lucas Cranach the Elder. Both squat atop a ridge overlooking Meissen's handsome Altstadt (old town).

Since 1863, porcelain production has taken place in a custom-built factory, about 1km south of the Altstadt. Next to it is the **Erlebniswelt Haus Meissen** (☎03521-468 208; www.meissen.com; Talstrasse 9; adult/concession €10/6; ⏰9am-6pm May-Oct, to 5pm Nov-Apr), a vastly popular porcelain museum where you can witness the astonishing artistry and craftsmanship that makes Meissen porcelain unique. Note that entry is timed and only in groups, so you may have to wait a while during high season.

For details and further information about the town, stop by the **tourist office** (☎03521-419 40; www.touristinfo-meissen.de; Markt 3; ⏰10am-6pm Mon-Fri, to 4pm Sat & Sun Apr-Oct, to 5pm Mon-Fri, to 3pm Sat Nov, Dec, Feb & Mar).

Half-hourly S1 trains run to Meissen from Dresden's Hauptbahnhof and Neustadt train stations (€6, 20 minutes). For the Erlebniswelt, get off at Meissen-Triebischtal. Boats operated by **Sächsische Dampfschiffahrt** (☎03521-866 090; www.saechsische-dampfschiffahrt.de; one way/return €16.50/21.50; ⏰May-Sep) make the trip to Meissen from the Terrassenufer in Dresden in two hours. Consider going one way by boat and the other by train.

Gewandhaus Hotel BOUTIQUE HOTEL €€€
(☎0351-494 90; www.gewandhaus-hotel.de; Ringstrasse 1; d from €157; P ❄ @ 📶 🏊) Revamped as a boutique hotel a few years ago, the stunning Gewandhaus, an 18th-century trading house of tailors and fabric merchants that burned down in 1945, boasts sleek public areas, beautiful and bright rooms, and a breakfast that sets a high bar for the city.

Little India INDIAN €€
(☎0351-3232 6400; www.littleindia-dresden.de; Louisenstrasse 48; mains €10-15; ⏰11am-2.30pm & 5-11pm Tue-Sat, to 10pm Sun; 🌿) Bright, minimalist and informal, this fantastic Indian restaurant is a world away from most in Dresden, and its popularity is obvious (be prepared to wait for a table when it's busy). The large menu (available in English) includes superb tandoori dishes and an entire vegetarian section, as well as standard chicken, lamb and pork mains. The naan is heavenly.

★**Restaurant Genuss-Atelier** GERMAN €€€
(☎0351-2502 8337; www.genuss-atelier.net; Bautzner Strasse 149; mains €15-27; ⏰5-11pm Wed-Fri, noon-3.30pm & 5-11pm Sat & Sun; 🚊11 to Waldschlösschen) Lighting up Dresden's culinary scene is this fantastic place that's well worth the trip on the 11 tram. The creative menu is streets ahead of most offerings elsewhere, although the best way to experience the 'Pleasure-Atelier' is to book a surprise menu (three/four/five courses €39/49/59) and let the chefs show off their craft. Reservations essential.

☆ Entertainment

Semperoper Dresden OPERA
(☎0351-491 1705; www.semperoper.de; Theaterplatz 2; ⏰ticket office 10am-6pm Mon-Fri, to 5pm Sat & Sun) Dresden's famous opera house is the home of the Sächsische Staatsoper Dresden, which puts on brilliant performances that usually sell out.

ℹ Information

There are tourist office branches inside the **Hauptbahnhof** (☎0351-501 501; www.dresden.de; Wiener Platz; ⏰8am-8pm) and near the **Frauenkirche** (☎0351-501 501; www.dresden.de; QF Passage, Neumarkt 2; ⏰10am-7pm Mon-Fri, to 6pm Sat, to 3pm Sun). Both book rooms and tours and rent out audioguides.

ℹ Getting There & Away

Dresden International Airport (DRS; ☎0351-881 3360; www.dresden-airport.de; Flughafenstrasse) is about 9km north of the city centre and linked by the S2 train several times hourly (€2.30, 20 minutes).

Fast trains make the trip to Dresden from Berlin-Hauptbahnhof in two hours (€40) and Leipzig in 1¼ hours (€19.90). The S1 local train runs half-hourly to Meissen (€6.20, 40 minutes) and Bad Schandau in Saxon Switzerland (€6.20, 45 minutes).

Leipzig & Western Saxony

The more industrialised western part of Saxony centres on Leipzig, a green, hip and vibrant city with many stories to tell and places to enjoy. Hugely important in the history of music, it was home to Johann Sebastian Bach and Richard Wagner.

Leipzig

0341 / POP 590,300

Hypezig! cry the papers. The New Berlin, says just about everybody. Yes, Leipzig is Saxony's coolest city, a playground for nomadic young creatives who have been displaced even by the fast gentrifying German capital. But Leipzig is also a city of enormous history and is known as the *Stadt der Helden* (City of Heroes) for its leading role in the 1989 'Peaceful Revolution' that helped bring the Cold War to an end. The city is solidly in the sights of classical music lovers due to its intrinsic connection to the lives and work of Bach, Mendelssohn and Wagner.

Sights

★Museum der Bildenden Künste MUSEUM
(0341-216 990; www.mdbk.de; Katharinenstrasse 10; adult/concession €10/7, audio guide €2; 10am-6pm Tue & Thu-Sun, noon-8pm Wed) This imposing modernist glass cube is the home of Leipzig's fine art museum and its world-class collection of paintings from the 15th century to today, including works by Caspar David Friedrich, Cranach, Munch and Monet. Highlights include rooms dedicated to native sons Max Beckmann, Max Klinger and Neo Rauch. Exhibits are playfully juxtaposed and include sculpture, installation and religious art. The collection is enormous, so set aside at least two hours to do it justice.

★Nikolaikirche CHURCH
(Church of St Nicholas; www.nikolaikirche.de; Nikolaikirchhof 3; 10am-6pm Mon-Sat, to 4pm Sun) This church has Romanesque and Gothic roots, but since 1797 has sported a striking neoclassical interior with palm-like pillars and cream-coloured pews. While the design is certainly gorgeous, the church is most famous for playing a key role in the nonviolent movement that led to the downfall of the East German government. As early as 1982 it hosted 'peace prayers' every Monday at 5pm (still held today), which over time inspired and empowered local citizens to confront the injustices plaguing their country.

Asisi Panometer GALLERY
(0341-355 5340; www.asisi.de; Richard-Lehmann-Strasse 114; adult/concession €11.50/10; 10am-5pm Mon-Fri, to 6pm Sat & Sun; 16 to Richard-Lehmann/Zwickauer Strasse) The happy marriage of a *pan*orama (a giant 360-degree painting) and a gas*ometer* (a giant gas tank) is a panometer. The unusual concept is the brainchild of Berlin-based artist Yadegar Asisi, who uses paper and pencil and computer technology to create bafflingly detailed monumental scenes drawn from nature or history. Each work is about 100m long and 30m high.

Sleeping & Eating

★Steigenberger Grandhotel Handelshof HOTEL €€€
(0341-350 5810; www.steigenberger.com; Salzgässchen 6; r from €182;) Behind the imposing historic facade of a 1909 municipal trading hall, this exclusive boutique luxury joint outclasses most of Leipzig's hotels with its super-central location, charmingly efficient team and modern rooms with crisp white-silver-purple colours, high ceilings and marble bathrooms. The stylish bi-level spa is the perfect bliss-out station.

★Stadtpfeiffer INTERNATIONAL €€€
(0341-217 8920; www.stadtpfeiffer.de; Augustusplatz 8; 4-/6-course menu €108/128; 6-11pm Tue-Sat) Petra and Deflef Schlegel give deceptively simple-sounding dishes the star treatment, and were deservedly the first in Leipzig to get the Michelin nod. Pairing punctilious artisanship with bottomless imagination, they create such exquisitely calibrated dishes as smoked Arctic char with foie gras or warm chocolate cake with lavender ice cream. It's a relaxed spot inside the Gewandhaus concert hall.

Auerbachs Keller GERMAN €€€
(0341-216 100; www.auerbachs-keller-leipzig.de; Mädlerpassage, Grimmaische Strasse 2-4; mains Keller €16-28, Weinstuben €33-35; Keller noon-11pm daily, Weinstuben 6-11pm Mon-Sat) Founded in 1525, Auerbachs Keller is one of Germany's best-known restaurants. It's cosy and touristy, but the food's actually quite good and the

setting memorable. There are two sections: the vaulted Grosser Keller for hearty Saxonian dishes and the four historic rooms of the Historische Weinstuben for upmarket German fare. Reservations are highly advised.

☆ Entertainment

Gewandhausorchester CLASSICAL MUSIC
(☎0341-127 0280; www.gewandhausorchester.de; Augustusplatz 8) Led by Latvian conductor Andris Nelsons, the Gewandhaus is one of Europe's finest and oldest civic orchestras. With a history harking back to 1743, it became an orchestra of European renown a century later under music director Felix Mendelssohn-Bartholdy.

ℹ Information

Tourist Office (☎0341-710 4260; www.leipzig.travel; Katharinenstrasse 8; ⊙10am-6pm Mon-Fri, to 4pm Sat, to 3pm Sun) Room referral, ticket sales, maps and general information. Also sells the **Leipzig Card** (one/three days €11.90/23.50), which is good for free or discounted admission to attractions, plus free travel on public transport.

ℹ Getting There & Away

Leipzig-Halle Airport (LEJ; ☎0341-2240; www.leipzig-halle-airport.de) is about 21km west of Leipzig.

High-speed trains frequently serve Frankfurt (€88, 3¾ hours), Dresden (€26.50, 1¼ hours) and Berlin (€49, 1¼ hours), among other cities.

CENTRAL GERMANY

Crucial to its culture, science, industry and history, Mitteldeutschland is Germany's beating heart. It is studded with cities whose historical importance matches their modern vitality (Weimar, Erfurt and Kassel are just the first names on this list). Ridged by low, forested mountains that loom large in German mythology, it's also edified by museums, cathedrals and castles without number.

Weimar

☎03643 / POP 64,426

Historical epicentre of the German Enlightenment, Weimar is an essential stop for anyone with a passion for German history and culture. A pantheon of intellectual and creative giants lived and worked here: Goethe, Schiller, Bach, Cranach, Liszt, Nietzsche, Gropius, Herder, Feininger, Kandinsky...the list goes on. In summer, Weimar's many parks and gardens lend themselves to quiet contemplation of the town's intellectual and cultural onslaught, or to taking a break from it.

Sights

★**Gedenkstätte Buchenwald** MEMORIAL
(☎03463-4300; www.buchenwald.de; Buchenwald; ⊙9am-6pm Apr-Oct, to 4pm Nov-Mar; P) Between 1937 and 1945, hidden from Weimarers and surrounding villagers, 250,000 men, women and children were incarcerated here, some 56,500 of whom were murdered. Buchenwald ('Beech Forest') has been preserved almost untouched as a memorial, with visitors encouraged to wander quietly and freely around the numerous structures, including the crematorium. Tours, pamphlets and books in English are available, as are excellent multilanguage audio guides (€3, or €5 with images). Last admission is 30 minutes before closing.

★**Goethe-Nationalmuseum** MUSEUM
(☎03643-545 400; www.klassik-stiftung.de; Frauenplan 1; adult/concession €12.50/9; ⊙9.30am-6pm Tue-Sun Apr-Oct, to 4pm Nov-Mar) This is the world's leading museum on Johann Wolfgang von Goethe, Germany's literary colossus. It incorporates his home of 50 years, gifted by Duke Carl August to keep him in Weimar, and left largely as it was upon his death in 1832. This is where Goethe worked, studied, researched, and penned *Faust* and other immortal works. In a modern annexe, documents and objects shed light on the man and his achievements in literature, art, science and politics.

★**Herzogin Anna Amalia Bibliothek** LIBRARY
(☎03643-545 400; www.klassik-stiftung.de; Platz der Demokratie 1; adult/concession €8/6.50; ⊙9.30am-2.30pm Tue-Sun) Assembled by Duchess Anna Amalia (1739–1807), the power (and purse) behind Weimar's classical florescence, this Unesco-listed library has been beautifully reconstructed after a fire in 2004 destroyed much of the building and its priceless contents. Some of the most precious tomes are housed in the magnificent Rokokosaal (Rococo Hall), and were once used by Goethe, Schiller, Christoph Wieland, Johann Herder and other Weimar hot shots, whose various busts and paintings still keep watch over the collection.

Sleeping & Eating

Labyrinth Hostel HOSTEL €

(☎03643-811 822; www.weimar-hostel.com; Goetheplatz 6; dm/d €18/48, linen €2; @📶) This super-friendly, professionally run hostel offers imaginative, artist-designed rooms. In one double the bed perches on stacks of books, while the 'purple room' features a wooden platform bed. There are en suites and shared bathrooms, plus a communal kitchen and lovely rooftop terrace. Breakfast costs €4, and the hostel will buy ingredients for guests to cook shared meals from their home countries.

★**Design Apartments Weimar** APARTMENT €€

(☎017 2356 2210; www.hier-war-goethe-nie.de; Fuldaer Strasse 85; 1-/2-/3-bedroom apt from €60/95/95; 📶) Get in quick to snap up one of these enormous, self-contained, fully renovated heritage apartments run by charming and generous hosts. The three apartments (with one, two or three bedrooms) are designed by Bauhaus University graduates: if you like their choice in fittings, they're available from the online shop. The ideal base from which to explore the delights of Weimar.

Gretchen's Cafe & Restaurant CAFE €€

(☎03643-457 9877; http://gretchens-weimar.de; Seifengasse 8; mains €19-20; ⏲9am-11pm; 👪) Located on the ground floor of the Familienhotel, and thus family friendly, this passionately locavore cafe offers great alternatives to the Thuringian standards available across Weimar. For those intent only on snacking and chatting, it serves great cakes, tea and coffee, but the meals (including great-value €7.50 midday specials such as salmon en papillote, with abundant salad) are wholesome and delightful.

Information

Tourist Office (☎03643-7450; www.weimar.de; Markt 10; ⏲9.30am-6pm Mon-Sat, to 2pm Sun Apr-Oct, 9.30am-5pm Mon-Fri, to 2pm Sat & Sun Nov-Mar) Pick up a great-value **Weimar Card** (€30 for two days) for free admission to most museums, free iGuides, free travel on city buses and discounted tours.

Getting There & Away

Frequent regional trains go from Weimar Hauptbahnhof, 1km north of Goetheplatz, to Erfurt (€5.80, 15 minutes), Jena (€5.80, 15 minutes), Gotha (€10, 40 minutes) and Eisenach (€16, one hour).

Erfurt

☎0361 / POP 212,988

A little river courses through this Instagram-pretty medieval pastiche of sweeping squares, time-worn alleyways, a house-lined bridge (Krämerbrücke) and lofty church spires. Erfurt also boasts one of Germany's oldest universities, founded by rich merchants in 1392, where Martin Luther studied philosophy before becoming a monk at the local monastery. It's a refreshingly untouristed spot and well worth exploring

Sights

Erfurt's main sights cluster in the old town, about a 10-minute walk from the train station (or quick ride on tram 3, 4 or 6).

★**Erfurter Dom** CATHEDRAL

(Mariendom; ☎0361-646 1265; www.dom-erfurt.de; Domplatz; ⏲9.30am-6pm Mon-Sat, 1-6pm Sun May-Oct, to 5pm Nov-Apr) FREE Erfurt's cathedral, where Martin Luther was ordained a priest, grew over the centuries from a simple 8th-century chapel into the stately Gothic pile of today. Standouts in its treasure-filled interior include the stained-glass windows; the 'Wolfram' (an 850-year-old bronze candelabrum in the shape of a man); the 'Gloriosa' (the world's largest free-swinging medieval bell); a Romanesque stucco Madonna; Cranach's *The Mystic Marriage of St Catherine*; and the intricately carved choir stalls. Group tours start at €4.50 per person.

★**Zitadelle Petersberg** FORTRESS

(☎0361-664 00; Petersberg 3; tour adult/concession €8/4; ⏲7pm Fri & Sat May-Oct) Situated on the Petersberg hill northwest of Domplatz, this 36-hectare citadel ranks among Europe's largest and best-preserved Baroque fortresses. While most interior buildings are closed to the public (and daubed with stencils by guerrilla artists), it sits above a honeycomb of tunnels that can be explored on two-hour guided tours (in German), run by the tourist office. Otherwise, it's free to roam the external grounds, and to enjoy fabulous views over Erfurt.

Sleeping & Eating

Opera Hostel HOSTEL €

(☎0361-6013 1360; www.opera-hostel.de; Walkmühlstrasse 13; dm €15-22, s/d/tr €50/60/80, linen €2.50; @📶) This upmarket hostel in an 18th-century hotel scores big with

WORTH A TRIP

WARTBURG CASTLE

On the edge of the Thuringian forest, Eisenach is the birthplace of Johann Sebastian Bach, but even the town's **museum** (☎03691-793 40; www.bachhaus.de; Frauenplan 21; adult/concession €9.50/5; ⊙10am-6pm) dedicated to the great composer plays second fiddle to its main attraction: the awe-inspiring 11th-century **Wartburg** (☎03691-2500; www.wartburg-eisenach.de; Auf der Wartburg 1; tour adult/concession €9/5, museum & Luther study only €5/3; ⊙tours 8.30am-5pm Apr-Oct, 9am-3.30pm Nov-Mar, English tour 1.30pm) castle.

Perched high above the town (views!), the humungous pile hosted medieval minstrel song contests and was the home of Elisabeth, a Hungarian princess later canonised for her charitable deeds. Its most famous resident, however, was Martin Luther, who went into hiding here in 1521 after being excommunicated and placed under papal ban. During this 10-month stay, he translated the New Testament from Greek into German, contributing enormously to the development of the written German language. His modest study is part of the guided tour. Back in town, there's an exhibit about the man and his historical impact in the **Lutherhaus** (☎03691-298 30; www.lutherhaus-eisenach.com; Lutherplatz 8; permanent & special collections adult/concession €8/6; ⊙10am-5pm, closed Mon Nov-Mar), where he lived as a schoolboy.

In summer, arrive before 11am to avoid the worst of the crowds. From April to October, bus 10 runs hourly from 9am to 5pm from the Hauptbahnhof to the Eselstation stop, from where it's a steep 10-minute walk up to the castle.

Regional trains run frequently to Erfurt (€14, 45 minutes) and Weimar (€15, one hour). The tourist office can help with finding accommodation.

wallet-watching global nomads, especially as reception's open round the clock and there's no lockout or curfew. Rooms are bright and spacious, many with sofas. Make friends in the communal kitchen and on-site lounge-bar, or pedal around the city on one of the hostel's bikes (€10 per day).

★Hotel Brühlerhöhe BOUTIQUE HOTEL **€€**
(☎0361-241 4990; www.hotel-bruehlerhoehe-erfurt.de; Rudolfstrasse 48; s/d from €80/95; P 🛜) This Prussian officers' casino turned chic city hotel gets high marks for its opulent breakfast spread (€12.50) and smiling, quick-on-their-feet staff. Rooms are cosy and modern with chocolate-brown furniture, solid timberwork, thick carpets and sparkling baths. It's a short ride on tram 4 (from the Justizzentrum stop) into central Erfurt.

Faustfood BARBECUE **€**
(☎0361-6443 6300; www.faustfood.de; Waagegasse 1; mains €10; ⊙11am-11pm Wed-Sat, to 7pm Sun) Despite its casual, student-y vibe, this rambunctious grill house is a great place for traditional Thuringian grills (*Rostbrätel* and bratwurst), plus more international meaty treats such as spare ribs, steak and cheeseburgers. Dine in (under the canopy of grill-smoke that hangs below the rafters of what was a medieval barn) or take away, but head elsewhere if you're vegetarian!

★Zum Wenigemarkt 13 GERMAN **€€**
(☎0361-642 2379; www.wenigemarkt-13.de; Wenigemarkt 13; mains €13-18; ⊙11.30am-11pm) This upbeat restaurant in a delightful spot (an 18th-century house on the small marketplace at the eastern end of the Krämerbrücke) serves traditional and updated takes on Thuringian cuisine, starring regionally hunted and gathered ingredients where possible. Tender neck fillets of pork with sauerkraut and Thuringian dumplings and roasted char with potato-coconut purée are both menu stars.

ℹ Information

Tourist Office Erfurt (☎0361-664 00; www.erfurt-tourismus.de; Benediktsplatz 1; ⊙10am-6pm Mon-Sat, to 3pm Sun) Sells the 48-hour **ErfurtCard**, available in two configurations: the Classic (€13) provides a free tour (in German) entry to the Alte Synagoge and discounts to all major attractions, while the Mobil (€18) also includes free use of the city's transport.

ℹ Getting There & Away

Direct IC/ICE trains connect Erfurt with Berlin (from €40, two hours), Dresden (from €25, two hours) and Frankfurt (from €30, 2½ hours). Direct regional trains also run regularly to Weimar (€5.80, 15 minutes) and Eisenach (€14, 45 minutes).

BAVARIA

POP 12.4 MILLION

From the cloud-shredding Alps to the fertile Danube plain, Bavaria (Bayern) is a place that keeps its clichéd promises. Storybook castles bequeathed by an oddball king poke through dark forest, cowbells tinkle in flower-filled meadows, the thwack of palm on Lederhosen accompanies the clump of frothy stein on timber, and medieval walled towns go about their time-warped business.

But there's so much more than the chocolate-box idyll. Learn about Bavaria's state-of-the-art motor industry in Munich, discover its Nazi past in Nuremberg and Berchtesgaden, sip world-class wines in Würzburg or take a mindboggling train ride up Germany's highest mountains.

Munich

089 / POP 1.46 MILLION / ELEV 520M

If you're looking for Alpine clichés, they're all here, but Munich also has plenty of unexpected cards down its Dirndl. Munich's walkable centre retains a small-town air but holds some world-class sights, especially art galleries and museums. Throw in royal Bavarian heritage, an entire suburb of Olympic legacy and a kitbag of dark tourism, and it's clear why southern Germany's metropolis is such a favourite among those who seek out the past but like to hit the town once they're done.

Sights

Munich's major sights cluster around the Altstadt, with the main museum district just north of the Residenz. However, it will take another day or two to explore bohemian Schwabing, the sprawling Englischer Garten and trendy Haidhausen to the east. Northwest of the Altstadt you'll find cosmopolitan Neuhausen, the Olympiapark and Schloss Nymphenburg.

Altstadt

Munich Residenz PALACE

(089-290 671; www.residenz-muenchen.de; Max-Joseph-Platz 3; Museum & Schatzkammer each adult/concession/under 18yr €7/6/free, combination ticket €11/9/free; 9am-6pm Apr–mid-Oct, 10am-5pm mid-Oct–Mar, last entry 1hr before closing; U Odeonsplatz) Generations of Bavarian rulers expanded a medieval fortress into this vast and palatial compound that served as their primary residence and seat of government from 1508 to 1918. Today it's an Aladdin's cave of fanciful rooms and collections through the ages, which can be seen on an audio-guided tour of what is called the **Residenzmuseum** (Residenzstrasse 1). Allow at least two hours to see everything at a gallop.

LOCAL KNOWLEDGE

BEER HALLS & BEER GARDENS

Beer drinking is not just an integral part of Munich's entertainment scene– it's a reason to visit. A few enduring faves:

Augustiner Bräustuben (089-507 047; www.braeustuben.de; Landsberger Strasse 19; 10am-midnight; Holzapfelstrasse) Depending on the wind, an aroma of hops envelops you as you approach this traditional beer hall inside the Augustiner brewery. The Bavarian fare is superb, especially the *Schweinshaxe* (pork knuckle). Due to the location the atmosphere in the evenings is slightly more authentic than that of its city-centre cousins, with fewer tourists at the long tables.

Chinesischer Turm (089-383 8730; www.chinaturm.de; Englischer Garten 3; 10am-11pm late Apr-Oct; Chinesischer Turm, Tivolistrasse) This one's hard to ignore because of its English Garden location and pedigree as Munich's oldest beer garden (open since 1791). Camera-toting tourists and laid-back locals, picnicking families and businessmen sneaking a sly brew clomp around the wooden pagoda, showered by the strained sounds of possibly the world's drunkest oompah band.

Hofbräuhaus (089-290 136 100; www.hofbraeuhaus.de; Am Platzl 9; 9am-midnight; Kammerspiele, S Marienplatz, U Marienplatz) Every visitor to Munich should make a pilgrimage to this mothership of all beer halls, if only once. Within this major tourist attraction you'll discover a range of spaces in which to do your mass lifting: the horse chestnut–shaded garden, the main hall next to the oompah band, tables opposite the industrial-scale kitchen and quieter corners.

Central Munich

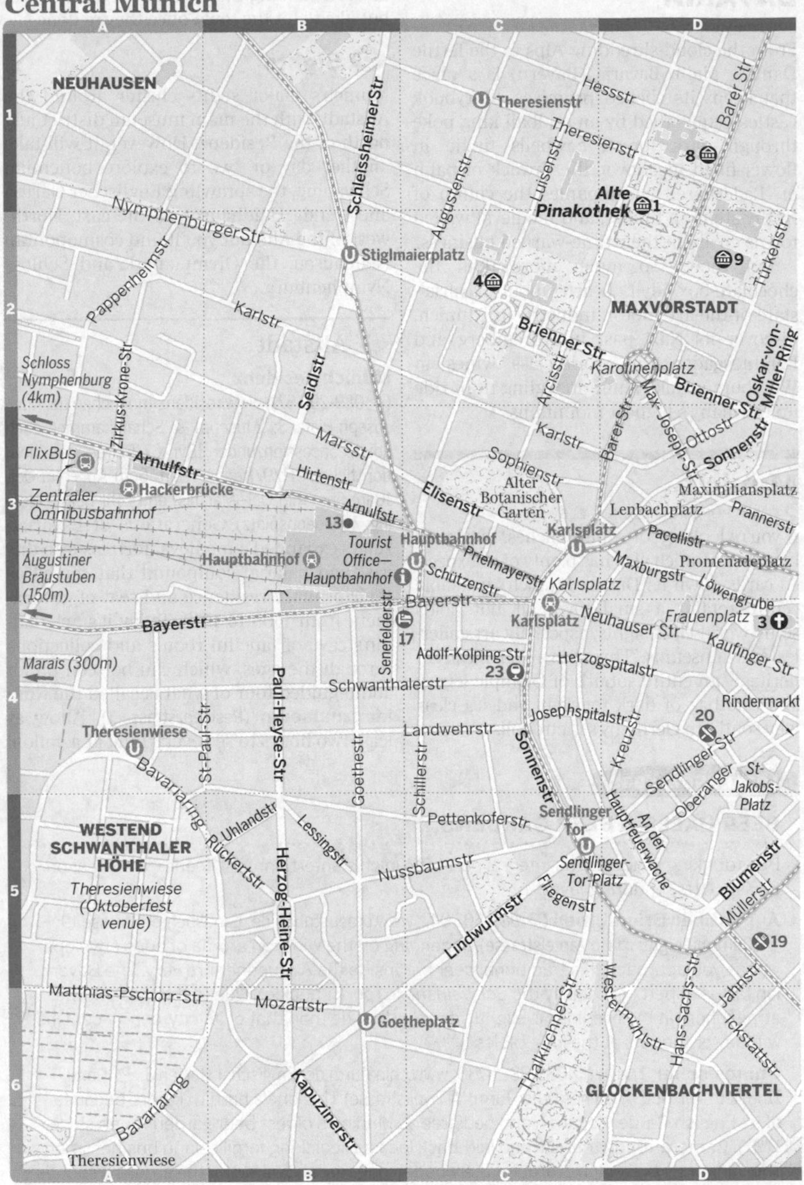

Highlights include the fresco-smothered **Antiquarium** banqueting hall and the exuberantly rococo **Reiche Zimmer** (Ornate Rooms). The **Schatzkammer** (Treasure Chamber) displays a veritable banker's bonus worth of jewel-encrusted bling of yesteryear, from golden toothpicks to finely crafted swords, from miniatures in ivory to gold-entombed cosmetics trunks.

Marienplatz SQUARE

(S Marienplatz, U Marienplatz) The epicentral heart and soul of the Altstadt, Marienplatz is a popular gathering spot and packs a lot

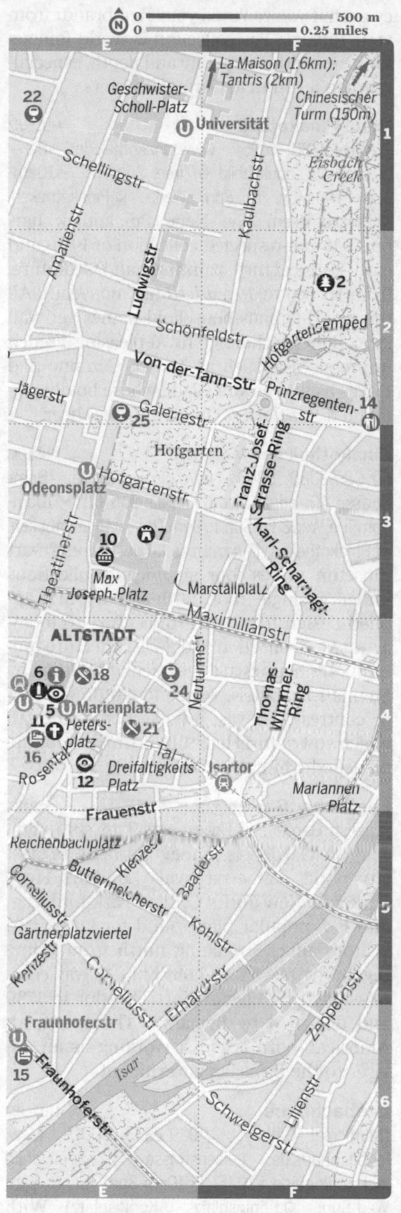

Central Munich

of personality into a compact frame. It's anchored by the **Mariensäule** (St Mary's Column), built in 1638 to celebrate victory over Swedish forces during the Thirty Years' War. This is the busiest spot in all Munich, with throngs of tourists swarming across its expanse from early morning till late at night. Many walking tours leave from here.

Frauenkirche CHURCH
(Church of Our Lady; www.muenchner-dom.de; Frauenplatz 1; 7.30am-8.30pm; S Marienplatz)
The landmark Frauenkirche, built between 1468 and 1488, is Munich's spiritual heart and the Mt Everest among its churches. No other building in the central city may stand taller than its onion-domed twin towers, which reach a skyscraping 99m. The south tower can be climbed, but has been under urgent renovation for several years.

St Peterskirche CHURCH
(Church of St Peter; Rindermarkt 1; church free, tower adult/child €3/2; tower 9am-6pm Mon-Fri, from 10am Sat & Sun; U Marienplatz, S Marienplatz)
Some 306 steps divide you from the best view of central Munich via the 92m tower of St Peterskirche, central Munich's oldest church

DON'T MISS

OKTOBERFEST

Hordes come to Munich for **Oktoberfest** (www.oktoberfest.de; mid-Sep–early Oct), running the 15 days before the first Sunday in October. Reserve accommodation well ahead and go early in the day so you can grab a seat in one of the hangar-sized beer tents spread across the Theresienwiese grounds, about 1km southwest of the Hauptbahnhof. While there is no entrance fee, those €11 1L steins of beer (called *Mass*) add up fast. Although its origins are in the marriage celebrations of Crown Prince Ludwig in 1810, there's nothing regal about this beery bacchanalia now: expect mobs, expect to meet new and drunken friends, expect decorum to vanish as night sets in and you'll have a blast.

(1150). Inside awaits a virtual textbook of art through the centuries. Worth a closer peek are the Gothic St-Martin-Altar, the baroque ceiling fresco by Johann Baptist Zimmermann and rococo sculptures by Ignaz Günther.

Viktualienmarkt MARKET
(Mon-Fri & morning Sat; U Marienplatz, S Marienplatz) Fresh fruit and vegetables, piles of artisanal cheeses, tubs of exotic olives, hams and jams, chanterelles and truffles – Viktualienmarkt is a feast of flavours and one of central Europe's finest gourmet markets.

Maxvorstadt, Schwabing & Englischer Garten

North of the Altstadt, Maxvorstadt is home to Munich's main university and top-drawer art museums. It segues into equally cafe-filled Schwabing, which rubs up against the vast Englischer Garten. Note that many major museums, including all the Pinakothek galleries, charge just €1 admission on Sundays.

★Alte Pinakothek MUSEUM
(089-238 0516; www.pinakothek.de; Barer Strasse 27; adult/concession/child €7/5/free, Sun €1, audio guide €4.50; 10am-8pm Tue, to 6pm Wed-Sun; Pinakotheken, Pinakotheken) Munich's main repository of Old European Masters is crammed with all the major players who decorated canvases between the 14th and 18th centuries. This neoclassical temple was masterminded by Leo von Klenze and is a delicacy even if you can't tell your Rembrandt from your Rubens. The collection is world famous for its exceptional quality and depth, especially when it comes to German masters.

Neue Pinakothek MUSEUM
(089-2380 5195; www.pinakothek.de; Barer Strasse 29; adult/child €7/free, Sun €1; 10am-6pm Thu-Mon, to 8pm Wed; Pinakotheken, Pinakotheken) The Neue Pinakothek harbours a well-respected collection of 19th- and early-20th-century paintings and sculpture, from rococo to *Jugendstil* (art nouveau). All the world-famous household names get wall space here, including crowd-pleasing French impressionists such as Monet, Cézanne and Degas as well as Van Gogh, whose boldly pigmented *Sunflowers* (1888) radiates cheer.

Pinakothek der Moderne MUSEUM
(089-2380 5360; www.pinakothek.de; Barer Strasse 40; adult/child €10/free, Sun €1; 10am-6pm Tue, Wed & Fri-Sun, to 8pm Thu; Pinakotheken, Pinakotheken) Germany's largest modern-art museum unites four significant collections under a single roof: 20th-century art, applied design from the 19th century to today, a graphics collection and an architecture museum. It's housed in a spectacular building by Stephan Braunfels, whose four-storey interior centres on a vast eye-like dome through which soft natural light filters throughout the blanched-white galleries.

Englischer Garten PARK
(English Garden; U Universität) The sprawling English Garden is among Europe's biggest city parks – it even rivals London's Hyde Park and New York's Central Park for size – and is a popular playground for locals and visitors alike. Stretching north from Prinzregentenstrasse for about 5km, it was commissioned by Elector Karl Theodor in 1789 and designed by Benjamin Thompson, an American-born scientist working as an adviser to the Bavarian government.

Lenbachhaus MUSEUM
(Municipal Gallery; 089-2333 2000; www.lenbachhaus.de; Luisenstrasse 33; adult/child incl audioguide €10/5; 10am-8pm Tue, to 6pm Wed-Sun; Königsplatz, U Königsplatz) With its fabulous wing added by noted architect Norman Foster, this glorious gallery is the go-to place to admire the vibrant canvases of Wassily Kandinsky, Franz Marc, Paul Klee and other members of ground-breaking modernist group Der Blaue Reiter (The Blue Rider), founded in Munich in 1911.

Further Afield

★Schloss Nymphenburg PALACE

(www.schloss-nymphenburg.de; castle adult/child €6/free, all sites €11.50/free; 9am-6pm Apr–mid-Oct, 10am-4pm mid-Oct–Mar; Schloss Nymphenburg) This commanding palace and its lavish gardens sprawl around 5km northwest of the Altstadt. Begun in 1664 as a villa for Electress Adelaide of Savoy, the stately pile was extended over the next century to create the royal family's summer residence. Franz Duke of Bavaria, head of the once-royal Wittelsbach family, still occupies an apartment here.

BMW Museum MUSEUM

(www.bmw-welt.de; Am Olympiapark 2; adult/child €10/7; 10am-6pm Tue-Sun; U Olympiazentrum) This silver, bowl-shaped museum comprises seven themed 'houses' that examine the development of BMW's product line and include sections on motorcycles and motor racing. Even if you can't tell a head gasket from a crankshaft, the interior design – with its curvy retro feel, futuristic bridges, squares and huge backlit wall screens – is reason enough to visit.

Tours

★Radius Tours & Bike Rental TOURS

(089-543 487 7740; www.radiustours.com; Arnulfstrasse 3, Hauptbahnhof; 8.30am-8pm; Hauptbahnhof, U Hauptbahnhof, S Hauptbahnhof) Entertaining and informative English-language tours include the two hour Discover Munich walk (€15), the fascinating 2½-hour Third Reich tour (€17.50) and the three-hour Bavarian Beer tour (€36). The company also runs popular excursions to Neuschwanstein, Salzburg and Dachau, and has hundreds of bikes for hire (€14.50 per day).

New Europe Munich WALKING

(www.neweuropetours.eu; tours 10am, 10.45am & 2pm; S Marienplatz, U Marienplatz) Departing from Marienplatz, these English-language walking tours tick off all Munich's central landmarks in three hours. Guides are well informed and fun, though they are under pressure at the end of the tour to get as much as they can in tips. The company also runs (paid) tours to Dachau (€24) and Neuschwanstein (€40).

Sleeping

Room rates in Munich tend to be high, and they skyrocket during the Oktoberfest. Book well ahead.

Wombats City Hostel Munich HOSTEL €

(089-5998 9180; www.wombats-hostels.com; Senefelderstrasse 1; dm/d from €25/95; P @ ; Hauptbahnhof, U Hauptbahnhof) Munich's top hostel is a professionally run affair with a whopping 300 dorm beds plus private rooms. Dorms are painted in cheerful pastels and outfitted with wooden floors, en suite facilities, sturdy lockers and comfy pine bunks, all in a central location near the train station.

★Flushing Meadows DESIGN HOTEL €€

(089-5527 9170; www.flushingmeadowshotel.com; Fraunhoferstrasse 32; studios around €150; P ; S Fraunhoferstrasse) Urban explorers keen on up-to-the-minute design cherish this new contender on the top two floors of a former postal office in hip Glockenbachviertel. Each of the 11 concrete-ceilinged lofts reflects the vision of a locally known personality, while three of the five penthouse studios have a private terrace. Breakfast costs €10.50.

Hotel Laimer Hof HOTEL €€

(089-178 0380; www.laimerhof.de; Laimer Strasse 40; s/d from €65/85; P ; Romanplatz) A mere a five-minute aristocratic amble from Schloss Nymphenburg, this commendably tranquil refuge is run by a friendly team who take time to get to know their guests. No two of the 23 rooms are alike, but all boast antique touches, oriental carpets and golden beds. Free bike rental, and coffee and tea in the lobby. Breakfast costs €12.

La Maison DESIGN HOTEL €€

(089-3303 5550; www.hotel-la-maison.com; Occamstrasse 24; r from €109; P ; U Münchner Freiheit) Situated in the cool area of Schwabing, this discerningly retro hotel comes immaculately presented in shades of imperial purple and ubercool grey. Rooms at this sassy number wow with heated oak floors, jet-black washbasins and starkly con-

NO WAVE GOODBYE

Possibly the last sport you might expect to see being practised in Munich is surfing, but go to the southern tip of the English Garden at Prinzregentenstrasse and you'll see scores of people leaning over a bridge to cheer on wetsuit-clad daredevils as they hang on an artificially created wave in the **Eisbach** (www.eisbachwelle.de; Prinzregentenstrasse; Nationalmuseum/Haus der Kunst). It's only a single wave, but it's a damn fine one!

trasting design throughout – though the operators can't resist putting a pack of gummy bears on the expertly ruffed pillows! Cool bar on ground level.

Louis Hotel HOTEL €€€

(☎089-411 9080; www.louis-hotel.com; Viktualienmarkt 6/Rindermarkt 2; r €179-320; 📶; S Marienplatz) An air of relaxed sophistication pervades the scene-savvy Louis, where 72 good-sized rooms are furnished in nut and oak, natural stone and elegant tiles. Rooms come equipped with the latest technology. All have small balconies facing either the courtyard or the Viktualienmarkt. Views are also terrific from the rooftop bar and restaurant.

Eating

Marais CAFE €

(www.cafe-marais.de; Parkstrasse 2; dishes €5-13; ⏰8am-8pm Tue-Sat, 10am-6pm Sun; 📝; 🚊Holzapfelstrasse) Is it a junk shop, a cafe or a sewing shop? Well, Westend's oddest coffee house is in fact all three, and everything you see in this converted haberdashery – the knick-knacks, the cakes and the antique chair you're sitting on – is for sale.

Weisses Brauhaus BAVARIAN €€

(☎089-290 1380; www.weisses-brauhaus.de; Tal 7; mains €7-20; ⏰8am-12.30am; S Marienplatz, U Marienplatz) One of Munich's classic beer halls, this place is charged in the evenings with red-faced, ale-infused hilarity, with Alpine whoops accompanying the rabble-rousing oompah band. The *Weisswurst* (veal sausage) here sets the standard for the rest to aspire to; sluice down a pair with the unsurpassed Schneider *Weissbier,* but only before noon. Understandably very popular and reservations are recommended after 7pm.

★ Fraunhofer BAVARIAN €€

(☎089-266 460; www.fraunhofertheater.de; Fraunhoferstrasse 9; mains €5-20; ⏰4.30pm-1am; 📝; 🚊Müllerstrasse) With its screechy parquet floors, stuccoed ceilings, wood panelling and virtually no trace that the last century even happened, this wonderfully characterful inn is perfect for exploring the region with a fork. The menu is a seasonally adapted checklist of southern German favourites, but also features at least a dozen vegetarian dishes and the odd exotic ingredient. Cash only.

Prinz Myshkin VEGETARIAN €€

(☎089-265 596; www.prinzmyshkin.com; Hackenstrasse 2; mains €9-20; ⏰11am-12.30am; 📝; S Marienplatz, U Marienplatz) This place is proof, if any were needed, that the vegetarian experience has well and truly left the sandals, beards and lentils era. Ensconced in a former brewery, Munich's premier meat-free dining spot occupies a gleamingly whitewashed, vaulted space where health-conscious eaters come to savour imaginative dishes such as curry-orange-carrot soup, unexpectedly good curries and 'wellness desserts'.

Alois Dallmayr DELI €€

(☎089-213 50; www.dallmayr.de; Dienerstrasse 14; ⏰9.30am-7pm Mon-Sat; S Marienplatz, U Marienplatz) A pricey gourmet delicatessen right in the thick of the Altstadt action, Alois Dallmayr is best known for its coffee but has so much more, including cheeses, ham, truffles, wine, caviar and exotic foods from every corner of the globe.

Tantris INTERNATIONAL €€€

(☎089-361 9590; www.tantris.de; Johann-Fichte-Strasse 7; menu from €100; ⏰noon-3pm & 6.30pm-1am Tue-Sat Oct-Dec, closed Tue Jan-Sep; 📶; U Dietlindenstrasse) Tantris means 'the search for perfection' and here, at one of Germany's most famous restaurants, it's not far off it. The interior design is full-bodied '70s – all postbox reds, truffle blacks and illuminated yellows. The food is sublime and the service is sometimes as unobtrusive as it is efficient. The wine cellar is probably Germany's best. Reservations essential.

Drinking & Nightlife

Generally speaking, student-flavoured places abound in Maxvorstadt and Schwabing, while traditional beer halls and taverns cluster in the Altstadt. Haidhausen attracts trendy types, and the Gärtnerplatzviertel and Glockenbachviertel are alive with gay bars and hipster haunts.

★ Schumann's Bar BAR

(☎089-229 060; www.schumanns.de; Odeonsplatz 6-7; ⏰8am-3am Mon-Fri, 6pm-3am Sat & Sun;

GAY & LESBIAN MUNICH

In Munich, the rainbow flag flies especially proudly along Müllerstrasse and the adjoining Glockenbachviertel. Keep an eye out for the freebie mags *Our Munich* and *Sergej,* which contain up-to-date listings and news about the community and gay-friendly establishments around town.

WORTH A TRIP

DACHAU CONCENTRATION CAMP

Officially called the **KZ-Gedenkstätte Dachau** (Dachau Concentration Camp Memorial Site; ☎08131-669 970; www.kz-gedenkstaette-dachau.de; Peter-Roth-Strasse 2a, Dachau; ⊙9am-5pm) FREE, the first Nazi concentration camp opened in 1933 in a bucolic village about 16km northwest of central Munich. All in all, it 'processed' more than 200,000 inmates, killing at least 43,000, and is now a haunting memorial. Expect to spend two to three hours exploring the grounds and exhibits. For deeper understanding, pick up an audioguide (€4), join a 2½-hour tour (€3.50) or watch the 22-minute English-language documentary at the main museum. From the Hauptbahnhof take the S2 to Dachau station (two-zone ticket; €5.80, 22 minutes), then catch frequent bus 726 (direction: Saubachsiedlung) to the camp.

S Odeonsplatz) Urbane and sophisticated, Schumann's shakes up Munich's nightlife with libational flights of fancy and an impressive range of concoctions. It's also good for weekday breakfasts. Cash only.

★Alter Simpl PUB
(☎089-272 3083; www.altersimpl.com; Türkenstrasse 57; ⊙11am-3am Mon-Fri, to 4am Sat & Sun; 🚋Schellingstrasse) Thomas Mann and Hermann Hesse used to knock 'em back at this well-scuffed and wood-panelled thirst parlour. A bookish ambience still pervades, making this an apt spot at which to curl up with a weighty tome over a few Irish ales. The curious name is an abbreviation of the satirical magazine *Simplicissimus*.

Harry Klein CLUB
(☎089-4028 7400; www.harrykleinclub.de; Sonnenstrasse 8; ⊙from 11pm; 🚋Karlsplatz, S Karlsplatz, U Karlsplatz) Follow the gold-lined passageway off Sonnenstrasse to what some regard as one of the best *Elektro-clubs* in the world. Nights here are an amazing alchemy of electro sound and visuals, with live video art projected onto the walls Kraftwerk-style and blending to awe-inspiring effect with the music.

☆ Entertainment

★FC Bayern München FOOTBALL
(☎089-6993 1333; www.fcbayern.de; Allianz Arena, Werner-Heisenberg-Allee 25, Fröttmaning; U Fröttmaning) Germany's most successful team both domestically and on a European level plays home games at the impressive Allianz Arena, built for the 2006 World Cup. Tickets can be ordered online.

ℹ Information

Tourist office branches include **Hauptbahnhof** (☎089-21 800; www.muenchen.de; Bahnhofplatz 2; ⊙9am-8pm Mon-Sat, 10am-6pm Sun; 🚋Hauptbahnhof, U Hauptbahnhof, S Hauptbahnhof) and **Marienplatz** (☎089-2339 6500; www.muenchen.de; Marienplatz 2; ⊙9am-7pm Mon-Fri, to 4pm Sat, 10am-2pm Sun; U Marienplatz, S Marienplatz).

ℹ Getting There & Away

AIR

Munich Airport (MUC; ☎089-975 00; www.munich-airport.de) is about 30km northeast of town and linked to the Hauptbahnhof every 10 minutes by S-Bahn (S1 and S8; €10.80, 40 minutes) and every 20 minutes by the **Lufthansa Airport Bus** (€10.50, 45 minutes, between 5.15am and 7.55pm).

Allgäu Airport (FMM; ☎08331-984 2000; www.allgaeu-airport.de; Am Flughafen 35, Memmingen) The Allgäu Airport Express also leaves from Arnulfstrasse at the Hauptbahnhof, making the trip up to seven times a day. The journey takes one hour 40 minutes and the fare is €13 (return €19.50).

BUS

The **Zentraler Omnibusbahnhof** (Central Bus Station, ZOB; www.muenchen-zob.de; Arnulfstrasse 21; S Hackerbrücke), next to the Hackerbrücke S-Bahn station, handles the vast majority of international and domestic coach services. The main operator is the low-cost coach company **Flixbus** (☎030 300 137 300; www.flixbus.com; Zentraler Omnibusbahnhof, Arnulfstrasse 21), which links Munich to countless destinations across Germany and beyond.

TRAIN

All services leave from the **Hauptbahnhof** (Central Station). Staffed by native English speakers, **Euraide** (www.euraide.de; Desk 1, Reisezentrum, Hauptbahnhof; ⊙10am-7pm Mon-Fri Mar-Apr & Aug-Dec, 9.30am-8pm May-Jul; 🚋Hauptbahnhof, U Hauptbahnhof, S Hauptbahnhof) is a friendly agency.

Frequent fast and direct services include trains to Nuremberg (€40 to €60, one hour), Frankfurt (€105, 3¼ hours), Berlin (€150, 5¼ hours) and Vienna (€99, four hours), and thrice daily services to Zürich (€84, 4¾ hours).

Getting Around

Central Munich is compact enough to explore on foot. The outlying suburbs are easily reachable by public transport, which is extensive and efficient, if showing its age slightly.

S-Bahn Reaches out into the suburbs and beyond. All *S-Bahn* trains follow the Stammstrecke (central line) through central Munich.

U-Bahn Serves the centre and the inner suburbs.

Tram These link the centre with the suburbs.

For public transport information, consult MVV (www.mvv-muenchen.de).

Bavarian Alps

Stretching west from Germany's remote southeastern corner to the Allgäu region near Lake Constance, the Bavarian Alps (Bayerische Alpen) form a stunningly beautiful natural divide along the Austrian border. Ranges further south may be higher, but these mountains shoot up from the foothills so abruptly that the impact is all the more dramatic.

Garmisch-Partenkirchen

☎08821 / POP 27,024

A paradise for skiers and hikers, Garmisch-Partenkirchen is blessed with a fabled setting a snowball's throw from Germany's highest peak, the 2962m-high Zugspitze. Garmisch has a more cosmopolitan feel, while Partenkirchen retains an old-world Alpine village vibe. The towns were merged for the 1936 Winter Olympics.

Sights

★Zugspitze MOUNTAIN

(www.zugspitze.de; return adult/child €56/32; ⏲train 8.15am-2.15pm) On good days, views from Germany's rooftop extend into four countries. The return trip starts in Garmisch aboard a cogwheel train (Zahnradbahn) that chugs along the mountain base to the Eibsee, an idyllic forest lake. From here, the Eibsee-Seilbahn, a super-steep cable car, swings to the top at 2962m. When you're done admiring the views, the Gletscherbahn cable car takes you to the Zugspitze glacier at 2600m, from where the cogwheel train heads back to Garmisch.

Partnachklamm CANYON

(www.partnachklamm.eu; adult/child €5/2; ⏲8am-6pm May & Oct, 6am-10pm Jun-Sep, 9am-6pm Nov-Apr) A top attraction around Garmisch is this narrow and dramatically beautiful 700m-long gorge with walls rising up to 80m. The trail hewn into the rock is especially spectacular in winter when you can walk beneath curtains of icicles and frozen waterfalls.

Sleeping & Eating

Reindl's Partenkirchner Hof HOTEL €€

(☎08821-943 870; www.reindls.de; Bahnhofstrasse 15; s/d €100/150; P ☎) Reindl's may not look worthy of its five stars from street level, but this elegant, tri-winged luxury hotel is stacked with perks, a wine bar and a top-notch gourmet restaurant. Renovated to perfection on a rolling basis, the rooms are studies in folk-themed elegance and some enjoy gobsmacking Alpine views to get you in the mood.

Gasthof Fraundorfer BAVARIAN €€

(☎08821-9270; www.gasthof-fraundorfer.de; Ludwigstrasse 24; mains €5-23; ⏲7am-midnight Thu-Mon, from 5pm Wed) If you've travelled to the Alps to experience yodelling, knee slapping and beetroot-faced locals squeezed into Lederhosen, you just arrived at the right address. Steins of frothing ale fuel the increasingly raucous atmosphere as the evening progresses and monster portions of plattered pig meat push belt buckles to the limit. Decor ranges from baroque cherubs to hunting trophies and the 'Sports Corner'. Unmissable.

Information

Tourist Office (☎08821-180 700; www.gapa.de; Richard-Strauss-Platz 2; ⏲9am-5pm Mon-Fri, to 3pm Sat) Friendly staff hand out maps, brochures and advice.

Getting There & Away

Numerous tour operators run day trips to Garmisch-Partenkirchen from Munich, but there's also at least hourly direct train services (€22, 80 minutes).

Berchtesgaden

☎08652 / POP 7791

Plunging deep into Austria and framed by six high-rise mountain ranges, the Berchtesgadener Land is a drop-dead-gorgeous corner of Bavaria steeped in myths and legends. Framed by Germany's second-highest mountain, the Watzmann (2713m), its dreamy, fir-lined valleys are filled with gurgling streams and peaceful Alpine villages. Much of the area is protected within the 210-sq-km Berchtesgaden National Park, a Unesco Biosphere Reserve. The village of Berchtesgaden is the obvious base for hiking circuits into the park.

Sights & Activities

Berchtesgaden's main sights are all a car or bus ride away from town. Seeing everything in a day without your own transport is virtually impossible.

★Eagle's Nest HISTORIC SITE
(Kehlsteinhaus; ☎08652-29 69; www.kehlsteinhaus.de; Obersalzberg; tour €30.50; ⊙buses 8.30am-4.50pm mid-May–Oct) At 1834m above sea level, the Eagle's Nest was built as a mountaintop retreat for Hitler, and gifted to him on his 50th birthday. It took around 3000 workers a mere two years to carve the precipitous 6km-long mountain road, cut a 124m-long tunnel and a brass-panelled lift through the rock, and build the lodge itself (now a restaurant). It can only be reached by special shuttle bus from the Kehlsteinhaus bus station.

★Königssee LAKE
(Schönau am Königsee) Gliding serenely across the wonderfully picturesque, emerald-green Königssee makes for some unforgettable memories and photo opportunities. Cradled by steep mountain walls some 5km south of Berchtesgaden, the Königssee is Germany's highest lake (603m), with drinkably pure waters shimmering into fjordlike depths. Bus 841/843 makes the trip out here from the Berchtesgaden train station roughly every hour. **Boat tours** (☎08652-963 60; www.seenschifffahrt.de; Schönau; return boat €15; ⊙boats 8am-5.15pm mid-Jun–mid-Sep, shorter hours rest of the year) run up to every 30 minutes in both directions.

Dokumentation Obersalzberg MUSEUM
(☎08652-947 960; www.obersalzberg.de; Salzbergstrasse 41, Obersalzberg; adult/child €3/free, audioguide €2; ⊙9am-5pm daily Apr-Oct, 10am-3pm Tue-Sun Nov-Mar, last entry 1hr before closing) In 1933 the tranquil Alpine settlement of Obersalzberg (3km from Berchtesgaden) in essence became the second seat of Nazi power after Berlin, a dark period that's given the full historical treatment at this superb exhibition. Various rooms document the forced takeover of the area, the construction of the compound and the daily life of the Nazi elite. All facets of Nazi terror are dealt with, including Hitler's near-mythical appeal, his racial politics, the resistance movement, foreign policy and the death camps.

Sleeping & Eating

★Hotel Reikartz Vier Jahreszeiten HOTEL €€
(☎08652-9520; www.hotel-vierjahreszeiten-berchtesgaden.de; Maximilianstrasse 20; r from €70; ⊙reception 7am-11pm; P) For a taste of Berchtesgaden's storied past, stay at this traditional lodge where Bavarian royalty once crumpled the sheets. Rooms are very well kept and the south-facing (more-expensive) quarters offer dramatic views of the peaks. After a day's sightseeing, dinner in the hunting lodge–style Hubertusstuben restaurant is a real treat.

Bräustübl BAVARIAN €€
(☎08652-976 724; www.braeustueberl-berchtesgaden.de; Bräuhausstrasse 13; mains €7-17; ⊙10am-midnight) Past the vaulted entrance painted in Bavaria's white and blue diamonds, this lively but cosy beer hall–beer garden is run by the local brewery. Expect a carnivorous feast with favourites such as pork roast and the house speciality: breaded calf's head (tastes better than it sounds). On Friday and Saturday, an oompah band launches into knee-slapping action.

Information

Tourist Office (☎08652-896 70; www.berchtesgaden.com; Königsseer Strasse 2; ⊙8.30am-6pm Mon-Fri, 9am-5pm Sat, shorter hours mid-Oct–Mar) Near the train station, this very helpful office has detailed information on the entire Berchtesgaden region.

Getting There & Away

Travelling from Munich by train involves a change from Meridian to BLB (Berchtesgadener Land Bahn) trains at Freilassing (€36.40, 2½ hours, at least hourly connections). The best option between Berchtesgaden and Salzburg is RVO bus 840 (45 minutes).

Füssen

☎08362 / POP 15,558

In the foothills of the Alps, Füssen itself is a charming town, although most visitors skip it and head straight to Schloss Neuschwanstein and Hohenschwangau, the two most famous castles associated with King Ludwig II. You can see both on a long day trip from Munich, although only when spending the night, after all the day-trippers have gone, will you sense a certain Alpine serenity.

Sights

★Schloss Neuschwanstein CASTLE
(☎tickets 08362-930 830; www.neuschwanstein.de; Neuschwansteinstrasse 20; adult/child €13/free, incl Hohenschwangau €25/free; ⏲9am-6pm Apr–mid-Oct, 10am-4pm mid-Oct–Mar) Appearing through the mountaintops like a mirage, Schloss Neuschwanstein was the model for Disney's *Sleeping Beauty* castle. King Ludwig II planned this fairy-tale pile himself, with the help of a stage designer rather than an architect. He envisioned it as a giant stage on which to recreate the world of Germanic mythology, inspired by the operatic works of his friend Richard Wagner. The most impressive room is the **Sängersaal** (Minstrels' Hall), whose frescos depict scenes from the opera *Tannhäuser*.

Schloss Hohenschwangau CASTLE
(☎08362-930 830; www.hohenschwangau.de; Alpseestrasse 30; adult/child €13/free, incl Neuschwanstein €25/free; ⏲8am-5pm Apr–mid-Oct, 9am-3pm mid-Oct–Mar) King Ludwig II grew up at the sun-yellow Schloss Hohenschwangau and later enjoyed summers here until his death in 1886. His father, Maximilian II, built this palace in a neo-Gothic style atop 12th-century ruins left by Schwangau knights. Far less showy than Neuschwanstein, Hohenschwangau has a distinctly lived-in feel where every piece of furniture is a used original. After his father died, Ludwig's main alteration was having stars, illuminated with hidden oil lamps, painted on the ceiling of his bedroom.

CASTLE TICKETS & TOURS

Schloss Neuschwanstein and Schloss Hohenschwangau can only be visited on guided tours (in German or English), which last about 35 minutes each (Hohenschwangau is first). Strictly timed tickets are available from the **Ticket Centre** (☎08362-930 830; www.hohenschwangau.de; Alpenseestrasse 12; ⏲7.30am-5pm Apr–mid-Oct, 8.30am-3pm mid-Oct–Mar) at the foot of the castles. In summer, come as early as 8am to ensure you get in that day.

Enough time is left between tours for the steep 30- to 40-minute walk between the castles. Alternatively, you can take a horse-drawn carriage, which is only marginally quicker.

Sleeping & Eating

Hotel Sonne DESIGN HOTEL €€
(☎08362-9080; www.hotel-fuessen.de; Prinzregentenplatz 1; s/d from €90/110; P 📶) Although traditional looking from outside, this Altstadt favourite offers an unexpected design-hotel experience within. Themed rooms feature everything from swooping bed canopies to big-print wallpaper, and huge pieces of wall art to sumptuous fabrics. The public spaces are littered with pieces of art, period costumes and design features – the overall effect is impressive and slightly unusual for this part of Germany.

Zum Hechten BAVARIAN €€
(Ritterstrasse 6; mains €8-19; ⏲10am-10pm) Füssen's best hotel restaurant has six different spaces to enjoy and keeps things regional with a menu of Allgäu staples like schnitzel and noodles, Bavarian pork-themed favourites, and local specialities such as venison goulash from the Ammertal.

Information

Tourist Office (☎08362-938 50; www.fuessen.de; Kaiser-Maximilian-Platz; ⏲9am-5pm Mon-Fri, 9.30am-3.30pm Sat) Can help find rooms.

Getting There & Away

Füssen is the southern terminus of the Romantic Road Coach.

If you want to do the castles in a single day from Munich, you'll need to start very early. The first train leaves Munich at 4.48am (€28.40, change in Kaufbeuren), reaching Füssen at 6.49am. Otherwise, direct trains leave Munich once every two hours throughout the day.

RVO buses 78 and 73 (www.rvo-bus.de) serve the castles from Füssen Bahnhof (€4.40 return, eight minutes, at least hourly).

The Romantic Road

Stretching 400km from the vineyards of Würzburg to the foot of the Alps, the Romantic Road (Romantische Strasse) is by far the most popular of Germany's holiday routes. This well-trodden trail cuts through a cultural and historical cross-section of southern Germany as it traverses Franconia and clips Baden-Württemberg in the north before plunging into Bavaria proper to end at Ludwig II's crazy castles.

Getting There & Away

Frankfurt and Munich are the most popular gateways for exploring the Romantic Road. The ideal way to travel is by car, though many prefer to take the **Romantic Road Coach** (www.romanticroadcoach.de), which can get incredibly crowded in summer. From April to October this special coach runs daily in each direction between Frankfurt and Füssen (for Neuschwanstein); the entire journey takes around 12 hours. There's no charge for breaking the journey and continuing the next day.

Tickets are available for the entire route or for short segments, and reservations are only necessary during peak-season weekends.

Rothenburg ob der Tauber

09861 / POP 11,106

With its jumble of half-timbered houses enclosed by Germany's best-preserved ramparts, Rothenburg ob der Tauber lays on the medieval cuteness with a trowel. It's an essential stop on the Romantic Road but, alas, overcrowding can detract from its charm. Visit early or late in the day (or, ideally, stay overnight) to experience this historic wonderland sans crowds.

Sights

Jakobskirche CHURCH

(Church of St Jacob; Klingengasse 1, adult/child €2.50/1.50; 9am-5pm Apr-Oct, shorter hours Nov-Mar) One of the few places of worship in Bavaria to charge admission, Rothenburg's Lutheran parish church was begun in the 14th century and finished in the 15th. The building sports some wonderfully aged stained-glass windows, but the top attraction is Tilman Riemenschneider's **Heilig Blut Altar** (Altar of the Holy Blood). The gilded cross above the main scene depicting the Last Supper incorporates Rothenburg's most treasured reliquary – a rock crystal capsule said to contain three drops of Christ's blood.

Rathausturm HISTORIC BUILDING

(Town Hall Tower; Marktplatz; adult/child €2/0.50; 9.30am-12.30pm & 1-5pm Apr-Oct, 10.30am-2pm & 2.30-6pm Sun-Thu, to 7pm Fri & Sat Dec, noon-3pm Sat & Sun Jan-Mar & Nov) The Rathaus on Marktplatz was begun in Gothic style in the 14th century and was completed during the Renaissance. Climb the 220 steps of the medieval town hall to the viewing platform of the Rathausturm to be rewarded with widescreen views of the Tauber.

Festivals & Events

Christmas Market CHRISTMAS MARKET

(www.rothenburg.de; Advent) The Rothenburger Reiterlesmarkt, as it's officially known, is the town's Christmas market and one of the most romantic in Germany. It's set out around the central Marktplatz during Advent.

Sleeping & Eating

Altfränkische Weinstube HOTEL €€

(09861-6404; www.altfraenkische.de; Klosterhof 7; d €80 130;) This very distinctive, 650-year-old inn has eight wonderfully romantic, realistically priced rural-style rooms with exposed half-timber, bath-tubs and four-poster or canopied beds in most rooms. From 6pm onwards, the tavern serves up sound regional fare with a dollop of medieval cheer.

Burg-Hotel HOTEL €€€

(09861 948 90; www.burghotel.eu; Klostergasse 1-3; s €100-135, d €125-195; P) Each of the 17 elegantly furnished guest rooms at this boutique hotel built into the town walls has its own private sitting area. The lower floors shelter a decadent spa with tanning beds, saunas and rainforest showers, and a cellar with a Steinway piano; while phenomenal valley views unfurl from the breakfast room and stone terrace.

Zur Höll FRANCONIAN €€

(09861-4229; www.hoell.rothenburg.de; Burggasse 8; mains €7-20; 5-11pm Mon-Sat) This medieval wine tavern is in the town's oldest original building, with sections dating back to AD 900. The menu of regional specialities is limited but refined, though it's the superb selection of Franconian wines that people really come for.

Information

Tourist Office (09861-404 800; www.tourismus.rothenburg.de; Marktplatz 2; 9am-6pm Mon-Fri, 10am-5pm Sat & Sun May-Oct, 9am-5pm Mon-Fri, 10am-1pm Sat Nov-Apr) Helpful office offering free internet access.

Getting There & Away

The Romantic Road Coach pauses in town for 45 minutes.

You can go anywhere by train from Rothenburg as long as it's Steinach. Change there for services to Würzburg (€15.70 – 70 minutes). Travel to and from Munich (from €29, three to four hours) can involve up to three different trains.

Würzburg

0931 / POP 126,635

Straddling the Main River, scenic Würzburg is renowned for its art, architecture and delicate wines. The definite highlight is the Residenz, one of Germany's finest baroque buildings and a Unesco World Heritage Site, though there's plenty more to see besides.

Sights

★Würzburg Residenz PALACE

(www.residenz-wuerzburg.de; Balthasar-Neumann-Promenade; adult/child €7.50/free; 9am-6pm Apr-Oct, 10am-4.30pm Nov-Mar, 45min English tours 11am & 3pm, plus 1.30pm & 4.30pm Apr-Oct) The vast Unesco-listed Residenz, built by 18th-century architect Balthasar Neumann as the home of the local prince-bishops, is one of Germany's most important and beautiful baroque palaces. Top billing goes to the brilliant zigzagging **Treppenhaus** (staircase) lidded by what still is the world's largest fresco, a masterpiece by Giovanni Battista Tiepolo depicting allegories of the four then-known continents (Europe, Africa, America and Asia).

Dom St Kilian CHURCH

(www.dom-wuerzburg.de; Domstrasse 40; 8am-7pm Mon-Sat, to 8pm Sun) FREE Würzburg's highly unusual cathedral has a Romanesque core that has been altered many times over the centuries. The elaborate stucco work of the chancel contrasts starkly with the bare whitewash of the austere Romanesque nave that is capped with a ceiling that wouldn't look out of place in a 1960s bus station. The whole mishmash creates quite an impression and is possibly Germany's oddest cathedral interior. The Schönbornkapelle by Balthasar Neumann returns a little baroque order to things.

Festung Marienberg FORTRESS

(tour adult/child €3.50/free; tours 11am, 2pm, 3pm & 4pm Tue-Sun, plus 10am & 1pm Sat & Sun mid-Mar–Oct, 11am, 2pm & 3pm Sat & Sun Nov–mid-Mar) Enjoy panoramic city and vineyard views from this hulking fortress whose construction was initiated around 1200 by the local prince-bishops who governed here until 1719. Dramatically illuminated at night, the structure was only penetrated once, by Swedish troops during the Thirty Years' War, in 1631. Inside, the **Fürstenbaumuseum** (closed November to mid-March) sheds light on its former residents' opulent lifestyle, while the Mainfränkisches Museum presents city history and works by local late-Gothic master carver Tilman Riemenschneider and other famous artists.

Sleeping & Eating

Babelfish HOSTEL €

(0931-304 0430; www.babelfish-hostel.de; Haugerring 2; dm/s/d €25/65/80; reception 8am-midnight;) With a name inspired by a creature in Douglas Adams' novel *The Hitchhiker's Guide to the Galaxy,* this uncluttered and spotlessly clean hostel has 74 beds spread over two floors and a sunny rooftop terrace. The communal areas are inviting places to down a few beers in the evening and there's a well-equipped guest kitchen. Breakfast costs €5.90.

Hotel Zum Winzermännle HOTEL €€

(0931-541 56; www.winzermaennle.de; Domstrasse 32; s €60-80, d €90-110; P) This family-run converted winery is a feel-good retreat in the city's pedestrianised heart. Rooms are well furnished, if a little on the old-fashioned side; some among those facing the quiet courtyard have balconies. Communal areas are bright and often seasonally decorated. Breakfast costs €7.

★Bürgerspital Weinstube FRANCONIAN €€

(0931-352 880; www.buergerspital-weinstuben.de; Theaterstrasse 19; mains €7-25; 10am-midnight) If you are going to eat out just once in Würzburg, the aromatic and cosy nooks of this labyrinthine medieval place probably provide the top local experience. Choose from a broad selection of Franconian wines (some of Germany's best) and wonderful regional dishes and snacks, including *Mostsuppe* (a tasty wine soup). Buy local whites in the adjoining wine shop.

Information

Tourist Office (0931-372 398; www.wuerzburg.de; Marktplatz 9; 10am-6pm Mon-Fri, to 3pm Sat, to 2pm Sun May-Oct, closed Sun & slightly shorter hours Nov-Apr) Within the attractive Falkenhaus, this efficient office can help you with room reservations and tour booking.

Getting There & Away

Frequent trains run to Bamberg (€22, one hour), Frankfurt (€20 to €36, one hour), Nuremberg (€20, one hour) and Rothenburg ob der Tauber (via Steinach; €15.70, one hour).

Nuremberg & Franconia

Nuremberg

☎0911 / POP 511,600

Nuremberg (Nürnberg) woos visitors with its wonderfully restored medieval Altstadt, its grand castle and, in December, its magical *Christkindlmarkt* (Christmas market). The town played a key role during the Nazi years. It was here that the fanatical party rallies were held, the boycott of Jewish businesses began and the anti-Semitic Nuremberg Laws were enacted. After WWII the city was chosen as the site of the Nuremberg Trials of Nazi war criminals.

Sights

Nuremberg's city centre is best explored on foot, but the Nazi-related sights are a tram ride away.

★Kaiserburg CASTLE
(Imperial Castle; ☎0911-244 6590; www.kaiserburg-nuernberg.de; Auf der Burg; adult/child incl Sinwell Tower €7/free, Palas & Museum €5.50/free; ⏲9am-6pm Apr-Sep, 10am-4pm Oct-Mar) This enormous castle complex above the Altstadt poignantly reflects Nuremberg's medieval might. The main attraction is a tour of the renovated residential wing (Palas) to see the lavish Knights' and Imperial Hall, a Romanesque double chapel and an exhibit on the inner workings of the Holy Roman Empire. This segues to the Kaiserburg Museum, which focuses on the castle's military and building history. Elsewhere, enjoy panoramic views from the Sinwell Tower or peer 48m down into the Deep Well.

Deutsche Bahn Museum MUSEUM
(☎0800 3268 7386; www.dbmuseum.de; Lessingstrasse 6; adult/child €6/3; ⏲9am-5pm Tue-Fri, 10am-6pm Sat & Sun) Forget Dürer and wartime rallies: Nuremberg is a railway town at heart. Germany's first passenger trains ran between here and Fürth, a fact reflected in the unmissable German Railways Museum, which explores the history of Germany's legendary rail system. The huge exhibition that continues across the road is one of Nuremberg's top sights, especially if you have a soft spot for things that run on rails.

Memorium Nuremberg Trials MEMORIAL
(☎0911-3217 9372; www.memorium-nuremberg.de; Bärenschanzstrasse 72; adult/child incl audioguide €6/1.50; ⏲9am-6pm Mon & Wed-Fri, 10am-6pm Sat & Sun Apr-Oct, slightly shorter hours Nov-Mar) Göring, Hess, Speer and 21 other Nazi leaders were tried for crimes against peace and humanity by the Allies in Schwurgerichtssaal 600 (Court Room 600) of this still-working courthouse. Today the room forms part of an engaging exhibit detailing the background, progression and impact of the trials using film, photographs, audiotape and even the original defendants' dock. To get here, take the U1 towards Bärenschanze and get off at Sielstrasse.

Reichsparteitagsgelände HISTORIC SITE
(Luitpoldhain; ☎0911-231 7538; www.museen.nuernberg.de/dokuzentrum; Bayernstrasse 110; grounds free, Documentation Centre adult/child incl audio guide €6/1.50; ⏲grounds 24hr, Documentation Centre 9am-6pm Mon-Fri, 10am-6pm Sat & Sun) If you've ever wondered where the infamous B&W images of ecstatic Nazi supporters hailing their Führer were taken, it was here in Nuremberg. Much of the grounds were destroyed during Allied bombing raids, but enough remain to get a sense of the megalomania behind it, especially after visiting the excellent **Dokumentationszentrum** (Documentation Centre). It's served by tram 8 from the Hauptbahnhof.

Sleeping

Five Reasons HOSTEL €
(☎0911-9928 6625; www.five-reasons.de; Frauentormauer 42; dm/d from €18/50; @📶) This crisp, 21st-century 90-bed hotel-hostel boasts spotless dorms, the trendiest hostel bathrooms you are ever likely to encounter, premade beds, card keys, fully equipped kitchen, a small bar and very nice staff. Breakfast is around €5 extra depending on what option you choose. Overall a great place to lay your head in a very central location.

★Hotel Deutscher Kaiser HOTEL €€
(☎0911-242 660; www.deutscher-kaiser-hotel.de; Königstrasse 55; s/d from €90/110; 📶) Aristocratic in its design and service, this centrally located treat of a historic hotel has been in the same family since the turn of the 20th century. Climb the castle-like granite stairs to find rooms of understated simplicity, flaunting oversize beds, Italian porcelain, silk lampshades and real period furniture (*Biedermeier* and *Jugendstil*).

Eating & Drinking

Don't leave Nuremberg without trying its famous finger-sized *Nürnberger Bratwürste*. You'll find them everywhere around town.

★Albrecht Dürer Stube FRANCONIAN €€
(☎0911-227 209; www.albrecht-duerer-stube.de; cnr Albrecht-Dürer-Strasse & Agnesgasse; mains €6-15.50; ⊙6pm-midnight Mon-Sat plus 11.30am-2.30pm Fri & Sun) This unpretentious and intimate restaurant has a Dürer-inspired dining room, prettily laid tables, a ceramic stove keeping things toasty and a menu of Nuremberg sausages, steaks, sea fish, seasonal specials, Franconian wine and *Landbier* (regional beer). There aren't many tables so booking ahead at weekends is recommended.

Kloster PUB
(Obere Wörthstrasse 19; ⊙5pm-1am) One of Nuremberg's best drinking dens is all dressed up as a monastery replete with ecclesiastic knick-knacks, including coffins emerging from the walls. The monks here pray to the god of *Landbier* (regional beer) and won't be up at 5am for matins, that's for sure.

Information

Tourist Office Hauptmarkt (☎0911-233 60; www.tourismus.nuernberg.de; Hauptmarkt 18; ⊙9am-6pm Mon-Sat, 10am-4pm Sun)

Tourist Office Künstlerhaus (☎0911-233 60; www.tourismus.nuernberg.de; Königstrasse 93; ⊙9am-7pm Mon-Sat, 10am-4pm Sun)

Getting There & Away

Nuremberg is connected by train to Berlin (from €80, three to 3½ hours, hourly), Frankfurt (€30 to €60, 2¼ hours, at least hourly), Hamburg (from €80, 4½ hours, hourly) and Munich (€40 and €60, one hour, twice hourly).

Bamberg

☎0951 / POP 75,743

Off the major tourist routes, Bamberg is one of Germany's most delightful and authentic towns. It has a bevy of beautifully preserved historic buildings, palaces and churches in its Unesco-recognised Altstadt, plus a lively student population and its own style of beer.

Sights

★Bamberger Dom CATHEDRAL
(www.erzbistum-bamberg.de; Domplatz; ⊙9.30am-6pm Apr-Oct, to 5pm Nov-Mar) Beneath the quartet of spires, Bamberg's cathedral is packed with artistic treasures, most famously the slender equestrian statue of the **Bamberger Reiter** (Bamberg Horseman), whose true identity remains a mystery. It overlooks the tomb of cathedral founders, Emperor Heinrich II and his wife Kunigunde, splendidly carved by Tilmann Riemenschneider. The marble tomb of Clemens II in the west choir is the only papal burial site north of the Alps. Nearby, the Virgin Mary altar by Veit Stoss also warrants closer inspection.

Altes Rathaus HISTORIC BUILDING
(Old Town Hall; Obere Brücke; adult/child €6/5; ⊙10am-4.30pm Tue-Sun) Like a ship in dry dock, Bamberg's 1462 Old Town Hall was built on an artifical island in the Regnitz River, allegedly because the local bishop had refused to give the town's citizens any land for its construction. Inside you'll find the Sammlung Ludwig, a collection of precious porcelain, but even more enchanting are the richly detailed frescos adorning its facades – note the cherub's leg cheekily protruding from the eastern facade.

Neue Residenz PALACE
(New Residence; ☎0951-519 390; Domplatz 8; adult/child €4.50/free; ⊙9am-6pm Apr-Sep, 10am-4pm Oct-Mar) This splendid episcopal palace gives you an eyeful of the lavish lifestyle of Bamberg's prince-bishops who, between 1703 and 1802, occupied its 40-odd rooms that can only be seen on guided 45-minute tours (in German). Tickets are also good for the **Bavarian State Gallery**, with works by Lucas Cranach the Elder and other Old Masters. The baroque Rose Garden delivers fabulous views over the town.

Tours

BierSchmecker Tour WALKING
(www.bier.bamberg.info; adult €22.50) Possibly the most tempting tour of the amazingly varied offerings at the tourist office is the self-guided BierSchmecker Tour. The price includes entry to the Fränkisches Brauereimuseum (depending on the route taken), plus five beer vouchers valid in five pubs and breweries, an English information booklet, a route map and a souvenir stein. Not surprisingly, it can take all day to complete the route.

Sleeping & Eating

Obere Sandstrasse near the cathedral and Austrasse near the university are both good eat and drink streets. Try Bamberg's unique style of beer called *Rauchbier* (smoked beer).

★Hotel Sankt Nepomuk HOTEL €€
(☎0951-984 20; www.hotel-nepomuk.de; Obere Mühlbrücke 9; s/d from €90/130; P 🛜) Aptly named after the patron saint of bridges, this is a classy establishment in a half-timbered

former mill right on the Regnitz. It has a superb restaurant (mains €15 to €30) with a terrace, and 24 new-fangled rooms of recent vintage. Breakfast is an extra €5.

Hotel Residenzschloss HOTEL €€
(☎0951-609 10; www.residenzschloss.com; Untere Sandstrasse 32; r from €100; P 📶) Bamberg's grandest digs occupy a palatial building formerly used as a hospital. But have no fear, as the swanky furnishings – from the Roman-style steam bath to the flashy piano bar – have little in common with institutional care. High-ceilinged rooms are business standard though display little historical charm. Take bus 916 from the ZOB.

Klosterbräu PUB FOOD €
(Obere Mühlbrücke 1-3; mains €7-13; ⏲11.30am-10pm Mon-Sat, to 2pm Sun) This beautiful half-timbered brewery is Bamberg's oldest. It draws *Stammgäste* (regulars) and tourists alike who wash down filling slabs of meat and dumplings with its excellent range of ales in the unpretentious dining room.

★Schlenkerla GERMAN €
(☎0951-560 60; www.schlenkerla.de; Dominikanerstrasse 6; mains €7-13; ⏲9.30am-11.30pm) Beneath wooden beams as dark as the superb *Rauchbier* poured straight from oak barrels, locals and visitors gather around a large ceramic stove to dig into scrumptious Franconian fare at this legendary flower-festooned tavern. Staff will pass beers through a tiny window in the entrance for those who just want to taste a beer but not sit.

Information

Tourist Office (☎0951-297 6200; www.bamberg.info; Geyerswörthstrasse 5; ⏲9.30am-6pm Mon-Fri, to 4pm Sat, to 2.30pm Sun) Staff sell the **Bambergcard** (€14.90), valid for three days of free bus rides and free museum entry.

Getting There & Away

Getting to and from Bamberg by train usually involves a change in Würzburg.

Regensburg & the Danube

Regensburg

☎0941 / POP 150,894

In a scene-stealing locale on the wide Danube River, Regensburg has relics of historical periods reaching back to the Romans, yet doesn't get the tourist mobs you'll find in other equally attractive German cities. Though big on the historical wow factor, today's Regensburg is a laid-back and unpretentious student town with a distinct Italianate flair.

CHRISTMAS MARKETS

Beginning in late November every year, central squares across Germany are transformed into Christmas markets or *Christkindlmarkt* (also known as *Weihnachtsmärkte*). Folks stamp about between the wooden stalls, perusing seasonal trinkets (from hand-carved ornaments to plastic angels) while warming themselves with *Glühwein* (mulled, spiced red wine) and grilled sausages. Locals love 'em and, not surprisingly, the markets are popular with tourists, so bundle up and carouse for hours. Markets in Nuremberg, Dresden, Cologne and Munich are especially famous.

Sights

★Dom St Peter CHURCH
(www.bistum-regensburg.de; Domplatz; ⏲6.30am-7pm Jun-Sep, to 6pm Apr, May & Oct, to 5pm Nov-Mar) It takes a few seconds for your eyes to adjust to the dim interior of Regensburg's soaring landmark, the Dom St Peter, one of Bavaria's grandest Gothic cathedrals with its stunning kaleidoscopic stained-glass windows and an opulent, silver-sheathed main altar. The cathedral is home of the Domspatzen, a 1000-year-old boys' choir that accompanies the 10am Sunday service (only during the school year). The Domschatzmuseum (Cathedral Treasury) brims with monstrances, tapestries and other church treasures.

Altes Rathaus HISTORIC BUILDING
(Old Town Hall; Rathausplatz; adult/child €7.50/4; ⏲tours in English 3pm Easter-Oct, 2pm Nov & Dec, in German every 30min) From 1663 to 1806, the Reichstag (imperial assembly) held its gatherings at Regensburg's old town, an important role commemorated by an exhibit in today's Reichstagsmuseum. Tours take in the lavish assembly hall and the original torture chambers in the cellar. Buy tickets at the tourist office in the same building. Note that access is by tour only. Audioguides are available for English speakers in January and February.

Steinerne Brücke BRIDGE
(Stone Bridge) An incredible feat of engineering for its day, Regensburg's 900-year-old

Stone Bridge was at one time the only fortified crossing of the Danube. Damaged and neglected for centuries (especially by the buses that once used it) the entire expanse has undergone renovation in recent years.

Sleeping & Eating

★**Elements Hotel** HOTEL €€
(☎941-2007 2275; www.hotel-elements.de; Alter Kornmarkt 3; d from €105; 📶) Four elements, four rooms, and what rooms they are! 'Fire' blazes in plush crimson; while 'Water' is a wellness suite with a hot tub; 'Air' is playful and light and natural wood; and stone and leather reign in colonial-inspired 'Earth'. Breakfast in bed costs an extra €10.

Hotel Orphée HOTEL €€
(☎0941-596 020; www.hotel-orphee.de; Untere Bachgasse 8; s €40-120, d €80-155; 📶) Behind a humble door lies a world of genuine charm, unexpected extras and ample attention to detail. The striped floors, wrought-iron beds, original sinks and common rooms with soft cushions and well-read books give the feel of a lovingly attended home. Check-in and breakfast is nearby in the Cafe Orphée at Untere Bachgasse 8. Additional rooms are available above the cafe.

Historische Wurstkuchl GERMAN €
(☎0941-466 210; www.wurstkuchl.de; Thundorferstrasse 3; 6 sausages €9.60; ⏰9am-7pm) Completely submerged several times by the Danube's fickle floods, this titchy eatery has been serving the city's traditional finger-size sausages, grilled over beech wood and dished up with its own sauerkraut and sweet grainy mustard, since 1135 and lays claim to being the world's oldest sausage kitchen.

★**Dicker Mann** BAVARIAN €€
(☎0941-573 70; www.dicker-mann.de; Krebsgasse 6; mains €9-21; ⏰9am-1am; 📶) The 'Chubby Chappy', a stylish, tranquil and very traditional inn, is one of the oldest restaurants in town, allegedly dating back to the 14th century. All the staples of Bavarian sustenance are plated up, plus a few other dishes for good measure. On a balmy eve, be sure to bag a table in the lovely beer garden out the back.

Information

Tourist Office (☎0941-507 4410; https://tourismus.regensburg.de; Rathausplatz 4; ⏰9am-6pm Mon-Fri, to 4pm Sat, 9.30am-4pm Sun Apr-Oct, to 2.30pm Sun Nov-Mar; 📶) In the historic Altes Rathaus. Sells tickets, tours, rooms and an audioguide for self-guided tours.

Getting There & Away

Frequent trains leave for Munich (€29.70, 1½ hours) and Nuremberg (€23.20, one to two hours), among other cities.

STUTTGART & THE BLACK FOREST

POP 12.6 MILLION

The high-tech urbanite pleasures of Stuttgart, one of the engines of the German economy, form an appealing contrast to the historical charms of Heidelberg, home to the country's oldest university and a romantic ruined castle. Beyond lies the myth-shrouded Black Forest (Schwarzwald in German), a pretty land of misty hills, thick forest and cute villages with youthful and vibrant Freiburg as its only major town.

Stuttgart

☎0711 / POP 628,032

Stuttgart residents enjoy an enviable quality of life that's to no small degree rooted in its fabled car companies – Porsche and Mercedes – which show off their pedigree in two excellent museums. Hemmed in by vine-covered hills the city also has plenty in store for fans of European art.

Sights

Königsstrasse, a long, pedestrianised shopping strip, links the Hauptbahnhof to the city centre with the Schloss and the art museums. The Mercedes-Benz Museum is about 5km northeast and the Porsche Museum 7km north of here.

★**Staatsgalerie Stuttgart** GALLERY
(☎0711-470 400; www.staatsgalerie.de; Konrad-Adenauer-Strasse 30-32; adult/concession €7/5; ⏰10am-6pm Tue, Wed & Fri-Sun, to 8pm Thu; Ⓤ Staatsgalerie) The neoclassical-meets-contemporary Staatsgalerie bears British architect James Stirling's curvy, colourful imprint. Alongside big-name exhibitions, the gallery harbours a stellar collection of European art from the 14th to the 21st centuries, and American post-WWII avant-gardists. Highlights include works by Miró, Picasso, Matisse, Kandinsky and Klee. Special billing goes to masterpieces such as Dalí's

The Sublime Moment (1938), Rembrandt's pensive, chiaroscuro *Saint Paul in Prison* (1627), Max Beckmann's utterly compelling, large-scale *Resurrection* (1916) and Monet's diffuse *Fields in the Spring* (1887).

Schlossgarten GARDENS

(U Neckartor) A terrific park for a wander right in the heart of the city, Stuttgart's sprawling Schlossgarten threads together the **Mittlerer Schlossgarten** (Middle Palace Garden; U Neckartor), with its fine beer garden for summer imbibing, the sculpture-dotted **Unterer Schlossgarten** (Lower Palace Garden; U Stöckach), and the **Oberer Schlossgarten** (Upper Palace Garden; U Charlottenplatz), home to stately landmarks such as the **Staatstheater** (☎0711-202 090; www.staatstheater-stuttgart.de; Oberer Schlossgarten 6; U Schlossplatz) and the glass-fronted **Landtag** (State Parliament; U Charlottenplatz).

Mercedes-Benz Museum MUSEUM

(☎0711-173 0000; www.mercedes-benz.com; Mercedesstrasse 100; adult/concession €10/5; ⏲9am-6pm Tue-Sun, last admission 5pm; S Neckarpark) A futuristic swirl on the cityscape, the Mercedes-Benz Museum takes a chronological spin through the Mercedes empire. Look out for legends such as the 1885 Daimler Riding Car (the world's first petrol-powered vehicle) and the record-breaking Lightning Benz that hit 228km/h at Daytona Beach in 1909.

Porsche Museum MUSEUM

(☎0711-9112 0911; www.porsche.com/museum; Porscheplatz 1; adult/concession €8/4; ⏲9am-6pm Tue-Sun; S Neuwirtshaus) Like a pearly white spaceship preparing for lift-off, the barrier-free Porsche Museum is a car-lover's dream. Audioguides race you through the history of Porsche from its 1948 beginnings. Stop to glimpse the 911 GT1 that won Le Mans in 1998. Call ahead for details of the factory tours that can be combined with a museum visit.

Sleeping

Hostel Alex 30 HOSTEL €

(☎0711-838 8950; www.alex30-hostel.de; Alexanderstrasse 30; dm €25-29, s/d €43/64; P 📶; U Olgaeck) Fun-seekers on a budget should thrive at this popular hostel within walking distance of the city centre. Rooms are kept spick and span, and the bar, sun deck and communal kitchen are ideal for swapping stories with fellow travellers. Light sleepers might want to pack earplugs for the thin walls and street noise. Breakfast costs €8.

> LOCAL KNOWLEDGE
>
> **BOHEMIAN BEANS**
>
> To really slip under Stuttgart's skin, mosey through the **Bohnenviertel** (Bean District), one of the city's lesser-known neighbourhoods. Walk south to Hans-im-Glück Platz, centred on a fountain depicting the caged Grimm's fairy-tale character Lucky Hans, and you'll soon reach the boho-flavoured Bohnenviertel, named after beans introduced in the 16th century. Back then they were grown everywhere as the staple food of the poor tanners, dyers and craftsmen who lived here.

Aloft DESIGN HOTEL €€

(☎0711-8787 5000; www.aloftstuttgarthotel.com; Milaneo Shopping Mall, Heilbronner Strasse 70; d €95-293; 📶; U Stadtbibliothek) It looks pretty nondescript from outside but don't be fooled – this newcomer to Stuttgart's hotel scene is a slick, open-plan design number, with lots of retro-cool touches, pops of bright colour and terrific views. Rooms ramp up the modern-living factor with creature comforts from Bliss Spa toiletries to coffee-making facilities.

Eating & Drinking

Reiskorn INTERNATIONAL €€

(☎0711-664 7633; www.das-reiskorn.de; Torstrasse 27; mains €11-15.50; ⏲5-10pm Tue-Sat; 🖉; U Rathaus) With an easygoing vibe and bamboo-green retro interior, this imaginative culinary globetrotter serves everything from celery schnitzel with mango-gorgonzola cream to meltingly tender beef braised in chocolate-clove sauce, and banana and yam curry. There are plenty of vegetarian and vegan choices. It's always busy.

★**Weinstube am Stadtgraben** GERMAN €€€

(☎0711-567 006; www.weinstube-stadtgraben.de; Am Stadtgraben 6, Stuttgart-Bad Cannstatt; 4-course menu €45; ⏲6-10pm; U Daimlerplatz) The Swabian food served at this warm, rustic, wood-beamed wine tavern in Bad Cannstatt is the real deal, albeit with a refined touch. Expect dishes that go with the seasons – be it spot-on suckling pig in dark beer sauce, fresh fish with pumpkin purée or duck breast with red cabbage and spinach dumplings. The wines hail from local vines.

Kraftpaule MICROBREWERY

(www.kraftpaule.de; Nikolausstrasse 2; ⏲4-10pm Tue-Fri, 11am-10pm Sat; U Stöckach) Competition is stiff but for our money this might just be Stuttgart's coolest new-wave craft microbrewery and bar. The bartenders really know their stuff, the selection of beers – from IPAs to stouts, single hop brews and wheat beers – is *wunderbar*, and the vibe easygoing in the bare-wood-tabled and terracotta-tiled interior. Check the website for details on tastings.

Information

Tourist Office (☎0711-222 80; www.stuttgart-tourist.de; Königstrasse 1a; ⏲9am-8pm Mon-Fri, to 6pm Sat, 10am-5pm Sun) Can help with room bookings (for a €3 fee). There's also a branch at the **airport** (☎0711-222 8100; Stuttgart Airport; ⏲8am-7pm Mon-Fri, 9am-1pm & 1.45-4.30pm Sat, 10am-1pm & 1.45-5.30pm Sun).

Getting There & Around

Stuttgart Airport (SGT; ☎0711-9480; www.stuttgart-airport.com), a major hub for Eurowings, is 13km south of the city and linked to the Hauptbahnhof by S2 and S3 trains (€4.20, 30 minutes).

There are train services to all major German cities, including Frankfurt (€50 to €66, 1¼ hours) and Munich (€54, 2¼ hours).

Heidelberg

☎06221 / POP 159,914

Germany's oldest and most famous university town is renowned for its lovely Altstadt, its plethora of pubs and its evocative half-ruined castle. Millions of visitors are drawn each year to this photogenic assemblage, thereby following in the footsteps of Mark Twain who kicked off his European travels in 1878 in Heidelberg, later recounting his bemused observations in *A Tramp Abroad*.

Sights

★Schloss Heidelberg CASTLE
(☎06221-658 880; www.schloss-heidelberg.de; Schlosshof 1; adult/child incl Bergbahn €7/4, tours €5/2.50, audioguide €5; ⏲grounds 24hr, castle 8am-6pm, English tours hourly 11.15am-4.15pm Mon-Fri, from 10.15am Sat & Sun Apr-Oct, fewer tours Nov-Mar) Towering over the Altstadt, Heidelberg's ruined Renaissance castle cuts a romantic figure, especially across the Neckar River when illuminated at night. Along with fabulous views, attractions include the **Deutsches Apotheken-Museum** (German Pharmacy Museum; incl in Schloss Heidelberg ticket; ⏲10am-6pm Apr-Oct, to 5.30pm Nov-Mar). The castle is reached either via a steep, cobbled trail in about 10 minutes or by taking the **Bergbahn** (cogwheel train) from Kornmarkt station. The only way to see the less-than-scintillating interior is by tour. After 6pm you can stroll the grounds for free.

Alte Brücke BRIDGE
(Karl-Theodor-Brücke) Heidelberg's 200m-long 'old bridge', built in 1786, connects the Altstadt with the river's right bank and the Schlangenweg (Snake Path), whose switchbacks lead to the **Philosophenweg** (Philosophers' Walk; Neckar River north bank). Next to the tower gate on the Altstadt side of the bridge, look for the brass sculpture of a monkey holding a mirror. It's the 1979 replacement of the original 17th-century sculpture.

Studentenkarzer HISTORIC SITE
(Student Jail; ☎06221-541 2813; www.uni-heidelberg.de; Augingergasse 2; adult/child incl Universitätsmuseum €3/2.50; ⏲10am-6pm Tue-Sun Apr-Oct, to 4pm Mon-Sat Nov-Mar) From 1823 to 1914, students convicted of misdeeds such as public inebriation, loud nocturnal singing, freeing the local pigs or duelling were sent to this student jail for at least 24 hours. Judging by the inventive wall graffiti, some found their stay highly amusing. Delinquents were let out to attend lectures or take exams. In certain circles, a stint in the Karzer was considered a rite of passage.

Sleeping

★Hotel Villa Marstall HISTORIC HOTEL €€
(☎06221-655 570; www.villamarstall.de; Lauerstrasse 1; s/d/ste from €115/135/165; ⏲reception 7am-10pm Mon-Sat, 8am-6pm Sun; ❄📶) A 19th-century neoclassical mansion directly overlooking the Neckar River, Villa Marstall is a jewel with cherrywood floors, solid-timber furniture and amenities including a lift. Its 18 exquisite rooms are decorated in whites, creams and bronzes, and come with in-room fridges (perfect for chilling a bottle of regional wine). A sumptuous breakfast buffet (€12) is served in the red-sandstone vaulted cellar.

Arthotel Heidelberg BOUTIQUE HOTEL €€
(☎06221-650 060; www.arthotel.de; Grabengasse 7; s €109-172, d €125-198; P❄📶) This charmer is a winning blend of historic setting and sleek contemporary design. Equipped with huge bathrooms (tubs!), the 24 rooms are spacious and modern – except for three that sport painted ceilings from 1790. There's a courtyard as well as a roof garden (but avoid

rooms below it in summer, when you can hear people walking above). Breakfast costs €13.50.

Eating & Drinking

Schnitzelbank GERMAN €€

(☎06221-211 89; www.schnitzelbank-heidelberg.de; Bauamtsgasse 7; mains €15-22; ⊙5pm-11.30pm Mon-Fri, from 11.30am Sat & Sun, bar to 1am) Small and often jam-packed, this cosy wine tavern has you sampling the local tipples (all wines are regional) and cuisine while crouched on wooden workbenches from the time when this was still a cooperage. It's these benches that give the place its name, incidentally, not the veal and pork schnitzel on the menu.

Zum Roten Ochsen PUB

(Red Ox Inn; www.roterochsen.de; Hauptstrasse 217; ⊙5pm-midnight Mon-Wed, from 11.30am Thu-Sat) Fronted by a red-painted, blue-grey-shuttered facade, Heidelberg's most historic student pub has black-and-white frat photos on the dark wooden walls and names carved into the tables. Along with German luminaries, visitors who've raised a glass here include Mark Twain, John Wayne and Marilyn Monroe. Live piano plays from 7.30pm, with plenty of patrons singing along.

Information

Tourist Office – Hauptbahnhof (☎06221-5844 444; www.heidelberg-marketing.de; Willy-Brandt-Platz 1; ⊙9am-7pm Mon-Sat, 10am-6pm Sun Apr-Oct, 9am-6pm Mon-Sat Nov-Mar) Right outside the main train station.

Tourist Office – Marktplatz (www.heidelberg-marketing.de; Marktplatz 10; ⊙8am-5pm Mon-Fri) In the old town.

Getting There & Away

From the **Hauptbahnhof** (Willy-Brandt-Platz), 3km west of the Schloss, there are up to three services per hour to/from Frankfurt (€19.90 to €29.90, one to 1½ hours) and Stuttgart (€23.90 to €39.90, 40 minutes to one hour).

The Black Forest

As deep, dark and delicious as its famous cherry gateau, the Black Forest gets its name from its canopy of evergreens. With deeply carved valleys, thick woodlands, luscious meadows, stout timber farmhouses and wispy waterfalls, it looks freshly minted for a kids' bedtime story. Many of the Black Forest's most impressive sights are in the triangle delimited by the lively university city of Freiburg, 15km east of the Rhine in the southwest; Triberg, cuckoo-clock capital in the north; and the river-valley city of St Blasien in the southeast.

Baden-Baden

☎07221 / POP 54,160

The northern gateway to the Black Forest, Baden-Baden is one of Europe's most famous spa towns and its mineral-rich waters have reputedly cured the ills of celebs from Queen Victoria to Victoria Beckham. An air of old-world luxury hangs over this beautiful town that's also home to a palatial casino.

Activities

★**Friedrichsbad** SPA

(☎07221-275 920; www.carasana.de; Römerplatz 1; 3hr ticket €25, incl soap-&-brush massage €37; ⊙9am-10pm, last admission 7pm) If it's the body of Venus and the complexion of Cleopatra you desire, abandon modesty to wallow in thermal waters at this palatial 19th-century marble-and-mosaic-adorned spa. As Mark Twain said, 'after 10 minutes you forget time; after 20 minutes, the world', as you slip into the regime of steaming, scrubbing, hot-cold bathing and dunking in the Roman-Irish bath.

Caracalla Spa SPA

(☎07221-275 940; www.carasana.de; Römerplatz 11; 2/3hr €16/19, day ticket €23; ⊙8am-10pm, last admission 8pm) This modern, glass-fronted spa has a cluster of indoor and outdoor pools, grottoes and surge channels, making the most of the mineral-rich spring water. For those who dare to bare, saunas range from the rustic 'forest' to the roasting 95°C 'fire' variety.

Sleeping & Eating

Hotel am Markt HISTORIC HOTEL €€

(☎07221-270 40; www.hotel-am-markt-baden.de; Marktplatz 18; s €65-88, d €105-128, apt €110-138; P 🛜) Sitting pretty in front of the **Stiftskirche** (Marktplatz; ⊙8am-6pm), this hotel, which is almost three centuries old, has 23 homey, well-kept rooms. It's quiet up here apart from your wake-up call of church bells, but then you wouldn't want to miss out on the great breakfast.

Weinstube im Baldreit GERMAN €€

(☎07221-231 36; Küferstrasse 3; mains €12.50-19; ⊙5-10pm Tue-Sat) Well hidden down cobbled lanes, this wine-cellar restaurant is tricky to find, but worth looking for. Baden-Alsatian fare such as *Flammkuchen* (Alsatian pizza) topped with Black Forest ham, Roquefort and pears is expertly matched with local wines. Eat in the ivy-swathed courtyard in summer, and the vaulted interior in winter.

Information

Main Tourist Office (07221-275 200; www.baden-baden.com; Schwarzwaldstrasse 52, B500; 9am-6pm Mon-Sat, to 1pm Sun) Situated 2km northwest of the centre.

Branch Tourist Office (Kaiserallee 3; 10am-5pm Mon-Sat, 2-5pm Sun;) In the Trinkhalle. Sells events tickets.

Getting There & Away

Karlsruhe-Baden-Baden Airport (Baden Airpark; 07229-662 000; www.badenairpark.de), 15km west of Baden-Baden, is served by Ryanair.

Twice-hourly trains run to destinations including Freiburg (€23.70 to €40, 45 to 90 minutes) and Karlsruhe (€11 to €16, 15 to 30 minutes).

Triberg

07722 / POP 4771

Cuckoo-clock capital, Black Forest–cake pilgrimage site and Germany's highest waterfall – Triberg is a torrent of Schwarzwald superlatives and attracts gushes of guests.

Sights

★Triberger Wasserfälle WATERFALL
(adult/concession €5/4.50) Niagara they ain't but Germany's highest waterfalls do exude their own wild romanticism. The Gutach River feeds the seven-tiered falls, which drop a total of 163m and are illuminated until 10pm. A paved trail accesses the cascades. Pick up a bag of peanuts at the ticket counter to feed the tribes of inquisitive red squirrels. Entry is cheaper in winter. The falls are in central Triberg.

Sleeping & Eating

Gasthaus Staude GUESTHOUSE €€
(07722-4802; http://gasthaus-staude.com; Obertal 20, Triberg-Gremmelsbach; s €55, d €86-104; P) A beautiful example of a 17th-century Black Forest farmhouse, with its hip roof, snug timber-clad interior and wonderfully rural setting in the forest, Gasthaus Staude is worth going the extra mile for. The rooms are silent and countrified, with chunky wood furnishings – the most romantic one has a four-poster bed. It's a 15-minute drive east of town on the B500.

Information

Tourist Office (07722-866 490; www.triberg.de; Wallfahrtstrasse 4; 9am-5pm Mon-Fri, 10am-5pm Sat & Sun) Inside the Schwarzwald-Museum.

Getting There & Away

From the Bahnhof (train station), 1.5km north of the centre, trains loop southeast to Konstanz (€27.50, 1½ hours, hourly), and northwest to Offenburg (€13.50, 46 minutes, hourly).

Freiburg

0761 / POP 229,636

Sitting plump at the foot of the Black Forest's wooded slopes and vineyards, Freiburg is a sunny, cheerful university town whose Altstadt is a storybook tableau of gabled town houses, cobblestone lanes and cafe-rimmed plazas. Party-loving students spice up the local nightlife and give Freiburg its relaxed air.

Sights

★Freiburger Münster CATHEDRAL
(Freiburg Minster; www.freiburgermuenster.info; Münsterplatz; tower adult/concession €2/1.50; 10am-5pm Mon-Sat, 1-7pm Sun, tower 9.30am-5pm Mon-Sat, 1-5pm Sun) With its lacy spires, cheeky gargoyles and intricate entrance portal, Freiburg's 11th-century minster cuts an impressive figure above the central market square. It has dazzling kaleidoscopic stained-glass windows that were mostly financed by medieval guilds and a high altar with a masterful triptych by Dürer protégé Hans Baldung Grien. Square at the base, the tower becomes an octagon higher up and is crowned by a filigreed 116m-high spire. On clear days you can spy the Vosges Mountains in France.

Augustinermuseum MUSEUM
(0761-201 2501; www.freiburg.de; Augustinerplatz 1; adult/concession/child €7/5/free; 10am-5pm Tue-Thu, Sat & Sun, to 7pm Fri) Dip into the past as represented by artists working from the Middle Ages to the 19th century at this superb museum in a sensitively modernised monastery. The Sculpture Hall on the ground floor is especially impressive for its fine medieval sculptures and masterpieces by Renaissance artists

Hans Baldung Grien and Lucas Cranach the Elder. Head upstairs for eye-level views of mounted gargoyles.

Sleeping

Green City Hotel Vauban HOTEL €€
(0761-888 5740; http://hotel-vauban.de; Paula-Modersohn-Platz 5; d €96-116, apt €150;) This ecofriendly hotel fits in neatly to Freiburg's Vauban neighbourhood, a shining model of sustainability with its PlusEnergy housing and car-free streets. The light, bright rooms are furnished with local woods and plump white bedding. The pick of the doubles have balconies. To reach it, take tram 3 from Freiburg Hauptbahnhof to Freiburg Paula-Modersohn-Platz.

The Alex BOUTIQUE HOTEL €€
(0761-296 970; www.the-alex-hotel.de; Rheinstrasse 29; d €94-148; P) The Alex stands head and shoulders above most hotels in town. Its clean, contemporary aesthetic includes lots of plate glass, blond wood, natural materials and a muted palette of colours. Besides modern rooms with rain showers, there's a bar, Winery29, where you can try locally produced wines.

Eating & Drinking

Markthalle MARKET €
(www.markthalle-freiburg.de; Martinsgasse 235; light meals €4-8; 8am-8pm Mon-Thu, to midnight Fri & Sat) Eat your way around the world – from curry to sushi, oysters to antipasti – at the food counters in this historical market hall, nicknamed 'Fressgässle'.

Gasthaus zum Kranz GERMAN €€
(0761-217 1967; www.gasthauszumkranz.de; Herrenstrasse 40; mains €15-26; 11.30am-3pm Mon, 11.30am-3pm & 5.30pm-midnight Tue-Sat, noon-3pm & 5.30pm-midnight Sun) There's always a good buzz at this rustic, quintessentially Badisch tavern. Pull up a hefty chair at one of the even heftier timber tables for well-prepared regional favourites such as roast suckling pig, *Maultaschen* (pork and spinach ravioli) and *Sauerbraten* (beef pot roast with vinegar, onions and peppercorns).

★**Kreuzblume** INTERNATIONAL €€€
(0761 311 94; www.hotel-kreuzblume.de; Konviktstrasse 31; mains €18-32, 3-course menu €42.50; 6-11pm Wed-Sun;) On a flower-festooned lane, this pocket-sized restaurant with clever backlighting, slick monochrome decor and a menu fizzing with bright, sunny flavours attracts a rather food-literate clientele. Each dish combines just a few hand-picked ingredients in bold and tasty ways: apple, celery and chestnut soup, say, or roast duck breast with wild herb salad. Service is tops.

Hausbrauerei Feierling MICROBREWERY
(www.feierling.de; Gerberau 46; 11am-midnight Sun-Thu, to 1am Fri & Sat) This stream-side microbrewery and beer garden is a relaxed spot to quaff a cold one under the chestnut trees in summer or next to the copper vats in winter. Pretzels and sausages (€3 to €9.50) soak up the malty, organic brews.

SOARING ABOVE THE FOREST

Freiburg seems tiny as you drift up above the city and over a tapestry of meadows and forest on the **Schauinslandbahn** (www.schauinslandbahn.de; Schauinslandstrasse, Oberried; return adult/child €12.50/8, one way €9/6; 9am-5pm Oct-Jun, to 6pm Jul-Sep) to the 1284m **Schauinsland** (www.bergwelt-schauinsland.de) peak, great for hiking, downhill scooter racing or simply surveying the view, which reaches all the way to the Rhine Valley and Alps on clear days. The lift provides a speedy link between Freiburg and the Black Forest highlands.

Information

Tourist Office (0761-388 1880; www.visit.freiburg.de; Rathausplatz 2-4; 8am-8pm Mon-Fri, 9.30am-5pm Sat, 10.30am-3.30pm Sun Jun-Sep, 8am-6pm Mon-Fri, 9.30am-2.30pm Sat, 10am-noon Sun Oct-May) Pick up the three-day **WelcomeKarte** (€26) at Freiburg's central tourist office.

Getting There & Away

There are frequent departures from the Hauptbahnhof for destinations such as Basel (€19.10 to €26.60, 45 minutes) and Baden-Baden (€23.70 to €40, 45 minutes to 1½ hours).

SOUTHERN RHINELAND

Defined by the mighty Rhine, fine wines, medieval castles and romantic villages, Germany's heartland speaks to the imagination

Frankfurt-am-Main

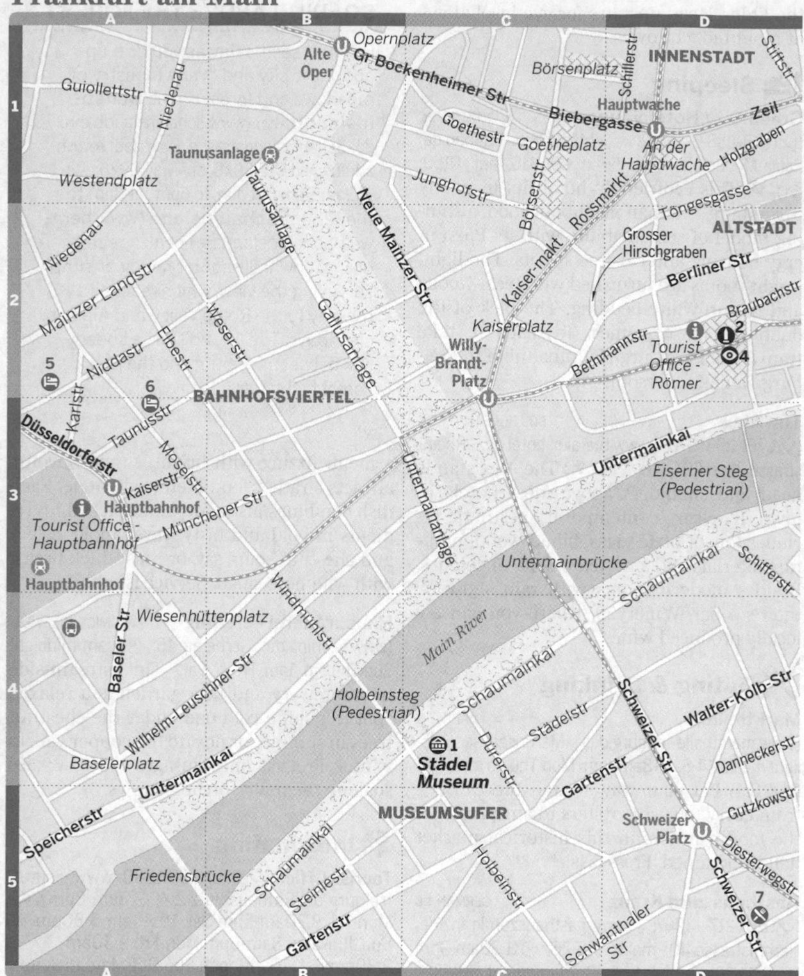

Even Frankfurt, which may seem all buttoned-up business, reveals itself as a laidback metropolis with fabulous museums and pulsating nightlife.

Frankfurt am Main

069 / POP 732,688

Unashamedly high-rise, Frankfurt-on-the-Main (pronounced 'mine') is a true capital of finance and business and hosts some of Europe's key trade fairs. But despite its business demeanour, Frankfurt consistently ranks highly among Germany's most liveable cities thanks to its rich collection of museums, expansive parks and greenery, a lively student scene and excellent public transport.

Sights

★ Städel Museum

MUSEUM

(069-605 098; www.staedelmuseum.de; Schaumainkai 63; adult/child €16/14; 10am-7pm Tue, Wed, Sat & Sun, to 9pm Thu & Fri; 15|16 Otto-Hahn-Platz) Founded in 1815, this world-renowned art gallery has an outstanding collection of European art from masters including Dürer, Rembrandt, Rubens, Renoir, Picasso and Cézanne, dating from the Middle Ages to today. More contemporary works by artists including Francis Bacon and Ger-

hard Richter are showcased in a subterranean extension lit by circular skylights. Admission prices can vary according to temporary exhibitions. Queues can be lengthy, so save time by pre-booking tickets online.

Kaiserdom CATHEDRAL
(Imperial Frankfurt Cathedral; www.dom-frankfurt.de; Domplatz 1; tower adult/child €3/1.50; church 9am-8pm Sun-Thu, from 1pm Fri, tower 9am-6pm Apr-Oct, 10am-5pm Nov-Apr; U Dom|Römer) Frankfurt's red-sandstone cathedral is dominated by a 95m-high Gothic tower, which can be climbed via 328 steps. Construction began in the 13th century; from 1356 to 1792, the Holy Roman Emperors were elected (and, after 1562, consecrated and crowned) in the *Wahlkapelle* at the end of the right aisle (look for the 'skull' altar). The cathedral was rebuilt both after an 1867 fire and after the bombings of 1944, which left it a burnt-out shell.

Frankfurt-am-Main

Top Sights
1 Städel Museum.......C4

Sights
2 Gerechtigkeitsbrunnen.......D2
3 Kaiserdom.......E2
4 Römerberg.......D2

Sleeping
5 25hours Hotel by Levi's.......A2
6 Five Elements.......A3

Eating
7 Adolf Wagner.......D5
8 Dauth-Schneider.......F4
9 Kleinmarkthalle.......E1

Drinking & Nightlife
10 Fichtekränzi.......F4

Römerberg SQUARE
(U Dom|Römer) The Römerberg is Frankfurt's old central square. Ornately gabled half-timbered buildings, reconstructed after WWII, give an idea of how beautiful the city's medieval core once was. In the square's centre is the **Gerechtigkeitsbrunnen** (Fountain of Justice; Römerberg).

Sleeping

If a big trade show is in town (and it often is) prices can triple. In general, rates drop on weekends.

Five Elements HOSTEL €
(069-2400 5885; www.5elementshostel.de; Moselstrasse 40; dm/s/d/apt from €22.50/34.50/82.90/134.50; ; Hauptbahnhof) The location mightn't be Frankfurt's most salubrious, but once you're inside the turn-of-the-20th-century gabled building it's a sanctuary of parquet floors, boldly coloured walls and designer furniture. Facilities include a laundry and 24-hour bar with a billiard table; breakfast costs €6.50. The apartment, sleeping up to four people, has a private bathroom and kitchen.

25hours Hotel by Levi's DESIGN HOTEL €€
(069-256 6770; www.25hours-hotels.com; Niddastrasse 58; d from €112; P ; Hauptbahnhof)

APPLE-WINE TAVERNS

Apple-wine taverns are Frankfurt's great local tradition. They serve *Ebbelwei* (Frankfurt dialect for *Apfelwein*), an alcoholic apple cider, along with local specialities like Handkäse mit Musik (literally, 'hand-cheese with music'). This is a round cheese soaked in oil and vinegar and topped with onions; your bowel supplies the music. Anything with *Grüne Sosse*, a herb sauce, is also a winner. **Fichtekränzi** (www.fichtekraenzi.de; Wallstrasse 5; ⏲5pm-1am Mon-Sat, from 4pm Sun; 🚋14|18 Frankensteiner Platz) and **Adolf Wagner** (☎069-612 565; www.apfelwein-wagner.com; Schweizer Strasse 71; mains €10-19.50; ⏲11am-midnight; Ⓤ Schweizer Platz) in Alt-Sachsenhausen are recommended traditional taverns.

Inspired by Levi's (yes, the jeans brand), this hip hotel has a rooftop terrace, free bike hire and a Gibson Music Room for jamming on drums and guitars. Its 76 rooms are themed by decade, from the 1930s (calm colours) to the 1980s (tiger-print walls, optical-illusion carpets). Be aware that its denim-blue bathrooms have no doors. Breakfast costs €18.

★Villa Orange BOUTIQUE HOTEL €€
(☎069-405 840; www.villa-orange.de; Hebelstrasse 1; s/d from €140/170; P❄📶; 🚋12|18 Friedberger Platz) 🌿 Offering a winning combination of tranquillity, modern German design and small-hotel comforts (such as a quiet corner library), this century-old, tangerine-coloured villa has 38 spacious rooms, some with free-standing baths and four-poster beds. Everything is organic – the sheets, the soap and the bountiful buffet breakfast (included in the rate) – with bikes also available to hire.

Eating & Drinking

The pedestrian strip west of Hauptwache square is nicknamed Fressgass (literally 'Grazing Street') thanks to its many (average) eateries. Cosy apple-wine taverns cluster in Alt-Sachsenhausen south of the Main.

Kleinmarkthalle MARKET €
(www.kleinmarkthalle.de; Hasengasse 5-7; ⏲8am-6pm Mon-Fri, to 4pm Sat; Ⓤ Dom|Römer) 🌿 Aromatic stalls inside this bustling traditional market hall sell artisanal smoked sausages, cheeses, roasted nuts, breads, pretzels, loose-leaf teas, pastries, cakes and chocolates, along with fruit, vegetables, spices, fresh pasta, olives, meat, poultry and, downstairs, fish. It's unmissable for picnickers or self-caterers, or anyone wanting to experience Frankfurt life. The upper-level wine bar opens onto a terrace.

★Zu den 12 Aposteln GERMAN €€
(☎069-288 668; www.12aposteln-frankfurt.de; Rosenbergerstrasse 1; mains €9-24; ⏲11.30am-1am; Ⓤ Konstablerwache) Glowing with sepia-toned lamplight, the 12 Apostles has ground-floor and cellar dining rooms serving traditional German dishes: *Matjes* (herring) with sour cream, apple and fried onion; roast pork knuckle with pickled cabbage; Frankfurter schnitzel with *Grüne Sosse* (green sauce); and *Käsespätzle* (handmade cheese noodles with onions). It brews its own light and dark beers on the premises.

Dauth-Schneider GERMAN €€
(☎069-613 533; www.dauth-schneider.de; Neuer Wall 5; mains €8-13.50; ⏲11.30am-midnight; Ⓢ Lokalbahnhof) With a history stretching back to 1849 (the basement housed an apple winery), this convivial tavern is a wonderful place to sample both the local drop and classic regional specialities such as *Sulz Fleisch* (cold meat and jelly terrine), *Gekochte Haspel* (pickled pork knuckle) with sauerkraut, and various tasting platters. Tables fill the tree-shaded terrace in summer.

Information

Tourist office locations include: **Hauptbahnhof** (☎069-2123 8800; www.frankfurt-tourismus.de; Main Hall, Hauptbahnhof; ⏲8am-9pm Mon-Fri, 9am-6pm Sat & Sun; Ⓢ Hauptbahnhof) and **Römer** (☎069-2123 8800; www.frankfurt-tourismus.de; Römerberg 27; ⏲9.30am-5.30pm Mon-Fri, to 4pm Sat & Sun; Ⓤ Dom|Römer), a smallish office in the central square.

Getting There & Around

AIR

Frankfurt Airport (FRA; www.frankfurt-airport.com; Hugo-Eckener-Ring; 📶; Ⓢ Flughafen Regionalbahnhof), 12km southwest of the city centre, is Germany's busiest. S-Bahn lines S8 and S9 shuttle between the airport and city centre (one way €4.90, 11 minutes, every 15 minutes).

BUS

Eurolines (www.eurolines.de) and Flixbus (www.flixbus.com) can take you inexpensively to cities across Germany and Europe. Both operate from the main **bus station** (Mannheimer Strasse 15; Hauptbahnhof).

TRAIN

There are direct trains to pretty much everywhere, including Berlin (€90, four hours), Cologne (€39, 1¼ hours) and Munich (€60, 3¼ hours, hourly).

Romantic Rhine Valley

Between Rüdesheim and Koblenz, the Rhine cuts deeply through the Rhenish slate mountains, meandering between hillside castles and steep fields of wine-producing grapes. This is Germany's landscape at its most dramatic – forested hillsides alternate with craggy cliffs and near-vertical terraced vineyards. Idyllic villages appear around each bend, their half-timbered houses and Gothic church steeples seemingly plucked from the world of fairy tales.

Bacharach

06743 / POP 1880

One of the prettiest of the Rhine villages, tiny Bacharach – 24km downriver from Bingen – conceals its considerable charms behind a 14th-century wall. From the B9, pass through one of the thick arched gateways under the train tracks to reach its medieval old town filled with half-timbered buildings.

For gorgeous views of village, vineyards and river, take a stroll atop the **medieval ramparts**, which are punctuated by guard towers. An especially scenic panorama unfolds from the **Postenturm** at the north end of town, from where you can also spy the filigreed ruins of the **Wernerkapelle**, a medieval chapel, and the turrets of the 12th-century hilltop **Burg Stahleck** (06743-1266; www.jugendherberge.de; Stahleckstrasse; dm/s/d from €22.50/34.50/69; P @), a castle turned youth hostel.

Dating from 1421, the olde-worlde tavern **Zum Grünen Baum** (www.weingut-bastian-bacharach.de; Oberstrasse 63; noon-10pm Apr-Oct, shorter hours Nov-Mar) serves some of Bacharach's best whites; the Weinkarussel (€22.50) lets you sample 15 of them.

Trains link Bacharach with Koblenz (€11.60, 35 minutes) and Mainz (€13.70, 40 minutes).

Loreley & St Goar Region

POP 4457

The most fabled spot along the Romantic Rhine, **Loreley** is an enormous, almost vertical slab of slate that owes its fame to a mythical maiden whose siren songs are said to have lured sailors to their death in the river's treacherous currents. Heinrich Heine told the tale in his 1824 poem *Die Lorelei*.

The nearby village of **St Goarshausen**, 2.5km north, is lorded over by the sprawling ruins of **Burg Rheinfels** (06741-7753; www.st-goar.de; Schlossberg 47; adult/child €5/2.50, guided mine tour €7/free; 9am-6pm Apr-Oct, to 5pm Mar & Nov, guided mine tours by reservation), once the mightiest fortress on the Rhine. It's linked by car ferry with its twin across the river, St Goar.

A classy spot to spend the night is **Romantik Hotel Schloss Rheinfels** (06741-8020; www.schloss-rheinfels.de; Schlossberg 47; s/d/ste from €110/140/270; P), right by the castle. Its three restaurants enjoy a fine reputation, but there are plenty more down in the village.

Koblenz is linked by train with St Goarshausen (€8.10, 30 minutes hourly).

EXPLORING THE ROMANTIC RHINE

Each mode of transport on the Rhine has its own advantages and all are equally enjoyable. Try combining several.

Boat From about Easter to October (winter services are very limited), passenger ships run by **Köln-Düsseldorfer** (KD; 0221-208 8318; www.k-d.com) link villages on a set timetable. You're free to get on and off as you like.

Car No bridges span the Rhine between Koblenz and Bingen, but you can easily change banks by using a car ferry *(Autofähre)*. There are five routes: Bingen–Rüdesheim, Niederheimbach–Lorch, Boppard–Filsen, Oberwesel–Kaub and St Goar–Goarshausen.

Train Villages on the Rhine's left bank (eg Bacharach and Boppard) are served regularly by local trains on the Koblenz–Mainz run. Right-bank villages such as Rüdesheim, St Goarshausen and Braubach are linked hourly to Koblenz' Hauptbahnhof and Frankfurt by the RheingauLinie train.

ROMANCING THE RHINE

The Romantic Rhine Valley villages have plenty more charmers that deserve at least a quick spin. Just pick one at random and make your own discoveries. Here are some teasers:

Boppard Roman ruins and a cable car to the stunning Vierseenblick viewpoint (left bank).

Oberwesel Famous for its 3km-long medieval town wall punctuated by 16 guard towers (left bank).

Assmannhausen Relatively untouristed village known for its red wines, sweeping views and good hikes (right bank).

Rüdesheim Day-tripper-deluged but handy launch pad for the mighty Niederwalddenkmal monument and Eberbach Monastery (right bank).

Koblenz

☎0261 / POP 112,586

Founded by the Romans, Koblenz sits at the confluence of the Rhine and Moselle Rivers, a point known as **Deutsches Eck** (German Corner) and dominated by a bombastic 19th-century statue of Kaiser Wilhelm I on horseback. On the right Rhine bank high above the Deutsches Eck – and reached by an 850m-long **Seilbahn** (cable car; ☎0261-2016 5850; www.seilbahn-koblenz.de; Rheinstrasse 6; adult/child return €9.90/4.40, incl Festung Ehrenbreitstein €13.80/6.20; ⏱9.30am-7pm Jul-Sep, to 6pm Easter-Jun & Oct, 10am-5pm Nov-Easter) – is the **Festung Ehrenbreitstein** (☎0261-6675 4000; www.tor-zum-welterbe.de; adult/child €7/3.50, incl cable car €13.80/6.20, audioguide €2; ⏱10am-6pm Apr-Oct, to 5pm Nov-Mar), one of Europe's mightiest citadels. Views are great and there's a restaurant and a regional museum inside.

Moselle Valley

Like a vine right before harvest, the Moselle hangs heavy with visitor fruit. Castles and towns with half-timbered buildings are built along the sinuous river below steep, rocky cliffs planted with vineyards. It's one of Germany's most evocative regions, with stunning views revealed at every river bend. Unlike the Romantic Rhine, it's spanned by plenty of bridges. The most scenic section unravels between Bernkastel-Kues and Cochem, 50km apart and linked by the B421. At the head of the valley is whimsically turreted **Burg Eltz** (☎02672-950 500; www.burg-eltz.de; Burg-Eltz-Strasse 1, Wierschem; tour adult/child €9/6.50; ⏱9.30am-5.30pm Apr-Oct), one of Germany's most romantic medieval castles.

Cochem

☎02671 / POP 5332

Cochem is one of the most popular destinations on the Moselle thanks to its fairy-tale-like **Reichsburg** (☎02671-255; www.reichsburg-cochem.de; Schlossstrasse 36; tours adult/child €6/3; ⏱tours 9am-5pm mid-Mar–Oct, shorter hours Nov–mid-Mar). The 40-minute tours (some in English; leaflet/audioguide otherwise available) take in decorative rooms reflecting 1000 years' worth of tastes and styles.

To taste and buy exceptional wines made from grapes grown on the hillside behind, stop by **VinoForum** (☎02671-917 1777; www.vinoforum-ernst.de; Moselstrasse 12-13, Ernst; ⏱10am-6pm Apr-Oct, 1-5pm Nov-Mar).

The **tourist office** (☎02671-600 40; www.ferienland-cochem.de; Endertplatz 1; ⏱9am-5pm Mon-Sat, 10am-3pm Sun mid-Jun–Sep, shorter hours Oct–mid-Jun) can suggest local wineries and hikes, and provide transport advice.

Cochem is 55km from Koblenz via the scenic B327 and B49. By train, destinations include Koblenz (€11.80, 40 minutes) and Trier (€14.90, 55 minutes).

Beilstein

☎02673 / POP 140

Picture-perfect Beilstein is little more than a cluster of higgledy-piggledy houses surrounded by steep vineyards. Its historic highlights include the **Marktplatz** and the ruined hilltop castle **Burg Metternich** (☎02673-936 39; www.burg-metternich.de; adult/child €2.50/1; ⏱9am-6pm Apr-Nov). The **Zehnthauskeller** (☎02673-900 907; www.zehnthauskeller.de; Marktplatz 1; ⏱11am-10pm Tue-Sat, from noon Sun; 📶) houses a romantically dark, vaulted wine tavern owned by the same family that also runs two local hotels.

Buses link Beilstein with Cochem (€3.80, 20 minutes, every two hours).

Bernkastel-Kues

☎06531 / POP 6987

These charming twin towns are the hub of the *Mittelmosel* (Middle Moselle) region. Bernkastel, on the right (eastern) bank, is a symphony in half-timber, stone and slate, and teems with wine taverns.

Get your heart pumping by hoofing it up to **Burg Landshut** (06531-972 770; www.burglandshut.de; Bernkastel; noon-9pm Thu-Tue), a ruined 13th-century castle on a bluff above town. Allow 30 minutes to be rewarded with glorious valley views. The castle contains a **restaurant** (mains €14-25; noon-2pm & 6-9pm Thu-Tue Easter-Nov) dishing up modern German cuisine.

Christiana's Wein & Art Hotel (06531-6627; www.wein-arthotel.de; Lindenweg 18, Kues; s/d/ste from €69/89/111; P) is a charming boutique base, with each of the 17 rooms named after a Moselle vineyard.

The **tourist office** (06531-500 190; www.bernkastel.de; Gestade 6; audioguides 3 hrs/1 day €6/8; 9am-5pm Mon-Fri, from 10am Sat, to 1pm Sun May-Oct, 9.30am-4pm Mon-Fri Nov-Apr) is in Bernkastel. Coming from Trier, drivers should follow the B53. Buses run to Bullay (€12.60, 1¼ hours) and Trier (€11.55, 2¼ hours).

Trier

0651 / POP 114, 914

With an astounding nine Unesco World Heritage Sites, Germany's oldest city shelters the country's finest ensemble of Roman monuments, among them a mighty gate, amphitheatre, elaborate thermal baths, an imperial throne room and the country's oldest bishop's church, which retains Roman sections. Architectural treasures from later ages include Germany's oldest Gothic church, and Karl Marx' baroque birthplace.

Sights

★Porta Nigra ROMAN SITE
(adult/child €4/2.50; 9am-6pm Apr-Sep, to 5pm Mar & Oct, to 4pm Nov-Feb) Trier's most famous landmark, this brooding 2nd-century Roman city gate – blackened by time, hence the name, which is Latin for 'black gate' – is a marvel of engineering, since it's held together by nothing but gravity and iron clamps. In the 11th century, the structure was turned into a church to honour Simeon, a Greek hermit who spent six years walled up in its east tower. After his death in 1134, he was buried inside the gate and later became a saint.

Konstantin Basilika ROMAN SITE
(Constantine's Throne Room; 0651-9949 1200; www.konstantin-basilika.de; Konstantinplatz 10; 10am-6pm Mon-Sat, 1-6pm Sun Apr-Oct, shorter hours rest of year) FREE Constructed around AD 310 as Constantine's throne room, this brick-built basilica is now an austere Protestant church. With built-to-impress dimensions (some 67m long, 27m wide and 33m high), it's the largest single-room Roman structure still in existence. Its organ, with 87 registers and 6500 pipes, generates a seven-fold echo.

Liebfrauenbasilika CHURCH
(Church of Our Lady; www.trierer-dom.de; Liebfrauenstrasse; 10am-6pm Mon-Fri, to 4.30pm Sat, 12.30-6pm Sun Apr-Oct, shorter hours rest of year) Germany's oldest Gothic church was built in the 13th century. It has a cruciform structure supported by a dozen pillars symbolising the 12 Apostles (look for the black stone from where all 12 articles of the Apostle's Creed painted on the columns are visible) and some colourful post-war stained glass.

★Trierer Dom CATHEDRAL
(0651-979 0790; www.trierer-dom.de; Liebfrauenstrasse 12; 6.30am-6pm Apr-Oct, to 5.30pm Nov-Mar) Looming above the Roman palace of Helena (Emperor Constantine's mother), this cathedral is Germany's oldest bishop's church and still retains Roman sections. Today's edifice is a study in nearly 1700 years of church architecture with Romanesque, Gothic and baroque elements. Intriguingly, its floorplan is of a 12-petalled flower, symbolising the Virgin Mary.

To see some dazzling ecclesiastical equipment and peer into early Christian history, head upstairs to the **Domschatz** (Cathedral Treasury; 0651-710 5378; www.trierer-dom.de/bauwerk/domschatz; adult/child €1.50/0.50; 10am-5pm Mon-Sat, from 12.30pm Sun Apr-Oct & Dec, 11am-4pm Tue-Sat, from 12.30pm Sun Nov & Jan-Mar) or around the corner to the **Museum am Dom Trier** (0651-710 5255; www.bistum-trier.de/museum; Bischof-Stein-Platz 1, adult/child €3.50/2; 9am-5pm Tue-Sat, from 1pm Sun).

Kaiserthermen ROMAN SITE
(Imperial Baths; Weberbachstrasse 41; adult/child €4/2.50; 9am-6pm Apr-Sep, to 5pm Mar & Oct, to 4pm Nov-Feb) Get a sense of the layout of this vast Roman thermal bathing complex with its striped brick-and-stone arches from the corner lookout tower, then descend into an underground labyrinth consisting of cavernous hot and cold water baths, boiler rooms and heating channels.

Amphitheatre ROMAN SITE
(Olewiger Strasse; adult/child €4/2.50; 9am-6pm Apr-Sep, to 5pm Mar & Oct, to 4pm Nov-Feb)

Trier's mighty Roman amphitheatre could accommodate 20,000 spectators for gladiator tournaments and animal fights. Beneath the arena are dungeons where prisoners sentenced to death waited next to starving beasts for the final showdown.

Sleeping

★Hotel Villa Hügel BOUTIQUE HOTEL €€
(☎0651-937 100; www.hotel-villa-huegel.de; Bernhardstrasse 14; s/d from €118/163; P@☎) You can begin the day with sparkling wine over breakfast at this chic 1914-built hillside villa, and end it luxuriating in the indoor or rooftop pools and Finnish sauna. The 45 rooms are decorated with honey-toned woods; higher-category 'relax' rooms have balconies. Panoramic views extend from its glass-walled gourmet restaurant and flower-filled summer terrace.

Becker's DESIGN HOTEL €€
(☎0651-938 080; www.beckers-trier.de; Olewiger Strasse 206; hotel s €95-125, d €140-190, ste €210-240, Weinhaus s/d €85/110; P❄@☎) In the peaceful wine district of Olewig, across the creek from the old monastery church, 3km southeast of the centre, classy Becker's pairs supremely tasteful rooms – ultramodern in its hotel; rustically traditional in its Weinhaus – with stellar **dining** (1-/3-course lunch menu €18/28, 3-/4-course dinner menu €45/58, mains €21-34; ⊙noon-2pm & 6-10pm Tue-Sun).

Eating & Drinking

★Weinwirtschaft Friedrich-Wilhelm GERMAN €€
(☎0651-994 7480; www.weinwirtschaft-fw.de; Weberbach 75; mains €12.50-27.50; ⊙11.30am-2.30pm & 5.30-10pm Mon-Fri, 11.30am-10pm Sat & Sun) A historical former wine warehouse with exposed brick and joists now houses this superb restaurant. Creative dishes incorporate local wines, such as trout poached in sparkling white wine with mustard sauce and white asparagus, or local sausage with Riesling sauerkraut and fried potatoes. Vines trail over the trellis-covered garden; the attached wine shop is a great place to stock up.

Alt Zalawen GERMAN €€
(☎0651-286 45; www.altzalawen.de; Zurlaubener Ufer 79; mains €6-18; ⊙kitchen 11am-10pm, closed Sun Nov-Mar; ☎) The pick of the cluster of bar-restaurants right on the riverfront, with terraces extending to the path running along the grassy bank, timber-panelled Alt Zalawen is a picturesque spot for traditional German specialities (schnitzels, sausages, *Spätzle*) and local Trierer Viez cider.

Information

Tourist Office (☎0651-978 080; www.trier-info.de; An der Porta Nigra; ⊙9am-6pm Mon-Sat, 10am-5pm Sun Mar-Dec, 10am-5pm Mon-Sat Jan & Feb)

Getting There & Away

Trier has frequent train connections to Saarbrücken (€20.90, one to 1½ hours) and Koblenz (€24, 1½ to two hours). There are also regular trains to Luxembourg City (€19.40, 50 minutes).

COLOGNE & NORTHERN RHINELAND

POP 17.9 MILLION (NORTH RHINE–WESTPHALIA)

Cologne's iconic Dom has twin towers that might as well be exclamation marks after the word 'welcome'. Flowing behind the cathedral, the Rhine provides a vital link for some of the region's highlights – Düsseldorf, with its great nightlife, architecture and shopping; and Bonn, the former capital, which hums to Beethoven. Away from the river, Aachen still echoes to the beat of the Holy Roman Empire and Charlemagne.

Cologne

☎0221 / POP 1.07 MILLION

Cologne (Köln) offers lots of attractions, led by its famous cathedral whose filigree twin spires dominate the skyline. The city's museum landscape is especially strong when it comes to art, but also has something in store for fans of chocolate, sports and Roman history. Its people are well known for their joie de vivre and it's easy to have a good time right along with them year-round in the beer halls of the Altstadt.

Sights

★Kölner Dom CATHEDRAL
(Cologne Cathedral; ☎0221-9258 4720; www.koelner-dom.de; Domkloster 4; tower adult/concession €4/2; ⊙6am-9pm May-Oct, to 7.30pm Nov-Apr, tower 9am-6pm May-Sep, to 5pm Mar, Apr & Oct, to 4pm Nov-Feb; 🚇5, 16, 18 Dom/Hauptbahnhof) Cologne's geographical and spiritual heart – and its single-biggest tourist draw – is the magnificent Kölner Dom. With its soaring twin spires, this is the Mt Everest of cathedrals, jam-packed with art and treasures. For an exercise fix, climb the 533 steps up the Dom's

south tower to the base of the steeple that dwarfed all buildings in Europe until Gustave Eiffel built a certain tower in Paris. The Domforum visitor centre is a good source of info and tickets.

Römisch-Germanisches Museum MUSEUM
(Roman Germanic Museum; ☎0221-2212 4438; www.roemisch-germanisches-museum.de; Roncalliplatz 4; adult/concession/under 18yr €6.50/3.50/free; ⏲10am-5pm Tue-Sun; 🚊5, 16, 18 Dom/Hauptbahnhof) Sculptures and ruins displayed outside the entrance are merely the overture to a full symphony of Roman artefacts found along the Rhine. Highlights include the giant Poblicius tomb (AD 30–40), the magnificent 3rd-century Dionysus mosaic, and astonishingly well-preserved glass items. Insight into daily Roman life is gained from toys, tweezers, lamps and jewellery, the designs of which have changed surprisingly little since Roman times.

Museum Ludwig MUSEUM
(☎0221-2212 6165; www.museum-ludwig.de; Heinrich-Böll-Platz; adult/concession €12/8, more during special exhibits; ⏲10am-6pm Tue-Sun; 🚊5, 16, 18 Dom/Hauptbahnhof) A mecca of modern art, Museum Ludwig presents a tantalising mix of works from all major genres. Fans of German expressionism (Beckmann, Dix, Kirchner) will get their fill here as much as those with a penchant for Picasso, American pop art (Warhol, Lichtenstein) and Russian avant-garde painter Alexander Rodchenko. Rothko and Pollock are highlights of the abstract collection, while Gursky and Tillmanns are among the reasons the photography section is a must-see.

Wallraf-Richartz-Museum & Fondation Corboud MUSEUM
(☎0221-2212 1119; www.wallraf.museum; Obenmarspforten; adult/concession €9/5.50; ⏲10am-6pm Tue-Sun; 🚊1, 7, 9 Heumarkt, 🚊5 Rathaus) One of Germany's finest art museums, the Wallraf-Richartz presents a primo collection of European art from the 13th to the 19th centuries in a minimalist cube designed by the late OM Ungers. All the marquee names are here – Rubens and Rembrandt to Manet and Monet – along with a prized sampling of medieval art, most famously Stefan Lochner's *Madonna in Rose Bower*, nicknamed the 'Mona Lisa of Cologne'.

Schokoladenmuseum MUSEUM
(Chocolate Museum; ☎0221-931 8880; www.schokoladenmuseum.de; Am Schokoladenmuseum 1a; adult/student/child €11.50/9/7.50; ⏲10am-6pm Tue-Fri, 11am-7pm Sat & Sun, last entry 1hr before closing; 🚌133 Schokoladenmuseum) This boat-shaped, high-tech temple to the art of chocolate making has plenty of engaging exhibits on the 5000-year cultural history of the 'elixir of the gods' (as the Aztecs called it) as well as on the cocoa-growing process. The walk-through tropical forest is a highlight, although most visitors are more enthralled by the glass-walled miniature production facility and a sample at the chocolate fountain.

DON'T MISS

CARNIVAL IN COLOGNE

Carnival in Cologne is one of the best parties in Europe and a thumb in the eye of the German work ethic. It all starts with *Weiberfastnacht*, the Thursday before Ash Wednesday, when women rule the day (and do things like chop off the ties of their male colleagues and bosses). The party continues through the weekend, with more than 50 parades of ingenious floats and wildly dressed lunatics dancing in the streets. By the time it all comes to a head with the big parade on *Rosenmontag* (Rose Monday), the entire city has become unglued. Those still capable of swaying and singing will live it up one last time on Shrove Tuesday before the curtain comes down on Ash Wednesday.

Sleeping & Eating

There are plenty of beer halls and restaurants in the tourist-adored Altstadt, but for a more local vibe head to student-flavoured Zülpicher Viertel or the Belgisches Viertel, both in the city centre. Local breweries turn out a variety called *Kölsch*, which is relatively light and served in skinny 200mL glasses.

★**25hours Hotel The Circle** HOTEL €€
(☎0221-162 530; www.25hours-hotels.com; Im Klapperhof 22-24; d €120-220; P ⊖ ❄ 📶; U Friesenplatz) The Cologne edition of this mod lifestyle hotel chain occupies a listed circular building (a former insurance company headquarters) and is bathed in a retro-futuristic design theme. Past the vast lobby with bike rental and DJ corner are good-sized rooms that bulge with quirks, character and zeitgeist-capturing amenities such as Bluetooth speakers.

Cologne

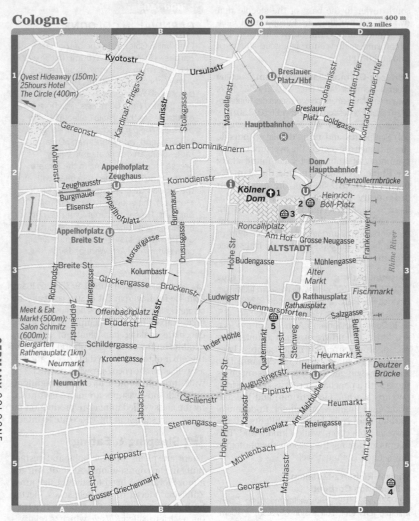

Cologne

Top Sights

1 Kölner Dom C2

Sights

2 Museum Ludwig C2
3 Römisch-Germanisches Museum C2
4 Schokoladenmuseum D5
5 Wallraf-Richartz-Museum & Fondation Corboud C3

Qvest Hideaway DESIGN HOTEL €€€
(☎0221-278 5780; www.qvest-hotel.com; Gereonskloster 12; d from €150; ; Christophstrasse/Mediapark) This dazzling alchemy of historical setting and up-to-the-minute design touches is hidden within the neo-Gothic ribbed vaults and stone pillars of the former city archives. The carefully chosen art, design classics, midcentury furniture and amenities are likely to inspire loads of decorating ideas (hint: there's a shop that sells some of the objects). Optional breakfast is €20.

Meet & Eat Markt MARKET €
(www.meet-and-eat.koeln; Rudolfplatz; 4-9pm Thu; U Rudolfplatz) A combination of farmers market and street-food fair, Meet & Eat draws locals of all ages to Rudolfplatz on Thursday evenings. Aside from fresh produce, you can pick up homemade pesto, chutney, organic cheeses and other artisanal products or sit down at a covered table for a vegan sausage or succulent burger.

★**Salon Schmitz** EUROPEAN €€
(0221-139 5577; www.salonschmitz.com; Aachener Strasse 28-34; mains from €10; 9am-1am Sun-Thu, open end Fri & Sat; 1, 7, 12, 15 Rudolfplatz) Spread over three historical row houses, the Schmitz empire is your one-stop shop for excellent food and drink. Greet the day with a lavish breakfast in the retro-hip 1950s and '60s setting of the Salon; order cake, quiche or a hot dish in the Metzgerei, a historical butcher's shop turned deli; or indulge in a fine brasserie-style dinner in the art nouveau–styled Bar.

★**Biergarten Rathenauplatz** BEER GARDEN
(0221-801 7349; www.rathenauplatz.de/biergarten; Rathenauplatz 30; noon-11.30pm Apr-Sep; 9, 12, 15 Zülpicher Platz) A large, leafy park has one of Cologne's best places for a drink: a community-run beer garden. Tables sprawl under huge old trees, while simple snacks such as salads and very good *Frikadelle* (spiced hamburger) issue forth from a cute little hut.

Information

Tourist Office (0221-346 430; www.cologne-tourism.com; Kardinal-Höffner-Platz 1; 9am-8pm Mon-Sat, 10am-5pm Sun; U Köln Dom/Hauptbahnhof) Excellent; near the cathedral. The app is well done.

Getting There & Around

AIR

Köln Bonn Airport (CGN; Cologne Bonn Airport; 02203-404 001; www.koeln-bonn-airport.de; Kennedystrasse; Köln/Bonn Flughafen) is about 18km southeast of the city centre and connected to the Hauptbahnhof by the S-Bahn S13 train every 20 minutes (€2.80, 15 minutes).

TRAIN

From Cologne's **Hauptbahnhof** (www.bahnhof.de/bahnhof-de/Köln_Hbf-1032796; Trankgasse 11; 16, 18 Breslauer Platz/Hauptbahnhof, 5 Dom/Hauptbahnhof), services are fast and frequent in all directions and include fast Thalys and ICE trains to Brussels (€59, two hours) where you can connect to the Eurostar for London and Paris.

Northern Rhineland

North of Koblenz, the scenery bordering the Rhine is not quite as romantic as along the Middle Rhine further south. Instead the river takes on the mightiness of an urban stream as it courses through such cities as Bonn and Düsseldorf. Many towns in the region started out as Roman settlements some 2000 years ago, and it was also the Romans who gave the Rhine its name (*rhenus* in Latin).

Düsseldorf

0211 / POP 628,000

Düsseldorf dazzles with boundary-pushing architecture, zinging nightlife and an art scene to rival many a metropolis. It's a posh and modern city whose economy is dominated by banking, advertising, fashion and telecommunications. However, a couple of hours of partying in the boisterous pubs of the Altstadt, the historical quarter along the Rhine, is all you need to realise that locals have no problem letting their hair down once they slip out of those Boss jackets.

Sights

★**K20 Grabbeplatz** MUSEUM
(0211 838 1204; www.kunstsammlung.de; Grabbeplatz 5; adult/concession/child €12/10/2.50; 10am-6pm Tue-Fri, 11am-6pm Sat & Sun; U Schadowstrasse) A collection that spans the arc of 20th-century artistic vision gives the K20 an enviable edge in the art world. It encompasses major works by Picasso, Matisse and Mondrian and more than 100 paintings and drawings by Paul Klee. Americans represented include Jackson Pollock, Andy Warhol and Jasper Johns. Düsseldorf's own Joseph Beuys has a major presence as well.

K21 Ständehaus MUSEUM
(0211-838 1204; www.kunstsammlung.de; Ständehausstrasse 1; adult/concession/child €12/10/2.50; 10am-6pm Tue-Fri, 11am-6pm Sat & Sun, U Graf-Adolf-Platz) A stately 19th-century parliament building forms a fabulously

dichotomous setting for the cutting-edge art of the K21 – a collection only showcasing works created after the 1980s. Large-scale film and video installations and groups of works share space with site-specific rooms by an international cast of artists including Andreas Gursky, Candida Höfer, Bill Viola and Nam June Paik.

Medienhafen ARCHITECTURE
(Am Handelshafen; 726, 732 Erftstrasse/Grand Bateau) Where sweat once dripped off dockland workers' foreheads, creative minds now forge ad campaigns and newspaper headlines. The Medienhafen (Media Harbour) is Düsseldorf's most spectacular urban revitalisation project, an old commercial harbour transformed by such architectural heavyweights as Richard Meier, Helmut Jahn and Claude Vasconi into a tableau of avant-garde buildings. Top billing goes to Frank Gehry's Neuer Zollhof, a trio of sculptural high-rises sheathed in stainless steel, red brick and white plaster, respectively.

Sleeping

Backpackers Düsseldorf HOSTEL €
(0211-302 0848; www.backpackers-duesseldorf.de; Fürstenwall 180; dm €18.50-25, s/d €32/50; reception 8am-10pm; Kirchplatz) Düsseldorf's adorable indie hostel sleeps 60 in clean four- to 10-bed dorms outfitted with individual backpack-sized lockers. Bathrooms are shared. It's a low-key place with a kitchen and a relaxed lounge where cultural and language barriers melt quickly. The vending machine is filled with beer. Rates include a small breakfast; linen costs €3.

Hotel Orangerie HOTEL €€
(0211-866 800; www.hotel-orangerie-mcs.de; Bäckergasse 1; r €130-250; Benrather Strasse) Ensconced in a neoclassical mansion in a quiet corner of the Altstadt, this place puts you within staggering distance of pubs, the river and museums, yet offers a serene and stylish refuge to retire to. Some of the 27 minimalist rooms skimp somewhat on size, but all are as bright, modern and uncluttered as the lobby and breakfast room.

Eating & Drinking

★**Brauerei im Füchschen** GERMAN €€
(0211-137 4716; www.fuechschen.de; Ratinger Strasse 28; mains €9-17; 9am-1am Mon-Thu, to 2am Fri & Sat, to midnight Sun; Tonhalle/Ehrenhof) Boisterous, packed and drenched with local colour, the 'Little Fox' in the Altstadt is all you expect a Rhenish beer hall to be. The kitchen is especially famous for its mean *Schweinshaxe* (roast pork leg) served in a high-ceilinged interior that echoes with the mirthful roar of people enjoying their meals.

Zum Uerige BEER HALL
(0211-866 990; www.uerige.de; Berger Strasse 1; 10am-midnight; Heinrich-Heine-Allee) Local colour by the bucketful (despite the high tourist contingent) is what awaits at this cavernous *Altbier* brewpub. The suds flow so quickly from giant copper vats that the waiters – called *Köbes* – simply carry huge trays of brew and plonk down a glass whenever they spy an empty. Even on a cold day, the outside tables are alive with merriment.

Information

Tourist Office – Altstadt (0211-1720 2840; www.duesseldorf-tourismus.de; cnr Marktstrasse & Rheinstrasse; 10am-6pm; Heinrich-Heine-Allee) Right in the heart of the old centre.

Tourist Office – Hauptbahnhof (0211-1720 2844; www.duesseldorf-tourismus.de; Immermannstrasse 65b; 9.30am-7pm Mon-Fri, to 5pm Sat; Hauptbahnhof) The main tourist office, across from the train station; has a currency exchange window.

Getting There & Around

Düsseldorf International Airport (DUS; 0211-4210; www.dus.com; Düsseldorf Flughafen), 10km north of the **Hauptbahnhof** (www.bahnhof.de/bahnhof-de/Düsseldorf_Hbf-1021118; Konrad-Adenauer-Platz 14; Hauptbahnhof), is linked to the city centre by S-Bahn.

ICE/IC trains departing from the Hauptbahnhof head to Berlin (€116, 4¼ hours), Hamburg (€86, 3½ hours), Frankfurt (€86, 1¾ hours) and many other destinations.

Aachen

0241 / POP 254,000

Aachen makes for an excellent day trip from Cologne or Düsseldorf as well as a worthy overnight stop. The Romans nursed their war wounds and stiff joints in the steaming waters of Aachen's mineral springs, but it was Charlemagne who put the city firmly on the European map. His legacy lives on in the stunning Dom, which in 1978 became Germany's first Unesco World Heritage Site, as well as the **Centre Charlemagne** (0241-432 4956; www.centre-charlemagne.eu; Katschhof 1; adult/concession €6/3; 10am-5pm Tue-Sun).

Sights

★ Aachener Dom CATHEDRAL

(☎0241-4770 9110; www.aachendom.de; Münsterplatz; tours adult/concession €4/3; ⏲7am-7pm Apr-Dec, to 6pm Jan-Mar) It's impossible to overestimate the significance of Aachen's magnificent cathedral. The burial place of Charlemagne, it's where more than 30 German kings were crowned and where pilgrims have flocked since the 12th century. Before entering the church, stop by **Dom Information** (☎0241-4770 9145; Johannes-Paul-II-Strasse 1; ⏲10am-5pm Jan-Mar, to 6pm Apr-Dec) for info and tickets for tours and the cathedral **treasury** (Cathedral Treasury; ☎0241-4770 9127; Johannes-Paul-II-Strasse 2; adult/concession €5/4; ⏲10am-2pm Mon, to 5pm Tue-Sun Jan-Mar, 10am-2pm Mon, to 6pm Tue-Sun Apr-Dec). English tours run daily at 2pm.

Rathaus HISTORIC BUILDING

(Town Hall; ☎0241-432 7310; http://rathaus-aachen.de; Markt; adult/concession/under 22yr incl audioguide €6/3/free; ⏲10am-6pm) Fifty life-sized statues of German rulers, including 30 kings crowned in Aachen between AD 936 and 1531, adorn the facade of Aachen's splendid Gothic town hall. Inside, the undisputed highlight is the vaulted coronation hall where the post-ceremony banquets were held. Note the epic 19th-century frescoes and replicas of the imperial insignia: a crown, orb and sword (the originals are in Vienna).

Sleeping & Eating

Aachen's students have their own 'Latin Quarter' along Pontstrasse northeast of the Markt.

Hotel Drei Könige HOTEL €€

(☎0241-483 93; www.h3k-aachen.de; Büchel 5; d €129-169;) The sunny Mediterranean design and quirky touches are an instant mood-lifter at this family-run favourite with its super-central location. Some of the 10 rooms are a tad wee. Breakfast, on the 4th floor, comes with dreamy views over the rooftops and the cathedral.

★ Am Knipp GERMAN €€

(☎0241-331 68; www.amknipp.de; Bergdriesch 3; mains €9-24; ⏲5-10.30pm Mon & Wed-Fri, 6-10.30pm Sat & Sun;) Hungry grazers have stopped by this traditional inn since 1698, and you too will have a fine time enjoying hearty German cuisine served amid a flea market's worth of knick-knacks or, if weather permits, in the big beer garden.

★ Café zum Mohren CAFE €

(☎0241-352 00; www.cafezummohren.de; Hof 4; mains €4.50-10; ⏲10am-7pm) This darling cafe just off the tourist trail is famous for its cakes, especially a wicked chocolate one called *Krippekratz* (local slang for 'devil') and sumptuous ice-cream cakes. Also a good spot for breakfast or light meals. Outside tables overlook a courtyard flanked by Roman columns.

Information

Tourist Office (☎0241-180 2950; www.aachen-tourist.de; Friedrich-Wilhelm-Platz; ⏲10am-6pm Mon-Fri, to 2pm Sat & Sun Apr-Dec, shorter hours Jan-Mar)

Getting There & Away

Regional trains to Cologne (€17.50, one hour) run twice hourly from the Hauptbahnhof, with some proceeding beyond. Aachen is a stop for high-speed trains to/from Brussels (€40, 1¼ hours) and Paris.

Bonn

☎0228 / POP 322,000

South of Cologne on the Rhine River, Bonn served as West Germany's capital from 1949 until 1990. For visitors, the birthplace of Ludwig van Beethoven has plenty in store, not least the great composer's birth house, a string of top-rated museums and the lovely riverside setting.

Sights

★ Beethoven-Haus Bonn MUSEUM

(Beethoven House; ☎0228-981 7525; www.beethoven-haus-bonn.de; Bonngasse 20; adult/concession €6/4.50; ⏲10am-6pm Apr-Oct, 10am-5pm Mon-Sat, 11am-5pm Sun Nov-Mar) Star composer Ludwig van Beethoven was born in 1770 in this rather humble townhouse, where today original scores, letters, paintings and instruments, including his last grand piano, offer insight into his work, routines and feelings. Of special note are the huge ear trumpets he used to combat his growing deafness. Tickets are also good for the new media exhibit in the adjacent building, where you can experience the composer's genius during a spacey, interactive 3D multimedia tour.

Haus der Geschichte MUSEUM

(Museum of History; ☎0228-916 5400; www.hdg.de; Willy-Brandt-Allee 14; ⏲9am-7pm Tue-Fri, 10am-6pm Sat & Sun; P; 🚊16, 63, 66 Heussallee/Museumsmeile) FREE The Haus der Geschichte der Bundesrepublik Deutschland presents a smart, fun romp through recent German history, starting from the end of WWII. Walk through the fuselage of a Berlin airlift *Rosinenbomber* plane, watch classic clips in a 1950s cinema, imagine free love in a VW microbus, examine Erich Honecker's arrest warrant, stand in front of a piece of the Berlin Wall or watch John F Kennedy's famous '*Ich bin ein Berliner*' speech.

Sleeping & Eating

Brauhaus Bönnsch GERMAN €€
(0228-650 610; www.boennsch.de; Sterntorbrücke 4; mains €10-22; 11am-1am Mon-Thu, to 3am Fri & Sat;) The unfiltered ale is a must at this congenial brewpub adorned with photographs of famous politicians great and failed, from Willy Brandt to, yes, Arnold Schwarzenegger. Schnitzel, Rhenish specialities and fry-ups dominate the menu, but the *Flammkuchen* (tarte flambée) is always a crowd-pleaser.

Information

Bonn Tourist Office (0228-775 000; www.bonn-region.de; Windeckstrasse 1; 10am-6pm Mon-Fri, to 4pm Sat, to 2pm Sun) Lots of free information and combined bus-and-walking tours in English (adult/concession €16/8).

Getting There & Away

Bonn is linked to Cologne many times hourly by U-Bahn lines U16 and U18 (€7.90, 54 minutes).

NORTHERN GERMANY

POP 6.5 MILLION

Germany's windswept and maritime-flavoured north is dominated by Hamburg, a metropolis shaped by water and commerce since the Middle Ages. Bremen is a fabulous stop with fairy-tale character, and not only because of the famous Brothers' Grimm fairy tale starring a certain donkey, dog, cat and rooster. Those with a sweet tooth should not miss a side trip to Lübeck, renowned for its superb marzipan.

Hamburg

040 / POP 1.8 MILLION

Hamburg's historic label, 'The gateway to the world', might be a bold claim, but Germany's second-largest city and biggest port has never been shy. Hamburg has engaged in business with the world ever since it joined the Hanseatic League back in the Middle Ages. Its maritime spirit infuses the entire city; from architecture to menus to the cry of gulls, you always know you're near the water. The city has given rise to vibrant neighbourhoods awash with multicultural eateries, as well as the gloriously seedy Reeperbahn red-light district. Hamburg nurtured the early promise of the Beatles, and today its distinctive live- and electronic-music scene thrives in unique harbourside venues.

Sights

The seven-storey red-brick warehouses lining the **Speicherstadt** archipelago are a famous Hamburg symbol and they're increasingly filled with fine museums. **HafenCity,** crowned by the superlative Elbphilharmonie, is Hamburg's most architecturally dynamic corner, with a world seemingly being created before your eyes.

★**Elbphilharmonie** ARTS CENTRE
(Elbe Philharmonic Hall; 040-3576 6666; www.elbphilharmonie.de; Platz der Deutschen Einheit 4; 9am-11.30pm; S Baumwall) FREE Welcome to one of the most Europe's most exciting recent architectural creations. A squat brown-brick former warehouse at the far west of HafenCity was the base for the architecturally bold Elbphilharmonie, a major concert hall and performance space, not to mention architectural icon. Pritzker Prize-winning Swiss architects Herzog & de Meuron were responsible for the design, which captivates with details like 1096 individually curved glass panes.

Hamburger Kunsthalle MUSEUM
(040-428 131 200; www.hamburger-kunsthalle.de; Glockengiesserwall; adult/child €14/free, Thu evening €8/free; 10am-6pm Tue, Wed & Fri-Sun, to 9pm Thu; U Hauptbahnhof-Nord) A treasure trove of art from the Renaissance to the present day, the Kunsthalle spans two buildings linked by an underground passage. The main building houses works ranging from medieval portraiture to 20th-century classics, such as Klee and Kokoschka. There's also a memorable room of 19th-century landscapes by Caspar David Friedrich. Its stark white modern cube, the Galerie der Gegenwart, showcases contemporary German artists.

LOCAL KNOWLEDGE

ST PAULI & THE REEPERBAHN

No discussion of Hamburg is complete without mentioning St Pauli, home to one of Europe's most (in)famous red-light districts. Sex shops, table-dance bars and strip clubs still line its main drag, the Reeperbahn, and side streets, but the popularity of prostitution has declined dramatically in the internet age. Today St Pauli is Hamburg's main nightlife district, drawing people of all ages and walks of life to live music and dance clubs, chic bars and theatres. In fact, street walkers are not even allowed to hit the pavement before 8pm and then are confined to certain areas, the most notorious being the gated Herbertstrasse (no women and men under 18 years allowed). Nearby, the cops of the Davidwache police station keep an eye on the lurid surrounds. A short walk west is the side street called Grosse Freiheit, where the Beatles cut their teeth at the Indra Club (No 64) and the Kaiserkeller (No 36). Both are vastly different venues today, but there's a small monument to the Fab Four in a courtyard behind No 35.

Rathaus HISTORIC BUILDING

(040-428 3124; Rathausmarkt 1; tours adult/under 14yr €5/free; tours half-hourly 11am-4pm Mon-Fri, 10am-5pm Sat, to 4pm Sun, English tours depend on demand; U Rathausmarkt, Jungfernstieg, S Jungfernstieg) With its spectacular coffered ceiling, Hamburg's baroque Rathaus is one of Europe's most opulent, and is renowned for its Emperor's Hall and Great Hall. The 40-minute tours take in only a fraction of this beehive of 647 rooms. A good secret to know about is the inner courtyard, where you can take a break from exploring the Rathaus on comfy chairs with tables.

St Michaelis Kirche CHURCH

(Church of St Michael; 040-376 780; www.st-michaelis.de; Englische Planke 1; tower adult/child €5/3.50, crypt €4/2.50, combo ticket €7/4, church only €2; 9am-7.30pm May-Oct, 10am-5.30pm Nov-Apr, last entry 30min before closing; U Rödingsmarkt) 'Der Michel', as it is affectionately called, is one of Hamburg's most recognisable landmarks and northern Germany's largest Protestant baroque church. Ascending the tower (by steps or lift) rewards visitors with great panoramas across the city and canals. The crypt has an engaging multimedia exhibit on the city's history.

Mahnmal St-Nikolai MEMORIAL

(Memorial St Nicholas; 040-371 125; www.mahnmal-st-nikolai.de; Willy-Brandt-Strasse 60; adult/child €5/3; 10am-6pm May-Sep, to 5pm Oct-Apr; U Rödingsmarkt) St Nikolai church was the world's tallest building from 1874 to 1876, and it remains Hamburg's second-tallest structure (after the TV tower). Mostly destroyed in WWII, it is now called Mahnmal St-Nikolai. You can take a glass lift up to a 76.3m-high viewing platform inside the surviving spire for views of Hamburg's centre, put into context of the wartime destruction. The crypt houses an unflinching underground exhibit on the horrors of war.

★ **Fischmarkt** MARKET

(Grosse Elbstrasse 9; 5am-9.30am Sun Apr-Oct, from 7am Nov-Mar; 112 to Fischmarkt, S Reeperbahn) Here's the perfect excuse to stay up all Saturday night. Every Sunday in the wee hours, some 70,000 locals and visitors descend upon the famous Fischmarkt in St Pauli. The market has been running since 1703, and its undisputed stars are the boisterous *Marktschreier* (market criers) who hawk their wares at full volume. Live bands also entertainingly crank out cover versions of ancient German pop songs in the adjoining **Fischauktionshalle** (Fish Auction Hall).

Auswanderermuseum BallinStadt MUSEUM

(Emigration Museum; 040-3197 9160; www.ballinstadt.de; Veddeler Bogen 2; adult/child €13/7; 10am-6pm Apr-Oct, to 4.30pm Nov-Mar; Veddel) Sort of a bookend for New York's Ellis Island, Hamburg's excellent emigration museum looks at the conditions that drove about five million people to leave Germany for the USA and South America in search of better lives from 1850 until the 1930s. Multilingual displays address the hardships endured before and during the voyage and upon arrival in the New World. About 4km southeast of the city centre, BallinStadt is easily reached by S-Bahn.

Chilehaus HISTORIC BUILDING

(040-349 194 247; www.chilehaus.de; Fischertwiete 2; S Messberg) One of Hamburg's most beautiful buildings is the crowning gem

Hamburg

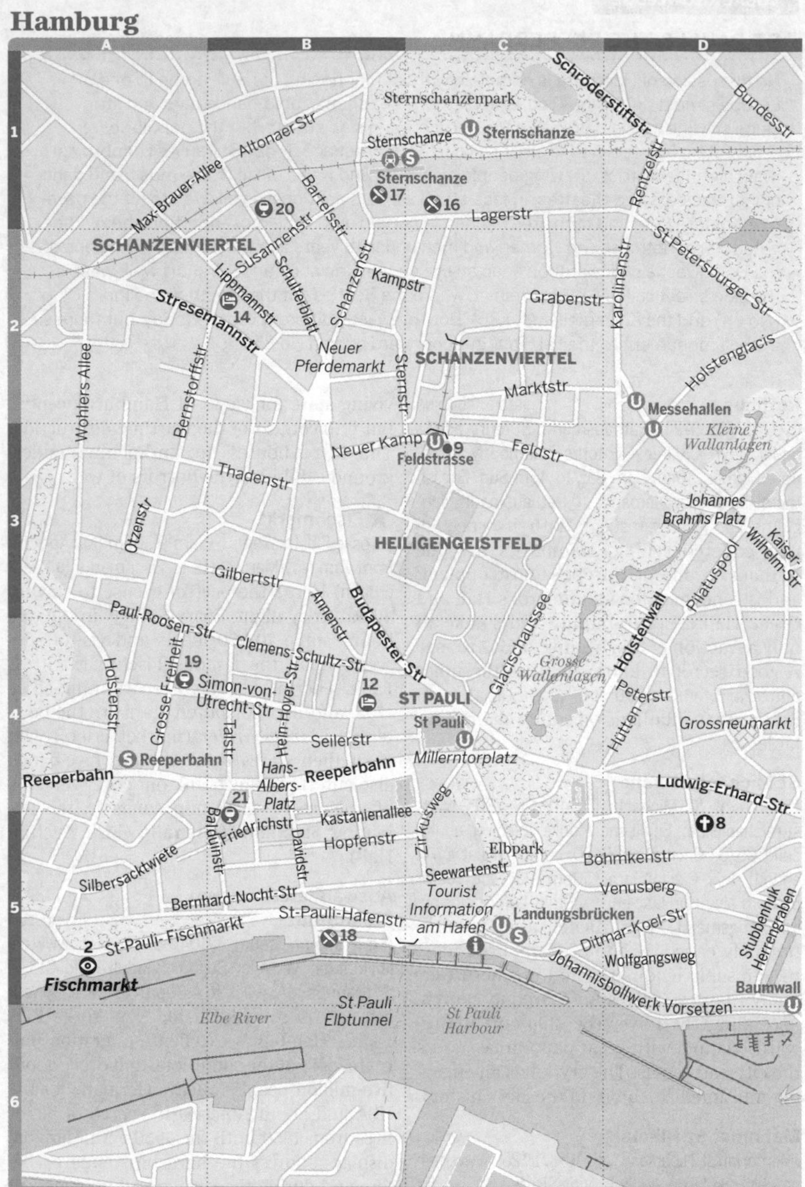

of the new Unesco-anointed Kontorhaus District. The brown-brick 1924 Chilehaus is shaped like an ocean liner, with remarkable curved walls meeting in the shape of a ship's bow and staggered balconies that look like decks. It was designed by architect Fritz Höger for a merchant who derived his wealth from trading with Chile. Casual visitors are not really welcome inside, but it's the exterior that you come here to see.

Miniatur Wunderland MUSEUM
(☎040-300 6800; www.miniatur-wunderland.de; Kehrwieder 2; adult/child €15/7.50; ⌚hours

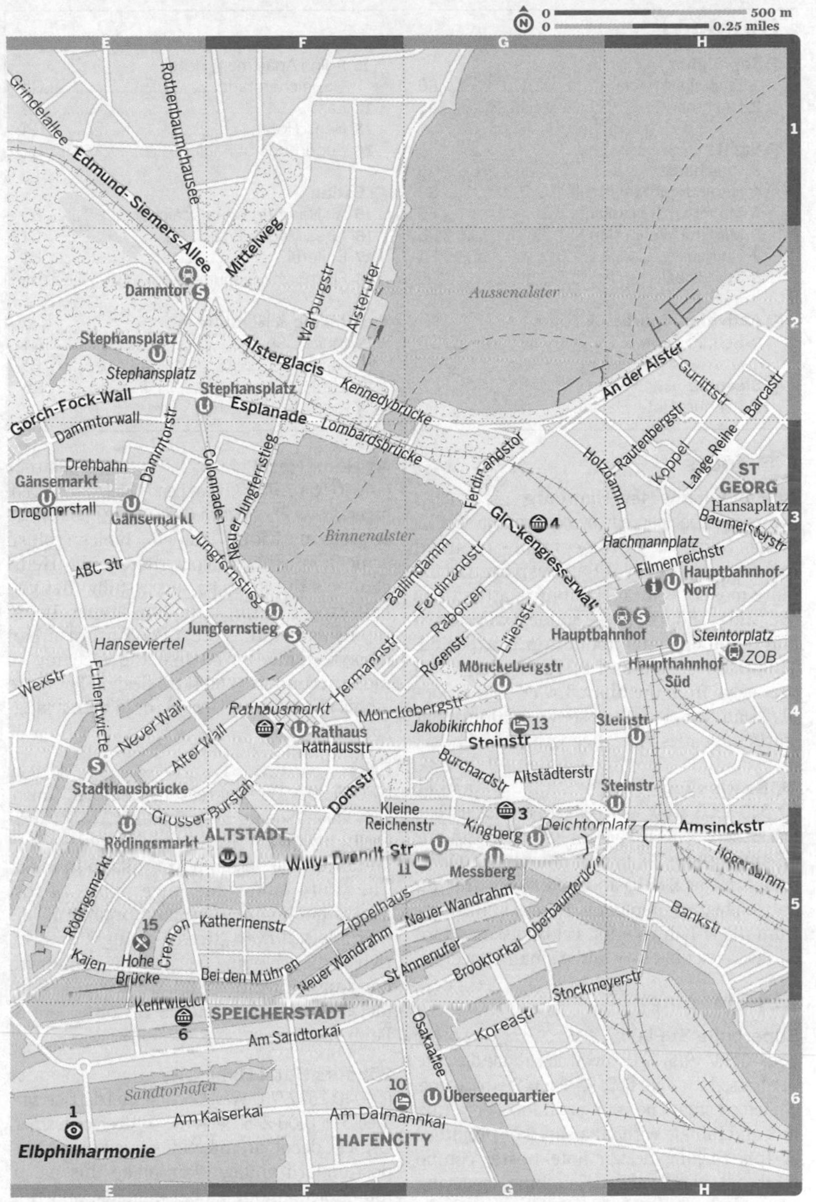

vary; Ⓤ Baumwall) Even the worst cynics are quickly transformed into fans of this vast miniature world that goes on and on. The model trains wending their way through the Alps are impressive, if slightly predictable, but when you see a model A380 swoop out of the sky and land at the fully functional model of Hamburg's airport, you can't help but gasp! On weekends and in summer holidays, pre-purchase your ticket online to skip the queues.

The current display is a mind-numbing 1300 sq metres; tiny details abound as days change to night.

Hamburg

Top Sights
1 Elbphilharmonie....E6
2 Fischmarkt....A5

Sights
3 Chilehaus....G5
4 Hamburger Kunsthalle....G3
5 Mahnmal St-Nikolai....F5
6 Miniatur Wunderland....E6
7 Rathaus....F4
8 St Michaelis Kirche....D5

Activities, Courses & Tours
9 Beatles Tour....C3

Sleeping
10 25hours Hotel HafenCity....F6
11 Adina Apartment Hotel Speicherstadt....G5
12 East....B4
13 Henri Hotel....G4
14 Superbude St Pauli....B2

Eating
15 Alt Hamburger Aalspeicher....E5
16 Altes Mädchen....C1
17 Bullerei....B1
18 Fischbrötchenbude Brücke 10....B5

Drinking & Nightlife
19 Indra Club....A4
20 Katze....B1
21 Zum Silbersack....B5

Tours

★Sandemans New Hamburg TOURS
(www.neweuropetours.eu; by donation up to €12; 11am & 2pm daily) These highly regarded free city tours begin at Rathausplatz and explore most of central Hamburg's attractions over three hours. These guides work hard and if you enjoy the tour, a tip is expected. They also run tours of St Pauli (€12, 7pm) that leave from the Clock Tower, and a popular Hamburg Pub Crawl (€12, 9.30pm) that starts in Beatles Platz, Reeperbahn.

★Beatles Tour WALKING
(040-3003 3790; www.hempels-musictour.com; tour €28; 6pm Sat Apr-Nov; U Feldstrasse) For an entertaining look at the Beatles in Hamburg, try this Beatles tour offered by the fun and engaging Stephanie Hempel. It starts from the U-Bahn station Feldstrasse and includes museum entry and a small concert.

Sleeping

Superbude St Pauli HOTEL €
(040-807 915 820; www.superbude.de; Juliusstrasse 1-7; r from €65; ; U Sternschanze, S Sternschanze) The young and forever-young mix and mingle without a shred of prejudice at this rocking design hotel-hostel combo that's all about living, laughing, partying and, yes, even sleeping well. All rooms have comfy beds and sleek private bathrooms, breakfast is served until noon and there's even a 'rock star suite' with an Astra beer as a pillow treat.

★Henri Hotel HOTEL €€
(040-554 357 557; www.henri-hotel.com; Bugenhagenstrasse 21; s/d from €98/118; ; S Mönckebergstrasse) Kidney-shaped tables, plush armchairs, vintage typewriters – the Henri channels the 1950s so successfully that you half expect to run into Don Draper. Its 65 rooms and studios are a good fit for urban lifestyle junkies who like the alchemy of modern comforts and retro design. For more elbow room get an L-sized room with a king-size bed.

East HOTEL €€
(040-309 933; www.east-hamburg.de; Simon-von-Utrecht-Strasse 31; r €100-225; ; U St Pauli) In an old iron foundry, East's bold and dramatic design never fails to impress. The walls, lamps and huge pillars of this hotel's public areas emulate organic forms – droplets, flowers, trees – giving it a warm, rich and enveloping feel. Rooms come with handmade furniture and are accented with tactile fabrics and leather. It's on a cool St Pauli street.

25hours Hotel HafenCity HOTEL €€
(040-257 7770; www.25hours-hotel.de; Überseeallee 5; r €100-225; P; U Überseequartier) Offbeat decor, an infectious irreverence and postmodern vintage flair make this pad a top choice among global nomads. Sporting maritime flourishes, the decor channels an old-timey seaman's club in the lobby, the excellent restaurant and the 170 cabin-style rooms. Enjoy views of the emerging HafenCity neighbourhood from the rooftop sauna.

★Adina Apartment Hotel Speicherstadt APARTMENT €€
(☎040-334 6080; www.adinahotels.com/hotel/hamburg-speicherstadt; Willy-Brandt-Strasse 25; r from €144; P❄📶🏊; U Messberg) An excellent addition to the Adina portfolio, this sophisticated place ticks all the boxes when it comes to location (within easy walking distance to most attractions), price (much more reasonable than many Hamburg apartment hotels) and comfort (the studio rooms are large, stylish and exceptionally soundproof). The swimming pool, gym and sauna are all nice touches. Multinight stays attract discounts.

Eating

Fischbrötchenbude Brücke 10 SEAFOOD €
(☎040-3339 9339; www.bruecke-10.de; Landungsbrücken, Pier 10; sandwiches €3-9.50; ⏲10am-10pm; S Landungsbrücken, U Landungsbrücken) There are a gazillion fish sandwich vendors in Hamburg, but we're going to stick our neck out and say that this vibrant, clean and contemporary outpost makes the best. Try a classic *Bismarck* (pickled herring) or *Matjes* (brined herring), or treat yourself to a bulging shrimp sandwich. Lovely tables outside.

Altes Mädchen EUROPEAN €€
(☎040-800 077 750; www.altes-maedchen.com; Lagerstrasse 28b; mains €6-29; ⏲noon-late Mon-Sat, 10am-late Sun; S Sternschanze, U Sternschanze) The lofty red-brick halls of a 19th-century animal market have been upcycled into a hip culinary destination that includes a coffee roastery, a celebrity chef restaurant, and this beguiling brewpub with a central bar, in-house bakery and garden.

Bullerei INTERNATIONAL €€
(☎040-3344 2110; www.bullerei.com; Lagerstrasse 34b; mains €10-25; ⏲11am-11pm; S Sternschanze) One of the coolest dining spaces in the city, Bullerei inhabits a converted former slaughterhouse with lovely high ceilings and a real buzz that bounces off the walls – don't come here for a quiet romantic dinner. Service is cool and attentive, and the menu revolves around steak dishes and Italian-inflected choices.

★Alt Hamburger Aalspeicher GERMAN €€€
(☎040-362 990; www.aalspeicher.de; Deichstrasse 43; mains €13-27; ⏲noon-11pm Wed-Sun; U Rödingsmarkt) Despite its tourist-friendly location, the knick-knack-filled dining room and warm service at this restaurant, in a 400-year-old canalside building, make you feel like you're dining in your *Oma's* (grandma's) house – it's a real slice of old Hamburg where you'd least expect it. Smoked eel from its own smokehouse is a speciality.

Drinking & Nightlife

Partying in Hamburg concentrates on the Schanzenviertel and St Pauli, a few streets further south.

★Strandperle BAR
(☎040-8809 9508; www.strandperle-hamburg.de; Oevelgönne 60; ⏲10am-11pm Mon-Fri, from 9am Sat & Sun May-Sep, shorter hours & Fri-Sun only Oct-Apr; 🚌112) Hamburg's original beach bar is a must for primo beer, burgers and people-watching. All ages and classes gather, mingle and wriggle their toes in the sand, especially at sunset, right on the Elbe, as huge freighters glide past. Get here by taking ferry 62 from Landungsbrücken or bus 112 from Altona station to Neumühlen/Oevelgönne.

★Katze COCKTAIL BAR
(☎040-5577 5910; Schulterblatt 88; ⏲1pm-3am Mon-Sat, to midnight Sun; S Sternschanze) Small and sleek, this 'kitty' (*Katze* = cat) gets the crowd purring for well-priced cocktails (the best caipirinhas in town) and great music (there's dancing on weekends). It's one of the most popular among the watering holes on this main Schanzenviertel booze strip.

★Zum Silbersack PUB
(☎040-314 589; www.facebook.com/zumsilbersack1949; Silbersackstrasse 9; ⏲5pm-1am Sun, to 3am Mon-Wed, to 4am Thu, 3pm-5am Fri & Sat; S Reeperbahn) A real St Pauli icon, Zum Silbersack is one of our favourites in the area. It's the sort of place where you'll find students, junkies, executives, greenies, millionaires and sex workers. Anything seems possible and it can be a little rough around the edges, but it's *very* St Pauli.

Indra Club CLUB
(www.indramusikclub.com; 64 Grosse Freiheit; ⏲9pm-late Wed-Sun; S Reeperbahn) The Beatles' small first venue is open again and has live acts some nights. The interior is vastly different from the 1960s and there is a fine beer garden.

Information

Tourist Information am Hafen (☎040-3005 1701; www.hamburg-travel.com; btwn piers 4 & 5, St Pauli Landungsbrücken; ⊙9am-6pm Sun-Wed, to 7pm Thu-Sat; **S** Landungsbrücken) No hotel bookings, but plenty of information.

Tourist Information Hauptbahnhof (☎040-3005 1701; www.hamburg-travel.com; Hauptbahnhof, near Kirchenallee exit; ⊙9am-7pm Mon-Sat, 10am-6pm Sun; 🚆Hauptbahnhof, **U** Hauptbahnhof) Busy all the time.

Getting There & Away

AIR

Hamburg Airport (Flughafen Hamburg Helmut Schmidt; HAM; ☎040-507 50; www.hamburg-airport.de; Flughafenstrasse; 🚆Hamburg Airport) is linked to the city centre every 10 minutes by the S-Bahn line S1 (€3.30, 25 minutes). A taxi takes about a half-hour and cost around €30.

BUS

The **ZOB** (Zentraler Omnibusbahnhof, Central Bus Station; ☎040-247 576; www.zob-hamburg.de; Adenauerallee 78; 🚆Hauptbahnhof, **U** Hauptbahnhof-Süd), southeast of the Hauptbahnhof, has many domestic and international departures by Eurolines, Flixbus and many other operators.

TRAIN

Frequent trains serve regional and long-distance destinations from Hamburg. There are two main-line stations worth noting: **Hamburg Hauptbahnhof** (Main Train Station; www.hamburger-hbf.de; 🚆Hauptbahnhof) and **Hamburg Altona** (**S** Altona).

Frequent trains serve Lübeck (from €14.50, 45 minutes), Bremen (from €20, one hour), Berlin-Hauptbahnhof (from €30, 1¾ hours), Cologne (from €36, four hours) and many other cities.

Getting Around

For public transport information, go to **HVV** (☎040-194 49; www.hvv.de). The city is divided into zones. Fare zone A covers the city centre, inner suburbs and airport.

Schleswig-Holstein

Sandy beaches, jaunty red-and-white striped lighthouses, deep fjords carved by glaciers, and wildlife like sandpipers and seals have made this sweeping peninsula between the North and Baltic Seas Germany's most elite summer retreat. Don't miss Lübeck, the magnificently preserved medieval headquarters of the Hanseatic League. Flensburg, too, is a lively harbour town.

Lübeck

☎0451 / POP 218,523

Compact and charming Lübeck makes for a great day trip from Hamburg. Looking like a pair of witches' hats, the pointed towers of its landmark Holstentor (Holsten Gate) form the gateway to its historic centre that sits on an island embraced by the arms of the Trave River. The Unesco-recognised web of cobbled lanes flanked by gabled merchants' homes and spired churches is an enduring reminder of Lübeck's role as the one-time capital of the medieval Hanseatic League trading power. Today it enjoys fame as Germany's marzipan capital, best sampled at **Niederegger** (☎0451-530 1126; www.niederegger.de; Breite Strasse 89; ⊙9am-7pm Mon-Fri, 9am-6pm Sat, 10am-6pm Sun).

Sights

★Holstentor LANDMARK

(Holsten Gate) Built in 1464 and looking so settled-in that it appears to sag, Lübeck's charming red-brick city gate is a national icon. Its twin pointed cylindrical towers, leaning together across the stepped gable that joins them, captivated Andy Warhol (his print is in the St Annen Museum), and have graced postcards, paintings, posters and marzipan souvenirs. Discover this and more inside the **Museum Holstentor** (☎0451-122 4129; www.museum-holstentor.de; Holstentor; adult/child €7/2.50; ⊙10am-6pm Apr-Dec, 11am-5pm Tue-Sun Jan-Mar), which sheds light on the history of the gate and on Lübeck's medieval mercantile glory days.

★Museumsquartier St Annen MUSEUM

(Museum Quarter St Annen; ☎0451-122 4137; www.museumsquartier-st-annen.de; St-Annen-Strasse; adult/child €12/6; ⊙10am-5pm Tue-Sun Apr-Dec, from 11am Jan-Mar) This museum quarter includes an old synagogue, church and medieval buildings along its uneven streets. The namesake **St Annen Museum** details the diverse history of the neighbourhood as it traces 700 years of art and culture. The adjoining **St Annen Kunstalle** has ecclesiastical art (including Hans Memling's 1491 *Passion Altar)* and contemporary art, including Andy Warhol's print of Lübeck's Holstentor. There's a chic little cafe in the courtyard.

★Europäisches Hansemuseum MUSEUM

(European Hanseatic Museum; ☎0451-809 0990; www.hansemuseum.eu; An der Untertrave 1; adult/child €12.50/7.50; ⊙10am-6pm) Opened in

OFF THE BEATEN TRACK

ANNE FRANK & BERGEN-BELSEN

Nazi-built **Bergen-Belsen** (Bergen-Belsen Memorial Site; 05051-475 90; www.bergen-belsen.de; Anne-Frank-Platz, Lohheide; Documentation Centre 10am-6pm Apr-Sep, to 5pm Oct-Mar, grounds until dusk) FREE began its existence in 1940 as a POW camp, but became a concentration camp after being taken over by the SS in 1943, initially to imprison Jews as hostages in exchange for German POWs held abroad. In all, 70,000 prisoners perished here, most famously Anne Frank. A modern Documentation Centre chronicles the fates of the people who passed through here. A small section deals with Anne Frank, and there's also a memorial grave stone for her and her sister, Margot, near the cemetery's Jewish Monument. The memorial site is in the countryside about 60km northeast of Hanover and a bit complicated to reach if you don't have your own wheels. See the website for detailed driving and public transport directions.

2015, this brilliant museum tells the remarkable story of the Hanseatic League, Lübeck and the region. For 600 years, city states in northern Europe and along the Baltic discovered that shared interests in trade made everybody's life better than war. Transfixing exhibits use every modern technology to tell a story as dramatic as anything on *Game of Thrones*. The complex includes the beautifully restored medieval **Castle Friary**.

Rathaus HISTORIC BUILDING
(Town Hall; 0451-122 1005; Breite Strasse 62; adult/concession €4/2; tours 11am, noon & 3pm Mon-Fri, 1.30pm Sat & Sun) Sometimes described as a 'fairy tale in stone', Lübeck's 13th- to 15th-century Rathaus is widely regarded as one of the most beautiful in Germany. Inside, a highlight is the *Audienzsaal* (audience hall), a light-flooded hall decked out in festive rococo.

Sleeping & Eating

★Hotel Haase BOUTIQUE HOTEL €€
(0451-7074 90 1; www.hotel-haase-luebeck.de; Glockengießerstrasse 24; s/d from €100/116;) Gorgeous rooms with exposed brick walls and polished hardwood floors inhabit this beautifully restored 14th-century home in the heart of town. The public areas in particular sparkle with character, and service never misses a beat.

Klassik Altstadt Hotel BOUTIQUE HOTEL €€
(0451-702 980; www.klassik-altstadt-hotel.de; Fischergrube 52; s/d from €55/120;) Each of the 29 rooms at this elegantly furnished boutique hotel are dedicated to a different, mostly German, writer or artist, such as Thomas Mann or Johann Sebastian Bach. Single rooms (some share baths and are great value) feature travelogues by famous authors.

Grenadine BISTRO €€
(0451-307 2950; www.grenadine-hl.de; Wahmstrasse 40; mains €10-23; 9am-4pm Mon, to 10pm Tue-Thu, to midnight Fri & Sat, to 3pm Sun;) This narrow, elongated bar leads through to a garden out the back. Enjoy bistro fare amid chic, retro-minimalist style. The long drinks menu goes well with tapas choices. Sandwiches, salads and pasta, plus a gorgeous breakfast buffet (€14.50 to €17.50), are served.

★Im Alten Zolln PUB
(0451-723 95; www.alter-zolln.de; Mühlenstrasse 93-95; 11am-late;) This classic pub inhabits a 16th-century customs post. There's an excellent beer selection. Patrons people-watch from terrace and pavement tables in summer and watch bands (rock and jazz) inside in winter. Fortify yourself with schnitzel and Lübeck's best roast potatoes.

Information

Tourist Office (0451-889 9700; www.luebeck-tourismus.de; Holstentorplatz 1; 9am-7pm Mon-Fri, 10am-4pm Sat, 10am-3pm Sun Jun-Aug, shorter hours Sep-Apr) One of Schleswig-Holstein's better tourist offices, with a cafe and internet terminals.

Getting There & Away

Lübeck is reached via the A1 from Hamburg. Lübeck has connections every hour to Hamburg (€14.50, 45 minutes) and Kiel (from €18.70, 1¼ hours).

LOWER SAXONY & BREMEN

POP 7.9 MILLION (LOWER SAXONY), 671,489 (BREMEN)

Lower Saxony (Niedersachsen) is the largest German state after Bavaria. West to east, it stretches from the World Heritage–listed Wattenmeer tidal flats and the East Frisian Islands to Wolfsburg. Bremen, the smallest of the German states, packs a punch for its size. At the mouth of the Weser, its port city of Bremerhaven upholds a rich seafaring tradition.

Bremen City

☎0421 / POP 568,006

It's a shame the donkey, dog, cat and rooster in Grimm's *Town Musicians of Bremen* never actually made it here – they would have fallen in love with the place. This little city is big on charm, from the fairy-tale character statue to a jaw-dropping expressionist laneway and impressive town hall. On top of that, the Weser riverside promenade is a relaxing, bistro- and beer garden–lined refuge and the lively student district ('Das Viertel') along Ostertorsteinweg is filled with indie boutiques, cafes, art-house cinemas and alt-flavoured cultural venues.

Sights & Activities

Bremen's Unesco World Heritage–protected **Marktplatz** is striking, especially for its ornate, gabled and sculpture-adorned **Rathaus**. On the town hall's western side is a sculpture of the animal quartet of lore, the **Town Musicians of Bremen** (Stadtmusikanten).

★Kunsthalle GALLERY

(☎0421-329 080; www.kunsthalle-bremen.de; Am Wall 207; adult/child €9/free; ⏲10am-5pm Wed-Sun, to 9pm Tue; 🚊2, 3 to Theater am Goetheplatz) For art lovers, the highlight of Bremen's *Kulturmeile* (Cultural Mile) is the Kunsthalle, which presents a large permanent collection of paintings, sculpture and copperplate engravings from the Middle Ages into the modern era – some of the masterpieces here are more than 600 years old. The collection includes work by van Dyck, Rubens, Monet, Van Gogh and Picasso, as well as 10 sculptures by Rodin. Rotating exhibitions display both classical and contemporary art.

Böttcherstrasse STREET

(www.boettcherstrasse.de) The charming medieval coopers lane was transformed into a prime example of mostly expressionist architecture in the 1920s at the instigation of coffee merchant Ludwig Roselius. Its red-brick houses sport unique facades, whimsical fountains, statues and a carillon; many house artisanal shops and art museums. Its most striking feature is Bernhard Hoetger's golden **Lichtbringer** (Bringer of Light) relief, which keeps an eye on the north entrance.

Dom St Petri CHURCH

(St Petri Cathedral; ☎0421-334 7142; www.stpetridom.de; Sandstrasse 10-12; tower adult/child €2/1, museum free; ⏲10am-5pm Mon-Fri, to 2pm Sat, 2-5pm Sun Oct-May, Mon-Fri & Sun to 6pm Jun-Sep) Bremen's Protestant main church has origins in the 8th century, though its ribbed vaulting, chapels and two high towers date from the 13th century. Aside from the imposing architecture, the intricately carved pulpit and the baptismal font in the western crypt deserve a closer look. For panoramic views, climb the 265 steps to the top of the south **tower** (April to October). The Dom museum displays religious artefacts and treasures found here in a 1970s archaeological dig.

WORTH A TRIP

BACK TO THE ROOTS IN BREMERHAVEN

Standing on the spot where more than 7.2 million emigrants set sail for the USA, South America and Australia between 1830 and 1942, the spectacular **Deutsches Auswandererhaus** (German Emigration Centre; ☎0471-902 200; www.dah-bremerhaven.de; Columbusstrasse 65; adult/child €14.80/8.80; ⏲10am-6pm Mar-Oct, to 5pm Nov-Feb) museum does a superb job commemorating some of their stories. The visitor relives stages of their journey, which begins at the wharf where passengers huddle together before boarding 'the ship', clutching the biographical details of one particular traveller and heading towards their new life. A second exhibit, opened in 2012, reverses the theme and tells of immigration to Germany since the 17th century. Everything is available in both German and English. Bremerhaven is some 70km north of Bremen and is served by regional train (€12.95, 40 minutes). From the station, take bus 502, 505, 506, 508 or 509 to 'Havenwelten' to get to the museum and the harbour with its many old vessels (including a WWII sub) and striking contemporary architecture.

Beck's Brewery Factory Tour BREWERY
(☎0421-5094 5555; www.becks.de/besucherzentrum; Am Deich 18/19; tours €12.90; ⏲tours 1pm, 3pm & 4.30pm Mon-Wed, 10am, 11.30am, 1pm, 3pm, 4.30pm & 6pm Thu-Sat; 🚋1, 2, 3 to Am Brill) Two-hour tours of one of Germany's most internationally famous breweries must be booked online through either the Beck's or tourist office websites. Expect a tasting at the end. The 3pm tour is also in English. Minimum age 16. Meet at the brewery's visitor centre; take the tram to Am Brill, cross the river, then turn right onto Am Deich.

Sleeping & Eating

Tourist-oriented places to eat cluster around Markt, which is pretty dead after dark. Das Viertel has an alternative, student-flavoured feel, while the waterfront promenade, Schlachte, is pricier and more mainstream.

Atlantic Grand HOTEL €€
(☎0421-620 620; www.atlantic-hotels.de; Bredenstrasse 2; r from €119) The simple but effortlessly stylish, dark-wood rooms pitched around a central courtyard and the top-notch service from attentive staff make this classy hotel an excellent choice. It's moments from Bremen's quirky Böttcherstrasse and steps from the riverside Schlacte.

Hotel Überfluss DESIGN HOTEL €€
(☎0421-322 860; www.designhotel-ueberfluss.de; Langenstrasse 72; s/d from €111/116; ; 🚋1, 2, 3 to Am Brill) Just metres above river level, this cutting-edge-cool hotel is a good choice for design-minded urban nomads. Black, white and chrome create a sleek, postmodern vibe that extends to the rooms (those with views are €15 more). There's one suite (from €328) with a river view and a private sauna and hot tub – perfect for a honeymoon. Breakfast costs €14.50.

Engel Weincafe CAFE €
(☎0421-6964 2390; www.engelweincafe-bremen.de; Ostertorsteinweg 31; dishes €4.50-15.60; ⏲9am-1am Mon-Fri, from 10am Sat & Sun; ; 🚋2, 6 to Wulwesstrasse) Situated on a sunny corner in Das Viertel, this popular hang-out exudes the nostalgic vibe of the old-fashioned pharmacy it once was. The menu features breakfast, a hot lunch special, crispy *Flammkuchen* (like a French pizza, with crème fraiche), carpaccio, or just some cheese and a glass of wine from the international list.

★**Bremer Ratskeller** GERMAN €€
(☎0421-321 676; www.ratskeller-bremen.de; Am Markt 11; mains €9-30; ⏲11am-midnight;) Ratskellers were traditionally built underneath the Rathaus (town hall) in every German town to keep the citizens and civil servants fed. Bremen's – in business since 1405! – is quite the experience, with high vaulted ceilings, private booths in little cubbies (the better to discuss town business), and good, heavy, no-fuss German food and beer. Service is attentive and friendly.

Information

Tourist office branches include **Böttcherstrasse** (☎0421-308 0010; www.bremen-tourism.de; Böttcherstrasse 4; ⏲9.30am-6.30pm Mon-Fri, to 5pm Sat, 10am-4pm Sun;), a full-service tourist office with friendly staff near Marktplatz, and **Hauptbahnhof** (☎0421-308 0010; www.bremen-tourism.de; Hauptbahnhof; ⏲9am-6.30pm Mon-Fri, 9.30am-5pm Sat & Sun;), handily located at the main train station. These offices can help book tours and offer free wi-fi.

Getting There & Around

Bremen Airport (BRE; ☎0421-559 50; www.airport-bremen.de) is about 3.5km south of the city and well connected to the city by the line 6 tram (€2.80, 15 minutes).

Frequent IC trains go to Hamburg (€30, one hour), Hanover (€31, one hour) and Cologne (€69, three hours). Less frequent IC trains go to Berlin (€93, three hours).

SURVIVAL GUIDE

Directory A-Z

ACCOMMODATION

Outside of high season, around holidays and during major trade shows it's generally not necessary to book accommodation in advance.

DISCOUNT CARDS

Many towns offer free guest cards *(Gästekarte)*, available from your hotel at the time of check-in, which entitle visitors to discounts on museums, sights and tours, plus sometimes the use of local public transport.

INTERNET ACCESS

➡ Some cafes and bars have wi-fi hot spots that let customers hook up for free, although you usually need to ask for a password.

- Wi-fi is available for a fee on select ICE train routes, including Berlin to Cologne and Frankfurt to Munich and in DB Lounges (free in 1st class).
- Locate wi-fi hot spots at www.hotspot-locations.com.

LGBTIQ+ TRAVELLERS

Germany is a magnet for *schwule* (gay) and *lesbische* (lesbian) travellers, with the rainbow flag flying especially proudly in Berlin and Cologne.

- Same-sex marriage is legal.
- Gay pride marches are held throughout Germany in springtime, the largest are in Cologne and Berlin.
- Attitudes tend to be more conservative in the countryside, among older people and in the eastern states.

MONEY

- ATMs (*Geldautomat*) are widely available in cities and towns, but rarely in villages. Most are linked to international networks such as Cirrus, Plus, Star and Maestro.
- Cash is king in Germany. Always carry some with you and plan to pay cash almost everywhere.
- Credit cards are becoming more widely accepted, but it's best not to assume you'll be able to use one – ask first.

OPENING HOURS

The following are typical opening hours; these may vary seasonally and between cities and villages. We've provided those applicable in high season. For specifics, see individual listings.

Banks 9am–4pm Monday to Friday, extended hours usually Tuesday and Thursday, some open Saturday

Bars 6pm–1am

Cafes 8am–8pm

Clubs 11pm to early morning

Post offices 9am–6pm Monday to Friday, 9am–1pm Saturday

Restaurants 11am–11pm (food service often stops at 9pm in rural areas)

Major stores and supermarkets 9.30am–8pm Monday to Saturday (shorter hours outside city centres)

PUBLIC HOLIDAYS

The following are *gesetzliche Feiertage* (public holidays):

Neujahrstag (New Year's Day) 1 January

Ostern (Easter) March/April; Good Friday, Easter Sunday and Easter Monday

Christi Himmelfahrt (Ascension Day) Forty days after Easter

Maifeiertag/Tag der Arbeit (Labour Day) 1 May

Pfingsten (Whit/Pentecost Sunday & Monday) Fifty days after Easter

Tag der Deutschen Einheit (Day of German Unity) 3 October

Weihnachtstag (Christmas Day) 25 December

Zweiter Weihnachtstag (Boxing Day) 26 December

TELEPHONE

German phone numbers consist of an area code (three to six digits), starting with 0, and the local number (three to nine digits). If dialling from a landline within the same city, you don't need to dial the area code. You must dial it if using a mobile.

Country code ☎ 49

International access code ☎ 00

TOURIST INFORMATION

German National Tourist Office (www.germany.travel) Should be your first port of call for travel in Germany.

Transport

GETTING THERE & AWAY

Air

Huge Frankfurt Airport (p304) is Germany's busiest, with Munich (p287) a close second and Düsseldorf (p312) getting a good share of flights as well. Airports in Berlin (p273), Hamburg (p320) and Cologne are comparatively small.

Bus

Long-distance coach travel to Germany from such cities as Milan, Vienna, Amsterdam and Copenhagen has become a viable option thanks to a new crop of companies offering good-value connections aboard comfortable buses with snack bars and free wi-fi. Major operators include **MeinFernbus** (☎ 030-300 137 300; www.meinfernbus.de), **Flixbus** (☎ 030-300 137 300; https://global.flixbus.com), **Megabus** (☎ UK 0900 1600 900; www.megabus.com) and **Eurolines** (☎ in the UK 08717-818177; www.eurolines.com). For routes, times and prices, check www.busliniensuche.de (also in English).

Car & Motorcycle

When bringing your own vehicle to Germany, you need a valid driving licence, car registration and proof of third-party insurance. Foreign cars must display a nationality sticker unless they have official European plates. You also need to carry a warning (hazard) triangle and a first-aid kit.

Train

- Germany has an efficient railway network with excellent links to other European destinations. Ticketing is handled by **Deutsche Bahn** (Germany Railways; ☎ 0180-699 66 33; www.bahn.de).
- Seat reservations are a good idea for Friday and Sunday travel on long-distance trains and highly recommended during the peak summer season and around major holidays.

➡ Eurail and Interrail passes are valid on all German national trains.

Sea

Germany's main ferry ports are Kiel and Travemünde (near Lübeck) in Schleswig-Holstein, and Rostock and Sassnitz (on Rügen Island) in Mecklenburg–Western Pomerania. All have services to Scandinavia. For details and tickets, go to www.ferrysavers.com.

GETTING AROUND

Germans are whizzes at moving people around, and the public transport network is one of the best in Europe. The best ways of getting around the country are by car and by train.

Air

Unless you're flying from one end of the country to the other, say from Berlin or Hamburg to Munich, planes are only marginally quicker than trains once you factor in the check-in and transit times.

Bicycle

➡ Cycling is allowed on all roads and highways but not on the autobahns (motorways).

➡ Bicycles may be taken on most trains but require a separate ticket *(Fahrradkarte)* and a reservation if travelling on an IC/EC train. They are not allowed on ICE trains.

➡ **Call a Bike** (www.callabike-interaktiv.de) is an automated cycle-hire scheme operated by Deutsche Bahn (German Rail) in some 50 German towns and cities.

Boat

From April to October, boats operate on set timetables along sections of the Rhine, the Elbe and the Danube.

Bus

➡ Buses are cheaper and slower than trains and have a growing long-haul network. Regional bus services fill the gaps in areas not served by rail. **Flixbus** (www.flixbus.com) is the dominant operator.

➡ In some rural areas buses may be your only option for getting around without your own vehicle. Commuter-geared routes offer limited or no service in the evenings and on weekends.

➡ In cities, buses generally converge at the Busbahnhof or Zentraler Omnibus Bahnhof (ZOB; central bus station), which is often near the Hauptbahnhof (central train station).

Car & Motorcycle

➡ Driving is on the right side of the road.

➡ Unless posted otherwise, speed limits are 50km/h in cities, 100km/h on country roads and no limit on the autobahn.

➡ With few exceptions, no tolls are charged on public roads.

TIPPING

Hotels €1 per bag is standard. It's also nice to leave a little cash for the room cleaners, say €1 or €2 per day.

Restaurants Restaurant bills always include *Bedienung* (service charge), but most people add 5% or 10%.

Bars About 5%, rounded to the nearest euro. For drinks brought to your table, tip as for restaurants.

Taxis Tip about 10%, rounded to the nearest euro.

Toilet attendants Loose change.

➡ Cars are impractical in urban areas. Leaving your car in a central Parkhaus (car park) can cost €20 per day or more.

➡ Visitors from most countries do not need an International Driving Permit to drive in Germany. Automatic transmissions are rare and must be booked well in advance.

Local Transport

➡ Bigger cities, such as Berlin and Munich, integrate buses, trams, U-Bahn (underground, subway) trains and S-Bahn (suburban) trains into a single network.

➡ Fares are determined by zones or time travelled, sometimes by both. A multi-ticket strip *(Streifenkarte* or *4-Fahrtenkarte)* or day pass *(Tageskarte)* generally offers better value than a single-ride ticket.

➡ Normally, tickets must be stamped upon boarding in order to be valid. Fines are levied if you're caught without a valid ticket.

Train

➡ Of the several train types, ICE trains are the fastest and most comfortable. IC trains (EC if they cross borders) are almost as fast but older and less snazzy. RE and RB trains are regional. S-Bahn are suburban trains operating in large cities and conurbations.

➡ At larger stations, you can store your luggage in a locker *(Schliessfach)* or a left-luggage office *(Gepäckaufbewahrung)*.

➡ Seat reservations for long-distance travel are highly recommended, especially if you're travelling on a Friday or Sunday afternoon, during holiday periods or in summer. Reservations can be made online and at ticket counters as late as 10 minutes before departure.

➡ Buy tickets online (www.bahn.de) or at stations from vending machines or ticket offices *(Reisezentrum)*. Only conductors on ICE and IC/EC trains sell tickets on board at a surcharge.

Greece Ελλάδα

POP 10.7 MILLION

Includes ➡

Best Places to Eat

- Klimataria (p368)
- Seychelles (p334)
- Bougatsa Iordanis (p358)
- Marco Polo Cafe (p361)

Best Places to Stay

- Athens Was (p333)
- Bella Venezia (p367)
- Caravan (p344)
- Aroma Suites (p352)
- Casa Leone (p358)

Why Go?

It's easy to understand how so many myths of gods and giants originated in the vast and varied wonderland of Greece, with its wide skies, island-speckled ocean and stunning terrain. Meander along Byzantine footpaths and shores, through villages, lush forests and olive groves. Swim in gorgeous clear waters. Lose yourself in sun-bleached ancient ruins – Acropolis, Delphi, Delos and Knossos. Greece is a treasure chest where socially spirited families and friends gather in cafes and play late into the summer evenings in plazas. Passionate about politics and art, the population embraces culture, and dances and festivals abound. Its celebrated cuisine highlights regional produce from local gardens, herbs and mountain greens, and the world's best olives and tomatoes; prepared as they have been for generations, or adapted into fabulous modern dishes. Ultimately, however, the locals themselves are the highlight. Think *filoxenia* (hospitality) personified. Greece is a legendary destination indeed.

When to Go

Athens

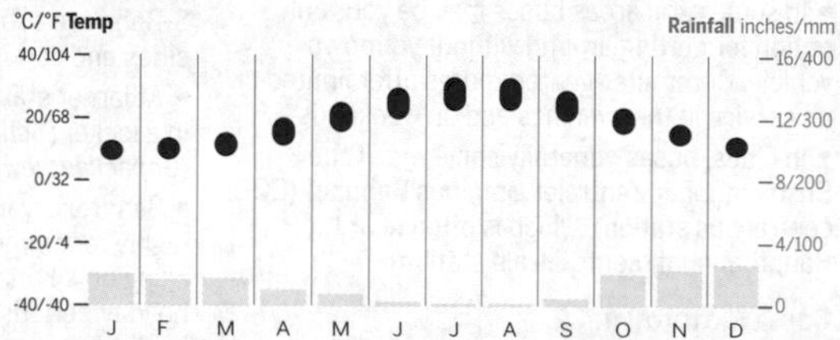

May–Aug Sights, tours and transport are running full tilt. Accommodation prices can double.

Apr, Sep & Oct Crowds thin, temperatures are more mild, and island ferries have reduced schedules.

Nov–Mar Many hotels, sights and restaurants shut down, especially on the islands.

Entering the Country

Greece is easy to reach by aeroplane or ferry – particularly in summer when it opens its arms (and schedules) wide. Getting to or from Greece overland takes more planning, but isn't impossible. Most visitors to Greece arrive by air, which tends to be the fastest and cheapest option, if not the most environmentally friendly.

ITINERARIES

Two Weeks

Begin in Athens (p328), visiting the grand sites plus cool bars, markets and cutting-edge eateries. Fly to Hania (p356), a vibrant Cretan town, then explore the Minoan ruins of Knossos (p356).

It's island hopping and ferry time. Take a ferry to Rhodes Town (p360) and get lost in the medieval old town. Then head to Kos (p361) and spend a couple days on the lovely sandy Kefalos Bay (p362), or Kos Town (p362). Next stop? Samos (p363), to spend a night or two bar-hopping in the small but active capital, Vathy (p363). The final island is Lesvos (p364). Chill out here for a few days, exploring the island's olive groves, the delightful village of Molyvos (p366) and the petrified forests of the island's barren eastern half.

Three Weeks

Fly direct to Thessaloniki (p342) and immerse yourself in the city's vibrant arts scene, fabulous local cuisine and funky accommodation. Head inland to Meteora (p342), to marvel at the extraordinary pinnacles and monasteries. Head next to Ancient Delphi (p341) and (pretend to) consult the oracle at this magical, ancient site. Go west via Patras to the Peloponnese Peninsula to take in the ancient site of Olympia (p341), where the first Olympic games played out. Wander east to your last stop, Nafplio (p339). This was Greece's former capital, a gorgeous town on the water featuring extraordinary Ottoman and Venetian architecture and three fortresses.

Essential Food & Drink

Tzatziki Yoghurt, cucumber and garlic.

Gyros Pork or chicken shaved from a revolving stack of sizzling meat and wrapped in pitta bread with tomato, onion, fried potatoes and lashings of *tzatziki*.

Mousakas Layers of aubergine and mince, topped with béchamel sauce and baked.

Baklava Thin layers of pastry filled with honey and nuts.

Pastitsio Baked dish of macaroni with minced meat and béchamel sauce.

Yemista Either tomatoes or green peppers stuffed with minced meat and rice.

AT A GLANCE

Area 131,944 sq km

Capital Athens

Country Code 30

Currency euro (€)

Emergency 112

Language Greek

Time Eastern European Time (GMT/UTC plus two hours) and three hours on daylight-saving time.

Visas Generally not required for stays up to 90 days. Schengen rules apply.

Sleeping Price Ranges

The following price ranges refer to a double room in high season (May to August). For the Cyclades, the price ranges are based on the rates in July and August. Unless otherwise stated, all rooms have private bathroom facilities.

€ less than €60 (less than €90 in Athens; less than €110 in Mykonos and Santorini)

€€ €60–150 (€90–180 in Athens; €110–250 in Mykonos and Santorini)

€€€ more than €150 (more than €185 in Athens; more than €250 in Mykonos and Santorini)

Eating Price Ranges

The following price ranges refer to the average cost of a main course (not including service charges):

€ less than €10

€€ €10–20

€€€ more than €20

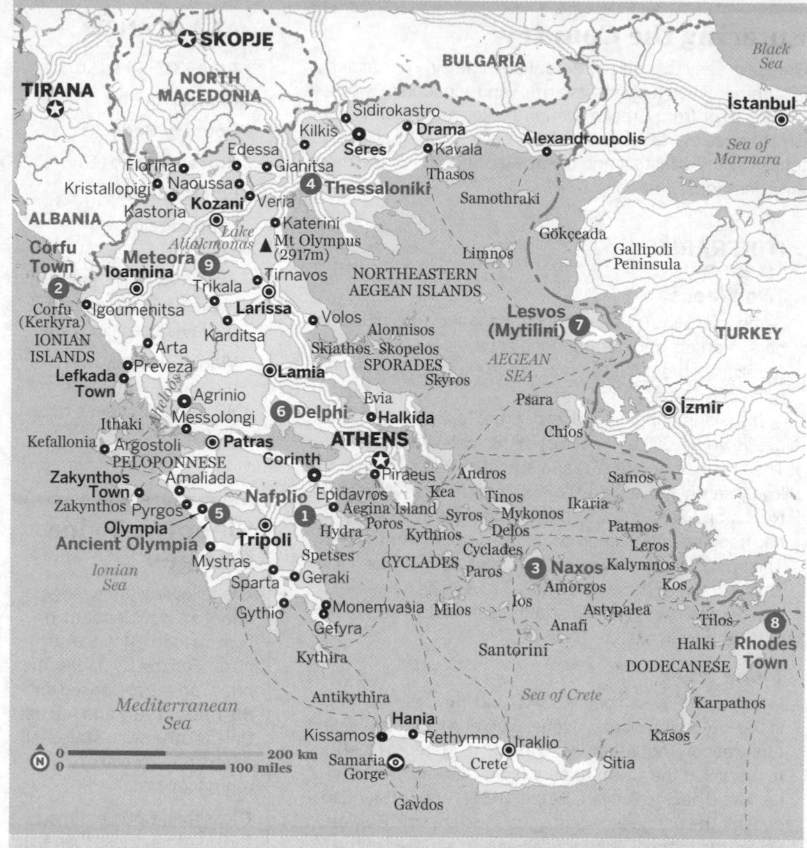

Greece Highlights

1 Nafplio (p339) Basing yourself in this quaint town and exploring fabulous Peloponnesian sites nearby.

2 Corfu Town (p366) Getting lost in the back alleys of the Venetian-style old town.

3 Naxos (p348) Choosing between swimming, visiting ruins or enjoying the local delights of this diverse island.

4 Thessaloniki (p342) Getting your taste buds to go 'high-end Greek' in this thriving city.

5 Ancient Olympia (p341) Rubbing shoulders with ghosts of great athletes at this atmospheric site.

6 Delphi (p341) Imagining yourself as a pilgrim and consulting the oracle at this historic place.

7 Lesvos (p364; Mytilini) Sipping ouzo while munching grilled octopus on this olive-tree-covered island.

8 Rhodes Town (p360) Meandering through the old town and imagining yourself as a player in its medieval past.

9 Meteora (p342) Heading out on foot for an alternative perspective of the lofty, monastery-strewn rock pinnacles.

ATHENS ΑΘΗΝΑ

POP 3.1 MILLION

With equal measures of grunge and grace, Athens is a heady mix of history and edginess. Iconic monuments mingle with first-rate museums, bustling shops and stylish, alfresco dining. Even in the face of financial struggles, Athens is more cosmopolitan than ever with hip hotels, artsy-industrial neighbourhoods and entertainment quarters showing its modern face.

Sights

★Acropolis HISTORIC SITE

(☎210 321 4172; http://odysseus.culture.gr; adult/concession/child €20/10/free; ⏲8am-8pm May-Sep, reduced hours in winter, last entry 30min before closing; Ⓜ Akropoli) The Acropolis is the most important ancient site in the Western world. Crowned by the Parthenon, it stands sentinel over Athens, visible from almost everywhere within the city. Its monuments and sanctuaries of white Pentelic marble gleam in the midday sun and gradually take on a honey hue as the sun sinks, while at night they stand brilliantly illuminated above the city. A glimpse of this magnificent sight cannot fail to exalt your spirit.

★Acropolis Museum MUSEUM

(☎210 900 0900; www.theacropolismuseum.gr; Dionysiou Areopagitou 15, Makrygianni; adult/child €10/free; ⏲8am-4pm Mon, to 8pm Tue-Sun, to 10pm Fri Apr-Oct, reduced hours rest of year; Ⓜ Akropoli) This dazzling museum at the foot of the Acropolis' southern slope showcases its surviving treasures. The collection covers the Archaic period to the Roman one, but the emphasis is on the Acropolis of the 5th century BC, considered the apotheosis of Greece's artistic achievement. The museum reveals layers of history: ruins are visible in its floor, and, through floor-to-ceiling windows, the Acropolis is always visible above. The surprisingly good-value restaurant has superb views; there's also a fine museum shop.

Benaki Museum of Greek Culture MUSEUM

(☎210 367 1000; www.benaki.gr; Koumbari 1, cnr Leoforos Vasilissis Sofias, Kolonaki; adult/student/child €9/7/free, 6pm-midnight Thu free; ⏲9am-5pm Wed & Fri, to midnight Thu & Sat, to 4pm Sun; Ⓜ Syntagma, Evangelismos) Antonis Benakis, a politician's son born in Alexandria, Egypt, in the late 19th century, endowed what is perhaps the finest museum in Greece. Its three floors showcase impeccable treasures from the Bronze Age up to WWII. Especially gorgeous are the Byzantine icons and the extensive collection of Greek regional costumes, as well as complete sitting rooms from Macedonian mansions, intricately carved and painted. Benakis had such a good eye that even the agricultural tools are beautiful.

Museum of Islamic Art MUSEUM

(☎210 325 1311; www.benaki.gr; Agion Asomaton 22, Keramikos; adult/student/child €9/7/free; ⏲10am-6pm Thu-Sun; Ⓜ Thissio) While not particularly large, this museum houses one of the world's most significant collections of Islamic art. Four floors of a mansion display, in ascending chronological order, exceptionally beautiful weaving, jewellery, porcelain and even a marble-floored reception room from a 17th-century Cairo mansion. It's all arranged for maximum dazzle, with informative signage. In the basement, part of Athens' ancient Themistoklean wall is exposed, and the top floor has a small cafe with a view of Kerameikos.

★National Archaeological Museum MUSEUM

(☎213 214 4800; www.namuseum.gr; Patision 44, Exarhia; adult/child €10/free mid Apr-Oct; €5/free Nov-mid Apr; ⏲8am-8pm Wed-Mon, 12.30am-8pm Tue mid Apr-Oct, reduced hours Nov-mid Apr; 🚌2, 3, 4, 5 or 11 to Polytechnio, Ⓜ Viktoria) This is one of the world's most important museums, housing the world's finest collection of Greek antiquities in an enormous neoclassical building. Treasures offering a view of Greek art and history – dating from the Neolithic era to Classical periods, including the Ptolemaic era in Egypt – include exquisite sculptures, pottery, jewellery, frescoes and artefacts found throughout Greece. The beautifully presented exhibits are displayed mainly thematically.

Temple of Olympian Zeus TEMPLE

(Olympieio; ☎210 922 6330; http://odysseus.culture.gr; Leoforos Vasilissis Olgas; adult/student/child €6/3/free; ⏲8am-3pm Oct-Apr, to 8pm May-Sep; Ⓜ Akropoli, Syntagma) A can't miss on two counts: it's a marvellous temple, the largest in Greece, and it's smack in the centre of Athens. The temple is impressive for the sheer size of its 104 Corinthian columns (17m high with a base diameter of 1.7m), of which 15 remain – the fallen column was blown down in a gale in 1852.

Roman Agora HISTORIC SITE

(☎210 324 5220; http://odysseus.culture.gr; Dioskouron, Monastiraki; adult/student/child €6/3/free; ⏲8am-3pm Mon-Fri, to 5pm Sat & Sun, mosque from 10am; Ⓜ Monastiraki) This was the city's market area under Roman rule, and it occupied a much larger area than the current site borders. You can see a lot from outside the fence, but it's worth going in for a closer look at the well-preserved **Gate of Athena Archegetis**, the propylaeum (entrance gate) to the market, as well as an Ottoman mosque and the ingenious and beautiful **Tower of the Winds**, on the east side of the site.

Central Athens

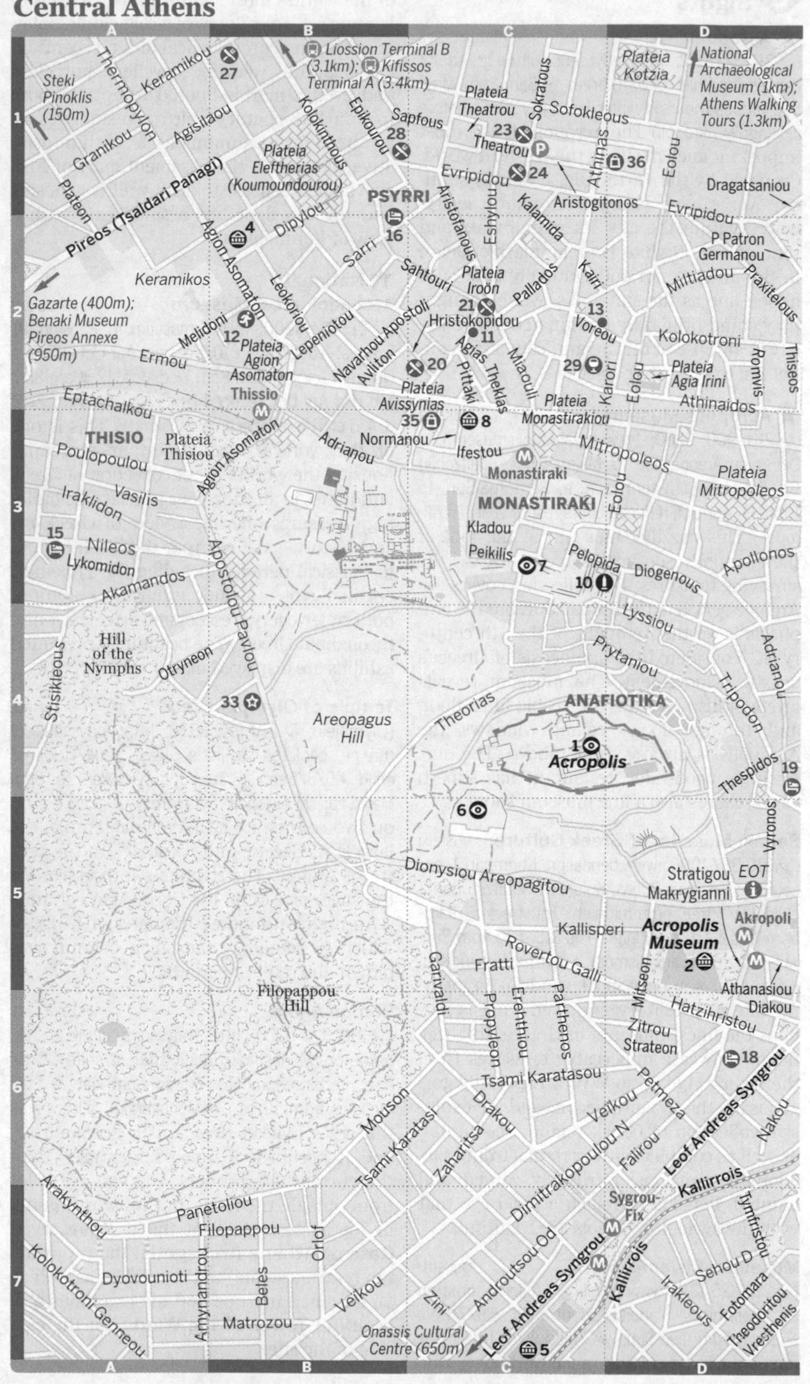

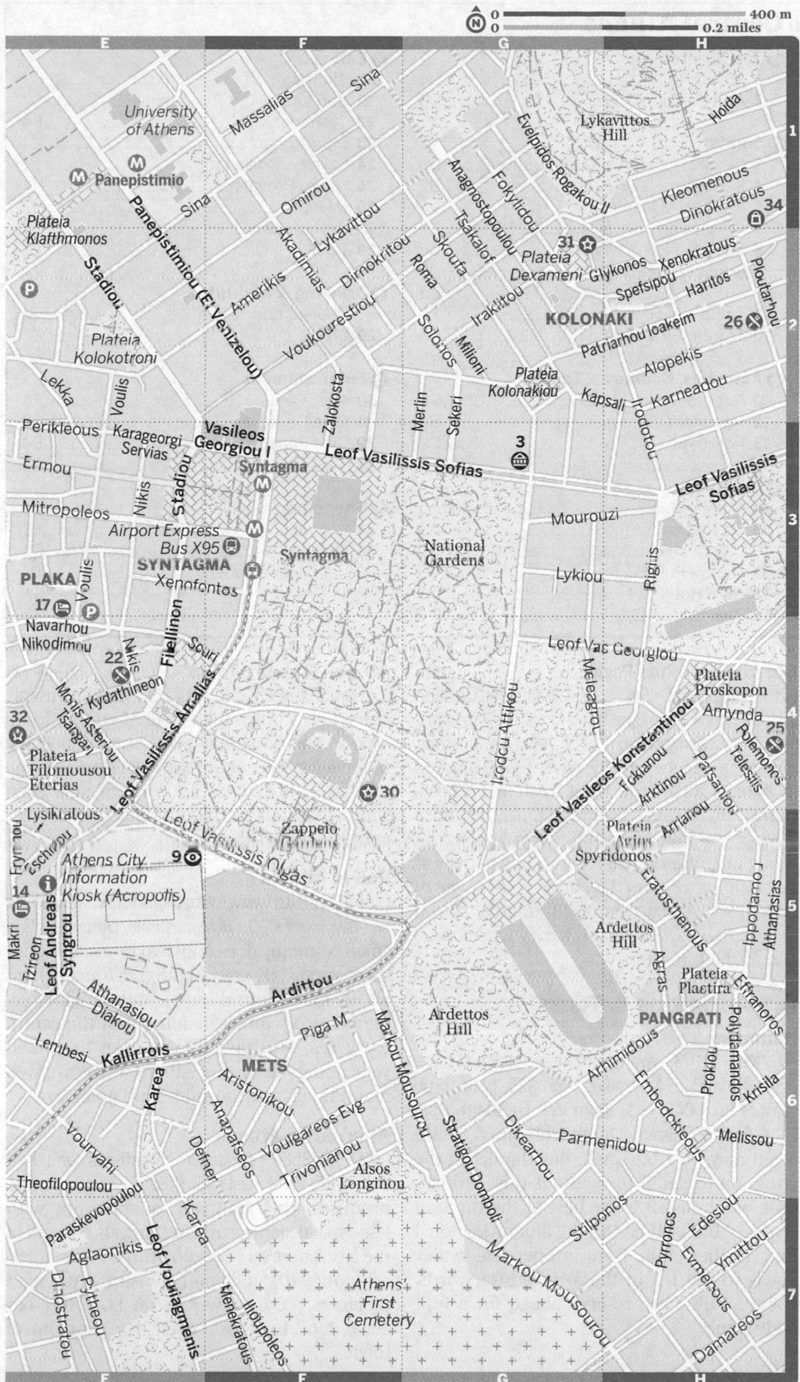
0 400 m
0 0.2 miles
University of Athens
Panepistimio
Plateia Klafthmonos
Stadiou
Panepistimiou (El Venizelou)
Sina
Massalias
Omirou
Akadimias
Lykavittou
Amerikis
Dimokritou
Voukourestiou
Roma
Skoufa
Tsakalof
Anagnostopoulou
Fokylidou
Evelpidos Rogakou II
Lykavittos Hill
Hoida
Kleomenous
Dinokratous
Plateia Dexameni
Glykonos
Xenokratous
Spefsipou
Haritos
Ploutarhou
KOLONAKI
Patriarhou Ioakeim
Alopekis
Irakleitou
Solonos
Milioni
Plateia Kolonakiou
Kapsali
Karneadou
Irodotou
Plateia Kolokotroni
Lekka
Voulis
Perikleous
Karageorgi Servias
Vasileos Georgiou I
Zalokosta
Merlin
Sekeri
Leof Vasilissis Sofias
Syntagma
Ermou
Nikis
Mitropoleos
Airport Express Bus X95
SYNTAGMA
Xenofontos
National Gardens
Mourouzi
Lykiou
Rigilis
PLAKA
Navarhou Nikodimou
Filellinon
Souri
Kydathineon
Leof Vasilissis Amalias
Leof Vas Georgiou
Meleagrou
Irodou Attikou
Plateia Proskopon
Amynda
Polemonos
Telesilis
Leof Vasileos Konstantinou
Fokianou
Arktinou
Pafsaniou
Arrianou
Plateia Filomousou Eterias
Lysikratous
Zappeio Gardens
Leof Vasilissis Olgas
Athens City Information Kiosk (Acropolis)
Spyridonos
Eratosthenous
Ardettos Hill
Ippodamou
Athanasias
Agras
Plateia Plastira
Eftranoros
Makri
Tzireon
Leof Andreas Syngrou
Athanasiou Diakou
Arditou
Piga M
Markou Mousourou
PANGRATI
Arhimidous
Polydamandos
Proklou
Krisila
Kallirrois
METS
Karea
Aristonikou
Anapafseos
Voulgareos Evg
Stratigou Domboli
Dikearhou
Embedokleous
Parmenidou
Melissou
Vourvahi
Theofilopoulou
Trivonianou
Alsos Longinou
Stilponos
Pyrronos
Edesiou
Ymittou
Evmenous
Paraskevopoulou
Aglaonikis
Leof Vouliagmenis
Menekratous
Iliopoleos
Athens' First Cemetery
Damareos
Dinostratou
Pytheou
GREECE

Central Athens

Stavros Niarchos Park PARK

(www.snfcc.org; Syngrou 364, Kallithea; 6am-midnight Apr-Oct, to 8pm Nov-Mar; 550 to Onasseio, 10 to Epaminonda) FREE Athens is short on green spaces, so this vast park, opened in 2016, is a true breath of fresh air. A large central lawn hosts free dance and exercise classes, as well as midnight movie marathons in summer, while rambling paths cut through patches of lavender and rows of olive trees. A playground, interactive sound installations and rental bikes (€1 per hour) add to the fun.

Activities & Tours

Hammam SPA

(210 323 1073; www.hammam.gr; Melidoni 1, cnr Agion Asomaton, Keramikos; 1hr €25, bath-scrub combos from €45; 11-10pm Mon-Fri, 10am-10pm Sat & Sun; M Thissio) The marble-lined steam room may be a bit small, but thanks to the attention to detail throughout this Turkish-style bathhouse it is the best of the three in central Athens. It has all the amenities you'd find further east, from proper-size water bowls to hot tea in the lounge afterwards. For the full effect, reserve ahead for a full-body scrub.

Athens Walking Tours TOURS

(694 585 9662, 210 884 7269; www.athenswalkingtours.gr) Runs a full range of guided tours around and outside the city, but is especially notable for its cooking class (€77) in a Thisio taverna, which cuts no corners and even shows you how to roll out your own filo for *spanakopita* (spinach pie).

Roll in Athens CYCLING

(6974231611; www.rollinathens.tours; Voreou 10; half-day tours €30; M Monastiraki, Omonia) This small company does only two tours, and does them very well: a city highlights tour, around all the main central sights, and – highly recommended – an excursion out of the centre to the sea, which is a pleasant way to expand your understanding of Athens. Bikes are well maintained, and the guides are great.

Alternative Athens TOURS

(6951518589; www.alternativeathens.com; Karaïskaki 28; M Monastiraki, Thissio) As the name promises, this company offers tours with less-typical slants, covering various corners of the city. There's a very good three-hour street-art tour (€40), and another visiting Athenian designers (€50), as well as an LGBTIQ+ bar crawl, food tours and even day trips out of town.

Festivals & Events

Athens & Epidaurus Festival PERFORMING ARTS
(Hellenic Festival; 210 928 2900; www.greekfestival.gr; Jun-Aug) The ancient **Theatre of Epidavros** (adult/concession €12/6; 8am-8pm Apr-Aug, reduced hours rest or year) and Athens' **Odeon of Herodes Atticus** (Herodeon; 210 324 1807; M Akropoli) are the headline venues for Greece's annual cultural festival, running since 1955 and featuring a top line-up of local and international music, dance and theatre.

Sleeping

Book well ahead for July and August.

City Circus HOSTEL €
(213 023 7244; www.citycircus.gr; Sarri 16, Psyrri; dm incl breakfast €27-31.50, s/d incl breakfast from €36/72; M Thissio, Monastiraki) It's not the cheapest hostel going, but with its jaunty style and helpful staff, City Circus does lift the spirit more than most ultra-budget lodgings. Its bright, well-designed rooms have modern bathrooms; some have kitchens. Book on its website for free breakfast at the chic bistro downstairs.

Phaedra HOTEL €
(210 323 8461; www.hotelphaedra.com; Herefontos 16, Plaka; s/d/tr from €60/80/90; M Akropoli) Almost all the rooms at this small, family-run hotel have balconies overlooking a church or the Acropolis. The rooms are basic and range from small to snug; a few have private bathrooms across the hall. Given the rooftop terrace, the friendly staff and the unbeatable location, it's one of the best deals in Plaka.

Hera Hotel BOUTIQUE HOTEL €€
(210 923 6682; www.herahotel.gr; Falirou 9, Makrygianni; d/ste incl breakfast from €145/280; M Akropoli) Behind its elegant neoclassical facade, this boutique hotel has been totally rebuilt. But the formal interior design stays true to exterior style, with lots of brass and dark wood. It's a short walk to the Acropolis and Plaka, and the rooftop Peacock restaurant and bar have fine views and good service. Northside rooms, away from an adjacent music bar, are preferable.

Be My Guest Athens HOTEL €€
(213 044 9929; www.bemyguestathens.gr; Nileos 33, Thisio; d/tr/ste with breakfast €102/126/150; M Thissio) This newly built hotel (opened in 2017) is for those seeking calm: the minimalist black-white-and-grey colour scheme is soothing, and its residential location (about 15 minutes' walk to the Acropolis) is quiet. The cheapest double rooms don't have balconies, but it's not much to upgrade. The suites have kitchens (handy grocery store downstairs).

★ **Athens Was** BOUTIQUE HOTEL €€€
(210 924 9954; www.athenswas.gr; Dionysiou Areopagitou 5, Makrygianni; d/ste incl breakfast from €390/465; M Akropoli) The location, a three-minute walk to the Acropolis east gate, couldn't be better. Staff are friendly, adding a warm touch to the minimalist decor, and standard rooms have big balconies overlooking the pedestrianised street. Korres amenities are another plus. Breakfast is excellent and the terrace has a magnificent view. Suites on the 5th and 6th floors also have Acropolis views.

Electra Palace LUXURY HOTEL €€€
(210 337 0000; www.electrahotels.gr; Navarhou Nikodimou 18, Plaka; d/ste incl breakfast from €255/440; M Syntagma) This classically elegant place is for the romantics: have breakfast under the Acropolis on your balcony (in higher-end rooms) and dinner in the chic rooftop restaurant. The well-appointed rooms are buffered from the sounds of the city streets. There's a gym and an indoor swimming pool, as well as a rooftop pool with Acropolis views.

CHEAPER BY THE HALF-DOZEN

A €30 unified ticket from the Acropolis (valid for five days) includes entry to the other significant ancient sites: Ancient Agora, Roman Agora, Keramikos, Temple of Olympian Zeus and the Theatre of Dionysos. For museums, a €15 ticket covers the National Archaeological Museum, the Byzantine & Christian Museum, the Epigraphic Museum and the Numismatic Museum. It's valid for three days.

Enter the sites free on the first Sunday of the month from November to March, and on certain holidays. Anyone aged under 18 years or with an EU student card gets in free.

Eating

Diporto Agoras TAVERNA €
(☎210 321 1463; Sokratous 9 & Theatrou; plates €5-7; ⏰7am-7pm Mon-Sat, closed 1-25 Aug; Ⓜ Omonia, Monastiraki) This quirky old taverna is an Athens dining gem. There's no signage – two doors lead to a rustic cellar where there's no menu, just a few dishes that haven't changed in years. The house speciality is *revythia* (chickpeas), usually followed by grilled fish and paired with wine from one of the giant barrels lining the wall.

Bougatsadiko I Thessaloniki PIES €
(☎210 322 2088; Plateia Iroön 1, Psyrri; pita €2; ⏰24hr; Ⓜ Monastiraki) Unexpected for its location on a key nightlife square in Psyrri, this place makes excellent *pitta* (pies), with filo crust that's 'opened' (rolled out by hand) every day. *Bougatsa* (filo with custard) is great for breakfast, the meat pies are a treat after drinks and *spanakopita* (spinach pie) hits the spot anytime.

Cremino ICE CREAM €
(Nikis 50a, Plaka; scoops €2.20; ⏰11.30am-6.30pm, later in spring & summer; Ⓜ Syntagma, Akropoli) The lovely proprietress at Cremino makes gelato and sorbet that's both intensely flavoured and incredibly light, using cow and buffalo milk. Flavours change daily, but look for creamy-chewy kaïmaki, a classic recipe with Chios mastic resin and orchid root.

CONTEMPORARY ART

Athens is not all about ancient art. For a taste of the contemporary, visit the following:

TAF (The Art Foundation; ☎210 323 8757; www.theartfoundation.gr; Normanou 5, Monastiraki; ⏰noon-9pm Mon-Sat, to 7pm Sun, cafe-bar open late; Ⓜ Monastiraki) Eclectic art and music gallery.

Onassis Cultural Centre (p336) Multimillion-euro visual and performing-arts centre.

National Museum of Contemporary Art (EMST; ☎211 101 9000; www.emst.gr; Kallirrois & Frantzi, Koukaki-Syngrou; Ⓜ Sygrou-Fix) In spectacularly renovated quarters, with top-notch rotating exhibits.

Oikeio MEDITERRANEAN €
(☎210 725 9216; www.facebook.com/oikeio/?rf=170935649625545; Ploutarhou 15, Kolonaki; mains €10-12; ⏰12.30pm-midnight Mon-Thu, to 1am Fri & Sat, to 6pm Sun; Ⓜ Evangelismos) With excellent home-style cooking, this modern taverna lives up to its name (meaning 'homey'). It's decorated like a cosy bistro, and tables on the footpath allow people-watching without the usual Kolonaki bill. Pastas, salads and international fare are tasty, but try the daily *mayirefta* (ready-cooked meals), such as the excellent stuffed zucchini. Book ahead on weekends.

Mavro Provato MEZEDHES €
(Black Sheep; ☎210 722 3466; www.tomauroprovato.gr; Arrianou 31-33, Pangrati; dishes €6-17.50; ⏰1pm-1am Mon-Sat, until 7pm Sun; Ⓜ Evangelismos) Book ahead for this wildly popular modern *mezedhopoleio* (mezedhes restaurant) in Pangrati, where tables line the footpath and delicious small (well, small for Greece) plates are paired with regional Greek wines.

★ **Seychelles** GREEK €€
(☎210 118 3478; www.seycheles.gr; Kerameikou 49, Metaxourgio; mains €8.50-14.50; ⏰2pm-12.30am Sun-Thu, until 1am Fri & Sat; Ⓜ Metaxourgio) Gutsy, fresh food, an open kitchen, earnest service, a handwritten daily menu and David Bowie on the soundtrack: Seychelles may be the Platonic ideal of a restaurant. Dishes can look simple – meaty pan-fried mushrooms with just a sliver of sheep's cheese, say, or greens with fish roe – but the flavour is incomparable. Go early or book ahead; it's deservedly popular.

Telis TAVERNA €€
(☎210 324 9582; Evripidou 86, Psyrri; meal with salad €13; ⏰noon-midnight Mon-Sat; Ⓜ Thissio) A fluorescent-lit beacon of good food and kind service on a grimy block, Telis has been serving up simplicity since 1978. There's no menu, just a set meal: a small mountain of charcoal-grilled pork chops atop chips, plus a side vegetable. Greek salad is optional, as is beer or rough house wine.

Akordeon MEZEDHES €€
(☎210 325 3703; Hristokopidou 7, Psyrri; dishes €6-16; ⏰7pm-1am Thu, to 2am Fri & Sat, 1-8pm Sun Sep-May; Ⓜ Monastiraki, Thissio) Slide into this charming butter-yellow house across from a church in a quiet Psyrri side street for a warm welcome by musician-chefs Pepi and Achilleas (and their spouses), who run this excellent venue for local music and mezedhes. They'll help you order authentic Greek fare, then surround you with their soulful songs.

Karamanlidika tou Fani GREEK €€
(☎210 325 4184; www.karamanlidika.gr; Sokratous 1, Psyrri; dishes €7-18; ⏰11am-midnight; Ⓜ Monastiraki) At this modern-day *pastomageireio* (combo tavern-deli) tables are set alongside the deli cases, and staff offer tasty morsels while you're looking at the menu. Beyond the Greek cheeses and cured meats, there's good seafood, such as marinated anchovies, as well as rarer wines and craft beers. Service is excellent, as is the warm welcome from Fani herself.

Drinking & Nightlife

One local favoured pastime is going for coffee. Athens' ubiquitous, packed cafes have some of Europe's most expensive coffee – you're essentially hiring the chair and can linger for hours. Many daytime cafes and restaurants turn into bars and clubs at night.

The city's hottest scene masses around Kolokotroni north of Plateia Syntagmatos, and around Plateia Agia Irini in Monastiraki. A cafe-thick area in Monastiraki is Adrianou, along the Ancient Agora, where people fill shady tables. Psyrri has seen a recent resurgence, while Kolonaki steadfastly attracts the trendier set, and Gazi remains tried and true. For the best dancing in summer, cab it to beach clubs along the coast near Glyfada – city locations close earlier.

English-language entertainment information appears daily in the 'Kathimerini' supplement in the *International Herald Tribune*. For comprehensive events listings, with links to online ticket sales points, try the following: www.elculture.gr, www.tickethour.com, www.tickethouse.gr and www.ticketservices.gr.

★Gazarte LIVE MUSIC
(☎210 346 0347; www.gazarte.gr; Voutadon 32-34, Gazi; tickets from €10; Ⓜ Kerameikos) At this varied arts complex, you'll find a cinema-sized screen playing videos, amazing city views taking in the Acropolis, mainstream music and a trendy 30-something crowd. A ground-level theatre hosts music and comedy. There's occasional live music and a restaurant to boot.

★Couleur Locale BAR
(☎216 700 4917; www.couleurlocaleathens.com; Normanou 3, Monastiraki; ⏰10am-2am Sun-Thu, to 3am Fri & Sat; Ⓜ Monastiraki) Look for the entrance to this rooftop bar down a narrow pedestrian lane, then inside the arcade. From there, a lift goes to the 3rd floor and its lively all-day bar-restaurant. It's a go-to spot for Athenians who love a chill coffee or a louder evening, all in view of their beloved Acropolis.

★Six d.o.g.s. BAR
(☎210 321 0510; www.sixdogs.gr; Avramiotou 6-8, Monastiraki; ⏰10am-late; Ⓜ Monastiraki) The core of this supercreative events space is a rustic, multilevel back garden, a great place for quiet daytime chats over coffee or a

LOCAL KNOWLEDGE

TO MARKET, TO MARKET...

Most Athens neighbourhoods have a weekly *laïki agora*, a street market for fruit, veg and household miscellany, and **Kolonaki's** (www.laikesagores.gr; Xenokratous; ⏰7am-2pm Fri; Ⓜ Evangelismos) is a good one. Local regulars come to buy fresh fruit, vegetables, fish, olives, honey, handmade products and flowers. **Varvakios Agora** (Athens Central Market; Athinas, btwn Sofokleous & Evripidou, Omonia; ⏰7am-6pm Mon-Sat; Ⓜ Panepistimio, Omonia) is a huge old wrought-iron market hall dedicated to fish and meat, with row upon row of lamb carcasses, hanging in just-barely-EU-compliant glass cases. In the surrounding streets are olives, cheeses and spices. For Monastiraki Flea Market (p336), head to Plateia Avyssinias where dusty *palaiopoleia* ('old-stuff sellers') rule. For the best rummaging, come on Sunday mornings, when the bric-a-brac explodes out onto the pavements, including on Astingos and even across Ermou in Psyrri.

relaxed drink. From there, you can head in to one of several adjoining buildings to see a band, art show or other generally cool happening.

Entertainment

★ Stavros Niarchos Foundation Cultural Center CULTURAL CENTRE

(☎216 809 1001; www.snfcc.org; Leoforos Syngrou 364, Kallithea; 🚌550 to Onasseio, 10 to Epaminonda) FREE Spreading its winged roof on a hill above Faliron Bay, this Renzo Piano building, surrounded by a vast park (p332), made a big splash on the Athens cultural scene when it opened in 2017. Architecture buffs will love seeing the structure. Otherwise, check the schedule for arts events by the grand pool or at the National Opera of Greece, inside the complex.

Theatro Skion Tasou Konsta PUPPET THEATRE

(☎210 322 7507; www.fkt.gr; Flisvos Park, Palaio Faliro; €3.50; ⏰8.30pm Fri-Sun Jun-Sep; 👪; 🚊Park Flisvou) Greece's wise fool, Karagiozis, gave his name to the art of shadow puppetry *(karagiozi)*, and they're on beautiful display in this tiny outdoor theatre every summer. Sure it's all in Greek, but the humour is slapstick and there's plenty of music in the various shows. After the 45-minute performance, kids can file backstage to see how the magic happens.

Onassis Cultural Centre CULTURAL CENTRE

(☎info & tickets 210 900 5800; www.sgt.gr; Leoforos Syngrou 107-109, Neos Kosmos; 🚌10 or 550 to Panteio, MSygrou-Fix, 🚊Kassomouli) This eye-catching visual- and performing-arts centre livens up the dull urbanity of Leoforos Syngrou. Cloaked in a net of white marble, it glows at night when it hosts big-name productions, installations and lectures. Check the schedule for free events. It's 1.5km southwest of the Sygrou-Fix metro station.

Steki Pinoklis TRADITIONAL MUSIC

(☎210 577 7355; www.facebook.com/pinoklis; Megalou Alexandrou 102, Keramikos; ⏰5pm-3am Mon-Sat, 2-1am Sun; MKerameikos) Although this taverna opened only in 2017, its musical taste and style skews much older. This is an excellent place to hear *rembetika* (blues) songs from Smyrna and other traditional Greek music, with a band playing most nights (starting at 9.30pm or 10pm) and Sunday afternoons (usually from 4pm). Food is average, but not expensive.

REMBETIKA

Athens has some of the best *rembetika* (Greek blues) in intimate, evocative venues. Performances usually include both *rembetika* and *laïka* (urban popular music), start at around 11.30pm and do not have a cover charge, though drinks can be expensive. Most close May to September, so in summer try live-music tavernas around Plaka, Psyrri and Exarhia.

Shopping

Central Athens is the city's original commercial district, and is still one big shopping hub, with an eclectic mix of shops. The area is still organised roughly by category – lace and buttons on one block, light bulbs on the next.

Find boutiques around Syntagma, from the Attica department store past Voukourestiou and on Ermou; designer brands and cool shops in Kolonaki; and souvenirs, folk art and leather in Plaka and Monastiraki with its fun **Monastiraki Flea Market** (Plateia Avyssinias; ⏰daily May-Oct, Sun-Wed & Fri Nov-Apr; MMonastiraki).

Information

SAFE TRAVEL

Since the financial crisis, crime has risen in Athens. But this is a rise from almost zero, and violent street crime remains relatively rare. Nonetheless, travellers should be alert. Stay aware of your surroundings at night, especially in streets southwest of Omonia, where sex workers and junkies gather, as well as by the Mavromateon bus terminal, as the adjacent park is a rather grim homeless encampment.

➡ Pickpockets favour the metro, particularly the Piraeus–Kifisia line, and crowded streets around Omonia, Athinas and the Monastiraki Flea Market.

➡ Athens taxi drivers have a reputation for mistreating foreigners with the usual tricks: failing to turn on the meter; setting the night rate (tariff set to '2' rather than '1') by day; claiming you gave them a smaller bill than you did; taking the longer route etc.

➡ Bar scams are commonplace, particularly in Plaka and Syntagma. Beware the over-friendly!

TOURIST INFORMATION

EOT (Greek National Tourism Organisation; ☎210 331 0347, 210 331 0716; www.visitgreece.gr; Dionysiou Areopagitou 18-20, Makrygianni; ⏲8am-8pm Mon-Fri, 10am-4pm Sat & Sun May-Sep, 9am-7pm Mon-Fri Oct-Apr; Ⓜ Akropoli) Free Athens map, current site hours, and bus and train information.

Athens City Information Kiosks Airport (☎210 353 0390; www.athensconventionbureau.gr/en/content/info-kiosk-athens-international-airport; Eleftherios Venizelos International Airport; ⏲8am-8pm; Ⓜ Airport), Acropolis (www.thisisathens.org; Syntagma; Ⓜ Syntagma) Maps, transport information and all Athens info.

Getting There & Away

AIR

Athens' modern **Eleftherios Venizelos International Airport** (ATH; ☎210 353 0000; www.aia.gr) is 27km east of Athens.

BOAT

Most ferry, hydrofoil and high-speed catamaran services to the islands leave from the massive port at **Piraeus** (☎210 455 0000, €0.89 per 1min 14541; www.olp.gr), southwest of Athens. Purchase tickets online at **Greek Ferries** (☎2810 529000; www.greekferries.gr), over the phone or at booths on the quay next to each ferry. Travel agencies selling tickets also surround each port; there is no surcharge.

Some services for Evia and the Cyclades arrive at/depart from the small port of Rafina, due east of Athens and the airport. To reach Athens from Rafina, take a KTEL bus (€2.60, one hour, approx half-hourly 6am to 10.45pm), which arrives at the Mavromateon Terminal, north of Athens centre.

BUS

Athens has two main intercity bus stations, 5km and 7km north and west of Omonia, plus a small bay for buses bound for south and east Attica. Pick up timetables at the tourist office, or see the relevant KTEL operator's website. Find a master list of KTEL companies at www.ktelbus.com; **KTEL Attikis** (☎210 880 8000; www.ktelattikis.gr) covers the Attica peninsula; **KTEL Argolida** (☎210 513 4588; www.ktelargolida.gr; one way €13) serves Epidavros, with dedicated buses during the summer festival season. Advance tickets for most buses can be purchased at the **ticket office** (☎210 523 3810; Sokratous 59, Omonia; ⏲7am-5.15pm Mon-Fri; Ⓜ Omonia) near Omonia.

DON'T MISS

SUMMER CINEMA

One of the delights of Athens is the enduring tradition of open-air cinema, where you can watch the latest Hollywood or art-house flick in the warm summer air. The settings are old-fashioned gardens and rooftops, with modern sound and projection. Cinemas start up in early May and usually close in September. Try **Thission** (☎210 342 0864; www.cine-thisio.gr; Apostolou Pavlou 7, Thisio; tickets €6-8; ⏲May-Oct; Ⓜ Thissio), **Cine Dexameni** (☎210 362 3942; www.cinedexameni.gr; Plateia Dexameni, Kolonaki; adult/child €8/5,; Ⓜ Evangelismos), **Cine Paris** (☎210 322 0721; www.cineparis.gr; Kydathineon 22, Plaka; ⏲May-Oct; Ⓜ Syntagma) or **Aegli Cinema** (☎210 336 9300; www.aeglizappiou.gr; Zappeio Gardens; adult/child €8.50/6.50; ⏲screenings at 9pm & 11pm May-Oct; Ⓜ Syntagma).

For international buses (from Bulgaria, Turkey etc), there is no single station; some come to Kifissos, while others stop between Plateia Karaïskaki and Plateia Omonias. **Tourist Service** (www.tourist-service.com) is one operator from Piraeus and Athens to Bulgaria.

CAR & MOTORCYCLE

The airport has all major car hire companies, and the north end of Leoforos Syngrou, near the Temple of Olympian Zeus, is dotted with firms. Expect to pay €45 per day, less for three or more days.

TRAIN

Intercity (IC) trains to central and northern Greece depart from the central Larisis train station, about 1km northwest of Plateia Omonias.

For the Peloponnese, take the suburban rail to Kiato and change for a bus there. The Patra train line is chronically closed for repairs, so OSE buses, via Kiato, replace its services. Because of this, it's easier to just take a bus from Athens' Kifissos Bus Terminal A to your ultimate destination.

Getting Around

TO/FROM THE AIRPORT

Bus

Express buses operate 24 hours between the airport and key points in the city. At the airport, buy tickets (€6; not valid for other forms of public transport) at the booth near the stop.

Plateia Syntagmatos Bus **X95** (tickets €6; ⏱24hr), one to 1½ hours, every 20 to 30 minutes. The Syntagma stop is on Othonos St.

Kifissos Terminal A and Liossion Terminal B bus stations Bus X93, one hour (terminal B) to 1½ hours (terminal A), every 20 to 30 minutes (60 minutes at night).

Piraeus Bus X96, 1½ hours, every 20 minutes. To Plateia Karaïskaki.

Metro

Metro line 3 goes from the airport to the city centre. Trains run every 30 minutes, leaving the airport between 6.30am and 11.30pm, on the hour and half-hour. Coming from the centre, trains leave Monastiraki between 5.40am and 11pm; some terminate early at Doukissis Plakentias, so disembark and wait for the airport train (displayed on the train and platform screen).

Tickets from the airport are priced separately from the rest of the metro. The cost is €10 per adult or €18 return (return valid seven days). A €22 pass, good for three days, includes a return-trip airport service and all other transit in the centre.

Taxi

From the airport to the centre, fares are flat day/night €38/54 rates; tolls are included. The ride takes 30 to 45 minutes. For Piraeus (one hour), expect day/night €50/60.

To the airport, drivers will usually propose a flat fare of €40 from the centre. You can insist on the meter, but with all the legitimate add-ons – tolls, airport fee, luggage fees – it usually works out the same.

To prebook a taxi, contact **Welcome Pickups** (www.welcomepickups.com), at the same flat rate as regular taxis.

PUBLIC TRANPORT

The transit system uses the unified Ath.ena Ticket, a reloadable paper card available from ticket offices and machines in the metro. You can load it with a set amount of money or buy a number of rides (€1.40 each; discounted when you buy five or 10) or a 24-hour/five-day travel pass for €4.50/9.

Children under six travel free; people under 18 or over 65 are technically eligible for half-fare, but you must buy the Ath.ena Ticket from a person at a ticket office.

Swipe the card at metro turnstiles or, on buses and trams, validate the ticket in the machine as you board, and keep it with you in case of spot-checks. One swipe is good for 90 minutes, including any transfers or return trips.

Bus & Trolleybus

Local express buses, regular buses and electric trolleybuses operate every 15 minutes from 5am to midnight. In lieu of maps, use Google Maps for directions or the trip planner at the website of the bus company, **OASA** (Athens Urban Transport Organisation; ☎11185; www.oasa.gr; ⏱6.30am-11.30pm Mon-Fri, from 7.30am Sat & Sun) (click 'Telematics'). The most useful lines for tourists are trolleybuses 2, 5, 11 and 15, which run north from Syntagma past the National Archaeological Museum. For all buses, board at any door; swipe your ticket on validation machines.

Metro

The metro works well and posted maps have clear icons and English labels. Trains operate from 5.30am to 12.30am, every four minutes during peak periods and every 10 minutes off-peak. On Friday and Saturday, lines 2 and 3 run till 2.30am. Get information at www.stasy.gr. All stations have wheelchair access.

Taxi

Athens' taxis are excellent value and can be the key for efficient travel on some routes. But it can be tricky getting one, especially during rush hour, so it can be much easier to use the mobile

WORTH A TRIP

ISLANDS IN A DAY: AEGINA & HYDRA

For islands within easy reach of Athens, head to the Saronic Gulf. **Aegina** (*eh*-yee-nah; www.aeginagreece.com), just a half-hour from Piraeus, is home to the impressive **Temple of Aphaia**, said to have served as a model for the construction of the Parthenon. The catwalk queen of the Saronics, **Hydra** (ee-drah; www.hydra.gr, www.hydraislandgreece.com) is a delight, an hour and a half from Piraeus. Its picturesque horseshoe-shaped harbour town with gracious stone mansions stacked up the rocky hillsides is known as a retreat for artists, writers and celebrities. There are no motorised vehicles – apart from sanitation trucks – leading to unspoilt trails along the coast and into the mountains.

From Hydra, you can return to Piraeus, or carry on to Spetses and the Peloponnese (Metohi, Ermione and Porto Heli). Check Hellenic Seaways (www.hsw.gr) and Aegina Flying Dolphins (www.aegeanflyingdolphins.gr).

> **PIRAEUS PORT**
>
> Greece's main port and ferry hub fills seemingly endless quays with ships, hydrofoils and catamarans heading all over the country. All ferry companies have online timetables and booths on the quays. Schedules are reduced in April, May and October and are radically cut in winter, especially to smaller islands. When buying tickets, confirm the departure point – some Cyclades boats leave from Rafina or Lavrio, and Patras port serves Italy and the Ionian Islands.
>
> The fastest and most convenient link between the Great Harbour and Athens is the metro (€1.40, 30 minutes, every 10 minutes, 5am to midnight), near the ferries at the northern end of Akti Kalimassioti.
>
> A new metro line is planned to open in 2022 between the airport and the centre of Piraeus.

app **Beat** (www.thebeat.co/gr) or **Taxiplon** (☎18222; www.taxiplon.gr) – you can pay in cash. Or call a taxi from dispatchers such as **Athina 1** (☎210 921 0417, 210 921 2800, www.athens1.gr), **Enotita** (☎6980666720, 18388, 210 649 5099; www.athensradiotaxienotita.gr) or **Parthenon** (☎210 532 3300; www.radiotaxi-parthenon.gr). Short trips around central Athens cost about €5; there are surcharges for luggage and pick-ups at transport hubs. At night and during holidays, the fare is about 60% higher.

Train

Suburban rail (Proastiakos; ☎14511; www.trainose.gr) is fast, but not commonly used by visitors – though it goes to the airport and as far as Piraeus and the northern Peloponnese. The airport–Kiato line (€14, 1½ hours) connects to the metro at Doukissis Plakentias and Neratziotissa. Two other lines cross the metro at Larisis station.

PELOPONNESE

ΠΕΛΟΠΟΝΝΗΣΟΣ

The Peloponnese offers lofty, snowcapped mountains, vast gorges, sandy beaches and azure waters. *Filoxenia* (hospitality) is strong here; the food is among Greece's best; and the region's vineyards are contributing to Greece's wine renaissance.

Nafplio Ναύπλιο

POP 33,000

Nafplio is one of Greece's prettiest and most romantic towns. It occupies a knockout location, on a small port beneath the towering Palamidi fortress, and is graced with attractive narrow streets, elegant Venetian houses, neoclassical mansions and interesting museums. The town is an ideal base from which to explore many nearby ancient sites.

Sights

★Palamidi Fortress FORTRESS

(☎27520 28036; adult/concession €8/4; ⊙8am-8pm May-Aug, reduced hours Sep-Apr) This vast, spectacular citadel, reachable either by steep ascent on foot or a short drive, stands on a 216m high outcrop of rock that gives all-encompassing views of Nafplio and the Argolic Gulf. It was built by the Venetians between 1711 and 1714, and is regarded as a masterpiece of military architecture in spite of being successfully stormed in one night by Greek troops in 1822, causing the Turkish garrison within to surrender without a fight.

★Archaeological Museum MUSEUM

(☎27520 27502; Plateia Syntagmatos; adult/child €6/3; ⊙8am-3pm Tue-Sun) Inside a splendid Venetian building, this museum traces the social development of Argolis, from the hunter-gatherers of the Fracthi cave to the sophisticated Mycenaean-era civilisations, through beautifully presented archaeological finds from the surrounding area. Exhibits include Paleolithic fire middens (32,000 BC), elaborately painted amphorae (c 520 BC) plus – a real highlight – the only existing bronze armour from near Mycenae (3500 years old, with helmet and boar tusk). Excellent audio guides are available in several languages (leave a government-issued ID).

Peloponnesian Folklore Foundation Museum MUSEUM

(☎27520 28379; www.pli.gr; Vasileos Alexandrou 1; adult/concession €5/3; ⊙9am-2.30pm Mon-Sat, 9.30am-3pm Sun) Established by its philanthropic owner, Nafplio's award-winning museum is a beautifully arranged collection of folk costumes and household items from Nafplio's 19th- and early-20th-century history. Be wowed by the intricate embroidery of traditional costumes and the heavy silver adornments, admire the turn-of-the-20th-century couture and look out for the cute horse-tricycle. The gift shop sells high-quality local crafts.

Sleeping & Eating

★**Pension Marianna** HOTEL €€
(☎27520 24256; www.hotelmarianna.gr; Potamianou 9; s/d/tr/q incl breakfast €55/80/90/105; P ❄ ☕) Vibrant Pension Marianna is one of Nafplio's long-standing and outstanding favourites; you can't do better for value, Greek authenticity, and setting (all fabulous). Many of the bright and airy, squeaky-clean rooms provide superb vistas from the hilltop position. The welcoming Zotos family epitomises Greek *filoxenia* (hospitality), and serves up conviviality, travel advice and delicious breakfasts (using their own farm produce).

Pidalio GREEK €
(☎27520 22603; 25 Martiou 5; mains €7-9; ⏲12.30pm-midnight Wed-Mon) One of several excellent new spots in the 'new town' frequented mainly by locals who might steer clear of those in the more touristy 'old town', this lovely taverna serves excellent Greek fare at fair prices. It's warm and lively, and you'll smell the aromas before you spot it.

To Omorfo Tavernaki GREEK €€
(☎27520 25944; Olgas 1; mains €7-15; ⏲1pm-late Fri-Wed; ☑) Ample servings of homemade delights are served in a convivial restaurant adorned with antique oddments. The mezedhes (starters) – zucchini balls, feta with honey, tzatziki etc – are particularly good, as are the meat dishes, including the slow-cooked pork belly. If meat isn't your thing, it has some fabulous contemporary-style salads as well.

Information

Staikos Tours (☎27520 27950; www.rentacarnafplio.gr; Bouboulinas 50; ⏲8.30am-2.30pm & 5.30-9pm) Run by the personable, English-speaking Christos. Offers full travel services, including ferry tickets, plus Sixt rental cars.

Getting There & Away

The **KTEL Argolis bus station** (☎27520 27323; www.ktelargolida.gr; Syngrou) has buses to Athens (€14.40, 2½ hours, 11 to 13 daily). Other services include the following:

Argos (€1.80, 30 minutes, hourly)

Epidavros (€4.20, 45 minutes, six Monday to Friday, four Saturday, one Sunday)

Mycenae (€3.20, one hour, three Monday to Friday, two Saturday)

DON'T MISS

MYSTRAS ΜΥΣΤΡΑΣ

The captivating ruins of churches, libraries, strongholds and palaces in the fortress town of Mystras, a World Heritage–listed site, spill from a spur of the Taÿgetos Mountains 7km west of Sparta. It's among the most important historical sites in the Peloponnese. This is where the Byzantine Empire's richly artistic and intellectual culture made its last stand before an invading Ottoman army, almost 1000 years after its foundation.

Traveller facilities are split between Mystras village, 1km or so below the main gate of ancient Mystras, and Pikoulianika village, 1.3km from Mystras' fortress gate.

Mycenae Μυκήνες

In the barren foothills of Mt Agios Ilias (750m) and Mt Zara (600m) stand the sombre and mighty ruins of **Ancient Mycenae** (☎27510 76585; http://odysseus.culture.gr; adult/concession €12/6; ⏲8am-8pm May-Aug, reduced hours Sep-Apr), home of the mythical Agamemnon. For 400 years (1600–1200 BC) this kingdom was the most powerful in Greece, holding sway over the Argolid and influencing other Mycenaean kingdoms.

Two to three daily buses (excluding Sundays) head to Mycenae from Nafplio (€3.20, one hour) and Argos (€1.80, 30 minutes). Buses stop both in the village and at the ancient site.

Epidavros Επίδαυρος

In its day **Epidavros** (☎27530 22009; http://odysseus.culture.gr; adult/concession €12/6; ⏲8am-8pm May-Aug, reduced hours Sep-Apr; P), 30km east of Nafplio, was famed and revered as far away as Rome as a place of miraculous healing. Visitors came great distances to the tranquil **Sanctuary of Asclepius** (adult/concession €12/6; ⏲8am-8pm Apr-Aug, reduced hours rest of year), the god of medicine, to seek a cure for their ailments. Today the World Heritage Site's amazingly well-preserved theatre (p333) remains a venue during the **Athens & Epidavros Festival** (☎21092 82900; www.greekfestival.gr/en; ⏲Jul & Aug) for Classical Greek plays, which were first performed here up to 2000 years ago.

There are buses from Nafplio to Epidavros (€4.20, 45 minutes, six Monday to Friday, three Saturday, one Sunday).

Olympia Ολυμπία

The compact village of Olympia, lined with souvenir shops and eateries, caters to the coach-loads of tourists who pass through on their way to the most famous sight in the Peloponnese: Ancient Olympia. This is where myth and fact merge. According to one (of many different) legends, Zeus held the first Olympic Games to celebrate beating his father Cronos at wrestling. This is the birthplace of the ideal that still brings states together, differences aside, for the sake of friendly athletic competition, just as it did more than 4000 years ago.

Just 500m south of the village, across the Kladeos River, are the remains of **Ancient Olympia** (☎26240 22517; adult/concession €12/6; ⊙8am-8pm Apr-Sep, to 6pm Oct, to 3pm Nov-Mar). As you walk around, or stand at the starting line of the ancient stadium, contemplate the influence of this site through millennia.

The Olympic Games took place here every four years for at least 1000 years, until their abolition by Emperor Theodosius I in AD 393. The Olympic flame is still lit here for the modern Games. Thanks to the destruction ordered by Theodosius II and various subsequent earthquakes, little remains of the magnificent temples and athletic facilities, but enough exists to give you a hint of this World Heritage–listed sanctuary's former glory. Ticket includes entry to the remarkable **archaeological museum** (adult/concession incl site €12/6; ⊙8am-8pm, to 3pm Nov-Apr).

Buses depart from the train station in the middle of town, one block east of the main street. There are services to Pyrgos (€2.30, 30 minutes, eight to 13 daily), with three handy Athens connections (€30.10, four hours).

CENTRAL GREECE
ΚΕΝΤΡΙΚΗ ΕΛΛΑΔΑ

Central Greece's dramatic landscape of deep gorges, rugged mountains and fertile valleys is home to the magical stone pinnacle-topping monasteries of Meteora and the iconic ruins of ancient Delphi, where Alexander the Great sought advice from the Delphic oracle. Established in 1938, **Parnassos National Park** (☎22340 23529; http://en.parnassosnp.gr), to the north of Delphi, attracts naturalists, hikers (it's part of the E4 European long-distance path) and skiers.

Delphi Δελφοί

POP 2370

Modern Delphi and its adjoining ruins hang stunningly on the slopes of Mt Parnassos overlooking the shimmering Gulf of Corinth.

According to mythology, Zeus released two eagles at opposite ends of the world and they met here, thus making Delphi the centre of the world. By the 6th century BC, **Ancient Delphi** (☎22650 82312; http://ancient-greece.org/history/delphi.html; combined ticket for site & museum adult/student/child, €12/6/free; ⊙8am-8pm Apr-Sep, to 6pm Oct, to 3pm Nov-Mar) had become the Sanctuary of Apollo. Thousands of pilgrims flocked here to consult the female oracle who sat at the mouth of a fume-emitting chasm. After sacrificing a sheep or goat, pilgrims would ask a question, and a priest would translate the oracle's response into verse. Wars, voyages and business transactions were undertaken on the strength of these prophecies.

In the town centre, **Rooms Pitho** (☎22650 82850; www.pithohotel.gr; Vasileon Pavlou & Friderikis 40a; s/d/tr incl breakfast from €45/55/70;) and **Fedriades Hotel** (☎22650 82370; www.fedriades.com; Vasileon Pavlou & Friderikis 46; s/d/tr/ste incl breakfast €45/55/65/130;) are both friendly,

MT OLYMPUS

Just as it did for the ancients, Greece's highest mountain, **Olympus** (Όρος Όλυμπος), the cloud-covered lair of the Greek pantheon, fires the visitor's imagination today. The highest of Olympus' eight peaks is **Mytikas** (2917m), which is popular with trekkers, who use **Litohoro** (305m), 5km inland from the Athens–Thessaloniki highway, as their base. The main route up takes two days, with a stay overnight at one of the refuges. Good protective clothing is essential, even in summer. **EOS Litohoro** (Greek Alpine Club; ☎23520 84544, 23520 82444; http://eoslitohorou.blogspot.com; ⊙9.30am-12.30pm & 6-8pm Mon-Sat Jun-Sep) has information.

tidy bets, the latter offering breakfast and bikes. Fill up on traditional dishes at the excellent, family-run **Taverna Vakhos** (☎22650 83186; www.vakhos.com; Apollonos 31; mains €8-16; ⏲noon-10:30pm; 📶👪).

Getting There & Away

Buses depart from the eastern end of Vasileon Pavlou and Friderikis, next to the In Delphi restaurant, where tickets can be purchased between 9am and 8pm (the bus system's closing time). If you're taking an early bus, plan ahead and buy tickets the day before. This especially applies in high season when buses fill up quickly. Travellers to Kalambaka/Meteora will find better connections via Lamia and Trikala, rather than Larissa.

Meteora Μετέωρα

The World Heritage–listed Meteora (meh-teh-o-rah) is an extraordinary place and one of the most visited in all of Greece. The massive pinnacles of smooth rock are the perfect setting for a science-fiction or fantasy tale. The monasteries atop them add to the strange and beautiful landscape.

Sights & Activities

While there were once monasteries on all 24 pinnacles, only six are still occupied: **Megalou Meteoro** (Grand Meteoron; €3; ⏲9am-4pm Wed-Mon Apr-Oct, to 3pm Thu-Mon Nov-Mar), **Varlaam** (€3; ⏲9am-4pm Sat-Thu Apr-Oct, to 3pm Sat-Wed Nov-Mar), **Agiou Stefanou** (St Stephen's; €3; ⏲9am-1.30pm & 3.30-5.30pm Tue-Sun Apr-Oct, 9am-1pm & 3-5pm Tue-Sun Nov-Mar), **Agias Triados** (Holy Trinity; €3; ⏲9am-5pm Fri-Wed Apr-Oct, to 4pm Fri-Tue Nov-Mar), **Agiou Nikolaou** (Monastery of St Nikolaou Anapafsa; €3; ⏲9am-4pm Sat-Thu) and **Agias Varvaras Rousanou** (€3; ⏲9am-5pm Thu-Tue Apr-Oct, to 2pm Thu-Tue Nov-Mar).

Strict dress codes apply (no bare shoulders or knees and women must wear skirts; you can borrow a long skirt at the door). Walk the footpaths between monasteries, drive the asphalt road, or take the bus that departs from Kalambaka and Kastraki at 9am and returns at 1pm (12.40pm on weekends).

Meteora's stunning rocks are also a climbing paradise. **Visit Meteora** (☎24320 23820; www.visitmeteora.travel; Patriarchou Dimitriou 2; ⏲9am-9pm) offers some excellent opportunities with professional guides, including hiking and walking tours.

Sleeping

Much of the best lodging around the Meteora is in the village of **Kastraki**, often with amazing close-up views. It's just 2km from Kalambaka.

Pyrgos Adrachti BOUTIQUE HOTEL **€€**
(☎24320 22275; www.hotel-adrachti.gr; d/tr incl breakfast from €90/108; P⊖❄📶) Slick and cool sums up this place – think subtle designer-style touches throughout the 14 rooms, bar and common areas, and an up-close-and-personal rock experience. Plus there's a tidy garden to relax in post-activities. It feels remote, but in fact it's a short stroll to the village square. A boutique hotel for real. Follow the signs.

Getting There & Away

Kalambaka's **KTEL bus station** (☎24320 22432; www.ktel-trikala.gr; Ikonomou) is 50m down from Plateia Dimarhiou (the town-hall square) and the large fountain, and is the arrival/departure point for regular Trikala bus connections. For Delphi, travellers should go via Trikala (not Larissa). The trip requires three straightforward bus changes: Kalambaka to Trikala, Trikala to Lamia, Lamia to Amfissa, and finally Amfissa to Delphi. It sounds fiddly, but the buses all connect; enquire at the station.

Trains depart from the Kalambaka **train station** (☎24320 22451; www.trainose.gr). For trains to Athens and Thessaloniki you may need to change at Paleofarsalos. For Volos you must change at Larissa.

NORTHERN GREECE
ΒΟΡΕΙΑ ΕΛΛΑΔΑ

Diversity should be northern Greece's second name – the region stretches across more cultures and terrains than any other in the country. Mighty civilisations, including Macedonians, Thracians, Romans, Byzantines, Slavs and Turks, have left traces here and this is nowhere more apparent than in Greece's second city, Thessaloniki.

Thessaloniki Θεσσαλονίκη

POP 788,952

Thessaloniki is easy to fall in love with – it has beauty, chaos, history and culture, a remarkable cuisine and wonderful, vast sea views. When you climb up to the Byzantine

Thessaloniki

Thessaloniki

Top Sights

1 Archaeological Museum D4

Sights

2 Museum of Byzantine Culture D4
3 Rotunda of Galerius D2
4 Thessaloniki Museum of Photography A2

Sleeping

5 Caravan B1
6 Colors Rooms & Apartments A1
7 Rent Rooms Thessaloniki D2

Eating

8 Chatzis B2
9 I Nea Follia C1
10 Mourga C2

walls and take in the whole of Thessaloniki at sunset, you see what a sprawling, organic city it is. Old and new cohabit wonderfully while Thessaloniki's most famous sight, the White Tower, anchors a waterfront packed with cocktail bars.

Sights

★ Archaeological Museum MUSEUM

(☎2310 830 538; www.amth.gr; Manoli Andronikou 6; adult/concession €8/4; ⏲8am-8pm Apr-Oct, 9am-4pm Nov-Mar) Macedonia's major prehistoric and ancient Macedonian and Hellenistic finds are housed in this museum (except for Vergina's gold tomb finds, which are exhibited in Vergina). Highlights include the **Derveni Crater** (330–320 BC), a huge, ornate Hellenistic bronze-and-tin vase. Used for mixing wine and water, and later as a funerary urn, it's marked by intricate relief carvings of Dionysos, along with mythical figures, animals and ivy vines. The **Derveni**

WORTH A TRIP

ZAGOROHORIA & VIKOS GORGE
ΤΑ ΖΑΓΟΡΟΧΩΡΙΑ & ΧΑΡΑΔΡΑ ΤΟΥ ΒΙΚΟΥ

Try not to miss the spectacular **Zagori region**, with its deep gorges, abundant wildlife, dense forests and snowcapped mountains. Some 46 charming villages, famous for their grey-slate architecture, and known collectively as the Zagorohoria, are sprinkled across a large expanse of the Pindos Mountains north of Ioannina. These beautifully restored gems were once only connected by stone paths and arching footbridges, but paved roads now wind between them. Get information on walks from Ioannina's **EOS** (Greek Alpine Club; 26510 22138; www.orivatikos.gr; Smyrnis 15; hours vary) office.

Monodendri is a popular departure point for treks through dramatic 12km-long, 900m-deep **Vikos Gorge**, with its sheer limestone walls. Exquisite inns with attached tavernas abound in remote (but popular) twin villages **Megalo Papingo** and **Mikro Papingo**. It's best to explore by rental car from Ioannina.

Treasure contains Greece's oldest surviving papyrus piece (320–250 BC).

Museum of Byzantine Culture MUSEUM
(2313 306 400; www.mbp.gr; Leoforos Stratou 2; adult/student Apr-Oct €8/4, Nov-Mar €4; 8am-8pm Apr-Oct, 9am-4pm Nov-Mar) This fascinating museum has plenty of treasures to please Byzantine buffs, plus simple explanations to introduce the empire to total beginners. More than 3000 Byzantine objects, including mosaics, intriguing tomb paintings, jewellery and glassware, are showcased with characterful asides about daily life. You'll be confidently discerning early-Christian from late-Byzantine icons in no time.

Rotunda of Galerius HISTORIC BUILDING
(2310 204 868; Plateia Agiou Georgiou; €2; 9am-5pm Nov-Mar, 8am-7pm Apr-Oct) FREE In AD 306 Roman emperor Galerius built this stocky 30m-high brick structure as his future mausoleum. But instead of being laid to rest within the 6m-thick walls of the Rotunda, he was buried in today's Serbia after succumbing to an unpleasant disease that still puzzles historians. Later, Constantine the Great made the Rotunda Thessaloniki's first church (Agios Georgios; observe dragon-slaying St George above the door). The Ottomans made it a mosque (note the restored minaret).

Thessaloniki Museum of Photography MUSEUM
(2310 566 716; www.thmphoto.gr; Warehouse A, Port; adult/concession €2/1; 11am-7pm Tue-Thu, Sat & Sun, to 10pm Fri) This 1910 port warehouse is home to thought-provoking exhibitions of historic and contemporary photography. These temporary displays change every four months or so.

Sleeping & Eating

Colors Rooms & Apartments APARTMENT €
(2310 502 280; www.colors.com.gr; Valaoritou 21; s/d from €86/89;) Two words: fabulous value. These 15 sparkling and uber-spacious apartments (some self-catering) with colourful minimalist decor rival more expensive hotel rooms. It can feel slightly institutional and there's no breakfast, but we're being ultra-picky. At weekends it's perfect for night owls exploring the surrounding bars (but ask for a room in the rear if you don't want street noise).

★**Caravan** HOTEL €€
(2313 062 780; www.thecaravan.gr; cnr Rebelou & Vamvaka; d/ste incl breakfast €70/150;) This beautiful hotel is a mix between a travellers' haven and contemporary design hotel – with luxury thrown in. Opened by three friends from Thessaloniki who love travel, the aim here is to make guests feel at home. Therefore, you get smart rooms in cool colours, a friendly common area and plenty of advice on where to go from fabulous reception staff.

Rent Rooms Thessaloniki HOSTEL €€
(2310 204 080; www.rentrooms-thessaloniki.com; Konstantinou Melenikou 9; dm/s/d/tr/q incl breakfast €25/69/79/90/100;) What it lacks in contemporary style, it makes up for with services: a charming back-garden cafe, where you can tuck into a choice of filling breakfasts with views of the Rotunda of Galerius; super-friendly and helpful staff; and a can-do attitude. It's handily located near the university. Dorms and adequate private rooms are available plus security lockers and luggage storage.

★Mourgá GREEK €
(☎2310 268 826; Christopoulou 12; mains €5-14; ⏲1pm-late) This has to be the place that will linger in your sensory memory for decades – elegant and relaxed, Mourgá will make you fall in love with Greek food, Thessaloniki style. Taste the buttery pan-fried shrimp, fava bean purée with preserved caper leaves that melt on your tongue, incredible Cretan seaweed, a fantastic cheese selection and local wine.

Chatzis SWEETS €
(☎2310 221 655; http://chatzis.gr; Mitropoleos 24; sweets €1.40-4; ⏲8am-midnight) Glistening syrup-soaked treats have been luring dessert fans into Chatzis since 1908, back when Thessaloniki was still an Ottoman city. Try the moist, sugar-rush-inducing *revani* (syrupy semolina cake), chickpea and raisin halva, or *rizogalo* (rice pudding) scented with cinnamon.

★I Nea Follia GREEK €€
(☎2310 960 383; cnr Aristomenous & Haritos; mains €7.50-12; ⏲2pm-late Sep-Jun; ✎) I Nea Follia is nothing special to look at, but once you sit down to a table and get served a beetroot and pistachio salad, an excellent veal steak or a juicy set of shrimp, you'll be coming back over and over again. The chef-owner, Girogos Hlazas, specialises in classic Greek fare with a contemporary twist.

Information

Tourism Office (☎2310 229 070; www.thessaloniki.travel; Plateia Aristotelous; ⏲10am-5pm) A very helpful tourism office on Plateia Aristotelous with maps, brochures and local information. Can also provide lists of hotels and assist with tours and excursions beyond Thessaloniki.

Getting There & Away

Thessaloniki is northern Greece's transport hub and gateway to the Balkans. Major European airlines and budget airlines fly to Thessaloniki and within Greece.

AIR

Besides Greece's **Aegean Airlines** (https://en.aegeanair.com), many foreign carriers use Thessaloniki for domestic and international flights. Prices and routes are fluid, so ascertain which companies are currently flying from the **Makedonia International Airport** (SKG; ☎2310 985 000; www.thessalonikiairport.com) website. Then visit a travel agent or book online.

If you're visiting Thessaloniki briefly, you can store luggage with Sky Bag at the airport.

BOAT

Ferries from Thessaloniki port are limited and change annually. To access the Sporades, you must depart from Volos (all year) or Agios Konstantinos further south during the summer period only. With private yacht charters you can sail to Italy, Turkey and Albania.

See www.ferries.gr for details and booking options for ferries from Thessaloniki.

BUS

Thessaloniki's main bus station, **KTEL Makedonia** (☎2310 595 444; www.ktelmacedonia.gr; Giannitson 244), is 3km west of the city centre. Each destination has its own specific ticket counter, signposted in Greek and English.

For Athens *only*, avoid the trip by going instead to **Monastiriou bus station** (☎2310 500 111; http://ktelthes.gr; Monastiriou 67) – next to the train station – where Athens-bound buses start before calling in at KTEL Makedonia.

Buses leave for Halkidiki from the eastern Thessaloniki **Halkidiki bus terminal** (☎2310 316 555; www.ktel-chalkidikis.gr; Km 9 Thessaloniki-Halkidiki road). The terminal is out towards the airport, reached via city buses 45A or 45B.

TRAIN

Direct ICE trains serve Athens (€55.40, 5¼ hours, seven daily), Paleofasala (for Meteora; €24.50, one hour, 10 daily) and Larissa (€14 to €22, two hours, 15 daily). Regular trains also serve Veria, Edessa and Florina (mostly via Platy). Only two daily trains currently serve Xanthi, Komotini and Alexandroupoli in Thrace.

Thessaloniki's **train station** (☎2310 121 530; www.trainose.gr; Monastiriou) has ATMs, card phones and small modern eateries, plus an Orthodox chapel. Self-serve luggage storage lockers start from €3.

Getting Around

TO/FROM THE AIRPORT

Buses X1 (during the day) and N1 (at night) run half-hourly from the airport (17km southeast of town), heading west through the city to the main bus station (KTEL Makedonia) via the train station. Tickets cost €2 from the airport to the bus station; €1 for short journeys.

Taxis to the airport cost around €20 – it is a set rate, even if the meter reads a lower fee (this allows for airport charges and the differences in central locations). Call in advance if you need them to pick you up from town; the operator speaks English.

BUS

Bus 1 connects the main bus station (KTEL Makedonia) and the train station. From the train station, major points on Egnatia are constantly served by buses such as 10 and 14.

Buy tickets at *periptera* (street kiosks) for €1, or from on-board blue ticket machines (€1.10). Validate the former in the orange machines. Machines neither give change nor accept bills; when boarding, be sure you have the right change and buy your ticket immediately. Thessaloniki's ticket police pounce at any sign of confusion. If they nab you, you'll pay €60.

TAXI

Thessaloniki's blue-and-white taxis carry multiple passengers, and only take you if you're going the same way. The minimum fare is €3.40. A more expensive 'night rate' takes effect from midnight until 5am. To book a cab for an airport transfer, try **Taxi Way** (☎2310 214 900, 2310 866 866; www.taxiway.gr).

CYCLADES ΚΥΚΛΑΔΕΣ

On a quest to find the Greek island of your dreams? Start, here, in the Cyclades, with rugged, sun-drenched outcrops of rock, anchored in azure seas and liberally peppered with snow-white villages and blue-domed churches, this is Greece straight from central casting, with stellar archaeological sites and dozens of postcard-worthy beaches. Throw in a blossoming food scene, some renowned party destinations and a good dose of sophistication, and you really do have the best of Greece's ample charms.

Mykonos Μύκονος

POP 10,134

Mykonos is the great glamour island of Greece and flaunts its sizzling St-Tropez-meets-Ibiza style and party-hard reputation. The high-season mix of hedonistic holidaymakers, cruise-ship crowds and posturing fashionistas throngs Mykonos Town (aka Hora), a traditional whitewashed Cycladic maze, delighting in its cubist charms and its chichi cafe-bar-boutique scene.

There are a few provisos about visiting here. Come only if you are prepared to pay top dollar, jostle with street crowds and sit bum cheek to cheek with oiled-up loungers at the packed main beaches.

Sights

The island's most popular beaches, thronged in summer, are on the southern coast. About 5km southwest of Hora are family-oriented **Agios Ioannis** (where *Shirley Valentine* was filmed) and **Kapari**. The nearby packed and noisy **Ornos** and the package-holiday resort of **Platys Gialos** have boats for the glitzier beaches to the east. In between these two is **Psarou**, a magnet for the Greek cognoscenti.

Approximately 1km south of Platys Gialos you'll find **Paraga Beach**, which has a small gay section. Party people should head about 1km east to famous **Paradise**. **Elia** is a long, lovely stretch of sand. A few minutes' walk west from here is the secluded **Agrari**. Further east, **Kalafatis** is a hub for water sports (including diving and windsurfing), and **Lia** has a remote, end-of-the-road feel.

Hora (also known as Mykonos), the island's well-preserved port and capital, is a warren of narrow alleyways and whitewashed buildings overlooked by the town's famous windmills. In the heart of the waterfront Little Venice quarter, tiny flower-bedecked churches jostle with glossy boutiques, and there's a cascade of bougainvillea around every corner.

Sleeping & Eating

It's best not to arrive in July or August without a reservation, as there will be few vacancies. Some places insist on a minimum stay during the peak period. Noise levels in Hora and popular resorts are high in summer.

Pension Kalogera PENSION €
(☎6972483263, 22890 24709; www.pensionkalogeramykonos.webs.com; Mavrogenous; s/d/tr/q €100/140/180/200; ❄📶) For a town with so few options for the budget traveller, this comes as welcome relief and a delightful surprise. The ultra-kind and hospitable owner, Aggeliki, runs a simple, clean and super-central place and is a wealth of information. She also restores faith that the town is not out to squeeze every last dollar of your beer money.

Fresh Hotel BOUTIQUE HOTEL €€
(☎22890 24670; www.hotelfreshmykonos.com; Kalogera 31; d incl breakfast from €200; ❄📶) In the heart of town, with a lush and leafy garden and highly regarded on-site restaurant, Fresh comes with a bit of attitude; it is indeed fresh, but with compact and stylishly minimalist rooms. Rates fall to around €90 in the low season.

Kadena CAFE €€
(☎22890 29290; mains €10-23; ⏰7am-late; 📶) Less pretentious than many other eateries, this place has a small menu of Mediterra-

WORTH A TRIP

DELOS

Southwest of Mykonos, the island of **Delos** (☎22890 22259; museum & site adult/concession €12/6; ⏰8am-8pm Apr-Oct, to 2pm Nov-Mar), a Unesco World Heritage Site, is the Cyclades' archaeological jewel. The mythical birthplace of twins Apollo and Artemis, splendid Ancient Delos was a shrine-turned-sacred treasury and commercial centre. It was inhabited from the 3rd millennium BC and reached its apex of power around the 5th century BC.

Overnight stays are forbidden (as is swimming) and boat schedules allow a maximum of four hours at Delos. A simple cafe is located by the museum, but it pays to bring water and food. Weat a hat, sunscreen and walking shoes.

Boats from Mykonos to Delos (€20 return, 30 minutes) go between 9am and 5pm in summer, and return between 12.15pm and 8pm. Departure/return times are posted at the **Delos Boat Ticket Kiosk** (☎22890 28603; www.delostours.gr; adult/child return ticket €20/10), at the foot of the jetty at the southern end of the old harbour, as well as online. Buy tickets online or from the kiosk or various travel and transport agencies. When buying tickets, establish which boat you can return on.

nean dishes, good breakfasts, friendly staff, and protection from the north wind.

★M-Eating MEDITERRANEAN €€€
(☎22890 78550; www.m-eating.gr; Kalogera 10; mains €24-64; ⏰7pm-1am; 📶) A classy act, run by a chef-husband and wife team. Attentive service, soft lighting and relaxed luxury are the hallmarks of this creative restaurant specialising in fresh Greek produce prepared with flair. Sample anything from sea bass tartare to rib-eye veal with honey truffle. Don't miss the dessert of Mykonian honey pie.

Drinking & Nightlife

Night action in Hora starts around 11pm and warms up by 1am. From posh cocktail spots to the colourful bars of Hora's Little Venice (where there are also some hip clubs), Hora has the lot. Another prime spot is the Tria Pigadia (Three Wells) area on Enoplon Dynameon. Outside of town, each major beach has at least one beach bar that gets going during the day. Bring a bankroll – the high life doesn't come cheap. Beach clubs are generally open June to September, but July and August is when the scene is most intense. See websites for events and ticket info.

Cavo Paradiso CLUB
(☎22890 26124; www.cavoparadiso.gr; Paradise Beach; ⏰11.30pm-7am) When dawn gleams just over the horizon, hard-core bar-hoppers move from Hora to Cavo Paradiso at Paradise Beach, the open-air clifftop mega-club that has featured top international DJs since 1994.

ℹ Getting There & Away

AIR

Mykonos Airport (☎22890 79000; www.mykonos-airport.com), 3km southeast of the town centre, has flights year-round to Athens with Sky Express (www.skyexpress.gr) and Aegean Airlines (https://en.aegeanair.com), among others, and to Thessaloniki with Aegean Airlines.

BOAT

Year-round ferries serve mainland ports Piraeus and Rafina (the latter is usually quicker if you are coming directly from Athens airport). In the high season, Mykonos is well connected with all neighbouring islands, including Paros and Santorini. Hora is loaded with ticket agents.

Mykonos has two ferry quays: the **Old Port**, 400m north of town, where a couple of fast ferries dock, and the **New Port**, 2km north of town, where the bigger fast ferries and all conventional ferries dock. When buying outgoing tickets, double-check which quay your ferry leaves from.

Excursion boats for Delos depart from the quay just off the waterfront of Mykonos Town.

ℹ Getting Around

TO/FROM THE AIRPORT

Buses from the southern bus station serve Mykonos' airport (€2). Some hotels and guesthouses offer free airport and port transfers. Otherwise, arrange airport transfer with your accommodation (around €10) or take a taxi to town (€10 or €15 depending on which side of town you are on).

BOAT

Mykonos Cruises (☎22890 23995; www.mykonos-cruises.gr; ⏰8am-7pm Apr-Oct) is an association of sea-taxi operators offering services to the island's best beaches. See the timetables online. The main departure point is **Platys Gialos**, with drop-offs and pick-ups at Ornos, Paraga, Paradise, Super Paradise, Agrari and Elia beaches (return trips cost between €5 and €7). Cruises and personalised itineraries can also be arranged.

The **Sea Bus** (☎6978830355; www.mykonos-seabus.gr; one way €2) water-taxi service connects the New Port with Hora, running hourly from 9am to 10pm (more frequently when a cruise ship is in port).

BUS

The **KTEL Mykonos** (☎22890 26797, 22890 23360; www.mykonosbus.com) bus network has two main terminals plus pick-up points at the Old and New Ports.

Low-season services are much reduced, but buses in high season run frequently; the fare is €1 to €2 depending on the distance travelled. Timetables are on the website. In July and August, some bus services run until 2am or later from the beaches.

Terminal A, the **southern bus station** (www.mykonosbus.com; Fabrika Sq), known as Fabrika, serves Ornos and Agios Ioannis Beach, Platys Gialos, Paraga and Super Paradise beaches.

Terminal B, the **northern bus station** (www.mykonosbus.com), sometimes called Remezzo, is behind the OTE office and has services to Agios Stefanos via Tourlos, Ano Mera, and Kalo Livadi, Kalafatis and Elia beaches.

CAR & MOTORCYCLE

Hire cars start at €45 per day in high season and €30 in low season. Scooters/quads are around €20/40 in high season and €15/30 in low season.

Avis and Sixt are among the agencies at the airport, and there are dozens of hire places all over the island, particularly near the ports and bus stations (which is where the large public car parks are found – you can't drive into Hora proper).

TAXI

Taxis (☎22890 23700, 22890 22400) queue at Hora's Plateia Manto Mavrogenous (Taxi Sq), bus stations and ports, but waits can be long in high season. All have meters, and the minimum fare is €3.50 (plus €0.50 per bag and €3.30 for phone booking).

Approximate fares from Hora include New Port (€6), Ornos (€10), Platys Gialos (€10), Paradise (€11), Kalafatis (€18) and Elia (€18).

Naxos ΝΑΞΟΣ

POP 18,900

The largest of the Cyclades, Naxos packs a lot of bang for its buck. Its main city of Hora (known also as Naxos) has a gorgeous waterfront and a web of steep cobbled alleys below its hilltop *kastro,* all filled with the hubbub of tourism and shopping. You needn't travel far, though, to find isolated beaches, atmospheric mountain villages and ancient sites.

Sights

★Kastro — AREA

The most alluring part of Hora is the 13th-century residential neighbourhood of Kastro, which Marco Sanudo made the capital of his duchy in 1207. Behind the waterfront, get lost in the narrow alleyways scrambling up to its spectacular hilltop location. Venetian mansions survive in the centre of Kastro, and you can see the remnants of the castle, the **Tower of Sanoudos**. To see the Bourgos area of the old town, head into the winding backstreets behind the northern end of Paralia.

★Temple of Apollo — ARCHAEOLOGICAL SITE

(The Portara; ⏲24hr) FREE From Naxos Town harbour, a causeway leads to the Palatia islet and the striking, unfinished Temple of Apollo, Naxos' most famous landmark (also known as the Portara, or 'Doorway'). Simply two marble columns with a crowning lintel, it makes an arresting sight, and people gather at sunset for splendid views.

Panagia Drosiani — CHURCH

(donations appreciated; ⏲10am-7pm May–mid-Oct) Located 2.5km north of Halki, just below Moni, the small, peaceful Panagia Drosiani is among the oldest and most revered churches in Greece. Inside is a series of cavelike chapels. In the darkest chapels, monks and nuns secretly taught Greek language and religion to local children during the Turkish occupation. Several frescoes still grace the walls, and date from the 7th century.

Look for the depiction of Mary in the eastern chapter; the clarity and expression is incredible.

Beaches

The popular beach of **Agios Georgios** is just a 10-minute walk south from the main waterfront.

Beaches south of here include beautiful **Agios Prokopios**, which is sandy and shallow and lies in a sheltered bay to the south of the headland of Cape Mougkri. It merges with **Agia Anna**, a stretch of shining white sand that's quite narrow but long enough to feel uncrowded towards its southern end.

Sandy beaches continue as far as Pyrgaki, passing the beautiful turquoise waters of the long, dreamy **Plaka Beach** and gorgeous sandy bays punctuated with rocky outcrops. You'll find plenty of restaurants, accommodation and bus stops along this stretch.

At **Mikri Vigla**, golden granite slabs and boulders divide the beach into two. This beach is becoming an increasingly big deal on the kitesurfing scene, with reliable wind conditions.

Villages

Heading north from the mountains inland, the roads wind and twist like spaghetti, eventually taking you to the somewhat scrappy seaside village of **Apollonas**. Tavernas line the waterfront and serve the freshest of fish. In an ancient quarry on the hillside above the village is a colossal 7th-century BC **kouros** (youth) statues. Follow the small signs to get here.

Apiranthos seems to grow out of the stony flanks of rugged Mt Fanari (883m), about 25km east of Hora. The village's unadorned stone houses and marble-paved streets reflect a rugged individualism that is matched by the villagers themselves. Many of them are descendants of refugees who migrated from Crete. Apiranthos people have always been noted for their spirited politics and populism, and the village is peppered with quirky shops, galleries and cafes.

Halki is a vivid reflection of historic Naxos, with the handsome facades of old villas and tower houses a legacy of its wealthy past as the island's long-ago capital. Today it's home to a small but fascinating collection of shops and galleries, drawing artists and culinary wizards. Halki lies at the heart of the Tragaea mountainous region, about 20 minutes' drive (15km) from Hora.

Sleeping

Hotel Galini HOTEL €€

(☎22850 22114; www.hotelgalini.com; d incl breakfast from €100; ❄📶) A nautical theme lends this super-friendly, family-run place loads of character. Updated, spacious rooms have small balconies, plus some rooms have creative decor fashioned from seashells and driftwood. The location is first-rate – close to the old town and the beach – and the breakfast is hearty. Prices drop significantly outside high season.

DON'T MISS

KITRON-TASTING IN HALKI

The historic village of **Halki** is a top spot to try *kitron*, a liqueur unique to Naxos. While the exact recipe is top secret, visitors can taste it and stock up on supplies at **Vallindras Distillery** (☎22850 31220; ⏲10am-10pm Jul & Aug, to 6pm May-Jun & Sep-Oct) in Halki's main square. There are free tours of the old distillery's atmospheric rooms, which contain ancient jars and copper stills. *Kitron* tastings round out the trip.

Xenia Hotel HOTEL €€

(☎22850 25068; www.hotel-xenia.gr; Plateia Pigadakia; s/d/tr incl breakfast from €95/120/130; ❄📶) Sleek and minimalist, this hotel is in the heart of the action in the old-town, close to everything, and the staff are attentive. Balconies overlook the bustle of the streets, but thick glass keeps the noise out when you decide to call it a night. Restaurants and cafes are right outside the front door.

Eating & Drinking

★Doukato GREEK €

(☎22850 27013; www.facebook.com/doukatonaxos; Old Town; mains €8-16; ⏲6pm-late May-Oct; dinner Fri & Sat, lunch Sun Nov-Apr) One of the Cyclades' best eating experiences, in a magical setting that has been a monastery, church and a school, Doukato is rightly capturing attention. Owner Dimitris grows much of the produce, or sources it locally. The result? Top Naxian specialities such as *gouna* (sun-dried mackerel), *kalogeras* (beef, eggplant and cheese) and their unbelievably delicious Doukato 'Special' souvlaki.

Naxos Cafe BAR

(☎22850 26343; Old Market St; ⏲8pm-2am) If you want to drink but don't fancy the club scene, here's your answer. This atmospheric, traditional bar is small and candlelit and spills into the cobbled Bourgos street. Drink Naxian wine with the locals.

Getting There & Around

AIR

The **airport** (JNX; www.naxos.net/airport) is 3km south of Hora. There's no shuttle bus, but buses to Agios Prokopios Beach and Agia Anna pass close by. A taxi costs around €15; luggage costs extra. There are daily flights to/from Athens (around €95, 40 minutes) with Olympic Air (www.olympicair.com), Agean Airlines (https://en.aegeanair.com/) and Sky Express (www.skyexpress.gr).

BOAT

Like Paros, Naxos is something of a ferry hub in the Cyclades, with a similar number of conventional and fast ferries making regular calls to/from Piraeus, plus the mainland port of Rafina via the northern Cyclades.

PUBLIC TRANSPORT

Frequent buses run to Agios Prokopios Beach and Agia Anna from Hora. Several buses daily serve Filoti via Halki, Apiranthos and Apollonas (€6.20), Pyrgaki (€2.30) and Melanes.

Buses leave from the end of the ferry quay in Hora; timetables are posted outside the **bus information office** (☎22850 22291; www.naxosdestinations.com; Harbour), diagonally left and across the road from the bus stop. You have to buy tickets from the office or from the machine outside (not from the bus driver).

Santorini ΣΑΝΤΟΡΙΝΗ

POP 15,550

You'll either love or hate Santorini. Its magnet, the multicoloured cliffs that soar above the sea-drowned caldera, are amazing indeed. The main towns of Fira and Oia – a snow-drift of white Cycladic houses that line the cliff tops and spill like icy cornices down the terraced rock – will take your breath away. And then there's the island's fascinating history, best revealed at the Minoan site of Akrotiri.

Santorini's main town of Fira is a vibrant place, if bursting at its seams. Its caldera edge is layered with swish hotels, cave apartments, infinity pools, all backed by a warren of narrow streets packed with shops, more bars and restaurants. And people.

DON'T MISS

ANCIENT AKROTIRI

In 1967, excavations in the southwest of Santorini uncovered **Ancient Akrotiri** (☎22860 81366; http://odysseus.culture.gr; adult/concession €12/6; ⏰8am-8pm May-Sep, to 3pm Oct-Apr), an ancient Minoan city buried deep beneath volcanic ash from the catastrophic eruption of 1613 BC. Housed within a cool, protective structure, wooden walkways allow you to pass through the city. Peek inside three-storey buildings that survived, and see roads, drainage systems and stashes of pottery.

Sights

★Museum of Prehistoric Thera MUSEUM
(☎22860 22217; www.santorini.com/museums; Mitropoleos; adult/child €3/free; ⏰8.30am-3pm Wed-Mon) Opposite the bus station, this well-presented museum houses extraordinary finds excavated from Akrotiri and is all the more impressive when you realise just how old they are. Most remarkable is the glowing gold ibex figurine, dating from the 17th century BC and in mint condition. Also look for fossilised olive tree leaves from within the caldera, which date back to 60,000 BC.

★Art Space GALLERY
(☎22860 32774; www.artspace-santorini.com; Exo Gonia; ⏰11am-sunset Apr-Oct) FREE This atmospheric gallery is on the way to Kamari, in Argyros Canava, one of the oldest wineries on the island. The atmospheric old wine caverns are hung with some superb artworks, while sculptures transform lost corners and niches. The collection features around 32 Greek and international modern artists. Winemaking is still in the owner's blood, and part of the complex produces some stellar vintages under the Art Space Wines label. Tastings (from €10) enhance the experience.

Ancient Thira ARCHAEOLOGICAL SITE
(☎22860 25405; http://odysseus.culture.gr; adult/child €4/free; ⏰8am-3pm Tue-Sun) First settled by the Dorians in the 9th century BC, Ancient Thira consists of Hellenistic, Roman and Byzantine ruins and is an atmospheric and rewarding site to visit. The ruins include temples, houses with mosaics, an *agora* (market), a theatre and a gymnasium. Views are splendid. If you're driving, take the narrow, switchbacked road from Kamari for 3km. From Perissa, a hike up a dusty path takes a bit over an hour to reach the site.

Oia

Perched on the northern tip of the island, the village of Oia reflects the renaissance of Santorini after the devastating earthquake of 1956. Restoration work has whipped up beauty. You will struggle to find a more stunning spot in the Cyclades. Built on a steep

Santorini

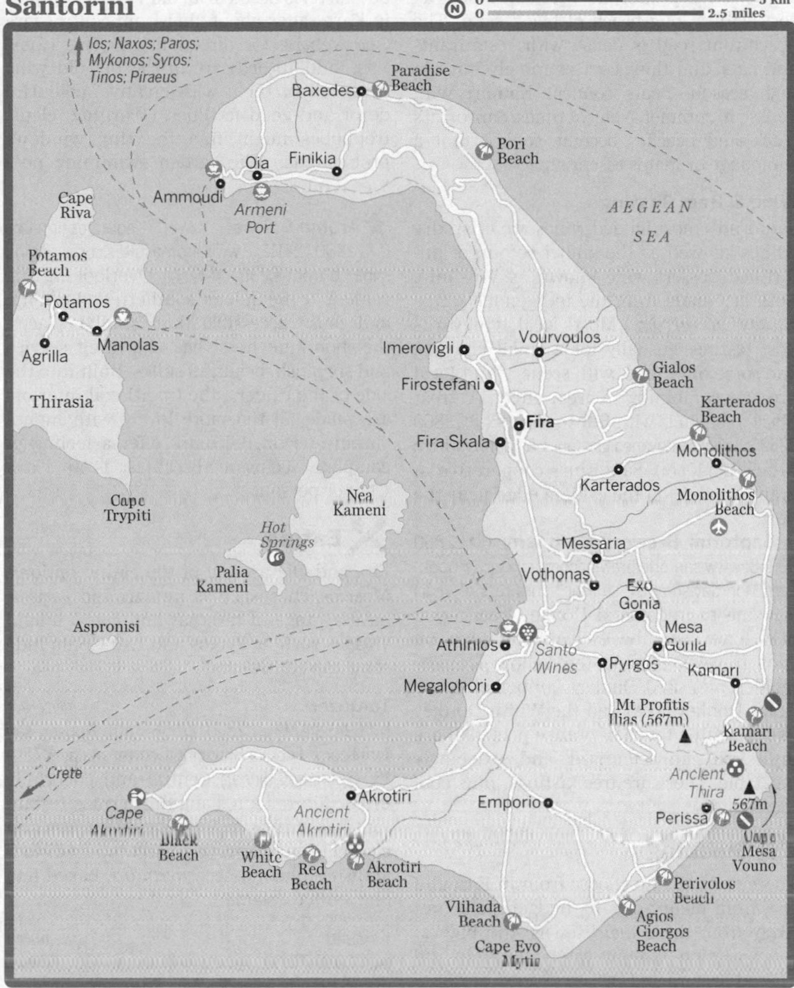

slope of the caldera, many of its dwellings nestle in niches hewn into the volcanic rock.

Not surprisingly, Oia draws enormous numbers of tourists, and overcrowding is the price it pays for its good looks. Try to visit in the morning or spend the night here; afternoons and evenings often bring busloads from the cruise ships moored in the bay.

Activities

Beaches

Santorini's best beaches are on the east and south coasts. Sunbeds, beach bars and water-sports operators are here to serve.

The long stretch of black sand, pebbles and pumice stones at **Perissa**, **Perivolos** and **Agios Georgios** is backed by bars, tavernas, hotels and shops, and remains fairly relaxed.

Red (Kokkini) Beach, near Ancient Akrotiri in the south, has impressive red cliffs. Caïques from **Akrotiri Beach** can take you there and on to **White (Aspri)** and **Black (Mesa Pigadia) Beaches** for about €5 return.

Vlihada, also on the south coast, has a beach backed by weirdly eroded cliffs as well as tavernas; it also has a photogenic fishing harbour.

Kamari is Santorini's best-developed resort, with a long beach of black sand. The beachfront road is dense with restaurants and bars, and things get extremely busy in high season. Boats connect Kamari with Perissa in summer. Note: at times, Santorini's black-sand beaches become so hot that a sunlounge or mat is essential.

Wine & Beer Tasting

Santorini's most lauded wines are crisp dry whites, as well as the amber-coloured, unfortified dessert wine known as Vinsanto. Both are made from the indigenous grape variety, *assyrtiko*. Most local vineyards host tastings (usually for a small charge), and some offer food, with scenery and local produce combining to great effect. A great place to begin is with **SantoWines** (22860 22596; www.santowines.gr; tours & tastings from €11; 9am-10pm), Santorini's cooperative of grape-growers on the caldera edge near the port.

Santorini Brewery Company (22860 30268; www.santorinibrewingcompany.gr; noon-5pm Mon-Sat summer, shorter hours rest of year) is home to in-demand Donkey beers (you may have seen the eye-catching logo on your travels). Sample the Yellow Donkey (golden ale), Red Donkey (amber ale), the Crazy Donkey (IPA) and the White Donkey (wheat with a touch of orange peel). All are unfiltered, unpasteurised and extremely palatable. There are free tastings, plus cool merchandise.

Sleeping

There's so much to choose from in Fira and Oia, from luxury digs to 'budget' pensions. Away from these main towns, the biggest concentration of rooms can be found in and around Kamari and Perissa (a good option if you are on a budget).

Zorzis Hotel BOUTIQUE HOTEL **€**

(22860 81104; www.santorinizorzis.com; Perissa; d incl breakfast from €99;) Behind a huge bloom of geraniums on Perissa's main street, Hiroko and Spiros (a Japanese-Greek couple) run an immaculate 10-room hotel. It's a pastel-coloured sea of calm (no kids), with delightful garden, pool and eye-catching mountain backdrop.

Karterados Caveland Hostel HOSTEL **€**

(22860 22122; www.cave-land.com; Karterados; dm from €26, d incl breakfast €100, apt €200; Mar-Oct; P) This fabulous, chilled-out hostel is based in an old winery complex in Karterados about 2km from central Fira (see website for directions). Dorms (four-, six- and 10-bed) are in the big old wine caves, all of them with creative, colourful decor and good facilities. (Warning: claustrophobes might find the tiny windows problematic.) The garden swimming pool tops it off.

★ **Aroma Suites** BOUTIQUE HOTEL **€€**

(22860 24112; www.aromasuites.com; Agiou Mina; d from €230; @) Overlooking the caldera at the quieter southern end of Fira, and more accessible than similar places, this boutique hotel has charming service and six plush, beautiful suites. Built into the side of the caldera, the traditional interiors are made all the more lovely with monochrome decor. Balconies offer a feeling of complete seclusion. Breakfast is an extra €12 per person.

Eating

Fira and Oia are full of top eating options. Most beaches, such as Kamari and Perissa, have a range of tavernas and cafes. Inland villages such as Pyrgos and Exo Gonia hide some top eating spots.

To Ouzeri TAVERNA **€**

(6945849921, 22860 21566; http://ouzeri-santorini.com; Fabrika Shopping Centre; mains €7.50-15; lunch & dinner) Central and cheerfully dressed in red gingham, this terrace restaurant has surprisingly reasonable prices and a good local following. Expect top traditional dishes like mussels *saganaki,* baked feta and stuffed calamari.

Krinaki TAVERNA **€€**

(22860 71993; www.krinaki-santorini.gr; Finikia; mains €17-27; noon-late) All-fresh, all-local ingredients go into top-notch taverna dishes at this homey spot in tiny Finikia, just east of Oia. Local beer and wine, plus a sea (but not caldera) view looking north to Ios.

Information

Dakoutros Travel (22860 22958; www.dakoutrostravel.gr; Fira; 8.30am-midnight Jul & Aug, 9am-9pm Sep-Jun) Helpful travel agency and de facto tourist office on the main street, just before Plateia Theotokopoulou. Ferry and air tickets sold; assistance with excursions, accommodation and transfers.

Getting There & Away

AIR

Santorini Airport (JTR; ☎22860 28400; www.santoriniairport.com) has flights year-round to/from Athens (from €65, 45 minutes) with Olympic Air (www.olympicair.com) and Aegean Airlines (https://en.aegeanair.com). Seasonal European connections from London, Rome, Geneva and Milan are plentiful with some budget carriers.

Give yourself plenty of time when flying back out as tourism infrastructure hasn't kept up with the island's growing popularity and it can be mayhem at the small airport terminal.

BOAT

There are plenty of ferries each day to and from Piraeus and many Cyclades islands.

Santorini's main port, Athinios, stands on a cramped shelf of land at the base of sphinx-like cliffs. It's a scene of marvellous chaos (that works itself out), except when ferries have been cancelled and arrivals and departures merge. Advice? Be patient. It clears, if eventually. Buses (and taxis) meet all ferries and then cart passengers up the towering cliffs through an ever-rising series of S-bends to Fira. Accommodation providers can usually arrange transfers (to Fira per person is around €10 to €15).

Getting Around

TO/FROM THE AIRPORT

There are frequent bus connections between Fira's bus station and the airport, 5km east of Fira (€1.80, 20 minutes, 7am to 9pm). Most accommodation providers will arrange paid transfers.

BUS

KTEL Santorini Buses (☎22860 25404; http://ktel-santorini.gr) has a good website with schedules and prices. Tickets are purchased on the bus.

In summer buses leave Fira regularly for Oia, with more services pre sunset (€1.80). There are also numerous daily departures for Akrotiri (€1.80), Kamari (€1.80), Perissa and Perivolos Beach (€2.40), and a few to Monolithos (€1.80).

Buses leave Fira for the port of Athinios (€2.30, 30 minutes) a half-dozen times per day, but it's wise to check times in advance. Buses for Fira meet all ferries, even late at night.

CAR & MOTORCYCLE

A car is the best way to explore the island during high season, when buses are intolerably overcrowded and you'll be lucky to get on one at all. Be very patient and cautious when driving – the narrow roads and heavy traffic, especially in and around Fira, can be a nightmare.

There are representatives of all the major international car-hire outfits, plus dozens of local operators in all tourist areas. You'll pay from around €65 per day for a car and €35/50 for a scooter/four-wheeler in high season, but it pays to shop around.

CRETE ΚΡΗΤΗ

POP 623,000

There's something undeniably artistic in the way the Cretan landscape unfolds, from the sun-drenched beaches in the north to the rugged canyons spilling out at the cove-carved and cliff-lined southern coast. Trek through Europe's longest gorge, hike to the cave where Zeus was born or cycle among orchards on the Lasithi Plateau. Leave time to plant your footprints on a sandy beach, and boat, kayak or snorkel in the crystal waters.

Crete's natural beauty is equalled only by the richness of its history. The island is the birthplace of the Minoans, the first advanced society on European soil, and you'll find evocative vestiges like the famous Palace of Knossos. History imbues Hania and Rethymno, where labyrinthine lanes are lorded over by mighty fortresses, restored Renaissance mansions, mosques and Turkish bathhouses.

Iraklio ΗΡΑΚΛΕΙΟ

POP 140,730

Crete's capital city, Iraklio (also called Heraklion), is Greece's fifth-largest city and the island's economic and administrative hub. It's also home to Crete's blockbuster sights. Take the time to explore its layers and wander its backstreets. You'll discover a low-key urban sophistication with a thriving restaurant scene. A revitalised waterfront invites strolling and the newly pedestrianised historical centre is punctuated by bustling

DON'T MISS

IRAKLIO MARKET

An Iraklio institution, just south of the Lion Fountain, narrow **Odos 1866** (1866 St) is part market, part bazaar and, despite being increasingly tourist-oriented, a fun place to browse and stock up on picnic supplies from fruit and vegetables, creamy cheeses and honey to succulent olives and fresh breads. Other stalls sell pungent herbs, leather goods, hats, jewellery and some souvenirs.

Crete

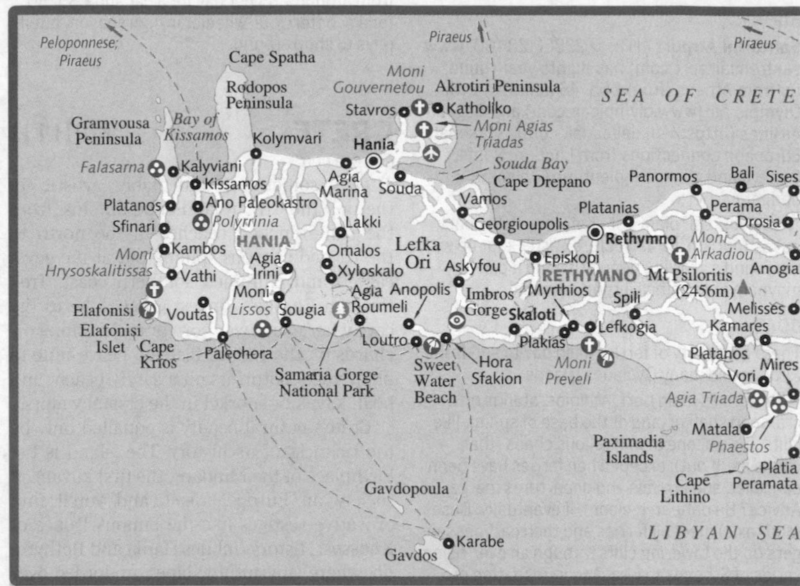

squares flanked by buildings from the time when Christopher Columbus first set sail.

Sights & Activities

★Heraklion Archaeological Museum

MUSEUM

(www.heraklionmuseum.gr; Xanthoudidou 2; adult/reduced/child €10/5/free, with Palace of Knossos adult/reduced €16/8; ⏲8am-8pm Mon & Wed-Sun, 10am-8pm Tue mid-Apr-Oct, 8am-4pm Nov-mid-Apr) This state-of-the-art museum is one of the largest and most important in Greece. The two-storey revamped 1930s Bauhaus building makes a gleaming showcase for artefacts spanning 5500 years from Neolithic to Roman times, including a Minoan collection of unparalleled richness. The rooms are colour coded and displays are arranged both chronologically and thematically, and presented with descriptions in English.

A visit here will greatly enhance your understanding of Crete's rich history. Don't skip it.

Cretan Adventures

OUTDOORS

(☎6944790771; www.cretanadventures.gr) This well-regarded local company run by friendly and knowledgeable English-speaking Fondas organises hiking tours, mountain biking and extreme outdoor excursions. It also coordinates fabulous week-long self-guided hiking tours including detailed hiking instructions, accommodation with breakfast and luggage transfer (from around €800). Fondas' office is up on the 3rd floor and easy to miss.

Sleeping & Eating

Hotel Mirabello

HOTEL €

(☎28102 85052; www.mirabello-hotel.gr; Theotokopoulou 20; s/d from €40/50;) Despite its dated Plain-Jane looks, this friendly and low-key hotel offers excellent value for money. Assets include squeaky-clean rooms with modern bathrooms, beds with individual reading lamps, a fridge and kettle plus a location close to, well, everything. The nicest units have a balcony.

Olive Green Hotel

HOTEL €€

(☎28103 02900; www.olivegreenhotel.com; cnr Idomeneos & Meramvellou; d incl breakfast €109-126;) This 'contemporary chic' and uber-smart place is one of Iraklio's newcomers to the hotel scene. Its clean rooms feature minimalistic white and olive-green decor, with separate shower and toilet (as opposed to the usual Greek-style all-in-one bathroom). It promotes itself as 'eco-friendly' but this seems to be limited to solar panels and low-impact building materials. Helpful reception staff.

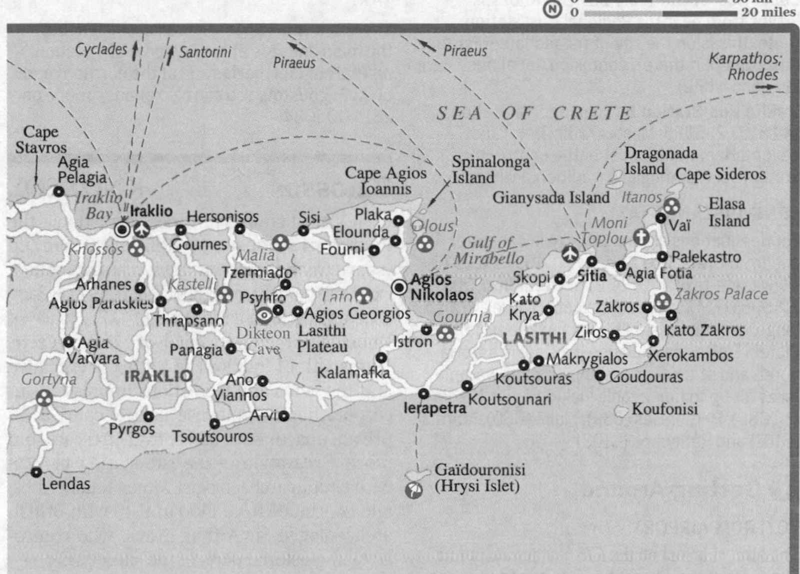

Phyllo Sofies CAFE €
(www.phyllosophies.gr; Plateia Venizelou 33; mains €3.50-12.50; 6am-midnight;) With tables sprawling out towards the Morosini Fountain, this is a great place to sample *bougatsa* (creamy semolina pudding wrapped in a pastry envelope and sprinkled with cinnamon and sugar). The less-sweet version is made with *myzithra* (sheep's-milk cheese).

★ **Merastri** CRETAN €€
(28102 21910; www.facebook.com/merastri; Chrisostomou 17; mains €7-13; 7pm-late) If there's a reason to come to Iraklio, it's to enjoy one of the most authentic Cretan meals, served in this stunning home, a former music building. The family of owners is passionate about their products (they use whatever they produce – oil and wine), and will conjure up everything from slow-cooked lamb to porterhouse steak with sage and wine.

Ippokambos SEAFOOD €€
(28102 80240; Sofokli Venizelou 3; mains €7-17; 12.30am-midnight Mon-Sat;) This long-running *ouzerie* (place that serves ouzo and light snacks) specialises in fish – freshly caught (if not, they state if it's frozen), simply but expertly prepared and sold at fair prices. In summer, park yourself on the covered waterfront terrace.

Getting There & Away

AIR

About 5km east of Iraklio city centre, the **Nikos Kazantzakis International Airport** (HER; 28103 97800; www.ypa.gr/en/our-airports/kratikos-aerolimenas-hrakleioy-n-kazantzakhs) has an ATM, a duty-free shop and a cafe-bar.

BOAT

The **ferry port** (28103 38000; www.portheraklion.gr) is 500m to the east of the Koules Fortress and old harbour. The Regional Bus Station is about 500m south, while the local bus terminal is outside the port entrance. Iraklio is a major port for access to many of the islands, though services are spotty outside high season. Tickets can be purchased online or through local travel agencies, including central **Paleologos** (28103 46185; www.paleologos.gr; 25 Avgoustou 5; 9am-8pm Mon-Fri, to 3pm Sat). Daily ferries from Iraklio's port include services to Piraeus and faster catamarans to Santorini and other Cycladic islands. Ferries sail east to Rhodes via Sitia, Kasos, Karpathos and Halki.

BUS

Regional Bus Station (28102 46530; www.ktelherlas.gr; Leoforos Ikarou 9;) East of Koules Fortress on Ikarou, this depot serves major destinations in eastern and western Crete, including Hania, Rethymno, Agios Nikolaos, Sitia and the Lassithi Plateau.

Local Bus Station City bus 2 to Knossos leaves from near the Regional Bus Station (note: this is on the site of the old long-distance bus station; if there's confusion, local buses are blue and white).

Iraklio Bus Station B (Chanioporta Station; 28102 255965; Machis Kritis 3;) Just beyond Hania Gate, west of the centre, this station serves Anogia, a traditional village.

LONG-DISTANCE TAXI

For destinations around Crete, you can order a cab from **Crete Taxi Services** (6970021970; www.crete-taxi.gr; 24hr) or **Heraklion Taxi** (6955171473; www.crete.cab). There are also long-distance cabs waiting at the airport, at Plateia Eleftherias (outside the Capsis Astoria hotel) and at the Regional Bus Station. Sample fares for up to four people include Agios Nikolaos (€85), Hersonisos (€39), Malia (€50), Matala (€101) and Rethymno (€108).

Getting Around

TO/FROM AIRPORT

The airport is just off the E75 motorway, about 5km east of the city centre. City buses connects it with the city centre, including the port, the regional (and local) bus stations and Plateia Eleftherias, every few minutes. These include bus numbers 6, 8, 10, 11, 12 and 31. The bus stop is to the left as you exit the terminal. Taxis wait outside the departures terminal with official fares posted. The fare into town is about €20.

CAR

Iraklio's streets are narrow and chaotic so it's best to drop your vehicle in a car park (about €6 per day) and explore on foot. All the international car-hire companies have branches at the airport. Local outlets line the northern end of 25 Avgoustou.

PHAESTOS ΦΑΙΣΤΟΣ

Phaestos (28920 42315; http://odysseus.culture.gr; Iraklio-Phaestos Rd; adult/concession/under 18yr €8/4/free; 8am-8pm Apr-Oct, 8am-3pm Nov-Mar; P), 63km southwest of Iraklio, is Crete's second-most important Minoan palatial site. More unreconstructed and moody than Knossos, Phaestos (fes-*tos*) is also worth a visit for its stunning views of the surrounding Mesara plain and Mt Psiloritis (2456m; also known as Mt Ida). The smaller site of **Agia Triada** (28920 91564; www.interkriti.org; off Phaestos-Matala Rd; adult/concession/under 18yr €4/2/free; 9am-4pm; P) is 3km west.

TAXI

There are small taxi stands all over town, but the main ones are at the Regional Bus Station, on **Plateia Eleftherias** and at the northern end of 25 Avgoustou. You can also phone for one on 2814 003084.

Knossos ΚΝΩΣΣΟΣ

Crete's most famous historical attraction is the **Palace of Knossos** (2810 231940; http://odysseus.culture.gr; Knossos; adult/concession €15/8, incl Heraklion Archaeological Museum €16/8; 8am-8pm Apr-Aug, to 5pm Sep-Mar; P; 2) Palace of Knossos, the grand capital of Minoan Crete, 5km south of Iraklio. The setting is evocative and the ruins and recreations impressive, incorporating an immense palace, courtyards, private apartments, baths, lively frescoes and more. Excavation of the site started in 1878 with Cretan archaeologist Minos Kalokerinos, and continued from 1900 to 1930 with British archaeologist Sir Arthur Evans, who controversially restored parts of the site.

To beat the crowds and avoid the heat, get to Knossos before 10am when tour buses start arriving, or later in the afternoon when it's cooler and the light is good for photographs. Budget a couple of hours to do the place justice.

Optional guided tours last about 1½ hours and leave from the little kiosk past the ticket booth. Most tours are in English, though other languages are available too. Prices vary according to group numbers (€10 per person in a group with an eight-person minimum). Private tours cost €80 with a maximum of six people.

Getting There & Away

Getting to Knossos is easy. City bus 2 runs from Iraklio's city centre – from the Regional Bus Station or from outside Hotel Capsis Astoria – every 15 minutes. Tickets cost €1.70 if purchased from a kiosk or vending machine and €2.50 from the bus driver. If driving, from Iraklio or the coastal road there are signs directing you to Knossos. There is free parking across from the souvenir shops, but the spaces fill quickly.

Hania ΧΑΝΙΑ

POP 54,000

Hania (also spelled Chania) is Crete's most evocative city, with its pretty Venetian quarter, criss-crossed by narrow lanes, culminating at a magnificent harbour. Remnants of

WORTH A TRIP

SOUTHWEST COAST VILLAGES

Crete's southern coastline at its western end is dotted with remote, attractive little villages that are brilliant spots to take it easy for a few days.

Paleohora Isolated on a peninsula with a sandy beach to the west and a pebbly beach to the east. On summer evenings the main street is closed to traffic and the tavernas move onto the road.

Sougia At the mouth of the **Agia Irini gorge**, Sougia (soo-yah) is a laid-back and refreshingly undeveloped spot with a wide curve of sand-and-pebble beach. The 14.5km (six hours) walk from Paleohora is popular, as is the Agia Irini gorge walk that ends (or starts) in Sougia.

Loutro This tiny village is a particularly picturesque spot, curled around the only natural harbour on the southern coast of Crete. With no vehicle access, the only way in is by boat or on foot. The village beach, great walks, rental kayaks, and boat transfers to excellent Sweetwater Beach fill peaceful days.

Hora Sfakion Renowned in Cretan history for its people's rebellious streak, this is the place where thousands of Allied troops were evacuated by sea after the Battle of Crete. Hora Sfakion's seafront tavernas serve fresh seafood and *Sfakianes pites*, which look like crêpes filled with sweet or savoury local cheese.

Venetian and Turkish architecture abound, with old townhouses now transformed into atmospheric restaurants and boutique hotels. Although all this beauty means the old town is deluged with tourists in summer, it's still a great place to unwind. The Venetian Harbour is super for a stroll, indie boutiques provide good shopping and, with a multitude of creative restaurants, you'll eat very well here. It's an excellent base for exploring nearby idyllic beaches and a spectacular mountainous interior.

Sights

★Venetian Harbour HISTORIC SITE
(24hr) FREE There are few places where Hania's historic charm and grandeur is more palpable than in the old Venetian Harbour. It's lined by pastel-coloured buildings that punctuate a maze of narrow lanes lined with shops and tavernas. The eastern side is dominated by the domed **Mosque of Kioutsouk Hasan** (Mosque of the Janissaries), now an exhibition hall, while a few steps further east, the impressively restored Grand Arsenal houses the **Centre for Mediterranean Architecture**.

★Hania Archaeological Museum MUSEUM
(28210 90334; http://chaniamuseum.culture.gr; Halidon 28; adult/concession/child €4/2/free; 8.30am-8pm Wed-Mon Apr-Oct, to 4pm Wed-Mon Nov-Mar) The setting alone in the beautifully restored 16th-century Venetian Church of San Francisco is reason to visit this fine collection of artefacts from Neolithic to Roman times. Late-Minoan sarcophagi catch the eye as much as a large glass case with an entire herd of clay bulls (used to worship Poseidon). Other standouts include Roman floor mosaics out the back, Hellenistic gold jewellery, clay tablets with Linear A and Linear B script, and a marble sculpture of Roman emperor Hadrian.

★Maritime Museum of Crete MUSEUM
(28210 91875; www.mar-mus-crete.gr; Akti Koundourioti; adult/concession €3/2; 9am-5pm Mon-Sat, 10am-6pm Sun May-Oct, 9am-3.45pm Mon-Sat Nov-Apr) Part of the hulking Venetian-built **Firkas Fortress** (8am-2pm Mon-Fri) at the western port entrance, this museum celebrates Crete's nautical tradition with model ships, naval instruments, paintings, photographs, maps and memorabilia. One room is dedicated to historical sea battles, while upstairs there's thorough documentation on the WWII-era Battle of Crete.

Sleeping & Eating

Hania's Venetian quarter brims with chic boutique hotels and family-run atmospheric pensions in restored Venetian buildings. Most hotels have no lift. They tend to be open year-round, but it's a good idea to book ahead for weekends and in summer.

Pension Theresa PENSION €
(28210 92798; www.pensiontheresa.gr; Angelou 8; d €50-80;) This creaky old Venetian

house with a long and steep winding staircase and antique furniture delivers eight snug rooms with character aplenty. The location is excellent, the ambience rustic and convivial, and the views lovely from the rooftop terrace, plus there's a communal kitchen stocked with basic breakfast items. It's close to plenty of bars and restaurants.

★**Casa Leone** BOUTIQUE HOTEL €€€
(☎28210 76762; www.casa-leone.com; Parodos Theotokopoulou 18; d/ste incl breakfast from €135/190; ❄📶) This Venetian residence has been converted into a lovely romantic family-run boutique hotel. The rooms are spacious and well appointed, with drape-canopy beds and sumptuous curtains, though some show ever-so-slight signs of wear and bathrooms are small. Some have balconies overlooking the harbour. The central salon is delightful; it sits above the harbour.

★**Bougatsa Iordanis** CRETAN €
(☎28210 88855; www.iordanis.gr; Apokoronou 24; bougatsa €3; ⏲6am-2.30pm Mon-Sat, to 1.30pm Sun; 👪) Locals start salivating at the mere mention of this little bakery-cafe dedicated to making the finest *bougatsa* since 1924. The flaky treat, filled with sweet or savoury cheese, is cooked fresh in enormous slabs and carved up in front of your eyes. Pair it with a coffee and you're set for the morning. There's nothing else on the menu!

Kouzina EPE CRETAN €
(☎28210 42391; www.facebook.com/kouzinaepe; Daskalogianni 25; mezhedes €4-9.50; ⏲noon-7.30pm Mon-Sat) This cheery lunch spot gets contemporary designer flair from the concrete floor, country-white tables and groovy lighting. It hands-down wins the area's 'local favourite' by serving great-value, delicious blackboard-listed *mayirefta* (ready-cooked meals) prepared by the owner; you can inspect what you're about to eat in the open kitchen.

To Maridaki SEAFOOD €€
(☎28210 08880; www.tomaridaki.gr; Daskalogianni 33; mezhedes €4-14; ⏲noon-midnight Mon-Sat) This modern seafood *mezedhopoleio* (restaurant specialising in mezedhes) is often packed to the gills with chatty locals. Dishes straddle the line between tradition and innovation with to-die-for mussels *saganaki* and crisp and delicious house white wine. The complimentary panna cotta is a worthy finish.

🍷 Drinking & Entertainment

The cafe-bars around the Venetian Harbour are nice places to sit, but charge top euro. For a more local vibe, head to Plateia 1821 in the Splantzia quarter, to the interior streets near Potie, or to alt-flavoured Sarpidona on the eastern end of the harbour.

★**Fagotto Jazz Bar** LIVE MUSIC
(☎28210 71877; Angelou 16; ⏲8.30am-noon & 9pm-late) Established in 1978, this Hania institution in a Venetian building offers smooth (mostly recorded but occasionally live) jazz, soft rock and blues in a setting brimming with jazz paraphernalia, including a saxophone beer tap. The action picks up after 10pm. It morphs into a cafe too, and serves breakfasts.

ℹ Getting There & Away

AIR

Hania's **airport** (☎28210 83800; www.chania-airport.com) is 14km east of town on the Akrotiri Peninsula, and is served year-round from Athens and Thessaloniki and seasonally from throughout Europe. Carriers include Aegean Airlines and Ryanair.

BOAT

Hania's port is at Souda, 7km southeast of town (and the site of a NATO base). The port is linked to town by bus (€2, or €2.50 if bought aboard) and taxi (around €12). Hania buses meet each boat, as do buses to Rethymno.

Anek Lines (☎28210 24000; www.anek.gr; Leoforos Karamanlis 70; ⏲7.30am-3.30pm Mon-Fri) runs a nightly overnight ferry between Piraeus and Hania (from €38, nine hours). Buy tickets online or at the port; reserve ahead for cars.

BUS

Hania's **KTEL bus station** (☎info 28210 93052, tickets 28210 93306; http://e-ktel.com; Kelaidi 73-77; 📶) has an information kiosk with helpful staff and timetables, plus a cafeteria, mini-market and left-luggage service. Check the excellent website for the current schedule.

ℹ Getting Around

Hania town is best navigated on foot, since most of it is pedestrianised.

TO/FROM THE AIRPORT

KTEL (www.e-ktel.com) buses link the airport with central Hania roughly every 30 minutes, with the last departure at around 11pm (€2.50, 25 minutes). Taxis between any place in the city and the airport cost €25.

WORTH A TRIP

PREVELI

Head south from the coastal city of **Rethymno** (reth-im-no), itself an architectural treasure, through the **Kourtaliotiko Gorge** towards Crete's southern coast. Here, a smooth ribbon of road soars up to the historic **Moni Preveli** (Μονή Πρεβέλης; ☎28320 31246; www.preveli.org; Koxaron-Moni Preveli Rd; €2.50; ⏲9am-6pm Apr & May, 9am-1pm & 3.30-7pm Jun-Oct; Ⓟ), which cuts an imposing silhouette high above the Libyan sea. Like most Cretan monasteries, it was a centre of resistance during the Turkish occupation and also played a key role in WWII when hiding trapped Allied soldiers from the Nazis until they could escape to Egypt by submarine.

Below stretches **Preveli Beach** (Παραλία Πρέβελη), one of Crete's most celebrated strands. At the mouth of the gorge, where the river Megalopotamos empties into the Libyan Sea, the palm-lined river banks have freshwater pools good for a dip. The beach is backed by rugged cliffs and punctuated by a heart-shaped boulder at the water's edge. A steep path leads down to the beach (10 minutes) from a car park (€2), 1km before Moni Preveli.

BUS

Local buses are operated by **Chania Urban Buses** (☎28210 98115; http://chaniabus.gr). Zone A/B tickets cost €1.20/1.70 if bought from a kiosk or vending machine and €2/2.50 from the driver.

A handily central stop for Souda port, Halepa, Nea Hora and other local destinations is on Giannari, near the *agora* market hall.

CAR & MOTORCYCLE

Major car-hire outlets are at the airport or on Halidon. There's free parking just west of Firkas Fortress and along the waterfront towards Nea Hora beach, or by the eastern edge of the harbour off Kyprou; but avoid areas marked residents-only.

Samaria Gorge
ΦΑΡΑΓΓΙ ΤΗΣ ΣΑΜΑΡΙΑΣ

Hiking the 16km-long **Samaria Gorge** (☎28210 45570; www.samaria.gr; Omalos; adult/child €5/free; ⏲6am-4pm May–mid-Oct) is considered one of Crete's must-do experiences, which is why you'll rarely be without company. Nevertheless, there's an undeniable raw beauty to Samaria, where vertical walls soar up to 500m and are just 3m apart at the narrowest point (150m at the broadest). The hike begins at 1230m at Xyloskalo just south of Omalos and ends in the coastal village of Agia Roumeli. It's especially scenic in April and May when wildflowers brighten the trail.

In peak season, up to 3000 people a day tackle the stony trail, and even in spring and autumn, there's rarely fewer than 1000 hikers. The vast majority arrive on organised coach excursions from the big northern resorts. You'll encounter a mix of serious trekkers and less-experienced types attempting the trail in flip-flops.

Samaria is home to the *kri-kri,* a rarely seen endangered wild goat. The gorge was made a national park in 1962 to save the *kri-kri* from extinction. You are unlikely to see these shy animals, which show a marked aversion to hikers, but you might spot golden eagles overhead.

ℹ Getting There & Away

Most people hike Samaria one way going north–south on an organised day trip from every sizeable town and resort in Crete. Confirm that tour prices include the €5 admission to the gorge or the boat ride from Agia Roumeli to Sougia or Hora Sfakion.

With some planning, it's possible to do the trek on your own. There are early-morning public buses to Omalos from Hania. Check www.e-ktel.com for the seasonally changing schedule. Taxis are another option. At the end of the trail, in Agia Roumeli, ferries go to Sougia or Hora Sfakion; some are met by public buses to Hania.

DODECANESE
ΔΩΔΕΚΑΝΗΣΑ

Strung out along the coast of western Turkey, the 12 main islands of the Dodecanese (*dodeca* means 12) have suffered a turbulent past of invasions and occupations that have endowed them with a fascinating diversity. Conquered successively by the Romans, the Arabs, the Knights of St John, the Turks and the Italians, then liberated from the Germans by British and Greek commandos in

1944, the Dodecanese became part of Greece in 1947. These days, tourists rule.

Rhodes ΡΟΔΟΣ

POP 115,500

By far the largest and historically the most important of the Dodecanese islands, Rhodes (*ro*-dos) abounds in beaches, wooded valleys and ancient history. Whether you arrive in search of buzzing nightlife, languid sun worshipping, diving in crystal-clear waters, or to embark on a culture-vulture journey through past civilisations, it's all here.

Rhodes Town

POP 90,000

Rhodes Town is really two distinct and very different towns. The **Old Town** lies within but utterly apart from the New Town, sealed like a medieval time capsule behind a double ring of high walls and a deep moat. Nowhere else in the Dodecanese can boast so many layers of architectural history, with ruins and relics of the Classical, medieval, Ottoman and Italian eras entangled in a mind-boggling maze of twisting alleys. Strolling its hauntingly pretty cobbled lanes, especially at night, is an experience no traveller should miss. Half the fun is letting yourself get lost. The **New Town**, to the north, boasts upmarket shops and waterfront bars servicing the package crowd, along with the city's best beach, while bistros and bars lurk in the backstreets.

Sights

A wander around Rhodes' Unesco World Heritage–listed Old Town is a must. It is reputedly the world's finest surviving example of medieval fortification, with 12m-thick walls. A mesh of Byzantine, Turkish and Latin architecture, the Old Town is divided into the Kollakio (the Knights' Quarter, where the Knights of St John lived during medieval times), the Hora and the Jewish Quarter. The Knights' Quarter contains most of the medieval historical sights while the Hora, often referred to as the Turkish Quarter, is primarily Rhodes Town's commercial sector with shops and restaurants, thronged by tourists.

The Knights of St John lived in the **Knights' Quarter** in the northern end of the Old Town. The cobbled Avenue of the Knights (Ippoton) is lined with magnificent medieval buildings, the most imposing of which is the **Palace of the Grand Master** (☎22410 23359, 22413 65270; €6; ⏲8am-8pm Apr-Oct, to 3pm Nov-Mar), which was restored, but never used, as a holiday home for Mussolini. From the palace, explore the **D'Amboise Gate**, the most atmospheric of the fortification gates that takes you across the moat.

The beautiful 15th-century Knights' Hospital, closer to the seafront, now houses the excellent **Archaeological Museum** (☎22413 65200; Plateia Mousiou; adult/child €8/free; ⏲8am-8pm daily Apr-Oct, to 3pm Tue-Sun Nov-Mar). The splendid building was restored by the Italians and has an impressive collection that includes the ethereal marble statue *Aphrodite of Rhodes*.

The pink-domed **Mosque of Süleyman**, at the top of Sokratous, was built in 1522 to commemorate the Ottoman victory against the knights, then rebuilt in 1808.

Sleeping & Eating

The most magical sleeping options are all in the Old Town. In summer it's essential to reserve ahead. In winter most budget options close altogether. Be warned, too, that most Old Town hotels are not accessible by taxi, so you'll have to haul your luggage along the narrow, cobbled lanes.

★**Marco Polo Mansion** BOUTIQUE HOTEL €€
(☎22410 25562; www.marcopolomansion.gr; Agiou Fanouriou 40; d incl breakfast €80-160, apt €130-180; ⏲Apr-Oct; ❄📶) With its stained-glass windows, dark-wood furniture, wood floors and raised beds, Marco Polo lovingly recreates an Ottoman ambience with verve and style, and is unlike anything else in the Old Town. This former 15th-century pasha's house is like a journey back in time. There are two apartments (with kitchenettes) too. Breakfast is served in the stunning flowering courtyard.

★**Spirit of the Knights** BOUTIQUE HOTEL €€€
(☎22410 39765; www.rhodesluxuryhotel.com; Alexandridou 14; s/d incl breakfast from €160/200; 🚭❄📶) This gorgeously finished boutique hotel has six stunning suites dripping with medieval atmosphere. Imagine thick rugs, dark woods, stained-glass windows and a sense of tranquillity. Perfectly isolated down a side street close to the Old Town walls, this fine hotel is a work of passion and vision. There's a library and a fragrant garden courtyard to read in and take breakfast.

★Marco Polo Cafe MEDITERRANEAN €€
(☎22410 25562; www.marcopolomansion.gr; Agiou Fanouriou 40-42; mains €15-25; ⏰7-11pm Apr-Oct) Don't be surprised if you are asked to taste a wine or culinary creation, a possible new addition to the menu that includes gourmet treats like skewered lamb with rosemary and pistachio, pork loin with figs, or octopus in sea-urchin sauce. It's served up with sincerity and style in a lemon-fragrant garden courtyard. Reserve ahead to ensure you don't miss out.

Nireas SEAFOOD €€
(☎22410 21703; Sofokleous 45-47; mains €10-17; ⏰noon-late Mar-Oct; ❄) Nireas' status as one of Rhodes' better seafood restaurants owes much to the sheer verve of enthusiastic owner Theo, from Symi – that and the well-prepared food served beneath a vine-shaded canopy outside, in the Jewish Quarter. Be sure to sample the Symi shrimp, salted mackerel and, if you're in the mood, the 'Viagra' salad of small shellfish.

Getting There & Away

AIR

Diagoras Airport (RHO; ☎22410 88700; www.rhodes-airport.org) is 16km southwest of Rhodes Town. Taxis cost €25; the local bus €2.50.

Olympic Air (☎22410 24571; www.olympicair.com; Ierou Lohou 9) connects the island with Athens and destinations throughout Greece, including several Dodecanese islands.

Sky Express (☎28102 23800; www.skyexpress.gr) flies up to six days a week to Herakion on Crete (€90, one hour) and once weekly to Samos (€73, 45 minutes).

BOAT

Inter-island ferries use the **Commercial Harbour** (aka Akandia), while catamarans use **Kolona Harbour**. Excursion boats and private yachts are based at Mandraki Harbour.

Two inter-island companies operate from Rhodes Old Town. **Dodekanisos Seaways** (☎22410 70590; www.12ne.gr/en; Afstralias 3, Rhodes Town) sails from Kolona Harbour immediately beyond the walls, with daily high-speed catamarans running north up the chain of the Dodecanese. **Blue Star Ferries** (☎22410 22461; www.bluestarferries.com; Amerikis 111, Rhodes Town; ⏰9am-8pm), operating from the Commercial Harbour, a five-minute taxi from the Old Town, provides slower and less frequent services to several of the same islands, continuing west to Astypalea and Piraeus. It also heads southwest to Karpathos and east to Kastellorizo. Anek Lines (www.anek.gr) runs to Kasos and Crete. Tickets are available at the dock and from travel agents in Rhodes Town.

In addition, daily excursion boats head to Symi from Mandraki Harbour in summer (around €20).

DON'T MISS

LINDOS

Your first glimpse of the ancient and unbelievably pretty town of Lindos is guaranteed to steal your breath away: the towering Acropolis radiant on the cypress-silvered hill, and the sugar-cube houses of the whitewashed town tumbling below it towards the aquamarine bay. Entering the town itself, you'll find yourself in a magical warren of hidden alleys, packed with the ornate houses of long-vanished sea captains that now hold appetising tavernas, effervescent bars and cool cafes. Pick your way past donkeys as you coax your calves up to the Acropolis and one of the finest views in Greece.

Getting Around

Two bus terminals, a block apart in Rhodes Town, serve half the island each. There is regular transport across the island all week, with fewer services on Saturday and only a few on Sunday. Pick up schedules from the kiosks at either terminal, or from the EOT (Greek National Tourist Organisation; www.visitgreece.gr) office.

Rhodes Town's main **taxi** rank is east of Plateia Rimini, on the northern edge of the Old Town. There are two zones on the island for taxi meters: zone one is Rhodes Town and zone two (for which rates are slightly higher) is everywhere else. Rates double between midnight and 5am. Set taxi fares are posted at the rank.

Kos ΚΩΣ

POP 33,400

Fringed by the finest beaches in the Dodecanese, dwarfed beneath mighty crags, and blessed with lush valleys, Kos is an island of endless treasures. Visitors soon become blasé at sidestepping the millennia-old Corinthian columns that poke through the rampant wildflowers – even in Kos Town, the lively capital, ancient Greek ruins are scattered everywhere you turn, and a mighty medieval castle still watches over the harbour.

Sights & Activities

★ Asklepieion ARCHAEOLOGICAL SITE

(☎22420 28763; adult/child €8/free; ⏰8am-7.30pm Apr-Oct, 8am-2.30pm Tue-Sun Nov-Mar) The island's most important ancient site stands on a pine-covered hill 3km southwest of Kos Town, commanding lovely views across towards Turkey. A religious sanctuary devoted to Asclepius, the god of healing, it was also a healing centre and a school of medicine. It was founded in the 3rd century BC, according to legend by Hippocrates himself, the Kos-born 'father' of modern medicine. He was already dead by then, though, and the training here simply followed his teachings.

Kefalos Bay

Enormous Kefalos Bay, a 12km stretch of high-quality sand, lines the southwest shoreline of Kos. For most of its length the beach itself is continuous, but the main road runs along a crest around 500m inland, so each separate section served by signposted tracks has its own name. Backed by scrubby green hills and lapped by warm water, these are the finest and emptiest beaches on the island. Kamari, at the western extremity of this black-pebbled beach, is a low-key resort with plenty of cafes, tavernas and accommodation, as well as decent water sports.

The most popular stretch of sand is **Paradise Beach**, while the least developed is **Exotic Beach**. **Langada Beach** (which you may also see referred to as Banana Beach) makes a good compromise, but the best of the lot is **Agios Stefanos Beach**, at the far western end. A small beachfront promontory here is topped by a ruined 5th-century basilica, while the absurdly photogenic islet of **Kastri** stands within swimming distance immediately offshore.

Buses to and from Kos Town (€4.40, three to four daily) stop nearby at Kamari Beach.

Kos Town

A handsome harbour community, fronted by a superb medieval castle and somehow squeezed amid a mind-blowing array of ancient ruins from the Greek, Roman and Byzantine eras, Kos Town is the island's capital, main ferry port and only sizeable town. In the lovely cobblestoned Plateia Platanou, you can pay your respects to the **Hippocrates' plane tree**, under which Hippocrates is said to have taught his pupils.

Long, sandy **Kritika Beach**, in easy walking distance of the town centre, is lined with hotels and restaurants. Southeast of the harbour the thin strip of sand known as **Kos Town Beach** is dotted with parasols in summer and offers deep water for swimming.

Sleeping & Eating

Nowhere else on the island has the culinary diversity of Kos Town: *ouzeries* (places that serve ouzo and light snacks), seafood restaurants, *kafeneia* (coffee houses) and upmarket dining.

★ Hotel Afendoulis HOTEL €

(☎22420 25321; www.afendoulishotel.com; Evripilou 1; s/d/tr from €35/50/60; ⏰Mar-Nov; ❄@📶) This family-run hotel has sparkling rooms with TVs, balconies, hairdryers and comfy beds. Downstairs, the open breakfast room and breezy terrace have wrought-iron tables and chairs for reading or enjoying the memorable breakfast that features homemade jams and much more. There may be plusher hotels in Kos, but none with the soul of the Afendoulis, where nothing is too much trouble.

Hotel Sonia HOTEL €€

(☎22420 28798; www.hotelsonia.gr; Irodotou 9; d/tr/f incl breakfast €80/95/140; ❄📶) A block from the waterfront on a peaceful backstreet, this pension offers 14 sparkling rooms with tiled floors, fridges and smart bathrooms. Rooms 4 and 5 have the best sea views; around five rooms have balconies. If you want to, you can have breakfast outside in the rear garden. There's a decent book exchange. Prices are significantly reduced outside high season.

★ Pote Tin Kyriaki TAVERNA €

(☎6930352099; Pisandrou 9; mezhedes 2.50-8; ⏰7pm-2am Mon-Sat) Named 'Never on a Sunday' to reflect its opening hours (yes, that's its day of rest), this traditional rough-and-ready *ouzerie* serves delicious specialities such as stuffed zucchini flowers, dolmadhes and steamed mussels. Come late, and you'll be cheek by jowl with the locals.

★ Elia GREEK €€

(☎22420 22133; Appelou Ifestou 27; mains €9-16; ⏰12.30pm-late; ❄📶🍷👶) With its traditional wood-beamed ceiling and partly exposed stone walls covered in murals of the gods of the pantheon, Elia is earthy and friendly, while its small menu is fit for a hard-to-please local deity. At the time of research, there were plans to introduce a more Greek fusion and Mediterranean-focused menu. Whatever the plans, they should be good.

Getting There & Away

AIR

Kos' **airport** (KGS; 22420 56000; www.kosairportguide.com) is in the middle of the island, 24km southwest of Kos Town. Aegean Airlines (https://en.aegeanair.com) and Olympic Air (www.olympicair.com) offer up to four daily flights to Athens (from €100, 55 minutes) and regular flights to Rhodes (€80, 30 minutes) and Leros (€100, 55 minutes). Flights to some other islands, such as Naxos, go via Athens.

BOAT

From the island's main ferry port, in front of the castle in Kos Town, Dodekanisos Seaways (p361) runs catamarans up and down the archipelago, southeast to Rhodes via Nisyros, Tilos, Halki and Symi, and north to Samos, with stops including Kalymnos, Leros and Patmos. Blue Star Ferries (p361) also sails to Rhodes, as well as west to Astypalea and Piraeus.

The **Panagia Spiliani** (Diakomihalis Travel & Shipping Agency; 22420 31015; www.visitnisyros.gr/en; Mandraki), which also runs day trips from Nisyros to Kos in summer, carries passengers and cars to Nisyros on sailings that leave from Kos Town three to four days a week, and from Kardamena on the other three days.

Eight daily ferries also connect Mastihari with Kalymnos (€4.50, 50 minutes); see www.12ne.gr, www.anekalymnou.gr and www.anemferries.gr.

Getting Around

TO/FROM THE AIRPORT

The airport is served by several daily buses to and from Kos Town's bus station (€3.20). A taxi to Kos Town costs around €37. Note that Kefalos-bound buses stop at the big roundabout near the airport entrance.

The airport is so far from Kos Town that if you're planning to rent a car anyway, it's worth doing so when you first arrive. All the international chains have airport offices.

BICYCLE

Cycling is very popular, so you'll be tripping over bicycles for hire. Prices range from as little as €5 per day for a boneshaker, up to €20 for a decent mountain bike.

BUS

The island's main **bus station** (22420 22292; www.ktel-kos.gr; Kleopatras 7; Information office 8am-9pm Mon-Sat Apr-Oct, to 3pm Mon-Fri Nov-Mar) is well back from the waterfront in Kos Town. It is the base for KTEL, which has services to all parts of the island, including the airport and south-coast beaches.

NORTHEASTERN AEGEAN ISLANDS
ΤΑ ΝΗΣΙΑ ΤΟΥ ΒΟΡΕΙΟ ΑΝΑΤΟΛΙΚΟ ΑΙΓΑΙΟΥ

One of Greece's best-kept secrets, these far-flung islands are strewn across the northeastern corner of the Aegean, closer to Turkey than mainland Greece. They harbour unspoilt scenery, welcoming locals and fascinating independent cultures, and remain relatively calm even when other Greek islands are bulging with tourists at the height of summer.

Samos ΣΑΜΟΣ

POP 33,000

A lush mountainous island only 3km from Turkey, Samos has a glorious history as the legendary birthplace of Hera, wife and sister of god of all gods Zeus. Samos was an important centre of Hellenic culture, and the mathematician Pythagoras and storyteller Aesop are among its sons. The island has beaches that bake in summer, and a hinterland that is superb for hiking. Spring brings with it pink flamingos, wildflowers, and orchids that the island grows for export, while summer brings throngs of package tourists.

Vathy Βαθύ Σάμου

POP 1900

The island's capital, Vathy (also called Samos) enjoys a striking setting within the fold of a deep bay, where its curving waterfront is lined with bars, cafes and restaurants. The historical quarter of Ano Vathy, filled with steep, narrow streets and red-tiled, 19th-century, hillside houses, brims with atmosphere.

The first-rate **Archaeological Museum** (22730 27469; adult/concession €4/2, 1st Sun of month Nov-Mar free; 8am-3pm Tue-Sun) is one of the best in the islands and the **Museum of Samos Wines** (22730 87510, ext 548; www.samoswine.gr; €2; 10am-5pm May-Oct; P) FREE offers tours and taste-testing with one of the island's best vinters. On the hilltop, the bright rooms at **Pension Dreams** (22730 24350, 6976425195; Areos 9; d €35-40, tr €45-50; P) have large terraces over a lush garden. Elegant **Ino Village Hotel** (22730 23241; www.inovillagehotel.com; Kalami; d incl breakfast €60-125; P) in the hills north of the ferry quay has **Elea Restaurant** with terrace views over town and the harbour.

ITSA Travel, opposite the quay, is helpful with travel enquiries, excursions, accommodation and luggage storage.

Getting Around

The **bus station** (22730 27262; www.samospublicbusses.gr; Themistokleous Sofouli) and nearby **taxi rank** (22730 28404) serve as a departure point to destinations all around the island.

Pythagorio Πυθαγόρειο

POP 1330

Little Pythagorio, 11km south of Vathy, is where you'll disembark if you've come by boat from Patmos. It is a small, enticing town with a yacht-lined harbour and a busy, holiday atmosphere, which is overwhelming to some.

The 1034m-long **Evpalinos Tunnel** (22730 61400; www.eupalinos-tunnel.gr; adult/child €8/4; 8.40am-2.40pm Tue-Sun Mar-Dec), built in the 6th century BC, was dug by political prisoners and used as an aqueduct to bring water from Mt Ampelos (1140m).

Heraion (adult/child €6/3; 8am-3pm Tue-Sun), the legendary birthplace of the goddess Hera, is 8km west of Pythagorio. The temple at this World Heritage Site was enormous – four times the size of the Parthenon – though only one column remains.

The impeccable **Pension Despina** (22730 61677, 6936930381; A Nikolaou; studio/apt €35/40;) is a relaxing spot with a garden, while **Polyxeni Hotel** (22730 61590; www.polyxenihotel.com; s/d incl breakfast from €65/72;) is in the heart of the waterfront action. Tavernas and bars line the waterfront.

Getting There & Away

There are five buses daily to Vathy (25 minutes) and five buses daily to Ireon (15 minutes) for Heraion. A taxi to the airport costs €10 to/from Pythagorio and €25 to/from Vathy. Taxis also ply the route between Pythagorio and Vathy (useful for ferry arrivals and departures) for around €20.

Northern Samos

Northern Samos is a wonderful mix of stunning sea and mountain scenery, marble gravel beaches and quirky villages favoured as a base by local and foreign artisans. The relatively remote, hence uncrowded **Potami Beach** is the area's crown jewel, especially as it is a short trek away from waterfalls and pools of cool crystal water beneath the thick canopy of a broadleaf forest.

Getting There & Around

AIR

Samos' airport is 4km west of Pythagorio. Aegean Airlines (https://en.aegeanair.com), Olympic Air (www.olympicair.com) and Sky Express (www.skyexpress.gr) all serve Samos and have offices at the airport.

Buses run to/from the airport three to four times daily (€2.30). Taxis from the airport cost €25 to Vathy, or €10 to Pythagorio, from where there are local buses to Vathy.

Boat

Samos is home to three ports – Vathy (aka Samos), Pythagorio and Karlovasi.

By Ship Travel (22730 62285; www.byshiptravel.gr) has an office in Pythagorio; check ferry and catamaran schedules with them. Alternatively, ask the **port police** (22730 61225).

In Karlovasi, **By Ship Travel** (22730 35252) will help you with travel tickets, including to Turkey.

Lesvos ΛΕΣΒΟΣ

POP 86,436

Lesvos, or Mytilini as it is often called, tends to do things in a big way. The third-largest of the Greek islands after Crete and Evia, Lesvos produces half the world's ouzo and is home to over 11 million olive trees. Mountainous yet fertile, the island has world-class local cuisine, and presents excellent hiking and birdwatching opportunities, but

SAPPHO, LESBIANS & LESVOS

Sappho, one of Greece's great ancient poets, was born on Lesvos during the 7th century BC. Most of her work was devoted to love and desire, and the objects of her affection were often female. Because of this, Sappho's name and birthplace have come to be associated with female homosexuality.

These days, Lesvos is visited by many lesbians paying homage to Sappho. The whole island is very gay-friendly, in particular the southwestern beach resort of **Skala Eresou**, which is built over ancient Eresos, where Sappho was born. The village is well set up to cater to lesbian needs and has a **Women Together** festival held annually in September. See www.womensfestival.eu and www.sapphotravel.com for details.

remains refreshingly untouched in terms of tourism.

Mytilini Town Μυτιλήνη

POP 29,650

The capital and main port, Mytilini, is a lively student town with great eating and drinking options, plus eclectic churches and grand 19th-century mansions and museums. It is built between two harbours (north and south) with an imposing fortress on the promontory to the east. All ferries dock at the southern harbour, and most of the town's action is found around this waterfront.

Sights

★Teriade Museum MUSEUM

(☎22510 23372; http://museumteriade.gr; Varia; €3; ⏲9am-2pm Tue-Sun) Extraordinary. It's worth coming to Lesvos just for this museum and its astonishing collection of paintings by artists including Picasso, Chagall, Miró, Le Corbusier and Matisse. The museum honours the Lesvos-born artist and critic Stratis Eleftheriadis, who brought the work of primitive painter and Lesvos native Theophilos to international attention. Located in Varia, 4km south of Mytilini.

Fortress FORTRESS

(Kastro; €2; ⏲8am-3pm Tue-Sun) Mytilini's imposing early-Byzantine fortress was renovated in the 14th century by Genoese overlord Francisco Gatelouzo, and then the Turks enlarged it again. Flanked by pine trees, it's popular for a stroll, with some good views included.

Sleeping & Eating

Theofilos Paradise Boutique Hotel BOUTIQUE HOTEL €€

(☎22510 43300; www.theofilosparadise.gr; Skra 7; d incl breakfast €114, ste €140-160, f €160; P❄@☜≋) This smartly restored 100-year-old mansion is elegant and good value, with modern amenities and a traditional *hammam*. The 22 swanky rooms (plus two luxe suites) are spread among three adjacent buildings surrounding an inviting courtyard.

Cafe P CAFE €

(☎22510 55594; Samou 2; mains €3-7; ⏲11am-3am) This hip back-alley bistro draws a crowd mostly from the university for its unusual and well-priced small plates, eclectic music mix and all-round chilled atmosphere. Sautéed shrimps, served with a draught beer, costs around €8. Cheap daily special too. It's about 50m in from Plateia Sapphou (Sappho Sq). Look for a sign with a single Greek letter, 'Π'.

Getting There & Around

The **airport** (Mitiline Airport; ☎22510 38700, 22510 61212; www.mjt-airport.gr/en) is 8km south along the coast.

Mytilini Town is the island's main port, with connections to other northeastern Aegean Islands and Piraeus (Athens).

The **long-distance bus station** (KTEL; ☎22510 28873; www.ktel-lesvou.gr; El Venizelou) is beside Irinis Park, near the domed church. Travelling between smaller places often requires changing in Kalloni, which receives one to three buses daily (except Sunday) from Mytilini (€4.90, 45 minutes). Two to three daily buses also go north from Mytilini Town to Mantamados (for Moni Taxiarhon; €4.50, one hour).

Mytilini's **local bus station** (KTEL; ☎22510 46436; Pavlou Kountourioti), near Plateia

Sapphou, serves in-town destinations and nearby Loutra, Skala Loutron and Tahiarhis.

Molyvos Μόλυβος

POP 1500

Molyvos, also known as Mithymna, is a well-preserved Ottoman-era town of narrow cobbled lanes and stone houses, with jutting wooden balconies wreathed in flowers, overlooking a sparkling pebble beach below. Its grand 14th-century Byzantine castle, some good nearby beaches and its north-central island location make it a great launch pad from which to explore Lesvos.

Sights

Byzantine-Genoese Castle CASTLE

(22530 71803; €2; 8am-3pm Tue-Sun) This handsome 14th-century castle stands guard above Molyvos. A steep climb is repaid by sweeping views over the town and sea – even across to Turkey, shimmering on the horizon. In summer the castle hosts several festivals.

Sleeping

Nadia Apartments & Studios PENSION €

(22530 71345; www.apartments-molivos.com; studio/apt €43/60;) On the road to Sikamenea and a short walk from the Old Town, these large motel-style rooms surrounding an expansive shady courtyard are owned by the organised Nadia. Her trademark cakes are complimentary; it's open all year.

Getting There & Away

At least one to two buses daily connect Molyvos with Mytilini Town (€7.50, 1½ hours).

Around Lesvos

Hire a car and tour the incredible countryside. Southern Lesvos is dominated by **Mt Olympus** (968m), and grove-covered valleys. Visit wonderful mountain village **Agiasos**, with its artisan workshops making everything from handcrafted furniture to pottery. **Plomari** in the far south is the land of ouzo distilleries; tour fascinating **Varvagianni Ouzo Museum** (22520 32741; www.barbayanni-ouzo.com; 9am-4pm Mon-Fri Apr-Oct, 10am-2pm Mon-Fri Nov-Mar, by appointment Sat & Sun) FREE.

Western Lesvos is known for its **petrified forest** (22510 47033; www.petrifiedforest.gr; entry fee varies; park 9am-5pm Jul-Sep, 8.30am-4.30pm Oct-Jun), with petrified wood at least 500,000 years old, and for the gay-friendly town of **Skala Eresou**, the birthplace of Sappho. You can stay over in peaceful **Sigri**, with its broad beaches, to the southwest.

IONIAN ISLANDS

ΤΑ ΕΠΤΑΝΗΣΑ

With their cooler climate, abundant olive and cypress trees, and forested mountains, the Ionians are a lighter, greener variation on the Greek template. Venetian, French and British occupiers have all helped to shape the islands' architecture, culture and (excellent) cuisine, and contributed to the unique feel of Ionian life. The Ionians hold something new for adventure seekers, food lovers, culture vultures and beach bums alike.

Corfu ΚΕΡΚΥΡΑ

POP 102,070

Still recognisable as the idyllic refuge where the shipwrecked Odysseus was soothed and sent on his way home, Corfu continues to welcome weary travellers with its lush scenery, bountiful produce and pristine beaches. While certain regions of the island have succumbed to overdevelopment, particularly those close to Corfu Town, Corfu is large enough to make it possible to escape the crowds.

Corfu Town Κέρκυρα

POP 30,000

Imbued with Venetian grace and elegance, historic Corfu Town (also known as Kerkyra) stands halfway down the island's east coast. The name Corfu, meaning 'peaks', refers to its twin hills, each topped by a massive fortress built to withstand Ottoman sieges. Sitting between the two, the Old Town is a tight-packed warren of winding lanes, majestic architecture, high-class museums and no fewer than 39 churches.

Sights

★**Palaio Frourio** FORTRESS

(Old Fort; 26610 48310; adult/concession €6/3; 8am-8pm Apr-Oct, 8.30am-3pm Nov-Mar) The rocky headland that juts east from Corfu Town is topped by the Venetian-built 14th-century Palaio Frourio. Before that, already enclosed within massive stone walls, it cradled the entire Byzantine city. A solitary bridge crosses its seawater moat.

Only parts of this huge site, which also holds later structures from the British era, are accessible to visitors; wander up to the **lighthouse** on the larger of the two hills for superb views.

Palace of St Michael & St George PALACE
(adult/concession €6/3; ⌚8am-8pm Apr-Oct, 9am-4pm Tue-Sun Nov-Mar) Beyond the northern end of the Spianada, the smart Regency-style Palace of St Michael & St George was built by the British from 1819 onwards, to house the High Commissioner and the Ionian Parliament. It's now home to the prestigious **Corfu Museum of Asian Art** (☎26610 30443; www.matk.gr; adult/child incl palace entry €6/3). Two municipal art galleries **I** (☎26610 48690, www.artcorfu.com; Palace of St Michael & St George; €3; ⌚10am-4pm Tue-Sun) and **II** (free entry) are housed in one annex, and its small formal **gardens** make a pleasant refuge.

Mon Repos Estate PARK
(Kanoni Peninsula, ⌚8am-3pm Tue-Sun) FREE This park-like wooded estate 2km around the bay south of the Old Town was the site of Corfu's most important ancient settlement, Palaeopolis. More recently, in 1921, the secluded neoclassical villa that now holds the **Museum of Palaeopolis** (☎26610 41369; Mon Repos, Kanoni Peninsula; adult/concession €4/2; ⌚8am-3pm Tue-Sun) was the birthplace of Prince Philip of Greece, who went on to marry Britain's Queen Elizabeth II. Footpaths lead through the woods to ancient ruins, including those of a Doric temple atop a small coastal cliff.

Antivouniotissa Museum MUSEUM
(Byzantine Museum; ☎26610 38313; www.antivouniotissamuseum.gr; off Arseniou; adult/concession €4/2; ⌚8am-3pm Tue-Sun) Home to an outstanding collection of Byzantine and post-Byzantine icons and artefacts, the exquisite, timber-roofed **Church of Our Lady of Antivouniotissa** doubles as both church and museum. It stands atop a short, broad stairway that climbs from shore-front Arseniou, and frames views out towards the wooded Vidos island.

Sleeping & Eating

★ Bella Venezia BOUTIQUE HOTEL €€
(☎26610 46500; www.bellaveneziahotel.com; N Zambeli 4; d incl breakfast from €130; ❄📶) Enter this neoclassical, historic villa, set in a peaceful central street, and you'll be seduced by its charms. It features an elegant lobby with candelabras, velvet chairs and a piano. The plush, high-ceilinged rooms (some with balconies) have fine city or garden views, while the garden breakfast area is delightful. The cheaper loft rooms have horizontal windows but no outlook.

Siorra Vittoria BOUTIQUE HOTEL €€€
(☎26610 36300; www.siorravittoria.com; Stefanou Padova 36; d incl breakfast from €205; P❄📶) Expect luxury and style at this quiet 19th-century Old Town mansion, where restored traditional architecture meets modern amenities; marble bathrooms, crisp linens and genteel service make for a relaxed stay. Breakfast is served either in your room or beneath an ancient magnolia in the peaceful garden.

Pane & Souvlaki GRILL €
(☎26610 20100; www.panesouvlaki.com; Guilford 77; mains €6-13.50; ⌚noon-1am) Arguably the Old Town's best-value budget option (the locals rave), with outdoor tables on the Town Hall square, this quick-fire restaurant does exactly what its name suggests, serving up three skewers of chicken or pork with chunky chips, dipping sauce and warm pitta in individual metal trays. The salads and burgers are good too.

Starenio BAKERY €
(☎26610 47370; www.facebook.com/stareniobakery; Guilford 59; sweets & pastries from €2; ⌚8am-8pm Mon-Sat) This magical little bakery, dripping with bougainvillea, is where in-the-know locals linger at little tables on the sloping pedestrian street to savour cakes, coffee, pastries, and delicious fresh pies with vegetarian fillings such as mushrooms or nettles.

To Tavernaki tis Marinas TAVERNA €€
(☎26611 00792; Velissariou 35; mains €8-15; ⌚noon-11.30pm) The stone walls, hardwood floors and cheerful staff lift the ambience of this taverna. As locals will tell you, check the daily specials or choose anything from

WORTH A TRIP

IONIAN PLEASURES

Paxi (Πάξοι) Paxi lives up to its reputation as one of the Ionians' most idyllic and picturesque islands. At only 10km by 4km it's the smallest of the main holiday islands and makes a fine escape from Corfu's quicker-paced pleasures.

Kefallonia (Κεφαλλονιά) Tranquil cypress- and fir-covered Kefallonia, the largest Ionian island, is breathtakingly beautiful with rugged mountain ranges, rich vineyards, soaring coastal cliffs and golden beaches. Not yet overrun with package tourism, it remains low-key outside resort areas and is a perfect spot for kayaking.

Ithaki (Ιθάκη) Odysseus' long-lost home in Homer's *Odyssey*, Ithaki (ancient Ithaca) remains a verdant, pristine island blessed with cypress-covered hills and beautiful turquoise coves. It's a walkers' paradise, best reached from Kefallonia.

Lefkada (Λευκάδα) Lefkada has some of the best beaches in Greece, if not the world, and an easygoing way of life.

mousakas (baked layers of eggplant or zucchini, minced meat and potatoes topped with cheese sauce) or sardines-in-the-oven to steak. Accompany it all with a dram of ouzo or *tsipouro* (distilled spirit similar to raki).

Getting There & Around

Corfu Town is at the centre of an efficient network of local buses, and you can get pretty much anywhere on the island from the **long-distance bus station** (☎26610 28900; https://greenbuses.gr; Lefkimmis 13) in the New Town.

Most Corfu Town car-rental companies are based along the northern waterfront.

Local blue buses depart from the **local bus station** (☎26610 31595; www.astikoktelkerkyras.gr; Plateia G Theotoki) in Corfu Old Town. Journeys cost €1.20 or €1.70. Buy tickets at the booth on Plateia G Theotiki, or on the bus itself. All trips are less than 30 minutes. Service is reduced on weekends.

Around Corfu

To explore the island fully your own transport is best. Much of the coast just north of Corfu Town is overwhelmed with beach resorts, while the south is quieter and the west has a beautiful, if popular, coastline. **The Corfu Trail** (ww.thecorfutrail.com) traverses the island north to south.

North of CorfuTown, in **Kassiopi**, picturesque **Manessis Apartments** (☎6973918416; www.manessiskassiopi.com; Kassiopi; 4-person apt €110; ❄📶) offers water-view apartments. South of Corfu Town, **Achillion Palace** (☎26610 56245; www.achillion-corfu.gr; Gastouri; adult/concession €8/6; ⏲8am-8pm Apr-Nov, to 4pm Dec-Mar) pulls 'em in for over-the-top royal bling. Don't miss a dinner at one of the island's best tavernas, **Klimataria** (☎26610 71201; www.klimataria-restaurant.gr; Benitses; mains €8-15; ⏲dinner Mon-Sat, lunch Sun Jun-Sep, lunch Sun mid-Feb–May & Oct-Nov), in nearby **Benitses**.

To gain an aerial view of the gorgeous cypress-backed bays around **Paleokastritsa**, the west coast's main resort, go to the quiet village of **Lakones**. For beautiful rooms just 20m from the pretty beach, check in to **Hotel Zefiros** (☎26630 41244; www.zefiroscorfuhotel.gr; Paleokastritsa; d/tr/q from €95/130/155; ❄📶). Further south good beaches surround tiny **Agios Gordios**.

Getting There & Around

AIR

Corfu's **airport** (CFU; ☎26610 89600; www.corfu-airport.com) is on the southwestern fringes of Corfu Town, just over 2km southwest of the Old Town.

Aegean Airlines (https://en.aegeanair.com) has direct flights to Athens and European destinations.

Sky Express (www.skyexpress.gr) operates a thrice-weekly island-hopping route to Preveza, Kefallonia and Zakynthos. It flies twice weekly to Thessaloniki.

Taxis between the airport and Corfu Town cost around €12, while local bus 15 runs to both Plateia G Theotoki (Plateia San Rocco) in town and the Neo Limani (New Port) beyond.

BOAT

Ferries depart from **Neo Limani** (New Port), northwest of Corfu Town's Old Town.

Ticket agencies line Ethnikis Antistaseos in Corfu Town, facing the Neo Limani.

SURVIVAL GUIDE

Directory A-Z

ACCESSIBLE TRAVEL

Travel Guide to Greece (www.greecetravel.com/handicapped) Links to local articles, resorts and tour groups catering for tourists with physical disabilities.

Sailing Holidays (www.charterayachtingreece.com/dryachting/index.html) Two-day to two-week sailing trips around the Greek islands in fully accessible yachts.

Sirens Resort (☎27410 91161; www.disableds-resort.gr; Skalouma) Family-friendly resort with accessible apartments, tours and ramps into the sea.

LEGAL MATTERS

Greek citizens are presumed always to have identification on them and the police presume foreign visitors do too. If you are arrested by police insist on an interpreter (*dierminéas;* say '*the*-lo dhi-ermi-*nea*') and/or a lawyer (*dikigóros;* say '*the*-lo dhi-ki-*go*-ro').

Greek drug laws are among the strictest in Europe. Greek courts make no distinction between possession and pushing. Possession of even a small amount of marijuana is likely to land you in jail.

LGBTIQ+ TRAVELLERS

In a country where the Church still plays a prominent role in shaping society's views on issues such as sexuality, it comes as no surprise that homosexuality is generally frowned upon by many locals – especially outside major cities. While there is no legislation against homosexual activity, it pays to be discreet.

Some areas of Greece are, however, extremely popular destinations for LGBTIQ+ travellers, including Athens, Mykonos and Lesvos (Mytilini).

MONEY

- The main credit cards are MasterCard and Visa, both of which are widely accepted.
- ATMs are found in most towns and almost all the tourist areas.
- Be aware that ATMs on the islands can lose their connection for a day or two at a time, making it impossible to withdraw money. It's useful to have a backup source of money.
- Automated foreign-exchange machines are common in major tourist areas.

OPENING HOURS

Opening hours vary throughout the year. High-season opening hours are provided below; hours decrease significantly in the shoulder and low seasons, when many places shut completely. Shops in tourist locations tend to have a licence for longer or alternative operating hours to those listed.

Banks 8.30am–2.30pm Monday to Thursday, 8am–2pm Friday

Restaurants 11am–3pm and 7pm–1am

Cafes 10am–midnight

Bars 8pm–late

Clubs 10pm–4am

Post offices 7.30am–2pm Monday to Friday (rural); 7.30am–8pm Monday to Friday, 7.30am–2pm Saturday (urban)

Shops 8am–2pm Monday, Wednesday and Saturday; 8am–2pm and 5pm–9pm Tuesday, Thursday and Friday

PUBLIC HOLIDAYS

New Year's Day 1 January

Epiphany 6 January

First Sunday in Lent February

Greek Independence Day 25 March

Good Friday 22 April 2022, 14 April 2023

Orthodox Easter Sunday 24 April 2022, 16 April 2023

May Day (Protomagia) 1 May

Whit Monday (Agiou Pnevmatos) 13 June 2022, 5 June 2023

Feast of the Assumption 15 August

Ohi Day 28 October

Christmas Day 25 December

St Stephen's Day 26 December

TELEPHONE

Mobile Phones

There are several mobile service providers in Greece, among which Cosmote, Vodafone and Wind are the best known. Of these three, Cosmote tends to have the best coverage in remote areas. All offer 2G connectivity and pay-as-you-talk services for which you can buy a rechargeable SIM card and have your own Greek mobile number.

TOILETS

- Public toilets at transport terminals (bus and train) sometimes have Ottoman/Turkish squat-style toilets.
- The Greek plumbing system can't handle toilet paper; the pipes are often too narrow and anything larger than a postage stamp seems to cause a problem. Toilet paper etc must be placed in the small bin provided next to every toilet.

TOURIST INFORMATION

The Greek National Tourist Organisation (www.visitgreece.gr) is known as GNTO abroad and EOT within Greece. The quality of service from office to office varies dramatically; in some you'll get information aplenty and in others you'll be hard-pressed to find anyone behind the desk. EOT offices can be found in major tourist locations. In some regions, such as the Peloponnese, tourist offices are run by the local government/municipality.

Transport

GETTING THERE & AWAY

Air

Aegean Airlines (A3; ☎801 112 0000; https://en.aegeanair.com) and its subsidiary, **Olympic Air** (☎801 801 0101; www.olympicair.com), have flights between Athens and destinations throughout Europe, as well as to Cairo, İstanbul, Tel Aviv and Toronto.

Land

Make sure you have all of your visas sorted out before attempting to cross land borders into or out of Greece. Before travelling, also check the status of borders with the relevant embassies.

Border Crossings

Albania Kakavia (60km northwest of Ioannina); Krystallopigi (14km west of Kotas); Mertziani (17km west of Konitsa); Sagiada/Mavromati (28km north of Igoumenitsa)

Bulgaria Exohi (50km north of Drama); Ormenio (41km from Serres); Promahonas (109km northeast of Thessaloniki)

North Macedonia Doïrani (31km north of Kilkis); Evzoni (68km north of Thessaloniki); Niki (16km north of Florina)

Turkey Kastanies (139km northeast of Alexandroupoli); Kipi (43km east of Alexandroupoli)

Train

The railways organisation **OSE** (Organismos Sidirodromon Ellados; ☎14511; www.trainose.gr) runs daily trains from Thessaloniki to Sofia, Skopje and Belgrade (with connection services to European cities from Belgrade).

Sea

Check ferry routes and schedules at www.greekferries.gr and www.openseas.gr. If you are travelling on a rail pass, check to see if ferry travel between Italy and Greece is included. Some ferries are free; others give a discount. On some routes you will need to make reservations.

Albania

For Saranda, **Petrakis Lines** (☎26610 38690; www.ionian-cruises.com) has daily hydrofoils to Corfu (25 minutes).

Italy

Routes vary so check online.

Ancona Patra (20 hours, three daily, summer)

Bari Patra (15 hours, daily) via Corfu (10 hours) and Keffalonia (14 hours); also to Igoumenitsa (11½ hours, daily)

Brindisi Patra (15 hours, April to early October) via Igoumenitsa (11 hours)

Venice Patra (30 hours, up to 12 weekly, summer) via Corfu (25 hours)

Turkey

Boat services operate between Turkey's Aegean coast and the Greek islands.

GETTING AROUND

Air

The vast majority of domestic mainland flights are handled by the country's national carrier Aegean Airlines and its subsidiary, Olympic Air. You'll find offices wherever there are flights, as well as in other major towns. There are also a number of smaller Greek carriers, including **Sky Express** (☎28102 23800; www.skyexpress.gr).

Bicycle

Cycling is not popular among Greeks – but it's gaining popularity, plus kudos with tourists. You'll need strong leg muscles to tackle the mountains; or you can stick to some of the flatter coastal routes. Bike lanes are rare to non-existent; helmets are not compulsory. The island of Kos is about the most bicycle-friendly place in Greece.

➡ You can hire bicycles in most tourist places. Prices range from €10 to €15 per day, depending on the type and age of the bike.

➡ Bicycles are carried free on ferries but cannot be taken on the fast ferries (catamarans and the like).

Boat

Greece has an extensive network of ferries – the only means of reaching many of the islands. Schedules are often subject to delays due to poor weather (note: this is a safety precaution) plus the occasional industrial action, and prices fluctuate regularly. Timetables are not announced until just prior to the season due to competition for route licences. In summer, ferries run regular services between all but the most out-of-the-way destinations; however, services seriously slow down in winter (and in some cases stop completely).

Be flexible. Boats seldom arrive early, but often arrive late. And some don't come at all. You may have the option of 'deck class', which is the cheapest ticket, or 'cabin class' with air-con assigned seats. On larger ferries there are lounges and restaurants for everyone serving fast food or snacks. Tickets can be bought at the dock, but in high season, boats are often full – plan ahead. Check www.openseas.gr or www.gtp.gr for schedules, costs and links to individual boat company websites. The Greek Ships app for smartphones tracks ferries in real time.

SAFE TRAVEL

If you take the usual precautions, Greece is a safe place to travel and you're more likely to suffer from heat exhaustion or sunburn than from any kind of crime.

- An unhealthy economy has led to an increase in pickpocketing; always be vigilant in busy bus stations, markets or on crowded streets.
- Watch out for adulterated drinks made from cheap illegal imports, and drink spiking, especially at party resorts.
- If you have an issue, go first to the *touristikíastynomía* (tourist police) in cities and popular tourist destinations; at least one staff member will speak English.

Bus

The bus network is comprehensive. All long-distance buses, on the mainland and the islands, are operated by regional collectives known as **KTEL** (www.ktelbus.com). Within towns and cities, different companies run inter-urban services. The fares are fixed by the government; bus travel is reasonably priced. All have good safety records.

Car & Motorcycle

No one who has travelled on Greece's roads will be surprised to hear that the road-fatality rate is still a lot higher than the EU average. Overtaking is listed as the greatest cause, along with speed. Heart-stopping moments aside, your own car is a great way to explore off the beaten track. The road network has improved enormously in recent years. There are regular (if costly) car-ferry services to almost all islands.

Car Hire

- All the big multinational companies are represented in Athens; most have branches in major towns and the majority of islands have at least one outlet.
- High-season weekly rates with unlimited mileage start at about €280 for the smallest models (eg a Fiat Seicento), dropping to about €150 per week in winter.
- On the islands, you can rent a car for the day for around €35 to €60, including all insurance and taxes.
- The minimum driving age in Greece is 18 years, but most car-hire firms require you to be at least 21 (or 23 for larger vehicles).

The major car-hire companies in Greece:

Avis (www.avis.gr)

Budget (www.budget.gr)

Europcar (www.europcar.gr)

Moped & Motorcycle Hire

- These are available for hire wherever there are tourists to rent them.
- You must produce a licence that shows proficiency to ride the category of bike you wish to rent.
- Rates start from about €20 per day for a moped or 50cc motorcycle, ranging to €35 per day for a 250cc motorcycle.

Road Rules

- Outside built-up areas, unless signed otherwise, traffic on a main road has right of way at intersections. In towns, vehicles coming from the right have right of way. This includes roundabouts – even if you're in the roundabout, you must give way to drivers coming on to the roundabout to your right.
- Seatbelts must be worn in front seats, and in back seats if the car is fitted with them.
- Children under 12 years of age are not allowed in the front seat.
- A blood-alcohol content of 0.05% can incur a fine, while over 0.08% is a criminal offence.

Local Transport

All the major towns have local buses.

Athens has a good underground system, and Thessaloniki is in the process of constructing one too (expected to open in 2023).

Taxi

Taxis are widely available in Greece, except on very small or remote islands. They are reasonably priced by European standards. City cabs are metered, with rates doubling between midnight and 5am. Additional costs are charged for trips from an airport or a bus, port or train station, as well as for each piece of luggage over 10kg.

Train

Trains are operated by the railways organisation OSE (p370; now an Italian-run company). The railway network is extremely limited with lines closed in recent years in areas such as the Peloponnese. OSE's northern line is the most substantial. Standard-gauge services run from Athens to Dikea in the northeast via Thessaloniki and Alexandroupoli. There are also connections to Florina and the Pelion Peninsula. The Peloponnese network runs only as far as Kiato, with bus services to Plata for ferry connections.

Due to financial instability, prices and schedules are very changeable. When you can, double-check on the OSE website. Information on departures from Athens or Thessaloniki are also available by calling 1440.

Ireland

POP REPUBLIC OF IRELAND 4.76 MILLION; NORTHERN IRELAND 1.87 MILLION

Includes ➡

Best Traditional Pubs

- ➡ Kyteler's Inn (p383)
- ➡ O'Connor's (p387)
- ➡ Peadar O'Donnell's (p399)
- ➡ Crane Bar (p392)

Best Places to Eat

- ➡ Fade Street Social (p379)
- ➡ Market Lane (p385)
- ➡ Oscar's (p391)

Why Go?

Few countries have an image so plagued by cliché. From shamrocks and *shillelaghs* (Irish fighting sticks) to leprechauns and lovable rogues, there's a plethora of platitudes to wade through before you reach the real Ireland.

The Emerald Isle is one of Europe's gems, a scenic extravaganza of lakes, mountains, sea and sky. From picture-postcard County Kerry to the rugged coastline of Northern Ireland (part of the UK, distinct from the Republic of Ireland), there are countless opportunities to get outdoors and explore, whether cycling the Causeway Coast or hiking the hills of Killarney and Connemara.

There are cultural pleasures too in the land of James Joyce and William Butler Yeats, U2 and the Undertones. Dublin, Cork and Belfast all have world-class art galleries and museums, and you can enjoy foot-stomping traditional music in the bars of Galway and Killarney. So push aside the shamrocks, and experience the real Ireland.

When to Go

Dublin

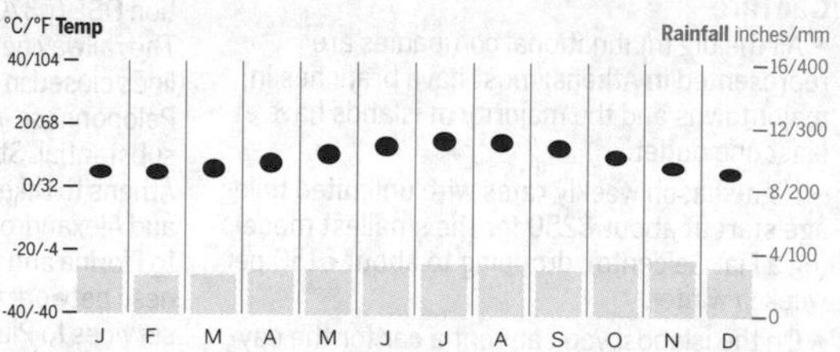

Late Mar Spring flowers are everywhere and St Patrick's Day festivities beckon.

Jun Best chance of dry weather, with long summer evenings. Bloomsday celebrates Joyce's *Ulysses* in Dublin.

Sep–Oct Summer crowds thin. Autumn colours reign and surf's up on the west coast.

Entering the Country

Dublin Airport Private coaches run every 10 to 15 minutes to the city centre (€7). Taxis take 30 to 45 minutes and cost €20 to €25.

Dun Laoghaire Ferry Port Public bus takes around 45 minutes to the centre of Dublin; DART (suburban rail) takes about 25 minutes. Both cost €3.25.

Dublin Port Terminal Buses are timed to coincide with arrivals and departures; they cost €3 to the city centre.

Belfast International Airport Airport Express 300 bus runs hourly from Belfast International Airport (one way/return £7.50/10.50, 30 to 55 minutes). A taxi costs around £30.

George Best Belfast City Airport Airport Express 600 bus runs every 20 minutes from George Best Belfast City Airport (one way/return £2.50/3.80, 15 minutes). A taxi costs around £10.

ITINERARIES

One Week

Spend a couple of days in Dublin (p375) ambling through the excellent national museums, and gorging yourself on Guinness and good company in Temple Bar. Get medieval in Kilkenny (p382) before heading on to Cork (p383) and discovering why they call it 'The Real Capital'. Head west for a day or two exploring the scenic Ring of Kerry (p388) and enchanting Killarney (p387).

Two Weeks

Follow the one-week itinerary, then make your way north from Killarney to bohemian Galway (p389). Using Galway as your base, explore the alluring Aran Islands (p392) and the hills of Connemara (p393). Finally head north to see the Giant's Causeway (p397) and experience the optimistic vibe in fast-changing Belfast (p393).

Essential Food & Drink

Potatoes Still a staple of most traditional meals and presented in a variety of forms.

Meat and seafood Beef, lamb and pork are common options. Seafood is widely available in restaurants and is often excellent, especially in the west. Oysters, trout and salmon are delicious, particularly if they're direct from the sea or a river rather than a fish farm.

Soda bread The most famous Irish bread is made with bicarbonate of soda to make up for soft Irish flour that traditionally didn't take well to yeast.

The fry Who can say no to a plate of fried bacon, sausages, black pudding, white pudding, eggs and tomatoes? For the famous Ulster fry, common throughout the North, simply add fadge (potato bread).

AT A GLANCE

Area 84,421 sq km

Capitals Dublin (Republic of Ireland), Belfast (Northern Ireland)

Country code Republic of Ireland 353, Northern Ireland 44

Currency euro (€) in Republic of Ireland; pound sterling (£) in Northern Ireland

Emergency 112

Languages English, Irish Gaelic

Time Winter: Greenwich Mean Time (UTC/GMT+00:00); Summer (UTC/GMT+01:00)

Visas Schengen rules do not apply

Sleeping Price Ranges

The following price ranges are based on a double room with private bathroom in high season (Republic/Dublin/Northern Ireland).

€/£ less than €80/€150/£50

€€/££ €80–180/€150–250/£50–120

€€€/£££ more than €180/€250/£12

Eating Price Ranges

The following price ranges refer to the cost of a main course at dinner (Republic/Dublin/Northern Ireland).

€/£ less than €12/€15/£12

€€/££ €12–25/€15–28/£12–20

€€€/£££ more than €25/€28/£20

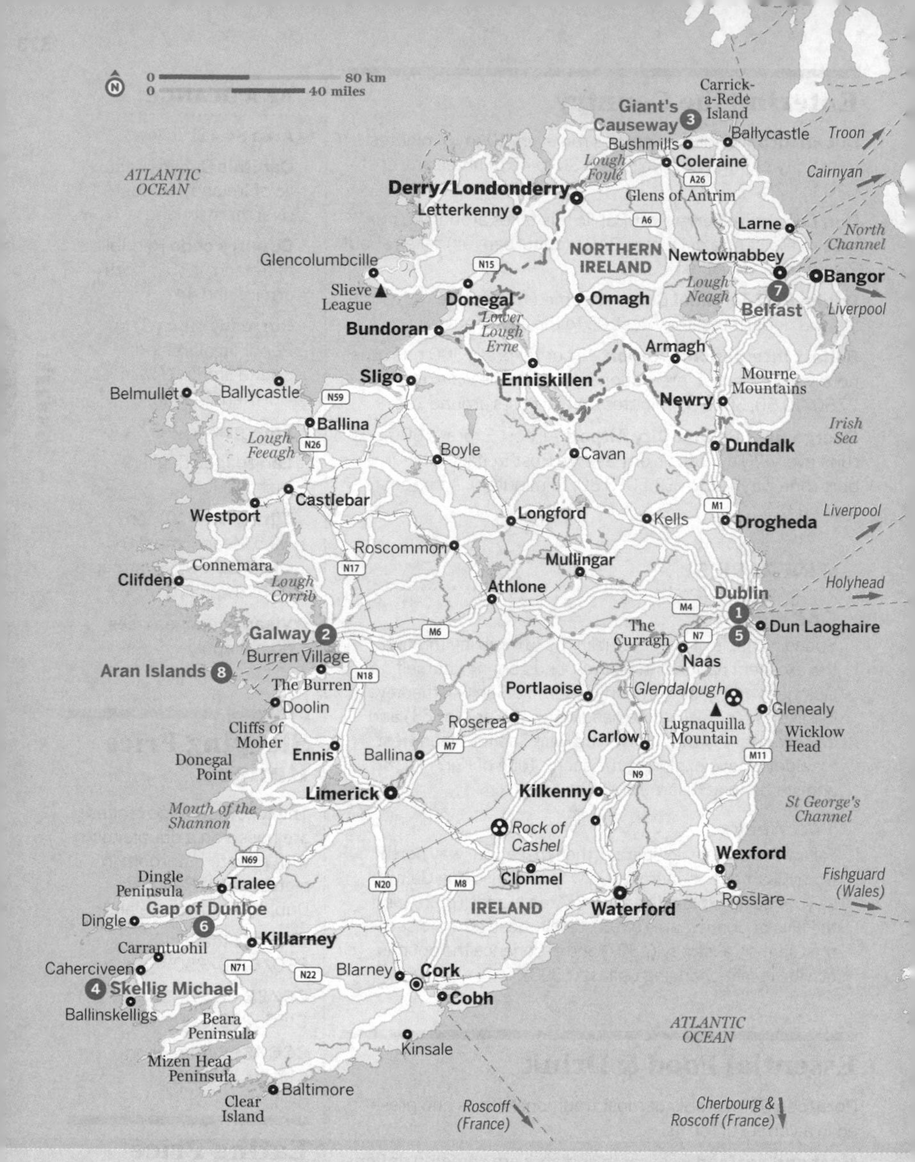

Ireland Highlights

❶ **Dublin** (p375) Meandering through museums, pubs and literary haunts.

❷ **Galway** (p389) Hanging out in bohemian Galway, with its hip cafes and live-music venues.

❸ **Giant's Causeway** (p397) Hiking along the Causeway Coast.

❹ **Skellig Michael** (p388) Taking a boat trip to the 6th-century monastery perched atop this wild rocky islet.

❺ **Irish pubs** Supping a pint of Guinness while tapping your toes to a live-music session.

❻ **Gap of Dunloe** (p387) Cycling through the spectacular lake and mountain scenery of the Gap of Dunloe.

❼ **Titanic Belfast** (p395) Discovering the industrial history of the city that built the famous ocean liner.

❽ **Aran Islands** (p392) Wandering the wild, limestone shores of the remote and craggy Aran Islands.

DUBLIN

POP 1.3 MILLION

Sultry rather than sexy, Dublin exudes the personality of a city that has managed to turn careworn into carefree. The halcyon days of the Celtic Tiger (the Irish economic boom of the late 1990s), when cash cascaded like a free-flowing waterfall, have long since disappeared, and the city has once again been forced to grind out a living. But Dubliners know how to enjoy life. They do so through their music, art and literature – cultural riches that Dubs often take for granted but generate immense pride. Dublin has world-class museums, superb restaurants and the best range of entertainment available anywhere in Ireland – and that's not including its pubs, the ubiquitous centre of the city's social life and an absolute must for any visitor. And should you wish to get away from it all, the city has a handful of seaside towns at its edges that make for wonderful day trips.

Sights

Dublin's relatively compact size means that the vast majority of sights – including most of the big hitters – are within walking distance of each other, on either side of the Liffey in the city centre. The exceptions are the Guinness Storehouse, the Irish Museum of Modern Art and Kilmainham Gaol, which are clustered together on the western edge of the city south of the river; they're easily reached by tram or bus, and conveniently they're also on all the the hop on, hop off bus itineraries, so you can take your time with each attraction. On the north side of the river, also west of the centre, the decorative arts branch of the National Museum is just a handful of stops away on the tram line.

★Trinity College HISTORIC BUILDING

(01-896 1000; www.tcd.ie; College Green; 8am-10pm; all city centre, Westmoreland or Trinity) FREE Ireland's most prestigious university is a 16th-century bucolic retreat in the heart of the city. Ambling about its cobbled squares, it's easy to imagine it in those far-off days when all good gentlemen (for they were only men until 1904) came equipped with a passion for philosophy and a love of empire. The student body is a lot more diverse these days, even if the look remains the same.

★National Museum of Ireland – Archaeology MUSEUM

(www.museum.ie; Kildare St; 10am-5pm Tue-Sat, 1-5pm Sun; all city centre) FREE Ireland's most important cultural institution was established in 1877 as the primary repository of the nation's archaeological treasures. These include the most famous of Ireland's crafted artefacts, the Ardagh Chalice and the Tara Brooch, dating from the 12th and 8th centuries respectively. They are part of the Treasury, itself part of Europe's finest collection of Bronze and Iron Age gold artefacts, and the most complete assemblage of medieval Celtic metalwork in the world.

★Guinness Storehouse BREWERY, MUSEUM

(www.guinness-storehouse.com; St James's Gate, South Market St; adult/child from €18.50/16, Connoisseur Experience €55; 9.30am-7pm Sep-Jun, 9am to 8pm Jul & Aug; ; 13, 21A, 40, 51B, 78, 78A, 123 from Fleet St, James's) The most popular visit in town is this multimedia homage to Guinness in a converted grain storehouse that is part of the 26-hectare brewery. Across its seven floors you'll discover everything about Guinness before getting to taste the brew in the top-floor Gravity Bar, with panoramic views. The floor directly below has a very good restaurant. Pre-booking your tickets online will save you time and money.

★Chester Beatty Library MUSEUM

(01-407 0750; www.cbl.ie; 10am-5pm Mon-Fri, 11am-5pm Sat & Sun Mar-Oct, 10am-5pm Tue-Fri, 11am-5pm Sat & Sun Nov-Feb; all city centre) FREE This world-famous library, in the grounds of **Dublin Castle** (01-645 8813; www.dublincastle.ie; Dame St; guided tours adult/child €12/6, self-guided tours €8/4; 9.45am-5.45pm, last admission 5.15pm; all city centre), houses the collection of mining engineer Sir Alfred Chester Beatty (1875–1968), bequeathed to the Irish State on his death. Spread over two floors, the breathtaking collection includes more than 20,000 manuscripts, rare books, miniature paintings, clay tablets, costumes and other objects of artistic, historical and aesthetic importance. Free tours run at 1pm Wednesdays, 2pm Saturdays and 3pm Sundays.

★Kilmainham Gaol MUSEUM

(01-453 5984; www.kilmainhamgaolmuseum.ie; Inchicore Rd; adult/child €9/5; 9am-7pm Jun-Aug, 9.30am-5.30pm Oct-Mar, 9am-6pm Apr, May & Sep; 69, 79 from Aston Quay, 13, 40 from O'Connell St) If you have *any* desire to understand Irish history – especially the long-running resistance to British rule – then a visit to this former prison is an absolute must. A threatening grey building, built in 1796, it's played a role in virtually every act of Ireland's painful

Dublin

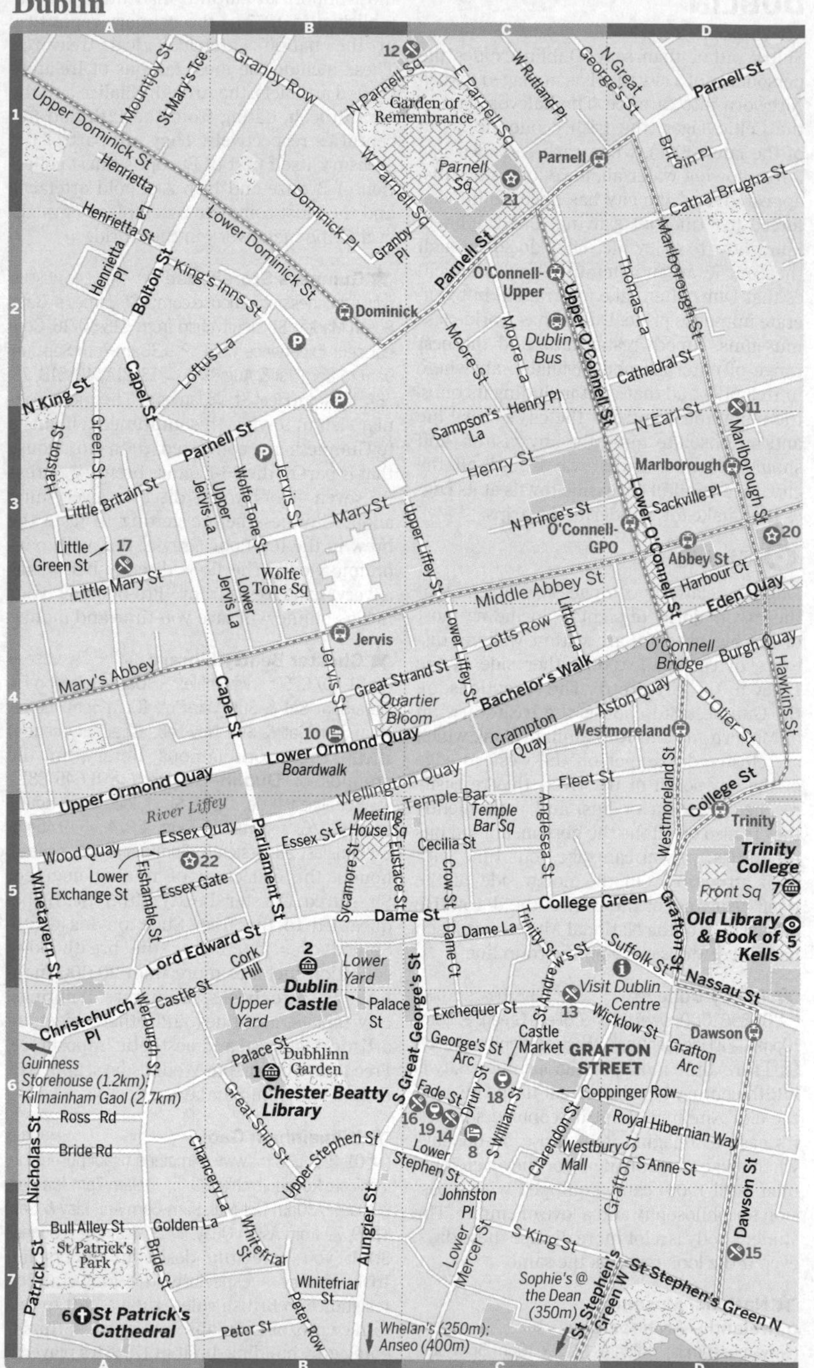
A
B
C
D
1
2
3
4
5
6
7
Mountjoy St
St Mary's Tce
Granby Row
12
N Parnell Sq
Garden of Remembrance
E Parnell Sq
W Rutland Pl
N Great George's St
Parnell St
Upper Dominick St
Henrietta La
Henrietta St
Henrietta Pl
Lower Dominick St
W Parnell Sq
Dominick Pl
Parnell Sq
21
Parnell
Britain Pl
Cathal Brugha St
Granby Pl
Parnell St
O'Connell-Upper
Thomas La
Marlborough St
Bolton St
King's Inns St
Dominick
Upper O'Connell St
Dublin Bus
Moore St
Moore La
Loftus La
Cathedral St
N King St
Capel St
Green St
Halston St
Parnell St
Sampson's La
Henry Pl
N Earl St
11
Marlborough
Marlborough St
Jervis St
Wolfe Tone St
Upper Jervis La
Henry St
Little Britain St
Mary St
Upper Liffey St
Lower O'Connell St
Sackville Pl
N Prince's St
O'Connell-GPO
20
Little Green St
17
Wolfe Tone Sq
Little Mary St
Lower Jervis La
Abbey St
Harbour Ct
Middle Abbey St
Eden Quay
Litton La
Jervis
Lotts Row
Lower Liffey St
O'Connell Bridge
Burgh Quay
Mary's Abbey
Jervis St
Great Strand St
Bachelor's Walk
Aston Quay
D'Olier St
Hawkins St
Quartier Bloom
Capel St
10
Crampton Quay
Westmoreland
Lower Ormond Quay
Boardwalk
Upper Ormond Quay
Wellington Quay
Fleet St
Westmoreland St
College St
River Liffey
Temple Bar
Temple Bar Sq
Trinity
Meeting House Sq
Essex Quay
Essex St E
Cecilia St
Anglesea St
Trinity College
Wood Quay
22
Lower Exchange St
Fishamble St
Essex Gate
Parliament St
Sycamore St
Eustace St
Crow St
Front Sq
7
Winetavern St
Dame St
College Green
Grafton St
Old Library & Book of Kells
5
Lord Edward St
Dame La
Dame Ct
Trinity St
St Andrew's St
Suffolk St
Nassau St
Cork Hill
2
Lower Yard
Dublin Castle
Visit Dublin Centre
Christchurch Pl
Castle St
Werburgh St
Upper Yard
Palace St
S Great George's St
Exchequer St
13
St Andrew's St
Wicklow St
Dawson
Castle Market
George's St Arc
GRAFTON STREET
Grafton Arc
Guinness Storehouse (1.2km); Kilmainham Gaol (2.7km)
Palace St
Dubhlinn Garden
1
Chester Beatty Library
Fade St
Drury St
18
Coppinger Row
16
19
14
8
S William St
Clarendon St
Royal Hibernian Way
Ross Rd
Great Ship St
Bride Rd
Chancery La
Upper Stephen St
Lower Stephen St
Westbury Mall
S Anne St
Grafton St
Dawson St
Nicholas St
Johnston Pl
Aungier St
Bull Alley St
Golden La
Whitefriar St
St Patrick's Park
Lower Mercer St
S King St
15
Patrick St
Bride St
Whitefriar St
St Stephen's Green N
Sophie's @ the Dean (350m)
St Stephen's Green W
6
St Patrick's Cathedral
Peter Row
Peter St
Whelan's (250m); Anseo (400m)

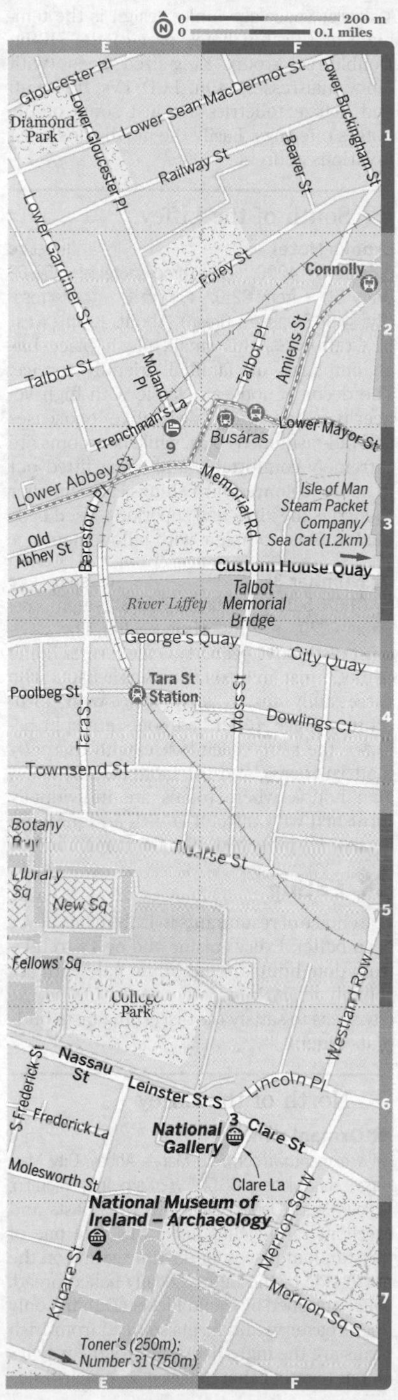

Dublin

Top Sights

path to independence, and even today, despite closing in 1924, it still has the power to chill. Book online as far in advance as possible to get your preferred visiting time.

National Gallery MUSEUM

(www.nationalgallery.ie; W Merrion Sq; ⌚9.15am-5.30pm Tue-Wed, Fri & Sat, to 8.30pm Thu, 11am-5.30pm Sun-Mon; 🚌4, 7, 8, 39A, 46A from city centre) FREE A magnificent Caravaggio and a breathtaking collection of works by Jack B Yeats – William Butler's younger brother – are the main reasons to visit the National Gallery, but not the only ones. Its excellent collection is strong in Irish art, and there are also high-quality collections of every major European school of painting.

St Patrick's Cathedral CATHEDRAL

(☎01-453 9472; www.stpatrickscathedral.ie; St Patrick's Close; adult/student €8/7; ⌚9.30am-5pm Mon-Fri, 9am-6pm Sat, 9-10.30am, 12.30-2.30pm & 4.30-6pm Sun Mar-Oct, shorter hours rest of year; 🚌50, 50A, 56A from Aston Quay, 54, 54A from Burgh Quay) Ireland's largest church, St Patrick's Cathedral was built between 1191 and 1270 on the site of an earlier church that had stood since the 5th century. It was here that St Patrick himself reputedly baptised the local Celtic chieftains, making this bit of ground some fairly sacred turf: the well in question is in the adjacent St Patrick's Park, which was once a slum but is now a lovely spot to sit and take a load off.

Sleeping

A surge in tourist numbers and a relative lack of beds means hotel prices are higher than they were during the Celtic Tiger years. There are good midrange options north of the Liffey, but the biggest spread of accommodation is south of the river, from midrange Georgian townhouses to the city's top hotels. Budget travellers rely on the selection of decent hostels.

North of the Liffey

★Isaacs Hostel HOSTEL €

(01-855 6215; www.isaacs.ie; 2-5 Frenchman's Lane; dm/tw from €22/99; @ ; all city centre, Connolly) The northside's best hostel – actually for atmosphere alone it's the best in town – is in a 200-year-old wine vault just around the corner from the main bus station. With summer barbecues, live music in the lounge, internet access, colourful dorms and even a sauna, this terrific place generates consistently good reviews from backpackers and other travellers.

Morrison Hotel HOTEL €€€

(01-887 2400; www.morrisonhotel.ie; Lower Ormond Quay; r €350; P @ ; all city centre, Jervis) Space-age funky design is the template at this hip hotel, part of the Hilton Doubletree group. King-sized beds (with fancy mattresses), 40in LCD TVs, free wi-fi and deluxe toiletries are just some of the hotel's offerings. Easily the northside's most luxurious address.

South of the Liffey

Brooks Hotel HOTEL €€

(01-670 4000; www.brookshotel.ie; 59-62 Drury St; r from €210; P @ ; all cross-city, St Stephen's Green) About 120m west of Grafton St, this small, plush place has an emphasis on familial, friendly service. The decor is nouveau classic with high veneer-panelled walls, decorative bookcases and old-fashioned sofas, while bedrooms are extremely comfortable and come fitted out in subtly coloured furnishings. The clincher though is the king- and superking-sized beds in all rooms, complete with pillow menu.

★Number 31 GUESTHOUSE €€

(01-676 5011; www.number31.ie; 31 Leeson Close; r from €220; P ; all city centre) The city's most distinctive property is the former home of modernist architect Sam Stephenson, who successfully fused 1960s style with 18th-century grace. Its 21 bedrooms are split between the retro coach house, with its coolly modern rooms, and the more elegant Georgian house, where rooms are individually furnished with tasteful French antiques and big, comfortable beds. Breakfast included.

Eating

The choice of restaurants in Dublin has never been better. Every cuisine and every trend – from doughnuts on the run to kale with absolutely everything – is catered for, as the city seeks to satisfy the discerning taste buds of its diners.

North of the Liffey

★Oxmantown CAFE €

(www.oxmantown.com; 16 Mary's Abbey, City Markets; sandwiches €6.50; 8am-4pm Mon-Fri; Four Courts, Jervis) Delicious breakfasts and excellent sandwiches make this cafe one of the standout places for daytime eating on the north side of the Liffey. Locally baked bread, coffee supplied by Cloud Picker (Dublin's only microroastery) and meats sourced from Irish farms are the ingredients, but it's the way it's all put together that makes it so worthwhile.

BOOK OF KELLS

The world-famous **Book of Kells** (www.tcd.ie; Library Sq; adult/student/family €11/11/28, fast-track €14/11/28; 8.30am-5pm Mon-Sat, 9.30am-5pm Sun May-Sep, 9.30am-5pm Mon-Sat, noon-4.30pm Sun Oct-Apr; all city centre, Westmoreland or Trinity) contains the four gospels of the New Testament, written in Latin, as well as prefaces, summaries and other text. If it were merely words, the *Book of Kells* would simply be a very old book – it's the extensive and amazingly complex illustrations (the illuminations) that make it so wonderful. The superbly decorated opening initials are only part of the story, for the book has smaller illustrations between the lines.

101 Talbot MODERN IRISH €€

(www.101talbot.ie; 100-102 Talbot St; mains €17-24; noon-3pm & 5-10pm Tue-Thu, to 11pm Fri-Sat; all city centre) This Dublin classic has expertly resisted every trendy wave and has been a stalwart of good Irish cooking since opening more than two decades ago. Its speciality is traditional meat-and-two-veg dinners but with Mediterranean influences: pan-fried sea bass with garlic new potatoes; squid and chorizo salad; and confit duck with peach and goat's cheese salad. Superb.

★ **Chapter One** MODERN IRISH €€€

(01-873 2266; www.chapteronerestaurant.com; 18 N Parnell Sq; 2-course lunch €36.50, 4-course dinner €80; 12.30-2pm Fri, 5-10.30pm Tue-Sat; 3, 10, 11, 13, 16, 19, 22 from city centre) Flawless haute cuisine and a relaxed, welcoming atmosphere make this Michelin-starred restaurant in the basement of the Dublin Writers Museum our choice for the best dinner experience in town. The food is French-inspired contemporary Irish; the menus change regularly; and the service is top-notch. The three-course pre-theatre menu (€42) is great if you're going to the **Gate** (01-874 4045; www.gatetheatre.ie; 1 Cavendish Row; performances 7.30pm Tue-Fri, 2.30pm & 7.30pm Sat; all city centre) around the corner.

South of the Liffey

Cornucopia VEGETARIAN €

(www.cornucopia.ie; 19-20 Wicklow St; salads €6-10, mains €13-15; 8.30am-9pm Mon, to 10pm Tue-Sat, noon-9pm Sun; ; all city centre) Dublin's best-known vegetarian restaurant is a terrific eatery that serves three sizes of wholesome salads, sandwiches, and a selection of hot main courses from a daily changing menu. There's live musical accompaniment on Thursday and Friday evenings. The 2nd-floor dining-room windows to the street below are good spots for people-watching.

Fade Street Social MODERN IRISH €€

(01-604 0066; www.fadestreetsocial.com; 4-6 Fade St; mains €20-36, tapas €6-17; 5-10.30pm Mon-Wed, 12.30-3pm & 5-10.30pm Thu, to 11pm Fri-Sat, to 10.30pm Sun; ; all city centre) Two eateries in one, courtesy of renowned chef Dylan McGrath: at the front, the buzzy tapas bar, which serves up gourmet bites from a beautiful open kitchen. At the back, the more muted restaurant specialises in Irish cuts of meat – from veal to rabbit – served with home-grown, organic vegetables. There's a bar upstairs too. Reservations recommended.

Sophie's @ the Dean ITALIAN €€

(01-607 8100; www.sophies.ie; 33 Harcourt St; mains €14-34; 7am-10.30pm Mon-Wed, to 1.30am Thu-Fri, 8am-1.30am Sat, 8am-10.30pm Sun; 10, 11, 13, 14, 15A, Harcourt) There's perhaps no better setting in all of Dublin – a top-floor glasshouse restaurant with superb views of the city – in which to enjoy this quirky take on Italian cuisine. Delicious pizzas come with nontraditional toppings (pulled pork with barbecue sauce?) and the fillet steak is done to perfection. A good spot for breakfast too.

★ **Greenhouse** SCANDINAVIAN €€€

(01-676 7015; www.thegreenhouserestaurant.ie; Dawson St; 2-/3-course lunch menu €45/55, 4-/6-course dinner menu €110/129; noon-2pm & 6-9.30pm Tue-Sat; all city centre, St Stephen's Green) Chef Mickael Viljanen might just be the most exciting chef working in Ireland today thanks to his Scandi-influenced tasting menus, which have made this arguably Dublin's best restaurant. Wine selections are in the capable hands of Julie Dupouy, who in 2017 was voted third-best sommelier in the world, just weeks before the restaurant was awarded a Michelin star. Reservations necessary.

Drinking & Nightlife

If there's one constant about life in Dublin, it's that Dubliners will always take a drink. Come hell or high water, the city's pubs will never be short of customers, and we suspect that exploring a variety of Dublin's legendary pubs and bars ranks pretty high on the list of reasons you're here.

★ **Toner's** PUB

(01-676 3090; www.tonerspub.ie; 139 Lower Baggot St; 10.30am-11.30pm Mon-Thu, to 12.30am Fri & Sat, 11.30am-11.30pm Sun; 7, 46 from city centre) Toner's, with its stone floors and antique snugs, has changed little over the years and is the closest thing you'll get to a country pub in the heart of the city. Next door, Toner's Yard is a comfortable outside space. The shelves and drawers are reminders that it once doubled as a grocery shop.

★ **Grogan's Castle Lounge** PUB

(www.facebook.com/groganscastlelounge; 15 S William St; 10.30am-11.30pm Mon-Thu, to 12.30am Fri & Sat, 12.30-11pm Sun; all city centre) Known simply as Grogan's (after the original owner), this is a city-centre institution. It has long been a favourite haunt of Dublin's writers and painters, as well as others from the alternative bohemian set, who enjoy a fine Guinness while they wait for that inevitable moment when they're discovered.

No Name Bar BAR

(www.nonamebardublin.com; 3 Fade St; ⌚1.30-11.30pm Mon-Wed, to 1am Thu, 12.30-2.30am Fri & Sat, noon-11pm Sun; 🚌all city centre) A low-key entrance just next to the trendy French restaurant **L'Gueuleton** (☎01-675 3708; www.lgueuleton.com; 1 Fade St; mains €20-31; ⌚12.30-4pm & 5.30-10pm Mon-Wed, to 10.30pm Thu-Sat, noon-4pm & 5.30-9pm Sun) leads upstairs to one of the nicest bar spaces in town, consisting of three huge rooms in a restored Victorian townhouse plus a sizeable heated patio area for smokers. There's no sign or a name – folks just refer to it as the No Name Bar.

Anseo BAR

(18 Lower Camden St; ⌚4-11.30pm Mon-Thu, to 12.30am Fri & Sat, to 11pm Sun; 🚌14, 15, 65, 83) Unpretentious, unaffected and incredibly popular, this cosy alternative bar – which is pronounced 'an-*shuh*', the Irish for 'here' – is a favourite with those who live by the credo that to try too hard is far worse than not trying at all. The pub's soundtrack is an eclectic mix; you're as likely to hear Peggy Lee as Lee Perry.

☆ Entertainment

Believe it or not, there is life beyond the pub. There are comedy clubs and classical concerts, recitals and readings, marionettes and music – lots of music. The other great Dublin treat is the theatre, where you can enjoy a light-hearted musical alongside the more serious stuff by Beckett, Yeats and O'Casey – not to mention a host of new talent.

Smock Alley Theatre THEATRE

(☎01-677 0014; www.smockalley.com; 6-7 Exchange St; 🚌all city centre) One of the city's most diverse theatres is hidden in this beautifully restored 17th-century building. It boasts a diverse program of events (expect anything from opera to murder mystery nights, puppet shows and Shakespeare) and many events also come with a dinner option.

Whelan's LIVE MUSIC

(☎01-478 0766; www.whelanslive.com; 25 Wexford St; 🚌16, 122 from city centre) Perhaps the city's most beloved live-music venue is this mid-sized room attached to a traditional bar. This is the singer-songwriter's spiritual home: when they're done pouring out the contents of their hearts on stage, you can find them filling up in the bar along with their fans.

Abbey Theatre THEATRE

(☎01-878 7222; www.abbeytheatre.ie; Lower Abbey St; 🚌all city centre, 🚋Abbey) Ireland's national theatre was founded by WB Yeats in 1904 and was a central player in the development of a consciously native cultural identity. In 2021 it appointed Caitríona McLaughlin and Mark O'Brien as its new directors, and they have promised a program that will promote new voices and new perspectives.

ℹ Information

A handful of official-looking tourism offices on Grafton and O'Connell Sts are actually privately run enterprises where members pay to be included.

Visit Dublin Centre (www.visitdublin.com; 25 Suffolk St; ⌚9am-5.30pm Mon-Sat, 10.30am-3pm Sun; 🚌all city centre) The main tourist information centre, with free maps, guides and itinerary planning, plus booking services for accommodation, attractions and events.

Grafton Medical Centre (☎01-671 2122; www.graftonmedical.ie; 34 Grafton St; ⌚8.30am-6pm Mon-Thu, to 5pm Fri; 🚌all city centre) One-stop shop with male and female doctors as well as physiotherapists. You'll usually need to give a day's advance notice, but same-day appointments are often available.

Hickey's Pharmacy (☎01-679 0467; 21 Grafton St; ⌚8am-8pm Mon-Wed & Fri, to 8.30pm Thu, 9am-8pm Sat, 10am-7pm Sun; 🚌all city centre) Well-stocked pharmacy on Grafton St.

St James's Hospital (☎01-410 3000; www.stjames.ie; James's St; 🚋James's) Dublin's main 24-hour accident and emergency department.

ℹ Getting There & Away

AIR

Dublin Airport (p400), about 13km north of the city centre, is Ireland's major international gateway, with direct flights from Europe, North America and Asia. Most international flights (including most US flights) use Terminal 2; Ryanair and select others use Terminal 1.

BOAT

The **Dublin Port Terminal** (☎01-855 2222; Alexandra Rd; 🚌53 from Talbot St) is 3km northeast of the city centre.

Irish Ferries (☎0818 300 400; www.irishferries.com; Ferryport, Terminal Rd South) Holyhead in Wales (€200 return, three hours)

Isle of Man Steam Packet Company/Sea Cat (www.steam-packet.com; Terminal 1, Dublin Port; ⌚4.30am-10pm; 🚌53 from city centre) Isle of Man (€110 return, 1½ hours)

P&O Irish Sea (☎01-686 9467; www.poferries.com; Terminal 3) Liverpool (€180 return, 8½ hours or four hours on fast boat)

BUS

Dublin's central bus station, **Busáras** (☎01-836 6111; www.buseireann.ie; Store St; Connolly) is just north of the river behind the Custom House. It has different-sized luggage lockers costing from €6 to €10 per day.

It's possible to combine bus and ferry tickets from major UK centres to Dublin on the bus network. The journey between London and Dublin takes about 12 hours and costs from €29 return (but note it's €42 for one way). For details in London, contact **Eurolines** (☎01-836 6111; https://eurolines.buseireann.ie).

From Dublin, Bus Éireann (p401) buses serve the whole national network, including buses to towns and cities in Northern Ireland.

TRAIN

All trains in the Republic are run by Irish Rail (p401). Dublin has two main train stations. **Heuston Station** (☎01-836 6222; Heuston), on the western side of town near the Liffey; and **Connolly Station** (☎01-703 2359; Connolly, Connolly Station), a short walk northeast of Busáras, behind the Custom House.

Connolly Station is a stop on the DART line into town; the Luas Red Line serves both Connolly and Heuston stations.

Getting Around

TO/FROM THE AIRPORT

Aircoach (www.aircoach.ie) Buses every 10 to 15 minutes between 6am and midnight, then hourly from midnight until 6am (one way/return €7/12).

Airlink Express (☎01-873 4222; www.dublinbus.ie; one way/return €7/12) Bus 747 runs every 10 to 20 minutes from 5.45am to 12.30am between the airport, central bus station (Busáras) and the Dublin Bus Office on Upper O'Connell St. Bus 757 runs every 15 to 30 minutes from 5am to 12.25am between the airport and various stops in the city, including Grand Canal Dock, Merrion Sq and Camden St.

Taxi There is a taxi rank directly outside the arrivals concourse of both terminals. It should take about 45 minutes to get into the city centre and cost about €25, including an initial charge of €3.60 (€4 between 10pm and 8am and on Sundays and bank holidays). Make sure the meter is switched on.

BICYCLE

Typical rental for a hybrid or touring bike is around €25 a day or €140 a week.

Dublinbikes (www.dublinbikes.ie) A public bicycle-rental scheme with more than 100 stations spread across the city centre. Purchase a €10 smart card (as well as pay a credit-card deposit of €150) or a three-day card online or at any station before 'freeing' a bike for use, which is then free of charge to use for the first 30 minutes and €0.50 for each half-hour thereafter.

Cycleways (www.cycleways.com; 31 Ormond Quay Lwr; 8.30am-6pm Mon-Fri, 10am-6pm Sat; all city centre) An excellent bike shop that rents out hybrids and touring bikes during the summer months (May to September).

PUBLIC TRANSPORT

Bus

The **Dublin Bus Office** (☎01-873 4222; www.dublinbus.ie; 59 Upper O'Connell St; 9am-5.30pm Tue-Fri, to 2pm Sat, 8.30am-5.30pm Mon; all city centre) has free single-route timetables for all its services. Buses run from around 6am (some start at 5.30am) to about 11.30pm.

Fares are calculated according to stages (stops):

Stages	Cash Fare (€)	Leap Card Fare (€)
1-3	2.10	1.50
4-13	2.85	2.15
more than 13	3.30	2.60

A **Leap Card** (www.leapcard.ie), available from most newsagents, is not just cheaper but also more convenient as you don't have to worry about tendering exact fares. Register the card online and top it up with whatever amount you need. When you board a bus, DART, Luas (light rail) or suburban train, just swipe your card and the fare is automatically deducted. If paying with cash, you will need to tender the exact fare; otherwise, you will get a receipt for reimbursement, which is only possible at the Dublin Bus main office.

If you're travelling within the College Green Bus Corridor (roughly between Parnell Sq to the north and St Stephen's Green to the south) you can use the €0.50 special City Centre fare.

Train

Dublin Area Rapid Transport (DART; ☎01-836 6222; www.irishrail.ie) provides quick rail access to the coast as far north as Howth (about 30 minutes) and as far south as Greystones in County Wicklow. Pearse and Tara St stations are convenient for central Dublin south of the Liffey, and Connolly Station for north of the Liffey. Single fares cost €2.50 to €6; a one-day pass costs €12.

Tram

The **Luas** (www.luas.ie) light-rail system has two lines: the green line (running every five to 15 minutes) connects St Stephen's Green with Sandyford in south Dublin via Ranelagh and Dundrum; and the red line (every 20 minutes) runs from the Point Village to Tallaght via the north quays and Heuston Station. The new cross-city line connects the green and red lines with a route from

St Stephen's Green through Dawson St, around Trinity College and over the river. A typical short-hop fare (around four stops) is €2.50.

Taxi

All taxi fares begin with a flagfall of €3.60 (€4 from 10pm to 8am), followed by €1.10 per km thereafter (€1.40 from 10pm to 8am). For taxi service, call **National Radio Cabs** (01-677 2222; www.nrc.ie).

THE SOUTHEAST

Kilkenny

POP 26,500

Kilkenny is the Ireland of many visitors' imaginations. Built from dark-grey limestone flecked with fossil seashells, Kilkenny (from the Gaelic 'Cill Chainnigh', meaning the Church of St Canice) is also known as 'the marble city'. Its picturesque 'Medieval Mile' of narrow lanes and historical buildings strung between castle and cathedral along the bank of the River Nore is one of the southeast's biggest tourist draws. It's worth braving the crowds to soak up the atmosphere of one of Ireland's creative crucibles – Kilkenny is a centre for arts and crafts, and home to a host of fine restaurants, cafes, pubs and shops.

Sights

★Kilkenny Castle CASTLE

(056-770 4100; www.kilkennycastle.ie; The Parade; adult/child €8/4; 9am-5.30pm Jun-Aug, 9.30am-5.30pm Apr, May & Sep, 9.30am-5pm Mar, 9.30am-4.30pm Oct-Feb) Rising above the River Nore, Kilkenny Castle is one of Ireland's most visited heritage sites. Stronghold of the powerful Butler family, it has a history dating back to the 12th century, though much of its present look dates from Victorian times.

During the winter months (November to January) visits are by 40-minute guided tours only, which shift to self-guided tours from February to October. Highlights include the Long Gallery with its painted roof and carved marble fireplace. There's an excellent tearoom in the former castle kitchens.

★St Canice's Cathedral CATHEDRAL

(056-776 4971; www.stcanicescathedral.ie; Coach Rd; cathedral/round tower/combined adult €4.50/4/7, child €3.50/4/6.50; 9am-6pm Mon-Sat, 1-6pm Sun Jun-Aug, shorter hours Sep-May) Ireland's second-largest medieval cathedral (after St Patrick's in Dublin) has a long and fascinating history. The first monastery was built here in the 6th century by St Canice, Kilkenny's patron saint. The present structure dates from the 13th to 16th centuries, with extensive 19th-century reconstruction, its interior housing ancient grave slabs and the tombs of Kilkenny Castle's Butler dynasty. Outside stands a 30m-high round tower, one of only two in Ireland that you can climb.

National Design & Craft Gallery GALLERY

(056-779 6147; www.ndcg.ie; Castle Yard; 10am-5.30pm Tue-Sat, from 11am Sun) FREE Contemporary Irish crafts are showcased at these imaginative galleries, set in former stables across the road from Kilkenny Castle, next to the shops of the **Kilkenny Design Centre** (056-772 2118; www.kilkennydesign.com; 9am-6pm). Ceramics dominate, but exhibits often feature furniture, jewellery and weaving from the members of the Crafts Council of Ireland. Family days are held the third Saturday of every month, with a tour of the gallery and free hands-on workshops for children. For additional workshops and events, check the website.

Festivals & Events

Kilkenny hosts several world-class events throughout the year, attracting thousands of revellers.

Kilkenny Rhythm & Roots MUSIC

(www.kilkennyroots.com; Apr-May) More than 30 pubs and other venues participate in hosting this major music festival in late April/early May, with an emphasis on country and 'old-time' American roots music.

Kilkenny Arts Festival ART

(www.kilkennyarts.ie; Aug) In August the city comes alive with theatre, cinema, music, literature, visual arts, children's events and street spectacles for 10 action-packed days.

Sleeping

Kilkenny Tourist Hostel HOSTEL €

(056-776 3541; www.kilkennyhostel.ie; 35 Parliament St; dm/tw/q from €18/48/88; @) Inside an ivy-covered 1770s Georgian townhouse, this fairly standard 60-bed IHH hostel has a sitting room warmed by an open fireplace, and a timber- and leadlight-panelled dining room adjoining the self-catering kitchen. Excellent location, but a place for relaxing rather than partying.

Celtic House B&B €
(☎056-776 2249; www.celtic-house-bandb.com; 18 Michael St; d from €85;) Artist and author Angela Byrne extends one of Ireland's warmest welcomes at this homey and comfortable B&B. Some of the brightly decorated bedrooms have sky-lit bathrooms, others have views of the castle, and Angela's landscapes adorn many of the walls. Book ahead.

★**Rosquil House** GUESTHOUSE €€
(☎056-772 1419; www.rosquilhouse.com; Castlecomer Rd; d/tr/f from €95/120/130, 2-person apt from €80; P) Rooms at this immaculately maintained guesthouse are decorated with dark-wood furniture and pretty paisley fabrics, while the guest lounge is similarly tasteful with sink-into sofas, brass-framed mirrors and leafy plants. The breakfast is above average, with homemade granola and fluffy omelettes. There's also a well-equipped and comfortable self-catering apartment (minimum three-night stay).

Eating & Drinking

Gourmet Store SANDWICHES €
(☎056-777 1727; www.facebook.com/gourmetstorekk; 56 High St; sandwiches €4.50; ⊙8am-5.30pm Mon-Sat) In this crowded little deli, takeaway sandwiches are assembled from choice imported meats and cheeses (plus a few top-notch local varieties).

★**Foodworks** BISTRO, CAFE €€
(☎056-777 7696; www.foodworks.ie; 7 Parliament St; mains €17.50-26.50, 3-course dinner menus €26-29; ⊙noon-9pm Wed & Thu, to 9.30pm Fri & Sat, to 5pm Sun;) The owners of this cool and casual bistro keep their own pigs and grow their own salad leaves, so it would be churlish not to try their pork belly stuffed with black pudding, or confit pig's trotter – and you'll be glad you did. Delicious food, excellent coffee and friendly service make this a justifiably popular venue; it's best to book a table.

★**Kyteler's Inn** PUB
(☎056-772 1064; www.kytelersinn.com; 27 St Kieran's St; ⊙11am-11.30pm Mon-Fri, to 2am Fri & Sat, 12.15pm-midnight Sun) Dame Alice Kyteler's old house was built back in 1224 and has seen its share of history: she was charged with witchcraft in 1323. Today the rambling bar includes the original building, complete with vaulted ceiling and arches. There is a beer garden, a courtyard and a large upstairs room for live bands (nightly from March to October), ranging from trad to blues.

Entertainment

Watergate Theatre THEATRE
(☎box office 056-776 1674; www.watergatetheatre.com; Parliament St) Kilkenny's top theatre venue hosts drama, comedy and musical performances. If you're wondering why intermission lasts 18 minutes, it's so patrons can nip across to **John Cleere's pub** (☎056-776 2573; www.cleeres.com; 28 Parliament St; ⊙noon-12.30am) for a pint.

Information

Kilkenny Tourist Office (☎056-775 1500; www.visitkilkenny.ie; Rose Inn St; ⊙9am-5pm Mon-Sat, 10am-4pm Sun) Stocks guides and walking maps. Located in Shee Alms House, dating from 1582 and built in local stone by benefactor Sir Richard Shee to help the poor.

Getting There & Away

BUS

Bus Éireann (p401) and DublinCoach (www.dublincoach.ie) services stop (Dublin Rd) at the train station and on Ormonde Rd (nearer the town centre); JJ Kavanagh (www.jjkavanagh.ie) buses to Dublin airport stop on Ormonde Rd only.

Cork (€15, 2½ hours, every two hours)

Dublin (€19, 3½ hours, four daily) Bus Éireann X4.

TRAIN

Kilkenny's **MacDonagh train station** (Dublin Rd) is a 10-minute walk northeast of the town centre. Trains run to Dublin Heuston (€13, 1½ hours, six daily) and Waterford (€7.50, 40 minutes, seven daily).

THE SOUTHWEST

Cork

POP 208,670

Ireland's second city is first in every important respect – at least according to the locals, who cheerfully refer to it as the 'real capital of Ireland'. The compact city centre is surrounded by interesting waterways and is chock-full of great restaurants fed by arguably the best foodie scene in the country.

Sights

★**English Market** MARKET
(www.englishmarket.ie; main entrance Princes St; ⊙8am-6pm Mon-Sat) It could just as easily be called the Victorian Market for its ornate vaulted ceilings and columns, but the English Market is a true gem, no matter what

Cork

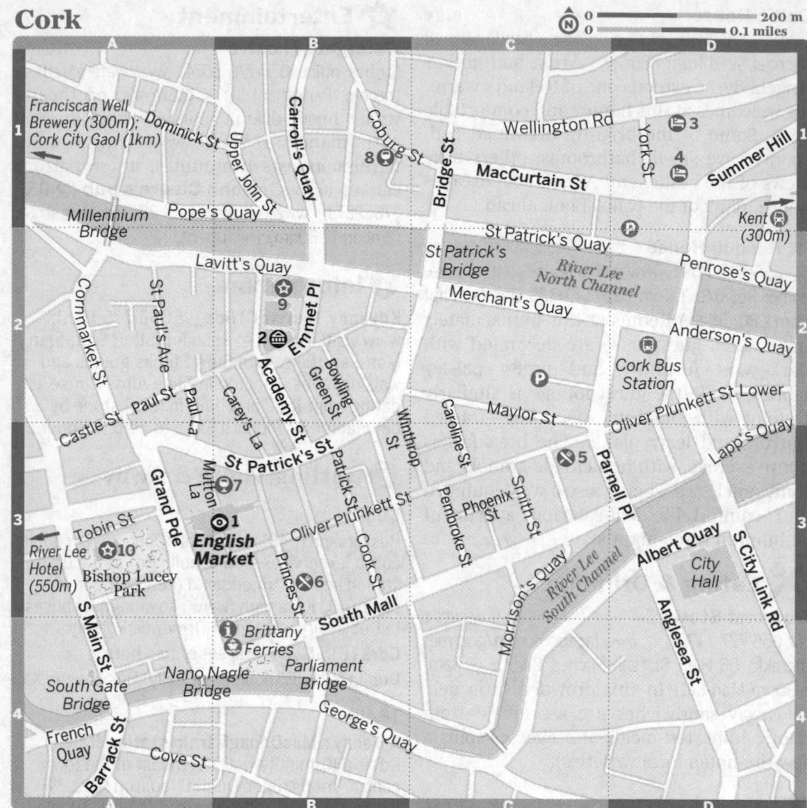

Cork

Top Sights
1 English Market B3

Sights
2 Crawford Art Gallery B2

Sleeping
3 Auburn House D1
4 Brú Bar & Hostel D1

Eating
Farmgate Cafe .... (see 1)
5 Market Lane C3
6 Nash 19 .... B3

Drinking & Nightlife
7 Mutton Lane Inn B3
8 Sin É B1

Entertainment
9 Cork Opera House B2
Half Moon Theatre .... (see 9)
10 Triskel Arts Centre A3

you name it. Scores of vendors set up colourful and photogenic displays of the region's very best local produce, including meat, fish, fruit, cheeses and takeaway food. On a sunny day, take your lunch to nearby Bishop Lucey Park, a popular alfresco eating spot.

★Cork City Gaol MUSEUM

(☎021-430 5022; www.corkcitygaol.com; Convent Ave; adult/child €10/6; ⌚9.30am-5pm Apr-Sep, 10am-4pm Oct-Mar) This imposing former prison is well worth a visit, if only to get a sense of how awful life was for prisoners a century ago. An audio tour (€2 extra) guides you around the restored cells, which feature models of suffering prisoners and sadistic-looking guards. Take a bus to UCC, and from there walk north along Mardyke Walk, cross the river and follow the signs uphill (10 minutes).

Crawford Art Gallery GALLERY

(☎021-480 5042; www.crawfordartgallery.ie; Emmet Pl; ⌚10am-5pm Mon-Wed, Fri & Sat, to 8pm Thu, 11am-4pm Sun) FREE Cork's public gallery houses a small but excellent permanent collection covering the 17th century through to the modern day. Highlights include works by Sir John Lavery, Jack B Yeats and Nathaniel Hone, and a room devoted to Irish women artists from 1886 to 1978 – don't miss the pieces by Mainie Jellet and Evie Hone.

Sleeping & Eating

Brú Bar & Hostel HOSTEL €

(021-455 9667; www.bruhostel.com; 57 MacCurtain St; dm/tw from €20/57;) This buzzing hostel has its own internet cafe, with free access for guests, and a fantastic bar, popular with backpackers and locals alike. The dorms (each with a bathroom) have four to six beds and are clean and stylish – ask for one on the upper floors to avoid bar noise. Breakfast is included.

★**Auburn House** B&B €€

(021-450 8555; www.auburnguesthouse.com; 3 Garfield Tce, Wellington Rd; s/d/tr €58/90/135;) There's a warm family welcome at this neat B&B, which has smallish but well-kept rooms brightened by window boxes. Try to bag one of the back rooms, which are quieter and have sweeping views over the city. Breakfast includes vegetarian choices, and the location near the fun of MacCurtain St is a plus.

★**River Lee Hotel** HOTEL €€€

(021-425 2700; www.doylecollection.com; Western Rd; r from €185;) This modern riverside hotel brings a touch of luxury to the city centre. It has gorgeous public areas with huge sofas, a designer fireplace, a stunning five-storey glass-walled atrium and superb service. There are well-equipped bedrooms (nice and quiet at the back, but request a corner room for extra space) and possibly the best breakfast buffet in Ireland.

★**Farmgate Cafe** CAFE, BISTRO €

(021-427 8134; www.farmgate.ie; Princes St, English Market; mains €8-14; 8.30am-5pm Mon-Sat) An unmissable experience at the heart of the English Market (p383), the Farmgate is perched on a balcony overlooking the food stalls below, the source of all that fresh local produce on your plate – everything from crab and oysters to the lamb in your Irish stew. Go up the stairs and turn left for table service, or right for counter service.

★**Market Lane** IRISH, INTERNATIONAL €€

(021-427 4710; www.marketlane.ie; 5 Oliver Plunkett St; mains €12-28; noon-9.30pm Mon-Wed, to 10pm Thu, to 10.30pm Fri & Sat, 1-9.30pm Sun;) It's always hopping at this bright corner bistro. The menu is broad and hearty, changing to reflect what's fresh at the English Market: perhaps roast cod with seaweed butter sauce, or pea and barley risotto with goat's cheese. No reservations for fewer than six diners; sip a drink at the bar till a table is free. Lots of wines by the glass.

★**Nash 19** INTERNATIONAL €€

(021-427 0880; www.nash19.com; Princes St; mains €10-17; 7.30am-4pm Mon-Fri, from 8.30am Sat) A superb bistro and deli where locally sourced food is honoured at breakfast and lunch, either sit-in or takeaway. Fresh scones draw crowds early; daily lunch specials (soups, salads, desserts etc), free-range chicken pie and platters of smoked fish from **Frank Hederman** (021-481 1089; www.frankhederman.com; Belvelly; free for individuals, charge for groups; by reservation 10am-5pm Mon-Fri) keep them coming for lunch – the Producers Plate, a sampler of local produce, is sensational.

Drinking & Nightlife

In Cork pubs, locally brewed Murphy's and Beamish stouts, not Guinness, are the preferred pints.

Given the city's big student population, the small selection of nightclubs does a roaring trade. Entry ranges from free to €15; most are open until 2am on Fridays and Saturdays.

★**Sin É** PUB

(021-450 2266; www.facebook.com/sinecork; 8 Coburg St; noon-11.30pm Mon-Thu, to 12.30am Fri & Sat, to 11pm Sun) You could easily spend an entire day at this place, which is everything a craic-filled pub should be – long on atmosphere and short on pretension (Sin É means 'that's it!'). There's music every night from 6.30pm May to September, and regular sessions Tuesday, Friday and Sunday during the rest of the year, many of them traditional but with the odd surprise.

★**Mutton Lane Inn** PUB

(021-427 3471; www.facebook.com/mutton.lane; Mutton Lane; 10.30am-11.30pm Mon-Thu, to 12.30am Fri & Sat, 12.30-11pm Sun) Tucked down the tiniest of alleys off St Patrick's St, this inviting pub, lit by candles and fairy lights, is one of Cork's most intimate drinking holes. It's minuscule, so try to get in early to bag the snug, or perch on the beer kegs outside.

★**Franciscan Well Brewery** PUB

(021-439 3434; www.franciscanwellbrewery.com; 14 North Mall; 1-11.30pm Mon-Thu, to 12.30am Fri

WORTH A TRIP

ROCK OF CASHEL

The **Rock of Cashel** (www.heritageireland.ie; adult/child €8/4; ⌚9am-7pm early Jun–mid-Sep, to 5.30pm mid-Mar–early Jun & mid-Sep–mid-Oct, to 4.30pm mid-Oct–mid-Mar) is one of Ireland's most spectacular historical sites: a prominent green hill, banded with limestone outcrops, rising from a grassy plain and bristling with ancient fortifications. Sturdy walls circle an enclosure containing a complete round tower, a 13th-century Gothic cathedral and the finest 12th-century Romanesque chapel in Ireland, home to some of the land's oldest frescoes.

Cashel Lodge & Camping Park (☎062-61003; www.cashel-lodge.com; Dundrum Rd; sites per person €10, s/d from €45/85; P 📶) is a good place to stay, with terrific views of the Rock and Hore Abbey. Bus Éireann runs eight buses daily between Cashel and Cork (€26.60, 1¾ hours).

& Sat, to 11pm Sun; 📶) The copper vats gleaming behind the bar give the game away: the Franciscan Well brews its own beer. The best place to enjoy it is in the enormous beer garden at the back. The pub holds regular beer festivals together with other small independent Irish breweries.

☆ Entertainment

Cork's cultural life is generally of a high calibre. To see what's happening, grab *WhazOn?* (www.whazon.com), a free monthly leaflet available from the tourist office, news agencies, shops, hostels and B&Bs.

★Cork Opera House OPERA

(☎021-427 0022; www.corkoperahouse.ie; Emmet Pl; tickets €30-50; ⌚box office 10am-5.30pm Mon-Sat, pre-show to 7pm Mon-Sat & 6-7pm Sun) Given a modern makeover in the 1990s, this leading venue has been entertaining the city for more than 150 years with everything from opera and ballet to stand-up comedy, pop concerts and puppet shows. Around the back, the **Half Moon Theatre** (tickets €5-15) presents contemporary theatre, dance, art and occasional club nights.

★Triskel Arts Centre ARTS CENTRE

(☎021-472 2022; www.triskelart.com; Tobin St; tickets €8-15; ⌚box office 10am-5pm Mon-Sat, 1-9pm Sun; 📶) A fantastic cultural centre housed partly in a renovated church building. Expect a varied program of live music, installation art, photography and theatre at this intimate venue. There's also a cinema (from 6.30pm) and a great cafe.

ℹ Information

Cork City Tourist Office (☎1850 230 330; www.discoverireland.ie/corkcity; Grand Pde; ⌚9am-5pm Mon-Sat year-round, plus 10am-5pm Sun Jul & Aug) Souvenir shop and information desk. Sells Ordnance Survey maps.

ℹ Getting There & Around

BICYCLE

Cycle Scene (☎021-430 1183; www.cyclescene.ie; 396 Blarney St; per day/week from €15/85) rents out bikes and accessories, including good-quality road-racing bikes (€45 a day).

BOAT

Brittany Ferries (☎021-427 7801; www.brittanyferries.ie; 42 Grand Pde) sails to Roscoff (France) weekly from the end of March to October. The ferry terminal is at Ringaskiddy, about 15 minutes by car southeast of the city centre along the N28.

BUS

Aircoach (☎01-844 7118; www.aircoach.ie) provides a direct service to Dublin city (€12.50) and Dublin Airport (€21.30) from St Patrick's Quay (3½ hours, hourly).

Cork bus station (cnr Merchant's Quay & Parnell Pl), east of the city centre, has services to the following:

Dublin €15.70, 3¾ hours, six daily

Kilkenny €15.70, 3½ hours, two daily

Killarney €18, 1½ hours, hourly

TRAIN

Cork's **Kent train station** (☎021-450 6766) is across the river. Destinations include the following:

Dublin €30, 2¼ hours, eight daily

Galway €20, four to six hours, seven daily, one or two changes

Killarney €12, 1½ to two hours, nine daily

Around Cork

If you need proof of the power of a good yarn, then join the queue to get into **Blarney Castle** (☎021-438 5252; www.blarneycastle.ie; Blarney; adult/child €18/8; ⌚9am-7pm Mon-Sat, to 6pm Sun Jun-Aug, shorter hours Sep-May; P), a 15th-century castle, one of Ireland's most popular tourist attractions. Everyone's here, of course, to plant their lips on the **Blarney Stone**, which supposedly gives one the gift of gab – a cliché that has entered every lexicon and tour route. Blarney is 8km northwest of Cork and buses run hourly from Cork bus station (€7.80 return, 20 minutes).

Killarney

POP 14,500

In the tourism game for more than 250 years, Killarney is a well-oiled machine set in the midst of sublime scenery that spans lakes, waterfalls and woodland beneath a skyline of 1000m-plus peaks. Competition keeps standards high and visitors on all budgets can expect to find good restaurants, great pubs and comfortable accommodation.

Mobbed in summer, Killarney is perhaps at its best in the late spring and early autumn when the crowds are manageable, but the weather is still good enough to enjoy its outdoor activities.

Sights & Activities

Most of Killarney's attractions are just outside the town. The mountain backdrop is part of **Killarney National Park** (www.killarneynationalpark.ie), which takes in beautiful Lough Leane (the Lower Lake or 'Lake of Learning'), Muckross Lake and the Upper Lake, as well as the Mangerton, Torc, Shehy and Purple Mountains. In addition to Ross Castle and Muckross House, the park also has much to explore by foot, bike or boat.

The **Gap of Dunloe** is a wild and scenic mountain pass studded with crags and bejewelled with lakes and waterfalls – that lies to the west of Killarney National Park, squeezed between Purple Mountain and the high summits of Macgillycuddy's Reeks (Ireland's highest mountain range).

Sleeping

★Fleming's White Bridge Caravan & Camping Park CAMPGROUND €
(064-663 1590; www.killarneycamping.com; White Bridge, Ballycasheen Rd; unit plus 2 adults €28, hiker/cyclist €12; mid-Mar–Oct;) A lovely sheltered family-run campground 2.5km southeast of the town centre off the N22, Fleming's has a games room, bike hire, campers' kitchen, laundry and free trout fishing on the river that runs alongside. Your man Hillary at reception can arrange bus, bike and boat tours.

★Crystal Springs B&B €€
(064-663 3272; www.crystalspringsbandb.com; Ballycasheen Cross, Woodlawn Rd; s/d from €98/120;) The timber deck of this wonderfully relaxing B&B overhangs the River Flesk, where trout anglers can fish for free. Rooms are richly furnished with patterned wallpapers and walnut timber; private bathrooms (most with spa baths) are huge. The glass-enclosed breakfast room also overlooks the rushing river. It's about a 15-minute stroll into town.

Eating & Drinking

Jam CAFE €
(064-663 7716; www.jam.ie; Old Market Lane; mains €4-11; 8am-5pm Mon-Sat;) Duck down the alley to this local hideout for deli sandwiches, coffee and cake, and a changing menu of hot lunch dishes such as shepherd's pie. It's all made with locally sourced produce. There are a few tables set up out the front in summer.

Treyvaud's IRISH €€
(064-663 3062; www.treyvaudsrestaurant.com; 62 High St; mains €10-30; 5-10pm Mon, noon-10pm Tue-Thu & Sun, noon 10.30pm Fri & Sat) Mustard-fronted Treyvaud's has a strong reputation for subtle dishes that merge trad Irish with European influences. The seafood chowder – a velvet stew of mussels, prawns and Irish salmon – makes a filling lunch; dinner mains incorporating local ingredients include cod with horseradish mash and tomato-and-caper salsa, and a hearty bacon and cabbage platter.

★O'Connor's PUB
(www.oconnorstraditionalpub.ie; 7 High St; noon-11.30pm Sun-Thu, to 12.30am Fri & Sat;) Live music plays every night at this tiny traditional pub with leaded-glass doors – one of Killarney's most popular haunts. In warmer weather, the crowds spill out onto the adjacent lane.

Courtney's PUB
(www.courtneysbar.com; 24 Plunkett St; 2-11.30pm Sun-Thu, to 12.30am Fri & Sat Jun-Sep, from 5pm Mon-Thu Oct-May) Inconspicuous on the outside, this cavernous 19th-century pub bursts at the seams with regular Irish music sessions (nightly in summer). Rock, blues, reggae and indie bands perform year-round on Fridays, with DJs taking over on Saturdays. This is where locals come to see their

WORTH A TRIP

SKELLIG MICHAEL

Portmagee (an 80km drive west of Killarney) is the jumping-off point for an unforgettable experience: the Skellig Islands, two tiny rocks 12km off the coast. The vertiginous climb up uninhabited **Skellig Michael** inspires an awe that monks could have clung to life in the meagre beehive-shaped stone huts that cluster on the tiny patch of level land on top. Skellig Michael famously featured as Luke Skywalker's Jedi temple in *Star Wars: The Force Awakens* (2015) and *Star Wars: The Last Jedi* (2017), attracting a whole new audience to the island's dramatic beauty. From spring to late summer, weather permitting, boat trips run from Portmagee to Skellig Michael; the standard rate is around €80 per person, with boats departing in the morning and returning at 3pm. Advance booking is essential; there are a dozen boat operators, including **Sea Quest** (☎087 236 2344; www.skelligsrock.com; per person €100; ⊙mid-May–Sep).

old mates perform and to kick off a night on the town.

Information

Tourist Office (☎064-663 1633; www.killarney.ie; Beech Rd; ⊙9am-5pm Mon-Sat; 📶) Killarney's tourist office can handle most queries and is especially good with transport intricacies.

Getting There & Around

BUS

Bus Éireann operates from the bus station on Park Rd.

Cork €18, 2½ hours, hourly
Galway €24.70, 5½ hours, every two hours
Limerick €14.25, two hours, every two hours
Rosslare Harbour €26.60, six hours, six daily
Tralee €10.45, 40 minutes, six daily

TAXI

The town taxi rank is on College St. Taxi companies include **Killarney Taxi & Tours** (☎085 280 3333; www.killarneytaxi.com).

TRAIN

Killarney's **train station** (☎064-663 1067; Fair Hill) is behind the Malton Hotel, just east of the centre.

There are one or two direct services per day to Cork and Dublin; otherwise you'll have to change at Mallow.

Cork €12, 1½ hours
Dublin €31, 3¼ hours

Ring of Kerry

The Ring of Kerry, a 179km circuit around the dramatic coastal scenery of the Iveragh Peninsula (pronounced eev-raa), is one of Ireland's premier tourist attractions. Most travellers tackle the Ring by bus on guided day trips from Killarney, but you could spend days wandering here.

The Ring is dotted with picturesque villages (**Sneem** and **Portmagee** are worth a stop), **prehistoric sites** (ask for a guide at Killarney tourist office) and spectacular **viewpoints**, notably at Beenarourke just west of Caherdaniel, and Ladies' View (between Kenmare and Killarney). The **Ring of Skellig**, at the end of the peninsula, has fine views of the Skellig Rocks and is not as busy as the main route. You can forgo driving completely by walking part of the 200km **Kerry Way** (www.kerryway.com), which winds through the Macgillycuddy's Reeks mountains past Carrauntoohill (1040m), Ireland's highest mountain.

Sights

Kerry Bog Village Museum MUSEUM
(www.kerrybogvillage.ie; Ballincleave, Glenbeigh; adult/child €6.50/4.50; ⊙9am-6pm; P) This museum recreates a 19th-century bog village, typical of the small communities that carved out a precarious living in the harsh environment of Ireland's ubiquitous peat bogs. You'll see the thatched homes of the turfcutter, blacksmith, thatcher and labourer, as well as a dairy, and meet Kerry bog ponies (a native breed) and Irish wolfhounds. It's on the N70, 8.3km southwest of Killorglin near Glenbeigh; buy a ticket at the neighbouring Red Fox Inn if no one's at the gate.

Old Barracks Heritage Centre MUSEUM
(☎066-401 0430; www.theoldbarrackscahersiveen.com; Bridge St; adult/child €4/2; ⊙10am-5pm Mon-Sat, 11am-4pm Sun Mar-Nov; P) Established in response to the Fenian Rising of 1867, the Royal Irish Constabulary barracks at Cahersiveen were built in an eccentric Bavarian-Schloss style, complete with pointy turret and stepped gables. Burnt down in 1922 by anti-Treaty forces, the imposing

building has been restored and now houses fascinating exhibitions on the Fenian Rising and the life and works of local hero Daniel O'Connell.

★Derrynane National Historic Park HISTORIC SITE
(☎066-947 5113; http://derrynanehouse.ie; Derrynane; adult/child €5/3; ⏱10.30am-6pm mid-Mar–Sep, 10am-5pm Oct, 10am-4pm Sat & Sun Nov–early-Dec; P) Derrynane House was the home of Maurice 'Hunting Cap' O'Connell, a notorious local smuggler who grew rich on trade with France and Spain. He was the uncle of Daniel O'Connell, the 19th century campaigner for Catholic emancipation, who grew up here in his uncle's care and inherited the property in 1825, when it became his private retreat. The house is furnished with O'Connell memorabilia, including the impressive triumphal chariot in which he lapped Dublin after his release from prison in 1844.

Sleeping & Eating

There are plenty of hostels and B&Bs along the Ring. It's wise to book ahead, as some places are closed out of season and others fill up quickly.

★Mannix Point Camping & Caravan Park CAMPGROUND €
(☎066-947 2806; www.campinginkerry.com; Mannix Point, Cahersiveen; hikers €8.50, vehicle plus 2 adults from €26; ⏱late Apr–mid-Sep;) Mortimer Moriarty's award-winning waterfront campground is one of Ireland's finest, with 42 pitches, an inviting kitchen, a campers' sitting room with peat fire (no TV, but regular music sessions and instruments if you haven't brought your own), laundry facilities, squeaky-clean showers (€1), a barbecue area and even a birdwatching platform. Sunsets here are stunning.

Moorings GUESTHOUSE €€
(☎066-947 7108; www.moorings.ie; s/d/tr from €90/120/165;) The Moorings is a friendly local hotel, **bar** (⏱8am-11.30pm Mon-Sat, 8am-11pm Sun;) and **restaurant** (mains €24-35; ⏱6-10pm Wed-Sun Apr-Oct;). It has 16 rooms, split between modern sea-view choices and simpler options, most refreshingly white in decor. Cots and pull-out sofas are available for kids.

★Smuggler's Inn MODERN IRISH €€
(☎066-947 4330; www.smugglersinn.ie; Cliff Rd; 3-course lunch & early-bird menu €30, mains €20-27; ⏱noon-2.45pm & 6-9.30pm;) At this diamond find near Waterville Golf Links, owner and chef Henry Hunt's gourmet creations incorporate fresh seafood and locally farmed poultry and meat, followed by artistic desserts (including homemade ice cream), served in a glass atrium dining room. Half-board deals are available at the inn's upstairs rooms (doubles from €85); cooked-to-order breakfasts include a catch of the day.

★Quinlan & Cooke SEAFOOD €€
(☎066-947 2244; www.qc.ie; 3 Main St; mains €18-27; ⏱food served 6-9pm, bar 3-10pm Thu-Mon Easter-Sep, shorter hrs Oct-Easter;) This is a modern take on a classic pub and as such is open pub hours for pints and craic. Some of the finest food on the Ring also pours forth, particularly locally sourced seafood from its own fishing fleet, such as Valentia crab and prawn bisque. Upstairs there are six boutique B&B bedrooms (doubles from €170).

Getting Around

Bus Éireann runs a once-daily Ring of Kerry bus service (No 280; €23.50) from late June to late August. Buses leave Killarney at 11.30am, arriving back at Killarney at 4.45pm. En route, stops include (in order):

Killorglin €8, 30 minutes
Cahersiveen €17.50, 1½ hours
Waterville €20, 1¾ hours
Caherdaniel €21.80, 2¼ hours

The road is narrow and windy in places. Tour buses travel the Ring in an anticlockwise direction. Getting stuck behind one is tedious, so consider driving clockwise; just watch out on blind corners.

THE WEST COAST

Galway

POP 79,930

Arty and bohemian, Galway (Gaillimh) is legendary around the world for its entertainment scene. Students make up a quarter of the city's population and brightly painted pubs heave with live music on any given night. Here, street life is more important than sightseeing – cafes spill out onto cobblestone streets filled with a frenzy of fiddles, banjos, guitars and *bodhráns* (hand-held goatskin drums), while jugglers,

Galway City

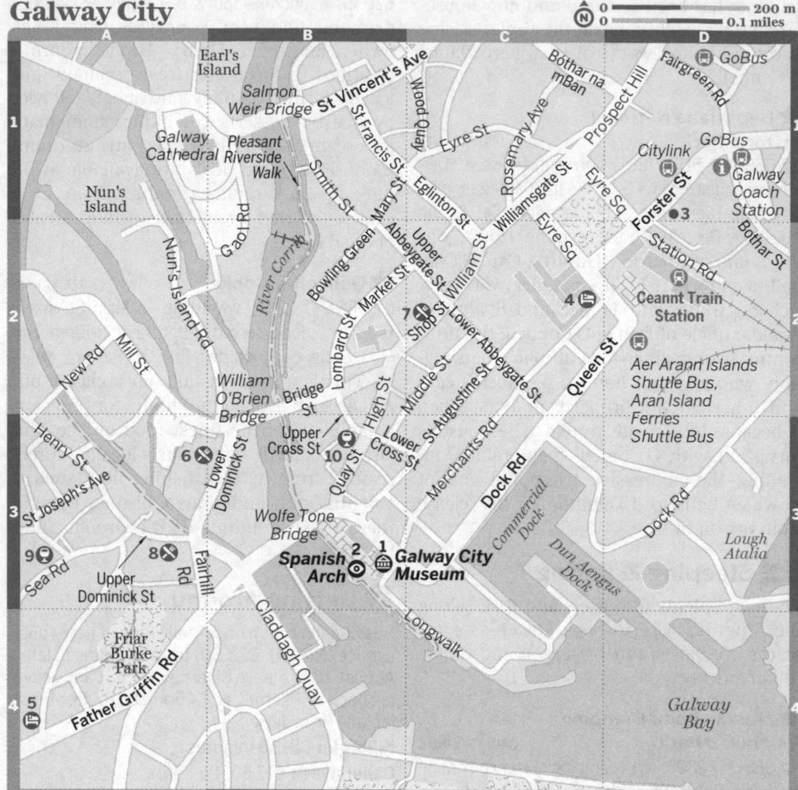

Galway City

Top Sights

1 Galway City Museum B3
2 Spanish Arch B3

Activities, Courses & Tours

3 Lally Tours D1

Sleeping

4 Kinlay House C2
5 Stop A4

Eating

6 Aniar A3
7 McCambridge's C2
8 Oscar's A3

Drinking & Nightlife

9 Crane Bar A3
10 Tigh Neachtain B3

painters, puppeteers and magicians in outlandish masks enchant passers-by.

Sights

★Galway City Museum MUSEUM

(☎091-532 460; www.galwaycitymuseum.ie; Spanish Parade; ⏲10am-5pm Tue-Sat, plus noon-5pm Sun Easter-Sep) FREE Exhibits at this modern, three-floor museum engagingly convey the city's archaeological, political, cultural and social history. Look out for an iconic Galway hooker fishing boat, a collection of *currachs* (boats made of a framework of laths covered with tarred canvas) and sections covering Galway's role in the revolutionary events that shaped the Republic of Ireland.

★Spanish Arch HISTORIC SITE

The Spanish Arch is thought to be an extension of Galway's medieval city walls, designed to protect ships moored at the nearby quay while they unloaded goods from Spain. It was partially destroyed by the tsunami that followed the 1755 Lisbon earthquake. Today it reverberates with buskers and drummers, and the lawns and riverside form a gathering place for locals and visitors on sunny days, as kayakers negotiate the tidal rapids of the River Corrib.

Festivals

Galway International Arts Festival ART
(www.giaf.ie; mid-late Jul) Catch performances and exhibits by top drama groups, musicians and bands, comedians, artists and much more during this two-week fiesta of theatre, comedy, music and art.

Galway International Oyster & Seafood Festival FOOD & DRINK
(www.galwayoysterfest.com; South Park; late Sep) Going strong since 1954, the world's oldest oyster festival draws thousands of visitors in late September. Events include the World Oyster Opening Championships, live music, a masquerade carnival and family activities.

Sleeping

★**Kinlay House** HOSTEL €
(091-565 244; www.kinlaygalway.ie; Merchants Rd, Eyre Sq; dm/d €25/70;) Easygoing staff and a brilliant location right by Eyre Sq make this large, brightly lit hostel a winner. Freshly renovated in 2017, superb amenities include a self-catering kitchen and a cosy TV lounge with a pool table. The four- to eight-bed dorms and private rooms come with electric sockets and USB points; dorms have curtains screening each bunk.

★**Stop** B&B €€
(091-586 736; www.thestopbandb.com; 38 Father Griffin Rd; s/d/tr/f from €50/100/150/200;) Done up with contemporary artworks, stripped floorboards and bold colours, this 11-room house pulls out all the stops. The rooms are individually decorated and space – at a premium – is wisely used, so there are no wardrobes (just hangers), small work desks and no TV, but comfy beds. Breakfast includes freshly squeezed orange juice. There's a handy supermarket right across the street.

★**Glenlo Abbey Hotel** HISTORIC HOTEL €€€
(091-519 600; www.glenloabbeyhotel.ie; Kentfield Bushy Park, N59; d/ste from €382/485;) Situated on the shores of Lough Corrib, 4km northwest of Galway, this 1740-built stone manor is the ancestral home of the Ffrench family, one of Galway's 14 tribes. Exceptionally preserved period architectural features are complemented by antique furnishings, sumptuous marble bathrooms, duck-down duvets and king-size pillows, along with lavish breakfasts. Its fine-dining **Pullman Restaurant** (2-/3-course menus €57/65; 6.30-10pm daily Mar-Oct, 6.30-9.30pm Fri & Sat Nov-Feb) occupies original *Orient Express* train carriages.

Eating & Drinking

McCambridge's CAFE, DELI €
(www.mccambridges.com; 38/39 Shop St; dishes €5-16; cafe 8.30am-5.30pm Mon-Thu, to 7pm Fri & Sat, 10am-4pm Sun, deli 8am-7pm Mon-Thu, to 8pm Fri & Sat, 10.30am-6pm Sun) Superb prepared salads are among the perfect picnic ingredients at this gourmet food emporium. All high ceilings, blond wood and busy staff, the upstairs cafe is lovely with a changing menu of modern Irish fare such as Galway Hooker beef stew, and more than 100 craft beers from Ireland's west. Brunch is served until 4.30pm on Sundays.

★**Oscar's** SEAFOOD €€
(091-582 180; www.oscarsseafoodbistro.com; Upper Dominick St; mains €16-26; 6-9.30pm Mon-Fri, 5.30-9.30pm Sat) The menu changes daily at this outstanding seafood restaurant, but it might include monkfish poached in saffron and white wine and served with cockles; seaweed-steamed Galway Bay lobster with garlic-lemon butter; or lemon sole with samphire. From Monday to Thursday before 6.30pm, the two-course early-bird menu (€19.50) is a steal.

★**Aniar** MODERN IRISH €€€
(091-535 947; www.aniarrestaurant.ie; 53 Lower Dominick St; 6/8/10 courses €72/89/99, with wine pairings €107-169; 6-9.30pm Tue-Thu, 5.30-9.30pm Fri & Sat) Terroir specialist Aniar is passionate about the flavours and food producers of Galway and West Ireland. Owner and chef JP McMahon's multicourse tasting menus have earned him a Michelin star, yet the casual spring-green dining space remains refreshingly down to earth. The wine list favours small producers. Reserve at least a couple of weeks in advance.

★**Tigh Neachtain** PUB
(www.tighneachtain.com; 17 Upper Cross St; 11.30am-midnight Mon-Thu, to 1am Fri, 10.30am-1am Sat, 12.30-11.30pm Sun) Painted a bright cornflower blue, this 19th-century corner pub – known simply as Neáchtain's (*nocktans*) or Naughtons – has a wraparound terrace for watching Galway's passing parade,

WORTH A TRIP

CLIFFS OF MOHER

In good visibility, the Cliffs of Moher (Aillte an Mothair, or Ailltreacha Mothair) are staggeringly beautiful. The entirely vertical cliffs rise to a height of 214m, their edge abruptly falling away into a ceaselessly churning Atlantic.

A progression of vast heads, the dark limestone marches in a rigid formation. Views stretch to the Aran Islands and the hills of Connemara. Sunsets here see the sky turn a kaleidoscope of amber, amethyst, rose-pink and deep garnet-red.

One of Ireland's blockbuster sights, it includes a high-tech visitor centre, 19th-century lookout tower and wealth of walking trails.

The **Cliffs of Moher Visitor Centre** (☎065-708 6141; www.cliffsofmoher.ie; R478; adult/child incl parking €8/free; ⏰8am-9pm May-Aug, 8am-7pm Mar, Apr, Sep & Oct, 9am-5pm Nov-Feb; 📶) has a spiralling exhibition covering the fauna, flora, geology and climate of the cliffs, and an interactive genealogy board with information on local family names. A number of bus tours leave Galway every morning for the Cliffs of Moher.

and a timber-lined interior with a roaring open fire, snugs and atmosphere to spare. Along with perfectly pulled pints of Guinness and 130-plus whiskeys, it has its own range of beers brewed by Galway Hooker.

★**Crane Bar** PUB
(www.thecranebar.com; 2 Sea Rd; ⏰10.30am-11.30pm Mon-Thu, to 1am Fri, 12.30pm-1am Sat, to 11.30pm Sun) West of the Corrib, this atmospheric, always-crammed two-storey pub is the best spot in Galway to catch an informal *céilidh* (traditional music and dancing session). Music on both levels starts at 9.30pm.

ℹ Information

Galway Tourist Office (☎091-537 700; www.discoverireland.ie; Forster St; ⏰9am-5pm Mon-Sat) Galway's large, efficient tourist office can help arrange tours and has reams of information on the city and region.

ℹ Getting There & Around

BICYCLE

Galway's bike-share scheme (www.bikeshare.ie/galway.html) has 16 stations around town. For visitors, €3 (with €150 deposit) gets you a three-day pass. The first 30 minutes of each hire is free; up to two hours costs €1.50.

On Yer Bike (☎091-563 393; www.onyourbikecycles.com; 42 Prospect Hill; bike rental per day from €20; ⏰9.30am-7pm Mon-Fri, 11am-4pm Sat) offers bike rental.

BUS

Bus Éireann services depart from outside the train station. **Citylink** (www.citylink.ie; 17 Forster St; ⏰office 9am-6pm Mon-Sat, 10am-6pm Sun; 📶) and **GoBus** (www.gobus.ie; 📶) use the **coach station** (New Coach Station; Fairgreen Rd) a block northeast. Citylink has buses to Clifden (€16, 1½ hours, six daily) and Dublin (€16, 2½ hours, hourly).

TRAIN

From the **train station** (www.irishrail.ie), just off Eyre Sq, there are up to 10 direct trains daily to/from Dublin's Heuston Station (from €17, 2½ hours), and five daily to Ennis (€7.50, 1¼ hours). Connections with other train routes can be made at Athlone (from €10.50, one hour).

Aran Islands

The windswept Aran Islands are one of western Ireland's major attractions. As well as their rugged beauty – they are an extension of The Burren's limestone plateau – the Irish-speaking islands have some of the country's oldest Christian and pre-Christian ruins.

There are three main islands in the group, all inhabited year-round. Most visitors head for the long and narrow (14.5km by a maximum 4km) **Inishmore** (Inis Mór). The land slopes up from the relatively sheltered northern shores and plummets on the southern side into the raging Atlantic. **Inishmaan** and **Inisheer** are much smaller and receive far fewer visitors.

The **tourist office** (☎099-61263; www.aranislands.ie; Kilronan; ⏰10am-5pm, to 6pm Jul & Aug) operates year-round at Kilronan, the arrival point and major village of Inishmore. You can leave your luggage here and change money. Around the corner is a Spar supermarket with an ATM (note, many places do not accept credit cards).

Inishmore

Three spectacular forts stand guard over Inishmore, each believed to be around 2000 years old. Chief among them is **Dún Aengus** (Dún Aonghasa; ☎099-61008; www.heritageireland.ie; adult/child €5/3; ⏲9.30am-6pm Apr-Oct, to 4pm Nov-Mar), which has three massive drystone walls that run right up to sheer drops to the ocean below. It is protected by remarkable *chevaux de frise,* fearsome and densely packed defensive stone spikes. A small visitor centre has displays that put everything in context. A slightly strenuous 900m walkway wanders uphill to the fort itself.

Kilronan Hostel (☎099-61255; www.kilronanhostel.com; Kilronan; dm from €24; ⏲late Feb-late Oct; @📶), perched above Tí Joe Mac's pub, is a friendly hostel just a two-minute walk from the ferry. **Kilmurvey House** (☎099-61218; www.aranislands.ie/kilmurvey-house; Kilmurvey; s/d from €60/95; ⏲Apr-mid-Oct; 📶) offers B&B in a grand 18th century stone mansion on the path leading to Dún Aengus.

Getting There & Away

AIR

Aer Arann Islands (☎091-593 034; www.aerarannislands.ie; one way/return €25/49) Aer Arann Islands has flights to each of the islands up to six times a day; the flights take about 10 minutes. A connecting shuttle bus (☎091-593 034; www.aerarannislands.ie) links Galway city with Connemara Regional Airport (Aerfort Réigiúnach Chonamara; NNR; ☎091-593 034; Inverin).

BOAT

Aran Island Ferries (☎091-568 903; www.aranislandferries.com; one way/return €15/25) Aran Island Ferries has sailings to Inishmore (40 minutes, two to three daily), Inishmaan (45 minutes, two daily) and Inisheer (55 minutes, two daily). Crossings are subject to cancellation in high seas. Boats leave from Rossaveal Ferry Terminal, 37km west of Galway city and linked by shuttle bus (☎091-568 903; www.aranislandferries.com; Queen St). Contact the company in advance to arrange bike transport.

NORTHERN IRELAND

☎028

An exploding food scene, hip cities and the stunning Causeway Coast: there's plenty to pull visitors to the North. When you cross from the Republic into Northern Ireland you'll notice a couple of changes: the road signs are in miles and the prices are in pounds sterling – you're in the UK. At the time of research, there was no border checkpoint and not even a sign to mark the crossing point.

Belfast

POP 280,900

Belfast is in many ways a brand-new city. Once shunned by travellers unnerved by tales of the Troubles and sectarian violence, in recent years it has pulled off a remarkable transformation from bombs-and-bullets pariah to a hip-hotels-and-hedonism party town.

WORTH A TRIP

CONNEMARA

With its shimmering black lakes, pale mountains, lonely valleys and more than the occasional rainbow, Connemara in the northwestern corner of County Galway is one of the most gorgeous pockets of Ireland. It's prime hill-walking country with plenty of wild terrain, none more so than the Twelve Bens, a ridge of rugged mountains that form part of **Connemara National Park** (☎076-100 2528; www.connemaranationalpark.ie; off N59; ⏲24hr) FREE.

Connemara's 'capital', **Clifden** (An Clochán), is an appealing Victorian-era town with an oval of streets offering evocative strolls. Right in the centre of town is charmingly old-fashioned **Ben View House** (☎095-21256; www.benviewhouse.com; Bridge St; s €50-75 d €70-100; 📶), and the gorgeous **Dolphin Beach B&B** (☎095-21204; www.dolphinbeachhouse.com; Lower Sky Rd; r from €110; P📶) is 5km west of town.

From Galway, **Lally Tours** (☎091-562 905; www.lallytours.com; 4 Forster St; tours adult/child €30/20) runs day-long coach tours of Connemara.

Belfast

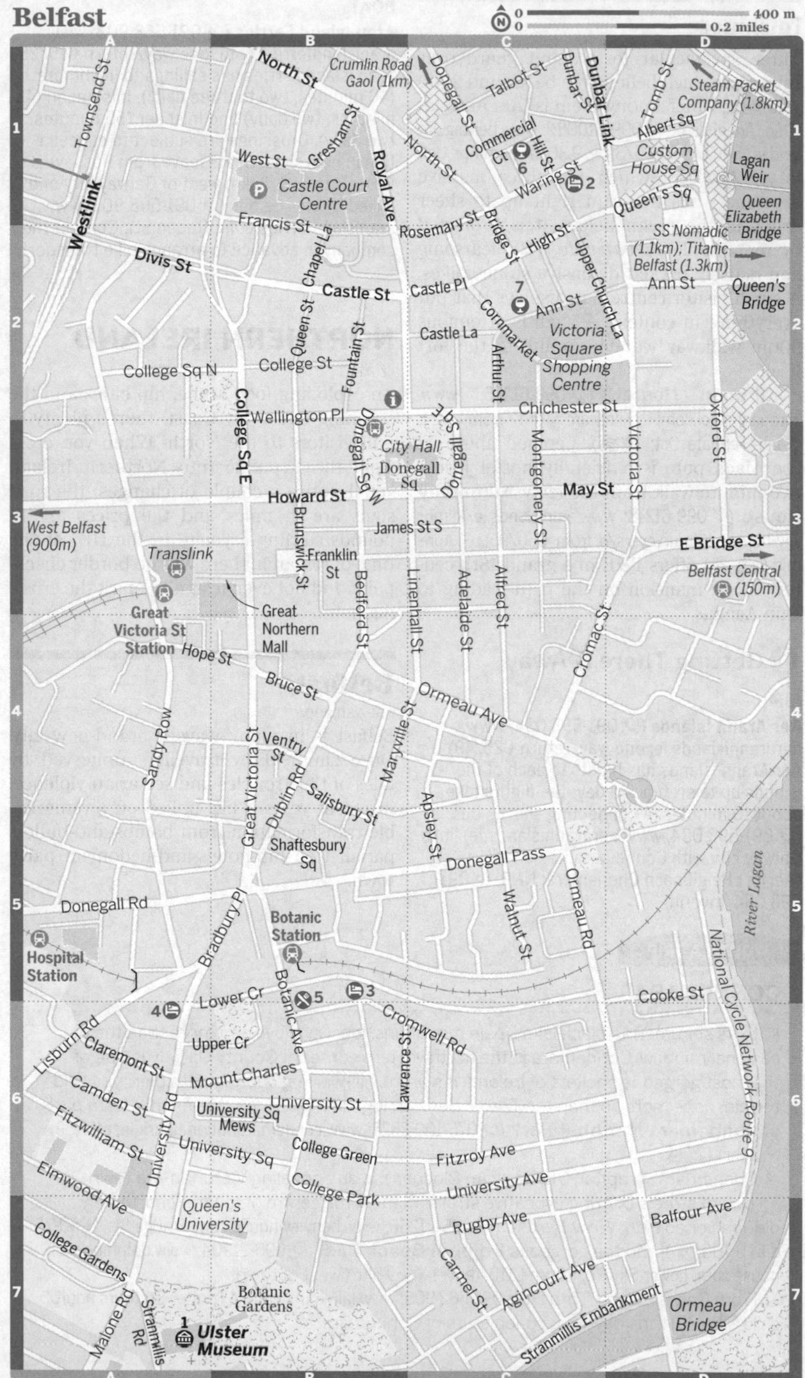

0 400 m
0 0.2 miles
North St
Crumlin Road Gaol (1km)
Donegall St
Talbot St
Dunbar St
Dunbar Link
Tomb St
Steam Packet Company (1.8km)
Townsend St
Gresham St
Royal Ave
North St
Commercial Ct
Hill St
Albert Sq
Custom House Sq
Lagan Weir
West St
Castle Court Centre
Waring St
Queen's Sq
Queen Elizabeth Bridge
Westlink
Francis St
Rosemary St
Bridge St
High St
SS Nomadic (1.1km); Titanic Belfast (1.3km)
Divis St
Chapel La
Upper Church La
Ann St
Queen's Bridge
Castle St
Castle Pl
Ann St
Queen St
Fountain St
Castle La
Cornmarket
Victoria Square Shopping Centre
College Sq N
College St
Arthur St
Wellington Pl
Chichester St
Oxford St
College Sq E
Donegall Sq W
City Hall
Donegall Sq E
Montgomery St
Victoria St
Donegall Sq
Howard St
May St
West Belfast (900m)
Brunswick St
James St S
E Bridge St
Translink
Franklin St
Bedford St
Linenhall St
Adelaide St
Alfred St
Belfast Central (150m)
Great Victoria St Station
Great Northern Mall
Cromac St
Hope St
Bruce St
Ormeau Ave
Sandy Row
Great Victoria St
Ventry St
Maryville St
Dublin Rd
Salisbury St
Apsley St
Shaftesbury Sq
Donegall Pass
Ormeau Rd
River Lagan
Donegall Rd
Bradbury Pl
Botanic Station
Walnut St
Hospital Station
Lower Cr
Botanic Ave
Cooke St
Lisburn Rd
Claremont St
Upper Cr
Cromwell Rd
Lawrence St
National Cycle Network Route 9
Camden St
Mount Charles
University St
University Sq Mews
Fitzwilliam St
University Rd
University Sq
College Green
Fitzroy Ave
Elmwood Ave
College Park
University Ave
Queen's University
Rugby Ave
Balfour Ave
College Gardens
Carmel St
Agincourt Ave
Malone Rd
Stranmillis Rd
Botanic Gardens
Ulster Museum
Stranmillis Embankment
Ormeau Bridge

Sights

★Titanic Belfast MUSEUM
(www.titanicbelfast.com; Queen's Rd; adult/child £18.50/8; 9am-7pm Jun & Jul, to 8pm Aug, to 6pm Apr, May & Sep, 10am-5pm Oct-Mar; G2) The head of the slipway where the RMS *Titanic* was built is now occupied by the gleaming, angular edifice of Titanic Belfast, an unmissable multimedia extravaganza that charts the history of Belfast and the creation of the world's most famous ocean liner. Cleverly designed exhibits enlivened by historical images, animated projections and soundtracks chart Belfast's rise to turn-of-the-20th-century industrial superpower, followed by a high-tech ride through a noisy, smells-and-all recreation of the city's shipyards. Tickets also include entry to the SS Nomadic.

SS Nomadic HISTORIC SITE
(www.nomadicbelfast.com; Hamilton Dock, Queen's Rd; adult/child £7/5; 10am-7pm Sun-Thu, to 8pm Fri & Sat Jul & Aug, 10am-7pm Jun, 10am-6pm Apr, May & Jun, 11am-5pm Oct-Mar; G2) Built in Belfast in 1911, the SS *Nomadic* is the last remaining vessel of the White Star Line. The little steamship ferried 1st- and 2nd-class passengers between Cherbourg Harbour and the ocean liners that were too big to dock at the French port. On 10 April 1912 it delivered 172 passengers to the ill-fated RMS *Titanic*. Don't miss the luxurious 1st-class toilets. Entry to the SS *Nomadic* (valid for 24 hours) is included in the ticket for Titanic Belfast.

★Ulster Museum MUSEUM
(www.nmni.com; Botanic Gardens; 10am-5pm Tue-Sun; ; 8A to 8D) FREE You could spend hours browsing this state-of-the-art museum, but if you're pressed for time don't miss the Armada Room, with artefacts retrieved from the 1588 wreck of the Spanish galleon Girona; the Egyptian Room, with Takabuti, a 2500-year-old Egyptian mummy unwrapped in Belfast in 1835; and the Early Peoples Gallery, with the bronze Bann Disc, a superb example of Celtic design from the Iron Age.

★Crumlin Road Gaol HISTORIC BUILDING
(028-9074 1500; www.crumlinroadgaol.com; 53-55 Crumlin Rd; tour adult/child £12/7.50; 10am-5.30pm, last tour 4.30pm; Agnes St) Guided tours of Belfast's notorious Crumlin Road Gaol take you from the tunnel beneath Crumlin Rd, built in 1850 to convey prisoners from the courthouse across the street (and allegedly the origin of the judge's phrase 'take him down'), through the echoing halls and cramped cells of C-Wing, to the truly chilling execution chamber. Advance tour bookings are recommended. The jail's pedestrian entrance is on Crumlin Rd; the car park entrance is reached via Cliftonpark Ave to the north.

Sleeping

Most budget and midrange accommodation is south of the centre in the leafy university district around Botanic Ave, University Rd and Malone Rd, around a 20-minute walk from City Hall. Business hotels and luxury boutiques proliferate in the city centre.

★Vagabonds HOSTEL €
(028-9023 3017; www.vagabondsbelfast.com; 9 University Rd; dm £15-18, d & tw £50; @; Shaftesbury Sq) Comfy bunks, lockable luggage baskets, private shower cubicles, a beer garden, a pool table and a relaxed atmosphere are what you get at one of Belfast's best hostels, run by a couple of experienced travellers. It's conveniently located close to both Queen's and the city centre.

Tara Lodge GUESTHOUSE €€
(028-9059 0900; www.taralodge.com; 36 Cromwell Rd; s/d from £75/80; P@; Upper Crescent Queens University) In a great location on a quiet side street just a few paces from the

buzz of Botanic Ave, this guesthouse feels more like a boutique hotel with its clean-cut, minimalist decor, friendly and efficient staff, and 34 bright and cheerful rooms. Delicious breakfasts include porridge with Bushmills whiskey.

★Merchant Hotel HOTEL €€€
(028-9023 4888; www.themerchanthotel.com; 16 Skipper St; d/ste from £160/350; P@; Queen's Sq) Belfast's most flamboyant hotel occupies the palatial former Ulster Bank head office. Rooms are individually decorated with a fabulous fusion of contemporary styling and old-fashioned elegance; those in the original Victorian building have opulent floor-length silk curtains while newer rooms have an art deco–inspired theme. Facilities include a luxurious spa and an eight-person rooftop hot tub.

Eating & Drinking

In recent years, Belfast's restaurant scene has been totally transformed by a wave of new restaurants whose standards compete with the best eateries in Europe.

Belfast's pub scene is lively and friendly, with the older traditional pubs complemented by a rising tide of stylish designer bars.

Maggie May's CAFE €
(028-9066 8515; www.maggiemaysbelfastcafe.co.uk; 50 Botanic Ave; mains £4.50-7.50; 8am-10pm Mon-Fri, 9am-11pm Sat & Sun; ; 7A to 7D) This is a classic little cafe with cosy wooden booths, murals of old Belfast and a host of hungover students wolfing down huge Ulster fry-ups. The all-day breakfast menu includes French toast and pancake stacks, while lunch can be soup and a sandwich or a burger.

★Duke of York PUB
(028-9024 1062; www.dukeofyorkbelfast.com; 11 Commercial Ct; 11.30am-11pm Mon, to 1am Tue & Wed, to 2am Thu & Fri, to midnight Sat, 3-9pm Sun; Queen's Sq) In a cobbled alleyway off buzzing Hill St, the snug, traditional Duke feels like a living museum. There's regular live music; local band Snow Patrol played some of their earliest gigs here. Outside on Commercial Ct, a canopy of umbrellas leads to an outdoor area covered with murals depicting Belfast life; it takes on a street-party atmosphere in warm weather.

★Love & Death Inc COCKTAIL BAR
(www.loveanddeathbelfast.com; 10A Ann St; 4pm-1am; Victoria Sq) More like a cool inner-city house party, speakeasy-style Love & Death Inc is secreted up a flight of stairs above a pizza joint. Its living-room-style bar has outrageous decor, feisty Latin American–influenced food, feistier cocktails and a wild nightclub in the attic on weekends.

Information

Visit Belfast Welcome Centre (028-9024 6609; www.visitbelfast.com; 9 Donegall Sq N; 9am-7pm Mon-Sat, 11am-4pm Sun Jun-Sep, 9am-5.30pm Mon-Sat, 11am-4pm Sun Oct-May; ; Donegall Sq) Provides stacks of information about the whole of Northern Ireland, and books accommodation. Services include left luggage (not overnight), currency exchange and free wi-fi. There's also a gift shop selling local crafts and souvenirs.

Getting There & Away

AIR

Belfast International Airport (Aldergrove; 028-9448 4848; www.belfastairport.com; Airport Rd) is 30km northwest of the city, and has flights from the UK, Europe and the USA.

George Best Belfast City Airport (BHD; 028-9093 9093; www.belfastcityairport.com; Airport Rd) is 6km northeast of the city centre, with flights from the UK and Europe.

BOAT

In addition to services with **Stena Line** (08447 707070; www.stenaline.co.uk; Victoria Terminal, 4 West Bank Rd; trips from £89; 96) and **Steam Packet Company** (08722 992 992; www.steam-packet.com; Albert Quay; return fares from £98), car ferries to and from Scotland and England dock at Larne, 37km north of Belfast. Trains to the terminal at Larne Harbour depart from Great Victoria St station.

BUS

Europa Bus Centre, Belfast's main bus station, is behind the Europa Hotel and next door to Great Victoria St train station; it's reached via the Great Northern Mall beside the hotel. It's the main terminus for buses to Derry, Dublin and destinations in the west and south of Northern Ireland.

Ballycastle £12.50, 1¾ to 3¼ hours, hourly

Derry £12.50, 1¾ hours, half-hourly

Dublin £15.70, 2½ hours, hourly

Aircoach (www.aircoach.ie) operates a service from Glengall St, near Europa Bus Centre, to Dublin city centre and Dublin Airport.

TRAIN

For information on train fares and timetables, contact **Translink** (☎028-9066 6630; www.translink.co.uk; Europa Bus Centre).

Belfast Central Station (East Bridge St) East of the city centre. Trains run to Dublin and all destinations in Northern Ireland.

Great Victoria St Station (Great Victoria St, Great Northern Mall) Next to the Europa Bus Centre. Trains run to Portadown, Lisburn, Bangor, Larne Harbour and Derry.

Northern Ireland Railways (NIR; ☎028-9066 6630; www.translink.co.uk/Services/NI-Railways) Runs four routes from Belfast. One links with the system in the Republic via Newry to Dublin; the other three go east to Bangor, northeast to Larne and northwest to Derry via Coleraine.

Getting Around

BICYCLE

Belfast Bikes (☎034-3357 1551; www.belfastbikes.co.uk; registration per 3 days £6, bikes per 30min/1hr/2hr/3hr free/£0.50/1.50/2.50; ⏲6am-midnight) has 45 docking stations across the city centre. Register as a casual user for £6 through the website, app or on a terminal. The first 30 minutes of each trip are free.

BUS

Metro (☎028-9066 6630; www.translink.co.uk) operates the bus network in Belfast. Most city services depart from various stops on and around Donegall Sq, at City Hall and along Queen St. You can pick up a free bus map (and buy tickets) from the **Metro kiosk** (Donegall Sq; ⏲8am-5.30pm Mon-Fri) at the northwest corner of the square.

You can also buy your ticket from the driver (change given); fares within the city zone are £2.

The Causeway & Antrim Coasts

Ireland isn't short of scenic coastlines, but the Causeway Coast between Portstewart (Port Stíobhaird) and Ballycastle (Baile an Chaibil) – climaxing in the spectacular rock formations of the Giant's Causeway – and the Antrim Coast between Ballycastle and Belfast, are as magnificent as they come.

GAME OF THRONES TOURS

If you're driving around Northern Ireland, you'll discover *Game of Thrones* filming locations aplenty; alternatively there are day-long bus tours departing from Belfast. Visit www.discovernorthernireland.com/gameofthrones for details.

From April to September the **Ulsterbus** (☎028-9066 6630; www.translink.co.uk) Antrim Coaster (bus 252) links Larne with Coleraine via the Glens of Antrim, Ballycastle, the Giant's Causeway, Bushmills, Portrush and Portstewart.

From Easter to September the Causeway Rambler (bus 402) links Coleraine and Carrick-a-Rede (£9, 40 minutes, 12 daily) via Bushmills Distillery, the Giant's Causeway, White Park Bay and Ballintoy. The ticket allows unlimited travel in both directions for one day.

There are several hostels along the coast, including **Sheep Island View Hostel** (☎028-2076 9391; www.sheepislandview.com; 42A Main St; dm/s/tw from £18/25/45; P @), **Ballycastle Backpackers** (☎077-7323 7890; www.ballycastlebackpackers.net; 4 North St; dm £17.50, d with/without bathroom £60/40; P @) and **Bushmills Youth Hostel** (☎028 2073 1222; www.hini.org.uk; 49 Main St; dm £16-20, s £30-35, tw £50-60, tr £60-75; ⏲closed 11.30am-2.30pm Jul & Aug, 11.30am-3.30pm Mar-Jun, Sep & Oct; @).

Sights

★Giant's Causeway LANDMARK

(www.nationaltrust.org.uk; ⏲dawn-dusk) FREE This spectacular rock formation – Northern Ireland's only Unesco World Heritage Site – is one of Ireland's most impressive and atmospheric landscape features, a vast expanse of regular, closely packed, hexagonal stone columns looking for all the world like the handiwork of giants. The phenomenon is explained in the **Giant's Causeway Visitor Experience** (☎028-2073 1855; 60 Causeway Rd; adult/child £12.50/6.25; ⏲9am-7pm Jun-Sep, to 6pm Mar-May & Oct, to 5pm Nov-Feb;), housed in a new, ecofriendly building half-hidden in a hillside above the sea.

★**Carrick-a-Rede Rope Bridge** BRIDGE
(☎028-2073 3335; www.nationaltrust.org.uk/carrick-a-rede; 119 Whitepark Rd, Ballintoy; adult/child £9/4.50; ⏲9.30am-6pm Apr-Oct, to 3.30pm Nov-Mar) This 20m-long, 1m-wide bridge of wire rope spans the chasm between the sea cliffs and the little island of Carrick-a-Rede, swaying 30m above the rock-strewn water. Crossing the bridge is perfectly safe, but frightening if you don't have a head for heights, especially if it's breezy (in high winds the bridge is closed). From the island, views take in Rathlin Island and Fair Head to the east.

There's a small National Trust information centre and cafe at the car park.

Derry (Londonderry)

POP 107,900

Northern Ireland's second-largest city continues to flourish as an artistic and cultural hub. Derry's city centre was given a striking makeover for its year as the UK City of Culture 2013, with the construction of the Peace Bridge to Ebrington Sq, and the redevelopment of the waterfront and Guildhall area making the most of the city's splendid riverside setting.

There's lots of history to absorb here, from the Siege of Derry to the Battle of the Bogside and Bloody Sunday. A stroll around the 17th-century city walls that encircle the city is a must, as is a tour of the Bogside murals, along with taking in the burgeoning live-music scene in the city's lively pubs.

Sights

★**Derry's City Walls** WALLS
(⏲dawn-dusk) FREE The best way to get a feel for Derry's layout and history is to walk the 1.5km circumference of the city's walls. Completed in 1619, Derry's city walls are 8m high and 9m thick, and are the only city walls in Ireland to survive almost intact. The four original gates (Shipquay, Ferryquay, Bishop's and Butcher's) were rebuilt in the 18th and 19th centuries, when three new gates (New, Magazine and Castle) were added.

★**Tower Museum** MUSEUM
(www.derrystrabane.com/towermuseum; Union Hall Pl; adult/child £3/1.50; ⏲10am-5.30pm, last entry 4pm) Head straight to the 5th floor of this award-winning museum inside a replica 16th-century tower house for a view from the top. Then work your way down through the excellent **Armada Shipwreck** exhibition, and the **Story of Derry**, where well-thought-out exhibits and audiovisuals lead you through the city's history, from the founding of the monastery of St Colmcille (Columba) in the 6th century to the Battle of the Bogside in the late 1960s. Allow at least two hours.

People's Gallery Murals PUBLIC ART
(Rossville St) The 12 murals that decorate the gable ends of houses along Rossville St, near Free Derry Corner, are popularly referred to as the People's Gallery. They are the work of 'the Bogside Artists' (Kevin Hasson, Tom Kelly, and Will Kelly, who passed away in 2017). The three men lived through the worst of the Troubles in Bogside. The murals can be clearly seen from the northern part of the City Walls.

Sleeping

★**Merchant's House** B&B €€
(☎028-7126 9691; www.thesaddlershouse.com; 16 Queen St; d from £75; @📶) This historical, Georgian-style townhouse is a gem of a B&B. It has an elegant lounge and dining room with marble fireplaces and antique furniture, TV, coffee-making facilities, homemade marmalade at breakfast and bathrobes in the bedrooms (some rooms have shared bathroom). Call at **Saddler's House** (36 Great James St; d from £75; 📶) first to pick up a key.

Abbey B&B B&B €€
(☎028-7127 9000; www.abbeyaccommodation.com; 4 Abbey St; s/d/tr from £50/70/90; 📶) There's a warm welcome waiting at this family-run B&B just a short walk from the walled city, on the edge of the Bogside. Rooms are spacious and modern.

Eating & Drinking

★**Pyke 'n' Pommes** STREET FOOD €
(The POD; www.pykenpommes.ie; behind Foyle Marina, off Baronet St; mains £4-16; ⏲noon-8.30pm Fri & Sat, to 6pm Sun-Thu; 🌱) Derry's single-best eatery is this quayside shipping container. Chef Kevin Pyke's delectable, mostly organic burgers span his signature Notorious PIG (pulled pork, crispy slaw, beetroot and crème fraiche) and Veganderry (chickpeas, lemon and coriander) to his Legenderry Burger (Wagyu beef, pickled onions and honey-mustard mayo). His Pykeos fish tacos are another hit. Seasonal specials might include mackerel or oysters.

★ **Peadar O'Donnell's** PUB
(www.facebook.com/Peadarsderry/; 59-63 Waterloo St; ⊙11.30am-1.30am Mon-Sat, 12.30pm-12.30am Sun) Done up as a typical Irish pub and grocery (with shelves of household items, shopkeeper's scales on the counter and a museum's-worth of old bric-a-brac), Peadar's has rowdy traditional-music sessions every night and often on weekend afternoons as well. Its adjacent **Gweedore Bar** (www.facebook.com/GweedoreRocks) hosts live rock bands every night, and a Saturday-night disco upstairs.

Information

Visit Derry Information Centre (☎028-7126 7284; www.visitderry.com; 44 Foyle St; ⊙9am-7pm Mon-Fri, 9am-6pm Sat, 10am-5pm Sun Jun-Aug, shorter hours Sep-May; 🛜) A large tourist information centre with helpful staff and stacks of brochures for attractions in Derry and beyond. Also sells books and maps, and can book accommodation. Claudy Cycles (☎028-7133 8128; www.claudycycles.com; bike hire per half-/full day £8/12) can be rented here.

Getting There & Away

BUS

The **bus station** (☎028-7126 2261; Foyle St) is just northeast of the walled city. Services include the following:

Belfast £12, 1¾ hours, half-hourly
Dublin £20, four hours, every two hours daily

TRAIN

Derry's train station (always referred to as Londonderry in Northern Ireland timetables) is on the eastern side of the River Foyle; a free Rail Link bus connects with the bus station. Services run to Belfast (£12, 2½ hours) hourly Monday to Saturday, with six on Sunday.

SURVIVAL GUIDE

Directory A–Z

ACCOMMODATION

Hostels in Ireland can be booked solid in summer.

From June to September a dorm bed at most hostels costs €12 to €25 (£10 to £20), except for the more expensive hostels in Dublin, Belfast and a few other places.

Typical B&Bs cost around €40 to €60 (£35 to £50) per person per night (sharing a double room), though more luxurious B&Bs can cost upwards of €70 (£60) per person. Most B&Bs are small, so in summer they quickly fill up.

Commercial campgrounds typically charge €15 to €25 (£12 to £20) for a tent or campervan and two people. Unless otherwise indicated, prices quoted for 'sites' are for a tent, car and two people.

Useful resources:

An Óige (www.anoige.ie) Hostelling International (HI)–associated national organisation with 23 hostels scattered around the Republic.

HINI (www.hini.org.uk) HI-associated organisation with four hostels in Northern Ireland.

Independent Holiday Hostels of Ireland (www.hostels-ireland.com) Fifty-five tourist-board-approved hostels throughout all of Ireland.

Independent Hostel Owners of Ireland (www.independenthostelsireland.com) Independent hostelling association.

MONEY

The Republic of Ireland uses the euro (€). Northern Ireland uses the pound sterling (£), although the euro is also accepted in many places.

Tipping

Hotels €1/£1 per bag is standard; tip cleaning staff at your discretion.

Pubs Not expected unless table service is provided, then €1/£1 for a round of drinks.

Restaurants For decent service 10%; up to 15% in more expensive places.

Taxis Tip 10% or round up fare to the nearest euro/pound.

Toilet attendants Loose change, no more than €0.50/50p.

OPENING HOURS

Banks 10am–4pm Monday to Friday (to 5pm Thursday)

Pubs 10.30am–11.30pm Monday to Thursday, 10.30am–12.30am Friday and Saturday, noon–11pm Sunday (30 minutes 'drinking up' time allowed); closed Christmas Day and Good Friday

Restaurants noon–10.30pm; many close one day of the week

Shops 9.30am–6pm Monday to Saturday (to 8pm Thursday in cities), noon–6pm Sunday

PUBLIC HOLIDAYS

The main public holidays in the Republic of Ireland and Northern Ireland:

New Year's Day 1 January

St Patrick's Day 17 March

Easter (Good Friday to Easter Monday inclusive) March/April

May Holiday First Monday in May

Christmas Day 25 December

St Stephen's Day (Boxing Day) 26 December

Northern Ireland

Spring Bank Holiday Last Monday in May

Orangemen's Day 12 July
August Holiday Last Monday in August

Republic of Ireland

June Holiday 1st Monday in June
August Holiday 1st Monday in August
October Holiday Last Monday in October

TELEPHONE

The mobile-phone network in Ireland runs on the GSM 900/1800 system, which is compatible with the rest of Europe and Australia, but not the USA. Mobile numbers in the Republic begin with 085, 086 or 087; in Northern Ireland it's 07. A local pay-as-you-go SIM for your mobile will cost from around €10, but may work out free after the standard phone-credit refund (make sure your phone is compatible with the local provider).

To call Northern Ireland from the Republic, do not use 0044 as for the rest of the UK. Instead, dial 048 and then the local number. To dial the Republic from Northern Ireland, however, use the full international code, 00 353, then the local number.

VISAS

If you're a European Economic Area (EEA) national, you don't need a visa to visit (or work in) either the Republic or Northern Ireland. Citizens of Australia, Canada, New Zealand, South Africa and the USA can visit the Republic for up to three months, and Northern Ireland for up to six months. They are not allowed to work unless sponsored by an employer.

Full visa requirements for visiting the Republic are available online at www.dfa.ie; for Northern Ireland's visa requirements see www.gov.uk/government/organisations/uk-visas-and-immigration.

Getting There & Away

AIR

There are nonstop flights from Britain, Continental Europe and North America to Dublin, Shannon and Belfast International, and nonstop connections from Britain and Europe to Cork. International departure tax is included in the price of your ticket.

International airports in Ireland:

Belfast International Airport (Aldergrove; ☎028-9448 4848; www.belfastairport.com; Airport Rd) Located 30km northwest of the city. Flights serve the UK, Europe, and the USA (New York and Boston).

Dublin Airport (☎01-814 1111; www.dublinairport.com) Dublin Airport, 13km north of the centre, is Ireland's major international gateway airport. It has two terminals: most international flights (including most US flights) use the newer Terminal 2; Ryanair and select others use Terminal 1. Both terminals have the usual selection of pubs, restaurants, shops, ATMs and car-hire desks.

George Best Belfast City Airport (BHD; ☎028-9093 9093; www.belfastcityairport.com; Airport Rd) Located 6km northeast of Belfast city centre; flights serve the UK and Europe.

Shannon Airport (SNN; ☎061-712 000; www.shannonairport.ie; wi-fi) Ireland's third-busiest airport has ATMs, currency exchange, car-rental desks, taxis and a tourist office (☎061-712 000; www.shannonregiontourism.ie; Shannon Airport; ⊙7am-11pm) near the arrivals area. Numerous flights serve North America (with US pre-clearance facilities), the UK and Europe.

SEA

The main ferry routes between Ireland and the UK and mainland Europe:

- Belfast to Liverpool (England; eight hours)
- Belfast to Cairnryan (Scotland; 2½ hours)
- Cork to Roscoff (France; 14 hours; April to October only)
- Dublin to Liverpool (England; fast ferry – four hours, slow ferry – 8½ hours)
- Dublin to Holyhead (Wales; fast ferry – two hours, slow ferry – 3½ hours)
- Larne to Cairnryan (Scotland; two hours)
- Rosslare to Cherbourg/Roscoff (France; 18/20½ hours)
- Rosslare to Fishguard and Pembroke (Wales; 3½ hours)

Competition from budget airlines has forced ferry operators to discount heavily and offer flexible fares.

A useful website is www.aferry.co.uk, which covers all sea-ferry routes and operators to Ireland.

Main operators include the following:

Brittany Ferries (www.brittanyferries.com) Cork to Roscoff; March to October.

Irish Ferries (www.irishferries.com) Dublin to Holyhead ferries (up to five per day year-round); and France to Rosslare (twice per week).

P&O Ferries (www.poferries.com) Daily sailings year-round from Dublin to Liverpool, and Larne to Cairnryan.

Stena Line (www.stenaline.com) Daily sailings from Holyhead to Dublin Port, from Belfast to Liverpool and Cairnryan, and from Rosslare to Fishguard.

Getting Around

The big decision in getting around Ireland is whether to go by car or use public transport. Your own car will make the best use of your time and help you reach even the most remote of places. It's usually easy to get very cheap rentals –

BUS & RAIL PASSES

There are a few bus, rail and bus-and-rail passes worth considering:

Irish Explorer Offers customers five days of unlimited Irish Rail travel within 15 consecutive days (adult/child €160/80).

Open Road Pass Three days' travel within six consecutive days (€60) on Bus Éireann; extra days cost €16.50.

Sunday Day Tracker One day's unlimited travel (adult/child £7/3.75) on Translink buses and trains in Northern Ireland; Sunday only.

Trekker Four Day Four consecutive days of unlimited travel (€110) on Irish Rail.

Note that Eurail's one-country pass for Ireland is a bad deal in any of its permutations.

€10 per day or less is common – and if two or more are travelling together, the fee for rental and petrol can be cheaper than bus fares.

The bus network, made up of a mix of public and private operators, is extensive and generally quite competitive – although journey times can be slow and lots of the points of interest outside towns are not served. The rail network is quicker but more limited, serving only some major towns and cities. Both buses and trains get busy during peak times; you'll need to book in advance to be guaranteed a seat.

BICYCLE

Ireland's compact size and scenic landscapes make it a good cycling destination. However, dodgy weather, many very narrow roads and some very fast drivers are major concerns. Special tracks such as the 42km **Great Western Greenway** in County Mayo are a delight. A good tip for cyclists in the west is that the prevailing winds make it easier to cycle from south to north.

Trains will carry bikes, but bear the following in mind:

- Bikes are carried free on Intercity and off-peak commuter trains.
- Book in advance (www.irishrail.ie), as there's only room for two bikes per service.

BUS

Private buses compete – often very favourably – with Bus Éireann in the Republic and also run where the national buses are irregular or absent.

Distances are not especially long: few bus journeys will last longer than five hours. Bus Éireann bookings can be made online, but you can't reserve a seat for a particular service. Dynamic pricing is in effect on many routes: book early to get the lowest fares.

Note the following:

- Bus routes and frequencies are slowly contracting in the Republic.
- The National Journey Planner app by Transport for Ireland is very useful for planning bus and train journeys.

The main bus services in Ireland:

Bus Éireann (☎1850 836 6111; www.buseireann.ie) The Republic's main bus line.

Translink (☎028-9066 6630; www.translink.co.uk) Northern Ireland's main bus service; includes Ulsterbus and Goldline.

CAR & MOTORCYCLE

The majority of hire companies won't rent you a car if you're under 23 years of age and haven't had a valid driving licence for at least a year.

TRAIN

Given Ireland's relatively small size, train travel can be quick and advance-purchase fares are competitive with buses. Worth noting:

- Many of the Republic's most beautiful areas, such as whole swaths of the Wild Atlantic Way, are not served by rail.
- Most lines radiate out from Dublin, with limited ways of interconnecting between lines, which can complicate touring.
- There are four routes from Belfast in Northern Ireland; one links with the system in the Republic via Newry to Dublin.
- True 1st class only exists on the Dublin–Cork and Dublin–Belfast lines. On all other trains, seats are the same size as in standard class, despite any marketing come-ons such as 'Premier' class.

Irish Rail (Iarnród Éireann; ☎01-836 6222; www.irishrail.ie) Operates trains in the Republic.

Translink NI Railways (☎028-9066 6630; www.translink.co.uk) Operates trains in Northern Ireland.

Italy

POP 62.14 MILLION

Includes ➡

Best Places to Eat

➡ Antiche Carampane (p447)

➡ Trattoria Mario (p457)

➡ Concettina Ai Tre Santi (p466)

➡ All'Osteria Bottega (p450)

Best Museums & Galleries

➡ Vatican Museums (p411)

➡ Galleria degli Uffizi (p452)

➡ Museo Archeologico Nazionale (p463)

➡ Museo del Novecento (p432)

➡ Museo e Galleria Borghese (p414)

Why Go?

A favourite destination since the days of the 18th-century Grand Tour, Italy may appear to hold few surprises. Its iconic monuments and masterpieces are known the world over, while cities like Rome, Florence and Venice need no introduction.

Yet Italy is far more than the sum of its sights. Its fiercely proud regions maintain centuries-old customs and culinary traditions, meaning enthralling festivals and delectable food appear at every turn. And then there are those timeless landscapes, from Tuscany's gentle hills to icy Alpine peaks, vertiginous coastlines and spitting volcanoes.

Drama is never far away in Italy and its streets and piazzas provide endless people-watching, ideally over a lazy lunch or *aperitivo* (evening drink). This is, after all, the land of *dolce far niente* (sweet idleness) where simply hanging out is a pleasure and time seems to matter just that little bit less.

When to Go

Rome

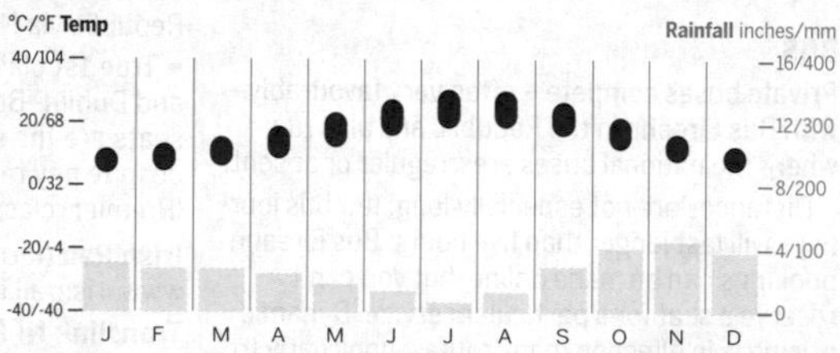

Apr–May Perfect spring weather; ideal for exploring vibrant cities and blooming countryside.

Jun–Jul Summer means beach weather and a packed festival calendar.

Sep–Oct Enjoy mild temperatures, autumn cuisine and the *vendemia* (grape harvest).

Entering the Country

Entering Italy from most other parts of the EU is generally uncomplicated, with no border checkpoints and no customs thanks to the Schengen Agreement. Document and customs checks remain standard if arriving from (or departing to) a non-Schengen country. A plethora of airlines link Italy with the rest of the world, and cut-rate carriers have significantly driven down the cost of flights from other European countries. Excellent rail and bus connections, especially with northern Italy, offer efficient overland transport, while car and passenger ferries run to ports throughout the Mediterranean.

ITINERARIES

One Week

A one-week whistle-stop tour of Italy is enough to take in the country's three most famous cities. After a couple of days exploring the unique canalscape of Venice (p440), head south to Florence (p452), Italy's great Renaissance city. Two days will whet your appetite for the artistic and architectural treasures that await in Rome (p405).

Two Weeks

After the first week, continue south for some sea and southern passion. Spend a day admiring art and lapping up the raw, high-octane energy of soul-stirring Naples (p463), a day investigating the ruins at Pompeii (p468), and a day or two enjoying the glitz and dramatic scapes of the Amalfi Coast (p470). Then backtrack to Naples for a ferry to Palermo (p474) and the gastronomic delights of Sicily.

Essential Food & Drink

Italian cuisine is highly regional in nature and wherever you go you'll find local specialities. That said, some staples are ubiquitous:

Pizza There are two varieties: Roman, with a thin crispy base; and Neapolitan, with a higher, more doughy base. The best are always prepared in a *forno a legna* (wood-fired oven).

Pasta Comes in hundreds of shapes and sizes and is served with everything from thick meat-based sauces to fresh seafood.

Gelato Classic flavours include *fragola* (strawberry), *pistacchio* (pistachio), *nocciola* (hazelnut) and *stracciatella* (milk with chocolate shavings).

Wine Ranges from big-name reds such as Piedmont's Barolo and Tuscany's Brunello di Montalcino to sweet Sicilian Malvasia and sparkling prosecco from the Veneto.

Caffè Italians take their coffee seriously, drinking cappuccino only in the morning, and espressos whenever, ideally standing at a bar.

AT A GLANCE

Area 302,073 sq km

Capital Rome

Country code ☎39

Currency euro (€)

Emergency ☎112

Language Italian

Time Central European Time (GMT/UTC plus one hour)

Visas Schengen rules apply

Sleeping Price Ranges

The following price ranges refer to a double room with private bathroom (breakfast included) in high season.

€ less than €110

€€ €110–200

€€€ more than €200

Eating Price Ranges

The following price ranges refer to a meal of two courses (antipasto/primo and secondo), a glass of house wine, and coperto (cover charge) for one person.

€ less than €25

€€ €25–45

€€€ more than €45

Resources

Lonely Planet (www.lonelyplanet.com/italy) Destination information.

ENIT (www.italia.it) Official tourism website.

The Local (www.thelocal.it) News from Italy.

Italy Highlights

1. **Rome** (p405) Facing up to awe-inspiring art and iconic monuments.
2. **Venice** (p440) Taking to the water and cruising past Gothic palaces, domed churches and crumbling piazzas.
3. **Florence** (p452) Exploring this exquisite Renaissance time capsule.
4. **Naples** (p463) Working up an appetite for the world's best pizza in Naples' baroque backstreets.
5. **Turin** (p431) Visiting Turin's regal palaces and magnificent museums.
6. **Siena** (p461) Admiring glorious Gothic architecture and Renaissance art.
7. **Amalfi Coast** (p470) Basking in the Amalfi Coast's inspiring sea views.
8. **Verona** (p439) Enjoying an open-air opera in one of Italy's most romantic cities.

ROME

POP 2.87 MILLION

Ever since its glory days as an ancient superpower, Rome has been astonishing visitors. Its historical cityscape, piled high with haunting ruins and iconic monuments, is achingly beautiful, and its museums and basilicas showcase some of Europe's most celebrated masterpieces. But no list of sights and must-sees can capture the sheer elation of experiencing Rome's operatic streets and baroque piazzas, of turning a corner and stumbling across a world-famous fountain or a colourful neighbourhood market. Its street-side cafes are made for idling and elegant Renaissance *palazzi* (mansions) provide the perfect backdrop for romantic alfresco dining.

Sights

Ancient Rome

The neighbourhood's main sights are concentrated in a tightly packed area. Starting in the southeast, the Colosseum, Palatino and Roman Forum are all covered by a single ticket and are all within comfortable walking distance of each other.

★Colosseum AMPHITHEATRE

(Colosseo; Map p406; ☎06 3996 7700; www.parcocolosseo.it; Piazza del Colosseo; adult/reduced incl Roman Forum & Palatino €16/7.50, Full Experience ticket €22/13.50; ⏲8.30am-1hr before sunset; MColosseo) Rome's great gladiatorial arena is the most thrilling of the city's ancient sights. Inaugurated in AD 80, the 50,000-seat Colosseum, also known as the Flavian Amphitheatre, was originally clad in travertine and covered by a huge canvas awning. Inside, tiered seating encircled the arena, itself built over an underground complex where animals were caged and stage sets prepared. Games involved gladiators fighting wild animals or each other.

Two thousand years on and it's Italy's top tourist attraction.

★Palatino ARCHAEOLOGICAL SITE

(Palatine Hill; Map p406; ☎06 3996 7700; www.parcocolosseo.it; Via di San Gregorio 30, Piazza di Santa Maria Nova; adult/reduced incl Colosseum & Roman Forum €12/7.50, SUPER ticket €18/13.50; ⏲8.30am-1hr before sunset; some SUPER ticket sites Mon, Wed, Fri & morning Sun only; MColosseo) Sandwiched between the Roman Forum and the Circo Massimo, the Palatino (Palatine Hill) is one of Rome's most spectacular sights, a beautiful, atmospheric area of towering pine trees, majestic ruins and unforgettable views. This is where Romulus supposedly founded the city in 753 BC and Rome's emperors lived in palatial luxury. Look out for the **stadio** (stadium), the ruins of the **Domus Flavia** (imperial palace), and grandstand views over the Roman Forum from the **Orti Farnesiani**.

★Roman Forum ARCHAEOLOGICAL SITE

(Foro Romano; Map p406; ☎06 3996 7700; www.parcocolosseo.it; Largo della Salara Vecchia, Piazza di Santa Maria Nova; adult/reduced incl Colosseum & Palatino €12/7.50, SUPER ticket €18/13.50; ⏲8.30am-1hr before sunset; SUPER ticket sites Tue, Thu, Sat & afternoon Sun only; 🚌Via dei Fori Imperiali) An impressive – if rather confusing – sprawl of ruins, the Roman Forum was ancient Rome's showpiece centre, a grandiose district of temples, basilicas and vibrant public spaces. The site, originally a marshy burial ground, was first developed in the 7th century BC, growing over time to become the social, political and commercial hub of the Roman empire. Signature sights include the **Arco di Settimio Severo** (Arch of Septimius Severus), the **Curia**, the **Tempio di**

COLOSSEUM & SUPER TICKETS

➡ If queues are long, get your ticket at the Palatino, about 250m away at Via di San Gregorio 30.

➡ Other queue-jumping tips: book your ticket online at www.coopculture.it (plus a €2 booking fee); get the Roma Pass; or join an official English-language tour (€5 on top of the regular ticket price).

➡ You'll need to book a guided tour if you want to visit the underground area (hypogeum) and/or upper floors (Belvedere). These cost €9 (or €15 for both) plus the normal Colosseum ticket.

➡ If you plan on visiting the Palatino and Roman Forum too, buy a SUPER ticket and plan carefully. The combo ticket, valid for all three sights for two consecutive days, is the only way to access internal sites at the Palatino and Roman Forum – all open a variety of different hours and days. Check schedules carefully to avoid missing out.

Ancient Rome

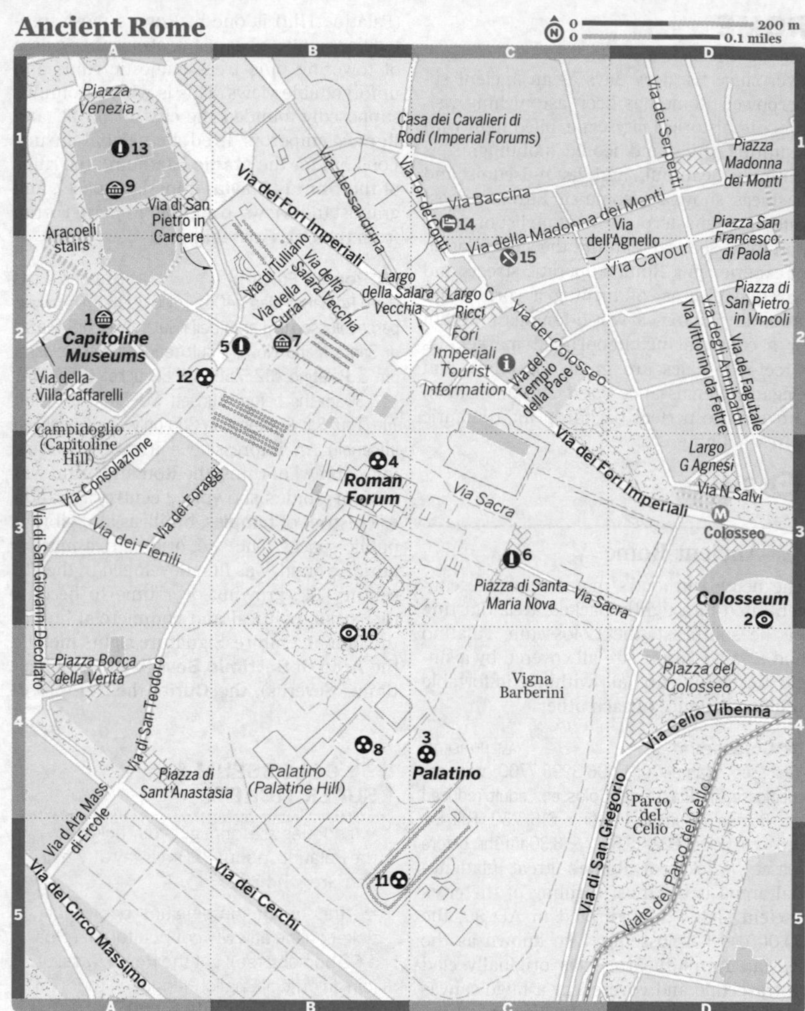

Saturno (Temple of Saturn) and the **Arco di Tito** (Arch of Titus).

★Capitoline Museums — MUSEUM

(Musei Capitolini; Map p406; ☎06 06 08; www.museicapitolini.org; Piazza del Campidoglio 1; adult/reduced €11.50/9.50; ⌚9.30am-7.30pm, last admission 6.30pm; 🚌Piazza Venezia) Dating from 1471, the Capitoline Museums are the world's oldest public museums. Their collection of classical sculpture is one of Italy's finest, boasting works such as the iconic *Lupa Capitolina* (Capitoline Wolf), a life-size bronze of a she-wolf suckling Romulus and Remus, and the *Galata morente* (Dying Gaul), a moving depiction of a dying warrior. There's also a formidable gallery with masterpieces by the likes of Titian, Tintoretto, Rubens and Caravaggio.

Ticket prices increase when there's a temporary exhibition on.

Vittoriano — MONUMENT

(Victor Emanuel Monument; Map p406; Piazza Venezia; ⌚9.30am-5.30pm summer, to 4.30pm winter; 🚌Piazza Venezia) **FREE** Love it or loathe it, as many Romans do, you can't ignore the Vittoriano (aka the Altare della Patria, Altar of the Fatherland), the colossal mountain of white marble that towers over Piazza Venezia. Built

Ancient Rome

Top Sights
1 Capitoline Museums...A2
2 Colosseum...D3
3 Palatino...C4
4 Roman Forum...B3

Sights
5 Arco di Settimio Severo...B2
6 Arco di Tito...C3
7 Curia...B2
8 Domus Flavia...B4
9 Museo Centrale del Risorgimento...A1
10 Orti Farnesiani...B4
11 Stadio...B5
12 Tempio di Saturno...A2
13 Vittoriano...A1

Sleeping
14 Residenza Maritti...C1

Eating
15 Alle Carrette...C2

at the turn of the 20th century to honour Italy's first king, Vittorio Emanuele II – who's immortalised in its vast equestrian statue – it provides the dramatic setting for the **Tomb of the Unknown Soldier** and, inside, the small **Museo Centrale del Risorgimento** (Map p406; 06 679 35 98; www.risorgimento.it; adult/reduced €5/2.50; 9.30am-6.30pm), documenting Italian unification.

Bocca della Verità MONUMENT
(Mouth of Truth; Map p408; Piazza Bocca della Verità 18; voluntary donation; 9.30am-5.50pm summer, to 4.50pm winter; Piazza Bocca della Verità) A bearded face carved into a giant marble disc, the *Bocca della Verità* is one of Rome's most popular curiosities. Legend has it that if you put your hand in the mouth and tell a lie, the Bocca will slam shut and bite it off.

The mouth, which was originally part of a fountain, or possibly an ancient manhole cover, now lives in the portico of the **Chiesa di Santa Maria in Cosmedin**, a handsome medieval church.

Centro Storico

Bound by the River Tiber and Via del Corso, the *centro storico* is made for aimless wandering. Even without trying you'll come across some of Rome's great sights: the Pantheon, Piazza Navona and Campo de' Fiori, as well as a host of monuments, museums and churches. To the south, the lively Ghetto has been home to Rome's Jewish community since the 2nd century BC.

★ **Pantheon** CHURCH
(Map p408; www.pantheonroma.com; Piazza della Rotonda; 8.30am-7.30pm Mon-Sat, 9am-6pm Sun; Largo di Torre Argentina) FREE A striking 2000-year-old temple, now a church, the Pantheon is the best preserved of Rome's ancient monuments and one of the most influential buildings in the Western world. Built by Hadrian over Marcus Agrippa's earlier 27 BC temple, it has stood since around AD 125, and while its greying, pockmarked exterior might look its age, it's still a unique and exhilarating experience to pass through its vast bronze doors and gaze up at the largest unreinforced concrete dome ever built.

Piazza Navona PIAZZA
(Map p408; Corso del Rinascimento) With its showy fountains, baroque *palazzi* and colourful cast of street artists, hawkers and tourists, Piazza Navona is central Rome's elegant showcase square. Built over the 1st-century **Stadio di Domiziano** (Domitian's Stadium; Map p408; 06 6880 5311; www.stadiodomiziano.com; Via di Tor Sanguigna 3; adult/reduced €8/6; 10am-6.30pm Sun-Fri, to 7.30pm Sat), it was paved over in the 15th century and for almost 300 years hosted the city's main market. Its grand centrepiece is Bernini's **Fontana dei Quattro Fiumi** (Fountain of the Four

ROME FOR FREE

Holders of the **Roma Pass** are entitled to free public transport. Some of Rome's most famous sights are free:

- Trevi Fountain
- Spanish Steps
- Pantheon
- St Peter's Basilica and all of Rome's churches
- Vittoriano
- Vatican Museums, the last Sunday of the month from 9am to 2pm
- All state-run museums are *gratis* on the first Sunday of the month between October and March.

To take a free guided city tour check out www.newromefreetour.com.

Centro Storico & Trastevere

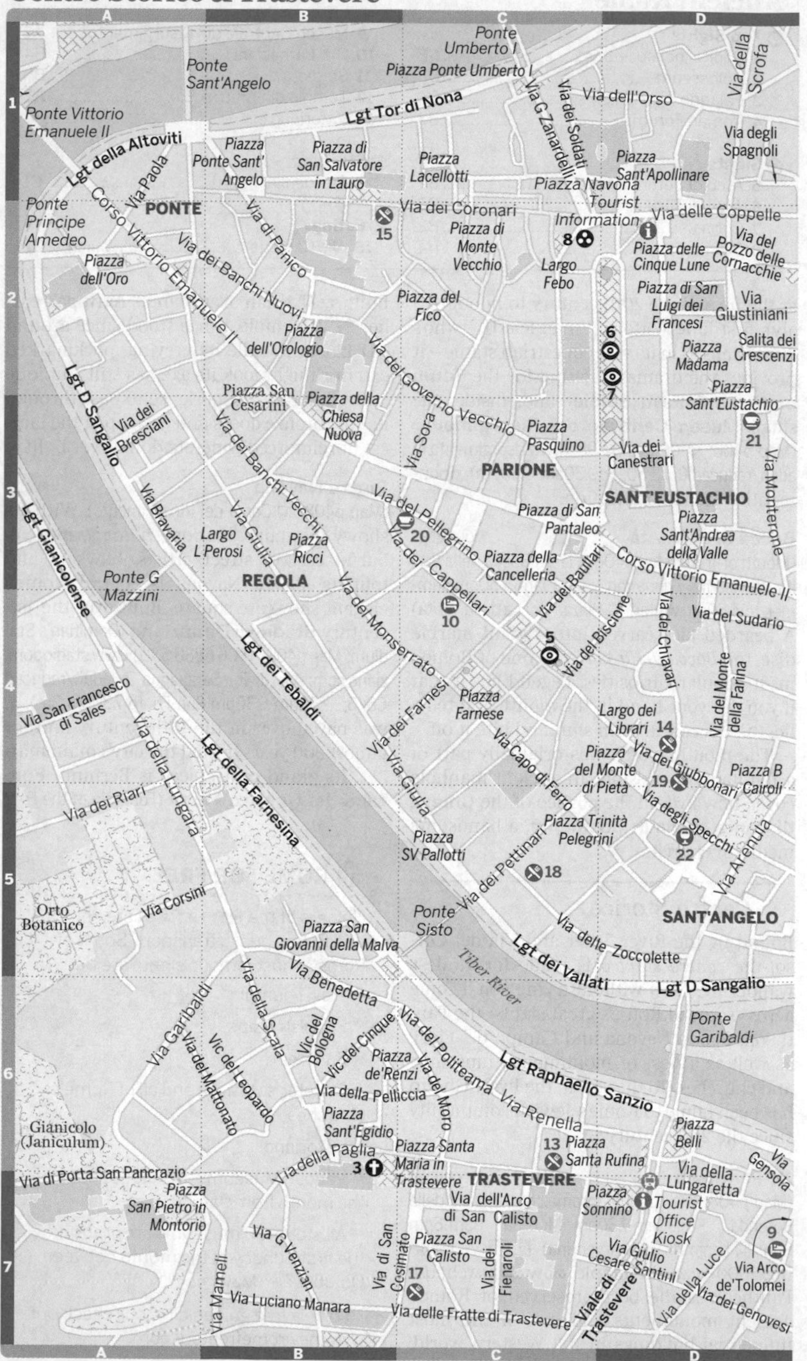

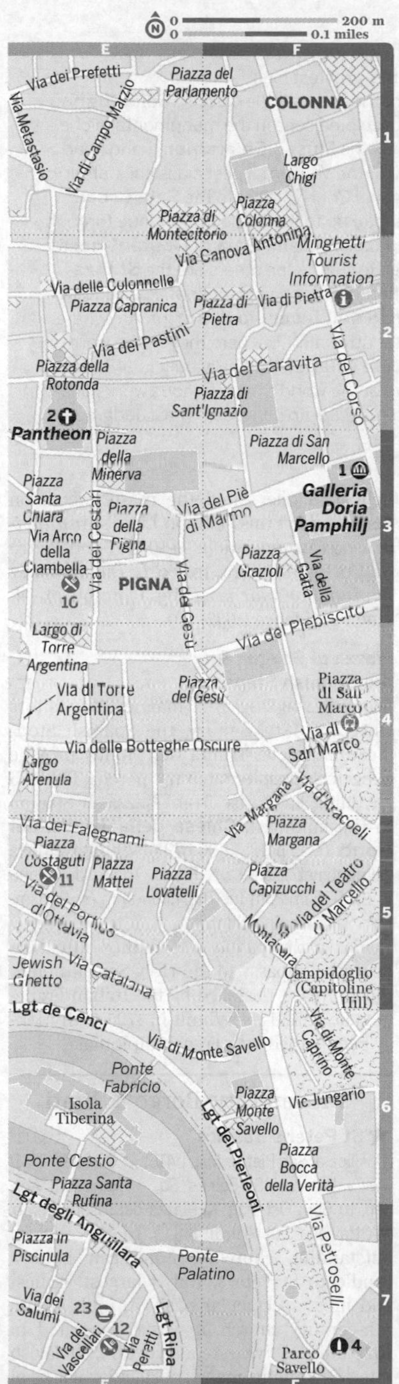

Centro Storico & Trastevere

Top Sights

1 Galleria Doria Pamphilj F3
2 Pantheon E2

Sights

3 Basilica di Santa Maria in Trastevere B6
4 Bocca della Verità F7
5 Campo de' Fiori C4
6 Fontana dei Quattro Fiumi D2
7 Piazza Navona D2
8 Stadio di Domiziano C2

Sleeping

9 Arco del Lauro D7
10 Navona Essence C4

Eating

11 Antico Forno Urbani E5
12 Da Enzo E7
13 Fior di Luna C6
14 Forno Roscioli D4
15 Gelateria del Teatro B2
16 La Ciambella E3
17 Otaleg C7
18 Pianostrada C5
19 Salumeria Roscioli D4

Drinking & Nightlife

20 Barnum Cafe C3
21 Caffè Sant'Eustachio D3
22 Open Baladin D5
23 Terra Satis E7

Rivers; Map p408; Piazza Navona), a flamboyant fountain featuring an Egyptian obelisk and muscular personifications of the rivers Nile, Ganges, Danube and Plate.

Campo de' Fiori PIAZZA

(Map p408; Corso Vittorio Emanuele II) Colourful and always busy, *Il Campo* is a major focus of Roman life: by day it hosts one of the city's best-known markets; by night it heaves with tourists and young drinkers who spill out of its many bars and restaurants. For centuries the square was the site of public executions. It was here that philosopher Giordano Bruno was burned for heresy in 1600, now marked by a sinister statue of the hooded monk, created by Ettore Ferrari in 1889.

★ **Galleria Doria Pamphilj** GALLERY

(Map p408; 06 679 73 23; www.doriapamphilj.it; Via del Corso 305; adult/reduced €12/8; 9am-7pm, last entry 6pm; Via del Corso) Hidden behind the grimy grey exterior of Palazzo Doria Pamphilj, this wonderful gallery

VATICAN MUSEUMS ITINERARY

Follow this three-hour itinerary for the museums' greatest hits:

At the top of the escalator after the entrance, head out to the **Cortile della Pigna**, a courtyard named after the Augustan-era bronze pine cone in the monumental niche. Cross the courtyard into the long corridor that is the **Museo Chiaramonti** and head left up to the **Museo Pio-Clementino**, home of the Vatican's finest classical statuary. Follow through the **Cortile Ottagono** (Octagonal Courtyard) onto the **Sala Croce Greca** (Greek Cross Room) from where stairs lead up to the 1st floor. Continue through the **Galleria delle Carte Geografiche** (Map Gallery) to the **Sala di Costantino**, the first of the four **Stanze di Raffaello** (Raphael Rooms) – the others are the **Stanza d' Eliodoro**, the **Stanza della Segnatura**, home to Raphael's superlative *La scuola di Atene* (The School of Athens), and the **Stanza dell'Incendio di Borgo**. Anywhere else these frescoed chambers would be the star attraction, but here they're the warm-up act for the museums' grand finale, the **Sistine Chapel**. Originally built in 1484 for Pope Sixtus IV, this towering chapel boasts two of the world's most famous works of art: Michelangelo's ceiling frescoes (1508–12) and his *Giudizio universale* (Last Judgment; 1535–41).

boasts one of Rome's richest private art collections, with works by Raphael, Tintoretto, Titian, Caravaggio, Bernini and Velázquez, as well as several Flemish masters. Masterpieces abound, but the undisputed star is Velázquez' portrait of an implacable Pope Innocent X, who grumbled that the depiction was 'too real'. For a comparison, check out Gian Lorenzo Bernini's sculptural interpretation of the same subject.

★Trevi Fountain — FOUNTAIN

(Fontana di Trevi; Map p412; Piazza di Trevi; Ⓜ Barberini) The Fontana di Trevi, scene of movie star Anita Ekberg's late-night dip in *La Dolce Vita,* is a flamboyant baroque ensemble of mythical figures and wild horses taking up the entire side of the 17th-century Palazzo Poli. Following a Fendi-sponsored restoration that finished in 2015, the fountain gleams brighter than it has for years. The tradition is to toss a coin into the water, thus ensuring that you'll return to Rome – on average about €3000 is thrown in every day.

Gallerie Nazionali: Palazzo Barberini — GALLERY

(Galleria Nazionale d'Arte Antica; Map p412; ☎06 481 45 91; www.barberinicorsini.org; Via delle Quattro Fontane 13; adult/reduced €12/6; ⏲8.30am-6pm Tue-Sun; Ⓜ Barberini) Commissioned to celebrate the Barberini family's rise to papal power, this sumptuous baroque palace impresses even before you view its breathtaking art collection. Many high-profile architects worked on it, including rivals Bernini and Borromini; the former contributed a square staircase, the latter a helicoidal one. Amid the masterpieces on display, don't miss Filippo Lippi's *Annunciazione* (Annunciation; 1440–45) and Pietro da Cortona's ceiling fresco *Il Trionfo della Divina Provvidenza* (The Triumph of Divine Providence; 1632–39).

Piazza di Spagna & the Spanish Steps — PIAZZA

(Map p412; Ⓜ Spagna) A magnet for visitors since the 18th century, the Spanish Steps (Scalinata della Trinità dei Monti) provide a perfect people-watching perch. The 135 gleaming steps rise from Piazza di Spagna to the landmark **Chiesa della Trinità dei Monti** (Map p412; ☎06 679 41 79; http://trinitadeimonti.net/it/chiesa/; Piazza Trinità dei Monti 3; ⏲10.15am-8pm Tue-Thu, noon-9pm Fri, 9.15am-8pm Sat, 9am-8pm Sun).

Piazza di Spagna was named after the Spanish Embassy to the Holy See, although the staircase, designed by the Italian Francesco de Sanctis, was built in 1725 with money bequeathed by a French diplomat.

Vatican City, Borgo & Prati

★St Peter's Basilica — BASILICA

(Basilica di San Pietro; Map p416; ☎06 6988 3731; www.vatican.va; St Peter's Sq; ⏲7am-7pm Apr-Sep, to 6pm Oct-Mar; 🚌 Piazza del Risorgimento, Ⓜ Ottaviano-San Pietro) FREE In this city of outstanding churches, none can hold a candle to St Peter's, Italy's largest, richest and most spectacular basilica. Built atop a 4th-century church, it was consecrated in 1626 after 120 years' construction. Its lavish interior contains many spectacular works of art, including three of Italy's most celebrated masterpieces: Michelangelo's *Pietà,* his soaring dome, and Bernini's 29m-high baldachin over the papal altar.

Expect queues and note that strict dress codes are enforced (no shorts, miniskirts or bare shoulders).

★Vatican Museums MUSEUM
(Musei Vaticani; Map p416; ☎06 6988 4676; www.museivaticani.va; Viale Vaticano; adult/reduced €17/8; ⏲9am-6pm Mon-Sat, to 2pm last Sun of month, last entry 2hr before close; 🚌Piazza del Risorgimento, Ⓜ Ottaviano-San Pietro) Founded by Pope Julius II in the early 16th century and enlarged by successive pontiffs, the Vatican Museums boast one of the world's greatest art collections. Exhibits, which are displayed along about 7km of halls and corridors, range from Egyptian mummies and Etruscan bronzes to ancient busts, old masters and modern paintings. Highlights include the spectacular collection of classical statuary in the **Museo Pio-Clementino**, a suite of rooms frescoed by Raphael, and the Michelangelo-painted **Sistine Chapel**.

Castel Sant'Angelo MUSEUM, CASTLE
(Map p416; ☎06 681 91 11; www.castelsantangelo.beniculturali.it; Lungotevere Castello 50; adult/reduced €14/7, free 1st Sunday of the month Oct-Mar; ⏲9am-7.30pm, ticket office to 6.30pm; 📶; 🚌Piazza Pia) With its chunky round keep, this castle is an instantly recognisable landmark. Built as a mausoleum for the emperor Hadrian, it was converted into a papal fortress in the 6th century and named after an angelic vision that Pope Gregory the Great had in 590. Nowadays, it is a moody and dramatic keep that houses the **Museo Nazionale di Castel Sant'Angelo** and its grand collection of paintings, sculpture, military memorabilia and medieval firearms.

Monti & Esquilino

Museo Nazionale Romano: Palazzo Massimo alle Terme MUSEUM
(Map p412; ☎06 3996 7700; www.coopculture.it; Largo di Villa Peretti 1; adult/reduced €10/5; ⏲9am-7.45pm Tue-Sun; Ⓜ Termini) One of Rome's preeminent museums, this treasure trove of classical art is a must-see when you're in the city. The ground and 1st floors are devoted to sculpture, with some breathtaking pieces – don't miss *The Boxer,* a 2nd-century-BC Greek bronze excavated on the Quirinale Hill in 1885, and the *Dying Niobid,* a 4th-century-BC Greek marble statue. But it's the magnificent and vibrantly coloured Villa Livia and Villa Farnesia frescoes on the 2nd floor that are the undisputed highlight.

Basilica di Santa Maria Maggiore BASILICA
(Map p412; ☎06 6988 6800; Piazza Santa Maria Maggiore; basilica free, adult/reduced museum €3/2, loggia €5; ⏲7am-6.45pm, loggia guided tours 9.30am-5.45pm; Ⓜ Termini or Cavour) One of Rome's four patriarchal basilicas, this 5th-century church stands on Esquiline Hill's summit, on the spot where snow is said to have miraculously fallen in the summer of AD 358. Every year on 5 August the event is recreated during a light show in Piazza Santa Maria Maggiore. Much altered over the centuries, the basilica is an architectural hybrid with 14th-century Romanesque campanile, Renaissance coffered ceiling, 18th-century baroque facade, largely baroque interior and a series of glorious 5th-century mosaics.

Trastevere

Trastevere is one of central Rome's most vivacious neighbourhoods, an old-world warren of ochre *palazzi,* ivy-clad facades and cobbled lanes. Originally working class, it's now a trendy hang-out full of bars and restaurants – its very name, 'across the Tiber' *(tras tevere),* evokes both its geographical location and sense of difference.

Basilica di Santa Maria in Trastevere BASILICA
(Map p408; ☎06 581 48 02; Piazza Santa Maria in Trastevere; ⏲7.30am-9pm Sep-Jul, 8am-noon & 4-9pm Aug; 🚌Viale di Trastevere, 🚋Belli) Nestled in a quiet corner of Trastevere's focal square, this is said to be the oldest church dedicated to the Virgin Mary in Rome. In its original

> **SKIP THE LINE AT THE VATICAN MUSEUMS**
>
> ➡ Book tickets online at http://biglietteriamusei.vatican.va/musei/tickets/do (plus €4 booking fee).
>
> ➡ Minimise crowds: Tuesdays and Thursdays are quietest; Wednesday mornings are good as everyone is at the pope's weekly audience; afternoon is better than the morning; and avoid Mondays when many other museums are shut.

Termini, Esquiline and Quirinal

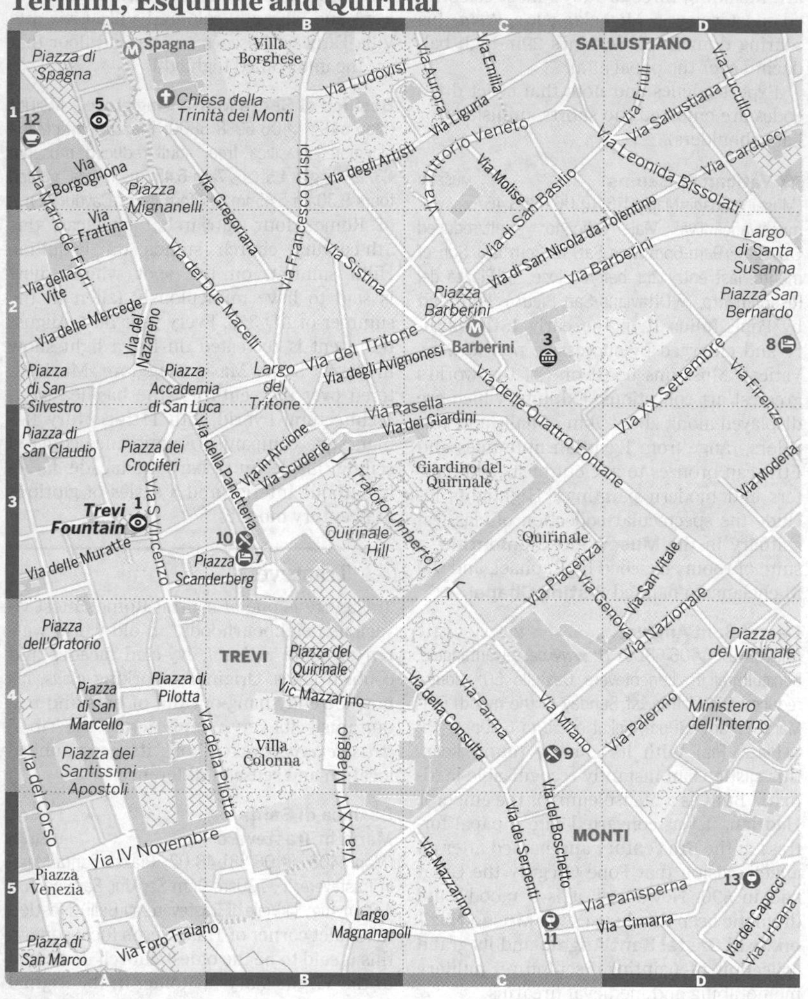

Termini, Esquiline and Quirinal

Top Sights

1 Trevi Fountain A3

Sights

2 Basilica di Santa Maria Maggiore F5
3 Gallerie Nazionali: Palazzo Barberini C2
4 Museo Nazionale Romano: Palazzo Massimo alle Terme F3
5 Piazza di Spagna & the Spanish Steps A1

Sleeping

6 Beehive H2
7 Palazzo Scanderbeg B3
8 RomeHello D2

Eating

9 La Barrique C4
10 Piccolo Arancio B3

Drinking & Nightlife

11 Ai Tre Scalini C5
12 Antico Caffè Greco A1
13 Blackmarket Hall D5

Entertainment

14 Teatro dell'Opera di Roma E3

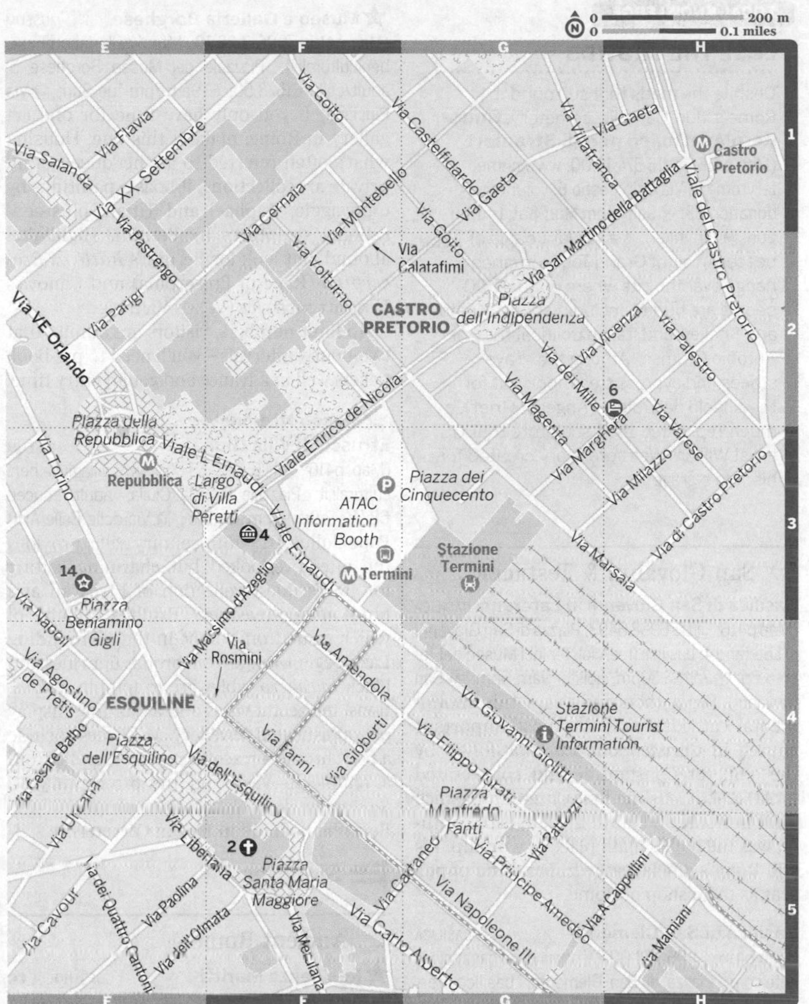

form, it dates from the early 3rd century, but a major 12th-century makeover saw the addition of a Romanesque bell tower and a glittering facade. The portico came later, added by Carlo Fontana in 1702. Inside, the 12th-century mosaics are the headline feature.

★Basilica di Santa Cecilia in Trastevere BASILICA

(Map p416; ☎06 4549 2739; www.benedettinesantacecilia.it; Piazza di Santa Cecilia 22; fresco & crypt each €2.50; ⏰basilica & crypt 10am-12.30pm & 4-6pm Mon-Sat, 11.30am-12.30pm & 4.30-6.30pm Sun, fresco 10am-12.30pm Mon-Sat, 11.30am-12.30pm Sun; 🚌Viale de Trastevere, 🚋Belli) The last resting place of the patron saint of music features Pietro Cavallini's stunning 13th-century fresco, in the nuns' choir of the hushed convent adjoining the church. Inside the church itself, Stefano Maderno's mysterious sculpture depicts St Cecilia's miraculously preserved body, unearthed in the Catacombs of San Callisto in 1599. You can also visit the excavations of Roman houses, one of which was possibly Cecilia's. The church is fronted by a gentle fountain surrounded by roses.

LOCAL KNOWLEDGE

LOSE THE CROWDS

Despite the roads that surround it, Rome's 'non-Catholic' cemetery, **Cimitero Acattolico per gli Stranieri** (Map p416; ☎06 574 19 00; www.cemeteryrome.it; Via Caio Cestio 6; voluntary donation €3; ⏰9am-5pm Mon-Sat, to 1pm Sun; Ⓜ Piramide), is a verdant oasis of peace. An air of Grand Tour romance hangs over the site where up to 4000 people are buried, including poets Keats and Shelley, and Italian political thinker Antonio Gramsci. Among the gravestones and cypress trees, look out for the Angelo del Dolore (Angel of Grief), a much-replicated 1894 sculpture that US artist William Wetmore Story created for his wife's grave.

San Giovanni & Testaccio

Basilica di San Giovanni in Laterano BASILICA
(Map p416; ☎06 6988 6493; Piazza di San Giovanni in Laterano 4; basilica free, cloister incl Museo del Tesoro €5; ⏰7am-6.30pm, cloister 9am-6pm; Ⓜ San Giovanni) For a thousand years this monumental cathedral was the most important church in Christendom. Commissioned by the emperor Constantine and consecrated in AD 324, it was the first Christian basilica built in Rome and, until the late 14th century, was the pope's main place of worship. It's still Rome's official cathedral and the pope's seat as the bishop of Rome.

Basilica di San Clemente BASILICA
(Map p416; ☎06 774 00 21; www.basilicasanclemente.com; Piazza di San Clemente; basilica free, excavations adult/reduced €10/5; ⏰9am-12.30pm & 3-6pm Mon-Sat, 12.15-6pm Sun; 🚌Via Labicana) Nowhere better illustrates the various stages of Rome's turbulent past than this fascinating multilayered church. The ground-level 12th-century basilica sits atop a 4th-century church, which, in turn, stands over a 2nd-century pagan temple and a 1st-century Roman house. Beneath everything are foundations dating from the Roman Republic.

Villa Borghese

Accessible from Piazzale Flaminio, Pincio Hill and the top of Via Vittorio Veneto, Villa Borghese is Rome's best-known park.

★Museo e Galleria Borghese MUSEUM
(Map p416; ☎06 3 28 10; http://galleriaborghese.beniculturali.it; Piazzale del Museo Borghese 5; adult/child €15/8.50; ⏰9am-7pm Tue-Sun; 🚌Via Pinciana) If you only have time for one art gallery in Rome, make it this one. Housing what's often referred to as the 'queen of all private art collections', it boasts paintings by Caravaggio, Raphael and Titian, plus sensational sculptures by Bernini. Highlights abound, but look for Bernini's *Ratto di Proserpina* (Rape of Proserpina) and Canova's *Venere vincitrice* (Venus Victrix).

To limit numbers, visitors are admitted at two-hourly intervals – you'll need to pre-book tickets well in advance and get an entry time.

★Museo Nazionale Etrusco di Villa Giulia MUSEUM
(Map p416; ☎06 322 65 71; www.villagiulia.beniculturali.it; Piazzale di Villa Giulia; adult/reduced €8/4; ⏰9am-8pm Tue-Sun; 🚋Via delle Belle Arti) Pope Julius III's 16th-century villa provides the often-overlooked but charming setting for Italy's finest collection of Etruscan and pre-Roman treasures. Exhibits, many of which came from tombs in the surrounding Lazio region, range from bronze figurines and black *bucchero* tableware to temple decorations, terracotta vases and a dazzling display of sophisticated jewellery. Must-sees include a polychrome terracotta statue of Apollo from a temple in Veio, and the 6th-century-BC *Sarcofago degli Sposi* (Sarcophagus of the Betrothed), found in 1881 in Cerveteri.

Sleeping

Ancient Rome

★Residenza Maritti GUESTHOUSE €€
(Map p406; ☎06 678 82 33; www.residenzamaritti.com; Via Tor de' Conti 17; s €100, d €130-180, tr €150-200, q €170-210; ❄📶; Ⓜ Cavour) Boasting stunning views over the nearby forums and Vittoriano, this hidden gem has 13 rooms spread over three floors. Some are bright and modern; others are more cosy with antiques, original tiled floors and family furniture. There's a fully equipped kitchen and a buffet breakfast is served in the bistro next door.

Centro Storico

Navona Essence BOUTIQUE HOTEL €€
(Map p408; ☎06 8760 5186; www.navonaessencehotel.it; Via dei Cappellari 24; d €70-200; ❄📶;

(Corso Vittorio Emanuele II) Bed down in the heart of the action at this snug boutique hotel. Situated on a narrow backstreet near Campo de' Fiori, it's something of a squeeze but its location is handy for pretty much everywhere and its rooms are attractive, sporting a pared-down modern look and designer bathrooms.

Casa Fabbrini: Campo Marzio B&B €€
(Map p416; 06 324 37 06; https://campomarzio.casafabbrini.it; Vicolo delle Orsoline 13; r from €155; ; Spagna) There are only four B&B rooms on offer in this 16th-century townhouse secreted in a pedestrianised lane near the Spanish Steps, ensuring an intimate stay. Owner Simone Fabbrini has furnished these with a mix of antiques and contemporary pieces, and the result is quite delightful. Common areas include a mezzanine lounge and a kitchen where breakfast is served.

★Palazzo Scanderbeg BOUTIQUE HOTEL €€€
(Map p412; 06 8952 90 01; www.palazzoscanderbeg.com; Piazza Scanderbeg 117; r/ste from €360/1000; ; Barberini) Suite hotels are a dime a dozen in central Rome, but few are as attractive and comfortable as this boutique offering in a 15th-century *palazzo* near the Trevi Fountain. All of the guest rooms are spacious and elegantly appointed; suites have kitchens. Enjoy breakfast in the chic breakfast room or have the butler bring it to your room.

Vatican City, Borgo & Prati

Le Stanze di Orazio BOUTIQUE HOTEL €€
(Map p416; 06 3265 2474; www.lestanzediorazio.com; Via Orazio 3; r €80-200; ; Via Cola di Rienzo, Lepanto) This five-room boutique hotel makes for an attractive home away from home in the heart of the elegant Prati district, a single metro stop from the Vatican. The rooms have refined decor from a modern colour palette. There are top-end luxuries and well-appointed bathrooms. The breakfast area is small and stylish.

Monti & Esquilino

★RomeHello HOSTEL €
(Map p412; 06 9686 00 70; https://theromehello.com/; Via Torino 45; dm/r from €15/45; ; Repubblica) Funnelling all of its profits into worthy social enterprises, this street-art adorned hostel is the best in the city. It offers 200 beds, a communal kitchen, courtyard, lounge and laundry. Dorms max out at 10 beds (most have four) and have good mattresses and en suite bathrooms; each bed has a locker, reading light, USB plug and power point.

★Beehive HOSTEL €
(Map p412; 06 4470 4553; www.the-beehive.com; Via Marghera 8; dm from €25, s/d €70/100; without bathroom €50/80; reception 7am-11pm; ; Termini) More boutique chic than backpacker grungy, this small and stylish hostel has a glorious summer garden and a friendly traveller vibe. Dynamic American owners Linda and Steve exude energy and organise yoga sessions, storytelling evenings and tri-weekly vegetarian and organic dinners around a shared table (€10). Private rooms come with or without bathrooms and air-con; dorms are mixed or female-only.

Trastevere

★Arco del Lauro GUESTHOUSE €€
(Map p408; 06 9784 0350; www.arcodellauro.it; Via Arco de' Tolomei 27; r €120-175; ; Viale di Trastevere, Viale di Trastevere) Perfectly placed on a peaceful cobbled lane on the 'quiet side' of Trastevere, this ground-floor guesthouse sports six gleaming white rooms with parquet floors, a modern low-key look and well-equipped bathrooms. Guests share a fridge, a complimentary fruit bowl and cakes. Breakfast (€5) is served in a nearby cafe. Daniele and Lorenzo, who run the place, could not be friendlier or more helpful.

Relais Le Clarisse HOTEL €€
(Map p416; 06 5833 4437; www.leclarissetrastevere.com; Via Cardinale Merry del Val 20; r €120-200; ; Viale di Trastevere, Trastevere/Mastai) Set around a pretty internal courtyard with a gnarled old olive tree, orange trees and a scattering of tables, this is a peaceful 18-room oasis in Trastevere's bustling core. In

LOCAL KNOWLEDGE

THE SACROSANCT PASSEGGIATA

The *passeggiata* (traditional evening stroll) is a quintessential Roman experience. It's particularly colourful at weekends when families, friends and lovers take to the streets to strut up and down, slurp on gelato and window-shop. To join in, head to Via del Corso around 6pm. Alternatively, park yourself on the Spanish Steps and watch the theatrics unfold beneath you on Piazza di Spagna (p410).

Greater Rome

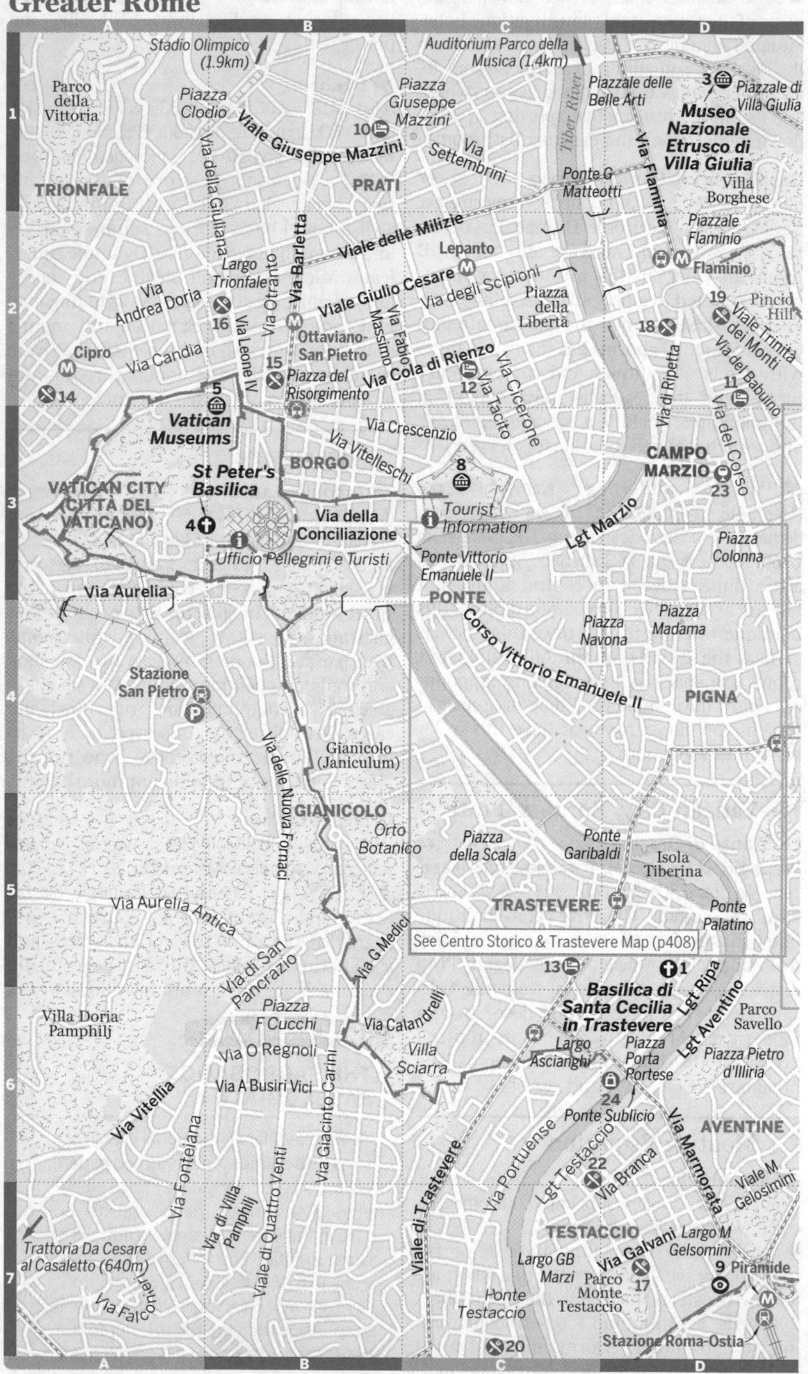

A
B
C
D
1
2
3
4
5
6
7
Stadio Olimpico (1.9km)
Auditorium Parco della Musica (1.4km)
Parco della Vittoria
Piazza Clodio
Piazza Giuseppe Mazzini
Viale Giuseppe Mazzini
Via Settembrini
Tiber River
Piazzale delle Belle Arti
Piazzale di Villa Giulia
Museo Nazionale Etrusco di Villa Giulia
Via Flaminia
Villa Borghese
TRIONFALE
PRATI
Ponte G Matteotti
Via della Giuliana
Via Barletta
Viale delle Milizie
Piazzale Flaminio
Flaminio
Lepanto
Largo Trionfale
Via Otranto
Viale Giulio Cesare
Via degli Scipioni
Piazza della Libertà
Via Andrea Doria
Via Leone IV
Via Fabio Massimo
Pincio Hill
Viale Trinità dei Monti
Via del Babuino
Cipro
Via Candia
Ottaviano-San Pietro
Via Cola di Rienzo
Via di Ripetta
Piazza del Risorgimento
Via Tacito
Via Cicerone
Via del Corso
Vatican Museums
Via Crescenzio
Via Vitelleschi
BORGO
CAMPO MARZIO
VATICAN CITY (CITTÀ DEL VATICANO)
St Peter's Basilica
Via della Conciliazione
Tourist Information
Lgt Marzio
Ufficio Pellegrini e Turisti
Ponte Vittorio Emanuele II
Piazza Colonna
Via Aurelia
PONTE
Piazza Navona
Piazza Madama
Corso Vittorio Emanuele II
Stazione San Pietro
PIGNA
Via delle Nuova Fornaci
Gianicolo (Janiculum)
GIANICOLO
Orto Botanico
Piazza della Scala
Ponte Garibaldi
Isola Tiberina
Via Aurelia Antica
TRASTEVERE
Ponte Palatino
Via G Medici
See Centro Storico & Trastevere Map (p408)
Via di San Pancrazio
Basilica di Santa Cecilia in Trastevere
Lgt Ripa
Lgt Aventino
Parco Savello
Villa Doria Pamphilj
Piazza F Cucchi
Via Calandrelli
Via O Regnoli
Villa Sciarra
Largo Ascianghi
Piazza Porta Portese
Piazza Pietro d'Illiria
Via A Busiri Vici
Via Giacinto Carini
Ponte Sublicio
Via Marmorata
AVENTINE
Via Vitellia
Via Fonteiana
Viale di Trastevere
Via Portuense
Lgt Testaccio
Via Branca
Viale M Gelosimini
Via di Villa Pamphilj
Viale di Quattro Venti
TESTACCIO
Largo M Gelsomini
Trattoria Da Cesare al Casaletto (640m)
Via Galvani
Largo GB Marzi
Parco Monte Testaccio
Piramide
Via Folconieri
Ponte Testaccio
Stazione Roma-Ostia
1
3
4
5
8
9
10
11
12
13
14
15
16
17
18
19
20
22
23
24

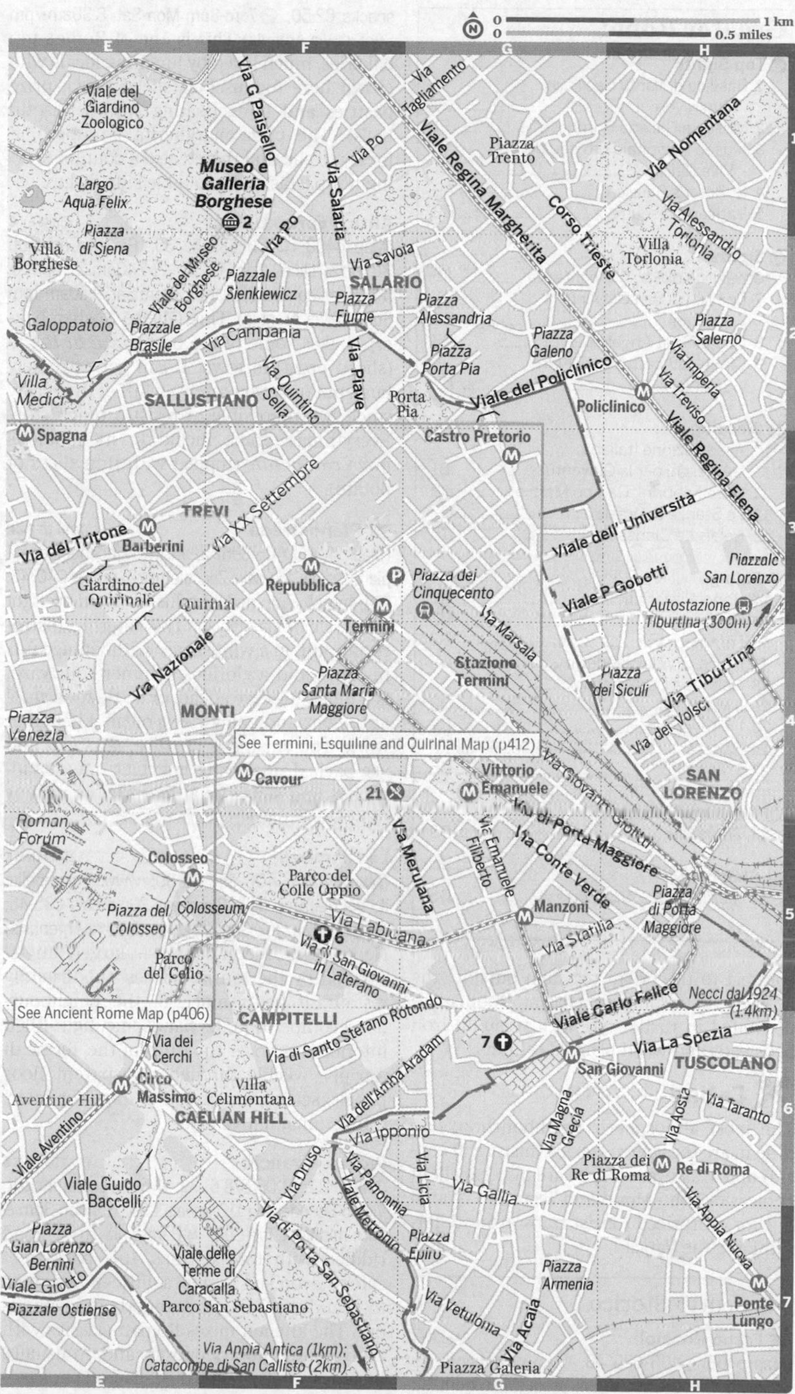

0 1 km
0 0.5 miles
Viale del Giardino Zoologico
Largo Aqua Felix
Piazza di Siena
Villa Borghese
Museo e Galleria Borghese
2
Via G Paisiello
Via Po
Via Salaria
Viale del Museo Borghese
Piazzale Sienkiewicz
Galoppatoio
Piazzale Brasile
Via Campania
Villa Medici
SALLUSTIANO
Via Quintino Sella
Via Piave
SALARIO
Via Savoia
Piazza Fiume
Piazza Alessandria
Piazza Porta Pia
Porta Pia
Via Tagliamento
Viale Regina Margherita
Piazza Trento
Corso Trieste
Via Nomentana
Via Alessandro Torlonia
Villa Torlonia
Piazza Galeno
Piazza Salerno
Via Imperia
Via Treviso
Viale Regina Elena
Viale del Policlinico
Policlinico
Spagna
Castro Pretorio
TREVI
Via XX Settembre
Via del Tritone
Barberini
Repubblica
Giardino del Quirinale
Quirinal
Piazza dei Cinquecento
Termini
Via Marsala
Stazione Termini
Viale dell' Università
Viale P Gobetti
Piazzale San Lorenzo
Autostazione Tiburtina (300m)
Via Nazionale
Piazza Santa Maria Maggiore
MONTI
Piazza Venezia
Piazza dei Siculi
Via Tiburtina
Via dei Volsci
See Termini, Esquiline and Quirinal Map (p412)
Cavour
21
Vittorio Emanuele
Via Giovanni Giolitti
SAN LORENZO
Via di Porta Maggiore
Via Conte Verde
Via Emanuele Filiberto
Via Merulana
Roman Forum
Colosseo
Parco del Colle Oppio
Piazza del Colosseo
Colosseum
Via Labicana
6
Via di San Giovanni in Laterano
Manzoni
Via Statilia
Piazza di Porta Maggiore
Parco del Celio
See Ancient Rome Map (p406)
CAMPITELLI
Via di Santo Stefano Rotondo
Viale Carlo Felice
Necci dal 1924 (1.4km)
Via dei Cerchi
7
Via dell'Amba Aradam
Via La Spezia
San Giovanni
TUSCOLANO
Circo Massimo
Aventine Hill
Villa Celimontana
CAELIAN HILL
Viale Aventino
Via Ipponio
Via Magna Grecia
Via Aosta
Via Taranto
Viale Guido Baccelli
Via Druso
Via Pannonia
Viale Metronio
Via Licia
Via Gallia
Piazza dei Re di Roma
Re di Roma
Via Appia Nuova
Piazza Gian Lorenzo Bernini
Viale Giotto
Piazzale Ostiense
Viale delle Terme di Caracalla
Parco San Sebastiano
Via di Porta San Sebastiano
Piazza Epiro
Via Vetulonia
Piazza Armenia
Via Acaia
Ponte Lungo
Via Appia Antica (1km); Catacombe di San Callisto (2km)
Piazza Galeria
ITALY

Greater Rome

Top Sights

1 Basilica di Santa Cecilia in Trastevere D5
2 Museo e Galleria Borghese F1
3 Museo Nazionale Etrusco di Villa Giulia D1
4 St Peter's Basilica A3
5 Vatican Museums B2

Sights

6 Basilica di San Clemente F5
7 Basilica di San Giovanni in Laterano G6
8 Castel Sant'Angelo C3
9 Cimitero Acattolico per gli Stranieri D7

Sleeping

10 Associazione Italiana Alberghi per la Gioventù B1
11 Casa Fabbrini: Campo Marzio D2
12 Le Stanze di Orazio C2
13 Relais Le Clarisse C5

Eating

14 Bonci Pizzarium A2
15 Fa-Bìo B2
16 Fatamorgana B2
17 Flavio al Velavevodetto D7
18 Gelateria Dei Gracchi D2
19 Il Margutta D2
20 La Tavernaccia C7
21 Panella F4
22 Trapizzino C6

Drinking & Nightlife

23 Zuma Bar D3

Shopping

24 Mercado de Porta Portese D6

contrast to the urban mayhem outside, the hotel is all farmhouse charm. Rooms are decorated in rustic style with wrought-iron bedsteads and wood-beamed ceilings.

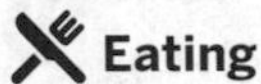

Eating

The most atmospheric neighbourhoods to dine in are the *centro storico* (historical centre) and Trastevere. There are also excellent choices in boho Monti and Testaccio. Watch out for overpriced tourist traps around Termini and the Vatican.

Centro Storico

★Forno Roscioli BAKERY €
(Map p408; ☎06 686 40 45; www.anticofornoroscioli.it; Via dei Chiavari 34; pizza slices from €2, snacks €2.50; ⊙7am-8pm Mon-Sat, 8.30am-7pm Sun; 🚋Via Arenula) This is one of Rome's top bakeries, much loved by lunching locals who crowd here for luscious sliced pizza, prize pastries and hunger-sating *supplì* (risotto balls). The pizza margherita is superb, if messy to eat, and there's also a counter serving hot pastas and vegetable side dishes.

Antico Forno Urbani BAKERY €
(Map p408; ☎06 689 32 35; Piazza Costaguti 31; pizza slices from €1.50; ⊙7.40am-2.30pm & 5-7.45pm Mon-Fri, 8.30am-1.30pm Sat, 9.30am-1pm Sun; 🚋Via Arenula) This Ghetto kosher bakery makes some of the best *pizza al taglio* (sliced pizza) in town. It can get extremely busy, but once you catch a whiff of the yeasty smell it's impossible to resist a quick stop. Everything's good, including its fabulous pizza *con patate* (topped with thin slices of potato).

★Pianostrada RISTORANTE €€
(Map p408; ☎06 8957 2296; www.facebook.com/pianostrada; Via delle Zoccolette 22; meals €40-45; ⊙1-4pm & 7pm-midnight Tue-Fri, 10am-midnight Sat & Sun; 🚋Via Arenula) This uberhip bistro-restaurant, in a white space with vintage furnishings and a glorious summer courtyard, is a must. Reserve ahead, or settle for a stool at the bar and enjoy views of the kitchen at work. The cuisine is creative, seasonal and veg-packed, including gourmet open sandwiches and sensational focaccia, as well as full-blown mains.

La Ciambella ITALIAN €€
(Map p408; ☎06 683 29 30; www.la-ciambella.it; Via dell'Arco della Ciambella 20; meals €35-45; ⊙noon-11pm Tue-Sun; 🚌Largo di Torre Argentina) Near the Pantheon but as yet largely undiscovered by the tourist hordes, this friendly restaurant beats much of the neighbourhood competition. Its handsome, light-filled interior is set over the ruins of the Terme di Agrippa, visible through transparent floor panels, setting an attractive stage for interesting, imaginative food.

Piccolo Arancio TRATTORIA €€
(Map p412; ☎06 678 61 39; www.piccoloarancio.it; Vicolo Scanderbeg 112; meals €38; ⊙noon-3pm & 7pm-midnight Tue-Sun; Ⓜ Barberini) In a 'hood riddled with tourist traps, this backstreet eatery – tucked inside a little house next to grandiose Palazzo Scanderberg – stands out. The kitchen mixes Roman classics with more contemporary options and, unusually, includes a hefty number of seafood choices –

the *linguini alla pescatora* (handmade pasta with shellfish and baby tomatoes) is sensational. Bookings essential.

Il Margutta VEGETARIAN €€
(Map p416; ☎06 3265 0577; www.ilmargutta.bio; Via Margutta 118; lunch buffet weekdays/weekends €15/25, meals €35; ⏰8.30am-11.30pm; ✎; Ⓜ Spagna) This chic art-gallery-bar-restaurant is packed at lunchtime with Romans feasting on its good-value, eat-as-much-as-you-can buffet deal. Everything on its menu is organic, and the evening menu is particularly creative – vegetables and pulses combined and presented with care and flair. Among the various tasting menus is a vegan option.

★ **Salumeria Roscioli** RISTORANTE €€€
(Map p408; ☎06 687 52 87; www.salumeriaroscioli.com; Via dei Giubbonari 21; meals €55; ⏰12.30-4pm & 7pm-midnight Mon-Sat; 🚋Via Arenula) The name Roscioli has long been a byword for foodie excellence in Rome, and this deli-restaurant is the place to experience it. Tables are set alongside the counter, laden with mouth-watering Italian and foreign delicacies, and in a small bottle-lined space behind. The food, including traditional Roman pastas, is top notch and there are some truly outstanding wines. Reservations essential.

Vatican City, Borgo & Prati

Fa-Bio SANDWICHES €
(Map p416; ☎06 3974 6510; Via Germanico 71; meals €5-7; ⏰10.30am-5.30pm Mon-Fri, to 4pm Sat; 🚌Piazza del Risorgimento, Ⓜ Ottaviano-San Pietro) 🍃 Sandwiches, wraps, salads and fresh juices are all prepared with speed, skill and fresh organic ingredients at this busy takeaway. Locals, Vatican tour guides and in-the-know visitors come here to grab a quick lunchtime bite. If you can't find room in the small interior, there are stools along the pavement.

★ **Bonci Pizzarium** PIZZA €
(Map p416; ☎06 3974 5416; www.bonci.it; Via della Meloria 43; pizza slices €5; ⏰11am-10pm Mon-Sat, from noon Sun; Ⓜ Cipro) Pizzarium, the takeaway of Gabriele Bonci, Rome's acclaimed pizza emperor, serves Rome's best sliced pizza, bar none. Scissor-cut squares of soft, springy base are topped with original combinations of seasonal ingredients and served for immediate consumption. Often jammed, there are only a couple of benches and stools for the tourist hordes; head across to the plaza at the metro station for a seat.

Monti & Esquilino

★ **Alle Carrette** PIZZA €
(Map p406; ☎06 679 27 70; www.facebook.com/allecarrette; Via della Madonna dei Monti 95; pizza €5.50-9; ⏰11.30am-4pm & 7pm-midnight; Ⓜ Cavour) Authentic pizza, super-thin and swiftly cooked in a wood-burning oven, is what this traditional Roman pizzeria on one of Monti's prettiest streets has done well for decades. Romans pile in here at weekends for good reason – it's cheap, friendly and delicious. All of the classic toppings are available, as well as gourmet choices such as anchovy and zucchini flower (yum!).

Panella BAKERY €
(Map p416; ☎06 487 24 35; www.panellaroma.com; Via Merulana 54; meals €7-15; ⏰7am-11pm Mon-Thu & Sun, to midnight Fri & Sat; Ⓜ Vittorio Emanuele) Freshly baked pastries, fruit tartlets, *pizza al taglio* (pizza by the slice) and focaccia fill display cases in this famous bakery, and there's also a *tavola calda* ('hot table') where an array of hot dishes are on offer. Order at the counter and eat at bar

WORTH A TRIP

VIA APPIA ANTICA

Completed in 190 BC, the Appian Way connected Rome with Brindisi on Italy's Adriatic coast. It's now a picturesque area of ancient ruins, grassy fields and towering pine trees. But it has a dark history – this is where Spartacus and 6000 of his slave rebels were crucified in 71 BC, and where the ancients buried their dead. Well-to-do Romans built elaborate mausoleums while the early Christians went underground, creating a 300km network of subterranean burial chambers – the catacombs.

Highlights include the **Catacombe di San Sebastiano** (☎06 785 03 50; www.catacombe.org; Via Appia Antica 136; adult/reduced €8/5; ⏰10am-5pm Mon-Sat Jan-Nov; 🚌Via Appia Antica) and the nearby **Catacombe di San Callisto** (☎06 513 01 51; www.catacombe.roma.it; Via Appia Antica 110-126; adult/reduced €8/5; ⏰9am-noon & 2-5pm Thu-Tue Mar-Jan; 🚌Via Appia Antica).

To get to the Via, take bus 660 from Colli Albani metro station (line A) to the end of the line near Capo di Bove.

Roman Forum

A HISTORICAL TOUR

In ancient times, a forum was a market place, civic centre and religious complex all rolled into one, and the greatest of all was the Roman Forum (Foro Romano). Situated between the Palatino (Palatine Hill), ancient Rome's most exclusive neighbourhood, and the Campidoglio (Capitoline Hill), it was the city's busy, bustling centre. On any given day it teemed with activity. Senators debated affairs of state in the ❶ **Curia**, shoppers thronged the squares and traffic-free streets and crowds gathered under the ❷ **Colonna di Foca** to listen to politicians holding forth from the ❷ **Rostri**. Elsewhere, lawyers worked the courts in basilicas including the ❸ **Basilica di Massenzio**, while the Vestal Virgins quietly went about their business in the ❹ **Casa delle Vestali**.

Special occasions were also celebrated in the Forum: religious holidays were marked with ceremonies at temples such as ❺ **Tempio di Saturno** and ❻ **Tempio di Castore e Polluce**, and military victories were honoured with dramatic processions up Via Sacra and the building of monumental arches like ❼ **Arco di Settimio Severo** and ❽ **Arco di Tito**.

The ruins you see today are impressive but they can be confusing without a clear picture of what the Forum once looked like. This spread shows the Forum in its heyday, complete with temples, civic buildings and towering monuments to heroes of the Roman Empire.

TOP TIPS

➡ Get grandstand views of the Forum from the Palatino and Campidoglio.

➡ Visit first thing in the morning or late afternoon; crowds are worst between 11am and 2pm.

➡ In summer it gets hot in the Forum and there's little shade, so take a hat and plenty of water.

Colonna di Foca & Rostri
The free-standing, 13.5m-high Column of Phocus is the Forum's youngest monument, dating to AD 608. Behind it, the Rostri provided a suitably grandiose platform for pontificating public speakers.

Campidoglio (Capitoline Hill)

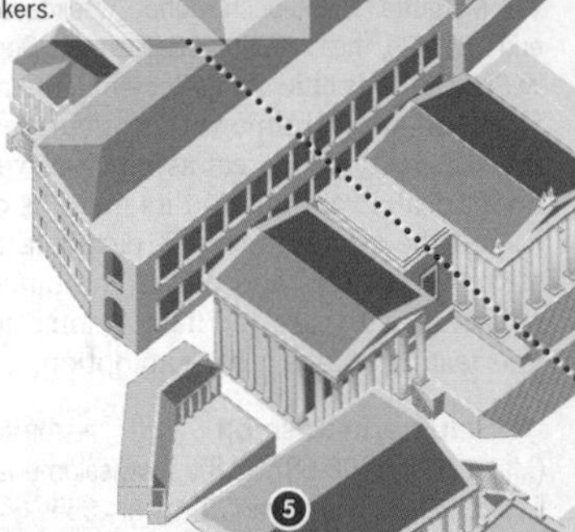

ADMISSION

SUPER tickets are valid for two consecutive days and cover the Roman Forum, Colosseum and Palatino.

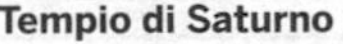

Tempio di Saturno
Ancient Rome's Fort Knox, the Temple of Saturn was the city treasury. In Caesar's day it housed 13 tonnes of gold, 114 tonnes of silver and 30 million sestertii worth of silver coins.

IASCIC/SHUTTERSTOCK ©

VIACHESLAV LOPATIN/SHUTTERSTOCK ©

Tempio di Castore e Polluce
Only three columns of the Temple of Castor and Pollux remain. The temple was dedicated to the Heavenly Twins after they supposedly led the Romans to victory over the Latin League in 496 BC.

Arco di Settimio Severo

One of the Forum's signature monuments, this imposing triumphal arch commemorates the military victories of Septimius Severus. Relief panels depict his campaigns against the Parthians.

Curia

This big barn-like building was the official seat of the Roman Senate. Most of what you see is a reconstruction, but the interior marble floor dates to the 3rd-century reign of Diocletian.

Basilica di Massenzio

Marvel at the scale of this vast 4th-century basilica. In its original form the central hall was divided into enormous naves; now only part of the northern nave survives.

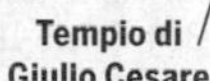

JULIUS CAESAR

Julius Caesar was cremated on the site where the Tempio di Giulio Cesare now stands.

Arco di Tito

Said to be the inspiration for the Arc de Triomphe in Paris, the well-preserved Arch of Titus was built by the emperor Domitian to honour his elder brother Titus.

Casa delle Vestali

White statues line the grassy atrium of what was once the luxurious 50-room home of the Vestal Virgins. The virgins played an important role in Roman religion, serving the goddess Vesta.

stools between shelves of gourmet groceries, or sit on the terrace for waiter service.

★**La Barrique** ITALIAN €€
(Map p412; ☎06 4782 5953; www.facebook.com/la.barrique.94/; Via del Boschetto 41b; meals €40; ⊙1-2.30pm & 7.30-11pm Mon-Fri, 7.30-11.30pm Sat; Ⓜ Cavour) This traditional *enoteca* is a classy yet casual place to linger over a meal. There's a large wine list, mostly sourced from small producers, with lots of natural wines to choose from. A small menu of creative pastas and mains provide a great accompaniment – this is one of the best places to eat in Monti. Bookings recommended.

Trastevere

★**Da Enzo** TRATTORIA €€
(Map p408; ☎06 581 22 60; www.daenzoal29.com; Via dei Vascellari 29; meals €30-35; ⊙12.30-3pm & 7.30-11pm Mon-Sat; 🚌 Lungotevere Ripa, 🚋 Belli) Vintage ochre walls, yellow-checked tablecloths and a traditional menu featuring all the Roman classics are here, but what makes this tiny and staunchly traditional trattoria exceptional is its careful sourcing of local, quality products, many from nearby farms in Lazio. The seasonal, deep-fried Jewish artichokes and the *pasta cacio e pepe* (cheese-and-black-pepper pasta) are among the best in Rome.

★**La Tavernaccia** TRATTORIA €€
(Map p416; ☎06 581 27 92; www.latavernacciaroma.com; Via Giovanni da Castel Bolognese 63; meals €30-45; ⊙12.45-3pm & 7.30-11pm Thu-Tue; 🚋 Stazione Trastevere) This family-run trattoria bustles every minute it's open. Book in advance to get one of Rome's most sought-after tables. Roman classics get stellar treatment here. First courses include various preserved meats and hams that melt away in your mouth. Besides pastas there are many roasts. Staff are cheery and helpful.

> **ROMA PASS**
>
> A cumulative sightseeing and transport card, available online or from tourist information points and participating museums, the **Roma Pass** (www.romapass.it) comes in two forms:
>
> **72 hours** (€38.50) Provides free admission to two museums or sites, as well as reduced entry to extra sites, unlimited city transport, and discounted entry to other exhibitions and events.
>
> **48 hours** (€28) Gives free admission to one museum or site, and then as per the 72-hour pass.

★**Trattoria Da Cesare al Casaletto** TRATTORIA €€
(☎06 53 60 15; www.trattoriadacesare.it; Via del Casaletto 45; meals €25-50; ⊙12.45-3pm & 8-11pm Thu-Tue; 🚋 Casaletto) Rome's best trattoria? Many think so and you will too after an amazing meal of Roman standards where virtually every dish is prepared just *so*. The restaurant is simplicity itself, with dozens of tables in a plain setting – in summer outside under a vine-covered arbour on a vast terrace. The food is rightfully the star. The service is efficient and relaxed.

San Giovanni & Testaccio

Trapizzino FAST FOOD €
(Map p416; ☎06 4341 9624; www.trapizzino.it; Via Branca 88; trapizzini from €3.50; ⊙noon-1am Tue-Sun; 🚌 Via Marmorata) The original of what is now a growing countrywide chain, this is the birthplace of the *trapizzino,* a kind of hybrid sandwich made by stuffing a cone of doughy focaccia with fillers like *polpette al sugo* (meatballs in tomato sauce) or *pollo alla cacciatore* (stewed chicken). They're messy to eat but quite delicious.

★**Flavio al Velavevodetto** ROMAN €€
(Map p416; ☎06 574 41 94; www.ristorantevelavevodetto.it; Via di Monte Testaccio 97-99; meals €30-35; ⊙12.30-3pm & 7.45-11pm; 🚌 Via Galvani) The pick of Testaccio's trattorias, this casual spot is celebrated locally for its earthy, no-nonsense *cucina romana* (Roman cuisine). For a taste, start with *carciofo alla giudia* (deep-fried artichoke) before moving onto *rigatoni alla carbonara* (pasta tubes wrapped in a silky egg sauce spiked with morsels of cured pig's cheek) and finishing up with tiramisu.

Drinking & Nightlife

Much of the drinking action is in the *centro storico*: Campo de' Fiori is popular with students, while the area around Piazza Navona hosts a more upmarket scene. Over the river, Trastevere is another favoured spot with dozens of bars and pubs. Rome's clubbing scene is centred on Testaccio and

ROME'S BEST GELATO

Fatamorgana (Map p416; ☎06 3751 9093; www.gelateriafatamorgana.it; Via Leone IV 52; gelato €2.50-5; ⏰noon-11pm summer, to 9pm winter; Ⓜ Ottaviano-San Pietro) Rome's finest artisanal flavours, now in multiple central locations.

Gelateria del Teatro (Map p408; ☎06 4547 4880; www.gelateriadelteatro.it; Via dei Coronari 65; gelato from €3; ⏰11am-8pm winter, 10am-10.30pm summer; 🚌Via Zanardelli) Around 40 choices of delicious ice cream, all made on-site.

Otaleg (Map p408; ☎338 6515450; www.otaleg.com; Via di San Cosimato 14a; gelato from €2; ⏰noon-midnight; 🖉; 🚋Trastevere/Mastai) Classic and experimental flavours.

Gelateria Dei Gracchi (Map p416; ☎06 322 47 27; www.gelateriadeigracchi.it; Via di Ripetta 261; cones & tubs €2.50-5.50; ⏰noon-10pm Tue-Sun; Ⓜ Flaminio) A taste of heaven in several locations across Rome.

Fior di Luna (Map p408; ☎06 6456 1314; http://fiordiluna.com; Via della Lungaretta 96; gelato from €2.50; ⏰1-8pm Sun & Mon, 1-11pm Tue-Sat; 🚌Belli, 🚋Viale di Trastevere) Great artisanal ice cream in Trastevere.

the Ostiense area, although you'll also find places in Trastevere and the *centro storico*. Admission to clubs is often free, but drinks are expensive.

Barnum Cafe CAFE

(Map p408; ☎06 6476 0483; www.barnumcafe.com; Via del Pellegrino 87; ⏰9am-10pm Mon, 8.30am-2am Tue-Sat; 📶; 🚌Corso Vittorio Emanuele II) A laid-back *Friends*-style cafe, evergreen Barnum is the sort of place you could quickly get used to. With its shabby-chic furniture and white bare-brick walls, it's a relaxed spot for a breakfast cappuccino, a light lunch or a late-afternoon drink. Come evening, a coolly dressed-down crowd sips expertly mixed craft cocktails.

★Caffè Sant'Eustachio COFFEE

(Map p408; ☎06 6880 2048; www.santeustachioilcaffe.it; Piazza Sant'Eustachio 82; ⏰7.30am-1am Sun-Thu, to 1.30am Fri, to 2am Sat; 🚌Corso del Rinascimento) Always busy, this workaday cafe near the Pantheon is reckoned by many to serve the best coffee in town. To make it, the bartenders sneakily beat the first drops of an espresso with several teaspoons of sugar to create a frothy paste to which they add the rest of the coffee. The result is superbly smooth.

★Open Baladin CRAFT BEER

(Map p408; ☎06 683 89 89; www.openbaladinroma.it; Via degli Specchi 6; ⏰noon-2am; 📶; 🚋Via Arenula) This modern pub near Campo de' Fiori has long been a leading light in Rome's craft-beer scene, and with more than 40 beers on tap and up to 100 bottled brews (many from Italian artisanal microbreweries) it's a top place for a pint. As well as great beer, expect a laid-back vibe and a young, international crowd.

Antico Caffè Greco CAFE

(Map p412; ☎06 679 17 00; www.facebook.com/AnticoCaffeGreco; Via dei Condotti 86; ⏰9am-9pm; Ⓜ Spagna) Rome's oldest cafe, open since 1760, is still working the look with the utmost elegance: staff in black tails and bow tie or frilly white pinnies, scarlet flock walls and age-spotted gilt mirrors. Prices reflect this amazing heritage: pay €9 for a cappuccino sitting down or join locals for the same (€2.50) standing at the bar.

★Zuma Bar COCKTAIL BAR

(Map p416; ☎06 9926 6622; www.zumarestaurant.com; Via della Fontanella di Borghese 48, Palazzo Fendi; ⏰6pm-1am Sun-Thu, to 2am Fri & Sat; 📶; Ⓜ Spagna) Dress up for a drink on the rooftop terrace of Palazzo Fendi of fashion-house fame – few cocktail bars in Rome are as sleek, hip or achingly sophisticated as this. City rooftop views are predictably fabulous; cocktails mix exciting flavours like shiso with juniper berries, elderflower and prosecco. DJs spin Zuma playlists at weekends.

Ai Tre Scalini WINE BAR

(Map p412; ☎06 4890 7495; www.facebook.com/aitrescalini; Via Panisperna 251; ⏰12.30pm-1am; Ⓜ Cavour) A firm favourite since 1895, the 'Three Steps' is always packed, with predominantly young patrons spilling out of its bar area and into the street. Its a perfect spot to enjoy an afternoon drink or a sim-

DON'T MISS

NEIGHBOURHOOD SPECIALITIES

Most entrenched in culinary tradition is the Jewish Ghetto area, with its hearty Roman-Jewish cuisine. Deep-frying is a staple of *cucina ebraico-romanesca* (Roman-Jewish cooking), which developed between the 16th and 19th centuries when the Jews were confined to the city's ghetto. To add flavour to their limited ingredients – those spurned by the rich, such as courgette (zucchini) flowers – they began to fry everything from mozzarella to *baccalà* (salted cod). Particularly addictive are the locally grown artichokes, which are flattened out to form a kind of flower shape and then deep-fried to a golden crisp and salted to become *carciofo alla giudia* (Jewish-style artichokes). By contrast, *carciofo alla romana* (Roman-style artichokes) are stuffed with parsley, mint and garlic, then braised in an aromatic mix of broth and white wine until they're soft.

For the heart (and liver and brains) of the *cucina romana*, head to Testaccio, a traditional working-class district clustered around the city's former slaughterhouse. In the past, butchers who worked in the city abattoir were often paid in cheap cuts of meat as well as money. The Roman staple *coda alla vaccinara* translates as 'oxtail cooked butcher's style'. This is cooked for hours to create a rich sauce with tender slivers of meat. A famous Roman dish that's not for the faint-hearted is pasta with *pajata*, made with the entrails of young veal calves, considered a delicacy since they contain the mother's congealed milk. If you see the word *coratella* in a dish, it means you'll be eating *lights* (lungs), kidneys and hearts.

ple meal of cheese, salami and dishes such as *polpette al sugo* (meatballs with sauce), washed down with superb choices of wine or beer.

Blackmarket Hall COCKTAIL BAR
(Map p412; ☎339 7351926; www.facebook.com/blackmarkethall/; Via de Ciancaleoni 31; ⏲6pm-3am; Ⓜ Cavour) One of Monti's best bars, this multi-roomed speakeasy in a former monastery has an eclectic vintage-style decor and plenty of cosy corners where you can enjoy a leisurely, convivial drink. It serves food up till midnight (burgers €12 to €15) and hosts live music – often jazz – on weekends. There's a second venue nearby on Via Panisperna 101.

Necci dal 1924 CAFE
(☎06 9760 1552; www.necci1924.com; Via Fanfulla da Lodi 68; ⏲8am-1am Sun-Thu, to 2am Fri & Sat; 📶👪; 🚋Prenestina/Officine Atac) An all-round hybrid in Pigneto, iconic Necci opened as a gelateria in 1924 and later became a favourite drinking destination of film director Pier Paolo Pasolini. These days it caters to a buoyant hipster crowd, offering a laid-back vibe, retro interior and all-day food. Huge kudos for the fabulous summertime terrace, which is very family friendly.

Terra Satis CAFE, WINE BAR
(Map p408; ☎06 9893 6909; Piazza dei Ponziani 1a; ⏲7am-1am Mon-Thu, to 2am Fri & Sat; 📶; 🚌Viale di Trastevere, 🚋Belli) This hip neighbourhood cafe and wine bar in Trastevere has it all: newspapers, great coffee and charming bar staff, not to mention vintage furniture, comfy banquette seating and really good snacks. On warm days the laid-back action spills out onto its bijou, vine-covered terrace on cobbled Piazza di Ponziani. Good wine and beer selection.

☆ Entertainment

Rome has a thriving cultural scene, with a year-round calendar of concerts, performances and festivals. Upcoming events are also listed on www.turismoroma.it and www.inromenow.com.

★ Auditorium Parco della Musica CONCERT VENUE
(☎06 8024 1281; www.auditorium.com; Viale Pietro de Coubertin; 🚋Viale Tiziano) The hub of Rome's thriving cultural scene, the Auditorium is the capital's premier concert venue. Its three concert halls offer superb acoustics, and together with a 3000-seat open-air arena stage everything from classical music concerts to jazz gigs, public lectures and film screenings.

The Auditorium is also home to Rome's world-class Orchestra dell'Accademia Nazionale di Santa Cecilia (www.santa cecilia.it).

Teatro dell'Opera di Roma OPERA
(Map p412; ☎06 48 16 01; www.operaroma.it; Piazza Beniamino Gigli 1; ⏰box office 10am-6pm Mon-Sat, 9am-1.30pm Sun; Ⓜ Repubblica) Rome's premier opera house boasts a dramatic red-and-gold interior, a Fascist 1920s exterior and an impressive history: it premiered both Puccini's *Tosca* and Mascagni's *Cavalleria rusticana*. Opera and ballet performances are staged between November and June.

Shopping

Rome boasts the usual cast of flagship chain stores and glitzy designer outlets, but what makes shopping here fun is its legion of small, independent shops: family run delis, small-label fashion boutiques, artisans' studios and neighbourhood markets.

Mercado de Porta Portese MARKET
(Map p416; Piazza Porta Portese; ⏰6am-2pm Sun; 🚌 Viale di Trastevere, 🚋 Trastevere/Min P Istruzione) Head to this mammoth flea market to see Rome bargain-hunting. Thousands of stalls sell everything from rare books and fell-off-a-lorry bikes to Peruvian shawls and off-brand phones. It's crazily busy and a lot of fun. Keep your valuables safe and wear your haggling hat for the inevitable discovery of a treasure amid the dreck.

Information

MEDICAL SERVICES

Farmacia Gruppo Farmacrimi (☎06 474 54 21; https://farmacrimi.it; Via Marsala 29; ⏰7am-10pm) Pharmacy in Stazione Termini, next to Platform 1.

Policlinico Umberto I (☎06 4 99 71; www.policlinicoumberto1.it; Viale del Policlinico 155; Ⓜ Policlinico, Castro Pretorio) Rome's largest hospital is near Stazione Termini.

SAFE TRAVEL

Rome is not a dangerous city, but petty theft can be a problem. Watch out for pickpockets around the big tourist sites, at Stazione Termini and on crowded public transport – the 64 Vatican bus is notorious.

TOURIST INFORMATION

There are tourist information points at Fiumicino (p426) and Ciampino (p426) airports, as well as locations across the city. Each can provide city maps and sell the Roma Pass (p422). Online visit Rome's official tourist website, Turismo Roma (www.turismoroma.it).

Information points:

Pazza delle Cinque Lune (Map p408; ⏰9.30am-7pm; 🚌 Corso del Rinascimento) Near Piazza Navona.

Stazione Termini (Map p412; ☎06 06 08; www.turismoroma.it; Via Giovanni Giolitti 34; ⏰8am-6.45pm) In the hall adjacent to platform 24.

Imperial Forums (Map p406; Via dei Fori Imperiali; ⏰9.30am-7pm, to 8pm Jul & Aug; 🚌 Via dei Fori Imperiali)

Via Marco Minghetti (Map p408; ☎06 06 08; www.turismoroma.it; ⏰9.30am-7pm; 🚌 Via del Corso) Between Via del Corso and the Trevi Fountain.

Castel Sant'Angelo (Map p416; www.turismo roma.it; Piazza Pia; ⏰9.30am-7pm summer, 8.30am-6pm winter; 🚌 Piazza Pia)

Trastevere (Map p408; www.turismoroma.it; Piazza Sonnino; ⏰10.30am-8pm; 🚌 Viale di Trastevere, 🚋 Belli)

For information about the Vatican, contact the **Ufficio Pellegrini e Turisti** (Map p416; ☎06 6988 1662; www.vatican.va; St Peter's Sq; ⏰8.30am-6.30pm Mon-Sat; 🚌 Piazza del Risorgimento, Ⓜ Ottaviano-San Pietro).

The **Comune di Roma** (☎06 06 08; www.060608.it; ⏰9am-7pm) runs a free multilingual tourist information phone line providing info on culture, shows, hotels, transport etc. Its website is also an excellent resource.

LOCAL KNOWLEDGE

A ROMAN PASSION

Football is a Roman passion, with support divided between the two local teams: Roma and Lazio. Both play their home games at the **Stadio Olimpico** (☎06 3685 7563; Viale dei Gladiatori 2, Foro Italico; 🚌 Lungotevere Maresciallo Cadorna), Rome's impressive Olympic stadium. If you go to a game, make sure you get it right – Roma play in red and yellow and its supporters stand in the *Curva Sud* (South Stand); Lazio plays in sky blue and its fans fill the *Curva Nord* (North Stand).

WORTH A TRIP

DAY TRIPS FROM ROME

Ostia Antica

An easy train ride from Rome, Ostia Antica is one of Italy's most under-appreciated archaeological sites. The ruins of ancient Rome's main seaport, the **Scavi Archeologici di Ostia Antica** (☎06 5635 8099; www.ostiaantica.beniculturali.it; Viale dei Romagnoli 717; adult/reduced €10/5; ⊙8.30am-7.15pm Tue-Sun summer, last admission 6.15pm, shorter hours winter), are spread out and you'll need a few hours to do them justice.

From Rome, take the Roma–Lido train from Stazione Porta San Paolo (Piramide metro station) to Ostia Antica (every 15 minutes). The 25-minute trip is covered by a standard Rome public transport ticket (€1.50).

Tivoli

Tivoli, 30km east of Rome, is home to two Unesco-listed sites. Five kilometres from Tivoli proper, the ruins of the emperor Hadrian's sprawling **Villa Adriana** (☎0774 38 27 33; www.villaadriana.beniculturali.it; Largo Marguerite Yourcenar 1; adult/reduced €10/5; ⊙8.30am-1hr before sunset) are quite magnificent. Up in Tivoli's hilltop centre, the Renaissance **Villa d'Este** (☎0774 33 29 20; www.villadestetivoli.info; Piazza Trento 5; adult/reduced €10/5; ⊙8.30am-7.45pm Tue-Sun, from 2pm Mon, gardens close sunset, ticket office closes 6.45pm) is famous for its elaborate gardens and fountains.

Tivoli is accessible by Cotral bus (€1.30, 50 minutes, at least wtice-hourly) from Ponte Mammolo metro station.

Getting There & Away

AIR

Rome's main international airport, **Leonardo da Vinci** (☎06 6 59 51; www.adr.it/fiumicino), better known as Fiumicino, is on the coast 30km west of the city.

The much smaller **Ciampino Airport** (⊙8.30am-6pm), 15km southeast of the city centre, is the hub for European low-cost carrier Ryanair.

BOAT

The nearest port to Rome is at Civitavecchia, about 80km north.

Ferries sail here from Spain and Tunisia, as well as Sicily and Sardinia. Book tickets at travel agents or online at www.traghettiweb.it. You can also buy tickets directly at the port.

Half-hourly trains connect Civitavecchia with Roma Termini (€4.60 to €16, 45 minutes to 1½ hours).

BUS

Long-distance national and international buses use the **Autostazione Tibus** (Autostazione Tiburtina; ☎06 44 25 95; www.tibusroma.it; Largo Guido Mazzoni; Ⓜ Tiburtina). Get tickets at the bus station or at travel agencies.

CAR & MOTORCYCLE

Rome is circled by the Grande Raccordo Anulare (GRA), to which all *autostrade* (motorways) connect, including the main A1 north–south artery, and the A12, which runs to Civitavecchia. Car hire is available at the airport and Stazione Termini.

TRAIN

Rome's main station is **Stazione Termini** (www.romatermini.com; Piazza dei Cinquecento; Ⓜ Termini). It has regular connections to other European countries, all major Italian cities and many smaller towns.

Left luggage (1st 5hr €6, 6-12hr per hour €1, 13hr & over per hour €0.50; ⊙6am-11pm) is by platform 24 on the Via Giolitti side of the station.

Getting Around

TO/FROM THE AIRPORTS

Fiumicino

The easiest way to get to/from Fiumicino is by train, but there are also bus services. The set taxi fare to the city centre is €48 (valid for up to four people with luggage).

Leonardo Express Train (www.trenitalia.com; one way €14) Runs to/from Stazione Termini. Departures from Fiumicino airport every 30 minutes between 6.08am and 11.23pm; from Termini between 5.20am and 10.35pm. Journey time is approximately 30 minutes. Wheelchair accessible.

FL1 Train (www.trenitalia.com; one way €8) Connects to Trastevere, Ostiense and Tiburtina stations, but not Termini. Departures from Fiumicino airport every 15 minutes (half-hourly on Sundays and public holidays) between 5.57am and 10.42pm; from Tiburtina every 15 to 30 minutes between 5.01am and 10.01pm.

Ciampino

The best option from Ciampino is to take one of the regular bus services into the city centre. The set taxi fare to the city centre is €30.

SIT Bus – Ciampino (☎06 591 68 26; www.sitbusshuttle.com; to/from airport €6/5, return €9) Regular departures from the airport to Via Marsala outside Stazione Termini between 7.45am and 12.15am; from Termini between 4.30am and 9.30pm. Get tickets online, on the bus or at the desk at Ciampino. Journey time is 45 minutes.

Schiaffini Rome Airport Bus – Ciampino (☎06 713 05 31; www.romeairportbus.com; Via Giolitti; one way/return €5.90/9.90) Regular departures to/from Via Giolitti outside Stazione Termini. From the airport, services run between 4am and 11.45pm; from Via Giolitti, buses run from 4.20am to midnight. Buy tickets onboard, online, at the airport or at the bus stop. Journey time is approximately 40 minutes.

PUBLIC TRANSPORT

Rome's public transport system includes buses, trams, metro and a suburban train network.

Tickets are valid on all forms of public transport, except for routes to Fiumicino airport. They come in various forms:

BIT (€1.50) Valid for 100 minutes and one metro ride.

Roma 24h (€7) Valid for 24 hours.

Roma 48h (€12.50) Valid for 48 hours.

Roma 72h (€18) Valid for 72 hours.

Buy tickets at *tabacchi* (tobacconist shops), news-stands or from vending machines.

Bus

- Rome's buses and trams are run by **ATAC** (☎06 5 70 03; www.atac.roma.it).
- The main bus station is in front of Stazione Termini on Piazza dei Cinquecento, where there's an **information booth** (Map p412; ⌚8am-8pm).
- Other important hubs are at Largo di Torre Argentina and Piazza Venezia.
- Buses generally run from about 5.30am until midnight, with limited services throughout the night.

Metro

- Rome has two main metro lines, A (orange) and B (blue), which cross at Termini.
- Trains run between 5.30am and 11.30pm (to 1.30am on Fridays and Saturdays).

TAXI

- Official licensed taxis are white with an ID number and *Roma Capitale* on the sides.
- Always go with the metered fare, never an arranged price (the set fares to and from the airports are exceptions).
- There are taxi ranks at the airports, Stazione Termini, Piazza della Repubblica, Piazza Barberini, Piazza di Spagna, Piazza Venezia, the Pantheon, the Colosseum, Largo di Torre Argentina, Piazza Belli, Piazza Pio XII and Piazza del Risorgimento.

NORTHERN ITALY

Italy's well-heeled north is a fascinating area of historical wealth and natural diversity. Bordered by the northern Alps and boasting some of the country's most spectacular coastline, it also encompasses Italy's largest lowland area, the fertile Po valley plain. Glacial lakes in the far north offer stunning scenery, while cities such as Venice, Milan and Turin harbour artistic treasures and lively cultural scenes.

Genoa

POP 583,600

Genoa (Genova) is an absorbing city of aristocratic *palazzi,* dark, malodorous alleyways, Gothic architecture and industrial sprawl. Formerly a powerful maritime republic known as *La Superba* (Christopher Columbus was born here in 1451), it's still an important transport hub, with ferry links to destinations across the Med and train links to the Cinque Terre.

Sights

★Palazzo Reale PALACE

(☎010 271 02 36; www.palazzorealegenova.beniculturali.it; Via Balbi 10; adult/reduced €6/3; ⌚9am-7pm Tue-Fri, 1.30-7pm Sat & Sun) If you only get the chance to visit one of the Palazzi dei Rolli (group of palaces belonging to the city's most eminent families), make it this one. A former residence of the Savoy dynasty, it has terraced gardens, exquisite furnishings, a fine collection of 17th-century art and a gilded Hall of Mirrors that is worth the entry fee alone.

★Musei di Strada Nuova MUSEUM

(Palazzi dei Rolli; ☎010 557 21 93; www.museidigenova.it; Via Garibaldi; combined ticket adult/reduced €9/7; ⌚9am-7pm Tue-Fri, 10am-7.30pm Sat & Sun summer, to 6.30pm winter) Skirting the northern edge of the old city limits,

A BRIEF HISTORY OF ITALY

Ancient Times

The Etruscans were the first major force to emerge on the Italian peninsula. By the 7th century BC they dominated central Italy, rivalled only by the Greeks from the southern colony of Magna Graecia. Both thrived until the emerging city of Rome began to flex its muscles.

Founded in the 8th century BC (legend has it by Romulus), Rome flourished, becoming a republic in 509 BC and growing to become the dominant force in the Western world. The end came for the Republic when internal rivalries led to the murder of Julius Caesar in 44 BC and his great-nephew Octavian took power as Augustus, the first Roman emperor.

The empire's golden age came in the 2nd century AD, but a century later it was in decline. Diocletian split the empire into eastern and western halves, and when his successor, Constantine (the first Christian emperor), moved his court to Constantinople, Rome's days were numbered. In 476 the western empire fell to Germanic tribes.

City States & the Renaissance

The Middle Ages was a period of almost constant warfare as powerful city states fought across central and northern Italy. Eventually Florence, Milan and Venice emerged as regional powers. Against this fractious background, art and culture thrived, culminating in an explosion of intellectual and artistic activity in 15th-century Florence – the Renaissance.

Unification

By the end of the 16th century most of Italy was in foreign hands – the Austrian Habsburgs in the north and the Spanish Bourbons in the south. Three centuries later, Napoleon's brief Italian interlude inspired the unification movement, the Risorgimento. With Count Cavour providing the political vision and Guiseppe Garibaldi the military muscle, the movement brought about the 1861 unification of Italy. Ten years later Rome was wrested from the papacy to become Italy's capital.

Birth of a Republic

Italy's brief fascist interlude was a low point. Mussolini gained power in 1925 and in 1940 entered WWII on Germany's side. Defeat ensued and *Il Duce* was killed by partisans in April 1945. A year later, Italians voted in a national referendum to abolish the monarchy and create a constitutional republic.

The Modern Era

Italy's postwar era has been largely successful. A founding member of the European Economic Community, it survived a period of domestic terrorism in the 1970s and enjoyed sustained economic growth in the 1980s. But the 1990s heralded a period of crisis as corruption scandals rocked the nation, paving the way for billionaire media mogul Silvio Berlusconi to enter the political arena.

More recently, political debate has centred on the nation's sluggish economy and issues surrounding immigration. This culminated in the 2018 general election that gave rise to western Europe's first populist government, a coalition of the anti-establishment Five Star Movement and right-wing League party.

pedestrianised Via Garibaldi (formerly Strada Nuova) was planned by Galeazzo Alessi in the 16th century. It quickly became the most sought-after quarter, lined with the palaces of Genoa's wealthiest citizens. Three of these *palazzi* – **Rosso**, **Bianco** and **Doria-Tursi** – today comprise the Musei di Strada Nuova. Between them, they hold the city's finest collection of old masters. Whether you visit the actual museums or not, the street is a must to wander.

Cattedrale di San Lorenzo CATHEDRAL
(Piazza San Lorenzo; ⏰8am-noon & 3-7pm) Genoa's zebra-striped Gothic-Romanesque

cathedral owes its continued existence to the poor quality of a British WWII bomb that failed to detonate here in 1941; it still sits on the right side of the nave like an innocuous museum piece.

The cathedral, fronted by three arched portals, twisting columns and crouching lions, was first consecrated in 1118. The two bell towers and cupola were added in the 16th century.

Sleeping & Eating

Hotel Cairoli HOTEL €

(☎010 246 14 54; www.hotelcairoligenova.com; Via Cairoli 14/4; d €76-116, tr €104-149, q €122-172; ❄@📶) For five-star service at three-star prices, book at this artful hideaway. Rooms, on the 3rd floor of a towering *palazzo*, are themed on modern artists and feature works inspired by the likes of Mondrian, Dorazio and Alexander Calder. Add in a library, chill-out area, small gym and terrace, and you have the ideal bolt-hole. Cheaper rates are available without breakfast.

★**Palazzo Grillo** DESIGN HOTEL €€

(☎010 247 73 56; www.hotelpalazzogrillo.it; Piazza delle Vigne 4; d €160-295; ❄📶) Genovese locals Matteo and Laura have created the extraordinary place to stay that Genoa has been crying out for in a once-derelict *palazzo*. Stunning public spaces are dotted with spot-on contemporary design pieces, character-filled vintage finds and – look in any direction – original 15th-century frescoes. Rooms are simple but super-stylish with Vitra TVs and high ceilings.

★**Trattoria Rosmarino** TRATTORIA €€

(☎010 251 04 75; www.trattoriarosmarino.it; Salita del Fondaco 30; meals €30-35; ⏲12.30-2.30pm & 7.30-10.30pm Mon-Sat) Rosmarino cooks up the standard local specialities, yes, but the straightforwardly priced menu has an elegance and vibrancy that sets it apart. With two nightly sittings, there's always a nice buzz (though there are also enough nooks and crannies that a romantic night for two isn't out of the question). Call ahead for an evening table.

Information

Tourist Office (☎010 557 29 03; www.visitgenoa.it; Via Garibaldi 12r; ⏲9am-6.20pm) Helpful office in the historical centre.

Getting There & Around

AIR

Genoa's **Cristoforo Colombo Airport** (☎010 6 01 51; www.airport.genova.it) is 6km west of the city.

To get to/from it, the **Volabus** (☎848 000 030; www.amt.genova.it; one-way €6) shuttle connects with Stazione Brignole and Stazione Principe. Buy tickets on board.

BOAT

Ferries sail to Spain, Sicily, Sardinia, Corsica, Morocco and Tunisia from the international passenger terminals, west of the city centre.

Grandi Navi Veloci (GNV; ☎010 209 45 91; www.gnv.it) Ferries to Sardinia (Porto Torres from €45) and Sicily (Palermo from €53). Also to Barcelona (Spain, from €51) and Tunis (Tunisia, from €77).

Moby Lines (☎199 30 30 40; www.moby.it) Ferries year-round to the Sardinian ports of Olbia (from €58) and Porto Torres (from €42).

BUS

Buses to international cities depart from **Piazza della Vittoria**, as does a daily bus to/from Milan's Malpensa airport (€25, three hours, 6am) and other interregional services. Tickets are sold at **Geotravels** (☎010 58 71 81; Piazza della Vittoria 57; ⏲9am-12.30pm & 3-7pm Mon-Fri, to noon Sat).

TRAIN

Genoa's Stazione Principe and Stazione Brignole are linked by very frequent trains to Milan (€13.45 to €21.50, 1½ to two hours), Pisa (€27, two hours), Rome (€63.50, five hours) and Turin (€12.40, two hours).

Stazione Principe tends to have more trains, particularly going west to San Remo (€12 to €18, two hours, eight daily) and Ventimiglia (€13.90 to €21, 2¼ hours, 10 daily).

Cinque Terre

Liguria's eastern Riviera boasts some of Italy's most dramatic coastline, the highlight of which is the Unesco-listed **Parco Nazionale delle Cinque Terre** (Cinque Terre National Park) just west of La Spezia. Running for 18km, this awesome stretch of plunging cliffs and vine-covered hills is named for its five tiny villages: Riomaggiore, Manarola, Corniglia, Vernazza and Monterosso.

Activities

The Cinque Terre offers excellent hiking with a 120km network of paths. The best known is the 12km **Sentiero Azzurro** (Blue

Trail), a one-time mule trail that links all five villages. To walk it (or any of the national park's trails) you'll need a **Cinque Terre Treking Card** (one/two days €7.50/14.50), or a **Cinque Terre Treno Card** (one/two days €16/29), which also provides unlimited train travel between La Spezia and the five villages. Both cards are available at park offices.

At the time of writing, two legs of the Sentiero Azzurro were closed for repair work – Riomaggiore to Manarola (the so-called Via dell'Amore) and Manarola to Corniglia. Check www.parconazionale5terre.it for the current situation.

If water sports are more your thing, you can hire snorkelling gear and kayaks at the **Diving Center 5 Terre** (☎ 0187 92 00 11; www.5terrediving.it; Via San Giacomo; ⊙ 10am-4pm Apr-Oct) in Riomaggiore.

ℹ Information

Parco Nazionale Offices (www.parconazionale5terre.it; ⊙ 8am-8pm summer, 8.30am-12.30pm & 1-5.30pm winter) Offices in the train stations of all five villages and La Spezia station; has comprehensive information about hiking trail closures.

ℹ Getting There & Away

BOAT

Golfo Paradiso SNC (☎ 0185 77 20 91; www.golfoparadiso.it) In summer, Golfo Paradiso runs boats to the Cinque Terre from Genoa (one way/return €21/36).

Consorzio Marittimo Turistico Cinque Terre Golfo dei Poeti (☎ 0187 73 29 87; www.navigazionegolfodeipoeti.it) From late March to October, this operator runs daily shuttle boats between all of the Cinque Terre villages (except Corniglia), costing €18 to €22 one way, €26 including all stops, or €35 for an all-day unlimited ticket.

TRAIN

From Genoa Brignole, direct trains run to Riomaggiore (€9.50, 1½ to two hours, at least 10 daily), stopping at each of the villages.

From La Spezia, one to three trains an hour run up the coast between 4.37am and 11.10pm. If you're using this route and want to stop at all the villages, get the Cinque Terre Treno Card.

Monterosso

The largest and most developed of the villages, Monterosso boasts the coast's only sandy beach, as well as a wealth of eating and accommodation options.

Ristorante Belvedere SEAFOOD €€
(☎ 0187 81 70 33; www.ristorante-belvedere.it; Piazza Garibaldi 38; meals €30; ⊙ noon-2.30pm & 6.30-10pm Wed-Mon) With tables overlooking the beach, this unpretentious seafood restaurant is a good place to try the local bounty. Start with *penne con scampi* (pasta tubes with scampi) before diving into *zuppa di pesce* (fish soup). Or partake of the speciality, the amphora Belvedere, where lobsters, mussels, clams, octopus and swordfish are stewed in a herb-scented broth in traditional earthenware.

Vernazza

Perhaps the most attractive of the five villages, Vernazza overlooks a small, picturesque harbour.

From near the harbour, a steep, narrow staircase leads up to **Castello Doria** (€1.50; ⊙ 10am-7pm summer, to 6pm winter), the oldest surviving fortification in the Cinque Terre. Dating from around 1000, it's now largely ruined except for the circular tower in the centre of the esplanade, but the castle is well worth a visit for the superb views it commands.

To overnight in Vernazza, try **La Mala** (☎ 334 2875718; www.lamala.it; Via San Giovanni Battista 29; d €160-250; ❄ 📶), a contemporary boutique hotel in the cliffside heights of the village.

Corniglia

Corniglia, the only village with no direct sea access, sits atop a 100m-high rocky promontory surrounded by vineyards. To reach the village proper from the train station you must first tackle the **Lardarina**, a 377-step brick stairway, or jump on a shuttle bus (one way €2.50).

Once up in the village, you can enjoy dazzling 180-degree sea views from the **Belvedere di Santa Maria**, a heart-stopping lookout point at the end of Via Fieschi.

Manarola

One of the busiest of the villages, Manarola tumbles down to the sea in a helter-skelter of pastel-coloured buildings, cafes, trattorias and restaurants. Bequeathed with more grapevines than any other Cinque Terre village, it is famous for its sweet Sciacchetrà wine.

Riomaggiore

The Cinque Terre's largest and easternmost village, Riomaggiore acts as the unofficial HQ.

For a taste of classic seafood and local wine, search out **Dau Cila** (☎0187 76 00 32; www.ristorantedaucila.com; Via San Giacomo 65; meals €40-45; ⏲12.30-3pm & 7-10.30pm), a smart restaurant-wine bar perched overlooking the twee harbour.

Turin

POP 886,800

With its regal *palazzi*, baroque piazzas, cafes and world-class museums, Turin (Torino) is a dynamic, cultured city. For centuries, it was the seat of the royal Savoy family, and between 1861 and 1864 it was Italy's first post-unification capital. Its now-booming contemporary art and architecture, live-music scene and innovative food and wine culture are definitely aspects you'll want to discover.

Sights

★Museo Egizio MUSEUM

(Egyptian Museum; ☎011 440 69 03; www.museoegizio.it; Via Accademia delle Scienze 6; adult/reduced €15/11; ⏲9am-6.30pm Tue-Sun, 9am-2pm Mon) Opened in 1824 and housed in the austere Palazzo dell'Accademia delle Scienze, this Turin institution houses the most important collection of Egyptian treasure outside Cairo. Among its many highlights are a statue of Ramses II (one of the world's most important pieces of Egyptian art) and a vast papyrus collection.

There are also 500 funerary and domestic items from the tomb of royal architect Kha and his wife Merit, dating from 1400 BC and found in 1906.

Mole Antonelliana LANDMARK

(www.gtt.to.it/cms/turismo/ascensore-mole; Via Montebello 20; lift adult/reduced €8/6, incl Museo €15/12; ⏲lift 9am-8pm Sun, Mon & Wed-Fri, to 11pm Sat) The symbol of Turin, this 167m tower with its distinctive aluminium spire appears on the Italian two-cent coin. It was originally intended as a synagogue when construction began in 1862, but was never used as a place of worship, and nowadays houses the **Museo Nazionale del Cinema** (☎011 813 85 63; www.museocinema.it; adult/reduced €11/9, incl lift €15/12; ⏲9am-8pm Sun, Mon & Wed-Fri, to 11pm Sat). For dazzling 360-degree views, take the **panoramic lift** up to the 85m-high outdoor viewing deck.

Cattedrale di San Giovanni Battista CATHEDRAL

(☎011 436 15 40; www.duomoditorino.it; Via XX Settembre 87; ⏲7am-12.30pm & 3-7pm) Turin's cathedral was built between 1491 and 1498 on the site of three 14th-century basilicas and, before that, a Roman theatre. Plain interior aside, as home to the **Shroud of Turin** (still alleged to be the burial cloth in which Jesus' body was wrapped, despite years of controversy), this is a highly trafficked church. The famous cloth is not on display, but you can see where it is kept and watch explanatory video presentations.

Piazza Castello PIAZZA

Turin's central square is lined with museums, theatres and cafes. The city's Savoy heart, although laid out from the mid-1300s, was mostly constructed from the 16th to 18th centuries. Dominating it is the part-medieval, part-baroque **Palazzo Madama**, the original seat of the Italian parliament. To the north, is the exquisite facade of the **Palazzo Reale**, the royal palace built for Carlo Emanuele II in the mid-1600s.

Sleeping & Eating

★Via Stampatori B&B €

(☎339 2581330; www.viastampatori.com; Via Stampatori 4; s/d €90/110; ❄📶) This utterly lovely B&B occupies the top floor of a frescoed Renaissance building, one of Turin's oldest. Its bright, stylish and individually furnished rooms overlook either a sunny

WORTH A TRIP

MUSEO NAZIONALE DELL'AUTOMOBILE

As the historical birthplace of one of the world's leading car manufacturers – the 'T' in Fiat stands for Torino – Turin is the obvious place for a car museum. **Museo Nazionale dell'Automobile** (☎011 67 76 66; www.museoauto.it; Corso Unità d'Italia 40; adult/reduced €12/10; ⏲10am-2pm Mon, to 7pm Tue-Sun; Ⓜ Lingotto), a dashing modern museum, roughly 5km south of the city centre, doesn't disappoint with its precious collection of more than 200 automobiles – everything from an 1892 Peugeot to a 1980 Ferrari 308 (in red, of course).

terrace or a leafy inner courtyard. The owner's personal collection of 20th-century design is used throughout, including in the two serene common areas. It's central but blissfully quiet.

DuParc Contemporary Suites DESIGN HOTEL €€
(☎011 012 00 00; www.duparcsuites.com; Corso Massimo D'Azeglio 21; r from €115; P❄📶) A business-friendly location doesn't mean this isn't a great choice for all travellers. Staff are young, clued-up and friendly, and the building's iconic modern lines are matched with a fantastic contemporary art collection and comfortable furnishings, along with stunning Italian lighting. Best of all, even the cheapest rooms here are sumptuously large, with king beds, huge baths and floor-to-ceiling windows.

★**Banco vini e alimenti** PIEDMONTESE €€
(☎011 764 02 39; www.bancovinialimenti.it; Via dei Mercanti 13f; meals €30-35; ⏲12.30pm-12.30am Tue-Sat, from 6.30pm Mon) A hybrid restaurant-bar-deli, this smartly designed, low-key place does clever small-dish dining for lunch and dinner. While it might vibe casual wine bar, with young staff in T-shirts, don't underestimate the food: this is serious Piedmontese cooking. Open all day, you can also grab a single-origin pour-over here in the morning, or a herbal house *spritz* in the late afternoon.

Drinking & Nightlife

Aperitivi and more substantial *apericenas* are a Turin institution. If you're on a tight budget, you can fill up on a generous buffet of bar snacks for the cost of a drink.

Nightlife concentrates in the riverside area around Piazza Vittoria Veneto, the Quadrilatero Romano district and the southern neighbourhoods of San Salvarino and Vanchiglia.

Information

Piazza Castello Tourist Office (☎011 53 51 81; www.turismotorino.org; Piazza Castello; ⏲9am-6pm) Central and multilingual.

Getting There & Around

From **Turin Airport** (☎011 567 63 61; www.aeroportoditorino.it; Strada Aeroporto 12), 16km northwest of the city centre in Caselle, airlines fly to Italian and European destinations.

Sadem (☎800 801600; www.sadem.it; one way €7.50) runs an airport shuttle (€7.50, 50 minutes, half-hourly) to/from Piazza Carlo Felice near Porta Nuova train station.

Trains connect with Milan (€12.45 to €34, one to 1¾ hours, more than 30 daily), Florence (€71, three hours, 11 daily), Genoa (€12.40 to €27, 2¼ hours, up to 16 daily) and Rome (€98, 4½ hours, up to 21 daily).

Milan

POP 1.35 MILLION

Few Italian cities polarise opinion like Milan, Italy's financial and fashion capital. Some people love the cosmopolitan, can-do atmosphere, the vibrant cultural scene and sophisticated shopping; others grumble that it's dirty, ugly and expensive. Certainly, it lacks the picture-postcard beauty of many Italian towns, but in among the urban hustle are some truly great sights – Leonardo da Vinci's *Last Supper*, the immense Duomo and La Scala opera house.

Sights

The **Civic Museum Card** (€12; www.turismo.milano.it) is a three-day ticket allowing a single admission to each of Milan's nine civic museums. Tickets can be purchased online or at any of the museums.

★**Duomo** CATHEDRAL
(☎02 7202 3375; www.duomomilano.it; Piazza del Duomo; adult/reduced Duomo €3/2, roof terraces via stairs €10/5, lift €14/7, archaeological area €7/3 (incl Duomo); ⏲Duomo 8am-7pm, roof terraces 9am-7pm, archaeological area 9am-7pm; MDuomo) A vision in pink Candoglia marble, Milan's extravagant Gothic cathedral, 600 years in the making, aptly reflects the city's creativity and ambition. Its pearly white facade, adorned with 135 spires and 3400 statues, rises like the filigree of a fairy-tale tiara, wowing the crowds with its extravagant detail. The interior is no less impressive, punctuated by three enormous stained-glassed apse windows, while in the crypt saintly Carlo Borromeo is interred in a rock-crystal casket.

★**Museo del Novecento** GALLERY
(☎02 8844 4061; www.museodelnovecento.org; Piazza del Duomo 8; adult/reduced €5/3; ⏲2.30-7.30pm Mon, from 9.30am Tue, Wed, Fri & Sun, to 10.30pm Thu & Sat; 📶; MDuomo) Overlooking Piazza del Duomo, with fabulous views of the cathedral, is Mussolini's Arengario, from where he would harangue huge crowds in his heyday. Now it houses Milan's museum

of 20th-century art. Built around a futuristic spiral ramp (an ode to the Guggenheim), the museum's lower floors are cramped, but the heady collection, which includes the likes of Boccioni, Campigli, Giorgio de Chirico and Marinetti, more than distracts.

Pinacoteca di Brera GALLERY
(☎02 7226 3264; www.pinacotecabrera.org; Via Brera 28; adult/reduced €12/8; ⊙8.30am-7.15pm Tue-Sun; Ⓜ Lanza, Montenapoleone) Located upstairs from one of Italy's most prestigious art schools, this gallery houses Milan's collection of Old Masters, much of it 'lifted' from Venice by Napoleon. Rubens, Goya and Van Dyck all have a place, but you're here for the Italians: Titian, Tintoretto, Veronese and the Bellini brothers. Much of the work has tremendous emotional clout, most notably Mantegna's brutal *Lamentation over the Dead Christ.*

★**The Last Supper** ARTWORK
(Il Cenacolo; ☎02 9280 0360; www.cenacolovinciano.net; Piazza Santa Maria delle Grazie 2; adult/reduced €10/5, plus booking fee €2; ⊙8.15am-7pm Tue-Sun; Ⓜ Cadorna) Milan's most famous mural, Leonardo da Vinci's *The Last Supper*, is hidden away on a wall of the refectory adjoining the **Basilica di Santa Maria delle Grazie** (☎02 467 61 11; www.legraziemilano.it; ⊙7am-12.55pm & 3-7.30pm Mon-Sat, 7.30am-12.30pm, 3.30-9pm Sun) FREE. Depicting Christ and his disciples at the dramatic moment when Christ reveals he's aware of his betrayal, it's a masterful psychological study and one of the world's most iconic images. You may very well kick yourself if you miss it, so book in advance or sign up for a guided city tour.

Museo Nazionale Scienza e Tecnologia Leonardo da Vinci MUSEUM
(☎02 48 55 51; www.museoscienza.org; Via San Vittore 21; adult/child €10/7.50, submarine tours €8; ⊙9.30am-5pm Tue-Fri, to 6.30pm Sat & Sun; 🛜👶; Ⓜ Sant'Ambrogio) Kids and would-be inventors will go goggle-eyed at Milan's science museum, the largest of its kind in Italy. It is a fitting tribute in a city where arch-inventor Leonardo da Vinci did much of his finest work. The 16th-century monastery where it's housed features a collection of more than 15,000 items, including models based on da Vinci's sketches, with outdoor hangars housing steam trains, planes and Italy's first submarine, *Enrico Toti* (tours available in English and Italian).

DON'T MISS

QUADRILATERO D'ORO

A stroll around the **Quadrilatero d'Oro** (Golden Quadrilateral; Ⓜ Monte Napoleone), the world's most famous shopping district, is a must. This quaintly cobbled quadrangle of streets – bounded by Via Monte Napoleone, Via Sant'Andrea, Via della Spiga and Via Manzoni – has always been synonymous with elegance and money (Via Monte Napoleone was where Napoleon's government managed loans). Even if you don't have the slightest urge to sling a swag of glossy carriers, the window displays and people-watching are priceless.

Sleeping

Finding a room in Milan (let alone a cheap one) isn't easy, particularly during trade fairs and fashion weeks when rates skyrocket. The tourist office distributes *Milano Hotels,* a free annual listings guide to Milan's hotels.

★**Ostello Bello** HOSTEL €
(☎02 3658 2720; www.ostellobello.com; Via Medici 4; dm €45-50 d €145-175; ❄🛜; 🚊2, 3, 14) A breath of fresh air in Milan's stiffly suited centre, this is the best hostel in town (and hands down the most social). Entrance is through its lively bar-cafe, where you're welcomed with a complimentary drink. Beds are in bright mixed dorms or private rooms, and there's a kitchen, sunny terrace, and basement lounge with board games and table football.

Babila Hostel HOSTEL €
(☎02 3658 8490; www.babilahostel.it; Via Conservatorio 2a; dm €30-42, d €89-159, q 120-176; ❄🛜; Ⓜ San Babila) Set in a beautifully restored neo-Gothic *palazzo* with high, vaulted halls and steel-grey marble fireplaces, this is finally a design hostel worthy of Milan. Colourful Scandinavian furniture, Hugo Pratt prints, a music room and playroom (with table football) add comfort and character, and there's a gorgeous outdoor terrace, a good restaurant and a popular bar that serves cocktails and craft beer.

★**Atellani Apartments** APARTMENT €€
(☎375 528 99 22; www.atellaniapartments.com; Corso Magenta 65; 1-bed apt €170-230, 2-bed apt

Central Milan

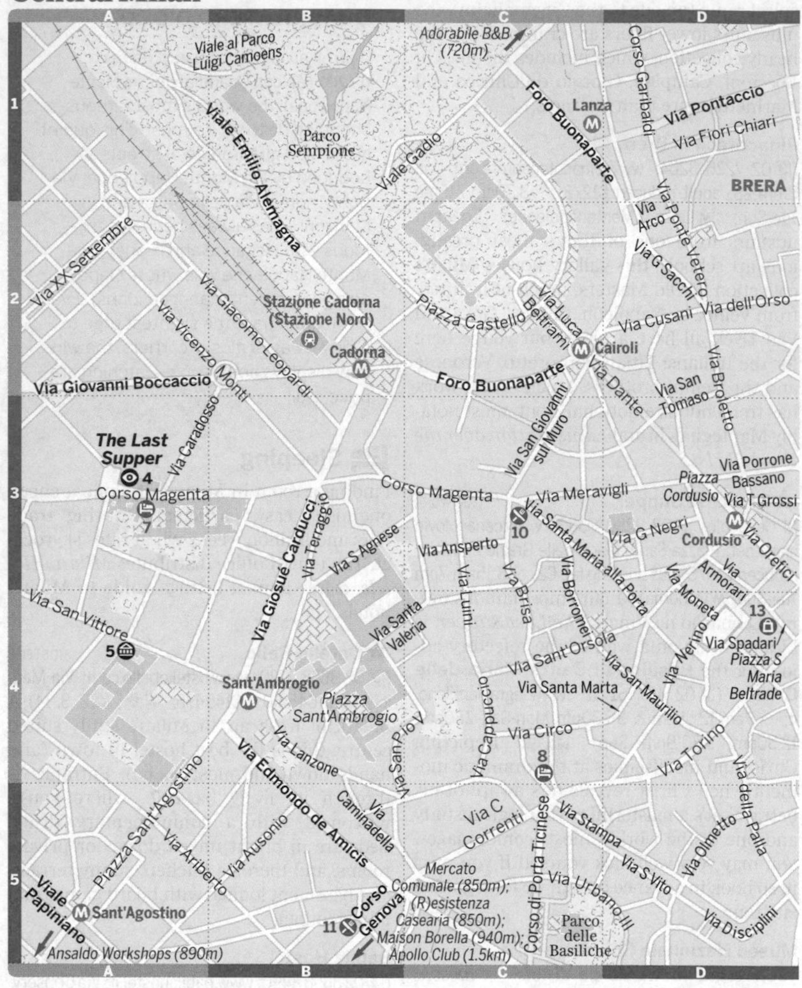

€260-300; P ❄ 📶; M Conciliazione, 🚌16) Now you can bed down in the 15th-century *palazzo* where Leonardo himself lodged while painting *The Last Supper*. Six boutique apartments run by Portaluppi's grandchildren feature the architect's inspired modernist design, parquet floors, slick contemporary decor by local artisans and views over the Santa Maria delle Grazie. Guests can also access the house museum and resplendent garden with Leonardo's own vineyard.

★ **Adorabile B&B** B&B €€
(☎391 114 2490; www.adorabile.it; Via Bramante 14; d €120; M Moscova) Step back in time in this beautiful 1930s apartment with rosette floor tiles, cast-iron radiators and Ariel Soule artworks. Host Franz Iacono has impeccable taste (check out those Hästen beds) and has created four characterful rooms. It's a great place to plug into the city (don't miss the 6pm *aperitivo*) in one of Milan's most up-and-coming neighbourhoods.

★ **Maison Borella** BOUTIQUE HOTEL €€€
(☎02 5810 9114; www.hotelmaisonborella.com; Alzaia Naviglio Grande 8; d €195-260, ste €350-600; P ❄ 📶; M Porta Genova) With balconies overhanging the Naviglio Grande and striking vintage furniture selected by collector

Raimondo Garau, this canalside hotel offers a touch of class in a dedicated bohemian neighbourhood. Converted from an old *casa di ringhiera,* its main rooms are arranged around an inner courtyard draped in ivy and offer charming features such as parquet floors and elegant *boiserie* (sculpted panelling).

Eating & Drinking

Local specialities include *risotto alla milanese* (saffron-infused risotto cooked in bone marrow stock) and *cotoletta alla milanese* (breaded veal cutlet).

Central Milan

Top Sights
1 Duomo E3
2 Museo del Novecento E4
3 Quadrilatero d'Oro F2
4 The Last Supper A3

Sights
Basilica di Santa Maria delle Grazie .... (see 4)
5 Museo Nazionale Scienza e Tecnologia Leonardo da Vinci A4
6 Pinacoteca di Brera E1

Sleeping
7 Atellani Apartments A3
8 Ostello Bello C4

Eating
9 Luini E3
10 Pasticceria Marchesi C3
11 Tokuyoshi B5

Entertainment
12 Teatro alla Scala E2

Shopping
13 Peck D4

★**(R)esistenza Casearia** CHEESE €
(☎02 3598 2848; Piazza XXIV Maggio; cheese boards €10-25; ⏲9am-10pm Tue-Thu, to midnight Fri-Sun; 🚇9) Street-food guru Giuseppe Zen has done it again with this spectacular cheese bar in the **Mercato Comunale** (⏲8.30am-1pm & 4-7.30pm Tue-Sat, 8.30am-1pm Mon). Let them arrange a tasting plate of some of the finest raw-milk cheeses in Lombardy, all of which come from heritage producers with high-mountain pastures. Make a meal of it with a glass of biodynamic wine and the house-made tiramisu.

Luini FAST FOOD €
(☎02 8646 1917; www.luini.it; Via Santa Radegonda 16; panzerotti €2.80; ⏲10am-3pm Mon, to 8pm Tue-Sat; 👪; Ⓜ Duomo) This historical joint is the go-to place for *panzerotti,* delicious pizza-dough parcels stuffed with a combination of mozzarella, spinach, tomato, ham or spicy salami, and then fried or baked in a wood-fired oven. Queues may be long but they move fast.

★**Pasticceria Marchesi** PASTRIES €
(☎02 86 27 70; www.pasticceriamarchesi.it; Via Santa Maria alla Porta 11/a; ⏲7.30am-8pm Tue-Sat, 8.30am-1pm Sun; Ⓜ Cairoli, Cordusio) Since 1824 the original Marchesi *pasticceria* (pastry

shop) has been charming customers with its refined 20th-century features and picture-perfect petit fours. Indulge your sweet tooth with any number of *bignes* (cream puffs), pralines, sugared almonds and fruit gels, and get your hands on some of the best *panettone* in Milan. The dining area out the back also makes for an elegant pit stop.

★Trattoria del Pescatore SEAFOOD **€€**
(☎02 5832 0452; www.trattoriadelpescatore.it; Via Atto Vannucci 5; meals €40-45; ⏲12.30-2.30pm & 8-11pm Mon-Sat; Ⓜ Porta Romana) Milan's finest fish restaurant hides modestly behind a row of green awnings. At the helm are Sardinian couple Giuliano and Agnese and their son, who interned at three-Michelin-starred Arzak in San Sebastián. The pasta is handmade in their home town and the unmissable signature dish is the Catalan lobster drowned in Camone tomatoes and Tropea onions. Finish with green-apple sorbet and Sardinian cheeses.

Tipografia Alimentare ITALIAN **€€**
(☎02 8353 7868; www.tipografiaalimentare.it; Via Dolomiti 1; meals €20-35; ⏲9am-10pm Wed-Mon; ; Ⓜ Turro) Take a break from Milan at this laid-back food hub on the Martesana Canal. Run by fresh-food warriors Martina and Mattia, its vegetarian-focused menu showcases sustainable producers both on the plate and through wine tastings and food events. Matteo's grasp of texture and flavour is outstanding, resulting in layered dishes such as orzo topped with earthy beets and sprinkled with crunchy hazelnuts.

★Tokuyoshi FUSION **€€€**
(☎02 8425 4626; www.ristorantetokuyoshi.com; Via San Calocero 3; meals €50-75; tasting menu €135; ⏲7-10.30pm Tue-Sat, 12.30-2.30pm & 7-10.30pm Sun; 🚋2, 14) Take a creative culinary voyage from Japan to Italy with Yoji Tokuyoshi at the helm. One-time sous-chef of world-renowned Osteria Francescana, this talented chef has already received a Michelin star for his efforts. Expect the unexpected, such as Parmesan tiramisu or cod-filled Sicilian *cannoli* (pastry shells).

☆ Nightlife & Entertainment

The tourist office stocks English-language entertainment guide *Hello Milano* (www.hello milano.it); while online Easy Milano (www.easymilano.it) serves the English-speaking community in Milan.

Apollo Club CLUB
(☎02 3826 0176; www.apollomilano.com; Via Giosuè Borsi 9; cocktails €8-10, meals €33-77; ⏲7pm-3am Wed-Thu, to 4am Fri & Sat, noon-1am Sun; 🚋3) Milan's creative crowd loves to hang at this multifunctional space incorporating a handsome vintage-style bar with club chairs and chesterfields, plus a 30-seat restaurant, a games room and a dance hall illuminated with a twinkling disco ball. Come for aperitif, dinner or brunch, but don't miss Friday's Rollover night, when a thousand people pack the dance floor thanks to international DJ talent.

Check out their Facebook posts for news and events (www.facebook.com/apolloclub milano).

LOCAL KNOWLEDGE

URBAN CHILLING

Conceived as a community hub by architect Luigi Secchi in 1939, **I Bagni Misteriosi** (☎02 8973 1800; www.bagnimisteriosi.com; Via Carlo Botta 18; adult €7-15, reduced €5-12 depending on time of day; ⏲10am-6pm Sun-Mon & Wed, 10am-midnight Thu, 10am-10pm Fri & Sat; ; Ⓜ Porta Romana) is a modernist *lido* with enormous heated pools, close-cropped lawns, shaded porticos, bistro and bar that has been painstakingly restored and is once again a favourite summer retreat. Besides the swimming, there's t'ai chi, art classes, evening *aperitivo*, and dance and music concerts hosted by the adjoining **Teatro Franco Parenti** (☎02 5999 5206; www.teatrofrancoparenti.it; Via Pier Lombardo 14; Ⓜ Porta Romana).

One of the pools, featuring a fountain with flamingos, is dedicated to children, while the other, Olympic-sized pool is adults only. There are hammocks for snoozing, a hip background playlist, tip-top changing rooms and on-duty lifeguards. Both the bar and bistro are accessible from Via Sabina without having to pay the entry fee.

In winter the complex is made over into an ice-skating rink, while future renovations will return the tennis court to use. The best time to visit is between 6.30pm and 9pm for an unforgettable *aperitivo* around the pools.

Teatro alla Scala OPERA
(La Scala; ☎02 7200 3744; www.teatroallascala.org; Piazza della Scala; tickets €30-300; Ⓜ Duomo) One of the most famous opera stages in the world, La Scala's season runs from early December to July. You can also see theatre, ballet and classical music concerts here year-round (except August). Buy tickets online or by phone up to two months before the performance, or from the **box office** (☎02 7200 3744; Largo Ghiringhelli; ⏲10.30am-6pm Mon-Sat, noon-6pm Sun; Ⓜ Duomo). Heavily discounted same-day tickets are also available from the box office.

San Siro Stadium FOOTBALL
(Stadio Giuseppe Meazza; ☎02 4879 8201; www.sansiro.net; Piazzale Angelo Moratti; tickets from €35; Ⓜ San Siro Stadio, 🚋16) San Siro Stadium wasn't designed to hold the entire population of Milan, but on a Sunday afternoon amid 80,000 football-mad citizens it can certainly feel like it. The city's two clubs, AC Milan and FC Internazionale Milano (aka Inter), play on alternate weeks from September to May.

Guided tours of the 1920s-built stadium take you behind the scenes to the players' locker rooms and include a visit to the **San Siro Museum** (☎02 404 24 32; Piazzale Angelo Moratti, Gate 8; museum & tour adult/reduced €15/11; ⏲9.30am-6pm Nov-Mar, to 7pm Apr-Oct), a shrine of memorabilia and film footage.

You can buy tickets for games on the clubs' websites (www.acmilan.com and www.inter.it).

Shopping

Beyond the hallowed streets of the Quadrilatero d'Oro, designer outlets and chains can be found along Corso Buenos Aires and Corso Vercelli; younger, hipper labels live along Via Brera and Corso Magenta; while Corso di Porta Ticinese and Navigli are home of the Milan street scene and subculture shops.

★**Peck** FOOD & DRINKS
(☎02 802 31 61; www.peck.it; Via Spadari 9; ⏲3-8pm Mon, from 9am Tue-Sat; 📶; Ⓜ Duomo) Milan's historical deli is a bastion of the city's culinary heritage, with the huge ground floor turning out a colourful cornucopia of fabulous foods. It showcases a mind-boggling selection of cheeses, chocolates, pralines, pastries, freshly made gelato, pasta, seafood, meat, caviar, pâté, olive oils and balsamic vinegars; it also has a downstairs wine cellar.

BACKSTAGE

Fashion alert: reserve ahead for fascinating behind-the-scenes **tours** (☎02 4335 3521; www.teatroallascala.org; Via Bergognone 34; per person €25; ⏲9am-noon & 2-4pm Tue & Thu; Ⓜ Porta Genova) of La Scala's costume and craft workshops.

Information

Milan Tourist Office (☎02 8845 5555; www.turismo.milano.it; Galleria Vittorio Emanuele II 11-12; ⏲9am-7pm Mon-Fri, 10am-5.30pm Sat & Sun; Ⓜ Duomo) Centrally located in the Galleria with helpful English-speaking staff and lots of useful maps, brochures and information on new exhibitions and events. They also support the useful website www.yesmilano.it, which features the latest events in the city.

Getting There & Away

AIR

Aeroporto Linate (LIN; ☎02 23 23 23; www.milanolinate-airport.com; Viale Forlanini) Located 7km east of Milan city centre; domestic and European flights only. Services at the airport include an exchange office, luggage storage and a VAT refund office.

Aeroporto Malpensa (MXP; ☎02 23 23 23; www.milanomalpensa-airport.com; 🚆Malpensa Express) Northern Italy's main international airport is about 50km northwest of Milan city. Services include car rental, banks, a VAT refund office and free wi-fi.

Orio al Serio (☎035 32 63 23; www.sacbo.it) Low-cost carriers link Bergamo airport with a wide range of European cities. There are direct transport links to Milan.

TRAIN

Regular fast trains depart Stazione Centrale for Venice (€45, 2½ hours), Bologna (€34.50 to €46, one to two hours), Florence (€56, 1¾ hours), Rome (€92, three hours) and other Italian and European cities.

Most regional trains also stop at Stazione Nord in Piazzale Cadorna.

Getting Around

TO/FROM THE AIRPORT

Linate

Airport Bus Express (☎02 3008 9000; www.airportbusexpress.it; one way/return €5/9; Ⓜ Centrale) The Autostradale express airport bus departs from Milan's Stazione Centrale for Linate airport every half-hour between 5.30am and 10pm. Buses from the airport to Milan start at 7.45am and run until 10.45pm. Buses from Milan depart from Piazza Luigi di Savoia on the east side of the station. Tickets are sold on board.

Malpensa

Malpensa Shuttle (☎02 5858 3185; www.malpensashuttle.it; one way/return €10/16; Ⓜ Centrale) This Malpensa airport shuttle runs at least half-hourly between 5.15am and 10.45pm from Stazione Centrale, and roughly hourly throughout the rest of the night. The journey time is 50 minutes and buses depart from Piazza IV Novembre on the west side of the station. Terminal 2 stops need to be requested.

Malpensa Express (☎02 7249 4949; www.malpensaexpress.it; one way €13) Half-hourly trains run from Malpensa airport to Cadorna Stazione Nord (40 minutes) and Stazione Centrale (60 minutes). Services to Cadorna run between 5.40am and 12.20am; to Stazione Centrale from 5.37am to 10.37pm. The train also serves both airport terminals.

Orio al Serio

Orio Shuttle (☎035 31 93 66; www.orioshuttle.com; adult/reduced €7/5; Ⓜ Centrale) This shuttle bus service departs Piazza Luigi di Savoia at Stazione Centrale approximately every half-hour between 2.45am to 10.40pm, and from Orio al Serio airport between 7.45am and 12.15am. The journey takes 50 minutes.

PUBLIC TRANSPORT

Milan's metro, buses and trams are run by **ATM** (Azienda Trasporti Milano; ☎02 4860 7607; www.atm.it). Tickets (€1.50) are valid for one underground ride and up to 90 minutes' travel on city buses and trams. A day ticket costs €4.50.

The Lakes

Ringed by snowcapped mountains, gracious towns and landscaped gardens, the Italian lake district is an enchanting corner of the country.

Lago Maggiore

Snaking across the Swiss border, Lago Maggiore, the westernmost of the three main lakes, retains the belle époque air of its 19th-century heyday when it was a popular retreat for artists and writers.

Its headline sights are the Borromean islands, accessible from **Stresa** on the lake's western bank. **Isola Bella** is dominated by the 17th-century **Palazzo Borromeo** (☎0323 93 34 78; www.isoleborromee.it; Isola Bella; adult/child €16/8.50, incl Palazzo Madre €21/10; ⌚9am-5.30pm mid-Mar–mid-Oct), a grand baroque palace with a wonderful art collection and beautiful tiered gardens. Over the water, **Palazzo Madre** (☎0323 93 34 78; www.isoleborromee.it; adult/child €13/6.50, incl Palazzo Borromeo €21/10; ⌚9am-5.30pm mid-Mar–mid-Oct) lords it over **Isola Madre**.

In Stresa's pedestrianised centre, **Ristorante Il Vicoletto** (☎0323 93 21 02; www.ristorantevicoletto.com; Vicolo del Pocivo 3; meals €30-45; ⌚noon-2pm & 7-10pm Fri-Wed) is a refined restaurant serving excellent regional cooking. Nearby, the **Hotel Saini Meublè** (☎0323 93 45 19; www.hotelsaini.it; Via Garibaldi 10; s/d €75/102; 📶) has warm, spacious rooms.

For further information, contact Stresa's **tourist office** (☎0323 3 13 08; www.stresaturismo.it; Piazza Marconi 16; ⌚10am-12.30pm & 3-6.30pm summer, closed Sat afternoon & Sun winter).

ℹ Getting There & Around

The easiest way to get to Stresa is by train from Milan (€8.60 to €12.90, 1¼ hours, up to 20 daily).

Between April and September, **SAF** (☎0323 55 21 72; www.safduemila.com) operates an Alibus shuttle to/from Malpensa airport (€15, 1½ hours, six daily).

Navigazione Lago Maggiore (☎800 551801; www.navigazionelaghi.it) operates ferries across the lake. From Stresa, a return ticket to Isola Bella costs €6.80; to Isola Madre it's €10.

Lago di Como

Lago di Como, overshadowed by steep wooded hills and snowcapped peaks, is the most spectacular and least visited of the lakes. At its southwestern tip, **Como** is a prosperous town with an imposing **Duomo** (Cattedrale di Como; ☎031 331 22 75; Piazza del Duomo; ⌚9.30am-5.30pm Mon-Fri, 10.45am-4.30pm Sat, 1-4.30pm Sun) FREE and a charming medieval core.

For lunch head to the characterful **Osteria del Gallo** (☎031 27 25 91; www.osteriadelgallo-como.it; Via Vitani 16; meals €26-32; ⌚12.30-3pm Mon-Sat & 7-9pm Tue-Sat).

Also in the medieval centre, the modish **Avenue Hotel** (☎031 27 21 86; www.avenuehotel.it; Piazzolo Terragni 6; d €165-210, ste €250-290; P❄📶) offers slick four-star accommodation.

You can get more information at the **tourist office** (☎342 0076403; www.visitcomo.eu;

VERONA

Wander Verona's atmospheric streets and you'll understand why Shakespeare set *Romeo and Juliet* here – this is one of Italy's most beautiful and romantic cities. Known as *piccola Roma* (little Rome) for its importance in ancient times, its heyday came in the 13th and 14th centuries when it was ruled by the Della Scala (aka Scaligeri) family, who built *palazzi* and bridges, sponsored Giotto, Dante and Petrarch, oppressed their subjects, and feuded with everyone else.

Roman Arena (045 800 32 04; Piazza Brà; adult/reduced €10/7.50; 8.30am-7.30pm Tue-Sun, 1.30-7.30pm Mon) Built of pink-tinged marble in the 1st century AD, Verona's Roman amphitheatre survived a 12th-century earthquake to become the city's legendary open-air opera house, with seating for 30,000 people. You can visit the arena year-round, though it's at its best during the summer opera festival. In winter months, concerts are held at the **Teatro Filarmonico** (045 800 28 80; www.arena.it; Via dei Mutilati 4; opera/concerts from €23/25). From October to May, admission is €1 on the first Sunday of the month.

Giardino Giusti (045 803 40 29; Via Giardino Giusti 2; adult/reduced €8.50/5; 9am-7pm) Across the river from the historical centre, these sculpted gardens are considered a masterpiece of Renaissance landscaping, and are named after the noble family that has tended them since opening the gardens to the public in 1591. The vegetation is an Italianate mix of the manicured and natural, graced by soaring cypresses, one of which the German poet Goethe immortalised in his travel writings.

Casa di Giulietta (Juliet's House; 045 803 43 03; Via Cappello 23; adult/reduced €6/4.50, free with VeronaCard; 1.30-7.30pm Mon, 8.30am-7.30pm Tue-Sun) Juliet's house is a spectacle, but not for the reasons you might imagine – entering the courtyard off Via Cappello, you are greeted by a young multinational crowd, everyone milling around in the tiny space trying to take selfies with the well-rubbed bronze of Juliet. The walls are lined up to 2m high with love notes, many attached with chewing gum. Above you is the famous balcony, with tourists taking their turn to have pics taken against the 'romantic background'.

Verona Villafranca Airport (045 809 56 66; www.aeroportoverona.it) is 12km outside town and accessible by ATV Aerobus to/from the train station (€6, 15 minutes, every 20 minutes 5.15am to 11.30pm).

From the station, buses 11, 12 and 13 (90, 92, 96, 97 and 98 evenings and Sundays) run to Piazza Brà.

Trains connect with Milan (€12.75 to €25, 1¼ to two hours, up to three hourly), Venice (€9 to €27, 1¼ to 2¼ hours, at least twice hourly) and Bologna (€10 to €25, 50 minutes to 1½ hours, 20 daily).

Como San Giovanni, Piazzale San Gottardo; 9am-5pm summer, 10am-4pm Wed-Mon winter) at San Giovanni train station.

Getting There & Around

Regional trains run to Como San Giovanni from Milan's Stazione Centrale and Porta Garibaldi (€4.80, 40 minutes, 19 daily).

Navigazione Lago di Como (800 551801; www.navigazionelaghi.it; Lungo Lario Trento) operates year-round ferries from the jetty near Piazza Cavour.

Lago di Garda

The largest and most developed of the lakes, Lago di Garda straddles the border between Lombardy and the Veneto.

A good base is **Sirmione**, a picturesque village on its southern shores. Here you can investigate the **Grotte di Catullo** (030 91 61 57; www.polomuseale.lombardia.beniculturali.it/index.php/grotte-di-catullo; Piazzale Orti Manara 4; adult/reduced €8/4; 8.30am-7.30pm Mon & Wed-Sat & 9.30am-7pm Sun summer, 8.30am-5pm Mon & Wed-Sat & to 2pm Sun winter), a ruined Roman villa, and enjoy views over the lake's placid blue waters.

There is an inordinate number of eateries crammed into Sirmione's historical centre. One of the best is **La Fiasca** (030 990 61 11, www.trattorialafiasca.it; Via Santa Maria Maggiore 11; meals €30-35; noon-2.30pm & 6.45-10.15pm Thu-Tue), an authentic trattoria serving flavoursome lake fish.

Grand Canal

A WATER TOUR

The 3.5km route of vaporetto (passenger ferry) No 1, which passes some 50 palazzi (mansions), six churches and scene-stealing backdrops featured in four James Bond films, is public transport at its most glamorous.

The Grand Canal starts with controversy: ❶ **Ponte di Calatrava** a luminous glass-and-steel bridge that cost triple the original €4 million estimate. Ahead are castle-like ❷ **Fondaco dei Turchi**, the historic Turkish trading-house; Renaissance ❸ **Palazzo Vendramin**, housing the city's casino; and double-arcaded ❹ **Ca' Pesaro**. Don't miss ❺ **Ca' d'Oro**, a 1430 filigree Gothic marvel.

Points of Venetian pride include the ❻ **Pescaria**, built in 1907 on the site where fishmongers have been slinging lagoon crab for 600 years, and neighbouring ❼ **Rialto Market** stalls, overflowing with island-grown produce. Cost overruns for 1592 ❽ **Ponte di Rialto** rival Calatrava's, but its marble splendour stands the test of time.

The next two canal bends could cause architectural whiplash, with Sanmicheli-designed Renaissance ❾ **Palazzo Grimani** and Mauro Codussi's ❿ **Palazzo Corner-Spinelli** followed by Giorgio Masari-designed ⓫ **Palazzo Grassi** and Baldassare Longhena's baroque jewel box, ⓬ **Ca' Rezzonico**.

Wooden ⓭ **Ponte dell'Accademia** was built in 1930 as a temporary bridge, but the beloved landmark remains. Stone lions flank the ⓮ **Peggy Guggenheim Collection**, where the American heiress collected ideas, lovers and art. You can't miss the dramatic dome of Longhena's ⓯ **Chiesa di Santa Maria della Salute** or ⓰ **Punta della Dogana**, Venice's triangular customs warehouse reinvented as a contemporary art showcase. The Grand Canal's grand finale is pink Gothic ⓱ **Palazzo Ducale** and its adjoining ⓲ **Ponte dei Sospiri**.

PHOTOGOLFER / SHUTTERSTOCK ©

Palazzo Grassi
French magnate François Pinault scandalised Paris when he relocated his contemporary art collection here, to be displayed in galleries designed by Gae Aulenti and Tadao Ando.

Ca' Rezzonico
See how Venice lived in baroque splendour at this 18th-century art museum with Tiepolo ceilings, silk-swagged boudoirs and even an in-house pharmacy.

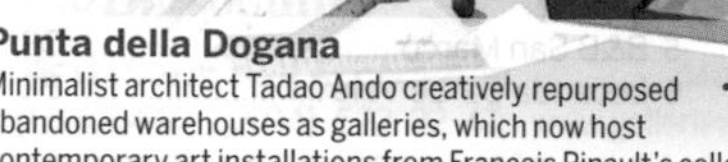

Punta della Dogana
Minimalist architect Tadao Ando creatively repurposed abandoned warehouses as galleries, which now host contemporary art installations from François Pinault's collection.

MUSICIANJZ/SHUTTERSTOCK ©

VERONA

Wander Verona's atmospheric streets and you'll understand why Shakespeare set *Romeo and Juliet* here – this is one of Italy's most beautiful and romantic cities. Known as *piccola Roma* (little Rome) for its importance in ancient times, its heyday came in the 13th and 14th centuries when it was ruled by the Della Scala (aka Scaligeri) family, who built *palazzi* and bridges, sponsored Giotto, Dante and Petrarch, oppressed their subjects, and feuded with everyone else.

Roman Arena (045 800 32 04; Piazza Brà; adult/reduced €10/7.50; 8.30am-7.30pm Tue-Sun, 1.30-7.30pm Mon) Built of pink-tinged marble in the 1st century AD, Verona's Roman amphitheatre survived a 12th-century earthquake to become the city's legendary open-air opera house, with seating for 30,000 people. You can visit the arena year-round, though it's at its best during the summer opera festival. In winter months, concerts are held at the **Teatro Filarmonico** (045 800 28 80; www.arena.it; Via dei Mutilati 4; opera/concerts from €23/25). From October to May, admission is €1 on the first Sunday of the month.

Giardino Giusti (045 803 40 29; Via Giardino Giusti 2; adult/reduced €8.50/5; 9am-7pm) Across the river from the historical centre, these sculpted gardens are considered a masterpiece of Renaissance landscaping, and are named after the noble family that has tended them since opening the gardens to the public in 1591. The vegetation is an Italianate mix of the manicured and natural, graced by soaring cypresses, one of which the German poet Goethe immortalised in his travel writings.

Casa di Giulietta (Juliet's House; 045 803 43 03; Via Cappello 23; adult/reduced €6/4.50, free with VeronaCard; 1.30-7.30pm Mon, 8.30am-7.30pm Tue-Sun) Juliet's house is a spectacle, but not for the reasons you might imagine – entering the courtyard off Via Cappello, you are greeted by a young multinational crowd, everyone milling around in the tiny space trying to take selfies with the well-rubbed bronze of Juliet. The walls are lined up to 2m high with love notes, many attached with chewing gum. Above you is the famous balcony, with tourists taking their turn to have pics taken against the 'romantic background'.

Verona Villafranca Airport (045 809 56 66; www.aeroportoverona.it) is 12km outside town and accessible by ATV Aerobus to/from the train station (€6, 15 minutes, every 20 minutes 5.15am to 11.30pm).

From the station, buses 11, 12 and 13 (90, 92, 96, 97 and 98 evenings and Sundays) run to Piazza Brà.

Trains connect with Milan (€12.75 to €25, 1¼ to two hours, up to three hourly), Venice (€9 to €27, 1¼ to 2¼ hours, at least twice hourly) and Bologna (€10 to €25, 50 minutes to 1½ hours, 20 daily).

Como San Giovanni, Piazzale San Gottardo; 9am-5pm summer, 10am-4pm Wed-Mon winter) at San Giovanni train station.

Getting There & Around

Regional trains run to Como San Giovanni from Milan's Stazione Centrale and Porta Garibaldi (€4.80, 40 minutes, 19 daily).

Navigazione Lago di Como (800 551801; www.navigazionelaghi.it; Lungo Lario Trento) operates year-round ferries from the jetty near Piazza Cavour.

Lago di Garda

The largest and most developed of the lakes, Lago di Garda straddles the border between Lombardy and the Veneto.

A good base is **Sirmione**, a picturesque village on its southern shores. Here you can investigate the **Grotte di Catullo** (030 91 61 57; www.polomuseale.lombardia.beniculturali.it/index.php/grotte-di-catullo; Piazzale Orti Manara 4; adult/reduced €8/4; 8.30am-7.30pm Mon & Wed-Sat & 9.30am-7pm Sun summer, 8.30am-5pm Mon & Wed-Sat & to 2pm Sun winter), a ruined Roman villa, and enjoy views over the lake's placid blue waters.

There is an inordinate number of eateries crammed into Sirmione's historical centre. One of the best is **La Fiasca** (030 990 61 11; www.trattorialafiasca.it; Via Santa Maria Maggiore 11; meals €30-35; noon-2.30pm & 6.45-10.15pm Thu-Tue), an authentic trattoria serving flavoursome lake fish.

Sirmione can be visited on a day trip from Verona, but if you want to overnight, **Meublé Grifone** (☎030 91 60 14; www.gardalakegrifonehotel.eu; Via Gaetano Bocchio 4; s €65-80, d €80-115;) boasts a superb lakeside location and relaxing views.

Get information from the **tourist office** (☎030 374 87 21; iat.sirmione@provincia.brescia.it; Viale Marconi 8; ⏲10am-12.30pm & 3-6pm Mon-Fri, 9.30am-12.30pm Sat) outside the medieval walls.

Getting There & Around

Regular buses run to Sirmione from Verona (€3.60, one hour, hourly).

Navigazione Lago di Garda (☎800 551801; www.navigazionelaghi.it) operates the lake's ferries.

Venice

POP 261,905

Venice (Venezia) is a hauntingly beautiful city. At every turn you're assailed by unforgettable images – tiny bridges arching over limpid canals; chintzy gondolas sliding past working barges; and towers and distant domes silhouetted against the watery horizon. Its celebrated sights are legion, and its labyrinthine alleyways exude a unique, almost eerie atmosphere, redolent of cloaked passions and dark secrets.

Sights

San Marco

★Basilica di San Marco CATHEDRAL

(St Mark's Basilica; Map p446; ☎041 270 83 11; www.basilicasanmarco.it; Piazza San Marco; ⏲9.30am-5pm Mon-Sat, 2-5pm Sun summer, to 4.30pm Sun winter; San Marco) FREE With a profusion of domes and over 8000 sq metres of luminous mosaics, Venice's cathedral is unforgettable. It was founded in the 9th century to house the corpse of St Mark after wily Venetian merchants smuggled it out of Egypt in a barrel of pork fat. When the original building burnt down in 932 Venice rebuilt the basilica in its own cosmopolitan image, with Byzantine domes, a Greek cross layout and walls clad in marble from Syria, Egypt and Palestine.

Campanile TOWER

(Map p446; www.basilicasanmarco.it; Piazza San Marco; adult/reduced €8/4; ⏲8.30am-9pm summer, 9.30am-5.30pm winter, last entry 45min before closing; San Marco) The basilica's 99m-tall bell tower has been rebuilt twice since its initial construction in AD 888. Galileo Galilei tested his telescope here in 1609, but modern-day visitors head to the top for 360-degree lagoon views and close encounters with the **Marangona**, the booming bronze bell that originally signalled the start and end of the working day for the *marangoni* (artisans) at the Arsenale shipyards. Today it rings twice a day, at noon and midnight.

Palazzo Ducale MUSEUM

(Ducal Palace; Map p446; ☎041 271 59 11; www.palazzoducale.visitmuve.it; Piazzetta San Marco 1; adult/reduced incl Museo Correr €20/13, with Museum Pass free; ⏲8.30am-7pm summer, to 5.30pm winter; San Zaccaria) Holding pride of place on the waterfront, this pretty Gothic confection is an unlikely setting for the political and administrative seat of a great republic, but an exquisitely Venetian one. Beyond its dainty colonnades and geometrically patterned facade of white Istrian stone and pale pink Veronese marble lie grand rooms of state, the Doge's private apartments and a large complex of council chambers, courts and prisons.

Ponte dei Sospiri BRIDGE

(Bridge of Sighs; Map p446; San Zaccaria) One of Venice's most photographed sights, the Bridge of Sighs connects the Palazzo Ducale to the 16th-century Priggione Nove (New Prisons). Its improbable popularity is due to British libertine Lord Byron (1788–1824), who mentioned it in one of his long narrative poems *Childe Harold's Pilgrimage*. Condemned prisoners were said to sigh as they passed through the enclosed bridge and glimpsed the beauty of the lagoon. Now the sighs are mainly from people trying to dodge the snapping masses.

Dorsoduro

★Gallerie dell'Accademia GALLERY

(Map p446; ☎041 522 22 47; www.gallerieaccademia.it; Campo de la Carità 1050; adult/reduced €12/2; ⏲8.15am-2pm Mon, to 7.15pm Tue-Sun; Accademia) Venice's historical gallery traces the development of Venetian art from the 14th to 19th centuries, with works by all of the city's artistic superstars. The complex housing the collection maintained its serene composure for centuries until Napoleon installed his haul of art trophies here in 1807 –

Greater Venice

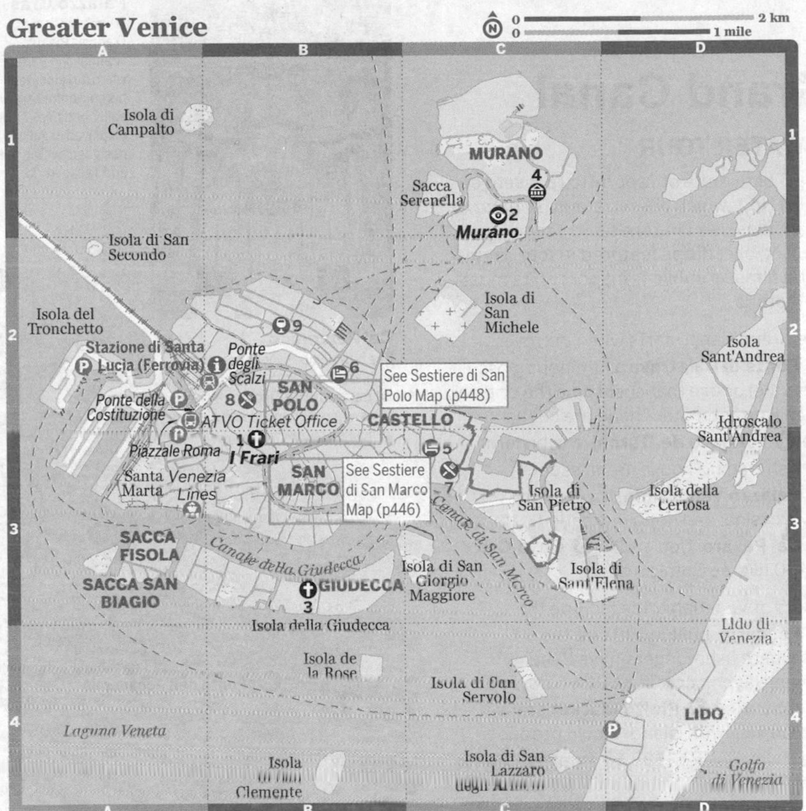

Greater Venice

Top Sights
1 I Frari B3
2 Murano C1

Sights
3 Chiesa del Santissimo Redentore B3
4 Museo del Vetro C1

Sleeping
5 B&B San Marco C3
6 Locanda Ca' Le Vele B2

Eating
7 CoVino C3
8 Osteria Trefanti B2

Drinking & Nightlife
9 Al Timon B2

looted from various religious institutions around town. Since then there's been non-stop visual drama on its walls. Note that the gallery is in the midst of a major refurbishment; some rooms may be closed.

★ Peggy Guggenheim Collection MUSEUM

(Map p446; ☎041 240 54 11; www.guggenheim-venice.it; Calle San Cristoforo 701; adult/reduced €15/9; ⏲10am-6pm Wed-Mon; Accademia) After losing her father on the *Titanic*, heiress Peggy Guggenheim became one of the great collectors of the 20th century. Her palatial canalside home, Palazzo Venier dei Leoni, showcases her stockpile of surrealist, futurist and abstract expressionist art with works by up to 200 artists, including her ex-husband Max Ernst, Jackson Pollock (among her many rumoured lovers), Pablo Picasso and Salvador Dalí.

Basilica di Santa Maria della Salute BASILICA

(Our Lady of Health Basilica; Map p446; www.basilicasalutevenezia.it; Campo de la Salute 1; sacristy adult/reduced €4/2; ⏲9.30am-noon & 3-5.30pm;

Grand Canal

A WATER TOUR

The 3.5km route of vaporetto (passenger ferry) No 1, which passes some 50 palazzi (mansions), six churches and scene-stealing backdrops featured in four James Bond films, is public transport at its most glamorous.

The Grand Canal starts with controversy: ❶ **Ponte di Calatrava** a luminous glass-and-steel bridge that cost triple the original €4 million estimate. Ahead are castle-like ❷ **Fondaco dei Turchi**, the historic Turkish trading-house; Renaissance ❸ **Palazzo Vendramin**, housing the city's casino; and double-arcaded ❹ **Ca' Pesaro**. Don't miss ❺ **Ca' d'Oro**, a 1430 filigree Gothic marvel.

Points of Venetian pride include the ❻ **Pescaria**, built in 1907 on the site where fishmongers have been slinging lagoon crab for 600 years, and neighbouring ❼ **Rialto Market** stalls, overflowing with island-grown produce. Cost overruns for 1592 ❽ **Ponte di Rialto** rival Calatrava's, but its marble splendour stands the test of time.

The next two canal bends could cause architectural whiplash, with Sanmicheli-designed Renaissance ❾ **Palazzo Grimani** and Mauro Codussi's ❿ **Palazzo Corner-Spinelli** followed by Giorgio Masari-designed ⓫ **Palazzo Grassi** and Baldassare Longhena's baroque jewel box, ⓬ **Ca' Rezzonico**.

Wooden ⓭ **Ponte dell'Accademia** was built in 1930 as a temporary bridge, but the beloved landmark remains. Stone lions flank the ⓮ **Peggy Guggenheim Collection**, where the American heiress collected ideas, lovers and art. You can't miss the dramatic dome of Longhena's ⓯ **Chiesa di Santa Maria della Salute** or ⓰ **Punta della Dogana**, Venice's triangular customs warehouse reinvented as a contemporary art showcase. The Grand Canal's grand finale is pink Gothic ⓱ **Palazzo Ducale** and its adjoining ⓲ **Ponte dei Sospiri**.

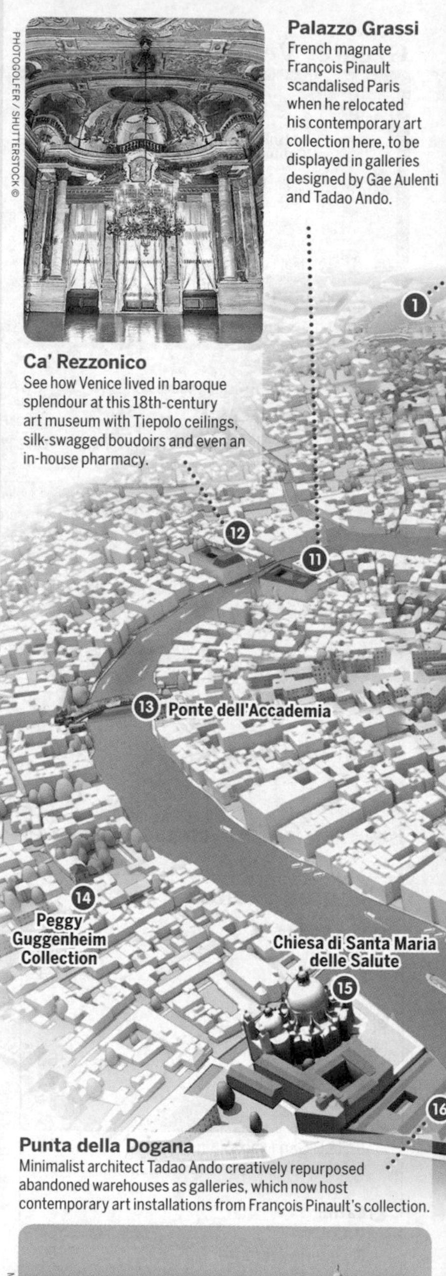

PHOTOGOLFER / SHUTTERSTOCK ©

Palazzo Grassi
French magnate François Pinault scandalised Paris when he relocated his contemporary art collection here, to be displayed in galleries designed by Gae Aulenti and Tadao Ando.

Ca' Rezzonico
See how Venice lived in baroque splendour at this 18th-century art museum with Tiepolo ceilings, silk-swagged boudoirs and even an in-house pharmacy.

Punta della Dogana
Minimalist architect Tadao Ando creatively repurposed abandoned warehouses as galleries, which now host contemporary art installations from François Pinault's collection.

MUSICIANJZ/SHUTTERSTOCK ©

PETR JILEK/SHUTTERSTOCK ©

Ponte di Calatrava
With its starkly streamlined fish-fin shape, the 2008 bridge was the first to be built over the Grand Canal in 75 years.

Fondaco dei Turchi
Recognisable by its double colonnade, watchtowers, and dugout canoe parked at the Museo di Storia Naturale's ground-floor loggia.

JAIONE GARCIA/SHUTTERSTOCK ©

Ca' d'Oro
Behind the triple Gothic arcades are priceless masterpieces: Titians looted by Napoleon, a rare Mantegna and semiprecious stone mosaic floors.

4
5

Palazzo Grimani 9

10 Palazzo Corner-Spinelli

8 Ponte di Rialto

Ponte dei Sospiri 18

Palazzo Ducale 17

Ca' Pesaro
Originally designed by Baldassare Longhena, this palazzo was bequeathed to the city in 1898 to house the Galleria d'Arte Moderna and Museo d'Arte Orientale.

Ponte di Rialto
Antonio da Ponte beat out Palladio for the commission of this bridge, but construction costs spiralled to 250,000 Venetian ducats – about €19 million today.

KIEVVICTOR/SHUTTERSTOCK ©

NAVIGATING VENICE

Venice is not an easy place to navigate and even with a smartphone and satellite mapping you're bound to get lost. The main area of interest lies between Santa Lucia train station (signposted as the *ferrovia*) and Piazza San Marco (St Mark's Sq). The path between the two – Venice's main drag – is a good 40- to 50-minute walk. It also helps to know that the city is divided into six *sestieri* (districts): Cannaregio, Castello, San Marco, Dorsoduro, San Polo and Santa Croce.

Salute) FREE Baldassare Longhena's magnificent basilica is prominently positioned near the entrance to the Grand Canal, its white stones, exuberant statuary and high domes gleaming spectacularly under the sun. The church makes good on an official appeal by the Venetian Senate directly to the Madonna in 1630, after 80,000 Venetians had been killed by plague.

The Senate promised the Madonna a church in exchange for her intervention on behalf of Venice – no expense or effort spared.

San Polo & Santa Croce

★I Frari BASILICA

(Basilica di Santa Maria Gloriosa dei Frari; Map p441; 041 272 86 18; www.basilicadeifrari.it; Campo dei Frari 3072, San Polo; adult/reduced €3/1.50, with Chorus Pass free; 9am-6pm Mon-Sat, 1-6pm Sun; San Tomà) A soaring Gothic church, the Friary's assets include marquetry choir stalls, Canova's pyramid mausoleum, Bellini's achingly sweet *Madonna with Child* triptych in the sacristy, and Longhena's creepy Doge Pesaro funereal monument.

Upstaging them all, however, is Titian's 1518 *Assunta* (Assumption) altarpiece, in which a radiant red-cloaked Madonna reaches heavenward, steps onto a cloud and escapes this mortal coil. Titian himself – lost to the plague in 1576 at the age 94 – has his memorial here.

Giudecca

Chiesa del Santissimo Redentore CHURCH

(Church of the Most Holy Redeemer; Map p441; www.chorusvenezia.org; Campo del SS Redentore 194, Giudecca; adult/reduced €3/1.50, with Chorus Pass free; 10.30am-4.30pm Mon-Sat; Redentore) Built to celebrate the city's deliverance from the Black Death, Palladio's *Il Redentore* was completed under Antonio da Ponte (of Rialto Bridge fame) in 1592. The theme is taken up in Paolo Piazza's monochrome *Venice's Offering for Liberation from the Plague of 1575–77* (1619), high above the entry door. Look for Tintoretto's *The Flagellation of Christ* (1588) on the third altar to the right.

The Islands

★Murano ISLAND

(Map p441; Faro) Murano has been the home of Venetian glass-making since the 13th century. Today artisans continue to ply their trade at workshops dotted around the island. To learn about local manufacturing traditions and view a collection of historical glass, visit the **Museo del Vetro** (Glass Museum; Map p441; 041 243 49 14; www.museovetro.visitmuve.it; Fondamenta Giustinian 8; adult/reduced €12/9.50, free with Museum Pass; 10am-5pm; Museo).

★Burano ISLAND

(Burano) Burano, with its cheery pastel-coloured houses, is renowned for its handmade lace, which once graced the décolletages and ruffs of European aristocracy. These days, with a couple of notable exceptions, much of the lace sold in local shops is imported. Still, tourists head here in droves to snap photos of the brightly painted houses reflecting in the canals – clogging up the bridges and driving the locals to distraction in the process. It's a much more peaceful place in the evening.

Torcello ISLAND

(Torcello) Torcello, the republic's original island settlement, was largely abandoned due to malaria and now counts only around 14 permanent residents. Its mosaic-clad Byzantine church, the **Basilica di Santa Maria Assunta** (041 73 01 19; Piazza Torcello; adult/reduced €5/4, incl museum & campanile €12/10; 10.30am-5.30pm), is Venice's oldest.

Activities

The official rate for a gondola tour is €80 for 30 minutes (for up to six people). After 7pm it's €100 for 35 minutes.

Festivals & Events

Carnevale CARNIVAL

(www.carnevale.venezia.it; ⌚Jan/Feb) Masquerade madness stretches over two weeks in January or February before Lent. A Cannaregio Canal flotilla marks the outbreak of festivities, which feature masked balls, processions, public parties in every *campo* (square) and all manner of dressing up.

★**La Biennale di Venezia** ART

(www.labiennale.org; Giardini della Biennale; ⌚mid-May–Nov; ⛴Giardini Biennale) Europe's premier arts showcase since 1907 is something of a misnomer: the Biennale is now actually held every year, but the spotlight alternates between art (odd-numbered years) and architecture (even-numbered years). Running alongside the two main events are annual showcases of dance, theatre, cinema and music.

Venice International Film Festival FILM

(Mostra Internazionale d'Arte Cinematografica; www.labiennale.org/en/cinema; Lungomare Marconi, Lido; ⌚Aug-Sep) The only thing hotter than a Lido beach in August is the Film Festival's star-studded red carpet, usually rolled out from the last weekend in August through to the first week of September.

Regata Storica CULTURAL

(www.regatastoricavenezia.it; ⌚Sep) Sixteenth-century costumes, eight-oared gondolas and ceremonial barques feature in this historical procession (usually held in early September) along the Grand Canal, which re-enacts the arrival of the Queen of Cyprus and precedes gondola races.

Sleeping

B&B San Marco B&B €

(Map p441; ☎041 522 75 89; www.realvenice.it; Fondamente San Giorgio dei Schiavoni 3385l; r €135, without bathroom €105-135; ❄; ⛴San Zaccaria) Alice and Marco welcome you warmly to their home overlooking Carpaccio's frescoed Scuola Dalmata. The 3rd-floor apartment (no lift), with its parquet floors and large windows, is furnished with family antiques and offers photogenic views over the terracotta rooftops and canals. The hosts live upstairs, so they're always on hand with great recommendations.

Oltre Il Giardino BOUTIQUE HOTEL €€

(Map p448; ☎041 275 00 15; www.oltreilgiardino-venezia.com; Fondamenta Contarini 2542; d/ste from €180/280; ❄📶; ⛴San Tomà) Live the dream in this garden villa, the 1920s home of Alma Mahler, the composer's widow. Hidden behind a lush walled garden, its six high-ceilinged guest rooms and suites marry historical charm with modern comfort: marquetry composer's desks, candelabras and 19th-century poker chairs sit alongside flat-screen TVs and designer bathrooms, while outside, pomegranate trees flower.

★**Locanda Ca' Le Vele** B&B €€

(Map p441; ☎041 241 39 60; www.locandalevele.com; Calle de le Vele 3969; d €122-148, ste €165-183; ❄📶; ⛴Ca' d'Oro) The lane may be quiet and the house might look demure, but inside it's Venetian glam all the way. The six guestrooms are a surprisingly stylish riot of terrazzo floors, damask furnishings, Murano glass sconces and ornate gilded beds with busy covers. Pay a little extra for a canal view.

Eating

★**Osteria Trefanti** VENETIAN €€

(Map p441; ☎041 520 17 89; www.osteriatrefanti.it; Fondamenta del Rio Marin o dei Garzoti 888; meals €40-45; ⌚noon-2.30pm & 7-10.30pm Tue-Sun; 📶; ⛴Riva de Biasio) La Serenissima's spice trade lives on at simple, elegant Trefanti, where gnocchi might get an intriguing kick from cinnamon and turbot is flavoured with almond and coconut. Seafood is the focus; try the 'doge's fettucine', with mussels, scampi and clams. Furnished with recycled copper

VENICE DISCOUNT PASSES

Civic Museum Pass (www.visitmuve.it; adult/reduced €24/18) Valid for single entry to 11 civic museums, or just four sites around Piazza San Marco (€20/13). Buy online or at participating museums.

Chorus Pass (www.chorusvenezia.org; adult/reduced €12/8) Covers admission to 16 churches. Buy online or at participating sites.

VeneziaUnica (www.veneziaunica.it) A universal pass covering museum admission, transport, wi-fi and more. There's no standard pass; instead you tailor it to your needs and pay according to the services you include on it. See the website for details.

Sestiere di San Marco

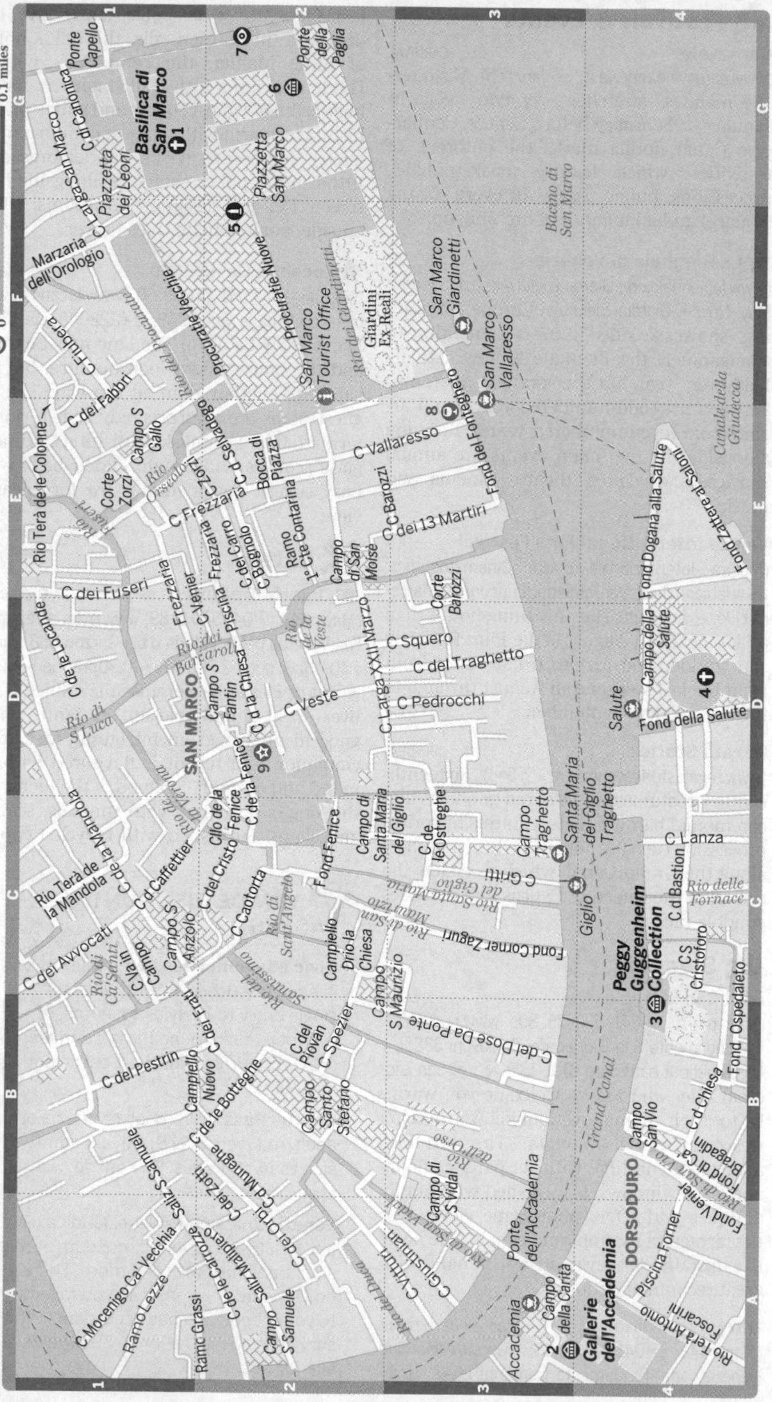

0 200 m
0 0.1 miles

Basilica di San Marco 1
Piazzetta San Marco
Procuratie Vecchie
Procuratie Nuove
San Marco Tourist Office
Giardini Ex Reali
Rio dei Giardinetti
San Marco Giardinetti
San Marco Vallaresso
Bacino di San Marco
Canale della Giudecca
Grand Canal
SAN MARCO
DORSODURO
Gallerie dell'Accademia 2
Peggy Guggenheim Collection 3
Ponte dell'Accademia
Campo della Carità
Accademia
Santa Maria del Giglio Traghetto
Giglio
Salute
Campo della Salute
Fond Dogana alla Salute
Fond della Salute
Fond Zattere al Saloni
Ponte della Paglia
Ponte Capello
Piazzetta dei Leoni
Marzaria dell'Orologio
C Larga San Marco
C di Canonica
C Fiubera
C dei Fabbri
Rio Terà de le Colonne
Campo S Gallo
Corte Zorzi
C dei Fuseri
C de le Locande
Frezzaria
C Venier
C Frezzaria
C Zorzi
C d Selvadego
Bocca di Piazza
Ramo 1° Cte Contarina
C del Carro
C Bognolo
Piscina Frezzaria
Campo S Fantin
C d la Chiesa
C de la Fenice
Cllo de la Fenice
C del Cristo
C Caotorta
C d Caffettier
C de la Mandola
Rio Terà de la Mandola
C dei Avvocati
C Va in Campo
Campo S Anzolo
C dei Frati
Campiello Nuovo
C del Pestrin
C de le Botteghe
C dei Zotti
C d Muneghe
C dei Orbi
Saliz Malipiero
C de le Carrozze
Saliz S Samuele
Campo S Samuele
Ramo Grassi
Ramo Lezze
C Mocenigo Ca' Vecchia
Campo Santo Stefano
C del Piovan
C Spezier
Campiello Drio la Chiesa
Campo S Maurizio
Fond Fenice
C Veste
Campo di San Moisè
C Larga XXII Marzo
Campo di Santa Maria del Giglio
C de le Ostreghe
C Pedrocchi
C del Traghetto
C Squero
Corte Barozzi
C dei 13 Martiri
C Barozzi
C Vallaresso
Fond del Fontegheto
C Gritti
Campo Traghetto
Fond Corner Zaguri
C del Dose Da Ponte
C Vitturi
C Giustinian
Campo di S Vidal
Rio del Duca
Rio di San Vidal
Rio dell'Orso
Rio del Santissimo
Rio di Sant'Angelo
Rio di San Maurizio
Rio Santa Maria del Giglio
Rio de la Veste
Rio dei Barcaroli
Rio di S Luca
Rio de la Verona
Rio di Ca'Santi
Rio Fuseri
Rio Orseolo
Rio del Procurate
Campo San Vio
Piscina Forner
Rio Terà Antonio Foscarini
Fond Venier
Rio di San Vio
Fond di Ca' Bragadin
C d Chiesa
Fond Ospedaleto
C S Cristoforo
C d Bastion
C Lanza
Rio delle Fornace

Sestiere di San Marco

Top Sights
1 Basilica di San Marco....G1
2 Gallerie dell'Accademia....A3
3 Peggy Guggenheim Collection....B4

Sights
4 Basilica di Santa Maria della Salute....D4
5 Campanile....F2
6 Palazzo Ducale....G2
7 Ponte dei Sospiri....G2

Drinking & Nightlife
8 Harry's Bar....E3

Entertainment
9 Teatro La Fenice....D2

lamps, the space is small and deservedly popular – so book ahead.

★CoVino VENETIAN €€
(Map p441; ☎041 241 27 05; www.covinovenezia.com; Calle del Pestrin 3829; fixed-price menu lunch €27-36, dinner €40; ⏰12.45-2.30pm & 7pm-midnight Thu-Mon; ; Arsenale) Tiny CoVino has only 14 seats but demonstrates bags of ambition with its inventive, seasonal menu inspired by the Venetian terroir. Speciality products are selected from Slow Food Foundation producers, and the charming waitstaff make enthusiastic recommendations from the wine list. Only a three-course set menu is available at dinner, but you can choose from two fixed-price options at lunch.

Osteria La Zucca ITALIAN €€
(Map p448; ☎041 524 15 70; www.lazucca.it; Calle del Tentor 1762; meals €32-38; ⏰noon-2.30pm & 7-10.30pm Mon-Sat; ; San Stae) With its menu of seasonal vegetarian creations and classic meat dishes, this cosy, woody restaurant consistently hits the mark. Herbs and spices are used to great effect in dishes such as nutmeg-tinged pumpkin and smoked ricotta flan. The small interior can get toasty, so reserve canalside seats in summer. Even in winter you're best to book ahead.

★Antiche Carampane VENETIAN €€€
(Map p448; ☎041 524 01 65; www.anticheca rampane.com; Rio Terà de le Carampane 1911; meals €55-63; ⏰12.45-2.30pm & 7.30-10.30pm Tue-Sat; San Stae) Hidden in the once-dodgy lanes behind Ponte de le Tette, this culinary indulgence is hard to find but worth the effort. Once you do, say hello to a market-driven menu of Venetian classics including *fegato alla veneziana* (veal liver with onions) and lots of seafood. Never short of a smart, convivial crowd, it's a good idea to book ahead.

Drinking & Nightlife

Al Prosecco WINE BAR
(Map p448; ☎041 524 02 22; www.alprosecco.com; Campo San Giacomo da l'Orio 1503; ⏰10am-8pm Mon-Fri, to 5pm Sat; San Stae) Positioned on Venice's loveliest *campo* (square), this wine bar specialises in *vini naturali* (natural-process wines) – organic, biodynamic, wild-yeast fermented – from Italian winemakers. Order a glass of unfiltered 'cloudy' prosecco and toast the view over a plate of *cicheti*.

★Al Timon WINE BAR
(Map p441; ☎041 524 60 66; www.altimon.it; Fondamenta dei Ormesini 2754; ⏰5pm-1am; San Marcuola) Find a spot in the wood-lined interior or, in summer, on the boat moored out the front along the canal and watch the motley parade of drinkers and dreamers arrive for steak platters and quality wines by the *ombra* (half-glass) or carafe.

Musicians play sets canalside when the weather obliges.

Harry's Bar BAR
(Map p446; ☎041 528 57 77; www.cipriani.com; Calle Vallaresso 1323; ⏰10.30am-11pm; San Marco) Aspiring auteurs hold court at tables well scuffed by Ernest Hemingway, Charlie Chaplin, Truman Capote and Orson Welles, enjoying the signature €21 bellini (Giuseppe Cipriani's original 1948 recipe: white peach juice and *prosecco*) with a side of reflected glory.

Entertainment

To find out what's on during your visit, check listings in free mags distributed city-wide and online at Venezia da Vivere (www.veneziadavivere.com) and 2Venice (www.2venice.it).

★Teatro La Fenice OPERA
(Map p446; ☎041 78 66 54; www.teatrolafenice.it; Campo San Fantin 1977; tickets €25-250; Giglio) One of Italy's top opera houses, La Fenice stages a rich roster of opera, ballet and classical music. The main opera season runs from January to July and September to October. The cheapest seats (€25) are in the boxes at the top. The view is extremely

Sestiere di San Polo

0 200 m
0 0.1 miles

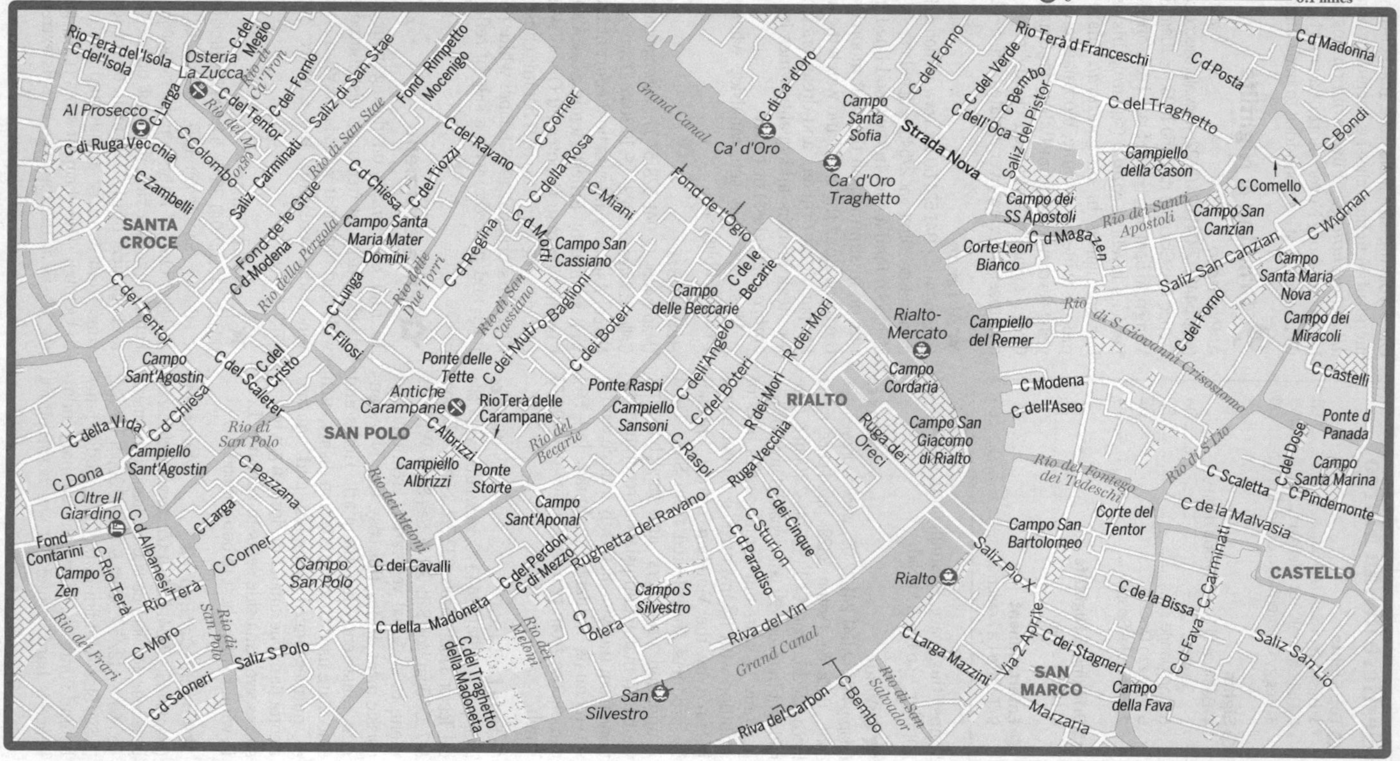

SANTA CROCE
SAN POLO
RIALTO
SAN MARCO
CASTELLO
Grand Canal
Rio Terà dell'Isola
C dell'Isola
C del Megio
Osteria La Zucca
Rio di Ca' Tron
Rio del Megio
C del Forno
Saliz di San Stae
Fond Rimpetto Mocenigo
Al Prosecco
C Larga
C del Tentor
C di Ruga Vecchia
C Colombo
Saliz Carminati
Rio di San Stae
C del Ravano
C Corner
C Zambelli
Fond de le Grue
C d Modena
Rio della Pergola
C d Chiesa
C del Tiozzi
Campo Santa Maria Mater Domini
C della Rosa
C Miani
C d Regina
Rio delle Due Torri
C d Morti
Campo San Cassiano
C Lunga
C Filosi
Rio di San Cassiano
C dei Mutr o Baglioni
C dei Boteri
Fond de l'Ogio
C de le Becarie
Campo delle Beccarie
C del Tentor
Campo Sant'Agostin
C del Scaleter
C del Cristo
Ponte delle Tette
Antiche Carampane
RioTerà delle Carampane
C Albrizzi
Ponte Raspi
Campiello Sansoni
C dell'Angelo
C del Boteri
R dei Mori
C della Vida
C d Chiesa
Rio di San Polo
Campiello Sant'Agostin
C Pezzana
Campiello Albrizzi
Ponte Storte
Rio del Becarie
C Raspi
Ruga Vecchia
Ruga dei Oreci
Campo San Giacomo di Rialto
Campo Cordaria
Rialto-Mercato
C Dona
Oltre Il Giardino
C d Albanesi
C Larga
Rio dei Meloni
Campo Sant'Aponal
Rughetta del Ravano
C dei Cinque
C Sturion
C d Paradiso
Fond Contarini
C Rio Terà
Campo Zen
Rio Terà
C Corner
Campo San Polo
C dei Cavalli
C del Perdon
C di Mezzo
Campo S Silvestro
Rio del Frari
C Moro
Rio di San Polo
Saliz S Polo
C della Madoneta
C del Traghetto della Madoneta
Rio dei Meloni
C Dolera
Riva del Vin
C d Saoneri
San Silvestro
Riva del Carbon
C Bembo
Rio di San Salvador
Rialto
C Larga Mazzini
Via 2 Aprile
Saliz Pio X
Campo San Bartolomeo
Corte del Tentor
Rio del Fontego dei Tedeschi
C Modena
C dell'Aseo
Campiello del Remer
Corte Leon Bianco
C d Magazen
Campo dei SS Apostoli
Ca' d'Oro
C di Ca' d'Oro
Campo Santa Sofia
Ca' d'Oro Traghetto
Strada Nova
C del Forno
C del Verde
C dell'Oca
C Bembo
Saliz del Pistor
Rio Terà d Franceschi
C del Traghetto
Campiello della Cason
C d Posta
C d Madonna
C Bondi
C Comello
Rio dei Santi Apostoli
Campo San Canzian
C Widman
Saliz San Canzian
Campo Santa Maria Nova
Campo dei Miracoli
Rio di S Giovanni Crisostomo
C del Forno
C Castelli
Ponte d Panada
C del Dose
Campo Santa Marina
C Pindemonte
Rio di S Lio
C Scaletta
C de la Malvasia
C Carminati
C de la Bissa
C d Fava
C dei Stagneri
Campo della Fava
Marzaria
Saliz San Lio

LOCAL KNOWLEDGE

CICHETI

Venice's answer to tapas, *cicheti* are served at lunch and from around 6pm to 8pm with sensational Veneto wines by the glass. They range from basic bar snacks (spicy meatballs, fresh tomato and basil bruschetta) to highly inventive small plates: think white Bassano asparagus and plump lagoon shrimp wrapped in pancetta, pungent gorgonzola paired with spicy peperoncino (chilli) jam, wild boar salami, or fragrant, bite-sized bread rolls crammed with tuna, chicory and horseradish.

Prices start at €1 for meatballs and range from €3 to €6 for gourmet offerings, typically devoured standing up or perched atop stools at the bar.

restricted, but you will get to hear the music, watch the orchestra, soak up the atmosphere and people-watch.

Information

Marco Polo Airport Tourist Office (041 24 24; www.veneziaunica.it; Arrivals Hall, Marco Polo Airport; 8.30am-7pm) Multilingual tourist information at the airport. It can help with information on transport to the city and offers a city map for €3.

Ospedale SS Giovanni e Paolo (041 529 43 11; www.aulss3.veneto.it; Campo Zanipolo 6777; Ospedale) Venice's main hospital; for emergency care.

San Marco Tourist Office (Map p446; 041 24 24; www.veneziaunica.it; Piazza San Marco 71f; 9am-7pm; San Marco) Sells tickets for transport, concerts and sights, including the Museum Pass and Tourist City Pass.

Stazione Santa Lucia Tourist Office (Map p441; 041 24 24; www.veneziaunica.it; 7am-9pm; Ferrovia) Near platform 2, this office grudgingly dispenses information and sells maps, museum passes and tickets for public transport and concerts.

Getting There & Away

AIR

Most flights arrive at and depart from **Marco Polo Airport** (flight information 041 260 92 60; www.veniceairport.it; Via Galileo Gallilei 30/1, Tessera), 12km outside Venice.

Ryanair flies to/from **Treviso Airport** (0422 31 51 11; www.trevisoairport.it; Via Noalese 63), about 30km away.

BOAT

Anek (041 528 65 22; www.anekitalia.com; Via Dell 'Elettronica, Fusina) runs regular ferries between Venice and Greece, and **Venezia Lines** (Map p441; 041 847 09 03; www.venezialines.com; 9am-5pm daily May-Sep, Mon-Fri Oct-Apr; San Basilio) runs high-speed boats to/from Croatia in summer.

BUS

ACTV (Azienda del Consorzio Trasporti Veneziano; 041 272 2111; http://actv.avmspa.it/en) buses service surrounding areas. Get tickets and information at the **bus station** (Piazzale Roma).

TRAIN

Regular trains serve Venice's **Stazione di Santa Lucia** from Padua (€4.25 to €18, 25 minutes) and Verona (€9 to €27, 50 minutes to 2¼ hours) as well as Bologna, Milan, Rome and Florence.

Getting Around

TO/FROM THE AIRPORT

Marco Polo Airport

Alilaguna (041 240 17 01; www.alilaguna.it; airport transfer one-way €15) operates four water shuttles that link the airport with various parts of Venice at a cost of €8 to Murano and €15 to all other landing stages. It takes approximately 1¼ hours to reach Piazza San Marco. Lines include the following:

Linea Blu (Blue Line) Stops at Lido, San Marco, Cruise Terminal and points in between.

Linea Rossa (Red Line) Serves Murano, Lido, San Marco and Giudecca.

Linea Arancia (Orange Line) Arrives at Santa Maria del Giglio via Rialto and the Grand Canal.

An **ATVO** (Map p441; 0421 59 46 71; www.atvo.it; Piazzale Roma 497g; 6.40am-7.30pm; Piazzale Roma) shuttle bus goes to/from Piazzale Roma (one way/return €8/15, 25 minutes, half-hourly), as does ACTV bus 5 (one way/return €8/15, 25 minutes, every 15 minutes).

Treviso Airport

ATVO buses run to/from Piazzale Roma (one way/return €12/22, 70 minutes, at least 13 daily).

BOAT

The city's main mode of public transport is the *vaporetto* (water bus).

Tickets, available from booths at major landing stations and on Piazzale Roma, cost €7.50 for a single trip. Passes are available for 24/48/72 hours at €20/30/40.

Useful routes:

1 Piazzale Roma to the train station and down the Grand Canal to San Marco and the Lido.

2 San Marco to Piazzale Roma and the train station, then along the Grand Canal to Rialto and the Lido.

4.1 Joins Murano to Fondamente Nove, then circles the perimeter of Venice.

Bologna

POP 388,400

Bologna is one of Italy's great unsung destinations. Its medieval centre is an eye-catching ensemble of red-brick *palazzi,* Renaissance towers and 40km of arcaded porticoes, and there are enough sights to excite without exhausting. A university town since 1088 (Europe's oldest), it's also a prime foodie destination, home to the eponymous bolognese sauce *(ragù)* as well as *tortellini,* lasagne and *mortadella* (Bologna sausage).

Sights

★Basilica di San Petronio CHURCH

(☎051 648 06 11; www.basilicadisanpetronio.org; Piazza Maggiore; photo pass €2; ⏰7.45am-1.30pm & 3-6.30pm Mon-Fri, 7.45am-6.30pm Sat & Sun) Bologna's hulking Gothic basilica is Europe's sixth-largest church, measuring 132m by 66m by 47m. Work began on it in 1390, but it was never finished and still today its main facade remains incomplete. Inside, look for the huge sundial that stretches 67.7m down the eastern aisle. Designed in 1656 by Gian Cassini and Domenico Guglielmi, this was instrumental in discovering the anomalies of the Julian calendar and led to the creation of the leap year.

Le Due Torri TOWER

(The Two Towers; Piazza di Porta Ravegnana) Standing sentinel over Piazza di Porta Ravegnana, Bologna's two leaning towers are the city's main symbol. The taller of the two, the 97.2m-high **Torre degli Asinelli** (www.duetorribologna.com; adult/reduced €5/3; ⏰9.30am-7.30pm Mar-5 Nov, to 5.45pm 6 Nov-Feb) is open to the public, while the neighbouring 47m Torre Garisenda is sensibly out of bounds given its drunken 3.2m tilt.

★Basilica di Santo Stefano CHURCH

(www.abbaziasstefano.wixsite.com/abbaziasstefano; Via Santo Stefano 24; ⏰9.15am-7.15pm Apr-Sep, to 6pm Oct-Mar) Bologna's most compelling religious site is this atmospheric labyrinth of interlocking ecclesiastical structures, whose architecture spans centuries of Bolognese history and incorporates Romanesque, Lombard and even ancient Roman elements. Originally there were seven churches – hence the basilica's nickname Sette Chiese – but only four remain intact today: Chiesa del Crocefisso, Chiesa della Trinità, Chiesa del Santo Sepolcro and Santi Vitale e Agricola.

Sleeping & Eating

★Bologna nel Cuore B&B €€

(☎329 2193354; www.bolognanelcuore.it; Via Cesare Battisti 29; s €90-120, d €125-145, apt €130-145; P ❄ 📶) This centrally located, immaculate and well-loved B&B features a pair of bright, high-ceilinged rooms with pretty tiled bathrooms and endless mod cons, plus two comfortable, spacious apartments with kitchen and laundry facilities. Owner and art historian Maria generously shares her knowledge of Bologna and serves breakfasts featuring jams made with fruit picked near her childhood home in the Dolomites.

Le Serre dei Giardini Margherita BAR

(☎370 3336439; www.vetro.kilowatt.bo.it; Via Castiglione 134; ⏰8am-1am Mon-Fri, 9am-1am Sat-Sun Mar-Dec, to 8pm Mon-Wed, to midnight Thu-Sat, 9am-8pm Sun Jan-Feb; 📶) 🍃 Bologna's best time: parking yourself down with an Aperol spritz (€4) in hand among the cool kids and digital nomads at these formerly abandoned city greenhouses that have been transformed into an immensely cool and highly recommended co-working space, vegetarian/vegan restaurant (Vetro) and community gardens in the heart of Giardini Margherita, the city's largest green space.

★All'Osteria Bottega OSTERIA €€

(☎051 58 51 11; Via Santa Caterina 51; meals €36-41; ⏰12.30-2.30pm & 8-10.30pm Tue-Sat) At Bologna's temple of culinary content, owners Daniele and Valeria lavish attention on every table between trips to the kitchen for astonishing plates of *culatello di Zibello* ham, tortellini in capon broth, Petroniana-style veal cutlets (breaded and fried, then topped with Parma ham and *parmigiano reggiano* and finished in broth), off-menu speciality pigeon and other Slow Food delights.

Information

Bologna Welcome (Tourist Office; ☎051 658 31 11; www.bolognawelcome.it; Piazza Maggiore 1e; ⏰9am-7pm Mon-Sat, 10am-5pm

THE MOSAICS OF RAVENNA

A rewarding and worthwhile day trip from Bologna, Ravenna is famous for its Early Christian mosaics. These Unesco-listed treasures have been impressing visitors since the 13th century, when Dante described them in his *Divine Comedy* (much of which was written here). They are spread over five sites in the centre: the Basilica di San Vitale, the Mausoleo di Galla Placidia, the Basilica di Sant'Appollinare Nuovo, the Museo Arcivescovile and the Battistero Neoniano. These are covered by a single ticket (five-site combo ticket €9.50), available at any of the sites. The website www.ravennamosaici.it gives further information.

On the northern edge of the *centro storico*, the sombre exterior of the 6th-century **Basilica di San Vitale** (Via San Vitale; 9am-7pm Mar-Oct, 10am-5pm Nov-May) hides a dazzling interior with mosaics depicting Old Testament scenes. In the same complex, the small **Mausoleo di Galla Placidia** (Via San Vitale; 5-site combo ticket €9.50 plus summer-only surcharge €2; 9am-7pm Mar-Oct, 10am-5pm Nov-May) contains the city's oldest mosaics.

Adjoining Ravenna's unremarkable cathedral, the **Museo Arcivescovile** (Piazza Arcivescovado 1; 9am-7pm Mar-Oct, 10am-5pm Nov-May) boasts an exquisite 6th-century ivory throne, while next door in the **Battistero Neoniano** (Piazza del Duomo 1; 9am-7pm Mar-Oct, 10am-5pm Nov-May), the baptism of Christ is represented in the domed roof mosaic.

To the east, the **Basilica di Sant'Apollinare Nuovo** (Via di Roma 52; 9am-7pm Mar-Oct, 10am-5pm Nov-May) boasts, among other things, a superb mosaic depicting a procession of martyrs headed towards Christ and his apostles.

Five kilometres southeast of the city, the apse mosaic of the **Basilica di Sant'-Apollinare in Classe** (Via Romea Sud 224; adult/reduced €5/2.50; 8.30am-7.30pm Mon-Sat, 1-7.30pm Sun) is a must-see. Take bus 4 from the train station.

Regional trains run to/from Bologna (€7.35, 1½ hours, twice hourly) and destinations on the east coast.

Sun) Bologna's official tourist information hub offers daily, two-hour morning and afternoon walking tours (€15), among other excursions; can help with bookings; puts out a handy daily news and events brochure in English; and sells the Bologna Welcome Card (www.bolognawelcome.com/en/richiedicard; Easy/Plus card €25/40) and 24-hour bus passes (€5). Also has an office at the airport (Tourist Office; 051 647 22 01; www.bolognawelcome.com; Via Triumvirato 84, Guglielmo Marconi Airport; 9am-7.30pm Mon-Sat, to 5pm Sun) and is an affiliate at FICO Eataly World (www.bolognawelcome.com; Via Paolo Canali 8, FICO Eataly World; 10am-10pm).

Getting There & Around

AIR

European and domestic flights serve **Guglielmo Marconi Airport** (051 647 96 15; www.bologna-airport.it; Via Triumvirato 84), 8km northwest of the city.

From the airport, an **Aerobus shuttle** (€6, 20 minutes, every 10 to 30 minutes) connects with the train station.

BUS

Bologna has an efficient bus system, run by **TPER** (051 29 02 90; www.tper.it).

Minibus A is the most direct of several buses that connect the bus station with the city centre.

TRAIN

Bologna is a major rail hub. From the station on Piazza delle Medaglie d'Oro, there are regular high-speed trains to Milan (€28.50 to €55, one to 2½ hours), Venice (€12.60 to €34, 1½ to 2½ hours), Florence (€28, 35 minutes) and Rome (€47.50 to €62, two to four hours).

TUSCANY & UMBRIA

Tuscany and its lesser-known neighbour, Umbria, are two of Italy's most beautiful regions. Tuscany's fabled landscape of rolling vine-covered hills dotted with cypress trees and stone villas has long been considered the embodiment of rural chic, while its historical cities and hilltop towns are home to a significant portfolio of the world's medieval and Renaissance art.

To the south, the predominantly rural region of Umbria, dubbed the 'green heart of Italy', harbours some of the country's best-preserved historical *borghi* (villages) and many important artistic, religious and architectural treasures.

Florence

POP 382,300

Visitors have been rhapsodising about Florence (Firenze) for centuries, and still it looms large on Europe's 'must-sees' list. Tourists flock here to feast on world-class art and explore its historical streets, laden with grand palaces, jewel-box churches, trattorias, wine bars and elegant boutiques. Cradle of the Renaissance and home of Machiavelli, Michelangelo and the Medici, it's a magnetic, romantic and brilliantly absorbing place.

Sights

Piazza del Duomo

★Duomo CATHEDRAL

(Cattedrale di Santa Maria del Fiore; 055 230 28 85; www.museumflorence.com; Piazza del Duomo; 10am-5pm Mon-Wed & Fri, to 4.30pm Thu & Sat, 1.30-4.45pm Sun) FREE Florence's Duomo is the city's most iconic landmark. Capped by Filippo Brunelleschi's red-tiled cupola, it's a staggering construction whose breathtaking pink, white and green marble facade and graceful *campanile* (bell tower) dominate the Renaissance cityscape. Sienese architect Arnolfo di Cambio began work on it in 1296, but construction took almost 150 years and it wasn't consecrated until 1436. In the echoing interior, look out for frescoes by Vasari and Zuccari and up to 44 stained-glass windows.

★Cupola del Brunelleschi LANDMARK

(Brunelleschi's Dome; 055 230 28 85; www.museumflorence.com; Piazza del Duomo; adult/reduced incl baptistry, campanile, crypt & museum €18/3; 8.30am-7pm Mon-Fri, to 5pm Sat, 1-4pm Sun) A Renaissance masterpiece, the Duomo's cupola – 91m high and 45.5m wide – was built between 1420 and 1436. Filippo Brunelleschi, taking inspiration from the Pantheon in Rome, designed a distinctive octagonal form of inner and outer concentric domes that rests on the drum of the cathedral rather than the roof itself. Four million bricks were used, laid in consecutive rings according to a vertical herringbone pattern. Advance time-slot reservations, made online or at the cathedral's Piazza di San Giovanni ticket office, are obligatory.

★Campanile TOWER

(Bell Tower; 055 230 28 85; www.museumflorence.com; Piazza del Duomo; adult/reduced incl baptistry, cupola, crypt & museum €18/3; 8.15am-7pm) The 414-step climb up the cathedral's 84.7m-tall *campanile,* begun by Giotto in 1334, rewards with staggering city views. The first tier of bas-reliefs around the base of its elaborate Gothic facade are copies of those carved by Pisano depicting the Creation of Man and *attività umane* (arts and industries). The second tier depicts the planets, the cardinal virtues, the arts and the seven sacraments. The sculpted Prophets and Sibyls in the upper-storey niches are copies of works by Donatello and others.

Battistero di San Giovanni LANDMARK

(Baptistry; 055 230 28 85; www.museumflorence.com; Piazza di San Giovanni; adult/reduced incl campanile, cupola, crypt & museum €18/3; 8.15-10.15am & 11.15am-7.30pm Mon-Fri, 8.15am-6.30pm Sat, 8.15am-1.30pm Sun) This 11th-century baptistry – the oldest religious building on the vast cathedral square – is a Romanesque, octagonal-striped structure of white-and-green marble with three sets of doors conceived as panels illustrating the story of humanity and the Redemption. Most celebrated are Lorenzo Ghiberti's gilded bronze doors at the eastern entrance, the *Porta del Paradiso* (Gate of Paradise). What you see today are copies – the originals are in the Museo dell'Opera del Duomo. Buy tickets online or at the ticket office at Piazza di San Giovanni 7, opposite the main Baptistry entrance.

Piazza della Signoria & Around

★Galleria degli Uffizi GALLERY

(Uffizi Gallery; 055 29 48 83; www.uffizi.it; Piazzale degli Uffizi 6; adult/reduced Mar-Oct €20/10, Nov-Feb €12/6; 8.15am-6.50pm Tue-Sun) Home to the world's greatest collection of Italian Renaissance art, Florence's premier gallery occupies the vast U-shaped Palazzo degli Uffizi (1560-80), built as government offices. The collection, bequeathed to the city by the Medici family in 1743 on condition that it never leave Florence, contains some of Italy's best-known paintings, including a room full of Botticelli masterpieces.

ITALIAN ART & ARCHITECTURE

Italy is littered with architectural and artistic reminders of its convoluted history. Etruscan tombs and Greek temples tell of glories long past, Roman amphitheatres testify to ancient blood lust and architectural brilliance, and Byzantine mosaics reveal influences sweeping in from the East.

The Renaissance left an indelible mark, giving rise to some of Italy's greatest masterpieces: Filippo Brunelleschi's dome atop Florence's Duomo, Botticelli's *The Birth of Venus*, and Michelangelo's Sistine Chapel frescoes. Contemporaries Leonardo da Vinci and Raphael further brightened the scene.

Caravaggio revolutionised the late-16th-century art world with his controversial and highly influential painting style. He worked in Rome and the south, where baroque art and architecture flourished in the 17th century.

In the late 18th and early 19th centuries neoclassicism saw a return to sober classical lines. Its main Italian exponent was sculptor Antonio Canova.

In sharp contrast to backward-looking neoclassicism, early 20th-century futurism sought new ways to express the dynamism of the machine age, while Italian rationalism saw the development of a linear, muscular style of architecture.

Continuing in this modernist tradition are Italy's two contemporary starchitects: Renzo Piano, the visionary behind Rome's Auditorium, and Rome-born Massimiliano Fuksas.

A combined ticket (valid three days) with Palazzo Pitti, Giardino di Boboli and Museo Archeologico is available for €38/21 (€18/11 November to February).

★Palazzo Vecchio MUSEUM

(☎055 276 85 58; www.musefirenze.it; Piazza della Signoria; adult/reduced museum €12.50/10, tower €12.50/10, museum & tower €17.50/15, museum & archaeological tour €16/13.50, archaeological tour €4, combination ticket €19.50/17.50; ⏰museum 9am-11pm Fri-Wed, to 2pm Thu summer, 9am-7pm Fri-Wed, to 2pm Thu winter, tower 9am-9pm Fri Wed, to 2pm Thu summer, 10am-5pm Fri-Wed, to 2pm Thu winter; 📶) This fortress palace, with its crenellations and 94m-high tower, was designed by Arnolfo di Cambio between 1298 and 1314 for the *signoria* (city government). Today it is home to the mayor's office and the municipal council. From the top of the **Torre d'Arnolfo** (tower), you can revel in unforgettable views. Inside, Michelangelo's *Genio della Vittoria* (Genius of Victory) sculpture graces the Salone dei Cinquecento, a magnificent painted hall created for the city's 15th-century ruling Consiglio dei Cinquecento (Council of 500).

Piazza della Signoria PIAZZA

(Piazza della Signoria) The hub of local life since the 13th century, Florentines flock here to meet friends and chat over early-evening *aperitivi* at historical cafes. Presiding over everything is Palazzo Vecchio, Florence's city hall, and the 14th-century **Loggia dei Lanzi**, an open-air gallery showcasing Renaissance sculptures, including Giambologna's *Rape of the Sabine Women* (c 1583), Benvenuto Cellini's bronze *Perseus* (1554) and Agnolo Gaddi's *Seven Virtues* (1384–89).

★Museo del Bargello MUSEUM

(☎055 238 86 06; www.bargellomusei.beniculturali.it; Via del Proconsolo 4; adult/reduced €8/4; ⏰8.15am-2pm, closed 2nd & 4th Sun, 1st, 3rd & 5th Mon of month) It was behind the stark walls of Palazzo del Bargello, Florence's earliest public building, that the *podestà* (governing magistrate) meted out justice from the 13th century until 1502. Today the building safeguards Italy's most comprehensive collection of Tuscan Renaissance sculpture, with some of Michelangelo's best early works and several by Donatello. Michelangelo was just 21 when a cardinal commissioned him to create the drunken grape-adorned *Bacchus* (1496–97). Unfortunately the cardinal didn't like the result and sold it.

San Lorenzo

★Museo delle Cappelle Medicee MAUSOLEUM

(Medici Chapels; ☎055 238 86 02; www.bargellomusei.beniculturali.it/musei/2/medicee; Piazza Madonna degli Aldobrandini 6; adult/reduced €8/4; ⏰8.15am-2pm, closed 2nd & 4th Sun, 1st, 3rd & 5th Mon of month) Nowhere is Medici conceit expressed so explicitly as in the Medici Chapels. Adorned with granite, marble, semi-precious stones and some of Michelangelo's most beautiful sculptures, it is the

Florence

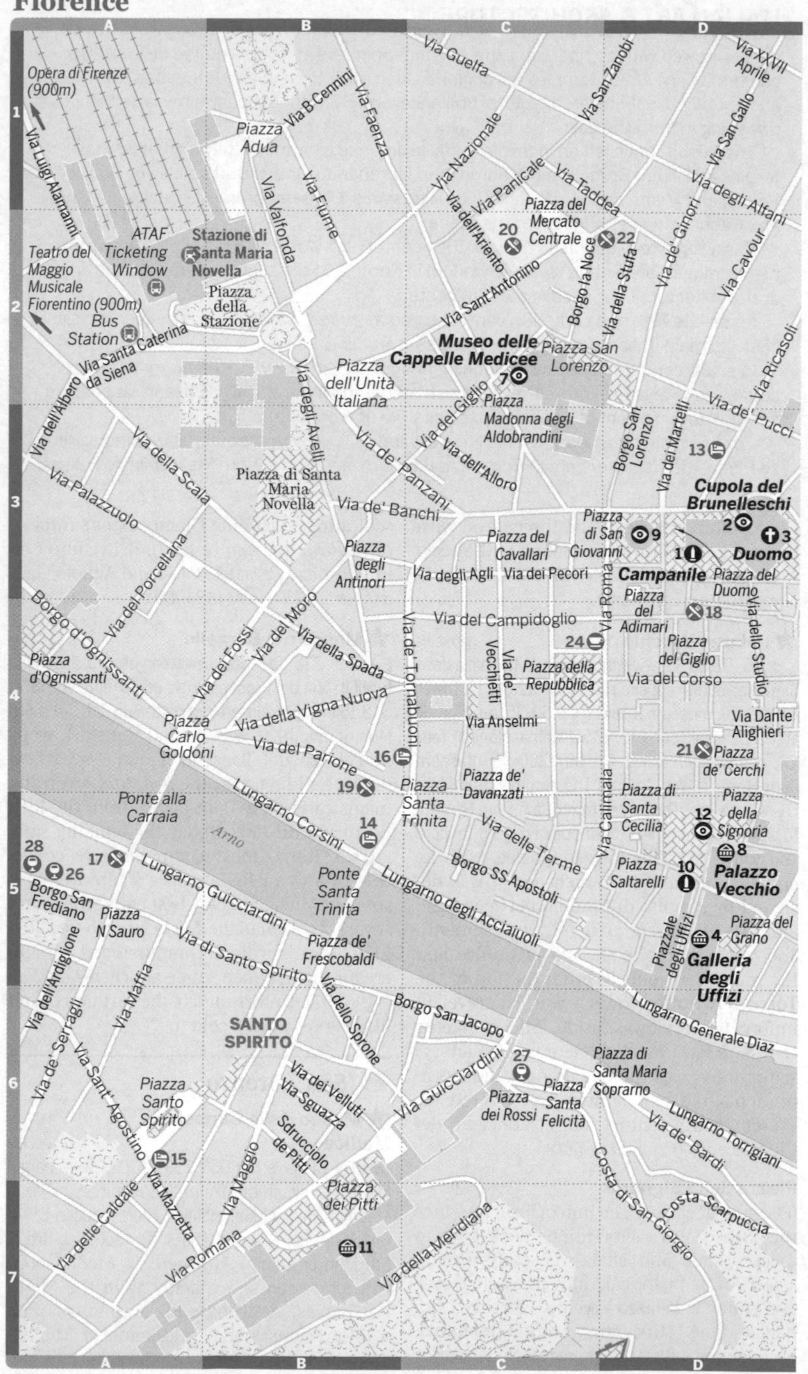

Stazione di Santa Maria Novella
Museo delle Cappelle Medicee
Cupola del Brunelleschi
Duomo
Campanile
Palazzo Vecchio
Galleria degli Uffizi
Piazza di Santa Maria Novella
Piazza della Repubblica
Piazza della Signoria
Piazza San Lorenzo
Piazza del Mercato Centrale
Piazza Santo Spirito
Piazza dei Pitti
Ponte Santa Trìnita
Ponte alla Carraia
Arno
SANTO SPIRITO
ATAF Ticketing Window
Bus Station
Opera di Firenze (900m)
Teatro del Maggio Musicale Fiorentino (900m)

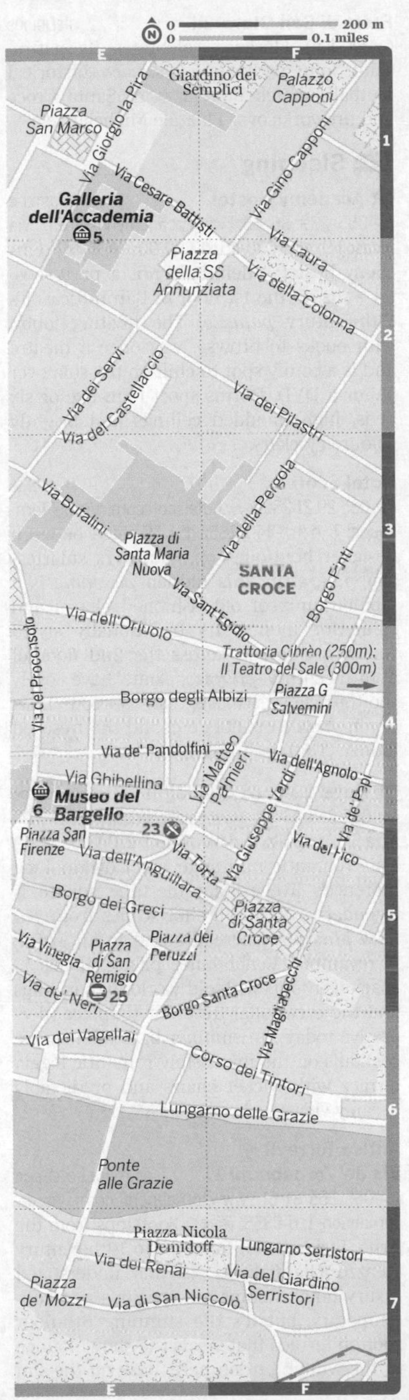

Florence

Top Sights

1	Campanile	D3
2	Cupola del Brunelleschi	D3
3	Duomo	D3
4	Galleria degli Uffizi	D5
5	Galleria dell'Accademia	E1
6	Museo del Bargello	E4
7	Museo delle Cappelle Medicee	C2
8	Palazzo Vecchio	D5

Sights

9	Battistero di San Giovanni	D3
10	Loggia dei Lanzi	D5
11	Palazzo Pitti	B7
12	Piazza della Signoria	D5

Sleeping

13	Academy Hostel	D3
14	Antica Torre di Via de' Tornabuoni 1	B5
15	Hotel Palazzo Guadagni	A6
16	Hotel Scoti	B4

Eating

17	Gelateria La Carraia	A5
18	Grom	D4
19	Mariano	B4
20	Mercato Centrale	C2
21	Osteria Il Buongustai	D4
22	Trattoria Mario	D2
23	Vivoli	E5

Drinking & Nightlife

24	Caffè Gilli	C4
25	Ditta Artigianale	E5
26	La Cité	A5
27	Le Volpi e l'Uva	C6
28	Mad Souls & Spirits	A5

burial place of 49 dynastic members. Francesco I lies in the dark, imposing **Cappella dei Principi** (Chapel of Princes) alongside Ferdinando I and II and Cosimo I, II and III. Lorenzo il Magnifico is buried in the graceful **Sagrestia Nuova** (New Sacristy), which was Michelangelo's first architectural work.

San Marco

★Galleria dell'Accademia GALLERY

(☎055 238 86 09; www.galleriaaccademiafirenze.beniculturali.it; Via Ricasoli 60; adult/reduced €12/6; ⏲8.15am-6.50pm Tue-Sun) A queue marks the door to this gallery, built to house one of the Renaissance's most iconic masterpieces, Michelangelo's *David*. But the world's most famous statue is worth the wait. The subtle detail – the veins in his sinewy arms, the leg muscles, the change in expression as you move around the statue –

BEST OF THE UFFIZI

Cut to the quick of the gallery's collection and start by getting to grips with pre-Renaissance Tuscan art in **Room 2**, home to several shimmering alterpieces by Giotto et al. Then work your way on to **Room 8** and Piero della Francesca's iconic profile portrait of the Duke and Duchess of Urbino. More familiar images await in the **Sala di Botticelli** (Rooms 10 to 14), including the master's great Renaissance masterpiece, *La nascita di Venere* (The Birth of Venus). Continue on to **Room 35** for Leonardo da Vinci's *Annunciazione* (Annunciation; 1472) and **Room 41** for Michelangelo's *Doni tondi* (The Holy Family).

is impressive. Carved from a single block of marble, Michelangelo's most famous work was his most challenging – he didn't choose the marble himself and it was veined.

Oltrarno

Palazzo Pitti MUSEUM

(☎055 29 48 83; www.uffizi.it/en/pitti-palace; Piazza dei Pitti; adult/reduced Mar-Oct €16/8, Nov-Feb €10/5, combined ticket with Uffizi Mar-Oct €38, Nov-Feb €18; ⊙8.15am-6.50pm Tue-Sun) Commissioned by banker Luca Pitta in 1458, this Renaissance palace was later bought by the Medici family. Over the centuries, it was a residence of the city's rulers until the Savoys donated it to the state in 1919. Nowadays it houses an impressive collection of silver and jewellery, a couple of art museums and a series of rooms recreating life in the palace during House of Savoy times. Stop by at sunset when its entire facade is coloured a vibrant pink.

Festivals & Events

Scoppio del Carro FIREWORKS

(⊙Mar/Apr) A cart of fireworks is exploded in front of the cathedral on Piazza del Duomo at 11am on Easter Sunday.

Maggio Musicale Fiorentino PERFORMING ARTS

(www.maggiofiorentino.com; ⊙Apr-Jun) Italy's oldest arts festival features world-class performances of theatre, classical music, jazz, opera and dance. Events are staged at the **Teatro del Maggio Musicale Fiorentino** (☎055 200 12 78; Piazzale Vittorio Gui 1; ⊙box office 10am-6pm Mon-Sat).

Festa di San Giovanni RELIGIOUS

(⊙24 Jun) Florence celebrates its patron saint, John, with a *calcio storico* (historical football) match on Piazza di Santa Croce and fireworks over Piazzale Michelangelo.

Sleeping

★Academy Hostel HOSTEL €

(☎055 239 86 65; www.academyhostel.eu; Via Ricasoli 9; dm €30-45, d €70-90; ❄@📶) This classy hostel – definitely not a party hostel – sits on the 1st floor of Baron Ricasoli's 17th-century *palazzo*. The inviting lobby, with books to browse, was once a theatre and is a comfy spot to chill on the sofa over TV or a DVD. Dorms sport four, five or six beds, high moulded ceilings and brightly coloured lockers.

Hotel Scoti PENSION €

(☎055 29 21 28; www.hotelscoti.com; Via de' Tornabuoni 7; d/tr €140/165; 📶) Wedged between designer boutiques on Florence's smartest shopping strip, this hidden *pensione* is a fabulous mix of old-fashioned charm and value for money. Its traditionally styled rooms are spread across the 2nd floor of a 16th-century *palazzo;* some have lovely rooftop views. Guests can borrow hairdryers, bottle openers etc, and the frescoed lounge (1780) is stunning.

★Hotel Palazzo Guadagni HOTEL €€

(☎055 265 83 76; www.palazzoguadagni.com; Piazza Santo Spirito 9; d/tr/q €250/270/310; ❄📶) This romantic midrange hotel overlooking Florence's liveliest summertime square is legendary – Zeffirelli shot scenes from *Tea with Mussolini* here. Housed in an artfully revamped Renaissance palace, it has 15 spacious rooms with old-world high ceilings and the occasional fresco or fireplace (decorative today). In summer bartenders serve cocktails on the impossibly romantic loggia terrace with wicker chairs and predictably dreamy views.

Antica Torre di Via de' Tornabuoni 1 BOUTIQUE HOTEL €€€

(☎055 265 81 61; www.tornabuoni1.com; Via de' Tornabuoni 1; d €355; ❄📶) Footsteps from the Arno, inside beautiful 13th- to 19th-century Palazzo Gianfigliazzi, is this understated luxury hotel. Rooms are spacious and contemporary, but it's the stunning 6th-floor rooftop terrace that steals the show: lounge in the winter garden here, bask on the sun terrace, drink at the bar and swoon over Florence graciously laid out at your feet.

Eating

Mercato Centrale FOOD HALL €

(055 239 97 98; www.mercatocentrale.it; Piazza del Mercato Centrale 4; dishes €5-15; market 7am-3pm Mon-Fri, to 5pm Sat, food hall 8am-midnight;) Wander the maze of stalls rammed with fresh produce at Florence's oldest and largest food market, on the ground floor of an iron-and-glass structure designed by architect Giuseppe Mengoni in 1874. Head to the 1st floor's buzzing, thoroughly contemporary food hall with dedicated cookery school and artisan stalls cooking steaks, burgers, tripe *panini,* vegetarian dishes, pizza, gelato, pastries and pasta.

★Trattoria Mario TUSCAN €

(055 21 85 50; www.trattoria-mario.com; Via Rosina 2; meals €25; noon-3.30pm Mon-Sat, closed 3 weeks Aug) Arrive by noon to ensure a spot at this noisy, busy, brilliant trattoria – a legend that retains its soul (and allure with locals) despite being in every guidebook. Charming Fabio, whose grandfather opened the place in 1953, is front of house while big brother Romeo and nephew Francesco cook with speed in the kitchen. No advance reservations; cash only.

★Osteria Il Buongustai OSTERIA €

(055 29 13 04; www.facebook.com/ibuongustaifirenze; Via dei Cerchi 15r; meals €15-20; 9.30am-3.30pm Mon-Sat) Run with breathtaking speed and grace by Laura and Lucia, 'The Gourmand' is unmissable. Lunchtimes heave with locals and savvy students who flock here to fill up on tasty Tuscan home cooking at a snip of other restaurant prices. The place is brilliantly no-frills – watch women in hair caps at work in the kitchen, share a table and pay in cash.

Mariano SANDWICHES €

(055 21 40 67; Via del Parione 19r; panini €3.50-6; 8am-3pm & 5-7.30pm Mon-Fri, 8am-3pm Sat) A local favourite for its simplicity and correct prices, it's been around since 1973. From sunrise to sunset, this brick-vaulted, 13th-century cellar gently buzzes with Florentines propped at the counter sipping coffee or wine or eating salads and *panini.* Come here for a coffee-and-pastry breakfast, light lunch, an *aperitivo* with cheese or salami tasting platter (€13 to €17), or a *panino* to eat on the move.

★Il Teatro del Sale TUSCAN €€

(055 200 14 92; www.teatrodelsale.com; Via dei Macci 111r; brunch/dinner €20/30; noon-2.30pm & 7-11pm Tue-Fri, noon-3pm & 7-11pm Sat, noon-3pm Sun, closed Aug) Florentine chef Fabio Picchi is one of Florence's living treasures who steals the Sant' Ambrogio show with this eccentric, good-value, members-only club (everyone welcome; membership €7) inside an old theatre. He cooks up brunch and dinner, culminating at 9.30pm in a live performance of drama, music or comedy arranged by his wife, artistic director and comic actress Maria Cassi.

Trattoria Cibrèo TUSCAN €€

(www.cibreo.com; Via dei Macci 122r; meals €30-35; 12.50-2.30pm & 6.50-11pm, closed Aug) Dine at chez Fabio Picchi and you'll instantly understand why a queue gathers outside before it opens. Once inside, revel in top-notch Tuscan cuisine: perhaps *pappa al pomodoro* (a thick soupy mash of tomato, bread and basil) followed by *polpettine di pollo e ricotta* (chicken and ricotta meatballs). No reservations, no credit cards, no pasta and arrive early.

Drinking & Nightlife

★Le Volpi e l'Uva WINE BAR

(055 239 81 32; www.levolpieluva.com; Piazza dei Rossi 1; 11am-9pm summer, 11am-9pm Mon-Sat winter) This humble wine bar remains as appealing as the day it opened over a decade ago. Its food and wine pairings are first class – taste and buy boutique wines by small Italian producers, matched perfectly with cheeses, cold meats and the finest crostini in town; the warm, melt-in-your-mouth *lardo di Cinta Sienese* (wafer-thin slices of aromatic of pork fat) is absolutely extraordinary.

CUT THE QUEUES

➡ Book tickets for the Uffizi and Galleria dell'Accademia, as well as several other museums, through **Firenze Musei** (Florence Museums; www.firenzemusei.it). Note that this entails a booking fee of €3 per museum (€4 for the Uffizi and Galleria dell'Accademia).

➡ Alternatively, the **Firenze Card** (€85, valid for 72 hours) allows you to bypass both advance booking and queues. Check details at www.firenzecard.it.

★**Mad Souls & Spirits** COCKTAIL BAR
(☎055 627 16 21; www.facebook.com/madsoulsandspirits; Borgo San Frediano 38r; ⏲6pm-2am; 📶) At this uber-cool bar in San Frediano, cult alchemists Neri Fantechi and Julian Biondi woo a discerning crowd with their expertly crafted cocktails, served in a tiny aqua-green and red-brick space that couldn't be more spartan. A potted cactus decorates each scrubbed wood table and the humorous cocktail menu is the height of irreverence.

Check the 'Daily Madness' blackboard for specials.

★**Ditta Artigianale** CAFE
(☎055 274 15 41; www.dittaartigianale.it; Via de' Neri 32r; ⏲8am-10pm Mon-Thu, to midnight Fri, 9am-midnight Sat, to 11pm Sun; 📶) With industrial decor and laid-back vibe, this ingenious coffee roastery is a perfect place to hang at any time of day. The creation of three-times Italian barista champion Francesco Sanapo, it's famed for its first-class coffee and outstanding gin cocktails. If you're yearning a flat white, cold brew tonic or cappuccino made with almond milk, come here.

La Cité BAR
(www.facebook.com/lacitelibreriacafe; Borgo San Frediano 20r; ⏲10am-2am Mon-Sat, from 2pm Sun; 📶) A hip cafe-bookshop with an eclectic choice of vintage seating, La Cité makes a wonderful, intimate venue for book readings, after-work drinks and fantastic live music – jazz, swing, world music. Check its Facebook page for the week's events.

Caffè Gilli CAFE
(☎055 21 38 96; www.gilli.it; Piazza della Repubblica 39r; ⏲7.30am-1am) Popular with locals who sip coffee standing up at the long marble bar, this is the most famous of the historical cafes on the city's old Roman forum. Gilli has been serving delectable cakes, chocolates, fruit tartlets and *millefoglie* (lighter-than-light vanilla or custard slice) since 1733. It moved to this square in 1910 and has a beautifully preserved art nouveau interior.

FLORENCE'S BEST GELATO

Grom (☎055 21 61 58; www.grom.it; Via del Campanile 2; cones & tubs €2.60-5.50; ⏲10am-midnight Sun-Fri, to 1am Sat summer, 10.30am-10.30pm winter) Top-notch gelato, including outstanding chocolate, near the Duomo.

Vivoli (☎055 29 23 34; www.vivoli.it; Via dell'Isola delle Stinche 7; tubs €2-10; ⏲7.30am-midnight Tue-Sat, from 9am Sun, to 9pm winter) Vintage classic for coffee and cakes as well as gelato.

Gelateria La Carraia (☎055 28 06 95; www.lacarraiagroup.eu; Piazza Nazario Sauro 25r; cones & tubs €1.50-6; ⏲11am-midnight) Florentine favourite on the other side of the river.

ℹ Information

24-Hour Pharmacy (☎055 21 67 61; Stazione di Santa Maria Novella; ⏲24hr) All-hours pharmacy inside Florence's central train station; at least one member of staff usually speaks English.

Dr Stephen Kerr: Medical Service (☎335 8361682, 055 28 80 55; www.dr-kerr.com; Piazza Mercato Nuovo 1; ⏲3-5pm Mon-Fri, or by appointment 9am-3pm Mon-Fri) Resident British doctor.

ℹ Getting There & Away

AIR

Florence airport (Aeroporto Amerigo Vespucci; ☎055 306 18 30, 055 3 06 15; www.aeroporto.firenze.it; Via del Termine 11) is 5km northwest of the city centre.

Pisa International Airport (Galileo Galilei Airport; ☎050 84 93 00; www.pisa-airport.com) in Pisa, 80km west of Florence, serves flights to Italian destinations and major European cities.

BUS

Services from the **bus station** (Autostazione Busitalia-Sita Nord; ☎800 373760; www.fsbusitalia.it; Via Santa Caterina da Siena 17r; ⏲5.45am-8.40pm Mon-Sat, 6.25am-8.30pm Sun), just west of Piazza della Stazione, are limited; the train is better. Destinations served include Siena (€8.40, 1¼ hours, at least hourly) and Greve in Chianti (€4.50, one hour, hourly).

TRAIN

Florence's **Stazione di Santa Maria Novella** (www.firenzesantamarianovella.it; Piazza della Stazione) is on the main Rome–Milan line. There are regular direct services to/from Pisa (€8.60, 1¼ hours, every 15 minutes), Rome (€22 to €36, 1½ to 3¾ hours, at least twice hourly), Venice (€26 to €43, two hours, at least hourly) and

WORTH A TRIP

PISA

A handsome university city, Pisa is best known as the home of an architectural project gone terribly wrong. However, the Leaning Tower is just one of a number of noteworthy sights in its compact medieval centre.

Pisa's golden age came in the 12th and 13th centuries when it was a maritime power to rival Genoa and Venice.

Leaning Tower (Torre Pendente; ☎050 83 50 11; www.opapisa.it; Piazza dei Miracoli; €18; ⏰8.30am-10pm Jun-Aug, 9am-8pm Apr-May & Sep, to 7pm Oct & Mar, to 6pm Nov-Feb) One of Italy's signature sights, the Torre Pendente truly lives up to its name, leaning a startling 5.5 degrees off the vertical. The 58m-high tower, officially the Duomo's *campanile* (bell tower), took almost 200 years to build, but was already listing when it was unveiled in 1372. Over time, the tilt, caused by a layer of weak subsoil, steadily worsened until it was finally halted by a major stabilisation project in the 1990s.

Duomo (Duomo di Santa Maria Assunta; ☎050 83 50 11; www.opapisa.it; Piazza dei Miracoli; ⏰10am-8pm Apr-Sep, to 7pm Oct & Mar, to 6pm Nov-Feb) Pisa's magnificent Romanesque Duomo was begun in 1064 and consecrated in 1118. Its striking tiered exterior, with cladding of green-and-cream marble bands, conceals a vast columned interior capped by a gold wooden ceiling. The elliptical dome, the first of its kind in Europe at the time, was added in 1380.

Admission is free but you need a ticket from another Piazza dei Miracoli sight to get in or a fixed-timed free pass issued by **ticket offices** (⏰8am-7.30pm summer, to 5.30pm winter) behind the Leaning Tower or inside **Museo delle Sinopie** (€5, combination ticket with Battistero & Camposanto €8; ⏰8am-8pm Apr-Sep, 9am-7pm Oct & Mar, to 6pm Nov-Feb).

Battistero (Battistero di San Giovanni; ☎050 83 50 11; www.opapisa.it; Piazza dei Miracoli; €5, with Camposanto & Museo €8; ⏰8am-8pm Apr-Sep, 9am-7pm Oct & Mar, to 6pm Nov-Feb) Pisa's unusual round baptistery has one dome piled on top of another, each roofed half in lead, half in tiles, and topped by a gilt bronze John the Baptist (1395). Construction began in 1152, but it was remodelled and continued by Nicola and Giovanni Pisano more than a century later and finally completed in the 14th century. Inside, the hexagonal marble pulpit (1260) by Nicola Pisano is the highlight.

Ristorante Galileo (☎050 2 82 87; www.ristorantegalileo.com; Via San Martino 6-8; meals €25-35; ⏰12.30-3pm & 7.30-10.30pm) For good, honest, unpretentious Tuscan cooking, nothing beats this classical old-timer. From the cork-covered wine list to the complimentary plate of warm homemade focaccia and huge platters of tempting *cantuccini* (almond-studded biscuits), Galileo makes you feel welcome. Fresh pasta is strictly hand- and homemade, and most veggies are plucked fresh that morning from the restaurant's garden.

Pisa International Airport (Galileo Galilei Airport; ☎050 84 93 00; www.pisa-airport.com) is linked to the city centre by the **PisaMover** (www.pisa-mover.com) shuttle, which runs to Pisa Centrale train station (€2.70, five minutes, every seven to 15 minutes from 4.30am to 1.30am).

Frequent trains run to Lucca (€3.60, 30 minutes, half-hourly), Florence (€8.60, 1¼ hours, every 15 minutes) and La Spezia (€7.80 to €15.50, one to 1½ hours, half-hourly) for the Cinque Terre.

Milan (€37 to €46, 1¾ hours to four hours, at least hourly).

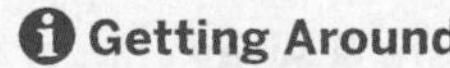

Getting Around

TO/FROM THE AIRPORT

Volainbus (☎800 373760; www.fsbusitalia.it) The Volainbus shuttle runs between Florence airport and the bus station on Via Santa Catarina da Siena, across from the train station. Going to the airport, departures are roughly half-hourly between 5am and 8.30pm and then hourly until 12.10am; from the airport between 5.30am and 8.30pm then hourly until 12.30am. Journey time is 20 to 30 minutes and a single/return ticket costs €6/10; drivers sell tickets.

PUBLIC TRANSPORT

City buses are operated by ATAF. Tickets are valid for 90 minutes (no return journeys), cost €1.50 (€2.50 on board) and are sold at the **ATAF ticketing window** (800 424500; www.ataf.net; Stazione di Santa Maria Novella, Piazza della Stazione; 6.45am-8pm) at Santa Maria Novella train station, at tobacconists and at kiosks.

Lucca

POP 88,400

Lucca is a love-at-first-sight type of place. Hidden behind monumental Renaissance walls, its historical centre is chock-full of handsome churches, alluring piazzas and excellent restaurants. Founded by the Etruscans, it became a city state in the 12th century and stayed that way for 600 years. Most of its streets and monuments date from this period.

Sights

★City Wall WALLS

Lucca's monumental *mura* (wall) was built around the old city in the 16th and 17th centuries and remains in almost perfect condition. It superseded two previous walls, the first built from travertine stone blocks in the 2nd century BC. Twelve metres high and 4.2km long, today's ramparts are crowned with a tree-lined footpath looking down on the historical centre and – by the **Baluardo San Regolo** (San Regolo Bastion) – the city's vintage **Orto Botanico** (Botanical Garden; 0583 58 30 86; www.lemuradilucca.it/orto-botanico; Casermetta San Regolo; adult/reduced €4/3; 10am-7pm Jul-Sep, to 6pm May & Jun, to 5pm Mar, Apr & Oct) with its magnificent cedar trees.

★Cattedrale di San Martino CATHEDRAL

(0583 49 05 30; www.museocattedralelucca.it; Piazza San Martino; €3, incl campanile, Museo della Cattedrale & Chiesa e Battistero dei SS Giovanni & Reparata adult/reduced €9/6; 9.30am-6pm Mon-Fri, to 6.45pm Sat, noon-6pm Sun summer, shorter hours winter) Lucca's predominantly Romanesque cathedral dates from the 11th century. Its stunning facade was constructed in the prevailing Lucca-Pisan style and designed to accommodate the pre-existing *campanile* (bell tower). The reliefs over the left doorway of the portico are believed to be by Nicola Pisano, while inside, treasures include the **Volto Santo** (literally, Holy Countenance) crucifix sculpture and a wonderful 15th-century tomb in the **sacristy**. The cathedral interior was rebuilt in the 14th and 15th centuries with a Gothic flourish.

Sleeping & Eating

Piccolo Hotel Puccini HOTEL €

(0583 5 54 21; www.hotelpuccini.com; Via di Poggio 9; s/d €75/100;) In a brilliant central location, this welcoming three-star hotel hides behind a discreet brick exterior. Its small guest rooms are attractive with wooden floors, vintage ceiling fans and colourful, contemporary design touches. Breakfast, optional at €3.50, is served at candlelit tables behind the small reception area. Rates are at least 30% lower in winter.

Da Felice PIZZA €

(0583 49 49 86; www.pizzeriadafelice.it; Via Buia 12; focaccia €1-4, pizza slices €1.40; 10am-8.30pm Mon-Sat) This buzzing spot behind Piazza San Michele is where the locals come for wood-fired pizza, *cecina* (salted chickpea pizza) and *castagnacci* (chestnut cakes). Eat in or take away, *castagnacci* come wrapped in crisp white paper, and my, they're good married with a chilled bottle of Moretti beer.

★Ristorante Giglio TUSCAN €€

(0583 49 40 58; www.ristorantegiglio.com; Piazza del Giglio 2; meals €40-50; 12.15-2.45pm & 7.30-10.30pm Thu-Mon, 7.30-10.30pm Wed) Splendidly at home in the frescoed 18th-century Palazzo Arnolfini, Giglio is stunning. Sip a complimentary *prosecco,* watch the fire crackle in the marble fireplace and savour traditional Tuscan with a modern twist: think fresh artichoke salad served in an edible parmesan-cheese wafer 'bowl', or risotto simmered in Chianti. End with Lucchese *buccellato* (sweet bread) filled with ice cream and berries.

Information

Tourist Office (0583 58 31 50; www.turismo.lucca.it; Piazzale Verdi; 9am-6.30pm) Offers free hotel reservations, left-luggage service (two bags €1.50/3 per hour/half-day) and two-hour guided city tours in English (€10 per person, under 15 years free) departing at 2pm daily, April to October, and on Saturdays and Sundays the rest of the year.

Getting There & Away

Regional trains run to/from Florence (€7.80 to €9.90, 1¾ hours) via Pisa (€3.60, 30 minutes, half-hourly).

Siena

POP 53,800

Siena is one of Italy's most enchanting medieval towns. Its walled centre is a beautifully preserved warren of dark lanes punctuated with Gothic *palazzi,* and at its heart is Piazza del Campo (Il Campo), the sloping square that is the venue for the city's famous annual horse race, Il Palio.

In the Middle Ages, the city was a political and artistic force to be reckoned with, a worthy rival for its larger neighbour Florence.

Sights

★Piazza del Campo — PIAZZA

Popularly known as 'Il Campo', this sloping piazza has been Siena's social centre since being staked out by the ruling Consiglio dei Nove (Council of Nine) in the mid-12th century. Built on the site of a Roman marketplace, its paving is divided into nine sectors representing the number of members of the *consiglio* and these days acts as a carpet on which young locals meet and relax. The cafes around its perimeter are the most popular coffee and *aperitivi* spots in town.

Palazzo Pubblico — HISTORIC BUILDING

(Palazzo Comunale, Piazza del Campo) Built to demonstrate the enormous wealth, proud independence and secular nature of Siena, this 14th-century Gothic masterpiece is the visual focal point of the Campo, itself the true heart of the city. Architecturally clever (notice how its concave facade mirrors the opposing convex curve) it has always housed the city's administration and been used as a cultural venue. Its distinctive bell tower, the **Torre del Mangia** (☎0577 29 26 15; www.enjoysiena.it/it/attrattore/Torre-del-Mangia; €10; ⏲10am-6.15pm summer, to 3.15pm winter), provides magnificent views to those who brave the steep climb to the top.

★Museo Civico — MUSEUM

(Civic Museum; ☎0577 29 26 15; www.enjoysiena.it/it/attrattore/Museo-Civico; Palazzo Pubblico, Piazza del Campo 1; adult/reduced €9/8; ⏲10am-6.15pm summer, to 5.15pm winter) Entered via the Palazzo Pubblico's **Cortile del Podestà** (Courtyard of the Podestà), this wonderful museum showcases rooms richly frescoed by artists of the Sienese school. Commissioned by the city's governing body rather than by the Church, some of the frescoes depict secular subjects – highly unusual at the time. The highlights are two huge frescoes: Ambrogio Lorenzetti's *Allegories of Good and Bad Government* (c 1338–40) and Simone Martini's celebrated *Maestà* (*Virgin Mary in Majesty;* 1315).

★Duomo — CATHEDRAL

(Cattedrale di Santa Maria Assunta; ☎0577 28 63 00; www.operaduomo.siena.it; Piazza Duomo; summer/winter €5/free, when floor displayed €8; ⏲10.30am-7pm Mon-Sat, 1.30-6pm Sun summer, to 5.30pm winter) Consecrated on the former site of a Roman temple in 1179 and constructed over the 13th and 14th centuries, Siena's majestic *duomo* (cathedral) showcases the talents of many great medieval and Renaissance architects and artists: Giovanni Pisano designed the intricate white, green and red marble facade; Nicola Pisano carved the elaborate pulpit; Pinturicchio painted the frescoes in the extraordinary **Libreria Piccolomini** (Piccolomini Library; ☎0577 28 63 00; summer/winter free/€2; ⏲10.30am-7pm summer, to 5.30pm winter); and Michelangelo, Donatello and Gian Lorenzo Bernini all produced sculptures.

★Museale Santa Maria della Scala — MUSEUM

(☎0577 28 63 00; www.santamariadellascala.com; Piazza Duomo 2; adult/reduced €9/7; ⏲10am-7pm Fri-Wed, to 10pm Thu summer, shorter hours winter) Built as a hospice for pilgrims travelling the Via Francigena, this huge complex opposite the Duomo dates from the 13th century. Its highlight is the upstairs **Pellegrinaio** (Pilgrim's Hall), featuring vivid 15th-century frescoes by Lorenzo di Pietro (aka Vecchietta), Priamo della Quercia and Domenico di Bartolo. All laud the good works of the hospital and its patrons; the most evocative is di Bartolo's *Il governo degli infermi* (Caring for the Sick; 1440–41), which depicts many activities that occurred here.

Festivals & Events

Palio — PARADE

(Piazza del Campo; ⏲2 Jul & 16 Aug) Dating from the Middle Ages, this spectacular annual event includes a series of colourful pageants and a wild horse race in Piazza del Campo. Ten of Siena's 17 *contrade* (town districts) compete for the coveted *palio* (silk banner). Each *contrada* has its own traditions, symbol and colours, plus its own church and *palio* museum.

Sleeping & Eating

Hotel Alma Domus HOTEL €

(☎0577 4 41 77; www.hotelalmadomus.it; Via Camporegio 37; s €46-55, d €83-140; ❄@📶) Your chance to sleep in a convent: Alma Domus is owned by the church and is still home to several Dominican nuns. The economy rooms, although comfortable, are styled very simply and aren't as soundproofed as many would like. But the superior ones are lovely, with a stylish decor and modern fittings; many have mini-balconies with uninterrupted Duomo views.

★Pensione Palazzo Ravizza BOUTIQUE HOTEL €€€

(☎0577 28 04 62; www.palazzoravizza.it; Pian dei Mantellini 34; r €110-320; P❄📶) Occupying a Renaissance-era *palazzo* in a quiet but convenient corner of Siena, this gorgeous hotel offers rooms perfectly melding heritage features and modern amenities; the best face the large rear garden, which has a panoramic terrace. The breakfast buffet is generous, on-site parking is free and room rates are remarkably reasonable (especially in the low season).

Morbidi DELI €

(☎0577 28 02 68; www.morbidi.com; Via Banchi di Sopra 75; lunch €12, aperitivo buffet from €8; ⊙8am-8pm Mon-Wed, to 9pm Thu & Fri, to 3pm Sat) A classy deli famed for its top-quality produce, Morbidi's excellent-value basement lunch buffet (€12; 12.15pm to 2.30pm Monday to Saturday) allows you to choose from freshly prepared antipasti, salads, risotto, pasta and dessert. Bottled water is supplied; wine and coffee cost extra. Buy your ticket upstairs before heading down. It also offers regular *aperitivo* buffets on Thursday and Friday evenings.

Enoteca I Terzi TUSCAN €€

(☎0577 4 43 29; www.enotecaiterzi.it; Via dei Termini 7; meals €35-40; ⊙12.30-3pm & 7.30-11pm Mon-Sat) Close to the Campo but off the well-beaten tourist trail, this *enoteca* (wine bar) is located in a vaulted medieval building but has a contemporary feel. It's popular with sophisticated locals, who linger over working lunches, *aperitivi* sessions and slow-paced dinners featuring Tuscan *salumi* (cured meats), delicate handmade pasta, grilled meats and wonderful wines (many available by the glass).

Information

Tourist Office (☎0577 28 05 51; www.enjoysiena.it; Piazza Duomo 2, Santa Maria della Scala; ⊙9am-6pm summer, to 5pm winter) Siena's tourist information office is in the Museale Santa Maria della Scala, and can provide free maps of the city. The entrance is on the right (western) side of the museum building.

Getting There & Away

Buses run by **Tiemme** (☎800 922984; www.tiemmespa.it) link Siena with Florence (€8.40, 1¼ hours, at least hourly) and San Gimignano (€6.20, 1¼ hours, up to 17 daily), either direct or via Poggibonsi.

WORTH A TRIP

ORVIETO

Strategically located on the main train line between Rome and Florence, this spectacularly sited hilltop town has one major draw: its extraordinary Gothic **Duomo** (☎0763 34 24 77; www.opsm.it; Piazza Duomo 26; admission €4, incl Museo dell'Opera del Duomo di Orvieto €5; ⊙9.30am-7pm Mon-Sat, 1-5.30pm Sun summer, shorter hrs winter), built over 300 years from 1290. The facade is stunning, and the beautiful interior contains Luca Signorelli's awe-inspiring *Giudizio universale* (The Last Judgment) fresco cycle.

The **tourist office** (☎0763 34 17 72; Piazza Duomo 24; ⊙8.15am-1.50pm & 4-7pm Mon-Fri, 10am-6pm Sat & Sun) is opposite the cathedral; nearby sits **I Sette Consoli** (☎0763 34 39 11; www.isetteconsoli.it; Piazza Sant'Angelo 1a; meals €40-45, tasting menu €45; ⊙12.30-3pm & 7.30-10pm, closed Wed & Sun dinner), one of Umbria's best restaurants – its pasta and risotto are simply sublime. **Bottega Vera** (☎349 4300167; www.casaveraorvieto.it/it/bottega.html; Via del Duomo 36; ⊙8.30am-8.30pm Mon-Fri & Sun, to 10pm Sat; 📶) is an excellent and non-touristy *enoteca* (wine bar).

Orvieto is a mere one-hour drive from both Montepulciano and Arezzo. Trains run to/from Florence (€16.70 to €25, 2½ hours, hourly) and Rome (€8.15 to €17.50, 1½ hours, hourly). From the train station you'll need to take the **funicular** (tickets €1.30; ⊙every 10min 7.15am-8.30pm Mon-Sat, every 15min 8am-8.30pm Sun) up to the town centre.

WORTH A TRIP

ASSISI

The birthplace of St Francis (1182–1226), the medieval town of Assisi is a major destination for millions of pilgrims. The main sight is the Basilica di San Francesco, one of Italy's most visited churches, but the hilltop historical centre is also well worth a look.

Basilica di San Francesco (www.sanfrancescoassisi.org; Piazza di San Francesco; ⏲ basilica superiore 8.30am-6.50pm, basilica inferiore 6am-6.50pm summer, shorter hours winter) Visible for miles around, the Basilica di San Francesco is the crowning glory of Assisi's Unesco listed historical centre. The 13th-century complex comprises two churches: the Gothic Basilica Superiore (Upper Church), with its celebrated cycle of Giotto frescoes, and beneath, the older Basilica Inferiore (Lower Church) where you'll find works by Cimabue, Pietro Lorenzetti and Simone Martini. Also here, in the **Cripta di San Francesco**, is St Francis' much-venerated tomb.

Basilica di Santa Chiara (www.assisisantachiara.it; Piazza Santa Chiara; ⏲ 6.30am-noon & 2-7pm summer, to 6pm winter) Built in a 13th-century Romanesque style, with muscular flying buttresses and a striking pink-and-white striped facade, this church is dedicated to St Clare, a spiritual contemporary of St Francis and founder of the *Sorelle Povere di Santa Chiara* (Order of the Poor Ladies), now known as the Poor Clares. She is buried in the church's crypt, alongside the original **Crocifisso di San Damiano**, a Byzantine cross before which St Francis was praying when he is said to have received his mission from God in 1205.

Tourist Office (☎ 075 813 86 80; www.visit-assisi.it; Piazza del Comune 10; ⏲ 9am-7pm) Stop by here for maps, leaflets and accommodation lists.

Sena (☎ 0861 199 19 00; www.sena.it) operates services to/from Rome Tiburtina (€15 to €23, three to 3¾ hours, 10 daily), Milan (€24 to €31, 4½ to 8¾ hours, seven daily), Perugia (€11, 1½ hours, one daily) and Venice (€21 to €25, five to 5¾ hours, three daily).

Ticket offices are in the basement under the bus station on Piazza Gramsci.

SOUTHERN ITALY

A sun-bleached land of spectacular coastlines and rugged landscapes, southern Italy is a robust contrast to the more genteel north. Its stunning scenery, baroque towns and classical ruins exist alongside ugly urban sprawl and scruffy coastal development, sometimes in the space of just a few kilometres.

Yet for all its flaws, *il mezzogiorno* (the midday sun, as southern Italy is known) is an essential part of every Italian itinerary, offering charm, culinary good times and architectural treasures.

Naples

POP 966,145

A love-it-or-loathe-it sprawl of regal palaces, bombastic churches and chaotic streets, Naples (Napoli) is totally exhilarating. Founded by Greek colonists, it became a thriving Roman city and was later the Bourbon capital of the Kingdom of the Two Sicilies. In the 18th century it was one of Europe's great cities, something you'll readily believe as you marvel at its art-crammed museums and great baroque buildings.

Sights

★Museo Archeologico Nazionale MUSEUM
(☎ 848 800 288; www.museoarcheologiconapoli.it; Piazza Museo Nazionale 19; adult/reduced €15/7.50; ⏲ 9am-7.30pm Wed-Mon; Ⓜ Museo, Piazza Cavour) Naples' National Archaeological Museum serves up one of the world's finest collections of Graeco-Roman artefacts. Originally a cavalry barracks and later the seat of the city's university, the museum was established by the Bourbon king Charles VII in the late 18th century to house the antiquities he inherited from his mother, Elisabetta Farnese, as well as treasures looted from Pompeii and Herculaneum. Star exhibits include the celebrated *Toro Farnese* (Farnese Bull) sculpture and awe-inspiring mosaics from Pompeii's **Casa del Fauno** (House of the Faun).

★Cappella Sansevero CHAPEL
(☎ 081 551 84 70; www.museosansevero.it; Via Francesco de Sanctis 19; adult/reduced €7/5;

Central Naples

0 — 400 m
0 — 0.2 miles

A B C D
1 2 3 4 5 6 7

Museo di Capodimonte (1.9km)
Museo Archeologico Nazionale
2
Museo
Piazza Cavour
Via Maria Longo
Piazza Cavour
Concettina Ai Tre Santi (650m)
Via Santissimi Apostoli
Via S Guiseppe dei Nudi
Piazza Museo Nazionale
5
Via Santa Maria di Costantinopoli
Via Anticaglia
Via Tommasi
Largo Regina Coeli
Via Pisanelli
Vico Giganti
Via Duomo
3
Via Broggia
Via San Paolo
Via dei Tribunali
Via della Zite
Via Francesco Saverio Correra
Via Enrico Pessina
Via della Sapienza
Via Atri
Vico Zuroli
Via Bellini
Via del Sole
Piazza San Gaetano
Vico Domenico Soriano
Via G Brombeis
4
Piazza Luigi Miraglia
Vico Giuseppe Maffei
Via Vicaria Vecchia
Piazza Bellini
Via dei Tribunali
Via Nilo
Via Port'Alba
Cappella Sansevero
1
Via San Biagio dei Librai
Piazza Museo Filangieri
Dante
Piazza Dante
Via San Sebastiano
Palazzo dei Di Sangrio
Piazzetta del Nilo
Vico S Severino
Via d'Alagno
Via Montesanto
Via Tarsia
Via Benedetto Croce
Duomo
Via Pellegrini
Via B Capasso
Piazza Nicola Amore
Funicolare di Montesanto (170m); Certosa e Museo di San Martino (1.5km)
Piazza del Gesù Nuovo
7
Via Mezzocannone
Via G Paladino
Alibus (Stazione Central Stop) (850m); Metropark Napoli Centrale (1.1km); Circumvesuviana (1.2km); Stazione Centrale (1.2km)
Via S Anna dei Lombardi
Via Santa Chiara
Largo Giusso
Via Pasquale Scura
Via T Caravita
Largo Banchi Nuovi
Corso Umberto I
Piazetta Orefici
Via Pignasecca
Via S Liborio
Via Formale
Piazza Carità
Via Monteoliveto
Via Donnalbina
Via Sedile di Porto
Via Nuova Marina
Via G Simonelli
Vico P Galluppi
Via C Battisti
Piazza Matteotti
Via D Cerriglio
Piazza Bovio
Università
Via G C Cortese
Via Concezione a Montecalvario
Via Bracco
Via A Diaz
6
Via dei Fiorentini
Via Graziella
Via Alside De Gasperi
Tirrenia
Toledo
Via A Depretis
Calata Porta di Massa
Varco Immacolatella
Via Potracarrese a Montecalvario
Via S Tommaso d'Aquino
Via F Gioia
Via S Nicola alla Dogana
Via Cristoforo Colombo
Via S Bartolomeo
Via Speranzella
Via S Giacomo
Via Medina
Via Toledo
Piazza del Municipio
Via P E Imbriani
Piazza Francese
Via G Melisurgo
Bacino del Piliero
Via G Verdi
Municipio
Via Santa Brigida
Via Vittorio Emanuele III
Vico d'Aflitto
Funicolare Centrale
Molo Angioino
Via San Carlo
Parco Castello
Piazza Trieste e Trento
9
Alilauro
SNAV
Caremar
Via Chiaia
8
Pescheria Mattiucci (760m); L'Antiquario (820m); Pasticceria Mennella (1km)
Molo Beverello
Porto Immacolatella
Via A F Acton
Da Ettore (170m)

ITALY NAPLES

Central Naples

9am-7pm Wed-Mon; Ⓜ Dante) It's in this Masonic-inspired baroque chapel that you'll find Giuseppe Sanmartino's incredible sculpture, *Cristo velato* (Veiled Christ), its marble veil so realistic that it's tempting to try to lift it and view Christ underneath. It's one of several artistic wonders that include Francesco Queirolo's sculpture *Disinganno* (Disillusion), Antonio Corradini's *Pudicizia* (Modesty) and riotously colourful frescoes by Francesco Maria Russo, the latter untouched since their creation in 1749.

Duomo CATHEDRAL
(081 44 90 97; Via Duomo 149; cathedral/baptistry free/€2; cathedral 8.30am-1.30pm & 2.30-7.30pm Mon-Sat, 8.30am-1.30pm & 4.30-7.30pm Sun, baptistry 8.30am-12.30pm & 3.30-6.30pm Mon-Sat, 8.30am-1pm Sun, Cappella di San Gennaro 8.30am-1pm & 3-6.30pm Mon-Sat, 8.30am-1pm & 4.30-7pm Sun; 147, 182, 184 to Via Foria, Ⓜ Piazza Cavour) Whether you go for Giovanni Lanfranco's fresco in the Cappella di San Gennaro (Chapel of St Janarius), the 4th-century mosaics in the baptistry, or the thrice-annual 'miracle' of San Gennaro, do not miss Naples' cathedral. Kick-started by Charles I of Anjou in 1272 and consecrated in 1315, it was largely destroyed in a 1456 earthquake. It has had copious nips and tucks over the subsequent centuries.

Certosa e Museo di San Martino MONASTERY, MUSEUM
(081 229 45 03; www.polomusealecampania.beniculturali.it/index.php/certosa-e-museo; Largo San Martino 5; adult/reduced €6/3; 8.30am-7.30pm Tue & Thu-Sat, to 6.30pm Sun; Ⓜ Vanvitelli, Montesanto to Morghen) The high point (quite literally) of the Neapolitan baroque, this charterhouse-turned-museum was built as a Carthusian monastery between 1325 and 1368. Centred on one of the most beautiful cloisters in Italy, it has been decorated, adorned and altered over the centuries by some of Italy's finest talent, most importantly architect Giovanni Antonio Dosio in the 16th century and baroque sculptor Cosimo Fanzago a century later. Nowadays, it's a superb repository of Neapolitan and Italian artistry.

★ **Museo di Capodimonte** MUSEUM
(081 749 91 11; www.museocapodimonte.beniculturali.it; Via Miano 2; adult/reduced €12/8; 8.30am-7.30pm Thu-Tue; ; R4, 178 to Via Capodimonte, Shuttle Capodimonte) Originally designed as a hunting lodge for Charles VII of Bourbon, the monumental Palazzo di Capodimonte was begun in 1738 and took more than a century to complete. It's now home to the **Museo di Capodimonte**, southern Italy's largest and richest art gallery. Its vast collection – much of which Charles inherited from his mother, Elisabetta Farnese – was moved here in 1759 and ranges from exquisite 12th-century altarpieces to works by Botticelli, Caravaggio, Titian and Warhol.

Sleeping

★ **Magma Home** B&B €
(320 4360272, 338 3188914; http://magmahome.it; Via San Giuseppe dei Nudi 18; d €70-150; ; Ⓜ Museo) Contemporary artworks, cultural soirées and impeccable hospitality plug you straight into Naples' cultural scene at Magma. Its eight rooms – each designed by a local artist – intrigue with their mix of Italian design classics, upcycled materials and specially commissioned artworks. There's a large, contemporary communal kitchen and living area, plus two inviting rooftop terraces with views of the city and Mt Vesuvius.

Neapolitan Trips HOSTEL €€
(B&B 081 551 8977, hostel 081 1836 6402, hotel 081 1984 5933; www.neapolitantrips.com; Via dei Fiorentini 10; hostel dm €15-35, B&B d €45-90, hotel d €80-160; ; Ⓜ Toledo) Neapolitan Trips is a unique beast, with a clean, next-gen hostel on one floor, and both B&B and hotel rooms on another. The hostel is the standout, boasting a hip communal lounge-bar complete with electric guitars, amps and a piano for impromptu evening jams, a modern guest kitchen with complimentary pasta

THE ARTECARD

The **Campania Artecard** (www.campaniartecard.it) offers discounted museum admission and transport. It comes in various forms, of which the most useful are the following:

Napoli (€21, valid for three days) Gives free entry to three sights in Naples, then discounts on others, as well as free city transport.

Tutta la regione (€34, valid for seven days) Provides free entry to five sights across the region and discounts on others.

Cards can be purchased online or at participating sites and museums.

to cook, and mixed-gender dorms with USB ports by each bed.

While the hostel floor has a buzzy outdoor terrace, hostel guests are also welcome to use the spectacular rooftop terrace, complete with sweeping city views, an upmarket restaurant and hot tubs. The work of emerging and established Neapolitan photographers grace the property, and the hostel also offers two triple rooms with communal bathroom. On-site laundry facilities are available, as well as a handy in-house 'shop' selling everything from phone chargers to batteries and portable tripods.

★Hotel Piazza Bellini BOUTIQUE HOTEL €€
(081 45 17 32; www.hotelpiazzabellini.com; Via Santa Maria di Costantinopoli 101; d €90-190; ; Dante) Only steps from the bars and nightlife of Piazza Bellini, this sharp, hip hotel occupies a 16th-century *palazzo*, its pure-white spaces spiked with original maiolica tiles, vaulted ceilings and *piperno*-stone paving. Rooms are modern and functional, with designer fittings, fluffy duvets and chic bathrooms with excellent showers. Four rooms on the 5th and 6th floors feature panoramic terraces.

Eating

★Concettina Ai Tre Santi PIZZA €
(081 29 00 37; www.pizzeriaoliva.it; Via Arena della Sanità 7; pizzas from €5; noon-midnight Mon-Sat, to 5pm Sun; ; Piazza Cavour, Museo) Head in by noon (or 7.30pm at dinner) to avoid a long wait at this hot-spot pizzeria, made famous thanks to its young, driven *pizzaiolo* Ciro Oliva. The menu is an index of fastidiously sourced artisanal ingredients, used to top Ciro's flawless, wood-fired bases. Traditional Neapolitan pizza aside, you'll also find a string of creative seasonal options.

Pasticceria Mennella PASTRIES €
(081 42 60 26; www.pasticceriamennella.it; Via Carducci 50-52; pastries from €1.50; 6.30am-9.30pm Mon-Fri, to 10.30pm Sat, 7am-9.30pm Sun; Piazza Amedeo) If you eat only one sweet treat in Naples (good luck with that!), make it Mennella's spectacular *frolla al limone*, a shortbread pastry filled with heavenly lemon cream. Just leave room for the *mignon* (bite-size) version of its *sciù* (choux pastry) with *crema di nocciola* (hazelnut cream). Before you go feeling guilty, remember that everything is free of preservatives and artificial additives.

★Salumeria NEAPOLITAN €€
(081 1936 4649; www.salumeriaupnea.it; Via San Giovanni Maggiore Pignatelli 34/35; sandwiches from €5.50, charcuterie platters from €8.50, meals around €30; 12.30-5pm & 7.15pm-midnight Thu-Tue; ; Dante) Small producers, local ingredients and contemporary takes on provincial Campanian recipes drive bistro-inspired Salumeria. Nibble on quality charcuterie and cheeses or fill up on artisanal *panini*, hamburgers or Salumeria's sublime *ragù napoletano* (pasta served in a rich tomato-and-meat sauce slow-cooked over two days). Even the ketchup here is made in-house, using DOP Piennolo tomatoes from Vesuvius.

★Da Ettore NEAPOLITAN €€
(081 764 35 78; Via Gennaro Serra 39; meals €25; 1-3pm & 8-10pm Tue-Sat, 1-3pm Sun; ; R2 to Via San Carlo, Chiaia-Monte di Dio) This homey, eight-table trattoria has an epic reputation. Scan the walls for famous fans like comedy great Totò, and a framed passage from crime writer Massimo Siviero, who mentions Ettore in one of his tales. The draw is solid regional cooking, which includes one of the best *spaghetti alle vongole* (spaghetti with clams) in town. Book two days ahead for Sunday lunch.

Pescheria Mattiucci SEAFOOD €€
(081 251 2215; www.pescheriamattiucci.com; Vico Belledonne a Chiaia 27; crudo €25, cooked dishes €12-15; 12.30-3pm & 7 10.30pm Tue-Sat; E6 to Piazza dei Martiri, Piazza Amedeo) Run by brothers Francesco, Gennaro and Luigi, this local Chiaia fishmonger transforms daily

into a wonderfully intimate, sociable seafood eatery. Perch yourself on a bar stool, order a vino, and watch the team prepare your super-fresh, tapas-style *crudo* (raw seafood) to order. You'll also find a number of simple, beautifully cooked surf dishes.

Drinking & Nightlife

★Caffè Gambrinus CAFE

(☎081 41 75 82; www.grancaffegambrinus.com; Via Chiaia 1-2; ⏰7am-1am Sun-Fri, to 2am Sat; 🚌R2 to Via San Carlo, Ⓜ Municipio) Gambrinus is Naples' oldest and most venerable cafe, serving superlative Neapolitan coffee under flouncy chandeliers. Oscar Wilde knocked back a few here and Mussolini had some rooms shut to keep out left-wing intellectuals. Sit-down prices are steep, but the *aperitivo* nibbles are decent and sipping a *spritz* or a luscious *cioccolata calda* (hot chocolate) in its belle époque rooms is something worth savouring.

★L'Antiquario COCKTAIL BAR

(☎081 764 53 90; www.facebook.com/AntiquarioNapoli; Via Gaetani 2; ⏰7.30pm-2.30am; 🚌151, 154 to Piazza Vittoria) If you take your cocktails seriously, slip into this sultry, speakeasy-inspired den. Wrapped in art nouveau wallpaper, it's the domain of Neapolitan barkeep Alex Frezza, a finalist at the 2014 Bombay Sapphire World's Most Imaginative Bartender Awards. Straddling classic and contemporary, the drinks are impeccable, made with passion and meticulous attention to detail. Live jazz-centric tunes add to the magic on Wednesdays.

Entertainment

★Teatro San Carlo OPERA, BALLET

(☎box office 081 797 23 31; www.teatrosancarlo.it; Via San Carlo 98; ⏰box office 10am-9pm Mon-Sat, to 6pm Sun; 🚌R2 to Via San Carlo, Ⓜ Municipio) San Carlo's opera season runs from November or December to June, with occasional summer performances. Sample prices: a place in the 6th tier (from €35), the stalls (€75 to €130) or the side box (from €40). Ballet season runs from late October to April or early May; tickets range from €30 to €110.

Information

Naples is a relatively safe place, but be careful about walking alone late at night near Stazione Centrale and Piazza Dante. Also watch out for pickpockets (especially on public transport and at markets) and scooter thieves.

Loreto Mare Hospital (Ospedale San Maria di Loreto Nuovo; ☎081 254 21 11; www.aslnapoli1centro.it/818; Via Vespucci 26; 🚌154 to Via Vespucci) Central city hospital with an emergency department.

Police Station (Questura; ☎081 794 11 11, emergencies 112; Via Medina 75; Ⓜ Università) If your car has been clamped or removed, call 081 795 28 66.

Tourist Information Office (☎081 551 27 01; www.inaples.it; Piazza del Gesù Nuovo 7; ⏰9am-5pm Mon-Sat, to 1pm Sun; Ⓜ Dante) Tourist office in the *centro storico*.

Tourist Information Office (☎081 40 23 94; www.inaples.it; Via San Carlo 9; ⏰9am-5pm Mon-Sat, to 1pm Sun; 🚌R2 to Via San Carlo, Ⓜ Municipio) Tourist office at Galleria Umberto I, directly opposite Teatro San Carlo.

Getting There & Away

AIR

Naples International Airport (Capodichino) (☎081 789 62 59; www.aeroportodinapoli.it; Viale F Ruffo di Calabria) Capodichino airport, 7km northeast of the city centre, is southern Italy's main airport. It's served by a number of major airlines and low-cost carriers, including easyJet, which operates flights to Naples from London, Paris, Amsterdam, Vienna, Berlin and several other European cities.

BOAT

Fast ferries and hydrofoils for Capri, Ischia, Procida and Sorrento depart from **Molo Beverello** (Ⓜ Municipio) in front of Castel Nuovo; hydrofoils for Capri, Ischia and Procida also sail from Mergellina.

Slow ferries for Sicily, the Aeolian Islands and Sardinia sail from **Molo Angioino** (Ⓜ Municipio) (right beside Molo Beverello) and neighbouring **Calata Porta di Massa** (Ⓜ Municipio).

As a rough guide, bank on about €22 for the 50-minute jet crossing to Capri, and €13 for the 35-minute sail to Sorrento.

Tickets for shorter journeys can be bought at the ticket booths on Molo Beverello, Calata Porta di Massa or at Mergellina. For longer journeys try the offices of the ferry companies or a travel agent.

Hydrofoil and ferry companies include the following:

Alilauro (☎081 497 22 38; www.alilauro.it; Molo Beverello)

Caremar (☎081 1896 6690; www.caremar.it; Molo Beverello)

Navigazione Libera del Golfo (NLG; ☎081 552 07 63; www.navlib.it; Marina Grande)

SNAV (☎081 428 55 55; www.snav.it; Molo Beverello, Naples)

WORTH A TRIP

POMPEII & HERCULANEUM

On 24 August AD 79, Mt Vesuvius erupted, submerging the thriving port of Pompeii in *lapilli* (burning fragments of pumice stone) and Herculaneum in mud. Both places were quite literally buried alive, leaving thousands of people dead. The Unesco-listed ruins of both provide remarkable models of working Roman cities, complete with streets, temples, houses, baths, forums, taverns, shops and even a brothel.

Pompeii

A stark reminder of the destructive forces that lie deep inside Vesuvius, the ruins of ancient **Pompeii** (☎081 857 53 47; www.pompeiisites.org; entrances at Porta Marina & Piazza Anfiteatro; adult/reduced €15/7.50, incl Oplontis & Boscoreale €18/9; ⏰9am-7.30pm Mon-Fri, from 8.30am Sat & Sun, last entry 6pm Apr-Oct, shorter hours Nov-Mar; 🚆Circumvesuviana to Pompei Scavi–Villa dei Misteri) make for one of Europe's most compelling archaeological sites. The remains first came to light in 1594, when the architect Domenico Fontana stumbled across them while digging a canal, but systematic exploration didn't begin until 1748. Since then 44 of Pompeii's original 66 hectares have been excavated.

There's a huge amount to see at the site. Start with the **Terme Suburbane**, a public bathhouse decorated with erotic frescoes just outside **Porta Marina**, the most impressive of the city's original seven gates. Once inside the walls, continue down **Via Marina** to the grassy **foro** (forum). This was the ancient city's main piazza and is today flanked by limestone columns and what's left of the **basilica**, the 2nd-century-BC seat of the city's law courts and exchange. Opposite the basilica, the **Tempio di Apollo** is the oldest and most important of Pompeii's religious buildings, while at the forum's northern end the **Granai del Foro** (forum granary) stores hundreds of amphorae and a number of body casts. These were made in the 19th century by pouring plaster into the hollows left by disintegrated bodies. A short walk away, the **Lupanare** (brothel) pulls in the crowds with its collection of red-light frescoes. To the south, the 2nd-century-BC **Teatro Grande** is a 5000-seat theatre carved into the lava mass on which Pompeii was originally built. Other highlights include the **Anfiteatro**, the oldest known Roman amphitheatre in existence; the **Casa del Fauno**, Pompeii's largest private house, where many of the mosaics now in Naples' Museo Archeologico Nazionale (p463) originated; and the **Villa dei Misteri**, home to the Dionysiac frieze, the most important fresco still on-site. To get to Pompeii, take the Circumvesuviana train to Pompeii Scavi–Villa dei Misteri (€2.80, 36 minutes from Naples; €2.40, 30 minutes from Sorrento) near the main Porta Marina entrance.

Herculaneum (Ercolano)

Smaller and less daunting than Pompeii, **Herculaneum** (☎081 777 70 08; http://ercolano.beniculturali.it; Corso Resina 187, Ercolano; adult/reduced €11/5.50; ⏰8.30am-7.30pm Apr-Oct, to 5pm Nov-Mar; 🅿; 🚆Circumvesuviana to Ercolano–Scavi) can reasonably be visited in a morning or afternoon.

A modest fishing port and resort for wealthy Romans, Herculaneum, like Pompeii, was destroyed by the Vesuvius eruption. But because it was much closer to the volcano, it drowned in a 16m-deep sea of mud and debris rather than in the *lapilli* and ash that rained down on Pompeii. This essentially fossilised the town, ensuring that even delicate items like furniture and clothing were well preserved. Excavations began after the town was rediscovered in 1709 and continue to this day.

There are a number of fascinating houses to explore. Notable among them are the **Casa d'Argo**, a noble residence centred on a porticoed, palm-treed garden; the aristocratic **Casa di Nettuno e Anfitrite**, named after the extraordinary mosaic of Neptune in the *nymphaeum* (fountain and bath); and the **Casa dei Cervi** with its marble deer, murals and beautiful still-life paintings. Marking the sites' southernmost tip, the 1st-century-AD **Terme Suburbane** is a wonderfully preserved baths complex with deep pools, stucco friezes and bas-reliefs looking down on marble seats and floors. To reach Herculaneum, take the Circumvesuviana train to Ercolano–Scavi (€2.20, 20 minutes from Naples; €2.90, 45 minutes from Sorrento), from where it's a 500m walk from the station – follow signs downhill to the *scavi* (ruins).

Tirrenia (☎199 303040; www.tirrenia.it; Calata Porta di Massa) Runs ferries from Naples to Cagliari in Sardinia (from €46) twice weekly. Also runs once daily from Naples to Palermo in Sicily (from €40).

BUS

Most national and international buses leave from **Metropark Napoli Centrale** (☎800 650006; Corso Arnaldo Lucci; Ⓜ Garibaldi), on the southern side of Napoli Centrale train station. The bus station is home to **Biglietteria Vecchione** (☎331 88969217; ⊙6.30am-9.15pm Mon-Fri, to 7pm Sat, 7am-7pm Sun), a ticket agency selling national and international bus tickets.

TRAIN

The city's main train station is **Napoli Centrale** (Stazione Centrale; ☎081 554 31 88; Piazza Garibaldi), just east of the *centro storico*. From here, the national rail company **Trenitalia** (☎892021; www.trenitalia.com) runs regular direct services to Rome (€13 to €48, 70 minutes to three hours, around 66 daily). High-speed private rail company **Italo** (☎892020; www.italotreno.it) also runs daily direct services to Rome (€15 to €40, 70 minutes, around 20 daily).

Getting Around

TO/FROM THE AIRPORT

Airport shuttle **Alibus** (☎800 639525; www.anm.it; one way €5) connects the airport to Piazza Garibaldi (Napoli Centrale) and Molo Beverello.

PUBLIC TRANSPORT

You can travel around Naples by bus, metro and funicular.

Tickets come in various forms: a 90-minute ticket costs €1.60, a day ticket is €4.50.

Note that these tickets are only valid for Naples city; they don't cover travel on Circumvesuviana trains to Herculaneum, Pompeii and Sorrento.

Capri

POP 14,120

The most visited of the islands in the Bay of Naples, Capri deserves more than a quick day trip. Beyond the glamorous veneer of chichi cafes and designer boutiques is an island of rugged seascapes, desolate Roman ruins and a surprisingly unspoiled rural inland.

Ferries dock at Marina Grande, from where it's a short funicular ride up to Capri, the main town. A further bus ride takes you up to Anacapri.

Sights

Grotta Azzurra CAVE

(Blue Grotto; €14; ⊙9am-5pm) Capri's most famous attraction is the Grotta Azzurra, an unusual sea cave illuminated by an otherworldly blue light. The easiest way to visit is to take a boat **tour** (☎081 837 56 46; www.motoscafisticapri.com; Private Pier 0; Grotta Azzurra/island trip €15/18) from Marina Grande; tickets include the return boat trip, but the rowing boat into the cave and admission are paid separately. Beautiful though it is, the Grotta is extremely popular in the summer, and the crowds coupled with long waiting times and tip-hungry guides can make the experience underwhelming for some.

Giardini di Augusto GARDENS

(Gardens of Augustus; €1; ⊙9am-7.30pm summer, reduced hours rest of year) As their name suggests, these gardens near the Certosa di San Giacomo were founded by Emperor Augustus. Rising in a series of flowered terraces, they lead to a lookout point offering breathtaking views over to the **Isole Faraglioni**, a group of three limestone stacks rising out of the sea.

★Villa Jovis RUINS

(Jupiter's Villa; Via A Maiuri; adult/reduced €6/4; ⊙10am-7pm Jun-Sep, to 6pm Apr, May & Oct, to 4pm Mar, Nov & Dec, closed Jan & Feb) Villa Jovis was the largest and most sumptuous of 12 Roman villas commissioned by Roman Emperor Tiberius (r AD 14–37) on Capri, and his main island residence. A vast complex, now reduced to ruins, it famously pandered to the emperor's supposedly debauched tastes, and included imperial quarters and extensive bathing areas set in dense gardens and woodland. It's located a 45-minute walk east of Capri Town along Via Tiberio.

★Seggiovia del Monte Solaro CABLE CAR

(☎081 837 14 38; www.capriseggiovia.it; Via Caposcuro; single/return €8/11; ⊙9.30am-5pm May-Oct, 9am-4pm Mar & Apr, to 3.30pm Nov-Feb) Sitting in an old-fashioned chairlift above the white houses, terraced gardens and hazy hillsides of Anacapri as you rise to the top of Capri's highest mountain, the silence broken only by a distant dog barking or your own sighs of contentment, has to be one of the island's most sublime experiences. The ride takes an all-too-short 13 minutes, but when you get there, the views, framed by dismembered classical statues, are outstanding.

★Villa Lysis HISTORIC BUILDING

(www.villalysiscapri.com; Via Lo Capo 12; €2; ⌚10am-7pm Thu-Tue Jun-Aug, to 6pm Apr, May, Sep & Oct, to 4pm Nov & Dec) This beautifully melancholic art nouveau villa is set on a clifftop on Capri's northeast tip and was the one-time retreat of French poet Jacques d'Adelsward-Fersen, who came to Capri in 1904 to escape a gay sex scandal in Paris. Unlike other stately homes, the interior has been left almost entirely empty; this is a place to let your imagination flesh out the details. It's a 40-minute walk from Piazza Umberto I and is rarely crowded.

Sleeping & Eating

★Casa Mariantonia BOUTIQUE HOTEL €€

(☎081 837 29 23; www.casamariantonia.com; Via Orlandi 80, Anacapri; d €120-300; ⌚late Mar-Oct; P❄📶🏊) A family-run boutique hotel with a history (*limoncello di Capri* was supposedly invented here), it boasts nine fabulous rooms, a giant swimming pool, prestigious restaurant and a heavyweight list of former guests – philosopher Jean-Paul Sartre among them. If the tranquillity, lemon groves and personal *pensione* feel doesn't soothe your existential angst, nothing will.

★È Divino ITALIAN €€

(☎081 837 83 64; www.edivinocapri.com/divino; Via Sella Orta 10a, Capri Town; meals €33-48; ⌚8pm-1am daily Jun-Aug, 12.30-2.30pm & 7.30pm-midnight Tue-Sun rest of year; 📶) Proudly eccentric (what other restaurant has a bed in its dining room?), this diligent purveyor of Slow Food is a precious secret to those who know it. Whether dining among lemon trees in the garden or among antiques, chandeliers, contemporary art (and that bed!) inside, expect a thoughtful, regularly changing menu dictated by what's fresh from the garden and market.

OTHER SOUTHERN SPOTS WORTH A VISIT

Lecce Known as the Florence of the south, it's a lively university town famous for its ornate baroque architecture.

Matera Europe's capital of culture 2019 is a prehistorical town set on two rocky ravines, known as *sassi,* studded with primitive cave dwellings.

Aeolian Islands An archipelago of seven tiny islands off Sicily's northeastern coast. Lipari is the largest and the main hub, while Stromboli is the most dramatic, with its permanently spitting volcano.

Information

Tourist Office (☎081 837 06 34; www.capritourism.com; Banchina del Porto; ⌚8.30am-4.15pm, closed Sat & Sun Jan-Mar & Nov) Can provide a map of the island, plus accommodation listings, ferry timetables and other useful information.

Getting There & Around

The two major ferry routes to Capri are from Naples and Sorrento, although there are also seasonal connections with Ischia and the Amalfi Coast (Amalfi, Positano and Salerno).

Caremar (☎081 837 07 00; www.caremar.it; Marina Grande) Operates hydrofoils and ferries to/from Naples (€12.50 to €18, 40 minutes to 1¼ hours, up to seven daily) and hydrofoils to/from Sorrento (€14.40, 25 minutes, four daily).

Navigazione Libera del Golfo (p467) Operates hydrofoils to/from Naples (from €19, 45 minutes, up to nine daily).

SNAV (☎081 428 55 55; www.snav.it; Marina Grande) Operates hydrofoils to/from Naples (from €22.50, 45 minutes, up to nine daily).

On the island, buses run from Capri Town to/from Marina Grande, Anacapri and Marina Piccola. Single tickets cost €2 (€2.50 if bought on board) on all routes, including the funicular.

Amalfi Coast

Stretching 50km along the southern side of the Sorrentine Peninsula, the Unesco-protected Amalfi Coast (Costiera Amalfitana) is a postcard-perfect vision of shimmering blue water fringed by vertiginous cliffs on which whitewashed villages and terraced lemon groves cling.

Sorrento

POP 16,400

Despite being a popular package-holiday destination, Sorrento manages to retain a laid-back southern Italian charm. There are very few sights to speak of, but there are wonderful views of Mt Vesuvius, and its small *centro storico* (historical centre) is an atmospheric place to explore. As the western gateway to the Amalfi, and close proximity to Pompeii and Capri, the town makes an excellent base for exploring the area.

Sights & Activities

Museo Correale di Terranova MUSEUM
(081 878 18 46; www.museocorreale.it; Via Correale 50; adult/reduced €8/5; 9.30am-6.30pm Mon-Sat, to 1.30pm Sat) East of the city centre, this wide-ranging museum is well worth a visit whether you're a clock collector, an archaeological egghead or into delicate ceramics. In addition to the rich assortment of 16th- to 19th-century Neapolitan art and crafts (including extraordinary examples of marquetry), you'll discover Japanese, Chinese and European ceramics, clocks, fans and, on the ground floor, ancient and medieval artefacts. Among these is a fragment of an ancient Egyptian carving uncovered in the vicinity of Sorrento's **Sedile Dominova** (Via San Cesareo).

Chiesa & Chiostro di San Francesco CHURCH
(081 878 12 69; Via San Francesco; 7am-7pm) Located next to the Villa Comunale Park, this church is best known for the peaceful 14th-century cloister abutting it, which is accessible via a small door from the church. The courtyard features an Arabic portico and interlaced arches supported by octagonal pillars. Replete with bougainvillea and birdsong, they're built on the ruins of a 7th-century monastery. Upstairs in the Sorrento International Photo School, the **Gallery Celentano** (344 0838503; www.raffaelecelentano.com; adult/reduced €3.50/free; 10am-9pm Mar-Dec) exhibits black-and-white photographs of Italian life and landscapes by contemporary local photographer Raffaele Celentano.

★ **Nautica Sic Sic** BOATING
(081 807 22 83; www.nauticasicsic.com; Via Marina Piccola 43, Marina Piccola; Apr-Oct) Seek out the best beaches by rented boat, with or without a skipper. This outfit rents out a variety of motor boats, starting at around €50 per hour or from €150 per day plus fuel. It also organises boat excursions and wedding shoots.

Sleeping & Eating

Ulisse HOSTEL €
(081 877 47 53; www.ulissedeluxe.com; Via del Mare 22; dm/d from €35/139; P) Although it calls itself a hostel, the Ulisse is about as far from a backpackers' pad as a hiking boot is from a stiletto. Most rooms are plush, spacious affairs with swish if bland fabrics, gleaming floors and large en suite bathrooms. There are two single-sex dorms, and quads for sharers. Breakfast is included in some rates but costs €10 with others.

Hotel Cristina HOTEL €€
(081 878 35 62; www.hotelcristinasorrento.it; Via Privata Rubinacci 6, Sant'Agnello; d/tr/q from €150/220/240; Mar-Oct; P) Located high above Sant'Agnello, this hotel has superb views, particularly from the swimming pool. The spacious rooms have sea-view balconies and combine inlaid wooden furniture with contemporary flourishes such as Philippe Starck chairs. There's an in-house restaurant and a free shuttle bus to/from Sorrento's Circumvesuviana train station.

★ **Da Emilia** TRATTORIA €€
(081 807 27 20; www.daemilia.it; Via Marina Grande 62; meals €22-30; noon-3pm & 6-10.30pm Mar-Nov) Founded in 1947 and still run by the same family, this is a friendly, fast-moving place overlooking the fishing boats in Marina Grande. There's a large informal dining room, complete with youthful photos of former patron Sophia Loren, a romantic terrace by lapping waves, and a menu of straightforward dishes such as mussels with lemon, clam spaghetti and grilled calamari.

★ **O'Puledrone** SEAFOOD €€
(081 012 41 34; www.opuledrone.com; Via Marina Grande 150; meals €25-30; noon-3pm & 6.30pm-late Apr-Oct) The best fish you eat in Sorrento might be one you caught – a viable proposition at this congenial joint on the harbour at Marina Grande run by a cooperative of

PATH OF THE GODS

The **Sentiero degli Dei** (Path of the Gods) is by far the best-known walk on the Amalfi Coast for two reasons: first, it's spectacular from start to finish; and second, unlike most Amalfi treks, it doesn't involve inordinate amounts of stair-climbing.

The walk commences in the heart of Praiano, where a thigh-challenging 1000-step start takes you up to the path itself. You'll eventually emerge at **Nocelle**, from where a series of steps will take you through the olive groves and deposit you on the road just east of Positano.

local fishermen. Let them take you out on a three-hour fishing trip (€70) and the chef will cook your catch and serve it to you with a carafe of wine.

Information

Main Tourist Office (081 807 40 33; www.sorrentotourism.com; Via Luigi de Maio 35; 9am-7pm Mon-Sat, to 1pm Sun Jun-Oct, 9am-4pm Mon-Fri, to 1pm Sat Nov-May;) In the Circolo dei Forestieri (Foreigners' Club); lists ferry and train times. Ask for the useful publication *Surrentum*, published monthly from March to October.

Getting There & Away

Circumvesuviana (800 211388; www.eavsrl.it) trains run half-hourly between Sorrento and Naples (€3.90, 70 minutes) via Pompeii (€2.40, 30 minutes) and Ercolano (€2.90, 50 minutes).

Regular **SITA** (www.sitasudtrasporti.it) buses leave from the bus station across from the entrance to the Circumvesuviana train station for the Amalfi Coast, stopping at Positano (€2, one hour) and Amalfi (€2.90, 1¾ hours).

From the **Ferry & Hydrofoil Terminal** (Via Luigi de Maio), hydrofoils run to Capri (€20.50, 20 minutes, up to 13 daily) and Naples (€13, 20 minutes, up to six daily). There are also twice-daily summer sailings to Positano (€20, 30 minutes) and Amalfi (€21, 50 minutes).

Positano

POP 3915

Approaching Positano by boat, you're greeted by an unforgettable view of colourful, steeply stacked houses clinging to near-vertical green slopes. In town, the main activities are hanging out on the small beach, drinking and dining on flower-laden terraces, and browsing the expensive boutiques.

The **tourist office** (089 87 50 67; www.aziendaturismopositano.it; Via Regina Giovanna 13; 8.30am-5pm Mon-Sat, to 3pm Sun) can provide information on walking in the densely wooded **Lattari Mountains.**

Sleeping & Eating

Villa Nettuno HOTEL €

(089 87 54 01; www.villanettunopositano.it; Viale Pasitea 208; d €80-150; Apr-Oct;) Hidden behind a barrage of perfumed foliage, lofty Villa Nettuno is not short on charm. Go for one of the original rooms in the 300-year-old part of the building, decked out in robust rustic decor and graced with a communal terrace. Bathrooms are a little old-fashioned, but this place is all about the view.

Albergo California HOTEL €€

(089 87 53 82; www.hotelcaliforniapositano.it; Via Cristoforo Colombo 141; d €150-190; Mar-mid-Oct; P) If you were to choose the best place to take a quintessential Positano photo, it might be from the balcony of this hotel. But the view isn't all you get. The rooms in the older part of this grand 18th-century palace are magnificent, with original ceiling friezes and decorative doors. New rooms are simply decorated but tasteful, spacious and minimalist.

★**C'era Una Volta** TRATTORIA, PIZZA €

(089 81 19 30; Via Marconi 127; meals €20-30; noon-3pm Wed-Mon, 6-11pm daily) Calling like a siren to any cash-poor budget traveller who thought Positano was for celebs only, this heroically authentic trattoria at the top of town specialises in honest, down-to-earth Italian grub. There's no need to look further than the *gnocchi alla sorrentina* (gnocchi in a tomato and basil sauce) and Caprese salad. Pizzas start at €4.50; beer is €2. In Positano, no less!

Amalfi

POP 5100

Amalfi, the main hub on the coast, makes a convenient base for exploring the surrounding coastline. It's a pretty place with a tangle of narrow alleyways, stacked whitewashed houses and sun-drenched piazzas, but it can get very busy in summer as day-trippers pour in to peruse its loud souvenir shops and busy eateries.

The **tourist office** (089 87 11 07; www.amalfitouristoffice.it; Corso delle Repubbliche Marinare 27; 8.30am-1pm & 2-6pm Mon-Sat Apr-Oct, 8.30am-1pm Mon-Sat Nov-Mar;) can provide information about sights, activities and transport.

Sights

★**Cattedrale di Sant'Andrea** CATHEDRAL

(089 87 35 58; Piazza del Duomo; adult/reduced €3/1 between 10am-5pm; 7.30am-8.30pm) A melange of architectural styles, Amalfi's cathedral is a bricks-and-mortar reflection of the town's past as an 11th-century maritime superpower. It makes a striking impression at the top of a sweeping 62-step staircase. Between 10am and 5pm, the cathedral is only accessible through the adjacent **Chi-**

ostro del Paradiso (☎089 87 13 24; adult/reduced €3/1; ⏲9am-7.45pm Jul-Aug, reduced hours Sep-Jun), part of a four-section museum incorporating the cloisters, the 9th-century Basilica del Crocefisso, the crypt of St Andrew and the cathedral itself. Outside these times, you can enter the cathedral for free.

Grotta dello Smeraldo CAVE
(€5; ⏲9am-4pm) Four kilometres west of Amalfi, this grotto is named after the eerie emerald colour that emanates from the water. Stalactites hang down from the 24m-high ceiling, while stalagmites grow up to 10m tall. Buses regularly pass the car park above the cave entrance (from where you take a lift or stairs down to the rowing boats). Alternatively, **Coop Sant'Andrea** (☎089 87 31 90; www.coopsantandrea.com; Lungomare dei Cavalieri 1) runs boats from Amalfi (€10 return, plus cave admission). Allow 1½ hours for the return trip.

Sleeping & Eating

Albergo Sant'Andrea HOTEL €
(☎089 87 11 45; www.albergosantandrea.it; Salita Costanza d'Avalos 1; s/d €70/100; ⏲Mar-Dec; ❄📶) Enjoy the atmosphere of busy Piazza del Duomo from the comfort of your own room. This modest two-star place has basic rooms with brightly coloured tiles and coordinating fabrics. Double glazing has helped cut down the piazza hubbub, which can reach fever pitch in high season – this is one place to ask for a room with a (cathedral) view.

★**DieciSedici** B&B €€
(☎089 87 22 52; www.diecisedici.it; Piazza Municipio 10-16; d from €145; ⏲Mar-Oct; ❄) DieciSedici (1016) dresses up an old medieval palace in the kind of style that only the Italians can muster. The half-dozen rooms dazzle with chandeliers, mezzanine floors, glass balconies and gorgeous linens. Two rooms (the Junior Suite and Family Classic) come with kitchenettes. All have satellite TV, aircon and Bose sound systems.

Trattoria Il Mulino TRATTORIA, PIZZA €
(☎089 87 22 23; Via delle Cartiere 36; pizzas €6-11, meals €20-30; ⏲11.30am-4pm & 6.30pm-midnight Tue-Sun) A TV-in-the-corner, kids-running-between-the-tables sort of place, this is about as authentic an eatery as you'll find in Amalfi. There are few surprises on the menu, just hearty, honest pastas, grilled meats and fish. For a taste of local seafood, try the octopus cake or pasta with swordfish. It's right at the top of the town under a simple plastic awning.

WORTH A TRIP

RAVELLO

Elegant Ravello sits high in the clouds overlooking the coast. From Amalfi's Piazza Flavio Gioia, it's a nerve-tingling half-hour bus ride (€1.30, up to three an hour), but once you've made it up, you can unwind in the ravishing gardens of **Villa Rufolo** (☎089 85 76 21; www.villarufolo.it; Piazza Duomo; adult/reduced €7/5; ⏲9am-9pm May-Sep, reduced hours Oct-Apr, tower museum 10am-6pm May-Sep, reduced hours Oct-Apr) and bask in awe-inspiring views at **Villa Cimbrone** (☎089 85 74 59; www.hotelvillacimbrone.com/gardens; Via Santa Chiara 26; adult/reduced €7/4; ⏲9am-sunset).

★**Ristorante La Caravella** ITALIAN €€€
(☎089 87 10 29; www.ristorantelacaravella.it; Via Matteo Camera 12; meals €50-90, tasting menus €50-135; ⏲noon-2.30pm & 7-11pm Wed-Mon) A restaurant of artists, art and artistry, Caravella once hosted Andy Warhol. It's no surprise that it doubles as a de-facto gallery with frescoes, creative canvases and a ceramics collection. And then there's the food on the seven-course tasting menu, prepared by some of the finest culinary Caravaggios in Italy.

Sicily

Everything about the Mediterranean's largest island is extreme, from the beauty of its rugged landscape to its hybrid cuisine and flamboyant architecture. Over the centuries Sicily has seen off a catalogue of foreign invaders, from the Phoenicians and ancient Greeks to the Spanish Bourbons and WWII Allies. All have contributed to the island's complex and fascinating cultural landscape.

Getting There & Away

AIR

Flights from mainland Italian cities and European destinations serve Sicily's two main airports: Palermo's **Falcone-Borsellino** (☎091 702 02 73, 800 541880; www.gesap.it) and Catania's **Fontanarossa** (☎095 723 91 11; www.aeroporto.catania.it; 📶).

BARI

Most travellers visit Puglia's regional capital to catch a ferry. And while there's not a lot to detain you, it's worth taking an hour or so to explore Bari Vecchia (Old Bari). Here, among the labyrinthine lanes, you'll find the **Basilica di San Nicola** (☎080 573 71 11; www.basilicasannicola.it; Piazza San Nicola; ⏲7am-8.30pm Mon-Sat, to 10pm Sun), the impressive home to the relics of St Nicholas (aka Santa Claus).

For lunch, **Terranima** (☎334 6608618, 080 521 97 25; www.terranima.com; Via Putignani 213; meals €30-35; ⏲noon-3pm daily & 7-11pm Mon-Sat) serves delicious Puglian food.

Regular trains run to Bari from Rome (€50 to €69, four to 6½ hours, five daily).

Ferries sail to Greece, Croatia, Montenegro and Albania from the port, accessible by bus 50 from the main train station.

BOAT

Regular car and passenger ferries cross to Sicily (Messina) from Villa San Giovanni and Reggio di Calabria.

Ferries also sail from Genoa, Livorno, Civitavecchia, Naples, Salerno and Cagliari, as well as Malta and Tunisia.

Main operators:

Caronte & Tourist (☎090 5737; www.carontetourist.it; Molo Norimberga) To Messina from Salerno.

Grandi Navi Veloci (☎010 209 45 91; www.gnv.it) To Palermo from Civitavecchia, Genoa, Naples and Tunis.

Grimaldi Lines (☎081 49 65 55, 091 611 36 91; www.grimaldi-lines.com; Molo Piave, Porto Stazione Marittima) To Palermo from Livorno, Salerno and Tunis.

Tirrenia (☎199 303040; www.tirrenia.it) To Palermo from Naples and Cagliari.

BUS

SAIS Trasporti (☎091 617 11 41; www.saistrasporti.it; Piazzetta Cairoli 2) operates long-distance buses between Sicily and Italian mainland destinations including Rome and Naples.

TRAIN

Trenitalia (☎892021; www.trenitalia.com) operates direct trains to Sicily from both Rome and Naples, along with direct night trains from Milan, Rome and Naples.

Palermo

POP 673,400

Still bearing the bruises of its WWII battering, Palermo is a compelling and chaotic city. It takes a little work, but once you've acclimatised to the congested and noisy streets you'll be rewarded with some of southern Italy's most imposing architecture, impressive art galleries and vibrant street markets, plus an array of tempting restaurants and cafes.

Sights

★Palazzo dei Normanni PALACE

(Palazzo Reale; ☎091 705 56 11; www.federicosecondo.org; Piazza del Parlamento; adult/reduced incl exhibition Fri-Mon €12/10, Tue-Thu €10/8; ⏲8.15am-5.40pm Mon-Sat, to 1pm Sun) Home to Sicily's regional parliament, this venerable palace dates from the 9th century. However, it owes its current look (and name) to a major Norman makeover, during which spectacular mosaics were added to its royal apartments and magnificent chapel, the Cappella Palatina. Visits to the apartments, which are off-limits from Tuesday to Thursday, take in the mosaic-lined **Sala dei Venti**, and **Sala di Ruggero II**, King Roger's 12th-century bedroom.

★Cappella Palatina CHAPEL

(Palatine Chapel; ☎091 705 56 11; www.federicosecondo.org; Piazza del Parlamento; adult/reduced incl exhibition Fri-Mon €12/10, Tue-Thu €10/8; ⏲8.15am-5.40pm Mon-Sat, to 1pm Sun) Designed by Roger II in 1130, this extraordinary chapel is Palermo's top tourist attraction. Located on the mid-level of Palazzo dei Normanni's three-tiered loggia, its glittering gold mosaics are complemented by inlaid marble floors and a wooden *muqarnas* ceiling, the latter a masterpiece of Arabic-style honeycomb carving reflecting Norman Sicily's cultural complexity.

Note that queues are likely, and you'll be refused entry if you're wearing shorts, a short skirt or a low-cut top.

Mercato di Ballarò MARKET

(Via Ballaro 1; ⏲7.30am-8.30pm) Snaking for several city blocks southeast of Palazzo dei Normanni is Palermo's busiest street market, which throbs with activity well into the early evening. It's a fascinating mix of noises, smells and street life, and the cheapest place for everything from Chinese padded bras to fresh produce, fish, meat, olives and cheese – smile nicely for *un assaggio* (a taste).

Cattedrale di Palermo CATHEDRAL
(☎329 3977513; www.cattedrale.palermo.it; Corso Vittorio Emanuele; cathedral free, royal tombs €1.50, treasury & crypt €3, roof €5, all-inclusive ticket adult/reduced €8/4; ⏰7am-7pm Mon-Sat, 8am-1pm & 4-7pm Sun; royal tombs, treasury, crypt & roof 9am-1.30pm Mon-Sat, royal tombs & roof also 9am-12.30pm Sun) A feast of geometric patterns, ziggurat crenellations, maiolica cupolas and blind arches, Palermo's cathedral has suffered aesthetically from multiple reworkings over the centuries, but remains a prime example of Sicily's unique Arab-Norman architectural style. The interior, while impressive in scale, is essentially a marble shell whose most interesting features are the **royal Norman tombs** (to the left as you enter), the **treasury** (home to Constance of Aragon's gem-encrusted 13th-century crown) and the panoramic views from the roof.

La Martorana CHURCH
(Chiesa di Santa Maria dell'Ammiraglio; Piazza Bellini 3; adult/reduced €2/1; ⏰9.30am-1pm & 3.30-5.30pm Mon-Sat, 9-10.30am Sun) On the southern side of Piazza Bellini, this luminously beautiful 12th century church was endowed by King Roger's Syrian emir, George of Antioch, and was originally planned as a mosque. Delicate Fatimid pillars support a domed cupola depicting Christ enthroned amid his archangels. The interior is best appreciated in the morning, when sunlight illuminates the magnificent Byzantine mosaics.

★Teatro Massimo THEATRE
(☎box office 091 605 35 80; www.teatromassimo.it; Piazza Giuseppe Verdi; guided tours adult/reduced €8/5; ⏰9.30am-6pm) Taking over 20 years to complete, Palermo's neoclassical opera house is the largest in Italy and the second-largest in Europe. The closing scene of *The Godfather: Part III,* with its visually arresting juxtaposition of high culture, crime, drama and death, was filmed here and the building's richly decorated interiors are nothing short of spectacular. Guided 30-minute tours are offered throughout the day in English, Italian, French, Spanish and German.

Sleeping

★Stanze al Genio Residenze B&B €
(☎340 0971561; www.stanzealgeniobnb.it; Via Garibaldi 11; s €85-100, d €100-120; ❄📶) Speckled with Sicilian antiques, this B&B offers four gorgeous bedrooms, three with 19th-century ceiling frescoes. All four are spacious and thoughtfully appointed, with Murano lamps, old wooden wardrobes, the odd balcony railing turned bedhead, and top-quality, orthopaedic beds. That the property features beautiful maiolica tiles is no coincidence; the B&B is affiliated with the wonderful **Museo delle Maioliche** (☎380 3673773; www.stanzealgenio.it; adult/reduced €9/8; ⏰guided tours in English 3pm Tue-Fri, 10am Sat, 11am Sun, in Italian 4pm Tue-Fri, 11am Sat & Sun) downstairs.

★BB22 Palace B&B €€
(☎091 32 62 14; www.bb22.it; cnr Via Roma & Via Bandiera; d €140-180, whole apt €700-1000) Occupying a flouncy *palazzo* in the heart of the city, BB22 Palace offers chic, contemporary rooms, each with its own style. Top billing goes to the Stromboli room, complete with spa bath and a bedroom skylight offering a glimpse of its 15th-century neighbour. Peppered with artworks, coffee-table tomes and an honour bar, the communal lounge makes for an airy retreat.

Eating & Drinking

★Trattoria al Vecchio Club Rosanero SICILIAN €
(☎349 4096880; Vicolo Caldomai 18; mains €3-12; ⏰1-3.30pm Mon-Sat & 8-11pm Thu-Sat; 📶) A veritable shrine to the city's football team (*rosa nero* refers to the team's colours, pink and black), cavernous Vecchio Club scores goals with its bargain-priced, flavour-packed grub. Fish and seafood are the real fortes here; if it's on the menu, order the *caponata e pesce spada* (caponata with swordfish), a sweet-and-sour victory. Head in early to avoid a wait.

Osteria Ballarò SICILIAN €€
(☎091 32 64 88; www.osteriaballaro.it; Via Calascibetta 25; meals €35-45; ⏰noon-3pm & 7-11pm) Bare stone columns, exposed brick walls and vaulted ceilings set an atmospheric scene at this buzzing restaurant-wine bar. Approved by the Slow Food movement, its graze-friendly menu celebrates island produce and cooking, from artisanal cheeses and salumi (charcuterie) to arresting *crudite di pesce* (local sashimi), seafood *primi* and memorable Sicilian *dolci* (sweets). Quality local wines top it off. Reservations recommended.

Enoteca Buonivini WINE BAR
(☎091 784 70 54; Via Dante 8; ⊙9.30am-1.30pm & 4pm-midnight Mon-Sat) Thirsty suits flock to this bustling, urbane *enoteca* (wine bar), complete with bar seating, courtyard and a generous selection of wines by the glass. There's no shortage of interesting local drops, not to mention artisanal cheese and charcuterie boards, beautiful pasta dishes and grilled meats.

When you're done, scan the shelves for harder-to-find craft spirits (Australian gin, anyone?) and Sicilian gourmet pantry essentials.

Information

Hospital (Ospedale Civico; ☎091 666 55 17; www.arnascivico.it; Via Tricomi; ⊙24hr) Has emergency facilities.

Municipal Tourist Office (☎091 740 80 21; http://turismo.comune.palermo.it; Piazza Bellini; ⊙8.45am-6.15pm Mon-Fri, from 9.45am Sat) The main branch of Palermo's city-run information booths. Other locations include Teatro Massimo, the Port of Palermo and Mondello, though these are only intermittently staffed, with unpredictable hours.

Police (Questura; ☎091 21 01 11; Piazza della Vittoria 8) Main police station.

Getting There & Away

AIR

Falcone-Borsellino Airport (p473) is at Punta Raisi, 35km northwest of Palermo on the A29 motorway. There are flights to mainland Italian airports and several European destinations.

BOAT

Numerous ferry companies operate from Palermo's port, just east of the city centre. These include the following:

Grandi Navi Veloci (☎010 209 45 91, 091 6072 6162; www.gnv.it; Molo Piave, Porto Stazione Marittima)

Grimaldi Lines (p474)

Tirrenia (☎091 611 65 18, 199 303040; www.tirrenia.it; Calata Marinai d'Italia)

BUS

The two main departure points are the **Piazzetta Cairoli bus terminal**, just south of the train station's eastern entrance, and the Intercity bus stop on Via Paolo Balsamo, two blocks due east of the train station.

Main bus companies:

Cuffaro (☎091 616 15 10; www.cuffaro.info; Via Paolo Balsamo 13) Services to Agrigento (€9, two hours, three to six daily).

Interbus (☎091 616 79 19; www.interbus.it; Piazzetta Cairoli Bus Terminal) To/from Syracuse (€13.50, 3½ hours, two to three daily).

SAIS Autolinee (☎091 616 60 28, 800 211020; www.saisautolinee.it; Piazzetta Cairoli Bus Terminal) To/from Catania (€13.50, 2¾ hours, nine to 14 daily) and Messina (€14, 2¾ hours, four to seven daily).

TRAIN

From Palermo Centrale station trains leave for Agrigento (€9, 2¼ hours, 10 daily) and Catania (€13.50 to €16.50, 3½ to five hours, five daily) via Messina (€12.80, three to 3¾ hours, 10 daily). There are also Intercity trains to Reggio di Calabria, Naples and Rome.

Getting Around

TO/FROM THE AIRPORT

Prestia e Comandè (☎091 58 63 51; www.prestiaecomande.it; one way/return €6.30/11) Runs an efficient half-hourly bus service between 5am and 12.30pm that transfers passengers from the airport to the centre of Palermo, dropping people off outside the Teatro Politeama Garibaldi (35 minutes) and Palermo Centrale train station (50 minutes). Get tickets from the office in the arrivals hall. Buses are parked to the right as you exit the hall.

BUS

Walking is the best way to get around Palermo's centre, but if you want to take a bus, most stop outside or near the train station. Tickets cost €1.40 (€1.80 on board) and are valid for 90 minutes.

Taormina

POP 10,900

Spectacularly perched on a clifftop terrace overlooking the Ionian Sea and Mt Etna, this sophisticated town has attracted socialites, artists and writers ever since Greek times. Its pristine medieval core, proximity to beaches, grandstand coastal views and chic social scene make it a hugely popular summer holiday destination.

Sights & Activities

★**Teatro Greco** RUINS
(☎0942 2 32 20; Via Teatro Greco; adult/reduced €10/5; ⊙9am-1hr before sunset) Taormina's premier sight is this perfect horseshoe-shaped theatre, suspended between sea and sky, with Mt Etna looming on the southern horizon. Built in the 3rd century BC, it's the most dramatically situated Greek theatre in the world and the second largest in Sicily (after Syracuse). In summer, it's used to

WORTH A TRIP

MT ETNA

The dark silhouette of Mt Etna (3329m) broods ominously over Sicily's east coast, more or less halfway between Taormina and Catania. One of Europe's highest and most volatile volcanoes, it erupts frequently, most recently in August 2018.

To get to Etna by public transport, take the AST bus from Catania. This departs from Piazza Papa Giovanni XXIII (opposite Catania's main train station) at 8.15am and drops you at the Rifugio Sapienza at 10.15am, where you can pick up the **Funivia dell'Etna** (☎095 91 41 41; www.funiviaetna.com; return €30, incl bus & guide €64; ⏰9am-4.15pm Apr-Nov, to 3.45pm Dec-Mar) to 2500m. From there buses courier you up to the crater zone (2920m). If you want to walk, allow up to four hours for the round trip. The return journey leaves Rifugio Sapienza at 4.30pm, arriving in Catania at 6.30pm.

Gruppo Guide Alpine Etna Sud (☎095 791 47 55, 389 3496086; www.etnaguide.eu) is one of many outfits offering guided tours. Bank on around €85 for a full-day excursion.

Further Etna information is available from Catania's **tourist office** (☎095 742 55 73; www.comune.catania.it/la-citta/turismo; Via Vittorio Emanuele 172; ⏰8am-7pm Mon-Sat, 8.30am-1.30pm Sun).

stage concerts and festival events. To avoid the high-season crowds try to visit early in the morning.

Corso Umberto I STREET

Taormina's chief delight is wandering this pedestrian-friendly, boutique-lined thoroughfare. Start at the tourist office in **Palazzo Corvaja** (⏰varies), which dates back to the 10th century, before heading southwest for spectacular panoramic views from **Piazza IX Aprile**. Facing the square is the early-18th-century **Chiesa San Giuseppe** (Piazza IX Aprile; ⏰closed for restoration). Continue west through the **Torre dell'Orologio**, the 12th-century clock tower, into **Piazza del Duomo**, home to an ornate baroque fountain (1635) that sports Taormina's symbol, a two-legged centaur with the bust of an angel.

Villa Comunale PARK

(Parco Duchi di Cesarò; Via Bagnoli Croce; ⏰8am-midnight summer, to 6pm winter) To escape the crowds, wander down to these stunningly sited public gardens. Created by Englishwoman Florence Trevelyan in the late 19th century, they're a lush paradise of tropical plants and delicate flowers, punctuated by whimsical follies. You'll also find a children's play area.

Sleeping & Eating

Le 4 Fontane B&B €

(☎333 6793876; www.le4fontane.com; Corso Umberto I 231; s €40-70, d €60-110; ❄📶) An excellent budget B&B on the top floor of an old *palazzo*, Le 4 Fontane is run by a friendly couple and has three homey rooms, two of which have views of Piazza del Duomo.

Isoco Guest House GUESTHOUSE €€

(☎0942 2 36 79; www.isoco.it; Via Salita Branco 2; r €78-220; ⏰Mar-Nov; P❄@📶) Each room at this welcoming, LGBTIQ-friendly guesthouse is dedicated to an artist, from Botticelli to Keith Haring. While the older rooms are highly eclectic, the newer suites are chic and subdued, each with a modern kitchenette. Breakfast is served around a large table, while a pair of terraces offer stunning sea views and a hot tub. Multinight or prepaid stays earn the best rates.

Tischi Toschi SICILIAN €€

(☎339 3642088; www.tischitoschitaormina.com; Vico Paladini 3; meals €35-45; ⏰12.30-2.30pm Wed-Sun & 7-10.30pm daily summer, 12.30-2.30pm & 7-10.30pm Wed-Sun winter) With only a handful of tables, this family-run, Slow Food–acclaimed trattoria offers a level of creativity and attention to detail that's generally lacking in touristy Taormina. The limited menu changes regularly based on what's in season, and is filled with less-common regional specialities, from succulent stewed rabbit with olives, carrots, pine nuts and celery, to heavenly wild-fennel 'meatballs'.

Information

Tourist Office (☎0942 2 32 43; Palazzo Corvaja, Piazza Santa Caterina; ⏰8.30am-2.15pm & 3.30-6.45pm Mon-Fri year-round, also 9am-1pm & 4-6.30pm Sat summer) Has plenty of practical information, including transport timetables and a free map.

WORTH A TRIP

VALLEY OF THE TEMPLES

Sicily's most enthralling archaeological site, **Valley of the Temples** (Valle dei Templi; ☎0922 62 16 11; www.parcovalledeitempli.it; adult/reduced €10/5, incl Museo Archeologico €13.50/7; ⊙8.30am-7pm year-round, plus 7.30-10pm Mon-Fri, 7.30-11pm Sat & Sun mid-Jul–mid-Sep) encompasses the ruined ancient city of Akragas, highlighted by the stunningly well-preserved Tempio della Concordia (Temple of Concordia), one of several ridge-top temples that once served as beacons for homecoming sailors. The 13-sq-km park, 3km south of Agrigento, is split into eastern and western zones. Ticket offices with car parks are at the park's southwestern corner (the main Porta V entrance) and at the northeastern corner near the Temple of Hera (Eastern Entrance).

For maps and information, ask at Agrigento's **tourist office** (☎0922 59 32 27; www.livingagrigento.it; Piazzale Aldo Moro 1; ⊙8am-7pm Mon-Fri, to 1pm Sat) in the Provincia building.

Getting There & Away

Bus is the easiest way to reach Taormina. The bus station is on Via Luigi Pirandello, 400m east of Porta Messina, the northeastern entrance to the old town. **Interbus** (☎0942 62 53 01; www.interbus.it; Via Luigi Pirandello) services leave daily for Messina (€4.30, 55 minutes to 1¾ hours, up to five daily), Catania (€5.10, 1¼ to two hours, twice hourly) and Catania airport (€8.20, 1½ hours, twice hourly). It also runs services to Castelmola (€1.90, 15 minutes, hourly).

Syracuse

POP 122,000

A tumultuous past has left Syracuse (Siracusa) a beautiful baroque centre and some of Sicily's finest ancient ruins. Founded in 734 BC by Corinthian settlers, it became the dominant Greek city state on the Mediterranean and was known as the most beautiful city in the ancient world. A devastating earthquake in 1693 destroyed most of the city's buildings, paving the way for a city-wide baroque makeover.

Sights

★Piazza del Duomo PIAZZA

Syracuse's showpiece square is a masterpiece of baroque town planning. A long, rectangular piazza flanked by flamboyant *palazzi*, it sits on what was once Syracuse's ancient acropolis (fortified citadel). Little remains of the original Greek building, but if you look along the side of the Duomo you'll see a number of thick Doric columns incorporated into the cathedral's structure.

★Parco Archeologico della Neapolis ARCHAEOLOGICAL SITE

(☎0931 6 62 06; Viale Paradiso 14; adult/reduced €10/5, incl Museo Archeologico €13.50/7; ⊙8.30am-1hr before sunset) For the classicist, Syracuse's real attraction is this archaeological park, home to the pearly white 5th century BC **Teatro Greco**. Hewn out of the rocky hillside, this 16,000-capacity amphitheatre staged the last tragedies of Aeschylus (including *The Persians*), first performed here in his presence. In late spring it's brought to life with an annual season of classical theatre.

★Museo Archeologico Paolo Orsi MUSEUM

(☎0931 48 95 11; www.regione.sicilia.it/beniculturali/museopaoloorsi; Viale Teocrito 66; adult/reduced €8/4, incl Parco Archeologico €13.50/7; ⊙9am-6pm Tue-Sat, to 1pm Sun) About 500m east of the archaeological park, this modern museum contains one of Sicily's largest and most interesting archaeological collections. Allow plenty of time to investigate the four sectors charting the area's prehistory, as well as Syracuse's development from foundation to the late Roman period.

Sleeping & Eating

★Hotel Gutkowski HOTEL €€

(☎0931 46 58 61; www.guthotel.it; Lungomare Vittorini 26; d €90-150, tr €150, q €160; ❄📶) Book well in advance for one of the sea-view rooms at this stylish, eclectic hotel on the Ortygia waterfront, at the edge of the Giudecca neighbourhood. Divided between two buildings, its rooms are simple yet chic, with pretty tiled floors, walls in teals, greys, blues and browns, and a sharply curated mix of vintage and industrial details.

Sicily PIZZA €

(☎392 9659949; www.sicilypizzeria.it; Via Cavour 67; pizzas €5.50-15; ⊙7pm-midnight Tue-

Sun; [wi-fi icon][family icon]) Experimenting with pizzas is something you do at your peril in culinary-conservative Sicily. But that's what is done, and done well, at this funky retro-chic pizzeria. So if you're game for wood-fired pizzas topped with more-ish combos such as sausage, cheese, Swiss chard, pine nuts, sun-dried tomatoes and raisins, this is the place for you.

★ **Bistrot Bella Vita** ITALIAN €€

(☎0931 46 49 38; Via Gargallo 60; meals €35-40; ⏲cafe 8.30am-3pm & 5-10.30pm, restaurant 12.30-2.30pm & 7.30-10.30pm Tue-Sun) This casually elegant cafe-restaurant is one of Ortygia's stars. Stop by for good coffee (soy milk available) and *cornetti, biscotti* and pastries (try the sour orange-and-almond tart). Or book a table in the intimate back dining room, where local, organic produce drives beautifully textured, technically impressive dishes.

ℹ Information

Tourist Office (☎800 055500; www.provincia.siracusa.it; Via Roma 31; ⏲7.30am-2pm Mon, Tue, Thu & Fri, to 4.30pm Wed) City maps and brochures.

ℹ Getting There & Around

Buses are generally faster and more convenient than trains, with long-distance buses arriving and departing from the **bus terminal** (Corso Umberto I), just 180m southeast of the train station.

Interbus (☎0931 6 67 10; www.interbus.it) runs buses to Noto (€3.60, 55 minutes, three to six daily), Catania (€6.20, 1½ hours, 10 to 17 daily) and its airport, and Palermo (€13.50, 3½ hours, two to three daily). You can buy tickets at the kiosk by the bus stops.

SURVIVAL GUIDE

ℹ Directory A–Z

ACCOMMODATION

- The bulk of Italy's accommodation is made up of *alberghi* (hotels) and *pensioni* (small, often family-run hotels). Other options are hostels, campgrounds, B&Bs, *agriturismi* (farm stays), mountain *rifugi* (Alpine refuges), monasteries and villa/apartment rentals.
- High-season rates apply at Easter, in summer (mid-June to August), and over the Christmas to New Year period.
- Many places in coastal resorts close between November and March.

ACTIVITIES

Cycling Tourist offices can provide details on trails and guided rides. The best time is spring. Favourite areas include Tuscany, the flatlands of Emilia-Romagna, and the peaks around Lago Maggiore and Lago del Garda.

Hiking Thousands of kilometres of *sentieri* (marked trails) criss-cross the country. The hiking season is from June to September. The Italian Parks organisation (www.parks.it) lists walking trails in Italy's national parks.

Skiing Italy's ski season runs from December through to March. Prices are generally high, particularly in the top Alpine resorts – the Apennines are cheaper. A popular option is to buy a *settimana bianca* (literally 'white week') package deal, covering accommodation, food and ski passes.

FOOD & DRINK

Eat Like an Italian

A full Italian meal consists of an *antipasto*, a *primo* (first course; pasta or rice dish), *secondo* (main course; usually meat or fish) with an *insalata* (salad) or *contorno* (vegetable side dish), *dolce* (dessert) and coffee. Most Italians only eat a meal this large at Sunday lunch or on a special occasion, and when eating out it's fine to mix and match and order, say, a *primo* followed by an *insalata* or *contorno*.

Italians are late diners, often not eating until after 8.30pm.

Where to Eat & Drink

Trattorias are traditional, often family-run places serving local food and wine; *ristoranti* (restaurants) are more formal, with a greater choice and smarter service; pizzerias, which usually open evenings only, often serve a full menu alongside pizzas.

At lunchtime bars and cafes sell *panini* (bread rolls), and many serve an evening *aperitivo* (aperitif) buffet. At an *enoteca* (wine bar) you can drink wine by the glass and snack on cheese and cured meats. Some also serve hot dishes. For a slice of pizza search out a *pizza al taglio* joint.

INTERNET ACCESS

- Numerous Italian cities and towns offer public wi-fi hotspots, including Rome, Bologna and Venice. To use them, you will need to register online using a credit card or an Italian mobile number. An easier option (no need for a local mobile number) is to head to a cafe or bar offering free wi-fi.

ROOM TAX

Most Italian hotels apply a room occupancy tax *(tassa di soggiorno)*, which is charged on top of your regular hotel bill. The exact amount, which varies from city to city, depends on several factors, including the type of accommodation, a hotel's star rating and the number of people under your booking. As a rough guide reckon on €1 to €7 per person per night.

Prices quoted in this chapter do not include the tax.

- Most hotels, B&Bs, hostels and *agriturismi* (farm stays) offer free wi-fi to guests, though signal quality can vary. There will sometimes be a computer for guest use.

LGBTIQ+ TRAVELLERS

Homosexuality is legal (over the age of 16) and even widely accepted, but Italy is notably conservative in its attitudes, largely keeping in line with those of the Vatican. Overt displays of affection by LGBTIQ+ couples can attract a negative response, especially in smaller towns.

There are gay venues in Rome, Milan and Bologna, and a handful in places such as Florence and Naples. Some coastal towns and resorts (such as the Tuscan town of Viareggio or Taormina in Sicily) are popular gay holiday spots in the summer.

Italy's main LGBTIQ+ organisation is **Arcigay** (☎051 095 7241; www.arcigay.it; Via Don Minzoni 18, Cassero LGBT Center, Bologna).

MONEY

ATMs Known as 'Bancomat', are widely available throughout Italy, and most will accept cards tied into the Visa, MasterCard, Cirrus and Maestro systems.

Credit cards Virtually all midrange and top-end hotels accept credit cards, as do most restaurants and large shops. Museums and some cheaper *pensioni*, trattorias and pizzerias often only accept cash. Major cards such as Visa, MasterCard, Eurocard, Cirrus and Eurocheques are widely accepted. Amex is also recognised, although it's less common.

Tipping If *servizio* is not included, leave up to 10% in restaurants and a euro or two in pizzerias. It's not necessary in bars or cafes, but many people leave small change (usually €0.10 per coffee) if drinking at the bar.

OPENING HOURS

Opening hours vary throughout the year. We've provided high-season opening hours, which will generally decrease in the shoulder and low seasons. 'Summer' times generally refer to the period from April to September or October, while 'winter' times generally run from October or November to March.

Banks 8.30am–1.30pm and 2.45pm–4.30pm Monday to Friday

Restaurants noon–3pm and 7.30pm–11pm or midnight

Cafes 7.30am–8pm, sometimes until 1am or 2am

Bars and clubs 10pm–4am or 5am

Shops 9am–1pm and 3.30pm–7.30pm (or 4pm–8pm) Monday to Saturday, some also open Sunday

PUBLIC HOLIDAYS

Most Italians take their annual holiday in August, with the busiest period occurring around 15 August, known locally as Ferragosto. As a result, many businesses and shops close for at least part of that month. Settimana Santa (Easter Holy Week) is another busy holiday period for Italians.

National public holidays include the following:

Capodanno (New Year's Day) 1 January

Epifania (Epiphany) 6 January

Pasquetta (Easter Monday) March/April

Giorno della Liberazione (Liberation Day) 25 April

Festa del Lavoro (Labour Day) 1 May

Festa della Repubblica (Republic Day) 2 June

Ferragosto (Feast of the Assumption) 15 August

Festa di Ognisanti (All Saints' Day) 1 November

Festa dell'Immacolata Concezione (Feast of the Immaculate Conception) 8 December

Natale (Christmas Day) 25 December

Festa di Santo Stefano (Boxing Day) 26 December

SAFE TRAVEL

Italy is generally a safe country, but watch out for pickpockets in popular tourist centres such as Rome, Florence, Venice and Naples.

TELEPHONE

- Area codes must be dialled even when calling locally.
- To call Italy from abroad, dial your international access number, then Italy's country code (39) followed by the relevant area code, including the leading 0, and the telephone number.
- To call abroad from Italy, dial 00, then the relevant country code followed by the telephone number.
- Italian mobile phone numbers begin with a three-digit prefix starting with a 3.

Mobile Phones

- The cheapest way of using your mobile is to buy a prepaid *(prepagato)* Italian SIM card. **TIM** (www.tim.it), **Wind** (www.wind.it), **Vodafone** (www.vodafone.it) and **Tre** (www.tre.it) all offer SIM cards and have retail outlets in most Italian cities and towns.
- All SIM cards must be registered in Italy, so make sure you have a passport or ID card with you when you buy one.
- You can easily top-up your Italian SIM with a recharge card *(ricarica)*, available from most tobacconists, some bars, supermarkets and banks.

Getting There & Away

AIR

Italy's main intercontinental gateway airports are Rome's Leonardo da Vinci (p426) and Milan's Aeroporto Malpensa (p437). Both are served by non-stop flights from around the world. Venice's Marco Polo Airport (p449) is also served by a handful of intercontinental flights.

Dozens of international airlines compete with the country's revamped national carrier, Alitalia, rated a three-star airline by UK aviation research company Skytrax. If you're flying from Africa or Oceania, you'll generally need to change planes at least once en route to Italy.

Intra-European flights serve plenty of other Italian cities; the leading mainstream carriers include Alitalia, Air France, British Airways, Lufthansa and KLM.

Cut-rate airlines, led by Ryanair and easyJet, fly from a growing number of European cities to more than two dozen Italian destinations, typically landing in smaller airports such as Rome's **Ciampino** (☎06 6 59 51; www.adr.it/ciampino).

LAND

Bus

Buses are the cheapest overland option to Italy, but services are less frequent, less comfortable and significantly slower than the train.

Eurolines (☎0861 199 19 00; www.eurolines.it) and **FlixBus** (www.flixbus.com) operate buses from European destinations to many Italian cities.

Train

Milan and Venice are Italy's main international rail hubs. International trains also run to/from Rome, Genoa, Verona, Padua, Bologna and Florence.

SEA

Multiple ferry companies connect Italy with countries throughout the Mediterranean. Many routes only operate in summer, when ticket prices also rise. Prices for vehicles vary according to their size.

The helpful website www.directferries.co.uk allows you to search routes and compare prices between the numerous international ferry companies servicing Italy. Another useful resource for ferries from Italy to Greece is www.ferries.gr.

International ferry companies that serve Italy include the following:

Adria Ferries (☎071 5021 1621; www.adriaferries.com)

Anek Lines (☎071 207 23 46; www.anekitalia.com)

GNV (Grandi Navi Veloci; ☎010 209 45 91; www.gnv.it)

Grimaldi Lines (☎081 49 64 44; www.grimaldi-lines.com)

Jadrolinija (☎071 228 41 00; www.jadrolinija.hr)

Minoan Lines (☎071 20 17 08; www.minoan.it)

Moby Lines (☎199 30 30 40; www.moby.it)

Montenegro Lines (☎Bar 382 3030 3469; www.montenegrolines.net)

SNAV (☎081 428 55 55; www.snav.it)

Superfast (☎Athens +30 210 891 97 00; www.superfast.com)

Venezia Lines (p449)

Ventouris (☎080 876 14 51; www.ventouris.gr; Nuova Stazione Marittima di Bari)

Virtu Ferries (☎095 703 12 11; www.virtuferries.com)

Getting Around

BICYCLE

- Bikes can be taken on regional and certain international trains carrying the bike logo, but you'll need to purchase a separate bicycle ticket *(supplemento bici)*, valid for 24 hours (€3.50 on regional trains, €12 on international trains).

ADMISSION PRICES

Admission to state-run museums, galleries and cultural sites is free to visitors under 18. EU citizens aged between 18 and 25 pay a token €2 to enter.

Between October and March admission to state-run museums and monuments is free to everyone on the first Sunday of each month. Watch out for other free days throughout the year, including six consecutive days during National Museum Week (first week in March).

- Bikes can be carried free if dismantled and stored in a bike bag.
- Check details at www.trenitalia.com/tcom-en/Services/Travelling-with-your-bike.
- Most ferries also allow free bicycle passage.

BOAT

Craft *Navi* (large ferries) service Sicily and Sardinia, while *traghetti* (smaller ferries) and *aliscafi* (hydrofoils) service the smaller islands. Most ferries carry vehicles; hydrofoils do not.

Routes Main embarkation points for Sicily and Sardinia are Genoa, Livorno, Civitavecchia and Naples. Ferries for Sicily also leave from Villa San Giovanni and Reggio di Calabria. Main arrival points in Sardinia are Cagliari, Arbatax, Olbia and Porto Torres; in Sicily they're Palermo, Catania, Trapani and Messina.

Timetables and tickets Comprehensive website **Direct Ferries** (www.directferries.co.uk) allows you to search routes, compare prices and book tickets for ferry routes in Italy.

Overnight ferries Travellers can book a two- to four-person cabin or a *poltrona*, which is an airline-type armchair. Deck class (which allows you to sit/sleep in lounge areas or on deck) is available only on some ferries.

MAIN INTERNATIONAL FERRY ROUTES

DESTINATION COUNTRY	DESTINATION PORT(S)	ITALIAN PORT(S)	COMPANY
Albania	Durrës	Bari	Ventouris, GNV
	Durrës	Bari, Ancona, Trieste	Adria Ferries
Croatia	Dubrovnik	Bari	Jadrolinija, Montenegro Lines
	Split, Stari Grad	Ancona	SNAV
	Split, Zadar, Stari Grad	Ancona	Jadrolinija
	Umag, Poreč, Rovinj, Pula	Venice	Venezia Lines
France (Corsica)	Bastia	Livorno, Genoa	Moby Lines
	Bonifacio	Santa Teresa di Gallura	Moby Lines
Greece	Corfu, Igoumenitsa, Patras	Bari	Superfast, Anek Lines
	Corfu, Igoumenitsa, Zakynthos, Cephalonia	Bari	Ventouris
	Igoumenitsa, Patras	Brindisi	Grimaldi Lines
	Igoumenitsa, Patras	Ancona	Superfast, Anek Lines, Grimaldi Lines, Minoan Lines
	Igoumenitsa, Patras	Venice	Superfast, Anek Lines, Grimaldi Lines, Minoan Lines
Malta	Valletta	Pozzallo	Virtu Ferries
Montenegro	Bar	Bari	Montenegro Lines, Jadrolinija
Morocco	Tangier	Genoa	GNV
	Tangier	Savona	Grimaldi Lines
Slovenia	Piran	Venice	Venezia Lines
Spain	Barcelona	Genoa	GNV
	Barcelona	Civitavecchia, Savona, Porto Torres	Grimaldi Lines
Tunisia	Tunis	Genoa, Civitaveccchia, Palermo	GNV
	Tunis	Civitavecchia, Palermo, Salerno	Grimaldi Lines

BUS

Routes Everything from meandering local routes to fast, reliable InterCity connections is provided by numerous bus companies.

Timetables and tickets These are available on bus-company websites and from local tourist offices. Tickets are generally competitively priced with the train and are often the only way to get to smaller towns. In larger cities most of the InterCity bus companies have ticket offices or sell tickets through agencies. In villages and even some good-sized towns, tickets are sold in bars or on the bus.

Advance booking Generally not required, but advisable for overnight or long-haul trips in high season.

CAR & MOTORCYCLE

Italy's extensive network of roads spans numerous categories. The main ones are as follows:

➡ Autostradas – An extensive, privatised network of motorways, represented on road signs by a white 'A' followed by a number on a green background. The main north–south link is the A1. Also known as the Autostrada del Sole (the 'Motorway of the Sun'), it extends from Milan to Naples. The main link from Naples south to Reggio di Calabria is the A3. There are tolls on most motorways, payable by cash or credit card as you exit.

➡ *Strade statali* (state highways) – Represented on maps by 'S' or 'SS'. Vary from toll-free, four-lane highways to two-lane main roads. The latter can be extremely slow, especially in mountainous regions.

➡ *Strade regionali* (regional highways) – Coded 'SR' or 'R'.

➡ *Strade provinciali* (provincial highways) – Coded 'SP' or 'P'.

➡ *Strade locali* – Often not even paved or mapped.

For information in English about distances, driving times and fuel costs, see https://en.mappy.com. Additional information, including traffic conditions and toll costs, is available at www.autostrade.it.

TRAIN

Italy has an extensive rail network. Most services are run by **Trenitalia** (☎892021; www.trenitalia.com), but Italo (www.italotreno.it) also operates high-speed trains.

➡ Reservations are obligatory on AV and Intercity trains. On other services they're not, and outside peak holiday periods you should be fine without them.

➡ Both Trenitalia and Italo offer a variety of advance purchase discounts. Basically, the earlier you book, the greater the saving. Discounted tickets are limited, and refunds and changes are highly restricted. For all ticket options and prices, see the Trenitalia and Italo websites.

➡ *Regionale* train tickets must be validated in the green machines (usually found at the head of platforms) just before boarding. Failure to do so can result in a fine.

The Netherlands

POP 17 MILLION

Includes ➡

Best Places to Eat

- Vleminckx (p491)
- D'Vijff Vlieghen (p492)
- Fouquet (p499)
- AJÍ (p503)
- Heron (p506)
- In den Doofpot (p498)

Best Places to Stay

- Cocomama (p490)
- Sir Albert Hotel (p491)
- Hotel Indigo (p498)
- Citizen M (p503)
- King Kong Hostel (p503)
- Mother Goose Hotel (p505)

Why Go?

Tradition and innovation intertwine in the Netherlands. The legacies of great Dutch artists Rembrandt, Vermeer and Van Gogh, beautiful 17th-century canals, vintage windmills, tulip fields and quaint candlelit brown cafes coexist with visionary contemporary architecture, ecological fashion and homewares, cutting-edge design and food scenes, phenomenal nightlife and a progressive mindset.

Much of the Netherlands is below sea level and two-wheeling along pancake-flat landscape is one of Dutch life's greatest pleasures. Rental outlets are ubiquitous across the country, which is criss-crossed with dedicated cycling paths.

Allow ample time to revel in the magical, multifaceted capital Amsterdam, before ventureing further afield to charming canal-laced towns like Leiden and Delft. Explore exquisite Maastricht, with its city walls, ancient churches and grand squares, and the pulsing port city of Rotterdam, Dutch hub of urban renaissance.

When to Go

Amsterdam

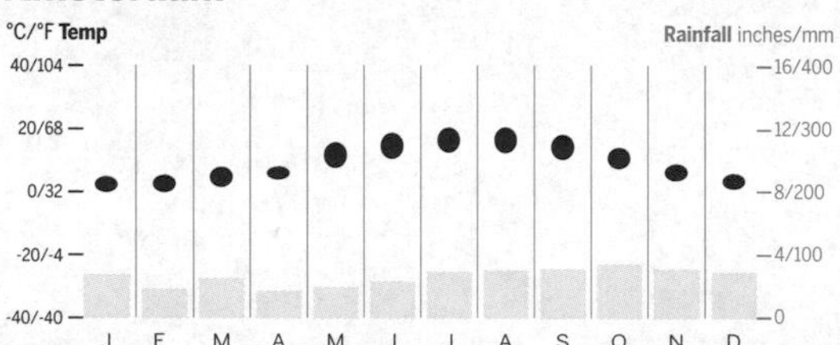

Jun–Aug High season: (the best odds for) balmy weather, alfresco cafe life and idyllic bike rides.

Mar–May See the world's largest flowering-bulb show in the Netherlands' fields.

Apr Europe's biggest street party celebrates the monarch's birthday on King's Day (Koningsdag).

Entering the Country

Schiphol International Airport (Amsterdam) Trains to Amsterdam Centraal Station cost €5.30 and take 15 minutes. Taxis to Amsterdam's centre (20 to 25 minutes) have a fixed rate of €39.

Duivendrecht and Sloterdijk bus stations Eurolines buses use Duivendrecht and FlixBus uses Sloterdijk; both have a fast metro or train link to Amsterdam Centraal.

Rotterdam The Hague Airport RET bus 33 (€3.50) makes the 20-minute run from the airport to Rotterdam Centraal Station every 15 minutes throughout the day; or hop off the bus at the Meijersplein metro station (line E) and continue by metro. Count on €25 for the 10-minute trip by taxi.

Eindhoven Airport Buses 400 and 401 travel up to six times hourly to/from Eindhoven train station (€3.50, 25 minutes).

ITINERARIES

One Week

Spend three days exploring canals, museum-hopping and cafe-crawling in Amsterdam (p487). Work your way through the ancient towns of the Randstad and edgy Rotterdam (p501); save a day for the grandeur of Maastricht (p506).

Two Weeks

Allow four days for Amsterdam's (p487) many delights, plus a day trip to the old towns of the north, and a day or two exploring some of the region's smaller towns. Then add a day each in beautiful Delft (p500), regal Den Haag (The Hague; p498), student-filled Utrecht (p504) and buzzing Rotterdam (p501). Finish off with two days in historic Maastricht (p506).

Essential Food & Drink

Vlaamse frites Iconic French fries smothered in mayonnaise or myriad other sauces.

Cheese Some Dutch say it makes them tall; others complain it causes nightmares. Nearly two-thirds of all Dutch *kaas* (cheese) sold is Gouda, classified by how long it's been aged. The tastiest hard, rich *oud* (old) varieties have strong, complex flavours.

Herring Street stalls sell raw, slightly salted *haring* (herring) cut into bite-sized pieces and served with onion and pickles.

Kroketten Croquettes are crumbed, deep-fried dough balls with various fillings, such as meat-filled *bitterballen*.

Jenever Dutch gin is made from juniper berries and drunk chilled from a tulip-shaped shot glass. *Jonge* (young) jenever is smooth; strongly flavoured *oude* (old) jenever can be an acquired taste.

AT A GLANCE

Area 41,543 sq km

Capital Amsterdam

Country Code ☎31

Currency euro (€)

Emergency ☎112

Language Dutch, English widespread

Time Central European Time (GMT/UTC plus one hour)

Visas Schengen rules apply

Sleeping Price Ranges

The following price ranges refer to a double room with bathroom in high season. Unless otherwise stated, breakfast is not included in the price.

€ less than €100

€€ €100–180

€€€ more than €180

Eating Price Ranges

The following price ranges refer to a main course.

€ less than €12

€€ €12–25

€€€ more than €25

Resources

Netherlands Tourism Board (www.holland.com)

Holland Cycling Routes (www.hollandcyclingroutes.com)

Dutch Review (https://dutchreview.com)

Dutch News (www.dutchnews.nl)

The Netherlands Highlights

❶ **Amsterdam** (p487) Canal-cruising, brown-cafe lounging and admiring world-class art.

❷ **Rotterdam** (p501) Marvelling at 20th-century and contemporary architecture.

❸ **Maastricht Underground** (p506) Exploring centuries-old tunnels below Maastricht.

❹ **Vermeer Centrum Delft** (p500) Learning about Vermeer's life and work in his evocative home town.

❺ **Den Haag** (p498) Discovering the beautiful tree-lined boulevards, museums and palatial Binnenhof buildings.

❻ **Keukenhof Gardens** (p497) Delving into Leiden's dazzling tulip displays at its nearby gardens.

❼ **Zaanse Schans** (p491) Watching windmills twirl at the delightful open-air museum.

❽ **Cycling** (p499) Uncovering canals and tulip fields along the world's best cycling-route network.

AMSTERDAM

☎020 / POP 854,047

World Heritage–listed canals lined by tilted gabled houses, candlelit cafes, whirring bicycles, lush parks, treasure-packed museums, colourful markets, diverse dining, quirky shopping and legendary nightlife make the free-spirited Dutch capital an essential port of call.

Amsterdam has been a liberal place since the Netherlands' Golden Age, when it was at the forefront of European art and trade. Centuries later, in the 1960s, it again led the pack – this time in the principles of tolerance, with broad-minded views on drugs and same-sex relationships taking centre stage.

Explore its many worlds-within-worlds, where nothing ever seems the same twice. Better still, do it by boat or bike. Two-wheeling is a way of life here and abundant bike-rental shops make it easy to gear up and take a wind-in-your-hair spin through one of Europe's wildest cities.

Sights

The **I Amsterdam City Card** (www.iamsterdam.com; per 24/48/72/96 hours €59/74/87/98) provides admission to more than 30 museums, a canal cruise, and discounts at shops, entertainment venues and restaurants. It also includes a public-transport pass. Enquire at the tourist office.

Medieval Centre

Crowned by the Royal Palace, the pigeon-, tourist- and busker-busy square that puts the 'Dam' in Amsterdam anchors the city's oldest quarter, which is also home to its infamous Red Light District.

★Royal Palace PALACE

(Koninklijk Paleis; Map p488; ☎020-522 61 61; www.paleisamsterdam.nl; Dam; adult/child €10/free; ⏲10am-5pm; 🚊4/14/24 Dam) Opened as a town hall in 1655, this resplendent building became a palace in the 19th century. The interiors gleam, especially the marble work – at its best in a floor inlaid with maps of the world in the great *burgerzaal* (citizens' hall) at the heart of the building. Pick up a free audioguide at the desk when you enter; it explains everything you see in vivid detail. King Willem-Alexander uses the palace only for ceremonies; check for periodic closures.

Begijnhof COURTYARD

(Map p488; www.nicolaas-parochie.nl; ⏲9am-5pm; 🚊2/11/12 Spui) FREE Dating from the early 14th century, this enclosed former convent is a surreal oasis of peace, with tiny houses and postage-stamp gardens around a well-kept courtyard off Gedempte Begijnensloot. The Beguines, a Catholic order of unmarried or widowed women who cared for the elderly, lived a religious life without taking monastic vows. The last Beguine died in 1971. Within the *hof* (courtyard) is the charming 1671 **Begijnhof Kapel** (Map p488; www.begijnhofkapelamsterdam.nl; Begijnhof 30; ⏲1-6.30pm Mon, 9am-6.30pm Tue-Fri, 9am-6pm Sat & Sun), and the **Engelse Kerk** (English Church; Map p488; www.ercadam.nl; Begijnhof 48; ⏲9am-5pm), built around 1392.

Canal Ring

Amsterdam's Canal Ring was built during the 17th century after the seafaring port grew beyond its medieval walls, and authorities devised a ground-breaking expansion plan.

Wandering here amid architectural treasures and their reflections on the narrow waters of the Prinsengracht, Keizersgracht and Herengracht can cause days to vanish.

★Anne Frank Huis MUSEUM

(Map p488; ☎020-556 71 05; www.annefrank.org; Prinsengracht 263-267; adult/child €10.50/5; ⏲9am-10pm Apr-Oct, 9am-7pm Sun-Fri, to 9pm Sat Nov-Mar; 🚊13/17 Westermarkt) The Anne Frank Huis draws more than one million

DON'T MISS

JORDAAN & THE WEST

If Amsterdam's neighbourhoods held a 'best personality' contest, the Jordaan (once the workers' quarter) would win. Its intimacy is contagious, with modest 17th- and 18th century merchants' houses and humble workers' homes, offbeat galleries and vintage shops peppering a grid of tiny lanes. This is the place for jovial bar sing-alongs and beery brown cafes (traditional Dutch pubs), the neighbourhood where you could spend a week wandering the narrow streets and still not discover all its hidden courtyards, tucked-away eateries and small-scale museums (cheese museum, tulip museum, houseboat museum). The 'hood abuts the West: industrial badlands that have transformed into an avant-garde cultural hub.

Central Amsterdam

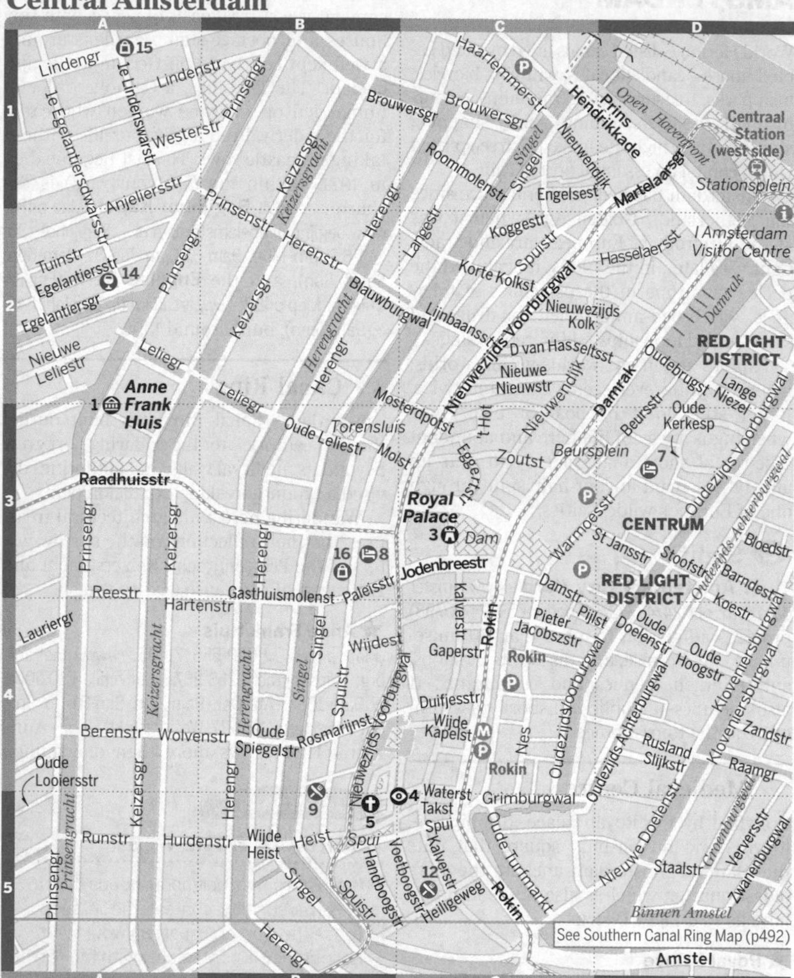

See Southern Canal Ring Map (p492)

visitors annually. With Anne's melancholy bedroom and her actual diary – sitting alone in its glass case, filled with sunnily optimistic writing tempered by quiet despair – it's a powerful experience. It's compulsory to choose a timeslot and prepurchase tickets online. Recent renovations include a new Westermarkt entrance and extensions to the museum.

Museumplein

Amsterdam's most famous museums cluster around Museumplein, an urban playground of a city square with its skateboard ramp, playground, ice-skating pond (in winter) and sky-high I Amsterdam sculpture (a favourite Instagram photo op).

★Rijksmuseum

MUSEUM

(National Museum; Map p492; 020-674 70 00; www.rijksmuseum.nl; Museumstraat 1; adult/child €17.50/free; 9am-5pm; 2/5/12 Rijksmuseum) The Rijksmuseum is among the world's finest art museums, packing works by local heroes Rembrandt, Vermeer and Van Gogh as well as 7500 other masterpieces over 1.5km of galleries. To avoid the biggest crowds, come before 10am or after 3pm. Prebooking tickets online provides fast-track entry.

Central Amsterdam

Top Sights
1 Anne Frank Huis A3
2 Museum het Rembrandthuis E4
3 Royal Palace C3

Sights
4 Begijnhof C5
5 Begijnhof Kapel B5
6 Centraal Station E1
Engelse Kerk .... (see 5)

Sleeping
7 St Christopher's at the Winston D3
8 W Amsterdam B3

Eating
9 D'Vijff Vlieghen B4
10 Greetje F4
11 Tokoman E5
12 Vleminckx C5

Drinking & Nightlife
13 SkyLounge E2
14 't Smalle A2
Winston Kingdom .... (see 7)

Shopping
15 Lindengracht Market A1
16 X Bank B3

Start on the 2nd floor, with the astounding Golden Age works. Intimate paintings by Vermeer and De Hooch allow insight into everyday life in the 17th century, while Rembrandt's *The Night Watch* (1642) takes pride of place.

★Van Gogh Museum MUSEUM
(Map p492; ☎020-570 52 00; www.vangoghmuseum.nl; Museumplein 6; adult/child €18/free, audioguide €5/3; ⏰9am-7pm Sun-Thu, to 10pm Fri, to 9pm Sat late Jun-Aug, shorter hours rest of year; 🚊2/3/5/12 Van Baerlestraat) It's a moving experience to visit this museum, which traces Van Gogh's life and development via the world's largest collection of his work, both familiar paintings and wonderful little-known pieces. It's fascinating to see his work change from tentative beginnings to giddily bright sunflowers, and on to his frenzy of creative brilliance towards the end of his life. There are also paintings by contemporaries Gauguin, Toulouse-Lautrec, Monet and Bernard. You must choose a timeslot and prepurchase tickets online.

Stedelijk Museum MUSEUM
(Map p492; ☎020-573 29 11; www.stedelijk.nl; Museumplein 10; adult/child €18.50/free; ⏰10am-6pm, to 10pm Fri; 🚊2/3/5/12 Van Baerlestraat) This fabulous museum houses the collection amassed by postwar curator Willem Sandberg. Displays rotate but you'll see an amazing selection featuring works by Picasso, Matisse, Mondrian, Van Gogh, Rothko, De Kooning, Warhol and more, plus an exuberant Karel Appel mural and great temporary exhibitions. The building was originally a bank, built in 1895 to a neo-Renaissance design by AM Weissman, and the modern extension is nicknamed 'the bathtub' for reasons that will be obvious when you see it.

Vondelpark PARK
(Map p492; www.hetvondelpark.net; 2 Amstelveenseweg) A private park for the wealthy until 1953, Vondelpark now occupies a special place in Amsterdam's heart. It's a magical escape, but also supplies a busy social scene, encompassing cycle ways, pristine lawns, ponds with swans, quaint cafes, footbridges and winding footpaths. On a sunny day, an open-air party atmosphere ensues when tourists, lovers, cyclists, in-line skaters, pram-pushing parents, cartwheeling children, football-kicking teenagers, spliff-sharing friends and champagne-swilling picnickers all come out to play.

Nieuwmarkt & Plantage

The streets around the Rembrandt House are prime wandering territory, offering a vibrant mix of old Amsterdam, canals and quirky shops and cafes.

★**Museum het Rembrandthuis** MUSEUM
(Rembrandt House Museum; Map p488; 020-520 04 00; www.rembrandthuis.nl; Jodenbreestraat 4; adult/child €14/5; 10am-6pm; M Waterlooplein) This evocative museum is housed in Rembrandt's former home, where the master painter spent his most successful years, painting big commissions such as *The Night Watch* and running the Netherlands' largest painting studio. It wasn't to last, however: his work fell out of fashion, he had some expensive relationship problems and bankruptcy came a-knocking. The inventory drawn up when he had to leave the house is the reason that curators have been able to refurnish the house so faithfully.

DON'T MISS

DE PIJP

Immediately south of the Canal Ring, villagey De Pijp is Amsterdam's most spontaneous and creative quarter. Bohemian cafes, restaurants and bars spill out around its festive street market, **Albert Cuypmarkt** (Map p492; www.albertcuyp-markt.amsterdam; Albert Cuypstraat, btwn Ferdinand Bolstraat & Van Woustraat; 9am-5pm Mon-Sat; M De Pijp, 24 Albert Cuypstraat). Amsterdam's largest and busiest market, this is *the* hot spot in the city for buying gadgets, homewares, flowers, fruit and veg, herbs and spices, clothing and other goods. Snack vendors tempt passers-by with raw-herring sandwiches, fries, *poffertjes* (tiny Dutch pancakes dusted with icing sugar) and caramel syrup–filled *stroopwafels*.

Tours

Amsterdam has more canals than Venice and getting on the water is one of the best ways to feel the pulse of the city – the waterways are, after all, are a Unesco World Heritage Site.

★**Rederji Lampedusa** BOATING
(http://rederijlampedusa.nl; Dijksgracht 6; 2hr canal tour €19; canal tours 11am & 1.30pm Sat May-Sep; 26 Muziekgebouw) Take a two-hour canal-boat tour around Amsterdam harbour in former refugee boats, brought from Lampedusa by Dutch founder Tuen. The tours are full of heart and offer a fascinating insight, not only into stories of contemporary migration, but also about how immigration shaped Amsterdam's history – especially the canal tour. Departs from next to Mediamatic.

Hungry Birds Street Food Tours WALKING, FOOD
(06 1898 6268; www.hungrybirds.nl; day/night tour per person €79/89; by reservation) Guides take you 'off the eaten track' to chow on Dutch and ethnic specialities. Tours visit around 10 spots over four hours in De Pijp, Utrechtsestraat, Rembrandtplein and the Spui, from family-run eateries to street vendors. Prices include all food. The meet-up location is given after you make reservations.

Festivals & Events

King's Day CULTURAL
(Koningsdag; 27 Apr) King's Day is a celebration of the House of Orange, with hundreds of thousands of orange-clad locals and visitors filling Amsterdam's streets for drinking and dancing. The city also becomes one big flea market, as people sell off all their unwanted junk.

Sleeping

Amsterdam has loads of hotels in wild and wonderful spaces. But charm doesn't come cheap, and places fill fast – reserve as far ahead as possible, especially for summer bookings and weekends at any time.

★**Cocomama** HOSTEL $
(Map p492; 020-627 24 54; www.cocomamahostel.com; Westeinde 18; dm/d from €42/120, minimum 2-night stay; ; 4 Stadhouderskade)

WORTH A TRIP

ZAANSE SCHANS

The working, inhabited village Zaanse Schans functions as an open-air **windmill gallery** (075-681 00 00; www.dezaanseschans.nl; Kalverringdijk; per windmill adult/child €4.50/2; most windmills 9am-5pm Apr-Oct, hours vary Nov-Mar) on the Zaan river. Popular with tourists, its mills are completely authentic and operated with enthusiasm and love. You can explore the windmills at will, seeing the vast moving parts first-hand. The impressive **Zaans Museum** (075-681 00 00; www.zaansmuseum.nl; Schansend 7; adult/child €10/6; 9am-5pm Apr-Sep, from 10am Oct-Mar) shows how wind and water were harnessed.

Trains (€3.20, 18 minutes, four per hour) run from Amsterdam Centraal Station (direction Alkmaar) to Koog Zaandijk, from where it's a well-signposted 1.5km walk.

Once a high-end brothel, this boutique hostel's doubles and dorms are light, bright and decorated with flair, with white walls and quirky designer Delftware or windmill themes. Amenities are way above typical hostel standard, with en suite bathrooms, in-room wi-fi, a relaxing back garden, a well-equipped kitchen, a book exchange and a super-comfy lounge open 24 hours. Breakfast is included.

St Christopher's at the Winston HOSTEL, HOTEL $
(Map p488; 020-623 13 80; www.st-christophers.co.uk; Warmoesstraat 129; dm/d from €47.80/150; ; 4/14/24 Dam) This place hops 24/7 with rock-and-roll rooms, a busy nightclub with live bands nightly, a bar and restaurant, a beer garden and a smoking deck downstairs. En suite dorms sleep up to eight. Local artists were given free rein on the rooms, with super-edgy (entirely stainless steel) to questionably raunchy results. Rates include breakfast (and earplugs!).

★Sir Albert Hotel DESIGN HOTEL $$
(Map p492; 020-710 72 58; www.sirhotels.com/albert; Albert Cuypstraat 2-6; d/ste from €170/320; ; De Pijp, 3/12/24 De Pijp) A 19th-century diamond factory houses this glitzy design hotel. Its 90 creative rooms and suites have high ceilings and large windows, with custom-made linens and Illy espresso machines; iPads are available for use in the Persian-rug-floored study. Energetic staff are helpful and professional. Of the 10 balcony rooms, west-facing *336*, *337* and *338* have sunset views over the canal.

W Amsterdam DESIGN HOTEL $$$
(Map p488; 020 811 25 00; www.wamsterdam.com; Spuistraat 175; d/ste from €380/567; ; 2/11/12/13/17 Dam) Designer hotel chain W opened its Amsterdam premises in two landmark buildings, the Royal Dutch Post's former telephone exchange and a former bank – part of which now houses Dutch design mega-store **X Bank** (Map p488; www.xbank.amsterdam; Spuistraat 172; 10am-8pm Mon-Sat, from noon Sun). Its 238 rooms (including connecting family rooms and 28 suites) combine design and vintage elements; there's also a state-of-the-art spa, a gym, an amazing rooftop lap pool, restaurants and bars.

Eating

Amsterdam abounds with eateries. Superb streets for hunting include Utrechtsestraat, near Rembrandtplein; Amstelveenseweg, along the Vondelpark's western edge; and any of the little streets throughout the western canals.

★Vleminckx FAST FOOD $
(Map p488; www.vleminckxdesausmeester.nl; Voetboogstraat 33; fries €3-5, sauces €0.70; noon-7pm Sun & Mon, 11am-7pm Tue, Wed, Fri & Sat, to 8pm Thu; 2/11/12 Koningsplein) Frying up *frites* (fries) since 1887, Amsterdam's best *friterie* has been based at this hole-in-the-wall takeaway shack near the Spui since 1957. The standard order of perfectly cooked crispy, fluffy *frites* is smothered in mayonnaise, though its 28 sauces also include apple, green pepper, ketchup, peanut, sambal and mustard. Queues almost always stretch down the block, but they move fast.

Braai BBQ Bar BARBECUE $
(020-221 13 76; www.braaiamsterdam.nl; Schinkelhavenkade 1; dishes €6.50-15.50; 4-9.30pm; 1/11/17 Surinameplein) Once a *haringhuis* (herring stand), this tiny place is now a street-food-style barbecue bar, with a great canal-side setting. Braai's speciality is

Southern Canal Ring

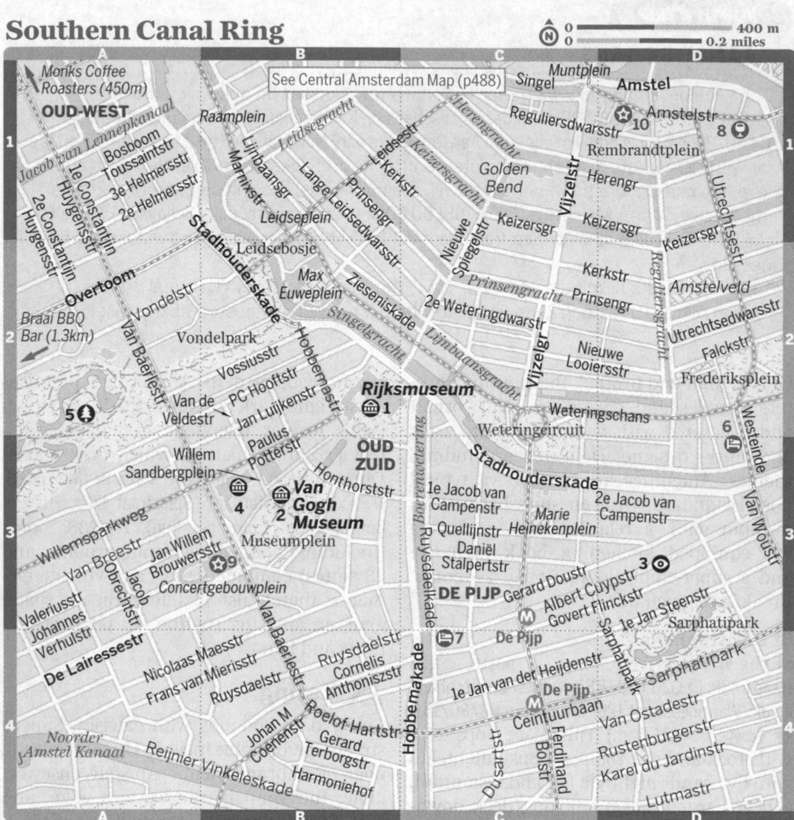

Southern Canal Ring

marinated, barbecued ribs (half or full rack) and roasted sausages, but there are veggie options too. Cards are preferred, but it accepts cash. Tables scatter under the trees alongside the water.

Tokoman SURINAMESE $

(Map p488; www.tokoman.nl; Waterlooplein 327; sandwiches €3.75-5.50, dishes €6.50-12.50; 11am-7pm, closed Sun; Waterlooplein) Queue with the folks getting their Surinamese spice on at Tokoman. It makes a sensational *broodje pom* (a sandwich filled with a tasty mash of chicken and a starchy Surinamese tuber). You'll want the *zuur* (pickled-cabbage relish) and *peper* (chilli) on it, plus a cold can of coconut water to wash it down.

★**D'Vijff Vlieghen** DUTCH $$

(Map p488; 020-530 40 60; www.vijffvlieghen.nl; Spuistraat 294-302; mains €19-26; 6-10pm; 2/11/12 Spui) Spread across five 17th-century canal houses, the 'Five Flies' is a jewel. Old-wood dining rooms overflow with character, featuring Delft-blue tiles and original works by Rembrandt; chairs have copper plates inscribed with the names of famous guests (Walt Disney, Mick Jagger...). Exquisite dishes range from goose breast with apple, sauerkraut and smoked butter to candied haddock with liquorice sauce.

Greetje DUTCH **$$$**

(Map p488; 020-779 74 50; www.restaurantgreetje.nl; Peperstraat 23-25; mains €24-29; 6-10pm; 22/48 Prins Hendrikkade) Greetje is Amsterdam's most creative Dutch restaurant, using the best seasonal produce to resurrect and re-create traditional Dutch recipes, like pickled beef, braised veal with apricots and leek *stamppot* (traditional mashed potatoes and vegetables), and pork belly with Dutch mustard sauce. Kick off with the Big Beginning (€17), a sampling of hot and cold starters.

Drinking & Nightlife

Amsterdam is one of the wildest nightlife cities in Europe and the world. Beyond the Red Light District and hotspots around Leidseplein and Rembrandtplein, the clubbing scene is also rapidly expanding thanks to 24-hour-licensed venues. Yet you can easily avoid a hardcore party scene: Amsterdam remains a *café* (pub) society where the pursuit of pleasure centres on cosiness and charm.

★ 't Smalle BROWN CAFE

(Map p488; www.t-smalle.nl; Egelantiersgracht 12; 10am-1am Sun-Thu, to 2am Fri & Sat; 13/17 Westermarkt) Dating back to 1786 as a *jenever* (Dutch gin) distillery and tasting house, and restored during the 1970s with antique porcelain beer pumps and lead-framed windows, locals' favourite 't Smalle is one of Amsterdam's most charming *bruin cafés*. Dock your boat right by the pretty stone terrace, which is wonderfully convivial by day and impossibly romantic at night.

Monks Coffee Roasters COFFEE

(www.monkscoffee.nl; Bilderdijkstraat 46; 8am-5pm Tue-Sun; ; 3/13/19 Bilderdijkstraat) Monks' phenomenal house blend, prepared with a variety of brewing methods, is hands down Amsterdam's best, but the cafe also serves superb coffee from small-scale specialists such as Amsterdam's Lot Sixty One and White Label Coffee, and Paris' Café Lomi. Its cavernous space is brilliant for brunch (try avocado toast with feta, chilli and lime, or banana bread with mascarpone and caramelised pineapple).

★ Brouwerij 't IJ BREWERY

(www.brouwerijhetij.nl; Funenkade 7; brewery 2-8pm, English tour 3.30pm Fri-Sun; 7 Hoogte Kadijk) Can you get more Dutch than drinking a craft beer beneath the creaking sails of the 1725 built De Gooyer Windmill? This is Amsterdam's leading microbrewery, with delicious standard, seasonal and limited-edition brews; try the smooth, fruity 'tripel' Zatte, their first creation back in 1985. Enjoy yours in the tiled tasting room, lined by an amazing bottle collection, or the plane-tree-shaded terrace.

Amsterdam Roest BEER GARDEN

(www.amsterdamroest.nl; Jacob Bontiusplaats 1; noon-midnight Sun-Wed, to 1am Thu, to 3am Fri & Sat; 22 Wittenburgergracht) This is one of those 'only in Amsterdam' places, and well worth the trip. Once-derelict shipyards now host an epically cool artist collective-bar-restaurant, Amsterdam Roest (Dutch for 'Rust'), with a canal-side terrace, mammoth playground of ropes and tyres, hammocks, street art, a sandy beach in summer and bonfires in winter.

RED LIGHT DISTRICT

Just southeast of Centraal Station, on and around the parallel neon-lit canals Oudezijds Voorburgwal and Oudezijds Achterburgwal, the warren of medieval alleyways making up Amsterdam's Red Light District (locally known as De Wallen), is a carnival of vice, seething with skimpily clad prostitutes in brothel windows, raucous bars, haze-filled 'coffeeshops', strip shows, sex shows, mind-boggling museums and shops selling everything from cartoonish condoms to S&M gear and herbal highs.

The area is generally safe, but keep your wits about you and don't photograph or film prostitutes in the windows – out of respect, and to avoid having your camera flung in a canal by their enforcers. Seriously.

COFFEESHOP & SMART SHOP DOS & DON'T

In the Netherlands, 'coffeeshops' are where one buys marijuana. 'Smart shops' sell mushroom truffles (psilocybin mushrooms, aka magic mushrooms, are now illegal in the Netherlands).

- Do ask coffeeshop staff for advice on what and how to consume, and heed it, even if nothing happens after an hour.
- Don't ask for hard (illegal) drugs.
- Don't drink alcohol – it's illegal in coffeeshops.
- Don't smoke tobacco, whether mixed with marijuana or on its own; it is forbidden inside all bars and restaurants, in accordance with the Netherlands' laws.

Pllek BAR

(www.pllek.nl; TT Neveritaweg 59; 9.30am-1am Sun-Thu, to 3am Fri & Sat; NDSM-werf) Ubercool Pllek is a Noord magnet, with hip things of all ages streaming over to hang out in its interior made of old shipping containers and lie out on its artificial sandy beach when the weather allows. It's a terrific spot for a waterfront beer or glass of wine.

★SkyLounge COCKTAIL BAR

(Map p488; 020-530 08 75; www.skyloungeamsterdam.com; Oosterdoksstraat 4; 11am-1am Sun-Tue, to 2am Wed & Thu, to 3am Fri & Sat; ; 2/4/11/12/13/14/17/24/26 Centraal Station) With wow-factor views whatever the weather, this bar offers a 360-degree panorama of Amsterdam from the 11th floor of the DoubleTree Amsterdam Centraal Station hotel – and it just gets better when you head out to its vast SkyTerrace, with an outdoor bar. Toast the view with a huge range of cocktails, craft beers and spirits. DJs regularly hit the decks from 9pm.

☆ Entertainment

Check what's on at I Amsterdam (www.iamsterdam.com).

Last Minute Ticket Shop sells same-day half-price tickets for concerts, performances and even club nights online. Events are handily marked 'LNP' (language no problem) if understanding Dutch isn't vital.

Pathé Tuschinskitheater CINEMA

(Map p492; www.pathe.nl; Reguliersbreestraat 26-34; 9.30am-12.30am; 14/24 Rembrandtplein) This fantastical cinema, with a facade that's a prime example of the Amsterdam School of architecture, is worth visiting for its sumptuous art deco interior alone. The *grote zaal* (main auditorium) is the most stunning; it generally screens blockbusters, while the smaller theatres play arthouse and indie films. Visit the interior on an audio tour (€10) when films aren't playing.

Concertgebouw CLASSICAL MUSIC

(Concert Hall; Map p492; 020-671 83 45; www.concertgebouw.nl; Concertgebouwplein 10; box office 1-7pm Mon-Fri, from 10am Sat & Sun; 3/5/12 Museumplein) The Concert Hall was built in 1888 by AL van Gendt, who managed to engineer its near-perfect acoustics. Bernard Haitink, former conductor of the Royal Concertgebouw Orchestra, remarked that the world-famous hall was the orchestra's best instrument. Free half-hour concerts take place Wednesdays at 12.30pm from September to June; arrive early. Try the **Last Minute Ticket Shop** (www.lastminuteticketshop.nl; online ticket sales from 10am on day of performance) for half-price seats to all other performances.

Shopping

Stumbling across offbeat little boutiques is one of the great joys of shopping in Amsterdam. The best areas are the nexus of the Western Canal Ring and Jordaan, along Haarlemmerstraat and Haarlemmerdijk. To the south the Negen Straatjes (Nine Streets) offers a satisfying browse among its pint-sized, one-of-a-kind shops. Staalstraat in Nieuwmarkt is another bountiful vein.

★Lindengracht Market MARKET

(Map p488; www.jordaanmarkten.nl; Lindengracht; 9am-4pm Sat; 3 Nieuwe Willemsstraat) Dating from 1895, Saturday's Lindengracht Market is a wonderfully local affair, with 232 stalls selling bountiful fresh produce, including fish and a magnificent array of cheese, as well as gourmet goods, clothing and homewares. Arrive as early as possible for the best pickings and thinnest crowds.

Information

I Amsterdam Visitor Centre (Map p488; ☎020-702 60 00; www.iamsterdam.com; Stationsplein 10; ⏰9am-5pm; 🚋2/4/11/12/13/14/17/24/26 Centraal Station) Located outside Centraal Station.

I Amsterdam Visitor Centre Schiphol (www.iamsterdam.com; ⏰7am-10pm) Inside Schiphol International Airport in the Arrivals 2 hall.

Getting There & Away

AIR

Most major airlines serve **Schiphol** (AMS; www.schiphol.nl), 18km southwest of the city centre.

BUS

Buses operated by Eurolines (www.eurolines.com) and FlixBus (www.flixbus.com) connect Amsterdam with all major European capitals and numerous smaller destinations. Book tickets online.

Eurolines buses use **Duivendrecht station** (Stationsplein 3, Duivendrecht; Ⓜ Duivendrecht), south of the centre, which has an easy metro link to Centraal Station (about a 20-minute trip via metros 50, 53 or 54).

FlixBus runs to/from **Sloterdijk train station**, west of the centre, which is linked to Centraal Station by metro number 50 (a six-minute trip).

TRAIN

Centraal Station (Map p488, Stationsplein; 🚋2/4/11/12/13/14/17/24/26 Centraal Station) is in the city centre, with easy onward connections.

NS (www.ns.nl), aka Dutch Railways, runs the nation's rail service. Trains are frequent from Centraal Station and serve domestic destinations such as Haarlem, Leiden and Delft several times per hour, making for easy day trips.

GAY AMSTERDAM

Amsterdam's gay scene is one of the largest in the world. Hubs include Warmoesstraat in the Red Light District and Reguliersdwarsstraat in the Southern Canal Ring. Gay Amsterdam (www.gayamsterdam.com) lists hotels, bars, clubs and more.

The main service centre to buy tickets for both national and international trains is on the station's west side.

Getting Around

TO/FROM THE AIRPORT

Trains to Centraal Station depart every 10 minutes or so from 6am to 12.30am, and hourly at other times; the trip takes 15 minutes and costs €5.30. Taxis take 20 to 30 minutes and cost €39.

BICYCLE

The vast majority of Amsterdammers get around town on their *fietsen* (bikes). Rental companies are all over town; bikes cost about €12 per day.

BOAT

Free ferries to Amsterdam Noord depart from piers behind Centraal Station.

PUBLIC TRANSPORT

Most public transport within the city is by tram. Tickets are not sold on board. Buy a disposable **OV-chipkaart** (www.ov-chipkaart.nl; 1hr €3) or a day pass (one to seven days €7.50 to €34.50) from the **GVB information office** (www.gvb.nl; Stationsplein 10; ⏰7am-9pm Mon-Fri, from 8am Sat & Sun; 🚋2/4/11/12/13/14/17/24/26 Centraal Station). When you enter *and* exit, wave your card at the machine to 'check in' and 'check out'.

THE RANDSTAD

One of the most densely populated places on the planet, the Randstad stretches from Amsterdam to Rotterdam and is crammed with classic Dutch towns and cities such as Den Haag, Utrecht, Leiden and Delft. A cycling network links the towns amid tulip fields.

Haarlem

☎023 / POP 159,556

This classic Dutch city of cobbled streets, historic buildings, grand churches, even grander museums, cosy bars, fine cafes and canals is just a 15-minute train ride from Amsterdam.

Sights

Flanked by historic buildings, restaurants and cafes, the large Grote Markt is the beating heart of Haarlem. Stalls crammed with market produce fill the square Monday and Saturday.

★ Frans Hals Museum – Hof MUSEUM

(www.franshalsmuseum.nl; Groot Heiligland 62; adult/child incl Frans Hals Museum – Hof €15/free; ⌚11am-5pm Tue-Sat, from noon Sun) A must for anyone interested in the Dutch Masters, this superb museum is located in the poorhouse where Hals spent his final years. The collection focuses on the 17th-century Haarlem School; its pride and joy are eight group portraits of the Civic Guard that reveal Hals' exceptional attention to mood and psychological tone. Other greats represented here include Pieter Bruegel the Younger and Jacob van Ruisdael. Tickets include admission to the modern- and contemporary-art **Frans Hals Museum – Hal** (☎023-511 57 75; Grote Markt 16; ⌚11am-5pm Tue-Sat, from noon Sun).

Grote Kerk van St Bavo CHURCH

(www.bavo.nl; Oude Groenmarkt 22; adult/child €2.50/1.25; ⌚10am-5pm Mon-Sat year-round, plus from noon Sun Jul & Aug) Topped by a towering 50m-high steeple, the Gothic Grote Kerk van St Bavo contains some fine Renaissance artworks, but the star attraction is its stunning Müller organ – one of the most magnificent in the world, standing 30m high and with about 5000 pipes, dating from 1738. It was played by Handel and a 10-year-old Mozart. Free hour-long **organ recitals** take place at 8.15pm Tuesday and 4pm Thursday from July to October, and on occasional Sundays at 2.30pm.

Eating & Drinking

Cafes and restaurants abound along Zijlstraat, Spaarne and especially Lange Veerstraat, but you'll find gems scattered all over town.

★ Restaurant Mr & Mrs BISTRO $$

(☎023-531 59 35; www.restaurantmrandmrs.nl; Lange Veerstraat 4; small plates €11-13, 4-/5-/6-course menu €40/48/56; ⌚5-10pm Tue-Sat) Unexpectedly gastronomic cooking at this tiny restaurant is artfully conceived and presented. Small hot and cold plates designed for sharing might include steak tartare with black truffles, white asparagus with honey-poached egg, mackerel with Dutch shrimp and rose petals, chorizo-stuffed quail with *fregola* (bead-like pasta), and desserts like passionfruit tart with mint meringue and mango salsa. Definitely book ahead.

★ Jopenkerk BREWERY

(www.jopenkerk.nl; Gedempte Voldersgracht 2; ⌚brewery & cafe 10am-1am, restaurant noon-3pm & 5.30-11pm; 👪) Haarlem's most atmospheric place to drink is this independent brewery inside a stained-glass-windowed 1910 church. Enjoy brews such as citrusy Hopen, fruity Lente Bier and chocolatey Koyt along with Dutch bar snacks – *bitterballen* (meat-filled croquettes) and cheeses – beneath the gleaming copper vats. Or head to the mezzanine for dishes made from locally sourced, seasonal ingredients and Jopenkerk's beers (pairings available).

DeDakkas ROOFTOP BAR

(www.dedakkas.nl; Parkeergarage de Kamp, 6th fl, De Witstraat; ⌚9am-11pm Tue, Wed & Sun, to midnight Thu-Sat; 📶) From the ground, it looks like any other multistorey car park, but taking the lift to the 6th floor brings you out at this fabulous rooftop with a greenhouse-style glass cafe and timber-decked terrace with sweeping views over Haarlem (you can see Amsterdam on a clear day). Regular events include barbecues, cinema screenings, yoga, DJs and live music gigs.

Information

Tourist Office (VVV; ☎023-531 73 25; www.haarlemmarketing.nl; Grote Markt 2; ⌚9.30am-5.30pm Mon-Fri, to 5pm Sat, noon-4pm Sun Apr-Sep, 1-5.30pm Mon, from 9.30am Tue-Fri, 10am-5pm Sat Oct-Mar)

Getting There & Away

Haarlem's 1908 art nouveau station is served by frequent trains to/from Amsterdam (€4.30, 15 minutes), Rotterdam (€12.40, one hour) and Den Haag (€8.50, 40 minutes).

Leiden

☎071 / POP 122,561

Vibrant Leiden is renowned for being Rembrandt's birthplace, the home of the Netherlands' oldest university (and 27,000 students) and the place America's pilgrims raised money to lease the *Mayflower* that took them to the New World in 1620. Beautiful 17th-century buildings line its canals.

Sights

As you walk five minutes southeast from Centraal Station, the city's traditional character unfolds, especially around the Pieterskerk and south. Leiden's district of histor-

DON'T MISS

KEUKENHOF GARDENS

One of the Netherlands' top attractions is 1km west of Lisse, between Haarlem and Leiden. **Keukenhof** (0252-465 555; www.keukenhof.nl; Stationsweg 166; 8am-7.30pm mid-Mar–mid-May;) is the world's largest bulb-flower garden, attracting around 1.4 million visitors during its eight-week season that coincides with the transient blooms in fields of multicoloured tulips, daffodils and hyacinths. Book ahead online to ensure a place.

In season, special buses link Keukenhof with Amsterdam's Schiphol Airport and Leiden's Centraal Station; combination tickets covering entry and transport are usually available.

ic waterways is worth at least a full day of wandering.

★ Museum Volkenkunde MUSEUM
(National Museum of Ethnology; www.volkenkunde.nl; Steenstraat 1; adult/student/child 4-18yr €14/8/6; 10am-5pm Tue-Sun) Cultural achievements by civilisations worldwide are on show at this splendid museum, which has a collection of more than 300,000 artefacts from across the globe. Permanent galleries are dedicated to the cultures of Africa; the Arctic and North America; Asia; Central and South America; China; Indonesia; Japan and Korea; and Oceania. Highlights include the atmospherically lit Buddha Room next to the Japan and Korea section and the 'Mountain of the Immortals' carving in the China section. Temporary exhibitions are also impressive.

★ Rijksmuseum van Oudheden MUSEUM
(National Museum of Antiquities; 071-516 31 63; www.rmo.nl; Rapenburg 28; adult/student/child 5-17yr €12.50/6/4; 10am-5pm Tue-Sun) Home to the Rijksmuseum's collection of Greek, Etruscan, Roman and Egyptian artefacts, this museum is best known for its Egyptian halls, which include the reconstructed **Temple of Taffeh**, a gift from Anwar Sadat to the Netherlands for helping to save ancient Egyptian monuments from flood. Other Egyptian exhibits include mastabas from Saqqara and a room of mummy cases. First-floor galleries are replete with Greek, Etruscan and Roman statuary and vases, as well as treasures from the ancient Near East.

Rijksmuseum Boerhaave MUSEUM
(071-751 99 99; www.rijksmuseumboerhaave.nl; Lange St Agnietenstraat 10; adult/student/child 4-17yr €12.50/7.50/5; 10am-5pm Tue-Sun) Named in honour of physician, botanist, chemist and University of Leiden teacher Herman Boerhaave (1668–1738), this impressive museum of science and medicine has exhibits profiling major discoveries in science in the Netherlands, and the doctors and scientists behind them. The museum is housed in a 15th-century convent that later became the first academic hospital in Northern Europe, and a multimedia introduction is presented in a recreated anatomical theatre. Teenagers will enjoy the opportunities for hands-on interaction in the Waterland exhibit.

Museum De Lakenhal MUSEUM
(www.lakenhal.nl; Oude Singel 28-32) Leiden's foremost museum, displaying works by native son Rembrandt among others, the Lakenhal has reopened its doors after undergoing a major renovation and expansion. Check online or with the tourist office for updates.

Sleeping & Eating

The city-centre canals and narrow old streets teem with choices. Market stalls line Botermarkt, Vismarkt, Aalmarkt and Nieuwe Rijn on Wednesday and Saturday.

★ Ex Libris B&B $$
(071 210 86 36; www.hotelexlibris.com; Kloksteeg 4; r €120-200;) There are plenty of boutique B&Bs in the Netherlands, but few are as stylish, comfortable and welcoming as this one. Occupying a former bookshop and adjoining house near the Pieterskerk, it offers five quiet rooms accessed via steep stairs; these have coffee/tea and a smart TV. The chic downstairs breakfast room offers a €17 cafe-style repast (smoothies, granola, eggs, pancakes, toasties).

Borgman & Borman CAFE
(071-566 55 37; www.borgmanborgman.nl; Nieuwe Rijn 41; 9am-5pm Mon, 8am-6pm Tue-Sat,10.30am-5pm Sun;) The Giesen roaster in the window signals that this hip cafe is serious about its coffee, and once you've ordered you'll find that the baristas deliver on this promise. There's also a small menu of breakfast dishes, sandwiches (€5 to €7) and toasties. Service is friendly and the music on the sound system is excellent – not a '70s or '80s pop song to be heard. Cash only.

★**In den Doofpot** EUROPEAN $$$
(☎071-512 24 34; www.indendoofpot.nl; Turfmarkt 9; mains €30, 3-/4-course lunch menu €39/45, 4-/5-/6-course dinner menu €55/65/75; ⌚12.30-3pm & 5.30-10pm Mon-Fri, 5.30-10pm Sat) Given the sky-high calibre of chef Patrick Brugman's food, In den Doofpot's prices are a veritable steal. This is extremely assured and creative cooking, as good to look at as it is to eat. Vegetarian menus are available on request, as are expert wine pairings by the glass (€8 per course). Highly recommended.

Information

Tourist Office (☎071-516 60 00; www.visitleiden.nl; Stationsweg 26; ⌚7am-7pm Mon-Fri, 10am-4pm Sat, 11am-3pm Sun; 📶)

Getting There & Away

Leiden's train station is 400m northwest of the centre. There are frequent trains to/from Amsterdam (€9.10, 35 minutes), Den Haag (€3.50, 15 minutes) and Rotterdam (€7.40, 35 minutes).

Den Haag

☎070 / POP 519,988

Flanked by wide, leafy boulevards, Den Haag (The Hague) is the Dutch seat of government. The city enjoys an exciting cultural scene and top-notch dining. The party precinct of Grote Markt and the much-loved Paard live-music venue are essential stops for every visitor.

Den Haag's seaside suburb of Scheveningen (pronounced as s'CHay-fuh-ninger), 4km west, has a loud and lively kitsch, and a long stretch of beach.

Sights

★**Mauritshuis** MUSEUM
(Royal Picture Gallery; ☎070-302 34 56; www.mauritshuis.nl; Plein 29; adult/student/child under 19yr €15.50/12.50/free; ⌚1-6pm Mon, 10am-6pm Tue, Wed & Fri-Sun, 10am-8pm Thu; 🚋Centrum) Offering a wonderful introduction to Dutch and Flemish art, this splendid museum is set in a 17th-century mansion built for wealthy sugar trader Johan Maurits. It became a museum housing the Royal Picture Collection in 1822, and acquired a swish modern wing in 2012–14. The 800-strong collection of paintings focuses on works created between the 15th and 18th centuries. It includes masterpieces such as Vermeer's *Girl with a Pearl Earring* (c1665) and Rembrandt's intriguing *The Anatomy Lesson of Dr Nicolaes Tulp* (1632).

Binnenhof PALACE
(🚋Centrum) Home to both houses of the Dutch government, this complex of buildings next to the **Hofvijver** (Court Pond) is arranged around a central courtyard that was once used for executions. Its splendid ceremonial **Ridderzaal** (Knights Hall) dates back to the 13th century. The 17th-century North Wing is still home to the Upper House, but the Lower House meets in a chamber in the modern eastern part of the complex. Visitor organisation **ProDemos** (☎070-757 02 00; www.prodemos.nl; Hofweg 1; Ridderzaal tour €5.50, Ridderzaal, House of Representatives & Senate tour €11; ⌚office 10am-5pm Mon-Sat, tours by reservation; 🚋Kneuterdijk, Centrum) conducts guided tours.

★**Escher in Het Paleis** MUSEUM
(☎070-427 77 30; www.escherinhetpaleis.nl; Lange Voorhout 74; adult/student/child 7-15yr/child under 7yr €10/8.50/6.50/free; ⌚11am-5pm Tue-Sun; 🚋Korte Voorhout) Once home to members of the Dutch royal family, the 18th-century Lange Voorhout Palace now houses a collection of the work of Dutch graphic artist MC Escher (1898–1972). The permanent exhibition features notes, letters, photos and plenty of woodcuts and lithographs from various points of his career, including everything from the early realism to the later phantasmagoria. All are fascinating exercises in the blending of different perspectives, and the conjunction of mathematical rules and artistic subject matter.

Sleeping

KingKool HOSTEL $
(☎070-215 83 39; www.kingkool.nl; Prinsegracht 51; dm €21-31, d with shared bathroom €55, d €69-76; 🅿📶; 🚋Brouwersgracht) Close to **Paard** (☎070-750 34 34; www.paard.nl; Prinsegracht 12; ⌚hours vary; 🚋Grote Markt) and the Grote Markt party precinct, this is Den Haag's backpacker central. The ground-floor bar is a popular gathering spot and the mixed dorms (sleeping eight to 12, some on three-tier bunks) are made cheerful with street-art-style murals; those on the 1st floor are best. Shared bathrooms are barracks-like but clean, with plenty of hot water.

★**Hotel Indigo** BOUTIQUE HOTEL $$$
(☎070-209 90 00; www.hotelindigo.com; Noordeinde 33; standard r €160-230, superior r €220-290; 📶; 🚋Kneuterdijk) A clever transformation of the former 1884 De Nederlandsche Bank headquarters, the Indigo is located on

DON'T MISS

THE NETHERLANDS BY BIKE

The Netherlands is the ultimate country to explore by *fiets* (bicycle). Cycling in the Netherlands (http://holland.cyclingaroundtheworld.nl) is a font of useful, inspiring information.

Cycling Routes & Maps

Bike routes web the country. Long-distance LF routes link one town to another and are well marked with distinctive, green-and-white signs. In 2017 work began on condensing the original 26 LP routes – comprising close to 4500km – into 12 longer themed routes. Expect to see changes to some LF routes.

Fietsersbond Routeplanner (https://en.routeplanner.fietsersbond.nl), powered by the Netherlands' national cycling federation, is a superb online route planner with an indispensable smartphone app.

The best overall maps are Falk/VVV *Fietskaart met Knooppuntennetwerk* maps (cycling network; www.falk.nl), with keys in English. Tourist offices often sell them.

Gearing Up

Rental shops are everywhere. Count on paying €12 per day. Many rent out e-bikes (electric bikes). Bikes always come with a lock. To brake on a traditional Dutch bicycle, back-pedal. Most Dutch cyclists don't wear a helmet, hence they're not standard with a rental.

Buy a day ticket for your bike (*dagkaart fiets;* €6.20) to take it on a train.

fashionable Noordeinde. Its 63 good-sized rooms are stylish, with smart furnishings and amenities – those in the attic have bags of character. Start the day with breakfast in the ground-floor cafe (included in the room rate) and finish with a cocktail in the basement speakeasy.

Eating & Drinking

The cobbled streets and canals off Denneweg continually host adventurous new openings. For cheap eats, head to Chinatown. The main cafe strips are Denneweg and Noordeinde.

Lola Bikes & Coffee CAFE
(www.facebook.com/LolaBikesandCoffee; Noordeinde 91; 8am-6pm Tue-Sun; Mauritskade) The owners and staff at this cafe are passionate cyclists, and operate a workshop at the rear where they repair racing bikes in between serving excellent coffee and cake to a host of regulars. Sit in the rear garden or relax in the shabby-chic front space. It's the home base of the Lola Cycling Club, which welcomes new members.

De Basiliek INTERNATIONAL **$$**
(070-360 61 44; www.debasiliek.nl; Korte Houtstraat 4a; mains €18-24, 3-course menu €37.50-42.50; noon-4pm & 6-10pm Mon-Fri, 6-10pm Sat; ; Kalvermarkt-Stadhuis) Moody lighting, comfortable seating and unobtrusive service set the scene for enjoyable meals at this classy choice. The menu is predominantly Italian and French, with a few Indian and Middle Eastern dishes thrown in as wildcards. The food is fresh and full of flavour, made with top-notch produce, and the stellar wine includes loads of by-the-glass options. Great coffee too.

★**Fouquet** DUTCH **$$$**
(070-360 62 73; www.fouquet.nl; Javastraat 31a; mains €25-28, 3-course menus €30-38; 6-9.30pm Mon-Sat; ; Javastraat, Javabrug) The three-course 'market fresh' menu at this elegant restaurant is an excellent and bargain-priced introduction to Sebastiaan de Bruijn's seasonally inspired French-Mediterranean fare. The menu changes daily, responding to what is fresh in the local markets, and is prepared with love and great expertise. Presentation, service and the wine list are all equally impressive.

Information

Tourist Office (VVV; 070-361 88 60; www.denhaag.com; Spui 68; noon-6pm Mon, 10am-6pm Tue-Fri, 10am-5pm Sat, noon-5pm Sun; ; Kalvermarkt-Stadhuis)

Getting There & Around

A one-hour/day pass for local trams costs €3.50/6.50.

Most trains use Den Haag **Centraal Station** (CS), but some through trains only stop at Den Haag **Hollands Spoor** (HS) station just south of the centre. Frequent trains serve Amsterdam (€11.70, 55 minutes) and Rotterdam (€4.70, 20 to 35 minutes). Den Haag's Centraal Station is also linked to Rotterdam by metro line E (€4.90, 30 minutes).

Delft

☎ 015 / POP 101,034

An easy day trip by bicycle or train from Den Haag or Rotterdam, historic Delft has changed little since Golden Age artist Johannes Vermeer, a born-and-bred Delft lad, painted his famous *View of Delft* in 1660–61. The town is synonymous with its blue-and-white-painted porcelain and is usually heaving with visitors by noon; arrive early to beat the crowds.

Sights

Delft is best seen on foot: almost all the interesting sights lie within a 1km radius of the vast Markt. Much of the town dates from the 17th century and is remarkably well preserved.

★Vermeer Centrum Delft MUSEUM

(☎015-213 85 88; www.vermeerdelft.nl; Voldersgracht 21; adult/student/child 12-17yr €9/7/5; ⏲10am-5pm) Johannes Vermeer was born in Delft in 1632 and lived here until his death in 1675, aged only 43. Sadly, none of his works remain in Delft, making it hard for the town to make the most of its connection to the great painter. Hence this centre, where reproductions of his works are exhibited, a short film about his life is screened and displays about 17th-century painting techniques and materials give context.

Nieuwe Kerk CHURCH

(New Church; ☎015-212 30 25; https://oudeennieuwekerkdelft.nl/; Markt 80; adult/child 6-11yr incl Oude Kerk €5/1, Nieuwe Kerk tower additional €4/2; ⏲9am-6pm Mon-Sat Apr-Oct, shorter hours rest of year) Construction of Delft's Nieuwe Kerk began in 1381; it was finally completed in 1655. The church has been the final resting place of almost every member of the House of Orange since 1584, including William of Orange (William the Silent), who lies in an over-the-top marble mausoleum designed by Hendrick de Keyser. Children under five are not permitted to climb the 109m-high tower, whose 376 narrow, spiralling steps lead to panoramic views.

Oude Kerk CHURCH

(Old Church; ☎015-212 30 15; https://oudeennieuwekerkdelft.nl/; Heilige Geestkerkhof 25; adult/child 6-11yr incl Nieuwe Kerk €5/1; ⏲9am-6pm Mon-Sat Apr-Oct, shorter hours rest of year) Founded c 1246, the Oude Kerk is a surreal sight: its 75m-high tower, which was erected c 1350, leans nearly 2m from the vertical due to subsidence caused by its canal location, hence its nickname Scheve Jan ('Leaning John'). The older section features an austere barrel vault; the newer northern transept has a Gothic vaulted ceiling. One of the tombs inside the church is that of painter Johannes Vermeer.

Royal Delft FACTORY

(Koninklijke Porceleyne Fles; ☎015-760 08 00; www.royaldelft.com; Rotterdamseweg 196; adult/child 13-18yr/child under 13yr €13.50/8.50/free; ⏲9am-5pm Mar-Oct, 9am-5pm Mon-Sat, noon-5pm Sun Nov-Feb) Pottery fans will love visiting Royal Delft, the town's most famous earthenware factory. The admission ticket includes an audio tour that leads you through a painting demonstration, the company museum and the factory's production process; there's a €3 discount if you have a Museumkaart (p507). For many, of course, the tour highlight is the final stop in the gift shop.

Eating & Drinking

There are plenty of cafes and restaurants on the Markt and surrounding streets. Drinking and partying unfolds in pubs on the Beestenmarkt and at renowned student hang-out **De Oude Jan** (☎015-214 53 63; www.oudejan.nl; Heilige Geestkerkhof 4; ⏲10am-1am Mon, to 4am Tue-Thu & Sun, to 3am Fri & Sat Easter-Oct, from noon Nov-Easter; 📶).

Kek CAFE $

(☎015-750 32 53; http://kekdelft.nl/; Voldersgracht 27; breakfast dishes €4-10, sandwiches €6-10; ⏲8.30am-6pm; 📶📝) 🌿 The baskets of organic fruit and vegetables at the front of this stylish cafe are a good indicator of what's on the menu – freshly squeezed juices, fruit smoothies and a tempting array of cakes, muffins, tarts and sandwiches made with local seasonal produce (sugar-free, vegan and gluten-free options available). Other draws include all-day breakfasts and coffee made using Giraffe beans.

Information

Tourist Information Point (☎015-215 40 51; www.delft.com; Kerkstraat 3; ⏲11am-3pm Sun & Mon, 10am-4pm Tue-Sat)

Getting There & Around

There are bike trails from Den Haag (11km northwest) and Rotterdam (28km southeast).

Delft By Cycle (06 2434 2610; https://delftbycycle.nl/en/; Phoenixstraat 112; per day €15; 9am-5pm) rents out bikes.

Regular train services to/from Delft include Amsterdam (€13.20 to €15.60, one hour), Den Haag (€2.50, 15 minutes) and Rotterdam (€3.40, 15 minutes).

ROTTERDAM WELCOME CARD

The **Rotterdam Welcome Card** (adult per 1/2/3 days €12/17/21) gives discounts of up to 25% on museum and attraction admission charges, as well as free public transport on RET metro, tram and bus services. Purchase it at Rotterdam's tourist offices.

Rotterdam

010 / POP 629,606

Futuristic architecture, a proliferation of art, and cutting-edge drinking, dining and nightlife scenes make Rotterdam one of Europe's most exhilarating cities right now. The Netherlands' second-largest metropolis has a diverse, multi-ethnic community, an absorbing maritime tradition centred on Europe's busiest port and a wealth of world-class museums.

The city was all but razed to the ground by WWII bombers, but rebuilding has continued unabated ever since with ingenuity and vision. Split by the vast Nieuwe Maas shipping channel, Rotterdam is crossed by a series of tunnels and bridges. On the north side of the water, the city centre is easily strolled – or pedalled around by bike.

Sights

Rotterdam's not just an open-air gallery of extraordinary architecture – it's also home to streets filled with art. For a full list of sculptures and an interactive map, visit Sculpture International Rotterdam (www.sculptureinternationalrotterdam.nl).

★Markthal NOTABLE BUILDING
(Market Hall; https://markthal.klepierre.nl/; Nieuwstraat; 10am-8pm Mon-Thu & Sat, to 9pm Fri, noon-6pm Sun; M Blaak, Blaak) One of the city's signature buildings, this extraordinary inverted-U-shaped market hall was designed by local architecture firm MVRDV and opened for business in 2014. It comprises highly sought-after glass-walled apartments arcing over a 40m-high market hall with a striking fruit-and-vegetable-muralled ceiling. Most of the stalls sell food to eat on the spot rather than produce to take home. There are also a number of sit-down eateries.

Huis Sonneveld ARCHITECTURE
(Sonneveld House; www.huissonneveld.nl; Jongkindstraat 25; adult/student/child under 18yr €10/6.50/free; 10am-5pm Tue-Sat; M Eendrachtsplein, Museumpark) When company director Albertus Sonneveld decided to commission an architect to design a contemporary home for his family, the obvious choice was Leendert van der Vlugt, who had designed the magnificent Van Nelle Factory. Working with Johannes Brinkman, Van der Vlugt designed a streamlined, state-of-the-art building that was hailed as an outstanding example of Dutch Functionalism as soon as its construction was completed in 1933. Replete with original fittings and furniture, it can now be visited with a fascinating audio tour.

Museum Rotterdam '40-'45 NU MUSEUM
(War & Resistance Museum; www.40-45nu.nl; Coolhaven 375; adult/child 4-17yr €7.50/2.50; 10am-5pm Sat, 11am-5pm Sun; M Coolhaven) Good things often come in small packages, and so it is with this small but excellent museum sheltered under a bridge on the Coolhaven. An eight-minute immersive multimedia experience outlines the terror and destruction caused by the bombing of Rotterdam on 14 May 1940, when 54 German aircraft dropped 1300 bombs on the city over a 13-minute period. Artefact-driven displays focus on all aspects of the wartime experience, interspersing tales of optimism and bravery among many sad stories.

★Van Nelle Fabriek NOTABLE BUILDING
(Van Nelle Factory; www.vannellefabriek.com; Van Nelleweg 1, Spaanse Polder; 38 & B9 from Centraal Station) Designed and built between 1925 and 1931, this modernist World Heritage–listed factory northwest of the city centre is an icon of 20th-century industrial architecture. Often described as a 'glass palace' (it's largely constructed of steel and glass), it functioned as a state-of-the-art coffee, tea and tobacco factory until the 1990s and now houses creative industries. Though closed to the public, the factory

Rotterdam

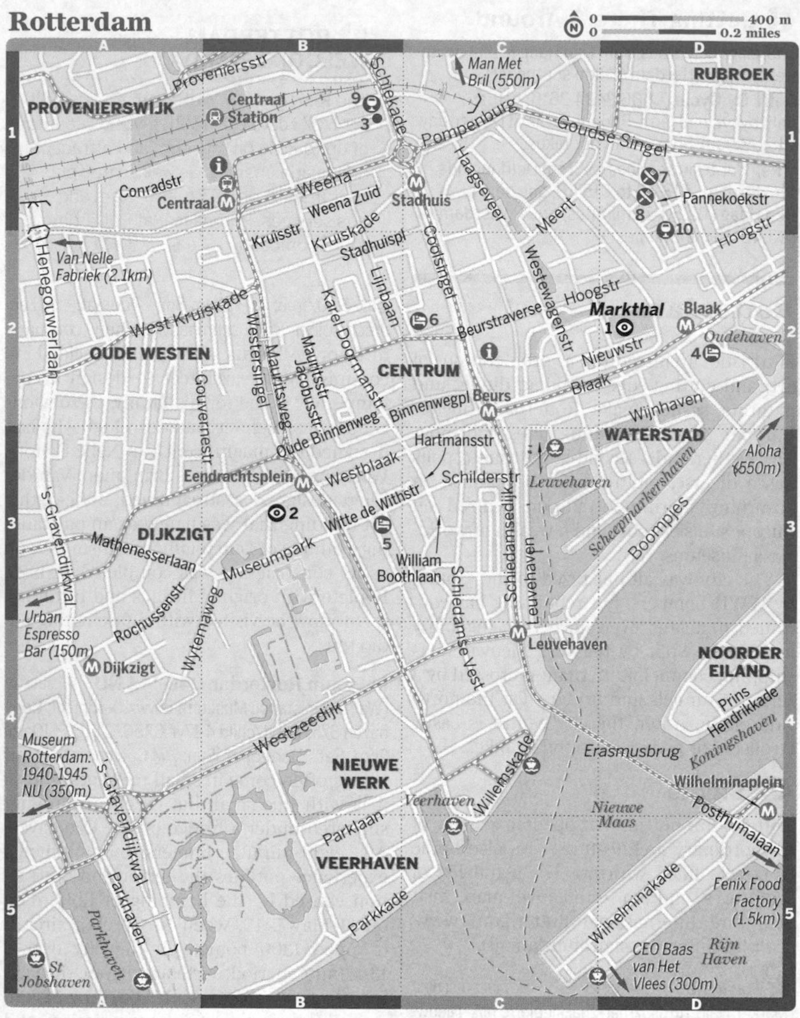

Rotterdam

Top Sights
1 Markthal D2

Sights
2 Huis Sonneveld B3

Activities, Courses & Tours
3 Urban Guides B1

Sleeping
4 Citizen M D2
5 King Kong Hostel B3
6 Urban Residences C2

Eating
7 AJÍ D1
8 Tante Nel D1

Drinking & Nightlife
9 Biergarten B1
10 Bokaal D1

sometimes offers guided tours on weekends at 1pm (adult/child under 13 years €8.50/5); check the factory website for details. **Urban Guides** (☎010-433 22 31; www.urbanguides.nl;

Schiekade 205; boat tour adult/child under 12yr €17/free; office 10am-6pm Mon-Sat, noon-5pm Sun; M Stadhuis, Pompenburg, Weena, Stadhuis) also runs one-hour guided tours (€15 per person) at noon on most Saturdays and Sundays (book ahead).

Sleeping

★**King Kong Hostel** HOSTEL $
(010-818 87 78; www.kingkonghostel.com; Witte de Withstraat 74; dm €19-26, d €75-105; ; M Beurs, Museumpark) There's plenty to like about this hip hostel in Rotterdam's major party precinct. Female and mixed-sex dorms sleep between four and 18, with bunks, under-bed lockers and plenty of power points. Shared bathrooms are modern and clean. Facilities include a laundry (€8 per load wash and dry), a luggage room, a communal kitchen, bike storage, a chill space and a ground-floor cafe.

★**Citizen M** BOUTIQUE HOTEL $$
(010-810 81 00; www.citizenm.com; Gelderse Plein 50; r from €66; P@; M Blaak, Blaak) A new-generation hostel for travellers who have progressed past dorms and shared bathrooms but want to recreate the casual conviviality of backpacker joints, Citizen M is as welcoming as it is well located. Capsule-like rooms are comfortable enough, with Smart TVs offering channels and free movies. The 1st floor bar, cafe and lounge are super-stylish spaces where you can relax or work.

Urban Residences APARTMENT $$
(010-414 32 99; www.urbanresidences.com; Hennekijnstraat 104; studio €95-150, 2-bedroom apt €220-280; P; M Beurs) You'll get a real taste of inner-city Rotterdam life when staying at these sleek apartments in the centre of town. Scattered over 15 floors of a recently constructed high-rise building, there are 76 generously sized apartments – many with impressive views. The Alessi interior fit-outs have a sternly minimalist decor but are very comfortable, offering couches, dining tables and well-equipped kitchens.

Eating

Rotterdam is replete with informal eateries and has two great food markets – the Markthal (p501) and **Fenix Food Factory** (www.fenixfoodfactory.nl; Veerlaan 19d, Katendrecht; 10am-7pm Tue-Thu, to 8pm Fri, to 6pm Sat, noon-6pm Sun, individual stall hours vary; ; M Rijnhaven) – with eateries alongside produce stalls.

★**Urban Espresso Bar** CAFE $
(UEB West; 010-477 01 88; www.urbanespressobar.nl; Nieuwe Binnenweg 263; sandwiches €5-6, mains €7-9; 9am-6pm Mon-Sat, 10am-6pm Sun; ; Claes de Vrieselaan) Could this be Rotterdam's best cafe? The coffee here is definitely a cut above most of its competitors (Giraffe beans, expert baristas), as is the food (artisanal breads and pastries, house-baked cakes, global flavours, organic ingredients). We can highly recommend the *tosties* (toasted sandwiches), soups and burgers, and we always enjoy chatting with fellow customers at the communal table. Cash only.

Tante Nel FAST FOOD $
(www.tante-nel.com; Pannekoekstraat 53a; fries €2.50-8.75; noon-10pm Mon-Sat, to 9pm Sun; Meent) Differing from traditional *patat* (fries) stands in a number of crucial ways, Tante Nel has pleasant street-side seating where its many and varied regulars settle in to enjoy treats such as hand-cut, expertly cooked fries with truffle mayonnaise or *patat stoofvlees* (fries topped with a rich meat stew), washed down with a gin and tonic, beer or milkshake.

★**AJÍ** INTERNATIONAL $$
(010-767 01 69; www.restaurantaji.nl; Pannekoekstraat 40a; snacks €5-24, small plates €10-24; noon-2pm & 5-10pm Tue-Thu, noon-11pm Fri & Sat; Meent) Good-quality Asian food is hard to source in Rotterdam, so we were thrilled to discover this chic bistro serving dishes inspired by Asia and the Mediterranean. Build a meal with a few small plates, or just pop in for drinks and a platter of oysters or Spanish cured meats. There are good wines by the glass and bottle too.

★**CEO Baas van Het Vlees** STEAK $$$
(010-290 94 54; www.ceobaasvanhetvlees.nl; Sumatraweg 1-3, Katendrecht; mains €21-39; 5-

DON'T MISS

WORLD-CLASS JAZZ FEST

North Sea Jazz Festival (www.northseajazz.nl; mid-Jul) One of the world's most respected jazz events sees hundreds of musicians perform. A free 'North Sea Round Town' festival in the weeks preceding the festival proper sees a variety of jazz acts performing in public spaces and concert halls around the city.

11pm Tue-Sat; Ⓜ Rijnhaven) Meat lovers should be sure to book a table at Rotterdam's best steakhouse. Working in their open kitchen, chefs cook spectacular cuts of beef to order. We love the fact that half portions of steak and delicious desserts are offered, and we have rarely been so impressed by a wine list (by both glass and bottle). Truly excellent.

Drinking & Nightlife

There's no lack of cafes, cocktail bars, microbreweries and pubs with alfresco summer seating. Witte de Withstraat is the main bar street.

★ Aloha BAR

(010-210 81 70; www.alohabar.nl; Maasboulevard 100; noon-11pm Sun-Thu, to 1am Fri & Sat; Ⓜ Oostplein) Sustainable, innovative and funky as anything, this bar-cafe in the former Tropicana baths has a large terrace boasting views across the Nieuwe Maas river. Operated by Blue City collective, a group of environmental entrepreneurs, it's a fabulous spot for summer lunches (sandwiches €6 to €9; snacks €5 to €13) or a drink accompanied by the house speciality, mushroom *bitterballen* (deep-fried croquette balls).

★ Biergarten BEER GARDEN

(010-233 05 56; www.biergartenrotterdam.nl; Schiestraat 18; noon-midnight or later; Ⓜ Centraal Station) A sun-bleached labyrinth of wooden tables, brightly painted stairs, exotic foliage and low-slung festoon lighting, the Biergarten throngs with thirsty locals enjoying ice-cold pilsner, homemade lemonade and a tempting selection of barbecued meats. On Fridays, DJs preside over the always-inclusive action.

Bokaal BAR

(010-720 08 98; www.bokaalrotterdam.nl; Nieuwemarkt 11; 11am-1am Sun-Thu, to 2am Fri & Sat; Meent) In a *bokaal* (trophy) location at the heart of the enclave around pedestrian Nieuwemarkt and Pannekoekstraat, Bokaal has an indoor bar and a huge all-day sun terrace that heaves with people on summer nights. Beer (craft and Trappist) is its speciality, with nine on tap, and more than 80 in bottles. There's a food menu, but many take advantage of on-site food trucks.

DON'T MISS

CRAFT COFFEE

Rotterdam's first artisanal coffee roastery (there are now 12), **Man Met Bril** (www.manmetbrilkoffie.nl; Vijverhofstraat 70; 8am-5pm Mon-Fri, 9pm-6pm Sat & Sun; ; Schiekade, Walenburgerweg) sources direct-trade, 90% organic beans from across the globe and then roasts them in this hip space under a railway viaduct north of Centraal Station. The on-site cafe offers expertly prepared brews, cakes and sandwiches. Arrive before 10am to take advantage of the generous and dirt-cheap breakfast deal (€6.66).

Information

Tourist Office (010-790 01 85; www.rotterdam.info; Coolsingel 114; 9.30am-6pm; ; Ⓜ Beurs) Main tourist office.

Tourist Office (www.rotterdam.info; Stationsplein 21, Centraal Station; 9am-5.30pm Sun-Wed, 9am-8pm Thu-Sat mid-Aug–early Jul, 9am-7pm early Jul–mid-Aug) Centraal Station branch.

Getting There & Around

Rotterdam's main train station is **Rotterdam Centraal** (www.ns.nl/stationsinformatie/rtd/rotterdam-centraal; Stationsplein 1; Ⓜ Centraal Station, Centraal) (CS). Major services include to/from Amsterdam (€15.40 to 17.80, 40 to 75 minutes), Schiphol airport (€12.40-14.80, 25-50 minutes) and Utrecht (€10.50, 40 minutes).

Rotterdam's tram, bus and metro services are provided by RET (www.ret.nl). Most converge near Rotterdam Centraal Station. A rechargeable two-hour ticket/day pass costs €3.50/13.50. **Zwann Bikes** (010-412 62 20; www.czwaan.nl; Weena 703-707; per day standard/electric bike €12.50/17.50; 7.30am-7.30pm Mon-Fri, 9am-7.30pm Sat & Sun) rents out bikes.

Utrecht

030 / POP 345,100

It's hard not to fall in love with Utrecht, one of the Netherlands' oldest urban centres and a vibrant university city. Its compact medieval core radiates out from the iconic 15th-century Domtoren, ringed by a loop of very pretty tree-lined canals. Their central sections have distinctive double-level sides inset with what were once medieval warehouses – many now form fascinating venues to eat, drink, dance or sleep with terrace-walkways that extend right to the

DON'T MISS

DELFSHAVEN

Just 3km southwest of Rotterdam's centre, Delfshaven, once the official seaport for the city of Delft, survived the war and retains a village-like atmosphere. Take trams 4 or 8, or the metro to the Delfshaven station.

waterside. The brilliant cafe culture goes well beyond the canals – Utrecht's vibrant concert schedules are a big draw.

Sights

There's plenty to see around **Domplein**, the heart of the city in a space where a cathedral should be. A tips-based three-hour 'free' walking tour starts outside Domtoren on Saturdays (noon) and Sundays (2pm).

Domtoren HISTORIC BUILDING
(Cathedral Tower; www.domtoren.nl; Domplein 9; tower tour adult/student/child €9/7.50/5; 11am-5pm Tue-Sat, noon-4pm Sun) Utrecht's most striking medieval landmark, this 112m tower is worth the 465-step climb for unbeatable city views: on a clear day you can see Amsterdam. Visits are by guided tour only, departing at least hourly on the hour. Buy tickets at the tourist office (p506) across the square or prebook online (advisable in summer). The tower was originally part of a splendid 14th or 15th-century **cathedral** (www.domkerk.nl; Achter de Dom 1; €2.50 donation; 11am-3.30pm or longer Mon-Sat, 12.30-4pm Sun) complex whose nave was blown down by a freak hurricane in 1674.

★**Dom Under** ARCHAEOLOGICAL SITE
(www.domunder.nl; Domplein 4; adult/child €12.50/10; tours hourly 11.30am-4.30pm Tue-Fri, from 10.30am Sat & Sun) Talented volunteer guides and fascinating educational films with CGI effects set the historical scene. Then it's your turn to become an amateur archaeologist as you're let loose in the subterranean half-dark beneath Domplein with your finger on the trigger of a smart-torch audio-gun. Finding clue-targets, you unravel the meaning of rubble-strata and the odd pottery piece, identifying relics of Utrecht's original Roman *castrum* and its early churches.

Museum Catharijneconvent MUSEUM
(030-231 38 35; www.catharijneconvent.nl; Lange Nieuwestraat 38; adult/senior/student & child €14/12.50/7; 10am-5pm Tue-Fri, from 11am Sat & Sun) Museum Catharijneconvent has the finest collection of medieval religious art in the Netherlands – virtually the history of Christianity, in fact – housed in a Gothic former convent and an 18th-century canal-side house. Marvel at the many beautiful illuminated manuscripts, look for the odd Rembrandt and enjoy the wide-ranging scope of the impressive special exhibitions.

★**Rietveld-Schröderhuis** HISTORIC BUILDING
(reservations 030-236 23 10; www.rietveldschroderhuis.nl; Prins Hendriklaan 50; €16.50; tours hourly 11am-4pm Tue-Sun, to 8pm some Fri; 8) Years ahead of its time, this small but uniquely conceived house was built in 1924 by celebrated Utrecht designer Gerrit Rietveld. He'd be amazed to find that it's now a Unesco-recognised monument. Visiting feels like walking into a 3D Piet Mondrian abstract, and things get especially interesting when the walls start to move. To see a contextualising video, arrive 20 minutes before your assigned tour time (booking ahead is mandatory; an eight-language audio guide is included).

Sleeping

Strowis Hostel HOSTEL $
(030-238 02 80; www.strowis.nl; Boothstraat 8; dm €22-28, s/d €72.50/82.50, s/d/tr without bathroom €62.50/72.50/95;) Utrecht's most appealing hostel occupies a high-ceilinged 17th-century building; the dorms don't feel overly cramped even in the 16-bunk room. In the basement, luggage lockers (free with a €10 deposit) are good-sized and some incorporate a charger plug. The appealing cafe-lounge area opens on to a quirky rear garden. The small but well-equipped kitchen closes at 10.30pm.

★**Mother Goose Hotel** HERITAGE HOTEL $$
(030-303 63 00; www.mothergoosehotel.com; Ganzenmarkt 26; r €120-250;) Sensitively restored from what was originally a fortified 13th-century mansion, this 23-room boutique hotel incorporates many salvaged historic details and time-stressed artefacts into rooms full of contemporary comforts. The chatty local staff add a very personal touch, and the reception is wonderfully homey – you might even find a handwritten welcome postcard on your bed.

Eating & Drinking

Wharf-side restaurants on the Oudegracht and terrace places along narrow Dreiharingstraat

WORTH A TRIP

DUTCH DAYS OUT

Other Netherlands highlights worth considering for day trips or longer visits:

Alkmaar Its cheese ceremony (Fridays from the first Friday of April to the first Friday of September) dates from the 17th century.

Hoge Veluwe National Park Beautiful landscape of forests, dunes and marshes, with a bonus of a Van Gogh-rich art museum on-site.

Kinderdijk & Dordrecht A good day trip by fast ferry from Rotterdam is to visit Kinderdijk's Unesco-listed windmills then Dordrecht's medieval canals.

Gouda The perfect cheesy Dutch town.

Texel Largest of the Frisian Islands, with endless walks along dune-backed beaches and excellent local seafood.

are appealing but tourist-centred. Increasingly fashionable, student-oriented Voorstraat has bargain-value takeaway, oriental and snack foods. Cheap pizza places compete on Nobelstraat.

★Heron EUROPEAN $$

(☎030-230 22 29; www.heronrestaurant.nl; Schalkwijkstraat 26-28; 1-/2-/3-/4-/5-course meals €22/33/35/40/45; ⊙5.30-9.30pm Tue-Sat) This adorable 'petit restaurant' presents expectant diners with a list of cryptic clues to a dinner that's brimming with imaginative flavours and is eminently seasonal. Expect 100% locally sourced fare including foraged plants collected by the forester owner. Six lucky guests get to sit right at the central cooking counter and watch every move of the expert chefs.

Olivier BROWN CAFE

(https://utrecht.cafe-olivier.be; Achter Clarenburg 6a; ⊙11am-midnight Sun-Wed, 10am-2am Thu-Sat) Located unpromisingly beside the ugly Hoog Catharijne building is this blessed beer heaven, an astonishingly slick yet super-characterful reworking of a large former church, complete with organ.

ℹ Information

Tourist Office (VVV; ☎030-236 00 04; www.visit-utrecht.com; Domplein 9; ⊙11.45am-5pm Mon, 10am-5pm Tue-Sat, noon-5pm Sun)

ℹ Getting There & Away

Regular direct services from Utrecht CS (Centraal Station) include Amsterdam (€7.60, 27 minutes), Den Haag (€11.20, 40 minutes), Maastricht (€23.90, two hours) and Rotterdam (€10.50, 37 minutes).

THE SOUTH

Actual hills rise on the Netherlands' southern edge, where Belgium and Germany are within range of a tossed wooden shoe. The star here is Maastricht.

Maastricht

☎043 / POP 122,500

Lively and energetic, Maastricht has Roman history, a maze of tunnel-caves and historical buildings aplenty, plus a Burgundian sophistication to its dining, a bacchanalian delight to its drinking culture, and a student-friendly street-life out of all proportion to its size. *Everything* stops for the orgy of partying and carousing during Carnaval in February or March.

Sights

Maastricht's greatest charm is exploring the compact area of narrow, cafe-filled streets on both sides of the pedestrianised Sint Servaasbrug, notably between the three main squares: Vrijthof, Markt and Onze Lieve Vrowplein.

★St Servaasbasiliek CHURCH

(www.sintservaas.nl; Keizer Karelplein 3; adult/child €4.50/3; ⊙10am-5pm Mon-Sat, from 12.30pm Sun) Built above and around the shrine of St Servaas (Servatius), the first bishop of Maastricht, the basilica presents an architectural pastiche whose earliest sections date from AD 1000. Its beautiful curved brick apse and towers dominate the Vrijthof. Tickets include access to the cloister garden and the four-room treasury whose star attractions are St Servaas' gilded bust and 11th-century sarcophagus.

Maastricht Underground CAVE

(☎043-325 21 21; www.maastrichtunderground.nl; Luikerweg 71; cave tour adult/child €6.25/5, combination tour €9.95/6.95) Maastricht Underground runs spooky, amusing and fascinating tours into sections of the vast tunnel network beneath St-Pietersberg massif. Departures run on a constantly shifting schedule, with up to five tours daily in summer, but very few in the off season – check the website.

Bonnefantenmuseum GALLERY
(☎043-329 01 90; www.bonnefanten.nl; Ave Cèramique 250; adult/child €12.50/free; ⏰11am-5pm Tue-Sun) Maastricht's star gallery has an excellent collection of early European painting and sculpture on the 1st floor, but is best known for contemporary art, with works by Limburg artists displayed upstairs; accessed via a dramatic sweep of stairs. There are regularly changing exhibitions.

Sleeping & Eating

Maastricht has many excellent dining addresses. Browse the eastern end of Tongersestraat and the little streets around the Vrijthof and Rechtstraat, just east of the river.

★**Kruisherenhotel** BOUTIQUE HOTEL $$$
(☎043-329 20 20; www.kruisherenhotel.nl; Kruisherengang 19-23; r weekday/weekend from €195/279; ❄@📶) This prize-winning design statement is housed inside the former Crutched Friar monastery complex, dating from 1483. Modern touches, such as moulded furniture and padded walls, accent the historical surroundings. Each of the 60 sumptuous rooms is unique. Some have murals and artwork; others are in the rafters of the old church. Breakfast is suitably heavenly.

★**Witloof** BELGIAN $$
(☎043-323 35 38; www.witloof.nl; Sint Bernardusstraat12; mains €17.50-21.50, 2-/3-course dinner €27/33; ⏰5.30-9.30pm Wed-Sun) A decade after hitting the *New York Times'* list of world's trendiest restaurant concepts, Witloof still cuts the mustard with top-quality Belgian traditional food, an astounding beer cellar (do take a look!) and a tongue-in-cheek humour with decor worthy of a 21st-century Magritte.

Information

Tourist Office (VVV; ☎043-325 21 21; www.vvvmaastricht.nl; Kleine Straat 1; ⏰10am-6pm Mon, 11am-5pm Sat & Sun)

Getting There & Away

There is an hourly international train service to Liège (€6.80, 33 minutes), from where fast trains depart for Brussels, Paris and Cologne. Domestic services include Amsterdam (€25.30, 2½ hours, two per hour) and Utrecht (€23.90, two hours, two per hour).

SURVIVAL GUIDE

Directory A–Z

ACCESSIBLE TRAVEL

The Netherlands ensures a certain level of accessibility for people with disabilities, particularly when it comes to public buildings, spaces and transport. However, older buildings may not be wheelchair-accessible and cobblestoned streets may be an issue for the mobility- or vision-impaired. The Dutch national organisation for people with a disability is **ANGO** (www.ango.nl).

ACCOMMODATION

Reserve ahead in high season (especially August) or during a big event.

B&Bs Very common in the countryside, and increasingly popular in towns and cities; some have automatic check-in.

Camping Campgrounds range from wild and remote to larger sites with luxury tents to rent and ample facilities.

Hostels Often design-driven, with dorms and private single and double rooms.

Hotels These embrace every budget. The bulk are standard and highly functional; a few are boutique.

DISCOUNT CARDS

Museumkaart (Museum Card; www.museumkaart.nl; adult/child €59.90/32.45, plus registration fee €4.95) offers free and discounted entry to some 400 museums all over the country, valid for one year, but strictly limited to five museum visits during the first 31 days. Purchase a temporary card at participating museums and validate online prior to initial one-month expiry.

INTERNET ACCESS

➡ Free wi-fi is widespread in hotels, restaurants, bars and coffeeshops, co-working cafes, tourist offices and other public places.

➡ In Amsterdam you can hire a pocket-sized mobile wi-fi device to carry around with you from **Pocket Wifi Amsterdam** (www.pocketwifi-amsterdam.com); order online and arrange delivery to your hotel or apartment or to Schiphol airport.

LEGAL MATTERS

➡ Technically, marijuana is illegal. However, possession of soft drugs (eg cannabis) up to 5g is tolerated. Larger amounts are subject to prosecution.

➡ In 2018 Den Haag became the first Dutch city to officially ban smoking cannabis in its city centre, train station and major shopping areas.

➡ Smoking (anything) is banned in all public places. In a uniquely Dutch solution, you can still smoke tobacco-free pot in coffeeshops.

➡ Possession of hard drugs is treated as a serious crime.

MONEY

ATMs are widely available. Credit cards are accepted in most hotels, but not all restaurants, cafes and shops. Non-European credit cards are quite often rejected.

OPENING HOURS

Banks 9am–4pm Monday to Friday, some Saturday morning

Cafes and bars Open noon (exact hours vary); most close 1am Sunday to Thursday, 3am Friday and Saturday

Museums 10am–5pm daily, some close Monday

Restaurants Lunch 11am–2.30pm, dinner 6–10pm

Shops 10am or noon to 6pm Tuesday to Friday, 10am–5pm Saturday and Sunday, noon or 1pm to 5pm or 6pm Monday (if at all)

Supermarkets 8am–8pm

PUBLIC HOLIDAYS

Nieuwjaarsdag (New Year's Day) 1 January. Parties and fireworks galore.

Goede Vrijdag Good Friday

Eerste Paasdag Easter Sunday

Tweede Paasdag Easter Monday

Koningsdag (King's Day) 27 April (26 April if the 27th is a Sunday)

Bevrijdingsdag (Liberation Day) 5 May. Not a universal holiday; government workers have the day off, but almost everyone else has to work.

Hemelvaartsdag (Ascension Day) Fortieth day after Easter Sunday

Eerste Pinksterdag (Whit Sunday; Pentecost) Fiftieth day after Easter Sunday

Tweede Pinksterdag (Whit Monday) Fiftieth day after Easter Monday

Eerste Kerstdag (Christmas Day) 25 December

Tweede Kerstdag ('Second Christmas' aka Boxing Day) 26 December

SAFE TRAVEL

The Netherlands is a safe country, but be sensible all the same and always lock your bike. Never buy drugs on the street: it's illegal. And don't light up joints just anywhere – stick to coffeeshops.

TELEPHONE

The Dutch phone network, **KPN** (www.kpn.com), is efficient. Prices are reasonable by European standards.

> #### HOLLAND OR THE NETHERLANDS?
>
> 'Holland' is a popular synonym for the Netherlands, yet it only refers to the combined provinces of Noord-Holland (North Holland) and Zuid-Holland (South Holland). The rest of the country is not Holland, even if the Dutch themselves often make the mistake.

Getting There & Away

AIR

Amsterdam's huge Schiphol International Airport (p495) is the country's main air-travel hub, with flights to/from cities all over the world. Within Europe, low-cost airlines land/take off in **Rotterdam** (RTM; ☎010-446 34 44; www.rotterdamthehagueairport.nl; wifi) and **Eindhoven** (EIN; www.vliegeindhovenairport.nl; Luchthavenweg 25; ⏲4.30am-midnight).

LAND

Bus

Eurolines (www.eurolines.com) Cheap international bus services to/from the Netherlands.

Busabout (www.busabout.com) From May to October, buses complete set circuits around Europe, stopping at major cities.

Flixbus (www.flixbus.com) Low-cost, intercity bus travel between 27 European countries aboard comfy buses.

IC Bus (www.dbicbus.com) Bus links between the Netherlands and Germany.

Car & Motorcycle

➡ Drivers need vehicle registration papers, third-party insurance and their domestic licence. Get a Green Card from your insurer to show you have coverage.

➡ **ANWB** (www.anwb.nl) provides information, maps, advice and services if you show a membership card from your own automobile association, like the AA or AAA.

➡ Hitching is uncommon.

Train

International train connections are good. All Eurail and Inter-Rail passes are valid on the Dutch national train service, **NS** (Nederlandse Spoorwegen; www.ns.nl). Many international services are operated by **NS International** (www.nsinternational.nl).

Thalys (www.thalys.com) fast trains serve Brussels (where you can connect to the Eurostar) and Paris. Twice-daily **Eurostar** (www.

 FARES, TICKETS & OV-CHIPKAARTS

The easiest and cheapest way to travel with a ticket on trains and public transport (buses, trams and metros) is with a credit-loaded, plastic smart card known as an OV-chipkaart (www.ov-chipkaart.nl).

- Purchase an OV-chipkaart (€7.50), valid for five years, as soon as you arrive in the Netherlands at a train station, public-transport information office, supermarket or newsagent. Online, buy one in advance at www.public-transport-holland.com.
- Two types of OV-chipkaarts exist: 'anonymous' OV-chipkaarts are aimed at tourists and short-term visitors; 'personal' OV-chipkaarts require an address of residence in the Netherlands, Belgium, Germany or Luxembourg.
- To travel using your card, you must charge it with credit (minimum €10 on buses, or €20 to use it on NS trains) at any public-transport or station information counter or ticketing machine; the card must have sufficient credit to cover the cost of your journey.
- When you enter and exit a bus, tram or metro station, hold the card against a reader at the doors or station gates. The system then calculates your fare and deducts it from the card. If you don't check out, the system will deduct the highest fare possible. At train stations, card readers are strategically placed at platform entrances and exits.
- Upon departure from the county, you can retrieve any leftover credit from your card at any public-transport or station information counter; you'll pay a €1 fee to do this.
- For single journeys, if you don't have an OV-chipkaart, you can effectively purchase a more expensive, single-use, disposable OV-chipkaart each time you board a bus or tram, or buy a train ticket. On trains, this translates in reality as a €1 surcharge per transaction on top of the regular train fare.
- Some trams have conductors responsible for ticketing, while on others the drivers handle tickets. It is no longer possible to pay by cash on public transport in Amsterdam.

eurostar.com) services link London St Pancras with Rotterdam (three hours) and Amsterdam (3¾ hours).

German ICE high-speed trains run daily between Amsterdam and Cologne (from €35.00, three hours). Many continue to Frankfurt (from €45.90, four to 4¾ hours) via Frankfurt Airport.

Reserve seats in advance during peak periods. Buy tickets online at **SNCB Europe** (www.b-europe.com).

SEA

Several companies operate car/passenger ferries between the Netherlands and the UK:

Stena Line (www.stenaline.co.uk) sails between Harwich and Hoek van Holland, 31km northwest of Rotterdam, linked to central Rotterdam by train (30 minutes).

P&O Ferries (www.poferries.com) operates an overnight ferry every evening (11¾ hours) between Hull and Europoort, 39km west of central Rotterdam. Book bus tickets (40 minutes) to/from Rotterdam when you reserve your berth.

DFDS Seaways (www.dfdsseaways.co.uk) sails between Newcastle and IJmuiden, 30km northwest of Amsterdam, linked to Amsterdam by bus; the 15-hour sailings depart daily.

 Getting Around

The Netherlands' compact size makes it a breeze to get around.

Bicycle Short- and long-distance bike routes lace the country and you are often pedalling through beautiful areas. All but the smallest train stations have bike-rental shops, as does every town and city.

Bus Cheaper and slower than trains but useful for remote villages not serviced by rail.

Car Good for visiting regions with minimal public transport. Drive on the right.

Train Service is fast, distances short, and trains frequent; buy an OV-chipkaart to get cheaper tickets and use on other forms of public transport too.

Portugal

POP 10.4 MILLION

Includes ➡

Best Places to Eat

- ➡ Alma (p518)
- ➡ Euskalduna Studio (p535)
- ➡ Taberna Típica Quarta Feira (p527)
- ➡ Antiga Confeitaria de Belém (p518)
- ➡ O Abocanhado (p540)

Best Places to Stay

- ➡ Casa do Príncipe (p517)
- ➡ Guest House Douro (p533)
- ➡ Albergaria do Calvario (p526)
- ➡ Dona Emilia (p537)
- ➡ Yeatman (p534)
- ➡ Moon Hill Hostel (p521)

Why Go?

With medieval castles, frozen-in-time villages, captivating cities and golden-sand bays, the Portuguese experience can mean many things. History, terrific food and wine, lyrical scenery and all-night partying are just the beginning. Portugal's cinematically beautiful capital, Lisbon, and its soulful northern rival, Porto, are two of Europe's most charismatic cities. Both are a joy to stroll, with gorgeous river views, rattling trams and tangled lanes hiding boutiques and vintage shops, new-wave bars, and a seductive mix of restaurants, fado (traditional Portuguese melancholic song) clubs and open-air cafes. Beyond the cities, Portugal's landscape unfolds in all its beauty. Here, you can stay overnight in converted hilltop fortresses fronting age-old vineyards, hike amid granite peaks or explore medieval villages in the little-visited hinterland. More than 800km of coast shelters some of Europe's best beaches.

When to Go

Lisbon

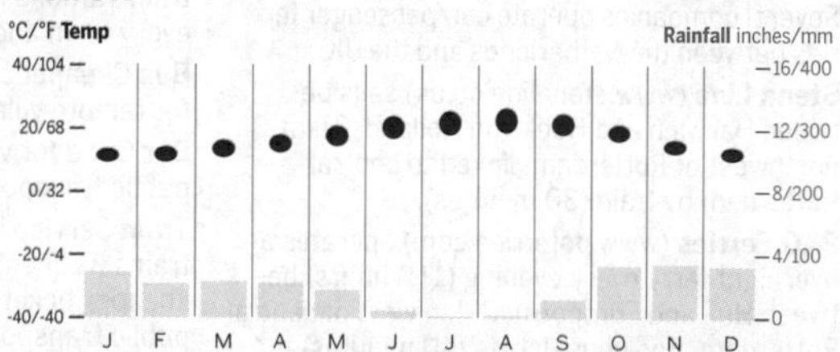

Apr & May Sunny days and wildflowers set the stage for hiking and outdoor activities.

Jun–Aug Lovely and lively, with a packed festival calendar and steamy beach days.

Late Sep & Oct Crisp mornings and sunny days; prices dip and crowds disperse.

Entering the Country

An increasingly popular destination, Portugal is well connected to North America and European countries by air. There are also handy overland links by bus and rail to and from Spain, from where you can continue on to other destinations on the continent – eg, the Sud Expresso train from Lisbon, which connects directly to Paris-bound TGV trains via the Spanish/French border at Irún/Hendaye.

ITINERARIES

One Week

Begin your journey in Porto (p532), gateway to the magical wine-growing region of the Douro valley (p533). Then head south to Coimbra (p530), Portugal's most venerable university town. Finish with three days to Lisbon (p513), including a night of fado in the Alfama, bar-hopping in Bairro Alto and pastry-eating in Belém.

Two Weeks

Explore Lisbon's environs, taking in the wooded wonderland of Sintra (p520), the crenellated charms of Óbidos (p528) and the Unesco-listed monastery at Tomar (p529). Next, head south, strolling the medieval lanes and Roman ruins of Évora (p526) before hitting the fabled beaches of the Algarve (p522). Follow the contours of Portugal's southern coast all the way to the dramatic end-of-the-continent cliffs at Sagres (p525) before flying home from Faro.

Essential Food & Drink

Cod for all seasons The Portuguese have dozens of ways to prepare *bacalhau* (dried salt cod). Try *bacalhau a brás* (grated cod fried with potatoes and eggs), *bacalhau espiritual* (cod soufflé) or *bacalhau com natas* (baked cod with cream and grated cheese).

Drink Port and red wines from the Douro valley, alvarinho and vinho verde (crisp, semi-sparkling wine) from the Minho and great, little-known reds from the Alentejo and the Beiras (particularly the Dão region).

Field and fowl *Porco preto* (sweet 'black' pork), *leitão* (roast suckling pig), *alheira* (bread and meat sausage – formerly Kosher), *cabrito assado* (roast kid) and *arroz de pato* (duck risotto).

Pastries The *pastel de nata* (custard tart) is legendary, especially in Belém. Other delicacies: *travesseiros* (almond and egg pastries) and *queijadas* (mini-cheese pastries).

Seafood Char-grilled *lulas* (squid), *polvo* (octopus) or *sardinhas* (sardines). Other treats: *cataplana* (seafood and sausage cooked in a copper pot), *caldeirada* (hearty fish stew) and *açorda de mariscos* (bread stew with shrimp).

AT A GLANCE

Area 88,323 sq km

Capital Lisbon

Country code ☎351

Currency euro (€)

Emergency ambulance, fire and police ☎112

Language Portuguese

Time GMT/UTC in winter, GMT/UTC plus one hour in summer.

Visas Schengen rules apply.

Sleeping Price Ranges

The following price ranges refer to a double room with bathroom in high season. Unless otherwise stated breakfast is included in the price.

€ less than €60

€€ €60–120

€€€ more than €120

Eating Price Ranges

The following price ranges refer to a main course.

€ less than €10

€€ €10–20

€€€ more than €20

Resources

Lonely Planet (www.lonelyplanet.com/portugal)

Portugal Tourism (www.visitportugal.com)

Wines of Portugal (www.winesofportugal.info)

Portugal Highlights

1 Alfama (p513) Following the sound of fado spilling from the lamplit lanes of this enchanting old-world neighbourhood in the heart of Lisbon.

2 Tavira (p523) Taking in the town's laid-back charms, before hitting some of the Algarve's prettiest beaches.

3 Coimbra (p530) Catching live music in a backstreet bar in this festive university town with a stunning medieval centre.

4 Sintra (p520) Exploring the wooded hills, studded with fairy tale palaces, villas and gardens.

5 Parque Nacional da Peneda-Gerês (p539) Conquering the park's ruggedly scenic trails.

6 Lagos (p524) Enjoying heady beach days in this surf-loving town with a vibrant drinking and dining scene.

7 Porto (p532) Exploring the Unesco World Heritage–listed city centre and sampling velvety ports at riverside wine lodges.

LISBON

POP 547,733

Spread across steep hillsides that overlook the Rio Tejo, Lisbon has captivated visitors for centuries. Windswept vistas at breathtaking heights reveal the city in all its beauty: Roman and Moorish ruins, white-domed cathedrals and grand plazas lined with sun-drenched cafes. The real delight of discovery, though, is delving into the narrow cobblestone lanes.

As bright-yellow trams clatter through curvy tree-lined streets, *lisboêtas* (residents of Lisbon) stroll through lamplit old quarters and exchange gossip over glasses of wine while fado singers perform in the background. In other parts of town, Lisbon reveals its youthful alter ego at stylish dining rooms and lounges, late-night street parties, riverside nightspots, and boutiques selling all things classic and cutting-edge.

Sights

★Castelo de São Jorge CASTLE

(www.castelodesaojorge.pt; adult/student/child €8.50/4/free; ⌚9am-9pm Mar-Oct, to 6pm Nov-Feb) Towering dramatically above Lisbon, the mid-11th-century hilltop fortifications of Castelo de São Jorge sneak into almost every snapshot. Roam its snaking ramparts and pine-shaded courtyards for superlative views over the city's red rooftops to the river. Three guided tours daily (in Portuguese, English and Spanish) at 10.30am, 1pm and 4pm are included in the admission price (additional tours available).

★Mosteiro dos Jerónimos MONASTERY

(www.mosteirojeronimos.pt; Praça do Império; adult/child €10/5, free Sun until 2pm for Portuguese citizens/residents only; ⌚10am-6.30pm Tue-Sun Jun-Sep, to 5.30pm Oct-May) Belém's undisputed heart-stealer is this Unesco-listed monastery. The *mosteiro* is the stuff of pure fantasy; a fusion of Diogo de Boitaca's creative vision and the spice and pepper dosh of Manuel I, who commissioned it to trumpet Vasco da Gama's discovery of a sea route to India in 1498.

★Museu Calouste Gulbenkian – Coleção do Fundador MUSEUM

(Founder's Collection; www.gulbenkian.pt; Av de Berna 45A; Coleção do Fundador/Coleção Moderna combo ticket adult/child €10/free, temporary exhibitions €3-6, free Sun from 2pm; ⌚10am-6pm Wed-Mon) Famous for its outstanding quality and breadth, the world-class Founder's Collection at Museu Calouste Gulbenkian showcases an epic collection of Western and Eastern art – from Egyptian treasures to Old Master and Impressionist paintings. Admission includes the separately housed **Coleção Moderna** (Modern Collection).

★Tram 28E TRAM

(Largo Martim Moniz) Don't leave the city without riding popular tram 28E from Largo Martim Moniz. This rickety, screechy, gloriously old-fashioned ride from Praça Martim Moniz to Campo de Ourique provides 45 minutes of mood-lifting views and absurdly steep climbs. With its polished wood panelling, bee-yellow paint job and chrome fittings, the century-old tram is like the full-scale model of a fastidious Hornby Railways collector.

Torre de Belém TOWER

(www.torrebelem.pt; Av de Brasília; adult/child €6/3, ⌚10am-6.30pm Tue-Sun May-Sep, to 5.30pm Oct-Apr) Jutting out onto the Rio Tejo, this Unesco World Heritage–listed fortress epitomises the Age of Discoveries. You'll need to breathe in to climb the narrow spiral staircase to the tower, which affords sublime views over Belém and the river.

Praça do Comércio PLAZA

(Terreiro do Paço; Praça do Comércio) With its grand 18th-century arcades, lemon-meringue facades and mosaic cobbles, the riverfront

HEAVENLY VIEWS

Lisbon's *miradouros* (lookouts) lift spirits with their heavenly views. Some have outdoor cafes for lingering.

Largo das Portas do Sol Moorish gateway with stunning views over Alfama's rooftops.

Miradouro da Graça (Largo da Graça) Pine-fringed square that's perfect for sundowners.

Miradouro da Senhora do Monte (Rua da Senhora do Monte) The highest lookout, with memorable castle views.

Miradouro de São Pedro de Alcântara (Rua São Pedro de Alcântara; ⌚viewpoint 24hr, kiosk 10am-midnight Sun-Wed, to 2am Thu-Sat) Drinks and sweeping views on the edge of Bairro Alto.

Miradouro de Santa Catarina (Rua de Santa Catarina; ⌚24hr) Youthful spot with guitar-playing rebels, artful graffiti and far-reaching views.

Central Lisbon

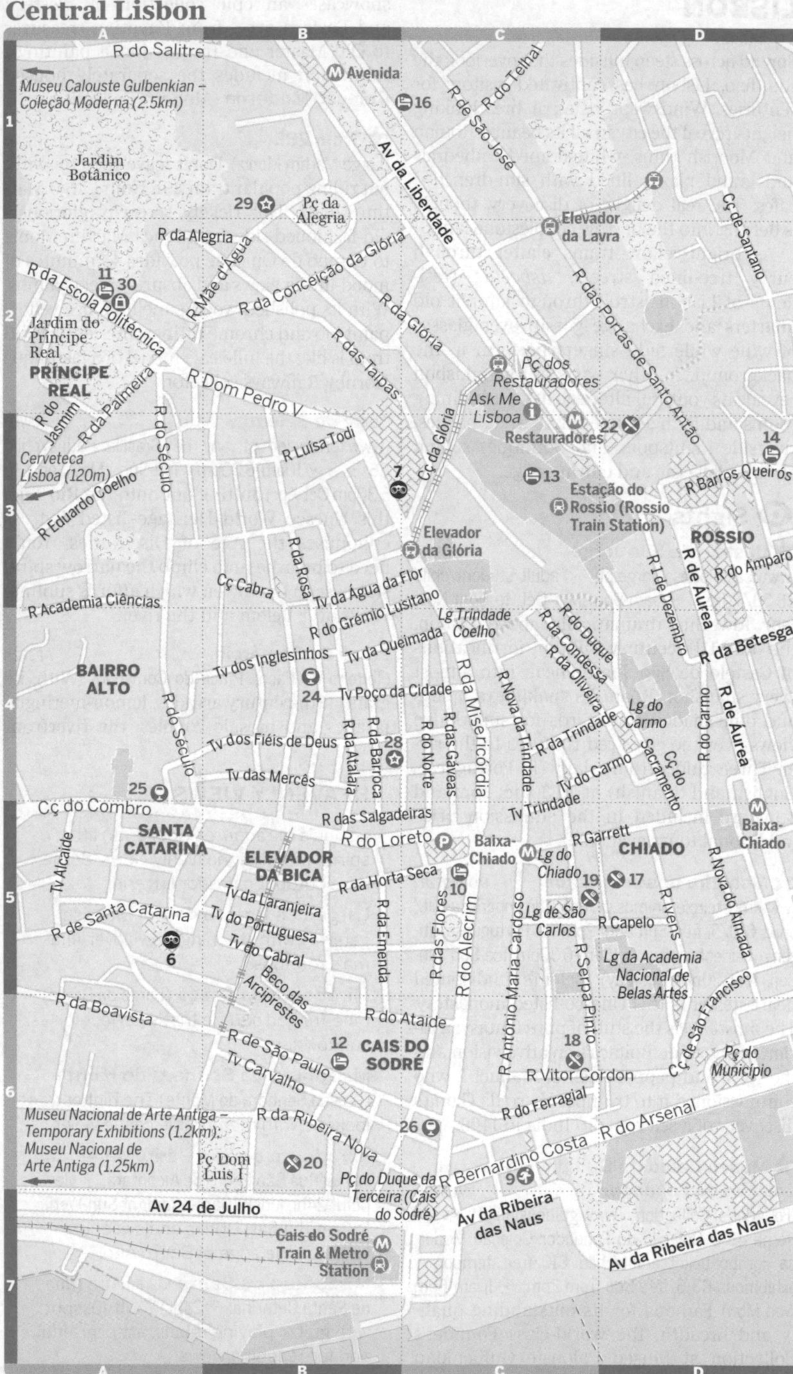

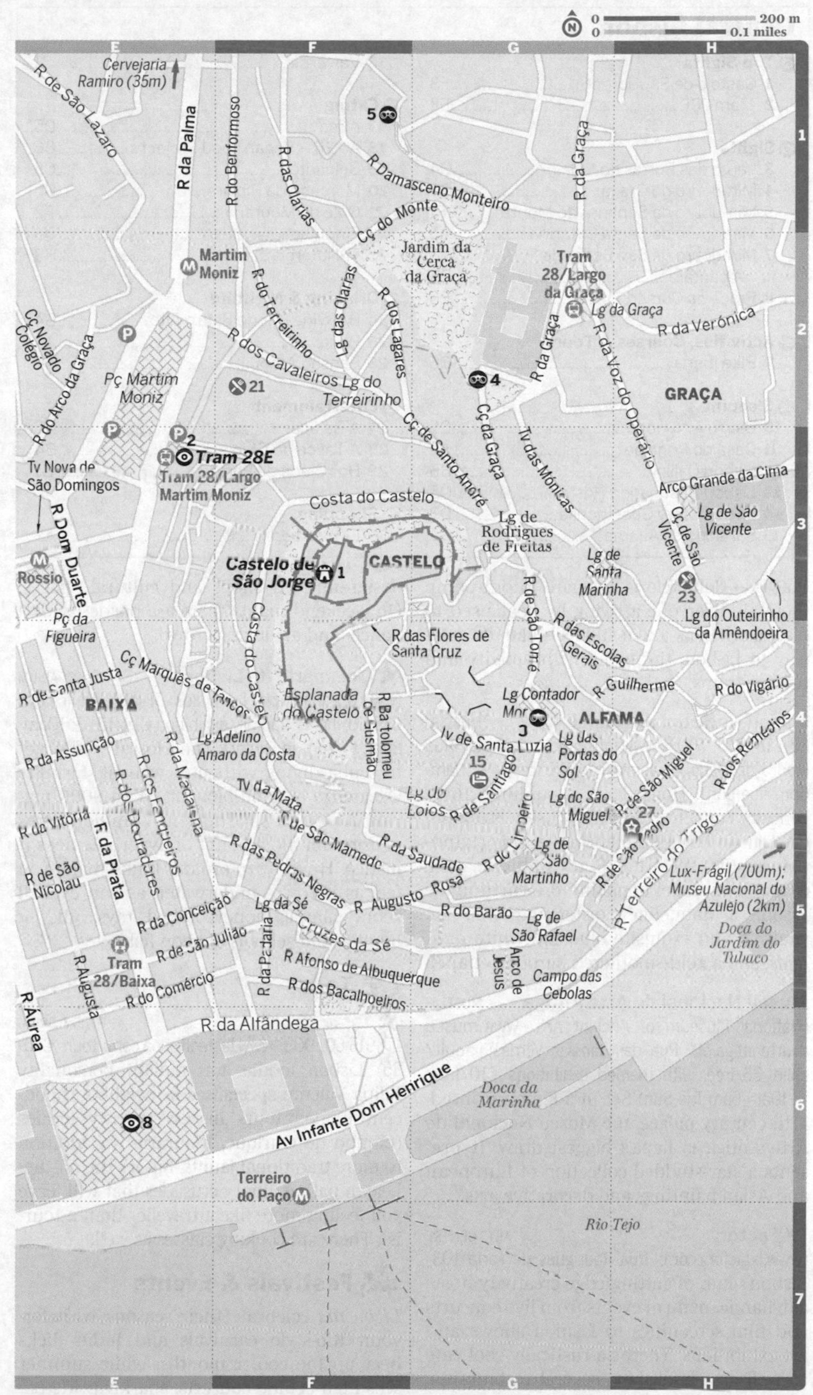
0 200 m
0 0.1 miles
Cervejaria Ramiro (35m)
R de São Lazaro
R da Palma
R do Benformoso
R das Olarias
R Damasceno Monteiro
Cç do Monte
R da Graça
Jardim da Cerca da Graça
Tram 28/Largo da Graça
Lg da Graça
R da Verónica
Martim Moniz
R do Terreirinho
Lg das Olarias
R dos Lagares
R dos Cavaleiros
Lg do Terreirinho
Cç Novado Colégio
R do Arco da Graça
Pç Martim Moniz
21
4
5
R da Graça
R da Voz do Operário
GRAÇA
Cç de Santo André
Cç da Graça
Tv das Mónicas
2
Tram 28E
Tram 28/Largo Martim Moniz
Tv Nova de São Domingos
Costa do Castelo
Arco Grande da Cima
Lg de São Vicente
Cç de São Vicente
Lg de Rodrigues de Freitas
R Dom Duarte
Rossio
Castelo de São Jorge
1
CASTELO
Lg de Santa Marinha
23
R de São Tomé
Lg do Outeirinho da Amêndoeira
Pç da Figueira
Costa do Castelo
R das Flores de Santa Cruz
R das Escolas Gerais
Cç Marquês de Tancos
R de Santa Justa
BAIXA
Esplanada do Castelo
R Bartolomeu de Gusmão
Lg Contador Mor
R Guilherme
R do Vigário
ALFAMA
R dos Remédios
Lg Adelino Amaro da Costa
Tv de Santa Luzia
Lg das Portas do Sol
R da Assunção
R da Madalena
R dos Fanqueiros
R dos Douradores
15
R de Santiago
R de São Miguel
Tv da Mata
Lg do Loios
Lg de São Miguel
27
R da Vitória
F. da Prata
R de São Mamede
R do Limoeiro
R de São Pedro
R Terreiro do Trigo
R das Pedras Negras
R da Saudade
Lg de São Martinho
Lux-Frágil (700m); Museu Nacional do Azulejo (2km)
R de São Nicolau
R Augusto Rosa
R da Conceição
Lg da Sé
R do Barão
Lg de São Rafael
Doca do Jardim do Tabaco
Cruzes da Sé
R de São Julião
Tram 28/Baixa
R da Padaria
R Afonso de Albuquerque
Arco de Jesus
Campo das Cebolas
R Augusta
R do Comércio
R dos Bacalhoeiros
R Áurea
R da Alfândega
Doca da Marinha
8
Av Infante Dom Henrique
Terreiro do Paço
Rio Tejo
PORTUGAL

Central Lisbon

Top Sights
1 Castelo de São Jorge....F3
2 Tram 28E....E3

Sights
3 Largo das Portas do Sol....G4
4 Miradouro da Graça....G2
5 Miradouro da Senhora do Monte....F1
6 Miradouro de Santa Catarina....A5
7 Miradouro de São Pedro de Alcântara....B3
8 Praça do Comércio....E6

Activities, Courses & Tours
9 Bike Iberia....C6

Sleeping
10 Bairro Alto Hotel....C5
11 Casa do Príncipe....A2
12 Lisbon Calling....B6
13 Lisbon Destination Hostel....C3
14 Lisbon Story Guesthouse....D3
15 Santiago de Alfama....G4
16 Valverde....C1

Eating
17 Alma....D5
18 Ao 26 – Vegan Food Project....C6
19 Belcanto....C5
20 Mercado da Ribeira....B6
21 O Zé da Mouraria....F2
22 Pinóquio....D3
23 Ti-Natércia....H3

Drinking & Nightlife
24 BA Wine Bar do Bairro Alto....B4
25 Park....A4
26 Pensão Amor....C6

Entertainment
27 A Baiuca....H5
28 A Tasca do Chico....B4
29 Hot Clube de Portugal....B1

Shopping
30 Embaixada....A2

Praça do Comércio is a square to out-pomp them all. Everyone arriving by boat used to disembark here, and it still feels like the gateway to Lisbon, thronging with activity and rattling trams.

Museu Nacional do Azulejo MUSEUM
(☎218 100 340; www.museudoazulejo.pt; Rua Madre de Deus 4; adult/child €5/free; ⏲10am-6pm Tue-Sun) Housed in a sublime 16th-century convent, Lisbon's Museu Nacional do Azulejo covers the entire *azulejo* (hand-painted tile) spectrum. Star exhibits feature a 36m-long panel depicting pre-earthquake Lisbon, a Manueline cloister with web-like vaulting and exquisite blue-and-white *azulejos,* and a gold-smothered baroque chapel.

Museu Nacional de Arte Antiga MUSEUM
(National Museum of Ancient Art; www.museudearteantiga.pt; Rua das Janelas Verdes; adult/child €6/free, with themed exhibitions €10/free; ⏲10am-6pm Tue-Sun) Set in a lemon-fronted, 17th-century palace, the Museu Nacional de Arte Antiga is Lapa's biggest draw. It presents a star-studded collection of European and Asian paintings and decorative arts.

LX Factory ARTS CENTRE
(www.lxfactory.com; Rua Rodrigues de Faria 103) Lisbon's hub of cutting-edge creativity hosts a dynamic menu of events from live concerts and film screenings to fashion shows and art exhibitions. There's a rustically cool cafe as well as a bookshop, several restaurants, design-minded shops and cultural spaces. On weekend nights there are parties with a dance- and art-loving crowd.

★ **Oceanário de Lisboa** AQUARIUM
(www.oceanario.pt; Doca dos Olivais; adult/child €15/10, incl temporary exhibition €18/12; ⏲10am-8pm, to 7pm in winter) The closest you'll get to scuba diving without a wetsuit, Lisbon's Oceanário is mind-blowing. With 8000 marine creatures splashing in 7 million litres of seawater, no amount of hyperbole does it justice. Huge wrap-around tanks make you feel as if you're underwater, as you eyeball zebra sharks, honeycombed rays, gliding mantas and schools of neon fish.

Tours

★ **Taste of Lisboa** FOOD & DRINK
(☎915 601 908; www.tasteoflisboa.com; tours €70-85) Lisbon foodie and radiant personality Filipa Valente specialises in neighbourhood-centric food tours in less touristy locales (Campo de Ourique, Mouraria) in addition to more traditional jaunts, but it's the off-the-beaten-path culinary crusades that will leave you feeling more like a traveller than a tourist. There are cooking classes as well.

Festivals & Events

Lisboêtas celebrate their seasons with fervour. Rio-style carnivals and indie flicks heat up the cooler months, while summer sees high-octane concerts, sparkly pride parading and saintly celebrations of feasting and matchmaking. *Fazer a festa* (partying) is considered a birthright in Portugal's live-wire capital. For up-to-date listings, pick up the tourist board's free magazine *Follow Me Lisboa* (www.visitlisboa.com/about-turismo-de-lisboa/publications).

Sleeping

★Lisbon Calling HOSTEL €
(☎213 432 381; www.lisboncalling.net; Rua de São Paulo 126, 3rd fl; dm from €20, d with/without bathroom from €75/55; @📶) This fashionable, unsigned backpacker favourite near Santa Catarina features original frescoes, *azulejos* and hardwood floors – all lovingly restored by friendly Portuguese owners. The bright, spacious dorms and a brick-vaulted kitchen are easy on the eye, but the private rooms – specifically room 1812 – will floor you. boutique-hotel-level dens of style and comfort that thunderously out-punch their price point.

Lisbon Destination Hostel HOSTEL €
(☎213 466 457; www.followyourdestination.com; Rossio train station, 2nd fl; dm €25, s/d without bathroom from €36/54, d from €107; @📶) Housed in Lisbon's loveliest train station, this world-class hostel has a glass ceiling that lights the spacious plant-filled common area. Rooms are crisp and well kept, and there are loads of activities (bar crawls, beach day trips etc). Facilities include a shared kitchen, game consoles, movie room (with popcorn) and a 24-hour self-service bar. The breakfast with crêpes and fresh fruit is top-notch.

Lisbon Story Guesthouse GUESTHOUSE €€
(☎218 879 392; www.lisbonstoryguesthouse.com; Largo de São Domingos 18; d €80-100, without bathroom €50-70, apt €110-120; @📶) 🍃 Overlooking Largo de São Domingos, Lisbon Story is a small, extremely welcoming guesthouse with nicely maintained, light-drenched rooms, all of which sport Portuguese themes (the Tejo, tram 28E, fado etc), plus working antique radios, record players and the like. The lounge, with throw pillows and low tables, is a great place to chill.

★Casa do Príncipe B&B €€
(☎218 264 183; www.casadoprincipe.com; Praça do Príncipe Real 23; d €108-209; ❄📶) Perfectly located and exquisitely restored (and accordingly priced to shock!), this 14-room B&B is housed inside what was once the same 19th-century neo-Moorish palace as **Embaixada** (www.embaixadalx.pt; Praça do Príncipe Real 26; ⊙noon-8pm Mon-Fri, 11am-7pm Sat & Sun, restaurants to 2am) next door. Original frescoes, *azulejos* and ornate moulded ceilings adorn the hardwood halls and spacious rooms, which are themed after the life of King Dom Pedro V. Indeed, you'll sleep like royalty here yourself.

Bairro Alto Hotel BOUTIQUE HOTEL €€€
(☎213 408 288; www.bairroaltohotel.com; Praça Luís de Camões 2; r from €380; P❄📶) On a pretty square is Lisbon's most storied luxury hotel, dating from 1921. It reopened in early 2019 after a massive €30 million redesign by Pritzker Prize–winning architect Eduardo Souto de Moura, who oversaw 32 new rooms, a redesigned reception and an entirely new 5th-floor restaurant (BAHR, by lauded chef Nuno Mendes) with a panoramic terrace for food and sundowners.

★Santiago de Alfama BOUTIQUE HOTEL €€€
(☎213 941 616; www.santiagodealfama.com; Rua de Santiago 10; d/ste from €285/660; ❄📶🏊) In 2015 Dutch hospitality dreamer Heleen Uitenbroek turned a ruined 15th-century palace into luxury sleeps at this 19-room bastion of style. It's airy and awash in light pinewoods and contemporary art, and exquisite attention to detail is everywhere, from the Santiago-cross-inspired tile flooring and textured bathroom tiling to an encased glass hallway revealing uncovered Roman steps.

Valverde BOUTIQUE HOTEL €€€
(☎210 940 300; www.valverdehotel.com; Av da Liberdade 164; d €302-410, ste €446-646; P❄@📶🏊) Exquisite Valverde feels like a boutique town house (which it once was). Its facade is not showy, but once inside, an urban oasis of discerning design and personalised service is subtly unveiled. Reached by black-dominated, hushed hallways, the

CYCLING THE TEJO

A cycling/jogging path courses along the Tejo for 7km, between Cais do Sodré and Belém. Complete with artful touches – including the poetry of Pessoa printed along parts of it – the path takes in ageing warehouses, weathered docks, and open-air restaurants and nightspots.

A handy place to rent bikes is a short stroll from Cais do Sodré: **Bike Iberia** (☎969 630 369; www.bikeiberia.com; Largo Corpo Santo 5; bike hire per hour/day from €5/15, e-bike €20/35; ⊙9.30am-5.30pm).

25 rooms elicit style, form and function, and feature cultured European art and unique mid-century-modern pieces.

Eating

Mercado da Ribeira MARKET €
(www.timeoutmarket.com; Av 24 de Julho; 10am-midnight Sun-Wed, to 2am Thu-Sat, traditional market 6am-2pm Mon-Sat;) Doing trade in fresh fruit and veg, fish and flowers since 1892, this domed market hall has been the word on everyone's lips since *Time Out* transformed half of it into a gourmet food court in 2014. Now it's Lisbon in chaotic culinary microcosm: Garrafeira Nacional wines, Café de São Bento steaks, Manteigaria Silva cold cuts and Michelin-star chef creations from Henrique Sá Pessoa.

Ti-Natércia PORTUGUESE €
(218 862 133; Rua Escola Gerais 54; mains €5.50-12; 7pm-midnight Tue-Fri, noon-3pm & 7pm-midnight Sat) 'Aunt' Natércia and her downright delicious Portuguese home cooking is a tough ticket: there are but a mere six tables and they fill up fast. She'll talk your ear off (and doesn't mince words – some have been rubbed the wrong way; vegetarians in particular should avoid) while you devour her excellent take on the classics. Reservations are essential (cash only).

Ao 26 – Vegan Food Project VEGAN €
(967 989 184; www.facebook.com/ao26veganfoodproject; Rua Vítor Cordon 26; mains €5.50-7.50; 12.30-6.30pm & 7.30-11pm Tue-Sat;) So good it even lures in devout carnivores, this small, hip and bustling vegan place offers two elaborate, daily-changing chalkboard specials (eg Manchurian meatballs with tomato, coconut and masala). There's a fixed menu of loaded lentil burgers, beet burgers and veg sandwiches on *bolo do caco* (round bread cooked on a basalt stone slab), plus Lisbon craft beer.

★**Antiga Confeitaria de Belém** PASTRIES €
(Pastéis de Belém; www.pasteisdebelem.pt; Rua de Belém 84-92; pastries from €1.10; 8am-11pm Oct-Jun, to midnight Jul-Sep) Since 1837 this patisserie has been transporting locals to sugar-coated nirvana with heavenly *pastéis de Belém*. The crisp pastry nests are filled with custard cream, baked at 200°C for that perfect golden crust, then lightly dusted with cinnamon. Admire *azulejos* in the vaulted rooms or devour a still-warm tart at the counter and try to guess the secret ingredient.

Pinóquio PORTUGUESE €€
(213 465 106; www.restaurantepinoquio.pt; Praça dos Restauradores 79; mains €17-26; noon-midnight;) Bustling Pinóquio is easy to miss as it's tucked into a *praça* corner partially obstructed by a souvenir kiosk. Dressed in white tablecloths against pea-green walls, it's distinctly old school, with indomitable waiters slinging a stunning slew of classic dishes: *arroz de pato* (duck rice), seafood *feijoada, arroz de bacalhau* (codfish rice), and pork chops with almonds and coriander.

★**O Zé da Mouraria** PORTUGUESE €€
(218 865 436; Rua João do Outeiro 24; mains for 2 €16.50-33.50; noon-4pm Mon-Sat;) Don't be fooled by the saloon-like doors, there's a typical Portuguese *tasca* (tavern) inside. With homey local cuisine, blue-and-white-tiled walls and chequered tablecloths it's one of Lisbon's best. The house-baked cod loaded with chickpeas, onions, garlic and olive oil is rightfully popular, and daily specials (duck rice on Wednesday!) make return trips tempting.

★**Alma** MODERN PORTUGUESE €€€
(213 470 650; www.almalisboa.pt; Rua Anchieta 15; mains €32-36, tasting menus €110-120; noon-3pm & 7-11pm Tue-Sun;) Two-Michelin-starred Henrique Sá Pessoa's flagship Alma is one of Portugal's destination restaurants and, in our humble opinion, Lisbon's best gourmet dining experience. The casual space exudes understated style amid the original stone flooring and gorgeous hardwood tables, but it's Pessoa's outrageously good nouveau Portuguese cuisine that draws the foodie flock from far and wide.

Cervejaria Ramiro SEAFOOD €€€
(www.cervejariaramiro.pt; Av Almirante Reis 1; seafood per kg €12-91; noon-12.30am Tue-Sun) Opened in 1956, Ramiro has legendary status among Lisbon's seafood lovers. Here you can feast on rich plates of giant tiger prawns, *percebes* (goose barnacles), lobster, crab and clams, and even juicy steak sandwiches.

Belcanto PORTUGUESE €€€
(213 420 607; www.belcanto.pt; Largo de São Carlos 10; mains €49.50, tasting menu €165-185 with 5/9 wines €100/120; 12.30-3pm & 7-11pm Tue-Sat;) José Avillez' two-Michelin-starred cathedral of cookery wows diners with painstaking creativity, polished service and a first-rate sommelier. Standouts among Lisbon's culinary adventure of a lifetime include suckling pig with orange purée; sea bass with seaweed and bivalves; and Avillez' masterstroke,

the Garden of the Goose that Laid the Golden Eggs (egg, crunchy bread and mushrooms). Paired wines sometimes date from the '70s!

Drinking & Nightlife

★Park BAR

(www.facebook.com/parklisboaofficial; Calçada do Combro 58; ⏱1pm-2am Tue-Sat, to 8pm Sun; 📶) If only all multistorey car parks were like this... Take the lift to the 5th floor, and head up and around to the top, which has been transformed into one of Lisbon's hippest rooftop bars, with sweeping views reaching right down to the Rio Tejo and over the bell towers of Igreja de Santa Catarina.

★Cerveteca Lisboa CRAFT BEER

(www.cervetecalisboa.com; Praça das Flores 62; ⏱3.30pm-1am Sun-Thu, to 2am Fri & Sat; 📶) Lisbon's best craft-beer bar is a boozy godsend: 14 oft-changing taps (including two hand pumps) focusing on local and Northern European artisanal brews, including numerous local microbreweries. Not only will hopheads rejoice at IPAs from Lisbon including standouts such as Dois Corvos and 8ª Colina, but having choice alone inspires cartwheels. *Adeus,* tasteless lagers!

Pensão Amor BAR

(www.pensaoamor.pt; Rua do Alecrím 19; ⏱2pm-3am Sun-Wed, to 4am Thu-Sat) Set inside a former brothel, this cheeky bar pays homage to its passion-filled past with colourful wall murals, a library of erotically tinged works, and a small stage where you can sometimes catch burlesque shows.

Lux-Frágil CLUB

(www.luxfragil.com; Av Infante D Henrique, Armazém A, Cais de Pedra; ⏱11pm-6am Thu-Sat) Lisbon's ice-cool, must-see club, glammy Lux hosts big-name DJs spinning electro and house. It was started by late Lisbon nightlife impresario Marcel Reis and is part-owned by John Malkovich. Grab a spot on the terrace to see the sun rise over the Rio Tejo, or chill like a king or queen on the throne-like giant interior chairs.

BA Wine Bar do Bairro Alto WINE BAR

(☎213 461 182; bawinebar@gmail.com; Rua da Rosa 107; ⏱6-11pm Tue-Sun; 📶) Reserve ahead unless you want to get shut out of Bairro Alto's best wine bar, where the genuinely welcoming staff will offer you three fantastic tasting choices based on your wine proclivities (wines from €5; tasting boards for one/four €13/47). The cheeses (from small artisanal producers) and charcuterie (melt-in-your-mouth black-pork *presuntos*) are not to be missed, either. Reservations are essential.

Entertainment

★Hot Clube de Portugal JAZZ

(☎213 460 305; www.hcp.pt; Praça da Alegria 48; ⏱10pm-2am Tue-Sat) As hot as its name suggests, this small, poster-plastered cellar (and newly added garden) has staged top-drawer jazz acts since the 1940s. It's considered one of Europe's best.

A Baiuca LIVE MUSIC

(☎218 867 284; Rua de São Miguel 20; ⏱8pm-midnight Thu-Mon) On a good night, walking into A Baiuca is like gate-crashing a family party. It's a special place with *fado vadio* (street fado), where locals take a turn and spectators hiss if anyone dares to chat during the singing. There's a €25 minimum spend, which is as tough to swallow as the food, though the fado is spectacular. Reserve ahead.

A Tasca do Chico LIVE MUSIC

(☎961 339 696; www.facebook.com/atasca.dochico; Rua do Diário de Notícias 39; ⏱7pm-1.30am Sun-Thu, to 3am Fri & Sat) This crowded dive (reserve ahead), full of soccer banners and spilling over with people of all ilks, is a fado free-for-all. It's not uncommon for taxi drivers to roll up, hum a few bars, and hop right back into their cabs, speeding off into the night.

Information

British Hospital (☎217 104 600; www.british-hospital.pt; Rua Tomás da Fonseca) English-speaking doctors and staff.

Farmácia Estácio (Praça Dom Pedro IV 62; ⏱8.30am-8pm Mon-Fri, 10am-7pm Sat & Sun) A central, English-speaking pharmacy.

Ask Me Lisboa (☎213 463 314; www.askmelisboa.com; Praça dos Restauradores, Palácio Foz; ⏱9am-8pm) Lisbon's largest and most helpful tourist office has maps and information, and books accommodation and rental cars.

Getting There & Away

AIR

Around 6km north of the centre, **Aeroporto de Lisboa** (Lisbon Airport; ☎218 413 500; www.ana.pt/pt/lis/home; Alameda das Comunidades Portuguesas) operates direct flights to international hubs including London, New York, Paris and Frankfurt.

BUS

Lisbon's main long-distance bus terminal is **Sete Rios** (Praça General Humberto Delgado, Rua das

Laranjeiras), adjacent to both Jardim Zoológico metro station and Sete Rios train station. The big carriers, **Rede Expressos** (☎707 223 344; www.rede-expressos.pt; Praça General Humberto Delgado, Terminal Rodoviário de Sete Rios; ⏰info booth 9am-1pm & 2-6pm Mon-Sat, 10am-2pm & 3-7pm Sun) and **Eva** (☎707 223 344; www.eva-bus.com; Praça General Humberto Delgado, Terminal Rodoviário de Sete Rios), run frequent services throughout Portugal.

The large bus terminal Gare do Oriente concentrates on services to the north and onto Spain and beyond. The biggest companies operating from here are **Renex/Rede Expressos/Citiexpress** (☎218 956 836; www.rede-expressos.pt; Via Recíproca 205, Gare do Oriente; ⏰7am-1pm) and Spanish operator **Avanza** (☎218 940 250; www.avanzabus.com; Av Dom João II, Gare do Oriente; ⏰8.30am-1pm & 2-8.15pm Mon-Fri, 8.30am-11am & 5-8.15pm Sat & Sun).

TRAIN

Gare do Oriente (Oriente Station; Av Dom João II) is Lisbon's biggest station. Trains to the Alentejo and the Algarve originate from here. **Santa Apolónia** is the terminal for trains from northern and central Portugal, **Cais do Sodré** serves Cascais and Estoril, and **Rossio** station offers frequent services to Sintra via Queluz. For fares and schedules, visit www.cp.pt.

Getting Around

TO/FROM THE AIRPORT

There's convenient metro access to the city centre from Aeroporto station; change at Alameda (green line) for Rossio and Baixa. A taxi for the 15-minute ride into central Lisbon costs around €16. Alternatively, buy a prepaid voucher to any address from Ask Me Lisboa in Arrivals. Uber and other app-based taxis pick up outside Departures (not Arrivals) and are considerably cheaper. You can also catch the Aerobus, which departs from outside Arrivals (adult/child €3.60/2, 25 to 35 minutes, every 20 minutes).

PUBLIC TRANSPORT

Public transport in Lisbon encompasses buses, trams, funiculars, lifts and a good metro system.

Metro Lisbon's subway is the quickest way around, running from 6.30am to 1am.

Tram The best way to get up into hilltop neighbourhoods (Alfama, Castelo, Graça) and western neighbourhoods (Estrela, Campo de Ourique). Runs from 5am/6am to about 10pm/11pm.

Bus An extensive network runs throughout the city. Buses operate from 5am/6am to about 10pm/11pm.

Elevadores and ascensors Lisbon's historic funiculars and lifts are the fastest way from lower neighbourhoods (Chiado, Baixa, Rossio) to hilltop neighbourhoods (Castelo, Glória, Graça).

Day passes (€6.40) allow unlimited travel over a 24-hour period on the entire bus, tram and metro network (€10.55 if you want to include Comboios de Portugal trains as well). If you're going to take more than five trips on the bus or metro on any given day, this is the best and easiest choice.

Lisboa Move-me (www.move-me.mobi; iOS/Android) and Lisboa Viagem by Transporlis (Android) are city-transportation apps for real-time routes and arrival/departure times.

AROUND LISBON

Sintra

POP 26,000

With its rippling mountains, dewy forests thick with ferns and lichen, exotic gardens and glittering palaces, Sintra is like a page torn from a fairy tale. Even Lord Byron waxed lyrical about Sintra's charms. Its Unesco World Heritage–listed centre, Sintra-Vila, is dotted with pastel-hued manors folded into luxuriant hills that roll down to the blue Atlantic. Sintra is *the* must-do side trip from Lisbon. Many do it in a day, but if time's not an issue, there's more than enough allure to keep you here for a few days.

Sights

★**Palácio Nacional de Sintra** PALACE
(www.parquesdesintra.pt; Largo Rainha Dona Amélia; adult/child €10/8.50; ⏰9.30am-7pm) The star of Sintra-Vila is this palace, with its iconic twin conical chimneys and lavish, whimsical interior, which is a mix of Moorish and Manueline styles, with arabesque courtyards, barley-twist columns and 15th- and 16th-century geometric *azulejos* (hand-painted tiles) that figure among Portugal's oldest.

Quinta da Regaleira NOTABLE BUILDING, GARDENS
(www.regaleira.pt; Rua Barbosa du Bocage; adult/child €6/4, tours €12/8; ⏰9.30am-7pm Apr-Sep, to 5pm Oct-Mar) This magical villa and gardens is a neo-Manueline extravaganza, dreamed up by Italian opera-set designer Luigi Manini, under the orders of Brazilian coffee tycoon António Carvalho Monteiro, aka 'Monteiro dos Milhões' ('Moneybags Monteiro'). The villa is surprisingly homey inside, despite its ferociously carved fireplaces, frescos and

Venetian-glass mosaics. Keep an eye out for mythological and Knights Templar symbols.

Castelo dos Mouros CASTLE

(www.parquesdesintra.pt; adult/child €8/6.50; ⏲9.30am-8pm) Soaring 412m above sea level, this mist-enshrouded ruined castle looms high above the surrounding forest. When the clouds peel away, the vistas over Sintra's palace-dotted hill and dale, across to the glittering Atlantic are – like the climb – breathtaking. The 10th-century Moorish castle's dizzying ramparts stretch across the mountain ridges and past moss-clad boulders the size of small buses. Tickets and info are available at the entrance (open 10am to 6pm).

Palácio Nacional da Pena PALACE

(www.parquesdesintra.pt; combined ticket with Parque da Pena adult/child €14/12.50; ⏲9.45am-7pm) Rising from a thickly wooded peak and often enshrouded in swirling mist, Palácio Nacional da Pena is a wacky confection of onion domes, Moorish keyhole gates, writhing stone snakes and crenellated towers in pinks and lemons. It is considered the greatest expression of 19th-century romanticism in Portugal.

Sleeping & Eating

★Moon Hill Hostel HOSTEL €

(☎219 243 755; www.moonhillhostel.com; Rua Guilherme Gomes Fernandes 17; dm €19-22, d with/without bathroom €75/55;) This design-forward, minimalist newcomer easily outshines the competition. Book a bed in a four-bed mixed dorm (with lockers), or a boutique-hotel-level private room, with colourful reclaimed-wood headboards and wall-covering photos of enchanting Sintra forest scenes (go for 10 or 14 for Palácio Nacional da Pena views; 12 or 13 for Moorish castle views). Either way, you're sleeping in high style.

Sintra 1012 B&B €€

(☎918 632 997; www.sintra1012.com; Rua Gil Vicente 10 & 12; dm €25, d €65-120, villas €120-150;) You'll probably need to go to war to book one of the eight spacious and smart rooms in this highly recommended guesthouse run by a young Portuguese-American couple. Behind original medieval walls, it's a modern minimalist retreat that, in Roman times, was Sintra's first theatre. Today it's all comfort and class, right down to the basement studio – an astonishing deal (€65).

Nau Palatina PORTUGUESE €€

(☎219 240 962; www.facebook.com/barnaupalatina; Calçada São Pedro 18, São Pedro de Penaferrim; tapas €1.50-11.90; ⏲6pm-midnight Tue-Sat;) Sintra's friendliest and most welcoming restaurant is a travel-highlight star in the making. Congenial owner Zé's creative tapas are as slightly off-centre as his location, a worthwhile 1km walk from Sintra centre in São Pedro de Penaferrim. Spice Route undertones are weaved throughout the small but tasty menu of tidbits, strongly forged from local and regional ingredients.

Information

Ask Me Sintra (☎219 231 157; www.visitlisboa.com; Praça da República 23; ⏲9.30am-6pm), near the centre of Sintra-Vila, is a helpful multilingual office with expert insight into Sintra and its surroundings. There's another small branch at **Sintra train station** (☎211 932 545; www.visitlisboa.com; Av Miguel Bombarda; ⏲9am-7pm).

Parques da Sintra – Monte da Lua (☎219 237 300; www.parquesdesintra.pt; Largo Sousa Brandão; ⏲9.30am-6pm Apr-Oct, 10am-5pm Nov-Mar), which manages most of Sintra's top sites, has a friendly information and ticket centre.

Getting There & Around

Trains run half-hourly between Sintra and Lisbon's Rossio station (€2.25, 40 minutes).

Scotturb (www.scotturb.com) bus 434 (€6.90) is handy for accessing the Castelo dos Mouros; it runs frequently from the train station via Sintra-Vila to the castle (10 minutes), Palácio Nacional da Pena (15 minutes) and back. One ticket gives you hop-on, hop-off access (in one direction; no backtracking).

Cascais

POP 35,000

Cascais (kush-*kaish*) has rocketed from sleepy fishing village to much-loved summertime playground of wave-frolicking *lisboêtas*. This 2018 European Youth Capital also boasts plenty of post-beach life, with winding lanes leading to small museums, cool gardens, a shiny marina and a pedestrianised old town dotted with designer boutiques, alfresco fish restaurants and lively bars.

Sights

Cascais' three sandy bays – **Praia da Conceição, Praia da Rainha** and **Praia da Ribeira** – are fine for a sunbake or a tingly Atlantic dip, but don't expect much towel space in summer. Atlantic waves pummel craggy **Boca do Inferno** (Mouth of Hell), 2km west of Cascais (about a 20-minute walk along the coast).

The best beach is wild, windswept **Praia do Guincho**, 9km northwest, a mecca to surfers and windsurfers with massive crashing rollers. The strong undertow can be dangerous for swimmers, but Guincho still lures nonsurfers with powder-soft sands, fresh seafood and magical sunsets.

Casa das Histórias Paula Rego MUSEUM
(www.casadashistoriaspaularego.com; Avenida da República 300; adult/child €5/free; 10am-6pm Tue-Sun, free 1st Sun of month) The Casa das Histórias Paula Rego showcases the disturbing, highly evocative paintings of Portugal's finest living artist. Biannually changing exhibits span Rego's career, from early work with collage in the 1950s to the twisted fairy tale–like tableaux of the 1980s, and up to the disturbing realism of more recent years.

Museu Condes de Castro Guimarães MUSEUM
(www.cm-cascais.pt/equipamento/museu-condes-de-castro-guimaraes; adult/child €4/free, free 1st Sun of month; 10am-6pm Tue-Sun) This whimsical early-19th-century mansion, complete with castle turrets and Arabic cloister, sits in the grounds of the **Parque Marechal Carmona** (www.cm-cascais.pt/equipamento/parque-marechal-carmona; Avenida Rei Humberto II; 8.30am-8pm Apr-Sep, to 6pm Oct-Mar).

Sleeping & Eating

Casa Vela GUESTHOUSE €€€
(218 093 996; www.casavelahotel.com; Rua dos Bem Lembrados 17; d from €155;) The friendly Casa Vela has it all: 29 bright and attractive rooms with modern furnishings in decor schemes set to spice, colonial or garden themes in two upmarket residential homes; deceptively large and grand gardens with trickling fountains, hidden nooks and two tranquil pools; and a Portuguese-by-birth, Mozambican-by-upbringing manager, João Paulo, who is the epitome of jovial hospitality. Paradise found.

★ **Bar do Guincho** PORTUGUESE €€
(214 871 683; www.bardoguincho.pt; Estrada do Abano, Praia do Guincho; mains €9-18; noon-7pm Sun & Tue-Thu, noon-11.45pm Fri & Sat, later hours Jul & Aug;) Sweeping the awards for most dramatic location in Cascais, this good-time bar-restaurant sits tucked behind a craggy ridge on the northern end of Guincho. From the sand, you would never know it's there, but it is – *and* it is packed! Revellers rake in the beach-friendly burgers, seafood and salads washed down with cold *cerveja* (beer). Settle in for the afternoon.

Café Galeria House of Wonders CAFE €€
(www.facebook.com/houseofwonders; Largo da Misericórdia 53; meals €4.75-14.75; 9am-10pm;) This fantastically whimsical, Dutch-owned cafe is tucked away in the old quarter. Its astonishingly good Middle Eastern/Mediterranean vegetarian plates, refreshing juices (€4), fabulous cakes (always at least one vegan and gluten-free option), warm, welcoming ambience and artwork-filled interior are unmissable.

Information

Cascais Visitor Center (Turismo; 912 034 214; www.visitcascais.com; Praça 5 de Outubro 45A; 9am-8pm May-Sep, to 6pm Oct-Apr) Has a handy map, events guide *(What's in Cascais)* and all sort of Cascais-branded merch.

Getting There & Away

Frequent trains run from Lisbon's Cais do Sodré station to Cascais (€2.25, 40 minutes) via Estoril.

THE ALGARVE

Soaring cliffs, sea caves, golden beaches, scalloped bays and sandy islands draw over four million visitors to the Algarve each year. In the south, tourist hotspots harbour holiday villas, brash resorts, splashy water parks, beach bars and sizzling nightclubs; elsewhere, the Algarve abounds in natural treasures, including the bird-filled lagoons and islands of the protected Parque Natural da Ria Formosa. Surrounded on two sides by the Atlantic, it's also a paradise for surfers, especially along the refreshingly undeveloped west coast.

Faro

POP 64,560

Exuding a more distinctly Portuguese feel than most resort towns, the Algarve's capital has an attractive marina, well-maintained parks and plazas, and a picturesque *cidade velha* (old town), ringed by medieval walls and home to museums, churches and al fresco cafes. On Faro's doorstep are the lagoons of the Parque Natural da Ria Formosa and the island beaches of Ilha de Faro and Ilha da Barreta.

★ Parque Natural da Ria Formosa NATURE RESERVE
(www.icnf.pt) Encompassing 18,000 hectares, this sizeable system of lagoons and islands stretches for 60km along the Algarve coastline from west of Faro to Cacela Velha. It encloses a vast area of *sapal* (marsh), *salinas* (salt pans), creeks and dune islands. The marshes are an important area for migrating and nesting birds. You can see a huge variety of wading birds, along with ducks, shorebirds, gulls and terns. It's the favoured nesting place of the little tern and the rare purple gallinule.

Formosamar CRUISE, KAYAKING
(☎918 720 002; www.formosamar.com; Avenida da República, Stand 1, Faro Marina) This recommended outfit promotes environmentally responsible tourism. Among its excellent tours are two-hour birdwatching trips around the Parque Natural da Ria Formosa (€25), dolphin watching (€45), cycling (€37) and a two-hour kayak tour negotiating some of the narrower lagoon channels (€35). All trips have a minimum number of participants (usually two to four).

Casa d'Alagoa HOSTEL €
(☎289 813 252; www.farohostel.com; Praça Alexandre Herculano 27; dm/d from €22/92;) A renovated mansion on a pretty square houses this cool, laid-back hostel. Great facilities include a lounge with long, sociable tables and beanbags, an upstairs terrace, barbecue and communal kitchen, plus on-site bike hire. There's a range of clean, spacious dorms (larger dorms have balconies) and en suite doubles.

Vila Adentro PORTUGUESE €€
(☎933 052 173; www.vilaadentro.pt; Praça Dom Afonso III 17; mains €9-17.50, cataplanas €39-49; ⏰9am-midnight;) With tables on the square in Faro's old town and a dining room decorated with floor-to-ceiling *azulejos* (hand-painted, blue-and-white tiles), this Moorish 15th-century building is a romantic spot for elevated Portuguese cuisine: pork, clam and lobster *cataplanas* (stew) for two, chargrilled octopus with fig and carob sauce, and tangerine-stuffed pork fillet. Wines hail from around the country.

O Castelo BAR
(www.facebook.com/OCasteloBar.CidadeVelha.Faro; Rua do Castelo 11; ⏰10.30am-4am Wed-Mon;) O Castelo is all things to all people: bar, restaurant, club and performance space. Its location atop the old town walls provides stunning Ria Formosa views, especially at sunset. Beer, wine and cocktails are accompanied by tapas such as flambéed chorizo and local cheeses.

ℹ Information

Turismo (www.visitalgarve.pt; Rua da Misericórdia 8; ⏰9.30am-1pm & 2-5.30pm;) Efficient office at the edge of the old town. There's another branch at the airport.

ℹ Getting There & Around

Faro Airport (FAO; ☎289 800 800; www.aeroportofaro.pt;), 7km west of the centre, has both domestic and international flights.

One or two buses per hour depart from the bus station for Faro Airport (€2.20, 15 minutes) and Praia de Faro (€2.30, 20 minutes).

Buses to Lisbon (€20, 3¼ hours, six per day) and Algarve coastal destinations depart from the **bus station** (☎289 899 760; Avenida da República 5), on the northern side of the marina. Most services are run by **Eva** (☎289 899 760, www.eva-bus.com).

Faro's train station is 500m northwest of the centre. There are five direct trains from Lisbon daily (€22.90, four hours), plus service every hour or two to nearby coastal destinations.

Tavira

POP 26,167

Set on either side of the meandering Rio Gilão, Tavira is arguably the Algarve's most charming town, with the ruins of a hilltop castle, an old Roman bridge and a smattering of Gothic and Renaissance churches. It's also the launching point for the stunning, unspoilt beaches of Ilha de Tavira.

Tavira is ideal for wandering; the warren of cobblestone streets hides leafy gardens and shady squares. There's a small, active fishing port and a modern market.

Maria Nova HOTEL €€€
(☎281 001 200; www.ap-hotelsresorts.com; Rua António Pinheiro 17; d/f from €122/180;) Tavira's best hotel is set on a hill; it's worth paying extra for a south-facing room, with views from the balcony over the vast, free-form pool (and poolside bar), palm-planted gardens and the town. Contemporary, sand toned rooms are up-to-the-minute; there's also an indoor pool spa, gym, gourmet restaurant and panoramic rooftop bar. Parking is first come, first served.

O Tonel PORTUGUESE €€
(963 427 612; Rua Dr Augo Silva Carvalho 6; tapas €3.50-7.50, mains €9-16; 6.30-10pm Mon-Sat) Contemporary Portuguese cuisine is complemented by a striking dining room of scarlet walls and *azulejos* (hand-painted tiles). Begin with *petiscos* (tapas-style sharing dishes) like chorizo sautéed in Medronho (local brandy) or clam-and-mackerel pâté served in a tin with crusty bread, before moving on to mains such as almond-crusted pork or carob-marinated lamb. Wines come from all over Portugal. Book ahead.

Fado Com História TRADITIONAL MUSIC
(966 620 877; www.fadocomhistoria.com; Rua Damião Augo de Brito Vasconcelos 4; adult/child €8/free; shows 12.15pm, 3.15pm & 5.15pm Mon-Fri, 12.15pm & 5.15pm Sat, museum 10am-6pm Mon-Sat) If you haven't experienced fado (traditional song), this comprehensive introduction is even more worthwhile. Space is limited, so buy your ticket a couple of hours ahead. The 35-minute show begins with an interesting film about fado's roots and history, followed by three live songs with explanations in English. On Saturdays the 3.15pm performance takes place at the **Igreja da Misericórdia** (www.diocese-algarve.pt; Largo da Misericórdia; church incl museum €2, fado performances €8; 10am-12.30pm & 3-6.30pm Tue-Sat Jul & Aug, shorter hours Sep-Jun, fado performances 3.15pm Sat year-round).

Information

Turismo (281 322 511; www.visitalgarve.pt; Praça da República 5; 9am-1pm & 2-5pm) Provides local and some regional information.

Getting There & Away

There are 12 trains daily to Faro (€3.20, 35 minutes).

Lagos

POP 22,000

As tourist towns go, Lagos *(lah-goosh)* has got the lot. Its old town's pretty, cobbled lanes and picturesque squares are enclosed by 16th-century walls, while some truly fabulous beaches lie just beyond. With a huge range of activities, excellent restaurants and a pumping nightlife, Lagos attracts travellers of all ages.

Numerous operators offer boat excursions, with ticket stands at the marina or along the promenade opposite. Lagos is also a popular centre for surfing, diving, windsurfing, kite-surfing and stand-up paddleboarding (SUP) .

Ponta da Piedade VIEWPOINT
(Point of Piety) Protruding 2.5km south of Lagos, Ponta da Piedade is a dramatic wedge of headland with contorted, polychrome sandstone cliffs and towers, complete with a lighthouse and, in spring, hundreds of nesting egrets, with crystal-clear turquoise water below. The surrounding area blazes with wild orchids in spring. On a clear day you can see east to Carvoeiro and west to Sagres. The only way to reach it is by car or on foot.

Lagos Atlantic Hotel HOTEL €€
(282 761 527; www.facebook.com/lagos.atlantic.hotel; Estrada do Monte Carapeto 9; d/f from €115/125; P) Most of the spacious rooms at this pristine, stylish hotel, face south and open to balconies overlooking the pool. Family rooms have pull-out sofa beds; kids under 12 stay free. Handy amenities include shaded lock-up parking and a barbecue area.

O Camilo SEAFOOD €€
(282 763 845; www.restaurantecamilo.pt; Praia do Camilo; mains €11.50-23.50; noon-4pm & 6-10pm Jun-Sep, to 9pm Oct-May;) Perched above pretty Praia do Camilo, this sophisticated restaurant is renowned for its high-quality seafood dishes. Specialities include razor clams, fried squid, lobster and oysters in season, along with grilled fish. The 40-seat dining room is light, bright and airy, and the large 28-seat terrace overlooks the ocean. Bookings are a good idea any time and essential in high season.

Bon Vivant BAR
(www.bonvivantbarinlagos.com; Rua 25 de Abril 105; 4pm-3.30am Mon-Thu, to 4am Fri-Sun;) Spread across five levels, including two underground rooms and a roof terrace, each with its own bar, cherry-red-painted Bon Vivant shakes up great house cocktails including the signature Mr Bonvivant (jenever, absinthe, strawberry-infused Aperol and bitters). Happy hour runs from 5pm to 9pm; DJs spin nightly downstairs.

Information

Turismo (282 763 031; www.visitalgarve.pt; Praça Gil Eanes 17; 9.30am-1pm & 2-5.30pm) Helpful office on Lagos' main square.

Getting There & Away

Eva (www.eva-bus.com) and Rede Expressos (www.rede-expressos.pt) depart frequently from the **bus station** (Rua Mercado de Levante) for other Algarve towns. Lagos is at the western end of the Algarve train line, with services to points east including Faro (€7.40, 1¾ hours, nine daily). For Lisbon (€22.15, four hours, five daily), change at Tunes.

Silves

POP 10,867

Silves' winding backstreets of whitewashed buildings topped by terracotta roofs climb the hillside above the banks of the Rio Arade. Crowning the hill, hulking red-stone walls enclose one of the Algarve's best-preserved castles. The town makes a good base if you're after a less hectic, non-coastal Algarvian pace.

Castelo CASTLE

(282 440 837; www.cm-silves.pt; Rua da Cruz de Portugal; adult/child €2.80/1.40, joint ticket with Museu Municipal de Arqueologia €3.90; 9am-10pm Jul & Aug, to 8pm Sep–mid-Oct, to 7pm Jun, to 5.30pm mid-Oct–May) This russet-coloured, Lego-like castle – originally occupied in the Visigothic period – has great views over the town and surrounding countryside. What you see today dates mostly from the Moorish era, though the castle was heavily restored in the 20th century. Walking the parapets and admiring the views is the main attraction, but you can also gaze down on the excavated ruins of the Almohad-era palace. The white-washed 12th-century water cisterns, 5m deep, now host temporary exhibitions.

Duas Quintas GUESTHOUSE €€

(282 449 311; www.duasquintas.com; Santo Estevão; d/studio €110/135;) Set amid 6 hectares of orange groves, with views over the rolling hills from the terrace, this restored farmhouse has six partially antique-furnished rooms (including a spacious three-person studio with a kitchenette and washing machine), a communal lounge room, terraces and landscaped natural pool. Cots and high chairs are available for tots. It's 6km north-east of Silves along the N124.

Restaurante O Barradas PORTUGUESE €€

(282 443 308; www.obarradas.com; Palmeirinha; mains €12.50-26.50, cataplanas €45-46; 6-10pm Thu-Tue) The star choice for foodies is this converted farmhouse 4.5km south of Silves, which utilises sustainably sourced fish and organic meat and vegetables in creations like slow-cooked suckling pig, char-grilled octopus with sweet potato, and fava bean and chorizo stew. The owner is a winemaker, whose wares appear on the wine list along-side vintages from Portugal's finest wineries.

Information

Centro de Interpretaçao do Património Islâmico (282 440 800; www.cm-silves.pt; Largo do Município; 10am-1pm & 2-5pm Mon-Fri) Municipal tourist office within the Islamic history interpretative centre.

Turismo (282 098 927; www.visitalgarve.pt; Parque Ribeirinho de Silves; 9.30am-1pm & 2-5.30pm Tue-Sat) Next to the main car park and bus stops.

Getting There & Away

The train station is 2km south of town; take a local bus or a taxi, as it's along a major highway. Nine trains daily serve Lagos (€2.95, 30 minutes) and Faro €5.20, one hour).

Sagres

POP 1909

Overlooking some of the Algarve's most dramatic scenery, the small, elongated village of Sagres has an end-of-the-world feel, with its sea-carved cliffs and wind-whipped fortress high above the frothing ocean. It's the only place in the world where white storks are known to nest on cliff faces. Sagres has milder temperatures than other parts of the Algarve, with Atlantic winds keeping the summers cool. Outside town are some splendid beaches that are increasingly popular with surfers, and the striking cliffs of **Cabo de São Vicente** – the southwestern-most point of the European mainland, and a spectacular spot for sunset.

Fortaleza de Sagres FORTRESS

(282 620 142; www.monumentosdoalgarve.pt; adult/child €3/1.50; 9.30am-8pm May-Sep, to 5.30pm Oct-Apr) Blank, hulking and forbidding, Sagres' fortress offers breathtaking views over the sheer cliffs, and all along the coast to Cabo de São Vicente. Legend has it that this is where Prince Henry the Navigator established his navigation school and primed the early Portuguese explorers. It's quite a large site, so allow at least an hour to see everything.

Mar Ilimitado WILDLIFE, CRUISE

(916 832 625; www.marilimitado.com; Porto da Baleeira) Mar Ilimitado's team of marine biologists lead a variety of highly recommended,

ecologically sound boat trips, from dolphin spotting (€35, 1½ hours) and seabird watching (€45, 2½ hours) to excursions up to Cabo de São Vicente (€25, one hour). Incredible marinelife you may spot includes loggerhead turtles, basking sharks, common and bottlenose dolphins, orcas, and minke and fin whales.

Pousada do Infante BOUTIQUE HOTEL €€€
(☎282 620 240; www.pousadas.pt; Rua Patrão António Faustino; d/ste from €150/230; P❄📶🏊) On the promontory's clifftop, this modern *pousada* (upmarket inn) occupies a never-to-be-outbuilt position. All rooms and suites (with king-size beds and whirlpool baths) have balconies, but those at the front face the car park, so it's definitely worth paying extra for one overlooking the fortress and ocean to take in the dazzling sunsets and swimming pool (romantically floodlit at night).

A Eira do Mel PORTUGUESE €€
(☎282 639 016; Estrada do Castelejo, Vila do Bispo; mains €11-22, cataplanas €27-35; ⏰noon-2.30pm & 7.30-10pm Tue-Sat) A rustic former farmhouse 9km north of Sagres is the atmospheric setting for José Pinheiro's lauded slow-food cooking. Seafood is landed in Sagres, with meats, vegetables and fruit sourced from local farms. Dishes such as octopus *cataplana* (seafood stew) with sweet potatoes, spicy piri-piri Atlantic wild shrimp, rabbit in red wine and *javali* (wild boar) are accompanied by regional wines.

ℹ Information

Turismo (☎282 624 873; www.visitalgarve.pt; Rua Comandante Matoso 75; ⏰9.30am-1pm & 2-7pm daily Jul & Aug, 9.30am-1pm & 2-5.30pm Tue-Sat Sep-Jun) Situated on a patch of green lawn, 100m east of Praça da República.

ℹ Getting There & Away

From the **bus stop** (Rua Comandante Matoso) by the *turismo*, buses travel to/from Lagos (€4, one hour, hourly Monday to Friday, fewer on weekends) via Salema. There are twice-daily services to Cabo de São Vicente (€2.10, 10 minutes) Monday to Friday. Buy tickets on the bus.

CENTRAL PORTUGAL

The vast centre of Portugal is a rugged swath of rolling hillsides, whitewashed villages, olive groves and cork trees. Richly historical, it is scattered with prehistoric remains and medieval castles. It's also home to one of Portugal's most architecturally rich towns, Évora, as well as several spectacular walled villages. There are fine local wines and, for the more energetic, plenty of outdoor exploring in the dramatic Beiras region.

Évora

POP 56,700

One of Portugal's most beautifully preserved medieval towns, Évora is an enchanting place to delve into the past. Inside the 14th-century walls, Évora's narrow, winding lanes lead to a striking Roman temple, a fortress-like medieval cathedral with rose granite towers, and a picturesque town square. Aside from its historical and aesthetic virtues, Évora is also a lively university town, surrounded by wineries and dramatic countryside.

★Templo Romano RUINS
(Temple of Diana; Largo do Conde de Vila Flor) Once part of the Roman Forum, the remains of this temple, dating from the 2nd or early 3rd century AD, are a heady slice of drama right in town. It's among the best-preserved Roman monuments in Portugal, and probably on the Iberian Peninsula. Though it's commonly referred to as the Temple of Diana, there's no consensus about the deity to which it was dedicated, and some archaeologists believe it may have been dedicated to Julius Caesar.

Capela dos Ossos CATACOMB
(Chapel of Bones; Praça 1 de Maio; adult/student €5/3.50; ⏰9am-6.30pm Jun-Sep, to 5pm Oct-May) One of Évora's most popular sights is also one of its most chilling. The walls and columns of this mesmerising *memento mori* (reminder of death) are lined with the bones and skulls of some 5000 people. This was the solution found by three 17th-century Franciscan monks for the overflowing graveyards of churches and monasteries.

Évora Inn HOSTEL €€
(☎266 744 500; www.evorainn.com; Rua da República 11; s/d/tr/q €40/50/80/95; 📶) This friendly 10-room guesthouse in a 120-year-old building brings a serious dose of style to Évora. Pop art adorns the rooms and corridors, along with eye-catching wallpaper, modular chairs, a bold colour scheme and unusual features (including a telescope in the Mirante room up top).

★ Albergaria do Calvario BOUTIQUE HOTEL €€€
(266 745 930; www.albergariadocalvario.com; Travessa dos Lagares 3; r €118-155; P ❄) Unpretentiously elegant, discreetly attentive and comfortable, this beautifully designed guesthouse has an ambience that travellers adore. The kind-hearted staff provide the best service in Évora, and breakfasts are outstanding, with locally sourced seasonal fruits, homemade cakes and egg dishes.

Salsa Verde VEGETARIAN €
(266 743 210; www.salsa-verde.org; Rua do Raimundo 93A; small plate €5; noon-3pm & 7-9.30pm Mon-Fri, noon-3pm Sat;) Vegetarians (and Portuguese livestock) will be thankful for this veggie-popping paradise. Pedro, the owner, gives a wonderful twist to traditional Alentejan dishes such as the famous bread dish, *migas*, prepared with mushrooms. Low-playing bossa nova and a cheerful airy design make a fine complement to the dishes – all made from fresh, locally sourced products (organic when possible).

★ Taberna Típica Quarta Feira PORTUGUESE €€€
(266 707 530; Rua do Inverno 16; dinner per person incl starters, house wine & dessert €30; 7.30-10pm Mon, 12.30-3pm & 7.30-10pm Tue-Sat) Don't bother asking for the menu since there's just one option on offer at this jovial eatery tucked away in the Moorish quarter. Luckily it's a stunner: slow-cooked black pork so tender it falls off the bone, plus freshly baked bread, grilled mushrooms (and other starters), dessert and ever-flowing glasses of wine – all served for one set price. Reserve ahead.

Information

Turismo (266 777 071; www.cm-evora.pt; Praça do Giraldo 73; 9am-7pm Apr-Oct, 9am-6pm Mon-Fri, 10am-2pm & 3-6pm Sat & Sun Nov-Mar) This central tourist office offers a great town map. Staff are more helpful if you have specific questions.

Getting There & Away

Évora station is outside the walls, 600m south of the Jardim Público. Two to five trains daily go to/from Lisbon (€13.70, two hours), Lagos (€25 to €28, 4¼ to five hours) and Faro (€26.20, 3½ to 4½ hours).

Peniche

POP 14,700

Popular for its nearby surf strands and also as a jumping-off point for the beautiful Ilhas Berlengas nature reserve, Peniche is spectacularly set on a headland surrounded by sea. It remains a working port, giving it a slightly grittier, more 'lived in' feel than its resort neighbours.

Dominating the south of the peninsula, the seaside **Fortaleza de Peniche** (262 780 116; Campo da República; 9am-12.30pm & 2-5.30pm Tue-Fri, from 10am Sat & Sun) FREE, where Salazar's regime detained political prisoners in the 20th century, is a must-see for anyone interested in Portuguese history.

Peniche is a renowned surfing destination. Northeast of town, the scenic island-village of **Baleal** is a paradise of challenging but above all consistent waves that make it an ideal learners' beach. Surf hostels and surf schools abound here. Well-established operators include **Baleal Surfcamp** (262 769 277; www.balealsurfcamp.com; Rua Amigos do Baleal 2; 2-/3-/7-day course with lodging €180/255/528) and **Peniche Surfcamp** (962 336 295; www.penichesurfcamp.com; Avenida do Mar 162, Casais do Baleal; 1/2/10 surf classes €30/50/145).

About 10km offshore, **Berlenga Grande** is a spectacular, rocky and remote island, with twisting, shocked-rock formations and gaping caverns. There are good opportunities for diving here. **AcuaSubOeste** (918 393 444; www.acuasuboeste.com; Armazém 3, Avenida do Porto de Pesca; 2 dives €70; 9-10am & 5-7pm) and **Haliotis** (262 781 160; www.haliotis.pt; Casal da Ponte S/N, Atouguia da Baleia; 2-tank dive €75; 9am-1pm & 2-6pm) both offer a range of PADI certification courses.

Kitesurfing is big in Peniche. On the far side of high dunes about 500m east of the walled town, **Peniche Kite & Surf Center** (919 424 951; www.penichesurfcenter.com; Avenida Monsenhor Bastos, Praia de Peniche de Cima; 9.30am-8pm Mar-Oct) offers lessons and equipment.

Casa das Marés B&B €€
(Casa 1 262 769 200, Casa 2 262 769 255, Casa 3 262 769 379; www.casadasmares1.com; Praia do Baleal; d/ste €70/120;) At the picturesque, windswept tip of Baleal stands one of the area's most distinctive accommodation options. Three sisters originally inherited this dramatically perched house from their parents and divided it into three parts – each of

which now serves as its own little B&B run by two surviving brothers-in-law and one of the sisters.

Information

Posto de Turismo (262 789 571; www.cm-peniche.pt; Rua Alexandre Herculano 70; 9am-1pm & 2-5pm)

Getting There & Away

Peniche's **bus station** (968 903 861; Rua Dr Ernesto Moreira) is served by served by Rodoviária do Oeste (www.rodoviariadooeste.pt), Rede Expressos (www.rede-expressos.pt) and Intercentro (www.internorte.pt). There are frequent services to Coimbra (€14.70, 2¾ hours), Lisbon (€9, 1½ hours) and Óbidos (€3.30, 40 minutes).

Óbidos

POP 3100

Surrounded by a classic crenellated wall, Óbidos' gorgeous historic centre is a labyrinth of cobblestone streets and flower-bedecked, whitewashed houses livened up by dashes of vivid yellow and blue paint. The 14th-century Porta da Vila gate leads directly into the main street, Rua Direita, which is lined with chocolate and sour cherry-liqueur shops. It's a delightful place to pass an afternoon, but overnight visitors will find its charms magnified after the tour buses leave, when you can explore Óbidos' nooks and crannies and wander along its imposing town walls in relative solitude.

Commanding centre-stage at the top of the village is **Castelo de Óbidos**, one of Dom Dinis' 13th-century creations. It's a stern edifice, with lots of towers, battlements and big gates. Converted into a palace in the 16th century (some Manueline touches add levity), it's now a deluxe **pousada** (210 407 630; www.pousadas.pt; Paço Real; d/ste from €200/320;).

The town's elegant main church, **Igreja de Santa Maria** (Praça de Santa Maria; 9.30am-12.30pm & 2.30-7pm summer, to 5pm winter), stands out for its interior, with a wonderful painted ceiling and walls done up in beautiful blue-and-white 17th-century *azulejos* (hand-painted tiles). Paintings by the renowned 17th-century painter Josefa de Óbidos are to the right of the altar.

★Muro de Óbidos HISTORIC SITE

Óbidos' dramatic, fully intact Moorish wall imposingly surrounds the historical centre of town and stretches in a completed loop of 1560m, all of which can be walked across the top, at a height of 13m in some spots (not including the towers). There are four staircases accessing the wall, but most folks climb up either at Porta da Vila or the castle. There are no guardrails here, so take care, especially with children or anyone prone to vertigo or spontaneous face plants.

Casa d'Óbidos HOTEL €€

(262 950 924; www.casadobidos.com; Quinta de São José; s/d €75/90, 2-/4-/6-person apt €90/140/175;) In a whitewashed, 1887 villa below town, this delightful option features spacious, breezy rooms with good modern bathrooms and period furnishings, plus a tennis court, swimming pool and lovely grounds with sweeping views of Óbidos' bristling walls and towers. Breakfast is served at a common dining table (fresh bread and breakfast fixings are delivered every morning to the apartments).

Ja!mon Ja!mon PORTUGUESE €€

(916 208 162; Rua da Biquinha S/N; mains €10-14; noon-3pm & 7-10pm Tue-Sat, noon-3pm Sun) With the cheery Andre, his family and a young, enthusiastic staff, the hospitality is oh-so Portuguese (read: happy and generous) at this excellent *tasca* (tavern) featuring a wonderful terrace with lush hillside views.

Information

Posto de Turismo (262 959 231; www.obidos.pt; Rua da Porta da Vila S/N; 9.30am-7.30pm May-Sep, to 6pm Oct-Apr) Just outside Porta da Vila, near the bus stop.

Getting There & Away

Rodoviária do Oeste (www.rodoviariadooeste.pt) runs frequent buses to Peniche (€3.30, 40 minutes) and Lisbon (€7.85, 65 minutes) from the bus stop on the main road near Porta da Vila.

Nazaré

POP 10,500

With a warren of narrow, cobbled lanes running down to a wide, cliff-backed beach, Nazaré is Estremadura's most picturesque coastal resort. Its sands are packed wall-to-wall with multicoloured umbrellas in July and August. Nazaré is also one of Portugal's top draws for New Year's Eve and Carnaval celebrations, and is renowned for the monster surfing waves that roll in north of town at Praia do Norte each winter.

The **beaches** here are superb, although swimmers should be aware of dangerous currents. Climb or take the funicular to the clifftop promontory of **Sitio**, with its cluster of fishermen's cottages and outstanding views.

You'll likely be hit up by elderly local women offering rooms for rent. It never hurts to bargain and see what the going rate is. Rates drop 30% to 50% outside July and August.

Lab Hostel HOSTEL €
(☎262 382 339; www.labhostel.pt; Rua de Rio Maior 14; dm €17.50-18.50, d €55-100;) One of Portugal's band of growing 'glostels' (glamorous hostels), stylish, minimal design, attention to detail and some of the whitest, brightest and cleanest rooms around make this worth a look. There's a female dorm, a family room and breakfast is included. It was a former laboratory (the owner's father in-law was a pharmacist), and old chemist jars and bottles make for fun *objets d'art*.

A Tasquinha SEAFOOD €€
(☎262 551 945; Rua Adrião Batalha 54; mains €7.50-17.50; noon-3pm & 7-10.30pm Tue-Sun Carnival-New Year) This exceptionally friendly family affair has been running for 50-plus years, serving high-quality seafood in a pair of snug but prettily tiled dining rooms. Solo travellers delight: *Arroz de Marisco* (shellfish rice) for one person (€17.50)!

Information

Posto de Turismo (☎262 561 194; www.cm-nazare.pt; Avenida Vieira Giumarães, Edifício do Mercado Municipal; 9.30am-1pm & 2.30-6pm Oct-Apr, to 7pm May, Jun & Sep, 9am-8pm Jul & Aug) In the front offices of the food market as well as next door to Igreja de Nossa Senhora da Nazaré in **Sítio** (☎930 424 860; www.cm-nazare.pt; Largo de Nossa Senhora da Nazaré; 9.30am-1pm & 2.30-6pm Oct-Apr, to 7pm May, Jun & Sep, 9am-8pm Jul & Aug). Helpful, multilingual staff.

Getting There & Away

Rodoviária do Oeste (www.rodoviariadooeste.pt) and Rede Expressos (www.rede-expressos.pt) run frequent buses to Lisbon (€12, 1¾ hours) and Peniche (€10, 70 minutes) from Nazaré's bus station, a couple of blocks in from the ocean.

Tomar

POP 16,000

Tomar is one of central Portugal's most appealing small towns. With its pedestrian-friendly historical centre, its pretty riverside park frequented by swans, herons and families of ducks, and its charming natural setting adjacent to the lush Mata Nacional dos Sete Montes (Seven Hills National Forest), it wins lots of points for aesthetics. Its crowning glory is the medieval hilltop Convento de Cristo, whose crenellated walls form a beautiful backdrop from almost any vantage point.

Just northwest of Tomar, the double-decker Aqueduto de Pegões with its 180 arches was built between 1593 and 1613 to supply water to thirsty monks. It's best seen just off the Leiria road, 2.3km from town.

★Convento de Cristo MONASTERY
(www.conventocristo.pt; Rua Castelo dos Templários; adult/under 12yr €6/free, with Alcobaça & Batalha €15; 9am-6.30pm Jun-Sep, to 5.30pm Oct-May) Wrapped in splendour and mystery, the Knights Templar held enormous power in Portugal from the 12th to 16th centuries, and largely bankrolled the Age of Discoveries. Their headquarters sit on wooded slopes above the town and are enclosed within 12th-century walls. The Unesco World Heritage–listed Convento de Cristo is a stony expression of magnificence, founded in 1160 by Gualdim Pais. It has chapels, cloisters and choirs in diverging styles, added over the centuries by successive kings and Grand Masters.

Hostel 2300 Thomar HOSTEL €
(☎249 324 256; www.hostel2300thomar.com; Rua Serpa Pinto 43; dm/s/d/tr/q €18/30/45/60/80;) One of Portugal's funkiest hostels, this cleverly renovated mansion right in the heart of town celebrates Portugal, with the rooms brightly decorated in an individual theme: from the Lisbon tram to sardines. Airy dorms (and doubles), lockers, modern bathrooms and a cool and fun living space are enough to convert those normally after luxe experiences into a backpacker.

Thomar Story BOUTIQUE HOTEL €€
(☎249 327 268; www.thomarstory.pt; Rua João Carlos Everard 53; s/d/tr €43/50/65;) A major refurbishment of an old house has created 12 light and pleasant rooms along the lines of the current trend in Portugal: funky wall decorations and mirrors, bright accessories and modern bathrooms. The

interior of each in some way reflects Tomar, from the town's convent to its synagogue. Breakfast costs €5. The best rooms have small patios and kitchenettes.

Restaurante Tabuleiro PORTUGUESE €€
(☎249 312 771; www.restaurantetabuleiro.wordpress.com; Rua Serpa Pinto 140; mains €15.80; ⊙noon-3pm & 7-10pm Mon-Sat;) Located just off Tomar's main square, this family-friendly local hang-out features warm, attentive service, good traditional food and ridiculous (read: more-than-ample) portions. A great spot to experience local fare. The cod pie is a standout.

Information

Posto de Turismo (☎249 329 823; www.cm-tomar.pt; Avenida Dr Cândido Madureira; ⊙9.30am-6pm Apr-Sep, 10am-5pm Oct-Mar) Offers a good town map, an accommodation list and information about a historical trail.

Getting There & Away

Trains run to Lisbon (€9.80 to €11.10, 1¾ to two hours) every hour or two.

Coimbra

POP 143,396

Rising scenically from the Rio Mondego, Coimbra is an animated city steeped in history. It was Portugal's medieval capital for more than a century and it's home to the country's oldest and most prestigious university, the Unesco-listed Universidade de Coimbra. Coimbra's steeply stacked historic centre dates from Moorish times and is wonderfully atmospheric with its dark cobbled lanes and monumental cathedral. On summer evenings, the city's old stone walls reverberate with the haunting metallic notes of the *guitarra* (Portuguese guitar) and the full, deep voices of fado singers.

Sights

★Biblioteca Joanina LIBRARY
(Baroque Library; ☎239 242 744; www.uc.pt/turismo; Pátio das Escolas, Universidade de Coimbra; adult/under 26yr/child incl Paço das Escolas, Capela de São Miguel & Museu da Ciência €12.50/10/free; ⊙9am-7.30pm Mar-Oct, 9am-1pm & 2pm-5pm Nov-Feb) The university's baroque library is Coimbra's headline sight. Named after King João V, who sponsored its construction between 1717 and 1728, it features a remarkable central hall decorated with elaborate ceiling frescoes and huge rosewood, ebony and jacaranda tables. Towering gilt chinoiserie shelves hold some 40,000 books, mainly on law, philosophy and theology. Curiously, the library also houses a colony of bats to protect the books – they eat potentially harmful insects.

Sé Velha CATHEDRAL
(Old Cathedral; ☎239 825 273; www.sevelha-coimbra.org; Largo da Sé Velha, Rua do Norte 4; €2.50; ⊙10am-6pm Mon-Sat, 1-6pm Sun) Coimbra's 12th-century cathedral is one of Portugal's finest examples of Romanesque architecture. The main portal and facade are particularly striking, especially on warm summer evenings when the golden stone seems to glow in the soft light. Its construction was financed by Portugal's first king, Afonso Henriques, and completed in 1184 at a time when the nation was still threatened by the Moors, hence its crenellated exterior and narrow, slit-like lower windows. Interior highlights include an ornate late-Gothic retable and a lovely 13th-century cloister.

Museu Nacional de Machado de Castro MUSEUM
(☎239 853 070; www.museumachadocastro.pt; Largo Dr José Rodrigues; adult/child €6/3, cryptoportico only €3; ⊙2pm-6pm Tue, 10am-6pm Wed-Sun) This great museum is a highlight of central Portugal. Housed in a 12th-century bishop's palace, it stands over the city's ancient Roman forum, remains of which can be seen in the maze of spooky tunnels under the building – the *cryptoporticus*. Once you emerge from this, you can start on the fascinating art collection, which runs the gamut from Gothic religious sculpture to 16th-century Flemish painting and ornately crafted furniture.

Sleeping & Eating

Serenata Hostel HOSTEL €
(☎239 853 130; www.serenatahostel.com; Largo da Sé Velha 21; dm €16, d €49-60, f €71;) Occupying an elegant townhouse overlooking Coimbra's old cathedral, this fabulous hostel sits in the heart of the historical centre. Rooms, spread over three floors, come in an array of shapes and sizes, ranging from 10-bed dorms to spacious family rooms. White walls and artistic stencils create a modern feel, while high ceilings and creaking wood floors add a period touch.

Quinta das Lágrimas LUXURY HOTEL €€€
(☎239 802 380; www.quintadaslagrimas.pt; Rua António Augusto Gonçalves; r €160-450; P) Coimbra's sole five-star hotel is charmingly

enconced in the romantic **Jardim Quinta das Lágrimas** (Rua Vilarinho Raposo; adult/under 15yr/family €2.50/1/5; ⏲10am-5pm Tue-Sun mid-Oct–mid-Mar, 10am-7pm mid-Mar–mid-Oct) on the west bank of the Mondego. Choose between classic richly furnished rooms in the original 18th-century palace, or go for something more minimalist in the modern annex. There's a formal fine-dining restaurant for gourmet dinners and a fully equipped spa.

Sete Restaurante MODERN PORTUGUESE €€
(☎239 060 065; www.facebook.com/seterestaurante; Rua Dr. Martins de Carvalho 10; mains €11-19; ⏲1-4pm & 7-midnight Wed-Mon) Squeezed into a corner behind the **Igreja de Santa Cruz** (Praça 8 de Maio; adult/child €3/free; ⏲9.30am-4.30pm Mon-Sat, 1-5pm Sun), this intimate restaurant is one of the most popular in town. Its casual wine bar vibe, personable service and modern take on Portuguese cuisine ensure it's almost always buzzing. Book ahead to avoid disappointment.

Loggia MODERN PORTUGUESE €€
(☎239 853 076; www.loggia.pt; Largo Dr José Rodrigues, Museu Nacional de Machado de Castro; mains €13-18; ⏲10am-6pm Tue & Sun, to 10.30pm Wed-Sat) As much as its confident modern cuisine, the Loggia's big draw is its setting, on a panoramic terrace overlooking the old town. There's open-air seating for romantic sunset dinners or you can sit inside and admire the views from its glass-walled dining room. Its lunch buffet (€9.50) is great value.

Drinking & Entertainment

Galeria Santa Clara BAR
(☎239 441 657; www.galeriasantaclara.com; Rua António Augusto Gonçalves 67; ⏲2pm-2am Sun-Thu, to 3am Fri & Sat) An arty tea room by day and chilled-out bar by night, this is a terrific place to hang out. Inside it's all mismatched vintage furniture, books and chandeliers, while out the back the garden terrace boasts lovely views over the river to the historical centre. The atmosphere is laid-back and can feel like a house party when things get going.

Fado ao Centro FADO
(☎239 837 060; www.fadoaocentro.com; Rua Quebra Costas 7; show incl drink €10; ⏲show 6pm) At the bottom of the old town, this friendly cultural centre is a good place to acquaint yourself with fado. The evening 6pm show includes plenty of explanation, in Portuguese and English, about the history of the music and the meaning of each song. It's tourist-oriented, but the performers enjoy it and do it well.

Information

Turismo Largo da Portagem (☎239 488 120; www.turismodecoimbra.pt; Largo da Portagem; ⏲9am-6pm Mon-Fri, 9.30am-1pm & 2-5.30pm Sat & Sun) Coimbra's main tourist office.

Getting There & Away

BUS

From the **bus station** (Av Fernão de Magalhães; ⏲ticket office 8am-10pm), a 15-minute walk

WORTH A TRIP

LUSO & MATA NACIONAL DO BUÇACO

A retreat from the world for almost 2000 years, the **Mata Nacional do Buçaco** (☎231 937 000; www.fmb.pt; per car/cyclist/pedestrian €5/free/free; ⏲8.30am-7pm Mon-Fri, to 8pm Sat & Sun) sits on the slopes of the Serra do Buçaco, some 30km north of Coimbra. This walled 105-hectare forest reserve harbours a network of paths and an astounding 700 plant species, from huge Mexican cedars to tree-sized ferns. Smack in the heart of the forest is the **Palace Hotel do Buçaco** (☎231 937 970; www.almeidahotels.pt/pt/hotel-coimbra-portugal; s €148-199, d €169-225; Ⓟ), a fairy-tale royal palace now converted into a splurge-worthy overnight accommodation.

Generations of writers have enshrined Buçaco in the national imagination with breathless hymns to its natural and spiritual beauty. Access to the forest is through the quaint spa town of Luso at the foot of the Serra. Famed for its thermal waters, Luso is an easy day trip from Coimbra, but it also has some decent accommodation and the recommended **Pedra de Sal** (☎231 939 405; www.restaurantepedradesal.com; Rua Francisco A Dinis 33; mains €9-20; ⏲noon-3pm & 7-10pm Wed-Mon) restaurant, specialising in succulent steak and Iberian pork.

Three weekday buses run from Coimbra's bus station to Luso (€3.75, 40 minutes) with two continuing on to Buçaco (€4, 50 minutes). Three daily trains run from Coimbra-B to Luso-Buçaco station (€2.55, 25 minutes). From here it's a 15-minute walk into town.

northwest of the centre, **Rede Expressos** (☎239 855 270; www.rede-expressos.pt) runs at least a dozen buses daily to Lisbon (€14.50, 2½ hours) and Porto (€12.50, 1½ hours), along with direct services to Braga (€14, 2¾ hours, six daily), and Faro (€28, six to 8½ hours, two daily).

TRAIN

Coimbra has two train stations: **Coimbra-B** and the more central **Coimbra A** (called just 'Coimbra' on timetables). Long-distance trains stop at Coimbra-B, 2km north of the city centre, from where local trains connect with Coimbra A – this connection is included in the price of tickets to/from Coimbra.

Coimbra has regular services to Lisbon (AP/IC €23.20/19.50, 1¾/two hours, hourly) and Porto (€17/13.40, one/1¼ hours, at least hourly).

THE NORTH

Beneath the edge of Spanish Galicia, northern Portugal is a land of lush river valleys, sparkling coastline, granite peaks and virgin forests. This region is also paradise for wine-lovers: it's home to Portugal's sprightly *vinho verde* (a young, slightly sparkling white or red wine) and ancient terraced Port vineyards along the dramatic Rio Douro. Gateway to the north is Porto, a beguiling riverside city blending both medieval and modern attractions. Smaller towns and villages also offer cultural allure, from majestic Braga, the country's religious heart, to seaside beauty Viana do Castelo.

Porto

☎22 / POP 237,600

Opening up like a pop-up book from the banks of the Rio Douro, edgy-yet-opulent Porto entices with its historical centre, sumptuous food and wine, and charismatic locals. A lively walkable city with chatter in the air and a tangible sense of history, Porto's old-world riverfront district is a Unesco World Heritage Site. Across the water twinkle the neon signs of Vila Nova de Gaia, headquarters of the major port wine manufacturers.

Sights

★Palácio da Bolsa HISTORIC BUILDING
(Stock Exchange; www.palaciodabolsa.com; Rua Ferreira Borges; tours adult/child €10/6.50; 9am-6.30pm Apr-Oct, 9am-12.30pm & 2-5.30pm Nov-Mar) This splendid neoclassical monument (built from 1842 to 1910) honours Porto's past and present money merchants. Just past the entrance is the glass-domed **Pátio das Nações** (Hall of Nations), where the exchange once operated. But this pales in comparison with rooms deeper inside; to visit these, join one of the half-hour guided tours, which set off every 30 minutes.

★Igreja de São Francisco CHURCH
(Jardim do Infante Dom Henrique; adult/child €6/5; 9am-8pm Jul-Sep, to 7pm Mar-Jun & Oct, to 5.30pm Nov-Feb) Igreja de São Francisco looks from the outside to be an austerely Gothic church, but inside it hides one of Portugal's most dazzling displays of baroque finery. Hardly a centimetre escapes unsmothered, as otherworldly cherubs and sober monks are drowned by nearly 100kg of gold leaf. If you see only one church in Porto, make it this one.

★Jardins do Palácio de Cristal GARDENS
(Rua Dom Manuel II; 8am-9pm Apr-Sep, to 7pm Oct-Mar;) Sitting atop a bluff, this gorgeous botanical garden is one of Porto's best-loved escapes, with lawns interwoven with sun-dappled paths and dotted with fountains, sculptures, giant magnolias, camellias, cypress and olive trees. It's actually a mosaic of small gardens that open up little by little as you wander – as do the stunning views of the city and Rio Douro.

★Serralves MUSEUM
(www.serralves.pt; Rua Dom João de Castro 210; adult/child museums & park €10/free, park only €5/free, 10am-1pm 1st Sun of the month free; 10am-7pm Mon-Fri, to 8pm Sat & Sun May-Sep, reduced hours Oct-Apr) This fabulous cultural institution combines a museum, a mansion and extensive gardens. Cutting-edge exhibitions, along with a fine permanent collection featuring works from the late 1960s to the present, are showcased in the **Museu de Arte Contemporânea**, an arrestingly minimalist, whitewashed space designed by the eminent Porto-based architect Álvaro Siza Vieira. The delightful, pink **Casa de Serralves** is a prime example of art deco, bearing the imprint of French architect Charles Siclis. One ticket gets you into both museums.

Museu Nacional Soares dos Reis MUSEUM
(www.museusoaresdosreis.pt; Rua Dom Manuel II 44; adult/child €5/free; 10am-6pm Tue-Sun) Porto's best art museum presents a stellar collection ranging from neolithic carvings to Portugal's take on modernism, all housed in the formidable Palácio das Carrancas.

Casa da Música LANDMARK
(☎220 120 220; www.casadamusica.com; Avenida da Boavista 604-610; guided tour €10; ⊙English guided tours 11am & 4pm) At once minimalist, iconic and daringly imaginative, the Casa da Música is the beating heart of Porto's cultural scene and the home of the Porto National Orchestra. Dutch architect Rem Koolhaas rocked the musical world with this crystalline creation – the jewel in the city's European Capital of Culture 2001 crown.

São Bento Train Station HISTORIC BUILDING
(Praça Almeida Garrett; ⊙5am-1am) One of the world's most beautiful train stations, beaux arts São Bento wings you back to a more graceful age of rail travel. Completed in 1903, it seems to have been imported from 19th-century Paris with its mansard roof. But the dramatic *azulejo* panels of historical scenes in the front hall are the real attraction. Designed by Jorge Colaço in 1930, some 20,000 tiles depict historic battles (including Henry the Navigator's conquest of Ceuta), as well as the history of transport.

Tours

Taste Porto FOOD & DRINK
(☎920 503 302; www.tasteporto.com; Downtown Food Tour adult/child €65/42, Vintage Food Tour €70/42; ⊙Downtown Food Tour 10.45am & 4pm Tue-Sat, Vintage Food Tour 10am & 4.15pm Mon-Sat, Photo Food Experience 9.45am daily) Loosen a belt notch for Taste Porto's superb Downtown Food Tours, where you'll sample everything from Porto's best slow-roast-pork sandwich to éclairs, fine wines, cheese and coffee. Friendly, knowledgeable guide André and his team lead these indulgent and insightful 3½-hour walking tours, which take in viewpoints and historical back lanes en route to restaurants, grocery stores and cafes.

Sleeping

Gallery Hostel HOSTEL €
(☎224 964 313; www.gallery-hostel.com; Rua Miguel Bombarda 222; dm/d/tr/ste from €20/59/75/80; ❄📶) A true travellers' hub, this hostel-gallery has clean and cosy dorms and doubles, a sunny, glass-enclosed back patio, a grassy terrace, a cinema room, a shared kitchen and a bar-music room. Throw in its free walking tours, homemade dinners on request, port-wine tastings and concerts, and you'll see why it's booked up so often – reserve ahead.

The Passenger HOSTEL €
(☎963 802 000; www.thepassengerhostel.com; Estação de São Bento, Praça Almeida Garrett; dm €22-27, d €55-90, tr €95-110, q €115-190) A night spent at the station is no longer a miserable prospect since the opening of this cool hostel in São Bento train station. Decorated with vintage furniture and one-of-a-kind Portuguese artworks, it sure is a step up from most backpacker digs. Besides upbeat staff, there's a shared kitchen and a bar with a Mac and piano.

Canto de Luz B&B €€
(☎225 492 142; www.cantodeluz.com; Rua do Almada 539; r €85-105; 📶) *Ah oui,* this French-run guesthouse, just a five-minute walk from Trindade metro, is a delight. Rooms are light, spacious and make the leap between classic and contemporary, with vintage furnishings used to clever effect. Your kindly hosts André and Brigitte prepare delicious breakfasts, with fresh-squeezed juice, pastries and homemade preserves. There's also a pretty garden terrace.

★**Guest House Douro** BOUTIQUE HOTEL €€€
(☎222 015 135; www.guesthousedouro.com; Rua da Fonte Taurina 99-101; r €160-230; ❄@📶) In

WORTH A TRIP

THROUGH THE GRAPEVINES OF THE DOURO

Portugal's best-known river flows through the country's rural heartland. In the upper reaches, port-wine grapes are grown on steep terraced hills, punctuated by remote stone villages and, in spring, splashes of dazzling white almond blossom. The Rio Douro is navigable right across Portugal. Highly recommended is the train journey from Porto to Pinhão (€11, 2½ hours, five daily), the last 70km clinging to the river's edge; from Pinhão, trains continue upstream as far as Pocinho (from Porto €13.30, 3¼ hours), or you can hop aboard a boat cruise for equally spellbinding perspectives on the river.

Cyclists and drivers can choose river-hugging roads along either bank – such as the N222 between Pinhão and Peso da Régua – and visit wineries along the way (check out www.dourovalley.eu for an extensive list of wineries open to visitors). You can also stay overnight in scenic wine lodges among the vineyards.

Porto

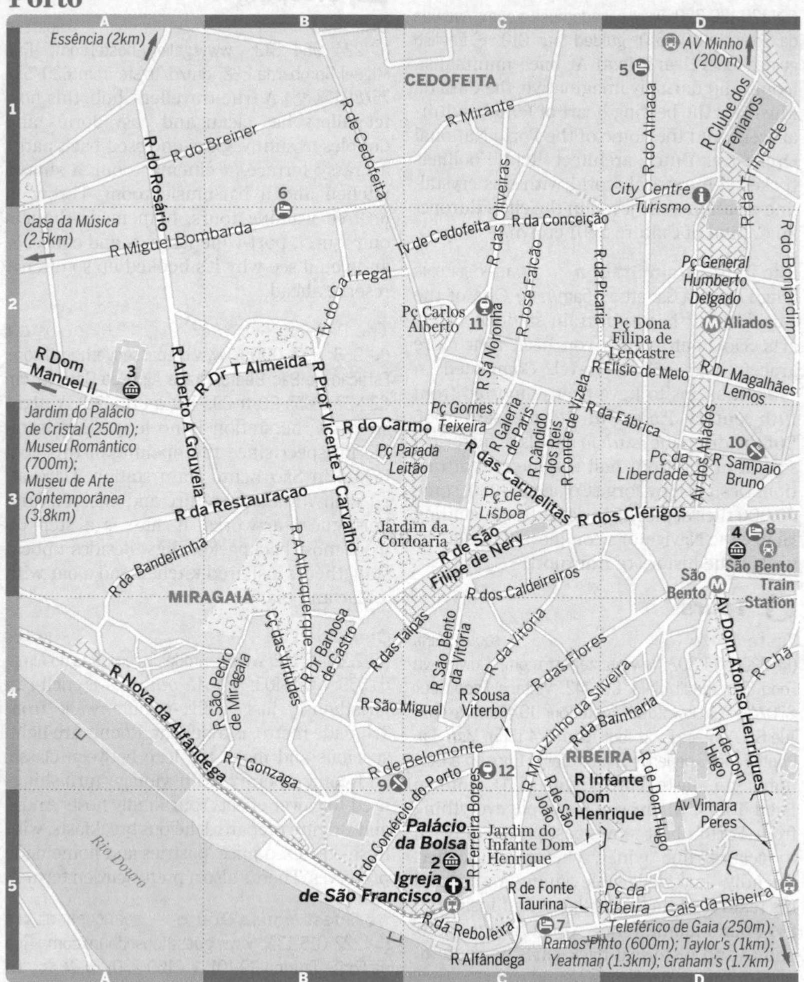

a restored relic overlooking the Rio Douro, these eight rooms have been blessed with gorgeous wooden floors, plush queen beds and marble baths; the best have dazzling river views. But it is the welcome that makes this place stand out from the crowd – your charming hosts Carmen and João bend over backwards to please.

★Yeatman RESORT **€€€**
(☎220 133 185; www.the-yeatman-hotel.com; Rua do Choupelo 88; d €255-315, ste €485-2370;) Named after one of port producer Taylor's original founders, the Yeatman is Porto's only true five-star resort, terraced and tucked into the Gaia hillside with expansive Douro and Porto views. There's a two-Michelin-starred restaurant; huge, sumptuous guest rooms and suites with private terraces; a decanter-shaped pool; sunken Roman baths in the fantastic Caudalie spa; and it's close to everything else you could possibly wish for.

Eating

Flor dos Congregados PORTUGUESE **€€**
(☎222 002 822; www.flordoscongregados.pt; Travessa dos Congregados 11; mains €8-16; ⏲7-10pm Mon-Wed, noon-3pm & 7-11pm Thu-Sat) Tucked away down a narrow alley, this softly

Porto

Top Sights
1 Igreja de São Francisco C5
2 Palácio da Bolsa C5

Sights
3 Museu Nacional Soares dos Reis A2
4 São Bento Train Station D3

Sleeping
5 Canto do Luz D1
6 Gallery Hostel B2
7 Guest House Douro C5
8 The Passenger D3

Eating
9 Belos Aires B4
10 Flor dos Congregados D3

Drinking & Nightlife
11 Aduela C2
12 Prova C4

lit, family-run restaurant brims with stone-walled, wood-beamed, art-slung nooks. The frequently changing blackboard menu goes with the seasons.

Belos Aires ARGENTINE €€
(☎223 195 661; www.facebook.com/belosairesrestaurante; Rua de Belomonte 104; mains €17-25; ⏰8-11.30am & 7pm-midnight Mon-Sat; 📶) At the heart of this intimate part-Argentine, part-Portuguese restaurant is Mauricio, a chef with a big personality and an insatiable passion for his homeland, revealed as you watch him dashing around in the open kitchen. The market-fresh menu changes frequently, but you'll always find superb steaks and to-die-for *empanadas* (savoury turnovers). Save an inch for the chocolate brownie with *dulce de leche*.

Essência VEGETARIAN €€
(☎228 301 813; www.essenciarestaurantevegetariano.com; Rua de Pedro Hispano 1190; mains €10.50-15; ⏰12.30-3pm & 8-10.30pm Mon-Thu, to midnight Fri & Sat; 🌿) This bright, modern brasserie is famous Porto-wide for its generous vegetarian (and nonvegetarian!) dishes, stretching from wholesome soups and salads to curries, pasta dishes, risotto and *feijoada* (pork and bean casserole). There's a terrace for warm-weather dining.

O Paparico PORTUGUESE €€€
(☎225 400 548; www.opaparico.com; Rua de Costa Cabral 2343; menus €90-120; ⏰7.30-11pm Tue-Sat) It's worth the taxi hop north of town to O Paparico. Portuguese authenticity is the name of the game here, from the romantically rustic interior of stone walls, beams and white linen to the menu that sings of the seasons. Dishes such as veal with wild mushrooms and monkfish are cooked with passion, served with precision and expertly paired with wines.

★ **Euskalduna Studio** GASTRONOMY €€€
(☎935 335 301; www.euskaldunastudio.pt; Rua de Santo Ildefonso 404; 10-course tasting menu €95-110; ⏰7-10pm Wed-Sat) Everyone loves surprises, especially edible ones prepared with flawless execution, experimental finesse and a nod to the seasons. Just 16 lucky diners (eight at the

DON'T MISS

TASTING PORT WINE

Sitting just across the Rio Douro from Porto, **Vila Nova da Gaia** is woven into the city's fabric by stunning bridges and a shared history of port-wine making. Since the mid-18th century, port-wine bottlers and exporters have maintained their lodges here. Today some 30 of these lodges clamber up the riverbank and most open their doors to the public for cellar tours and tastings. Among the best are **Taylor's** (☎223 772 973; www.taylor.pt; Rua do Choupelo 250; tours incl tasting adult/child €15/6; ⏰10am-6pm), **Graham's** (☎223 776 490, 223 776 492; www.grahams-port.com; Rua do Agro 141; tours incl tasting from €15; ⏰9.30am-6.30pm Apr-Oct, to 6pm Nov-Mar) and **Ramos Pinto** (☎967 658 980, 936 809 283; www.ramospinto.pt; Av Ramos Pinto 400; tours incl tasting €10; ⏰10am-6pm May-Oct, reduced hours Nov-Apr).

green marble counter peeking into the kitchen and eight at oak tables) get to sample Vasco Coelho Santos' stunning 10-course menus that allow flavours and textures to shine.

Drinking & Entertainment

★Prova WINE BAR
(www.prova.com.pt; Rua Ferreira Borges 86; ⏰5pm-1am Wed-Sun; 📶) Diogo, the passionate owner, explains the finer nuances of Portuguese wine at this chic, stone-walled bar, where relaxed jazz plays. Stop by for a two-glass tasting (€5), or sample wines by the glass – including beefy Douros, full-bodied Dãos and crisp Alentejo whites. These marry well with sharing plates of local hams and cheeses (€14). Diogo's port tonics are legendary.

Aduela BAR
(Rua das Oliveiras 36; ⏰3pm-2am Mon, 10am-2am Tue-Thu, to 4am Fri & Sat, 3pm-midnight Sun) Retro and hip but not self-consciously so, chilled Aduela bathes in the nostalgic orange glow of its glass lights, which illuminate the green walls and mishmash of vintage furnishings. Once a sewing machine warehouse, today it's where friends gather to converse over wine and appetising *petiscos* (€3 to €8).

Terraplana CAFE
(www.terraplanacafe.com; Avenida Rodrigues de Freitas 287; ⏰6pm-midnight Sun-Thu, to 3am Fri & Sat) Totally relaxed and boho-cool without trying, Terraplana is the bar of the moment in this neck of Porto. Murals adorn the arty, stone-walled interior, and there's a pretty patio for summer imbibing. Besides inventive cocktails (around €10 a pop), they also have a solid selection of wines, gins and beers. These marry well with super-tasty pizzas (€8.50 to €9.50).

★Casa da Música CONCERT VENUE
(House of Music; ☎220 120 220; www.casadamusica.com; Avenida da Boavista 604; ⏰box office 9.30am-7pm Mon-Sat, to 6pm Sun) Grand and minimalist, sophisticated yet populist, Porto's cultural behemoth boasts a shoebox-style concert hall at its heart, meticulously engineered to accommodate everything from jazz duets to Beethoven's Ninth.

ℹ Information

City Centre Turismo (☎300 501 920; www.visitporto.travel; Rua Clube dos Fenianos 25; ⏰9am-8pm May-Jul & Sep-Oct, to 9pm Aug, to 7pm Nov-Apr) The main city *turismo* has a detailed city map, a transport map and the *Agenda do Porto* cultural calendar, among other printed materials.

Santo António Hospital (☎222 077 500; www.chporto.pt; Largo Prof Abel Salazar) Has English-speaking staff.

ℹ Getting There & Away

AIR

Porto's gleaming, ultra-modern **Francisco de Sá Carneiro Airport** (☎229 432 400; www.aeroportoporto.pt; 4470-558 Maia), 16km northwest of the city centre, has excellent connections to international hubs including London, Brussels, Madrid, Frankfurt, New York and Toronto.

BUS

Bus services in Porto are regrettably dispersed, with no central bus terminal. On the plus side, there are frequent services to most places in northern Portugal, and express services to Coimbra, Lisbon and points south.

Renex-Rede Expressos (www.rede-expressos.pt; Campo 24 de Agosto) is the choice for Lisbon (€19, 3½ hours), with the most direct routes and eight to 12 departures daily, including one continuing on to the Algarve. Buses depart from Campo 24 de Agosto. **Transdev-Norte** (☎225 100 100; www.transdev.pt; Campo 24 de Agosto) runs to Braga (€6, one hour), and **AV Minho** (☎222 006 121; www.avminho.pt; Rua Régulo Maguanha 46) serves Viana do Castelo (€5.60, 2¼ hours).

TRAIN

Porto is northern Portugal's rail hub. Long-distance services start at **Campanhã** (Rua Monte da Estação) station, 3km east of the centre. Direct IC trains run hourly to Lisbon (€24.70 to €30.80, 2½ to three hours).

Most *urbano, regional* and *interregional* (IR) trains depart from **São Bento** (Praça Almeida Garrett) station, though they also pass through Campanhã.

Getting Around

TO/FROM THE AIRPORT

The Metro do Porto violet line E links the airport with central Porto. A one-way ticket costs €2 and the journey takes around 45 minutes. Taxis charge €20 to €25 for the hour-long trip to the centre.

PUBLIC TRANSPORT

Public transport is inexpensive, clean and efficient in Porto. For maximum convenience, Porto's transport agency, **STCP** (Sociedade de Transportes Colectivos do Porto; ☎808 200 166; www.stcp.pt), offers the rechargeable **Andante Card** (€0.60; www.linhandante.com), allowing smooth movement between tram, metro, funicular and many bus lines. A 24-hour ticket for the entire public transport network, excluding trams, costs €7. For timetables, routes and fares, see www.stcp.pt and www.metrodoporto.pt.

Bus

STCP's extensive bus system has central hubs at Praça da Liberdade (the south end of Avenida dos Aliados), Praça Almeida Garrett (in front of São Bento train station) and Cordoaria. A one-way ticket bought on the bus costs €1.95, or €1.20 with an Andante Card.

Funicular

The panoramic **Funicular dos Guindais** (one way adult/child €2.50/1.25; ⊙8am-10pm Sun-Thu, to midnight Fri & Sat Apr-Oct, to 8pm Sun-Thu, to 10pm Fri & Sat Nov-Mar) shuttles up and down a steep incline from Avenida Gustavo Eiffel to Rua Augusto Rosa.

Metro

Running from around 6am to 1am daily, Porto's newish, easy-to-navigate **metro system** (http://en.metrodoporto.pt) comprises six metropolitan lines that all converge at the Trindade stop. Tickets cost €1.20/1.60/2 for zone 2/3/4 with an Andante Card.

Tram

Only three Porto tram lines remain, but they're very scenic. The Massarelos stop, on the riverfront near Palácio de Cristal, is the system's hub. From here, the most useful line (tram 1E) trundles along the Douro towards Foz do Douro. Trams run half-hourly from 8am to 9pm. One-way tickets cost €3; a two-day adult/child pass costs €10/5.

Viana do Castelo

POP 37,972

The jewel of the Costa Verde, Viana do Castelo is blessed with an appealing medieval centre, an attractive riverfront and lovely beaches just outside town. Viana's old quarter showcases leafy 19th-century boulevards and narrow lanes crowded with Manueline manors and rococo palaces, all dramatically presided over by the pearly-white, neo-Byzantine Santa Luzia church on the hilltop high above town. The stately heart of town is Praça da República, with its delicate Renaissance fountain and grandiose mansions and monuments.

Monte de Santa Luzia HILL

There are two good reasons to visit Viana's 228m eucalyptus-clad hill. One is the wondrous view down the coast and up the Lima valley. The other is the fabulously over-the-top, 20th-century, neo-Byzantine **Templo do Sagrado Coração de Jesus** (Templo Monumento Santa Luzia, Temple of the Sacred Heart of Jesus; www.templosantaluzia.org; admission to dome €2; ⊙9am-6.45pm Apr-Oct, to 4.45pm Nov-Mar). You can get a little closer to heaven by climbing to the *zimbório* (lantern tower) atop its dome, via a lift, followed by an elbow-scraping stairway – take the museum entrance on the ground floor.

Praia do Cabedelo BEACH

This is one of the Minho's best beaches: a 1km-long arc of blond, powdery sand that folds into grassy dunes backed by a grove of wind-blown pines. It's across the river from town, best reached on a five-minute **ferry trip** (one way/return adult €1.40/2.80, child under 12yr/under 6yr half price/free; ⊙9am-6pm May-Sep) from the pier south of Largo 5 de Outubro.

★Dona Emília GUESTHOUSE €€

(☎917 811 392; www.dona-emilia.com; Rua Manuel Espregueira 6; d with shared/private bathroom from €55/75; 🛜) This phenomenal new B&B in a 19th-century town house commands front-row perspectives of Viana's historical centre from its luminous, high-ceilinged common areas and six guest rooms. Second-floor units have shared facilities, while suites under the eaves have beautifully tiled private bathrooms. All abound in period details; two have terraces with views over Viana's elegant main square or the leafy backyard.

O Marquês PORTUGUESE €

(Rua do Marquês 72; meals from €6; ⏰noon-3.30pm & 7-10pm Mon-Fri, noon-3.30pm Sat) A tremendous backstreet find, this place is absolutely jammed with locals for the *platos do dia* (daily specials; €6). Think baked cod with white beans or roasted turkey leg with potatoes and salad. It's a friendly, satisfying, family-run affair.

Confeitaria Natário BAKERY €

(☎258 822 376; Rua Manuel Espregueira 37; pastries from €1; ⏰9am-9pm Mon & Wed-Sat, 9am-1.30pm & 3.30-9pm Sun) This popular bakery is the place to try delicious *bolas de Berlim* (cream-filled doughnuts) – so good that you'll often have to wait in line. Get 'em warm from the oven at 11.30am and 4.30pm. Locals also convene here for *milfolhas* (flaky pastry filled with shrimp or meat), traditionally enjoyed with a glass of sparkling wine.

Information

Viana Welcome Centre (☎258 098 415; www.vivexperiencia.pt; Praça do Eixo Atlântico; ⏰10am-7pm Jul & Aug, 10am-1pm & 2-6pm Tue-Sun Sep-Oct & Mar-Jun, to 5pm Tue-Sun Nov-Feb) Centrally located down by the riverfront; offers tourist information, tours and activities.

Getting There & Away

Viana is linked to Porto by direct trains (€6.85 to €7.95, 1¼ to two hours) and AV Minho buses (€6.50, two hours).

Braga

POP 136,885

Portugal's third-largest city boasts an elegant historical centre laced with ancient pedestrian lanes, grand plazas and a splendid array of baroque churches. Packed with cafes, boutiques, restaurants and bars, and enlivened by a large student population, Braga is also famous throughout Portugal for its religious festivals – particularly the elaborately staged **Semana Santa** (Holy Week) leading up to Easter Sunday. Just east of Braga stands the magnificent hillside sanctuary of **Bom Jesus do Monte**, one of Portugal's most iconic tourist attractions.

★Sé CATHEDRAL

(www.se-braga.pt; Rua Dom Paio Mendes; ⏰9.30am-12.30pm & 2.30-6.30pm Apr-Oct, to 5.30pm Nov-Mar) Braga's extraordinary cathedral, the oldest in Portugal, was begun when the archdiocese was restored in 1070 and completed in the following century. It's a rambling complex made up of differing styles, and architecture buffs could spend half a day happily distinguishing the Romanesque bones from Manueline musculature and baroque frippery.

★Escadaria do Bom Jesus do Monte CHRISTIAN SITE

(Monte do Bom Jesus) Climbing dramatically to the hilltop pilgrimage site of Bom Jesus do Monte, 5km east of Braga, is this extraordinary staircase, with allegorical fountains, chapels and a superb view. City bus 2 runs frequently from Braga to the site, where you can climb the 580 steps (pilgrims sometimes do this on their knees) or ascend by funicular (one way/return €1.20/2).

Collector's Hostel HOSTEL €

(☎253 048 124; www.collectorshostel.com; Rua Francisco Sanches 42; dm €17-20, d/tr €44/62, s/d with shared bath €27/40) This lovely hostel is lovingly run by two well-travelled women (one of whom was born in the hostel's living room) who met in Paris, restored the family house and all the furniture inside, and turned the three floors into a cosy hideaway where guests feel like they're in their grandparents' home, with a twist.

Vila Galé Collection Braga LUXURY HOTEL €€€

(☎253 146 000; www.vilagale.com; Largo Carlos Amarante 150; r/ste from €144/195; P ❄ @ 📶 🏊) Braga's newest luxury hotel is this magnificent former hospital and convent dating from 1508, adopted by the Vila Galé hotel chain and reopened in 2018. Abounding in vaulted ceilings, interior courtyards, baroque fountains and other grandiose architectural touches, it houses 123 palatial rooms and suites with five-star amenities, complemented by a spa, two outdoor pools, two restaurants and a bar.

Livraria Centésima Página CAFE €

(Avenida Central 118-120; snacks €3-5; ⏰9am-7.30pm Mon-Sat) Tucked inside Centésima Página, an absolutely splendid bookshop with foreign-language titles, this charming cafe serves a rotating selection of tasty quiches along with salads and desserts, and has outdoor tables in the pleasantly rustic garden. Its lunch specials are a steal.

Casa de Pasto das Carvalheiras FUSION €€

(☎253 046 244; www.facebook.com/casadepastodascarvalheiras; Rua Dom Afonso Henriques 8;

small plates €5-15; ⏲noon-3pm & 7pm-midnight Mon-Fri, noon-midnight Sat & Sun) This colourful eatery with a long bar serves up delectable, weekly changing *pratinhos* (small plates), from codfish confit with bok choy and noodles, to mushrooms with creamy polenta, to tasty cakes of *alheira* (a light garlicky sausage of poultry or game) and turnip greens. Weekday lunch menus go for €9 or €12, depending on the number of dishes you order.

ℹ Information

Turismo (☎253 262 550; www.visitbraga.travel; Avenida da Liberdade 1; ⏲9am-6.30pm Mon-Fri, 9.30am-1pm & 2-5.30pm Sat & Sun) Braga's helpful tourist office is in an art deco–style building facing busy Praça da República.

ℹ Getting There & Away

Hourly trains go to Porto (€3.25, about one hour). Direct trains also serve Coimbra (€21, 1¾ to 2¾ hours, four to seven daily) and Lisbon (€34, four hours, two to four daily).

Airport Bus (☎253 262 371; www.getbus.eu) travels to Porto's airport (one way/return €8/14, 50 minutes, 10 daily). **Transdev** (☎225 100 100; www.transdev.pt) runs buses to Viana do Castelo (€4.55, 1¾ hours).

Parque Nacional da Peneda-Gerês

Spread across four impressive granite massifs, this vast park encompasses boulder-strewn peaks, precipitous valleys, gorse-clad moorlands and forests of oak and pine. It also shelters more than 100 granite villages that, in many ways, have changed little since Portugal's founding in the 12th century.

For nature lovers, the stunning scenery here is unmatched in Portugal for outdoor adventures. There are trails and footpaths through the park, some between villages with accommodation. In Campo do Gerês (16km west of Vila do Gerês), **Equi Campo** (☎914 848 094, 253 357 022; www.equicampo.com; ⏲9am-7pm May-Sep, by arrangement Oct-Apr) organises hikes and horse-riding trips. Rio Caldo, 8km south of Vila do Gerês, is the base for water sports on the Caniçada Reservoir. English-run **Água Montanha Lazer** (☎925 402 000; www.aguamontanha.com; Rua da Raposeira 31; per hr kayak/SUP/pedalo €6/10/12, motorboat €35-45; 4-/10-person cottage per day €80/160, per week €525/980) rents a variety of boats and organises kayaking trips.

Convenient overnight bases for exploring the park include the old-fashioned hot springs resort of Vila do Gerês and the picturesque village of Soajo – at the park's southern and western edges respectively. Both boast a variety of sleeping and eating options. More remote villages offering simple accommodation include Campo do Gerês, Pitões das Júnias and Castro Laboreiro. Rental cottages throughout the park are available through **Adere Peneda-Gerês** (☎258 452 250; www.adere-pg.pt; Rua Dom Manuel

DON'T MISS

FIVE GREAT HIKES IN PARQUE NACIONAL PENEDA-GERÊS

Here are five of the national park's best walks, with starting point in parentheses. Park offices can provide further details.

Via Geira Roman Road (Portela do Homem, 12km north of Vila do Gerês) Trace the ancients' footsteps past dozens of intact mileposts as you follow this venerable Roman road downriver through the dense Albergaria da Mata forest to the Albufeira do Homem reservoir.

Caminhos do Pão & Caminhos da Fé (Soajo) Experience first-hand the interplay between Portuguese mountain people and their natural setting on this 8km loop through terraced fields and past ancient water mills.

Castro Laboreiro Loop (Castro Laboreiro) Climb 1km to the ruins of a medieval hilltop castle for spectacular views of the park's rugged northern mountains.

Mosteiro de Santa Maria das Júnias Loop (Pitões das Júnias) This 2.5km loop descends to a secluded valley where a 13th-century Cistercian monastery slumbers in solitude.

Trilho Pertinho do Céu (http://trilhos.arcosdevaldevez.pt/activities/trilho-pertinho-do-ceu) (Gavieira) Loop through high pastures and picturesque stone villages on the 8km 'Close to Heaven Trail'.

l; ⌚9am-12.30pm & 2.30-6pm Mon-Fri) in Ponte da Barca.

★Casa do Adro INN €

(☎258 576 327; Largo do Eiró; r €50; P 📶) This manor house (rather than a cottage), off Largo do Eiró by Soajo's parish church, dates from the 18th century. Rooms are huge, furnished with antiques and blessed with sweet vineyard and village vistas. There is a minimum two-night stay in August.

Parque Campismo Lamas de Mouro CAMPGROUND €

(☎251 466 041; www.montesdelaboreiro.pt/parquecampismo.pdf; Lamas de Mouro; per adult/child/tent/car €4.20/2.80/3.70/3, 2-/4-/6-person bungalow €55/65/75) This tremendous private campground near boulder fields and flowering meadows has shady creekside tent sites plus four cosy pine-clad bungalows with kitchenettes. It rents out mountain bikes (€2.50/10 per hour/day) and offers treetop adventures, canyoning and hikes with shepherds. There are a couple of restaurants not too far away in the Lamas de Mouro village northwest of the park gate.

★O Abocanhado PORTUGUESE €€

(☎253 352 944; www.abocanhado.com; Brufe; mains €12-18; ⌚12.30-3.30pm & 7.30-9.30pm) With its stunning panoramic terrace high above the Rio Homem, this gorgeously situated restaurant is a temple to the finest ingredients that the surrounding countryside has to offer, including *javali* (wild boar), *veado* (venison) and *coelho* (rabbit), along with beef and goat raised in the adjacent fields. Finish with *requeijão* – a soft goat's cheese so fresh it's actually sweet.

Information

Park Information Centre (Centro de Educação Ambiental do Vidoeiro; ☎253 390 110; www.icnf.pt; Lugar do Vidoeiro 99; ⌚9am-1pm & 2-5pm Mon-Fri) About 1km north of Vila do Gerês. Other park offices, from northwest to southeast, are located in the villages of Lamas de Mouro, Lindoso, Mezio, Campo do Gerês and Montalegre.

Getting There & Away

Public transport within the park is extremely limited, so it's helpful to have your own wheels. You can rent cars from **Avic** (☎253 203 910; www.avic.pt; Rua Gabriel Pereira de Castro 28; ⌚9am-7pm Mon-Fri, 9am-12.30pm Sat) in Braga.

SURVIVAL GUIDE

Directory A–Z

ACCOMMODATION

Although you can usually show up in any town and find a room on the spot, it's worthwhile booking ahead, especially for July and August.

LGBTIQ+ TRAVELLERS

In 2010 Portugal legalised gay marriage, becoming the sixth European country to do so. Most Portuguese profess a laissez-faire attitude about same-sex couples, although how out you can be depends on where you are in Portugal. In Lisbon, Porto and the Algarve, acceptance has increased, whereas in most other areas, same-sex couples would be met with incomprehension. In this conservative Catholic country, homosexuality is still outside the norm. And while homophobic violence is extremely rare, discrimination has been reported in schools and workplaces.

Lisbon has the country's best LGBTIQ+network and nightlife. Lisbon and Porto hold Gay Pride marches, but outside these events the LGBTIQ+ community keeps a discreet profile.

MONEY

ATMs are widely available, except in the smallest villages. Credit cards are accepted in midrange and high-end establishments.

OPENING HOURS

Opening hours vary throughout the year. We provide high-season opening hours; hours will generally decrease in the shoulder and low seasons.

Banks 8.30am–3pm Monday to Friday

Bars 7pm–2am

Cafes 9am–7pm

Clubs 11pm–4am Thursday to Saturday

Restaurants noon–3pm and 7–10pm

Shopping malls 10am–10pm

Shops 9.30am–noon and 2–7pm Monday to Friday, 10am–1pm Saturday

PUBLIC HOLIDAYS

Banks, offices, department stores and some shops close on the public holidays listed here. On New Year's Day, Easter Sunday, Labour Day and Christmas Day, even *turismos* close.

New Year's Day 1 January

Carnaval Tuesday February/March – the day before Ash Wednesday

Good Friday March/April

Liberty Day 25 April

Labour Day 1 May

Corpus Christi May/June – ninth Thursday after Easter

Portugal Day 10 June – also known as Camões and Communities Day

Feast of the Assumption 15 August
Republic Day 5 October
All Saints' Day 1 November
Independence Day 1 December
Feast of the Immaculate Conception 8 December
Christmas Day 25 December

TELEPHONE

To call Portugal from abroad, dial the international access code (00), then Portugal's country code (351), then the number. All domestic numbers have nine digits, and there are no area codes. The main domestic mobile operators are Vodafone, Optimus and TMN; all sell prepaid SIM cards that can be used in unlocked European, Australian and quad-band US mobiles.

Getting There & Away

AIR

Most international flights arrive in Lisbon, though Porto and Faro also receive some. For more information, including live arrival and departure schedules, see www.ana.pt.

LAND

Portugal shares a land border only with Spain, but there is both bus and train service linking the two countries, with onward connections to the rest of mainland Europe.

Bus

The major long-distance carriers that serve European destinations are **Busabout** (www.busabout.com) and **Eurolines** (www.eurolines.eu); though these carriers serve Portugal, the country is not currently included in the multicity travel passes of either company.

For some European routes, Eurolines is affiliated with the big Portuguese operators **Internorte** (☎707 200 512; www.internorte.pt) and **Eva Transportes** (☎289 589 055; www.eva-bus.com).

Train

There is nightly sleeper service between Madrid and Lisbon. Spanish trains also run from Vigo (Galicia) to Porto. Purchase tickets online through **Renfe** (www.renfe.com).

The train journey from Paris (Gare de Montparnasse) to Lisbon takes 21 hours and stops in a number of Spanish cities along the way. Buy tickets direct from **SNCF** (www.oui.sncf).

Getting Around

AIR

TAP (www.flytap.com) has multiple daily Lisbon–Porto and Lisbon–Faro flights (taking less than one hour) year-round.

BUS

A host of small private bus operators, most amalgamated into regional companies, run a dense network of services across the country. Among the largest are **Rede Expressos** (☎707 223 344; www.rede-expressos.pt), **Rodonorte** (☎259 340 710; www.rodonorte.pt) and the Algarve-based Eva Transportes.

Bus services are of four general types.

Alta Qualidade A fast deluxe category offered by some companies.

Carreiras Marked 'CR'; slow, seemingly stopping at every crossroads.

Expressos Comfortable, fast buses between major cities.

Rápidas Quick regional buses.

Even in summer you'll have little problem booking an *expresso* ticket for the same or next day. Fares and schedules are available online or at bus stations.

CAR & MOTORCYCLE

Automobile Associations

Automóvel Club de Portugal (ACP; ☎219 429 113, 24hr emergency assistance 808 222 222; www.acp.pt), Portugal's national auto club, has a reciprocal arrangement with several foreign automobile clubs, and can provide medical, legal and breakdown assistance.

Hire

To rent a car in Portugal you must be at least 25 years old and have held your driving licence for more than a year. The widest choice of car-hire companies is at Lisbon, Porto and Faro airports. Scooters/motorcycles (from €30/60 per day) are available in larger cities and all over coastal Algarve.

Road Rules

Speed limits for cars and motorcycles are generally 50km/h in towns and villages, 90km/h outside built-up areas and 120km/h on motorways. The legal blood-alcohol limit is 0.05%, and there are fines of up to €2500 for drink-driving. It's also illegal in Portugal to drive while talking on a mobile phone.

TRAIN

Train travel in Portugal is extremely affordable, with a decent network between major towns. Visit **Comboios de Portugal** (☎707 210 220; www.cp.pt) for schedules and prices.

There are four main types of long-distance service. Note that international services are marked IN on timetables.

Regional (R) Slow; stop everywhere.

Interregional (IR) Reasonably fast.

Intercidade (IC) *Rápido* or express trains.

Alfa Pendular Deluxe Marginally faster than express and much pricier.

Spain

POP 46.7 MILLION

Includes ➡

Best Places to Eat

- Casa Delfín (p572)
- La Cuchara de San Telmo (p581)
- El Poblet (p588)
- Adolfo (p563)

Best Places to Stay

- Un Patio en Santa Cruz (p595)
- Balcón de Córdoba (p598)
- Barceló Raval (p570)
- Hotel Costa Vella (p585)

Why Go?

Passionate, sophisticated and devoted to living the good life, Spain is at once a stereotype come to life and a country more diverse than you ever imagined.

Spanish landscapes stir the soul, from the jagged Pyrenees and wildly beautiful cliffs of the Atlantic northwest to charming Mediterranean coves, while astonishing architecture spans the ages at seemingly every turn. Spain's cities march to a beguiling beat with cutting-edge architecture and unrivalled nightlife, even as time-capsule villages serve as beautiful signposts to Old Spain. And then there's one of Europe's most celebrated (and varied) gastronomic scenes.

But, above all, Spain lives very much in the present. Perhaps you'll sense it along a crowded after-midnight street when all the world has come out to play. Or maybe that moment will come when a flamenco performer touches something deep in your soul. Whenever it happens, you'll find yourself nodding in recognition: *this* is Spain.

When to Go

Madrid

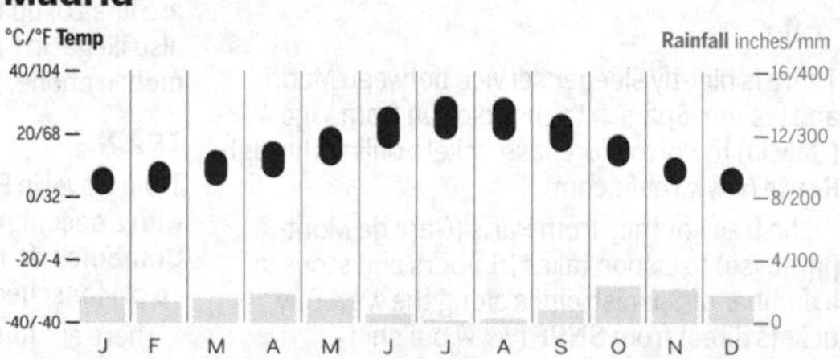

Mar & Apr Spring wildflowers, Semana Santa processions and mild southern temperatures.

May, Jun & Sep Balmy weather but without the crowds of high summer.

Jul & Aug Spaniards hit the coast in the summer heat, but quiet corners still abound.

Entering the Country

Immigration and customs checks usually involve a minimum of fuss, although there are exceptions. Your vehicle could be searched on arrival from Morocco; they're looking for controlled substances. Expect long delays at these borders, especially in summer. The tiny principality of Andorra is not in the EU, so border controls (and rigorous customs checks for contraband) remain in place.

ITINERARIES

One Week

Marvel at the art nouveau–influenced Modernista architecture and seaside style of Barcelona (p563) before taking the train to San Sebastián (p580). Head on to Bilbao (p582) for the Guggenheim Museum and end the trip living it up in the legendary night-life scene of Madrid (p546).

One Month

Fly into Seville (p592) and embark on a route exploring this and Andalucía's other magical cities, Granada (p599) and Córdoba (p597). Take the train to Madrid (p546), from where you can check out Toledo (p562), Salamanca (p557) and Segovia (p559). Make east for the coast and Valencia (p586). Head up to the Basque Country to see the epoch-making Guggenheim Museum in Bilbao (p582) and feast on some of the world's best food in San Sebastián (p580), then head east via the medieval villages of Aragón (p578) and the dramatic Pyrenees (p580) to Catalonia, spending time in Tarragona (p576) before reaching Barcelona (p563). Take a plane or boat for some R&R on the beautiful Balearic Islands (p589) before catching a flight home.

Essential Food & Drink

Tapas or pintxos Possibly the world's most ingenious form of snacking. Madrid's La Latina *barrio* (district), Zaragoza's El Tubo and most Andalucían cities offer rich pickings, but a *pintxo* (Basque tapas) crawl in San Sebastián's Parte Vieja is one of life's most memorable gastronomic experiences.

Chocolate con churros These deep-fried doughnut strips dipped in thick hot chocolate are a Spanish favourite for breakfast, afternoon tea or at dawn on your way home from a night out. Madrid's Chocolatería de San Ginés (p554) is the most famous purveyor.

Bocadillos Rolls filled with *jamón* (cured ham) or other cured meats, cheese or (in Madrid) deep fried calamari.

Pa amb tomaquet Bread rubbed with tomato, olive oil and garlic – a staple in Catalonia and elsewhere.

AT A GLANCE

Area 505,370 sq km

Capital Madrid

Country Code ☎34

Currency euro (€)

Emergency ☎112

Languages Spanish (Castilian), Catalan, Basque, Galician (Gallego)

Time Central European Time (GMT/UTC plus one hour)

Visas Schengen rules apply

Sleeping Price Ranges

The following price ranges refer to a double room with private bathroom (Madrid and Barcelona/rest of Spain):

€ less than €75/65

€€ €75–200/€65–140

€€€ more than €200/140

Eating Price Ranges

The following price ranges refer to a standard main dish:

€ less than €12

€€ €12–20

€€€ more than €20

Resources

Fiestas.net (www.fiestas.net)

Tour Spain (www.tourspain.org)

Turespaña (www.spain.info)

Paradores (www.parador.es)

Spain Highlights

❶ **Alhambra** (p599) Exploring the exquisite Islamic palace complex in Granada.

❷ **La Sagrada Família** (p567) Visiting Gaudí's singular work in progress in Barcelona, a cathedral that truly defies imagination.

❸ **Mezquita** (p597) Wandering amid the horseshoe arches of Córdoba's great medieval mosque, close to perfection wrought in stone.

❹ **San Sebastián** (p580) Eating your way through a food-lover's paradise with an idyllic setting.

❺ **Santiago de Compostela** (p584) Joining the pilgrims in Galicia's magnificent cathedral city.

❻ **Seville** (p592) Soaking up the scent of orange blossom, being carried away by the passion of flamenco and surrendering to the party atmosphere in this sunny southern city.

❼ **Madrid** (p546) Spending your days in some of Europe's best art galleries and nights amid its best nightlife.

Bordeaux
FRANCE
Avignon
Nîmes
Montpellier
Toulouse
BASQUE COUNTRY
San Sebastián
Bayonne
Bilbao
Irún
NAVARRA
Tarbes
Narbonne
CANTABRIA
Vitoria Gasteiz
Pamplona
PYRENEES
Golfe du Lion
Perpignan
Miranda de Ebro
Jaca
ANDORRA LA VELLA
ANDORRA
AP1
Logroño
Figueres
Calahorra
CATALONIA
Girona
Burgos
Huesca
Fornells
Costa Brava
AP68
Aranda de Duero
Soria
Lleida
Manresa
Tossa de Mar
A9
Zaragoza
AP2
Barcelona
CASTILLA Y LEÓN
Sitges
Tarragona
ARAGÓN
A1
A23
AP7
Guadalajara
Alcalá de Henares
Teruel
Ciutadella de Menorca
Menorca
Maó
Chinchón
Cuenca
Castellón de la Plana
Aranjuez
A3
Inca
Artà
Mallorca
Sagunto
Alcázar de San Juan
Palma de Mallorca
Manacor
Valencia
VALENCIA
Alginet
Balearic Islands
Albacete
Ibiza
Valdepeñas
Dénia
Benidorm
Formentera
A4
Alicante
Elche
Cieza
MURCIA
Murcia
Costa Blanca
MEDITERRANEAN SEA
A7
A91
Cartagena
Guadix
Granada
Mojácar
Costa Cálida
Almería
Adra
Salobreña
Costa De Almería
ALGERIA
Melilla (Spain)
0 200 km
0 100 miles

MADRID

POP 3.18 MILLION

Madrid is a beguiling place with an energy that carries one simple message: this city really knows how to live.

Sights

★Museo del Prado MUSEUM

(Map p552; www.museodelprado.es; Paseo del Prado; adult/child €15/free, 6-8pm Mon-Sat & 5-7pm Sun free, audio guide €3.50, admission plus official guidebook €24; ⌚10am-8pm Mon-Sat, to 7pm Sun; 📶; Ⓜ Banco de España) Welcome to one of the world's premier art galleries. More than 7000 paintings are held in the Museo del Prado's collection (of which only around 1500 are currently on display), acting like a window onto the historical vagaries of the Spanish soul, at once grand and imperious in the royal paintings of Velázquez, darkly tumultuous in *Las pinturas negras* (The Black Paintings) of Goya, and outward looking with sophisticated works of art from all across Europe.

★Centro de Arte Reina Sofía MUSEUM

(Map p552; ☎91 774 10 00; www.museoreinasofia.es; Calle de Santa Isabel 52; adult/concession €10/free, 1.30-7pm Sun, 7-9pm Mon & Wed-Sat free; ⌚10am-9pm Mon & Wed-Sat, to 7pm Sun; Ⓜ Atocha) Home to Picasso's *Guernica*, arguably Spain's most famous artwork, the Centro de Arte Reina Sofía is Madrid's premier collection of contemporary art. In addition to plenty of paintings by Picasso, other major drawcards are works by Salvador Dalí and Joan Miró.

The collection principally spans the 20th century up to the 1980s. The occasional non-Spanish artist makes an appearance (including Francis Bacon's *Lying Figure;* 1966), but most of the collection is strictly peninsular. Tickets are cheaper if purchased online.

★Plaza Mayor SQUARE

(Map p552; Ⓜ Sol) Madrid's grand central square, a rare but expansive opening in the tightly packed streets of central Madrid, is one of the prettiest open spaces in Spain, a winning combination of imposing architecture, picaresque historical tales and vibrant street life. At once beautiful in its own right and a reference point for so many Madrid days, it also hosts the city's main tourist office, a Christmas market in December and arches leading to laneways out into the labyrinth.

★Museo Thyssen-Bornemisza MUSEUM

(Map p552; ☎902 760511; www.museothyssen.org; Paseo del Prado 8; adult/child €12/free, Mon free; ⌚10am-7pm Tue-Sun, noon-4pm Mon; Ⓜ Banco de España) The Thyssen is one of the most extraordinary private collections of predominantly European art in the world. Where the Prado or Reina Sofía enable you to study the body of work of a particular artist in depth, the Thyssen is the place to immerse yourself in a breathtaking breadth of artistic styles.

Most of the big names are here, sometimes with just a single painting, but the Thyssen's gift to Madrid and the art-loving public is to have them all under one roof.

★Palacio Real PALACE

(Map p552; ☎91 454 87 00; www.patrimonionacional.es; Calle de Bailén; adult/concession €11/6, guide/audio guide €3, EU citizens free last 2hr Mon-Thu; ⌚10am-8pm Apr-Sep, to 6pm Oct-Mar; Ⓜ Ópera) Spain's lavish Palacio Real is a jewel box of a palace, although it's used only occasionally for royal ceremonies; the royal family moved to the modest Palacio de la Zarzuela years ago.

When the *alcázar* (Muslim fortress) burned down on Christmas Day 1734, Felipe V, the first of the Bourbon kings, decided to build a palace that would dwarf all its European counterparts. Felipe died before the palace was finished, which is perhaps why the Italianate baroque colossus has a mere 2800 rooms, just one-quarter of the original plan.

★Parque del Buen Retiro GARDENS

(Map p548; Plaza de la Independencia; ⌚6am-midnight Apr-Sep, to 10pm Oct-Mar; Ⓜ Retiro, Príncipe de Vergara, Ibiza, Atocha) The glorious gardens of El Retiro are as beautiful as any you'll find in a European city. Littered with marble monuments, landscaped lawns, the occasional elegant building (the Palacio de Cristal is especially worth seeking out) and abundant greenery, it's quiet and contemplative during the week but comes to life on weekends. Put simply, this is one of our favourite places in Madrid.

★Museo Lázaro Galdiano MUSEUM
(Map p548; ☎91 561 60 84; www.flg.es; Calle de Serrano 122; adult/concession/child €6/3/free, last hour free; ⊙10am-4.30pm Tue-Sat, to 3pm Sun; Ⓜ Gregorio Marañón) This imposing early-20th-century Italianate stone mansion, set discreetly back from the street, belonged to Don José Lázaro Galdiano (1862–1947), a successful businessman and passionate patron of the arts. His astonishing private collection, which he bequeathed to the city upon his death, includes 13,000 works of art and objets d'art, a quarter of which are on show at any time.

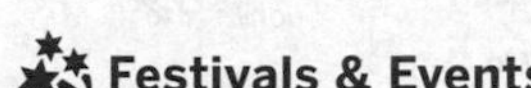

Festivals & Events

Fiestas de San Isidro Labrador CULTURAL
(www.esmadrid.com; ⊙May) Around 15 May Madrid's patron saint is honoured with a week of nonstop processions, parties and bullfights. Free concerts are held throughout the city, and this week marks the start of the city's bullfighting season.

Sleeping

Plaza Mayor & Royal Madrid

★Central Palace Madrid HOTEL €€
(Map p552; ☎91 548 20 18; www.centralpalacemadrid.com; Plaza de Oriente 2; d without/with view €145/200; ❄📶; ⓂÓpera) Now here's something special. The views alone would be reason enough to come to this hotel and definitely worth paying extra for – rooms with balconies look out over the Palacio Real and Plaza de Oriente. The rooms themselves are lovely and light filled, with tasteful, subtle faux-antique furnishings, comfortable beds, light wood floors and plenty of space.

La Latina

Posada del León de Oro BOUTIQUE HOTEL €€
(Map p552; ☎91 119 14 94; www.posadadelleondeoro.com; Calle de la Cava Baja 12; d/ste from €70/145; ❄📶; Ⓜ La Latina) This rehabilitated inn has muted colour schemes and generally large rooms. There's a *corrala* (traditional internal or communal patio) at its core and

MUSEO DEL PRADO ITINERARY: ICONS OF SPANISH ART

The collection of the Museo del Prado (p546) can be overwhelming in scope, and it's a good idea to come twice if you can – but if your time is limited, zero in on the museum's peerless collection of Spanish art.

Francisco José de Goya y Lucientes (Goya) is found on all three floors of the Prado but we recommend starting at the southern end of the ground or lower level. In room 65, Goya's *El dos de mayo* and *El tres de mayo* rank among Madrid's most emblematic paintings; they bring to life the 1808 anti-French revolt and subsequent execution of insurgents in Madrid. Alongside, in rooms 67 and 68, are some of his darkest and most disturbing works, *Las pinturas negras*; they are so called in part because of the dark browns and black that dominate, but more for the distorted animalesque appearance of their characters.

There are more Goyas on the 1st floor in rooms 34 to 37. Among them are two more of Goya's best-known and most intriguing oils: *La maja vestida* and *La maja desnuda*. These portraits, in room 37, of an unknown woman, commonly believed to be the Duquesa de Alba (who may have been Goya's lover), are identical save for the lack of clothing in the latter. There are further Goyas on the top floor.

Having studied the works of Goya, turn your attention to Velázquez. Of all his works, *Las meninas* (room 12) is what most people come to see. Completed in 1656, it is more properly known as *La família de Felipe IV* (The Family of Felipe IV). The rooms surrounding *Las meninas* contain more fine works by Velázquez: watch out in particular for his paintings of various members of royalty who seem to spring off the canvas – Felipe II, Felipe IV, Margarita de Austria (a younger version of whom features in *Las meninas*), El Príncipe Baltasar Carlos and Isabel de Francia – on horseback.

Further, Bartolomé Esteban Murillo, José de Ribera, the stark figures of Francisco de Zurbarán and the vivid, almost surreal works of El Greco should all be on your itinerary.

Madrid

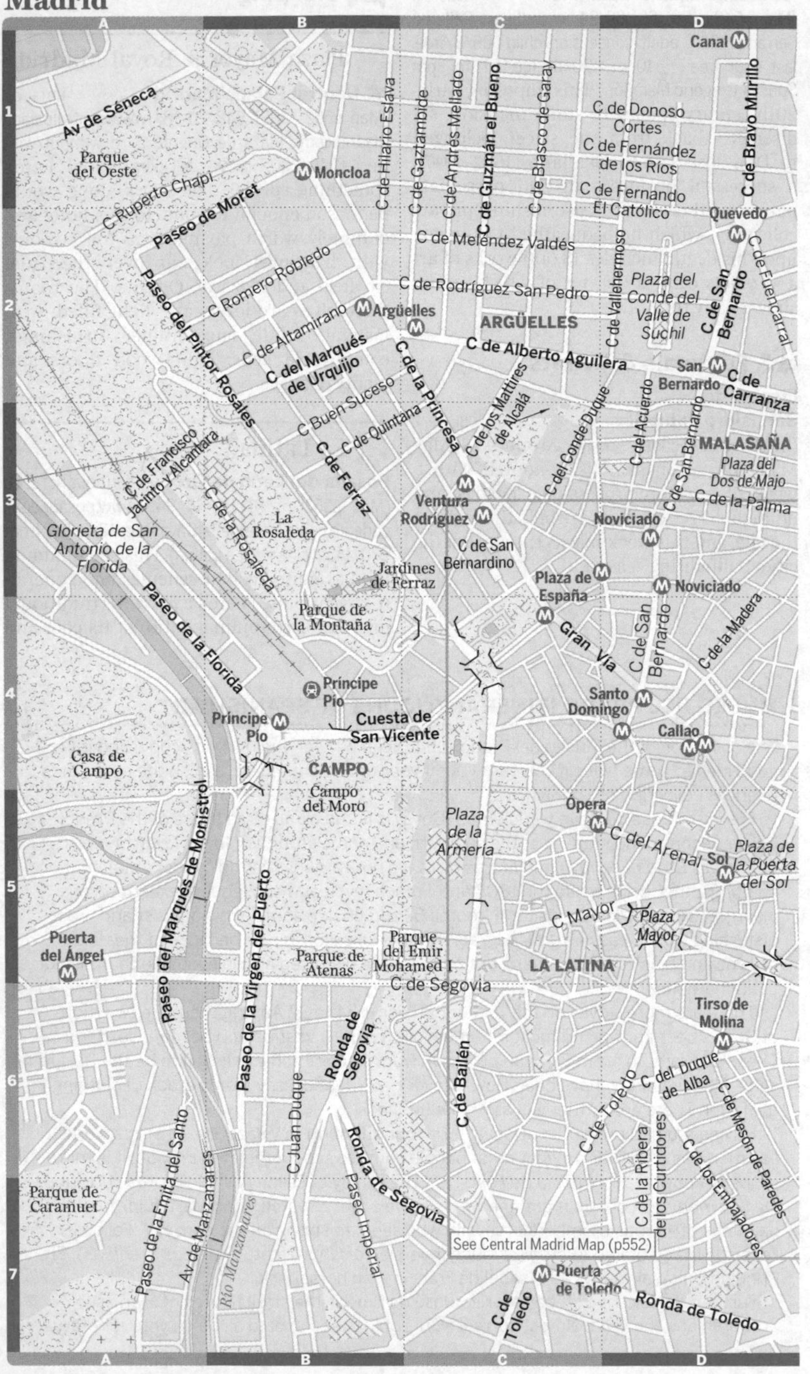
A
B
C
D
1
2
3
4
5
6
7
Av de Séneca
Parque del Oeste
C Ruperto Chapí
Paseo de Moret
Moncloa
C de Hilario Eslava
C de Gaztambide
C de Andrés Mellado
C de Guzmán el Bueno
C de Blasco de Garay
C de Donoso Cortes
C de Fernández de los Ríos
C de Fernando El Católico
Canal
C de Bravo Murillo
Quevedo
C de Fuencarral
C de Meléndez Valdés
C de Rodríguez San Pedro
C de Vallehermoso
Plaza del Conde del Valle de Suchil
C de San Bernardo
Paseo del Pintor Rosales
C Romero Robledo
C de Altamirano
Argüelles
ARGÜELLES
C de Alberto Aguilera
San Bernardo
C de Carranza
C del Marqués de Urquijo
C de la Princesa
C Buen Suceso
C de Quintana
C de los Mártires de Alcalá
C del Conde Duque
C del Acuerdo
MALASAÑA
Plaza del Dos de Mayo
C de la Palma
C de Ferraz
C de Francisco Jacinto y Alcántara
C de la Rosaleda
La Rosaleda
Ventura Rodríguez
Noviciado
Glorieta de San Antonio de la Florida
Paseo de la Florida
C de San Bernardino
Jardines de Ferraz
Plaza de España
Parque de la Montaña
Gran Vía
C de la Madera
Príncipe Pío
Cuesta de San Vicente
Santo Domingo
Callao
Casa de Campo
CAMPO
Campo del Moro
Plaza de la Armería
Ópera
C del Arenal
Sol
Plaza de la Puerta del Sol
Paseo del Marqués de Monistrol
Paseo de la Virgen del Puerto
C Mayor
Plaza Mayor
Puerta del Ángel
Parque de Atenas
Parque del Emir Mohamed I
C de Segovia
LA LATINA
Tirso de Molina
Ronda de Segovia
C Juan Duque
C de Bailén
C de Toledo
C del Duque de Alba
C de Mesón de Paredes
C de la Ribera de los Curtidores
C de los Embajadores
Paseo de la Emita del Santo
Av de Manzanares
Río Manzanares
Paseo Imperial
Parque de Caramuel
See Central Madrid Map (p552)
Puerta de Toledo
Ronda de Toledo

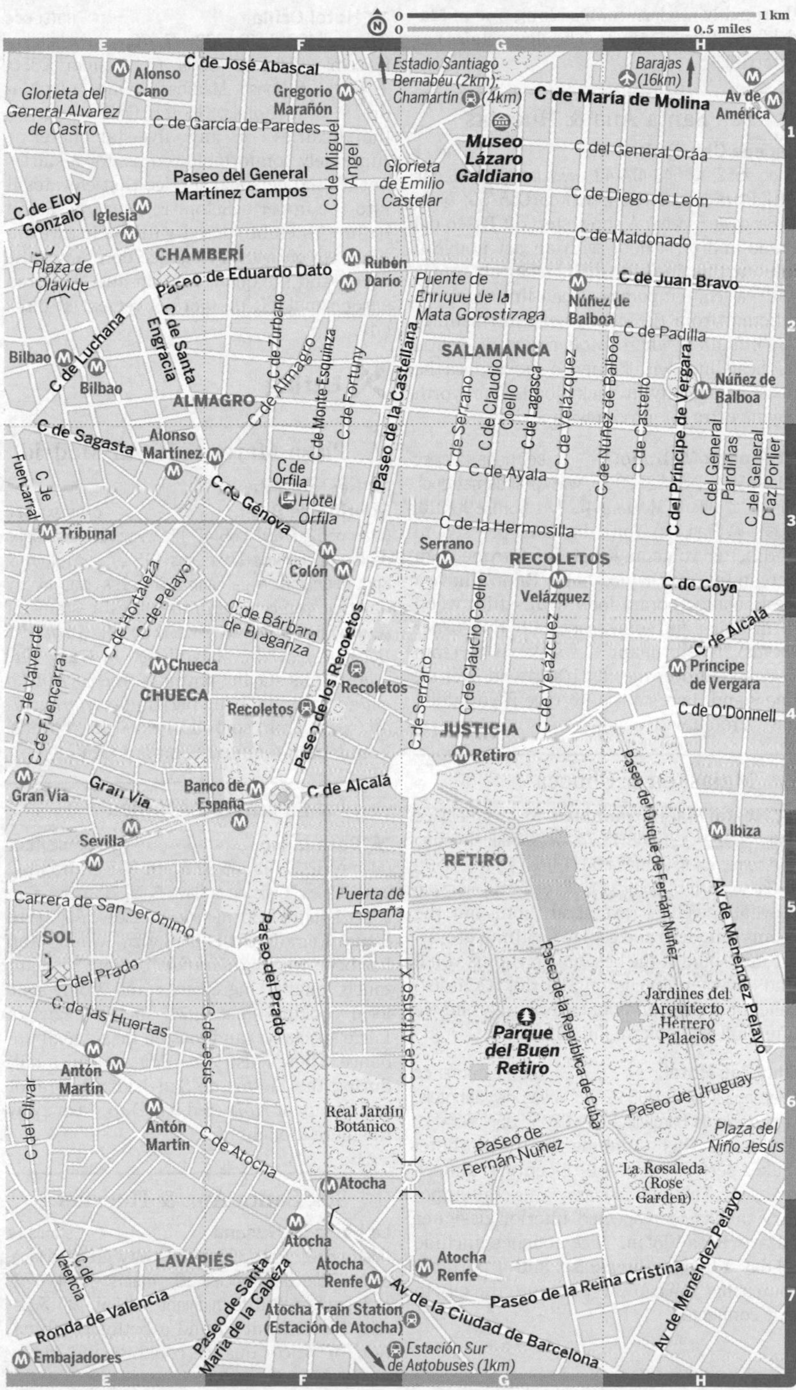
0 1 km
0 0.5 miles
E
F
G
H
C de José Abascal
Alonso Cano
Glorieta del General Alvarez de Castro
Gregorio Marañón
Estadio Santiago Bernabéu (2km); Chamartín (4km)
Barajas (16km)
C de María de Molina
Av de América
C de García de Paredes
Museo Lázaro Galdiano
C del General Oráa
Paseo del General Martínez Campos
C de Miguel Angel
Glorieta de Emilio Castelar
C de Diego de León
C de Eloy Gonzalo
Iglesia
C de Maldonado
CHAMBERÍ
Plaza de Olavide
Paseo de Eduardo Dato
Rubén Darío
Puente de Enrique de la Mata Gorostizaga
Núñez de Balboa
C de Juan Bravo
C de Padilla
C de Zurbano
C de Santa Engracia
C de Luchana
Bilbao
C de Almagro
C de Monte Esquinza
C de Fortuny
Paseo de la Castellana
SALAMANCA
C de Serrano
C de Claudio Coello
C de Lagasca
C de Velázquez
C de Núñez de Balboa
C de Castelló
C del Príncipe de Vergara
C del General Pardiñas
C del General Díaz Porlier
ALMAGRO
C de Sagasta
Alonso Martínez
C de Fuencarral
C de Orfila
Hotel Orfila
C de Ayala
C de Génova
Tribunal
C de la Hermosilla
Serrano
RECOLETOS
Colón
Velázquez
C de Goya
C de Hortaleza
C de Pelayo
C de Bárbara de Braganza
Paseo de los Recoletos
C de Alcalá
Príncipe de Vergara
Chueca
CHUECA
Recoletos
C de Valverde
C de O'Donnell
JUSTICIA
Retiro
Gran Vía
Banco de España
Paseo del Duque de Fernán Núñez
Ibiza
Sevilla
RETIRO
Av de Menéndez Pelayo
Carrera de San Jerónimo
Puerta de España
Paseo del Prado
SOL
Paseo de la República de Cuba
C del Prado
C de las Huertas
C de Jesús
C de Alfonso XII
Jardines del Arquitecto Herrero Palacios
Parque del Buen Retiro
Antón Martín
C del Olivar
Paseo de Uruguay
Real Jardín Botánico
Plaza del Niño Jesús
C de Atocha
Paseo de Fernán Nuñez
La Rosaleda (Rose Garden)
Atocha
LAVAPIÉS
C de Valencia
Atocha Renfe
Paseo de la Reina Cristina
Av de la Ciudad de Barcelona
Ronda de Valencia
Paseo de Santa María de la Cabeza
Atocha Train Station (Estación de Atocha)
Estación Sur de Autobuses (1km)
Embajadores
1
2
3
4
5
6
7

thoroughly modern rooms along one of Madrid's best-loved streets. The downstairs bar is terrific.

Sol, Santa Ana & Huertas

Lapepa Chic B&B B&B €

(Map p552; 648 474742; www.lapepa-bnb.com; 7th fl, Plaza de las Cortes 4; s/d from €55/60; ; Banco de España) A short step off Paseo del Prado and on a floor with an art nouveau interior, this fine little B&B has lovely rooms with a contemporary, clean-line look so different from the dour *hostal* furnishings you'll find elsewhere. Modern art or even a bedhead lined with flamenco shoes gives the place personality in bucketloads. It's worth paying extra for a room with a view.

★Praktik Metropol BOUTIQUE HOTEL €€

(Map p552; 91 521 29 35; www.praktikmetropol.com; Calle de la Montera 47; s/d from €90/110; ; Gran Vía) You'd be hard-pressed to find better value anywhere in Europe than here in this overhauled hotel. Rooms have a fresh, contemporary look with white wood furnishings, and some (especially the corner rooms) have brilliant views down to Gran Vía and out over the city. It's spread over six floors and there's a roof terrace if you don't have a room with a view.

Malasaña & Chueca

★Hostal Main Street Madrid HOSTAL €

(Map p552; 91 548 18 78; www.mainstreetmadrid.com; 5th fl, Gran Vía 50; r from €140; ; Callao, Santo Domingo) Excellent service is what travellers rave about here, but the rooms – modern and cool in soothing greys – are also some of the best *hostal* rooms you'll find anywhere in central Madrid. It's an excellent package, and not surprisingly they're often full, so book well in advance.

Only You Hotel BOUTIQUE HOTEL €€

(Map p552; 91 005 22 22; www.onlyyouhotels.com; Calle de Barquillo 21; d €205-285; @; Chueca) This stunning boutique hotel makes perfect use of a 19th-century Chueca mansion. The look is classy and contemporary thanks to respected interior designer Lázaro Rosa-Violán. Nice touches include all-day à la carte breakfasts and a portable router that you can carry out into the city to stay connected.

★Hotel Orfila HOTEL €€€

(Map p548; 91 702 77 70; www.hotelorfila.com; Calle de Orfila 6; r from €350; P; Alonso Martínez) One of Madrid's best hotels, Hotel Orfila has all the luxuries of any five-star hotel – supremely comfortable rooms, for a start – but it's the personal service that elevates it into the upper echelon; regular guests get bathrobes embroidered with their own initials. An old-world elegance dominates the decor, and the quiet location and sheltered garden make it the perfect retreat at day's end.

Eating

Plaza Mayor & Royal Madrid

★Restaurante Sobrino de Botín CASTILIAN €€€

(Map p552; 91 366 42 17; www.botin.es; Calle de los Cuchilleros 17; mains €18-27; 1-4pm & 8pm-midnight; La Latina, Sol) It's not every day that you can eat in the oldest restaurant in the world (as recognised by the *Guinness Book of Records* – established in 1725). The secret of its staying power is fine *cochinillo asado* (roast suckling pig) and *cordero asado* (roast lamb) cooked in wood-fired ovens. Eating in the vaulted cellar is a treat.

La Latina & Lavapiés

★Casa Lucio SPANISH €€€

(Map p552; 91 365 32 52, 91 365 82 17; www.casalucio.es; Calle de la Cava Baja 35; mains €18-29; 1-4pm & 8.30pm-midnight, closed Aug; La Latina) Casa Lucio is a Madrid classic and has been wowing *madrileños* with his light touch, quality ingredients and home-style local cooking since 1974, such as eggs (a Lucio speciality) and roasted meats in abundance. There's also *rabo de toro* (bull's tail) during the Fiestas de San Isidro Labrador and plenty of *rioja* (red wine) to wash away the mere thought of it.

Sol, Santa Ana & Huertas

La Finca de Susana SPANISH €

(Map p552; 91 369 35 57; www.grupandilana.com; Calle del Príncipe 10; mains €8-14; 1-11.30pm Sun-Wed, to midnight Thu-Sat; ; Sevilla) It's difficult to find a better combination of price, quality cooking and classy

MADRID'S BEST SQUARES

Plaza de Oriente (Map p552; Ⓜ Ópera) is a living, breathing monument to imperial Madrid. Here you'll find sophisticated cafes watched over by apartments that cost the equivalent of a royal salary; the **Teatro Real** (Map p552; ☎ 902 244848; www.teatro-real.com), Madrid's opera house and one of Spain's temples to high culture; and Palacio Real (p546), which once had aspirations to be the Spanish Versailles. Local legend has it that the marble statues surrounding the square get down off their pedestals at night to stretch their legs when no one's looking.

On the other hand, the intimate **Plaza de la Villa** (Map p552; Ⓜ Ópera) is one of Madrid's prettiest. Enclosed on three sides by wonderfully preserved examples of 17th-century *barroco madrileño* (Madrid-style baroque architecture – a pleasing amalgam of brick, exposed stone and wrought iron), it was the permanent seat of Madrid's city government from the Middle Ages until recent years, when Madrid's city council relocated to the grand Palacio de Cibeles on **Plaza de la Cibeles** (Map p552; Ⓜ Banco de España).

Plaza de Santa Ana (Map p552; Ⓜ Sevilla, Sol, Antón Martín) is a delightful confluence of elegant architecture and irresistible energy. It presides over the upper reaches of the Barrio de las Letras and this literary personality makes its presence felt with statues of the 17th-century writer Calderón de la Barca and poet Federico García Lorca, and in the **Teatro Español** (Map p552; ☎ 91 360 14 84; www.teatroespanol.es; Calle del Príncipe 25; Ⓜ Sevilla, Sol, Antón Martín), formerly the Teatro del Príncipe, at the plaza's eastern end. Apart from anything else, the plaza is the starting point for many a long Huertas night.

atmosphere anywhere in Huertas. The softly lit dining area has a sophisticated vibe and the sometimes-innovative, sometimes-traditional food draws a hip young crowd. The duck confit with plums, turnips and couscous is a fine choice. No reservations.

Malasaña & Chueca

Bazaar MODERN SPANISH €
(Map p552; ☎ 91 523 39 05; www.restaurantbazaar.com; Calle de la Libertad 21; mains €8-13; ⏲ 1pm-11.30pm Sun-Wed, to midnight Thu-Sat; 📶; Ⓜ Chueca) Bazaar's popularity among the well-heeled Chueca set shows no sign of abating. Its pristine white interior design, with theatre-style lighting and wall-length windows, may draw a crowd that looks like it's stepped out of the pages of *¡Hola!* magazine, but the food is extremely well priced and innovative, and the atmosphere is casual.

Yakitoro by Chicote JAPANESE, SPANISH €€
(Map p552; ☎ 91 737 14 41; www.yakitoro.com; Calle de la Reina 41; tapas €3-9; ⏲ 1pm-midnight; Ⓜ Banco de España) Based around the idea of a Japanese tavern, driven by a spirit of innovation and a desire to combine the best in Spanish and Japanese flavours, Yakitoro is a hit. Apart from salads, it's all built around brochettes cooked over a wood fire, with wonderful combinations of vegetable, seafood and meat.

Drinking & Nightlife

Nights in the Spanish capital are the stuff of legend. They're invariably long and loud most nights of the week, rising to a deafening crescendo as the weekend nears. And what Ernest Hemingway wrote of the city in the 1930s remains true to this day: 'Nobody goes to bed in Madrid until they have killed the night.'

Delic BAR
(Map p552; ☎ 91 364 54 50; www.delic.es; Costanilla de San Andrés 14; ⏲ 11am-2am Sun & Tue-Thu, to 2.30am Fri & Sat; Ⓜ La Latina) We could go on for hours about this long-standing cafe-bar, but we'll reduce it to its most basic elements: nursing an exceptionally good mojito or three on a warm summer's evening at Delic's outdoor tables on one of Madrid's prettiest plazas is one of life's great pleasures. Bliss.

★ **La Venencia** BAR
(Map p552; ☎ 91 429 73 13; Calle de Echegaray 7; ⏲ 12.30-3.30pm & 7.30pm-1.30am; Ⓜ Sol, Sevilla) La Venencia is a *barrio* classic, with *manzanilla* (chamomile-coloured sherry) from

Central Madrid

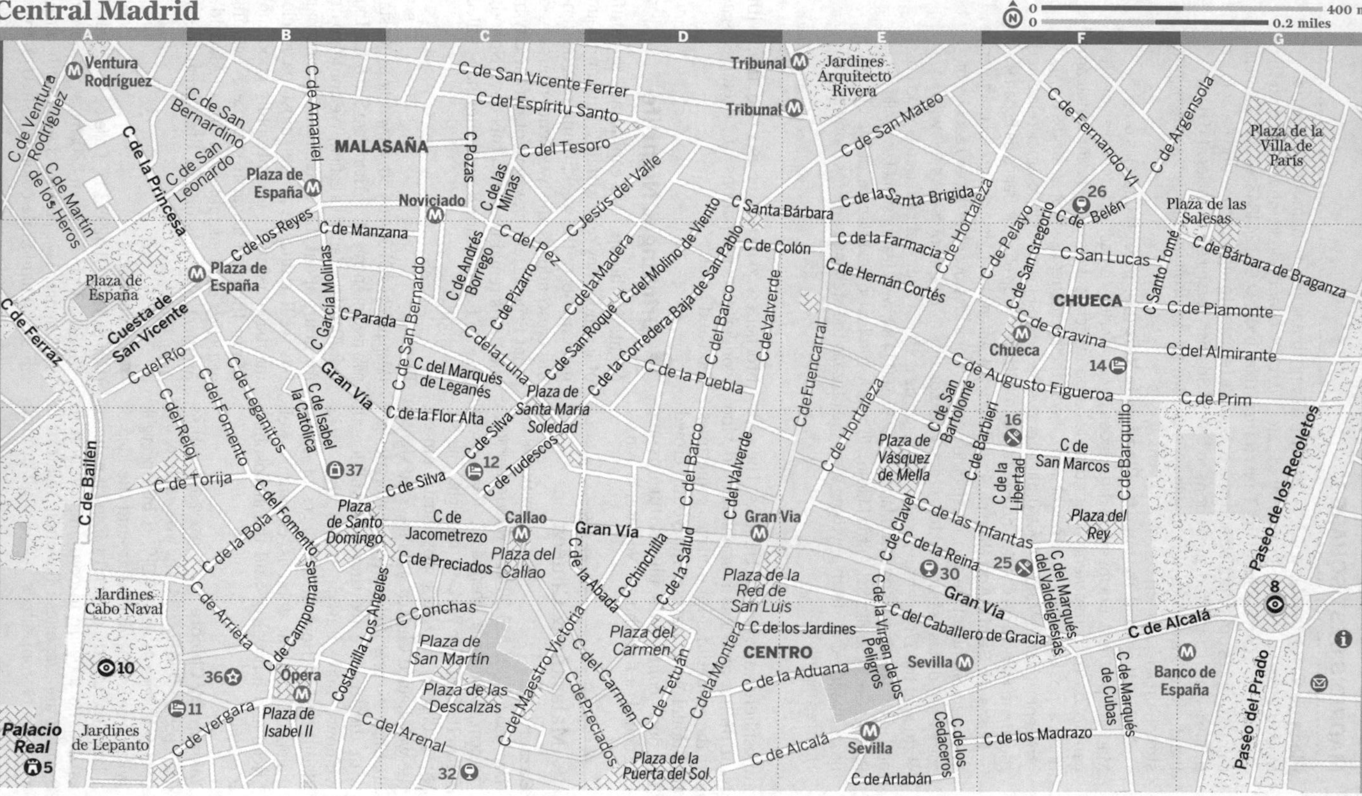

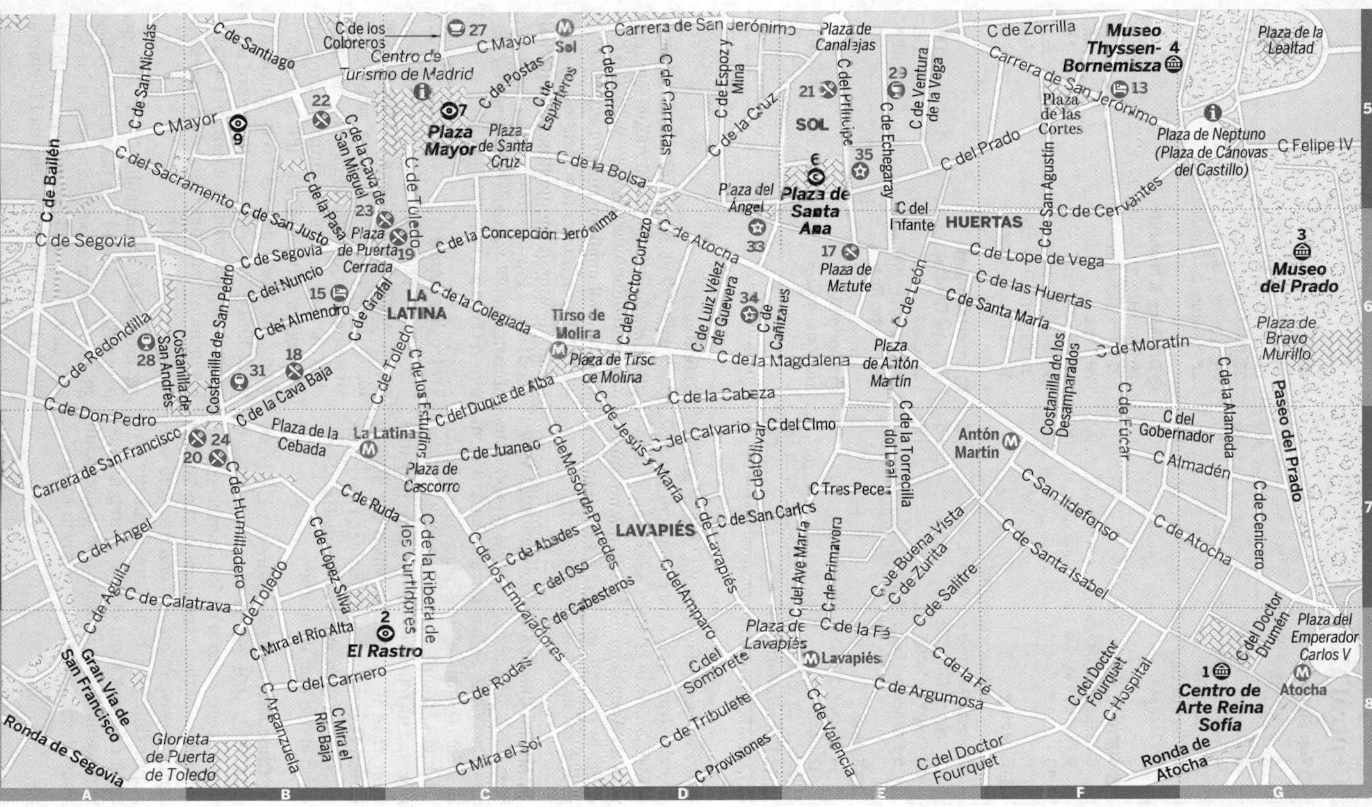
C de Santiago
C de los Coloreros
Centro de Turismo de Madrid
C Mayor
Sol
Carrera de San Jerónimo
Plaza de Canalejas
C de Zorrilla
Museo Thyssen-Bornemisza
Plaza de la Lealtad
C de San Nicolás
C de Postas
C de Esparteros
C del Correo
C de Carretas
C de Espoz y Mina
C de la Cruz
SOL
C del Príncipe
C de Echegaray
C de Ventura de la Vega
Carrera de San Jerónimo
Plaza de las Cortes
Plaza de Neptuno (Plaza de Cánovas del Castillo)
C Felipe IV
C Mayor
Plaza Mayor
Plaza de Santa Cruz
C de Bailén
C del Sacramento
C de la Cava de San Miguel
C de Toledo
C de la Bolsa
C de la Pasa
Plaza del Ángel
Plaza de Santa Ana
C del Prado
C del Infante
HUERTAS
C de San Agustín
C de Cervantes
C de Segovia
C de San Justo
Plaza de Puerta Cerrada
C de la Concepción Jerónima
C del Doctor Cortezo
C de Atocha
Plaza de Matute
C de Lope de Vega
Museo del Prado
C de Segovia
C del Nuncio
LA LATINA
C de la Colegiata
C de Luiz Vélez de Guevera
C de Cañizares
C de León
C de las Huertas
C de Santa María
C de Redondilla
Costanilla de San Andrés
Costanilla de San Pedro
C del Almendro
C de Grafal
Tirso de Molina
Plaza de Tirso de Molina
C de la Magdalena
Plaza de Antón Martín
Costanilla de los Desamparados
C de Moratín
Plaza de Bravo Murillo
C de la Alameda
Paseo del Prado
C de la Cava Baja
C de Toledo
C de los Estudios
C del Duque de Alba
C de la Cabeza
C de la Torrecilla del Leal
C de Fúcar
C del Gobernador
C de Don Pedro
Plaza de la Cebada
La Latina
C del Calvario
C del Olivar
C del Olmo
Antón Martín
C Almadén
Carrera de San Francisco
C de Humilladero
C de Juanelo
Plaza de Cascorro
C de Mesón de Paredes
C de Jesús y María
C Tres Peces
C San Ildefonso
C de Cenicero
C de Ruda
C de la Ribera de los Curtidores
C de Abades
LAVAPIÉS
C de San Carlos
C de Lavapiés
C de Buena Vista
C de Zurita
C de Santa Isabel
C de Atocha
C del Ángel
C de López Silva
C de los Embajadores
C del Oso
C de Cabestreros
C del Amparo
C del Ave María
C de Primavera
C de Salitre
C de Aguila
C de Calatrava
C de Toledo
C Mira el Río Alta
El Rastro
Plaza de Lavapiés
C de la Fé
C del Doctor Drumen
Plaza del Emperador Carlos V
Gran Vía de San Francisco
C del Carnero
C de Rodas
C del Sombrerete
Lavapiés
C de la Fé
C de Argumosa
C del Doctor Fourquet
C Hospital
Centro de Arte Reina Sofía
Atocha
Ronda de Segovia
Glorieta de Puerta de Toledo
C Arganzuela
C Mira el Río Baja
C Mira el Sol
C de Tribulete
C Provisiones
C de Valencia
C del Doctor Fourquet
Ronda de Atocha

Central Madrid

Top Sights
1 Centro de Arte Reina Sofía G8
2 El Rastro B8
3 Museo del Prado G6
4 Museo Thyssen-Bornemisza F5
5 Palacio Real A4
6 Plaza de Santa Ana E5
7 Plaza Mayor C5

Sights
8 Plaza de la Cibeles G4
9 Plaza de la Villa B5
10 Plaza de Oriente A4

Sleeping
11 Central Palace Madrid A4
12 Hostal Main Street Madrid C3
13 Lapepa Chic B&B F5
14 Only You Hotel F2
15 Posada del León de Oro B6

Eating
16 Bazaar F3
17 Casa Alberto E6
18 Casa Lucio B6
19 Casa Revuelta C6
20 Juana La Loca B7
21 La Finca de Susana E5
22 Mercado de San Miguel B5
23 Restaurante Sobrino de Botín C6
24 Txirimiri B7
25 Yakitoro by Chicote F3

Drinking & Nightlife
26 Café Belén F1
27 Chocolatería de San Ginés C5
28 Delic A6
29 La Venencia E5
30 Museo Chicote E3
31 Taberna El Tempranillo B6
32 Teatro Joy Eslava C4

Entertainment
33 Café Central D6
34 Casa Patas D6
35 Teatro Español E5
36 Teatro Real B4

Shopping
37 Antigua Casa Talavera B3

Sanlúcar and sherry from Jeréz poured straight from the dusty wooden barrels, accompanied by a small selection of tapas with an Andalucian bent. There's no music, no flashy decorations; here it's all about you, your *fino* (sherry) and your friends.

★ **Museo Chicote** COCKTAIL BAR
(Map p552; ☎91 532 67 37; www.museochicote.com; Gran Vía 12; ⏰7pm-3am Sun-Thu, to 3.30am Fri & Sat; Ⓜ Gran Vía) This place is a Madrid landmark, complete with its 1930s-era interior, and its founder is said to have invented more than 100 cocktails, which the likes of Ernest Hemingway, Ava Gardner, Grace Kelly, Sophia Loren and Frank Sinatra all enjoyed at one time or another.

★ **Chocolatería de San Ginés** CAFE
(Map p552; ☎91 365 65 46; www.chocolateriasangines.com; Pasadizo de San Ginés 5; ⏰24hr; Ⓜ Sol) One of the grand icons of the Madrid night, this *chocolate con churros* cafe sees a sprinkling of tourists throughout the day, but locals pack it out in their search for sustenance on their way home from a nightclub somewhere close to dawn. Only in Madrid…

Café Belén BAR
(Map p552; ☎91 308 27 47; www.elcafebelen.com; Calle de Belén 5; ⏰3.30pm-3am Tue-Thu, to 3.30am Fri & Sat, 7-10pm Sun; 📶; Ⓜ Chueca) Café Belén is cool in all the right places – lounge and chill-out music, dim lighting, a great range of drinks (the mojitos are especially good) and a low-key crowd that's the height of casual sophistication. It's one of our preferred Chueca watering holes.

Teatro Joy Eslava CLUB
(Joy Madrid; Map p552; ☎91 366 37 33; www.joy-eslava.com; Calle del Arenal 11; admission €10-18; ⏰11.30pm-6am; Ⓜ Sol) The only things guaranteed at this grand old Madrid dance club (housed in a 19th-century theatre) are a crowd and the fact that it'll be open (it claims to have operated every single day since 1981). The music and the crowd are a mixed bag, but queues are long and invariably include locals, tourists and the occasional *famoso* (celebrity).

★ **Taberna El Tempranillo** WINE BAR
(Map p552; ☎91 364 15 32; Calle de la Cava Baja 38; ⏰1-4pm Mon, 1-4pm & 8pm-midnight Tue-Sun; Ⓜ La Latina) You could come here for the tapas, but we recommend Taberna El Tempra-

nillo primarily for its wines, of which it has a selection that puts numerous Spanish bars to shame. It's not a late-night place, but it's always packed in the early evening and on Sunday after El Rastro. Many wines are sold by the glass.

☆ Entertainment

★Casa Patas FLAMENCO

(Map p552; 91 369 04 96; www.casapatas.com; Calle de Cañizares 10; admission incl drink €38; shows 10.30pm Mon-Thu, 8pm & 10.30pm Fri & Sat; Antón Martín, Tirso de Molina) One of the top flamenco stages in Madrid, this *tablao* (choreographed flamenco show) always offers flawless quality that serves as a good introduction to the art. It's not the friendliest place in town, especially if you're only here for the show, and you're likely to be crammed in a little, but no one complains about the standard of the performances.

★Café Central JAZZ

(Map p552; 91 369 41 43; www.cafecentralmadrid.com; Plaza del Ángel 10; admission €12-18; 11.30pm-2.30am Sun-Thu, to 3.30am Fri & Sat, performances 9pm; Antón Martín, Sol) In 2011 the respected jazz magazine *Down Beat* included this art deco bar on the list of the world's best jazz clubs, the only place in Spain to earn the prestigious accolade (said by some to be the jazz equivalent of earning a Michelin star). With well over 1000 gigs under its belt, it rarely misses a beat.

A TAPAS TOUR OF MADRID

Madrid's home of tapas is La Latina, especially along Calle de la Cava Baja and the surrounding streets.

Juana La Loca (Map p552; 91 366 55 00; www.juanalalocamadrid.com; Plaza de la Puerta de Moros 4; tapas from €4, mains €10-30; 1.30-5.30pm Tue-Sun, 7pm-midnight Sat Wed, to 1am Thu-Fri; La Latina) Juana La Loca does a range of creative tapas with tempting options lined up along the bar, and more on the menu that they prepare to order. But we love it above all for its brilliant *tortilla de patatas*, which is distinguished from others of its kind by the caramelised onions – simply wonderful.

Txirimiri (Map p552; 91 364 11 96; www.txirimiri.es; Calle del Humilladero 6; tapas from €3; noon-midnight; La Latina) This *pintxos* (Basque tapas) bar is a great little discovery just down from the main La Latina tapas circuit. Wonderful wines, gorgeous *pinchos* (the *tortilla de patatas* – potato and onion omelette – is superb) and fine risottos add up to a pretty special combination.

Mercado de San Miguel (Map p552; 91 542 49 36; www.mercadodesanmiguel.es; Plaza de San Miguel; tapas from €1.50; 10am-midnight Sun-Thu, to 1am Fri & Sat; Sol) This is one of Madrid's oldest and most beautiful markets, within early-20th-century glass walls and an inviting space strewn with tables. You can order tapas and sometimes more substantial plates at most of the counter bars, and everything here (from caviar to chocolate) is as tempting as the market is alive. Put simply, it's one of our favourite experiences in Madrid.

Casa Revuelta (Map p552; 91 366 33 32; Calle de Latoneros 3; tapas from €3; 10am-4pm & 7-11pm Tue-Sat, 10am-4pm Sun, closed Aug; Sol, La Latina) Casa Revuelta puts out some of Madrid's finest tapas of *bacalao* (cod) bar none – unlike elsewhere, *tajadas de bacalao* don't have bones in them and slide down the throat with the greatest of ease. Early on a Sunday afternoon, as the Rastro crowd gathers here, it's filled to the rafters. Other specialities include *torreznos* (bacon bits), *callos* (tripe) and *albóndigas* (meatballs).

Casa Alberto (Map p552; 91 429 93 56; www.casaalberto.es; Calle de las Huertas 18; tapas €3.25-10, raciones €7-16.50, mains €16-19; restaurant 1.30-4pm & 8pm-midnight Tue-Sat, 1.30-4pm Sun, bar noon-1.30am Tue-Sat, 12.30-4pm Sun, closed Sun Jul & Aug; Antón Martín) One of the most atmospheric old *tabernas* (taverns) of Madrid, Casa Alberto has been around since 1827 and occupies a building where Cervantes is said to have written one of his books. The secret to its staying power is vermouth on tap, excellent tapas at the bar and fine sit-down meals.

Estadio Santiago Bernabéu STADIUM
(☎tickets 90 232 43 24, tours 91 398 43 70; www.realmadrid.com; Avenida de Concha Espina 1; tours adult/child €25/18; ⏲tours 10am-7pm Mon-Sat, 10.30am-6.30pm Sun, except match days; Ⓜ Santiago Bernabéu) Football fans and budding Madridistas (Real Madrid supporters) will want to make a pilgrimage to the Estadio Santiago Bernabéu, a temple to all that's extravagant and successful in football. Self-guided tours take you up into the stands for a panoramic view of the stadium, then through the presidential box, press room, dressing rooms, players' tunnel and even onto the pitch. The tour ends in the extraordinary Exposición de Trofeos (trophy exhibit). Better still, attend a game alongside 80,000 delirious fans.

Shopping

Our favourite aspect of shopping in Madrid is the city's small boutiques and quirky shops. Often run by the same families for generations, they counter the over commercialisation of mass-produced Spanish culture with everything from fashions to old-style ceramics to rope-soled espadrilles or gourmet Spanish food and wine.

★ **El Rastro** MARKET
(Map p552; Calle de la Ribera de los Curtidores; ⏲9am-3pm Sun; Ⓜ La Latina) A Sunday morning at El Rastro flea market is a Madrid institution. You could easily spend an entire morning inching your way down the hill and the maze of streets. Cheap clothes, luggage, old flamenco records, even older photos of Madrid, faux-designer purses, grungy T-shirts, household goods and electronics are the main fare. For every 10 pieces of junk, there's a real gem (a lost masterpiece, an Underwood typewriter) waiting to be found.

Antigua Casa Talavera CERAMICS
(Map p552; ☎91 547 34 17; www.antiguacasatalavera.com; Calle de Isabel la Católica 2; ⏲10am-1.30pm & 5-8pm Mon-Fri, 10am-1.30pm Sat; Ⓜ Santo Domingo) The extraordinary tiled facade of this wonderful old shop conceals an Aladdin's cave of ceramics from all over Spain. This is not the mass-produced stuff aimed at a tourist market, but instead comes from the small family potters of Andalucía and Toledo, ranging from the decorative (tiles) to the useful (plates, jugs and other kitchen items). The elderly couple who run the place are delightful.

Information

SAFE TRAVEL

Madrid is generally safe, but as in any large European city, keep an eye on your belongings and exercise common sense.

➡ El Rastro, around the Museo del Prado and the metro are favourite pickpocketing haunts, as are any areas where tourists congregate in large numbers.

➡ Avoid park areas (such as the Parque del Buen Retiro) after dark.

➡ Keep a close eye on your taxi's meter and try to keep track of the route to make sure you're not being taken for a ride.

TOURIST INFORMATION

The Madrid government's **Centro de Turismo** (Map p552; ☎91 578 78 10; www.esmadrid.com; Plaza Mayor 27; ⏲9.30am-9.30pm; Ⓜ Sol) is terrific. Housed in the Real Casa de la Panadería on the northern side of the Plaza Mayor, it allows access to its outstanding website and city database, and offers free downloads of the metro map to your phone. Staff are also helpful.

Getting There & Away

AIR

Madrid's **Adolfo Suárez Madrid-Barajas** (☎902 404704; www.aena.es; Ⓜ Aeropuerto T1, T2 & T3, Aeropuerto T4) airport lies 15km northeast of the city, and it's Europe's sixth-busiest hub, with almost 50 million passengers passing through here every year. The airport has four terminals: terminal 4 (T4) deals mainly with flights of Iberia and its partners (eg British Airways, American Airlines and Vueling), while the remainder leave from the conjoined T1, T2 and (rarely) T3.

Direct flights connect the city with destinations across Europe, as well as the Americas, Asia and Africa.

BUS

Estación Sur de Autobuses (☎91 468 42 00; Calle de Méndez Álvaro 83; Ⓜ Méndez Álvaro), just south of the M30 ring road, is the city's principal bus station. It serves most destinations to the south and many in other parts of the country. Most bus companies have a ticket office here, even if their buses depart from elsewhere. Avanzabus has services to Cáceres (€23, four to five hours, seven daily), Salamanca (€21, 2½ to 3½ hours, hourly) and Valencia (€28, 4¼ hours, nine daily). There are also international buses to Lisbon (€42 to €46, seven to 7½ hours, three daily).

TRAIN

All trains are run by **Renfe** (☎912 320 320; www.renfe.com). High-speed AVE (Tren de Alta

Velocidad Española) services connect Madrid with Alicante, Barcelona, Córdoba, Huesca, León, Málaga, Seville, Valencia, Valladolid, Zaragoza and some towns en route.

North of the city centre, **Estación de Chamartín** (☎912 432 343; Paseo de la Castellana; Ⓜ Chamartín) has numerous long-distance rail services, especially those to/from northern Spain. This is also where long-haul international trains arrive from Paris and Lisbon.

Madrid's main train station **Puerta de Atocha** (www.renfe.es; Avenida de la Ciudad de Barcelona; Ⓜ Atocha Renfe) is at the southern end of the city centre. The bulk of trains for Spanish destinations depart from Atocha, especially those going south.

Getting Around

TO/FROM THE AIRPORT

Bus

The **Exprés Aeropuerto** (Airport Express; www.emtmadrid.es; per person €5; ⏲24hr; 📶) runs between Puerta de Atocha train station and the airport. From 11.55pm to 5.35am, departures are from the Plaza de Cibeles, not the train station. Services depart every 15 to 20 minutes from the station or every 35 minutes during the night from Plaza de Cibeles.

Metro

One of the easiest ways into town from the airport is line 8 of the metro to the Nuevos Ministerios transport interchange, which connects with lines 10 and 6 and the local overground *cercanías* (local trains serving suburbs and nearby towns). It operates from 6.05am to 1.30am. A single ticket costs €4.50 including the €3 airport supplement. If you're charging your public transport card with a 10-ride Metrobús ticket (€12.20), you'll need to top it up with the €3 supplement if you're travelling to/from the airport. The journey to Nuevos Ministerios takes around 15 minutes, around 25 minutes from T4.

Taxi

There is a fixed rate of €30 for taxis from the airport to the city centre (around 30 minutes, depending on traffic; 35 to 40 minutes from T4).

PUBLIC TRANSPORT

Madrid's modern metro (www.metromadrid.es), Europe's second largest, is a fast, efficient and safe way to navigate Madrid, and generally easier than getting to grips with bus routes. There are 11 colour-coded lines in central Madrid, in addition to the modern southern suburban MetroSur system, as well as lines heading east to the population centres of Pozuelo and Boadilla del Monte. Colour maps showing the metro system are available from any metro station or online. The metro operates from 6.05am to 1.30am.

TAXI

You can pick up a taxi at ranks throughout town or simply flag one down. From 7am to 9pm Monday to Friday, flag fall is €2.40 and you pay €1.05 per kilometre. The rest of the time flag fall is €2.90 and the per-kilometre charge is €1.20. Several supplementary charges, usually posted inside the taxi, apply; these include €3 from taxi ranks at train and bus stations.

CASTILLA Y LEÓN

Salamanca

POP 144,436

Whether floodlit by night or bathed in late-afternoon light, there's something magical about Salamanca. This is a city of rare beauty, awash with golden sandstone overlaid with ochre-tinted Latin inscriptions – an extraordinary virtuosity of plateresque and Renaissance styles. The monumental highlights are many and the exceptional Plaza Mayor is unforgettable. This is also Castilla's liveliest city, home to a massive Spanish and international student population that throngs the streets at night and provides the city with so much vitality.

Sights

★Plaza Mayor SQUARE

Built between 1729 and 1755, Salamanca's grand square is widely considered to be Spain's most beautiful central plaza. The square is particularly memorable at night when illuminated (until midnight) to magical effect. Designed by Alberto Churriguera, it's a remarkably harmonious and controlled baroque display. The medallions placed around the square bear the busts of famous figures.

★Universidad Civil HISTORIC BUILDING

(☎923 29 44 00, ext 1150; www.salamanca.es; Calle de los Libreros; adult/concession €10/5, audio guide €2; ⏲10am-7pm Mon-Sat mid-Sep–Mar, 10am-8pm Mon-Sat, to 2pm Sun Apr–mid-Sep) Founded initially as the Estudio General in 1218, the university reached the peak of its renown in the 15th and 16th centuries. The visual feast of the entrance facade is a tapestry in sandstone, bursting with images of mythical heroes, religious scenes and coats of arms. It's dominated by busts of Fernando and Isabel. Behind the facade, the highlight of an otherwise-modest collection of rooms lies upstairs: the extraordinary **university library**, the oldest in Europe.

Catedral Nueva CATHEDRAL

(☎923 21 74 76; www.catedralsalamanca.org; Plaza de Anaya; adult/child incl audio guide & Catedral Vieja €5/3; ⏰10am-8pm Apr-Sep, 10am-6pm Oct-Mar) The tower of this late-Gothic cathedral lords over the city centre, its compelling Churrigueresque (an ornate style of baroque architecture) dome visible from almost every angle. The interior is similarly impressive, with elaborate choir stalls, main chapel and retrochoir, much of it courtesy of the prolific José Churriguera. The ceilings are also exceptional, along with the Renaissance doorways – particularly the **Puerta del Nacimiento** on the western face, which stands out as one of several miracles worked in the city's native sandstone.

Museo de Art Nouveau y Art Decó MUSEUM

(Casa Lis; ☎923 12 14 25; www.museocasalis.org; Calle de Gibraltar; adult/under 12yr €4/free, 11am-2pm Thu free; ⏰11am-8pm Tue-Sun Apr-Oct, plus 11am-8pm Mon Aug, 11am-2pm & 4-8pm Tue-Fri, 11am-8pm Sat & Sun Nov–Mar; 👪) Utterly unlike any other Salamanca museum, this stunning collection of sculpture, paintings and art deco and art nouveau pieces inhabits a beautiful, light-filled Modernista (Catalan art nouveau) house. There's abundant stained glass and exhibits that include Lalique glass, toys by Steiff (inventor of the teddy bear), Limoges porcelain, Fabergé watches, fabulous bronze and marble figurines, and a vast collection of 19th-century children's dolls (some strangely macabre), which kids will love. There's also a cafe and an excellent gift shop.

Sleeping

Hostal Concejo HOSTAL €

(☎92 087 521; https://hostalconcejo.com; Plaza de la Libertad 1; s €30, d €40-45; P❄📶) A cut above the average *hostal*, the stylish Concejo has polished-wood floors, tasteful furnishings, light-filled rooms and a superb central location. Try to snag one of the corner rooms, such as No 104, which has a traditional, glassed-in balcony, complete with a table, chairs and people-watching views.

Microtel Placentinos BOUTIQUE HOTEL €€

(☎923 28 15 31; www.microtelplacentinos.com; Calle de Placentinos 9; s/d incl breakfast Sun-Thu €62/75, Fri & Sat €75/90; ❄📶) One of Salamanca's most charming boutique hotels, Microtel Placentinos is tucked away on a quiet street and has rooms with exposed stone walls and wooden beams. The service is faultless, and the overall atmosphere one of intimacy and discretion. All rooms have a hydromassage shower or tub and there's an outside whirlpool spa (summer only).

★**Don Gregorio** BOUTIQUE HOTEL €€€

(☎923 21 70 15; www.hoteldongregorio.com; Calle de San Pablo 80; r/ste incl breakfast from €200/310; P❄📶) A palatial hotel with part of the city's Roman wall flanking the garden. Rooms are decorated in soothing café-con-leche shades with crisp white linens and extravagant extras, including private saunas, espresso machines, complimentary minibar, king-size beds and vast hydromassage tubs. Sumptuous antiques and medieval tapestries adorn the public areas.

Eating & Drinking

La Cocina de Toño TAPAS €€

(☎923 26 39 77; www.lacocinadetoño.es; Calle Gran Via 20; tapas from €2, set menus €17-38, mains €18-23; ⏰11am-4.30pm & 8pm-midnight Tue-Sat, 11am-4.30pm Sun; 📶) This place owes its loyal following to its creative *pinchos* (tapas-like snacks) and half-servings of dishes such as escalope of foie gras with roast apple and passionfruit gelatin. The restaurant serves more traditional fare as befits the decor, but the bar is one of Salamanca's gastronomic stars. Slightly removed from the old city, it draws a predominantly Spanish crowd.

★**Victor Gutierrez** CONTEMPORARY SPANISH €€€

(☎923 26 29 73; www.restaurantevictorgutierrez.com; Calle de Empedrada 4; set menus €65-95; ⏰1.30-4pm & 8.30pm-midnight Tue-Sat, 1.30-4pm Sun; 📶) This is still the best table in town. Chef Victor Gutierrez has a Michelin star and his place has a justifiably exclusive vibe, with an emphasis on innovative dishes with plenty of colourful drizzle. The choice of what to order is largely made for you with some excellent set menus that change regularly. Reservations essential.

The Doctor Cocktail COCKTAIL BAR

(☎923 26 31 51; www.facebook.com/thedoctorsalamanca; Calle del Doctor Piñuela 5; ⏰4pm-late) Excellent cocktails, friendly bar staff and a cool crowd make for a fine mix just north of the Plaza Mayor. Apart from the creative list of cocktails, it has over 30 different kinds of

WORTH A TRIP

ÁVILA

Ávila's old city is one of Spain's best-preserved medieval bastions, surrounded by imposing city walls comprising eight monumental gates, 88 watchtowers and more than 2500 turrets. Ávila a deeply religious city that for centuries has drawn pilgrims to the cult of Santa Teresa de Ávila, with its many churches, convents and high-walled palaces. It's 1½ hours from Madrid by train or bus, and about halfway between Segovia and Salamanca.

Murallas (www.muralladeavila.com; adult/under 12yr €5/3.50; ⌚10am-8pm Apr-Jun & Sep-Oct, to 9pm Jul & Aug, to 6pm Tue-Sun Nov-Mar; 👪) Ávila's splendid 12th-century walls stretch for 2.5km atop the remains of earlier Roman and Muslim battlements and rank among the world's best-preserved medieval defensive perimeters. Two sections of the walls can be climbed – a 300m stretch that can be accessed from just inside the Puerta del Alcázar, and a longer (1300m) stretch from Puerta de los Leales that runs the length of the old city's northern perimeter. The admission price includes a multilingual audio guide.

Catedral del Salvador (☎920 21 16 41; Plaza de la Catedral; incl audio guide €6; ⌚10am-8pm Mon-Fri, to 9pm Sat, 11.45am-7.30pm Sun Apr-Jun, Sep & Oct, 10am-9pm Mon-Sat, 11.45am-9pm Sun Jul & Aug, 10am-6pm Mon-Fri, to 7pm Sat, to 5.30pm Sun Nov-Mar) Ávila's 12th-century cathedral is both a house of worship and an ingenious fortress: its stout granite apse forms the central bulwark in the historic city walls. The sombre, Gothic-style facade conceals a magnificent interior with an exquisite early-16th-century altar frieze showing the life of Jesus, plus Renaissance-era carved choir stalls. There is also a museum with an El Greco painting and a splendid silver monstrance by Juan de Arfe. (Push the buttons to illuminate the altar and the choir stalls.)

Hotel El Rastro (☎920 35 22 25; www.elrastroavila.com; Calle Cepedas; s/d €45/90; 🐾📶) This atmospheric hotel occupies a former 16th-century palace with original stone, exposed brickwork and a natural, earth-toned colour scheme exuding a calm, understated elegance. Each room has a different form, but most have high ceilings and plenty of space. Note that the owners also run a marginally cheaper *hostal* (budget hotel) of the same name around the corner.

gin to choose from and above-average tonic to go with it.

ℹ Information

Oficina de Turismo (☎923 21 83 42; www.salamanca.es; Plaza Mayor 32; ⌚9am-7pm Mon-Fri, 10am-7pm Sat, to 2pm Sun) The municipal tourist office shares its space with the regional office on Plaza Mayor. An audio guide to city sights can be accessed on your smartphone via www.audioguiasalamanca.es.

ℹ Getting There & Away

The bus and train stations are a 10- and 15-minute walk, respectively, from Plaza Mayor.

There are buses to Madrid (regular/express €15/24, 2½ to 3¼ hours, hourly) and Ávila (€7, 1½ hours, four daily).

Trains run to Madrid's Chamartín station (from €20, 1½ to 4½ hours, 13 daily), Ávila (€12.25, 1¼ hours, eight daily) and Valladolid (from €10.45, 1½ hours, eight daily).

Segovia

POP 51,756

Set amid the rolling hills of Castilla, Unesco World Heritage–listed Segovia is a city of warm terracotta and sandstone hues, with a stunning monument to Roman grandeur and a castle said to have inspired Walt Disney.

👁 Sights

★Acueducto LANDMARK

Segovia's most recognisable symbol is El Acueducto (Roman Aqueduct), an 894m-long engineering wonder that looks like an enormous comb plunged into Segovia. First raised here by the Romans in the 1st century AD, the aqueduct was built with not a drop of mortar to hold together more than 20,000 uneven granite blocks. It's made up of 163 arches and, at its highest point in Plaza del Azoguejo, rises 28m high.

★**Alcázar** CASTLE

(☎921 46 07 59; www.alcazardesegovia.com; Plaza de la Reina Victoria Eugenia; adult/concession/under 6yr €8/5.50/free, tower €2.50, audio guide €3; ⏰10am-6pm Nov-Mar, to 8pm Apr-Oct; 👪) Rapunzel towers, turrets topped with slate witches' hats and a deep moat at its base make the Alcázar a prototypical fairy-tale castle – so much so that its design inspired Walt Disney's vision of Snow White's castle. Fortified since Roman days, the site takes its name from the Arabic *al-qasr* (fortress). It was rebuilt in the 13th and 14th centuries, but the whole lot burned down in 1862. What you see today is an evocative, over-the-top reconstruction of the original.

Catedral CATHEDRAL

(☎921 46 22 05; www.turismodesegovia.com; Plaza Mayor; adult/concession €3/2.50, Sun morning free, tower tour €5; ⏰9am-9.30pm Apr-Oct, 9.30am-6.30pm Nov-Mar, tower tours 10.30pm, noon, 1.30pm & 4pm year-round) Started in 1525 on the site of a former chapel, Segovia's cathedral is a powerful expression of Gothic architecture that took almost 200 years to complete. The austere three-nave interior is anchored by an imposing choir stall and enlivened by 20-odd chapels, including the Capilla del Cristo del Consuelo, with its magnificent Romanesque doorway, and the Capilla de la Piedad, containing an important altarpiece by Juan de Juni. Join an hour-long guided tour to climb the tower for fabulous views.

Sleeping & Eating

Häb Urban Hostel HOSTAL €

(☎921 46 10 26; www.habhostel.com; Calle de Cervantes 16; r €60-90; ❄📶) This bright and welcoming *hostal* has doubles with private bathrooms rather than dorms with bunk beds, despite the name. It's modern and has a fine location just where the pedestrian street begins the climb up into the old town. Some rooms are on the small side, but the look is light and contemporary.

★**Hotel Palacio San Facundo** HISTORIC HOTEL €€

(☎921 46 30 61; www.hotelpalaciosanfacundo.com; Plaza San Facundo 4; s/d incl breakfast €95/145; ❄@📶) Segovia's hotels are proving adept at fusing stylishly appointed modern rooms with centuries-old architecture. This place is one of the best, with an attractive columned courtyard, a warm colour scheme, chic room decor and a central location. The breakfast buffet is more generous than most.

★**Restaurante El Fogón Sefardí** JEWISH €€

(☎921 46 62 50; www.lacasamudejar.com; Calle de Isabel la Católica 8; tapas from €3.75, mains €12-26, set menus €20-35; ⏰1.30-4.30pm & 8.30-11.30pm) Located within the Hospedería La Gran Casa Mudéjar, this is one of the most original places in town. Sephardic Jewish cuisine is served either on the intimate patio or in the splendid dining hall with original 15th-century Mudéjar flourishes. The theme in the bar is equally diverse. Stop here for a taste of the award-winning tapas. Reservations recommended.

★**Casa Duque** SPANISH €€€

(☎921 46 24 87; www.restauranteduque.es; Calle de Cervantes 12; mains €19.50-24, set menus €35-40; ⏰12.30-4.30pm & 8.30-11.30pm) *Cochinillo asado* (roast suckling pig) has been served at this atmospheric *mesón* (tavern) since the 1890s. For the uninitiated, try the *menú de degustación,* which includes *cochinillo.* Downstairs is the informal *cueva* (cave), where you can get tapas (snacks) and full-bodied *cazuelas* (stews). Reservations recommended.

Information

Centro de Recepción de Visitantes (☎921 46 67 21; www.turismodesegovia.com; Plaza del Azoguejo 1; ⏰10am-8pm Mon-Sat, to 7pm Sun Apr-Sep, 10am-6.30pm Mon-Sat, to 5pm Sun Oct-Mar) Segovia's main tourist office runs at least two guided tours of the city's monumental core daily (€10 to €17 per person), usually departing at 11am and 4pm (although check as this schedule can change). Reserve ahead.

Oficina de Turismo (☎921 46 03 34; www.segoviaturismo.es; Plaza Mayor 10; ⏰9.30am-2pm & 5-8pm Mon-Sat, 9.30am-5pm Sun Jul–mid-Sep, 9.30am-2pm & 4-7pm Mon-Sat, 9.30am-5pm Sun mid-Sep–Jun) On Plaza Mayor, with information on the wider region.

Getting There & Away

BUS

The bus station is just off Paseo de Ezequiel González. **La Sepulvedana** (☎902 11 96 99; www.lasepulvedana.es) buses run from Segovia to Madrid's Intercambiador de Moncloa (€4, one to 1½ hours, every 15 minutes). Buses also head to Ávila (€4.80, one hour, four daily) and Salamanca (€5.30, 3½ hours, two daily), among other destinations.

WORTH A TRIP

BURGOS & LEÓN: A TALE OF TWO CATHEDRALS

Burgos and León are cathedral towns par excellence, and both are well connected by train and bus to Madrid.

Burgos

Catedral (947 20 47 12; www.catedraldeburgos.es; Plaza del Rey Fernando; adult/under 14yr incl audio guide €7/2, from 4.30pm Tue free; 9.30am-7.30pm mid-Mar–Oct, 10am-7pm Nov–mid-Mar) This Unesco World Heritage–listed cathedral, once a former modest Romanesque church, is a masterpiece. Work began on a grander scale in 1221; remarkably, within 40 years most of the French Gothic structure had been completed. You can enter from Plaza de Santa María for free for access to the Capilla del Santísimo Cristo, with its much-revered 13th-century crucifix, and the Capilla de Santa Tecla, with its extraordinary ceiling. However, we recommend that you visit the cathedral in its entirety.

Rimbombín (947 26 12 00; www.rimbombin.com; Calle Sombrería 6; d/tr/apt from €35/52/70;) Opened in 2013, this 'urban *hostal*' has an upbeat, contemporary feel – its slick white furnishings and decor are matched with light-pine beams and modular furniture. Three of the rooms have balconies overlooking the pedestrian street. Conveniently, it's in the heart of Burgos' compact tapas district. The apartment is excellent value for longer stays, with the same chic modern look and two bedrooms.

Cervecería Morito (947 26 75 55; Calle de Diego Porcelos 1; tapas/raciones from €4/6; 12.30-3.30pm & 7-11.30pm) Cervecería Morito is the undisputed king of Burgos tapas bars and as such it's always crowded. A typical order is *alpargata* (lashings of cured ham with bread, tomato and olive oil) or the *revueltos Capricho de Burgos* (scrambled eggs served with potatoes, blood sausage, red peppers, baby eels and mushrooms) – the latter is a meal in itself.

León

Catedral (987 87 57 70; www.catedraldeleon.org; Plaza Regia, adult/concession/under 12yr €6/5/free, combined ticket with Claustro & Museo Catedralicio-Diocesano €9/8/free; 9.30am-1.30pm & 4-8pm Mon-Fri, 9.30am-noon & 2-6pm Sat, 9.30-11am & 2-8pm Sun May-Sep, 9.30am-1.30pm & 4-7pm Mon-Sat, 9.30am-2pm Sun Oct-Apr) León's 13th-century cathedral, with its soaring towers, flying buttresses and breathtaking interior, is the city's spiritual heart. Whether spotlit by night or bathed in glorious northern sunshine, the cathedral, arguably Spain's premier Gothic masterpiece, exudes a glorious, almost luminous quality. The show-stopping facade has a radiant rose window, three richly sculpted doorways and two muscular towers. The main entrance is lorded over by a scene of the Last Supper, while an extraordinary gallery of *vidrieras* (stained-glass windows) awaits you inside.

Panteón Real (www.turismoleon.org; Plaza de San Isidoro; adult/child €5/free; 10am-2pm & 4-7pm Mon-Sat, 10am-2pm Sun) Attached to the **Real Basílica de San Isidoro** (987 87 61 61; 7.30am-11pm), the stunning Panteón Real houses royal sarcophagi, which rest with quiet dignity beneath a canopy of some of the finest Romanesque frescos in Spain. Colourful motifs of biblical scenes drench the vaults and arches of this extraordinary hall, held aloft by marble columns with intricately carved capitals. The pantheon also houses a small **museum** where you can admire the shrine of San Isidoro, a mummified finger(!) of the saint and other treasures.

La Posada Regia (987 21 31 73; www.regialeon.com; Calle de Regidores 9-11; s €55-70, d €60-130;) This place has the feel of a *casa rural* (village or farmstead accommodation) despite being in the city centre. The secret is a 14th-century building, magnificently restored (with wooden beams, exposed brick and understated antique furniture), with individually styled rooms and supremely comfortable beds and bathrooms. As with anywhere in the Barrio Húmedo, weekend nights can be noisy.

TRAIN

There are a couple of services by train operated by **Renfe** (☎ 912 32 03 20; www.renfe.es): just three normal trains run daily from Madrid to Segovia (€8.25, two hours), leaving you at the main train station 2.5km from the aqueduct. The faster option is the high-speed Avant (€12.90, 28 minutes), which deposits you at the newer Segovia-Guiomar station, 5km from the aqueduct.

CASTILLA-LA MANCHA

Toledo

POP 83,741

Toledo is truly one of Spain's most magnificent cities. Dramatically sited atop a gorge overlooking the Río Tajo, it was known as the 'city of three cultures' in the Middle Ages, a place where – legend has it – Christian, Muslim and Jewish communities peacefully coexisted. Unsurprisingly, rediscovering the vestiges of this unique cultural synthesis remains modern Toledo's most compelling attraction. Horseshoe-arched mosques, Sephardic synagogues and one of Spain's finest Gothic cathedrals cram into its dense historical core. But the layers go much deeper. Further sleuthing will reveal Visigothic and Roman roots. Toledo's other forte is art, in particular the haunting canvases of El Greco, the influential, impossible-to-classify painter with whom the city is synonymous. Justifiably popular with day trippers, try to stay overnight to really appreciate the city in all its haunting glory.

Sights

★ Catedral de Toledo CATHEDRAL
(☎ 925 22 22 41; www.catedralprimada.es; Plaza del Ayuntamiento; incl Museo de Textiles y Orfebrería adult/child €12.50/free; ⏲ 10am-6.30pm Mon-Sat, 2-6.30pm Sun) Toledo's illustrious main church ranks among the top 10 cathedrals in Spain. An impressive example of medieval Gothic architecture, its enormous interior is full of the classic characteristics of the style, rose windows, flying buttresses, ribbed vaults and pointed arches among them. The cathedral's sacristy is a veritable art gallery of old masters, with works by Velázquez, Goya and – of course – El Greco.

★ Alcázar FORTRESS
(Museo del Ejército; ☎ 925 23 88 00; Calle Alféreces Provisionales; adult/child €5/free, Sun free; ⏲ 10am-5pm Thu-Tue) At the highest point in the city looms the foreboding Alcázar. Rebuilt under Franco, it has been reopened as a vast military museum. The usual displays of uniforms and medals are here, but the best part is the exhaustive historical section, with an in-depth examination of the nation's history in Spanish and English. The exhibition is epic in scale, but like a well-run marathon it's worth the physical (and mental) investment.

★ Sinagoga del Tránsito SYNAGOGUE, MUSEUM
(☎ 925 22 36 65; www.culturaydeporte.gob.es; Calle Samuel Leví; adult/child €3/1.50, after 2pm Sat & all day Sun free; ⏲ 9.30am-7.30pm Tue-Sat Mar-Oct, to 6pm Tue-Sat Nov-Feb, 10am-3pm Sun year-round) This magnificent synagogue was built in 1355 by special permission from Pedro I. The synagogue now houses the **Museo Sefardí** (http://museosefardi.mcu.es; ⏲ 9.30am-6pm Mon-Sat, 10am-3pm Sun). The vast main prayer hall has been expertly restored and the Mudéjar decoration and intricately carved pine ceiling are striking. Exhibits provide an insight into the history of Jewish culture in Spain, and include archaeological finds, a memorial garden, costumes and ceremonial artefacts.

Sleeping & Eating

La Posada de Manolo BOUTIQUE HOTEL €€
(☎ 925 28 22 50; www.laposadademanolo.com; Calle de Sixto Ramón Parro 8; r €75-90; ❄ 📶) This memorable hotel has themed each floor with furnishings and decor reflecting one of the three cultures of Toledo: Christian, Islamic and Jewish. Rooms vary in size and cost, depending on whether they are interior or exterior, and some have balconies. There are stunning views of the old town and cathedral from the terrace, where breakfast is served, weather permitting.

★ Hacienda del Cardenal HISTORIC HOTEL €€
(☎ 925 22 49 00; www.haciendadelcardenal.com; Paseo de Recaredo 24; r incl breakfast €90-135; ❄ 📶 🏊) This wonderful 18th-century former cardinal's mansion has pale ochre-coloured walls, Moorish-inspired arches and stately columns. Some rooms are grand and others are more simply furnished, but all come with dark furniture, plush fabrics and parquet floors.

Several overlook the glorious terraced gardens. Underground parking is available nearby (€15 per day).

★**Alfileritos 24** MODERN SPANISH €€
(☎925 23 96 25; www.alfileritos24.com; Calle de los Alfileritos 24; mains €18-21, bar food €5-12; ⏲1.30-4pm & 8-11.30pm) The 14th-century surroundings of columns, beams and barrel-vault ceilings are cleverly coupled with modern artwork and bright dining rooms in an atrium space spread over four floors. The menu demonstrates an innovative flourish in the kitchen, with dishes such as green rice with quail or loin of venison with baked-in-the-bag *reineta* (pippin) apple.

★**Adolfo** MODERN EUROPEAN €€€
(☎925 22 73 21; www.adolforestaurante.com; Callejón Hombre de Palo 7; mains €25-28, set menu €76; ⏲1-4pm & 8pm-midnight Mon-Sat) Toledo doffs its hat to fine dining at this temple of good food and market freshness. Run by notable La Mancha–born chef Adolfo Muñoz, the restaurant has been around for over 25 years, and in that time has morphed into one of Spain's best gourmet establishments. Partridge is the speciality.

Information

Located virtually across from the cathedral, the **main tourist office** (☎925 25 40 30; www.toledo-turismo.com; Plaza Consistorio 1; ⏲10am-6pm) could not be more central. There's an excellent free map and plenty of 'what's on' type of information.

Getting There & Away

To get to most major destinations, you'll need to backtrack to Madrid.

Buses run from Madrid's Plaza Elíptica to Toledo's **bus station** (☎925 21 58 50; www.alsa.es; Bajada Castilla La Mancha), and back, roughly every half-hour (€5.40, 45 minutes to 1½ hours); some go direct, some via villages.

High-speed trains run from Madrid's Puerta de Atocha station (one way/return €13/21, 33 minutes, hourly) to Toledo's pretty **train station** (☎902 240202; www.renfe.es; Paseo de la Rosa).

CATALONIA

Barcelona

POP 1.62 MILLION

Barcelona is one of Europe's coolest cities. Despite two millennia of history, it's a forward-thinking place, always at the cutting edge of art, design and cuisine. Whether you explore its medieval palaces and plazas, admire the Modernista masterpieces of Antoni Gaudí and others, shop for designer fashions along its bustling boulevards, sample its exciting nightlife or just soak up the sun on the beaches, you'll find it hard not to fall in love with this vibrant city.

As much as Barcelona is a visual feast, it will also lead you into culinary temptation. Anything from traditional Catalan cooking to the latest in avant-garde new Spanish cuisine will have your appetite in overdrive.

Sights & Activities

La Rambla & El Raval

★**La Rambla** STREET
(Map p568; Ⓜ Catalunya, Liceu, Drassanes) Barcelona's most famous street is both a tourist magnet and a window into Catalan culture, with cultural centres, theatres and intriguing architecture. Flanked by plane trees, the middle section of La Rambla is a broad pedestrian boulevard, crowded every day until the wee hours with a wide cross-section of society. Horrific terrorist attacks in 2017 did little to diminish its popularity either with the tourists or with the hawkers, pavement artists and handful of living statues.

★**Mercat de la Boqueria** MARKET
(Map p568; ☎93 318 20 17; www.boqueria.barcelona; La Rambla 91; ⏲8am-8.30pm Mon-Sat; Ⓜ Liceu) Mercat de la Boqueria is possibly La Rambla's most interesting building, not so much for its Modernista-influenced design – it was actually built over a long period, from 1840 to 1914, on the site of the former St Joseph Monastery – but for the action of the food market within.

Gran Teatre del Liceu ARCHITECTURE
(Map p568; ☎93 485 99 14; www.liceubarcelona.cat; La Rambla 51-59; tours adult/concession/under 7yr 30min €6/5/free, 45min €9/7.50/free; ⏲30min tours 1pm Mon-Sat, 45min tours hourly 2-5pm Mon-Fri, from 11am Sat; Ⓜ Liceu) If you can't catch a night at the opera, you can still have a look around one of Europe's greatest opera houses, known to locals as the Liceu. Smaller than Milan's La Scala but bigger than Venice's La Fenice, it can seat up to 2300 people in its grand auditorium.

Barri Gòtic

You could easily spend several days or even a week exploring the medieval streets of the

Barcelona

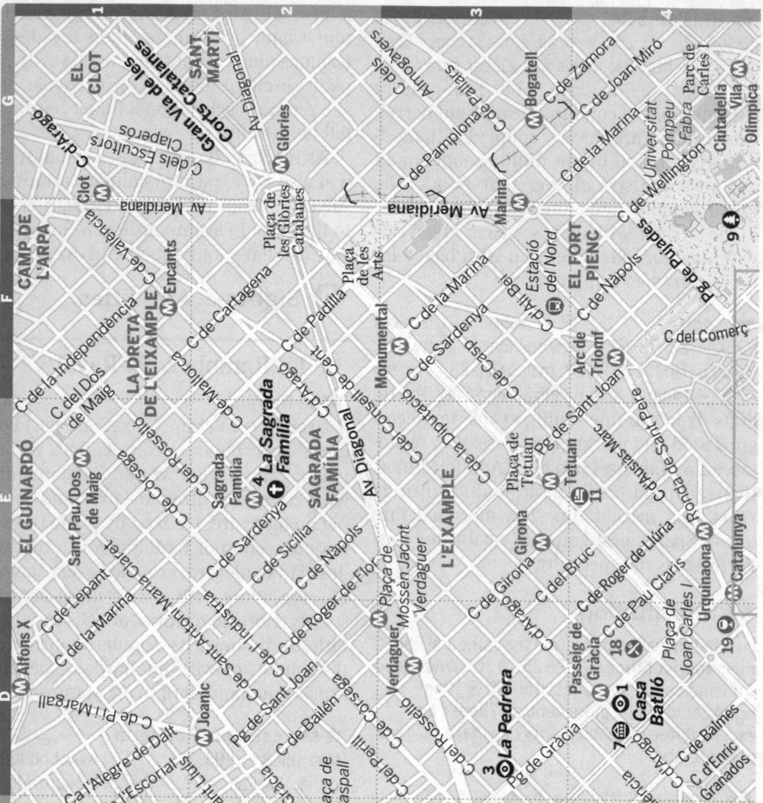

0.5 miles
1 km
EL CLOT
SANT MARTÍ
Gran Via de les Corts Catalanes
C d'Aragó
Av Diagonal
Glòries
C dels Escultors Claperós
Clot
Av Meridiana
Plaça de les Glòries Catalanes
CAMP DE L'ARPA
C de València
Encants
C de la Independència
LA DRETA DE L'EIXAMPLE
C de Cartagena
C de Mallorca
C del Dos de Maig
C de Padilla
Plaça de les Arts
C dels Almogàvers
C de Pallars
C de Pamplona
Bogatell
C de Zamora
C de Joan Miró
C de la Marina
Marina
Av Meridiana
Monumental
C del Consell de Cent
C de Sardenya
C de la Diputació
C de Casp
C d'Alí Bei
Estació del Nord
EL FORT PIENC
C de Nàpols
Arc de Triomf
Universitat Pompeu Fabra
Parc de Carles I
Ciutadella Vila Olímpica
C de Wellington
Pg de Pujades
9
C del Comerç
EL GUINARDÓ
Sant Pau/Dos de Maig
C del Rosselló
C de Còrsega
Sagrada Família
4 La Sagrada Família
SAGRADA FAMÍLIA
Av Diagonal
L'EIXAMPLE
Plaça de Tetuan
Tetuan
11
Pg de Sant Joan
C d'Ausiàs Marc
Ronda de Sant Pere
Alfons X
C de Lepant
C de la Marina
C de Sant Antoni Maria Claret
C de Sicília
C de Nàpols
C de l'Indústria
C de Roger de Flor
Plaça de Mossèn Jacint Verdaguer
Verdaguer
Girona
C de Girona
C del Bruc
C de Roger de Llúria
C de Pau Claris
Urquinaona
Catalunya
Plaça de Joan Carles I
18
19
Joanic
C de Pi i Margall
Pg de Sant Joan
C de Bailèn
C de Còrsega
C del Rosselló
C del Perill
3 La Pedrera
Pg de Gràcia
Passeig de Gràcia
7
1 Casa Batlló
C d'Aragó
C de Balmes
C d'Enric Granados
C de València
C de Ca l'Alegre de Dalt
C de l'Escorial
C de Sant Lluís
Plaça de Raspall
Travessera de Gràcia
GRÀCIA
C de Sant Salvador
C de Martí
C de l'Or
C del Robí
Plaça de Joan Carles I
8
Provença
C d'Enric Granados
C d'Aribau
C de Muntaner
EL CARMEL
Park Güell (200m)
Travessera de Dalt
C de Verdi
Fontana
C Gran de Gràcia
Via Augusta
Av Diagonal
20
14
Gràcia
Lesseps
Plaça de Lesseps
Plaça de la Torre
Vallcarca
Av de l'Hospital Militar
SANT GERVASI DE CASSOLES
C de Vallirana
C de Saragossa
Molina
C d'Alfons XII
C de Tuset
C d'Aribau
C de Muntaner
C de Casanova
C de Còrsega
Hospital Clínic
C de Londres
C de París
C de Viladomat
Pàdua
Sant Gervasi
C dels Madrazo
C de Tavern
C d'Amigó
C de Calvet
Muntaner
Ronda del General Mitre
C de Muntaner
Via Augusta
C de Loreto
C de Borí i Fontestà
Av Diagonal
Travessera de les Corts
Camp Nou (2km)
Av Tibidabo
C de Balmes
La Bonanova
C de Ganduxer

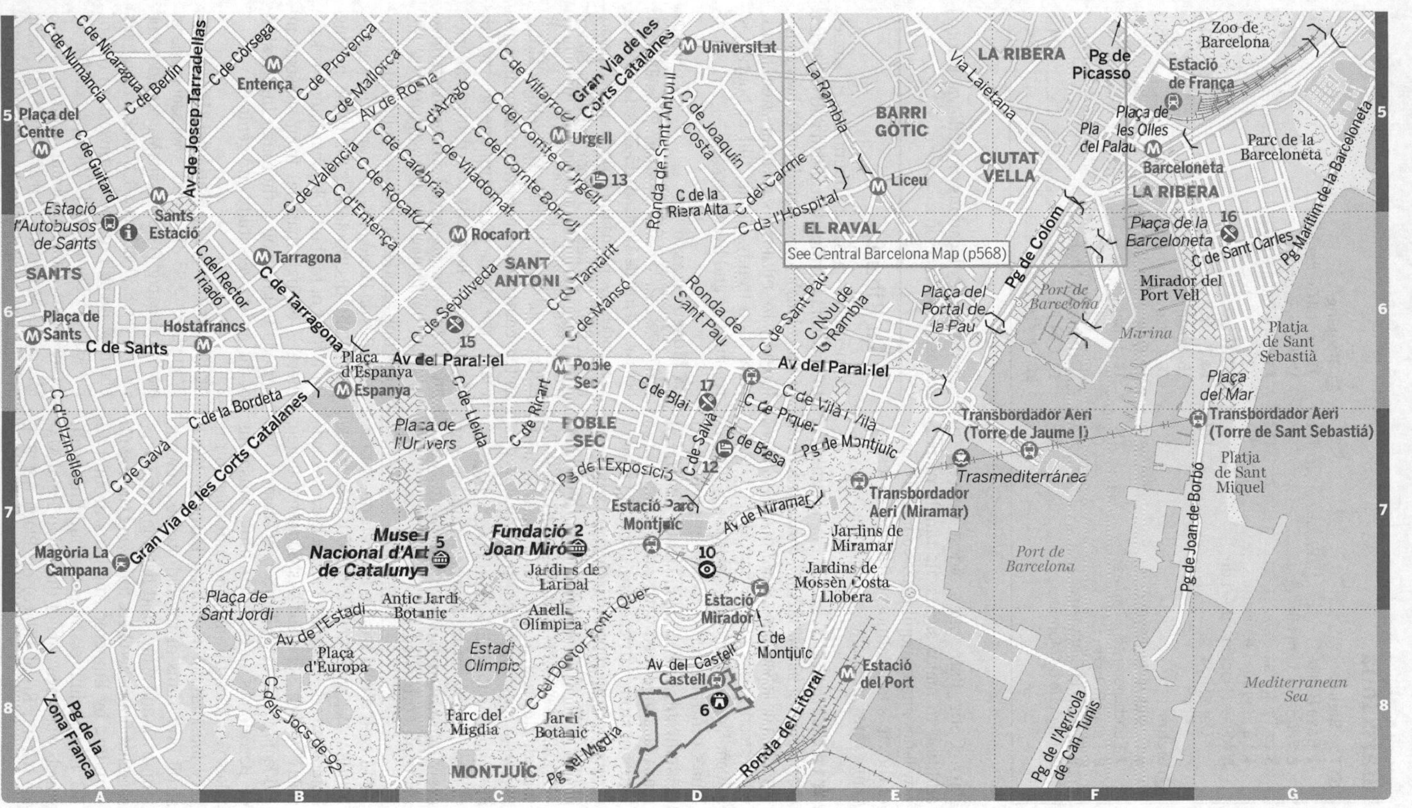

C de Nicaragua
C de Numància
C de Berlín
Av de Josep Tarradellas
C de Còrsega
Entença
C de Provença
C de Mallorca
Av de Roma
C d'Aragó
C de Villarroel
Gran Via de les Corts Catalanes
Universitat
Plaça del Centre
C de Guitard
C de València
C de Calàbria
C de Viladomat
C del Comte d'Urgell
Urgell
C del Comte Borrell
Ronda de Sant Antoni
C de Joaquín Costa
La Rambla
BARRI GÒTIC
Via Laietana
LA RIBERA
Pg de Picasso
Estació de França
Zoo de Barcelona
Plaça de les Olles
Pla del Palau
CIUTAT VELLA
Barceloneta
Parc de la Barceloneta
Pg Marítim de la Barceloneta
LA RIBERA
Estació d'Autobusos de Sants
Sants Estació
C de Rocafort
C d'Entença
13
C de la Riera Alta
C del Carme
C de l'Hospital
Liceu
EL RAVAL
See Central Barcelona Map (p568)
Pg de Colom
Plaça de la Barceloneta
16
C de Sant Carles
SANTS
Tarragona
Rocafort
SANT ANTONI
C del Rector Triadó
C de Tarragona
C de Tamarit
Mirador del Port Vell
Plaça de Sants
Hostafrancs
C de Sepúlveda
C de Manso
Ronda de Sant Pau
C de Sant Pau
C Nou de la Rambla
Plaça del Portal de la Pau
Port de Barcelona
Marina
Platja de Sant Sebastià
C de Sants
15
Plaça d'Espanya
Av del Paral·lel
Poble Sec
Av del Paral·lel
Espanya
C d'Olzinelles
C de la Bordeta
C de Lleida
C de Ricart
C de Blai
17
C de Vila i Vilà
C de Piquer
Plaça del Mar
Transbordador Aeri (Torre de Jaume I)
Transbordador Aeri (Torre de Sant Sebastià)
Plaça de l'Univers
POBLE SEC
C de Salvà
C de Blesa
Pg de Montjuïc
Platja de Sant Miquel
C de Gavà
Gran Via de les Corts Catalanes
Pg de l'Exposició
12
Trasmediterránea
Transbordador Aeri (Miramar)
Pg de Joan de Borbó
Estació Parc Montjuïc
Av de Miramar
Jardins de Miramar
Museu Nacional d'Art de Catalunya
5
Fundació Joan Miró
2
10
Port de Barcelona
Magòria La Campana
Jardins de Laribal
Jardins de Mossèn Costa i Llobera
Plaça de Sant Jordi
Antic Jardí Botànic
Anella Olímpica
C del Doctor Font i Quer
Estació Mirador
Av de l'Estadi
C de Montjuïc
Plaça d'Europa
Estadi Olímpic
Av del Castell
Castell
Estació del Port
Mediterranean Sea
Pg de la Zona Franca
C dels Jocs de 92
6
Parc del Migdia
Jardí Botànic
Ronda del Litoral
Pg de l'Agrícola
de Can Tunis
MONTJUÏC
Pg del Migdia

Barcelona

Top Sights
1 Casa Batlló D4
2 Fundació Joan Miró C7
3 La Pedrera D3
4 La Sagrada Família E2
5 Museu Nacional d'Art de Catalunya C7

Sights
6 Castell de Montjuïc D8
7 Fundació Antoni Tàpies D4
8 Palau Robert C3
9 Parc de la Ciutadella F4
10 Telefèric de Montjuïc D7

Sleeping
11 Hostal Center Inn E4
12 Hotel Brummell D7
13 Pars Tailor's Hostel D5

Eating
14 Disfrutar C4
15 Enigma C6
16 La Cova Fumada G6
17 Quimet i Quimet D6
18 Tapas 24 .... D4

Drinking & Nightlife
19 City Hall D4
20 Dry Martini C4

Barri Gòtic, Barcelona's oldest quarter. In addition to major sights, its tangle of narrow lanes and tranquil plazas conceals some of the city's most atmospheric shops, restaurants, cafes and bars.

★La Catedral CATHEDRAL
(Map p568; ☎93 342 82 62; www.catedralbcn.org; Plaça de la Seu; donation €7 or choir €3, roof €3; ⏰tourist visits 12.30-7.45pm Mon-Fri, 12.30-5.30pm Sat, 2-5.30pm Sun; Ⓜ Jaume I) Barcelona's central place of worship presents a magnificent image. The richly decorated main facade, dotted with gargoyles and the kinds of stone intricacies you would expect of northern European Gothic, sets it quite apart from other churches in Barcelona. The facade was actually added in 1870, although the rest of the building was built between 1298 and 1460. Its other facades are sparse in decoration, and the octagonal, flat-roofed towers are a clear reminder that, even here, Catalan Gothic architectural principles prevailed.

★Museu d'Història de Barcelona MUSEUM
(MUHBA; Map p568; ☎93 256 21 00; www.museuhistoria.bcn.cat; Plaça del Rei; adult/concession/child €7/5/free, 3-8pm Sun & 1st Sun of month free; ⏰10am-7pm Tue-Sat, to 8pm Sun; Ⓜ Jaume I) One of Barcelona's most fascinating museums takes you back through the centuries to the very foundations of Roman Barcino. You'll stroll over ruins of the old streets, sewers, laundries and wine- and fish-making factories that flourished here following the town's founding by Emperor Augustus around 10 BC. Equally impressive is the building itself, which was once part of the Palau Reial Major (Grand Royal Palace) on Plaça del Rei, among the key locations of medieval princely power in Barcelona.

La Ribera

In medieval days, La Ribera was a stone's throw from the Mediterranean and the heart of Barcelona's foreign trade, with homes belonging to numerous wealthy merchants. Now it's a trendy district full of boutiques, restaurants and lively bars.

★Museu Picasso MUSEUM
(Map p568; ☎93 256 30 00; www.museupicasso.bcn.cat; Carrer de Montcada 15-23; adult/concession/under 16yr permanent collection & temporary exhibit €14/7.50/free, 6-9.30pm Thu & 1st Sun of month free; ⏰9am-7pm Tue, Wed & Fri-Sun, to 9.30pm Thu; 📶; Ⓜ Jaume I) The setting alone, in five contiguous medieval stone mansions, makes the Museu Picasso unique (and worth the queues). The pretty courtyards, galleries and staircases preserved in the first three of these buildings are as delightful as the collection inside. While the collection concentrates on Pablo Picasso's formative years – potentially disappointing for those hoping for a feast of his better-known later works – there is enough material from subsequent periods to give you a thorough impression of the artist's versatility and genius.

★Basílica de Santa Maria del Mar CHURCH
(Map p568; ☎93 310 23 90; www.santamariadelmarbarcelona.org; Plaça de Santa Maria; guided tour €10; ⏰9am-8.30pm Mon-Sat, 10am-8pm Sun, tours 1-5pm; Ⓜ Jaume I) At the southwestern end of Passeig del Born stands the apse of Barcelona's finest Catalan Gothic church, Santa Maria del Mar (Our Lady of the Sea). Built in the 14th century with record-breaking

alacrity for the time (it took just 54 years), the church is remarkable for its architectural harmony and simplicity.

★Palau de la Música Catalana ARCHITECTURE

(Map p568; ☎93 295 72 00; www.palaumusica.cat; Carrer de Palau de la Música 4-6; adult/concession/under 10yr €20/11/free; ⊙guided tours 10am-3.30pm Sep-Jun, to 6pm Easter & Jul, 9am-6pm Aug; MUrquinaona) This concert hall is a high point of Barcelona's Modernista architecture, a symphony in tile, brick, sculpted stone and stained glass. Built by Domènech i Montaner between 1905 and 1908 for the Orfeo Català musical society, it was conceived as a temple for the Catalan Renaixença (Renaissance).

Parc de la Ciutadella PARK

(Map p564; Passeig de Picasso; ⊙10am-10.30pm; ; MArc de Triomf) Parc de la Ciutadella is perfect for winding down. Come for a stroll, a picnic, a boat ride on the lake or to inspect Catalonia's parliament in what is the most central green lung in the city.

L'Eixample

Modernisme, the Catalan version of art nouveau, transformed Barcelona's cityscape in the early 20th century. Most Modernista works, including Antoni Gaudí's unfinished masterpiece, La Sagrada Família, were built in the elegant, if traffic-filled, L'Eixample (pronounced 'lay-sham-pluh'), a grid-plan district that was developed from the 1870s on.

★La Sagrada Família CHURCH

(Map p564; ☎93 208 04 14; www.sagradafamilia.org; Carrer de la Marina; adult/child €15/free; ⊙9am-8pm Apr-Sep, to 7pm Mar & Oct, to 6pm Nov-Feb; MSagrada Família) If you have time for only one sightseeing outing, this should be it. La Sagrada Família inspires awe by its sheer verticality, and in the manner of the medieval cathedrals it emulates, it's still under construction. Work began in 1882 and is hoped (perhaps optimistically) to be completed in 2026, a century after the architect's death. Unfinished it may be, but it attracts more than 4.5 million visitors a year and is the most visited monument in Spain.

★La Pedrera ARCHITECTURE

(Casa Milà; Map p564; ☎93 214 25 76; www.lapedrera.com; Passeig de Gràcia 92; adult/child €25/14; ⊙9am-8.30pm & 9-11pm Mar-Oct, 9am-6.30pm & 7-9pm Nov-Feb; MDiagonal) This madcap Gaudí masterpiece was built in 1905–10 as a combined apartment and office block. Formally called Casa Milà, after the businessman who commissioned it, it is better known as La Pedrera (the Quarry) because of

DON'T MISS

LA SAGRADA FAMÍLIA HIGHLIGHTS

Roof The roof of La Sagrada Família is held up by a forest of extraordinary angled pillars. As the pillars soar towards the ceiling, they sprout a web of supporting branches, creating the effect of a forest canopy.

Nativity Facade The artistic pinnacle of the building. You can climb high up inside some of the four towers by a combination of lifts and narrow spiral staircases – a vertiginous experience.

Passion Facade The southwestern Passion Facade, on the theme of Christ's last days and death, was built between 1954 and 1978 based on surviving drawings by Gaudí, with four towers and a large, sculpture-bedecked portal by Josep Subirachs.

Glory Facade The Glory Facade is under construction and will, like the others, be crowned by four towers – the total of 12 representing the Twelve Apostles.

Museu Gaudí The Museu Gaudí, below ground level, includes interesting material on Gaudí's life and other works, as well as models and photos of La Sagrada Família.

Exploring La Sagrada Família Booking tickets online avoids what can be very lengthy queues. Although the church is essentially a building site, the completed sections and museum may be explored at leisure. Fifty-minute guided tours (€24) are offered. Alternatively, pick up an audio guide, for which you need ID. Enter from Carrer de Sardenya or Carrer de la Marina. Once inside, €14 (which includes the audio guide) will get you into lifts that rise up inside towers in the Nativity and Passion facades.

Central Barcelona

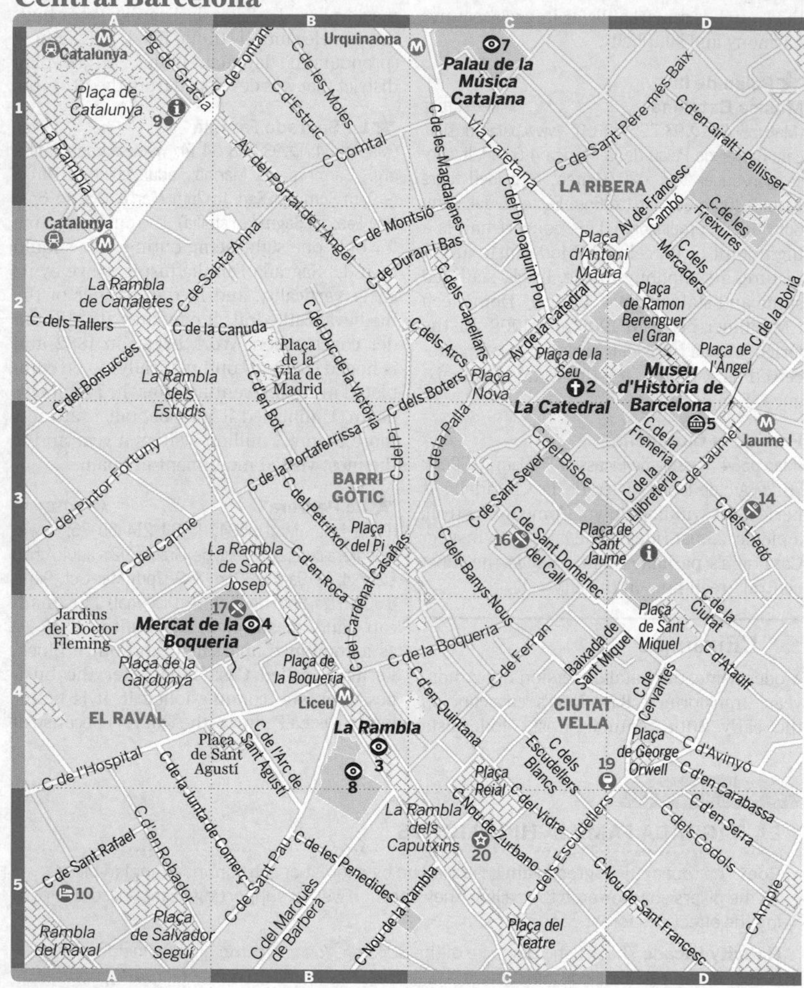

its uneven grey stone facade, which ripples around the corner of Carrer de Provença.

★ Casa Batlló — ARCHITECTURE

(Map p564; ☎93 216 03 06; www.casabatllo.es; Passeig de Gràcia 43; adult/child €28.50/25.50; ⏰9am-9pm, last admission 8pm; Ⓜ Passeig de Gràcia) One of the strangest residential buildings in Europe, this is Gaudí at his hallucinatory best. The facade, sprinkled with bits of blue, mauve and green tiles and studded with wave-shaped window frames and balconies, rises to an uneven blue-tiled roof with a solitary tower.

Fundació Antoni Tàpies — GALLERY

(Map p564; ☎93 487 03 15; www.fundaciotapies.org; Carrer d'Aragó 255; adult/child €7/5.60; ⏰10am-7pm Tue-Thu & Sat, to 9pm Fri, to 3pm Sun; Ⓜ Passeig de Gràcia) The Fundació Antoni Tàpies is both a pioneering Modernista building (completed in 1885) and the major collection of leading 20th-century Catalan artist Antoni Tàpies. Tàpies died in February 2012, aged 88; known for his esoteric work, he left behind a powerful range of paintings and a foundation intended to promote contemporary artists. Admission includes an audio guide.

Central Barcelona

Top Sights
1 Basílica de Santa Maria del Mar E3
2 La Catedral C2
3 La Rambla B4
4 Mercat de la Boqueria B4
5 Museu d'Història de Barcelona D3
6 Museu Picasso E2
7 Palau de la Música Catalana C1

Sights
8 Gran Teatre del Liceu B4

Activities, Courses & Tours
9 Barcelona Walking Tours A1

Sleeping
10 Barceló Raval A5
11 H10 Port Vell F4
12 Serras Hotel E5

Eating
13 Bormuth F2
14 Cafè de l'Acadèmia D3
15 Casa Delfín F2
16 La Vinateria del Call C3
17 Pinotxo Bar B4

Drinking & Nightlife
18 El Born Bar F2
19 Marula Café D4

Entertainment
20 Jamboree C5
Palau de la Música Catalana .... (see 7)

Shopping
21 Coquette F2
22 Custo Barcelona F3

★ **Park Güell** PARK

(☎93 409 18 31; www.parkguell.cat; Carrer d'Olot 7; adult/child €8.50/6; ⏲8am-9.30pm May-Aug, to 8.30pm Apr, Sep & Oct, to 6.15pm Nov–mid-Feb, to 7pm mid-Feb–Mar; 🚌24, 92, Ⓜ Lesseps, Vallcarca) North of Gràcia, Unesco-listed Park Güell is where architect Antoni Gaudí turned his hand to landscape gardening. It's a strange, enchanting place where his passion for natural forms really took flight and the artificial almost seems more natural than the natural.

The park is extremely popular, and access to the central area is limited to a certain number of people every half-hour – book ahead online (and you'll also save on the admission fee). The rest of the park is free and can be visited without booking.

Montjuïc

Southwest of the city centre, the hillside overlooking the port has some of the city's finest art collections, and also serves as a Central Park of sorts, and is a great place for a jog or stroll. The closest metro stops are Espanya, Poble Sec and Paral·lel. From Paral·lel a funicular railway runs up to Estació Parc Montjuïc, from where a cable car, the **Telefèric de Montjuïc** (Map p564; ☎93 328 90 03; www.telefericdemontjuic.cat; Avinguda de Miramar 30; adult/child one way €8.40/6.60; ⏲10am-9pm Jun-Sep, to 7pm Mar-May & Oct, to 6pm Nov-Feb; 🚌55, 150), climbs to the Castell de Montjuïc. Bus 150 loops from Plaça d'Espanya to Castell de Montjuïc.

★Museu Nacional d'Art de Catalunya MUSEUM

(MNAC; Map p564; ☎936 22 03 76; www.museunacional.cat; Mirador del Palau Nacional; adult/child €12/free, after 3pm Sat & 1st Sun of month free, rooftop viewpoint only €2; ⏰10am-8pm Tue-Sat, to 3pm Sun May-Sep, to 6pm Tue-Sat, to 3pm Sun Oct-Apr; 📶; 🚌55, Ⓜ Espanya) From across the city, the bombastic neobaroque silhouette of the Palau Nacional can be seen on the slopes of Montjuïc. Built for the 1929 World Exhibition and restored in 2005, it houses a vast collection of mostly Catalan art, spanning the early Middle Ages to the early 20th century. The high point is the collection of extraordinary Romanesque frescoes.

★Fundació Joan Miró MUSEUM

(Map p564; ☎93 443 94 70; www.fmirobcn.org; Parc de Montjuïc; adult/child €12/free; ⏰10am-8pm Tue, Wed, Fri & Sat, to 9pm Thu, to 3pm Sun Apr-Oct, 10am-6pm Tue, Wed & Fri, to 9pm Thu, to 8pm Sat, to 3pm Sun Nov-Mar; 📶; 🚌55, 150, 🚊Paral·lel) Joan Miró, the city's best-known 20th-century artistic progeny, bequeathed this art foundation to his home town in 1971. Its light-filled buildings, designed by close friend and architect Josep Lluís Sert (who also built Miró's Mallorca studios), are crammed with seminal works, from Miró's earliest timid sketches to paintings from his last years.

Castell de Montjuïc FORTRESS

(Map p564; ☎93 256 44 40; http://ajuntament.barcelona.cat/castelldemontjuic; Carretera de Montjuïc 66; adult/child €5/3, after 3pm Sun & all day 1st Sun of month free; ⏰10am-8pm Mar-Oct, to 6pm Nov-Feb; 🚌150, 🚡Telefèric de Montjuïc, Castell de Montjuïc) This forbidding *castell* (castle or fort) dominates the southeastern heights of Montjuïc and enjoys commanding views over the Mediterranean. It dates, in its present form, from the late 17th and 18th centuries. For most of its dark history, it has been used to watch over the city and as a political prison and killing ground.

La Barceloneta & the Waterfront

Since the late 20th century, Barcelona's formerly industrial waterfront has experienced a dramatic transformation, and now boasts sparkling beaches and seaside bars and restaurants, elegant sculptures, a 4.5km-long boardwalk, ultramodern high-rises and yacht-filled marinas. The gateway to the Mediterranean is the gridlike neighbourhood of Barceloneta, an old-fashioned fishing quarter full of traditional seafood restaurants, while to the northeast, post-industrial El Poblenou is worth a visit for its inviting roster of bars and places to eat.

Festivals & Events

Festes de Santa Eulàlia CULTURAL

(http://lameva.barcelona.cat/santaeulalia; ⏰Feb) Around 12 February this big winter fest celebrates Barcelona's first patron saint with a week of cultural events, including parades of *gegants* (giants), theatre, *correfocs* (fire runs) and *castells* (human castles). It's held in conjunction with Llum BCN (which takes place a few days later), during which light installations are set up across the city.

Festes de la Mercè CULTURAL

(www.bcn.cat/merce; ⏰Sep) The city's biggest party involves four days of concerts, dancing and street theatre held in various locations across town. There are also *castells* (human castles), a fireworks display synchronised with the Montjuïc fountains, a parade of giants, and *correfocs* – a parade of fireworks-spitting monsters and demons who run with the crowd. Held around 24 September.

Sleeping

Accommodation in Barcelona is more expensive than anywhere else in Spain except Madrid. La Rambla, the Barri Gòtic and El Raval can be noisy but are close to the action with a big selection of boxy hotels, glorious boutique options, hostels and fleapits. You'll find a few attractive boutique-style guesthouses and hostels in Poble Sec and up-and-coming Sant Antoni. L'Eixample has the greatest range of hotels in most classes, including some classic hotels and a long list of decent midrange places, though some are a bit far from the old city.

El Raval

★Barceló Raval DESIGN HOTEL €€

(Map p568; ☎93 320 14 90; www.barceloraval.com; Rambla del Raval 17-21; r from €185; ❄📶; Ⓜ Liceu) Part of the city's plans to pull the El Raval district up by the bootstraps, this cylindrical designer hotel tower makes a 21st-century splash. The rooftop terrace offers fabulous views and the B-Lounge bar-restaurant is a lively joint for meals and cocktails. Rooms have slick aesthetics (white with lime green or ruby red splashes of colour), coffee machines and iPod docks.

Barri Gòtic

Serras Hotel BOUTIQUE HOTEL €€€
(Map p568; 93 169 18 68; www.hoteltheserras barcelona.com; Passeig de Colom 9; r from €250; ; M Barceloneta) This fresh five-star has every comfort – including a rooftop bar with a small dipping pool and a terrific view over the port – but never feels stuffy. Rooms at the front are brighter and have a better view (from the bathtub, in some cases), but rooms at the side are spared the traffic noise.

Poble Sec & Sant Antoni

Pars Tailor's Hostel HOSTEL €
(Map p564; 93 250 56 84; www.parshostels.com; Carrer de Sepúlveda 146; dm €25-30; ; M Urgell) Decorated like a mid-20th-century tailor's shop, with rooms themed around different fabrics, this popular hostel's common areas have old sewing machines, lovingly framed brassieres and vintage fixtures. You can shoot a round on the old billiard table, hang out in the comfy lounge, cook a meal in the well-equipped kitchen or join one of the activities on offer.

★ **Hotel Brummell** BOUTIQUE HOTEL €€
(Map p564; 93 125 86 22; www.hotelbrummell.com; Carrer Nou de la Rambla 174; d from €140; ; M Paral·lel) Stylish Brummell has been turning heads since its 2015 opening. It's a thoughtfully designed hotel with a creative soul and great atmosphere. The 20 bright rooms have a minimalist design, and the best of the bunch have sizeable terraces with views and even outdoor soaking tubs. The cheapest (the 'poolside classic' rooms) feel a little tight.

L'Eixample

Hostal Center Inn HOSTAL €€
(Map p564; 93 265 25 60; www.centerinnbarcelona.com; Gran Via de les Corts Catalanes 688; s/d/f from €65/75/115; ; M Tetuan) Set across two historic buildings 50m apart, Hostal Center Inn's simple rooms – some with balconies or terraces – have quirky touches such as wrought-iron bedsteads, Moroccan mosaic tables, gilded mirrors and, in one room, an antique escritoire.

La Barceloneta & the Waterfront

H10 Port Vell BOUTIQUE HOTEL €€€
(Map p568; 93 310 30 65; www.h10hotels.com; Pas de Sota Muralla 9; d from €150; ; M Barceloneta) The location is excellent at this 58-room hotel within a short stroll of El Born and Barceloneta. Sleek, modern rooms have a trim, minimalist design with black-and-white bathrooms, and the best rooms (not all) have views over the marina. The rooftop terrace is the best feature, with sunloungers, a tiny plunge pool and evening cocktails.

Eating

Barcelona has a celebrated food scene fuelled by a combination of world-class chefs, imaginative recipes and magnificent ingredients fresh from farms and the sea. Catalan culinary masterminds like brothers Ferran and Albert Adrià, and Carles Abellán have become international icons, reinventing the world of haute cuisine, while classic old-world Catalan recipes continue to earn accolades in dining rooms and tapas bars across the city.

El Raval

Pinotxo Bar TAPAS €€
(Map p568; 93 317 17 31; www.pinotxobar.com; Mercat de la Boqueria, La Rambla 89; mains €9-17; 6.30am-4pm Mon-Sat; M Liceu) Pinotxo is arguably La Boqueria's, and even Barcelona's, best tapas bar. The ever-charming owner, Juanito, might serve up chickpeas with pine nuts and raisins, a soft mix of potato and spinach sprinkled with salt, soft baby squid with cannellini beans, or a quivering cube of caramel-sweet pork belly.

Barri Gòtic

La Vinateria del Call SPANISH €€
(Map p568; 93 302 60 92; www.lavinateriadelcall.com; Carrer Salomó Ben Adret 9; raciones €7-12; 7.30pm-1am; ; M Jaume I) In a magical setting in the former Jewish quarter, this tiny jewel-box of a wine bar serves up tasty Iberian dishes including Galician octopus, cider-cooked chorizo and the Catalan *escalivada* (roasted peppers, aubergine and onions) with anchovies. Portions are small and made for sharing, and there are over 160 varieties of wine to choose from.

Cafè de l'Acadèmia CATALAN €€

(Map p568; ☎93 319 82 53; Carrer dels Lledó 1; mains €8-20; ⊙1-3.30pm & 8-11.30pm Mon-Fri; 📶; MJaume I) Expect a mix of traditional Catalan dishes with the occasional creative twist. At lunchtime, local city hall workers pounce on the *menú del día* (€16). In the evening it is rather more romantic, as low lighting emphasises the intimacy of the beamed ceiling and stone walls. On warm days you can also dine in the pretty square at the front.

Poble Sec & Sant Antoni

Quimet i Quimet TAPAS €€

(Map p564; ☎93 442 31 42; www.facebook.com/quimetyquimet; Carrer del Poeta Cabanyes 25; tapas €4-10, montaditos €3-4; ⊙noon-4pm & 7-10.30pm Mon-Fri, noon-4pm Sat, closed Aug; MParal·lel) Quimet i Quimet is a family-run business that has been passed down from generation to generation. There's barely space to swing a *calamar* (squid) in this bottle-lined, standing-room-only place, but it is a treat for the palate, with *montaditos* (tapas on a slice of bread) made to order.

★Enigma GASTRONOMY €€€

(Map p564; ☎616 696322; www.enigmaconcept.es; Carrer de Sepúlveda 38-40; tasting menu €220; ⊙7-9.30pm Tue-Fri, 1-2.30pm & 7-9.30pm Sat; MEspanya) Resembling a 3D art installation, this conceptual offering from the famed Adrià brothers is a 40-course tour de force of cutting-edge gastronomy across six dining spaces. A meal takes 3½ hours and includes customised cocktail pairings (you can order additional drinks). There's a minimum of two diners; reserve months in advance. A €100 deposit per guest is required upon booking.

La Ribera

Bormuth TAPAS €

(Map p568; ☎93 310 21 86; www.facebook.com/bormuthbarcelona; Carrer del Rec 31; tapas €4-10; ⊙12.30pm-1.30am Sun-Thu, to 2.30am Fri & Sat; 📶; MJaume I) Bormuth is a popular tapas bar with traditional decor, clad in bare brick and recycled wood. It serves typical favourites from around Spain, including *pimientos de Padrón* (fried green peppers), *buñelos de bacalao* (cod fritters) and *patatas mojo picón* (Canary Island baked potatoes, smothered in a spicy sauce). Bormuth also specialises in homemade vermouth, which it has on tap.

Casa Delfín CATALAN €€

(Map p568; ☎93 319 50 88; www.casadelfinrestaurant.com; Passeig del Born 36; mains €12-18; ⊙noon-midnight Sun-Thu, to 1am Fri & Sat; 📶; MJaume I) One of Barcelona's culinary delights, Casa Delfín is everything you dream of when you think of Catalan (and Mediterranean) cooking. Start with salt-strewn *Padrón* peppers, moving on to plump anchovies from L'Escala in the Costa Brava, then tackle *suquet de los pescadores* (traditional Catalan fish stew; €14.50, minimum two people).

L'Eixample

Tapas 24 TAPAS €

(Map p564; ☎93 488 09 77; www.carlesabellan.com; Carrer de la Diputació 269; tapas €4-12; ⊙9am-midnight; 📶; MPasseig de Gràcia) Hotshot chef Carles Abellán runs this basement tapas haven known for its gourmet versions of old faves. Highlights include the *bikini* (toasted ham and cheese sandwich – here the ham is cured and the truffle makes all the difference) and zesty *boquerones al limón* (lemon-marinated anchovies). You can't book, and service can be slow, but it's worth the wait.

★Disfrutar MODERN EUROPEAN €€€

(Map p564; ☎93 348 68 96; www.disfrutarbarcelona.com; Carrer de Villarroel 163; tasting menus €150-190; ⊙1-2.30pm & 8-9.30pm Mon-Fri; MHospital Clínic) Disfrutar ('Enjoy' in Catalan) is among the city's finest restaurants, with two Michelin stars. Run by alumni of Ferran Adrià's game-changing (now closed) El Bulli restaurant, nothing is as it seems, such as black and green olives that are actually chocolate ganache with orange-blossom water.

La Barceloneta & the Waterfront

La Cova Fumada TAPAS €

(Map p564; ☎93 221 40 61; Carrer del Baluard 56; tapas €4-12; ⊙9am-3.15pm Mon-Wed, 9am-3.15pm & 6-8.15pm Thu & Fri, 9am-1pm Sat; MBarceloneta) There's no sign and the setting is decidedly downmarket, but this tiny, buzzing family-run tapas spot always packs in a crowd. The secret? Mouth-watering *pul-*

po (octopus), calamari, sardines, *bombas* (meat and potato croquettes served with aioli) and grilled *carxofes* (artichokes) cooked in the open kitchen. Everything is amazingly fresh.

 Drinking & Nightlife

Barcelona is a town for nightlife lovers, with an enticing spread of candlelit wine bars, old-school taverns, stylish lounges and kaleidoscopic nightclubs where the party continues until daybreak. For something a little more sedate, the city's atmospheric cafes and teahouses make a fine retreat when the skies turn grey.

 Barri Gòtic

Marula Café BAR

(Map p568; 93 318 76 90; www.marulacafe.com; Carrer dels Escudellers 49; cover up to €10; 11pm-5am Wed, Thu & Sun, to 6am Fri & Sat; M Liceu) A fantastic find in the heart of the Barri Gòtic, Marula will transport you to the 1970s and the best in funk and soul. James Brown fans will think they've died and gone to heaven. It's not, however, a mono-thematic place: DJs slip in other tunes, from breakbeat to house. Samba and other Brazilian dance sounds also penetrate here.

 La Ribera

El Born Bar BAR

(Map p568; 93 319 53 33; www.elbornbar.com; Passeig del Born 26; 10am-2.30am Mon-Thu, to 3am Fri, 11am-3am Sat, noon-2.30am Sun; ; M Jaume I) Moss-green paintwork, marble tables and a chequered black-and-white tiled floor create a timeless look for this popular little cafe-bar. A spiral wrought-iron staircase leads to a quieter room upstairs (the twisting steps mean that there is no table service and hot drinks can't be carried upstairs). El Born is ideal for either morning coffee, an afternoon vermouth or an evening cocktail.

 L'Eixample

Dry Martini BAR

(Map p564; 93 217 50 72; www.drymartiniorg.com; Carrer d'Aribau 162-166; 1pm-2.30am Mon-Thu, 1pm-3am Fri, 6.30pm-3am Sat, 6.30pm-2.30am Sun; FGC Provença) Waiters make expert cocktail suggestions, but the house drink, taken at the bar or on one of the plush green banquettes, is always a good bet. The gin and tonic comes in an enormous mug-sized glass – one will take you most of the night.

City Hall CLUB

(Map p564; 93 238 07 22; www.cityhallbarcelona.com; Rambla de Catalunya 2-4; cover from €10; midnight-5am Mon-Thu, to 6am Sat; M Catalunya) A long corridor leads to the dance floor of this venerable and popular club, located in a former theatre. Music styles, from house and techno to reggaeton, change nightly; check the agenda online. The cover charge includes a drink.

DON'T MISS

SEEING AN FC BARCELONA MATCH

Fútbol in Barcelona has the aura of religion, and for much of the city's population, support of FC Barcelona is an article of faith. FC Barcelona is traditionally associated with the Catalans and even Catalan nationalism.

Tickets to FC Barcelona matches are available at **Camp Nou** (902 189900; www.fcbarcelona.com; Carrer d'Arístides Maillol; M Palau Reial), online via FC Barcelona's official website, and at various city locations. Tourist offices sell them (the branch at Plaça de Catalunya is a centrally located option) as do FC Botiga shops. Tickets can cost anything from €39 to upwards of €250, depending on the seat and match. On match day the ticket windows (at gates 9 and 15) are open from 9.15am until kick-off.

Fans who can't get to a game will still enjoy the self-guided **stadium tour and museum** (902 189900; www.fcbarcelona.com; Gate 9, Avinguda de Joan XXIII; adult/child self-guided tour €29.50/23.50, guided tour €50/35; 9.30am-7.30pm mid-Apr–mid-Oct, 10am-6.30pm Mon-Sat, to 2.30pm Sun mid-Oct–mid-Apr; M Palau Reial).

☆ Entertainment

★Palau de la Música Catalana CLASSICAL MUSIC
(Map p568; ☎93 295 72 00; www.palaumusica.cat; Carrer de Palau de la Música 4-6; tickets from €18; ⏲box office 9.30am-9pm Mon-Sat, 10am-3pm Sun; Ⓜ Urquinaona) A feast for the eyes, this Modernista confection is also the city's most traditional venue for classical and choral music, although it has a wide-ranging program, including flamenco, pop and – particularly – jazz. Just being here for a performance is an experience. In the foyer, its tiled pillars all a-glitter, you can sip a pre-concert tipple.

Jamboree LIVE MUSIC
(Map p568; ☎93 319 17 89; www.masimas.com/jamboree; Plaça Reial 17; tickets €5-22; ⏲8pm-6am; Ⓜ Liceu) For over half a century, Jamboree has been bringing joy to the jivers of Barcelona, with high-calibre acts featuring jazz trios, blues, Afrobeats, Latin and big-band sounds. Two concerts are held most nights (at 8pm and 10pm), after which Jamboree morphs into a DJ-spinning club at 12.30am. Jamboree Jam sessions are held on Monday (entrance a mere €5).

Shopping

Most mainstream fashion stores are along a shopping 'axis' that runs from Plaça de Catalunya along Passeig de Gràcia, then left (west) along Avinguda Diagonal.

In La Ribera, El Born and Carrer del Rec are the places for cool designer boutiques that sell high-end fashion. There are plenty of shops scattered throughout the Barri Gòtic (stroll Carrer d'Avinyò). El Raval is a haven for vintage fashion (especially Carrer de la Riera Baixa) and all kinds of original and arty independent shops.

Coquette FASHION & ACCESSORIES
(Map p568; ☎93 310 35 35; www.coquettebcn.com; Carrer de Bonaire 5; ⏲11am-3pm & 5-9pm Mon-Fri, 11.30am-9pm Sat; Ⓜ Barceloneta) With its spare, cut-back and designer look, this friendly fashion store is attractive in its own right. Women can browse through casual, feminine wear by such designers as Humanoid, Vanessa Bruno, UKE and Hoss Intropia.

Custo Barcelona FASHION & ACCESSORIES
(Map p568; ☎93 268 78 93; www.custo.com; Plaça de les Olles 7; ⏲10am-8pm Mon-Sat; Ⓜ Barceloneta) The psychedelic decor and casual atmosphere lend this avant-garde Barcelona fashion store a youthful edge. Custo presents daring new women's and men's collections each year on the New York catwalks. The dazzling colours and cut of everything from dinner jackets to hot pants are for the uninhibited. It has three other shops around town.

ℹ Information

Purse snatching and pickpocketing are major problems, especially around Plaça de Catalunya, La Rambla and Plaça Reial. Report thefts to the **Guàrdia Urbana** (Local Police; ☎092, 93 256 24 77; www.bcn.cat/guardiaurbana; La Rambla 43; ⏲24hr; Ⓜ Liceu) on La Rambla. You're unlikely to recover your goods, but you will need to make this formal *denuncia* (police report) for insurance purposes. Avoid walking around El Raval and the southern end of La Rambla late at night.

Oficina d'Informació de Turisme de Barcelona (Map p568; ☎93 285 38 34; www.barcelonaturisme.com; Plaça de Catalunya 17-S, underground; ⏲8.30am-9pm; Ⓜ Catalunya) Barcelona's main tourist office is in Plaça de Catalunya. Helpful staff are clued up on the city. It also organises a great range of **walking tours** (Map p568; ☎93 285 38 32; www.barcelonaturisme.com; Plaça de Catalunya 17; Ⓜ Catalunya).

Palau Robert Regional Tourist Office (Map p564; ☎93 238 80 91; http://palaurobert.gencat.cat; Passeig de Gràcia 107; ⏲9am-8pm Mon-Sat, to 2.30pm Sun; Ⓜ Diagonal) Inside the Palau Robert, Catalonia's regional tourist office has a host of info including audiovisual resources, a bookshop and a branch of Turisme Juvenil de Catalunya (for youth travel).

ℹ Getting There & Away

AIR

Barcelona's **El Prat airport** (☎91 321 10 00; www.aena.es; 📶) lies 17km southwest of Plaça de Catalunya at El Prat de Llobregat. The airport has two main terminal buildings: the newer T1 terminal and the T2, itself divided into three terminal areas (A, B and C). While the majority of international flights arrive at El Prat airport, there are two other airports in nearby cities, which are used by some budget airlines.

BOAT

Barcelona has ferry connections to the Balearic Islands and Italy. Boats depart from the port just south of the old city.

Passenger and vehicular ferries operated by **Trasmediterránea** (Map p564; ☎902 454645; www.trasmediterranea.es; Moll de Sant Bertran; Ⓜ Drassanes) to/from the Balearic Islands dock around the Moll de Barcelona wharf in Port Vell. Information and tickets are available at the

WORTH A TRIP

GIRONA

A tight huddle of ancient arcaded houses, grand churches, cobbled streets and medieval baths, all enclosed by defensive walls and a lazy river, constitutes a powerful reason for visiting northern Catalonia's largest city, Girona (Castilian: Gerona). From Girona station there are trains to Figueres (€4.10 to €6.90, 30 to 40 minutes, at least 15 daily) and Barcelona (from €10, 40 minutes to 1¼ hours, 30 daily).

Catedral de Girona (www.catedraldegirona.cat; Plaça de la Catedral; adult/concession incl Basílica de Sant Feliu €7/5; 10am-7.30pm Jul & Aug, to 6.30pm Apr-Jun, Sep & Oct, to 5.30pm Nov-Mar) Towering over a flight of 86 steps rising from Plaça de la Catedral, Girona's imposing cathedral is far more ancient than its billowing baroque facade suggests. Built over an old Roman forum, parts of its foundations date from the 5th century. Today, 14th-century Gothic styling – added over an 11th-century Romanesque church – dominates, though a beautiful, double-columned Romanesque **cloister** dates from the 12th century. With the world's second-widest Gothic nave, it's a formidable sight to explore, but audio guides are provided.

Museu d'Història dels Jueus (www.girona.cat/call; Carrer de la Força 8; adult/child €4/free; 10am-8pm Mon-Sat, to 2pm Sun Jul & Aug, 10am-2pm Mon & Sun, to 6pm Tue-Sat Sep-Jun) Until 1492, Girona was home to Catalonia's second-most important medieval Jewish community, after Barcelona, and one of the country's finest Jewish quarters. This excellent museum takes pride in Girona's Jewish heritage, without shying away from less salubrious aspects such as Inquisition persecution and forced conversions. You also see a rare 11th-century *miqvé* (ritual bath) and a 13th-century Jewish house.

Bells Oficis (972 22 81 70; www.bellsoficis.com; Carrer dels Germans Busquets 2; r incl breakfast €45-100;) A lovingly restored 19th-century apartment towards the southern end of the old town, Bells Oficis makes a stylish, ultra-welcoming base. It's the former home of Catalan artist Jaume Busquets i Mollera, and retains period details in the five very different rooms (one of which is a teeny two-bunk pad). Three rooms share a bathroom; one en suite room has no bathroom door.

El Celler de Can Roca (972 22 21 57; www.cellercanroca.com; Carrer Can Sunyer 48; degustation menus €180-215; bookings 12.30-2pm & 8-9.30pm Wed-Sat) Ever-changing avant-garde takes on Catalan dishes have catapulted El Celler de Can Roca to global fame. Holding three Michelin stars, it was named the best restaurant in the world in 2013, 2015 and 2018 by The World's 50 Best. Each year brings new innovations, from molecular gastronomy to multi-sensory food-art interplay to sci-fi dessert trolleys, all with mama's home cooking as the core inspiration.

terminal buildings along Moll de Sant Bertran and on Moll de Barcelona or from travel agents. Fares vary enormously according to season, how far in advance you book and whether or not you want a cabin. Fares for a 'Butaca Turista' (seat) from Barcelona to any of the islands typically start around €60 on ferries in the summertime.

BUS

Long-distance buses leave from **Estació del Nord** (Map p564; 93 706 53 66; www.barcelonanord.cat; Carrer d'Ali Bei 80; M Arc de Triomf). A plethora of companies service different parts of Spain; many come under the umbrella of **ALSA** (902 422242; www.alsa.es). For other companies, ask at the bus station. There are frequent services (20 or more daily) to Madrid (seven to eight hours), Valencia (four to 4½ hours) and Zaragoza (3½ hours) and several daily departures to distant destinations such as Burgos, Santiago de Compostela and Seville. Fares vary hugely depending on what time of day you travel and how far in advance you book.

Eurolines (www.eurolines.es), in conjunction with local carriers all over Europe, is the main international carrier. Its website provides links to national operators; it runs services across Europe and to Morocco from Estació del Nord, and from **Estació d'Autobusos de Sants** (Map p564; Carrer de Viriat; M Sants Estació), next to Estació Sants Barcelona.

TRAIN

The main station is **Estació Sants** (912 432343; www.adif.es; Plaça dels Països Catalans; M Sants Estació), 2.5km west of La Rambla. Daily high-speed trains head for Madrid (€50 to more than €200, from 2½ hours, 30 daily) via

WORTH A TRIP

ANDORRA

This mini-country wedged between France and Spain offers by far the best ski slopes and resort facilities in all the Pyrenees. Once the snows melt, there's an abundance of great walking, ranging from easy strolls to demanding day hikes in the principality's higher, more remote reaches. Strike out above the tight valleys and you can walk for hours, almost alone.

The only way to reach Andorra is by road from Spain or France. If driving, fill up in Andorra; fuel is substantially cheaper there. There are buses to/from Barcelona's Estació del Nord, Estació Sants and airport, Lleida, La Seu d'Urgell and Toulouse (France). All bus services arrive at and leave from Andorra la Vella.

Zaragoza; book well ahead for the lowest fares. Other daily trains run to Valencia (€12 to €45, three to 4½ hours, up to 19 daily), Pamplona, San Sebastián, Bilbao, Santiago de Compostela, Seville and Málaga. Direct overnight trains from Paris, Geneva, Milan and Zürich also arrive at Estació Sants.

Getting Around

TO/FROM THE AIRPORT

Frequent *aerobúses* (www.aerobusbcn.com) run between both airport terminals and Plaça de Catalunya (€5.90, 35 minutes, every five or 10 minutes), from 6am to 1am.

PUBLIC TRANSPORT

Barcelona's metro system spreads its tentacles around the city in such a way that most places of interest are within a 10-minute walk of a station. It runs 5am to midnight Sunday to Thursday, till 2am on Friday and 24 hours on Saturday. Targeta T-10 (10-ride passes; €10.20) are the best value; otherwise, it's €2.20 per ride.

TAXI

Taxis charge €2.10 to €2.30 flagfall plus €1.10 to €1.30 per kilometre (the higher rates are for nights and weekends). You can flag a taxi down in the street, or call **Fonotaxi** (☎93 300 11 00; www.fonotaxi.net) or **Radio Taxi 033** (☎93 303 30 33; www.radiotaxi033.com). The call-out charge is €3.40 (€4.20 at night and on weekends).

Tarragona

POP 63,838

In this effervescent port city, Roman history collides with beaches, nightlife and a food scene that perfumes the air with freshly grilled seafood. The biggest lure is the wealth of remains from one of Spain's most important Roman cities, including mosaic-packed museums and a seaside amphitheatre. A roll-call of excellent places to eat gives you good reason to linger in the knot of lanes in the medieval centre, flanked by a broad cathedral with Gothic flourishes.

Sights

★Catedral de Tarragona CATHEDRAL
(www.catedraldetarragona.com; Plaça de la Seu; adult/child €5/3; ⏲10am-8pm Mon-Sat mid-Jun-mid-Sep, 10am-7pm Mon-Sat mid-Mar–mid-Jun & mid-Sep–Oct, 10am-5pm Mon-Fri, to 7pm Sat Nov-mid-Mar) Crowning the town, Tarragona's cathedral incorporates both Romanesque and Gothic features, as typified by the main facade. The flower-filled cloister has Gothic vaulting and Romanesque carved capitals, one of which shows rats conducting a cat's funeral... until the cat comes back to life! Chambers off the cloister display the remains of a Roman temple (unearthed in 2015) and the **Museu Diocesà**, its collection extending from Roman hairpins to 13th- and 14th-century polychrome Virgin woodcarvings. Don't miss the east nave's 14th-century frescos.

Passeig Arqueològic Muralles WALLS
(Avinguda de Catalunya; adult/child €3.30/free; ⏲9am-9pm Tue-Sat, to 3pm Sun Easter-Sep, 9am-7pm Tue-Fri, to 3pm Sun Oct-Easter) A peaceful walk takes you around the inland part of the old town's perimeter between two lines of city walls. The inner walls are mainly Roman and date back to the 3rd century BC, while the outer ones were put up by the British in 1709 during the War of the Spanish Succession. The earliest stretches are a mighty 4m thick. There's a helpful interpretation centre (Catalan, Spanish and English).

★Museu Nacional Arqueològic de Tarragona MUSEUM
(www.mnat.cat; Plaça del Rei 5; adult/child €4.50/free; ⏲8am-6pm Mon & Wed-Fri, 8am-3pm & 4-6.30 Tue Oct-May, 8am-3pm Mon-Fri Jun-Sep, 10am-2pm Sun year-round) This excellent museum does justice to the cultural and material

wealth of Roman Tarraco. The mosaic collection traces changing trends from simple black-and-white designs to complex full-colour creations; highlights include the fine 2nd- or 3rd-century *Mosaic de la Medusa* and the large, almost complete 3rd-century *Mosaic dels Peixos de la Pineda,* showing fish and sea creatures. Explanations are mostly in Catalan and Spanish, but there are English-language booklets across the galleries.

Sleeping & Eating

Look for tapas bars and inexpensive cafes on the Plaça de la Font. The quintessential Tarragona seafood experience can be had in Serrallo, the town's fishing port, where a dozen bars and restaurants sell the day's catch.

Tarragona Hostel HOSTEL €
(☎877 05 58 96; www.tarragonahostel.com; Carrer de la Unió 26; dm/tr €12/40; 📶) All the backpacker essentials are well executed at this friendly central hostel with chirpy staff, a leafy patio, a comfy common room, a shared kitchen and laundry facilities. Choose from two eight-bed dorms and a more modern four-bed dorm (all with air-con and personal lockers), or a private fan-cooled triple room.

Hotel Plaça de la Font HOTEL €€
(☎977 24 61 34; www.hotelpdelafont.com; Plaça de la Font 26; s/d/tr €60/80/100; ❄📶) Comfortable modern rooms, individually decorated with photos of local monuments, make this cheerful, convenient hotel one of Tarragona's most attractive options. Rooms at the front have tiny balconies and are well soundproofed from the sociable murmur on bustling Plaça de la Font below. With tables right on the square, the cafe is perfect for light breakfasts (€6).

Barquet SEAFOOD €€
(☎977 24 00 23; www.restaurantbarquet.com; Carrer del Gasòmetre 16; mains €12-22; ⏲12.30-3.30pm Mon, 12.30-3.30pm & 8.30-10pm Tue-Fri, 1-3.30pm & 8.30-10.00pm Sat) This popular neighbourhood restaurant is a short downhill stroll south from Tarragona centre. It's deservedly famous for its expertly concocted rice dishes bursting with maritime flavour, and also does great seafood *raciones* (large plates). Don't be fooled by the nautical warehouse interior: fish dishes and desserts are executed with finesse.

AQ MEDITERRANEAN, FUSION €€
(☎977 21 59 54; www.aq-restaurant.com; Carrer de les Coques 7; mains €11-24; ⏲1.30-3.30pm & 8.30-11pm) The crisp interior design of this palm-patterned restaurant promises fine dining and AQ amply delivers, with its impeccably crafted, playfully executed fusion dishes taking inspiration from Catalan, Italian and Asian cuisines. Treat your taste buds to squid-ink croquettes, chunky strips of *patatas bravas,* grilled Wagyu steak,

DALÍ'S CATALONIA

The only name that could come into your head when you set eyes on the red castle-like building in central **Figueres**, topped with giant eggs and stylised Oscar-like statues and studded with plaster-covered croissants, is Salvador Dalí. With its entrance watched over by medieval suits of armour balancing baguettes on their heads, the **Teatre-Museu Dalí** (www.salvador-dali.org; Plaça de Gala i Salvador Dalí 5; adult/child under 9yr €14/free; ⏲9am-8pm Apr-Jul & Sep, 9am-8pm & 10pm-1am Aug, 9.30am-6pm Tue-Sun Oct & Mar, 10.30am-6pm Tue-Sun Nov-Feb) is an entirely appropriate final resting place for the master of surrealism. 'Theatre-museum' is an apt label for this trip through the incredibly fertile imagination of one of the great showmen of the 20th century. It's full of surprises, tricks and illusions, and contains a substantial portion of Dalí's life's work.

Port Lligat, 1km northeast of Cadaqués, is a tiny settlement around a lovely cove, with fishing boats pulled up on its beach. The **Casa Museu Dalí** (☎972 25 10 15; www.salvador-dali.org; adult/child under 8yr €12/free; ⏲9.30am-9pm mid-Jun–mid-Sep, 10.30am-6pm mid-Sep–Jan & mid-Feb–mid-Jun, closed mid-Jan–mid-Feb, plus Mon Nov–mid-Mar) started life as a fisherman's hut, but was steadily enlarged by Dalí and his wife Gala during their residence here from 1930 to 1982 (apart from a dozen or so years abroad around the Spanish Civil War). It provides a fascinating insight into the lives of the (excuse the pun) surreal couple. We probably don't need to tell you that it's the house with a lot of little white chimneypots and two egg-shaped towers, overlooking the western end of the beach. You must book ahead.

cod-and-aubergine teriyaki or wok-fried mussels.

Information

The **tourist office** (☎977 25 07 95; www.tarragonaturisme.es; Carrer Major 39; ⌚10am-8pm late Jun-Sep, 10am-2pm & 3-5pm Mon-Fri, 10am-2pm & 3-7pm Sat, 10am-2pm Sun Oct-late Jun) is a good place for booking guided tours of the city. Opening hours are extended in high season.

Getting There & Away

BUS

The **bus station** (Plaça Imperial Tarraco) is 1.5km northwest of the old town along Rambla Nova. Destinations include Barcelona (€8.70, 1½ hours, seven daily) and Valencia (€22, three to 4½ hours, six daily).

TRAIN

Tarragona station is a 10-minute walk from the old town, while fast AVE trains stop at Camp de Tarragona station, 10km north. Departures from Tarragona station include trains to Barcelona (€10.50 to €17.30, one to 1½ hours, around every 30 minutes) and Valencia (€17 to €24, two to four hours, 15 to 17 daily).

ARAGÓN, BASQUE COUNTRY & NAVARRA

Zaragoza

POP 664,938

Zaragoza (Saragossa), on the banks of the mighty Río Ebro, is a vibrant, elegant and fascinating city. Its residents, who form over half of Aragón's population, enjoy a lifestyle that revolves around some superb tapas bars, great shopping and a vigorous nightlife. But Zaragoza is much more than just a good-time city: its host of historical sights spans all the great civilisations that have left their mark on the Spanish soul. This is also a good place to get acquainted with the artistic genius of Francisco de Goya, who was born a short horse-ride away in 1746.

Sights

★Basílica de Nuestra Señora del Pilar CHURCH

(www.basilicadelpilar.es; Plaza del Pilar; ⌚6.45am-8.30pm Mon-Sat, to 9.30pm Sun) Brace yourself for this great baroque cavern of Catholicism. The faithful believe that here on 2 January AD 40, the Virgin Mary appeared to Santiago (St James the Apostle) atop a *pilar* (pillar) of jasper, and left the pillar behind as a testament to her visit. A chapel was built around the pillar, followed by a series of ever more grandiose churches, culminating in the enormous basilica.

★Aljafería PALACE

(☎976 28 96 83; www.cortesaragon.es; Calle de los Diputados; adult/concession/child €5/1/free, Sun free; ⌚10am-2pm & 4.30-8pm Apr-Oct, 10am-2pm & 4-6.30pm Nov-Mar) The Aljafería is Spain's finest Islamic-era edifice outside Andalucía. Built as a fortified palace for Zaragoza's Islamic rulers in the 11th century, it underwent various alterations after 1118 when Zaragoza passed into Christian hands. In the 1490s the Reyes Católicos (Catholic Monarchs), Fernando and Isabel, tacked on their own palace. From the 1590s the Aljafería was developed into more of a fortress than a palace. Twentieth-century restorations brought it back to life, and Aragón's regional parliament has been housed here since 1987.

La Seo CATHEDRAL

(Catedral de San Salvador; ☎976 29 12 31; www.zaragozaturismo.es; Plaza de la Seo; adult/senior/child €4/3/free; ⌚10am-6.30pm & 7.30-9pm Mon-Thu, 10am-6.30pm Fri, 10am-noon, 3-8.30pm Sat, 10am-noon, 3-6.30pm & 7.30-9pm Sun mid-Jun–mid-Oct, 10am-2pm & 4-6.30pm Mon-Fri, 10am-noon & 4-6.30pm Sat & Sun mid-Oct–mid-Jun) Dominating the eastern end of Plaza del Pilar, La Seo is Zaragoza's finest work of Christian architecture, built between the 12th and 17th centuries and displaying a fabulous spread of styles from Romanesque to baroque. It stands on the site of Islamic Zaragoza's main mosque (which itself stood upon the temple of the Roman forum). The admission price includes La Seo's **Museo de Tapices** (⌚10am-6.30pm & 7.45-9pm Mon-Thu, 10am-6.30pm Fri, 10am-noon, 3-6.30pm & 7.45-9pm Sat & Sun mid-Jun–mid-Oct, 10am-2pm & 4-6.30pm mid-Oct–mid-Jun), a collection of Flemish and French tapestries considered the best of its kind in the world.

Museo Goya – Colección Ibercaja MUSEUM

(☎976 39 73 87; http://museogoya.ibercaja.es; Calle de Espoz y Mina 23; adult/senior & child €4/free, audio guide or tablet €2; ⌚10am-8pm Mon-Sat, to 2pm Sun Apr-Oct, 10am-2pm & 4-8pm Mon-Sat, 10am-2pm Sun Nov-Mar) Apart from Madrid's Museo del Prado, this exceedingly well-laid-out museum contains arguably the best exposé of the work of one of Spain's most revered artists. Each of the three floors has a different focus, the 2nd floor being the one that exhibits Goya's own work. Four complete sets of his prints are included, most notably the groundbreaking, sometimes grotesque *Desastres de la Guerra* (Disasters of War), a bitter attack on the cruelty and folly of war.

Museo del Teatro de Caesaraugusta MUSEUM
(☎976 72 60 75; www.zaragozaturismo.es; Calle de San Jorge 12; adult/student/senior & child €4/3/free; ⊙10am-2pm & 5-9pm Tue-Sat, 10am-2.30pm Sun) The finest in Zaragoza's quartet of Roman museums was discovered during excavation of a building site in 1972. Great efforts, including an entertaining 15-minute audiovisual, have been made to help visitors visualise the splendour of this theatre that accommodated 6000 spectators on more than 30 rows of seating. The theatre is visible from the surrounding streets and is protected by a huge polycarbonate roof, 25m above ground, that is set at the height of the top of the original building.

Sleeping

★Hotel Sauce HOTEL €
(☎976 20 50 50; www.hotelsauce.com; Calle de Espoz y Mina 33; s €47-55, d €50-70; ❄📶) This stylish small hotel with a great central location is a superb option for its fresh, cheerful, contemporary rooms with tasteful watercolours, outstandingly friendly and helpful staff, and pleasant 24-hour cafe serving excellent breakfasts, cakes and cocktails. Its prices are very reasonable given everything that the hotel provides.

Catalonia El Pilar HOTEL €€
(☎976 20 58 58; www.hoteles-catalonia.com; Calle de la Manifestación 16; s/d from €75/80; ❄@📶) Ten out of 10 for the facade, a handsome Modernista construction that has been artfully renovated to house this eminently comfortable contemporary hotel. Inside, rooms are spacious and decorated in restful, muted earth tones with elegant marble-clad bathrooms. Some of the beds are king-size. Breakfast costs €14.

Eating & Drinking

Head to the tangle of lanes in El Tubo, north of Plaza de España, for one of Spain's richest gatherings of tapas bars.

After the tapas bars close around midnight, late-night and music bars come into their own. There's a good scattering of these in the historic centre.

Méli Melo TAPAS €
(☎976 29 46 95; www.restaurantemelimelozaragoza.com; Calle Mayor 45; tapas €2.50-3; ⊙1-5pm & 8pm-midnight Mon-Sat, 1-4pm Sun) The creative tapas at this tightly packed spot are arrayed very temptingly along the bar: you can just select those that appeal most; maybe prawn-stuffed squid, or artichoke with ham, or a mini fish-and-shrimp burger. Or choose more substantial *raciones* from the board, such as *patatas a la gresca* (fried potato cubes) or *escalibada con bacalao* (baked veggies with cod).

Los Xarmientos ARAGONESE €€
(☎976 29 90 48; www.facebook.com/xarmientos; Calle de Espoz y Mina 25; mains €12-16, set menus €26.50-35; ⊙1.30-4pm & 8.30-11pm Wed-Sat, 1.30-4pm Tue & Sun) Aragonese meat dishes are a speciality at this artfully designed restaurant. It styles itself as a *parrilla*, meaning the dishes are cooked on a barbecue-style grill. It's a fine place to sample the local *ternasco* (lamb), Aragon's most emblematic dish, accompanied by a good Somontano wine and perhaps preceded by a spinach and goat's-cheese salad…or even some snails?

Information

Municipal Tourist Office (☎976 20 12 00; www.zaragozaturismo.es; Plaza del Pilar; ⊙10am-8pm; 📶) Has branch offices around town, including at the train station.

Oficina de Turismo de Aragón (☎976 28 21 81; www.turismodearagon.com; Plaza de España 1; ⊙9.30am-2.30pm & 4.30-7.30pm) Helpful place with plenty of brochures covering all of Aragón.

Getting There & Away

BUS

Dozens of bus lines fan out across Spain from the bus station attached to the Estación Intermodal Delicias train station, 3km west of the centre. **ALSA** (☎902 422242; www.alsa.es) runs to/from Madrid (from €16.80, three to four hours, 19 or more daily) and Barcelona (from €9.60, 3¾ hours, 16 or more daily). **Alosa** (☎974 21 07 00; www.avanzabus.com) runs buses to/from Huesca (€8, 1¼ hours, 14 or more daily) and Jaca (€16, 2½ hours, six or more daily).

TRAIN

Zaragoza's futuristic **Estación Intermodal Delicias** (Avenida de Navarra 80) is connected by around 20 daily high-speed AVE services to Madrid (€34 to €55, 1½ hours) and Barcelona (€37 to €60, 1¾ hours). Other destinations include Huesca (from €8, one hour, one or two daily), Jaca (€15, 3¼ hours, two daily) and Teruel (€20, 2½ hours, four daily).

Around Aragón

Aragón is a beautiful and fascinating region to explore if you have a few days to do so. In the south, little visited **Teruel** is home to some stunning Mudéjar architecture. Nearby, **Albarracín** is one of Spain's prettiest villages.

In the north, the **Parque Nacional de Ordesa y Monte Perdido** is the most spectacular stretch of the Spanish Pyrenees, with dramatic mountain scenery and superb hiking; the pretty village of **Torla** is the main gateway (though it gets overrun with visitors in July and August). En route to the mountains are several towns and villages with enchanting medieval quarters or fascinating medieval monuments, such as **Aínsa**, **Jaca** and **Huesca**.

In Aragón's northwest, **Sos del Rey Católico** is another gorgeous stone village draped along a ridge.

San Sebastián

POP 181,932

With Michelin stars apparently falling from the heavens onto its restaurants, not to mention a *pintxo* (tapas) culture almost unmatched anywhere else in Spain, stylish San Sebastián (Donostia in Basque) frequently tops lists of the world's best places to eat. Charming and well-mannered by day, cool and happening by night, the city has an idyllic location on the shell-shaped Bahía de la Concha, with crystalline waters, a flawless beach and green hills on all sides.

Sights

★Playa de la Concha BEACH

(Paseo de la Concha) Fulfilling almost every idea of how a perfect city beach should be formed, Playa de la Concha (and its westerly extension, Playa de Ondarreta) is easily among the best city beaches in Europe. Throughout the long summer months a fiesta atmosphere prevails, with thousands of tanned and toned bodies spread across the sands. The swimming is almost always safe.

Monte Igueldo VIEWPOINT

(www.monteigueldo.es; 10am-9pm Mon-Fri, to 10pm Sat & Sun Jul, 10am-10pm daily Aug, 10am-8pm Mon-Fri, to 9pm Sat & Sun Jun & Sep, shorter hours rest of year) The views from the summit of Monte Igueldo, just west of town, will make you feel like a circling hawk staring down over the vast panorama of the Bahía de la Concha and the surrounding coastline and mountains. The best way to get there is via the old-world **funicular railway** (Plaza del Funicular; return adult/child €3.15/2.35; 10am-9pm Jun-Aug, shorter hours rest of year) to the **Parque de Atracciones** (943 21 35 25; Paseo de Igeldo; 10am-9pm Mon-Fri, to 10pm Sat & Sun Jul & Aug, 10am-7pm Mon-Fri, to 8pm Sat & Sun Jun & Sep, shorter hours rest of year), a small, old-fashioned theme park at the top of the hill. Opening hours vary throughout the year; check the website for details.

San Telmo Museoa MUSEUM

(943 48 15 80; www.santelmomuseoa.com; Plaza Zuloaga 1; adult/concession/child €6/3/free, Tue free; 10am-8pm Tue-Sun) One of the best museums in the Basque Country, the San Telmo Museoa has a thought-provoking collection that explores Basque history and culture in all its complexity. Exhibitions are spread between a restored convent dating back to the 16th century and a cutting-edge newer wing that blends into its plant-lined backdrop of Mount Urgull. The collection ranges from historical artefacts to bold fusions of contemporary art. San Telmo also stages some outstanding temporary exhibitions.

Sleeping

Pensión Altair PENSIÓN €

(943 29 31 33; www.pension-altair.com; Calle Padre Larroca 3; s/d €60/110;) This *pensión* is in a beautifully restored town house, with unusual church-worthy arched windows and modern, minimalist rooms that are a world away from the fusty decor of the old-town *pensiones*. Interior rooms lack the grandiose windows but are much larger.

Pensión Amaiur BOUTIQUE HOTEL €€

(943 42 96 54; www.pensionamaiur.com; Calle 31 de Agosto 44; d with/without bathroom from €80/70;) A top-notch guesthouse in a prime old-town location, Amaiur has bright floral wallpapers and bathrooms tiled in Andalucian blue and white. The best rooms are

those that overlook the main street, where you can sit on a little balcony and be completely enveloped in blushing red flowers. Some rooms share bathrooms. Guest kitchen and free snacks add to the value.

Hotel de Londres y de Inglaterra HISTORIC HOTEL €€€
(☎943 44 07 70; www.hlondres.com; Calle de Zubieta 2; d €380; P ❄ 📶) Sitting pretty on the beachfront, Hotel de Londres y de Inglaterra (Hotel of London and England) is as proper as it sounds. Queen Isabel II set the tone for this hotel well over a century ago, and things have stayed pretty regal ever since. The place exudes elegance; some rooms have stunning views over Playa de la Concha.

Eating & Drinking

With 18 Michelin stars, San Sebastián stands atop a pedestal as one of the culinary capitals of the planet. As if that alone weren't enough, the city is overflowing with bars – almost all of which have bar tops weighed down under a mountain of *pintxos* that almost every Spaniard will tell you are the best in country.

Most of the city's bars mutate through the day from calm morning-coffee hang-outs to pintxo-laden delights, before finally finishing up as noisy bars full of writhing, sweaty bodies. Nights in San Sebastián start late and go on until well into the wee hours.

★La Fábrica BASQUE €€
(☎943 43 21 10; www.restaurantelafabrica.es; Calle del Puerto 17; mains €15-20, set menus from €30; ⏲1-4pm & 7.30-11.30pm) The red-brick interior walls and white tablecloths lend an air of class to this restaurant, whose modern takes on Basque classics have been making waves with San Sebastián locals in recent years. La Fábrica only works with multicourse *menús*, which means you'll get to sample various delicacies like wild mushroom ravioli with foie gras cream or venison in red wine sauce. Advance reservations essential.

★La Cuchara de San Telmo BASQUE €€
(☎943 44 16 55; www.lacucharadesantelmo.com; Calle de 31 de Agosto 28; pintxos from €2.50; ⏲7.30-11pm Tue, 12.30-5.30pm & 7.30-11.30pm Wed-Sun) This bustling, always-packed bar offers miniature *nueva cocina vasca* (Basque nouvelle cuisine) from a supremely creative kitchen. Unlike many San Sebastián bars, this one doesn't have any *pintxos* laid out on the bar top; instead you must order from the blackboard menu behind the counter.

Restaurante Kokotxa MODERN SPANISH €€€
(☎943 42 19 04; www.restaurantekokotxa.com; Calle del Campanario 11; mains €27-35, menús €85-115; ⏲1.30-3.30pm & 8.30-10.30pm Tue-Sat) This Michelin-star restaurant is hidden away down an overlooked alley in the old town, but the food rewards those who search. Most people opt for the *menú de mercado* (€85) and enjoy the flavours of the traders from the busy city market. It's closed from mid-February through March and for two weeks in late October.

SAN SEBASTIÁN SPLURGE

With three shining Michelin stars, acclaimed chef Juan Mari Arzak is king when it comes to *nueva cocina vasca* and his restaurant, **Arzak** (☎943 27 84 65; www.arzak.info; Avenida Alcalde Jose Elósegui 273; tasting menu €210; ⏲1.15-3.15pm & 8.45-10.30pm Tue-Sat, closed mid-Jun–early Jul & Nov) is considered one of the best in the world. Arzak is now assisted by his daughter Elena, and they never cease to innovate. Reservations, well in advance, are obligatory.

Information

The friendly **Oficina de Turismo** (☎943 48 11 66; www.sansebastianturismo.com; Alameda del Boulevard 8; ⏲9am-8pm Mon-Sat, 10am-7pm Sun Jul-Sep, 9am-7pm Mon-Sat, 10am 2pm Sun Oct-May) offers comprehensive information on the city and the Basque Country in general.

Getting There & Away

AIR

Aeropuerto de San Sebastián (EAS; ☎902 404704; www.aena.es) is 22km northeast of the city. There are no international flights here, though there are several daily connections to Barcelona (1½ hours) and Madrid (1¼ hours).

BUS

San Sebastián's **bus station** (Estación Donostia Geltokia; www.estaciondonostia.com; Paseo Federico García Lorca 1) is on the eastern side of the river, just across from the Renfe train station. Services leave for Bilbao (from €7, 1¼ hours, frequent), Bilbao Airport (€17, 1¼ hours, hourly), Biarritz (France; from €7, 1¼ hours, six to eight daily) and Pamplona (from €8, 1¼ hours).

TRAIN

The main **Renfe train station** (Paseo de Francia) is just across Río Urumea, on a line linking Paris to Madrid. There are services to Madrid (from €29, 5½ hours, several daily) and to Barcelona (from €32, six hours, two daily).

For France you must first go to the Spanish/French border town of Irún (or sometimes trains go as far as Hendaye; from €2.25, 27 minutes), which is also served by Eusko Tren/Ferrocarril Vasco (www.euskotren.es), and change there. Trains depart every half-hour from **Amara train station** (Easo Plaza 9), about 1km south of the city centre, and also stop in Pasajes (from €1.70, 12 minutes) and Irún/Hendaye (€2.45, 25 minutes). Another ET/FV railway line heads west to Bilbao via Zarautz, Zumaia and Durango, but it's painfully slow, so the bus is usually a better plan.

Bilbao

POP 345,100

The commercial hub of the Basque Country, Bilbao (Bilbo in Basque) is best known for the magnificent Guggenheim Museum. An architectural masterpiece by Frank Gehry, the museum was the catalyst of a turnaround that saw Bilbao transformed from an industrial port city into a vibrant cultural centre (without losing its down-to-earth soul). After visiting this must-see temple to modern art, spend time exploring Bilbao's Casco Viejo (Old Quarter), a grid of elegant streets dotted with shops, cafes, *pintxo* bars and several small but worthy museums.

Sights

★Museo Guggenheim Bilbao — GALLERY

(☎944 35 90 80; www.guggenheim-bilbao.es; Avenida Abandoibarra 2; adult/concession/child from €13/7.50/free; ⏲10am-8pm, closed Mon Sep-Jun) Shimmering titanium Museo Guggenheim Bilbao is one of modern architecture's most iconic buildings. It played a major role in helping to lift Bilbao out of its postindustrial depression and into the 21st century – and with sensation. It sparked the city's inspired regeneration, stimulated further development and placed Bilbao firmly in the international art and tourism spotlight.

★Museo de Bellas Artes — GALLERY

(☎944 39 60 60; www.museobilbao.com; Plaza del Museo 2; adult/concession/child €10/8/free, free 6-8pm; ⏲10am-8pm Wed-Mon) The Museo de Bellas Artes houses a compelling collection that includes everything from Gothic sculptures to 20th-century pop art. There are three main subcollections: classical art, with works by Murillo, Zurbarán, El Greco, Goya and van Dyck; contemporary art, featuring works by Gauguin, Francis Bacon and Anthony Caro; and Basque art, with works of the great sculptors Jorge Oteiza and Eduardo Chillida, and strong paintings by the likes of Ignacio Zuloaga and Juan de Echevarría.

Casco Viejo — OLD TOWN

The compact Casco Viejo, Bilbao's atmospheric old quarter, is full of charming streets, boisterous bars and plenty of quirky and independent shops. At the heart of the Casco are Bilbao's original seven streets, **Las Siete Calles**, which date from the 1400s.

Sleeping & Eating

The Bilbao tourism authority has a useful **reservations department** (☎946 94 12 12) for accommodation.

Pintxos (Basque tapas) are as good in Bilbao as they are in San Sebastián, and slightly cheaper (from around €2.50). Plaza Nueva, on the edge of the Casco Viejo, offers especially rich pickings, as do Calles de Perro and Jardines.

Casual Bilbao Gurea — PENSION €€

(☎944 16 32 99; www.casualhoteles.com; Calle de Bidebarrieta 14; s/d €75/85; 📶) The family-run Gurea has arty, modern rooms with wooden floors, good natural light and exceptionally friendly staff. It's set on the 3rd and 4th floors of a building in the old town, with great dining options just steps from the entrance.

Miró Hotel — DESIGN HOTEL €€€

(☎946 61 18 80; www.mirohotelbilbao.com; Alameda Mazarredo 77; d from €210; ❄@📶) This hip hotel facing the Museo Guggenheim Bilbao is the passion project of fashion designer Antonio Miró. It's filled with modern photography and art, quirky books, and minimalist decor – a perfect fit with art-minded Bilbao.

★La Viña del Ensanche — PINTXOS €

(☎944 15 56 15; www.lavinadelensanche.com; Calle de la Diputación 10; small plates €5-15, set menu €30; ⏲8.30am-11pm Mon-Fri, noon-1am Sat) Set with old-fashioned wood-panelled walls and framed postcards written by adoring fans over the years, La Viña del Ensanche maintains a reputation as one of Bilbao's best eating spots – no small achievement for a place that has been in business since 1927. Mouth-watering morsels of ham, tender oc-

PAMPLONA & SAN FERMINES

Immortalised by Ernest Hemingway in *The Sun Also Rises*, the pre-Pyrenean city of Pamplona (Iruña in Basque) is home of the wild Sanfermines festival, but it is also an extremely walkable city that's managed to mix the charm of old plazas and buildings with modern shops and a lively nightlife.

The **Sanfermines festival** is held from 6 to 14 July, when Pamplona is overrun with thrill-seekers, curious onlookers and, yes, bulls. *El encierro* (running of the bulls) begins at 8am daily, when bulls are let loose from the Coralillos Santo Domingo. The 875m run through the streets to the bullring lasts just three minutes.

Since records began in 1924, 16 people have died during Pamplona's bullrun. Many of those who participate are full of bravado (and/or drink) and have little idea of what they're doing. For dedicated *encierro* news, check out www.sanfermin.com.

Animal rights groups oppose bullrunning as a cruel tradition, and the participating bulls will almost certainly all be killed in the afternoon bullfight. PETA (www.peta.org.uk) organises eye-catching protests in Pamplona at every Sanfermines.

topus and crispy asparagus tempura are just a few of the many temptations.

Agape Restaurante BASQUE **€€**
(☎944 10 05 06; www.restauranteagape.com; Calle de Hernani 13; menú del día €13.50, menús €24-37; ⏲1-4pm Mon & Tue, 1-4pm & 9-11pm Wed-Sat; 📶) With a solid reputation among locals for good-value meals that don't sacrifice quality, this is a highly recommended place for a slice of real Bilbao culinary life. Think sea bass served over shrimp and leek risotto, lamb confit with roasted aubergines and stir-fried vegetables with almond and sesame pesto – all served in a stylish but rustic setting.

ℹ Information

The very helpful **main branch** (☎944 79 57 60; www.bilbaoturismo.net; Plaza Circular 1; ⏲9am-8pm; 📶) of the tourist office is near the Abando train station.

ℹ Getting There & Away

BUS

Bilbao's main bus station, **Termibus** (☎944 39 50 77; www.termibus.es; Gurtubay 1, San Mamés), is west of the centre. Services operate to San Sebastián (from €7, 1¼ hours, frequent), Madrid (from €32, four to five hours, 15 daily), Barcelona (from €36, 8½ hours, four daily), Pamplona (€15, 2½ hours, six daily) and Santander (from €7, 1¼ hours, frequent).

TRAIN

Two Renfe trains run daily to Madrid (from €20, five to seven hours) and Barcelona (from €27, seven hours) from the Abando station. Slow **Renfe Feve** (www.renfe.com/viajeros/feve) trains from Concordia station next door head west to Santander (from €9, three hours, three daily), where you can connect for places further west in Cantabria, Asturias and Galicia.

CANTABRIA, ASTURIAS & GALICIA

With a landscape reminiscent of parts of the British Isles, 'Green Spain' offers great walks and scenery in mountainous national and regional parks, seafood feasts in sophisticated towns or quaint fishing villages, and a spectacular coastline strung with oodles of beautiful beaches washed by the chilly waters of the north Atlantic.

Santillana del Mar

Thirty kilometres west of the Cantabrian capital, Santander, Santillana del Mar is a *bijou* medieval village and the obvious overnight base for visiting nearby Altamira. Buses run six times a day from Santander to Santillana del Mar.

Spain's finest prehistoric art, in the **Cueva de Altamira**, 2.5km southwest of Santillana, was discovered in 1879. It took more than 20 years, after further discoveries of cave art in France, before scientists accepted that these wonderful paintings of bison, horses and other animals really were the handiwork of primitive people many thousands of years ago. A replica cave here in the **Museo de Altamira** (☎942 81 80 05; http://museodealtamira.mcu.es; Avenida Marcelino Sanz de Sautuola, Santillana del Mar; adult/child €3/free, Sun & from 2pm Sat free; ⏲9.30am-8pm Tue-Sat May-Oct, to 6pm Tue-Sat Nov-Apr, to 3pm Sun &

WORTH A TRIP

PICOS DE EUROPA

These jagged mountains straddling corners of Asturias, Cantabria and Castilla y León amount to some of the finest walking country in Spain. They comprise three limestone massifs (the highest peak rises to 2648m). The 674-sq-km **Parque Nacional de los Picos de Europa** covers all three massifs and is Spain's second-biggest national park.

There are numerous places to stay and eat all around the mountains, with Cangas de Onís (Asturias) and Potes (Cantabria) the main centres for accommodation and information. Getting here and around by public transport can be slow going, but the Picos are accessible by bus from Oviedo and Santander (the former is easier).

The official websites, www.mapama.gob.es and www.parquenacionalpicoseuropa.es, are mostly in Spanish, but www.picosdeeuropa.com and www.liebanaypicosdeeuropa.com are useful for the Asturias and Cantabria sides respectively.

holidays year-round; P 👪) now enables everyone to appreciate the inspired, 13,000- to 35,000-year-old paintings – advance bookings are advisable.

Santiago de Compostela

POP 80,326

The supposed burial place of St James (Santiago), this unique cathedral city and goal of pilgrims for nearly 1200 years is a bewitching place. The hundreds of thousands who walk here every year along the Camino de Santiago are often struck mute with wonder on entering the city's medieval centre. Fortunately, they usually regain their verbal capacities over a celebratory nocturnal foray into the city's lively bar scene.

Sights & Activities

★Catedral de Santiago de Compostela CATHEDRAL

(http://catedraldesantiago.es; Praza do Obradoiro; ⏲7am-8.30pm) The grand heart of Santiago, the cathedral soars above the city in a splendid jumble of spires and sculpture. Built piecemeal over several centuries, its beauty is a mix of the original Romanesque structure (constructed between 1075 and 1211) and later Gothic and baroque flourishes. The tomb of Santiago beneath the main altar is a magnet for all who come here. The cathedral's artistic high point is the Pórtico de la Gloria inside the west entrance, featuring 200 masterly Romanesque sculptures.

★Cathedral Rooftop Tour TOURS

(☎881 55 79 45; www.catedraldesantiago.es; adult/concession/child €12/10/free, combined ticket with Museo da Catedral €15/12/free; ⏲tours hourly 10am-1pm & 4-7pm; 👪) For unforgettable bird's-eye views of the cathedral interior from its upper storeys, and of the city from the cathedral roof, take the rooftop tour, which starts in the **visitor reception centre** (Praza do Obradoiro; ⏲9am-8pm Apr-Oct, 10am-8pm Nov-Mar). The tours are popular, so book beforehand, either at the visitor reception centre for same-day visits, or on the cathedral website up to several weeks ahead. Tours are given in Spanish, but some guides also speak some English.

Praza do Obradoiro PLAZA

The grand square in front of the cathedral's western facade earned its name (Workshop Sq) from the stonemasons' workshops set up here while the cathedral was being built. It's free of both traffic and cafes, and has a unique, magical atmosphere.

Museo da Catedral MUSEUM

(Colección Permanente; www.catedraldesantiago.es; Praza do Obradoiro; adult/concession/child €6/4/free; ⏲9am-8pm Apr-Oct, 10am-8pm Nov-Mar) The Cathedral Museum spreads over four floors and incorporates the cathedral's large 16th-century Gothic/plateresque cloister. You'll see a sizeable section of Maestro Mateo's original carved-stone choir (destroyed in 1604 but pieced back together in 1999), an impressive collection of religious art (including the *botafumeiros* in the 2nd-floor library), the lavishly decorated 18th-century *sala capitular* (chapter house), a room of tapestries woven from designs by Goya, and, off the cloister, the Panteón de Reyes, with tombs of kings of medieval León.

Museo das Peregrinacións e de Santiago MUSEUM

(http://museoperegrinacions.xunta.gal; Praza das Praterías; adult/pilgrim & student/senior & child €2.40/1.20/free; ⏲9.30am-8.30pm Tue-Fri, 11am-7.30pm Sat, 10.15am-2.45pm Sun) The brightly displayed Museum of Pilgrimages & Santiago gives fascinating insights into the phenomenon of Santiago (man, city and pilgrimage) down the centuries. Much of the explanatory material is in English as well as Spanish and Galician. There are also great close-up views of some of the cathedral's towers from the 3rd-floor windows.

Sleeping & Eating

Hostal Suso HOSTAL €
(981 58 66 11; www.hostalsuso.com; Rúa do Vilar 65; r €42-80;) Stacked above a convenient cafe (with excellent-value breakfasts), the friendly, family-run 14-room Suso received a full makeover in 2016 and boasts immaculate, thoughtfully designed rooms in appealing greys and whites, with up-to-date bathrooms and firm beds. It's very good for the price. Everything is thoroughly soundproofed, too – the street outside is traffic-free but can get quite celebratory in summer.

Hotel Costa Vella BOUTIQUE HOTEL €€
(981 56 95 30; www.costavella.com; Rúa da Porta da Pena 17; s €50-60, d €55-95;) Tranquil, well-designed rooms (some with typically Galician *galerías* – glassed-in balconies), a friendly welcome, super helpful management and staff, and a lovely garden cafe make this family-run hotel a wonderful option. It's set in an old stone house just a 400m stroll from the cathedral; the €5 breakfast is substantial.

★ **Parador Hostal dos Reis Católicos** HISTORIC HOTEL €€€
(981 58 22 00; www.parador.es; Praza do Obradoiro 1; incl breakfast s €145-185, d €165-335;) Opened in 1509 as a pilgrims' hostel, and with a claim as the world's oldest hotel, this palatial *parador* occupies a wonderful building that is one of Santiago's major monuments in its own right. Even standard rooms are grand, if a little old-fashioned, with wooden floors, original art and good-sized bathrooms with big glass showers. Some have four-poster beds.

Café-Jardin Costa Vella CAFE €
(www.costavella.com; Rúa da Porta da Pena 17; breakfast €2.70-4.50; 8am-11pm;) The garden cafe of Hotel Costa Vella is the most delightful spot for breakfast (or a drink later in the day), with its fountain, a scattering of statuary and beautiful flowering fruit trees. And if the weather takes a Santiago-esque rainy turn, you can still enjoy it from the glass pavilion or the *galería*.

★ **Abastos 2.0** GALICIAN €€
(654 015937; www.abastoscompostela.com; Rúa das Ameas; dishes €6-13, menú from €30; noon-3.30pm & 8-11pm Mon-Sat) This highly original, incredibly popular marketside eatery offers new dishes concocted daily from the market's offerings, with an emphasis on seafood. Inside is one long 12-seat table where they serve a daily changing menu for €30-plus: reservations are highly advisable. Outside are a few tables (not reservable) where they serve small- to medium-size individual dishes. Almost everything in both sections is delicious.

★ **O Curro da Parra** GALICIAN, FUSION €€
(www.ocurrodaparra.com; Rúa do Curro da Parra 7; mains €17-23, starters & medias raciones €8-14; 1.30-3.30pm & 8.30-11.30pm Tue-Sun;) With a neat little stone-walled dining room upstairs and a narrow food-and-wine bar below, always-busy Curro da Parra serves thoughtfully created, market-fresh fare, changing weekly. Everything is delectable; typical offerings might include line-caught hake with cockles and green beans or beef tenderloin with shiitake mushrooms. The 2010 cheesecake has been a favourite ever since it opened.

Information

Turismo de Santiago (981 55 51 29; www.santiagoturismo.com; Rúa do Vilar 63; 9am-9pm May-Oct, 9am-7pm Mon-Fri, 9am-2pm & 4-7pm Sat & Sun Nov-Apr) is very efficient. Its website is a multilingual mine of information.

Getting There & Around

AIR

The busy **Santiago airport** (903 211 000; www.aena.es) has direct flights to/from some 20 European and Spanish cities, many of them operated by budget airlines easyJet, Ryanair and Vueling.

BUS

The **bus station** (981 54 24 16; Praza de Camilo Díaz Baliño;) is 1.5km northeast of the city centre. There are services to León (€31, six hours, one daily), Madrid (from €21, eight to 10 hours, four daily), Porto (Portugal; from €27, 4¼ hours, three daily), Santander (from €44, nine to 10 hours, two daily) and many places around Galicia.

TRAIN

From the **train station** (www.renfe.com; Rúa do Hórreo), plentiful trains run up and down the Galician coast as far as A Coruña and Vigo. There are regular services to Madrid (from €22, 5¼ hours).

Around Galicia

Galicia's dramatic coastline is one of Spain's best-kept secrets, with wild and precipitous cliffs, long inlets running far inland, splendid beaches and isolated fishing villages. The lively port city of **A Coruña** has a lovely city beach and fabulous seafood (a recurring Galician theme). It's also a gateway to the stirring landscapes of the **Costa da Morte** and **Rías Altas**; the latter's highlight among many is probably **Cabo Ortegal**. Inland Galicia is also worth exploring, especially the old town of **Lugo**, surrounded by what many consider the world's best preserved Roman walls.

VALENCIA

POP 787,808

Spain's third-largest city is a magnificent place, content for Madrid and Barcelona to grab the headlines while it gets on with being a wonderfully liveable city with thriving cultural, eating and nightlife scenes. The star attraction is the strikingly futuristic buildings of the Ciudad de las Artes y las Ciencias, designed by local boy Santiago Calatrava. Valencia also has an array of fabulous Modernista architecture, great museums and a large, characterful old quarter. Surrounded by fertile fruit-and-veg farmland, the city is famous as the home of rice dishes like paella, but its buzzy dining scene offers plenty more besides.

Sights & Activities

★Ciudad de las Artes y las Ciencias ARCHITECTURE

(City of Arts & Sciences; 961 97 46 86; www.cac.es; Avenida del Professor López Piñero;) This aesthetically stunning complex occupies a massive 350,000-sq-metre swath of the old Turia riverbed. It's occupied by a series of spectacular buildings that are mostly the work of world-famous, locally born architect Santiago Calatrava. The principal buildings are a majestic **opera house** (tours 672 062523; www.lesarts.com; guided visit adult/child €10.60/8.10; guided visits 10.45am, noon & 1.30pm daily, plus 3.45pm & 5pm Mon-Sat), a **science museum** (961 97 47 86; adult/child €8/6.20, with Hemisfèric €12.60/9.60; 10am-6pm or 7pm mid-Sep–Jun, 10am-9pm Jul–mid-Sep;), a **3D cinema** (sessions adult/child €8.80/6.85, incl Museo de las Ciencias Príncipe Felipe €12.60/9.60; from 10am) and an **aquarium** (960 47 06 47; www.oceanografic.org; Camino de las Moreras; adult/child €29.10/21.85, audio guide €3.70, combined ticket with Hemisfèric & Museo de las Ciencias Príncipe Felipe €37.40/28.40; 10am-6pm Sun-Fri, to 8pm Sat mid-Sep–mid-Jun, 10am-8pm mid-Jun–mid-Jul & early Sep, 10am-midnight mid-Jul–Aug;). Calatrava is a controversial figure for many Valencians, who complain about the expense and various design flaws. Nevertheless, if your taxes weren't involved, it's awe-inspiring and pleasingly family-oriented.

Catedral de Valencia CATHEDRAL

(963 91 81 27; www.catedraldevalencia.es; Plaza de la Virgen; adult/child €7/5.50; 10am-6.30pm Mon-Sat, 2-6.30pm Sun Apr-Oct, 10am-5.30pm Mon-Sat Nov-May;) Valencia's cathedral was built over a mosque after the 1238 reconquest. Its low, wide, brick-vaulted triple nave is mostly Gothic, with neoclassical side chapels. Highlights are its **museum** (incl in cathedral entry; 10am-6.30pm Mon-Sat, 2-6.30pm Sun Jun-Sep, 10am-5.30pm Mon-Sat, 10am-2pm Sun Oct-May, closed Sun Nov-Feb;), rich Italianate frescos above the altarpiece, a pair of Goyas in the Capilla de San Francisco de Borja, and in the flamboyant Gothic Capilla del Santo Cáliz, what's claimed to be the Holy Grail from which Christ sipped during the Last Supper. It's a Roman-era agate cup, later modified, so at least the date is right. Admission includes an audio guide.

La Lonja HISTORIC BUILDING

(962 08 41 53; www.valencia.es; Calle de la Lonja; adult/child €2/1, Sun free; 10am-7pm Mon-Sat, to 2pm Sun) This splendid building, a Unesco World Heritage Site, was originally Valencia's silk and commodity exchange, built in the late 15th century when the city was booming. It's one of Spain's finest examples of a civil Gothic building. Two main structures flank a citrus-studded courtyard: the magnificent Sala de Contratación, a cathedral of commerce with soaring twisted pillars, and the Consulado del Mar, where a maritime tribunal sat. The top floor boasts a stunning coffered ceiling brought here from another building.

Mercado Central MARKET
(☎963 82 91 00; www.mercadocentralvalencia.es; Plaza del Mercado; ⏰7.30am-3pm Mon-Sat) Valencia's vast Modernista covered market, constructed in 1928, is a swirl of smells, movement and colour. Spectacular seafood counters display cephalopods galore and numerous fish species, meat stalls groan under the weight of sausages and giant steaks, while the fruit and vegetables, many produced locally in Valencia's *huerta* (area of market gardens), are of special quality. A tapas bar lets you sip a wine and enjoy the atmosphere.

Museo de Bellas Artes GALLERY
(San Pío V; ☎963 87 03 00; www.museobellasartesvalencia.gva.es; Calle de San Pío V 9; ⏰10am-8pm Tue-Sun) FREE Bright and spacious, this gallery ranks among Spain's best. Highlights include a collection of magnificent late-medieval altarpieces, and works by several Spanish masters, including some great Goya portraits, a haunting Velázquez self-portrait, an El Greco *John the Baptist* and works by Murillos, Riberas and the Ribaltas, father and son.

Downstairs, an excellent series of rooms focuses on the great, versatile Valencian painter Joaquín Sorolla (1863–1923), who, at his best, seemed to capture the spirit of an age through sensitive portraiture.

Beaches

Valencia's town beaches are 3km from the centre. Playa de las Arenas runs north into Playa de la Malvarrosa and Playa de la Patacona, forming a wide strip of sand some 4km long. It's bordered by the Paseo Marítimo promenade and a string of restaurants and cafes. The marina and port area, refurbished for the 2007 Americas Cup, is south of here and backed by the intriguing and increasingly trendy fishing district of El Cabanyal, which makes for excellent exploration.

Sleeping

Russafa Youth Hostel HOSTEL €
(☎963 31 31 40; www.russafayouthhostel.com; Carrer del Padre Perera 5; dm €18-25, s with shared bathroom €30-50, d with shared bathroom €50-65; @ 📶) You'll feel instantly at home in this super-welcoming, cute hostel set over various floors of a venerable building in the heart of vibrant Russafa. It's all beds, rather than bunks, and with a maximum of three to a room, there's no crowding. Sweet rooms and spotless bathrooms make for a mighty easy stay.

WORTH A TRIP

LAS FALLAS

In mid-March, Valencia hosts one of Europe's wildest street parties: **Las Fallas de San José** (www.fallas.com). From 15 to 19 March the city is engulfed by an anarchic swirl of fireworks, music, festive bonfires and all-night partying. On the final night, hundreds of giant effigies *(fallas)*, many of them representing political and social personages, are torched. A popular vote spares the most-cherished *ninot* (figure), which gets housed for posterity in the **Museo Fallero** (☎962 08 46 25; www.valencia.es; Plaza Monteolivete 4; adult/child €2/free, Sun free; ⏰10am-7pm Mon-Sat, to 2pm Sun).

Hotel Sorolla Centro HOTEL €€
(☎963 52 33 92; www.hotelsorollacentro.com; Calle Convento Santa Clara 5; s/d from €55/70; ❄ 📶) Neat and contemporary but without any flashy design gimmicks, this hotel offers very solid value for comfortable, well-thought-out modern rooms with powerful showers and plenty of facilities. Staff are extremely helpful and the location, on a pedestrian street close to the main square, is fab.

★ **Caro Hotel** HOTEL €€€
(☎963 05 90 00; www.carohotel.com; Calle Almirante 14; r €165-325; P ❄ 📶) Housed in a sumptuous 19th-century mansion, this hotel sits atop two millennia of Valencian history, with restoration revealing a hefty hunk of the Arab wall, Roman column bases and Gothic arches. Each room is furnished in soothing dark shades, with a great king-size bed and varnished concrete floors. Bathrooms are tops. For special occasions, reserve the 1st-floor grand suite, once the ballroom.

Eating

The number of restaurants has to be seen to be believed! In the centre there are numerous traditional options, as well as trendy tapas choices. The main eating zones are the Barrio del Carmen, L'Eixample and, above all, the vibrant tapas-packed streets of Russafa.

L'Ostrería del Carme SEAFOOD €

(☎629 145026; www.laostreriadelcarmen.com; Plaza de Mossén Sorell; oysters €2-4; ⏲11am-3pm Mon-Sat, plus 5-8.30pm Thu & Fri) This little stall inside the **Mossén Sorell market** (⏲7.30am-3pm Mon-Sat, plus 5-8.30pm Thu & Fri except in Aug) is a cordial spot and a fabulous snack stop. It has oysters of excellent quality from Valencia and elsewhere; sit down with a glass of white wine and let them shuck you a few.

Navarro VALENCIAN €€

(☎963 52 96 23; www.restaurantenavarro.com; Calle del Arzobispo Mayoral 5; rices €14-17, set menu €22; ⏲1-4pm Mon-Sat;) A byword in the city for decades for its quality rice dishes, Navarro is run by the grandkids of the original founders and it offers plenty of choice, outdoor seating and a set menu, including one of the rices as a main.

★ **El Poblet** GASTRONOMY €€€

(☎961 11 11 06; www.elpobletrestaurante.com; Calle de Correos 8; degustation menus €85-125, mains €25-35; ⏲1.30-3.15pm & 8.30-10.15pm Mon & Wed-Sat;) This upstairs restaurant, overseen by famed Quique Dacosta and with Luis Valls as chef, offers elegance and fine gastronomic dining at prices that are very competitive for this quality. Modern French and Spanish influences combine to create sumptuous degustation menus. Some of the imaginative presentation has to be seen to be believed, and staff are genuinely welcoming and helpful.

Drinking & Nightlife

Russafa has the best bar scene, with a huge range of everything from family-friendly cultural cafes to quirky bars, as well as a couple of big clubs. The Barrio del Carmen is also famous nightlife territory. In summer the port area and Malvarrosa beach leap to life.

★ **La Fábrica de Hielo** CAFE

(☎963 68 26 19; www.lafabricadehielo.net; Calle de Pavia 37; ⏲5pm-midnight Tue & Wed, to 1am Thu, to 1.30am Fri, 11am-1.30am Sat, to midnight Sun) It's difficult to know how to classify this former ice factory, converted with great charm into a sizeable multi-purpose space that does cultural events, drinks and tapas just back from the beach. Just drop by and see what's going down – Sundays are loads of fun, with paella and dancing, but there's always a great atmosphere.

★ **Radio City** CLUB

(☎963 91 41 51; www.radiocityvalencia.es; Calle de Santa Teresa 19; ⏲10.30pm-4am Fri-Mon, from 10pm Tue, from 8pm Wed & Thu) Almost as much mini-cultural-centre as club, Radio City, which gets packed from around 1am, pulls in the punters with activities such as language exchange, and DJs or live music every night. There's everything from flamenco (Tuesday) to reggae and funk, and the crowd is eclectic and engaged.

L'Umbracle Terraza BAR, CLUB

(☎671 668000; www.umbracleterraza.com; Avenida del Professor López Piñero 5; admission €12; ⏲midnight-7.30am Thu-Sat) At the southern end of the Umbracle walkway within the Ciudad de las Artes y las Ciencias, this is a touristy but atmospheric spot to spend a hot summer night. After the queue and laughable door attitude, catch the evening breeze under the stars on the terrace. The downstairs club **Mya** is a sweatier experience. Admission covers both venues.

Information

Tourist Info Valencia – Paz (☎963 98 64 22; www.visitvalencia.com; Calle de la Paz 48; ⏲9am-6.50pm Mon-Sat, 10am-1.50pm Sun;) has information about the city and region.

Getting There & Away

AIR

Valencia's **airport** (☎902 404 704; www.aena.es) is 10km west of the city centre along the A3, towards Madrid. Flights, including many budget routes, serve major European destinations, including London, Paris and Berlin.

BOAT

Trasmediterránea (☎902 454645; www.trasmediterranea.es) operates car and passenger ferries to Ibiza, Mallorca and Menorca. **Baleària** (☎902 160180, from overseas 912 66 02 14; www.balearia.com; Moll de la Pansa) goes to Mallorca and Ibiza.

BUS

Valencia's **bus station** (☎963 46 62 66; Avenida Menéndez Pidal) is located beside the riverbed. Bus 8 connects it to Plaza del Ayuntamiento. **Avanza** (www.avanzabus.com) operates regular bus services to/from Madrid (€28 to €36, 4½ to five hours). **ALSA** (www.alsa.es) has services to/from Barcelona (€29 to €38, four to six hours, up to 10 daily) and Alicante (€21 to €25, 2½ to 5½ hours, more than 10 daily), most via Benidorm.

TRAIN

All fast trains now use the **Valencia Joaquín Sorolla station** (www.adif.es; Calle San Vicente Mártir 171), 800m south of the old town. It's meant to be temporary, but looks like sticking around for a long time. It's linked with nearby **Estación del Norte** (Calle de Xàtiva; 5.30am-midnight;), 500m away, by free shuttle bus. Estación del Norte has slow trains to Gandia, Alicante and Madrid, as well as local *cercanía* lines.

Major destinations include Alicante (€17 to €20, 1½ to 2¼ hours, 12 daily), Barcelona (€22 to €28, 3¼ to 5½ hours, 14 daily) and Madrid (€21 to €51, 1¾ to 7¾ hours, 18 daily).

Getting Around

Valencia has an integrated bus, tram and metro network. Rides are €1.50; one-/two-/three-day travel cards cost €4/6.70/9.70. Metro lines 3 and 5 connect the airport, central Valencia and the port. The tram is a pleasant way to get to the beach and port. Pick it up at Pont de Fusta or where it intersects with the metro at Benimaclet.

BALEARIC ISLANDS

The Balearic Islands (Illes Balears in Catalan) adorn the glittering Mediterranean waters off Spain's eastern coastline. Beach tourism destinations par excellence, each of the islands has a quite distinct identity and they have managed to retain much of their individual character and beauty. All boast beaches second to none in the Med, but each offers reasons for exploring inland too.

Check out websites like www.illesbalears.es and www.platgesdebalears.com.

Getting There & Away

AIR

In summer, charter and regular flights converge on Palma de Mallorca and Ibiza from all over Europe.

BOAT

The major ferry companies are Trasmediterránea (p574) and **Baleària** (902 16 01 80; www.balearia.com). Compare prices and look for deals at Direct Ferries (www.directferries.com).

The main ferry routes to the mainland, most operating only from Easter to late October, include the following:

Ibiza (Ibiza City) To/from Barcelona and Valencia (Trasmediterránea, Baleària) and Denia (Baleària)

Ibiza (Sant Antoni) To/from Valencia (Baleària)

Mallorca (Palma de Mallorca) To/from Barcelona and Valencia (Trasmediterránea, Baleària) and Denia (Baleària)

Mallorca (Port d'Alcúdia) To/from Barcelona (Baleària)

The main inter-island ferry routes include the following:

Ibiza (Ibiza City) To/from Palma de Mallorca (Trasmediterránea, Baleària)

Mallorca (Palma de Mallorca) To/from Ibiza City (Baleària) and Maó (Trasmediterránea)

Mallorca (Port d'Alcúdia) To/from Ciutadella (Trasmediterránea, Baleària)

Menorca (Ciutadella) To/from Port d'Alcúdia (Trasmediterránea, Baleària)

Menorca (Maó) To/from Palma de Mallorca (Trasmediterránea)

Mallorca

The ever-popular star of the Mediterranean, Mallorca has a sunny personality thanks to its ravishing beaches, azure views, remote mountains and soulful hill towns.

Palma de Mallorca

Palma de Mallorca is a graceful and historic Mediterranean city with some world-class attractions and equally impressive culinary, art and nightlife scenes.

POP 406,692

Sights

★Catedral de Mallorca CATHEDRAL

(La Seu; www.catedraldemallorca.org; Carrer del Palau Reial 9; adult/child €7/free; 10am-6.15pm Mon-Fri Jun-Sep, to 5.15pm Apr, May & Oct, to 3.15pm Nov-Mar, 10am-2.15pm Sat year-round) Palma's vast cathedral ('La Seu' in Catalan) is the city's major architectural landmark. Aside from its sheer scale and undoubted beauty, its stunning interior features, designed by Antoni Gaudí and renowned contemporary artist Miquel Barceló, make this unlike any cathedral elsewhere in the world. The awesome structure is predominantly Gothic, apart from the main facade, which is startling, quite beautiful and completely mongrel.

Palau de l'Almudaina PALACE

(https://entradas.patrimonionacional.es; Carrer del Palau Reial; adult/child €7/4, audio guide €3, guided tour €4; 10am-8pm Tue-Sun Apr-Sep, to 6pm Tue-Sun Oct-Mar) Originally an Islamic fort, this mighty construction opposite the cathedral was converted into a residence for the Mallorcan monarchs at the end of the 13th century. The King of Spain resides here still, at least symbolically. The royal family is rarely in residence, except for the occasional ceremony, as they prefer to spend summer in the Palau Marivent (in Cala Major). At other times you can wander through a series of cavernous stone-walled rooms that have been lavishly decorated.

★Palau March MUSEUM
(☎971 71 11 22; www.fundacionbmarch.es; Carrer del Palau Reial 18; adult/child €4.50/free; ⏲10am-6.30pm Mon-Fri Apr-Oct, to 5pm Nov-Mar, to 2pm Sat year-round) This house, palatial by any definition, was one of several residences of the phenomenally wealthy March family. Sculptures by 20th-century greats including Henry Moore, Auguste Rodin, Barbara Hepworth and Eduardo Chillida grace the outdoor terrace. Within lie many more artistic treasures from such luminaries of Spanish art as Salvador Dalí and Barcelona's Josep Maria Sert and Xavier Corberó. Not to be missed are the meticulously crafted figures of an 18th-century Neapolitan *belén* (nativity scene).

★Es Baluard GALLERY
(Museu d'Art Modern i Contemporani; ☎971 90 82 00; www.esbaluard.org; Plaça de Porta de Santa Catalina 10; adult/child €6/free; ⏲10am-8pm Tue-Sat, to 3pm Sun; 📶) Built with flair and innovation into the shell of the Renaissance-era seaward walls, this contemporary art gallery is one of the finest on the island. Its temporary exhibitions are worth viewing, but the permanent collection – works by Miró, Barceló and Picasso – gives the gallery its cachet. Entry on Friday is by donation, and anyone turning up on a bike, on any day, is charged just €2.

Sleeping & Eating

Misión de San Miguel BOUTIQUE HOTEL €€
(☎971 21 48 48; www.urhotels.com; Carrer de Can Maçanet 1A; d/ste from €110/175; P ❄ @ 📶) This boutique hotel, with its 32 stylish designer rooms gathered discreetly around a quiet inner courtyard, is a real bargain. Good-quality mattresses and rain shower heads are typical of a place where the little things are always done well, although some rooms open onto public areas and can be a tad noisy. Service is friendly and professional.

★Hotel Tres BOUTIQUE HOTEL €€€
(☎971 71 73 33; www.hoteltres.com; Carrer dels Apuntadors 3; s/d/ste €240/280/345; ❄ @ 📶 ≋) Hotel Tres swings joyously between 16th-century town palace and fresh-faced Scandinavian design. Centred on a courtyard with a single palm, the rooms are cool and minimalist, with cowhide benches, anatomy-inspired prints, and nice details like rollaway desks and Durance aromatherapy cosmetics. Head up to the roof terrace at sunset for a steam and dip as the cathedral begins to twinkle.

★Can Cera Gastro-Bar MEDITERRANEAN €€
(☎971 71 50 12; www.cancerahotel.com; Carrer del Convent de Sant Francesc 8; tapas €6-24; ⏲12.30-10.30pm) This restaurant spills onto a lovely inner patio at the Can Cera hotel, housed in a *palau* that dates originally from the 13th century. Dine by lantern light on tapas-sized dishes such as *frito mallorquín* (seafood fried with potato and herbs), Cantabrian anchovies, and pork ribs with honey and mustard. The vertical garden attracts plenty of attention from passers-by.

★Marc Fosh MODERN EUROPEAN €€€
(☎971 72 01 14; www.marcfosh.com; Carrer de la Missió 7A; menús lunch €30-40, dinner €72-90; ⏲1-3pm & 7.30-10pm) The flagship of Michelin-starred Fosh's burgeoning flotilla of Palma restaurants, this stylish gastronomic destination introduces novel twists to time-honoured Mediterranean dishes and ingredients, all within the converted refectory of a 17th-century convent. The weekly lunch *menú* is a very reasonable way to enjoy dishes such as foie gras and duck terrine, or truffled pasta with burrata.

Information

Consell de Mallorca Tourist Office (☎971 17 39 90; www.infomallorca.net; Plaça de la Reina 2; ⏲8.30am-8pm Mon-Fri, to 3pm Sat; 📶)

Around Palma de Mallorca

Mallorca's northwestern coast is a world away from the high-rise tourism on the other side of the island. Dominated by the dramatic, razorback Serra de Tramuntana, it's a beautiful region of olive groves, pine forests and small villages with shuttered stone buildings. There are a couple of highlights for drivers: the hair-raising road down to the small port of **Sa Calobra**, and the amaz ing trip along the peninsula at the island's northern tip, **Cap Formentor**.

Sóller is a good place to base yourself for hiking and the nearby village of **Fornalutx** is one of the prettiest on Mallorca.

From Sóller, it's a 10km walk to the beautiful hilltop village of **Deià**, where Robert Graves, poet and author of *I Claudius*, lived for most of his life. From the village, you can scramble down to the small shingle beach of **Cala de Deià**. The pretty streets of **Valldemossa**, further southwest down the coast, are crowned by a fine monastery.

Further east, **Pollença** and **Artà** are attractive inland towns. Nice beaches include those at **Cala Sant Vicenç**, **Platja des Coll Baix** hidden on Cap des Pinar, **Cala Agulla** and others near Cala Ratjada, **Cala Mondragó** and **Cala Llombards**.

Buses and/or trains cover much of the island, but hiring a car (in any town or resort) is best for exploring the remoter beaches, hill towns and mountains.

Ibiza

Ibiza (Eivissa in Catalan) is an island of extremes. Its formidable party reputation is completely justified, with some of the world's greatest clubs attracting hedonists from the world over. The interior and northeast of the island, however, are another world. Peaceful country drives, hilly green territory, a sprinkling of mostly laid-back beaches and coves, and some wonderful inland accommodation and eateries are light years from the throbbing all-night dance parties that dominate the west.

Ibiza Town

Sights

Ibiza Town's port and nightlife area **Sa Penya** is crammed with funky and trashy clothing boutiques and arty-crafty market stalls. From here, you can wander up into Dalt Vila, the atmospheric old walled town.

★Dalt Vila OLD TOWN

Its formidable, floodlit, 16th-century bastions visible from across southern Ibiza, Dalt Vila is a fortified hilltop first settled by the Phoenicans and later occupied by a roster of subsequent civilisations. Tranquil and atmospheric, many of its cobbled lanes are accessible only on foot. It's mostly a residential area, but contains moody medieval mansions and several key cultural sights. Enter via the Portal de Ses Taules gateway and wind your way uphill: all lanes lead to the cathedral-topped summit.

★Ramparts WALLS

Completely encircling Dalt Vila, Ibiza's colossal protective walls reach more than 25m in height and include seven bastions. Evocatively floodlit at night, these fortifications were constructed in the Renaissance era to protect Ibizans against the threat of attack by north African raiders and the Turkish navy. In under an hour, you can walk the entire 2km perimeter of the 16th-century ramparts, which were designed to withstand heavy artillery. Along the way, enjoy great views over the port and south across the water to Formentera.

Sleeping & Eating

Many of Ibiza City's hotels and *hostales* are closed in winter and heavily booked between April and October. Make sure you book ahead.

★Urban Spaces DESIGN HOTEL €€€

(☎601 199302; info@urbanspacesibiza.com; Carrer de la Via Púnica 32; r €240-295; ⏲Apr-early Jan; ❄📶) Some of the world's most prolific street artists (N4T4, INKIE, JEROM) have pooled their creativity in this design hotel with an alternative edge. The roomy, mural splashed suites sport clever backlighting, proper workstations and balconies with terrific views. Extras such as summer rooftop yoga and clubber-friendly breakfasts until 1pm are sure-fire people pleasers.

★S'Escalinata MEDITERRANEAN, CAFE €

(☎971 30 61 93; www.sescalinata.es; Carrer des Portal Nou 10; dishes €7-13; ⏲10am-3am Apr-Oct; 📶) With its low-slung tables and colourful cushions cascading down a steep stone staircase, this boho-chic cafe-bar-restaurant enjoys a magical location inside Dalt Vila. On the tempting menu are healthy breakfasts, tapas, *bocadillos* and delicious light dinners of hummus, tortilla or goat's-cheese salads. It's open late into the night, mixing up freshly squeezed juices, G&Ts and fruity cocktails.

Ca n'Alfredo IBIZAN €€€

(☎971 31 12 74; www.canalfredo.com; Passeig de Vara de Rey 16; mains €20-30; ⏲1-5pm & 8pm-1am Tue-Sat, 1-5pm Sun) Locals have been flocking to family-run Alfredo's on leafy Vara de Rey since 1934. It's a great place for the

CLUBBING IN IBIZA

Believe the hype. Despite being, essentially, a tiny island in the western Mediterranean, Ibiza can happily lay claim to being the world's queen of clubs. The globe's top DJs spin their magic here in summer, and the clubbing industry is very much the engine of the Ibizan economy. Sant Rafel, Ibiza Town, Platja d'en Bossa and Sant Antoni are the mega-club hubs. Expect to pay €15 to €20 for a *combinado* (spirit and mixer) and €10 to €12 for beer or water.

Pacha (www.pachaibiza.com; Avinguda 8 d'Agost; admission from €15; ⊙midnight-7am May-Sep) Going strong since 1973, Pacha is Ibiza's original megaclub and the islanders' party venue of choice. It's built around the shell of a farmhouse, boasting a multilevel main dance floor, a Funky Room (for soul and disco beats), a huge VIP section and myriad other places to dance or lounge.

Amnesia (www.amnesia.es; Carretera Eivissa–Sant Antoni Km 5; admission €40-70; ⊙midnight-6am late May-Oct) Amnesia is arguably Ibiza's most influential and legendary club, its decks welcoming such DJ royalty as Sven Väth, Paul Van Dyk, Paul Oakenfold, Tiësto and Avicii. There's a warehouse-like main room and a terrace topped by a graceful atrium. Big nights include techno-fests Cocoon and Music On, trance-mad Cream and foam-filled Espuma, which always draws a big local crowd.

Ushuaïa (☎971 92 81 93; www.ushuaiabeachhotel.com; Platja d'en Bossa 10; admission €45-75; ⊙3pm or 5pm-midnight May-Oct; 📶) Queen of daytime clubbing, ice-cool Ushuaïa is an open-air megaclub, packed with designer-clad hedonistas and waterside fun. The party starts early, with superstar DJs such as David Guetta, Martin Garrix, Luciano and Robin Schulz, and poolside lounging on Bali-style beds. Check out the Sky Lounge for sparkling sea views, or stay the night in the minimalist-chic hotel (r €390-840; ⊙May-Oct; P❄📶🏊).

freshest of seafood and other classic Ibizan dishes that are so good it's essential to book. Try John Dory fillets in almond sauce, or a traditional dish from the dedicated Ibizan cuisine menu, all accompanied by an impressive selection of Balearic wines.

Drinking & Nightlife

Sa Penya is the nightlife centre. Dozens of bars keep the port area jumping. Alternatively, various bars at Platja d'en Bossa combine sounds, sand, sea and sangria. Much cheaper than a taxi, the **Discobus** (www.discobus.es; per person €3-4; ⊙midnight-6am Jun-Sep) does an all-night whirl of the major clubs, bars and hotels in Ibiza City, Platja d'en Bossa, Sant Rafel, Es Canar, Santa Eulària and Sant Antoni.

Bar 1805 COCKTAIL BAR

(☎651 625972; www.bar1805ibiza.com; Carrer Baluard de Santa Llúcia 7; ⊙8pm-4am mid-Apr–Oct; 📶) Tucked away on a Sa Penya backstreet, this boho bar mixes some of the best cocktails in town, with lots of absinthe action on its beautifully illustrated menu. Try the signature Green Beast (served in a punch bowl) or a Gin-Basil Smash, which arrives in a teacup. Moules-frites, burgers, steaks, salads and other bites are served until 2am.

Bora Bora Beach Club BAR

(www.boraboraibiza.net; Carrer d'es Fumarell 1; ⊙4pm-late May-Sep) A long beachside bar where sun and fun worshippers work off hangovers and prepare new ones. Entry is free and the ambience moves from chilled to party fever. It can get pretty messy in here with hundreds of swimwear-clad partygoers and jets screaming overhead (the airport is *very* close). There are also sun loungers to rent (€15).

ANDALUCÍA

So many of the most powerful images of Spain emanate from Andalucía that it can be difficult not to feel a sense of déjà vu. It's almost as if you've already been there in your dreams: the flashing fire of a flamenco dancer, the scent of orange blossom, a festive summer fair and magical nights in the shadow of the Alhambra. In the bright light of day, the picture is no less magical.

Seville

POP 689,434

It takes a stony heart not to be captivated by stylish but ancient, proud yet fun-loving Seville – home to two of Spain's most colourful festivals, fascinating and distinctive *barrios* (neighbourhoods) such as the flower-decked Santa Cruz, great historic monuments, and a population that lives life to the fullest. Being out among the celebratory, happy crowds in the tapas bars and streets on a warm spring night in Seville is an unforgettable experience. But try to avoid July and August, when it's so hot that most locals flee to the coast.

Sights

★Real Alcázar PALACE

(☎954 50 23 24; www.alcazarsevilla.org; Plaza del Triunfo; adult/child €7/free; ⌚9.30am-7pm Apr-Sep, to 5pm Oct-Mar) A magnificent marriage of Christian and Mudéjar architecture, Seville's Unesco-listed palace complex is a breathtaking spectacle. The site, which was originally developed as a fort in 913, has been revamped many times over the 11 centuries of its existence, most spectacularly in the 14th century when King Pedro added the sumptuous Palacio de Don Pedro, still today the Alcázar's crown jewel. More recently, the Alcázar featured as a location for the *Game of Thrones* TV series.

★Catedral de Sevilla & Giralda CATHEDRAL

(☎902 09 96 92; www.catedraldesevilla.es; Plaza del Triunfo; adult/child €9/free, incl rooftop guided tour €15; ⌚11am-3.30pm Mon, to 5pm Tue-Sat, 2.30-6pm Sun) Seville's immense cathedral is awe-inspiring in its scale and majesty. The world's largest Gothic cathedral, it was built between 1434 and 1517 over the remains of what had previously been the city's main mosque. Highlights include the Giralda, the mighty bell tower, which incorporates the mosque's original minaret, the monumental tomb of Christopher Columbus, and the Capilla Mayor with an astonishing gold altarpiece. Note that children must be aged 11 years and over to access the rooftop tours. Audio guides cost €3.

Museo de Bellas Artes MUSEUM

(Fine Arts Museum; ☎955 54 29 42; www.museodebellasartesdesevilla.es; Plaza del Museo 9; €1.50; ⌚9am-9pm Tue-Sat, to 3pm Sun) Housed in the beautiful former Convento de la Merced, Seville's Fine Arts Museum provides an elegant showcase for a comprehensive collection of Spanish and Sevillan paintings and sculptures. Works date from the 15th to 20th centuries, but the onus is very much on brooding religious paintings from the city's 17th-century *Siglo de Oro* (Golden Age).

★Hospital de los Venerables Sacerdotes MUSEUM

(☎954 56 26 96; www.focus.abengoa.es; Plaza de los Venerables 8; adult/child €8/4, 1st Thu of month free; ⌚10am-2pm Thu-Sun) This gem of a museum, housed in a former hospice for ageing priests, is one of Seville's most rewarding. The artistic highlight is the Focus-Abengoa Foundation's collection of 17th-century paintings in the Centro Velázquez. It's not a big collection, but each work is a masterpiece of its genre – highlights include Diego Velázquez' *Santa Rufina,* his *Inmaculada Concepción,* and a sharply vivid portrait of *Santa Catalina* by Bartolomé Murillo.

Plaza de España SQUARE

(Avenida de Portugal, Parque de María Luisa) This bombastic plaza in the Parque de María Luisa was the most grandiose of the building projects completed for the 1929 Exposición Iberoamericana. A huge brick-and-tile confection, it's all very over the top, but it's undeniably impressive with its fountains, mini-canals and Venetian-style bridges. A series of gaudy tile pictures depict maps and historical scenes from each Spanish province.

Festivals & Events

Semana Santa RELIGIOUS

(www.semana-santa.org; ⌚Mar/Apr) Seville's Holy Week celebrations are legendary. Every day from Palm Sunday to Easter Sunday, large, life-size *pasos* (sculptural representations of events from Christ's Passion) are solemnly carried from the city's churches to the cathedral, accompanied by processions of marching *nazarenos* (penitents).

Feria de Abril FERIA

(www.turismosevilla.org; El Real de la Feria; ⌚Apr) The largest and most colourful of all Andalucía's *ferias* (fairs), Seville's weeklong spring fair is held in the second half of the month (sometimes edging into May) on El Real de la Feria, in the Los Remedios area west of the Río Guadalquivir. For six nights, *sevillanos* dress up in elaborate finery, parade around in horse-drawn carriages, eat, drink and dance till dawn.

Seville

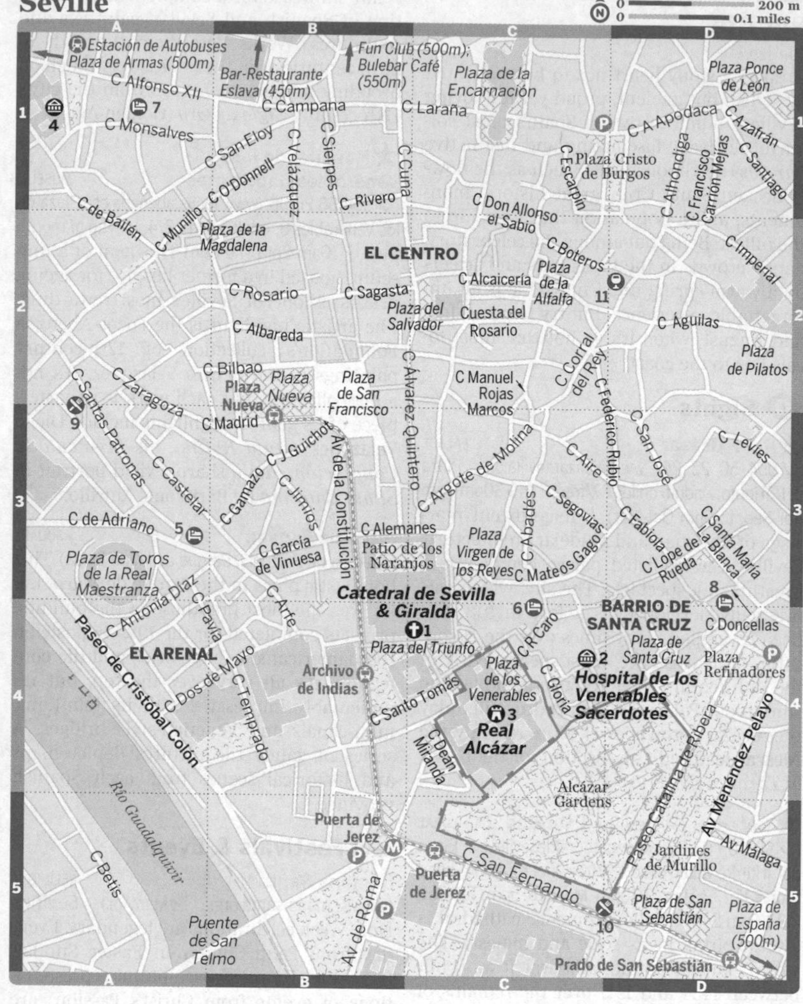

Seville

Top Sights
1 Catedral de Sevilla & Giralda C4
2 Hospital de los Venerables Sacerdotes C4
3 Real Alcázar C4

Sights
4 Museo de Bellas Artes A1

Sleeping
5 Hotel Adriano A3
6 Hotel Casa 1800 .... C4
7 Oasis Backpackers' Hostel A1
8 Un Patio en Santa Cruz D3

Eating
9 La Brunilda A3
10 Restaurante Oriza D5

Drinking & Nightlife
11 El Garlochi D2

Sleeping

Oasis Backpackers' Hostel HOSTEL €
(☎955 26 26 96; www.oasissevilla.com; Calle Almirante Ulloa 1; dm €15-32, d €70-160;) A veritable oasis in the busy city-centre district, this welcoming hostel is set in a palatial 19th-century mansion. There are various sleeping options ranging from mixed 14-person dorms to doubles with en suite bathrooms, and excellent facilities, including a cafe-bar, kitchen and rooftop deck with a small pool. Breakfast, not included in most rates, is available for €3.50.

Hotel Adriano HOTEL €€
(☎954 29 38 00; www.adrianohotel.com; Calle de Adriano 12; s €65-70, d €75-140; P) In the Arenal neighbourhood near the bullring, the three-star Adriano scores across the board with friendly staff, traditional, individually styled rooms and a lovely coffee shop, Pompeia, on the ground floor. Garage parking is available for €20 per day.

Un Patio en Santa Cruz HOTEL €€€
(☎807 31 70 70; www.patiosantacruz.com; Calle Doncellas 15; s €65-140, d €75-200;) Feeling more like a gallery than a hotel, this place has stark white walls hung with bright works of art and lofty pot plants. The summery rooms, complete with parquet and dashes of purple, are good looking and comfortable, staff are friendly, and there's a cool rooftop terrace with Moroccan-mosaic tables.

★**Hotel Casa 1800** LUXURY HOTEL €€€
(☎954 56 18 00; www.hotelcasa1800sevilla.com; Calle Rodrigo Caro 6; d €125-525;) A short hop from the cathedral in the heart of Santa Cruz, this stately *casa* (house) is positively regal. Setting the tone is the elegant, old-school decor – wooden ceilings, chandeliers, parquet floors and plenty of gilt – but everything about the place charms, from the helpful staff to the rooftop terrace and complimentary afternoon tea.

Eating

★**La Brunilda** TAPAS €
(☎954 22 04 81; www.labrunildatapas.com; Calle Galera 5; tapas €3.20-7.50; ⊙1-4pm & 8.30-11.30pm Tue-Sat, 1-4pm Sun) A regular fixture on lists of Seville's best tapas joints, this backstreet Arenal bar is at the forefront of the city's new wave of gourmet eateries. The look is modern casual with big blue doors, brick arches and plain wooden tables and the food is imaginative and good looking. The word is out, though, so arrive promptly or expect to queue.

★**Bar-Restaurante Eslava** FUSION, ANDALUCIAN €€
(☎954 90 65 68; www.espacioeslava.com; Calle Eslava 3; tapas €2.90-4.50, restaurant mains €16-24; ⊙bar 12.30-midnight Tue-Sat, 12.30-4pm Sun, restaurant 1-4pm & 8.30-midnight Tue-Sat, 1.30-4pm Sun) A hit with locals and savvy visitors, much-lauded Eslava shirks the traditional tilework and bullfighting posters of tapas-bar lore in favour of a simple blue space and a menu of creative contemporary dishes. Standouts include slow-cooked egg served on a mushroom cake, and memorable pork ribs in a honey and rosemary glaze. Expect crowds and a buzzing atmosphere.

Restaurante Oriza BASQUE €€€
(☎954 22 72 54; www.restauranteoriza.com; Calle San Fernando 41; tapas €2.80-4.80, mains €23-35; ⊙1-5pm & 8pm-1am Mon-Thu, 1pm-1am Fri & Sat, 1pm-5pm Sun) The fabulous flavours of the Basque Country come to town at this upmarket eatery near the Parque de María Luisa. For the full-on à la carte experience, book at the restaurant; for a more casual meal,

DON'T MISS

CATEDRAL HIGHLIGHTS

The enormous Gothic cathedral was completed by 1507 after a century's work.

Puerta del Perdón A legacy of the great mosque.

Sala del Pabellón Art by 17th-century Golden Age masters.

Tomb of Christopher Columbus Inside the south entrance.

Capilla Mayor The fabulous Gothic retable is reckoned to be the world's biggest altarpiece.

Sacristía de los Cálices Art treasures including Goya's *Santas Justa y Rufina*.

Giralda Climb up inside the minaret of the great mosque, now the cathedral's bell tower.

DON'T MISS

ALCÁZAR HIGHLIGHTS

Founded in AD 913 as a fort for Muslim Córdoba's local governors in Seville, the Alcázar (p593) has been revamped many times since. Muslim rulers built at least two palaces inside it and after the Christians took Seville in 1248 they made further major modifications.

Patio del León (Lion Patio) The garrison yard of an 11th-century Islamic palace within the Alcázar. Off here is the Sala de la Justicia (Hall of Justice), with beautiful Mudéjar plasterwork and an *artesonado* (ceiling of interlaced beams with decorative insertions).

Patio de la Montería The rooms surrounding this patio are filled with interesting artefacts from Seville's history.

Cuarto Real Alto The Cuarto Real Alto (Upper Royal Quarters; used by the Spanish royal family on visits to Seville) are open for tours several times a day. The 14th-century Salón de Audiencias is still the monarch's reception room.

Palacio de Don Pedro Built by the Castilian king Pedro I ('the Cruel') in the 1360s, this is the single most stunning building in Seville. At its heart is the wonderful Patio de las Doncellas (Patio of the Maidens), surrounded by beautiful arches, plasterwork and tiling. The Alcoba Real (Royal Quarters), on the patio's northern side, has stunningly beautiful ceilings. The little Patio de las Muñecas (Patio of the Dolls), the heart of the palace's private quarters, features delicate Granada-style decoration. The Salón de Embajadores (Hall of Ambassadors), at the western end of the Patio de las Doncellas, was the throne room. Its fabulous wooden dome of multiple star patterns, symbolising the universe, was added in 1427.

Salones de Carlos V Reached via a staircase at the southeastern corner of the Patio de las Doncellas, these are the much-remodelled rooms of Alfonso X's 13th-century Gothic palace.

Gardens From the Salones de Carlos V you can go out and wander in the Alcázar's large and sleepy gardens, some with pools and fountains.

head to the in-house Bar España, which serves tapas and a €12 weekday lunch menu comprising starter, main course, dessert, coffee and drink.

Drinking & Nightlife

Drinking and partying really get going around midnight on Friday and Saturday (daily when it's hot). Classic drinking areas include Plaza de la Alfalfa (cocktail and dive bars), the Barrio de Santa Cruz and the Alameda de Hércules. The latter is the hub for young *sevillanos* and the city's gay nightlife. In summer, dozens of open-air late-night bars *(terrazas de verano)* spring up along both banks of the river.

El Garlochi BAR

(Calle Boteros 26; ⌚9pm-3am Mon-Sat, to midnight Sun) There surely can't be many weirder places to drink than this dark temple of kitsch. Decked out in ultracamp religious decor, it's dedicated entirely to the iconography, smells and sounds of the Semana Santa (Holy Week). To get into the mood, try its signature cocktail, a Sangre de Cristo (Blood of Christ), made from grenadine, pink champagne and whisky.

Bulebar Café BAR

(☎955 29 42 12; www.facebook.com/bulebarcafe; Alameda de Hércules 83; ⌚12.30pm-2am) With its day-long opening hours and outdoor terrace overlooking the Alameda de Hércules, this friendly spot is good for a leisurely people-watching break. Come for a late breakfast, a chilled early evening pick-me-up or a beer or two into the early hours.

☆ Entertainment

Seville is arguably Spain's flamenco capital and there are many opportunities to experience live performances.

Fun Club LIVE MUSIC

(☎636 669023; www.funclubsevilla.com; Alameda de Hércules 86; €5-12; ⌚9.30pm-7am Thu-Sat) Positively ancient by nightlife standards, the iconic Fun Club has been entertaining the nocturnal Alameda de Hércules crowd since the late 1980s. It still packs them in, hosting club nights and regular gigs – indie, rock and hip-hop.

Getting There & Away

AIR

Seville's **airport** (Aeropuerto de Sevilla; 902 404704; www.aena.es; A4, Km 532) has a fair range of international and domestic flights.

BUS

Buses to Córdoba (€12, two hours, seven daily), Granada (€23 to €30, three hours, 10 daily), Málaga (€19 to €24, 2½ to four hours, 10 daily), Madrid (€23 to €33, 6½ hours, eight daily) and Lisbon (€45, seven to eight hours, five daily) go from the **Estación de Autobuses Plaza de Armas** (955 03 86 65; www.autobusesplazadearmas.es; Avenida del Cristo de la Expiración).

TRAIN

Seville's principal train station, **Estación Santa Justa** (Avenida Kansas City), is 1.5km northeast of the centre.

High-speed AVE trains go to/from Madrid (from €35, 2½ to 3¼ hours, hourly) and Córdoba (from €21, 45 minutes to 1¼ hours, 25 daily). Slower trains head to Cádiz (€16, 1¾ hours, 15 daily), Huelva (€12, 1½ hours, three daily), Granada (€30, four hours, four daily) and Málaga (€24 to €44, two to 2½ hours, 11 daily).

Córdoba

POP 293,485

A little over a millennium ago Córdoba was the capital of Islamic Spain and Western Europe's biggest, most cultured city, where Muslims, Jews and Christians coexisted peaceably. Its past glories place it among Andalucía's top draws today. The centrepiece is the mesmerising, multiarched Mezquita. Surrounding it is an intricate web of winding streets, geranium-sprouting flower boxes and cool intimate patios that are at their most beguiling in late spring.

Sights

★Mezquita MOSQUE, CATHEDRAL

(Mosque; 957 47 05 12; www.mezquita-catedraldecordoba.es; Calle Cardenal Herrero; adult/child €10/5; 10am-7pm Mon-Sat, 8.30-11.30am & 3-7pm Sun Mar-Oct, 8.30am-6pm Mon-Sat, 8.30-11.30am & 3-6pm Sun Nov-Feb, Mass 9.30am Mon-Sat, noon & 1.30pm Sun) It's impossible to overemphasise the beauty of Córdoba's great mosque, with its remarkably serene (despite tourist crowds) and spacious interior. One of the world's greatest works of Islamic architecture, the Mezquita hints, with all its lustrous decoration, at a refined age when Muslims, Jews and Christians lived side by side and enriched their city with a heady interaction of diverse, vibrant cultures.

★Palacio de Viana MUSEUM

(www.palaciodeviana.com; Plaza de Don Gome 2; whole house/patios €8/5; 10am-7pm Tue-Sat, to 3pm Sun Sep-Jun, 9am-3pm Tue-Sun Jul & Aug) A stunning Renaissance palace with 12 beautiful, plant-filled patios, the Viana Palace is a particular delight to visit in spring. Occupied by the aristocratic Marqueses de Viana until 1980, the large building is packed with art and antiques. You can just walk round the lovely patios and garden with a self-guiding leaflet, or take a guided tour of the rooms as well. The palace is an 800m walk northeast from Plaza de las Tendillas.

Alcázar de los Reyes Cristianos FORTRESS

(Fortress of the Christian Monarchs; 957 42 01 51; https://cultura.cordoba.es; Campo Santo de Los Mártires; adult/concession/child €4.50/2.25/free; 8.30am-2.30pm Tue-Sat, from 9.30am Sun mid-Jun–mid-Sep, 8.30am-8.45pm Tue-Fri, to 4.30pm Sat, to 3pm Sun mid-Sep–mid-Jun,) Built under Castilian rule in the 13th and 14th centuries on the remains of a Moorish predecessor, this fort-cum-palace was where the Catholic Monarchs, Fernando and Isabel, made their first acquaintance with Columbus in 1486. One hall displays some remarkable Roman mosaics, dug up from Plaza de la Corredera in the 1950s. The Alcázar's terraced gardens – full of fish ponds, fountains, orange trees and flowers – are a delight to stroll around.

★Centro Flamenco Fosforito MUSEUM

(Posada del Potro; 957 47 68 29; https://cultura.cordoba.es; Plaza del Potro; 8.30am-2.30pm Tue-Sat, from 9.30am Sun mid-Jun–mid Sep, 8.30am-7.30pm Tue-Fri, to 2.30pm Sat & Sun mid-Sep–mid-Jun) FREE Possibly the best flamenco museum in Andalucía, the Fosforito centre has exhibits, film and information panels in English and Spanish telling you the history of the guitar and all the flamenco greats. Touch-screen videos demonstrate the important techniques of flamenco song, guitar, dance and percussion – you can test your skill at beating out the *compás* (rhythm) of different *palos* (song forms). Regular free live flamenco performances are held here, too, often at noon on Sunday (see the website).

Sleeping

★Patio del Posadero BOUTIQUE HOTEL **€€**
(☎957 94 17 33; www.patiodelposadero.com; Calle Mucho Trigo 21; r incl breakfast €95-155; ❄📶🏊) A 15th-century building in a quiet lane 1km east of the Mezquita has been superbly converted into a welcoming boutique hideaway combining comfort and unique contemporary design with that old-Córdoba Moorish style. At its centre is a charming cobble-floored, brick-arched patio, with steps leading up to a lovely upper deck with plunge pool, where the first-class home-made breakfasts are served.

Balcón de Córdoba BOUTIQUE HOTEL **€€€**
(☎957 49 84 78; www.balcondecordoba.com; Calle Encarnación 8; incl breakfast s €185-275, d €200-350; ❄📶) Offering top-end boutique luxury a stone's throw from the Mezquita, the 10-room Balcón is a riveting place with a charming patio, slick rooms and ancient stone relics dotted around as if it were a wing of the nearby archaeological museum. Service doesn't miss a beat and the rooms have tasteful, soothing, contemporary decor with a little art but no clutter.

Eating

★Mercado Victoria FOOD HALL **€**
(www.mercadovictoria.com; Paseo de la Victoria; items €2-19; ⏲noon-1am Sun-Thu, noon-2am Fri & Sat mid-Jun–mid-Sep, 10am-midnight Sun-Thu, 10am-2am Fri & Sat mid-Sep–mid-Jun) The Mercado Victoria is, yes, a food court – but an unusually classy one, with almost everything, from Argentine empanadas and Mexican burritos to sushi and classic Spanish seafood and grilled meats, prepared fresh before your eyes. The setting is special too – a 19th-century wrought-iron-and-glass pavilion in the Victoria gardens just west of the old city.

La Boca FUSION **€€**
(☎957 47 61 40; www.facebook.com/restaurante.laboca; Calle de San Fernando 39; dishes €6-15; ⏲noon-midnight Wed-Mon; 📶) If oxtail tacos, red-tuna *tataki,* or a salad of duck-prosciutto and mango in walnut vinaigrette sound appetising, you'll like La Boca. This inventive eatery serves up global variations in half a dozen appealingly arty, rustic-style *taberna* rooms or in its marginally more formal restaurant section. It's very well done, though portions are not large. Reservations advisable at weekends.

DON'T MISS

MEZQUITA HIGHLIGHTS

Emir Abd ar-Rahman I founded the Mezquita (p597) in AD 785. Three later extensions nearly quintupled its original size and brought it to the form you see today – except for one major alteration: a 16th-century cathedral plonked right in the middle.

Torre del Alminar You can climb inside the 54m-tall bell tower (originally the Mezquita's minaret) for fine panoramas.

Patio de los Naranjos This lovely courtyard, with its orange and palm trees and fountains, was the site of ritual ablutions before prayer in the mosque.

Prayer hall Divided into 19 'naves' by lines of two-tier arches striped in red brick and white stone. Their simplicity and number give a sense of endlessness to the Mezquita.

Mihrab and Maksura The arches of the *maksura* (the area where the caliphs and their retinues would have prayed) are the mosque's most intricate and sophisticated, forming a forest of interwoven horseshoe shapes. The portal of the mihrab itself is a sublime crescent arch in glittering gold mosaic.

The cathedral A 16th-century construction in the Mezquita's heart.

JEWISH CÓRDOBA

Jews were among the most dynamic and prominent citizens of Islamic Córdoba. The medieval *judería* (Jewish quarter), extending northwest from the Mezquita almost to Avenida del Gran Capitán, is today a maze of narrow streets and whitewashed buildings with flowery window boxes. The **Sinagoga** (957 74 90 15; www.turismodecordoba.org; Calle de los Judíos 20; €0.30; 9am-9pm Tue-Sat, to 3pm Sun), built in 1315, is one of the few surviving testaments to the Jewish presence in Andalucía. Across the street is the **Casa de Sefarad** (957 42 14 04; www.casadesefarad.es; cnr Calles de los Judíos & Averroes; €4; 11am-6pm Mon-Sat, to 2pm Sun), an interesting museum on the Sephardic (Iberian Peninsula Jewish) tradition.

★Bodegas Campos ANDALUCIAN **€€**
(957 49 75 00; www.bodegascampos.com; Calle de Lineros 32; mains €12-24; 1.30-4pm & 8.30-11pm) This atmospheric warren of rooms and patios is a Córdoba classic, and is popular with *cordobeses* and visitors alike. The restaurant and more informal *taberna* (tavern) serve up delicious dishes putting a slight creative twist on traditional Andalucian fare – the likes of cod-and-cuttlefish ravioli or pork tenderloin in grape sauce. Campos also produces its own house Montilla.

Information

Centro de Visitantes (Visitors Centre; 902 201774; www.turismodecordoba.org; Plaza del Triunfo; 9am-7pm Mon-Fri, 9.30am-2.30pm Sat & Sun) The main tourist office has an exhibit on Córdoba's history, and some Roman and Visigothic remains downstairs.

Getting There & Away

BUS

The **bus station** (957 40 40 40; www.estacionautobusescordoba.es; Avenida Vía Augusta) is 2km northwest of the Mezquita, behind the train station. Destinations include Seville (€12, two hours, seven daily), Granada (€10, 2¾ hours, seven daily) and Málaga (€8 to €19, 2½ to 3½ hours, four daily).

TRAIN

Córdoba's **train station** (91 232 03 20; www.renfe.com; Plaza de las Tres Culturas) is on the high-speed AVE line between Madrid and Seville/Málaga. Rail destinations include Seville (€14 to €30, 45 minutes to 1¼ hours, more than 30 daily), Madrid (€33 to €66, 1¾ hours, 29 daily) and Málaga (€24 to €42, one hour, 18 daily). Trips to Granada (€24 to €36, two to 2¾ hours, four or more daily) include changing to a train or bus at Antequera.

Granada

ELEV 680M / POP 232,770

Granada's eight centuries as a Muslim city are symbolised in its keynote emblem, the remarkable Alhambra, one of the most graceful achievements of Islamic architecture. Granada is chock-full of history, the arts and life, with tapas bars filled to bursting and flamenco dives resounding to the heart-wrenching tones of the south.

Today, Islam is more present than it has been for many centuries, in the shops, tearooms and mosque of a growing North African community around the maze of the Albayzín.

Sights

★Alhambra ISLAMIC PALACE
(958 02 79 71, tickets 858 95 36 16; www.alhambra-patronato.es; adult/12-15yr/under 12yr €14/8/free, Generalife & Alcazaba adult/under 12yr €7/free; 8.30am-8pm Apr–mid-Oct, to 6pm mid-Oct–Mar, night visits 10-11.30pm Tue & Sat Apr–mid-Oct, 8-9.30pm Fri & Sat mid-Oct–Mar) The Alhambra is Granada's – and Europe's – love letter to Moorish culture. Set against a backdrop of brooding Sierra Nevada peaks, this fortified palace complex started life as a walled citadel before going on to become the opulent seat of Granada's Nasrid emirs. Their showpiece palaces, the 14th-century Palacios Nazaríes, are among the finest Islamic buildings in Europe and, together with the gorgeous Generalife gardens, form the Alhambra's great headline act.

★Capilla Real HISTORIC BUILDING
(Royal Chapel; 958 22 78 48; www.capillarealgranada.com; Calle Oficios; adult/concession/child €5/3.50/free; 10.15am-6.30pm Mon-Sat, 11am-6pm Sun) The Royal Chapel is the last resting

Granada

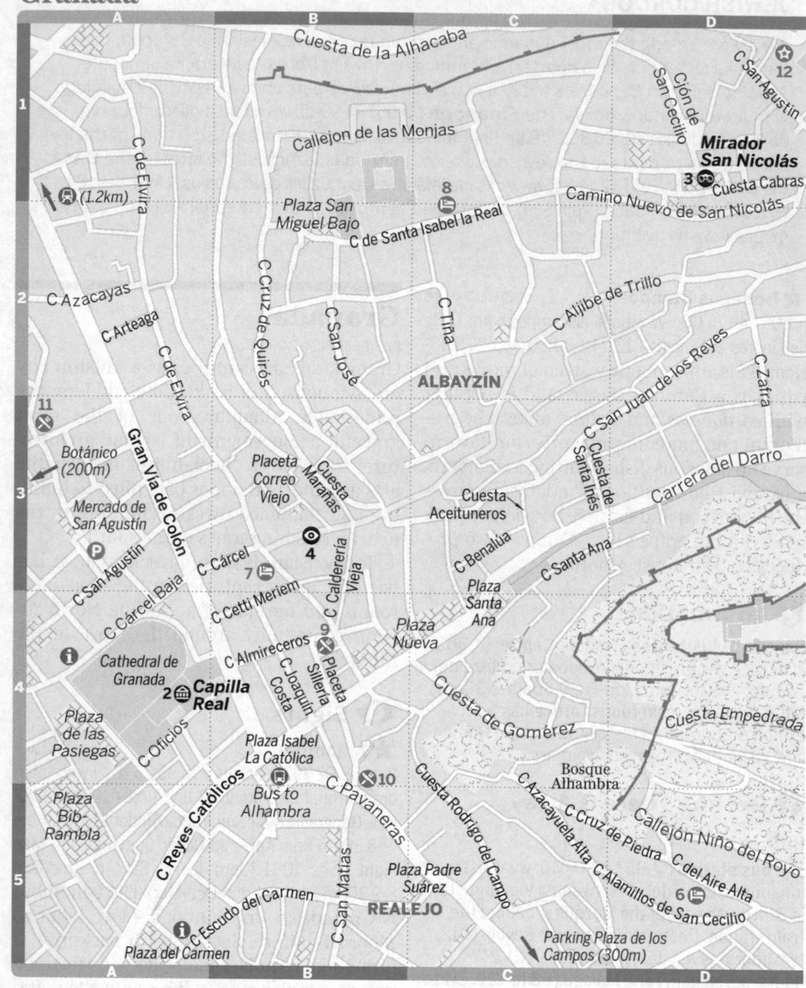

place of Spain's Reyes Católicos (Catholic Monarchs), Isabel I de Castilla (1451–1504) and Fernando II de Aragón (1452–1516), who commissioned the elaborate Isabelline-Gothic-style mausoleum that was to house them. It wasn't completed until 1517, hence their interment in the Alhambra's **Convento de San Francisco** (www.parador.es; Calle Real de la Alhambra) until 1521.

Their monumental marble tombs (and those of their heirs) lie in the chancel behind a gilded wrought-iron screen created by Bartolomé de Jaén in 1520.

Albayzín

On the hill facing the Alhambra across the Darro valley, the Albayzín is an open-air museum in which you can lose yourself for most of a day. The cobbled streets are lined with gorgeous *cármenes* (large mansions with walled gardens). It survived as the Muslim quarter for several decades after the Christian conquest in 1492.

Calle Calderería Nueva STREET

Linking the upper and lower parts of the Albayzín, Calle Calderería Nueva is a narrow

Granada

Top Sights
1 Alhambra ... E4
2 Capilla Real ... A4
3 Mirador San Nicolás ... D1

Sights
4 Calle Calderería Nueva ... B3
5 Convento de San Francisco ... F4

Sleeping
6 Carmen de la Alcubilla del Caracol ... D5
7 Hotel Posada del Toro ... B3
8 Santa Isabel La Real ... C2

Eating
9 Bodegas Castañeda ... B4
10 Carmela Restaurante ... B4
11 El Bar de Fede ... A3

Entertainment
12 Jardines de Zoraya ... D1
13 Peña La Platería ... E2

street famous for its *teterías* (tearooms). It's also a good place to shop for slippers, hookahs, jewellery and North African pottery from an eclectic cache of shops redolent of a Moroccan souk.

★Mirador San Nicolás VIEWPOINT
(Plaza de San Nicolás) This is the place for those classic sunset shots of the Alhambra sprawled along a wooded hilltop with the dark Sierra Nevada mountains looming in the background. It's a well-known spot, accessible via Callejón de San Cecilio, so expect crowds of camera-toting tourists, students and buskers. It's also a haunt of pickpockets and bag snatchers, so keep your wits about you as you enjoy the views.

Sleeping

Hotel Posada del Toro HOTEL €
(☎958 22 73 33; www.posadadeltoro.com; Calle de Elvira 25; s/d/ste from €45/50/70;) A lovely little hotel in the lively Albayzín quarter. Bullfighting posters line a small passageway that leads to the main body of the hotel where tasteful rooms are decked out with parquet floors, Alhambra-style stucco and rustic furniture. Rates are a bargain considering its central location.

Carmen de la Alcubilla del Caracol HISTORIC HOTEL €€
(☎958 21 55 51; www.alcubilladelcaracol.com; Calle del Aire Alta 12; r €165-185; closed mid-Jul–Aug;) This much-sought-after small hotel inhabits a traditional whitewashed *carmen* on the slopes of the Alhambra (p599). It feels more like a B&B than a hotel with its elegant homey interiors and seven quietly refined rooms washed in pale pastel colours. Outside, you can bask in fabulous views from the spectacular terraced garden.

★Santa Isabel La Real BOUTIQUE HOTEL €€€
(☎958 29 46 58; www.hotelsantaisabellareal.com; Calle de Santa Isabel La Real 19; r €115-210;

ALHAMBRA TICKETS

Up to 6600 tickets to the Alhambra are available each day. About one-third of these are sold at the entrance on the day, but they sell out early, and if you're here between March and October you need to start queuing by 7am to be reasonably sure of getting one. Fortunately, it's also possible to buy tickets up to three months ahead, online or by phone, from **Alhambra Advance Booking** (☎858 95 36 16; https://tickets.alhambra-patronato.es), for €0.85 extra per ticket.

Tickets purchased online or by phone can be collected from ATMs of La Caixa bank throughout Andalucía, or from ticket machines or ticket windows at the Alhambra entrance. You'll need your booking reference number and your payment card (or ID document if collecting at Alhambra ticket windows).

The Palacios Nazaríes are open for night visits, good for atmosphere rather than detail.

It's a pleasant (if uphill) walk of just over 1km from Plaza Nueva to the Alhambra's main entrance. Alternatively, buses C3 and C4 (€1.40) run every few minutes from Plaza Isabel La Católica. By car, follow 'Alhambra' signs from the highway to the car park, just uphill from the ticket office.

) Up in hilltop Albayzín, this welcoming small hotel occupies a whitewashed 16th-century building. Many original architectural features endure, including marble columns and flagged stone floors, while a fireplace and sofa add a homey touch in the communal area. The guest rooms, which are set around a central patio, are individually decorated with embroidered pictures and hand-woven rugs.

Eating

Granada is a bastion of that fantastic practice of free tapas with every drink, and some have an international flavour. The labyrinthine Albayzín holds a wealth of eateries tucked away in the narrow streets. Calle Caldería Nueva is a fascinating muddle of *teterías* (tearooms) and Arabic-influenced takeaways.

Bodegas Castañeda TAPAS €

(☎958 21 54 64; Calle Almireceros 1; tapas €2-5; 11.30am-4.30pm & 7.30pm-1am Mon-Thu, to 2am Fri-Sun) Eating becomes a contact sport at this traditional tapas bar where crowds of hungry punters jostle for food under hanging hams. Don't expect any experimental nonsense here, just classic tapas (and *raciones*) served lightning fast with booze poured from big wall-mounted casks.

Carmela Restaurante SPANISH €€

(☎958 22 57 94; www.restaurantecarmela.com; Calle Colcha 13; tapas €7, mains €11-20; 8am-midnight, kitchen noon-midnight) Traditional tapas updated for the 21st century are the star turn at this smart all-day cafe-restaurant at the jaws of the Realejo quarter. Bag a table in the cool brick-lined interior or on the outdoor terrace and bite into croquettes with black pudding and caramelised onion, or tuna *tataki* with soy reduction.

★El Bar de Fede INTERNATIONAL €€

(☎958 28 88 14; Calle Marqués de Falces 1; raciones €9-15; 9am-2am Mon-Thu, to 3am Fri & Sat, 11am-2am Sun) The 'Fede' in the name refers to home-town poet Federico García Lorca, whose free spirit seems to hang over this hip, gay-friendly bar. It's a good-looking spot with patterned wallpaper and high tables set around a ceramic-tiled island, and the food is a joy. Standouts include chicken pâté served with orange sauce and heavenly melt-in-your mouth grilled squid.

Drinking & Entertainment

The best street for drinking is the rather scruffy Calle de Elvira, but other chilled bars line the Río Darro at the base of the Albayzín and Calle Navas in Realejo.

Botánico BAR

(☎958 27 15 98; www.botanicocafe.es; Calle Málaga 3; 1pm-1am Mon-Thu, to 2am Fri & Sat, to 6pm Sun) Dudes with designer beards, students finishing off their Lorca dissertations, and bohemians with arty inclinations hang out at Botánico, a casual eatery by day, a cafe at *merienda* (afternoon snack) time (5pm to 7pm), and a buzzing bar come the evening.

Peña La Platería FLAMENCO

(☎958 21 06 50; www.laplateria.org.es; Placeta de Toqueros 7) Peña La Platería claims to be Spain's oldest flamenco club, founded in 1949. Unlike other more private clubs, it regularly opens its doors to nonmembers for performances on Thursday nights at 10pm. Tapas and drinks are available. Reservations recommended.

Jardines de Zoraya FLAMENCO

(☎958 20 62 66; www.jardinesdezoraya.com; Calle Panaderos 32; ticket €20, dinner from €29; ⊙shows 8pm & 10.30pm) Hosted in a restaurant in the Albayzín district, the Jardines de Zoraya appears, on first impression, to be a touristy *tablao* (choreographed flamenco show). But reasonable entry prices, talented performers and a highly atmospheric patio make it a worthwhile stop for any aficionado.

ℹ Information

Municipal Tourist Office (☎958 24 82 80; www.granadatur.com; Plaza del Carmen 9; ⊙9am-7pm Mon-Sat, 10am-2pm Sun) Helpful English-speaking staff can provide maps and useful city information.

Provincial Tourist Office (☎958 24 71 28; www.turgranada.es; Calle Cárcel Baja 3; ⊙9am-8pm Mon-Fri, 10am-7pm Sat, 10am-3pm Sun) For information on Granada province.

ℹ Getting There & Away

BUS

Granada's **bus station** (☎958 18 50 10; Avenida Juan Pablo II; ⊙6.30am-1.30am) is 3km northwest of the city centre. Destinations include Córdoba (€15 to €17, 2¾ hours, nine daily), Seville (€23 to €30, three hours, 10 daily), Málaga (€12 to €14, 1¾ hours, hourly) and Madrid (€19 to €45, five hours, 13 daily).

WORTH A TRIP

ANDALUCÍA BEYOND THE CITIES

The Andalucian countryside, with its white villages, rugged mountains, winding country roads and appealing small towns, is every bit as magical as the region's famed cities – and packs in huge variety.

On the south flank of the Sierra Nevada (mainland Spain's highest mountain range), the jumble of valleys known as **Las Alpujarras** juxtaposes arid mountainsides and deep ravines with oasis-like, Berber-style villages set amid orchards and woodlands. There's great walking, a unique ambience derived from the area's Moorish past, and plenty of good accommodation in and around scenic villages like **Capileira**, **Ferreirola**, **Trevélez** and **Cádiar**, one to two hours' drive south from Granada.

Further afield, 200km northeast from Granada, the **Parque Natural Sierras de Cazorla, Segura y Las Villas** is 2099 sq km of craggy mountains, remote hilltop castles and deep green river valleys with some of the most abundant and visible wildlife in Spain – including three types of deer, ibex, wild boar, mouflon (a wild sheep), griffon vultures and golden eagles. The picturesque medieval town of **Cazorla** is a great base, and en route you shouldn't miss the gorgeous towns of **Úbeda** and **Baeza**, which are World Heritage–listed for their outstanding Renaissance architecture.

If you're starting from Seville, it's about an hour's drive west to the vast wetlands of the **Parque Nacional de Doñana**, Western Europe's biggest roadless region, where flocks of flamingos tinge the sky pink, huge herds of deer and boar roam the woodlands, and the iberian lynx fights for survival. Four-hour minibus safaris into the park go from **El Rocío**, **Sanlúcar de Barrameda** and **El Acebuche** visitors centre.

Along back roads between Seville and Málaga, hung from the skies between the spectacular clifftop towns of **Arcos de la Frontera** and **Ronda**, the gorgeously green limestone gorges and crags of the **Sierra de Grazalema** are criss-crossed by beautiful, marked trails between charming white villages such as **Grazalema**, **Benaoján** and **Zahara de la Sierra**.

All these areas have plenty of good accommodation, including many charming country guesthouses or small hotels. They can be reached by bus with a bit of effort: a car is the ideal way to get to and around them.

TRAIN

The **train station** (☎958 27 12 72; Avenida de Andaluces) is 1.5km west of the centre. Services run to Seville (€30, 3¾ hours, four daily), Almería (€20, three hours, four daily), Madrid (€30 to €47, four hours, six daily) and Barcelona (€40 to €85, eight hours, two daily).

Málaga

POP 569,002

Málaga is a world apart from the adjoining, overdeveloped Costa del Sol: an exuberant, historic port city that has rapidly emerged as a city of culture, its so-called 'mile of art' being compared to Madrid, and its dynamism and fine dining to Barcelona.

The tastefully restored historic centre is a delight, with a Gothic cathedral surrounded by narrow pedestrian streets flanked by traditional and modern bars, and shops that range from idiosyncratic and family owned to urban-chic and contemporary. The city's terrific bars and nightlife, the last word in Málaga *joie de vivre,* stay open very late.

Sights

★Museo Picasso Málaga MUSEUM

(☎952 12 76 00; www.museopicassomalaga.org; Calle San Agustín 8; €8, incl temporary exhibition €12; ⏲10am-8pm Jul & Aug, to 7pm Mar-Jun, Sep & Oct, to 6pm Nov-Feb; 📶) This unmissable museum in the city of Picasso's birth provides a solid overview of the great master and his work, although, surprisingly, it only came to fruition in 2003 after more than 50 years of planning. The 200-plus works in the collection were donated and loaned to the museum by Christine Ruiz-Picasso (wife of Paul, Picasso's eldest son) and Bernard Ruiz-Picasso (Picasso's grandson) and catalogue the artist's sparkling career with a few notable gaps (the 'blue' and 'rose' periods are largely missing).

★Catedral de Málaga CATHEDRAL

(☎952 22 03 45; www.malagacatedral.com; Calle Molina Lario; cathedral & Ars Málaga €6, incl roof €10; ⏲10am-8pm Mon-Fri, to 6.30pm Sat, 2-6.30pm Sun Apr, May & Oct, 10am-9pm Mon-Fri, to 6.30pm Sat, 2pm-6.30pm Sun Jun-Sep, closes 6.30pm daily Nov-Mar) Málaga's elaborate cathedral was started in the 16th century on the site of the former mosque. Of the mosque, only the **Patio de los Naranjos** survives, a small courtyard of fragrant orange trees. Inside, the fabulous domed ceiling soars 40m into the air, while the vast colonnaded nave houses an enormous cedar-wood choir. Aisles give access to 15 chapels with gorgeous 18th-century retables and religious art. It's worth taking the guided tour up to the *cubiertas* (roof) to enjoy panoramic city views.

★Alcazaba CASTLE

(☎952 227 230; www.malagaturismo.com; Calle Alcazabilla; €3.50, incl Castillo de Gibralfaro €5.50; ⏲9am-8pm Apr-Oct, to 6pm Nov-Mar) No time to visit Granada's Alhambra? Then Málaga's Alcazaba can provide a taster. The entrance is next to the **Roman amphitheatre** (☎951 50 11 15; Calle Alcazabilla 8; ⏲10am-8pm) FREE, from where a meandering path climbs amid lush greenery: crimson bougainvillea, lofty palms, fragrant jasmine bushes and rows of orange trees. Extensively restored, this palace-fortress dates from the 11th-century Moorish period; the caliphal horseshoe arches, courtyards and bubbling fountains are evocative of this influential period in Málaga's history.

Centre Pompidou Málaga MUSEUM

(☎951 92 62 00; www.centrepompidou.es; Pasaje Doctor Carrillo Casaux, Muelle Uno; €7, incl temporary exhibition €9; ⏲9.30am-8pm Wed-Mon; 📶) Opened in 2015 in the port, this offshoot of Paris' Pompidou Centre is housed in a low-slung modern building crowned by a playful multicoloured cube. The permanent exhibition includes the extraordinary *Ghost,* by Kader Attia, depicting rows of Muslim women bowed in prayer and created from domestic aluminium foil, plus works by such modern masters as Frida Kahlo, Francis Bacon and Antoni Tàpies. There are also audiovisual installations, talking 'heads' and temporary exhibitions.

Castillo de Gibralfaro CASTLE

(☎952 22 72 30; www.malagaturismo.com; Camino de Gibralfaro; €3.50, incl Alcazaba €5.50; ⏲9am-8pm Apr-Sep, to 6pm Oct-Mar) One remnant of Málaga's Islamic past is the craggy ramparts of the Castillo de Gibralfaro, spectacularly located high on the hill overlooking the city. Built by Abd ar-Rahman I, the 8th-century Córdoban emir, and later rebuilt in the 14th century when Málaga was the main port for the emirate of Granada, the castle originally acted as a lighthouse and military barracks. Nothing much is original in the castle's interior, but the protective walkway around the ramparts affords the best views over Málaga.

Museo Automovilístico Málaga MUSEUM
(☎951 13 70 01; www.museoautomovilmalaga.com; Avenida Sor Teresa Prat 15; €8.50; ⏱10am-7pm; 📶) Fashion and old cars might seem like weird bedfellows, but they're an inspired combo when viewed through the prism of this slightly out-of-the-box museum in Málaga's erstwhile tobacco factory. The museum juxtaposes cars from the 1900s to the 1960s with haute couture from the same era. Imagine a 1936 Merc lined up next to a mannequin clothed in a Chanel jacket.

Sleeping

★Dulces Dreams HOSTEL €
(☎951 35 78 69; www.dulcesdreamshostel.com; Plaza de los Mártires 6; r incl breakfast €55-85; ❄📶) Managed by an enthusiastic young team, the rooms at Dulces (sweet) Dreams are, appropriately, named after desserts; 'Cupcake' is a good choice, with a terrace overlooking the imposing red-brick church across the way. This is an older building, so there's no lift and the rooms vary in size, but they're bright and whimsically decorated, using recycled materials as much as possible.

★Molina Lario HOTEL €€
(☎952 06 20 02; www.hotelmolinalario.com; Calle Molina Lario 20-22; r €170-210; ❄📶🏊) Perfect for romantic couples, this hotel has a sophisticated, contemporary feel, with spacious rooms decorated in a cool palette of earthy colours. There are crisp white linens, marshmallow-soft pillows and tasteful paintings, plus a fabulous rooftop terrace and pool with views to the sea. Situated within confessional distance of the cathedral.

Eating & Drinking

Málaga has a staggering number of tapas bars and restaurants, particularly around the historic centre (over 400 at last count). One of the city's biggest pleasures is a slow crawl round its numerous tapas bars and old bodegas (cellars). The best bar-hop areas are from Plaza de la Merced in the northeast to Calle Carretería in the northwest, plus Plaza Mitjana and Plaza de Uncibay.

ANDALUCÍA'S QUIETEST BEACHES

The coast east of Almería in eastern Andalucía is perhaps the last section of Spain's Mediterranean coast where you can (sometimes) have a beach to yourself. This is Spain's sunniest region – even in March it can be warm enough to strip off and take in the rays. The best thing about it is the wonderful coastline and semidesert scenery of the **Cabo de Gata** promontory. All along the 50km coast from El Cabo de Gata village to Agua Amarga, some of the most beautiful beaches on the Mediterranean, from long sandy strands to tiny rock-girt coves, alternate with precipitous cliffs and scattered villages. The main base is laid-back **San José**, with excellent beaches nearby, such as Playa de los Genoveses, Playa de Mónsul and the four isolated little beaches of the Calas de Barronal. The former gold-mining village of **Rodalquilar**, a few kilometres inland, is a bit of a boho-chic hideaway.

★El Mesón de Cervantes TAPAS, ARGENTINE €€
(☎952 21 62 74; www.elmesondecervantes.com; Calle Álamos 11; medias raciones €4.50-8.50, raciones €7.50-14; ⏱7pm-midnight Wed-Mon) Cervantes started as a humble tapas bar run by expat Argentine Gabriel Spatz, but has now expanded into four bar-restaurants (each with a slightly different bent), all within a block of each other. This one is the HQ, where pretty much everything on the menu is a show-stopper – lamb stew with couscous, pumpkin and mushroom risotto, and, boy, the grilled octopus!

★Óleo FUSION €€
(☎952 21 90 62; www.oleorestaurante.es; Edificio CAC, Calle Alemania; mains €14-22; ⏱1.15-4pm & 8.30pm-midnight Mon-Sat; 📶) Located at the city's **Centro de Arte Contemporáneo** (Contemporary Art Museum; www.cacmalaga.org; ⏱9am-2pm & 5-9pm Tue-Sun) FREE with white-on-white minimalist decor, Óleo provides diners with the unusual choice of Mediterranean or Asian food, with some subtle combinations such as duck breast with a side of seaweed with hoisin, as well as more purist Asian dishes and gourmet palate-ticklers such as candied roasted piglet.

Los Patios de Beatas WINE BAR
(☎952 21 03 50; www.lospatiosdebeatas.com; Calle Beatas 43; ⏲1-5pm & 8pm-midnight Mon-Sat, 1-6pm Sun; 📶) Two 18th-century mansions have metamorphosed into this sumptuous space where you can sample fine wines from a selection reputed to be the most extensive in town. Stained-glass windows and beautiful resin tables inset with mosaics and shells add to the overall art-infused atmosphere. Innovative tapas and *raciones* (full-plate servings) are also on offer.

☆ Entertainment

★Kelipe FLAMENCO
(☎692 829885; Muro de Puerta Nueva 10; shows €25; ⏲shows 9.30pm Thu-Sat) There are many flamenco clubs springing up all over Andalucía, but few are as soul-stirring as Kelipe. Not only are the musicianship and dancing of the highest calibre, but the talented performers create an intimate feel and a genuine connection with the audience.

ℹ Information

The **municipal tourist office** (☎951 92 60 20; www.malagaturismo.com; Plaza de la Marina; ⏲9am-8pm Apr-Oct, to 6pm Nov-Mar) offers a range of city maps and booklets. It also operates information kiosks at the Alcazaba entrance (Calle Alcazabilla), at the main train station (Explanada de la Estación), on Plaza de la Merced and on the eastern beaches (El Palo and La Malagueta).

ℹ Getting There & Around

AIR

Málaga's **airport** (AGP; ☎952 04 88 38; www.aena.es), 9km southwest of the city centre, is the main international gateway to Andalucía, served by top global carriers as well as budget airlines. Buses (€3, 15 minutes) and trains (€1.80, 12 minutes) run every 20 or 30 minutes between airport and city centre.

BUS

Málaga's **bus station** (☎952 35 00 61; www.estabus.emtsam.es; Paseo de los Tilos) is 1km southwest of the city centre. Destinations include Seville (€19, 2¾ hours, seven daily), Granada (€12, two hours, hourly) and Córdoba (€12, three to four hours, seven daily).

TRAIN

Málaga is the southern terminus of the Madrid–Málaga high-speed train line.

Málaga María Zambrano Train Station (☎902 43 23 43; www.renfe.com; Explanada de la Estación; ⏲6am-11pm) is near the bus station, a 15-minute walk from the city centre. Destinations include Córdoba (€27.50, one hour, 19 daily), Seville (€24, 2¾ hours, 11 daily) and Madrid (€80, 2¾ hours, 15 daily). Note that for Córdoba and Seville the daily schedule includes fast AVE trains at roughly double the cost.

EXTREMADURA

Cáceres

POP 95,917

Few visitors make it to the region of Extremadura, bordering Portugal, but those who do are rewarded with some true gems of old Spain, especially Roman Mérida and the 16th-century towns of Trujillo and Cáceres. The Ciudad Monumental, Cáceres' old centre, is truly extraordinary. Narrow cobbled streets twist and climb among ancient stone walls lined with palaces and mansions, while the skyline is decorated with turrets, spires, gargoyles and enormous storks' nests. Protected by defensive walls, it has survived almost intact from its 16th-century heyday.

👁 Sights

★Palacio de los Golfines de Abajo HISTORIC BUILDING
(☎927 21 80 51; www.palaciogolfinesdeabajo.com; Plaza de los Golfines; tours adult/child €2.50/free; ⏲tours hourly 10am-1pm & 5-7pm Tue-Sat, 10am-1pm Sun May-Sep, 10am-1pm & 4.30-6.30pm Tue-Sat, 10am-1pm Sun Oct-Apr) The sumptuous home of Cáceres' prominent Golfín family has been beautifully restored. Built piecemeal between the 14th and 20th centuries, it's crammed with historical treasures: original 17th-century tapestries and armoury murals, a 19th-century bust of Alfonso XII, and a signed 1485 troops request from the Reyes Católicos (Catholic Monarchs) to their Golfín stewards. But it's the detailed, theatrical tours (Spanish, English, French or Portuguese), through four richly decorated lounges, an extravagant chapel and a fascinating documents room, that make it a standout.

★Museo de Cáceres MUSEUM
(☎927 01 08 77; http://museodecaceres.juntaex.es; Plaza de las Veletas; €1.20; ⏲9.30am-2.30pm & 4pm-8pm Tue-Fri, 10am-2.30pm & 4pm-8pm

Sat, 10am-3pm Sun) The excellent Museo de Cáceres, spread across 12 buildings in a 16th-century mansion built over an evocative 12th-century *aljibe* (cistern), is the only surviving element of Cáceres' Moorish castle. The impressive archaeological section includes an elegant stone boar dated to the 4th to 2nd centuries BC, while the equally appealing fine-arts display (behind the main museum; open only in the mornings) showcases works by such greats as Picasso, Miró, Tàpies and El Greco. It's one of Spain's most underrated collections.

Sleeping & Eating

★Hotel Soho Boutique Casa Don Fernando BOUTIQUE HOTEL €€
(927 62 71 76; www.sohohoteles.com; Plaza Mayor 30; s/d from €55/70; P ❄ ☎) Cáceres' smartest midrange choice sits on Plaza Mayor right opposite the Arco de la Estrella. Boutique-style rooms, spread over four floors, are tastefully modern, with gleaming bathrooms through glass doors. Pricier 'superiors' enjoy the best plaza views (though weekend nights can be noisy), and attic-style top-floor rooms are good for families. Service hits that perfect professional-yet-friendly note.

★La Cacharrería TAPAS €€
(927 10 16 79; lacacharreria@live.com; Calle de Orellana 1; tapas €4.50, raciones €10-18; restaurant 1-4pm & 8.30pm-midnight Thu-Mon, cafe 4pm-1.30am Thu-Sat, 4-11pm Sun;) Local flavours and ingredients combine in exquisite, international-inspired concoctions at this packed-out, minimalist-design tapas bar tucked into an old-town house. *Solomillo* (tenderloin) in Torta del Casar cheese arrives in martini glasses. Delicious guacamole, hummus, falafel and 'salsiki' are a godsend for vegetarians. No advance reservations: get here by 1.45pm or 8.30pm.

Information

The **Oficina de Turismo** (927 25 55 97; www.turismocaceres.org; Palacio Carvajal, Calle Amargura 1; 8am-8.45pm Mon-Fri, 10am-1.45pm & 5-7.45pm Sat, 10am-1.45pm Sun) covers Cáceres city and province; it's inside the Palacio de Carvajal.

Getting There & Away

BUS

The **bus station** (927 23 25 50; www.estacionautobuses.es; Calle Túnez 1; 6.30am-10.30pm) has services to Madrid (from €23, four hours, seven daily) and Trujillo (€4, 45 minutes, six daily).

TRAIN

From the train station, 2.5km southwest of the old town, trains run to/from Madrid (€28 to €33, 3¾ hours to 4¼ hours, five daily), Mérida (€6 to €7, one hour, six daily) and Plasencia (€5 to €6, one hour, four daily).

SURVIVAL GUIDE

Directory A–Z

ACTIVITIES

Hiking

- Top walking areas include the Pyrenees, Picos de Europa, Las Alpujarras (Andalucía) and the Galician coast.
- The best season is June to September in most areas, but April to June, September and October in most of Andalucía.
- Region-specific walking guides are published by Cicerone Press (www.cicerone.co.uk).
- GR (*Gran Recorrido;* long distance) trails are indicated with red-and-white markers; PR (*Pequeño Recorrido*; short distance) trails have yellow-and-white markers.
- Good hiking maps are published by Prames (www.prames.com), Editorial Alpina (www.editorialalpina.com) and the Institut Cartogràfic de Catalunya (www.icgc.cat).
- The Camino de Santiago pilgrim route to Santiago de Compostela has many variations starting from all over Spain (and other countries). Most popular is the Camino Francés, running 783km from Roncesvalles, on Spain's border with France. Good websites: Caminolinks (www.santiago-compostela.net), Mundicamino (www.mundicamino.com) and Camino de Santiago (www.caminodesantiago.me).

Skiing

Skiing is cheaper but less varied than in much of the rest of Europe. The season runs from December to mid-April. The best resorts are in the Pyrenees, especially in northwest Catalonia and in Aragón. The Sierra Nevada in Andalucía offers the most southerly skiing in Western Europe.

Surfing, Windsurfing & Kitesurfing

The Basque Country has good surf spots, including San Sebastián, Zarautz and the legendary left at Mundaka. Tarifa in Andalucía, with its long beaches and ceaseless wind, is generally considered to be the kitesurfing and windsurfing capital of Europe.

INTERNET ACCESS

Wi-fi is available at most hotels and in some cafes, restaurants and airports; generally (but not always) free.

LGBTIQ+ TRAVELLERS

Homosexuality is legal in Spain. Same-sex marriage was legalised in 2005. Madrid, Barcelona, Sitges, Torremolinos and Ibiza have particularly active and lively gay scenes. Gay Iberia (www.gayiberia.com) has gay guides to the main destinations.

MONEY

- Many credit and debit cards can be used for withdrawing money from *cajeros automáticos* (ATMs) and for making purchases. The most widely accepted cards are Visa and MasterCard.
- Most banks will exchange major foreign currencies and offer the best rates. Ask about commissions and take your passport.
- Exchange offices, indicated by the word *cambio* (exchange), offer longer opening hours than banks, but have worse exchange rates and higher commissions.
- Value-added tax (VAT) is known as IVA (*impuesto sobre el valor añadido*). Non-EU residents are entitled to a refund of the 21% IVA on purchases to be taken back to their country.
- Menu prices include a service charge. Most people leave some small change as a tip. Taxi drivers don't have to be tipped, but a little rounding up won't go amiss.

OPENING HOURS

Banks 8.30am–2pm Monday–Friday; some also open 4–7pm Thursday and 9am–1pm Saturday
Central post offices 8.30am–9.30pm Monday–Friday, 8.30am–2pm Saturday; most other branches 8.30am–2.30pm Monday–Friday, 9.30am–1pm Saturday
Nightclubs Midnight or 1am–5am or 6am
Restaurants Lunch 1–4pm; dinner 8.30–11pm or midnight
Shops 10am–2pm and 4.30–7.30pm or 5–8pm Monday–Friday or Saturday; big supermarkets and department stores generally open 10am–10pm Monday–Saturday

PUBLIC HOLIDAYS

The two main periods when Spaniards go on holiday are Semana Santa (the week leading up to Easter Sunday) and July or August. At these times accommodation can be scarce and transport heavily booked.

There are at least 14 official holidays a year – some observed nationwide, some locally. When a holiday falls close to a weekend, Spaniards like to make a *puente* (bridge), meaning they take the intervening day off too. Occasionally when some holidays fall close, they make an *acueducto* (aqueduct)! Here are the national holidays:

Año Nuevo (New Year's Day) 1 January
Viernes Santo (Good Friday) March/April
Fiesta del Trabajo (Labour Day) 1 May
La Asunción (Feast of the Assumption) 15 August
Fiesta Nacional de España (National Day) 12 October
La Inmaculada Concepción (Feast of the Immaculate Conception) 8 December
Navidad (Christmas) 25 December

Regional governments set five holidays and local councils two more. Common dates include the following:

Epifanía (Epiphany) or **Día de los Reyes Magos** (Three Kings' Day) 6 January
Jueves Santo (Good Thursday) March/April; not observed in Catalonia and Valencia
Corpus Christi June; the Thursday after the eighth Sunday after Easter Sunday
Día de Santiago Apóstol (Feast of St James the Apostle) 25 July
Día de Todos los Santos (All Saints' Day) 1 November
Día de la Constitución (Constitution Day) 6 December

SAFE TRAVEL

Most visitors to Spain never feel remotely threatened, but you should be aware of the possibility of petty theft (which may of course not seem so petty if your passport, cash, credit card and phone go missing). Stay alert and you can avoid most thievery techniques. Barcelona, Madrid and Seville are the worst offenders, as are popular beaches in summer (never leave belongings unattended).

TELEPHONE

The once widespread, but now fast disappearing, blue payphones accept coins, *tarjetas telefónicas* (phonecards) issued by the national phone company Telefónica and, in some cases, various credit cards. Calling from your smartphone, tablet or computer using an internet-based service such as WhatsApp, Skype or FaceTime is generally the cheapest and easiest option.

Mobile Phones

Local SIM cards are widely available and can be used in unlocked European and Australian mobile phones, but are not compatible with many North American or Japanese systems. The Spanish mobile-phone companies (Telefónica's MoviStar, Orange and Vodafone) offer *prepagado* (prepaid) accounts for mobiles. The SIM card costs from €10, to which you add some prepaid phone time.

Phone Codes

Spain has no area codes. All numbers are nine digits and you just dial that nine-digit number.

Numbers starting with 900 are national toll-free numbers, while those starting 901 to 905 come with varying costs; most can only be dialled from within Spain.

TOURIST INFORMATION

Most towns and large villages of any interest have a helpful *oficina de turismo* (tourist office) where you can get maps and brochures.

Turespaña (www.spain.info) is the country's national tourism body.

VISAS

Spain is one of 26 member countries of the Schengen Convention and Schengen visa rules apply.

Citizens or residents of EU and Schengen countries No visa required.

Citizens or residents of Australia, Canada, Israel, Japan, NZ and the USA No visa required for tourist visits of up to 90 days out of every 180 days.

Other countries Check with a Spanish embassy or consulate.

To work or study in Spain A special visa may be required – contact a Spanish embassy or consulate before travel.

Getting There & Away

Flights, cars and tours can be booked online at lonelyplanet.com/bookings.

AIR

Flights from all over Europe (including numerous budget airlines), plus direct flights from North and South America, Africa, the Middle East and Asia, serve main Spanish airports. All of Spain's airports share the user-friendly website and flight information telephone number of **Aena** (☎91 321 10 00; www.aena.es), the national airports authority. Each airport's page on the website has details on practical information (such as parking and public transport) and a list of (and links to) airlines using that airport.

Madrid's airport (p556) is Europe's sixth-busiest airport. Other major airports include Barcelona's Aeroport del Prat and the airports of Palma de Mallorca, Málaga, Alicante, Ibiza, Valencia, Seville, Bilbao, Menorca and Santiago de Compostela.

LAND

Spain shares land borders with France, Portugal and Andorra.

Bus

Aside from the main cross-border routes, numerous smaller services criss-cross Spain's borders with France and Portugal. Regular buses connect Andorra with Barcelona (including winter ski buses and direct services to the airport) and other destinations in Spain (including Madrid) and France.

Eurolines (www.eurolines.com) is the main operator of international bus services to Spain from most of Western Europe and Morocco. Services from France include Nice to Madrid, and Paris to Barcelona.

Avanza (www.avanzabus.com) runs daily buses between Lisbon and Madrid (€41 to €46, eight hours, two to three daily).

Train

Paris to Barcelona (from €49, 6½ hours, two to four daily) A high-speed service runs via Valence, Nîmes, Montpellier, Beziers, Narbonne, Perpignan, Figueres and Girona. Also high-speed services run from Lyon (from €39, five hours) and Toulouse (from €39, three to four hours).

Paris to Madrid (from €145 to €210, 9¾ to 11¼ hours, eight daily) The slow route runs via Les Aubrais, Blois, Poitiers, Irún, Vitoria, Burgos and Valladolid. The quicker route uses high-speed French TGV trains between Paris and Barcelona, where you change to a high-speed Spanish AVE to reach Madrid.

Lisbon to Madrid (chair/sleeper class from €61/95, 10½ hours, one daily)

Lisbon to Irún (chair/sleeper class €70/94, 13½ hours, one daily)

Porto to Vigo (€15, 2½ hours, two daily)

SEA

Trasmediterránea (www.trasmediterranea.es) This Spanish company runs many Mediterranean ferry services.

Brittany Ferries (www.brittany-ferries.co.uk) Services between Spain and the UK.

Grandi Navi Veloci (www.gnv.it) High-speed luxury ferries between Barcelona and Genoa.

Grimaldi Lines (www.grimaldi-lines.com) Barcelona to Civitavecchia (near Rome), Savona (near Genoa) and Porto Torres (northwest Sardinia).

Getting Around

Students and seniors are eligible for discounts of 30% to 50% on most types of transport within Spain.

AIR

Air Europa (www.aireuropa.com) Madrid to A Coruña, Vigo, Bilbao and Barcelona, as well as other routes between Spanish cities.

Iberia (www.iberia.com) Spain's national airline has an extensive domestic network.

Ryanair (www.ryanair.com) Some domestic Spanish routes.

Volotea (www.volotea.com) Budget airline that flies domestically and internationally. Domestic routes take in Alicante, Bilbao, Málaga, Seville, Valencia, Zaragoza, Oviedo and the Balearics (but not Madrid or Barcelona).

Vueling (www.vueling.com) Spanish low-cost company with loads of domestic flights within Spain, especially from Barcelona.

BOAT

Regular ferries connect the Spanish mainland with the Balearic Islands.

BUS

Spain's bus network is operated by countless independent companies and reaches into the most remote towns and villages. Many towns and cities have one main bus station where most buses arrive and depart.

It is not necessary, and often not possible, to make advance reservations for local bus journeys. It is, however, a good idea to turn up at least 30 minutes before the bus leaves to guarantee a seat. For longer trips, you can and should buy your ticket in advance.

ALSA Countrywide bus network.

Avanza Buses from Madrid to Extremadura, western Castilla y León and Valencia.

Socibus Services between Madrid, western Andalucía and the Basque Country.

CAR & MOTORCYCLE

Spain's roads vary enormously but are generally good. Fastest are the *autopistas;* on some, you have to pay hefty tolls.

Every vehicle should display a nationality plate of its country of registration and you must always carry proof of ownership of a private vehicle. Third-party motor insurance is required throughout Europe. A warning triangle and a reflective jacket (to be used in case of breakdown) are compulsory.

Driving Licences

All EU member states' driving licences are recognised. Other foreign licences should be accompanied by an International Driving Permit (although in practice local licences are usually accepted). These are available from automobile clubs in your country and valid for 12 months.

Hire

To rent a car in Spain you have to have a licence, be aged 21 or over and have a credit or debit card. Rates vary widely: the best deals tend to be in major tourist areas, including airports. Prices are especially competitive in the Balearic Islands.

FERRIES TO SPAIN

A useful website for comparing routes and finding links to the relevant ferry companies is www.ferrylines.com.

From Italy

ROUTE	DURATION (HR)	FREQUENCY (WEEKLY)
Civitavecchia (near Rome) to Barcelona	20	6
Genoa to Barcelona	18	1-2
Porto Torres (Sardinia) to Barcelona	12	2-5
Savona (near Genoa) to Barcelona	20	1

From Morocco

ROUTE	DURATION	FREQUENCY
Nador to Almería	5-7hr	daily
Tangier to Barcelona	27-33hr	1-2 weekly
Tangier to Tarifa	35–40min	up to 15 daily
Tangier to Algeciras	1-2hr	up to 12 daily

From the UK

ROUTE	DURATION (HR)	FREQUENCY
Plymouth to Santander	20	weekly (mid-March to November)
Portsmouth to Bilbao	24	2 weekly
Portsmouth to Santander	24	3 weekly

Road Rules

- The blood-alcohol limit is 0.05%.
- The legal driving age for cars is 18. The legal driving age for motorcycles and scooters is 16 (80cc and over) or 14 (50cc and under). A licence is required.
- Motorcyclists must use headlights at all times and wear a helmet if riding a bike of 125cc or more.
- Drive on the right.
- In built-up areas, the speed limit is 50km/h (and in some cases, such as inner-city Barcelona, 30km/h), which increases to 100km/h on major roads and up to 120km/h on *autovías* and *autopistas* (toll-free and tolled dual-lane highways, respectively). Cars towing caravans are restricted to a maximum speed of 80km/h.

TRAIN

The national railway company is **Renfe** (☎91 232 03 20; www.renfe.com). Trains are mostly modern and comfortable, and late arrivals are the exception. The high-speed network is in constant expansion.

Passes are valid for all long-distance Renfe trains; Interrail users pay supplements on Talgo, InterCity and AVE trains. All pass-holders making reservations pay a small fee.

Types of Train

Among Spain's numerous types of train are the following:

Altaria, Alvia and Avant Long-distance intermediate-speed services.

AVE (Tren de Alta Velocidad Española) High-speed trains that link Madrid with Albacete, Alicante, Barcelona, Córdoba, Cuenca, Huesca, León, Lleida, Málaga, Palencia, Salamanca, Seville, Valencia, Valladolid and Zaragoza. There are also Barcelona–Seville, Barcelona–Málaga and Valencia–Seville services. In coming years, Madrid–Bilbao should also come on line, and travel times to Galicia should fall. The same goes for Madrid–Granada and Madrid–Badajoz.

Cercanías (rodalies in Catalonia) For short hops and services to outlying suburbs and satellite towns in Madrid, Barcelona and 11 other cities.

Euromed Similar to AVE trains, they connect Barcelona with Valencia and Alicante.

Regionales Trains operating within one region, usually stopping at all stations.

Talgo & intercity Slower long-distance trains.

Trenhotel Overnight trains with sleeper berths.

Classes & Costs

- Fares vary enormously depending on the service (faster trains cost considerably more) and, for many long-distance trains, on the time and day of travel and how far ahead you book (the earlier the better).
- Long-distance trains have 2nd and 1st classes, known as *turista* and *preferente*, respectively. The latter is 20% to 40% more expensive.
- Children aged between four and 14 years are entitled to a 40% discount; those aged under four travel for free (but on long- and medium-distance trains only if they share a seat with a fare-paying passenger).
- Buying a return ticket gives a 20% discount on most long- and medium-distance trains.
- Students and people up to 25 years of age with a Euro<26 or GO 25 card are entitled to 20% off most ticket prices.

Reservations

Reservations are recommended for long-distance trips; you can make them in train stations, Renfe offices and travel agencies, as well as online. In a growing number of stations, you can pick up pre-booked tickets from machines scattered about the station concourse.

Switzerland

POP 8.5 MILLION

Includes ➡

Best Places to Eat

- Chez Vrony (p622)
- Didi's Frieden (p630)
- Volkshaus Basel (p633)
- Cafe 3692 (p627)
- Zur Werkstatt (p625)
- Kraftwerk (p630)

Best Places to Stay

- Hotel Widder (p629)
- The Bed & Breakfast (p625)
- Float Inn (p616)
- Hotel Glacier (p627)

Why Go?

What giddy romance Zermatt, St Moritz and other glitterati-encrusted names evoke. This is Sonderfall Schweiz ('special-case Switzerland'), a privileged neutral country set apart from others, proudly idiosyncratic, insular and unique. It's blessed with gargantuan cultural diversity: its four official languages alone speak volumes.

The Swiss don't do half measures: Zürich, their most gregarious urban centre, has cutting-edge art, legendary nightlife and one of the world's highest living standards. The national passion for sharing the great outdoors provides access (by public transport, no less!) to some of the world's most inspiring panoramic experiences.

So don't depend just on your postcard images of Bern's and Lucerne's chocolate-box architecture, the majestic Matterhorn or those pristine lakes – Switzerland is a place so outrageously beautiful it simply must be seen to be believed.

When to Go

Bern

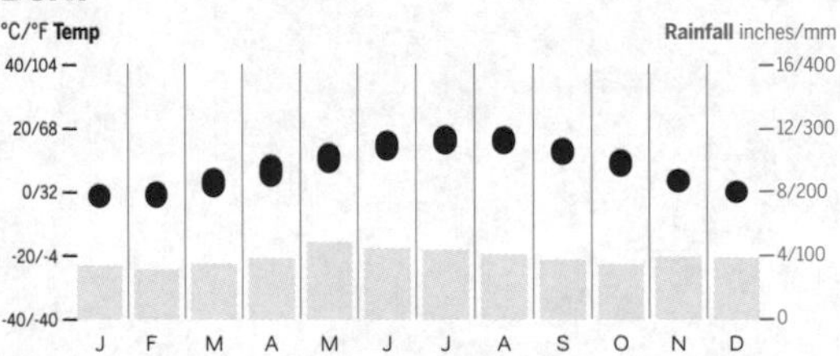

Dec–early Apr Carve through powder and eat fondue at an Alpine resort.

Jun–Sep Hike in the shadow of the mesmerising Matterhorn and be wowed by its perfection.

Aug Celebrate Swiss National Day on 1 August and witness Swiss national pride in full force.

Entering the Country

Formalities are minimal when arriving in Switzerland by air, rail or road thanks to the Schengen Agreement, which allows passengers coming from the EU to enter without showing a passport. When arriving from a non-EU country, you'll need your passport or EU identity card – and visa if required – to clear customs.

ITINERARIES

One Week

Starting in vibrant Zürich (p628), shop famous Bahnhofstrasse, then eat, drink and be merry. Next, head to the Jungfrau region (p627) to explore some kick-arse Alpine scenery, whether it be by hiking or skiing. Take a pit stop in beautiful Lucerne (p624) before finishing up in Switzerland's delightful capital, Bern (p622).

Two Weeks

As above, then head west for a French flavour in Geneva (p614) or lakeside Lausanne (p619). Stop in Gruyères (p620) to dip into a cheesy fondue and overdose on meringues drowned in thick double cream. Zip to Zermatt (p621) or across to St Moritz (p635) to frolic in snow or green meadows, then loop east to taste the Italian side of Switzerland at lakeside Lugano (p634).

Essential Food & Drink

Fondue Switzerland's best-known dish, in which melted Emmental and Gruyère cheese are combined with white wine in a large pot and eaten with small bread chunks.

Raclette Another popular artery-hardener of melted cheese served with potatoes.

Rösti German Switzerland's national dish of fried shredded potatoes is served with everything.

Veal Highly rated throughout the country; in Zurich, veal is thinly sliced and served in a cream sauce *(Zürcher Geschnetzeltes)*.

Bündnerfleisch Dried beef, smoked and thinly sliced.

Chocolate Good at any time of day and available seemingly everywhere.

AT A GLANCE

Area 41,285 sq km

Capital Bern

Country Code ☎41

Currency Swiss franc (Sfr)

Emergency Ambulance ☎144, fire ☎118, police ☎117

Languages French, German, Italian, Romansch

Time Central European Time (GMT/UTC plus one hour)

Visas Schengen rules apply

Sleeping Price Ranges

The following price ranges refer to a double room with a private bathroom. Quoted rates are for high season and include breakfast, unless otherwise noted.

$ less than Sfr170

$$ Sfr170–350

$$$ more than Sfr350

Eating Price Ranges

The following price ranges refer to a main course.

$ less than Sfr25

$$ Sfr25–50

$$$ more than Sfr50

Resources

My Switzerland (www.myswitzerland.com)

Swiss Info (www.swissinfo.ch)

SBB (www.sbb.ch)

Switzerland Highlights

❶ **Zürich** (p628) Discovering this zesty city via a daytime stroll along the city's sublime lake followed by a rollicking night out.

❷ **Zermatt** (p621) Marvelling at the iconic Matterhorn and wandering around this car-free Alpine village.

❸ **Bern** (p622) and **Lucerne** (p624) Enjoying the charm of these famous beauties: think medieval Old Town appeal, folkloric fountains and art.

❹ **Jungfraujoch** (p627) Being wowed by the Eiger's monstrous north face on a ride to the 'top of Europe', 3471m Jungfraujoch.

❺ **Geneva** (p614) Boarding a boat in this sophisticated city for a serene Lake Geneva cruise to medieval Lausanne.

❻ **Bernina Express** (p635) Riding one of Switzerland's legendary scenic trains, such as the Bernina Express.

❼ **Lugano** (p634) Going Italian at Lugano, with its lovely, temperate lake setting.

GENEVA

POP 198,979 / ELEV 375M

Like the swans that frolic on its eponymous Alpine lake (Europe's largest), Geneva (Genève) is a rare bird. Constantly perceived as the Swiss capital (it isn't), Switzerland's second-largest city is slick and cosmopolitan, and its people chatter in almost every language. The headquarters of the World Trade Organization, World Health Organization, International Committee of the Red Cross, and the second-largest branches of the United Nations and World Bank are here, along with an overload of luxury hotels, boutiques, jewellers, restaurants and chocolatiers.

Sights

The city centre is so compact it's easy to see many of the main sights on foot. Begin your explorations on the southern side of Lake Geneva and visit the **Jardin Anglais** (English Garden; Quai du Général-Guisan) to see the **Horloge Fleurie** (Flower Clock). Crafted from 6500 flowers, the clock has ticked since 1955 and sports the world's longest second hand (2.5m).

★Jet d'Eau FOUNTAIN

(Quai Gustave-Ador) When landing by plane, this lakeside fountain is your first dramatic glimpse of Geneva. The 140m-tall structure shoots up water with incredible force – 200km/h, 1360 horsepower – to create the sky-high plume, kissed by a rainbow on sunny days. At any one time, 7 tonnes of water are in the air, much of which sprays spectators on the pier beneath. Two or three times a year it is illuminated pink, blue or another colour to mark a humanitarian occasion.

CERN RESEARCH CENTRE

(☎022 767 84 84; www.cern.ch; Meyrin; ⏱guided tours in English 11am & 1pm Mon-Sat) FREE Founded in 1954, the European Organization for Nuclear Research (CERN), 8km west of Geneva, is a laboratory for research into particle physics. It accelerates protons down a 27km circular tube (the Large Hadron Collider, the world's biggest machine) and the resulting collisions create new matter. Come anytime to see the permanent exhibitions shedding light on its work, but for two-hour guided tours in English reserve online up to 15 days ahead and bring photo ID.

Musée International de la Croix-Rouge et du Croissant-Rouge MUSEUM
(International Red Cross & Red Crescent Museum; ☎022 748 95 11; www.redcrossmuseum.ch; Av de la Paix 17; adult/child Sfr15/7; ⏲10am-6pm Tue-Sun Apr-Oct, to 5pm Nov-Mar) Compelling multimedia exhibits at Geneva's fascinating International Red Cross and Red Crescent Museum trawl through atrocities perpetuated by humanity. The litany of war and nastiness, documented in films, photos, sculptures and soundtracks, is set against the noble aims of the organisation founded by Geneva businessmen Henry Dunant in 1863. Excellent temporary exhibitions command an additional entrance fee. To get here take bus 8 from **Gare CFF de Cornavin** (www.sbb.ch; Pl de Cornavin) to the Appia stop.

Cathédrale St-Pierre CATHEDRAL
(www.cathedrale-geneve.ch; Cour de St-Pierre; towers adult/child Sfr5/2; ⏲9.30am-6.30pm Mon-Sat, noon-6.30pm Sun Jun-Sep, 10am-5.30pm Mon-Sat, noon-5.30pm Sun Oct-May) Geneva's cathedral is predominantly Gothic with an 18th-century neoclassical facade. Between 1536 and 1564 Protestant John Calvin preached here; see his seat in the north aisle. Inside the cathedral, 96 steps spiral up to the **northern tower**, offering a fascinating glimpse at the cathedral's architectural construction. From here, another 60 steps climb into the **southern tower**, revealing close-up views of the bells and panoramic city vistas. From June to September, daily free carillon (5pm) and organ (6pm) concerts are a bonus.

Patek Philippe Museum MUSEUM
(☎022 707 30 10; www.patekmuseum.com; Rue des Vieux-Grenadiers 7; adult/child Sfr10/free; ⏲2-6pm Tue-Fri, 10am-6pm Sat) An ode to Swiss timing, this elegant museum by one of Switzerland's leading luxury watchmakers displays exquisite timepieces and enamels from the 16th century to the present, with some 2000 exhibits on display.

Activities

Genève Plage SWIMMING
(☎022 736 24 82; www.geneve-plage.ch; Quai de Cologny 5, Port Noir; adult/child Sfr7/3.50; ⏲10am-8pm mid-May–mid-Sep) This delightful swimming-pool complex, with its water slide and plenty of lawn to flop on, has been pleasing frolicking-in-the-sun Genevans since the 1930s. You can rent stand-up paddleboards for Sfr12 per hour, have fun surfing the artificial wave (Sfr10 per session) or get an Ayurvedic massage.

CGN Ferries & Cruises BOATING
(Compagnie Générale de Navigation; ☎0900 929 929; www.cgn.ch; Quai du Mont-Blanc; 👪) Lake Geneva's biggest ferry operator runs regular scheduled ferry services and a variety of themed lake cruises aboard beautiful belle époque steamers. Check the website for full details.

Festivals & Events

L'Escalade CARNIVAL
(⏲Dec) Smashing sweet marzipan-filled *marmites en chocolat* (chocolate cauldrons) and gorging on the broken pieces makes Geneva's biggest festival (second weekend of December) loads of fun. Torch-lit processions enliven the Vieille Ville and a bonfire is lit in the cathedral square to celebrate the defeat of Savoy troops in 1602.

Sleeping

When checking in, ask for your free Public Transport Card, covering public-transport travel for the duration of your hotel stay.

Le Jour et la Nuit B&B $$
(☎079 214 73 87; www.lejouretlanuit-bnb.com; Av du Mervelet 8; ⏲s/d Sfr210/230, ste Sfr250-270, apt Sfr135-250; P📶) Alain and Sylvie are your affable hosts at this highly tasteful

GRAND TOUR OF SWITZERLAND

Imagine if you could see all of Switzerland's highlights in one unforgettable road trip. Well, the Swiss have done just that with this new 1600km route (www.grandtour.myswitzerland.com), linking 12 Unesco World Heritage Sites and taking in glaciers, mountain passes, cities, medieval villages, lakes, castles, abbeys – you name it. It's also doable by electric vehicle, with charging points en route.

Geneva

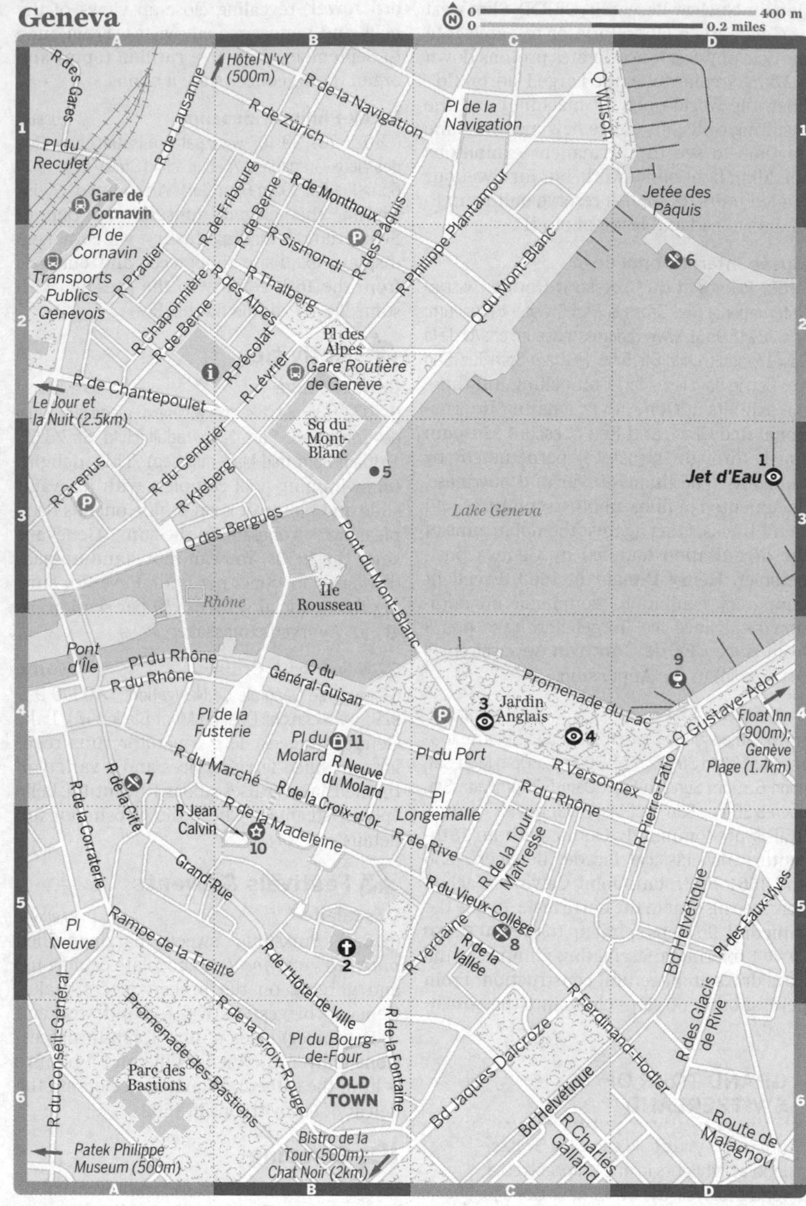

B&B, housed in a renovated 1920s villa. The three rooms and two apartments have been decorated with an eye for design, with Eames coat racks, Nespresso makers and Tivoli stereos. Generous breakfasts and a pretty garden are bonuses. Trams 14 and 18 to Bouchet stop close by.

Float Inn HOUSEBOAT **$$**

(☎078 797 51 97; www.floatinn.swiss; 55 Quai Gustave-Ador, Port des Eaux-Vives; d Sfr243; 📶) If you fancy spending the night adrift on Lake Geneva and waking up to eye-popping views of the Jet d'Eau, this catamaran turned luxe floating B&B makes that wish come true.

Geneva

Top Sights
1 Jet d'Eau D3

Sights
2 Cathédrale St-Pierre B5
3 Horloge Fleurie C4
4 Jardin Anglais C4

Activities, Courses & Tours
5 CGN Ferries & Cruises B3

Eating
6 Buvette des Bains D2
7 La Finestra A4
8 Three Kids Bagel C5

Drinking & Nightlife
9 La Buvette du Bateau D4

Entertainment
10 Alhambra B5

Shopping
11 Globus B4

Five portholed cabins with private bathrooms welcome guests, and there's also a bar, sun terrace and excellent home cooking.

Hôtel N'vY HOTEL $$
(022 544 66 66; www.hotelnvygeneva.com; Rue de Richemont 18; d/f/ste from Sfr169/299/337;) Contemporary flair abounds at this modish four-star place northeast of the train station, from the purple-lit bar downstairs to in-room amenities like international power outlets, Bluetooth connectivity and chromotherapy lighting. Among the five room categories, all but the standards come with big-screen TV, tea-making facilities and parquet wood floor. Upper-floor executive rooms have views of Lake Geneva and the Alps.

Eating

Eateries crowd Place du Bourg-de-Four, Geneva's oldest square, in the lovely Old Town. Otherwise, head down the hill towards the river and Place du Molard, packed with tables and chairs for much of the year. In Pâquis, there's a tasty line-up of more affordable restaurants on Place de la Navigation.

Three Kids Bagel BAGELS $
(022 311 24 24; www.threekids.ch; Rue du Vieux-Collège 10BIS; bagels Sfr9.50-16; 11am-3.30pm Mon-Sat) How can you elevate the humble bagel to an art form? According to Three Kids, the devil is in the detail: they take local sourcing seriously, baking bagels daily to chewy perfection using unbleached, organic, stone-ground flour, then getting creative with fillings like raclette, Grisons ham, pickles, paprika chips, onions and honey-mustard.

Buvette des Bains CAFETERIA $
(022 738 16 16; www.bains-des-paquis.ch; Quai du Mont-Blanc 30, Bains des Pâquis; mains Sfr14-23; 7am-10.30pm;) Meet Genevans at this earthy beach bar – rough and hip around the edges – at the Bains des Pâquis lakeside pool and sauna complex. Grab breakfast, a salad or the *plat du jour* (dish of the day), or dip into a *fondue au crémant* (sparkling-wine fondue). Dining is self-service on trays and alfresco in summer.

★**La Finestra** ITALIAN $$
(022 312 23 22; www.restaurant-lafinestra.ch/fr; Rue de la Cité 11; mains Sfr44-48, menus Sfr39-90; noon-2.30pm & 7-10.30pm Mon-Fri, 7-10.30pm Sat) This handsome little restaurant nestled in the heart of the Old Town rustles up authentic haute-Italian cuisine in a casual yet refined setting. The low beams and tiny tables wedged into the basement level of this historic building make for an intimate setting. Freshness and a passion for herbs show in dishes as simple as risotto with rocket pesto and scallops.

Bistro de la Tour BISTRO $$
(022 321 97 66; www.bistrodelatour.ch; Blvd de la Tour 2; mains Sfr29-38, 1-/2-/3-course lunch Sfr19/25/29; noon-2pm & 7-10pm Mon-Fri) Just a handful of tables await lucky diners at this intimate bistro and wine bar. And the menu? Succinct but *magnifique,* thanks to the combined passion of owners Philippe and Francis who source seasonal ingredients for homemade dishes as simple as bream with avocado, coriander and pomegranate, and succulent sirloin steak – all brilliantly cooked and matched with Swiss, Burgundy and Bordeaux wines.

Drinking & Nightlife

Pâquis, the district in between the train station and lake, is particularly well endowed with bars. For a dose of Bohemia, head to Carouge on tram 12. This shady quarter of 17th-century houses and narrow streets has galleries, funky shops and hip nightlife.

★**La Buvette du Bateau** BAR
(022 508 56 89; www.bateaugeneve.ch; Quai Gustave-Ador 1; 4.30pm-midnight Tue-Thu, to 2am Fri & Sat) Few terraces are as dreamy as this. Moored permanently by the quay

near Jet d'Eau, this fabulous belle époque paddle steamer, with flower boxes adorning its decks, sailed Lake Geneva's waters from 1896 until its retirement in 1974, and is now one of the busiest lounge bars in town in summer. Go for drinks, not food.

Chat Noir BAR
(☎ 022 307 10 40; www.chatnoir.ch; Rue Vautier 13, Carouge; ⏲ 5pm-2am Mon & Tue, to 4am Wed & Thu, to 5am Fri & Sat, 3pm-2am Sun) One of the busiest night spots in Carouge, the Black Cat is packed most nights thanks to its all-rounder vibe: arrive after work for an aperitif with a selection of tapas to nibble on, and stay until dawn for dancing, live music, jam sessions and DJ sets.

☆ Entertainment

★ L'Usine PERFORMING ARTS
(www.usine.ch; Pl des Volontaires 4) At the gritty heart of Geneva's alternative culture scene, this nonprofit collection of 18 arts-related initiatives is housed beside the Rhône in a former gold-processing factory. On any given night, expect to see cutting-edge theatre at **TU** (www.theatredelusine.ch), live music at **Le Zoo** (www.lezoo.ch) or up-and-coming VJ artists at **Kalvingrad** (www.kalvingrad.com).

Alhambra LIVE MUSIC
(☎ 078 966 07 97; www.alhambra-geneve.ch; Rue de la Rôtisserie 10) This gorgeous historic theatre with its cut-glass chandeliers, embossed silver ceilings and scarlet chairs makes a classy venue for live concerts ranging from Brazilian 'electrotropical' to African drumming, from disco to salsa, and from Afro-Caribbean to R&B.

Shopping

Designer shopping is wedged between Rue du Rhône and Rue de Rive; the latter has lots of chain stores. Grand-Rue in the Old Town and Carouge boast artsy boutiques. **Globus** (www.globus.ch/fr/store/116/globus-geneve; Rue du Rhône 48; ⏲ 9am-7pm Mon-Wed, to 9pm Thu, to 7.30pm Fri, to 6pm Sat, food hall 7.30am-10pm Mon-Fri, 8.30am-10pm Sat) is Geneva's main department store, also home to a top-notch food hall.

ℹ Information

Tourist Office (☎ 022 909 70 00; www.geneve.com; Rue du Mont-Blanc 18; ⏲ 9am-6pm Mon-Wed, Fri & Sat, 10am-6pm Thu, 10am-4pm Sun) Helpful, well-stocked office just downhill from the train station.

ℹ Getting There & Away

AIR

Geneva Airport (Aéroport International de Genève; www.gva.ch), 4km northwest of the town centre, is served by a wide variety of Swiss and international airlines.

BOAT

CGN (p615) runs up to four steamers per day from Jardin Anglais and Pâquis to other Lake Geneva villages, including Nyon (adult return Sfr50, 1¼ hours) and Yvoire (Sfr50, 1¾ hours).

BUS

Gare Routière de Genève (☎ 022 732 02 30; www.gare-routiere.com; Pl Dorcière) operates buses across the border into neighbouring France.

TRAIN

More-or-less-hourly connections run from Geneva's central train station, Gare CFF de Cornavin (p615), to most Swiss towns and cities.

Bern (Sfr51, 1¾ hours)
Geneva Airport (Sfr4, seven minutes)
Lausanne (Sfr22.80, 36 to 50 minutes)
Zürich (Sfr88, 2¾ hours)

ℹ Getting Around

TO/FROM THE AIRPORT

The quickest way to/from Geneva Airport is by train (Sfr4, seven minutes, several hourly); otherwise take bus 10 from the Rive stop (Sfr3, 30 minutes, four to nine hourly). When arriving at the airport, before leaving the luggage hall, grab a free public transport ticket from the machine next to the information desk.

A metered taxi into town costs Sfr35 to Sfr50 and takes about 15 minutes.

BICYCLE

Bike rental is available at **Genèveroule** (☎ 022 740 14 15; www.geneveroule.ch; Pl de Montbrillant 17; city/mountain/e-bikes per half-day Sfr8/12/17, full day Sfr12/18/25; ⏲ 8am-9pm May-Oct, to 6pm Nov-Apr), just outside the train station. A second office, known as Terrassière, is at Ruelle des Templiers 4 in the Eaux-Vives neighbourhood (left bank).

PUBLIC TRANSPORT

When you stay overnight in Geneva, you automatically receive a transport card, which enables you to use the entire public transport network (local trams, trains, buses, taxi-boats) for free. These are operated by **TPG** (TPG; www.tpg.ch; Rue de Montbrillant; ⏲ 7am-7pm Mon-Fri, 9am-6pm Sat).

LAKE GENEVA & VAUD

Western Europe's largest lake – known by the francophones who people its shores as Lac Léman, but the rest of the world as Lake Geneva – is anchored by the city that claims it, wrapping around its southern shore.

Lausanne

POP 137,810 / ELEV 495M

In a fabulous location overlooking Lake Geneva, Lausanne is an enchanting beauty with several distinct personalities: the former fishing village of Ouchy, with its lakeside bustle; the Vieille Ville (Old Town), with charming cobblestone streets and covered staircases; and Flon, a warehouse district of bars and boutiques.

Sights

★AQUATIS Aquarium & Vivarium AQUARIUM

(www.aquatis.ch/en; Rte de Berne 144, Lausanne-Vennes; adult/child Sfr29/19; 9am-7pm Apr-Oct, 10am-6pm Nov-Mar;) AQUATIS has given Lausanne a striking new landmark with a spherical facade that appears to be clad in shimmering fish scales. Using cutting-edge technology, it takes an immersive, eco-aware look at the world's freshwaters, whisking you around five continents, from Europe's glaciers to the Amazon.

★Musée Cantonal des Beaux Arts MUSEUM

(MCB-A; 021 316 34 45; www.mcba.ch; Plateforme10, Pl de la Gare 16; 10am-6pm Tue, Wed & Fri-Sun, to 8pm Thu) The Fine Arts Museum showcases works by Swiss and foreign artists, ranging from Ancient Egyptian art to cubism, but the core collection comprises works by landscape painter Louis Ducros (1748–1810). Admission is free, but a ticket needs to be booked via the website. There may be entry fees for individual exhibitions.

★Olympic Museum MUSEUM

(Musée Olympique; 021 621 65 11; www.olympic.org/museum; Quai d'Ouchy 1; adult/child Sfr18/10; 9am-6pm daily May–mid-Oct, 10am-6pm Tue-Sun mid-Oct–Apr;) Musée Olympique is easily Lausanne's most lavish museum and an essential stop for sports buffs (and kids). State-of-the-art installations recount the Olympic story from its inception to the present day through video, interactive displays, memorabilia and temporary themed exhibitions. Other attractions include tiered landscaped gardens, site-specific sculptural works and a fabulous cafe with champion lake views from its terrace.

★Cathédrale de Notre Dame CATHEDRAL

(021 316 71 60; www.patrimoine.vd.ch; Pl de la Cathédrale; 9am-7pm Apr-Sep, to 5.30pm Oct-Mar) Lausanne's Gothic cathedral, Switzerland's finest, stands proudly at the heart of the Old Town. Raised in the 12th and 13th centuries on the site of earlier, humbler churches, it lacks the lightness of French Gothic buildings but is remarkable nonetheless. Pope Gregory X, in the presence of Rudolph of Habsburg (the Holy Roman Emperor) and an impressive following of European cardinals and bishops, consecrated the church in 1275.

Sleeping & Eating

★Hôtel Beau-Rivage Palace HISTORIC HOTEL $$$

(021 613 33 33; www.brp.ch; Pl du Port 17-19; d from Sfr520;) Easily the most stunningly located hotel in Lausanne, this luxury lakeside address is sumptuous. A beautifully maintained early-19th-century mansion set in immaculate grounds, it tempts with magnificent lake and Alp views, a grand spa, and a number of bars and upmarket restaurants (including a superb gastronomic temple headed by Anne-Sophie Pic, the only French female chef with three Michelin stars).

Eat Me TAPAS $

(021 311 76 59; www.eat-me.ch; Rue Pépinet 3; small plates Sfr10-24; noon-2pm & 6pm-midnight Tue-Sat;) This fun, immensely popular and downright delicious resto-bar is all about global tapas, basically, with everything from baby burgers (sliders) to electric 'sashimiviche' (Sichuan sashimi à la ceviche!) and shrimp lollipops. Everything is well priced. Bring your friends!

Le Pointu CAFE $

(021 351 14 14; www.le-pointu.ch; Rue Neuve 2; snacks & light bites Sfr15-23, brunch items Sfr6-18; 7am-midnight Mon-Wed, to 1am Thu, to 2am Fri, 9am-2am Sat, 10am-3pm Sun) Lodged in a turreted belle époque building on a street corner, this cafe-restaurant is a talking point, with its boho-flavoured vibe, green ceiling lit by bare bulbs, beautiful tilework and

DON'T MISS

MONTREUX

This tidy lakeside town boasts Switzerland's most extraordinary castle. Originally constructed on the shores of Lake Geneva in the 11th century, **Château de Chillon** (021 966 89 10; www.chillon.ch; Av de Chillon 21; adult/child Sfr12.50/6; 9am-7pm Apr-Sep, 9.30am-6pm Mar & Oct, 10am-5pm Nov-Feb, last entry 1hr before close) was brought to the world's attention by Lord Byron and the world has been filing past ever since. Spend at least a couple of hours exploring its numerous courtyards, towers, dungeons and halls filled with arms, period furniture and artwork. The castle is a lovely 3km lakefront walk from Montreux. Alternatively, take bus 201 (10 minutes) or a CGN steamer (15 minutes). Crowds throng to the legendary (and not all-jazz) **Montreux Jazz Festival** (www.montreuxjazz.com; late Jun–mid-Jul). Free concerts take place every day (tickets for bigger-name artists cost anything from Sfr60 to Sfr450). There are frequent trains to Lausanne (Sfr13, 20 to 35 minutes) and other lakeside points. Montreux is also a stop on the scenic **GoldenPass** (021 989 81 90; www.goldenpass.ch/en) route into the Bernese Oberland.

vintage-style furniture. Drop by for a coffee, cocktail, gourmet salad or open sandwich. Weekend brunches are worth raving about, with the likes of blueberry pancakes and açaí smoothie bowls.

Information

Lausanne Tourisme (Gare) (021 613 73 73; www.lausanne-tourisme.ch; Pl de la Gare 9; 9am-7pm Jun-Aug, 9am-6pm Sep-May) At the train station.

Lausanne Tourisme (Ouchy) (021 613 73 73; www.lausanne-tourisme.ch; Av de Rhodanie 2; 9am-7pm Apr-Sep, to 6pm Oct-Mar) By the lakeside.

Getting There & Around

Remember to collect your free Lausanne Transport Card for unlimited use of public transport during your stay. For timetables, visit www.t-l.ch.

BOAT

The **CGN** (www.cgn.ch; Quai Jean-Pascal Delamuraz; leisure cruises from Sfr25) runs passenger boats (no car ferries) from Ouchy to destinations around Lake Geneva.

Destinations include Montreux (Sfr27, 1½ hours, up to six daily), Vevey (Sfr21, one hour, up to seven daily), Nyon (Sfr35, 2¼ hours, up to four daily) and Geneva (Sfr45, 3½ to four hours, up to five daily).

TRAIN

You can travel by train to and from Geneva (Sfr22.80, 36 to 50 minutes, up to six hourly), Geneva Airport (Sfr27, 45 to 56 minutes, up to four hourly) and Bern (Sfr34, 65 to 70 minutes, one or two hourly).

FRIBOURG, DREI-SEEN-LAND & THE JURA

Gruyères

POP 2203 / ELEV 830M

Cheese and featherweight meringues drowned in thick cream are what this dreamy village is all about. Named after the emblematic *gru* (crane) brandished by the medieval Counts of Gruyères, it is a riot of 15th- to 17th-century houses tumbling down a hillock. Its heart is cobbled, a castle is its crowning glory and hard AOC Gruyère (the village is Gruyères, but the 's' is dropped for the cheese) has been made for centuries in its surrounding Alpine pastures. Fondue-serving cafes line the main square.

Sights

★ **Château de Gruyères** CASTLE

(026 921 21 02; www.chateau-gruyeres.ch; Rue du Château 8; adult/child Sfr12/4; 9am-6pm Apr-Oct, 10am-5pm Nov-Mar) This bewitching turreted castle, home to 19 different counts of Gruyères, who controlled the Sarine Valley from the 11th to 16th centuries, was rebuilt after a fire in 1493. Inside you can view period furniture, tapestries and modern 'fantasy art', plus watch a 20-minute multimedia film about Gruyères' history. Don't miss the short footpath that weaves its way around the castle. Combined tickets covering the château and other area attractions are available.

La Maison du Gruyère FARM
(☎026 921 84 00; www.lamaisondugruyere.ch; Pl de la Gare 3, Pringy-Gruyères; adult/child Sfr7/6; ⏰9am-6.30pm Jun-Sep, to 6pm Oct-May) The secret behind Gruyère cheese is revealed in Pringy, directly opposite Gruyères train station (1.5km below town). Cheesemaking takes place three to four times daily between 9am and 11am, and 12.30pm and 2.30pm. A combined ticket for the dairy and Château de Gruyères (p620) costs Sfr16 (no child combo).

Eating

★Chez Boudji SWISS $$
(☎026 921 90 50; www.boudji.ch; Gite d'Avau 1, Broc; mains Sfr15-27; ⏰11.30am-2.30pm & 5.30-9pm May-Oct) Visitors love the authenticity of this Swiss mountain chalet with a panoramic terrace overlooking the Alps. Linger there in anticipation of the cheesy goodness you're about to consume. This is stodgy, hearty food: macaroni cheese, fondue, chalet soup and meringue with double cream for dessert! The rich flavour of the local cheese enlivening each simple dish is indescribably enjoyable.

Information

Pop in to see the friendly folks at **La Gruyère Tourisme** (☎084 842 44 24; www.la-gruyere.ch; Rue du Bourg 1; ⏰9.30am-5.30pm Jul & Aug, shorter hours rest of year) if you need clarification on the best way to use your time in this sprawling area.

Getting There & Away

Gruyères can be reached by hourly bus or train from Fribourg (Sfr16.80, 55 minutes, via Bulle) or Montreux (Sfr20.20, 1¼ hours, via Montbovon).

VALAIS

POP 335,700

This is Matterhorn country, an intoxicating land that seduces the toughest of critics with its endless panoramic vistas and breathtaking views. Switzerland's 10 highest mountains rise to the sky here, while snow fiends ski and board in one of Europe's top resorts, Zermatt.

Zermatt

POP 5643 / ELEV 1605M

Since the mid-19th century, Zermatt has starred among Switzerland's glitziest resorts. Today skiers cruise along well-kept pistes, spellbound by the scenery, while style-conscious darlings flash designer threads in the town's swish lounge bars. But all are smitten with the Matterhorn (4478m), an unfathomable monolith you can't quite stop looking at.

Sights & Activities

Zermatt is cruising heaven, with mostly long, scenic red runs, plus a smattering of blues for ski virgins and knuckle-whitening blacks for experts. The main skiing areas in winter are **Rothorn**, **Stockhorn** and **Klein Matterhorn** – 52 lifts and 360km of ski runs in all, with a link from Klein Matterhorn to the Italian resort of Cervinia and a **freestyle park** with a half-pipe for snowboarders. **Summer skiing** (20km of runs) and **boarding** (gravity park at Plateau Rosa on the Theodul glacier) is Europe's most extensive. One-/two-day summer ski passes cost Sfr84/125.

Zermatt is also excellent for **hiking**, with 400km of summer trails through some of the most incredible scenery in the Alps – the tourist office has trail maps. For Matterhorn close-ups, nothing beats the highly dramatic **Matterhorn Glacier Trail** (two hours, 6.5km) from Trockener Steg to Schwarzsee; 23 information panels en route tell you everything you could possibly need to know about glaciers and glacial life.

★Matterhorn Glacier Paradise CABLE CAR
(www.matterhornparadise.ch; Schluhmattstrasse; return adult/child Sfr100/50; ⏰8.30am-4.50pm) Views from Zermatt's cable cars are all remarkable, but the Matterhorn Glacier Paradise is the icing on the cake. Ride the world's highest-altitude 3S cable car to 3883m to gawp at 14 glaciers and 38 mountain peaks over 4000m from the **Panoramic Platform** (good weather only). Don't miss the **Glacier Palace**, an ice palace complete with glittering ice sculptures and an ice slide to swoosh down bum first. Finish with some exhilarating **snow tubing** outside in the snowy surrounds.

★Gornergratbahn RAIL
(www.gornergrat.ch; Bahnhofplatz 7; return adult/child Sfr98/49; ⏰7am-6.24pm) Europe's highest cogwheel railway has been climbing through staggeringly beautiful scenery to **Gornergrat** (3089m) – a 30-minute journey – since 1898. On the way up, sit on the right-hand side of the train to gaze at the Matterhorn. In summer an extra train runs once a week at sunrise and sunset – the most spectacular trips of all.

Sleeping & Eating

Most places close May to mid- (or late) June and again from October to mid-November.

Hotel Bahnhof HOTEL $
(027 967 24 06; www.hotelbahnhof.com; Bahnhofstrasse; dm Sfr35-50, s/d from Sfr80/120; closed May–mid-Jun & mid-Oct–Nov;) Opposite the train station, these budget digs have comfy beds, spotless bathrooms and family-perfect rooms for four. Dorms are cosy and there's a stylish lounge with armchairs to flop in and books to read. There's no breakfast, but feel free to prepare your own in the snazzy, open-plan kitchen. Ski-storage room, lockers and laundry are available.

Snowboat INTERNATIONAL $
(027 967 43 33; www.zermattsnowboat.com; Vispastrasse 20; mains Sfr22-39; 2pm-midnight Mon-Fri, from noon Sat & Sun;) This hybrid eating-drinking riverside address, with deckchairs sprawled across its rooftop sun terrace, is a blessing. When fondue tires, head here for barbecue-sizzled burgers (not just beef, but crab and veggie burgers, too), super-power creative salads (the Omega 3 buster is a favourite) and great cocktails. The vibe? Completely friendly, fun and funky.

★**Chez Vrony** SWISS $$
(027 967 25 52; www.chezvrony.ch; Findeln; breakfast Sfr15-28, mains Sfr25-45; 9.15am-5pm Dec-Apr & mid-Jun–mid-Oct) Ride the *Sunnegga Express* funicular to 2288m, then ski down or summer-hike 15 minutes to Zermatt's tastiest slope-side address in the Findeln hamlet. Delicious dried meats, homemade cheese and sausage come from Vrony's own cows, grazing away the summer on the high Alpine pastures (2100m) surrounding it, and the Vrony burger is legendary. Advance reservations essential in winter.

Information

The **tourist office** (027 966 81 00; www.zermatt.ch; Bahnhofplatz 5; 8.30am-8pm;) has a wealth of information, plus iPads to surf on and free wi-fi.

Getting There & Away

CAR

Zermatt is car-free. Motorists have to park in the **Matterhorn Terminal Täsch** (027 967 12 14; www.matterhornterminal.ch; Täsch; per 24hr Sfr15.50) and ride the Zermatt Shuttle train (return adult/child Sfr16.40/8.20, 12 minutes, every 20 minutes from 6am to 9.40pm).

TRAIN

Direct trains to Zermatt depart hourly from Brig (Sfr38, 1½ hours), stopping at Visp en route. Zermatt is also the start/end point of the **Glacier Express** (www.glacierexpress.ch; adult/child one way St Moritz-Zermatt Sfr153/76.50, obligatory seat reservation summer/winter Sfr33/13; 3 trains daily May-Oct, 1 daily mid-Dec–Feb) to/from St Moritz.

BERN

POP 142,479 / ELEV 540M

One of the planet's most underrated capitals, Bern is a fabulous find. With the genteel old soul of a Renaissance man and the heart of a high-flying 21st-century gal, the riverside city is both medieval and modern. The 15th-century Old Town is gorgeous enough to sweep you off your feet and make you forget the century (it's definitely worthy of its 1983 Unesco World Heritage Site status).

Sights & Activities

Bern's flag-bedecked **medieval centre** is an attraction in its own right, with 6km of covered arcades and cellar shops and bars descending from the streets. After a devastating fire in 1405, the wooden city was rebuilt in today's sandstone. The city's 11 **decorative fountains** (1545) depict historical and folkloric characters. Most are along Marktgasse as it becomes Kramgasse and Gerechtigkeitsgasse, but the most famous lies in Kornhausplatz: the **Kindlifresserbrunnen** (Ogre Fountain) of a giant snacking...on children.

★**Zentrum Paul Klee** MUSEUM
(031 359 01 01; www.zpk.org; Monument im Fruchtland 3; adult/child Sfr20/7; 10am-5pm Tue-Sun) Bern's answer to the Guggenheim, Renzo Piano's architecturally bold, 150m-long wave-like edifice houses an exhibition space that showcases rotating works from Paul Klee's prodigious and often playful career. Interactive computer displays and audioguides help interpret the Swiss-born artist's work. Next door, the fun-packed **Kindermuseum Creaviva** (031 359 01 61; www.creaviva-zpk.org) FREE lets kids experiment with hands-on art exhibits or create original artwork with the atelier's materials during the weekend program **Five Franc Studio** Sfr5; 10am-4.30pm Sat & Sun;). Bus 12 runs from Bubenbergplatz direct to the museum.

SWITZERLAND'S SCENIC TRAINS

Swiss trains, buses and boats are more than a means of getting from A to B. Stunning views invariably make the journey itself the destination. Switzerland boasts the following routes among its classic sightseeing journeys. You're able to choose just one leg of the trip. Also, scheduled services often ply the same routes for standard fares; these are cheaper than the named trains, which often have cars with extra-large windows and require reservations.

Bernina Express (www.rhb.ch) This unforgettable four-hour train ride cuts 145km through the Engadine's glaciated realms, linking Chur, St Moritz and Tirano, Italy. Between May and October, continue for 2½ hours by bus from Tirano to Lugano along Italy's Lake Como and Ticino's palm-fringed Lake Lugano.

Centovalli Express (www.centovalli.ch) An underappreciated gem of a line (two hours) that snakes along fantastic river gorges in Switzerland and Italy, from Locarno to Domodossola. Trains run through the day and it is easy to connect to Brig and beyond from Domodossola in Italy.

Glacier Express (www.glacierexpress.ch) Hop aboard this red train with floor-to-ceiling windows for the famous eight-hour journey between St Moritz and Zermatt. Scenic highlights include the climb through Alpine meadows to Oberalp Pass (2033m) – the journey's high point between Disentis/Mustér and Andermatt – and the crossing of the iconic 65m-high Landwasser Viaduct between St Moritz and Chur.

GoldenPass Line (www.goldenpass.ch) Travels between Lucerne and Montreux. The journey is in three legs, and you must change trains twice. Regular trains, without panoramic windows, work the whole route hourly.

Jungfrau Region (www.jungfrau.ch) You can spend days ogling stunning Alpine scenery from the trains, cable cars and more here.

Zytglogge TOWER

(Marktgasse) Bern's most famous Old Town sight, this ornate clock tower once formed part of the city's western gate (1191–1256). Crowds congregate to watch its revolving figures twirl at four minutes before the hour, after which the chimes begin. Tours enter the tower to see the clock mechanism from May to October; contact the tourist office for details. The clock tower supposedly helped Albert Einstein hone his special theory of relativity, developed while working as a patent clerk in Bern.

Münster CATHEDRAL

(www.bernermuenster.ch; Münsterplatz 1; tower adult/child Sfr5/2; ⏲10am-5pm Mon-Sat, 11.30am-5pm Sun Apr–mid-Oct, noon-4pm Mon-Fri, 10am-5pm Sat, 11.30am 4pm Sun mid-Oct–Mar) Bern's 15th-century Gothic cathedral boasts Switzerland's loftiest spire (100m); climb the 344-step spiral staircase for vertiginous views. Coming down, stop by the **Upper Bells** (1356), rung at 11am, noon and 3pm daily, and the three 10-tonne **Lower Bells** (Switzerland's largest). Don't miss the main portal's **Last Judgement**, which portrays Bern's mayor going to heaven, while his Zürich counterpart is shown into hell. Afterwards wander through the adjacent **Münsterplattform**, a bijou clifftop park with a sunny pavilion cafe.

Aare Tubing WATER SPORTS

(www.aaretubing.ch; ⏲Apr-Sep; 🚸) Urban swimming has become a big thing in Switzerland, and Bern is certainly in on the act. For even more action on the Aare River, this company will sort you out with tubes, inflatable rafts or stand-up paddleboards. Life jackets and safety instructions (phew!) are included. Visit the website for more details on locations, prices and bookings.

Sleeping & Eating

Am Pavillon B&B $

(☎079 198 62 83; www.ampavillon.ch; Pavillonweg 1a; s Sfr100-110, d Sfr150-180; 📶) An appealing conversion of a late-19th-century town house, this B&B is just a couple of minutes' stroll from the Hauptbahnhof. The rooms have plenty of original art nouveau charm (high ceilings, parquet floors and the like), and a palette of modern, neutral colours. Breakfast is served on the garden terrace when warm weather permits.

Hotel Landhaus HOTEL $

(☎031 348 03 05; www.landhausbern.ch; Altenbergstrasse 4; dm/s/d from Sfr38/90/130; P📶) Fronted by the river and Old Town spires, this well-run boho hotel offers a mix of stylish six-bed dorms, family rooms and doubles.

Its buzzing ground-floor cafe and terrace attracts a cheery crowd. Breakfast (included with private rooms) costs Sfr12 extra for dorm-dwellers.

★Kornhauskeller MEDITERRANEAN $$
(031 327 72 72; www.bindella.ch; Kornhausplatz 18; mains Sfr24-58; noon-2.30pm & 6pm-12.30am;) Fine dining takes place beneath vaulted frescoed arches at Bern's ornate former granary, now a stunning cellar restaurant serving Mediterranean cuisine. Beautiful people sip cocktails alongside historic stained-glass windows on the mezzanine, while in its neighbouring cafe, punters lunch in the sun on the busy pavement terrace. Children's menus are available.

Information

The **Bern Tourismus** (031 328 12 12; www.bern.com; Bahnhoftplatz 10a; 9am-7pm Mon-Sat, to 6pm Sun;) office at the train station is fully stocked with all you need to know about the capital. There's also a **branch** (031 328 12 12; www.bern.com; Grosser Muristalden 6, Bärengraben; 9am-6pm Jun-Sep, 10am-4pm Mar-May & Oct, 11am-4pm Nov-Feb) near the bear park.

Getting There & Around

Frequent trains connect to most Swiss cities, including Geneva (Sfr51, 13/4 hours), Basel (Sfr41, 55 minutes) and Zürich (Sfr51, 55 minutes to 11/2 hours).

Buses and trams are operated by BernMobil (www.bernmobil.ch); many depart from stops near Bahnhofplatz.

CENTRAL SWITZERLAND

POP 718,400

To the Swiss, Central Switzerland – green, mountainous and soothingly beautiful – is the essence of 'Swissness'. It was here that the pact that kick-started a nation was signed in 1291, and here that hero William Tell gave a rebel yell against Habsburg rule. Geographically, politically and spiritually, this is the heartland. Nowhere does the flag fly higher.

Lucerne

POP 81,592 / ELEV 435M

Recipe for a gorgeous Swiss city: take a cobalt lake ringed by mountains of myth, add a medieval Old Town and sprinkle with covered bridges, sunny plazas, candy-coloured houses and waterfront promenades. Bright, beautiful Lucerne has been Little Miss Popular since the likes of Goethe, Queen Victoria and Wagner savoured her views in the 19th century.

Sights & Activities

Your first port of call should be the medieval **Old Town**, with its ancient rampart walls and towers. Wander the cobblestone lanes and squares, pondering 15th-century buildings with painted facades and the two much-photographed covered bridges over the Reuss.

★Sammlung Rosengart MUSEUM
(041 220 16 60; www.rosengart.ch; Pilatusstrasse 10; adult/child Sfr18/10; 10am-6pm) Lucerne's blockbuster cultural attraction is the Sammlung Rosengart, occupying a graceful neoclassical pile in the heart of town. It showcases the outstanding stash of Angela Rosengart, a Swiss art dealer and close friend of Picasso. Alongside works by the great Spanish master are paintings and sketches by Klee, Cézanne, Renoir, Chagall, Kandinsky, Miró, Matisse, Modigliani and Monet, among others. Complementing this collection are some 200 photographs by David Douglas Duncan documenting the last 17 years of Picasso's life.

★Kapellbrücke BRIDGE
(Chapel Bridge) You haven't really been to Lucerne until you have strolled the creaky 14th-century Kapellbrücke, spanning the Reuss River in the Old Town. The octagonal water tower is original, but its gabled roof is a modern reconstruction, rebuilt after a disastrous fire in 1993. As you cross the bridge, note Heinrich Wägmann's 17th-century triangular roof panels, showing important events from Swiss history and mythology. The icon is at its most photogenic when bathed in soft golden light at dusk.

Lion Monument MONUMENT
(Löwendenkmal; Denkmalstrasse) By far the most touching of the 19th-century sights that lured so many British to Lucerne is the Lion Monument. Lukas Ahorn carved this 10m-long sculpture of a dying lion into the rock face in 1820 to commemorate Swiss soldiers who died defending King Louis XVI during the French Revolution. For *Narnia* fans, it often evokes Aslan at the stone table.

Verkehrshaus MUSEUM
(Swiss Museum of Transport; 0900 333 456; www.verkehrshaus.ch; Lidostrasse 5; adult/child

Sfr32/12; ⏲10am-6pm Apr-Oct, to 5pm Nov-Mar; 👪) A great kid-pleaser, the fascinating interactive Verkehrshaus is deservedly Switzerland's most popular museum. Alongside rockets, steam locomotives, aeroplanes, vintage cars and dugout canoes are hands-on activities, such as pedalo boats, flight simulators, broadcasting studios and a walkable 1:20,000-scale map of Switzerland.

The museum also shelters a **planetarium** (www.verkehrshaus.ch/en/planetarium; adult/child Sfr16/7; ⏲hours vary), Switzerland's largest **3D cinema** (www.filmtheater.ch; evening film adult/child Sfr19/8) and the **Swiss Chocolate Adventure** (www.verkehrshaus.ch/en/swiss-chocolate-adventure; adult/child Sfr16/7), a 20-minute ride that whirls visitors through multimedia exhibits on the origins, history, production and distribution of chocolate, from Ghana to Switzerland and beyond.

Sleeping

★ The Bed & Breakfast B&B $

(☎041 310 15 14; www.thebandb.ch; Taubenhausstrasse 34; s Sfr85-130, d Sfr120-130, tr Sfr165-180, q Sfr200-220; P 📶) This friendly B&B feels like home – with stylish, contemporary rooms, crisp white bedding and scatter cushions. Unwind in the garden or with a soak in the old-fashioned tub. Book ahead for the room under the eaves with private bathroom; all others share facilities. Take bus 1 to Eichhof or walk 15 minutes from the train station.

Backpackers Lucerne HOSTEL $

(☎041 360 04 20; www.backpackerslucerne.ch; Alpenquai 42; dm Sfr30-35, d Sfr72-90, tr Sfr99-117; ⏲reception 7.30-10am & 4-11pm; 📶) Just opposite the lake, a 15-minute walk southeast of Lucerne's train station, this is a soulful place to crash, with art-slung walls, bubbly staff and immaculate dorms with balconies. There's no breakfast, but guests have access to a well-equipped kitchen. Blades and mountain bikes for rent.

Hotel des Balances HOTEL $$

(☎041 418 28 28; www.balances.ch; Weinmarkt 4; s/d/ste from Sfr150/220/305; P 📶) Behind its elaborately frescoed facade, this perfectly positioned Old Town hotel flaunts a light and airy design ethos, with ice-white rooms, gilt mirrors and parquet floors. Suites have river-facing balconies. For the singles and doubles, expect to pay more for river-facing rooms. Breakfast is an additional Sfr35 per person.

Eating & Drinking

★ Zur Werkstatt INTERNATIONAL $$

(☎041 979 03 03; www.zurwerkstatt.ch; Waldstätterstrasse 18; lunch/dinner menus Sfr25/58; ⏲11.30am-1.30pm & 5pm-midnight Mon-Fri, 10am-2pm & 5pm-midnight Sat; 🌿👪) This funky, post-industrial, monochrome-toned restaurant revolves around a show kitchen and hip cocktail bar. Menus are kept simple (go meaty or veggie), but the food is anything but, singing of the seasons in dishes from mozzarella with wild asparagus and pomegranate to hand-cut steak tartare with crispy marrow and pumpkin chutney. It's popular – book ahead.

Wirtshaus Galliker SWISS $$

(☎041 240 10 02; Schützenstrasse 1; mains Sfr27-49; ⏲9.30am-midnight Tue-Sat) Passionately run by the Galliker family for over four generations, this old-style, wood-panelled tavern attracts a lively bunch of regulars. Motherly waitresses dish up Lucerne soul food – rösti, *Chögalipaschtetli* (veal pastry pie) and the like – that is batten-the-hatches filling.

Rathaus Bräuerei BREWERY

(☎041 410 61 11; www.rathausbrauerei.ch; Unter der Egg 2; ⏲9am-midnight Mon-Sat, to 11pm Sun) Sip home-brewed beer under the vaulted arches of this buzzy tavern near Kapellbrücke, or nab a pavement table and watch the river flow. You know this place is good as it's positively brimming with locals.

Information

Stamped by your hotel, the free **Lake Lucerne Region Visitors Card** entitles you to discounts on various museums, sporting facilities, cable cars and lake cruises.

Tourist Office (☎041 227 17 17; www.luzern.com; Zentralstrasse 5; ⏲8.30am-7pm Mon-Fri, 9am-7pm Sat, 9am-5pm Sun May-Oct, shorter hours Nov-Apr) Reached from Zentralstrasse or platform 3 of the Hauptbahnhof. Book day excursions around Lake Lucerne here.

Getting There & Around

Frequent trains connect Lucerne to Interlaken Ost (Sfr33, 1¾ hours), Bern (Sfr39, one to 1½ hours), Lugano (Sfr61, two hours) and Zürich (Sfr25, 45 minutes to one hour).

SNG (☎041 368 08 08; www.sng.ch; Alpenquai 11; pedalo/motorboat/pontoon boat per hour from Sfr30/60/90) operates extensive boat services on Lake Lucerne (including some paddle steamers). Rail passes are good for free or discounted travel.

BERNESE OBERLAND

POP 207,652

In the Bernese Oberland, nature works on an epic scale. Fittingly watched over by Mönch (Monk), Jungfrau (Virgin) and Eiger (Ogre), the Swiss Alps don't get more in-your-face beautiful than this.

Interlaken

POP 5673 / ELEV 570M

Once Interlaken made the Victorians swoon with mountain vistas from the chandelier-lit confines of grand hotels; today it makes daredevils scream with adrenaline-loaded activities. Straddling the glacier-fed Lakes Thun and Brienz and capped by the pearly white peaks of Eiger, Mönch and Jungfrau, the town is the gateway to Switzerland's fabled Jungfrau region and the country's hottest adventure destination bar none.

 Activities

Switzerland is the world's second-biggest adventure-sports centre and Interlaken is its busiest hub. Some sample prices for these activities: around Sfr120 to Sfr170 for rafting or canyoning; Sfr140 for hydrospeeding; Sfr130 to Sfr180 for bungee or canyon jumping; Sfr170 for tandem paragliding; Sfr180 for ice climbing; Sfr220 for hang-gliding; and Sfr400 to Sfr450 for skydiving.

A good one-stop shop is **Outdoor Interlaken** (☎033 826 77 19; www.outdoor-interlaken.ch; Hauptstrasse 15; ⏲8am-7pm).

Harder Kulm MOUNTAIN
(www.jungfrau.ch/harderkulm; adult/child Sfr32/16) For far-reaching views to the 4000m giants, take the eight-minute funicular ride to 1322m Harder Kulm. Many hiking paths begin here, and the vertigo-free can enjoy the panorama from the Zweiseensteg (Two Lake Bridge) jutting out above the valley. The wildlife park near the valley station is home to Alpine critters, including marmots and ibex.

Sleeping & Eating

Backpackers Villa Sonnenhof HOSTEL $
(☎033 826 71 71; www.villa.ch; Alpenstrasse 16; dm Sfr43-49; P 📶) Repeatedly voted one of Europe's best hostels, Sonnenhof is a slick, eco-friendly combination of ultramodern chalet and elegant art nouveau villa. Dorms are immaculate, and some have balconies with Jungfrau views. There's also a relaxed lounge, a well-equipped kitchen, a kids' playroom and a vast backyard for mountain gazing. Special family rates are available. Breakfast is included.

Hotel Alphorn HOTEL $$
(☎033 822 30 51; www.hotel-alphorn.ch; Rothornstrasse 29a; s Sfr140-160, d Sfr160-180, tr Sfr225-240; P 📶) Super-central yet peaceful, the Alphorn is a five-minute toddle from Interlaken West station. Decorated in cool blues and whites, the rooms are spotlessly clean, but you'll need to fork out an extra Sfr10 for a balcony.

The Barrel CAFE $
(www.craft-cafe.ch; Postgasse 10; snacks & light meals Sfr7.50-19.50; ⏲noon-10pm Wed-Sat) Swiftly becoming one of Interlaken's preferred haunts, this easygoing cafe makes a fine pit stop for coffee with homemade cake, lunch or a craft beer (there are some great ones on tap). They whip up good salads, burgers, quiches and sandwiches using locally sourced ingredients.

Information

Tourist Office (☎033 826 53 00; www.interlakentourism.ch; Marktgasse 1; ⏲8am-7pm Mon-Fri, to 5pm Sat, 10am-5pm Sun Jul & Aug, shorter hours Sep-Jun) Right in the centre of things, Interlaken's tourist office has stacks of information on the town and surrounds. It also has a booking service.

Getting There & Away

There are two train stations: Interlaken West and Interlaken Ost.

Trains to Lucerne (Sfr33, 1¾ to two hours), Brig (Sfr46, 1¼ hours) and Montreux (Sfr74, 2¼ to 2¾ hours, via Spiez/Visp or Bern/Lausanne) depart frequently from Interlaken Ost train station.

Many trains up to mountain resorts begin in Lauterbrunnen (Sfr7.60, 20 minutes).

Grindelwald

POP 3818 / ELEV 1034M

Grindelwald's charms were discovered by skiers and hikers in the late 19th century, making it one of Switzerland's oldest resorts and the Jungfrau's largest. It has lost none of its appeal over the decades, with archetypal Alpine chalets and verdant pastures set against the chiselled features of the Eiger north face.

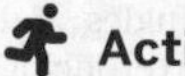

Stretching from Oberjoch at 2486m right down to the village, the region of First presents a fine mix of cruisey red and challenging black ski runs, plus 15.5km of well-groomed cross-country ski trails.

In summer, Grindelwald is outstanding hiking territory, with high-altitude trails commanding arresting views to massive mountain faces, crevassed glaciers and snowcapped peaks.

★Kleine Scheidegg Walk HIKING

One of the region's most stunning day hikes is the 15km trek from Grindelwald Grund to Wengen via Kleine Scheidegg, which heads up through wildflower-freckled meadows to skirt below the Eiger's north face and reach Kleine Scheidegg, granting arresting views of the 'Big Three': Eiger (3970m), Mönch (4107m) and Jungfrau (4158m). Allow around 5½ to six hours.

Grindelwald Sports ADVENTURE SPORTS

(☎033 854 12 80; www.grindelwaldsports.ch; Dorfstrasse 103; ⏲8.30am-7pm) Opposite the tourist office, this outfit arranges guided mountain climbing, glacier hikes, *vie ferrate* (protected climbing routes) and Alpine treks, plus ski and snowboard instruction in winter, and the heart-stopping canyon swing, a terrifying freefall at 120km/h between the canyon walls. It also houses a cosy cafe and sells walking guides.

Sleeping & Eating

Mountain Hostel HOSTEL $

(☎033 854 38 38; www.mountainhostel.ch; Grundstrasse 58; dm Sfr42-47, d Sfr90-110, q Sfr168-208; P 📶) In a bright-blue building halfway between Grindelwald Grund train station and the Männlichen cable-car station, this is an ideal base for sports junkies, with well-kept dorms and a helpful crew. There's a beer garden, ski storage, TV lounge and mountain-bike and e-bike rental. Breakfast (included in rates) comes with locally sourced cheese, yoghurt, bread and honey.

Hotel Glacier BOUTIQUE HOTEL $$

(☎033 853 10 04; www.hotel-glacier.ch; Endweg 55; d sfr280-450; P 📶) With astonishing views of the Eiger, this chic boutique hotel pays homage to its past as humble lodgings for the men who once harvested the ice from Grindelwald's glacier, with black-and-white photos, icicle lights and mountain murals. Retro-modern rooms in cool grey and blue tones come with hardwood floors, Marshall radios and Coco-Mat beds. The restaurant serves imaginative, region-driven food.

★Cafe 3692 CAFE $$

(☎033 853 16 54; www.cafe3692.ch; Terrassenweg 61; snacks & light meals Sfr7-25, mains Sfr35-38; ⏲8.30am-6pm Sun-Tue, to midnight Fri & Sat) Run by dream duo Myriam and Bruno, Cafe 3692 is a delight. Bruno is a talented carpenter and has let his imagination run riot – a gnarled apple tree is an eye-catching artwork, a mine-cart trolley cleverly transforms into a grill, and the ceiling is a wave of woodwork. Garden herbs and Grindelwald-sourced ingredients are knocked up into tasty specials.

Getting There & Away

There are frequent train connections to Interlaken (Sfr11.20, 34 minutes) and Lauterbrunnen via Zweilütschinen (Sfr9, 36 minutes).

Wengen

POP 1292 / ELEV 1274M

Photogenically poised on a mountain ledge, Wengen has celestial views of the glacier-capped giant peaks' silent majesty as well as the shimmering waterfalls spilling into the Lauterbrunnen Valley below.

The village is car-free and can only be reached by train. It's a fabulous hub for **hiking** for much of the year as well as **skiing** in winter.

From Wengen's train station, loop back under the tracks and head three minutes downhill to **Hotel Bären** (☎033 855 14 19; www.baeren-wengen.ch; s Sfr190-230, d Sfr220-390, f Sfr390-490, all incl half-board; 📶), a snug log chalet with bright, cosy rooms; the affable Brunner family serves a hearty breakfast and delicious seasonal cuisine in the attached restaurant. For superb regional fare in an even dreamier setting, check out the leafy mountain-facing terrace or the pine-clad, candlelit dining room at **Restaurant 1903** (☎033 855 34 22; www.hotel-schoenegg.ch; mains Sfr28-54; ⏲6.30-10pm, closed May & mid-Oct–mid-Dec), a 250m walk uphill from the station.

The highlight of Wengen's calendar is the world-famous **Lauberhorn** (www.lauberhorn.ch; ⏲mid-Jan) downhill ski race, where pros reach speeds of up to 160km/h.

Jungfraujoch

Jungfraujoch (3471m) is a once-in-a-lifetime trip and there's good reason why two million people a year visit Europe's highest train station. Clear good weather is essential; check www.jungfrau.ch for current conditions, and don't forget warm clothing, sunglasses and sunscreen.

From Interlaken Ost, the journey time is 2¼ to 2½ hours each way and the return fare is Sfr210.80. The last train back from Jungfraujoch leaves at 6.43pm in summer and 4.43pm in winter. From early May to late October you can qualify for a discounted Good Morning Ticket (Sfr145) by taking one of the first two trains from Interlaken Ost (6.35am or 7.05am) and boarding a return train from the summit no later than 1.13pm.

Gimmelwald

POP 101 / ELEV 1367M

Decades ago some anonymous backpacker scribbled these words in the guestbook at the Mountain Hostel: 'If heaven isn't what it's cracked up to be, send me back to Gimmelwald'. Enough said. When the sun is out in Gimmelwald, this pipsqueak of a village will simply take your breath away. Sit outside and listen to the distant roar of avalanches on the sheer mountain faces arrayed before you.

The charming **Esther's Guest House** (☎033 855 54 88; www.esthersguesthouse.ch; Kirchstatt; s Sfr60-90, d Sfr120-180, tr Sfr180, q Sfr200, apt Sfr240-250;) is run with love by Uri and his wife Dana, who extend a warm welcome and pay attention to guests' comfort.

Mürren

POP 418 / ELEV 1650M

Arrive on a clear evening when the sun hangs low on the horizon, and you'll think you've died and gone to heaven. Car-free Mürren is storybook Switzerland.

From the top station of Allmendhubel funicular, you can set out on many walks, including the spectacular **North Face Trail** (1½ hours), via Schiltalp, with big views to the glaciers and waterfalls of the Lauterbrunnen Valley and the monstrous Eiger north face. To up the challenge, try the head-spinning **Klettersteig** (☎033 856 86 86, tour bookings 033 854 12 80; www.klettersteig-muerren.ch; mid-Jun–Oct) *via ferrata*.

Sleeping options near the train station include **Eiger Guesthouse** (☎033 856 54 60; www.eigerguesthouse.com; s Sfr60-170, d Sfr130-200, q Sfr180-210;), with its downstairs pub serving tasty food, and **Hotel Eiger** (☎033 856 54 54; www.hoteleiger.com; s Sfr183-270, d Sfr280-435, ste Sfr410-715;), a huge wooden chalet with swimming pool and ravishing views.

Schilthorn

There's a tremendous 360-degree, 200-peak panorama from the 2970m Schilthorn, best appreciated from the Skyline view platform or Piz Gloria revolving restaurant. On a clear day, you can see from Titlis around to Mont Blanc, and across to the German Black Forest.

Note that this was the site of Blofeld's HQ in the 1969 James Bond film *On Her Majesty's Secret Service,* as explained at the interactive **Bond World 007** (www.schilthorn.ch; Schilthorn; free with cable-car ticket; 8am-6pm). The Skyline Walk is a glass-and-steel platform dangling over a precipice, providing dizzying perspectives of the snow-dusted Jungfrau massif.

From Interlaken, the grand round-trip excursion to Schilthorn costs Sfr131.40 and goes via Lauterbrunnen, Grütschalp and Mürren, returning via Stechelberg to Interlaken. Ask about discounts for early-morning trips.

CANTON OF ZÜRICH

Naturally, the lakeside city of Zürich is the canton's centre of attention, but within half an hour of the city you can try out walking trails or mountain-bike routes in the heights of 871m Uetliberg, or explore castle-topped Rapperswil and the cutting-edge galleries of Winterthur, something of a cultural hot spot.

Zürich

POP 409,241

Culturally vibrant, efficiently run and attractively set at the meeting of river and lake, Zürich is regularly recognised as one of the world's most liveable cities. Long known as a savvy, hard-working financial centre, Switzerland's largest and wealthiest metropolis has also emerged in the 21st century as one of central Europe's hippest destinations, with an artsy, post-industrial edge that is epitomised in its exuberant summer **Street Parade**.

Sights & Activities

The cobbled streets of the pedestrian Old Town line both sides of the river, while the bank vaults beneath Bahnhofstrasse, the city's most elegant shopping street, are said to be crammed with gold. On Sunday, seemingly all of Zürich strolls around the lake – on a clear day you'll glimpse the Alps in the distance.

★Fraumünster CHURCH
(www.fraumuenster.ch/en; Stadthausquai 19; Sfr5 incl audioguide; 10am-6pm Mar-Oct, to 5pm Nov-Feb; 6, 7, 10, 11, 14 to Paradeplatz) This 13th-century church is renowned for its stunning stained-glass windows, designed by the Russian-Jewish master Marc Chagall (1887–1985), who executed the series of five windows in the choir stalls in 1971 and the rose window in the southern transept in 1978. The rose window in the northern transept was created by Augusto Giacometti in 1945.

★Kunsthaus MUSEUM
(044 253 84 84; www.kunsthaus.ch; Heimplatz 1; adult/child Sfr16/free, Wed free; 10am-6pm Tue & Fri-Sun, to 8pm Wed & Thu; 5, 8, 9, 10 to Kunsthaus) Zürich's impressive fine-arts gallery boasts a rich collection of largely European art. It stretches from the Middle Ages through a mix of Old Masters to Alberto Giacometti stick figures, Monet and van Gogh masterpieces, Rodin sculptures, and other 19th- and 20th-century art. It also hosts rotating exhibitions of the highest calibre.

Schweizerisches Landesmuseum MUSEUM
(Swiss National Museum; 058 466 65 11; www.nationalmuseum.ch/e/zuerich; Museumstrasse 2; adult/child Sfr10/free; 10am-5pm Tue, Wed & Fri-Sun, to 7pm Thu; Zürich Hauptbahnhof, Zürich Hauptbahnhof) Inside a purpose-built cross between a mansion and a castle sprawls this eclectic and imaginatively presented museum. The permanent collection offers an extensive romp through Swiss history, with exhibits ranging from elaborately carved and painted sleds to domestic and religious artefacts, via a series of reconstructed historical rooms spanning six centuries. In 2016 the museum celebrated a major expansion with the opening of its archaeology section in a brand-new wing.

Lindenhof SQUARE
(4, 6, 7, 10, 11, 13, 14, 15, 17 to Rennweg) Spectacular views across the Limmat to the Grossmünster can be enjoyed from a tree-shaded hilltop park, smack in the heart of the Old Town. Bring a picnic and watch the *boules* players while you eat.

Seebad Utoquai SWIMMING
(044 251 61 51; www.bad-utoquai.ch; Utoquai 49; adult/child Sfr8/4; 7am-8pm mid-May–late Sep; 2, 4, 10, 11, 14, 15 to Kreuzstrasse) Just north of leafy Zürichhorn park, 400m south of Bellevueplatz, this is the most popular bathing pavilion on the Zürichsee's eastern shore.

Sleeping

SYHA Hostel HOSTEL $
(043 399 78 00; www.youthhostel.ch; Mutschellenstrasse 114; dm Sfr40.50, s Sfr82-118, d Sfr92-139; @; 7 to Morgental, S S8, S24 to Wollishofen) A pink 1960s landmark houses this busy, institutional hostel with 24-hour reception, dining hall, sparkling modern bathrooms and dependable wi-fi in the downstairs lounge. The included breakfast features miso soup and rice alongside all the Swiss standards. It's about 20 minutes south of the Hauptbahnhof.

LADYs FIRST HOTEL $$
(044 380 80 10; www.ladysfirst.ch; Mainaustrasse 24; d Sfr205-365, ste Sfr305-435; ; 2, 4, 10, 11, 14, 15 to Feldeggstrasse) Ladies come first here, as the name suggests, but gents are also welcome at this eco-aware, socially responsible hotel, housed in an art nouveau town house near the opera house and lake, though the spa and roof terrace are open to women only. The immaculate, generally spacious rooms abound in aesthetic touches such as traditional parquet flooring and designer furnishings.

Townhouse BOUTIQUE HOTEL $$
(044 200 95 95; www.townhouse.ch; Schützengasse 7; s Sfr195-365, d Sfr225-395, ste Sfr315-425; ; Zürich Hauptbahnhof, Zürich Hauptbahnhof) With a cracking location only steps from the train station and the shops of Bahnhofstrasse, this stylish five-storey hotel offers friendly service and a host of welcoming touches. The 26 rooms come in an assortment of sizes (from 15 to 35 sq metres), with luxurious wallpaper, wall hangings, parquet floors, retro furniture, DVD players and iPod docking stations.

★Hotel Widder BOUTIQUE HOTEL $$$
(044 224 25 26; www.widderhotel.ch; Rennweg 7; d/ste from Sfr470/870; P@; 4, 6, 7, 10, 11, 13, 14, 15, 17 to Rennweg) A supremely stylish boutique hotel in the equally grand district of Augustiner, the Widder is a pleasing fusion of five-star luxury and 12th-century charm. Rooms and public areas across the eight individually decorated town houses that make up this place are stuffed with designer furniture, art and original features – from oak beams to antique stoves and murals.

Eating

Traditional local cuisine is very rich, as epitomised by the city's signature dish, *Zürcher*

Zürich

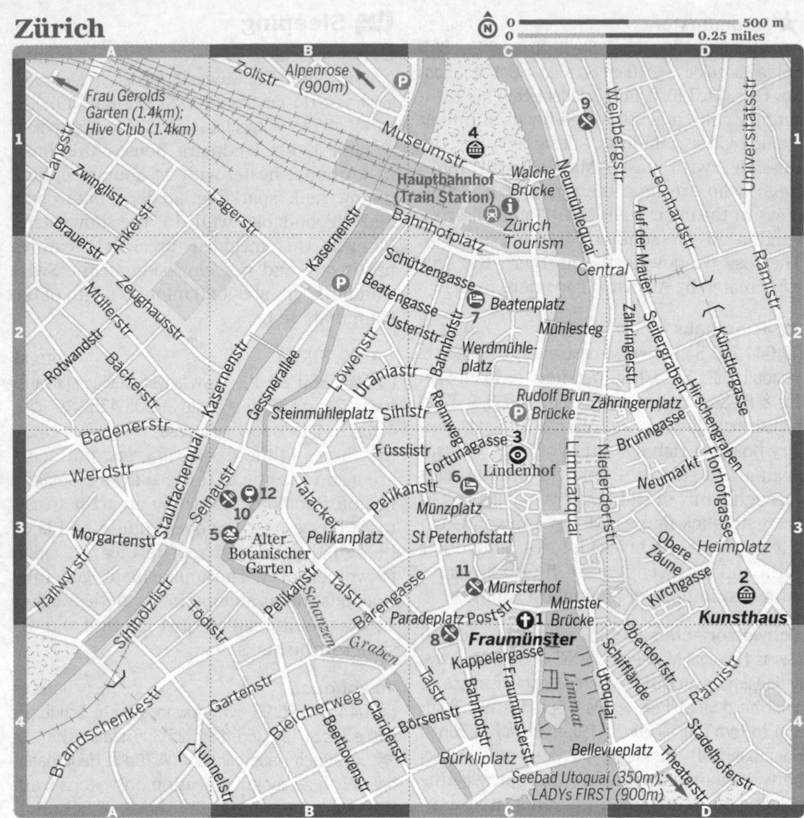

Geschnetzeltes (sliced veal in a creamy mushroom and white wine sauce).

★Kraftwerk INTERNATIONAL **$**

(☎079 817 07 03; www.kraftwerk.coffee; Selnaustrasse 25; sharing plates Sfr29-65, lunch specials Sfr15-16.50; ⊙8am-10pm Mon-Wed, to midnight Thu & Fri; 🚊2, 9 to Sihlstrasse) This born-again *kraftwerk* (power station) now pumps out excellent locally roasted coffee, delicious meze and lunch specials in uberhip industrial surrounds. Vintage furniture is scattered around the high-ceilinged, crate-lined hall, where you can nibble on season-driven bites from aubergine caviar to spinach with smoked mozzarella, and fennel salad with hazelnuts and orange. The vibe is sociable and the service clued up.

Café Sprüngli SWEETS **$**

(☎044 224 46 46; www.spruengli.ch; Bahnhofstrasse 21; sweets Sfr8-16; ⊙7.30am-6.30pm Mon-Fri, 8am-6pm Sat, 9.30am-5.30pm Sun; 🚊4, 6, 7, 10, 11, 13, 14, 15, 17 to Paradeplatz) Sit down for cakes, chocolate, ice cream and exquisite coffee drinks at this epicentre of sweet Switzerland, in business since 1836. You can have a light lunch too, but whatever you do, don't fail to check out its heavenly chocolate shop, where you can buy delectable pralines and truffles, plus the house speciality – rainbow-bright Luxemburgerli macarons – to take home.

★Didi's Frieden SWISS **$$**

(☎044 253 18 10; www.didisfrieden.ch; Stampfenbachstrasse 32; 4-/5-course menu Sfr98/108, mains Sfr24-49; ⊙11am-2.30pm & 5pm-midnight Mon-Fri, 6pm-midnight Sat; 🚊7, 11, 14, 17 to Stampfenbachplatz) With its unique blend of familiarity and refinement, Didi's Frieden features among Zürich's top tables. The look is understated elegance, with wood floors, white tablecloths and wine-glass chandeliers. Service is discreet yet attentive, while menus sing of the seasons in dishes like venison steak with wild mushrooms and red wine-shallot jus – big on integral flavours and presented with panache.

Zürich

Top Sights

Sights

Activities, Courses & Tours

Sleeping

Eating

Drinking & Nightlife

Alpenrose SWISS **$$**

(☎044 431 11 66; www.restaurantalpenrose.ch; Fabrikstrasse 12; mains Sfr24-38; ⏰9am-11.30pm Tue-Fri, from 5pm Sat & Sun; 🚋3, 4, 6, 10, 11, 13, 15, 17 to Quellenstrasse) With its tall, stencilled windows, warm wood panelling and stucco ceiling ornamentation, the Alpenrose exudes cosy Old World charm, and the cuisine here lives up to the promise. Hearty Swiss classics, such as herb-stuffed trout with homemade *Spätzli* (egg noodles) and buttered carrots, are exquisitely prepared and presented, and accompanied by a good wine list and a nice selection of desserts.

Zeughauskeller SWISS **$$**

(☎044 220 15 15; www.zeughauskeller.ch; Bahnhofstrasse 28a; lunch specials Sfr22.50, mains Sfr19-37; ⏰11.30am-11pm; ✎; 🚋4, 10, 11, 14, 15 to Paradeplatz) Tuck into the heartiest of Swiss grub under the heavy oak beams at this sprawling, atmospheric 15th-century beer hall with ample pavement seating. The menu (in eight languages) goes to town with a dozen varieties of sausage, along with other Swiss faves like pork roast with lashings of sauerkraut. Vegetarian options are also available.

Drinking & Entertainment

Options abound across town, but the bulk of the more animated drinking dens are in Züri-West, especially along Langstrasse in Kreis 4 and Hardstrasse in Kreis 5.

★ **Frau Gerolds Garten** BAR

(www.fraugerold.ch; Geroldstrasse 23/23a; ⏰barrestaurant 11am-midnight Mon-Sat, noon-10pm Sun Apr-Sep, 6pm-midnight Mon-Sat Oct-Mar, market & shops 11am-7pm Mon-Fri, to 6pm Sat year-round; **S** Hardbrücke) Hmm, where to start? The wine bar? The margarita bar? The gin bar? Whichever poison you choose, this wildly popular focal point of Zürich's summer drinking scene is pure unadulterated fun and one of the best grown-up playgrounds in Europe.

★ **Rimini Bar** BAR

(www.rimini.ch; Badweg 10; ⏰5-11pm Mon-Wed, to midnight Thu-Sat, to 10pm Sun; 🚋2, 8, 9, 13, 14, 17 to Sihlstrasse) Secluded behind a fence along the Sihl River, this bar at the **Männerbad** (☎044 211 95 94; ⏰11am-7pm Mon-Thu & Sun, to 6.30pm Fri, to 5.30pm Sat Jun-Sep) public baths is one of Zürich's most inviting openair drinking spots. Its vast wood deck is adorned with red-orange party lights, picnic tables and throw cushions for lounging, accompanied by the sound of water from the adjacent pools.

Open in good weather only.

Hive Club CLUB

(☎044 271 12 10; www.hiveclub.ch; Geroldstrasse 5; ⏰11pm-4am Thu, to 7am Fri, to 9am Sat; **S** Hardbrücke) Electronic music creates the buzz at this artsy, alternative club (cover Sfr35) adjacent to Frau Gerolds Garten in Kreis 5. Enter through an alley strung with multicoloured umbrellas, giant animal heads, mushrooms and watering cans. Big-name DJs keep things going into the wee hours three nights a week.

Rote Fabrik LIVE MUSIC

(☎044 485 58 58; www.rotefabrik.ch; Seestrasse 395; 🚌161, 165 to Rote Fabrik) With a fabulous lakeside location, this multifaceted performing-arts centre stages rock, jazz and hip-hop concerts, original-language films, and theatre and dance performances. There's also a bar and a restaurant. Take bus 161 or 165 from Bürkliplatz.

Information

In the main train station, **Zürich Tourism** (☎044 215 40 00, hotel reservations 044 215 40 40; www.zuerich.com; Hauptbahnhof; ⏰8am-8.30pm Mon-Sat, 8.30am to 6.30pm Sun May-Oct, 8.30am-7pm Mon-Sat, 9am-6pm Sun Nov-Apr) is an excellent first port of call.

Getting There & Away

AIR

Zürich Airport (☎043 816 22 11; www.zurich-airport.com) is 9km north of the city centre, with flights to most capitals in Europe as well as some in Africa, Asia and North America.

TRAIN

Direct trains run frequently to Stuttgart (Sfr70, three hours), Munich (Sfr102, 4½ to 5½ hours), Innsbruck (Sfr83, 3½ hours) and other international destinations. There are regular direct departures to most major Swiss destinations, such as Lucerne (Sfr25, 45 to 50 minutes), Bern (Sfr51, one to 1½ hours) and Basel (Sfr34, 55 minutes to 1¼ hours).

Getting Around

TO/FROM THE AIRPORT

Several trains an hour connect Zürich Airport with the Hauptbahnhof (Sfr6.80, 12 minutes) between around 5am and midnight. A taxi to the centre costs around Sfr60.

BICYCLE

Züri Rollt (☎044 415 67 67; www.schweizrollt.ch) is an innovative program that allows visitors to borrow or rent bikes from a handful of locations, including Velostation Nord, across the road from the north side of the Hauptbahnhof. Bring ID and leave Sfr20 as a deposit. Rental is free if you bring the bike back on the same day; it costs Sfr10 per day if you keep it overnight.

PUBLIC TRANSPORT

The comprehensive, unified bus, tram and S-Bahn public transit system **ZV** (☎0848 988 988; www.zvv.ch) includes boats plying the Limmat River. Short trips under five stops are Sfr2.70; typical trips are Sfr4.40. A 24-hour pass for the city centre is Sfr8.80.

NORTHWESTERN SWITZERLAND

With businesslike Basel at its heart, this region also prides itself on having the country's finest Roman ruins (at Augusta Raurica) and a gaggle of proud castles and pretty medieval villages scattered across the rolling countryside of Aargau Canton.

Basel

POP 175,940 / ELEV 273M

Tucked up against the French and German borders in Switzerland's northwest corner, Basel straddles the majestic Rhine. The town is home to art galleries, 40-odd museums and galleries, avant-garde architecture and an enchanting Old Town centre.

Sights

★Fondation Beyeler MUSEUM

(☎061 645 97 00; www.fondationbeyeler.ch; Baselstrasse 101, Riehen; adult/under 25yr Sfr25/free; ⏰10am-6pm Thu-Tue, to 8pm Wed; 🅿) This astounding private-turned-public collection, assembled by former art dealers Hildy and Ernst Beyeler, is housed in a long, low, light-filled, open-plan building designed by Italian architect Renzo Piano. The varied exhibits juxtapose 19th- and 20th-century works by Picasso and Rothko against sculptures by Miró and Max Ernst and tribal figures from Oceania; there are also regular visiting exhibitions. Take tram 6 to Riehen from Barfüsserplatz or Marktplatz.

★Museum Jean Tinguely MUSEUM

(☎061 681 93 20; www.tinguely.ch; Paul Sacher-Anlage 2; adult/student/child Sfr18/12/free; ⏰11am-6pm Tue-Sun; 🅿) Designed by leading Ticino architect Mario Botta, this museum showcases the playful, mischievous and downright wacky artistic concoctions of sculptor-turned-mad-scientist Jean Tinguely. Buttons next to some of Tinguely's 'kinetic' sculptures allow visitors to set them in motion. It's great fun to watch them rattle, shake and twirl, with springs, feathers and wheels radiating at every angle, or to hear the haunting musical sounds produced by the gigantic *Méta-Harmonies* on the upper floor. Catch bus 31 or 36 from Claraplatz.

Sleeping & Eating

Hotels are often full during Basel's trade fairs and conventions; book ahead. Head to the Marktplatz for a daily market and several stands selling excellent quick bites, such as local sausages and sandwiches.

SYHA Youth Hostel Basel HOSTEL $

(☎061 272 05 72; www.youthhostel.ch; St Alban-Kirchrain 10; dm/s/tw with shared bathroom from Sfr41/70/93, s/d from Sfr120/132; 📶) Designed by Basel-based architects Buchner & Bründler, this swanky, modern hostel in a very pleasant neighbourhood is flanked by tree-shaded squares and a rushing creek. It's only a stone's throw from the Rhine, and 15 minutes on foot from the SBB Bahnhof (or take tram 2 to Kunstmuseum and walk five minutes downhill).

WORTH A TRIP

LIECHTENSTEIN

If Liechtenstein didn't exist, someone would have invented it. A tiny German-speaking mountain principality in the heart of 21st-century Europe, it certainly has novelty value. Only 25km long by 12km wide (at its broadest point) – just larger than Manhattan – Liechtenstein is mostly visited by people who want a glimpse of the turreted castle in capital **Vaduz**. Stay a little longer and you can escape into its pint-sized Alpine wilderness. The 75km **Liechtenstein Trail** (www.tourismus.li/en/activities/the-liechtenstein-trail), beginning in Vaduz, showcases the principality's greatest hits, from hilltop castles to serene villages. The **Liechtenstein Center** (☎239 63 63; www.tourismus.li; Städtle 39, Vaduz; ⏰9am-5pm Nov-Apr, 9am-6pm May-Oct; 📶) offers brochures and souvenir passport stamps. From the Swiss border towns of Buchs (Sfr5.80, 27 minutes) and Sargans (Sfr7.20, 32 minutes), there are frequent buses to Vaduz.

Hotel Krafft HOTEL **$$**
(☎061 690 91 30; www.krafftbasel.ch; Rheingasse 12; s Sfr144-225, d Sfr248-450, ste Sfr292-490; 📶) Design-savvy urbanites gravitate to this renovated historic hotel for its smart, minimalist rooms that wonderfully fuse old and new; some have balconies. Free folding bikes, fresh fruit, tea and water stations impress, but the hotel's key feature is its prime riverside position, adjacent to Mittlere Brücke, peering out from Kleinbasel across the Rhine onto Grossbasel's gorgeous townscape. Ask for a room with a view.

★Volkshaus Basel BRASSERIE **$$**
(☎061 690 93 00; www.volkshaus-basel.ch/en; Rebgasse 12-14; mains Sfr32-46; ⏰restaurant 11.30am-2pm & 6-10pm Mon-Fri & 6-10pm Sat, bar 10am-midnight Mon-Wed, to 1am Thu-Sat) This stylish Herzog & de Meuron–designed venue is part resto bar, part gallery and part performance space. For relaxed dining, head for the atmospheric beer garden in a cobblestoned courtyard decorated with columns, vine-clad walls and light-draped rows of trees. The menu ranges from brasserie classics *(steak frites)* to more innovative offerings (salmon tartare with citrus fruits and gin cucumber).

ℹ Information

Pop into **Basel Tourismus** (☎061 268 68 68; www.basel.com; Centralbahnstrasse 10; ⏰8-6pm Mon-Fri, 9am-5pm Sat, 9am-3pm Sun) or **Basel Tourismus** (☎061 268 68 68; www.basel.com; Barfüsserplatz; ⏰9am-6.30pm Mon-Fri, to 5pm Sat, 10am-3pm Sun) for information and maps on the city and its surrounds.

ℹ Getting There & Around

Basel hotel guests automatically receive a 'mobility ticket' pass, providing free transport throughout the city, operated by **BVB** (☎061 685 14 14; www.bvb.ch/en).

AIR

The **EuroAirport** (☎+33 3 89 90 31 11; www.euroairport.com), 5km northwest of town in France, is the main airport for Basel. It offers flights to numerous European cities on a variety of low-cost carriers. **Airport Bus 50** links the airport and Basel's main train station SBB Bahnhof (Sfr4.70, 22 minutes).

TRAIN

Basel is a major European rail hub. The main station has TGVs to Paris (three hours) and fast ICEs to major cities in Germany.

Frequent direct trains run from SBB Bahnhof to Zurich (Sfr34, 55 minutes to 1¼ hours) and Bern (Sfr41, 55 minutes). Services to Geneva (Sfr76, 2¾ hours) require a change of train in Bern, Biel/Bienne or Olten.

TICINO

POP 351,946

Switzerland meets Italy: in Ticino the summer air is rich and hot, and the peacock-proud posers propel their scooters in and out of traffic. Italian weather, Italian style. Not to mention the Italian ice cream, Italian pizza, Italian architecture and Italian language.

Locarno

POP 16,122 / ELEV 205M

Italianate architecture and the northern end of Lago Maggiore, plus more hours of sunshine than anywhere else in Switzerland (2300 hours, to be precise), give this laid-back town a summer resort atmosphere. Locarno is on the northeastern corner of Lago Maggiore, which mostly lies in Italy's Lombardy region. **Navigazione Lago Maggiore** (www.navigazionelaghi.it/lago-maggiore) operates boats across the entire lake.

Sights

★ Santuario della Madonna del Sasso CHURCH

(www.madonnadelsasso.org; Via Santuario 2; ⌚7.30am-6.30pm) Overlooking the town, this sanctuary was built after the Virgin Mary supposedly appeared in a vision to a monk, Bartolomeo d'Ivrea, in 1480. There's a highly adorned church and several rather rough, near-life-size statue groups (including one of the Last Supper) in niches on the stairway. The best-known painting in the church is *La fuga in egitto* (Flight to Egypt), painted in 1522 by Bramantino.

Piazza Grande AREA

Locarno's Italianate Città Vecchia (Old Town) fans out from Piazza Grande, a photogenic ensemble of arcades and Lombard-style houses. A craft and fresh-produce market takes over the square every Thursday, and regular events are staged here during the warmer months.

Information

Locarno's **tourist office** (☎084 809 10 91; www.ascona-locarno.com; Piazza Stazione; ⌚9am-6pm Mon-Fri, 10am-6pm Sat, 10am-1.30pm & 2.30-5pm Sun) is housed in the train station. Ask about the free Ascona-Locarno Welcome Card.

Getting There & Around

Locarno is well linked to Ticino and the rest of Switzerland via Bellinzona, or take the scenic Centovalli Express (www.centovalli.ch) to Brig via Domodossola in Italy.

A **funicular** (one way/return adult Sfr4.80/7.20, child Sfr2.20/3.60; ⌚8am-10pm May, Jun & Sep, to midnight Jul & Aug, to 9pm Apr & Oct, to 7.30pm Nov-Mar) runs every 15 minutes from the Locarno town centre past the Santuario della Madonna del Sasso to Orselina.

Lugano

POP 63,932 / ELEV 270M

Ticino's lush, mountain-rimmed lake isn't its only liquid asset. Lugano is also the country's third-most-important banking centre. Suits aside, it's a vivacious city, with bars and pavement cafes huddling in the spaghetti maze of steep cobblestone streets that untangle at the edge of the lake and along the flowery promenade. The busy main square holds **markets** on Tuesday and Friday mornings.

Sights & Activities

Take the stairs or the **funicular** (Piazzale della Stazione; Sfr1.30; ⌚5am-midnight) from Lugano's train station down to the centre, a patchwork of interlocking *piazze*. Here, Lugano's early-16th-century cathedral **Cattedrale di San Lorenzo** (St Lawrence Cathedral; Via San Lorenzo; ⌚6.30am-6pm) conceals some fine frescos and ornate baroque statues behind its Renaissance facade. **Società Navigazione del Lago di Lugano** (☎091 971 52 23; www.lakelugano.ch; Riva Vela; ⌚Apr-Oct) runs hour-long cruises of the bay.

Museo d'Arte della Svizzera Italiana GALLERY

(MASI; www.masilugano.ch; LAC Lugano Arte e Cultura, Piazza Bernardino Luini 6; adult/child Sfr20/free; ⌚10am-6pm Tue, Wed, Fri-Sun, to 8pm Thu) The showpiece of Lugano's striking new **LAC cultural centre** (☎058 866 42 22; www.luganolac.ch), the MASI zooms in predominantly on 20th-century and contemporary art – from the abstract to the highly experimental, with exhibitions spread across three spaces. There is no permanent collection currently on display, but there is a high-calibre roster of rotating exhibitions. Recent focuses have included European pop art and the work of Belgian surrealist René Magritte.

Sleeping & Eating

Hotel & Hostel Montarina HOTEL, HOSTEL $

(☎091 966 72 72; www.montarina.ch; Via Montarina 1; dm/s/d Sfr29/105/140; P 🛜 🏊) Occupying a pastel-pink villa dating from 1860, this hotel-hostel duo extends a heartfelt welcome. Mosaic floors, high ceilings and wrought-iron balustrades are lingering traces of old-world grandeur. There's a shared kitchen-lounge, toys to amuse the kids, a swimming pool set in palm-dotted gardens and even a tiny vineyard.

★ Guesthouse Castagnola GUESTHOUSE $$

(☎078 632 67 47; www.gh-castagnola.com; Salita degli Olivi 2; apt Sfr120-200; P 🛜) Kristina and Maurizio bend over backwards to please at their B&B, lodged in a beautifully restored 16th-century town house. Exposed stone, natural fabrics and earthy colours dominate in four rooms kitted out with Nespresso coffee machines and flat-screen TVs. There's also a family-friendly apartment with a washing machine and full kitchen. Take bus 2 to Posta Castagnola, 2km east of the centre.

La Tinèra SWISS $

(☎091 923 52 19; Via dei Gorini 2; mains Sfr19-24; ⌚11.30am-3pm & 5.30-11pm Mon-Sat) Huddled down a backstreet near Piazza della Riforma, this convivial, rustic restaurant rolls out extremely tasty Ticinese home cooking. You might begin, say, with homemade *salumi* (cured meats), moving on to polenta with porcini mushrooms or meltingly tender osso buco. Simply pair with a good Merlot from the region.

Information

Lugano's main **tourist office** (058 220 65 00; www.lugano-tourism.ch; Piazza della Riforma, Palazzo Civico; 9am-6pm Mon-Fri, 9am-5pm Sat, 10am-4pm Sun) is the starting point for guided tours of the city. There is also a **branch** (058 220 65 04; Piazzale della Stazione; 9am-6pm Mon-Fri, 9am-1pm Sat) at the train station.

Getting There & Away

From Lugano's **train station** (Piazzale della Stazione) there are very frequent connections to Bellinzona (Sfr11, 30 minutes), with onward connections to destinations further north. Getting to Locarno (Sfr15.20, one hour) involves a change at Giubiasco.

GRAUBÜNDEN

POP 197,888

While you've probably heard about Davos' sensational downhill skiing, St Moritz' glamour and the tales of Heidi (fictionally born here), vast swaths of Graubünden remain little known and ripe for exploring. Strike into the Alps on foot or follow the lonely passes that corkscrew high into the mountains and the chances are you will be alone in exhilarating landscapes.

St Moritz

POP 5084 / ELEV 1856M

Switzerland's original winter wonderland and the cradle of Alpine tourism, St Moritz has been luring royals, celebrities and moneyed wannabes since 1864. With its shimmering aquamarine lake, emerald forests and aloof mountains, the town looks a million dollars.

Activities

Schweizer Skischule SKIING
(081 830 01 01; www.skischool.ch; Via Stredas 14; 8am-noon & 2-6pm Mon-Sat, 8-9am & 4-6pm Sun) The first Swiss ski school was founded in St Moritz in 1929. Today you can arrange skiing or snowboarding lessons here – check out the website for details.

Sleeping & Eating

Jugendherberge St Moritz HOSTEL $
(081 836 61 11; www.youthhostel.ch/st.moritz; Via Surpunt 60; dm/s/d/q Sfr42.50/135.50/170/220; P) On the edge of the forest, this modern hostel has clean, quiet four-bed dorms and doubles. Considered a top family hostel, there's a children's toy room, bike hire and laundrette. Bus 3 offers door-to-door connections with the town centre (five minutes) and train station (10 minutes).

Chesa Spuondas HOTEL $$
(081 833 65 88; www.chesaspuondas.ch; Via Somplaz 47; s/d/f incl half-board Sfr155/280/330; P) This family hotel nestles amid meadows at the foot of forest and mountains, 3km southwest of the town centre. Rooms have high ceilings, parquet floors and the odd antique. Kids are the centre of attention here, with dedicated meal times, activities and play areas, plus a children's ski school a 10-minute walk away.

Pizzeria Caruso PIZZA $
(081 836 06 29; www.laudinella.ch; Via Tegiatscha 17; pizza Sfr13.50-22.50; noon-1am;) Pizza lovers rave about the thin-crust Neapolitan numbers that fly out of the wood oven at Hotel Laudinella's pizzeria. These range from a simple Margherita to the gourmet Domenico with truffles and beef. Laudinella also offers a delivery service.

Information

The main **tourist office** (081 837 33 33; www.stmoritz.ch; Via Maistra 12; 9am-6.30pm Mon-Fri, 10am-6pm Sat) is in St Moritz-Dorf, but if you're coming by train, visit the **sub-office** (10am-2pm & 3-6.30pm) in the train station.

Getting There & Away

Trains run at least hourly from Zürich to St Moritz (Sfr76, three to 3½ hours), with one change (at Landquart or Chur).

Between mid-December and late October, one of Switzerland's most celebrated trains, the **Glacier Express** (www.glacierexpress.ch; one way adult/child Sfr153/76.50; mid-May–late Oct & mid-Dec–early May), makes the scenic eight-hour journey from St Moritz to Zermatt (one to three times daily).

The **Bernina Express** (www.berninaexpress.ch; one way Chur-Tirano Sfr77; mid-May–early Dec) provides seasonal links to Lugano from St Moritz, which include the stunning Unesco-recognised train line over the Bernina Pass to Tirano, Italy.

DON'T MISS

SWISS NATIONAL PARK

The Engadine's pride and joy is the **Swiss National Park** (www.nationalpark.ch) FREE, easily accessed from Scuol, Zernez and S-chanf. Spanning 172 sq km, Switzerland's only national park is a nature-gone-wild swath of dolomitic peaks, shimmering glaciers, larch woodlands, pastures, waterfalls and high moors strung with topaz-blue lakes. This was the first national park to be established in the Alps, on 1 August 1914, and more than 100 years later it remains true to its original conservation ethos, with the aims to protect, research and inform. Given that nature has been left to its own devices for a century, the park is a glimpse of the Alps before the dawn of tourism. There are some 80km of well-marked hiking trails, where, with a little luck and a decent pair of binoculars, ibex, chamois, marmots, deer, bearded vultures and golden eagles can be sighted. The **Swiss National Park Centre** (☎081 851 41 41; www.nationalpark.ch; exhibition adult/child Sfr7/3; ⊙8.30am-6pm Jun-Oct, 9am-noon & 2-5pm Nov-May) should be your first port of call for information on activities and accommodation. It sells an excellent 1:50,000 park map (Sfr14, or Sfr20 with guidebook), which covers 21 walks through the park.

You can easily head off on your own, but you might get more out of one of the informative guided hikes (Sfr25) run by the centre from late June to mid-October. These include wildlife-spotting treks to the Val Trupchun and high-alpine hikes to the Offenpass and Lakes of Macun. Most are in German, but many guides speak a little English. Book ahead by phone or at the park office in Zernez. Entry to the park and its car parks is free. Conservation is paramount here, so stick to footpaths and respect regulations prohibiting camping, littering, lighting fires, cycling, picking flowers and disturbing the animals. For an overnight stay in the heart of the park, look no further than **Il Fuorn** (☎081 856 12 26; www.ilfuorn.ch; s Sfr85-120, d Sfr130-196, tr Sfr180-195, q Sfr200-220, half-board extra Sfr35; ⊙closed Nov, 2nd half Jan & Easter-late Apr; P 📶), an idyllically sited guesthouse that serves fresh trout and game at its excellent on-site restaurant.

SURVIVAL GUIDE

Directory A–Z

INTERNET ACCESS

Free wi-fi hot spots can be found at airports, dozens of Swiss train stations and in many hotels and cafes. Public wi-fi, provided by **Swisscom** (www.swisscom.ch), costs from Sfr5 per day.

MONEY

- ATMs are at every airport, most train stations and on every second street corner in towns and cities; Visa, MasterCard and Amex are widely accepted.
- Swiss francs are divided into 100 centimes (Rappen in German-speaking Switzerland). Euros are accepted by many tourism businesses.
- Exchange money at large train stations.
- Tipping is not necessary, given that hotels, restaurants, bars and even some taxis are legally required to include service charge in bills. You can round up the bill after a meal for good service, as locals do.

OPENING HOURS

We list high-season opening hours for sights and attractions; hours tend to decrease during low season. Most businesses shut completely on Sunday.

Banks 8.30am–4.30pm Monday to Friday

Museums 10am–5pm, many close Monday and stay open late Thursday

Restaurants noon–2.30pm and 6pm–9.30pm; most close one or two days per week

Shops 10am–6pm Monday to Friday, to 4pm Saturday

PUBLIC HOLIDAYS

New Year's Day 1 January

Good Friday March/April

Easter Sunday and Monday March/April

Ascension Day 40th day after Easter

Whit Sunday and Monday (Pentecost) 7th week after Easter

National Day 1 August

Christmas Day 25 December

St Stephen's Day 26 December

TELEPHONE

- Search for phone numbers online at http://tel.local.ch/en.
- National telecom provider Swisscom (www.swisscom.ch) provides public phone booths that accept coins and major credit cards.
- Prepaid local SIM cards are available from network operators Salt (www.salt.ch), Sunrise (www.sunrise.ch) and Swisscom Mobile (www.swisscom.ch/mobile) for as little as Sfr10.

TOURIST INFORMATION

My Switzerland (www.myswitzerland.com) is an in-depth, multilingual Switzerland Tourism website.

Transport

GETTING THERE & AWAY

Air

The main international airports:

Geneva Airport (p618) Geneva's airport is 4km northwest of the town centre.

Zürich Airport (p632) The airport is 9km north of the centre, with flights to most European capitals as well as some in Africa, Asia and North America.

Bus

Eurolines (www.eurolines.com) has buses with connections across Western Europe.

Train

Eco-friendly Switzerland makes rail travel a joy.

- Zürich is Switzerland's busiest international terminus, with trains to Munich and Vienna, from where there are extensive onward connections to cities in Eastern Europe.
- Most connections from Germany pass through Zürich or Basel.
- Nearly all connections from Italy pass through Milan before branching off to Zürich, Lucerne, Bern or Lausanne.
- Book tickets and get train information from Rail Europe (www.raileurope.com).

GETTING AROUND

Marketed as the Swiss Travel System, the network has a useful website (www.swisstravelsystem.co.uk). Excellent free maps covering the country are available at train stations and tourist offices.

Bicycle

- For details on national, regional and local routes, rental, bike-friendly accommodation, guides and maps, visit www.schweizmobil.ch and click on 'Cycling in Switzerland'.
- **SBB Rent-a-Bike** (☎041 925 11 70; www.rentabike.ch; half-/full day from Sfr27/35), run by Swiss railways, offers bike hire at 100-odd train stations. For a Sfr10 surcharge they can be collected at one station and returned to another.
- Free bike hire is available from April to October through the eco-friendly initiative Schweiz Rollt, with outlets in Zürich and Geneva.

Boat

All the larger lakes are serviced by steamers operated by Swiss Federal Railways (www.sbb.ch). These include Lakes Geneva, Constance, Lucerne, Lugano, Neuchâtel, Biel, Murten, Thun, Brienz and Zug, but not Lago Maggiore.

Bus

- Yellow post buses (www.postauto.ch) supplement the rail network, linking towns to difficult-to-access mountain regions.
- Services are regular, and departures (usually next to train stations) are linked to train schedules.
- Swiss national travel passes are valid.
- Purchase tickets on board; some scenic routes over the Alps (eg the Lugano–St Moritz run) require reservations.

Car & Motorcycle

- Major car-rental companies have offices at airports and in major cities and towns.
- Public transport is excellent in city centres – unlike parking cars, which is usually hard work.
- Headlights must be on at all times, and dipped (set to low-beam) in tunnels.
- The speed limit is 50km/h in towns, 80km/h on main roads outside towns, 100km/h on single-lane freeways and 120km/h on dual-lane freeways.
- Purchase a Sfr40 *vignette* (toll sticker) at the border or the nearest petrol station to use Swiss freeways and semi-freeways.

Local Transport

The Swiss have many words to describe mountain transport: funicular (*Standseilbahn* in German, *funiculaire* in French, *funicolare* in Italian), cable car *(Luftseilbahn, téléphérique, funivia)*, gondola *(Gondelbahn, télécabine, telecabina)* and chairlift *(Sesselbahn, télésiège, seggiovia)*.

Always check what time the last cable car goes down the mountain – in winter it's as early as 4pm in mountain resorts.

Train

The Swiss rail network combines state-run and private operations. The Swiss Federal Railway (www.sbb.ch) is abbreviated to SBB in German, CFF in French and FFS in Italian.

- Second-class compartments are perfectly acceptable but are often close to full; 1st-class carriages are more spacious and have fewer passengers.
- Train schedules are available online and at train stations. For information, see www.sbb.ch.
- Larger train stations have 24-hour left-luggage lockers (Sfr3 to Sfr6 per day), usually accessible 6am to midnight.
- Seat reservations (Sfr5) are advisable for longer journeys, particularly in high season.
- While European rail passes such as Eurail and Interrail passes are valid on Swiss national railways, a Swiss Travel Pass is a better option for exploring scenic Switzerland.

Acropolis (p329), Greece

Survival Guide

Directory A–Z

Accessible Travel

Western Europe's historic buildings and streetscapes can pose problems for travellers with disabilities or limited mobility, due to steep hills, cobblestones, stairs and lack of lifts in many older buildings (it's worth asking if a freight lift is available). Bathrooms in restaurants may not be accessible for wheelchairs; check when making reservations. New buildings are required to be accessible under EU law.

Older public transport systems, such as underground rail networks, can also be problematic, but alternatives may include accessible buses or trams.

Audible pedestrian crossing signals are only available in a few places. Guide dogs are generally accepted everywhere.

The website **Sage Travelling** (www.sagetravelling.com) is an outstanding resource for European travel, with accessible travel agent links, planning guides, tips, hotel lists, guided tours and excursions, cruises and more.

Download Lonely Planet's free Accessible Travel guide from http://lptravel.to/AccessibleTravel.

Accommodation

Where you stay in Western Europe may be one of the highlights of your trip, with options as diverse as the region itself. Wherever you go, book ahead during peak holiday periods.

Hotels Range from simple to extravagant, historic to cutting-edge.

B&Bs and guesthouses Get a local perspective by staying in private homes.

Hostels Shared-facility options spanning Hostelling International (HI) premises though to designer flashpacker pads exist all over Western Europe.

Camping Magnificent scenery forms a backdrop to basic grounds though to luxury 'glamping' sites.

Resorts From spa and golf complexes and to beachfront havens, resorts provide easy living.

B&Bs & Guesthouses

In the UK and Ireland, B&Bs – providing bed and breakfast in a private home – can be real bargains.

Elsewhere, similar private accommodation – though often without breakfast – may go under the name of pension, guesthouse, *gasthaus, zimmerfrei, chambre d'hôte* and so on. Although the majority of guesthouses are simple affairs, there are plenty of luxurious ones around.

Check that accommodation is centrally located and not in a dull, distant suburb.

Camping

Camping – in tents, caravans/campervans or cabins – is immensely popular in Western Europe and provides the cheapest form of accommodation.

- There's usually a charge per tent or site, per person and per vehicle.
- National tourist offices provide details of their countries' campgrounds.
- In large cities, most campgrounds will be some distance from the centre, so it's best suited to those with their own transport. If you're on foot, the money you save can quickly be eaten up by the cost of commuting.
- Many campgrounds rent out cabins, bungalows or cottages accommodating two to eight people.
- Camping grounds often close outside the summer months.
- Camping other than at designated campgrounds is difficult; you usually need permission from the local authorities (the police or local council office) or from the owner of the land.
- In some countries, such as Austria, France and Germany, free camping (aka wild camping) is illegal on all but private land; in others, such as Greece, it's illegal altogether. Free camping is tolerated at some remote locations in Ireland and permissible most places in Scotland, though not in England or Wales.

Hostels

Hostels offer the cheapest secure roof over your head in Western Europe, and you generally don't have to be a youngster to use them.

HOSTELLING INTERNATIONAL

Most hostels are part of the national Youth Hostel Association (YHA), which is affiliated with **Hostelling International** (HI; www.hihostels.com).

- The HI website has links to all the national organisations and you can use it to book beds or rooms in advance.
- You can join YHA or HI in advance or at the hostels. Members usually pay about 10% less on rates.
- At a hostel, you get a bed in a dorm or a private room plus the use of communal facilities, which often include a kitchen where you can prepare your own meals.
- Hostels vary widely in character, but increased competition – particularly from privately owned hostels – have prompted many places to improve their facilities and cut back on rules and regulations.
- The trend is moving towards smaller dormitories with just four to six beds. Single and double rooms with private bathrooms are common and it's not unusual for families to stay at hostels.
- Female-only dorms are often available.
- Some more institutional hostels regularly host school groups, which means they can be booked out or can be noisy.

PRIVATE HOSTELS

There are many private hostelling organisations in Western Europe and hundreds of unaffiliated backpacker hostels. Private hostels have fewer rules (eg no curfew and no daytime lockout), more self-catering facilities and a much lower number of large, noisy school groups. They often also have a much more sociable, party-friendly vibe.

However, whereas HI hostels must meet minimum safety and cleanliness standards, private hostels do not, which means that facilities vary greatly. Dorms in some private hostels can be mixed gender. Most private hostels now have small dorm rooms of three to eight beds, and private singles and doubles.

Hotels

From castles and palaces to workaday cheapies, the range of hotels in Western Europe is immense. You'll often find inexpensive hotels clustered around bus and train station areas, but these can be charmless and scruffy, and the streets outside edgy. Look for moderately priced places closer to the interesting parts of town.

Check whether breakfast is included (often it's not). Wi-fi is almost always free.

Rental Accommodation

Rental properties can be both advantageous and fun for families travelling together or for those staying in one place for a few nights. You can have your own chic Left Bank apartment in Paris or a villa in Tuscany with a pool – and often at cheaper rates than hotels.

All rentals should be equipped with kitchens (or at least a kitchenette), which can save on the food bill and allow you to browse the neighbourhood markets and shops, eating like the locals do. Some come with laundry facilities and parking.

Booking websites abound; alternatively, check with local tourist offices.

Beware direct-rental scams: unless you book through a reputable agency, your property might not actually exist. Scammers often compile fake apartment advertisements at too-good-to-be-true prices. *Never* send payment to an untraceable account via a money transfer.

Resorts

From Irish mansions amid rambling grounds to grand Swiss spa hotels, golf resorts and beach properties with water sports and activities galore, Western Europe has many fabled resorts, where travellers try to avoid ever checking out. Ask about deals and all-inclusive packages.

Activities

Western Europe offers infinite opportunities to get active in its great outdoors. Its varied geography and climate means it offers the full range of pursuits: from swimming, surfing, windsurfing, paddleboarding and boating on its coastline, to skiing, snowboarding and mountaineering in its peaks, and fishing, hiking and cycling almost everywhere.

Boating

Europe's many lakes, rivers and diverse coastlines offer an incredible variety of boating options. You can houseboat in France, kayak in Switzerland, charter a yacht in Greece, row on a peaceful Alpine lake, join a cruise along the Rhine, Main and Danube rivers from Amsterdam to Vienna (and beyond), rent a sailing boat on the French Riviera, go white-water rafting in

PLAN YOUR STAY ONLINE

For more accommodation reviews by Lonely Planet authors, check out http://lonelyplanet.com/europe/hotels. You'll find independent reviews, as well as recommendations on the best places to stay.

Austria, or pilot a canal boat along the extraordinary canal network of Britain (or Ireland, or France) – the possibilities are endless.

Cycling

Along with hiking, cycling is ideal for getting up close to the scenery. It's also a superb way to get around many cities and towns.

Popular cycling areas include the Ardennes, spanning Belgium, northeastern France and Luxembourg; the west of Ireland; much of the Netherlands; the coasts of Sardinia and Puglia in Italy; anywhere in the Alps (for those fit enough); and the south of France.

Check with your airline about taking bikes in the cargo hold. Alternatively, places to hire a bicycle are myriad. Bikes can be carried on most European trains (some outside peak hours).

Hiking

Keen hikers can spend a lifetime exploring Western Europe's trails. Popular routes feature places to stay, often with jaw-dropping views.

Highlights include the following:

The Alps Spanning Switzerland, Austria, Germany and Italy, with bell-wearing dairy cows and trails organised with Swiss precision.

Pyrenees Follow trails through hills in both France and Spain.

Corsica and Sardinia Sun-drenched rugged beauty, with a Mediterranean view around every corner.

Northern Portugal A glass of port awaits after a day on the trail.

Connemara Prime hillwalking on the west coast of Ireland.

Scotland Vast tracts of wilderness.

In the UK, **Ramblers** (www.ramblers.org.uk) is a nonprofit organisation that promotes long-distance walking and can help you with maps and information. The British-based **Ramblers Holidays** (www.ramblersholidays.co.uk) offers hiking-oriented trips in Europe and elsewhere.

For shorter day hikes, local tourist offices are excellent resources.

Every country in Western Europe has national parks and other scenic areas or attractions. Guided hikes are often available.

Skiing & Snowboarding

In winter Europeans take to the pistes, flocking to hundreds of resorts in the Alps and Pyrenees for downhill skiing and snowboarding. Cross-country skiing is also very popular in some areas, such as around Switzerland's St Moritz.

Equipment hire (or even purchase) can be relatively cheap, and the hassle of bringing your own skis may not be worth it. **Intersport Rent** (www.intersportrent.com) has numerous outlets.

The ski season generally lasts from early December to late March, though at higher altitudes it may extend an extra month either side. Snow conditions can vary greatly from one year to the next and from region to region, but January and February tend to be the best (and busiest) months.

For comprehensive reports on ski conditions, try **OnTheSnow** (www.onthesnow.com).

Surfing & Windsurfing

Surfing hot spots include Ireland's west coast, France (especially around Biarritz), Spain (especially around San Sebastián) and Portugal. Gear rental and lessons are readily available.

Windsurfing is popular at Western Europe's breezy beaches and lakes. It's easy to rent sailboards in many tourist centres, and there are often courses for beginners.

Kitesurfing and SUP (stand-up paddleboarding) are also widely available.

Children

Europe is the home of Little Red Riding Hood, Cinderella, King Arthur, Tintin et al, and is a great place to travel with kids. Successful travel with young children requires some careful planning and effort. Don't try to overdo things; even for adults, packing too much sightseeing into your schedule can be counterproductive.

- Most car-hire firms in Western Europe have children's safety seats for hire at a nominal cost, but it's essential that you book in advance.
- High chairs and cots (cribs) are available in many restaurants and hotels but numbers are often limited.
- Disposable nappies (diapers) are widely available, as is formula.
- Babysitters are best sourced through your hotel.
- Attitudes to breastfeeding in public vary; ask locally for advice.

Customs Regulations

- Duty-free goods are not sold to those travelling from one EU country to another.
- For goods purchased at airports or on ferries *outside* the EU, allowances apply for tobacco (200 cigarettes, 50 cigars or 250g of loose tobacco) – although some countries have reduced this to curb smoking – and alcohol (1L of spirits or 2L of liquor with less than 22% alcohol by volume or 4L of wine or 16L of beer).
- The total value of other duty-free goods (perfume, electronic devices etc) cannot exceed €430 for air and sea travellers or €300 for other travellers.

Discount Cards

Camping Card International

Camping Card International (http://campingcardinternational.com) is a campground ID that can be used instead of a passport when checking into a campground and includes third-party insurance. Many campgrounds offer a small discount (usually 5% to 10%) if you sign in with one.

Senior Cards

Museums and various other sights and attractions (including public swimming pools and spas), as well as transport companies, frequently offer discounts to retired people, old-age pensioners and/or those aged over 60. Make sure you bring proof of age.

Student & Youth Cards

The **International Student Travel Confederation** (ISTC; www.istc.org) issues three cards for students, teachers and under-30s, offering thousands of worldwide discounts on transport, museum entry, youth hostels and even some restaurants.

ISIC (International Student Identity Card)

ITIC (International Teacher Identity Card)

IYTC (International Youth Travel Card).

Issuing offices include **STA Travel** (www.statravel.com). Most places, however, will also accept regular student identity cards from your home country.

The **European Youth Card** (www.eyca.org) has scores of discounts for under-30s. You don't need to be an EU citizen.

Electricity

Most of Europe runs on 220V/50Hz AC (as opposed to, say, North America, where the electricity is 120V/60Hz AC). Chargers for phones, iPods and laptops *usually* can handle any type of electricity. If in doubt, read the fine print.

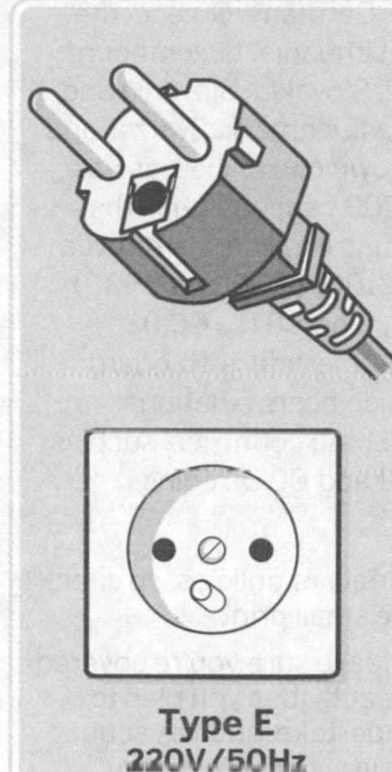

Type E
220V/50Hz

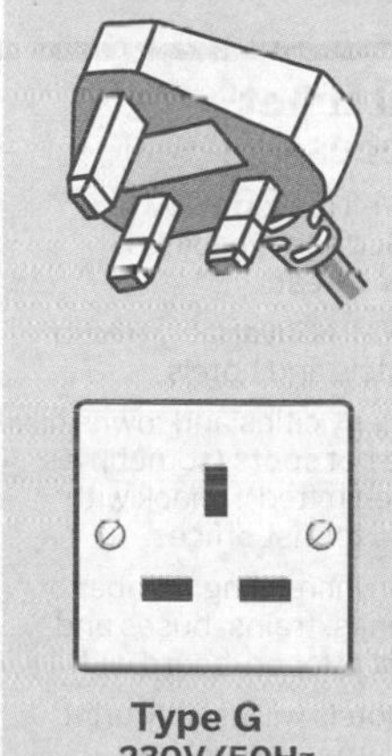

Type G
230V/50Hz

Embassies & Consulates

As a tourist, it is crucial that you understand what your own embassy (the embassy of the country of which you are a citizen) can and cannot do. Generally speaking, embassies won't be much help in emergencies if the trouble you're in is even remotely your fault.

Remember that you are bound by the laws of the country that you are in. Your embassy will show little sympathy if you end up in jail after committing a crime locally, even if such actions are legal in your own country.

In genuine emergencies you might get some assistance, but only if other channels have been exhausted. For example, if you need to get home urgently, the embassy would expect you to have insurance. If you have all your money and documents stolen, the embassy might assist with getting a new passport, but a loan for onward travel is almost always out of the question.

Locations

Embassies and consulates are located in Western European capitals and major cities.

You can find locations online at the following websites:

Australia (www.dfat.gov.au)

Canada (www.international.gc.ca)

New Zealand (www.mfat.govt.nz)

UK (www.gov.uk/fco)

USA (https://travel.state.gov)

Food

Western Europe has some phenomenal eating options; check individual destination coverage for more specific information. Popular and/or high-end restaurants should be booked up to a couple of months ahead. Western Europe is increasingly vegetarian- and vegan-friendly.

Restaurants Typically where you'll eat your evening meal, from cheap-and-cheerful to Michelin-starred, restaurants. Similarly Greek tavernas, Italian trattorias and French bistros also offer dinner.

Cafes In many destinations, cafes are a lunch spot serving sandwiches, simple meals and coffee. French *cafés* serve something more substantial and

EURO

The euro is the official currency used in Austria, Belgium, Cyprus, Estonia, Finland, France, Germany, Greece, the Republic of Ireland, Italy, Latvia, Lithuania, Luxembourg, Malta, the Netherlands, Portugal, Slovakia, Slovenia and Spain. Other EU countries such as Denmark, Switzerland and Sweden have retained their own currencies, as has the UK. The euro is divided into 100 cents and has the same value in all EU member countries. There are seven euro notes (€5, €10, €20, €50, €100, €200 and €500) and eight euro coins (€1 and €2, then €0.01, €0.02, €0.05, €0.10, €0.20 and €0.50). One side is standard for all euro coins and the other side bears a national emblem of participating countries. Some countries, such as the Netherlands, don't use €0.01 and €0.02 coins.

Austrian *kaffeehäuser* are grandiose coffee houses. Dutch *bruin cafés* ('brown cafes', ie pubs) often serve food.

Health

It is unlikely that you will encounter unusual health problems in Western Europe, and if you do, standards of care are world-class. It's vital to have health insurance for your trip.

No jabs are necessary for Western Europe. However, the World Health Organization (WHO) recommends that all travellers be covered for diphtheria, tetanus, measles, mumps, rubella and polio, regardless of their destination. Since most vaccines don't produce immunity until at least two weeks after they're given, visit a doctor at least six weeks before departure.

Insurance

It's foolhardy to travel without insurance to cover theft, loss and medical problems.

➡ Before you buy insurance, see what your existing insurance covers, be it medical, home owner's or renter's. You may find that some aspects of travel in Western Europe are covered.

➡ If you need to purchase coverage, there's a wide variety of policies, so check the small print.

➡ Make sure you're covered for activities you plan to undertake, such as scuba diving, skiing or surfing.

➡ Strongly consider a policy that covers you for the worst possible scenario.

Internet Access

➡ Wi-fi (called WLAN in Germany) access is widespread.

➡ Wi-fi is invariably free in hostels and hotels.

➡ Many cities and towns have free hot spots (sometimes time-limited); check with local tourist offices.

➡ An increasing number of airlines, trains, buses and taxis offer on-board wi-fi.

➡ Hotels will usually print documents (such as boarding passes) for guests.

➡ The number of internet cafes is plummeting. You'll occasionally still find them in tourist areas and around big train stations. Libraries may be another option. Tourist offices can provide advice.

Legal Matters

Most Western European police are friendly and helpful, especially if you have been a victim of a crime. You are required by law to prove your identity if asked by police, so always carry your passport, or an identity card if you're an EU citizen.

Illegal Drugs

Narcotics are sometimes openly available in Europe, but that doesn't mean they're legal.

➡ The Netherlands is famed for its liberal attitudes, including 'coffeeshops' selling cannabis. However, it's a case of the police turning a blind eye. Possession of cannabis is decriminalised but not legalised (except for medicinal use). Don't take this relaxed attitude as an invitation to buy harder drugs; if you get caught, you'll be punished.

➡ Austria, Belgium, Italy, Luxembourg and Switzerland have all decriminalised marijuana use; possession of small amounts will incur a fine but won't result in a criminal record.

➡ In Spain, cannabis has been decriminalised and is legal to use in private areas but not public spaces.

➡ In Portugal, the possession of *all* drugs has been decriminalised; however, selling is illegal.

LGBTIQ+ Travellers

In cosmopolitan centres in Western Europe you'll find very liberal attitudes towards homosexuality. Austria, Belgium, France, Germany, the Republic of Ireland, Luxembourg, the Netherlands, Portugal, Spain and the UK (except Northern Ireland) have legalised same-sex marriages. Many other countries allow civil partnerships that grant all or most of the rights of marriage.

London, Paris, Berlin, Madrid, Lisbon and Amsterdam have thriving gay communities and Pride events. The Greek islands of Mykonos and Lesvos are popular gay beach destinations.

Useful organisations:

Damron (www.damron.com) The USA's leading gay publisher offers guides to world cities.

Spartacus International Gay Guide (www.spartacusworld.com) A male-only directory of gay entertainment venues and hotels in Europe and the rest of the world.

Money

ATMs

- Most countries in Western Europe have international ATMs allowing you to withdraw cash directly from your home account. This is the most common way European travellers access their money.
- Always have a back-up option, however, as some travellers have reported glitches with ATMs in various countries, even when their card worked elsewhere across Western Europe. In some remote villages, ATMs might be scarce too.
- When you withdraw money from an ATM the amounts are converted and dispensed in local currency but there will be fees. Ask your bank for details.
- Don't forget your normal security procedures: cover the keypad when entering your PIN and make sure there are no unusual devices (which might copy your card's information) attached to the machine.
- If your card disappears and the screen goes blank before you've even entered your PIN, don't enter it – especially if a 'helpful' bystander tells you to do so. If you can't retrieve your card, call your bank's emergency number as soon as possible.

Cash

Nothing beats cash for convenience…or risk. If you lose it, it's gone forever and very few travel insurers will come to your rescue. Those that do will limit the amount to somewhere around €300 or £200.

If flying into Western Europe from elsewhere, you'll find ATMs and currency exchanges in the arrivals area of the airport. There is no reason to get local currency before arriving in Western Europe, especially as exchange rates in your home country are likely to be abysmal.

Credit Cards

- Credit cards are often necessary for major purchases such as air or rail tickets, and offer a lifeline in certain emergencies.
- Visa and MasterCard are much more widely accepted in Europe than Amex and Diners Club.
- There are regional differences in the general acceptability of credit cards. In the UK, for example, you can usually flash your plastic in the most humble of budget restaurants; in Germany some restaurants don't take credit cards. Cards are not widely accepted off the beaten track.
- As with ATM cards, banks have loaded up credit cards with hidden charges for foreign purchases. Cash withdrawals on a credit card are almost always a much worse idea than using an ATM card due to the fees and high interest rates. Plus, purchases in different currencies are likely to draw various conversion surcharges that are simply there to add to the bank's profit. These can run up to 5% or more. Check before leaving home.

Travel Money Cards

Prepaid cards – also called travel money cards, prepaid currency cards or cash passport cards – are a popular way of carrying money.

These enable you to load a card with as much foreign currency as you want to spend. You then use it to withdraw cash at ATMs – the money comes off the card and not out of your account – or to make direct purchases in the same way you would with a Visa or MasterCard. You can reload it via telephone or online.

International Transfers

In an emergency, it's quick and easy to have money wired via **Western Union** (www.westernunion.com) or **MoneyGram** (www.moneygram.com), but it can be quite costly.

MINIMISING ATM CHARGES

When you withdraw cash from an ATM overseas there are several ways you can get hit. Firstly, most banks add a hidden 2.75% loading to what's called the 'Visa/MasterCard wholesale' or 'interbank' exchange rate. In short, they're giving you a worse exchange rate than strictly necessary. Additionally, some banks charge their customers a cash withdrawal fee (usually 2% with a minimum €2 or more). If you're really unlucky, the bank at the foreign end might charge you as well. Triple whammy. If you use a credit card in ATMs you'll also pay interest – usually quite high – on the cash withdrawn.

If your bank levies fees, then making larger, less frequent withdrawals is better. It's also worth seeing if your bank has reciprocal agreements with banks where you are going that minimise ATM fees.

Taxes & Refunds

Sales tax applies to many goods and services in Western Europe (although the amount – 10% to 25% – is already built into the price of the item). When non-EU residents spend more than a certain amount (about €75) they can usually reclaim that tax when leaving the country.

Making a tax-back claim is straightforward:

➡ Make sure the shop offers duty-free sales (often a sign will be displayed reading 'Tax-Free Shopping').

➡ When making your purchase ask the shop attendant for a tax-refund voucher, filled in with the correct amount and the date.

➡ The voucher can be used to claim a refund directly at international airports (beware, however, of very long lines), or be stamped at ferry ports or border crossings and mailed back for a refund.

EU residents aren't eligible for this scheme. Even an American citizen living in Amsterdam is not entitled to a rebate on items bought in Paris. Conversely, an EU-passport holder living in New York is.

Safe Travel

On the whole, you should experience few problems travelling in Western Europe – even on your own – as the region is well developed and relatively safe. But do exercise common sense.

➡ Work out how friends and relatives can contact you in case of an emergency and keep in touch.

➡ Scanning your passport, driving licence and credit and ATM cards and storing them securely online gives you access from anywhere. If things are stolen or lost, replacement is much easier when you have the vital details available.

➡ Train stations in many Western European cities can be sketchy, particularly late at night.

Scams

Be aware of shopkeepers in touristy places who may shortchange you. The same applies to taxi drivers.

Never buy tickets other than from official vendors – they may turn out to be counterfeit.

Theft

Watch out for theft in Western Europe, including theft by other travellers. The most important things to secure are your passport, documents (such as a driving licence), tickets and money, in that order.

➡ Protect yourself from 'snatch thieves' who go for cameras and shoulder bags. They sometimes operate from motorcycles or scooters and expertly slash the strap before you have a chance to react. A small day pack is better, but watch your rear.

➡ At cafes and bars; loop the strap of your bag around your leg while seated. A jacket or bag left on the back of a chair is an invitation for theft; as is a phone left on a table where it's easily swiped.

➡ Pickpockets come up with endlessly creative diversions to distract you: tying friendship bracelets on your wrist, peddling trinkets, pretending to 'find' a gold ring on the ground that they've conveniently placed there, posing as beggars or charity workers brandishing petitions, or as tourists wanting you to take their photograph...ignore them.

➡ Beware of gangs of kids – whether dishevelled or well dressed – demanding attention, who may be trying to pickpocket you or overtly rob you.

➡ Pickpockets are most active in dense crowds, especially in busy train stations and on public transport during peak hours.

Smoking

Cigarette-smoking bans have been progressively introduced across Europe. Although outdoor seating has long been a tradition at European cafes, it's gained new popularity given that most Western European countries have banned smoking in public places, including restaurants and bars. Almost all hotel rooms are now non-smoking.

Telephone

Hotel phones notoriously have outrageous rates and hidden charges. Public phone booths have almost completely disappeared.

Mobile Phones

Travellers can cheaply and easily purchase prepaid mobile phones or SIM cards. GSM phones can be used throughout Western Europe. Mobile shops are everywhere.

You can bring your mobile phone from home and buy a local SIM card to enjoy cheap local calling rates if it is both unlocked and compatible with European GSM networks. Check first.

A great option is a **Toggle** (www.togglemobile.co.uk) multicountry SIM card. It allows you to have up to nine numbers in countries across much of Europe, allowing calls, text and data at local rates, plus you receive free incoming calls in some 20 countries. Purchase SIMs online or at certain phone shops; topping up online is easy.

If you plan to use your mobile phone from home:

➡ Check international roaming rates in advance; often they are very expensive.

➡ Check roaming fees for data/internet usage; users can get socked with huge fees. You may be able to buy a data package to limit your costs.

Time

Greenwich Mean Time/UTC UK, Ireland, Portugal, Canary Islands (Spain)

Central European Time (GMT/UTC plus one hour) Austria, Belgium, France, Germany, Italy, Luxembourg, the Netherlands, Spain (except Canary Islands), Switzerland

Eastern European Time (GMT/UTC plus two hours) Greece

Daylight Saving Time/Summer Time Last Sunday in March to the last Sunday in October

Tourist Information

Tourist offices in Western Europe are common and almost universally helpful. They can help find accommodation, issue maps, advise on sights, activities, nightlife and entertainment while you're visiting, and help with more obscure queries such as where to find laundry facilities.

Official tourism authority websites:

Austria Austria.info (www.austria.info)

Belgium Visit Belgium (www.visitbelgium.com)

Britain Visit Britain (www.visitbritain.com)

France France.fr (www.france.fr)

Germany Germany.travel (www.germany.travel)

Greece Visit Greece (www.visitgreece.gr)

Ireland Discover Ireland (www.discoverireland.ie)

Italy Italia (www.italia.it)

Luxembourg Visit Luxembourg (www.visitluxembourg.com)

The Netherlands Holland.com (www.holland.com)

Northern Ireland Discover Northern Ireland (www.discovernorthernireland.com)

Portugal Visit Portugal (www.visitportugal.com)

Spain Spain.info (www.spain.info)

Switzerland MySwitzerland.com (www.myswitzerland.com)

Visas

The Schengen Agreement (no passport controls at borders between member countries) applies to most areas; the UK and Ireland are exceptions.

Until late 2022, citizens of Australia, Canada, Japan, New Zealand and the USA don't need visas for tourist visits to the UK, Ireland or any Schengen country. With a valid passport you should be able to visit Western European countries for up to 90 days in a six-month period, provided you have some sort of onward or return ticket and/or 'sufficient means of support' (ie money).

From late 2022, non-EU nationals who don't require a visa for entry to the Schengen area will need prior authorisation to enter under the new European Travel Information and Authorisation System (ETIAS). Travellers can apply online; the cost will be €7 for a three-year, multi-entry authorisation. Visit www.eulisa.europa.eu for more information.

Nationals of other countries (eg China and India) will need a Schengen visa, which is good for a maximum stay of 90 days in a six-month period. For those who do require visas, it's important to remember that these will have a 'use-by' date, and you'll be refused entry after that period has elapsed. It may not be checked when entering these countries overland, but major problems can arise if it is requested during your stay or on departure and you can't produce it.

Schengen Visa Rules

As per the Schengen Agreement, there are no passport controls at borders between the following countries:

- Austria
- Belgium
- Czech Republic
- Denmark
- Estonia
- Finland
- France
- Germany
- Greece
- Hungary
- Iceland
- Italy
- Latvia
- Liechtenstein
- Lithuania
- Luxembourg
- Malta
- The Netherlands
- Norway
- Poland
- Portugal
- Slovakia
- Slovenia
- Spain
- Sweden
- Switzerland

New EU members Bulgaria, Croatia, Cyprus and Romania are required to join the Schengen zone. Dates for this are uncertain, although Croatia is expected to join in 2022.

Note that Ireland and the UK are outside the Schengen zone; they are part of the separate Common Travel Area border controls (along with the Bailiwick of Guernsey, Bailiwick of Jersey and Isle of Man).

Weights & Measures

The metric system is used throughout Western Europe. In the UK, however, nonmetric equivalents are prevalent (distances appear on road signs and odometers in miles, and beer is sold in pints, not litres).

Transport

GETTING THERE & AWAY

The beginning of your Western European adventure is deciding how to travel here, and in these days of cut-throat competition among airlines there are plenty of opportunities to find cheap tickets to a variety of gateway cities.

Flights, cars and tours can be booked online at lonely planet.com/bookings.

Air

Western Europe is well served by just about every major airline in the world Major cities have at least one airport.

Key intercontinental hubs include Amsterdam (Schiphol Airport), Frankfurt (Frankfurt Airport), London (Heathrow), Paris (Charles de Gaulle) and Rome (Leonardo da Vinci aka Flumicino).

Land

You can easily get to Western Europe from the rest of Europe by road, bus or train. The further away you're coming from, however, the more complicated it can be.

Train

It's possible to get to Western Europe by train from central and eastern Asia, but count on spending at least eight days doing it.

Four different train lines wind their way to Moscow: the Trans-Siberian (9259km from Vladivostok), the Trans-Mongolian (7621km from Beijing) and the Trans-Manchurian (8986km from Beijing) all use the same tracks across Siberia but have different routes east of Lake Baikal, while the Trans-Kazakhstan (another Trans-Siberian line) runs between Moscow and Urumqi in northwestern China. Prices vary enormously depending on where you buy the ticket and what's included; advertised 2nd-class fares cost €720/£555 from Beijing to Moscow.

There are many travel options between Western Europe and Moscow as well as other Eastern European countries. Poland, the Czech Republic and Hungary have myriad rail links.

There are also rail links between Germany and Denmark with connections to other Scandinavian countries.

Sea

Ferries

Numerous ferries cross the Mediterranean between Africa and Western Europe. Options include Spain–Morocco, France–Algeria, France–Morocco, France–Tunisia and Italy–Tunisia.

Other ferry destinations from Italy include Albania, Croatia, Montenegro, Morocco and Slovenia. There are also ferries linking Greece

CLIMATE CHANGE & TRAVEL

Every form of transport that relies on carbon-based fuel generates CO_2, the main cause of human-induced climate change. Modern travel is dependent on aeroplanes, which might use less fuel per kilometre per person than most cars but travel much greater distances. The altitude at which aircraft emit gases (including CO_2) and particles also contributes to their climate change impact. Many websites offer 'carbon calculators' that allow people to estimate the carbon emissions generated by their journey and, for those who wish to do so, to offset the impact of the greenhouse gases emitted with contributions to portfolios of climate-friendly initiatives throughout the world. Lonely Planet offsets the carbon footprint of all staff and author travel.

with Albania and Turkey. Ferries also connect Germany with Scandinavian countries.

Ferry Lines (www.ferrylines.com) is a useful resource for researching ferry routes and operators.

Passenger Ships

Cruise ships have occasional transatlantic crossings.

Cunard's *Queen Mary 2* (www.cunard.com) sails between New York, USA and Southampton, England several times a year; the trip takes seven days one way. Prices start from €2680 for two people in a standard double cabin. Deals abound.

DISCOUNT AIRLINES

With cheap fares come many caveats.

- Some of the bare-bones airlines are just that – expect nonreclining seats and nonexistent legroom.
- Baggage allowances are often minimal and extra baggage charges can be costly.
- At some small airports, customer service may be nonexistent.
- Convenience can be deceptive. If you really want to go to Carcassonne in the south of France, then getting a bargain-priced ticket from London will be a dream come true. But if you want to go to Frankfurt in Germany and buy a ticket to 'Frankfurt-Hahn', you will find yourself at a tiny airport 120km west of Frankfurt and almost two hours away by bus.
- Beware of discount airline websites showing nonstop flights that are actually connections.

GETTING AROUND

Air

Discount airlines are revolutionising the way people cover long distances within Europe. However, trains can sometimes work out to be quicker, taking you directly between city centres rather than further-flung airports, and are better for the environment.

Dozens of tiny airports across Europe now have airline services. For instance, a trip to Italy doesn't mean choosing between Milan and Rome, but rather scores of airports up and down the 'boot'.

It's possible to put together a practical itinerary that might bounce from London to the south of Spain to Italy to Amsterdam in a two-week period, all at an affordable price and avoiding endless train rides.

Airlines in Western Europe

Although many people first think of budget airlines when they consider a cheap ticket in Western Europe, you should compare all carriers, including established ones like British Airways and Lufthansa, which serve major airports close to main destinations. Deals crop up frequently.

Various websites compare fares across a range of airlines within Europe, including the following:

- www.cheapoair.com
- www.kayak.com
- www.skyscanner.net

Scores of smaller low-cost airlines serve Western Europe along with major budget airlines including the following:

easyJet (www.easyjet.com) Flies to major airports across Europe.

Eurowings (www.eurowings.com) Hubs in Germany; services across Europe.

Ryanair (www.ryanair.com) Flies to scores of destinations across Europe, but confirm your destination airport is not a deserted airfield out in the sticks.

Vueling (www.vueling.com) Serves a broad swath of Europe from its Spanish hubs.

Bicycle

A tour of Western Europe by bike may seem daunting but it can be a fantastic way to travel.

Cycling UK (www.cyclinguk.org) Offers members an information service on all matters associated with cycling, including cycling conditions, detailed routes, itineraries and maps.

Bike Tours (www.biketours.com) Has details of self-guided tours.

Wearing a helmet is not always compulsory but is advised. A seasoned cyclist can average about 80km a day, but this depends on the terrain and how much you are carrying.

The key to a successful cycling trip is to travel light. What you carry should be determined by your destination and the type of trip you're taking. Even for the most basic trip, it's worth carrying the tools necessary for repairing a puncture. Bicycle shops are found everywhere, but you still might want to pack the following if you don't want to rely on others:

- Allen keys
- Spanners
- Spare brake and gear cables

DEPARTURE TAX

All taxes are included in tickets; there's no separate departure tax from any Western European country.

- Spare spokes
- Strong adhesive tape

Hire

It's easy to hire bicycles in Western Europe and you can often negotiate good deals. Rental periods vary. Local tourist offices, hostels and hotels will have information on rental outlets. Occasionally you can drop off the bicycle at a different location so you don't have to double back on your route.

Urban bike-share schemes, where you check out a bike from one stand and return it to another after brief use, have taken off in cities and towns across Western Europe.

Purchase

For major cycling tours it's best to have a bike you're familiar with, so consider bringing your own rather than buying one on arrival. If you can't be bothered with the hassle of transporting it, there are plenty of places to buy bikes in Western Europe (shops sell them new and secondhand).

Transporting a Bicycle

Check with the airline for details of taking your bicycle with you on the plane before you buy your ticket as each one has a different policy.

Within Western Europe, bikes can often be taken on to a train with you (usually outside peak hours) for a small supplementary fee.

Boat

The main areas of ferry service for Western Europe travellers are between Ireland and Britain, France and Spain; Northern Ireland and Britain; England and the continent (especially France, but also Belgium, the Netherlands and Spain); and Italy and Greece.

Multiple ferry companies compete on the main ferry routes, and the resulting service is comprehensive but complicated.

- A ferry company can have a host of different prices for the same route, depending on the time of day or year, the validity of the ticket or the length of your vehicle.
- It's worth planning (and booking) ahead where possible as there may be special reductions on off-peak crossings and advance-purchase tickets.
- Most ferry companies adjust prices according to the level of demand (so-called 'fluid' or 'dynamic' pricing), so it may pay to try alternative travel dates.
- Vehicle tickets generally include the driver and a full complement of passengers.
- Access to your vehicle during the voyage is usually prohibited for safety reasons.
- Rail-pass holders are entitled to discounts or free travel on some lines.
- Compare fares and routes using **Ferrysavers** (www.ferrysavers.com).

Bus

Buses are invariably cheaper but slower and much less comfortable than trains, and not as quick (or sometimes as cheap) as airlines. There are many services, however, and it's possible to travel long distances for less than €100.

Eurolines (www.eurolines.com) A consortium of bus companies operates under the name Eurolines. Its various affiliates offer many national and regional bus passes.

FlixBus (www.flixbus.com) Rapidly expanding international bus company linking 900 destinations in 20 countries. On-board facilities include free wi-fi and plentiful power sockets.

Campervan

A popular way to tour Europe is to buy or rent a campervan.

Campervans usually feature a fixed high-top or elevating roof and two to five bunk beds. Apart from the essential gas cooker, professional conversions may include a sink, a fridge and built-in cupboards. Prices and facilities vary considerably and it's certainly worth getting advice from a mechanic to see if you are being offered a fair price. Getting a mechanical check is also a good idea.

London is the usual embarkation point. Good British websites to check for campervan purchases and rentals include the following.

Auto Trader (www.autotrader.co.uk)

Loot (http://loot.com)

Worldwide Motorhome Hire (www.worldwide-motorhome-hire.com)

It can be difficult for non-residents to get insurance; one company that offers a 'Walkabout' service is UK-based **Herts Insurance** (www.hertsinsurance.com).

Car

Travelling with your own vehicle allows increased flexibility and the option to get off the beaten track. Unfortunately, cars can be problematic in city centres when you have to negotiate one-way streets or find somewhere to park amid a confusing concrete jungle and a welter of expensive parking options.

In an effort to curb congestion and pollution, cities and larger towns in Western Europe often have restrictions for non-authorised traffic between certain hours and/or for vehicles with high emissions, so check ahead before driving in.

Remember to never leave valuables in the vehicle.

Driving Licences

Proof of ownership of a private vehicle should always be carried (a Vehicle Registration Document for British-registered cars). An EU driving licence is acceptable for driving throughout Europe.

Many non-EU driving licences are valid in Europe.

An International Driving Permit (IDP) is technically required in addition to a current driving licence for foreign drivers in some Western European countries (in practice, it's rare you'll be asked for it). Your national auto club can advise if you'll need one for the itinerary you plan to take and can sell you these multilingual documents.

Fuel

Fuel prices can vary enormously from country to country (though it's always more expensive than in North America or Australia) and may bear little relation to the general cost of living. For fuel prices across the EU, visit **AA Ireland** (www.theaa.ie/aa/motoring-advice/petrol prices.aspx).

Unleaded petrol and diesel are available across Western Europe. To reduce pollution, many cities are planning to ban diesel vehicles (and some, ultimately, petrol vehicles as well).

Charging points for electric cars are increasingly widespread.

Hire

Renting a vehicle is straightforward.

- All major international rental companies operate in Western Europe and will give you reliable service and a good standard of vehicle.
- Usually you will have the option of returning the car to a different outlet at the end of the rental period (for an additional fee).
- Rates vary widely, but expect to pay between €25 and €70 per day, not including insurance. Prebook for the lowest rates – if you walk into an office and ask for a car on the spot, you will pay much more.
- For really good deals, prepay for your rental. Fly/drive combinations and other programs are worth looking into.
- It's imperative to understand exactly what is included in your rental agreement (collision waiver etc). Make sure you are covered with an adequate insurance policy.
- Check whether mileage is unlimited or whether you'll be charged for additional kilometres beyond a particular threshold – extra mileage can quickly add up.
- Less than 4% of European cars have automatic transmissions. If you don't want to drive a manual (stick-shift), you'll need to book much further ahead, and expect to pay more than double for the car.
- The minimum age to rent a vehicle is usually 21 or even 23, and you'll need a credit card.
- If you get a ticket from one of Europe's thousands of hidden speeding cameras, they will track you down through your rental company.

RENTAL BROKERS

Rental brokers (clearing houses) can be a lot cheaper than the major car-rental firms, but always check what is and isn't included (insurance, mileage etc). Companies include the following:

Auto Europe (www.autoeurope.com)

AutosAbroad (www.autosabroad.com)

Car Rentals.co.uk (www.carrentals.co.uk)

Holiday Autos Car Hire (www.holidayautos.com)

Kemwel (www.kemwel.com)

Insurance

Third-party motor insurance is compulsory in Europe if you are driving your own car (rental cars usually come with insurance). Most UK motor-insurance policies automatically provide this for EU countries. Get your insurer to issue a Green Card (which may cost extra), which is an internationally recognised proof of insurance, and check that it lists all the countries you intend to visit.

It's a good investment to take out a European motoring-assistance policy, such as the **AA** (www.theaa.com) Five Star Service or the **RAC** (www.rac.co.uk) European Motoring Assistance.

Non-EU citizens might find it cheaper to arrange international coverage with their national motoring organisation before leaving home. Ask your motoring organisation for details about free services offered by affiliated organisations around Western Europe.

Every vehicle travelling across an international border should display a sticker (or number/licence plate) showing its country of registration. Car-rental/hire agencies usually ensure cars are properly equipped; if in doubt, ask

Purchase

Britain is probably the best place to buy a vehicle as secondhand prices are good and, whether buying privately or from a dealer, if you're an English speaker the absence of language difficulties will help you establish what you are getting and what guarantees you can expect in the event of a breakdown.

Bear in mind that you will be getting a car with the steering wheel on the right-hand side in Britain, whereas in Continental Europe the steering wheel is on the left.

Getting insurance can be difficult; one company offering a 'Walkabout' service to non-residents is **Herts Insurance** (www.hertsinsurance.com).

If you're driving a right-hand-drive car, by law you'll need adjust your headlamps to avoid blinding oncoming traffic.

Leasing

Leasing a vehicle involves fewer hassles and can work out much cheaper than hiring for longer than 17 days. This program is limited to certain new cars, including **Renault** (www.renault-eurodrive.com) and **Peugeot** (www.peugeot-openeurope.com), but you save money because short-term leasing is exempt from VAT and inclusive insurance plans are cheaper than daily insurance rates.

Leasing is also open to people as young as 18 years old. To lease a vehicle your permanent address must be outside the EU. The maximum lease is five-and-a-half months; it's possible to pick up the vehicle in one country and return it in another. Leases include all on-road taxes as well as theft and collision insurance.

Road Conditions

Conditions and types of roads vary across Western Europe, but it is possible to make some generalisations.

➡ The fastest routes are four- or six-lane dual carriageways/highways (motorway, autobahn, autoroute, autostrada etc).

➡ Motorways and other primary routes are great for speed and comfort but driving can be dull, with little or no interesting scenery.

➡ Some fast routes incur expensive tolls (eg in Italy, France and Spain) or have a general tax for usage (Switzerland and Austria), but there will usually be an alternative route you can take.

➡ Motorways and other primary routes are almost always in good condition.

➡ Road surfaces on minor routes are not perfect in some countries (eg Greece), although normally they will be more than adequate.

➡ Minor roads are narrower and progress is generally much slower. To compensate, you can expect much better scenery and plenty of interesting villages along the way.

Road Rules

➡ Automobile associations can supply members with country-by-country information about motoring regulations.

➡ With the exception of the UK and Ireland, driving is on the right-hand side of the road.

➡ Take care with speed limits, as they vary from country to country.

➡ You may be surprised at the apparent disregard of traffic regulations in some places (particularly in Italy and Greece), but as a visitor it is always best to be cautious.

➡ In many countries, driving infringements are subject to an on-the-spot fine; always ask for a receipt.

➡ European drink-driving laws are particularly strict. The blood-alcohol concentration (BAC) limit when driving is generally 0.05% but in certain cases it can be as low as 0%. The European Transport Safety Council (www.etsc.eu) lists the limits for each country.

➡ Some countries require compulsory in-car equipment, such as a portable breathalyser, warning triangle and fluorescent vest. These are supplied by rental companies, but you'll need to have them if you're driving your own vehicle.

➡ For some countries (eg Portugal) you'll need an electronic tag for road tolls. Hire companies generally supply them, but if you're bringing your own vehicle or travelling cross-border, check ahead for information on obtaining one.

➡ In Austria and Switzerland, motorists must buy a motorway tax sticker (*vignette* in German and French; *contrassegno* in Italian) to display on the windscreen. Buy *vignettes* in advance from motoring organisations or (in cash) at petrol stations, Austrian post offices and tobacconists at borders before crossing into the country.

Hitching

Hitching is never entirely safe in any country and we don't recommend it. Travellers who decide to hitch should understand that they are taking a small but potentially serious risk. Key points to remember:

➡ Hitch in pairs; it will be safer.

➡ Solo women should never hitch.

➡ Don't hitch from city centres; take public transport to suburban exit routes.

➡ Hitching is usually illegal on motorways – stand on the slip roads or approach drivers at petrol stations and truck stops.

➡ Look presentable and cheerful, and make a cardboard sign indicating your intended destination in the local language.

➡ Never hitch where drivers can't stop in good time or without causing an obstruction.

➡ At dusk, give up and think about finding somewhere to stay.

➡ It is sometimes possible to arrange a lift in advance via car-sharing agencies. Such agencies are particularly popular in Germany – visit www.blablacar.de.

Motorcycle

With its good-quality winding roads, stunning scenery and an active motorcycling scene, Western Europe is made for motorcycle touring.

➡ The weather is not always reliable, so make sure your wet-weather gear is up to scratch.

➡ Helmets are compulsory for riders and passengers

everywhere in Western Europe.

- On ferries, motorcyclists can sometimes be squeezed on board without a reservation, although booking ahead is advisable during peak travelling periods.
- Take note of local customs about parking motorcycles on footpaths, which is illegal in some countries.
- If you're thinking of touring on a motorcycle, contact **FEMA** (the Federation of European Motorcyclists Associations; www.fema-online.eu) or the **British Motorcyclists Federation** (www.bmf.co.uk) for help and advice.
- Motorcycle and moped rental is easy in countries such as Italy, Spain and Greece and in the south of France. In tourist areas just ask around for nearby rental agencies.

Local Transport

Most Western European cities have excellent public-transport systems, which comprise some combination of metros (subways), trains, trams and buses. Service is usually comprehensive. Major airports generally have fast-train or metro links to the city centre.

Taxi

Taxis in Western Europe are metered and rates are generally high. There might also be supplements (depending on the country) for things such as luggage, the time of day, the location at which you boarded and for extra passengers.

Good public transport networks make the use of taxis almost unnecessary, but if you need one in a hurry they can usually be found idling near train stations or outside big hotels.

Never take an unauthorised ('freelance') taxi.

Tours

A huge variety of tours – whether standard or tailor-made – are available.

Many people have had memorable trips on tours organised by cultural institutions such as the USA's **Smithsonian Institution** (www.smithsonianjourneys.org), which runs tours led by experts in fields such as art.

Boat

One of the biggest advantages of a liveaboard cruise is only having to unpack once.

CroisiEurope (www.croisieuroperivercruises.com) Cruises along Europe's great rivers and canals.

Viking Cruises (www.vikingcruises.co.uk) European river cruises and Mediterranean ocean cruises.

Bus

Bus tours vary enormously in price and corresponding comfort of nightly accommodation, from camping and hostels through to luxury hotels.

Contiki (www.contiki.com) Caters specifically for travellers aged 18 to 35. Expect a party atmosphere.

Globus Journeys (www.globusjourneys.com) Runs budget bus tours for all ages covering Western Europe's most famous attractions.

Insight Vacations (www.insightvacations.com) Operates tours at the high end of the market, attracting an older clientele.

Cycling

Western Europe covers a vast area so multicountry cycling tours are rare; most tours stick to a particular country or region. The website www.biketours.com lists hundreds of options throughout Western Europe.

Train

Escorted rail tours of Western Europe are another way to discover the region. The excellent website **Man in Seat Sixty-One** (www.seat61.com) recommends several options.

Great Rail (www.greatrail.com) offers a range of guided itineraries.

Train

Trains are an ideal way of getting around: they are comfortable, frequent and generally on time. The Channel Tunnel makes it possible to get from Britain to continental Europe using **Eurostar** (www.eurostar.com)

These days, Western Europe's fast, modern trains are

EURAIL & HIGH-SPEED TRAINS

Eurail likes to promote the 'hop-on/hop-off any train' aspect of their passes. But when it comes to the most desirable high-speed trains this is not always the case. Many require a seat reservation and the catch is that these are not always available to pass holders on all trains.

In addition, some of the high-speed services require a fairly hefty surcharge from pass users. For example, Thalys trains from Brussels to Amsterdam incur a 1st-/2nd-class surcharge of €20/15; German ICE trains from Paris to Munich incur a surcharge of €30/13; and Spanish AVE trains from Barcelona to Lyon have a surcharge of €26/19.

On some high-speed routes it may work out cheaper to buy a separate ticket rather than use your pass, especially if you can find a discount fare.

ONLINE TRAIN TICKETS & DISCOUNTS

Many railways offer cheap ticket deals through their websites. It's always worth checking online for sales including advance-purchase reductions, one-off promotions and special circular-route tickets.

How you actually receive the train tickets you've purchased online varies. Common methods include the following:

➡ The ticket is sent to the passenger either as an email or as a stored graphic on an app from the train company (increasingly widespread).

➡ A reservation number is issued with the reservation, which you use at a station ticket-vending machine (some UK lines).

➡ The credit card you used to purchase the tickets can be used to retrieve them at a station ticket-vending machine (in some cases, nonlocal credit- and debit-card holders must retrieve their tickets at a ticket window).

➡ If nonlocal credit and debit cards aren't accepted online and you can't buy the tickets at the station (the Netherlands), purchase them online from **SNCB Europe** (www.b-europe.com) instead.

➡ For multi-country and/or multi-journey tickets, the excellent website **Loco2** (www.loco2.com) accepts international credit and debit cards.

like much-more-comfortable versions of planes. Dining cars have mostly been replaced by snack bars or trolleys, although most people buy food before boarding.

Information

Every national railway has a website with a vast amount of schedule and fare information.

➡ Major national railway companies' smartphone apps are excellent for checking schedules. Many can be used to store tickets bought online. Instead of having to print electronic tickets, the conductor can scan your phone's screen.

➡ **DB Bahn** (www.bahn.de) provides excellent schedule and fare information in English for trains across Europe.

➡ **Man in Seat Sixty-One** (www.seat61.com) has invaluable train descriptions and comprehensive practical details of journeys to the far reaches of the continent.

➡ If you plan to travel extensively by train, the **European Rail Timetable** (www.europeanrailtimetable.eu), issued by Thomas Cook for 140 years and now produced independently, gives a condensed listing of train schedules that indicate where extra fees apply or where reservations are necessary. The timetable is updated monthly and is available online and at selected European bookshops.

High-Speed Trains

High-speed networks (300km/h or more) continue to expand and have given the airlines major competition on many routes.

Sample travel times:

ROUTE	DURATION (HR)
Amsterdam–London	4
Amsterdam–Paris	3¼
Barcelona–Madrid	2½
Brussels–Cologne	1¾
London–Paris	2¼
Milan–Rome	3
Nuremberg–Munich	1¼
Paris–Frankfurt	4
Paris–Marseille	3
Zürich–Milan	3¾

Major high-speed trains that cross borders include the following:

Eurostar (www.eurostar.com) Links beautiful St Pancras station in London to Brussels and Paris; direct services also include London to Marseille via Lyon and Avignon, and London to Amsterdam via Brussels, Antwerp, Rotterdam and Schiphol Airport.

ICE (www.bahn.de) The fast trains of the German railways span the country and extend to Paris, Brussels, Amsterdam, Vienna and Switzerland.

TGV (www.oui.sncf) France's fast trains reach Belgium, Luxembourg, Germany, Switzerland and Italy.

Thalys (www.thalys.com) Links Paris with Brussels, Amsterdam and Cologne.

Other Trains

NIGHT TRAINS

The romantic image of the European night train is disappearing with the popularity of budget airlines and budget constraints.

Night trains still in service include the following:

Caledonian Sleeper (www.scotrail.co.uk) Links London overnight with Scotland (as far north as Inverness and Aberdeen).

ÖBB Nightjet (www.nightjet.com) Routes include Vienna–Rome, Hamburg–Zürich and Munich–Milan.

Thello (www.thello.com) Night services between France and Italy include Paris–Venice.

Trenhotel (www.renfe.com) Services include Madrid–Lisbon and Hendaye–Lisbon (connect in Handaye, France, for Paris).

EXPRESS TRAINS

Slower but still reasonably fast trains that cross borders are often called EuroCity (EC) or InterCity (IC). Reaching speeds of up to 200km/h or more, they are comfortable and frequent. A good example is Austria's RailJet service, which reaches Munich and Zürich.

Reservations

- Some flexible tickets allow stopovers, but not all, so check carefully; alternatively book separate tickets for each leg.
- At weekends and during holidays and summer, it's a good idea to reserve seats on trains (which costs about €3 to €5). Standing at the end of the car for five hours is not what holiday dreams are made of, especially if you're travelling with kids or have reduced mobility.
- Pass holders should note that reservations are a good idea: just because your pricey pass lets you hop-on/hop-off at will, there's no guarantee that you'll have a seat.
- Tickets bought online may include an assigned seat on a train, but most regular tickets are good for any train on the route.
- You can usually reserve ahead of time using a ticket machine at stations or at a ticket window.
- On many high-speed trains – such as France's TGVs – reservations are mandatory.

Train Passes

Think carefully about purchasing a rail pass. Check the national railways' websites and determine what it would cost to do your trip by buying the tickets separately. Often you'll find that you'll spend less than if you buy a Eurail pass.

Shop around as pass prices can vary between different outlets. Once purchased, take care of your pass as it cannot be replaced or refunded if lost or stolen.

Passes get reductions on the Eurostar through the Channel Tunnel and on certain ferry routes (eg between France and Ireland).

In the USA, **Rail Europe** (www.raileurope.com) sells a variety of rail passes, as does Europe-based **OUI.sncf** (www.oui.sncf); note that individual train tickets tend to be more expensive than what you'll pay buying from railways online or in stations.

EURAIL

There are so many different **Eurail** (www.eurail.com) passes to choose from and such a wide variety of areas and time periods covered that you need to have a good idea of your itinerary before purchasing one.

These passes can only be bought by residents of non-European countries and are supposed to be purchased before arriving in Europe, but they can be delivered to a European address. Passes are available for children (aged four to 11), youths (12 to 27), adults (28 to 59) and seniors (60 and above). First-class tickets cost more.

Eurail passes are valid for unlimited travel on national railways and some private lines in 31 countries, including Austria, Belgium, Britain, France, Germany, Greece, Ireland (including Northern Ireland), Italy, Luxembourg, the Netherlands, Portugal, Spain and Switzerland. They are also valid on some ferries between Italy and Greece. Reductions are given on some other ferry routes and on river/lake steamer services in various countries and on the Eurostar to/from Britain.

Single-country passes are also available.

INTERAIL

The **InterRail** (www.interrail.eu) pass is available to European residents of more than six months' standing (passport identification is required), as well as citizens of Russia and Turkey. Terms and conditions vary slightly from country to country, but in the country of origin there is a discount of around 30% to 50% on the normal fares. The pass covers 31 countries; single country and 'global' (multi-country) passes are available.

InterRail passes are generally cheaper than Eurail, but most high-speed trains require that you also buy a seat reservation and pay a supplement of €3 to €40 depending on the route.

InterRail passes are also available for individual countries. Compare these to passes offered by the national railways.

NATIONAL RAIL PASSES

If you're intending to travel extensively within one country, check what national rail passes are available as these can sometimes save you a lot of money. In a large country such as Germany where you might be covering long distances, a pass can make sense, whereas in a small country such as the Netherlands it won't.

Language

This chapter offers basic vocabulary to help you get around Western Europe. If you read our coloured pronunciation guides as if they were English, you'll be understood.

Note that, in our pronunciation guides, the stressed syllables are indicated with italics. The abbreviations 'm' and 'f' indicate masculine and feminine gender respectively.

DUTCH

Dutch is spoken in The Netherlands and the northern part of Belgium (Flanders).

Vowels in Dutch can be long or short. Note that ew is pronounced as 'ee' with rounded lips, oh as the 'o' in 'note', uh as the 'a' in 'ago', and kh as the 'ch' in the Scottish *loch* (harsh and throaty).

Hello.	*Dag.*	dakh
Goodbye.	*Dag.*	dakh
Please.	*Alstublieft.*	al·stew·*bleeft*
Thank you.	*Dank u.*	dangk ew
Excuse me.	*Pardon.*	par·*don*
Sorry.	*Sorry.*	*so*·ree
Yes./No.	*Ja./Nee.*	yaa/ney
Help!	*Help!*	help
Cheers!	*Proost!*	prohst

Do you speak English?
Spreekt u Engels? — spreykt ew *eng*·uhls

I don't understand.
Ik begrijp het niet. — ik buh·*khreyp* huht neet

WANT MORE?

For in-depth language information and handy phrases, check out Lonely Planet's *Western Europe Phrasebook*. You'll find it at **shop.lonelyplanet.com**.

How much is it?
Hoeveel kost het? — hoo·*veyl* kost huht

Where's ...?
Waar is ...? — waar is ...

Can you show me (on the map)?
Kunt u het aanwijzen (op de kaart)? — kunt ew huht *aan*·wey·zuhn (op duh kaart)

I'm lost.
Ik ben de weg kwijt. — ik ben duh wekh kweyt

I'm ill.
Ik ben ziek. — ik ben zeek

Where are the toilets?
Waar zijn de toiletten? — waar zeyn duh twa·*le*·tuhn

FRENCH

French is spoken in France, Switzerland, Luxembourg and the southern part of Belgium (Wallonia).

French has nasal vowels (pronounced as if you're trying to force the sound through your nose), which are indicated in our guides with o or u followed by an almost inaudible nasal consonant sound m, n or ng. Note also that air is pronounced as in 'fair', ew as ee with rounded lips, r is a throaty sound, and zh is pronounced as the 's' in 'pleasure'. Syllables in French words are, for the most part, equally stressed.

Hello.	*Bonjour.*	bon·zhoor
Goodbye.	*Au revoir.*	o·rer·vwa
Please.	*S'il vous plaît.*	seel voo play
Thank you.	*Merci.*	mair·see
Excuse me.	*Excusez-moi.*	ek·skew·zay·mwa
Sorry.	*Pardon.*	par·don
Yes./No.	*Oui./Non.*	wee/non
Help!	*Au secours!*	o skoor
Cheers!	*Santé!*	son·tay

Do you speak English?
Parlez-vous anglais? par·lay·voo ong·glay

I don't understand.
Je ne comprends pas. zher ner kom·pron pa

How much is it?
C'est combien? say kom·byun

Where's ...?
Où est ...? oo ay ...

Can you show me (on the map)?
Pouvez-vous m'indiquer (sur la carte)? poo·vay·voo mun·dee·kay (sewr la kart)

I'm lost.
Je suis perdu/ perdue. (m/f) zher swee pair·dew

I'm ill.
Je suis malade. zher swee ma·lad

Where are the toilets?
Où sont les toilettes? oo son ley twa·let

GERMAN

The language of Germany, Austria and Liechtenstein also has official status, and is spoken in Switzerland, Luxembourg and Belgium.

Vowels in German can be short or long. Note that air is pronounced as in 'fair', aw as in 'saw', eu as the 'u' in 'nurse', ew as ee with rounded lips, ow as in 'now', kh as the 'ch' in the Scottish *loch* (pronounced at the back of the throat), and r is also a throaty sound.

Hello.		
(in general)	*Guten Tag.*	*goo*·ten taak
(Austria)	*Servus.*	*zer*·vus
(Switzerland)	*Grüezi.*	*grew*·e·tsi
Goodbye.	*Auf Wiedersehen.*	owf vee·der·zey·en
Please.	*Bitte.*	*bi*·te
Thank you.	*Danke.*	*dang*·ke
Excuse me.	*Entschuldigung.*	ent·*shul*·di·gung
Sorry.	*Entschuldigung.*	ent·*shul*·di·gung
Yes./No.	*Ja./Nein.*	yaa/nain
Help!	*Hilfe!*	*hil*·fe
Cheers!	*Prost!*	prawst

Do you speak English?
Sprechen Sie Englisch? *shpre*·khen zee *eng*·lish

I don't understand.
Ich verstehe nicht. ikh fer·*shtey*·e nikht

How much is it?
Wie viel kostet das? vee feel *kos*·tet das

Where's ...?
Wo ist ...? vaw ist ...

Can you show me (on the map)?
Können Sie es mir (auf der Karte) zeigen? *keu*·nen zee es meer (owf dair *kar*·te) *tsai*·gen

I'm lost.
Ich habe mich verirrt. ikh *haa*·be mikh fer·*irt*

I'm ill.
Ich bin krank. ikh bin krangk

Where are the toilets?
Wo ist die Toilette? vo ist dee to·a·*le*·te

GREEK

Greek is the language of mainland Greece and its islands (as well as a co-official language of Cyprus).

Note that dh is pronounced as the 'th' in 'that', and that gh and kh are both throaty sounds, similar to the 'ch' in the Scottish *loch*.

Hello.	Γεια σου.	yia su
Goodbye.	Αντίο.	a·*di*·o
Please.	Παρακαλώ.	pa·ra·ka·*lo*
Thank you.	Ευχαριστώ.	ef·kha·ri·*sto*
Excuse me.	Με συγχωρείτε.	me sing·kho·*ri*·te
Sorry.	Συγνώμη.	si·*ghno*·mi
Yes./No.	Ναι./Όχι.	ne/*o*·hi
Help!	Βοήθεια!	vo·*i*·thia
Cheers!	Στην υγειά μας!	stin i·*yia* mas

Do you speak English?
Μιλάς Αγγλικά; mi·*las* ang·gli·*ka*

I don't understand.
Δεν καταλαβαίνω. dhen ka·ta·la·*ve*·no

How much is it?
Πόσο κάνει; *po*·so *ka*·ni

Where's ...?
Που είναι ...; pu *i*·ne ...

Can you show me (on the map)?
Μπορείς να μου δείξεις (στο χάρτη); bo·*ris* na mu *dhik*·sis (sto *khar*·ti)

I'm lost.
Έχω χαθεί. *e*·kho kha·*thi*

I'm ill.
Είμαι άρρωστος/ άρρωστη. (m/f) *i*·me *a*·ro·stos/ *a*·ro·sti

Where are the toilets?
Που είναι η τουαλέτα; pu *i*·ne i tu·a·*le*·ta

ITALIAN

The language of Italy also has official status – and is spoken – in Switzerland.

Italian vowel are generally shorter than those in English. The consonants sometimes have a stronger, more emphatic pronunciation – if the word is written with a double consonant, pronounce them stronger. Note that r is rolled and stronger than in English.

Hello.	*Buongiorno.*	bwon·*jor*·no
Goodbye.	*Arrivederci.*	a·ree·ve·*der*·chee
Please.	*Per favore.*	per fa·*vo*·re
Thank you.	*Grazie.*	*gra*·tsye
Excuse me.	*Mi scusi.*	mee *skoo*·zee
Sorry.	*Mi dispiace.*	mee dees·*pya*·che
Yes./No.	*Sì./No.*	see/no
Help!	*Aiuto!*	ai·*yoo*·to
Cheers!	*Salute!*	sa·*loo*·te

Do you speak English?
Parla inglese? par·la een·*gle*·ze

I don't understand.
Non capisco. non ka·*pee*·sko

How much is it?
Quant'è? kwan·*te*

Where's ... ?
Dov'è ... ? do·*ve* ...

Can you show me (on the map)?
Può mostrarmi (sulla pianta)? pwo mos·*trar*·mee (*soo*·la *pyan*·ta)

I'm lost.
Mi sono perso/a. (m/f) mee *so*·no *per*·so/a

I'm ill.
Mi sento male. mee *sen*·to *ma*·le

Where are the toilets?
Dove sono i gabinetti? *do*·ve *so*·no ee ga·bee·*ne*·tee

PORTUGUESE

Most vowel sounds in Portugal's language have a nasal version (ie pronounced as if you're trying to force the sound through your nose), which is indicated in our pronunciation guides with ng after the vowel. Note also that oh is pronounced as the 'o' in 'note', ow as in 'how', and rr is a throaty sound.

Hello.	*Olá.*	o·*laa*
Goodbye.	*Adeus.*	a·de·*oosh*
Please.	*Por favor.*	poor fa·*vor*
Thank you.	*Obrigado.* (m) *Obrigada.* (f)	o·bree·*gaa*·doo o·bree·*gaa*·da
Excuse me.	*Faz favor.*	faash fa·*vor*
Sorry.	*Desculpe.*	desh·*kool*·pe
Yes./No.	*Sim./Não.*	seeng/nowng
Help!	*Socorro!*	soo·*ko*·rroo
Cheers!	*Saúde!*	sa·*oo*·de

Do you speak English?
Fala inglês? faa·la eeng·*glesh*

I don't understand.
Não entendo. nowng eng·*teng*·doo

How much is it?
Quanto custa? *kwang*·too *koosh*·ta

Where's ...?
Onde é ...? *ong*·de e ...

Can you show me (on the map)?
Pode-me mostrar (no mapa)? *po*·de·me moosh·*traar* (noo *maa*·pa)

I'm lost.
Estou perdido/perdida. (m/f) shtoh per·*dee*·doo/per·*dee*·da

I'm ill.
Estou doente. shtoh doo·*eng*·te

Where are the toilets?
Onde é a casa de banho? *ong*·de e a *kaa*·za de *ba*·nyoo

SPANISH

Spanish is the main language of Spain. Spanish vowels are generally pronounced short. Note that r is rolled and stronger than in English, and v is pronounced as a soft 'b'.

Hello.	*Hola.*	o·la
Goodbye.	*Adiós.*	a·*dyos*
Please.	*Por favor.*	por fa·*vor*
Thank you.	*Gracias.*	*gra*·thyas
Excuse me.	*Perdón.*	per·*don*
Sorry.	*Lo siento.*	lo *syen*·to
Yes./No.	*Sí./No.*	see/no
Cheers!	*¡Salud!*	sa·*loo*
Help!	*¡Socorro!*	so·*ko*·ro

Do you speak English?
¿Habla/Hablas inglés? (pol/inf) a·bla/a·blas een·*gles*

I don't understand.
Yo no entiendo. yo no en·*tyen*·do

How much is it?
¿Cuánto cuesta? *kwan*·to *kwes*·ta

Where's ...?
¿Dónde está ...? *don*·de es·*ta* ...

Can you show me (on the map)?
¿Me lo puede indicar (en el mapa)? me lo *pwe*·de een·dee·*kar* (en el *ma*·pa)

I'm lost.
Estoy perdido/a. (m/f) es·*toy* per·*dee*·do/a

I'm ill.
Estoy enfermo/a. (m/f) es·*toy* en·*fer*·mo/a

Where are the toilets?
¿Dónde están los servicios? *don*·de es·*tan* los ser·*vee*·thyos

Behind the Scenes

SEND US YOUR FEEDBACK

We love to hear from travellers – your comments keep us on our toes and help make our books better. Our well-travelled team reads every word on what you loved or loathed about this book. Although we cannot reply individually to your submissions, we always guarantee that your feedback goes straight to the appropriate authors, in time for the next edition. Each person who sends us information is thanked in the next edition – the most useful submissions are rewarded with a selection of digital PDF chapters.

Visit **lonelyplanet.com/contact** to submit your updates and suggestions or to ask for help. Our award-winning website also features inspirational travel stories, news and discussions.

Note: We may edit, reproduce and incorporate your comments in Lonely Planet products such as guidebooks, websites and digital products, so let us know if you don't want your comments reproduced or your name acknowledged. For a copy of our privacy policy visit lonelyplanet.com/privacy.

WRITER THANKS

Catherine Le Nevez

Thanks first and foremost to Julian, and to all of the locals, fellow travellers and tourism professionals across Western Europe for insights, inspiration and good times throughout the years. Huge thanks too to my Western Europe co-authors, and to Dan Fahey, Evan Godt and everyone at LP. As ever, *merci encore* to my parents, brother, *belle-soeur, neveu* and *nièce*.

ACKNOWLEDGEMENTS

Climate map data adapted from Peel MC, Finlayson BL & McMahon TA (2007) 'Updated World Map of the Köppen-Geiger Climate Classification', *Hydrology and Earth System Sciences*, 11, 1633–44.

Front cover: Castell Coch, Wales, Billy Stock/Getty Images ©

Illustrations p184–5, p188–9, p420–1 and p442–3 by Javier Zarracina.

THIS BOOK

This 15th edition of Lonely Planet's *Western Europe* guidebook was researched and written by Catherine Le Nevez, Kerry Christiani, Gregor Clark, Mark Elliott, Duncan Garwood, Korina Miller, Nicola Williams, Neil Wilson, Isabel Albiston, Kate Armstrong, Alexis Averbuck, Oliver Berry, Cristian Bonetto, Jean-Bernard Carillet, Fionn Davenport, Marc Di Duca, Belinda Dixon, Anthony Ham, Paula Hardy, Damian Harper, Anita Isalska, Ali Lemer, Virginia Maxwell, Hugh McNaughtan, Isabella Noble, John Noble, Lorna Parkes, Christopher Pitts, Leonid Ragozin, Kevin Raub, Simon Richmond, Daniel Robinson, Brendan Sainsbury, Andrea Schulte-Peevers, Helena Smith, Regis St Louis, Andy Symington, Benedict Walker and Greg Ward. This guidebook was produced by the following:

Destination Editors Jennifer Carey, Daniel Fahey, Niamh O'Brien, Tom Stainer, Anna Tyler, Brana Vladisavljevic, Clifton Wilkinson

Senior Product Editors Grace Dobell, Elizabeth Jones, Sandie Kestell

Product Editor Kate James

Senior Cartographers Mark Griffiths, Anthony Phelan

Book Designers Gwen Cotter, Clara Monitto

Assisting Editors Sarah Bailey, Andrew Bain, James Bainbridge, Judith Bamber, Imogen Bannister, Michelle Bennett, Nigel Chin, Katie Connolly, Lucy Cowie, Peter Cruttenden, Jacqueline Danam, Melanie Dankel, Andrea Dobbin, Bruce Evans, Samantha Forge, Carly Hall, Paul Harding, Jennifer Hattam, Gabrielle Innes, Kellie Langdon, Jodie Martire, Lou McGregor, Rosie Nicholson, Lauren O'Connell, Kristin Odijk, Susan Paterson, Monique Perrin, Sarah Reid, Tamara Sheward, Gabrielle Stefanos, Gina Tsarouhas, Fionnuala Twomey, Simon Williamson

Assisting Cartographers Julie Dodkins, Rachel Imeson, Valentina Kremenchutskaya, Katerina Pavkova

Cover Researcher Brendan Dempsey-Spencer

Thanks to Ben Buckner, Carolyn Boicos, Esme Fox, Sandra Henriques Gajjar, Evan Godt, Shona Gray, Alicia Johnson, Sonia Kapoor, Amy Lysen, Claire Naylor, Karyn Noble, Matt Phillips, Kirsten Rawlings, Kathryn Rowan, James Smart, Vicky Smith, Fiona Flores Watson

Index

Map Pages **000**
Photo Pages **000**

Map Pages **000**
Photo Pages **000**

N

O

P

Map Pages **000**
Photo Pages **000**

Map Pages **000**
Photo Pages **000**

Map Legend

Sights
- Beach
- Bird Sanctuary
- Buddhist
- Castle/Palace
- Christian
- Confucian
- Hindu
- Islamic
- Jain
- Jewish
- Monument
- Museum/Gallery/Historic Building
- Ruin
- Shinto
- Sikh
- Taoist
- Winery/Vineyard
- Zoo/Wildlife Sanctuary
- Other Sight

Activities, Courses & Tours
- Bodysurfing
- Diving
- Canoeing/Kayaking
- Course/Tour
- Sento Hot Baths/Onsen
- Skiing
- Snorkelling
- Surfing
- Swimming/Pool
- Walking
- Windsurfing
- Other Activity

Sleeping
- Sleeping
- Camping
- Hut/Shelter

Eating
- Eating

Drinking & Nightlife
- Drinking & Nightlife
- Cafe

Entertainment
- Entertainment

Shopping
- Shopping

Information
- Bank
- Embassy/Consulate
- Hospital/Medical
- Internet
- Police
- Post Office
- Telephone
- Toilet
- Tourist Information
- Other Information

Geographic
- Beach
- Gate
- Hut/Shelter
- Lighthouse
- Lookout
- Mountain/Volcano
- Oasis
- Park
- Pass
- Picnic Area
- Waterfall

Population
- Capital (National)
- Capital (State/Province)
- City/Large Town
- Town/Village

Transport
- Airport
- Border crossing
- Bus
- Cable car/Funicular
- Cycling
- Ferry
- Metro station
- Monorail
- Parking
- Petrol station
- S-Bahn/Subway station
- Taxi
- T-bane/Tunnelbana station
- Train station/Railway
- Tram
- U-Bahn/Underground station
- Other Transport

Routes
- Tollway
- Freeway
- Primary
- Secondary
- Tertiary
- Lane
- Unsealed road
- Road under construction
- Plaza/Mall
- Steps
- Tunnel
- Pedestrian overpass
- Walking Tour
- Walking Tour detour
- Path/Walking Trail

Boundaries
- International
- State/Province
- Disputed
- Regional/Suburb
- Marine Park
- Cliff
- Wall

Hydrography
- River, Creek
- Intermittent River
- Canal
- Water
- Dry/Salt/Intermittent Lake
- Reef

Areas
- Airport/Runway
- Beach/Desert
- Cemetery (Christian)
- Cemetery (Other)
- Glacier
- Mudflat
- Park/Forest
- Sight (Building)
- Sportsground
- Swamp/Mangrove

Note: Not all symbols displayed above appear on the maps in this book

Contributing Writers & Researchers

Isabel Albiston (Ireland)
Kate Armstrong (Greece)
Alexis Averbuck (France)
Oliver Berry (Britain & France)
Cristian Bonetto (Italy)
Jean-Bernard Carillet (France)
Fionn Davenport (Britain)
Marc Di Duca (Britain, Germany & Portugal)
Belinda Dixon (Britain)
Anthony Ham (Germany)
Paula Hardy (Italy)
Damian Harper (Britain & France)
Anita Isalska (France)
Ali Lemer (Germany)
Virginia Maxwell (The Netherlands)
Hugh McNaughtan (Britain, France & Germany)
Isabella Noble (Spain)
John Noble (Spain)
Lorna Parkes (Britain)
Christopher Pitts (France)
Leonid Ragozin (Germany)
Kevin Raub (Portugal)
Simon Richmond (Greece)
Daniel Robinson (France)
Brendan Sainsbury (Italy & Spain)
Andrea Schulte-Peevers (Germany)
Helena Smith (Belgium)
Regis St Louis (Belgium, France & Portugal)
Andy Symington (Britain)
Benedict Walker (Belgium & Germany)
Greg Ward (Britain & France)

Mark Elliott
Belgium (Ardennes; Northeast), The Netherlands (Southeastern; Utrecht) Mark Elliott had already lived and worked on five continents when, in the pre-Internet dark ages, he started writing travel guides. He has since authored (or co-authored) around 60 books including dozens for Lonely Planet. He also acts as a travel consultant, occasional tour leader, video presenter, speaker, interviewer and blues harmonicist.

Duncan Garwood
Italy, Portugal (The Beiras) From facing fast bowlers in Barbados to sidestepping hungry pigs in Goa, Duncan's travels have thrown up many unique experiences. These days he largely dedicates himself to the Mediterranean and Italy, his adopted homeland where he's been living since 1997. He's worked on more than 30 Lonely Planet titles, including guidebooks to Rome, Sardinia, Sicily, Spain and Portugal, and has contributed to books on food and epic drives. He's also written on Italy for newspapers, websites and magazines.

Korina Miller
Greece Korina grew up on Vancouver Island and has been exploring the globe independently since she was 16, visiting or living in 36 countries and picking up a degree in Communications and Canadian Studies, an MA in Migration Studies and a diploma in Visual Arts en route. As a writer and editor, Korina has worked on nearly 60 titles for Lonely Planet and has also worked with lonelyplanet.com, BBC, *The Independent, The Guardian,* BBC5 and CBC, as well as many independent magazines, covering travel, art and culture. She has currently set up camp back in Victoria, soaking up the mountain views and the pounding surf.

Nicola Williams
France (Atlantic Coast, Paris), The Netherlands (Central and Northeastern Netherlands) Border-hopping is a way of life for British writer, runner, foodie, art aficionado and mum-of-three Nicola Williams, who has lived in a French village on the southern side of Lake Geneva for more than a decade. Nicola has authored more than 50 guidebooks on Paris, Provence, Rome, Tuscany, France, Italy and Switzerland for Lonely Planet and covers France as a destination expert for the *Telegraph*. She also writes for the *Independent, Guardian,* lonelyplanet.com, *Lonely Planet Magazine, French Magazine, Cool Camping France* and others. Catch her on the road on Twitter and Instagram at @tripalong.

Neil Wilson
Britain (Scotland) Neil was born in Scotland and has lived there most of his life. Based in Perthshire, he has been a full-time writer since 1988, working on more than 80 guidebooks for various publishers, including the Lonely Planet guides to Scotland, England, Ireland and Prague. An outdoors enthusiast since childhood, Neil is an active hill-walker, mountain-biker, sailor, snowboarder, fly-fisher and rock-climber, and has climbed and tramped in four continents, including ascents of Jebel Toubkal in Morocco, Mount Kinabalu in Borneo, the Old Man of Hoy in Scotland's Orkney Islands and the Northwest Face of Half Dome in California's Yosemite Valley.

OUR STORY

A beat-up old car, a few dollars in the pocket and a sense of adventure. In 1972 that's all Tony and Maureen Wheeler needed for the trip of a lifetime – across Europe and Asia overland to Australia. It took several months, and at the end – broke but inspired – they sat at their kitchen table writing and stapling together their first travel guide, *Across Asia on the Cheap*. Within a week they'd sold 1500 copies. Lonely Planet was born.

Today, Lonely Planet has offices in the US, Ireland and China, with a network of over 2000 contributors in every corner of the globe. We share Tony's belief that 'a great guidebook should do three things: inform, educate and amuse'.

OUR WRITERS

Catherine Le Nevez

Plan and Survival Guide chapters, Britain (The Midlands), France (Paris; Lille & the Somme), Germany (Frankfurt & Southern Rhineland), Luxembourg, The Netherlands (Amsterdam), Portugal (The Algarve) Catherine's wanderlust kicked in when she road-tripped across Europe from her Parisian base aged four, and she's been hitting the road at every opportunity since, travelling to some 60 countries and completing her Doctorate of Creative Arts in Writing, Masters in Professional Writing, and postgrad qualifications in Editing and Publishing along the way. Over the past decade-and-a-half she's written scores of Lonely Planet guides and articles covering Paris, France, Europe and far beyond. Her work has also appeared in numerous online and print publications.

Kerry Christiani

Austria, France (Alsace & Lorraine; Champagne), Germany (Stuttgart & the Black Forest), Portugal (Porto), Switzerland Kerry is an award-winning travel writer, photographer and Lonely Planet author, specialising in Central and Southern Europe. Based in Wales, she has authored/co-authored more than a dozen Lonely Planet titles. An adventure addict, she loves mountains, cold places and true wilderness. She features her latest work at https://its-a-small-world.com and tweets @kerrychristiani.

Gregor Clark

France (Burgundy; Nice), Monaco, Portugal (the Douro & Trás-os-Montes; the Minho) Gregor Clark is a US-based writer whose love of foreign languages and curiosity about what's around the next bend have taken him to dozens of countries on five continents. Chronic wanderlust has also led him to visit all 50 states and most Canadian provinces on countless road trips through his native North America. Since 2000, Gregor has regularly contributed to Lonely Planet guides, with a focus on Europe and the Americas. Titles include *Italy, France, Brazil, Costa Rica, Argentina, Portugal, Switzerland, Mexico, South America on a Shoestring, Montreal & Quebec City, France's Best Trips, New England's Best Trips*, cycling guides to Italy and California and coffee-table pictorials such as *Food Trails, The USA Book* and *The Lonely Planet Guide to the Middle of Nowhere*.

OVER PAGE MORE WRITERS

Published by Lonely Planet Global Limited
CRN 554153
15th edition – May 2022
ISBN 978 1 78868 393 7

10 9 8 7 6 5 4 3 2 1
Printed in Singapore